The
World Book
Encyclopedia

W·X·Y·Z Volume 21

World Book–Childcraft International, Inc.
A subsidiary of The Scott & Fetzer Company
Chicago London Paris Sydney Tokyo Toronto

The World Book Encyclopedia

Copyright © 1980, U.S.A.
by
World Book–Childcraft International, Inc.

Ww

W is the 23rd letter of our alphabet. The letter developed from a symbol used by the Semites, who once lived in Syria and Palestine. They named it *waw*, meaning *hook*, and adapted an Egyptian *hieroglyphic*, or picture symbol. The Romans, who took it from the Greeks, gave it a V shape. They first pronounced it as we pronounce *W*, but later pronounced it as *V*. During the 1000's, French scribes doubled the *V*, as *VV*, in order to write the Anglo-Saxon letter *wen*, for which they had no letter in their alphabet. The *VV* was also written in a rounded form as *UU*. It later came to be called "double U" in English. See ALPHABET.

Uses. W or w is about the 19th most frequently used letter in books, newspapers, and other printed material in English. *W* is used to abbreviate *west*. In military titles, *W* often stands for *women* or *women's*, as in *WAC* for *Women's Army Corps*. In electricity, *w* is used for *watt*. In chemistry *W* is the symbol for the element tungsten.

Pronunciation. In English, *w* is pronounced by rounding the lips and raising the tongue toward the velum, or soft palate, in preparation for a vowel sound to follow. The velum is closed, and the vocal cords vibrate. *W* is silent in words such as *wrong* and *answer*. It rarely occurs in Scandinavian languages or in French and other Romance languages, except for a few words from other tongues. In German, it usually has the sound of *v*. See PRONUNCIATION. I. J. GELB and JAMES M. WELLS

Development of the Letter W

 The Ancient Egyptians drew this symbol of a supporting pole about 3000 B.C. The Semites adapted the symbol and named it *waw*, their word for *hook*.

 The Phoenicians used this symbol of a hook in their alphabet about 1000 B.C.

 The Greeks changed the symbol and added it to their alphabet about 600 B.C. They called their letter *upsilon*.

 The Romans gave the letter V its capital shape about A.D. 114.

 Medieval Scribes used VV as a letter about 1000. VV was also written UU, and the letter became known as "double U."

The Small Letter w came into use along with the capital during the 1000's. By the 1500's, the small letter had developed its present shape.

1000

Today

Special Ways of Expressing the Letter W

International Morse Code

Braille

International Flag Code

Semaphore Code

Sign Language Alphabet

Common Forms of the Letter W

Handwritten Letters vary from person to person. Manuscript (printed) letters, *left*, have simple curves and straight lines. Cursive letters, *right*, have flowing lines.

Roman Letters have small finishing strokes called *serifs* that extend from the main strokes. The type face shown above is Baskerville. The italic form appears at the right.

Sans-Serif Letters are also called *gothic letters*. They have no serifs. The type face shown above is called Futura. The italic form of Futura appears at the right.

Computer Letters have special shapes. Computers can "read" these letters either optically or by means of the magnetic ink with which the letters may be printed.

I

WAALS, JOHANNES DIDERIK VAN DER. See VAN DER WAALS, JOHANNES DIDERIK.

WABASH COLLEGE. See UNIVERSITIES AND COLLEGES (table).

WABASH RIVER is the main waterway of Indiana. It rises in western Ohio and flows northwest into Indiana to Huntington. Then it turns southwest to Covington, where it flows south to the Ohio River, at the Illinois-Indiana-Kentucky boundary line. The Wabash forms the boundary between Illinois and Indiana from near Terre Haute, Ind., to the Ohio River (see INDIANA [physical map]). Today, only small boats and ferries navigate the Wabash River. The old Wabash and Erie Canal runs parallel with the Wabash River from Terre Haute to Huntington, Ind. The river is 475 miles (764 kilometers) long, and drains an area of 33,150 square miles (85,858 square kilometers). Many songs about Indiana mention the Wabash River.   PAUL E. MILLION, JR.

WAC. See ARMY, UNITED STATES (Women in the Army).

WAC CORPORAL, a U.S. Army rocket. See ROCKET (High-Altitude Rockets).

WACO, *WAY koh,* Tex. (pop. 95,326; met. area pop. 147,553), is a leading cotton market of the United States and an industrial center of central Texas. Waco lies on the Brazos River about 100 miles (160 kilometers) south of Dallas (see TEXAS [political map]).

The city serves as the shipping center for a farm region which produces grain, hay, fruits, vegetables, livestock, and poultry. Waco industries manufacture dairy and cottonseed products, textiles, tents and awnings, glass products, furniture, wood products, and iron and steel products.

Baylor University and Paul Quinn College are in Waco. Waco was laid out in 1849 on the site of a former Waco Indian village. The city was incorporated in 1850. It is the seat of McLennan County. Waco has a council-manager government.   H. BAILEY CARROLL

WADI, *WAH dee,* in the Middle East and northern Africa, is a gully or ravine through which a stream flows in the rainy season. Wadis are often formed in desert sand. In Arabic the word *wadi* means *ravine.*

See also EGYPT (The Land).

WADSWORTH, JOSEPH. See CHARTER OAK.

WADSWORTH-LONGFELLOW HOUSE. See MAINE (Places to Visit; picture).

WAF. See AIR FORCE, UNITED STATES (Women in the Air Force).

WAGER is a bet, or anything which is risked on the outcome of an event or the answer to a question. Money or other property may be wagered, or it may be agreed that the loser of the bet shall do a certain thing. Laws do not enforce the payment of wagers, except in certain countries and states where that kind of gambling is lawful.   JOHN SCARNE

See also GAMBLING; LOTTERY.

WAGES AND HOURS. Wages are the price paid for the services of labor. They are usually figured per hour or per week.

Wages are the source of a worker's ability to buy goods and services. Wages are classified as money wages and real wages. *Money wages* are the actual amount of money a worker receives from an employer. *Real wages* are figured from the amount of goods and services workers can buy with their money wages.

Money wages depend upon the amount of money in circulation, government economic policies, and general business conditions in a country. Real wages depend upon money wages and workers' average output per worker-hour.

An employer can increase both the real and money wages of workers by giving them a raise in salary. Their real wages would rise even if the employer increased the price of the product to regain the money lost by paying higher salaries. But if every employer raised prices when increasing salaries, workers might lose the increase in real wages. For example, workers earning $100 a week may receive a raise of 10 per cent to $110 a week. But if the prices of the goods they buy also rise by 10 per cent, they are receiving the same real wage at $110 as they did at $100. Since 1900, money wages in the United States have risen about $3\frac{1}{2}$ times as much as real wages.

State minimum-wage laws and the Federal Fair Labor Standards Act of 1938—amended in 1949, 1955, 1961, 1966, 1974, and 1977—have helped raise the wages of the lowest paid workers in many industries.

Real wages per hour are closely related to *output per worker-hour.* Output per worker-hour shows the amount of goods a worker can produce in one hour. Output per worker-hour increases as workers become more skilled, and as machinery, tools, and factories become more efficient. From 1909 to 1947, output per

Greater Waco Chamber of Commerce

Baylor University's Main Campus, *above,* is in Waco. A statue there honors R. E. B. Baylor, who helped found the school.

Wages and Hours in the United States

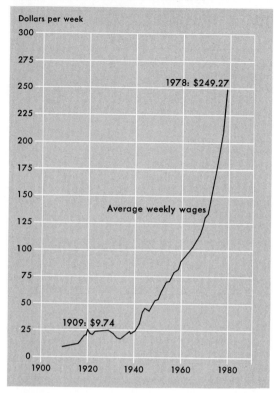

Dollars per week

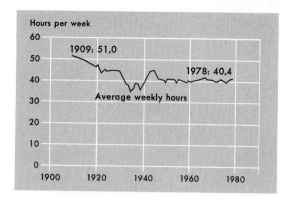

Hours per week

Average weekly gross wages (before social security and income tax deductions) have increased greatly during the 1900's, *above, left*. Average weekly working hours have decreased during the same period, *above, right*. Both graphs report statistics only for production workers in manufacturing industries. The figures include overtime and holiday pay and work.

Year	Weekly Wages	Weekly Hours
1909	$ 9.74	51.0
1914	10.92	49.4
1920	26.02	47.4
1925	24.11	44.5
1930	23.00	42.1
1935	19.91	36.6
1940	24.96	38.1
1945	44.20	43.5
1950	58.32	40.5
1955	75.70	40.7
1960	89.72	39.7
1965	107.53	41.2
1970	133.33	39.8
1971	142.44	39.9
1972	154.71	40.5
1973	166.46	40.7
1974	177.20	40.0
1975	190.79	39.5
1976	209.32	40.1
1977	228.50	40.3
1978	249.27	40.4

Source: U.S. Bureau of Labor Statistics.

worker-hour in the U.S. increased from 2 to 2½ per cent a year. From 1947 to the early 1970's, the output rose to 3¼ per cent.

Since 1945, employers have spent an increasing percentage of their labor costs on *fringe benefits*, rather than *take-home pay* for the worker. The most popular fringe benefits include pension plans, prepaid medical and dental care for employees, paid holidays, and paid rest time. Employers usually consider fringe benefits as a substitute for wages, rather than as an additional contribution to the workers.

Hours. Before the Industrial Revolution, most persons worked on farms where the workday ran from sunrise to sunset. Factory operators tried to enforce the same hours during the Industrial Revolution of the 1700's and early 1800's, despite the difference in working conditions and the type of work. Gradually, factories began adopting the 10-hour day and the 6-day week. This became the normal working period in the United States and Europe.

Labor began its demands for an 8-hour day in the 1880's. But the 8-hour day did not become common in the United States until after World War I. During the 1930's, the 5-day, 40-hour workweek came into general practice in the United States. In the 1960's, some

U.S. labor leaders talked of a 35-hour workweek for their union members.

Shorter workweeks provide additional leisure time for workers. This extra leisure time comes from a rising standard of living among workers, combined with an output per worker-hour that has been greatly increased over the years by more efficient mass-production methods.   MELVIN WARREN REDER

Related Articles in WORLD BOOK include:

Child Labor
Cost of Living
Labor,
    Department of
Labor Movement

Minimum Wage
Piecework
Profit Sharing
Unemployment
    Insurance

WAGNER, *WAG nuhr,* **HONUS,** *HOH nuhs* (1874-1955), is considered baseball's greatest shortstop by many experts. Wagner played for the Pittsburgh Pirates for 18 years. Later, he served many years as a coach for the Pirates. He had a lifetime batting average of .329 and led the National League in batting eight times, including four times in a row. Wagner batted .300 or better during 17 of his seasons in the National League, and held many batting records by the time he retired as an active player. He stole 61 bases in 1907, and led the league in stolen bases five times.

Historical Pictures Service

Richard Wagner

ance of Beethoven's ninth symphony in 1839. This renewed his faith in German music and inspired his first masterpiece, *A Faust Overture* for orchestra (1840). Wagner no longer believed in *Rienzi*. But he completed it anyway, because a successful production in Paris would ensure his reputation as an opera composer all over Europe. The opera was not produced, however, and Wagner ran out of money. During this period of misery in Paris, he wrote *The Flying Dutchman* (1841), returning to the German romantic style.

His fortunes revived in 1842 with an offer to conduct at the Dresden opera house. In Dresden, he composed *Tannhäuser* (1845) and *Lohengrin* (1848), two great artistic treatments of the romantic view of medieval life.

Meanwhile, social revolution brewed in Germany. Wagner was convinced that musicians were being treated unjustly and that the organization and operation of the theaters were poor. His resentment led to his participation in an unsuccessful revolution in 1849. Afterward, a warrant was issued for his arrest and he fled to Switzerland. He was not allowed to return to Germany for 12 years.

Later Career. During his first years in Switzerland, Wagner wrote no music. Instead, he examined his own philosophy of art and life and wrote on social and artistic problems. He also began the libretto for his greatest creation, *The Ring of the Nibelung*. He began work on the music for this cycle of four operas in 1853. He finished *The Rhine Gold* (*Das Rheingold*) in 1854, *The Valkyrie* (*Die Walküre*) in 1856, and the first two acts of *Siegfried* by 1857. Then he composed another work he had been planning, *Tristan and Isolde*. He did not compose the third act of *Siegfried* until 1869.

Tristan, completed in 1859, is a landmark in music because of the intensely *chromatic* style used to express the love interest in the story. This style increased the expressive nature of a melody or chord (see MUSIC [Sound in Music]). *Tristan* is a unique conception for the stage. It deals less with external events or actions than with the emotional lives of the characters, what Wagner called "soul states."

Getting *Tristan* produced was Wagner's chief concern after 1859. Debts piled up, and he was constantly threatened with financial ruin. In 1864, King Ludwig II of Bavaria came to his rescue. Wagner became the king's adviser in Munich and *Tristan* was finally produced there in 1865. Meanwhile, Wagner had started work on his only mature comedy, *The Mastersingers of Nuremberg* (*Die Meistersinger von Nürnberg*). He finished this in Switzerland in 1867. In 1874 he concluded the entire *Ring* cycle with the completion of *The Twilight of the Gods* (*Die Götterdämmerung*). About 1864, Wagner fell in love with Cosima von Bülow, the married daughter of composer Franz Liszt. Cosima became his mistress and they were married in 1870.

With the king's aid, Wagner finally built a theater of his own in Bayreuth in which to perform the *Ring*. The

Culver

Honus Wagner, a shortstop for the Pittsburgh Pirates, was one of the greatest hitters and fielders in baseball history.

Wagner was elected to the National Baseball Hall of Fame in 1936. His full name was John Peter Wagner. He was born in Carnegie, Pa.   ED FITZGERALD

WAGNER, *VAHG ner,* **RICHARD** (1813-1883), was a great German composer who fundamentally changed European musical, literary, and theatrical life. Wagner believed that the theater should be the center of a community's culture rather than merely a place of entertainment. He finally built his own theater and founded Europe's oldest summer music festival. He intended this festival and the ideal conditions it offered to performing artists to serve as a model for other theaters.

Wagner wrote his own opera *librettos* (words), basing his mature works on episodes from history and from medieval myths and legends. In the music of his earlier works, he used elements of the German, French, and Italian operatic styles of his time. He reached a climax in *Lohengrin*, which brought these diverse elements into complete unity. After *Lohengrin*, Wagner developed a new "musical language." Composers like Mozart tended to explore a twofold set of melodies with properly matched keys, as in a symphonic movement. Wagner moved to a greater variety of melodies (called motives) and keys, using new ways to blend them into the unity of his musical dramas.

Early Career. Wagner was born in Leipzig on May 22, 1813. He was educated at the best schools. Early in life, he showed a flair for the theater and might have become a great actor if he had not decided to become a musician. From 1833 to 1839, he worked as an opera conductor in several German cities. He wrote his first complete opera, *The Fairies* (1834), in the German romantic style. He abandoned this style in his next opera, *The Ban on Love* (1835), based on Shakespeare's *Measure for Measure*. In 1836, he married Minna Planer, an actress. It was a stormy marriage and the two lived apart in the last years before her death in 1866.

Wagner's next project was *Rienzi*, an opera in the imposing style called French grand opera. He interrupted his work on *Rienzi* after hearing a perform-

4

first festival was held there in 1876. Wagner composed his last work, the opera *Parsifal* (1882), especially to be performed in this theater.

Wagner's Philosophy. Wagner tried to find a new way of combining music and drama in the theater. He believed the basic error in opera was that music had become the sole end. Drama served merely as an excuse for the music. Wagner aimed at a work in which all the various elements in operatic composition were in perfect harmony and directed toward a single artistic end.

Wagner considered the orchestra the greatest artistic achievement of his time, and wanted to take greater advantage of its expressive possibilities. Wagner did not think the orchestra should accompany a vocal line with repeated chords like a "monstrous guitar." He believed it could be given a more elaborate musical texture in which the vocal line would be one independent strand. His use of recurrent motives permitted continuous music throughout an act, with no breaks or applause until the end. Wagner disliked "operatic" acting, and insisted that singers use only those movements and gestures required by the music.

Wagner waged one of the hardest battles ever fought in the cause of artistic freedom. His stormy and debt-ridden career forced many people to realize that creative artists deserve their support. Wagner's works were a dominant force in Western culture until World War I. He ranks with Bach, Mozart, and Beethoven as one of the world's greatest composers.   ROBERT BAILEY

See also OPERA; RING OF THE NIBELUNG, THE.

WAGNER, *WAG nuhr,* **ROBERT FERDINAND** (1877-1953), an American statesman, served in the New York legislature and showed special interest in welfare ques-

tions. He was justice of the Supreme Court of New York from 1919 to 1926, and from then until 1949 served as a United States Senator from New York. A Democrat, he introduced the National Labor Relations Act, or "Wagner Act," the National Industrial Recovery Act, the Social Security Act, and the U.S. Housing Act of 1937. He was born in Nastatten, near Wiesbaden, Germany. His son, Robert F. Wagner, Jr. (1910-   ), was mayor of New York City from 1954 to 1965.   HARVEY WISH

WAGNER ACT. See NATIONAL LABOR RELATIONS ACT.

WAGNER VON JAUREGG, JULIUS. See FEVER; NOBEL PRIZES (table: Nobel Prizes in Physiology or Medicine—1927).

WAGON. The wheel and the wagon developed at the same time. This was at least 5,000 years ago, when people first found that they could pull sledges more easily if they had them fitted with wheels that were solid pieces of wood. The Egyptians were among the earliest people to use wagons. The Scythians wandered over the plains of southeastern Europe as early as 700 B.C., carrying their possessions on two-wheeled carts covered with reeds. The Greeks and the Romans developed chariots which were lighter and faster than those of the Egyptians. The four-wheeled coach was developed in Germany during the Middle Ages.

English governors of American colonies introduced the first wagons in North America. Stagecoaches began to run over colonial roads about the time of George Washington. The *prairie schooner* (covered wagon), which was first built by the German farmers of Pennsyl-

Some Kinds of Wagons

Detail of the Bayeux Tapestry (1000's-1100's); Bayeux Museum, Bayeux, France (Giraudon)

A Wagon of the Middle Ages was used to carry weapons into battle.

Brown Brothers

The Conestoga Wagon carried pioneers westward over the Allegheny Mountains from the late 1700's until about 1850. It was drawn by a team of four to six horses.

Brown Brothers

The New England Buckboard Wagon was a popular American carriage of the early 1900's. These open wagons were used for short business and pleasure trips.

Brown Brothers

A Horse-Drawn Delivery Wagon was a common sight during the early 1900's.

vania, was used in the development of the American West. Farm wagons carried crops to market until the early 1900's. The present-day truck trailer is actually a kind of wagon. FRANKLIN M. RECK

See also CHUCK WAGON; CONESTOGA WAGON; PIONEER LIFE IN AMERICA (The Wagon Train); STAGECOACH; TRANSPORTATION (pictures).

WAGON TRAIN. See PIONEER LIFE IN AMERICA; WESTERN FRONTIER LIFE (Transportation).

WAHHABI. See IKHWAN; SAUDI ARABIA (History).

WAHL, ARTHUR CHARLES. See PLUTONIUM.

WAHOO is a fish that lives in the warm waters of all oceans. In American waters, it lives off Florida, Cuba, the West Indies, Panama, and the Galapagos Islands. The wahoo is a game fighter and a good food fish. It may grow to be 5 or 6 feet (1.5 or 1.8 meters) long and weigh over 140 pounds (64 kilograms). It has a pointed snout and a long dorsal fin. It is also called the *queenfish*, or the *peto*.

Scientific Classification. The wahoo belongs to the mackerel family, *Scombridae*. It is classified as genus *Acanthocybium*, species *A. solanderi*. LEONARD P. SCHULTZ

U.S. Dept. of Commerce

The Wahoo Provides Excellent Sport for Anglers.

WAIBLINGEN. See GUELPHS AND GHIBELLINES.

WAILING WALL is a high wall in Jerusalem. It is also called the *Western Wall*, because during Biblical times it formed the western wall of the courtyard of the Jews' holy Temple. The wall is about 160 feet (49 meters) long and about 40 feet (12 meters) high. Archaeologists have discovered that 19 rows of stones extend about 20 feet (6 meters) underground. The lower part of the wall contains stones said to be from Herod's Temple.

Beginning in the 700's, the Arabs permitted Jews to assemble at the wall on the evenings before their Sabbath and before their feast days. In services at the wall, the Jews recalled their traditions and sufferings.

Jews continued to use the wailing wall after the British won control of Jerusalem during World War I. In 1948, Jordan captured the section of Jerusalem where the wall was located, and prohibited Jews from the new state of Israel from using it. But the Jews regained access to the wall when Israel captured the Jordanian section of Jerusalem in the Arab-Israeli war of June, 1967. For location of the wailing wall, see JERUSALEM (map). BRUCE M. METZGER

See also ISRAEL (picture: The Wailing Wall); JERUSALEM (Holy Places; picture).

WAINWRIGHT, JONATHAN MAYHEW (1883-1953), was an American general whose courage made him a hero of World War II. After General Douglas MacArthur was ordered to leave the Philippines and go to Australia in March, 1942, Wainwright remained in command of the American and Filipino forces on Bataan Peninsula and Corregidor. He was forced to surrender in May, 1942, and was held a prisoner for three years by the Japanese. He was released in 1945, and participated in the surrender ceremony of the Japanese delegates aboard the U.S.S. *Missouri* in Tokyo Bay. On his return to the United States, he became a full general and received the Congressional Medal of Honor.

Wainwright was born in Walla Walla, Wash., and was graduated from the United States Military Academy in 1906. He became a cavalry officer and served in the Philippines in 1909 and 1910. During World War I, he served on the general staff of the 82nd Division in France. After World War II, he commanded the Fourth Army. He retired in 1947. MAURICE MATLOFF

See also BATAAN PENINSULA; WORLD WAR II (Burma and the Philippines).

WAITANGI, TREATY OF. See NEW ZEALAND (Colonization; picture).

WAITE, *wayt,* **MORRISON REMICK** (1816-1888), served as chief justice of the United States from 1874 until his death. In the Granger Cases, his opinions upheld the power of state governments to regulate business (see GRANGER CASES). Later in Waite's term, this doctrine lost favor when the Supreme Court developed broad powers to enforce the 14th Amendment. However, the doctrine of broad power to regulate business was revived in the 1930's.

Waite was born in Lyme, Conn. He was graduated from Yale University. In 1871 he was an American delegate to the Geneva Tribunal which considered the *Alabama* claims (see ALABAMA [ship]). Waite also helped found the Republican Party. JERRE S. WILLIAMS

WAKE is the custom of watching over a dead person before burial. In many countries, the custom is rarely observed today. But some form of the custom has been practiced in all parts of the world. In the traditional wake, family and friends gathered at the dead person's home. The custom probably began because people believed that evil spirits might possess an unburied corpse if it were left alone. CHARLES L. WALLIS

WAKE FOREST UNIVERSITY is a coeducational liberal arts school in Winston-Salem, N.C. It is affiliated with the Baptist Church. The school offers degrees in liberal arts, medicine, law, and business administration. It has an Army ROTC unit. It was founded in 1834 at Wake Forest, N.C. The move to Winston-Salem was completed in 1956. For enrollment, see UNIVERSITIES AND COLLEGES (table). RUSSELL BRANTLEY

WAKE ISLAND is a United States possession in the west-central Pacific Ocean. It is a natural crossroads for ships and airplanes crossing the Pacific. Wake is a triangular atoll made up of three small coral islets, Wake, Peale, and Wilkes. The islets cover a land area of about 3 square miles (8 square kilometers), and have a population of about 1,650. With a curving reef, they enclose a lagoon that is less than 4 square miles (10 square kilometers) in area. Wake lies 2,300 miles (3,700 kilometers) west of Honolulu and 1,985 miles (3,195 kilometers) southeast of Tokyo. It has no fresh water, and its vegetation consists mainly of shrubs and bushes.

Spaniards probably sighted Wake when they explored the Pacific in the late 1500's. The British schooner *Prince William Henry* landed at the island in 1796. In 1841, Commander Charles Wilkes of the United States Exploring Expedition surveyed the island with the aid of the naturalist Titian Peale. They found no indication that the island had ever been inhabited. The United States claimed Wake in 1899 because it lay on the cable route from San Francisco to Manila. In 1935, Wake became a base for Pacific air traffic.

Wake Island became a national defense area in 1941. For two weeks, a force of 400 United States Marines and about 1,000 civilians fought off a Japanese invasion. But the island finally was captured late in December, 1941. The Japanese garrison on Wake surrendered at the end of World War II.   EDWIN H. BRYAN, JR.

WAKE-ROBIN. See TRILLIUM.

WAKEFIELD, EDWARD GIBBON. See NEW ZEALAND (History).

WAKSMAN, *WAKS man,* **SELMAN ABRAHAM** (1888-1973), made outstanding contributions to soil microbiology and to the development of antibiotics. He taught and did research, especially on a group of microbes known as *actinomycetes.* He studied the effects of soil microbes on each other, on the fertility of the soil, and on the formation of humus.

In 1943 Waksman and his collaborators discovered the antibiotic, *streptomycin* (see STREPTOMYCIN). Waksman gave his share of the royalties to establish an Institute of Microbiology at Rutgers University. He retired as the director of the institute in 1958. He won the 1952 Nobel prize for physiology or medicine.

Waksman was born in Novaya Priluka, Russia. He moved to the United States in 1910.   MORDECAI L. GABRIEL

WAKULLA SPRINGS. See FLORIDA (The Land).

WALACHIA. See ROMANIA (History).

WALATA, *wah LAH tah,* was a leading trading city in West Africa from the late 1000's to the 1500's. Copper, swords, and other goods were traded there for gold and sometimes for slaves. Today, Walata is a small town in Mauritania called *Oualata.*

During the 1000's, Muslim traders from the south settled in Walata. The city became part of the Mali Empire in the 1300's. The Tuaregs of the south seized and occupied Walata in 1433. In the late 1400's, it became part of the Songhai Empire. After that empire fell, various peoples ruled Walata.   LEO SPITZER

WALD, GEORGE (1906-   ), an American biochemist, determined how chemical changes in the retina enable a person to see. He shared the 1967 Nobel prize for physiology or medicine.

Wald analyzed the *pigment* (coloring matter) of *rods,* the cells in the retina that respond to dim light. He found that light causes certain changes in *retinene,* a chemical in the pigment. These changes trigger a nerve impulse that transmits to the brain an image of what is seen. Wald discovered that the body makes retinene from vitamin A. This discovery explained why a deficiency of vitamin A reduces vision at night.

Wald was born in New York City and earned a Ph.D. at Columbia University in 1932. He joined the faculty of Harvard University in 1934. He became known as an outspoken opponent of the Vietnam War during the late 1960's and early 1970's.   ISAAC ASIMOV

WALD, LILLIAN D. (1867-1940), founded the first nonsectarian visiting nurse program in the United States. Her contacts with the poor in New York City in the depression of 1892-1893 inspired her to found the *Nurses' Settlement,* later known as the Henry Street Settlement. To her we owe our system of public-school

nursing. She also worked with the founder of the first "ungraded" class for mentally retarded children.

Henry Street Settlement Archives
Lillian D. Wald

She and social reformer Florence Kelley were the first to suggest to President William Howard Taft the idea of a national Children's Bureau to study the needs of children everywhere. Congress set up the Children's Bureau as an agency of the U.S. government in 1912. She was an ardent pacifist, and her views were held in high regard by President Woodrow Wilson and others who worked for peace. Lillian Wald was born in Cincinnati. She wrote *The House on Henry Street* and *Windows on Henry Street.*   ALAN KEITH-LUCAS

WALDENSES, *wahl DEN seez,* are members of a Christian religious group. The group was founded by Peter Waldo, a wealthy merchant of Lyon, France. In 1173, Waldo left his wife, gave his fortune to the Church and charity, and began preaching in the streets of Lyon. His message of poverty and religious devotion attracted many followers. The followers were called the *poor men of Lyon.* Pope Alexander III and the Archbishop of Lyon forbade them to preach because they were not priests and their teachings differed from those of the Church. For example, they denied the pope's authority and the existence of purgatory. The Waldenses continued to preach and were *excommunicated* (expelled) from the Church in 1184 by Pope Lucius III.

There are now about 50,000 members in Europe and North and South America. Waldensian headquarters are in Rome.   WILLIAM H. MAEHL

WALDHEIM, KURT (1918-   ), is an Austrian diplomat who became secretary-general of the United Nations (UN) in 1972. He replaced U Thant of Burma, who retired after holding the office for more than 10 years. Waldheim was the UN's fourth secretary-general. He was reelected in 1976.

When Waldheim began his first five-year term, the UN was deeply in debt. He stressed the need for additional funds and suggested that the UN reorganize its 4,000-member headquarters staff.

Waldheim was born near Vienna. He attended the Vienna Consular Academy and earned a law degree at the University of Vienna. Waldheim entered the Austrian foreign service in 1945. He became permanent Austrian observer at the UN in 1955 and headed Austria's first delegation to the UN that same year. From 1964 to 1968, and again from 1970 to 1971, he served as Austria's representative at the UN. Waldheim also served as Austrian minister to Canada from 1956 to 1958 and as ambassador to Canada from 1958 to 1960. He was Austria's foreign minister from 1968 to 1970. Waldheim ran for president of Austria in 1971 but lost to President Franz Jonas.   RAYMOND E. LINDGREN

See also UNITED NATIONS (The Secretariat [picture]).

WALDSEEMÜLLER, MARTIN. See MAP (Famous Map Makers).

Peter Baker Photography

Many Cottages in Northern Wales, such as the one above near Mount Snowdon, are small and built low to the ground.

G. R. Roberts from Carl Östman

A Love for Music is a famous characteristic of the Welsh people. The Welsh children shown above are playing recorders.

WALES

WALES is one of the four countries that make up the UNITED KINGDOM OF GREAT BRITAIN AND NORTHERN IRELAND. The other countries are England, Northern Ireland, and Scotland. Wales is slightly larger than the state of New Jersey. Cardiff is the capital and largest city of Wales.

Wales occupies a wide peninsula on the west coast of the island of Great Britain. It takes up about a tenth of the island. Much of Wales is a land of low, broad mountains and deep, green valleys.

Most of the Welsh people live in coal-mining regions and industrial cities and towns in southern Wales. The Welsh have great pride in their country. Although Wales has been united with England for more than 400 years, the Welsh have kept alive their own language, literature, and traditions.

This article tells about the people, geography, and economy of Wales. It also traces the country's history up to 1536, when Wales was united with England. For a discussion of Great Britain as a whole, of the relation of Wales to the other British countries, and of Britain's history, see the WORLD BOOK article on GREAT BRITAIN.

Government

Wales is part of Great Britain, a constitutional monarchy. Queen Elizabeth II is Britain's head of state, but a Cabinet of government officials called *ministers* actually rules the nation. The prime minister is the chief

governing official. Britain's laws are made by *Parliament*, which consists of the *House of Commons* and the *House of Lords*. Wales elects 36 of the 630 members of the House of Commons. Most members of the House of Lords are nobles who inherit their seats. For more information on the British government, see GREAT BRITAIN (Government).

The chief administrative official of Wales is the *secretary of state for Wales*, who is appointed by the British prime minister and is a member of the Cabinet. The secretary of state heads the *Welsh Office* in Cardiff. The

───────── **FACTS IN BRIEF** ─────────

Capital: Cardiff.

Official Languages: English and Welsh.

Form of Government: Constitutional monarchy; part of the United Kingdom of Great Britain and Northern Ireland (see GREAT BRITAIN [Government]).

Area: 8,019 sq. mi. (20,768 km²). *Greatest Distances—* north-south, 137 mi. (220 km); east-west, 116 mi. (187 km). *Coastline—*614 mi. (988 km).

Elevation: *Highest—*Snowdon, 3,561 ft. (1,085 m) above sea level. *Lowest—*sea level, along the coast.

Population: *Estimated 1980 Population—*2,800,000; distribution, 69 per cent urban, 31 per cent rural; density, 350 persons per sq. mi. (135 persons per km²). *1971 Census—*2,731,204. *Estimated 1985 Population—*2,843,000.

Chief Products: *Agriculture—*barley, cattle, hay, oats, potatoes, sheep, turnips. *Manufacturing—*aluminum, chemicals, electrical equipment, iron, motor vehicle parts, steel, synthetic fibers, tin plate. *Mining—*coal, limestone, slate.

Money: *Basic Unit—*pound. See MONEY (table: Exchange Rates [Great Britain]). See also POUND.

The contributors of this article are Norman Runnion, Editor of the Brattleboro (Vt.) Daily Reformer *and former London Correspondent of United Press International; Vernon F. Snow, Professor of History at Syracuse University; and J. Wreford Watson, Professor of Geography at Edinburgh University.*

Welsh Office carries out the day-to-day administration of Wales. It is responsible for housing, local government, national parks, public health, roads, town planning, water and sewerage systems, and welfare programs.

Wales is divided into various units for purposes of local government. The main units are *administrative counties* and *county boroughs*. The administrative counties are divided into *urban districts* (small towns) and *rural districts* (farming areas). The county boroughs are independent of administrative counties and are made up of cities and towns of more than 75,000 persons. Each unit of local government has its own elected council.

Some Welsh people are satisfied with their system of government, but others object to being governed by Great Britain. A Welsh nationalist party, the *Plaid Cymru*, seeks complete independence for Wales from Britain. Other Welsh people think that Wales should at least have its own legislative assembly to deal with

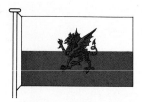 

The Unofficial Flag of Wales is more popular than the official one. The official flag includes the complete Welsh coat of arms.

The Welsh Coat of Arms. The dragon has been a Welsh symbol since the Romans occupied Wales nearly 2,000 years ago.

Wales occupies about a tenth of the island of Great Britain. The country is slightly larger than the state of New Jersey.

WORLD BOOK map

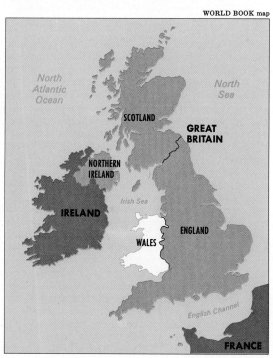

legislation that directly affects the country. In the 1970's, the British government worked out a plan under which Wales would be given this *home rule* power. In 1979, the Welsh people were given the opportunity to vote on the plan. They rejected it.

People

Ancestry and Population. Most of the Welsh are descended from peoples who began settling in the British Isles thousands of years ago. The earliest known settlers were the Iberians. Later, Celts, Romans, Anglo-Saxons, Vikings, Normans, and Englishmen invaded Wales. Struggles against these invaders, and efforts to earn a living from the harsh, rugged land, helped shape the strong, independent character of the Welsh people.

Wales has a population of about 2,800,000. About two-thirds of the people live in southeastern Wales, near large coal fields. The country has three cities with more than 100,000 persons. They are Cardiff, Swansea, and Newport, all on the southern coast. Cardiff, the capital and largest city, has a population of 276,880.

Language. Wales has two official languages, English and Welsh. About a fourth of the people speak Welsh. In some rural areas, almost three-fourths of the people speak it. Either English or Welsh may be used in the courts and for government business. Some newspapers are printed partly or entirely in Welsh, and radio and television programs are broadcast in both languages.

Welsh is a form of the ancient Celtic language and has been influenced by each group of invaders (see CELTS). The letters *j*, *k*, *q*, *v*, *x*, and *z* are not used in Welsh, and the letters *w* and *y* are sometimes used as vowels. Many Welsh words have a double *l* or a double *d*. The *ll* is pronounced like the *thl* in *athletics*. The *dd* is pronounced like the *th* in *this*.

Way of Life in industrial Welsh cities and towns is similar to that in industrial areas of England, Canada, and the United States. After working in a factory or office during the day, many Welsh people spend the evening watching television. Wales has two television networks—the British Broadcasting Corporation (BBC) and the Independent Television Authority (ITA). The British government regulates both networks, and television owners pay yearly fees. The fees help finance the BBC, which does not broadcast commercials.

Many Welsh people enjoy visiting the neighborhood *pub* (public house) in the evening. Pubs play an important part in social life throughout Great Britain. Friends gather in their favorite pubs to drink beer and talk.

In Welsh coal-mining regions, most people live crowded together in *row houses*, which are attached together in a row and are of the same design. The *pit* (mining) towns are known for being gloomy. But the areas around them are among the most scenic in Wales.

Welsh people in both the cities and the rural areas keep close family ties and are deeply religious. They love to sing—and to talk. The Welsh are famous for their excellent choirs and glee clubs.

A popular Welsh tradition is the *eisteddfod* (pronounced *ay STEHTH vahd*), a festival featuring poets, musicians, and singers. Eisteddfods began during the Middle Ages but died out. The Welsh started them again in the late 1800's to help keep their culture alive.

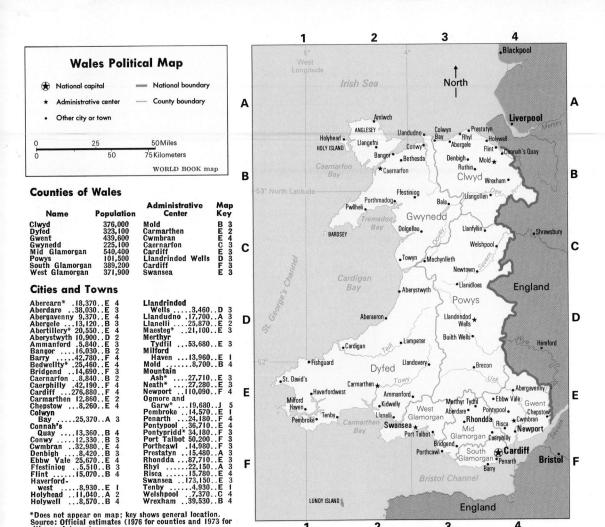

Wales Political Map

⊛ National capital — National boundary
★ Administrative center — — County boundary
• Other city or town

Miles: 0 — 25 — 50
Kilometers: 0 — 50 — 75

WORLD BOOK map

Counties of Wales

Name	Population	Administrative Center	Map Key
Clwyd	376,000	Mold	B 3
Dyfed	323,100	Carmarthen	E 2
Gwent	439,600	Cwmbran	E 4
Gwynedd	225,100	Caernarfon	C 3
Mid Glamorgan	540,400	Cardiff	E 3
Powys	101,500	Llandrindod Wells	D 3
South Glamorgan	389,200	Cardiff	F 3
West Glamorgan	371,900	Swansea	E 3

Cities and Towns

Abercarn*	18,370	E	4
Aberdare	38,030	E	3
Abergavenny	9,370	E	4
Abergele	13,120	B	3
Abertillery*	20,550	E	4
Aberystwyth	10,900	D	2
Ammanford	5,840	E	3
Bangor	16,030	B	2
Barry	42,780	F	4
Bedwellty*	25,460	E	4
Bridgend	14,690	F	3
Caernarfon	8,840	B	2
Caerphilly	42,190	F	4
Cardiff	276,880	F	4
Carmarthen	12,860	E	2
Chepstow	8,260	E	4
Colwyn Bay	25,370	A	3
Connah's Quay	13,360	B	4
Conwy	12,330	B	3
Cwmbran	32,980	E	4
Denbigh	8,420	B	3
Ebbw Vale	25,670	E	4
Ffestiniog	5,510	B	3
Flint	15,070	B	4
Haverfordwest	8,930	E	1
Holyhead	11,040	A	2
Holywell	8,570	B	4
Llandrindod Wells	3,460	D	3
Llandudno	17,700	A	3
Llanelli	25,870	E	2
Maesteg*	21,100	E	3
Merthyr Tydfil	53,680	E	3
Milford Haven	13,960	E	1
Mold	8,700	B	4
Mountain Ash*	27,710	E	3
Neath*	27,280	E	3
Newport	110,090	F	4
Ogmore and Garw*	19,680	J	5
Pembroke	14,570	E	1
Penarth	24,180	F	4
Pontypool	36,710	E	4
Pontypridd*	34,180	F	3
Port Talbot	50,200	F	3
Porthcawl	14,980	F	3
Prestatyn	15,480	A	3
Rhondda	87,710	E	3
Rhyl	22,150	A	3
Risca	15,780	E	4
Swansea	173,150	E	3
Tenby	4,930	E	1
Welshpool	7,370	C	4
Wrexham	39,530	B	4

*Does not appear on map; key shows general location.
Source: Official estimates (1976 for counties and 1973 for cities and towns).

Each year, the people hold two world-famous eisteddfods. The Royal National Eisteddfod takes place in August. It is held in various cities and towns, alternately in northern and southern Wales. Only the Welsh language is used during this event. The International Music Eisteddfod is held in July at Llangollen in northern Wales. Both festivals attract visitors from throughout the world.

Food. Most Welsh cooking is simple. The people like roast lamb, roast beef, and mutton stew. Their most famous dish is *Welsh rabbit*, also called Welsh *rarebit*. It consists of melted cheese and butter mixed with beer and served on toast. Especially tasty Welsh foods include salmon from Welsh rivers and *bara laver*, a vegetable dish made from seaweed.

Recreation. Rugby, a form of football, is one of the most popular sports in Wales. Many Welsh people travel great distances to watch matches between teams from Wales and other countries. See RUGBY FOOTBALL.

Another popular sport is *football*, or soccer. The Football Association of Wales supervises amateur teams. Professional teams belong to the 92-team Football League of England and Wales. See SOCCER.

Cricket, which is somewhat like baseball, and dog racing are popular in southern Wales (see CRICKET).

In rural areas of northern Wales, many people hunt foxes and rabbits. The rugged Welsh mountains, especially those in Snowdonia National Park in northwestern Wales, provide excellent climbing areas.

Education. Wales and England have the same school system. It is supervised by the Department of Education and Science, a department of the British government, and by local education authorities. The local authorities resemble local boards of education in the United States.

All Welsh children between the ages of 5 and 16 must attend school. For many years, every child had to take an *11-plus* examination at about the age of 11. This test determines whether a student will enter a grammar, secondary-modern, or technical school. *Grammar schools* prepare students for college entrance. *Secondary-modern schools* provide a general education. *Technical schools* offer vocational training. Many local education authorities no longer require the 11-plus examination. They are replacing the specialized schools with *comprehensive schools*, which provide all three types of education under one roof. The comprehensive schools are similar to high schools in the United States.

Wales has one university, the University of Wales. The university has colleges in Aberystwyth, Bangor,

Cardiff, and Swansea. It also includes the Welsh School of Medicine and the Institute of Science and Technology, both in Cardiff, and St. David's College in Lampeter. It has a total enrollment of about 13,500.

Religion. Nearly all the Welsh people are Protestants. The Methodist Church is the largest Protestant church in Wales. Others include the Anglican, Baptist, Congregational, and Presbyterian. The Roman Catholic Church has about 140,000 members in Wales.

The Church of England became the official Welsh church in 1536. But by 1811, so many Welsh people had joined the Methodist Church that Wales formally separated from the Church of England. The Welsh Church Act of 1914 declared that the Church of England was no longer the official church of Wales.

The Arts. Wales is a country of poets and singers. The traditions of Welsh literature and music date back more than 1,000 years to the *bards* (poet-singers) of the Middle Ages (see BARD).

One of the greatest Welsh poems, the *Gododdin*, was written about 600. It describes a battle in Yorkshire. During the 1100's, Geoffrey of Monmouth wrote poems that helped spread the legends of King Arthur. Welsh legends of the 1200's and 1300's are found in the *Mabinogion*, a collection of stories based on Celtic myths. During the 1300's, one of the greatest Welsh poets, Dafydd ap Gwilym, wrote about nature and love. The most famous Welsh poet of the 1900's has been Dylan Thomas. See MYTHOLOGY (Celtic Mythology).

Most Welsh people love to sing, either alone or in a group. According to an old saying, when two Welshmen get together, they form a chorus. Nearly all Welsh villages and churches have choirs. Welsh songs have a hymnlike quality. One of the most famous songs is "Ar Hyd y Nos" ("All Through the Night").

The Land

Wales occupies a broad peninsula on the west coast of Great Britain. It covers 8,019 square miles (20,768 square kilometers). England lies east of Wales. The Irish Sea on the north and St. George's Channel on the west separate Wales from Ireland. The Bristol Channel lies to the south.

Surface Features. The Cambrian Mountains cover about two-thirds of Wales. In northern Wales, the mountains are steep and rugged. The highest peak in the country, 3,561-foot (1,085-meter) Snowdon (called *Eryri* in Welsh), rises in northwestern Wales. In central and southern Wales, the Cambrian range becomes flatter and forms large plateaus cut deeply by valleys. On the plateaus are pastures, grassy plains, and *bogs* (swamplands). In many areas, gorges mark the steep slopes leading from the plateaus to the valleys. Many small lakes and waterfalls dot the mountain region.

Coastal plains and river valleys cover about a third of Wales. Low, narrow plains stretch along the south and west coasts. The broadest lowlands are along the Dee, Severn, and Wye rivers, near the English border.

A large island, the Isle of Anglesey (*Môn* in Welsh), lies off the northwest coast. The Menai Strait separates the island from the mainland.

Rivers and Coastline. The largest rivers in Wales are the Severn, 210 miles (338 kilometers) long, and the

Wye, 130 miles (209 kilometers) long. Both begin near Aberystwyth, flow eastward into England, and then turn south and empty into the Bristol Channel. The River Dee, which flows northeastward from Bala Lake into the Irish Sea, forms part of the boundary between Wales and England. See SEVERN, RIVER.

Much of the country's coastline is jagged and lined with cliffs. The coastline is 614 miles (988 kilometers) long. Many natural bays and harbors lie along the coast. Milford Haven, one of the natural harbors that have been developed as ports, is used by large ships that carry oil to Great Britain.

Economy

The economy of Wales depends mainly on mining and manufacturing. Coal mining and metal processing have been the country's most important industries since the Industrial Revolution began in Great Britain in the 1700's. Most of the mines and factories are in southern Wales.

Natural Resources. Coal is the most important natural resource of Wales. The largest and richest deposits lie in the valleys of southern Wales. These deposits have been mined for over 150 years, but they still have large reserves. A smaller coal field is in the north.

In northern Wales, the Cambrian Mountains contain limestone and slate. One of the largest slate quarries in the world is in the northwest. Copper ore, iron ore, and other minerals are also found in northern Wales.

One of the country's chief resources is its plentiful water supply. Many large reservoirs have been created

Wales Physical Map

Most of Wales, except the coastal plains and river valleys, is covered by the Cambrian Mountains. A region of low plains, called the Welsh Marches, extends along the English border. The Welsh coast is irregular and has many bays and harbors.

WORLD BOOK map

by damming and flooding the deep valleys. Water from the reservoirs is used to produce hydroelectric power. It is also sold to cities in central England.

Manufacturing. About a third of all Welsh workers are employed in manufacturing. The country's chief manufactured products are aluminum, iron, iron and copper tubing, steel, steel rails, tin plate, and other metals and metal products. The area around Cardiff and Swansea is one of the world's greatest producers of metals and metal products. Plants in this area produce about a fourth of Great Britain's steel, a third of its aluminum, and all its tin plate. Wales imports most of its iron ore from Spain and northern Africa.

Other products manufactured in Wales include asbestos, chemicals, electrical equipment, motor vehicle parts, plastics, and *synthetic* (man-made) fibers.

Agriculture. Most Welsh farms are in lowland areas —along the coasts and in the river valleys. The farms do not produce enough food for all the country's people, and so much food must be imported. The chief Welsh crops are barley, hay, oats, potatoes, and turnips. Most lowland farmers also raise beef and dairy cattle. Sheep are raised in mountain areas, where the land is too steep for growing crops. Wales exports much wool.

Mining. Coal mining is one of the most important industries in Wales, but it has declined steadily because of falling demand. Between 1947 and 1966, 115 coal mines closed in southern Wales. Today, about 60 mines remain open. They employ about 56,000 miners. Both iron and copper mining are also declining, because the deposits have been nearly worked out.

Limestone and slate are taken from stone quarries in the mountains. The limestone is used for building materials and to make lime, which has many industrial uses. Slate is exported for use as roofing material.

History

Scholars do not know how long men have lived in what is now Wales. But they do know that people called

Iberians lived there between about 6000 and 3000 B.C. These people used flint to make tools.

About 2000 B.C., people called the *Beaker folk* settled the Wales region. Their name comes from small clay containers called *beakers*, which they buried with their dead. The Beaker folk raised crops and made bronze tools. About 600 B.C., the Celts invaded and conquered the country. The Celts introduced the use of iron in Wales.

The Romans, who had conquered England in A.D. 43, conquered Wales between A.D. 60 and 75. They controlled the country for nearly 400 years and built roads, walls, cities, and castles throughout Wales.

Struggles Against the Anglo-Saxons. The Romans left Wales and England in the early 400's. Soon afterward, Angles and Saxons from northern Germany invaded eastern, southern, and central England. They conquered all the Celtic tribes in England except the Britons, who fled to Wales. For hundreds of years, the Britons succeeded in keeping Wales independent.

During their long struggle against the Anglo-Saxons, the Welsh frequently sent raiders into England. To stop the raids, Offa II, ruler of the kingdom of Mercia, built a boundary between Mercia and Wales in the late 700's. The boundary, called *Offa's Dike*, still stands. It

---

IMPORTANT DATES IN WALES

A.D. 60-75 Roman armies conquered Wales.

1071 William the Conqueror declared himself lord of Wales.

1282 English troops killed Llewelyn ap Griffith, Prince of Wales, in battle, crushing a Welsh revolt.

1301 Edward I gave the title Prince of Wales to his son.

1402-1410 Owen Glendower revolted against English rule.

1485 Henry Tudor, a Welsh prince, became King Henry VII of England.

1536 Henry VIII united Wales and England.
(For later dates, see ENGLAND [History]; GREAT BRITAIN [History]).

Welsh Mining Villages have long rows of attached houses. The villages are known for being dreary, but they are surrounded by beautiful green countryside.

consists of a ditch and earthen wall from the River Wye to the River Dee.

Revolts Against England. William the Conqueror and his Norman armies won control of England in 1066. In 1071, William declared himself lord of Wales. To keep the Welsh under control, he gave lands along the border between England and Wales to Norman barons. These borderlands were called the *Marches*, and the barons were known as *marcher lords*. The marcher lords built castles on their lands and gradually expanded their estates. They soon controlled most of central and southern Wales. The Welsh people were divided into various tribes headed by chieftains. Some chieftains accepted the barons so that they could stay on their land. But many others fought for their independence, and the Welsh regained much of their land during the 1100's.

During the 1200's, Llewelyn ap Griffith, a Welsh prince, won control of most of Wales. King Henry III of England recognized Llewelyn as Prince of Wales in 1267. In return, Llewelyn had to recognize Henry as his superior. But after Henry died in 1272, Llewelyn refused to accept his son, Edward I, as a superior. The dispute led the Welsh to revolt in 1282. Llewelyn was killed in battle, and the revolt collapsed.

In 1284, Edward I issued the Statute of Rhuddlan. This order placed northern Wales directly under English control and established royal courts at Caernarfon. It also divided central and southern Wales into counties under the control of English sheriffs. In 1301, Edward I gave the title Prince of Wales to his son, Edward, who was born at Caernarfon Castle. Since then, all English monarchs except Edward II have given the title to their oldest son.

During the 1300's, the Welsh revolted many times against English rule. In 1402, one rebel leader, Owen Glendower, drove the English out of much of Wales. But by 1410, the English regained control.

Union with England. In 1485, Henry Tudor, a Welsh prince, became King Henry VII of England. The Welsh people then gradually began to accept the idea of uniting with England. In 1536, Henry VII's son, Henry VIII, was able to join the two countries under one government. Welsh counties and some Welsh towns were given representation in the English Parliament. English became the official language of Wales, and the Church of England became the country's official church.

After 1536, the history of Wales thus became part of the history of England and, later, of Great Britain. For the story of England and Britain, see ENGLAND (History); GREAT BRITAIN (History).

NORMAN RUNNION, VERNON F. SNOW, and J. WREFORD WATSON

Related Articles in WORLD BOOK include:

BIOGRAPHIES

Bradley, Francis H.	Lloyd George, David
Geoffrey of Monmouth	Owen (Robert)
John, Augustus E.	Thomas, Dylan
Lawrence, T. E.	Williams, Emlyn

CITIES AND TOWNS

Aberystwyth	Cardiff	Swansea
Caernarfon	Merthyr Tydfil	

Llanfairpwllgwyngyllgogerychwyrndrobwllllantysiliogogogoch

Popperfoto

The Prince of Wales, traditionally the eldest son of the British monarch, officially receives his title in a colorful *investiture* ceremony. Prince Charles, son of Queen Elizabeth II, was invested by his mother at Caernarfon Castle in Caernarfon in 1969.

HISTORY

Celts	David, Saint	Prince of Wales

PHYSICAL FEATURES

Bristol Channel	Severn, River
Saint George's Channel	

OTHER RELATED ARTICLES

Bard	Leek
Clothing (picture: Traditional Costumes)	Saint David's
Great Britain (picture:	Day
Mountain Climbing)	

Outline

I. Government

II. People

A. Ancestry and Population	E. Recreation
B. Language	F. Education
C. Way of Life	G. Religion
D. Food	H. The Arts

III. The Land

A. Surface Features	B. Rivers and Coastline

IV. Economy

A. Natural Resources
B. Manufacturing
C. Agriculture
D. Mining

V. History

Questions

What is an *eisteddfod?*

What is the title of the chief administrative official of Wales?

Who were the *marcher lords?*

What mountain range covers most of Wales?

How are *ll* and *dd* pronounced in Welsh?

What is the *Plaid Cymru?*

Who has been the most famous Welsh poet of the 1900's?

How did union with England affect Wales?

On what two activities does the economy of Wales mainly depend?

What is the most famous Welsh dish?

What are the two official languages of Wales?

In what part of Wales do most of the Welsh people live?

WALES, PRINCE OF. See PRINCE OF WALES.

WALK. See HORSE (Gaits).

WALKER, DAVID (1785-1830), was a black American abolitionist who wrote a famous antislavery pamphlet. This pamphlet, called *An Appeal to the Colored Citizens of the World* (1829), urged American slaves to fight for their freedom. Its publication marked the beginning of the radical antislavery movement in the United States. The *Appeal* was the strongest attack on slavery made up to that time by a black writer.

Walker was born a free man in Wilmington, N.C. His father had been a slave, and his mother a free woman. Walker educated himself. In 1827, he settled in Boston and established a second-hand clothing business. He became a leader in Boston's Colored Association, which worked against slavery. He also wrote for and helped distribute *Freedom's Journal*, the first black newspaper in the United States.

After the publication of the *Appeal*, rumors circulated of large rewards being offered for Walker, dead or alive. Walker died under mysterious circumstances, reportedly of poisoning. Many abolitionists believed he had been murdered.   OTEY M. SCRUGGS

WALKER, JAMES JOHN (1881-1946), served as Democratic mayor of New York City from 1926 to 1932. Handsome and fun-loving, he came to symbolize the *Roaring Twenties*. In 1932, Governor Franklin D. Roosevelt called Walker to Albany to explain corruption in the city's affairs. Investigation showed that Walker had been more careless than crooked, but his reputation was injured, and he resigned as mayor. Walker, who was known by the nickname Jimmy, was born in New York City.   JOHN A. GARRATY

Wide World
Jimmy Walker

WALKER, JOHN. See MATCH (The First Matches).

WALKER, LEROY POPE (1817-1884), served in 1861 as the first Confederate secretary of war. He was appointed because he was a leading Alabama secessionist. As war secretary, he had little or no influence on military strategy, but he worked hard to raise troops and obtain war materials for the Confederacy. The success of the Confederate armies during the first year of the Civil War owed much to his efforts. Walker later became a Confederate brigadier general. He was born in Huntsville, Ala.   RICHARD N. CURRENT

WALKER, MARY EDWARDS (1832-1919), was the only woman to receive the Medal of Honor, the highest military award given by the United States government. She was a pioneer woman physician and a supporter of the women's rights movement of the late 1800's.

Walker served as a surgeon with the Union Army during the Civil War. In 1864, she was captured and held for four months in a Confederate prison. She was released in exchange for a Confederate officer. In 1865, she was awarded the Medal of Honor for her medical treatment of Union soldiers.

Walker helped lead a movement aimed at ending the social restrictions on the way women dressed. She believed that women should be allowed to wear whatever they pleased and became known for wearing trousers. Walker also campaigned to give women the right to vote. She wrote several books on the role of women in society, including *Hit* (1871) and *Unmasked, or the Science of Immorality* (1878).

Walker was born in Oswego, N.Y., and graduated from Syracuse Medical College. In 1917, a federal review board revoked her Medal of Honor, claiming that she had never actually served in the Army. The Army restored her award in 1977.   MIRIAM SCHNEIR

WALKER, WALTON HARRIS. See KOREAN WAR (The Land War).

WALKER, WILLIAM (1824-1860), an was American *filibuster* (military adventurer). He tried to make himself ruler of two Central American republics.

In 1853, Walker gathered a company of soldiers and tried to conquer Lower California and the state of Sonora, both in Mexico. His attempt failed, and United States officials arrested him for violating neutrality laws. He was freed, and in 1855 he led a successful revolution in Nicaragua. He ruled as president from 1856 to 1857, but then was forced to leave.

Walker tried to gain control of Honduras in 1860, but the Honduran government captured and executed him. He was born in Nashville, Tenn.   WAYNE GARD

WALKIE-TALKIE is a hand-held two-way radio that provides quick communication. Police officers, soldiers, sports enthusiasts, and workers use walkie-talkies.

Many walkie-talkies transmit with a power of less than one-tenth watt. They can send and receive messages over distances up to 1 mile (1.6 kilometers). Other walkie-talkies have from 1 to 4 watts of transmitted power, and can send and receive messages over maximum distances of 2 to 4 miles (3 to 6 kilometers). However, under certain conditions, walkie-talkie signals can travel over hundreds of miles or kilometers from the source. This happens when the signal *skips* (is reflected off the ionosphere). Electrical devices operating nearby, and such obstacles as buildings, may cut down a walkie-talkie's effective range.

Walkie-talkies of less than one-tenth watt that have been manufactured since Jan. 1, 1977, operate on frequencies between 49.82 and 49.90 megahertz. The more powerful types of walkie-talkies operate between 26.965 and 27.405 megahertz.

In the United States, a license is required to operate a walkie-talkie of more than one-tenth watt. Any citizen 18 years old or older may obtain a license from the Federal Communications Commission.   FOREST H. BELT

See also CITIZENS BAND RADIO.

WALKING, as a competitive sport, is a race between two or more persons, or against time. Most races are held at distances ranging from 20 kilometers to 50 kilometers. In one event, the winner is decided by which competitor covers the greatest distance in two hours.

Competitive walkers developed a method of walking called the "heel-and-toe." A long stride lands the foot on the heel and swings the walker forward to put weight quickly on the toe. The toe acts as a springboard for the next stride. At least part of one foot must always be on the ground and the leg must be completely straight, or *locked*, momentarily during each step. A nonracing walker covers 1 mile (1.6 kilometers) in 15 to 20 minutes. A heel-and-toe expert can do it in 6½ minutes, only 2½ minutes slower than a champion mile runner.

The walking contest was popular in England for hundreds of years before it was introduced into the United States during the 1870's. In the United States, contestants once competed in six-day marathons on indoor oval tracks. BERT NELSON

WALKING LEAF. See LEAF INSECT.

WALKING STICK is an insect that looks like a twig. The strange appearance of this insect hides it from its enemies. There are several kinds of these insects in the United States. The common walking stick of the Eastern states has long legs and a slender body that is 2

Lars Hedman

The Walking Stick's coloring makes it hard to see. It looks so much like a twig that it escapes the notice of its enemies.

to 3 inches (5 to 8 centimeters) long. Unlike most insects, it has no wings. It may be brown or green. It eats leaves, and sometimes harms trees. The female usually drops her eggs on the ground. The young are neglected, and few survive.

Scientific Classification. Walking sticks make up the walking stick family, *Phasmidae*. The common walking stick is genus *Diapheromera*, species *D. femorata*. URL LANHAM

See also LEAF INSECT.

WALKÜRE, DIE. See OPERA (*Ring of the Nibelung*).

WALL OF CHINA. See GREAT WALL OF CHINA.

WALL OF SHAME. See BERLIN (The Wall of Shame).

WALL PAINTING. See MURAL.

WALL STREET is a short, narrow street in New York City. Along with Broad and New Streets, it forms a triangle where the New York Stock Exchange and many great commercial houses and banks are located. For location, see NEW YORK CITY (map). The district is the heart of U.S. banking and business and an international

symbol of finance. See also NEW YORK CITY (Settlement); TREATY (picture).

WALLA WALLA, Wash. (pop. 23,619), is the trading and shipping center for the truck farms and ranches of southeastern Washington and northeastern Oregon (see WASHINGTON [political map]). *Walla Walla* is the Indian name for *place of many waters*. They gave this name to the region because of its many streams.

Large quantities of fruits and vegetables are produced on the farms near Walla Walla. Whitman Mission National Historic Site is to the southwest. The city is the home of Whitman College. Walla Walla College is nearby. Walla Walla was founded as a military post in 1855. The seat of Walla Walla County, the city has a council-manager government. HOWARD J. CRITCHFIELD

WALLABY. See KANGAROO; ANIMAL (picture).

WALLACE, ALFRED RUSSEL (1823-1913), was a British naturalist and explorer. He became famous by reaching independently the same explanation for evolution as Charles Darwin did. He also laid the basis for the study of animal geography. He spent five years in the Amazon Valley and nine in the East Indies collecting data on animals. He wrote *The Malay Archipelago* (1869), and *Geographical Distribution of Animals* (1876). He was born in Usk, England. LORUS J. and MARGERY MILNE

See also DARWIN, CHARLES R.; WALLACE'S LINE.

WALLACE, GEORGE CORLEY (1919-   ), an American political leader, gained national attention for his strong support of states' rights and his opposition to school integration. Wallace served as governor of Alabama from 1963 to 1967 and again from 1971 to 1979. Wallace was a presidential candidate in 1968, 1972, and 1976. While campaigning in 1972, he was shot and seriously wounded.

Wallace was born in Clio, Ala., and graduated from the University of Alabama Law School in 1942. He was captain of the university boxing team and won academic honors in college. After serving three years in the Army Air Forces, he entered politics. A Democrat, he served in the Alabama legislature from 1947 to 1953 and as state judge from 1953 to 1958. He ran for governor in 1958, but lost. He ran again in 1962 and won.

As governor of Alabama, Wallace opposed federal involvement in what he considered state problems, especially school integration. At his inauguration in 1963, he pledged: "Segregation now, segregation tomorrow, and segregation forever." He denounced federal court orders to end school segregation. His "stand in the doorway" at the University of Alabama in 1963, opposing the enrollment of two black students, made him a hero to opponents of integration. Actually, many Alabama schools became integrated during Wallace's first term.

Wallace's wife, Lurleen, ran for governor in 1966 because at that time Alabama law prohibited Wallace from serving two terms in a row. But most persons

The Wallace Campaign

George C. Wallace

understood that Wallace would continue to exercise the authority of governor. Mrs. Wallace won the election, but she died in office in 1968.

In 1968, Wallace was the presidential candidate of the American Independent Party (now called the American Party). He lost the election to Republican Richard M. Nixon and ran third behind Hubert H. Humphrey, the Democratic nominee. Wallace failed to achieve his goal of a deadlock in the Electoral College, which would have given him bargaining power to decide who became President. But he received almost 10 million votes. He carried five states and received 46 electoral votes. Wallace's running mate was retired Air Force General Curtis E. LeMay. See AMERICAN PARTY.

Wallace was again elected governor of Alabama in 1970. In 1971, he married Cornelia Ellis Snively, a niece of former Alabama Governor James E. Folsom. The Wallaces were divorced in 1978.

Wallace was the victim of an attempted assassination in May 1972, during his campaign for the 1972 Democratic presidential nomination. He was shot and seriously wounded in Laurel, Md. Arthur H. Bremer, a 21-year-old man from Milwaukee, was convicted of the shooting and sentenced to 53 years in prison. The shooting left Wallace's legs paralyzed. He did not win the Democratic nomination. He also failed to win the Democratic nomination in 1976.　　　DAVID S. BRODER

WALLACE, HENRY AGARD (1888-1965), served as Vice-President of the United States from 1941 to 1945 under President Franklin D. Roosevelt. He was also secretary of agriculture from 1933 to 1940 and secretary of commerce in 1945 and 1946. In 1948, he was the presidential nominee of the Progressive Party, a third political party. He was also an expert on plant culture, and developed a successful hybrid seed corn.

Wallace was one of the most controversial figures of the New Deal and Fair Deal periods (see NEW DEAL). He urged adoption of the Agricultural Adjustment Act, the first of many New Deal plans to regulate the farm problem by government planning. In 1946, President Truman asked him to resign as secretary of commerce because of Wallace's outspoken criticism of the U.S. "get-tough" policy toward Russia.

Wallace became the first Vice-President to take an active post in an administrative agency when Roosevelt appointed him chairman of the Board of Economic Warfare in 1941. The board was abolished in 1943 after a feud developed between Wallace and the Reconstruction Finance Corporation. Wallace was an important foreign policy adviser. He participated in the decisions that led to the development of the atomic bomb, and served as chairman of the Supply Priorities and Allocations Board. He was not renominated in 1944 because many powerful Democrats did not like his social idealism and internationalism.

Brown Bros.
Henry A. Wallace

Wallace was born in Adair County, Iowa. He was graduated from Iowa State College (now Iowa State University). When his father, Henry Cantwell Wallace (1866-1924), became United States secretary of agriculture in 1921, young Wallace took his place as editor of the family magazine, *Wallace's Farmer*. In 1950, he resigned from the Progressive Party because it had condemned U.S. intervention in Korea.　　IRVING G. WILLIAMS

WALLACE, HENRY C. See WALLACE, HENRY A.

WALLACE, LEW (1827-1905), was an American novelist, soldier, and politician. He wrote the novel *Ben-Hur: A Tale of the Christ* (1880). It sold more than 300,000 copies in 10 years, and helped popularize the historical novel as a literary form.

Born Lewis Wallace in Brookville, Ind., he worked as a court and legislative reporter, and studied law. He served as a volunteer in the Mexican War. After the war, he practiced law and entered politics. At the outbreak of the Civil War, Wallace became adjutant general of Indiana. He won promotion to the rank of major general of volunteers. In 1864, he temporarily stopped a Confederate offensive at the Battle of the Monocacy, an action that may have saved Washington, D.C., from capture. After the war, he served as governor of the New Mexico Territory from 1878 to 1881, and as minister to Turkey from 1881 to 1885.　　T. HARRY WILLIAMS

WALLACE, SIR WILLIAM (1272?-1305), was a Scottish patriot who led a revolt against King Edward I of England. The story of his life has stirred the national pride of Scots for more than 600 years.

In 1296, King Edward drove out the king of Scotland and stationed English soldiers in the country. Wallace, known for his strength and courage, became the leader of bands of Scottish patriots who carried on a bitter war against the invaders. The English raised an army and advanced against Wallace. He defeated them in the battle of Stirling Bridge. At that point, King Edward hurried home from France and led a great army against the rebels. His heavily armored soldiers defeated the Scottish clansmen at Falkirk. Wallace escaped and carried on the fight in the mountains. Seven years later, he was captured and executed for treason. PAUL M. KENDALL

WALLACE'S LINE is an imaginary line in the southwestern Pacific that divides the animal life of the Australian region from that of the Asiatic, or Oriental, region. The line begins at the Philippines and extends west, separating Celebes from Borneo and Bali from Lambok. Scientists named the line for Alfred Russel Wallace, an English naturalist. His researches convinced him that no two species are identical if they develop under different geographical and climatic conditions, even though they may be descended from a common ancestor. The animals of the southwest Pacific are supposedly different on the two sides of the line. See also WALLACE, ALFRED RUSSEL.　　GEORGE W. BEADLE

WALLACH, *VAHL ahk*, **OTTO** (1847-1931), a German chemist, worked out the nature of the complex mixtures found in ethereal oils of plants. He showed that they belonged to a group called *terpenes*. The nature of such products as perfumes and vitamins was discovered because of his work. Wallach received the 1910 Nobel prize for chemistry. He was born in Königsberg, East Prussia (now Kaliningrad, Russia).　　HENRY M. LEICESTER

WALLBOARD is a kind of board made of fibers of wood, cane, and other fibrous materials. It is used to cover walls and ceilings. Wallboard gives protection against fire and weather, and insulation against heat and cold. It absorbs sound and also serves as a decoration. Wallboard is made in sheets $\frac{1}{10}$ inch to 3 inches (2.5 to 76 millimeters) thick, depending on the kind of wallboard and its intended use. It is made in sections up to 8 feet (24 meters) wide and 20 feet (6 meters) long. A wall that is covered with wallboard rather than plaster is called a *dry wall*.

Fiberboard is made from masses of cane or wood fiber pressed into sheets (see FIBERBOARD). The fibers may be loosely compressed, leaving air spaces for good heat insulation and sound absorption. The surface of fiberboard is usually fibrous, but some is veneered with paper-thin sheets of mahogany and other woods. Fiberboard is used for interior surfaces and also for outside wall sheathing which is to be covered with wood siding or brick veneer. *Celotex* is the trade name of a well-known fiberboard made of cane fiber.

Hardboard is a variety of wallboard that is often used in making furniture. It is made by heating specially treated masses of wood fibers and placing them under great pressure to form a dense, hard board. *Tempered board* is made by further treatment of hard board with liquids and heat. *Plasterboard* has a core of gypsum that is sandwiched between layers of heavy paper.   GEORGE W. WASHA

WALLENSTEIN, *VAHL un shtyn,* **ALBRECHT WENZEL EUSEBIUS VON** (1583-1634), was one of the most important figures of the Thirty Years' War. He was the inspiration for Friedrich Schiller's tragedy, *Wallenstein*.

He was born in Bohemia of noble, Protestant parents. After he was expelled from the Lutheran school at Altdorf, he was converted to Catholicism and served with the Hungarian army. When the Thirty Years' War broke out, Wallenstein entered the service of Emperor Ferdinand II. He was rewarded with the Duchy of Friedland. He expanded the duchy, introduced agricultural reforms, and soon controlled a large prosperous area. He also recruited troops for the emperor, supplied them by plunder, and led them in battles in Denmark, Germany, and Bohemia.

Wallenstein believed he was destined to play a great political role. His goal was a huge central European empire that would dominate the Turks and western Europe. His great ambition and his intrigues with Protestant leader Gustavus Adolphus of Sweden alarmed the emperor and other Catholic princes. His officers deserted him, and he was murdered.   ROBERT G. L. WAITE

See also THIRTY YEARS' WAR.

WALLEYE. See FISH (picture: Fish of Temperate Fresh Waters); PERCH; PIKE.

WALLFLOWER is a fragrant plant that originated in southern Europe. It blooms in the spring, and bears clusters of single or double golden, maroon, or purple flowers. It is called *wallflower* because its stems often grow on walls and stony cliffs for support. The plants seem to thrive on the lime in cliffs. They grow well in England's cool climate and in warm southern areas of the United States. They are also called *gillyflowers*.

Scientific Classification. Wallflowers belong to the mustard family, *Cruciferae*. They are genus *Cheiranthus*, species *C. cheiri*.   ROBERT W. SCHERY

WALLIS AND FUTUNA ISLANDS are a French territory in the southwestern Pacific. They cover 106 square

miles (275 square kilometers) and have about 9,000 residents. They are made up of the Wallis Islands and the Hoorn Islands (Futuna and Alofi). The chief products are copra and timber.

WALLOONS, *wah LOONZ,* are a Celtic people who live in the provinces of southern Belgium. They are descendants of the ancient Belgae of Gaul who adopted Roman ways of life. Today, Walloon customs and language are much like those of the French.

WALLPAPER is decorative paper used to cover inside walls. Many wall coverings made of other materials—for example, burlap, linen, man-made fibers, plastics, and thin sheets of wood—are also considered wallpaper. A special paste, which is brushed onto the undecorated side of wallpaper, makes it stick to a wall. Manufacturers sell most wallpaper in rolls of sheets that measure about 30 feet (9.1 meters) long and $2\frac{1}{4}$ feet (69 centimeters) wide.

Most people use wallpaper to make a room more attractive. Colorful, lively patterned wallpaper can brighten a room at low cost. Soft pastels and small patterns can create a restful mood. Walls covered with shiny foil stripes, a delicate floral print, or other designs express the decorator's individuality.

Wallpaper also provides practical advantages. For example, it hides cracks, stains, and other flaws on walls. Paper made of plaster reinforced with plant fibers can be used to cover brick, concrete blocks, or rough plaster. Wallpaper made of a plastic material called *vinyl* can be scrubbed with a mild detergent and water. Its easy care makes it ideal for such areas as kitchens and children's playrooms, which become especially soiled. Many apartment dwellers and people who frequently redecorate use a special kind of wall covering called *strippable wallpaper*. It can be peeled off easily without damaging the wall.

How Wallpaper Is Made. Manufacturers make most wallpaper from softwoods, such as hemlock and spruce. Machines slice the wood into chips. The chips are cooked in a chemical solution until they form a soft mass called *sulfate pulp*. The pulp is then mixed with ground wood. This mixture goes through the same processes used in the manufacture of most other paper. Wallpaper is printed by a process called *gravure*. This process is also used to print wallpaper made of such woven fabrics as burlap and linen. See PAPER (How Paper Is Made); PRINTING (Printing by Gravure; Printing in Color).

After being printed, the wallpaper is put on racks to dry. Finally, it is measured into sheets, cut, wound onto rolls, and packed for shipment.

History. Scholars believe the first wallpaper was made in England, France, or The Netherlands during the 1500's. Artists designed patterned wallpaper as a cheaper substitute for the *tapestries* (woven wall hangings) that had decorated European palaces for centuries. Craftworkers painted designs on the paper by hand or printed them from carved blocks of wood. The Chinese began to make wallpaper in the early 1600's. They painted birds, flowers, and landscapes on rectangular sheets of rice paper. In the 1700's, the French decorated wallpaper with Chinese objects and patterns. This popular style became known as *chinoiserie*.

WALLPAPER

Wallpaper was first produced in the United States in Philadelphia in 1739. Landscapes, the architectural ruins of ancient Greece, and scenes from American life became favorite designs during the 1800's. In 1947, the B. F. Goodrich Chemical Company introduced a vinyl substance used in making washable, vinyl-covered wallpaper. Pre-pasted paper, which sticks to a wall when the paper is moistened with water, was developed in the 1950's. In 1975, Imperial Chemical Industries, Ltd., Great Britain's largest chemical company, began to sell wallpaper made of a kind of plastics called *polyethylene*. This paper is easy to hang because a special dripless paste is brushed directly onto the wall instead of onto the paper.   HOWARD A. RICKSPOONE

See also INTERIOR DECORATION.

L. W. Brownell

Pulpy Coverings called *hulls, above,* contain the nuts of a black walnut tree.

WORLD BOOK photo

The Nuts of the English Walnut Tree have a thin shell and a mild flavor.

U.S. Forest Service

The Bark of the black walnut tree has a rough texture and a dark color. The wood is dark purple-brown, with a fine grain and luster. Black walnut trees have yellow-green leaves.

Canada Dept. of Agriculture

The Black Walnut is a hardy tree that may grow 150 feet (46 meters) high. It is native to the Eastern United States and provides wood for furniture and gunstocks.

WALNUT is a forest tree that bears one of the most valuable of nuts. Several kinds of walnut trees grow in the United States. Two of these are native to the East, the *black walnut*, and the *white walnut*, also called the *butternut*. Another kind, the *English walnut* or *Persian walnut*, was brought to the United States from southern Europe. It is grown commercially in California and Oregon. Black and English walnut trees provide lumber for valuable furniture wood.

English Walnut trees bear walnuts that are the most valuable commercially. The trees have gray bark and usually are smaller than the American walnuts. They have large leaflets, soft wood, and a mild-flavored nut. The English walnut has been grown commercially in Europe since Roman times.

There are two kinds of English walnuts, the *Santa Barbara* and the *French*. The Santa Barbaras are less able to resist heat and cold and require a longer growing season than the French group. Santa Barbaras grow only along the coastal plains and the valleys of southern California. The French group resists extremes of heat and cold. It grows from central California to Oregon.

Neither kind of English walnuts grows well in the Southern States. These trees need deep, well-drained, fertile soil to give their best yield and quality. English walnut trees are also sensitive to alkali salts and must have pure irrigation water.

The English walnut produces small flowers, which may be cross-pollinated or self-pollinated. This thin-shelled nut tastes sweet. It contains fats and proteins.

Growers plant permanent trees at least 60 feet (18 meters) apart. They need no special care, except irrigation in some areas. When the nuts ripen, they are shaken down, hulled, and dried. At the packing houses, they are sorted, sized, bleached, blended, branded, and sacked for shipment. The poorer grades are shelled and used to make walnut oil and shell flour.

The United States leads in the production of walnuts, followed by France, Italy, India, and Turkey. California produces about 135,000 short tons (122,500 metric tons) per year. Oregon is next with about 2,000 short tons (1,800 metric tons) a year. The walnut industry is centered in the area around Stockton, Calif.

Black Walnut is a hardy Temperate Zone forest tree. It is grown mainly for lumber, although the nuts are also harvested and sold. These nuts have a distinctive and rich flavor, but their shell is hard and thick. They are usually shelled before they are sold. Growers have also developed a few thin-shelled varieties of these nuts.

Black walnut wood is dark purplish-brown, with a fine grain and luster. It is valuable for interior finishing, furniture, and gunstocks. This wood is becoming rare.

Scientific Classification. Walnuts belong to the walnut family, *Juglandaceae*. The English walnut is genus *Juglans*, species *J. regia*. The black walnut is *J. nigra*, and the butternut is *J. cinerea*. The two native California species are *J. hindsii* and *J. californica*.   THEODORE W. BRETZ

See also BUTTERNUT; TREE (Familiar Broadleaf and Needleleaf Trees [picture]).

WALNUT CANYON NATIONAL MONUMENT is in central Arizona. It contains 800-year-old cliff-dwelling ruins in shallow caves. The monument was established in 1915. For its area, see NATIONAL PARK SYSTEM (table: National Monuments).

WALPOLE is the family name of two famous Englishmen of the 1700's, father and son. They bore the title Earl of Orford. The father was a famous political leader, the son a noted writer.

Sir Robert Walpole (1676-1745) was the most influential politician in England during the first half of the 1700's. He became England's first prime minister, though the title was not official at the time. He sponsored no memorable legislation, and did nothing to raise the standard of conduct in government. But during the 21 years he governed Great Britain, he became famous for his ability to transact government business.

Walpole was born at Houghton, Norfolk, and was educated at Eton College and Cambridge University. He entered Parliament in 1701, and by 1710 was secretary at war and treasurer of the navy. He showed ability, but lost his offices when the Tories replaced the Whigs in 1710-1711. He then became the leader of the opposition in the House of Commons. The new government convicted him of graft and sent him to prison in 1712, but he returned to Parliament in 1713.

After George I became king in 1714, Walpole's political stature increased. He became first lord of the treasury in 1715, but resigned in 1717. During the next few years, he attacked the government and built up his influence in the House of Commons. His greatest triumph in this period came in 1718 when he defeated the Peerage Bill, which sought to limit the House of Lords to 216 members. He also profited politically from the collapse of the speculative South Sea Company in 1720, which disgraced the men in office.

In 1721, Walpole again became first lord of the treasury and chancellor of the exchequer. For the next 20 years, he was the most powerful person in Great Britain. His primary purpose was to govern Britain with as little excitement as possible. He left the direction of foreign affairs to others, and worked to control the House of Commons and build his personal interests. For years, Walpole defeated opposition by his debating skill, his power and influence, and his constant attendance in the House of Commons. Eventually Walpole lost

Sir Robert Walpole
Detail of an oil portrait (1740) by Jean-Baptiste van Loo; National Portrait Gallery, London

his vigor. In domestic affairs, his readiness to compromise and his preference for doing nothing brought criticism from William Pitt. Walpole was a man of peace who knew that in war even the victors lose. As the demand for war with Spain rose, his hold on the House of Commons declined. His loss of influence and failing health prompted him to resign in 1742. However, Walpole was almost immediately created Earl of Orford, and he influenced policies in the House of Lords until his death.   CHARLES F. MULLETT

Horace Walpole (1717-1797), the youngest son of the prime minister, was a letter writer, author, and art lover. Even at a time when personal letters were considered a minor art form, Walpole's huge correspondence is remarkable. His witty letters provide an entertaining documentary of life in English high society. They report social and political gossip, and express Walpole's opinions on literature and the arts.

As a scholar fascinated by medieval life, Walpole greatly influenced the Gothic revival of the late 1700's. He transformed Strawberry Hill, his house in Twickenham, into a miniature Gothic castle. He built a printing press nearby, and published many of his own writings. His most influential literary work is *The Castle of Otranto* (1764). This tale of terror and the supernatural was the first of what became known as Gothic novels.

Walpole was born in London. He served in Parliament from 1741 to 1768. In 1791, he succeeded to the family title as the fourth Earl of Orford.   MARTIN C. BATTESTIN

WALPOLE, SIR HUGH SEYMOUR (1884-1941), was one of the most popular British novelists in the early 1900's. His finest novels are probably the *Herries Chronicles* (1930-1933), a series of four historical novels set in England during the 1700's. The series includes *Rogue Herries, Judith Paris, The Fortress*, and *Vanessa*. Walpole wrote more than 30 other novels on a variety of subjects. In *The Dark Forest* (1916) and *The Secret City* (1919), he described his World War I experiences with the Red Cross in Russia. *The Cathedral* (1922) is based on his experiences as a clergyman's son. *Portrait of a Man with Red Hair* (1925) is a horror story about a brutal murderer.

Walpole was born in Auckland, New Zealand, and was sent to school in England at the age of five. He was knighted in 1937.   HARRY T. MOORE

WALPURGIS NIGHT, *vahl PUR gihs*, is the eve of May Day, when German people celebrate the feast of St. Walpurgis. According to legend, witches gather on this night and celebrate their Sabbath on mist-covered Brocken, the highest peak in the Harz Mountains.

WALRUS is a sea animal that lives in parts of the Arctic, North Atlantic, and North Pacific oceans. It has two ivory tusks, and its four feet are flattened into flippers. The flippers make the walrus a good swimmer.

During the winter and spring, walruses drift along on large floating fields of ice. In summer, some may rest on shore. A walrus spends much time in the water searching for food. It looks for clams, its favorite food, probably while skidding along the ocean bottom on its tusks. The animal uses its tongue to form a vacuum to suck clams into its mouth. A walrus has bristles on its upper lip. These bristles are sensitive to touch and probably help the walrus find food.

A Group of Walruses Rests on an Ice Floe in the Arctic. Each of the Larger Animals May Weigh over a Ton.

Scientists classify the walrus as a kind of large seal. An adult male grows about 12 feet (3.7 meters) long and weighs up to 3,000 pounds (1,400 kilograms).

The walrus is the only seal with tusks. The tusks, which are its upper canine teeth, point downward and may grow as long as 39 inches (99 centimeters). A walrus defends itself from polar bears with its tusks. It also uses them as hooks when climbing onto ice. Walruses do not attack man, but an angry, wounded walrus can injure a hunter and damage his boat with its tusks. A walrus makes a loud bellow that can be heard for $\frac{1}{2}$ mile (0.8 kilometer). This bellowing helps hunters find the animals.

Walruses are mammals. A female walrus usually has one calf every other year and cares for her young for about two years. Twins are very rare. Baby walruses are grayish-brown, and adults are rusty-brown. Some walruses live as long as 40 years.

Most walruses live in herds, but some live alone. Some Eskimos hunt walruses. They eat the meat, use the hides to make shelters or boats, and burn the blubber oil for heat and light. Some Eskimos carve walrus tusks into figures of animals and hunting scenes.

Scientific Classification. The walrus is in the order *Pinnipedia*. It forms the walrus family, *Odobenidae*. It is genus *Odobenus*, species *O. rosmarus*.   KARL W. KENYON

See also ANIMAL (color picture: Animals of the Polar Regions); SEAL.

WALT DISNEY WORLD. See FLORIDA (Places to Visit).

WALTER, *VAHL tur,* **BRUNO** (1876-1962), was one of the leading symphony orchestra and opera conductors of the 1900's. He became noted for the warmth and insight of his musical interpretations. He was also known for his support of the music of his friend Gustav Mahler (see MAHLER, GUSTAV).

Walter was born in Berlin, where he received his musical education. His real name was Bruno Walter Schlesinger. At the age of 18, he became an assistant to Mahler, who was director of the Hamburg Opera. Their association continued until Mahler died in 1911.

While still a young man, Walter became one of the most celebrated conductors in central Europe and held several important positions. He moved to the United States in 1939. He frequently conducted the New York Philharmonic Orchestra from 1941 to 1957 and at the Metropolitan Opera from 1941 to 1959. ROBERT C. MARSH

WALTER, THOMAS USTICK (1804-1887), an American architect, became noted for his buildings in the Greek Revival style. He is known chiefly as the architect of the United States Capitol from 1851 to 1865. He added the Senate and House wings, and the large cast-iron dome, painted to resemble stone. Walter was born in Philadelphia. With Richard Upjohn, he founded the American Institute of Architects.   HUGH MORRISON

WALTER REED ARMY MEDICAL CENTER, Washington, D.C., provides care for servicemen and government officials. It also conducts scientific research and trains doctors in advanced methods. It covers 113 acres (46 hectares) in Washington, and also includes 118 acres (48 hectares) in Forest Glen and 22 acres (9 hectares) in Glenhaven, both in Maryland. Major activities of the center are the Walter Reed General Hospital, Walter Reed Army Institute of Research, Biomechanical Research Laboratory, Institute of Dental Research, and Armed Forces Institute of Pathology. The center was named for Walter Reed, an Army surgeon who helped conquer typhoid fever and yellow fever (see REED, WALTER).   SAMUEL J. ZISKIND

WALTHER VON DER VOGELWEIDE, *foh gel VY duh* (1170?-1230?), was perhaps the greatest of the medieval *minnesingers* (love poets). Walther was born in Austria, and he lived during the period when the elegance and grace of aristocratic culture flourished. He was a poet in the court of Vienna but apparently had to leave when his patron died. He then moved from court to court until, late in life, he received a grant of land from German Emperor Frederick II.

Walther's love poetry differed from the conventions of courtly *minnesang,* which celebrated a hopeless love for some high-born lady. Walther praised the love for a village girl. He also raised poems of political commentary to a high art. His large and varied poetic production shows originality. His technique ranges from simple to highly complex forms.   JAMES F. POAG

WALTON, ERNEST THOMAS SINTON (1903-   ), an Irish physicist, shared the 1951 Nobel prize in physics with Sir John Cockcroft. They discovered jointly the transmutations of atomic nuclei by artificially accelerated particles in 1932. They constructed the first of the controlled particle accelerators, producing 600,000 volts. Their experiments confirmed Albert Einstein's theory that mass and energy are equivalent in nuclear reactions. Walton was born in Dungarvan. See also COCKCROFT, SIR JOHN DOUGLAS.

WALTON, GEORGE (1741-1804), a Georgia signer of the Declaration of Independence, served as governor and chief justice of Georgia several times. In 1775, he became secretary of the provincial congress and president of the council of safety. He served as a delegate to the Continental Congress from 1776 to 1781. Walton fought in the defense of Savannah in 1778, and was wounded and captured by the British. He was a United States senator in 1795 and 1796. He was born near Farmville, Va.   RICHARD B. MORRIS

WALTON, IZAAK (1593-1683), an English author, became known for his classic on fishing, *The Compleat Angler* (1653). It is written as a conversation between Piscator, a fisherman, and Venator, a hunter. Piscator, who is Walton himself, converts Venator to the joys of fishing and instructs him in how to catch trout, salmon, carp, and other English fish. The writing style breathes serenity and contentment.

Walton also wrote short biographies of five clergymen and authors whose holiness he admired. His best-known lives are those of John Donne and Richard Hooker. He acquired the material from the men themselves, their friends, and letters and records.

Walton was born in Stafford, and became a merchant or tradesman in London. He read widely, and his schooling was probably good, though he did not go to a university. He lived 90 years and went fishing until he was 83. The Izaak Walton League, a conservation organization, is named for him.   ARNOLD WILLIAMS

WALTON, SIR WILLIAM (1902-   ), a versatile British composer, achieved recognition in 1926 with his setting of Edith Sitwell's satirical poems, *Façade*. He composed *Viola Concerto* (1929); a brilliant oratorio, *Belshazzar's Feast* (1931); *Violin Concerto* (1939); an opera, *Troilus and Cressida* (1954); and the scores for several motion pictures. Walton was born at Oldham. HALSEY STEVENS

WALTZ is a round dance for couples in $\frac{3}{4}$ time. The waltz developed from the *Weller*, a German peasant dance, and the *Laendler*, an Austrian dance. Two famous types of the waltz are the fast *Viennese*, in which the couples turn in one direction, and the slower *Boston*, in which couples turn in several directions. The waltz was the most popular dance of the 1800's, and is still a favorite. Waltz music is also found in many operas and orchestral pieces. Hector Berlioz, Wolfgang Amadeus Mozart, Maurice Ravel, Richard Strauss, the Strauss family (including Johann, the younger Johann, and Joseph), and many others used light and airy waltz

music in the compositions they wrote. See also DANCING (The Rise of Romanticism; picture); STRAUSS (Johann, Jr.).   WALTER SORELL

WAMPANOAG INDIANS. See MASSASOIT; PHILIP, KING; INDIAN, AMERICAN (Table of Tribes); RHODE ISLAND (King Philip's War).

WAMPUM is a name for white, purple, or black beads made from shells. The Indians in the eastern part of North America once used wampum as money. They also used it as a decoration, and wore it on holidays. The Indians made wampum into belts or wove it into clothing to stand for wealth or power. The colors of the beads stood for certain things. The Indians believed that white stood for health, peace, and riches. Purple and black meant sorrow or sympathy with another's sorrow. Dark beads were often more valuable than white ones.

The beads were made from the insides of shells and were about $\frac{1}{4}$ inch (6 millimeters) long, and half that wide. They were often strung on a strip of animal skin.

Wampum served as money for trade between the Indians and the colonists in the early days of America. Most of the things bought or sold were exchanged on the basis of how much they were worth in wampum. Colonists set up a standard of value for wampum. Six beads were worth a penny in some places. A 6-foot (1.8-meter) string of beads was worth 5 to 10 shillings.

Indians and colonists often exchanged belts of wampum as a sign of good faith when treaties and agreements were made. In 1661, the use of wampum as money was stopped in many places because so much false wampum was in circulation. But strings of beads were considered valuable for exchange purposes until the 1700's. Shells have served as money in many lands and among many different peoples, especially in Asia, Polynesia, and Australia.   BURTON H. HOBSON

WANAMAKER, JOHN (1838-1922), was an American merchant and philanthropist. In 1860, he joined his brother-in-law in founding a clothing business in Philadelphia. This business grew into John Wanamaker & Company, one of the largest department stores in the United States. Wanamaker became active in politics and served as Postmaster General of the United States from 1889 to 1893. He contributed generously to colleges and churches in many parts of the world. He was born in Philadelphia.   W. H. BAUGHN

WANDERING JEW. An old Christian legend told of a Jew who was doomed to wander over the earth forever because he joined in the mocking of Jesus at the time of the Crucifixion.

WANDERING JEW is the common name for certain kinds of plants belonging to the spiderwort family. They

Field Museum of Natural History, Chicago (WORLD BOOK photo)

Wampum Necklaces Were Worn on Holidays by Some American Indians. The Indians also Used Wampum as Money.

WANG HUNG-WEN

The Wandering Jew's Striped Leaves and graceful flowers make it a favorite ornamental plant for indoor cultivation.

J. Horace McFarland

grow in the southern United States, Mexico, and South America. The name refers to the old legend of the Jew who was doomed to wander over the earth forever because he mocked Jesus as He carried the cross. These plants seem to wander all over and live indefinitely. They are grown as house plants for the beauty of their leaves, which have a silvery sheen. In the strong sunlight these leaves show white or cream stripes above, and reddish-purple beneath. The plants require much water and sunlight. They bear white or rose-red flowers.

Scientific Classification. The plants belong to the spiderwort family, *Commelinaceae*. They are genus *Tradescantia*, species *T. fluminensis*, with white flowers, and *Zebrina pendula* with rose-red flowers.   DONALD WYMAN

WANG HUNG-WEN, *wawng hoong wuhn* (1937?-), was second vice-chairman of the Central Committee of the Chinese Communist Party from 1973 to 1976. He rose to power after serving as a leading supporter of Party Chairman Mao Tse-tung during China's Cultural Revolution of the late 1960's. Mao and his followers organized this movement against government officials who were accused of disobeying Mao's teachings. Mao died in 1976, and Hua Kuo-feng succeeded him as party chairman. Hua and his followers publicly denounced Wang and three other leaders—including Mao's wife, Chiang Ch'ing—and accused them of failing to follow Mao's teachings. The four were removed from their leadership positions and reportedly arrested.

Historians know little about Wang's early life. He was probably born in Shanghai or in Kirin Province. During the Cultural Revolution, Wang became a leader of the city government of Shanghai.   DONALD W. KLEIN

WANG WEI (699-759) is remembered by Chinese art lovers as the first great Chinese landscape painter. No one thought of him that way in his own time. His reputation probably resulted from the fact that not only his pictures, but his whole way of life, seemed ideally beautiful. He made the best of two worlds—the busy court society where he had official duties, and the quiet countryside where his heart really lay. He was also a musician and poet. Wang Wei was born at T'ai-yüan.   ALEXANDER C. SOPER

WANKEL ENGINE is a gasoline engine that has a rotor instead of a piston. It is sometimes called a *rotary* engine. The engine was named for its inventor, Felix Wankel of Germany.

A Wankel engine operates more quietly and smoothly than a piston engine because it does not involve the *reciprocating* (back-and-forth) motion of pistons. It needs fewer moving parts, weighs less, and is smaller than a piston engine of the same power. A Wankel uses lower octane gasoline than a piston engine does, but it burns more fuel per mile or kilometer. Many engineers and environmental experts believe that the Wankel engine can help reduce air pollution from automobiles. Pollution control devices remove pollutants from the exhaust of a Wankel engine more easily than from the exhaust of a piston engine.

Manufacturers have built Wankel engines in a wide variety of sizes. These engines power automobiles and other vehicles, including boats, motorcycles, propeller airplanes, and snowmobiles.

How a Wankel Engine Works. The most important parts of a Wankel engine are its triangular rotor and specially shaped chamber. The rotor moves so that its tips always touch the walls of the chamber and divide the chamber into three areas. Different engine operations take place in each of these three areas. A Wankel engine may have several rotors, each with its own chamber.

A Wankel engine, like a four-stroke piston engine, goes through four steps to complete one cycle of operation: (1) *intake*, (2) *compression*, (3) *expansion* or *power*, and (4) *exhaust*. During the intake step, a combustible mixture of air and gasoline enters the chamber. This mixture is compressed into a smaller volume. One or two spark plugs then ignite the compressed mixture. The burning produces expanding gases that move the rotor. The exhaust step pushes the burned gases from the engine.

In a piston engine, each piston must move back and forth twice and stop four times to complete the cycle (see GASOLINE ENGINE [diagram: How a Four-Stroke Cycle Gasoline Engine Works]). The Wankel rotor turns

Mazda Motors of America, Inc.

A Small Wankel Engine can produce as much power as a larger and heavier piston engine. Wankel engines can power such vehicles as airplanes, automobiles, boats, and trucks.

HOW A WANKEL ENGINE WORKS

A Wankel engine uses triangular rotors instead of pistons in its specially shaped combustion chambers. As a rotor turns, each of its three sides goes through a four-step cycle that produces power in the engine. These steps are (1) intake, (2) compression, (3) expansion or power, and (4) exhaust.

WORLD BOOK diagram

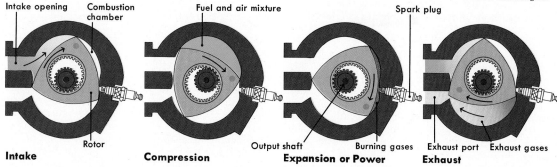

Intake

Fresh air mixed with fuel is drawn into the engine as a tip of the rotor, shown by a dot, passes the intake opening.

Compression

The rotor begins to compress the fuel and air mixture when the following tip of the rotor passes the intake opening.

Expansion or Power

The spark plug ignites the compressed mixture. The burning gases expand and move the rotor around the output shaft.

Exhaust

The burned gases leave the engine through the exhaust port after the rotor tip uncovers it. The cycle then begins again.

only once in its chamber to complete the cycle, and it never stops moving. The steps in the cycle occur at the same time in different areas of the chamber. Thus, a Wankel rotor produces three power strokes each time it rotates. The shaft connected to the rotor makes three revolutions for each turn of the rotor. As a result, the Wankel engine produces one power stroke per turn of its shaft. A piston engine, on the other hand, produces one power stroke every other time a piston moves down its cylinder. As a result, a small Wankel engine may generate the same power as a larger piston engine.

History. Felix Wankel developed the basic principles of his rotary engine during the early 1950's. By 1958, he and a team of researchers had worked out the present design of the engine. Automobile manufacturers rejected the engine at first because of its poor fuel economy, short operating life, and dirty exhaust. But after engineers began to solve some of these problems, the Wankel engine's simplicity and low cost caught the attention of the manufacturers. Since the mid-1960's, various automakers in Germany, Japan, and the United States have sought to develop efficient Wankel engines, but they have had only limited success. OTTO A. UYEHARA

WAPITI. See ELK; DEER (Kinds); MOOSE.

WAR. Since the dawn of history, people have fought against other people. Any struggle in which two large groups try to destroy or conquer each other is a war. There have been many kinds of wars. Families have fought against families, tribes against tribes, followers of one religion against followers of another. In modern times, wars have been fought between nations or groups of nations. Armies and navies once were almost the only factors in determining the outcome of wars. Now, civilians must join in the war effort if it is to succeed.

Wars have always caused great suffering and hardship. Most people hate war, yet for hundreds of years war has been going on somewhere in the world nearly all the time. Earthquakes and floods *happen* to people, but people *make* war themselves. To understand why wars go on when nearly everyone wants peace, we must look into the nature of war.

Causes of War. In modern times, no nation or group chooses war if it can get what it wants peacefully. The fighting starts when a nation wants something so badly that it is willing to go to war to get it. Sometimes war results from a disagreement between two nations, and sometimes from a desire for conquest. Some basic causes may be a desire for more land, a desire for more wealth, a desire for more power, or a desire for security.

War for Land to Live on. In ancient times, people often fought so that they could get enough to eat. When the pasture lands in Central Asia dried up, hungry tribes would make war on their neighbors in order to get new lands. The neighbors sometimes fought back. More often they gave up their lands and tried to seize those of a still weaker tribe.

Much of the fighting that went on between early American pioneers and American Indians was this kind of war. The Indians wanted to roam freely over the land, hunting, trapping, or fishing. The pioneers wanted to clear the land and plant it in crops. Indian fighting was dangerous, and no one who already had a good farm was likely to go out and fight the Indians for another. But landless people from abroad preferred the dangers of war to the horrors of poverty.

This type of war has not entirely disappeared, but it is no longer common or important. The early war for land to live on usually had these two important characteristics: those who did the fighting made the decision to fight, and the fighters wanted something for themselves.

War for Wealth. The peoples of ancient empires fought many wars for wealth. The decision to fight was made by the ruler and his or her advisers. The fighting was often done by hired armies. A ruler who sought to conquer new lands did not mean to drive the people out of the lands. Generally he or she just wanted to collect taxes from the people in the territory invaded.

When Alexander the Great led his armies against the Persian Empire, the common people of the invaded lands paid little attention, except to hope that their own property would not be destroyed. It usually made little difference to these people which ruler collected taxes.

WAR

Wars were fought solely by rulers and their armies.

In the Middle Ages, there were many wars for wealth. Often one noble would try to seize the property of another. He would use his own soldiers and perhaps hire other leaders and their soldiers to help him. Sometimes the conqueror of a city would take a large money payment in return for leaving the city in peace.

War for Power. The great European nations fought wars throughout the world to gain or increase their power. These wars united the people and strengthened the governments. Wars of conquest based on the ideas of a super-race or of a superior economic system are often wars to extend the power of a government.

War for Security. Most countries fear the possibility of attack, and maintain armed forces to defend themselves. Sometimes this fear may be directed toward a particular country. In that case a nation may decide to choose its own time and strike the first blow. Or it may decide to conquer some weaker neighbor, and thus increase its own resources as a defense against attack.

Differences Between Causes and Reasons. When a nation makes war, its government always states the *reasons* for the war. This is necessary if the people are to be united in the war effort. But the reasons given for a war need not be the same as its *causes*. For example, the government of the United States pointed to the British interference with American shipping and the impressment of American seamen as reasons for the War of 1812. A cause which was not stated was the desire on the part of some Americans to extend the United States into lands held by the British and their Spanish allies in North America. This was one of the important *causes* of the war, but it was not stated as a *reason*. The causes of war may be selfish, base, or even wicked, but the reasons stated are usually lofty and noble. Both sides in a war may show reasons which they consider to be valid.

War Means Absence of Law. War is not the only kind of struggle in which there may be some right on both sides. Almost every case that comes to trial before a court has this same quality. In a suit over property, both sides can usually show a claim of some sort. The court has to decide which is the *better* claim. If there were no court, both persons claiming the property might feel justified in fighting for it.

In frontier days many Westerners carried guns and settled their disputes by fighting. Until courts and police forces were established, they had no other way to settle quarrels in which both sides were partly right. People often joined forces against horse thieves and other "bad men," but they could not handle quarrels between honest men who disagreed about their rights.

Today a similar problem exists among nations. The people in any country are likely to see their own interests more clearly than they can see the interests of people in another country. People's own desires seem so reasonable and so important that the desires of people in another country are likely to look selfish and unreasonable. Laws and courts can take care of such disputes *within* a country, but there has as yet been no effective law *between* countries. That is why the use of force to settle a dispute is a *crime* within a country and a *war* between countries. War can exist only where there is no effective law.

Most Wars Have Several "Causes." In modern times, a nation usually does not make war for a single simple reason. There may be dozens or hundreds of causes for war. In every country there are groups of people with different aims and different hopes. When nearly all these groups are willing, each for its own reasons, to run the risk of war, war will almost certainly result.

For example, some groups in the United States wanted to enter World War I because they were angry at the Germans for invading Belgium. Some groups wanted to make sure that Great Britain and France would win the war, because of America's close economic and cultural ties with these countries. Some people feared that the German submarine campaign might halt trade relations between the United States and the Allied countries, and cause a depression. Some were indignant at the sinking of the *Lusitania*. Others simply believed that the Germans were wrong and the Allies were right, and wanted to help the right side. A few persons saw that it would not be safe for the United States to allow Germany to dominate Europe.

Depression and War. Some economists and historians think there is a close connection between war and economic depression. They argue that in a worldwide depression every country tries to protect itself at the expense of other countries. Each nation wants to cut down unemployment at home, and tries to make sure that little is bought from abroad which could be made by its own workers at home. This can easily be done by raising tariffs. It is sometimes called a way of "exporting unemployment" to other countries.

The chief concern of any government during a depression is to get people back to work. One way to do this is by building armaments. If anger can be stirred up against another country, or if people can be made to feel that they are in danger of attack, funds for military preparation are readily voted. Besides, the armed forces themselves give employment to many.

A modern democracy, such as the United States, would never risk war in order to end a depression or put people to work. But war may provide more employment and give many people a larger share of food, clothing, and other good things than they can have in depression. For this reason, a long depression makes war seem less dreadful to those who have lost all hope, and may drive them to follow such leaders as Adolf Hitler.

War Aims and Peace Aims. War seldom accomplishes the complete results any side has hoped for. Many people with different purposes may unite to make war, but they often start quarreling among themselves when the war is over. In order to hold a warring people or group of countries together, peace aims are usually stated in vague, general terms, so that everyone concerned can see in them a promise of what he wants. When the victory is won, general terms become specific, and usually do not satisfy all the winners.

Methods of Warfare. Changes in the ways of waging war have had a great effect on the way people live. Some historians think that the idea of human equality came to be widely accepted because guns took the place of spears, swords, and arrows as the chief weapons of war. They point out that an armored knight in feudal days was more than a match for dozens of men who had no armor. But, these historians point out, the minutemen of Lexington and Concord, with guns in their hands, were equal or nearly equal to the same number of British soldiers. Following their theory, the historians go on to point out that when one soldier became the equal of another, some people decided that voting was an easy way to tell how a fight over an issue would come out. The idea of human equality gained strength when people accepted each person's right to cast a vote that was just as important as any other person's vote.

Modern warfare has moved away from the days when soldiers with rifles were the most important part of an army. War has been mechanized until it is in large part a contest in producing machinery. In Thomas Jefferson's day, it made sense to protect "the right to keep and bear arms," so that people could overthrow a tyrannical government. Today, the private citizen cannot keep the kinds of weapons that would serve this purpose.

As the methods of warfare have changed, the cost of war has increased. For example, the War of 1812 cost the United States about $90 million. But World War II cost the nation about $263 billion.

The Atomic Bomb, used by the United States against Japan in 1945, has brought another great change into warfare. After the invention of the bomb, it seemed probable that future wars would be short and terribly destructive. Great cities could be destroyed and millions of people killed within a few hours. The only question was whether the nations of the world could change their habits fast enough to keep war from breaking out. See ATOMIC BOMB; HYDROGEN BOMB.

Total War is one in which a nation uses all its people, resources, and weapons. In such wars, civilians as well as military people take part in the war effort. For example, World Wars I and II were total wars in which entire populations took part. Civilians worked on such activities as civil defense and weapons manufacture, and many civilians were killed by bombs.

Limited War is one in which the warring nations limit the weapons they use, the targets they attack, or the areas involved. Since the invention of the atomic bomb, *limited war* has come to mean a war in which neither side uses atomic weapons. The Korean War (1950-1953) was a limited war in this sense. Only North and South Korea fought a total war. Neither Russia nor the United States used their nuclear weapons.

After World War II, several international disputes grew into wars. But fear of nuclear destruction prevented any of the wars from becoming total. These limited wars included the Vietnam War (1957-1975) and the Middle East wars of 1948, 1956, 1967, and 1973.

Is War "Normal"? Democratic countries take it for granted that peace is normal, and that war means some-

WARS INVOLVING THE UNITED STATES

Wars	U.S. Military Deaths	U.S. War Costs
Revolutionary War	25,324*	$101,100,000
War of 1812	2,260	$90,000,000
Mexican War	13,283	$71,400,000
Civil War		
Union Forces	364,511	$3,183,000,000
Confederate Forces	164,821	$2,000,000,000
Spanish-American War	2,446	$283,200,000
World War I	116,516	$18,676,000,000
World War II	405,399	$263,259,000,000
Korean War	54,246	$67,386,000,000
Vietnam War	56,480	$140,824,000,000

*Estimate.

WAR ACES

thing has gone wrong. But it is hard to say just where peace ends and war begins. Nations may be on unfriendly terms for years, building up their armies and navies, seeking allies, and trying to win control of each other's markets, without any actual clash of armed forces. It is debatable whether these countries are really at peace. They might be considered to be merely observing a rest period between wars. Many historians consider the years between World Wars I and II as a breathing spell in a single great war.   PAYSON S. WILD

Related Articles in WORLD BOOK include:

WARS

Boer War	Revolutionary War in
Chinese-Japanese Wars	America
Civil War	Russo-Japanese War
Cold War	Russo-Turkish Wars
Crimean War	Seven Weeks' War
Crusades	Seven Years' War
Franco-Prussian War	Spanish-American War
French and Indian Wars	Succession Wars
Hundred Years' War	Thirty Years' War
Indian Wars	Vietnam War
Korean War	War of 1812
Mexican War	Wars of the Roses
Peasants' War	World War I
Peloponnesian War	World War II
Punic Wars	

OTHER RELATED ARTICLES

Air Force	Draft, Military	Navy
Amphibious	Embargo	Neutrality
Warfare	Espionage	Peace
Army	Geneva Conventions	Prisoner of War
Blockade	Guerrilla Warfare	Propaganda
Censorship	Hostage	Psychological
Chemical-Biolog-	International Law	Warfare
ical-Radiologi-	Jingo	Siege
cal Warfare	Marine	Underground
Contraband	Military Science	Weapon

WAR ACES are airplane pilots who shoot down five or more enemy planes during a war. Each plane downed must be confirmed by eyewitnesses or gun-camera films to count as a *victory* or *kill*. Pilots often lose credit for planes shot down because there are no witnesses, or because the victims crash behind enemy lines.

In World War I (1914-1918), Captain Eddie Rickenbacker of the United States shot down 22 German planes and four balloons. Baron Manfred von Richthofen of Germany, called the *Red Baron* or the *Red Knight*, shot down 80 planes—more than any other pilot in the war. Captain René Fonck of France was credited with 75, Major Edward Mannock of Great Britain with 73, and Colonel Billy Bishop of Canada with 72.

In World War II (1939-1945), air power played a greater role than in World War I. Major Richard I. Bong of the U.S. Army Air Forces shot down 40 enemy planes. Air Force Major Thomas McGuire had 38. Other leading Air Force aces included Colonel Francis Gabreski and Major Robert Johnson. U.S. Navy Commander David McCampbell shot down 34, and Major Joseph Foss of the U.S. Marine Corps had 26. Another American, Major Gregory (Pappy) Boyington, shot down 28 planes—6 as a member of the Flying Tigers and 22 as a Marine pilot (see FLYING TIGERS).

Major Alexander Pokryshkin of Russia shot down 59 German planes, and Wing Commander J. E. Johnson of Great Britain had 38. Major General Adolf Galland was the most famous German ace of World War II.

In the Korean War (1950-1953), the Air Force had 39 jet aces. Captain Joe McConnell, Jr., shot down 16 enemy planes. Captain James Jabara shot down 15.

In the Vietnam War (1957-1975), the United States had five war aces. Air Force Captain Charles D. De-Bellevue shot down six enemy planes. Air Force Captains Jeffrey Feinstein and Richard S. Ritchie and Navy Lieutenants Randy Cunningham and William Driscoll shot down five enemy planes each.   WILBERT H. RUENHECK

See also Foss, JOSEPH J.; RICKENBACKER, EDDIE.

WAR AND PEACE is one of the greatest novels in Russian literature. It was written by Count Leo Tolstoy, and published in installments from 1865 to 1869 (see TOLSTOY, LEO N.). The story centers around the war in 1812 between Russia and France. The novel has over 500 characters. It deals with the problems of individuals caught up in the war and presents Tolstoy's theory that it is not heroes who make history, but destiny that produces heroes.   OLEG A. MASLENIKOV

WAR BETWEEN THE STATES. See CIVIL WAR.

WAR CORRESPONDENT is one of the most dramatic news reporting jobs. A reporter on a war front runs the risk of being killed or wounded. War correspondents have covered fighting in all parts of the world from Mexico in the 1840's to Vietnam in the 1970's.

Perhaps the first efforts to give readers quick and accurate news of a war were made by George W. Kendall, founder of the *New Orleans Picayune*. Kendall set up a system of messengers to speed the news of the Mexican War (1846-1848) back to the United States. Mathew B. Brady first used the camera for reporting during the Civil War (1861-1865). Walt Whitman sent stories of this war to New York City papers.

Stephen Crane was another great writer to gain fame as a war correspondent. He reported the war between Spain and Cuba in 1896. The first roving war correspondent to become well known was Richard Harding Davis. Beginning with the Spanish-American War (1898), he reported the happenings of six major conflicts.

Before World War I (1914-1918), reporters had remained behind the lines, getting their information from commanders. Beginning with World War I, they moved with the troops and wrote firsthand accounts. Ernie Pyle's descriptions of World War II (1939-1945) endeared him to readers in the United States. Pyle was killed by enemy fire in the Pacific.   GORDON A. SABINE

See also DAVIS, RICHARD HARDING; PYLE, ERNIE.

WAR CRIME is a military violation of the rules of warfare. Since World War II (1939-1945), the term has referred to any crime, atrocity, or persecution committed during the course of a war.

For thousands of years, certain rules and customs have governed the conduct of warfare. These rules developed partly from the customs of chivalry and diplomacy and partly from man's desire to limit the horror and destruction of war. Throughout history, many persons have been tried for war crimes.

Since the late 1800's, most nations have signed international treaties establishing rules of warfare. These rules deal with fair treatment of war prisoners, outlawing of gas and germ warfare, and humane treatment of civilians in areas occupied by military forces.

World War I. After World War I (1914-1918), the Treaty of Versailles required Germany to turn over about 900 persons for trial by the Allies as war criminals. But the Germans held their own trials instead. Only 13 of the 900 were tried, and the few who were convicted received light sentences.

World War II. In 1943, during World War II, the Allies set up the United Nations (UN) War Crimes Commission in London. The commission collected evidence and compiled lists of war criminals. After the war, the main war crimes trials took place in Nuremberg, Germany; and Tokyo, Japan. The defendants were charged with starting wars of conquest and violating the rules of war. See NUREMBERG TRIALS.

From 1945 to 1950, the Allies held many other war crimes trials in Europe and the Far East. Some countries that had been occupied by German or Japanese troops held their own trials of officers and occupation officials. West Germany also tried a number of Germans charged with war crimes committed during World War II. Some of these trials continued into the 1970's.

For years after World War II, Israeli agents sought Adolf Eichmann, a former German officer believed chiefly responsible for deporting Jews to Nazi extermination camps. In 1960, the agents found Eichmann in Argentina. They kidnaped him and took him to Israel, where a court found him guilty of war crimes and crimes against humanity. Eichmann was sentenced to death and hanged.

The Korean War. During the Korean War (1950-1953), the United States accused the Chinese and North Korean forces of war crimes against UN troops and South Korean civilians. In 1953, the UN General Assembly expressed "grave concern" over these reports. However, the war ended without any war crimes trials.

The Vietnam War. Beginning in 1965, the United States sent troops to Vietnam to aid South Vietnam against the Communist Viet Cong forces and the North Vietnamese. As the fighting grew heavier, each side accused the other of violating the rules of war. The United States and South Vietnam charged North Vietnam with violating the Geneva Conventions, which provide for humane treatment of war prisoners, wounded soldiers, and civilians (see GENEVA CONVENTIONS).

Late in 1969, it was disclosed that in March, 1968, U.S. troops had massacred hundreds of civilians in the village of My Lai. As a result, U.S. military courts-martial tried several officers and enlisted men for war crimes. One man, Lieutenant William L. Calley, Jr., was found guilty of murder and was sentenced to a long prison term.

The United Nations and War Crimes. The war crimes trials after World War II drew criticism from some scholars and statesmen. They felt that international law provided no basis for the trials. In 1947, the UN established the International Law Commission to develop a code of international laws, including those governing war crimes. The commission prepared a *Draft Code on Offences Against the Peace and Security of Mankind*. The UN has not yet adopted the code.

Many people believe that an international body, such as the UN, should conduct war crimes trials. They feel such a procedure would draw less criticism than trials held by individual nations.   TELFORD TAYLOR

See also GENOCIDE.

WAR DEBT was one of the most difficult problems left by World War I. Huge war costs had forced some countries to borrow from others. The borrowed sums came to be known as *inter-Allied debts*.

The United States was the chief lender during the war. It loaned more than $10 billion. In 1922, Congress organized the World War Foreign Debts Commission. By 1930, the commission had made agreements with all the debtor countries except Russia and Nicaragua. Cuba and Liberia had paid their small debts in full. The United States tried to make all settlements in accordance with each nation's ability to pay.

German Reparations. The Treaty of Versailles held Germany responsible for the losses that the Allied nations suffered during World War I. In 1921, a commission of Allied experts ordered Germany to make *reparations* (damage payments) of about $33 billion. It was to make some payments in money, and some in goods. Germany paid a few installments, but claimed that the payments were wrecking its economic system.

In 1924, an international committee headed by Charles G. Dawes worked out a payment and loan plan to ease the financial strain on Germany (see DAWES PLAN). But Germany insisted on a reduction in its payments. In 1929, an international commission of financial experts met in Paris to discuss German reparations. The outcome of the discussions was the Young Plan. This plan reduced the German debt to about $16 billion, and made payments easier. The members of the commission also established a Bank for International Settlements to handle payments. Meanwhile, general inflation and uncontrolled spending had led to a world-wide financial panic and depression. The panic threatened Germany with complete financial collapse.

The Hoover Moratorium. On June 30, 1931, President Herbert Hoover proposed that all intergovernmental debts be held up for one year. The purpose of this action, known as the *Hoover Moratorium*, was to provide a "breathing spell" for European countries. Germany took the opportunity to ask for a complete adjustment of all war debts.

The Lausanne Conference. In June, 1932, an international conference met in Lausanne, Switzerland. The conference agreed to cancel all German reparations until better conditions returned to Germany.

The worldwide depression greatly hindered the government debt problem. On June 15, 1933, debt payments to the United States amounted to about 8 per cent of the total due. Only Finland made full payment. In 1934, the war-debt agreements totally collapsed.

During World War II, the United States was again the great financial power. The Lend-Lease Act of 1941 replaced the huge lending system of World War I. According to this act, the United States loaned goods and materials to nations fighting Germany and Japan. After the war, no repayment terms were decided upon. The United States canceled some war debts outright. During the Korean War, the U.S. loaned its allies about $11 billion in military goods.   NORMAN D. PALMER

See also BANK FOR INTERNATIONAL SETTLEMENTS; LEND-LEASE.

WAR DEPARTMENT was an executive department of the United States government from 1789 to 1947. It was set up to supervise all military activities and all phases

of national defense. In 1798, Congress separated the naval forces from the land forces, creating a new Department of the Navy. The War Department retained control over the Army. The secretaries of both departments reported to the President, were members of the President's Cabinet, and cooperated through joint committees and conferences.

After World War II, government authorities decided that a unification of all three military services—the land, sea, and air forces—would result in greater national defense at lower cost. Congress passed the National Security Act in 1947, setting up the National Military Establishment (NME). The secretary of war became the secretary of the army, and lost his place in the President's Cabinet. A secretary of defense supervised the NME, which included the new Department of the Army and two other military departments. In 1949, the NME became the Department of Defense (see DEFENSE, DEPARTMENT OF).

The War Department was one of the first three departments established by the federal government. The secretary was chosen as an administrator, and not as a military expert. He relied on military officers for advice. He was assisted by the *War Council*, which included his undersecretary and the chief of staff of the army. The *War Department General Staff*, established in 1903 under the chief of staff, provided professional military advice to the secretary of war and the President.

The War Department's principal job was to manage the Army. It had to recruit men, provide them with weapons and supplies, transport them, and protect their health. It also had to build fortifications, direct the education of officers, and supervise the National Guard (see NATIONAL GUARD).

In its early years, the War Department also had important nonmilitary functions. It conducted a large construction program in improving rivers and harbors, building dams and reservoirs, and developing other public works. Other government agencies took over much of this public works program during the 1930's. The War Department also managed the affairs of the island possessions of the United States through its Department of Insular Affairs. This agency was abolished in 1939, and its duties were transferred to the Department of the Interior.

One of the War Department's biggest tasks in the years before World War II was the administration of the Civilian Conservation Corps (CCC), an organization of about 300,000 young men who worked on government conservation projects. For a limited time, the War Department also had the responsibility of transporting all air mail.

Many famous men held the office of secretary of war. Some of the best known included James Monroe, Jefferson Davis, Edwin M. Stanton, Elihu Root, William Howard Taft, Newton D. Baker, and Henry L. Stimson. Baker was secretary during World War I, and Stimson during World War II.   JOHN C. BOLLENS

See also ARMY, DEPARTMENT OF THE; AIR FORCE, DEPARTMENT OF THE.

WAR HAWKS. See WAR OF 1812 (Causes of the War).

WAR LABOR BOARD, NATIONAL. See ARBITRATION.

Detail of *Perry's Victory on Lake Erie*, an engraving by A. Lawson, after a painting by Thomas Birch, New-York Historical Society, New York City, Olds Collection (about 1813)

The Battle of Lake Erie in 1813 was won by U.S. naval forces under Master-Commandant Oliver H. Perry. During the battle, Perry was rowed from his sinking ship to another vessel, *above*.

WAR OF 1812

WAR OF 1812. The War of 1812 was in many ways the strangest war in United States history. It could well be named the War of Faulty Communication. Two days before war was declared, the British Government had stated that it would repeal the laws which were the chief excuse for fighting. If there had been telegraphic communication with Europe, the war might well have been avoided. Speedy communication would also have prevented the greatest battle of the war, which was fought at New Orleans fifteen days after a treaty of peace had been signed.

It is strange also that the war for freedom of the seas began with the invasion of Canada, and that the treaty of peace which ended the war settled none of the issues over which it had supposedly been fought.

The chief United States complaint against the British was interference with shipping. But New England, the great shipping section of the United States, bitterly opposed the idea of going to war. The demand for war came chiefly from the West and South, although these sections were not really hurt by British naval policy.

When we add that both sides claimed victory in the War of 1812, it becomes clear that the whole struggle was a confused mass of contradictions. These must be explained and cleared up before we can understand why the democratic United States sided with Napoleon I, the French dictator, in a struggle for world power.

Causes of the War

Napoleon Bonaparte, head of the French Government after 1799 and Emperor after 1804, had made himself the master of continental Europe. Except for one short breathing spell (1801-1803), Great Britain had been fighting France since 1793. Napoleon had long hoped to invade and conquer Britain, but in 1805 his navy was destroyed at the battle of Trafalgar. This forced Napoleon to give up the idea of taking an army across the English Channel. So he set out instead to ruin Great Britain by destroying British trade. Napoleon's Berlin and Milan Decrees (1806-1807) were an attempt to shut off Great Britain from all trade with Europe. (See CONTINENTAL SYSTEM; MILAN DECREE.) Great Britain, in turn, issued a series of Orders in Council which declared a blockade of French ports and of ports in Europe and elsewhere that were under French control. See ORDER IN COUNCIL.

Neither Napoleon nor the British Government intended that these measures should injure the United States. But the British and French blockades had disastrous effects on United States shipping. Before 1806, the United States was getting rich on the European war. United States ships took goods to both Great Britain and France, and the value of trade carried increased fourfold from 1791 to 1805. Now the picture had suddenly changed. A United States ship bound for French ports had to stop first at a British port for inspection and payment of fees. Otherwise the British were likely to seize the ship. But Napoleon ordered neutral ships not to stop at British ports for inspection, and he also announced that he would order his forces to seize any United States ships which they found had obeyed the British Orders in Council.

The British navy controlled the seas. So the easiest thing for United States vessels was to trade only with other neutrals and with Great Britain. A few adventurous spirits ran the British blockade for the sake of huge profits they could make, and continued the risky trade

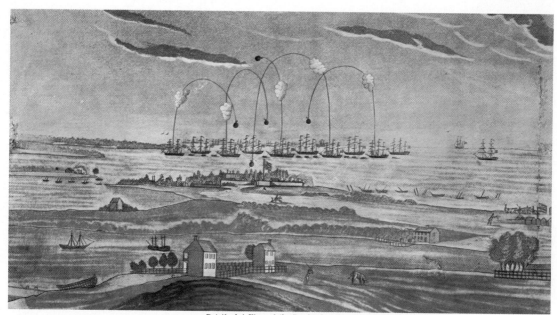

Detail of *A View of the Bombardment of Fort McHenry . . .*, an aquatint engraving by J. Bower,
The Peale Museum, Baltimore, Maryland, The Hambleton Collection (about 1817)

Bombs Burst in the Air over Fort McHenry in 1814 during a British attack on the Baltimore
area. Francis Scott Key wrote "The Star Spangled Banner" after watching this battle.

with continental Europe. The United States complained of both French and British policies as illegal
"paper blockades," because neither side could really enforce such an extensive blockade. See BLOCKADE (Paper
Blockade).

Impressment of Seamen. The British navy was always
in need of seamen. One reason for this need was that
hundreds of deserters from the British navy had found
work on United States ships. The British Government
claimed the right to stop neutral ships on the high seas,
remove sailors of British birth, and *impress*, or force,
them back into British naval service. The United States
objected strongly to this practice, partly because many
native-born Americans were impressed "by mistake,"
along with men who had actually been British seamen.
See JEFFERSON, THOMAS (The Struggle for Neutrality).

In June, 1807, Captain James Barron of the frigate
Chesapeake refused to let the British search his ship for
deserters. The British frigate *Leopard* fired on the *Chesapeake*, removed four men whom the British called deserters, and hanged one of them. Anti-British feeling in
the United States rose sharply. President Thomas Jefferson ordered all British naval vessels out of American
harbors. Four years later, the British apologized for the
incident and paid for the damage done, but the bitterness remained.

American Reaction. The United States tried several
times to get the British to change their policy toward
neutral shipping and toward impressment. In April,
1806, the United States Congress passed a Non-Impor-
tation Act, which shut out British goods from American
markets. The Act was not enforced until November,
and was followed by other Acts. But all American efforts to change British policy failed. In December, 1807,
Congress passed the Embargo Act. This act closed

Detail of *Washington*, an engraving by an unknown artist, from
The Stationer's Almanack, London, 1815 (Library of Congress)

The British Captured Washington, D.C., in 1814, *above.*
They burned the Capitol, the White House, and other buildings.

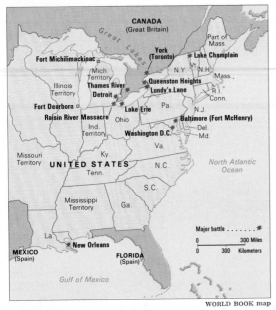

CANADA
(Great Britain)

Part of
Mass.

York
(Toronto)

Lake Champlain

Fort Michilimackinac

N.Y. Vt. N.H.

Mich.
Territory

Mass.

Illinois
Territory

Queenston Heights

Thames River

Lundy's Lane

R.I.

Detroit

Conn.

Fort Dearborn

Lake Erie

Pa.

Raisin River Massacre

N.J.

Ohio

Baltimore (Fort McHenry)

Ind.
Territory

Washington D.C.

Del.
Md.

Missouri
Territory

Va.

Ky.

UNITED STATES

N.C.

North Atlantic
Ocean

Tenn.

S.C.

Mississippi
Territory

Ga.

La.

Major battle . . . . ✷

0   300 Miles

New Orleans

0   300 Kilometers

MEXICO
(Spain)

FLORIDA
(Spain)

Gulf of Mexico

WORLD BOOK map

The War of 1812 was fought mainly in the northern United States and southern Canada. This map shows where the major land and water battles took place.

United States ports to all foreign ships, and forbade American ships to sail for any but other home ports.

The embargo did not produce anything like the results Congress desired. Overseas trade nearly stopped, almost ruining New England shipowners and putting many sailors out of work. Shipyards closed, and goods piled up in warehouses. The embargo also hurt Southern planters, who normally sold tobacco, rice, and cotton to Great Britain. Opponents of the embargo described its effects on the United States by spelling the word backwards. They called the embargo the "O-Grab-Me" act. Even with the hardships the embargo caused for the United States, it failed as a policy. It did little to hurt either the British or the French.

After 15 months, Congress gave up the embargo and tried a new device for hurting British and French commerce. It passed the Non-Intercourse Act in March, 1809, permitting American ships to trade with any countries but Great Britain and France. The act also opened American ports to all but British and French ships. But this plan also failed.

In 1810, Congress passed Macon's Bill No. 2, or the Macon Act, which removed all restrictions on trade. The law went on to say that if either Great Britain or France would give up its orders or decrees, the United States would immediately restore non-intercourse rules against the other nation, unless it also agreed to change its policy.

Macon's Bill really helped Napoleon, who was eager to get the United States into the war against Great Britain. He pretended to repeal his Berlin and Milan Decrees so far as they applied to United States ships. President James Madison at once shut off all trade with Great Britain. In the summer of 1811 further attempts were made to reach an agreement with the British. But

these attempts failed, and in November, Madison advised Congress to get ready for war.

The War Hawks. A group of young men known as "War Hawks" dominated Congress during this period. Henry Clay of Kentucky and John C. Calhoun of South Carolina were the outstanding leaders of the group. Clay was then Speaker of the House of Representatives. Like Clay and Calhoun, most of the War Hawks came from western and southern states, where many of the people were in favor of going to war with Great Britain.

The people of New England generally opposed going to war, because war with Great Britain would wipe out entirely the New England shipping trade which had already been heavily damaged. Another reason New England opposed war was because many New Englanders sympathized with Great Britain in its struggle against the dictator Napoleon.

Many historians believe that a leading motive of the War Hawks was a desire for expansion. The people of the Northwest were meeting armed resistance in their attempt to take more land from the Indians, and they believed that the Indians had considerable British support. An American army was attacked by Indians at the Battle of Tippecanoe in the Wabash Valley in November, 1811, and British guns were found on the battlefield. The Westerners, therefore, were anxious to drive the British out of Canada. Southerners looked longingly at Florida, which belonged to Great Britain's ally, Spain. The South had also suffered a serious loss of markets. But the deciding motive for war seems to have been a strong desire for more territory.

Progress of the War

Declaration of War. On June 1, 1812, President Madison asked Congress to declare war against Great Britain. He gave as his reasons the impressment of United States seamen and the interference with United States trade. He charged also that the British had stirred up Indian warfare in the Northwest. Congress declared war on June 18, 1812. Two days earlier, the British Foreign Minister had announced that the Orders in Council would be repealed, but word of this announcement did not reach America until after the war had begun.

――――― **IMPORTANT DATES IN THE WAR OF 1812** ―――――

1812 (June 18) The United States declared war on Great Britain.

1812 (Oct. 13) British forces won the Battle of Queenston Heights in Canada.

1813 (April 27) The Americans captured York (now Toronto), the capital of Upper Canada. They later burned some public buildings.

1813 (Sept. 10) American forces under Master-Commandant Oliver Hazard Perry won the Battle of Lake Erie.

1813 (Oct. 5) The Americans won the Battle of the Thames River in Moraviantown, an Indian village in Canada.

1814 (Aug. 24) British troops invaded Washington, D.C., and burned the Capitol and the White House.

1814 (Sept. 11) American forces won the Battle of Lake Champlain.

1814 (Dec. 24) The Americans and the British signed a peace treaty in Ghent, Belgium.

1815 (Jan. 8) American forces won the Battle of New Orleans. News of the peace treaty did not reach the United States until after this battle.

Because President Madison asked for the declaration of war, many Federalists blamed him for the conflict, calling it "Mr. Madison's war." But it was more the War Hawks' war than it was Madison's.

Attitude of the Nation. Congress had known for seven months that war was likely to come, but no real preparations had been made. There was little money in the Treasury. The regular army had only about 10,000 troops, and very few trained officers. The navy had fewer than twenty seagoing ships.

To make matters worse, a large minority, both in Congress and in the country, was opposed to war. The declaration of war had passed by a vote of only 79 to 49 in the House, and 19 to 13 in the Senate. New England, the richest section in the country, bitterly opposed the war, and interfered with its progress by withholding both money and troops.

The War at Sea. The position of the United States on the oceans was hopeless from first to last. Great Britain had more than a hundred battleships, while the United States had not a single vessel of that class. The seventeen frigates and sloops of war that made up the United States Navy were competing against nearly a thousand British fighting ships. Now and then an American vessel won a brilliant victory over a single British ship, but the British navy ruled the waves.

A British blockade was clamped on the United States coast, and United States trade almost disappeared. Because duties on imports were the chief source of Federal revenue, the Treasury drifted further and further into debt.

The only American naval victories that directly affected the course of the war were those won by Oliver Hazard Perry on Lake Erie, on September 10, 1813, and by Thomas Macdonough on Lake Champlain, on September 11, 1814. But United States naval vessels and privateers did some damage to British commerce, taking about 1,500 prize ships in all.

Land Campaign of 1812. The American plan of attack called for a three-way invasion of Canada. Invasion forces were to start from Detroit, from the Niagara River, and from the foot of Lake Champlain.

At Detroit, General William Hull led about 2,000 troops across the Detroit River into Canada. The British commander, General Sir Isaac Brock, drove Hull's forces back into Detroit, surrounded them, and captured both the city and Hull's entire army. British and Indians also captured Michilimackinac and Fort Dearborn (Chicago).

On the Niagara River, a United States force occupied Queenston Heights on the Canadian side. This force was defeated and captured when New York militia units refused to come to its support.

At Lake Champlain, the third United States army advanced from Plattsburgh, N.Y., to the Canadian frontier. Here, too, the militia refused to leave United States territory, and the army marched back again to Plattsburgh. Thus the first attempt to invade Canada failed completely.

Campaigns of 1813. In January, 1813, an American army advancing toward Detroit was defeated and captured at Frenchtown on the Raisin River. In April, York (now Toronto), the capital of Upper Canada, was cap-

tured by United States troops and held for a short time. Some of the public buildings were burned.

Perry's destruction of the British fleet on Lake Erie forced the British to pull out of Detroit, and much of Michigan Territory came under United States control. General William Henry Harrison was able to take his army across the lake and defeat the retreating British at the Battle of the Thames.

In the autumn, General James Wilkinson and General Wade Hampton undertook a campaign against Montreal. This attempt failed, and the United States armies retreated into northern New York. In December, the British crossed the Niagara River, captured Fort Niagara, and burned Buffalo and neighboring villages.

Campaigns of 1814. By 1814 Napoleon had been defeated in Europe. Great Britain was then able to send 18,000 veteran troops to Canada, thus ending all American hopes of conquest. But the United States had at last built up a well trained and disciplined army on the New York frontier. Under the able leadership of Major General Jacob Brown and Brigadier General Winfield Scott, this army crossed the Niagara River from Buffalo in July and defeated the British at the Battle of Chippewa. But soon after that the Americans were turned back at the Battle of Lundy's Lane. After holding Fort Erie in Canada for several months, the United States troops finally withdrew to the American side. This was the last attempt to invade Canada. Meanwhile, 11,000 British troops had moved into New York by way of Lake Champlain. They retreated hastily when the destruction of the British fleet on the lake injured their supply lines back to Canada.

Another British army, under General Robert Ross, was escorted by a fleet to Chesapeake Bay, scattered the United States troops at the Battle of Bladensburg, occupied Washington, D.C., and burned the Capitol, the White House, and other public buildings. Both the British army and the British fleet were driven back before Baltimore, Md. This engagement inspired Francis Scott Key to write "The Star-Spangled Banner" (see STAR-SPANGLED BANNER).

"The Needless Battle." The Battle of New Orleans was the last engagement of the war. It was fought on January 8, 1815. Like the declaration of war, this battle might have been prevented if there had been speedy communication. A treaty of peace had been signed at Ghent, Belgium, fifteen days before the battle took place, but it was not ratified by the United States until a month later.

The British had sent an army of more than 8,000 men to capture New Orleans. There were several possible routes to the city, but the British chose to march straight toward the entrenchments that had been prepared by General Andrew Jackson. American artillery and sharpshooting riflemen mowed down about 1,500 British soldiers, including the commanding officer, General Sir Edward Pakenham. The Americans lost few men.

Treaty of Ghent. The British public was tired of war and especially of war taxes. The British Government therefore proposed discussing terms. Commissioners of the two countries met at Ghent, Belgium, in August, 1814.

The British at first insisted that the United States should give up certain territory on the northern frontier,

Detail of *The Battle of New Orleans,* an 1867 engraving after a painting by D. M. Carter, Chicago Historical Society

American Troops Won the Battle of New Orleans 15 days after the War of 1812 had officially ended. Word of the peace settlement had not reached New Orleans when the battle took place.

and set up a large permanent Indian reservation in the Northwest. But American victories in the summer and fall of 1814 led the British to drop these demands. A treaty was finally signed on December 24, 1814, in Ghent, Belgium. By its terms, all land which had been captured by either party was to be given up. Everything was to be exactly as it was before the war, and commissions from both countries were to settle any disputed points about boundaries. Nothing whatever was said about impressments, blockades, or the British Orders in Council, which supposedly had caused the war. The treaty was formally ratified on February 17, 1815.

Results of the War

One important result of the War of 1812 was the rapid rise of manufacturing in the United States. During the war, United States citizens were unable to import goods from Great Britain, and had to begin making many articles for themselves. The war also increased national patriotism, and helped to unite the United States into one nation.

The war settled none of the issues over which the United States had fought. But most of these issues faded out during the following years. In the long period of peace after 1815, the British had no occasion to make use of impressments or blockades. Indian troubles in the Northwest were practically ended by the death of the chief Tecumseh and by the British surrender of Detroit and other posts. The United States occupied part of Florida during the war, and was soon able to buy the rest of it from Spain.

One indirect result of the War of 1812 was the later election to the Presidency of Andrew Jackson and of William Henry Harrison. Both of these men won military fame which had much to do with their elections. Another indirect result was the decline of Federalist power. New England leaders, most of them Federalists, met secretly in Hartford, Conn., to study amendments

to the Constitution. Their opponents charged that they had plotted treason, and the Federalists never recovered (see HARTFORD CONVENTION).

Chief Battles of the War

The War of 1812 was not an all-out struggle on either side. For the British, the war was just an annoying part of their struggle with Napoleon. For many Americans, it was an unjustified attempt to gratify the expansionist ambitions of the South and West.

The chief battles of the war are described below.

Lake Champlain (Sept. 11, 1814). The British had four ships and about a dozen rowing galleys on Lake Champlain to protect the flank of General Sir George Prevost's army. Prevost was advancing against Plattsburgh on the west shore of the lake. Master-Commandant Thomas Macdonough commanded the American fleet of four ships and ten rowing galleys. Macdonough anchored his ships across the mouth of Plattsburgh Bay, so that the British had to approach him head on. He also arranged the anchors and cables of his flagship, the *Saratoga,* so that he could turn the ship about to bring a fresh broadside to bear on the enemy at a critical point in the fighting. As a result of Macdonough's careful planning, the entire British fleet surrendered.

Lake Erie (Sept. 10, 1813). At Erie, Pa., Master-Commandant Oliver Hazard Perry had built two fine brigs, each carrying twenty guns. In addition, he had under his command a smaller brig captured from the British, and six small schooners, each armed with one or two heavy guns. With these nine ships, Perry blockaded the British fleet of six ships at the western end of the lake. The British came out to fight, and at first had the advantage. When Perry's flagship, the *Lawrence,* was disabled, he transferred in a small boat to the *Niagara,* which had suffered little damage in the battle. He went on to defeat the British fleet and capture it. Perry reported his victory to General Harrison in the famous words, "We have met the enemy and they are ours."

Lundy's Lane (July 25, 1814). This battle took place on Canadian soil, about 1 mile (1.6 kilometers) from Niagara Falls. The battle began when General Winfield Scott was advancing toward Queenston with about 1,300 men and came upon about 2,800 British troops. The American General Jacob Brown had some 2,700 men in Chippewa, about 3 miles (4.8 kilometers) away. The fighting began at about five o'clock in the afternoon. Before darkness fell General Brown had arrived on the field with reinforcements. The battle raged until midnight, and the losses were heavy.

Each side claimed victory in the battle. The Americans drove the British from their position and captured the chief British battery, but the British later retook the field and recaptured the guns. The battle of Lundy's Lane is remembered for brave fighting on both sides.

New Orleans (Jan. 8, 1815). This battle has already been described under the heading *The Needless Battle*. It had no effect on the outcome of the war, but it gave the United States government some political standing in Europe. The battle also brought great fame to General Andrew Jackson.

Queenston Heights (Oct. 13, 1812). This battle ended the second American attempt to invade Canada. General Sir Isaac Brock, the British commander, had about 1,500 men scattered along 36 miles (58 kilometers) of the Niagara River. The Americans, under Generals Stephen Van Rensselaer and Alexander Smyth, numbered more than 6,000. The Americans tried to cross the Niagara River from a point opposite Queenston Heights, 7 miles (11 kilometers) below the Falls. About 400 Americans got across the river, and were attacked by a force under Brock. Brock was fatally wounded in the battle.

Later in the day, after both sides had received reinforcements, the British drove the invaders down to the bank of the river. Here the United States troops stopped, because they could not get back across the stream. The entire American force of about 900 surrendered. The British victory was clouded by the death of General Brock, who was one of the finest officers in either army. A monument to his memory stands on the battlefield.

Raisin River Massacre (Jan. 22, 1813) took place in Frenchtown (now Monroe, Mich.) on the Raisin River. A detachment of Kentucky troops, sent to drive the British from Frenchtown, was defeated and captured by the British and Indians. After the battle the British departed with the able-bodied American prisoners, leaving the wounded Americans behind with the Indians. The Indians massacred wounded prisoners.

Thames River (Oct. 5, 1813), also known as the BATTLE OF MORAVIANTOWN. This battle was the direct result of Perry's naval victory on Lake Erie. The British had to abandon Detroit. British troops withdrew from Detroit and crossed into Canada. The British were accompanied by 600 Indians under their chief, Tecumseh. After the British had entered Canada, about 3,000 United States troops under General Harrison pursued them for several days.

The British finally halted in Moraviantown, on the Thames River in Kent County, Ontario, and offered battle. British General Proctor and many of his men fled soon after the first volley, but Tecumseh died on the battlefield. On the following day, the Americans burned Moraviantown, which was the home of the Moravian Indians. The death of Tecumseh, the leading Indian chief, broke the league of Indian tribes which had been allied to the British and practically ended the cooperation of the British and Indians on the northwestern frontier. A court-martial later publicly reprimanded General Proctor and suspended him. JULIUS W. PRATT

Related Articles in WORLD BOOK include:

BIOGRAPHIES

Brock, Sir Isaac	Key, Francis Scott
Brown, Jacob J.	Lawrence, James
Decatur, Stephen	Macdonough, Thomas
Forten, James	Madison, James ("Mr.
Harrison, William Henry	Madison's War")
Hull, Isaac	Perry (Oliver H.)
Jackson, Andrew	Scott, Winfield
(Jackson the Soldier)	

OTHER RELATED ARTICLES

Bank of the United States	Hartford Convention
Constitution (ship)	Non-Intercourse Act
Ghent, Treaty of	Star-Spangled Banner

Outline

I. Causes of the War
    A. Impressment of Seamen   C. The War Hawks
    B. American Reaction

II. Progress of the War
    A. Declaration of War   E. Campaigns of 1813
    B. Attitude of the Nation   F. Campaigns of 1814
    C. The War at Sea   G. "The Needless
    D. Land Campaign of   Battle"
       1812   H. Treaty of Ghent

III. Results of the War
IV. Chief Battles of the War

Questions

Why might the War of 1812 be called the War of Faulty Communication?

What were the Milan Decrees? The Orders in Council? Why were these measures declared?

What was *impressment?* Why did Americans object to it?

Who were the War Hawks? Why did they favor war with Great Britain?

What two American naval victories affected the course of the war?

When and by whom were these historic words written: "We have met the enemy and they are ours"?

When was the Capitol burned by the British?

What famous American patriotic song was written during the battle off Baltimore?

What battle of this war is known as "The Needless Battle"? Why?

WAR OF SECESSION. See CIVIL WAR.

WAR OF THE AMERICAN REVOLUTION. See REVOLUTIONARY WAR IN AMERICA.

WAR OF THE LEAGUE OF AUGSBURG. See RYSWICK, TREATY OF.

WAR ON POVERTY. See JOHNSON, LYNDON BAINES (The National Scene).

WAR PAINT. Warriors of many American Indian tribes painted their faces before going into battle. The paint made them look more terrifying. Indians also believed that it would bring them success and protect them from harm. Some warriors painted their entire faces bright red. Others applied stripes, circles, or dots in different colors. Plains Indians blackened their faces after killing an enemy, as a sign of their accomplishment. JOHN C. EWERS

WAR PRISONER. See PRISONER OF WAR.

WAR RISK INSURANCE

WAR RISK INSURANCE. See INSURANCE (History; Government Insurance); VETERANS ADMINISTRATION.

WAR SAVINGS BOND. See SAVINGS BOND.

WARBECK, PERKIN (1474?-1499), became one of the most famous "pretenders" in European history. He appeared suddenly in Ireland during the shaky reign of Henry VII of England. He claimed to be Richard, the younger of the two sons of the Yorkist king, Edward IV. Richard and his older brother, Edward V, had been imprisoned in the Tower of London by their uncle, Richard III, in 1483 and were never heard of again.

Perkin's claim was supported by many followers of the House of York in England, and by several European princes who were King Henry's enemies. Perkin tried to invade England in 1497, but he was captured and imprisoned. When he attempted to escape, Henry VII had him hanged. There is convincing evidence that Perkin was a Flemish youth of humble parentage. PAUL M. KENDALL

WARBLE FLY is a large, hairy fly similar to the botfly. The *larvae*, or young, of the warble fly live under the skin of animals. The

USDA
Adult Female Warble Fly

cattle warble, or *heel fly*, lays its eggs on the feet or legs of cattle. The larvae, called *cattle grubs*, work their way through the skin into the animal's body. Under the skin of the back, the larvae cause painful swellings, called *warbles*. See also BOTFLY.

Scientific Classification. Warble flies are in the order *Diptera*. They make up the family *Hypodermatidae*. The two cattle warbles in North America are genus *Hypoderma*, species *lineatum*, and *H. bovis*.   E. GORTON LINSLEY

WARBLER is the popular name of the small migratory songbirds of the wood warbler family. They live in the Americas from the tropics to the far north. Most of them are about $5\frac{1}{2}$ inches (14 centimeters) long. Warblers are hard to see because they are small and they keep close to the foliage of trees and bushes. Their feathers are of many beautiful colors. People enjoy the quick movements and abrupt, high-pitched songs of the warblers.

Many warblers winter in South and Central America, and migrate through the United States late in the spring. In May, they begin to appear in woods, in city parks, and in trees near buildings. Many species go on farther north for their nesting. Some warblers go as far north as the Hudson Bay and the Yukon Territory in Canada, but others nest in the Southern States.

Warblers build their nests in trees and bushes or on the ground. The nests are usually cup-shaped, and loosely built of twigs and grasses woven together, but some are compact structures of plant down. The female warbler lays from three to six eggs, which are whitish with brownish markings at the larger end.

Yellow Warbler
Dendroica petechia
Found from Canada to
northern South America
Body length: 4½ to 5¼ inches
(11.4 to 13.3 centimeters)

Blackburnian Warbler
Dendroica fusca
Found from Canada to
northern South America
Body length: 4½ to 5½ inches
(11.4 to 14.0 centimeters)

Yellow-Rumped Warbler
Dendroica coronata
Found in North and
Central America
Body length: 5 to 6 inches
(12.7 to 15.2 centimeters)

Hooded Warbler
Wilsonia citrina
Found in eastern and
midwestern United States
and in Central America
Body length: 5 to 6 inches
(12.7 to 15.2 centimeters)

Black-and-White Warbler
Mniotilta varia
Found from Canada to
northwestern South America
Body length: 4½ to 5½ inches
(11.4 to 14.0 centimeters)

WORLD BOOK illustrations by Albert Earl Gilbert

Many kinds of warblers have fine singing voices. Others sing only weak, lisping notes. There are more than 150 species and subspecies of warblers. Some of the better-known ones are the *yellow warbler*, the *black-and-white warbler*, and the *yellow-rumped warbler*. Yellow warblers are quite common in city parks. The black-and-white warbler likes to creep along the branches of trees. The yellow-rumped warbler has four yellow patches on its head, rump, and breast.

Another well-known warbler is the *American redstart*. It is colored a striking black with salmon markings, and looks somewhat like a small oriole. The redstart is one of the most active and graceful of American warblers. The *Blackburnian warbler* has a bright orange throat. Two other warblers are named for their colors. They are the *black-throated green warbler* and the *black-throated blue warbler*. The *ovenbird* has a yellowish-brown stripe on its head, a white breast marked with black, and an olive-green back. It is named for its ovenlike nest.

Warblers help farmers by killing insects that destroy fruits and strip trees of their leaves. Warblers search in tiny cracks in the bark and in fruit buds for insects that might escape larger birds.

Scientific Classification. Wood warblers make up the wood warbler family, *Parulidae*. The black-and-white warbler is genus *Mniotilta*, species *M. varia*. The American redstart is *Setophaga ruticilla*. The ovenbird is *Seiurus aurocapillus*. The yellow warbler is *Dendroica petechia*, and the yellow-rumped is *D. coronata*. The Blackburnian warbler is *D. fusca*, the black-throated green is *D. virens*, and the black-throated blue is *D. caerulescens*. ALBERT WOLFSON

See also BIRD (Foster Parents in the Bird World; color pictures: Birds' Eggs; Favorite Songbirds); CHAT; OVENBIRD; REDSTART; YELLOWTHROAT.

WARBURG, OTTO H. See NOBEL PRIZES (table: Nobel Prizes for Physiology or Medicine—1931).

WARD is a word that once had much the same meaning as the word *guard*. The relationship between the two words may be seen in two of the present meanings of *ward* that are described below.

In law, a ward is a person who needs to be guarded or protected, and so the court has appointed a guardian for the ward. Most wards are *minors* (persons under legal age). Spendthrifts or mentally unsound persons, however, may be legally considered wards. A guardian's duty is to protect the ward's interests and act in the place of a parent (*in loco parentis*) toward the ward.

In politics, a ward is a political division of a city. The early use of this name started when cities were divided into wards so that they might be guarded more easily. But today cities are divided into wards chiefly to simplify city government and city elections. For purposes of government, each ward elects one or two *aldermen*. The aldermen help govern the city and look after the ward. JOHN W. WADE

See also GUARDIAN.

WARD, AARON MONTGOMERY (1844-1913), an American businessman, pioneered in the mail-order business in the United States. As a traveling salesman in the Middle West, he conceived the idea of buying merchandise in large quantities from manufacturers for cash and selling it directly to farmers for cash.

In 1872, Ward and his partner, George R. Thorne, began in the mail-order business in a livery-stable loft with $2,400 capital and a single-sheet catalog listing a few dry goods items. When he died, annual sales had

risen to $40 million. Ward was born in Chatham, N.J., on Feb. 17, 1844. KENNETH WIGGINS PORTER

WARD, ARTEMAS (1727-1800), an American Revolutionary War commander, was the first commander in chief of the Massachusetts troops. When George Washington was given supreme command of all the American forces in 1775, Ward became second in command. In 1776, he resigned his commission because of ill health, but he remained active in politics for several years.

Ward was born in Shrewsbury, Mass., and was graduated from Harvard College. He was an officer in the French and Indian War. In 1762, he became a justice, and later chief justice, of the Worcester County Court of Common Pleas. He served in the Massachusetts legislature, in the Continental Congress, and in the U.S. House of Representatives. KENNETH R. ROSSMAN

WARD, ARTEMUS (1834-1867), was the pen name of Charles Farrar Browne, an American humorous writer and lecturer. He began a story about Artemus Ward, a traveling showman who exhibited waxworks, when he worked for the Cleveland *Plain Dealer*. His humor depended on amusing misspellings. Lincoln read a piece by Ward to his Cabinet in 1862 before reading a draft of the Emancipation Proclamation. Ward was born in Waterford, Me. He lectured on the Pacific Coast, where he encouraged young Mark Twain, and also lectured in England. EDWARD WAGENKNECHT

WARD, BARBARA (1914-   ), is a British economist and journalist. She became known for her books about the problems of economic development in developing nations. Ward argues for a more even distribution of the world's economic resources between the industrial and the developing countries. To achieve these goals, she favors international cooperation and programs to control population growth.

Barbara Mary Ward was born in York, England. She attended schools in Paris and in Germany before entering Oxford University in England in 1932. She graduated in 1935. Ward joined the staff of *The Economist*, an influential weekly British newspaper, in 1939. In 1950, she married Sir Robert G. A. Jackson, an Australian economist and United

V. Sladon
Barbara Ward

Nations official. She received the title Dame Commander of the British Empire in 1974. In 1976, she was made a life *peeress* (member of the nobility) with the title Baroness Jackson of Lodsworth.

Ward has written more than 12 books. They include *The Rich Nations and the Poor Nations* (1962) and *The Lopsided World* (1968). DANIEL R. FUSFELD

WARD, EBER B. See IRON AND STEEL (Famous People in Iron and Steel).

WARD, JOSEPH (1838-1889), was a noted clergyman and educator, and a leader in South Dakota's drive for statehood. In 1879, he helped form a group that worked for South Dakota's statehood.

WARD, LYND KENDALL

Ward became a Congregational minister in 1869, and became a missionary in Yankton, then capital of the Dakota Territory. Because of his missionary work, some people call him the *Father of Congregationalism in Dakota*. In 1881, he helped establish Yankton College, a private school associated with the Congregational church. He served as president and professor of philosophy at Yankton until his death.

Ward was born in Perry Centre, N.Y. A statue of him represents South Dakota in the United States Capitol in Washington, D.C.   RICHARD A. BARTLETT

WARD, LYND KENDALL (1905-   ), is an American artist. His reputation as a wood engraver was established with the publication of *God's Man* and five other novels in woodcut. They were the first such novels without text to be published in the United States. His works also appear in water color, oil, and lithography. He wrote and illustrated *The Biggest Bear* (1953), a children's book which received the Caldecott medal in 1953. Ward and his wife, May McNeer, received the 1975 Regina medal. Ward was born in Chicago. He graduated from Columbia University.   RUTH HILL VIGUERS

See also LITERATURE FOR CHILDREN (picture: The Biggest Bear).

WARD, SAMUEL A. See AMERICA THE BEAUTIFUL.

WARDEN. See PRISON.

WAREHOUSE is a storage place for goods and merchandise. It is usually a large, well-constructed, fireproof building or series of buildings. Storing goods in such places is called *warehousing*.

Warehousing helps to distribute goods between the manufacturer or importer and the consumer. Goods that cannot be sold immediately are stored in warehouses and used as needed. This regulates distribution, and equalizes supply with demand. Prices of goods would rise and fall out of proportion to value if all supplies were dumped on the market at the same time.

The modern form of warehousing began in the Middle Ages. Europeans imported goods that had to be protected until they could be sold. American merchants used warehouses during colonial times. They stored European shipments in large buildings in cities along the Atlantic Coast. Storage needs increased with the expansion of the railroads. They carried more goods than could be disposed of, so the railroads provided storage in freight depots and grain elevators.

Warehousing has become an industry since then. Warehouse owners make a profit from renting space and providing other services for industries and their retail customers. The Federal Warehouse Act of 1916 and certain state laws govern warehousing practices. These laws make the warehouse owner responsible for the condition of stored goods. They also provide for inspection and they regulate issuance of receipts, which are often used as security for loans.   JOHN H. FREDERICK

See also BONDED WAREHOUSE.

WARFARE. See WAR; GUERRILLA WARFARE.

WARHEAD. See BOMB; GUIDED MISSILE (The Warhead); TORPEDO.

WARHOL, ANDY (1930-   ), is an American artist whose work suggests the influence of the machine on art. He avoids any quality of feeling or emotion in his work, and presents his material with mechanical impersonality.

Warhol is not a painter in the traditional sense. He often uses a mechanical stencil process called *silk screen* in creating his pictures. Often he repeats the same image several times in a single work, suggesting the multiple copies of a newspaper illustration. Warhol's themes come from everyday life. They include soup cans, soft drink bottles, celebrities, and reproductions of newspaper pictures of automobile accidents. Warhol was born in Philadelphia.   ALLEN S. WELLER

See also CUNNINGHAM, MERCE (picture).

WARLOCK. See WITCHCRAFT.

WARM-BLOODED ANIMAL is an animal that almost always has about the same body temperature, regardless of the temperature of its surroundings. Birds and mammals, including human beings, are warm-blooded animals. Nearly all other kinds of animals are cold-blooded.

The body of a warm-blooded animal produces heat by burning food. Shivering and physical activity also generate body heat. Young warm-blooded animals and some adult small mammals have heat-producing organs, called *brown fat*, on their neck, chest, and back.

A layer of fat beneath the skin, plus a covering of hair, fur, or feathers, helps keep a warm-blooded animal warm. The animal's body can also conserve heat by reducing the flow of blood to the limbs and to uncovered skin. The body becomes cooler by such means as panting and sweating.   JAMES EDWARD HEATH

See also BIRD (Body Temperature); MAMMAL; COLD-BLOODED ANIMAL; TEMPERATURE, BODY.

WARM FRONT. See WEATHER (Fronts; diagram: Warm Front); CLOUD (Storms).

WARNER, POP (1871-1954), was one of America's greatest college football coaches for 47 years. He left his law practice in 1895 to coach at Iowa State College, the Carlisle (Pa.) Indian Industrial School, and Pittsburgh, Stanford, Georgia, Cornell, and Temple universities. Warner developed the wing-back formations and many clever offensive plays. At Carlisle, he coached Jim Thorpe, whom he called "the greatest football player of all time." Warner was born in Springville, N.Y. His full name was Glenn Scobey Warner.   FOREST EVASHEVSKI

WARNER, SETH (1743-1784), was an American soldier in the Revolutionary War. He is chiefly remembered for the part he played in forming and leading the famed regiment of Green Mountain Boys. His most important single contribution to winning the war was his timely arrival to help reinforce the colonial troops at the Battle of Bennington on Aug. 16, 1777. His support of John Stark clinched a decisive victory for the American forces. In recognition of his services, Warner was appointed a brigadier general in 1778. He was born in Roxbury, Conn.   CLINTON ROSSITER

See also GREEN MOUNTAIN BOYS.

WARP. See WEAVING (Types of Weaves).

WARRANT, *WAHR uhnt*, is a document authorizing a person to do something. A *search warrant* authorizes a law officer to search a house or other premises for goods held illegally. A *bench warrant* authorizes a law officer to arrest and bring before the court a person charged with a crime, misdemeanor, or contempt of court. Other warrants authorize persons to pay and receive money.   HUNTINGTON CAIRNS

See also ARREST; SEARCH WARRANT; WIRETAPPING.

WARRANT OFFICER. See RANK IN ARMED SERVICES.

WARRANTY. See DEED.

WARREN, Mich. (pop. 179,260), is a suburb of Detroit. Its main industries are automotive research and production. Warren was incorporated as a village in 1893. It became a city in 1955. Warren has a mayor-council government. For location, see MICHIGAN (political map).   WILLIS F. DUNBAR

WARREN, CHARLES (1868-1954), an American lawyer, gained fame for his definitive historical books on the Supreme Court of the United States and on the American bar. He wrote *A History of the American Bar* (1911) and won the 1923 Pulitzer prize in history for his three-volume *The Supreme Court in United States History* (1922). Warren served as assistant attorney general of the United States under President Woodrow Wilson. Warren was born in Boston.   H. G. REUSCHLEIN

WARREN, EARL (1891-1974), became chief justice of the United States in 1953. He submitted his resignation in June, 1968, but did not leave office. He remained on the court because a Senate filibuster prevented a vote on the nomination of associate justice Abe Fortas to succeed him as chief justice. Warren later agreed to remain in office until the end of the Supreme Court's term in the summer of 1969.

Warren had won recognition as a liberal and influential presiding officer. In 1954, he wrote the opinion for the unanimous ruling by the Supreme Court outlawing racial segregation in the public schools. He wrote the 1964 decision that states must apportion both houses of their legislatures on the basis of equal population. Also in 1964, he was chairman of a presidential committee that investigated the assassination of President John F. Kennedy (see WARREN REPORT).

Warren was born in Los Angeles, and received his law degree from the University of California. He served as attorney general of California from 1939 to 1943, and as governor of California from 1943 to 1953. In 1946, he became the first candidate for governor to win both the Republican and Democratic nominations. Warren was the Republican nominee for Vice-President in 1948.   MERLO J. PUSEY

WARREN, JOHN COLLINS (1778-1856), was an American surgeon. He is chiefly remembered for taking part, with dentist William Morton, in the first public demonstration of ether as a surgical anesthetic in 1846. He made the famous remark, "Gentlemen, this is no humbug," as he finished the operation. Warren was born in Boston, and was educated at Harvard College. Between 1815 and 1821, he helped found the Massachusetts General Hospital.   GEORGE ROSEN

WARREN, JOSEPH (1741-1775), was a leading Massachusetts statesman in the period before the Revolutionary War. He was among the first to die for the patriot cause when he was killed at the Battle of Bunker Hill. He spoke and wrote frequently for the colonial cause after 1765, and he helped draft some key Massachusetts protests against the British enactments. Warren's selection in 1775 as president of the Provincial Assembly and his election as major general in the Massachusetts forces reflected the respect he won. He was born in Roxbury, Mass. He studied at Harvard College and became a successful physician.   CLARENCE L. VER STEEG

WARREN, MERCY OTIS (1728-1814), was a colonial American writer. Her most important work was the

three-volume *History of the Rise, Progress, and Termination of the American Revolution* (1805). She had helped encourage prorevolutionary feelings by ridiculing the British colonial government in such plays as *The Adulateur* (1773), *The Defeat* (1773), and *The Group* (1775).

Warren had extensive knowledge of political affairs and was a close friend of many leaders of the revolution, who included her brother, James Otis, and her husband, James Warren. Mercy Otis Warren expressed her political convictions even when they were unpopular. For example, she opposed ratification of the United States Constitution because she felt it gave too much power to the federal government. She favored increased safeguards for individual liberties and equal opportunities for women in education and public affairs. Warren was born in Barnstable, Mass.   DEAN DONER

WARREN, ROBERT PENN (1905-   ), is an American novelist, poet, and literary critic. Warren won the 1947 Pulitzer prize for fiction for *All the King's Men* (1946). This novel describes the rise and fall of a ruthless Southern politician. Warren won the 1958 Pulitzer prize for poetry for his collection *Promises: Poems 1954-1956*, which was published in 1957. He also won the 1979 poetry prize for his collection *Now and Then: Poems 1976-1978*, which was published in 1978.

In addition to *All the King's Men*, Warren's major novels include *World Enough and Time* (1950), *The Cave* (1959), and *Meet Me in the Green Glen* (1971). These books reflect the author's Southern heritage. They also emphasize the interaction of past and present, and what Warren believes is each person's struggle to determine his or her identity. Warren's poetry explores the themes of time, the individual, and the nature of evil. His long poem *Brother to Dragons* (1953) is typical of his verse. Warren also co-edited, with the critic Cleanth Brooks, two influential textbooks—*Understanding Poetry* (1938) and *Understanding Fiction* (1943). Warren was born in Guthrie, Ky.   JOHN B. VICKERY

WARREN REPORT is a summary of events related to the assassination of President John F. Kennedy in Dallas, Tex., on Nov. 22, 1963. Issued by the Warren Commission in September 1964, it concluded that Lee Harvey Oswald, acting alone, shot Kennedy from a window on the sixth floor of the Texas School Book Depository building. The report also said that Jack Ruby acted alone in killing Oswald on Nov. 24, 1963, in a Dallas jail. It found no evidence of a conspiracy involving Oswald and Ruby. It criticized the Secret Service and Federal Bureau of Investigation (FBI), and asked for better measures in the future to protect the President.

President Lyndon B. Johnson named Chief Justice Earl Warren to head the commission. The other members were Senator Richard B. Russell, Democrat of Georgia; Senator John S. Cooper, Republican of Kentucky; Representative T. Hale Boggs, Democrat of Louisiana; Representative Gerald R. Ford, Republican of Michigan; Allen W. Dulles, former director of the Central Intelligence Agency (CIA); and John J. McCloy, former adviser to President Kennedy.

The commission was appointed on Nov. 29, 1963. During 10 months, it took testimony from 552 witnesses. But critics accused the commission of not probing deeply enough into the possibility of a conspiracy.

WARS OF SUCCESSION

During the late 1970's, a special committee of the U.S. House of Representatives reexamined the evidence. It concluded that Kennedy "was probably assassinated as a result of a conspiracy." See KENNEDY, JOHN F. (Assassination Controversy).　CAROL L. THOMPSON

WARS OF SUCCESSION. See SUCCESSION WARS.

WARS OF THE ROSES brought civil strife to England in the late 1400's. Two branches of the royal house fought for the English throne. The symbols adopted by each side gave the struggle its name. The House of York had long used a white rose as its emblem. The House of Lancaster became identified with a red rose, but historians are not certain when this took place. Some believe the red rose symbol did not appear until the final battle of the wars. The wars began in 1455 with the Battle of Saint Albans, and ended in 1485 with the Battle of Bosworth Field.

King Henry VI of the House of Lancaster held the throne when the Wars of the Roses began. His grandfather, Henry IV, had seized power in 1399. Richard, Duke of York, claimed that Henry VI had no right to be king. Richard was killed at the Battle of Wakefield in 1460. But his son Edward led York forces which crushed the Lancastrians at the Battle of Towton in 1461. Edward then became king as Edward IV.

In 1470, the forces of Lancaster drove Edward from England and brought back Henry VI. Edward returned seven months later, defeated the Lancaster forces at the battles of Barnet and Tewkesbury, and regained the throne. The House of York ruled until Richard III lost his throne to the Lancaster descendant, Henry Tudor, who became King Henry VII in 1485. Henry VII married Elizabeth, daughter of Edward IV, uniting the houses of Lancaster and York, and founding the Tudor dynasty.　PAUL KENDALL

See also ENGLAND (The Wars of the Roses); LANCASTER; TUDOR, HOUSE OF; YORK.

WARSAW, a name for black jewfish. See JEWFISH.

WARSAW, *WAWR saw* (pop. 1,317,000), is the capital and largest city of Poland. Its name in Polish is WARSZAWA. The city, a center of culture and industry, lies in east-central Poland, on both banks of the Vistula River. For location, see POLAND (political map).

Warsaw has been the capital of an independent country throughout much of its history. But Prussia, Russia, and Germany have each controlled the city at various times. During World War II (1939-1945), German troops occupied Warsaw. The war left the city in ruins, its population reduced by more than 60 per cent. Warsaw today is largely a city rebuilt from the ruins.

The City. Warsaw covers 174 square miles (450 square kilometers). The Vistula River divides the city. The left bank section lies west of the river, and the right bank section lies east of it. The center of Warsaw and most of the residential areas are on the left bank.

The Poles reconstructed many of Warsaw's historic buildings that had been damaged in the war. Churches and palaces built during the Middle Ages stand near modern hospitals, schools, and government buildings. Warsaw has spacious parks, and fine libraries, museums, and theaters. Statues of famous Poles stand throughout the city.

Famous landmarks, rebuilt since the war, include the Cathedral of St. John and the ancient city walls, both dating from the 1300's. Warsaw's opera house, also reconstructed since the war, is one of the largest in the world. The city's many monuments include the Column of King Sigismund. This monument, built in 1644, honors the king who moved the Polish capital from Kraków to Warsaw in 1596.

Warsaw has modern housing developments and office buildings. New stores line Marszałkowska Street, the heart of the city's main shopping district. The huge Palace of Culture and Science, a gift from the Soviet Union in 1954, stands in a modern part of Warsaw. The city's many educational and research institutions include the University of Warsaw and the headquarters of the Polish Academy of Science.

Numerous cultural events take place in the capital. Each fall, the Festival of Contemporary Music attracts musicians from all Europe. Every five years, pianists from many parts of the world play in Warsaw's Frédéric Chopin International Piano Competition.

The People. World War II severely reduced Warsaw's population. But after the war, the population grew so rapidly that serious housing shortages developed. The government built many housing projects and restricted the flow of new residents into Warsaw.

Almost all the people of Warsaw are Poles. They share the same cultural, national, and racial backgrounds. The great majority of the people are Roman Catholics, and religion plays an important role in their lives. Religious festivals, such as the Corpus Christi procession in May or June, rank as major events.

Economy. Warsaw is an important center of Polish industry. Major industries in the city include food processing and the manufacture of automobiles, electronic equipment, machines, metals, and textiles. Warsaw has long been a trading city, and it is one of the chief railroad centers of eastern Europe. Thousands of Warsaw's citizens work in agencies of the Polish government.

History. As early as the A.D. 900's, a small Slavic settlement existed in the area that is now Warsaw. During the late Middle Ages, from the 1200's to the 1500's, Warsaw was the home of the dukes of Mazovia. Mazovia entered the Polish kingdom in the 1500's, and King Sigismund III moved the capital from Kraków to Warsaw in 1596. Swedish forces invaded Poland in the mid-1600's and destroyed much of Warsaw in 1656. But Warsaw remained the capital of Poland until 1795. That year, Austria, Prussia, and Russia divided Poland among themselves, and Prussia took over Warsaw.

From 1807 to 1813, the city was the capital of the Duchy of Warsaw, a state created by the French emperor Napoleon. After Napoleon's defeat in eastern Europe, Russia gained control of Warsaw. The Poles rebelled against the Russians in 1830 and 1863, but these uprisings failed. During the late 1800's, the Russians tightened their control over Warsaw. World War I (1914-1918) brought an end to the Russian rule. Germany controlled Warsaw from 1915 to 1918, when Poland again became independent.

World War II (1939-1945) brought the almost total destruction of Warsaw. In 1939, the Germans held the city in a three-week siege that caused great damage. Warsaw surrendered to the Germans, but it became the heart of the Polish underground resistance movement. The people of Warsaw suffered under the ruthless ter-

Modern Stores and Office Buildings line the streets of downtown Warsaw. Marszałkowska Street, *left*, runs through the heart of the city's main shopping district.

ror of the German troops. The Nazis staged mass arrests and public executions, and they forced many of Warsaw's people to leave the city. They confined about 500,000 Jews to a section of the city called the *ghetto*. Many of the Jews died of hunger and disease. The Germans executed thousands of others. In April 1943, about 60,000 Jews who still remained in the ghetto revolted. The Germans killed almost all of them.

By the summer of 1944, Soviet armies had pushed the Germans out of Russia and had reached the outskirts of Warsaw. On Aug. 1, 1944, the people of Warsaw rose against the Germans. At first, the Poles seized large parts of the city. But the nearby Soviet troops did not come to their aid, and the Poles soon began to weaken. In spite of massive German counterattacks, the Poles held on to isolated areas on the left bank of the Vistula River. They finally surrendered on October 3. The Germans then evacuated the entire population of the left bank and systematically destroyed what remained of Warsaw. They burned and dynamited all the buildings that still stood. On Jan. 17, 1945, Soviet forces entered Warsaw. They set up a Polish Communist government in the city in February, and Warsaw became the capital of the Polish People's Republic.

Anti-Soviet demonstrations took place in Warsaw in 1956. In 1968, Warsaw students rioted in protest against government limits on cultural freedom.   ADAM BROMKE

See also POLAND (picture).

WARSAW PACT is a treaty which brought the Communist nations of Europe under a unified military command. Russia, Albania, Bulgaria, Czechoslovakia, East Germany, Hungary, Poland, and Romania signed the treaty at Warsaw in May 1955. They signed the alliance after the western countries had formed the North Atlantic Treaty Organization (see NORTH ATLANTIC TREATY ORGANIZATION). China did not sign the Warsaw Pact, but pledged its support to the Warsaw Pact countries. Albania withdrew from the pact in 1968. A Russian army marshal serves as supreme commander of Warsaw Pact forces. The command has headquarters in Moscow.

WARSHIP is a naval combat ship. Some kinds of warships attack enemy aircraft, surface ships, and sub-

marines. These warships are heavily armed with such weapons as guns, missiles, rockets, and torpedoes. Other types of warships serve as bases for planes or helicopters. Still others transport troops, weapons, and equipment to battle areas.

Warships range in size from small vessels with only a few crew members to huge ships that carry more than 6,000 persons. Most warships have radar and sonar to detect and locate enemy planes, surface ships, and submarines. Radar detects aircraft and surface ships, and sonar locates submarines.

In ancient times and until the 1600's, warships and cargo ships were almost identical. However, warships gradually become highly specialized vessels used only for military purposes.

This article provides general information on warships. See also the separate WORLD BOOK articles on the types of ships discussed.

Kinds of Warships

Large modern navies have many kinds of warships that are designed for certain combat operations. The United States Navy uses six principal types: (1) aircraft carriers, (2) amphibious warfare ships, (3) cruisers, (4) destroyers, (5) frigates, and (6) submarines. The U.S. fleet also includes various kinds of small warships called *small combatants*.

Aircraft Carriers are the largest and most powerful warships. They serve as bases for bomber and fighter planes. They also carry antisubmarine aircraft, helicopters, and small numbers of other kinds of planes. Aircraft carriers have few defensive weapons, and so they must depend on other warships to serve as protective escorts.

A carrier has a large, flat flight deck with equipment that enables planes to take off and land without a long runway. The aircraft are launched by four catapults, each of which can put a plane into the air every 30 seconds. The landing area of the flight deck has steel wires stretched across it. A hook attached to the bottom of each plane catches onto a wire, bringing the aircraft to a quick stop.

The powerful radars of an aircraft carrier not only

A Warship in Action. The frigate U.S.S. *Lockwood*, shown above, tests a missile for use against enemy surface ships and submarines. This ship is also armed with a 5-inch (127-millimeter) gun and antisubmarine torpedoes. It carries a helicopter for locating and attacking submarines.

detect enemy planes but also guide the carrier's own aircraft. Short-range radars are used to detect enemy missiles. These radars also help the crew keep track of nearby ships at night and navigate the carrier when close to shore.

Aircraft carriers are about 1,100 feet (335 meters) long and can carry from 85 to 95 planes. Carriers travel at speeds of more than 30 knots (nautical miles per hour).

Amphibious Warfare Ships land troops, weapons, and vehicles on beaches held by the enemy. Some of these ships remain far from shore and use small landing craft, amphibious tractors, or helicopters to land the troops and cargo. Such ships have closed-off areas at sea level called *docking wells*. The docking wells are flooded and opened into the sea so that landing craft and amphibious tractors can float out through them.

Some amphibious warfare ships serve chiefly as helicopter carriers. They resemble small aircraft carriers but do not have the launching and landing equipment needed for conventional planes. These ships carry from 20 to 30 helicopters, as well as troops and small vehicles. The ships also can serve as bases for *V/STOL aircraft*. V/STOL's can take off and land vertically or on a very short runway. Other amphibious warfare ships have command and communications facilities to coordinate air, shore, and surface operations.

Amphibious warfare ships measure up to 800 feet (250 meters) long and travel at speeds of about 20 knots. They carry few defensive weapons.

Cruisers escort aircraft carriers and defend them against air and submarine attacks. Modern cruisers

are called *guided missile cruisers*. They carry supersonic missiles that can be fired at aircraft that are from 15 to 85 miles (24 to 137 kilometers) from the ship. Cruisers also have antisubmarine rockets and torpedoes for use against enemy submarines. Some cruisers carry one or two helicopters. After an enemy submarine has been detected by sonar, the helicopters pinpoint its location and attack it. Some cruisers also carry 5-inch (127-millimeter) guns. Modern cruisers are about 600 feet (180 meters) long and travel at speeds of more than 30 knots.

Destroyers are used chiefly to defend aircraft carriers, amphibious ships, and merchant ships. They also perform various independent missions, such as bombarding enemy shores and conducting search and rescue operations at sea.

Modern destroyers have 5-inch (127-millimeter) guns, short-range antiaircraft missiles, and antisubmarine weapons. They also carry one or two helicopters to attack submarines. Destroyers range in length from about 375 to 560 feet (112$\frac{1}{2}$ to 171 meters). They can reach speeds of 30 to 33 knots.

Frigates are used primarily to defend amphibious ships and merchant ships against enemy submarines. Frigates carry torpedoes, nuclear depth charges, and other antisubmarine weapons. They also have a helicopter for locating and attacking submarines. In addition, most of these warships carry missiles and one or two guns for defense against air and surface attacks. Modern frigates measure up to 445 feet (136 meters) long. They travel at speeds of 27 to 30 knots.

Some navies have small frigates called *corvettes* to patrol coastal waters. Corvettes measure about 150 feet (46 meters) long. The U.S. Navy does not use corvettes.

Submarines search out and attack enemy submarines and surface ships. Some can also fire missiles at enemy cities and military bases. Modern submarines have nuclear power systems that enable them to remain underwater for months at a time. The U.S. Navy has two kinds of submarines, *attack submarines* and *ballistic missile submarines*.

Attack submarines have large sonars for detecting submarines and surface ships from long distances. They carry torpedoes that are fired from tubes inside the hull. Antisubmarine missiles can also be fired from the torpedo tubes. In addition, these tubes carry mines that are laid off an enemy coast. Attack submarines range in length from 250 to 360 feet (76 to 110 meters). Some can travel underwater at speeds of more than 30 knots.

Ballistic missile submarines carry long-range missiles that can hit targets up to 4,000 miles (6,400 kilometers) away. These submarines are designed chiefly to attack enemy cities. They also carry torpedoes for defense against enemy surface ships and submarines. Ballistic missile submarines measure from about 380 to 550 feet (115 to 168 meters) long. They reach speeds of about 20 knots underwater.

Small Combatants include such ships as minesweepers, missile boats, and patrol boats. Minesweepers locate and remove underwater explosives. Missile boats carry guided missiles that can attack enemy surface ships from 10 to 60 miles (16 to 97 kilometers) away. Patrol boats guard rivers and coastal waters.

Small combatants are generally operated near coasts. The U.S. Navy has few of these ships because it conducts chiefly long-range ocean operations.

History

Ships have been used in combat for at least 3,000 years. Until the 1600's, however, there were few differences between warships and cargo ships. Any ship that fought in combat might also transport goods or carry explorers on long voyages.

Early Warships. The ancient Greek and Roman navies used long, narrow wooden ships called *galleys*. These vessels were powered by oarsmen, who sat in one or more rows on each side. Galleys also had a rectangular sail called a *square sail*, which was used in a favorable wind. The bow of a galley ended in a long, sharp point that was rammed into the hull of an enemy ship.

During the A.D. 700's, the Vikings of northern Europe developed the *long ship*. It was powered by rowers and a square sail but weighed only about half as much as a galley. Long ships were strong and seaworthy, and they helped the Vikings control the seas until the 1000's.

Southern Europeans continued to use galleys in battle but gradually stopped attacking by ramming enemy ships. Instead, the rowers maneuvered their galley close to an enemy ship and then boarded it.

By the 1500's, most warships carried guns, and so battles no longer were fought aboard ship. Navies began to use warships as floating gun platforms and replaced galleys with larger, more heavily armed ships.

The Age of Sailing Ships. During the 1500's, Europeans began to build large, heavy sailing ships designed for long ocean voyages by explorers. Such ships included *galleons*, which were also used as warships.

The Spanish Navy built large galleons that sailed high on the water. English galleons were smaller, lower, and easier to maneuver. In 1588, the Spanish Navy tried to invade England. The Spaniards called their fleet the "Invincible Armada" because they were sure it could not be defeated. But the English won the battle, partly because their galleons were more maneuverable warships than those of the Spaniards.

After Spain's defeat, navies began to build specialized fighting ships. These vessels included *capital ships*, an important type of warship during the 1600's and 1700's. Capital ships were fairly easy to maneuver and large enough to carry more than 100 guns. They became known as *ships of the line* because they could serve in the line of battle.

Warships of the 1800's. In 1814, Robert Fulton, an American inventor, built the first steam-powered warship. Navies then began to use warships driven by steam, but the vessels were also powered by sails until the mid-1800's.

Naval guns that fired explosive shells, rather than solid cannon balls, were developed in the 1820's. The shells could easily tear huge holes in the sides of wooden ships. Therefore, navies began to build iron vessels and also *ironclad* ships, which were made of wood covered with iron. Ironclads could withstand attack far better than wooden ships could. The first battle between these new types of warships occurred in 1862, during the American Civil War. The North's iron *Monitor* fought the South's ironclad Merrimack (then called the *Virginia*) at Hampton Roads, Va. Neither ship won, but the battle marked the beginning of the age of steel ships. It was also one of the first battles between ships powered only by steam.

Rotating gun turrets were invented in the mid-1800's, and the *Monitor* was the first ship in the U.S. Navy to use them. They enabled guns to be turned in various directions and ended the need for extensive maneuvers by warships. Heavy rifles became standard armament on combat vessels and greatly improved the range and accuracy of naval gunfire.

The Birth of the Modern Battleship. In 1906, the British Navy introduced the *Dreadnought*, the first modern battleship. It was the forerunner of the massive battleships that ruled the seas for more than 35 years. The *Dreadnought* was faster, larger, and more heavily armed than any earlier warship.

During the early and mid-1900's, navies improved the basic design of the *Dreadnought* to make battleships larger and faster. Better communications methods developed within the ships increased the efficiency of their command. The battleship became the chief combat warship, and nations measured their power in the world by the number of battleships in their navies.

Warships in the Two World Wars. Battleships were the most powerful warships during World War I (1914-1918). However, the German Navy proved that submarines were also highly effective warships. German submarines, called *U-boats*, sank thousands of Allied merchant ships. These deadly attacks soon led to the development of sonar equipment and various antisubmarine ships.

Radar was perfected shortly before World War II be-

The Development of Warships

Ships have been used in battle since ancient times. But warships and cargo ships were almost identical until the 1600's, when navies began to build vessels designed only for combat. Today, large navies have many kinds of warships. Each type performs specific functions in battle. These illustrations show the development of some major warships from the 200's B.C. to modern times.

WORLD BOOK illustrations by George Suyeoka

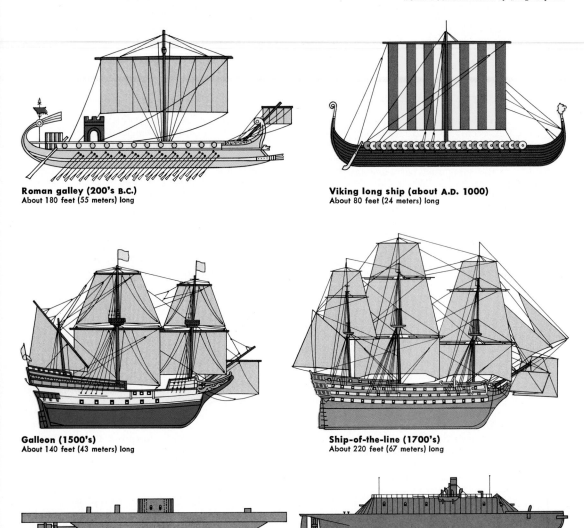

Roman galley (200's B.C.)
About 180 feet (55 meters) long

Viking long ship (about A.D. 1000)
About 80 feet (24 meters) long

Galleon (1500's)
About 140 feet (43 meters) long

Ship-of-the-line (1700's)
About 220 feet (67 meters) long

U.S. Civil War iron ship (1860's)
About 170 feet (52 meters) long

U.S. Civil War ironclad ship (1860's)
About 270 feet (82 meters) long

gan in 1939. It enabled warships to locate enemy aircraft and ships at night, through clouds, and at great distances. Improved *gun directors* were developed at about the same time. These devices quickly tracked moving aircraft and directed gunfire at them. Gun directors were used with *proximity fuzes*, which exploded a shell as it neared its target and eliminated the need for a direct hit.

Aircraft became the most effective military weapons of World War II. The importance of battleships declined, and navies began to concentrate on building aircraft carriers. They also built large numbers of cruisers and destroyers to protect the carriers and installed antiaircraft weapons on all warships.

The U.S. Navy built thousands of amphibious war-fare ships during World War II. One type, the *landing ship—tank* (*LST*), carried tanks and landed them on enemy beaches. Other amphibious warfare ships carried troops, landing craft, and military supplies. Still others used guns, mortars, and rockets to bombard enemy beaches before invasions.

Warships in the Nuclear Age. After World War II ended in 1945, the U.S. Navy began to develop nuclear-powered warships. It launched the first nuclear-powered submarine, the *Nautilus*, in 1954. The *Nautilus* could travel much faster than the diesel-powered submarines then in use. Its nuclear power system also enabled the submarine to travel hundreds of thousands of miles underwater without refueling.

The development of powerful, long-range guided mis-

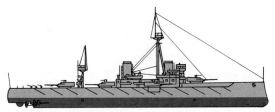

Dreadnought (early 1900's)
About 500 feet (150 meters) long

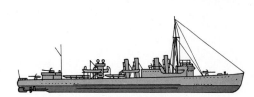

World War I destroyer (early 1900's)
About 300 feet (91 meters) long

World War II battleship (mid-1900's)
About 900 feet (274 meters) long

World War II submarine (mid-1900's)
About 300 feet (91 meters) long

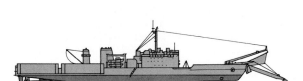

Modern landing ship—tank (LST)
About 500 feet (150 meters) long

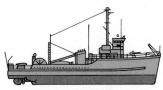

Minesweeper (1950's)
About 150 feet (46 meters) long

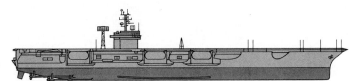

Modern nuclear-powered aircraft carrier
About 1,000 feet (300 meters) long

Modern missile boat
About 130 feet (40 meters) long

Modern nuclear-powered guided-missile cruiser
About 600 feet (180 meters) long

Modern nuclear-powered ballistic missile submarine
About 500 feet (150 meters) long

siles also increased the capabilities of warships. These missiles can be launched from almost every kind of warship to attack aircraft, surface ships, and submarines. In the early 1960's, the U.S. Navy developed the first ballistic missile submarine.

During the 1960's, the U.S. Navy also built nuclear-powered surface ships. In the 1970's, U.S. warships began to use gas turbine engines, which cost much less to build and operate than nuclear power systems. These engines operated almost as effectively in surface ships as did nuclear power systems.   NORMAN POLMAR

Related Articles in WORLD BOOK include:

WART

WART is a horny growth on the surface of the skin. Warts may appear anywhere, in a wide range of shapes, sizes, and numbers. Flat warts that grow on the sole of the foot look like corns and hurt like tacks. Warts on the face may form little beardlike projections. In moist parts of the body, warts may grow into masses like tiny cauliflowers. Warts can even appear on the lips or tongue. Warts are infections caused by viruses. If a wart is scratched open, the virus may spread by contact to another part of the body or to another person. Contrary to superstition, touching the skin of a toad will not cause warts.

The viruses that cause warts live in cells of the surface layer of the skin, and do not infect the deep layer. The thickened surface layer forms folds into which little blood vessels grow. Sometimes warts go away without treatment, perhaps because immunity to the infection develops. Wart vaccine cures infections in cattle, but it is not a practical treatment for human beings. Physicians often remove warts by burning off surface skin. This does little harm to the deep layers. X-ray treatment is sometimes useful. Treatment for any wart should be administered by a doctor.   RICHARD L. SUTTON, JR.

WART HOG is an African pig with large curved tusks protruding from its huge flattened head. These tusks may be as much as 2 feet (61 centimeters) long. Between the tusks and the eyes are three pairs of large "warts" from which the hog gets its name. The coarsely grained pale gray hide of the wart hog is thinly sprinkled with stiff, brownish-gray hairs. A thin mane of long bristly hair hangs over its back and head. A large boar may weigh over 200 pounds (91 kilograms) and it may be about 30 inches (76 centimeters) high.

The Boer farmers call the wart hog *vlakte-vark* (pig of the plains). It lives in dry, sandy country from southern Africa to Ethiopia and prefers open forest with plenty of thickets for protection. The wart hog travels in small family groups. Old boars, however, usually prefer to live by themselves. The sow may produce as many as six to eight young at a time. Ordinarily, only half that number are born at one time. Wart hogs often use burrows that have been made by other animals. They eat almost everything—roots, plants, birds' eggs, and even small mammals.

Scientific Classification. The wart hog belongs to the Old World pig family, *Suidae*. It is genus *Phacochoerus*, species *P. aetheopicus*.   VICTOR H. CAHALANE

New York Zoological Society
The Wart Hog Is Named for the Warts on Its Face.

WARTON, THOMAS. See POET LAUREATE.

WARWICK, *WAWR ihk* (pop. 83,694), is Rhode Island's second largest city and a chief commercial center of the state. Only Providence is larger. Warwick lies on the Pawtuxet River in east-central Rhode Island (see RHODE ISLAND [political map]). Warwick helps form a metropolitan area with 908,887 persons.

Warwick is the home of the Warwick Musical Theater. The city's industries produce textiles and metal products. The Theodore Francis Green State Airport, Rhode Island's largest airport, is in Warwick. Narragansett Bay, a summer resort, is nearby. Warwick received its city charter in 1931. It has a mayor-council form of government.

WARWICK, *WAWR ihk*, **EARL OF** (1428-1471), RICHARD NEVILLE, was a famous English soldier and statesman. He is known to English history as the *Kingmaker*, and as the *Last of the Barons*.

Warwick was one of the most powerful men in England during the Wars of the Roses. He commanded an army with great skill at the Battle of Saint Albans in 1455. In 1460 war broke out again. Warwick again took the field and won the Battle of Northampton, capturing King Henry VI. But later in the year the Yorkists were defeated at Wakefield. The Duke of York was captured and killed. Warwick became head of the Yorkists as guardian of his cousin, Prince Edward.

Another battle was fought at Saint Albans in 1461, and Warwick was defeated. But he boldly proclaimed Edward, the Duke of York, king of England, and succeeded in having him crowned. Edward and Warwick soon quarreled. In 1470, an army led by Warwick invaded England from France and forced King Edward to flee.

Warwick then restored Queen Margaret and Henry VI to the throne. But in 1471 Warwick met Edward in battle again, at Barnet, and was killed.   ANDRÉ MAUROIS

WARWICK, EARL OF (1587-1658), ROBERT RICH, was an English colonial administrator. He served as a member of the Virginia Company and of the Council of the New England Company. He helped found the colonies of Plymouth (Mass.), Connecticut, Virginia, and Rhode Island.

His ship, the *Treasurer*, engaged in privateering against the Spaniards, and in 1619 brought over some of the first blacks to Virginia. In 1643 Warwick was appointed Lord High Admiral and Governor-in-Chief of all the English royal colonies.   IAN C. C. GRAHAM

WARWICK, GUY OF. See GUY OF WARWICK.

WARWICKSHIRE. See ENGLAND (political map).

WASATCH RANGE, *WAW sach*, is a mountain range that extends for about 140 miles (225 kilometers) from southern Idaho into northern Utah. Its abrupt western face forms the western front of the Rocky Mountains and the eastern rim of the Great Basin.

Salt Lake City lies at the foot of the range. The range's average elevation is 10,000 feet (3,000 meters). Mount Timpanogos (11,750 feet, or 3,581 meters) is the highest peak. Steep narrow valleys cut the range's western side. The eastern slope is less steep (see UTAH [physical map]).   JOHN H. GARLAND

See also SALT LAKE CITY (picture); UTAH (picture: The Wasatch Range).

WASHAKIE (1804?-1900) was a chief of the eastern Shoshoni Indians in Utah and Wyoming. He was noted for his friendship toward whites and his relentless warfare against his tribal enemies.

Washakie furnished aid to many immigrants moving west over the Oregon Trail, and also sent some Indians to General George Crook in the 1870's to serve as scouts against the Sioux.

He spent his later years in splendor as the ruler, guide, and counselor of his people. Washakie renounced many of the old Indian customs and joined the Protestant Episcopal Church.   WILLIAM H. GILBERT

WASHBURN, ICHABOD. See IRON AND STEEL (Famous People in Iron and Steel).

WASHBURN, SHERWOOD LARNED (1911-   ), is an American anthropologist. He became noted for his studies of ape behavior and of human and ape anatomy. Washburn was one of the first scientists to study the behavior of apes in their natural surroundings. He taught at Columbia University and the University of Chicago, and he has taught at the University of California at Berkeley since 1959. He edited the *American Journal of Physical Anthropology* from 1955 to 1957. Washburn was born in Cambridge, Mass.   MORDECAI L. GABRIEL

WASHING MACHINE is a machine that quickly washes clothes, linens, and other items. Before the invention of the washing machine, people spent hours doing their laundry by hand. Some people soaked their clothes in streams and then beat them with rocks to get out the dirt. Later, people scrubbed their laundry on washboards. People in some parts of the world still use such methods today.

Most washing machines work automatically. The operator simply puts in laundry, pours in detergent, and sets the controls. One set of controls determines whether the machine uses hot, warm, or cold water. The water enters the machine through hoses connected to hot and cold water pipes. The operator also sets controls to select the length of washing and rinsing time and the speed at which the water moves through the laundry. The machine, which is powered by an electric motor, then operates automatically. Many automatic washing machines have special features, such as filters that remove lint, and automatic dispensers for bleach and fabric softener.

Most automatic washers have an inner tub that is surrounded by an outer tub. The washing takes place in the inner tub, called the *washbasket*. After the laundry has been washed and rinsed, the washbasket spins rapidly. The spinning removes most of the water from the various items and throws it into the outer tub. The water is then pumped out of the machine through a drain hose. Finally, the operator dries the laundry in a drying machine or hangs it on a clothesline or somewhere else to dry.

There are two types of automatic washers, *agitator machines* and *tumbler machines*. Most automatic washers are agitator machines.

The operator of an agitator machine puts in laundry by lifting the lid of the washer. A cone-shaped device called an *agitator* is mounted in the center of the washbasket. Most agitators have several projections called *fins*. As the agitator rotates, it continually reverses direction. This action moves the laundry through the water and forces water through the items.

A tumbler machine is loaded through a door on the front of the machine. The washbasket revolves, and the laundry tumbles through the water.

Some washing machines are not automatic. A *semiautomatic machine* has controls like those of an automatic machine, but the operator must set them more than once. A *spinner machine* has two tubs that are set apart from each other. The operator transfers laundry from the washtub to the second tub, which spins rapidly and throws the water into a surrounding chamber. A *wringer machine* has two rollers that squeeze water out of the laundry. The operator removes the items from the tub before passing them through the rollers.

One of the first mechanical washers was patented about 1860 by Hamilton E. Smith of Philadelphia. A crank on this machine turned paddles inside, pushing the laundry through the water. An electric-powered washer was invented in 1910, and an automatic washing machine was introduced in 1937.   HOWARD F. McBRIDE

See also LAUNDRY.

WASHING SODA. See SODA.

How an Agitator Washing Machine Works

Hot and cold water inlet hoses
Outer tub   Inner tub   Controls
Agitator

Drain hose

Drain outlet hose to sewer

Drain pump

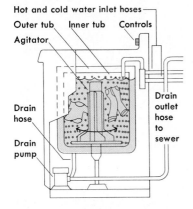
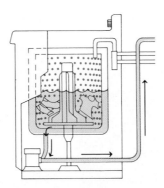
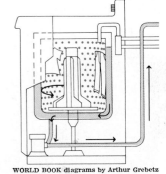

WORLD BOOK diagrams by Arthur Grebetz

Washing begins after water fills the tubs. The action of the agitator moves the laundry and forces water through it.

Rinsing takes place after the wash water is pumped out of the tubs. After the rinsing process, the rinse water is pumped out.

Spin Drying. As the inner tub spins, excess water from the laundry goes into the outer tub. The water is then pumped out.

Bob and Ira Spring
Mount Shuksan Rises Behind Picture Lake

Washington (blue) ranks 20th in size among all the states, and is the smallest of the Pacific Coast States (gray).

Ray Atkeson

A Field of Washington Daffodils

Bob and Ira Spring
Locks in Seattle

The contributors of this article are C. Brewster Coulter, Professor of History at the University of Puget Sound; and Howard J. Critchfield, Professor of Geography at Western Washington University.

44

WASHINGTON *THE EVERGREEN STATE*

WASHINGTON is the only state named for a President. It was named in honor of George Washington. The state lies on the Pacific Coast in the northwestern part of the United States. Its location makes it a gateway for land, sea, and air travel to Alaska and to Asian countries across the Pacific Ocean.

Washington is famous for scenery of breathtaking beauty and sharp contrasts. High mountains rise above thick evergreen forests and sparkling coastal waters. The junglelike forests of the Olympic Peninsula in the west are among the rainiest places in the world. But the flat semidesert land east of the Cascade Mountains stretches for long distances without a single tree.

Snow-covered peaks such as Mount Adams and Mount Saint Helens tower above the foothills and lowlands around them. Mount Rainier, the highest mountain in the state, appears to "float" on the horizon southeast of Seattle and Tacoma. On a clear day, persons in the Seattle area can also see Mount Baker to the north, the Olympic Mountains to the west, and the Cascades to the east. Lodges and chair lifts in the mountains attract thousands of tourists and skiers.

Washington's coastline has hundreds of bays and inlets that make excellent harbors. Ships from all parts of the world dock at Bellingham, Seattle, Tacoma, and other ports on Puget Sound. Washington also has important shipping centers on the Pacific Ocean and the Columbia River. Washington fishing fleets catch salmon, halibut, and other fishes in the chilly waters off the northern Pacific Coast. The state is famous for seafoods, especially chinook and sockeye salmon.

Washington's nickname, the *Evergreen State*, comes from its many firs, hemlocks, pines, and other evergreen trees. Washington has large areas of thick forests, especially on the western slopes of the Cascades. The state produces large amounts of lumber, pulp and paper, and other wood products. The state's nickname also suggests the lush green lowlands of western Washington. A mild, moist climate makes this region excellent for dairy farming and for the production of flower bulbs.

East of the Cascades, farmers raise livestock and wheat on large ranches. They grow fruits and vegetables in fertile, irrigated river valleys such as the Okanogan, Wenatchee, and Yakima. Delicious apples produced in these areas are a Washington specialty. Washington leads the states in apple production.

Giant dams on the Columbia River and its tributaries capture water for irrigation and power. The largest dam, Grand Coulee, is one of the engineering wonders of the world. Irrigation water is transforming the Columbia Basin, where farmers raise large crops of vegetables on land that once was dry and bare.

Washington contributes to the nuclear age with the Hanford Project of the U.S. Department of Energy, a nuclear energy center near Richland. Washington also has a part in the space age. The Boeing Company, a leading producer of commercial airliners and spacecraft, has headquarters in Seattle and plants in Auburn, Kent, Renton, and near Everett.

Olympia is the capital of Washington, and Seattle is the largest city. For the relationship of Washington to other states in its region, see PACIFIC COAST STATES.

FACTS IN BRIEF

Capital: Olympia.

Government: *Congress*—U.S. senators, 2; U.S. representatives, 7. *Electoral Votes*—9. *State Legislature*—senators, 49; representatives, 98. *Counties*—39.

Area: 68,192 sq. mi. (176,616 km²), including 1,622 sq. mi. (4,201 km²) of inland water but excluding 2,397 sq. mi. (6,208 km²) of Pacific coastal water, Puget Sound, and Straits of Georgia and Juan de Fuca; 20th in size among the states. *Greatest Distances*—east-west, 358 mi. (576 km); north-south, 240 mi. (386 km). *Coastline*—157 mi. (253 km).

Elevation: *Highest*—Mount Rainier, 14,410 ft. (4,392 m) above sea level. *Lowest*—sea level, along the Pacific Ocean.

Population: *Estimated 1975 Population*—3,544,000. *1970 Census*—3,409,169; 22nd among the states; distribution, 73 per cent urban, 27 per cent rural; density, 50 persons per sq. mi. (19 per km²).

Chief Products: *Agriculture*—wheat, milk, apples, beef cattle, forest products, hay, sugar beets, greenhouse and nursery products, eggs. *Fishing Industry*—salmon, oysters, tuna, crabs. *Manufacturing*—transportation equipment; lumber and wood products; food products; primary metals; paper products; fabricated metal products; chemicals; nonelectric machinery; stone, clay, and glass products; printed materials; petroleum and coal products; electric and electronic equipment; clothing; rubber and plastics products; furniture and fixtures. *Mining*—coal, sand and gravel, stone, zinc.

Statehood: Nov. 11, 1889, the 42nd state.

State Abbreviations: Wash. (traditional); WA (postal).

State Motto: *Alki* (Bye and Bye). This Indian word was first used by pioneers in Seattle. They called their settlement "New York-Alki."

State Song: "Washington, My Home." Words and music by Helen Davis.

Catching Crabs on the North Peninsula of Willapa Bay
Washington State Dept. of Commerce

Constitution. Washington is governed under its original constitution, adopted in 1889. The constitution has been amended over 50 times. Amendments to the constitution may be proposed by the state Legislature, or by a constitutional convention called by a majority of the legislators with the approval of a majority of the voters. All amendments must be approved by two-thirds of the legislators in both houses, and then by a majority of the voters in a statewide election.

Executive. The governor of Washington serves a four-year term and may be re-elected an unlimited number of times. The governor receives a yearly salary of $42,150. The governor has the power to appoint more than 350 lesser state officials. The governor may also fill vacancies that occur in elective executive offices and among the superior and Supreme Court judges. The governor may veto bills passed by the Legislature. Washington's governor, unlike those in most other states, also has the power to veto individual items in any bill without killing the whole bill. For a list of all the governors of Washington, see the *History* section of this article.

Other top state officials are the lieutenant governor, secretary of state, treasurer, auditor, attorney general, superintendent of public instruction, commissioner of public lands, and insurance commissioner. They serve four-year terms, and may be re-elected an unlimited number of times. The superintendent of public instruction is elected by *nonpartisan* (no-party) ballot.

Legislature consists of a 49-member Senate and a 98-member House of Representatives. By law, the House of Representatives cannot have less than 63 members or more than 99. The number of senators cannot be more than one-half or less than one-third of the number of representatives. The state has 49 legislative districts. Voters in each district elect one senator and two representatives. Senators serve four-year terms, and representatives serve two-year terms. Regular legislative sessions begin on the second Monday in January of odd-numbered years. The law limits these sessions to 60 days. The governor may call special legislative sessions.

In June 1964, the Supreme Court of the United States ruled that representation in both houses of a state's Legislature must be apportioned on the basis of equal population in all voting districts. On July 23, 1964, a federal court ordered the Washington Legislature to reapportion itself. The Legislature did so in 1965. In early 1972, state legislators failed to agree on a reapportionment plan for the 1970's. Later that year, a federal court redrew the legislative districts.

Courts. The highest court in Washington is the state Supreme Court. It has nine judges elected to six-year terms. The voters elect three Supreme Court judges in each general election, every two years. The judge with the shortest remaining term serves as chief justice. If two or more judges have equal terms remaining, the other judges decide which one will be chief justice.

Washington's next highest court is the state court of appeals. This court has 12 justices elected to six-year terms. Other Washington courts include district superior courts, headed by one or more judges elected for four years, and justice-of-the-peace courts, with justices elected for four years.

Local Government. A 1948 amendment to the Washington constitution gave counties the right to choose their own form of county government. In most of Washington's 39 counties, a three-member board of commissioners has both executive and lawmaking powers. The commissioners are elected to four-year terms. Other county officials include the prosecuting attorney, superintendent of schools, sheriff, clerk, and treasurer. A county may also have an auditor, assessor, coroner, health officer, relief administrator, and other officials.

Washington has 266 incorporated cities and towns. The state constitution provides that any city with a population of 20,000 or more may have *home rule*. That is, it may choose its own form of local government. About 10 Washington cities have home rule. Some of the home-rule cities have a council-manager form of government, some a commission form, and some a mayor-council form. Most smaller cities are governed by a mayor and a city council.

Taxation. The state government receives about 80 per cent of its income from state taxes. Almost all the

The Capitol Group in Olympia, *left,* forms the center of Washington's state government. The Capitol, the Supreme Court offices, the state library, and other government buildings share a 35-acre (14-hectare) plot overlooking Puget Sound. The governor's mansion, *below,* stands on a wooded hill behind the Capitol.

Merle Junk

The State Seal

Symbols of Washington, the state seal and flag, bear a portrait of George Washington, for whom the state was named. The date 1889 beneath the portrait is the year in which the state was admitted to the Union. The green field of the flag represents the green of Washington's forests. The seal was adopted in 1889, and the flag was adopted in 1925.

Bird and flower illustrations, courtesy of Eli Lilly and Company

rest comes from federal grants and other U.S. government programs. Washington's main source of tax income is a general retail sales tax. The state also receives a large share of its income from excise taxes, such as those on alcoholic beverages, motor fuels, and tobacco. There are also taxes on public utilities and insurance, and a license tax on motor vehicles.

Politics. In 1912, Washington cast its electoral votes for the candidates of the Progressive Party. Otherwise, the state has voted about evenly between Republican and Democratic presidential candidates. For the state's voting record in presidential elections since 1892, see ELECTORAL COLLEGE (table).

Voters of farm areas and suburbs have generally favored Republicans. People in the cities of western Washington have usually supported the Democrats.

State Capitol in Olympia, called the Legislative Building, was built between 1911 and 1928. Olympia has been the state capital since Washington achieved statehood in 1889.

Washington State Dept. of Commerce

The State Flag

The State Bird
Willow Goldfinch

The State Flower
Coast Rhododendron

The State Tree
Western Hemlock

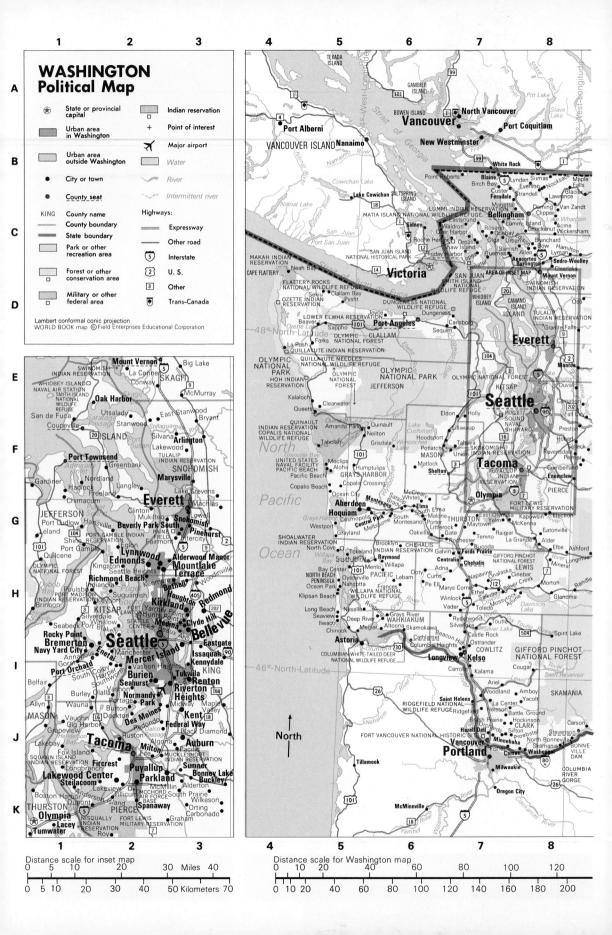

WASHINGTON
Political Map

Legend:
- ★ State or provincial capital
- ▢ Urban area in Washington
- ▢ Urban area outside Washington
- ● City or town
- ● County seat
- KING County name
- County boundary
- State boundary
- Park or other recreation area
- Forest or other conservation area
- Military or other federal area
- ▢ Indian reservation
- + Point of interest
- ✈ Major airport
- ~ Water
- ~ River
- ~ Intermittent river

Highways:
- Expressway
- Other road
- ⑤ Interstate
- ② U.S.
- ③ Other
- 🍁 Trans-Canada

Lambert conformal conic projection
WORLD BOOK map ©Field Enterprises Educational Corporation

Distance scale for inset map
0 5 10 20 30 Miles 40
0 5 10 20 30 40 50 Kilometers 70

Distance scale for Washington map
0 10 20 40 60 80 100 120
0 10 20 40 60 80 100 120 140 160 180 200

North

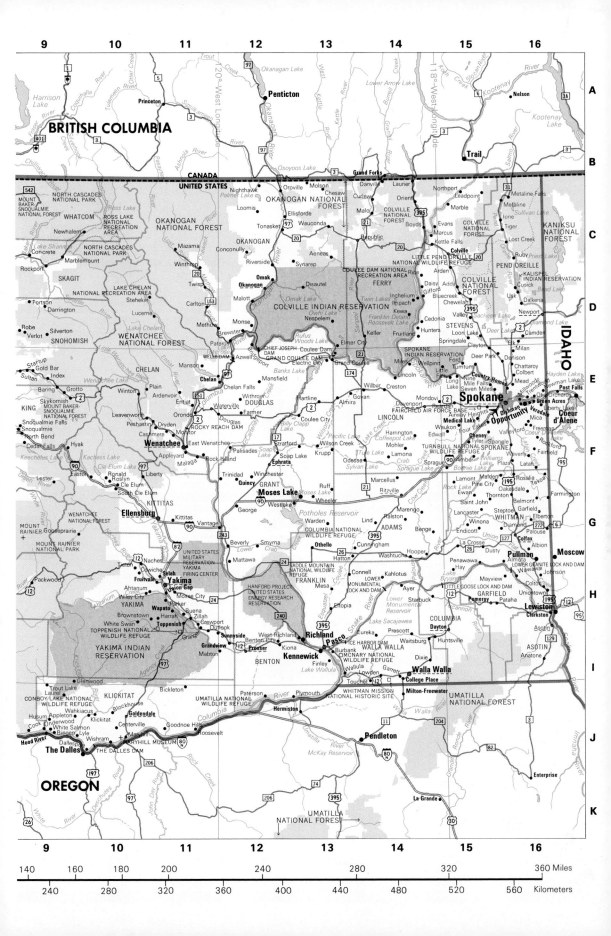

WASHINGTON MAP INDEX

Population

3,544,000 Estimate..1975
3,409,169 ..Census..1970
2,853,214 ....“....1960
2,378,963 ....“....1950
1,736,191 ....“....1940
1,563,396 ....“....1930
1,356,621 ....“....1920
1,141,990 ....“....1910
518,103 ....“....1900
357,232 ....“....1890
75,116 ....“....1880
23,955 ....“....1870
11,594 ....“....1860
1,201 ....“....1850

Metropolitan Areas

Portland (Ore.) 1,007,130 (878,676 in Ore.; 128,454 in Wash.)
Richland-Kennewick 93,356
Seattle-Everett 1,424,605
Spokane 287,487
Tacoma 412,344
Yakima 145,212

Counties

Adams .....12,014..G 14
Asotin .....13,799..I 16
Benton ....67,540..I 12
Chelan .....41,103..E 10
Clallam ...34,770..D 6
Clark .....128,454..J 8
Columbia ...4,439..H 15
Cowlitz ....68,616..I 7
Douglas ....16,787..E 12
Ferry ....3,655..D 14
Franklin ...25,816..H 14
Garfield ....2,911..H 15
Grant .....41,881..F 12
Grays Harbor ..59,553..F 5
Island .....27,011..D 7
Jefferson ...10,661..E 6
King ....1,159,369..E 9
Kitsap ....101,732..E 7
Kittitas ....25,039..G 11
Klickitat ...12,138..I 10
Lewis ......45,467..H 8
Lincoln .....9,572..F 14
Mason .....20,918..F 6
Okanogan ..25,867..C 12
Pacific .....15,796..H 6
Pend Oreille 6,025..C 16
Pierce ....412,344..G 8
San Juan ....3,856..D 7
Skagit .....52,381..D 9
Skamania ...5,845..I 8
Snohomish 265,236..D 9
Spokane ...287,487..F 15
Stevens .....17,405..D 15
Thurston ...76,894..G 7
Wahkiakum .3,592..H 6
Walla Walla ....42,176..I 14
Whatcom ..81,983..C 9
Whitman ..37,900..G 16
Yakima ...145,212..H 10

Cities and Towns

Aberdeen ..18,489..G 5
Acme ....C 8
Addy ....D 15
Adna ....H 7
Aeneas ....C 13
Ahtanum ....H 10
Airway Heights 744..E 15
Albion ....687..G 16
Alder ....G 8
Alderwood Manor ..H 3
Algona ......1,276..J 3
Allen ....C 8
Allyn ....J 1
Almira ......376..E 13
Aloha ....F 5
Altoona ....H 6
Amanda Park ......F 5
Amber ....F 15
Amboy ....I 7
Anacortes ...7,701..C 7
Anatone ....I 16
Anderson Island ...K 1
Appleton ....J 9
Appleyard ....F 11
Arden ....C 15
Ardenvoir ....E 11
Ariel ....I 7
Arlington ....2,261..F 3
Ashford ....G 8
Asotin ....637.°H 16
Auburn ....21,653..J 3
Ault Field* .1,478..D 7
Ayer ....H 14
Azwell ....E 12
Baring ....E 9
Battle Ground ...1,438..J 7
Bay Center ....H 5
Beacon Hill .1,263..I 7
Beaux Arts ...475..I 3
Beaver ....D 5
Belfair ....I 1
Bellevue ....61,196..I 3
Bellingham .39,375.°C 8
Belmont ....G 16
Benge ....G 15
Benton City .1,070..I 12
Beverly ....G 12
Bickleton ....I 11
Big Lake ....E 3
Bingen ......671..J 9
Birch Bay ....B 7
Black Diamond ..1,160..J 3
Blaine ......1,955..B 7
Blanchard ....C 8
Blockhouse ....J 10
Bluecreek ....D 15
Bonney Lake 2,700..K 3
Boston Harbor ......K 1
Bothell .....5,420..H 3
Bow ....C 8
Boyds ....C 14
Brady ....G 6
Bremerton .35,307..I 1
Brewster ....1,059..D 12
Bridgeport ....952..E 12
Brier* ......3,093..E 8
Brinnon ....H 1
Brownstown ....H 11
Brush Prairie ......J 7
Bryant ....F 3
Buckley .....3,446..K 3
Bucoda ......421..G 7
Buena ....H 11
Burbank ....I 13
Burien ....I 2
Burley ....I 1
Burlington ..3,138..C 8
Burton ....J 2
Camas ......5,790..J 8
Carbonado .....394..K 3
Carlsborg ....D 7
Carlton ....D 11
Carnation .....530..E 8
Carrolls ....I 7
Carson ....J 8
Cashmere ...1,976..F 11
Castle Rock .1,647..I 7
Cathlamet ....647.°I 6
Cedar Falls ....F 9
Cedonia ....D 14
Centerville ....J 10
Central Park 2,720..G 6
Centralia ..10,054..H 7
Chattaroy ....E 16
Chehalis .....5,727.°H 7
Chelan .....2,837..E 11
Chelan Falls ....E 12
Cheney .....6,358..F 15
Chesaw ....B 13
Chewelah ...1,365..D 15
Chimacum ....G 1
Chinook ....H 5
Chuckanut ....C 8
Cinebar ....H 7
Clallam Bay ....D 5
Clarkston ...6,312..H 16
Clayton ....E 15
Cle Elum ...1,725..F 10
Clearlake ....C 8
Clearwater ....E 5
Clinton ....G 2
Clipper ....C 8
Clyde Hill ..2,987..H 3
Colbert ....E 16
Colfax ......2,664.°G 16
College Place 4,510..I 14
Colton ......279..H 16
Columbia Heights ...1,572..I 7
Colville .....3,742.°C 15
Conconully ...122..C 12
Concrete .....573..C 9
Connell .....1,161..H 13
Conway ....E 2
Cook ....J 9
Copalis Beach ......F 5
Copalis Crossing ......G 5
Cosmopolis ..1,599..G 5
Coulee City .....558..F 13
Coulee Dam .1,425..E 13
Country Homes ......E 16
Coupeville ....678.°F 1
Cowiche ....H 10
Creston ....325..E 14
Crewport ....H 11
Cumberland ....F 8
Cunningham ....G 13
Curlew ....B 14
Curtis ....H 6
Cusick ....257..D 16
Custer ....B 7
Daisy ....D 14
Dalkena ....D 16
Dallesport ....J 10
Danville ....B 14
Darrington ..1,094..D 9
Davenport ..1,363.°E 14
Dayton ......2,596.°H 15
Decatur ....C 7
Deep River ....H 5
Deer Harbor ....C 7
Deer Park ...1,295..E 15
Deming ....C 8
Des Moines .3,951..J 2
Diamond ....G 16
Disautel ....D 13
Dishman ....9,079..E 16
Dixie ....I 15
Dockton ....J 2
Doebay ....C 7
Doty ....H 6
Douglas ....E 11
Dryden ....F 11
Dungeness ....D 7
Dupont ....384..K 1
Dusty ....G 15
Duvall ....607..E 8
East Olympia ......G 7
East Wenatchee ..913..F 11
East Wenatchee Bench* ...2,446..F 11
Eastgate ....I 3
Easton ....F 10
Eastsound ....C 7
Eatonville ....852..G 8
Edison ....C 8
Edmonds ...23,998..H 2
Edwall ....F 15
Eglon ....G 2
Elbe ....G 8
Elberton ....G 16
Electric City ..651..E 13
Electron ....G 8
Elk ....D 16
Ellensburg .13,568.°G 11
Ellisforde ....C 12
Elma ....2,227..G 6
Elmer City ....324..E 13
Eltopia ....H 13
Endicott ......333..G 15
Enetai ......2,878..I 1
Entiat ....355..E 11
Enumclaw ..4,703..F 8
Ephrata ....5,255.°F 12
Erlands Point* ....1,017..E 7
Ethel ....H 7
Eureka ....I 14
Evans ....C 15
Everett .....53,622.°E 8
Everson ....633..B 8
Ewan ....G 15
Fairchild* ..6,754..E 15
Fairfield ......469..F 16
Fairmont ....G 3
Fairview* ...2,111..H 11
Fall City ....F 8
Farmer ....E 12
Farmington ...140..G 16
Federal Way ......J 2
Ferndale ...2,164..C 7
Fife ....1,458..J 2
Finley ....I 13
Fircrest .....5,651..J 2
Fisher ....J 7
Ford ....E 15
Fords Prairie ...2,250..G 7
Forks ......1,680..E 5
Fort Lewis .38,054..F 7
Four Lakes ....F 15
Fox Island ....J 1
Frances ....H 6
Freeland ....G 2
Freeman ....F 16
Friday Harbor 803.°C 7
Fruitland ....D 14
Fruitvale ....3,275..H 11
Galvin ....G 7
Gardiner ....F 1
Garfield ......610..G 16
Garrett ......1,586..I 14
Gate ....G 6
Geiger Heights* ..1,424..E 16
George ....273..G 12
Gifford ....D 14
Gig Harbor ..1,657..J 2
Glacier ....B 8
Glenoma ....H 8
Glenwood ....I 9
Gold Bar ......504..E 9
Goldendale ..2,484.°J 10
Gooseprairie ....G 9
Gorst ....I 1
Govan ....E 13
Graham ....K 3
Grand Coulee ....1,302..E 13
Grandview ..3,605..I 12
Granger .....1,567..H 11
Granite Falls .813..D 8
Grapeview ....J 1
Grayland ....G 5
Grays River ....H 6
Green Acres .2,324..E 16
Greenbank ....F 2
Grisdale ....F 6
Grotto ....E 9
Guemes ....C 7
Hadlock ....G 1
Hamilton ......196..C 8
Hansville ....G 2
Harper ....I 2
Harrah ......305..H 11
Harrington ....489..F 14
Hartline ......189..E 13
Hatton ....60..G 13
Hay ....H 15
Heisson ....J 7
Highland, see West Clarkston-Highland
Hobart ....F 8
Hockinson ....J 7
Holly ....F 7
Hoodsport ....F 6
Hooper ....G 15
Hoquiam ...10,466..G 5
Humptulips ....F 5
Hunters ....D 14
Hunts Point ..578..H 3
Husum ....J 9
Hyak ....F 9
Ilwaco ....506..H 5
Inchelium ....D 14
Index ....169..E 9
Indianola ....H 2
Ione ....529..C 16
Issaquah ....4,313..I 3
Johnson ....H 16
Joyce ....D 6
Kahlotus .....308..H 14
Kalaloch ....E 5
Kalama .....1,106..I 7
Kapowsin ....G 8
Keller ....D 14
Kelso ......10,296.°I 7
Kenmore ....H 3
Kennewick .15,212..I 13
Kennydale ....I 3
Kent ......16,596..J 3
Kettle Falls ...893..C 15
Kewa ....D 14
Keyport ....H 1
Kingston ....H 2
Kiona ....I 12
Kirkland ....14,970..H 3
Kittitas ......637..G 11
Klickitat ....J 10
Klipsan Beach ......H 5
Krupp ....52..F 13
La Center .....300..J 7
Lacey ....9,696..K 1
La Conner ....639..E 2
La Crosse ....426..G 15
La Grande ....G 8
Lake Forest Park* .....2,530..E 8
Lake Stevens 1,283..G 3
Lakebay ....J 1
Lakes District* .48,195..F 7
Lakeview ....K 2
Lakewood ....F 3
Lakewood Center ...K 2
Lamona ....F 14
Lamont ....88..F 15
Langley ....547..G 2
La Push ....E 4
Latah ....169..F 16
Laurel ....I 9
Laurier ....B 14
Lawrence ....C 8
Leavenworth .1,322..F 10
Lebam ....H 6
Leland ....G 1
Lester ....F 9
Liberty ....F 10
Liberty Lake ....E 16
Lilliwaup ....F 7
Lincoln ....E 14
Lind ....622..G 14
Little Falls ....E 15
Littlerock ....G 7
Long Beach ...968..H 5
Long Lake ....E 15
Longbranch ....J 1
Longmire ....G 9
Longview ...28,373..I 7
Loomis ....C 12
Loon Lake ....D 15
Lopez ....C 7
Lost Creek ....C 16
Lowden ....I 14
Lucerne ....D 11
Lummi Island ......C 7
Lyle ....J 9
Lyman ....324..C 8
Lynden .....2,808..B 8
Lynnwood ..17,711..H 2
Mabton ....926..I 11
Machias ....G 3
Malaga ....F 11
Malden ....219..F 16
Malo ....C 14
Malone ....G 6
Malott ....D 12
Manchester ....I 2
Mansfield .....273..E 12
Manson ....E 11
Maple Falls ....B 8
Maple Valley ......J 3
Marble ....C 15
Marblemount ....C 9
Marcellus ....F 14
Marcus ....142..C 15
Marengo ....G 14
Marietta ....C 7
Marys Corner ......H 7
Marysville ...4,343..F 3
Matlock ....F 6
Mattawa ......180..H 12
Maytown ....G 7
Mazama ....C 11
McChord* ....6,515..K 2
McCleary ...1,265..G 6
McKenna ....G 7
McMillin ....K 3
McMurray ....E 3
Mead ....1,099..E 16
Medical Lake ......3,529..F 15
Medina .....3,455..I 3
Melbourne ....G 6
Menlo ....H 6
Mercer Island ...19,819..I 3
Mesa ....274..H 13
Metaline ....197..C 16
Metaline Falls 307..B 16
Methow ....D 11
Mica ....F 16
Milan ....E 16
Miles ....E 14
Millwood ....1,770..E 16
Milton ......2,607..J 2
Mineral ....H 8
Minnehaha ....J 7
Moclips ....F 5
Mohler ....F 14
Molson ....B 13
Mondovi ....E 15
Monitor ....F 11
Monroe .....2,687..E 8
Monse ....D 12
Montesano ...2,847.°G 6
Morton ......1,134..H 8
Moses Lake 10,310..G 13
Moses Lake North* .....2,672..G 13
Mossyrock .....409..H 7
Mount Vernon ....8,804.°D 8
Mountlake Terrace ...16,600..H 2
Moxee City ...600..H 11
Mukilteo ....1,369..G 2
Naches ....666..H 10
Nahcotta ....H 5
Napavine .....377..H 7
Naselle ....H 5
Navy Yard City ......2,827..I 1
Neah Bay ....D 4
Neilton ....F 5
Nespelem .....323..D 13
Newhalem ....C 10
Newman Lake ....E 16
Newport ....1,418.°D 16
Nighthawk ....B 12
Nine Mile Falls ....E 15
Nooksack .....322..B 8
Nordland ....F 1
Normandy Park .....4,208..I 2
North Bend .1,625..F 9
North Bonneville ..165..J 8
North Cove ....G 5
Northport .....423..B 15
Oak Harbor .9,167..E 1
Oakesdale ......447..G 16
Oakville ......460..G 6
Ocean City ....G 5
Ocean Park ....H 5
Ocean Shores .....768..F 5
Odessa ......1,074..F 14
Okanogan ...2,015.°D 12
Olalla ....I 2
Olga ....C 7
Olympia ....23,296.°G 7
Omak ......4,164..D 12
Onalaska ....H 7
Opportunity 16,604..E 16
Orcas ....C 7
Orchards ....J 7
Orient ....C 14
Orondo ....E 11
Oroville .....1,555..B 12
Orting ......1,643..K 3
Oso ....D 8
Ostrander ....I 7
Othello .....4,122..G 13
Otis Orchards ....E 16
Outlook ....H 11
Oysterville ....H 5
Pacific ......1,831..J 3
Pacific Beach ......F 5
Packwood ....H 9
Palisades ....F 12
Palmer ....F 8
Palouse ....948..G 16
Parker ....H 11
Parkland ...21,012..K 2
Pasco ......13,920.°I 13
Pasco West* .....3,809..I 13
Pateros ....472..D 12
Paterson ....I 12
Pe Ell ....582..H 6
Penawawa ....H 15
Peshastin ....F 11
Pine City ....F 15
Plain ....E 10
Plaza ....F 16
Plymouth ....I 13
Point Roberts ......B 7
Pomeroy ....1,823.°H 15
Port Angeles ..16,367.°D 6
Port Angeles East* .....1,523..D 6
Port Blakely ......I 2

Port Gamble ....G 2
Port Ludlow ....G 1
Port Orchard 3,904.°I 1
Port
 Townsend .5,241.°F 1
Portage ....J 2
Porter ....G 6
Potlatch ....F 6
Poulsbo ...1,856..H 1
Prescott ....242..I 14
Preston ....F 8
Proebstel ....J 7
Prosser ..2,954.°I 12
Pullman ..20,509..G 16
Puyallup ..14,742..K 2
Queets ....E 5
Quilcene ....H 1
Quinault ....F 5
Quincy ...3,237..F 12
Rainier ......382..G 7
Ralston ....G 14
Randle ....H 8
Ravensdale ....F 8
Raymond ..3,126..H 5
Reardan ......389..E 15
Redmond ..11,020..H 3
Redondo ....J 2
Renton ...25,878..I 3
Republic ....862.°C 13
Rice ....D 14
Richland ..26,290..I 13
Richmond Beach ....H 2
Ridgefield ..1,004..J 7
Ritzville ..1,876.°G 14
Riverside ....228..C 12
Riverton Heights ..I 3
Robe ....D 9
Roche Harbor ......C 7
Rochester ....G 7
Rock Island ..191..F 11
Rockford ....327..F 16
Rockport ....C 9
Rocky Point .1,733..H 1
Ronald ....F 10
Roosevelt ....J 11

Rosalia ....569..F 16
Rosario ....C 7
Rosburg ....H 6
Roslyn ....1,031..F 10
Roy ....381..K 2
Royal City* ..477..G 12
Ruby ....C 16
Ruff ....G 13
Ruston ....668..J 2
Ryderwood ....H 7
St. John ....575..G 15
Salkum ....H 7
Samish ....C 8
San de Fuca ....F 1
Sappho ....D 5
Satsop ....G 6
Seabeck ....H 1
Seahurst ....I 2
Seattle ....530,831.°E 8
Seattle Heights ...H 2
Seaview ....H 5
Sedro-
 Woolley ...4,598..C 8
Sekiu ....D 5
Selah .....3,311..H 11
Selleck ....F 9
Sequim ....1,549..D 7
Shaw Island ....C 7
Shelton ...6,515.°F 7
Shine ....G 1
Shoultes* ..4,754..D 8
Sifton ....J 7
Silvana ....F 3
Silver Creek ......H 8
Silverdale ....H 1
Silverlake ....H 7
Silverton ....D 9
Skamania ....J 7
Skamokawa ....H 6
Skykomish ....283..E 9
Snohomish ..5,174..G 3
Snoqualmie .1,260..F 9
Snoqualmie Falls ..F 9
Soap Lake .1,064..F 12
South Bend .1,795..H 5

South
 Broadway* 3,298..H 11
South Cle
 Elum ......374..G 10
South Colby ....I 2
South Prairie .206..K 3
Southworth ....I 2
Spanaway ..5,768..K 2
Spangle .....179..F 16
Spirit Lake ....I 8
Spokane .170,516.°E 16
Sprague .....550..F 15
Springdale ...215..D 15
Stanwood ..1,347..F 2
Starbuck .....216..H 15
Startup ....E 9
Stehekin ....D 10
Steilacoom .2,850..K 1
Steptoe ....G 16
Stevenson ...916.°J 8
Stratford ....F 13
Sultan ....1,119..E 9
Sumas ....689..B 8
Sumner ....4,325..J 3
Sunnyside .6,751..I 11
Suquamish ....H 2
Tacoma ...154,407.°F 8
Taholah ....F 5
Tahuya ....F 7
Tanglewilde, see
 Thompson Place-
 Tanglewilde
Tekoa ....808..F 16
Tenino ....962..G 7
Terrace
 Heights* ..1,033..H 11
Thompson
 Place-Tangle-
 wilde* ...3,423..G 7
Thornton ....G 16
Tieton ......415..H 10
Tiger ....G 5
Tillicum ....K 2
Tokeland ....G 5
Toledo ....654..H 7

Tonasket ....951..C 12
Toppenish ..5,744..H 11
Touchet ....I 14
Toutle ....H 7
Town and
 Country* ..6,484..E 16
Tracyton* ..1,413..E 7
Trentwood ....E 16
Trinidad ....F 12
Trout Lake ....I 9
Tukwila ...3,509..I 3
Tumtum ....E 15
Tumwater ..5,373..K 1
Twisp ....756..D 11
Tyler ....F 15
Underwood ....J 9
Union ....F 7
Union Gap .2,040..H 11
Uniontown ....310..H 16
University
 Place* ..13,230..F 7
Urban ....C 7
Usk ....D 16
Utsalady ....F 2
Vader ....387..H 7
Valley ....D 15
Valleyford ....F 16
Vancouver .41,859.°J 7
Vantage ....G 11
Van Zandt ....C 8
Vashon ....I 2
Vashon Heights ....I 2
Vaughn ....J 1
Veradale ....E 16
Verlot ....D 9
Wahkiacus ....J 10
Waitsburg ....953..I 14
Waldron ....C 7
Walla
 Walla ...23,619.°I 14
Walla Walla
 East* ...2,840..I 14
Wallula ....I 13
Wapato ....2,841..H 11
Warden ....1,254..G 13

Washougal ..3,388..J 8
Washtucna ...316..G 14
Waterville ...919.°E 11
Wauconda ....C 13
Waukon ....F 15
Wauna ....J 1
Waverly ....48..F 16
Wellpinit ....E 15
Wenatchee .16,912.°F 11
West
 Clarkston-
 Highland* 3,797..H 16
West
 Richland .1,107..I 13
West We-
 natchee* ..2,134..F 11
Westport ..1,364..G 5
Wheeler ....G 13
White
 Salmon ...1,585..J 9
White Swan ....H 10
Whites ....G 6
Wickersham ....C 8
Wilbur ....1,074..E 14
Wilkeson .....317..K 3
Willapa ....H 6
Wilson
 Creek ....184..F 13
Winchester ....F 12
Winlock .....890..H 7
Winona ....G 15
Winslow ...1,461..H 2
Winthrop .....371..C 11
Winton ....E 10
Wishram ....J 10
Withrow ....E 12
Woodinville ....H 3
Woodland ..1,622..I 7
Woodway* .....879..E 8
Yacolt ....488..J 8
Yakima ...45,588.°H 11
Yarrow
 Point ....1,101..H 3
Yelm ....628..G 7
Zillah ....1,138..H 11

*Does not appear on the map; key shows general location.
°County seat.

Sources: Latest census figures (1970 and special census); U.S. Army Corps of Engineers estimate. Places without population figures are unincorporated areas and are not listed in census reports.

George Hall

Tacoma, Washington's third largest city, lies on Commencement Bay on Puget Sound's east shore. The state's highest point, Mount Rainier, rises 14,410 feet (4,392 meters) southeast of the city.

The 1970 United States census reported that Washington had 3,409,169 persons. The population had increased 20 per cent over the 1960 census figure, 2,853,214. The U.S. Bureau of the Census estimated that by 1975 the population had reached about 3,544,000.

More than two-fifths of the people of Washington live in the Seattle-Everett metropolitan area in the western part of the state. Washington has six Standard Metropolitan Statistical Areas (see METROPOLITAN AREA). For the names and populations of these areas, see the *Index* to the political map of Washington.

Most of the larger Washington cities are in the western part of the state along Puget Sound. Seattle, the state's largest city, is in this region. It serves as an important shipping and manufacturing center. Tacoma, an industrial and port city, is about 28 miles (45 kilometers) south of Seattle. Both these cities began chiefly as ports for shipping lumber. Later, they became shipping centers for trade with Alaska and Asia.

Most of the cities in eastern Washington developed as centers for farm trade, lumbering, or mining. Spokane, the largest eastern city, is an important railroad, manufacturing, grain, and financial center. The "Tri-Cities" of Richland, Pasco, and Kennewick in south-central Washington grew in size and importance after World War II. At that time, the Hanford nuclear energy center was established nearby. See the separate articles on the cities of Washington listed in the *Related Articles* at the end of this article.

About 95 out of 100 Washingtonians, including those of Canadian and Oriental ancestry, were born in the United States. Canadians and Scandinavians are the largest foreign-born groups. Washington has over 33,000 Indians. About half of them live on the state's 22 reservations and 3 other areas granted by the United States government.

The Roman Catholic Church has the largest religious membership in Washington. Lutherans and Methodists are the largest Protestant groups. Other major religious groups in the state include Baptists, Disciples of Christ, Episcopalians, Mormons, and Presbyterians.

POPULATION

This map shows the *population density* of Washington, and how it varies in different parts of the state. Population density means the average number of persons who live in a given area.

Persons per sq. mi.	Persons per km²
More than 100	More than 40
25 to 100	10 to 40
10 to 25	4 to 10
Less than 10	Less than 4

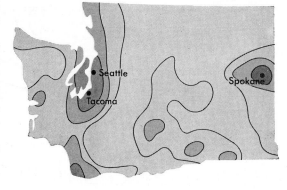

0   50   100 Miles
0   50   100   150 Kilometers

WORLD BOOK map

Washington State Department of Commerce News Bureau

A Thirsty Young Brave at the Ellensburg Rodeo reflects Washington's heritage as a center of Indian life. About half the state's large Indian population lives on 22 reservations.

Crowds Waiting for a Monorail Train in Seattle symbolize the busy city life of Washington today. About three-fourths of the people live in the state's six metropolitan areas.

Marshall Lockman, Black Star

Lyman Hall at Whitman College in Walla Walla stands at the east end of the campus. The college has the first charter granted to an institution by the territorial legislature.

The Pacific Science Center, in Seattle, features demonstrations and exhibits of modern science. Its buildings were constructed for the Century 21 Exposition, a world's fair held in 1962.

WASHINGTON/*Education*

Schools. The first school in Washington opened at Old Fort Vancouver in 1832. It was established for the children of employees of the Hudson's Bay Company, a British trading firm. In the 1830's, missionaries began teaching Indians in eastern Washington near present-day Spokane and Walla Walla. These early teachers included Marcus Whitman and his wife Narcissa, and Cushing Eells, Henry Spalding, and Elkanah Walker. In 1859, Whitman College, Washington's first institution of higher learning, was founded in Walla Walla. A statewide system of public schools began in 1895. A law passed that year provided state financial support for schools.

An elected state superintendent of public instruction and a state board of education supervise Washington's public school system. Children between the ages of 8 and 15 must attend school. Children between 15 and 16 must attend school unless they have a regular job. For the number of students and teachers in Washington, see EDUCATION (table).

Libraries. Washington's first library, the State Library in Olympia, began in 1853 as the Territorial Library. Today, about 75 public libraries and library systems serve the state. The Seattle Public Library has more than a million books, including collections on the Pacific Northwest and on aeronautics. Many Washington colleges and universities also include outstanding libraries. The Henry Suzzallo Library at the University of Washington has several famous collections, including historical material on the Pacific Northwest, oceanography, and the fisheries industry.

Museums. The Thomas Burke Memorial Washington State Museum on the campus of the University of Washington features exhibits on natural history. Museums with relics of Washington history include the Pacific Northwest Indian Center and the Cheney

Cowles Memorial Museum in Spokane, the Washington State Historical Society in Tacoma, and the Museum of History and Industry in Seattle. The Seattle Art Museum has a fine collection of Oriental art. The museum also features works by artists of the Pacific Northwest. The Charles and Emma Frye Free Public Art Museum displays paintings by European and American artists. The Pacific Science Center in Seattle has exhibits of modern science.

—— UNIVERSITIES AND COLLEGES ——

Washington has 20 universities and colleges accredited by the Northwest Association of Schools and Colleges. For enrollments and further information, see UNIVERSITIES AND COLLEGES (table).

Name	Location	Founded
City College	Seattle	1973
Central Washington University	Ellensburg	1890
Cornish Institute of Allied Arts	Seattle	1914
Eastern Washington University	Cheney	1890
Evergreen State College	Olympia	1967
Fort Wright College	Spokane	1907
Gonzaga University	Spokane	1887
Northwest College of the Assemblies of God	Kirkland	1949
Pacific Lutheran University	Tacoma	1894
Puget Sound, University of	Tacoma	1888
Saint Martin's College	Olympia	1895
Seattle Pacific University	Seattle	1891
Seattle University	Seattle	1891
Sulpician Seminary of the Northwest	Kenmore	1931
Walla Walla College	College Place	1892
Washington, University of	Seattle	1861
Washington State University	Pullman	1890
Western Washington University	Bellingham	1933
Whitman College	Walla Walla	1859
Whitworth College	Spokane	1890

Bob and Ira Spring

Space Needle and Monorail in Seattle

Ray Atkeson, Publix

Olympic National Park on the Olympic Peninsula

WASHINGTON/*A Visitor's Guide*

Washington is a paradise for persons who enjoy the outdoors. It offers some of the best hunting and fishing in the United States. People who fish for sport catch more than a million salmon each year off the state's Pacific coast. Every winter, skiers flock to the slopes of Mount Spokane and areas in the Cascade Range such

as Crystal Mountain, Mission Ridge, Mount Baker, Mount Rainier, Snoqualmie Pass, Stevens Pass, and White Pass. The main skiing season begins in December and lasts until late spring. In summer, rugged mountains and wilderness areas attract hikers and mountain climbers.

PLACES TO VISIT

Following are brief descriptions of some of Washington's many interesting places to visit.

Grand Coulee Dam, 92 miles (148 kilometers) west of Spokane, is the largest concrete dam in the United States (see GRAND COULEE DAM).

Lewis and Clark Interpretive Center, near Ilwaco, features maps and paintings that illustrate the Lewis and Clark expedition between Missouri and the Pacific Coast.

Maryhill Castle, in Maryhill, is an art museum in an elaborate mansion built in 1926 by multimillionaire Samuel Hill. The gray stone structure stands on a high bluff overlooking the scenic Columbia River Gorge.

Rocky Reach Dam, near Wenatchee, has a museum and an underground room where visitors can watch salmon swim upstream to lay their eggs.

San Juan Islands, near Canada's Vancouver Island, are vacation resorts noted for their scenic beauty (see SAN JUAN ISLANDS).

Seattle Center includes the Pacific Science Center from the Century 21 Exposition, a world's fair held in 1962. The Space Needle, a tower 607 feet (185 meters) high, is in the area. It has an observation deck. A monorail links the center and downtown Seattle.

National Parks and Forests. Washington has three national parks—Mount Rainier, North Cascades, and

The San Juan Islands near Bellingham   Bob and Ira Spring

Racing Event During the Seafair in Seattle
Ray Atkeson

Skiing in the Northern Cascade Mountains
Bob and Ira Spring, Publix

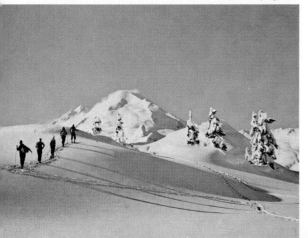

Olympic. These parks include some of the country's most scenic areas. Part of Klondike National Historical Park is in Washington. The other part is in Alaska. Washington has nine national forests. Seven of them lie entirely within the state. They are Okanogan, Gifford Pinchot, Mount Baker, Snoqualmie, Wenatchee, Olympic, and Colville. Kaniksu National Forest is shared by Washington, Idaho, and Montana. Umatilla National Forest, in the Blue Mountains, lies in both Washington and Oregon. In 1964, Congress set aside four areas in these forests as national wildernesses, to be preserved in their natural condition. For the area and chief features of each national park and forest, see NATIONAL PARK SYSTEM and NATIONAL FOREST (table).

National Historic Sites. Whitman Mission National Historic Site marks the spot of the Indian mission founded by Marcus Whitman and his wife in 1836. It was also the scene of the Indian massacre of 1847 in which the Whitmans and others lost their lives. The place became a national monument in 1936, and a historic site in 1963. Fort Vancouver National Historic Site was the western headquarters of the Hudson's Bay Company from 1825 to 1849. Established in 1948 as a national monument, the area became a national historic site in 1961. Each historic site has a separate article in WORLD BOOK.

State Parks. Washington has over a hundred developed parks and historic and geologic sites under the administration of the state parks and recreation commission. The park system includes several undeveloped tracts. For information on state parks, write to Director, Washington State Parks and Recreation Commission, P.O. Box 1128, Olympia, Washington 98504.

——————— ANNUAL EVENTS ———————

Washington's many annual events include Indian festivals, flower exhibitions, sports competitions, and regional fairs. Perhaps the outstanding annual event is the Seafair, held in Seattle in late July and early August. This show features parades, water carnivals, and boat races on Lake Washington. Other annual events in Washington include the following.

January-May: Seattle Boat Show (January); Ski-Jumping Tournament in Leavenworth (February); Trade Fair in Seattle (early April); Daffodil Festival in Puyallup (April); Apple Blossom Festival in Wenatchee (first week in May); Lilac Festival in Spokane (May); Blossom Time Festival in Bellingham (May); Rhododendron Festival in Port Townsend (late May).

June-August: Lummi Stommish Water Carnival near Bellingham (June); Toppenish Indian Pow Wow in Toppenish (July 3-4); International Cruiser Race from Puget Sound to Nanaimo, B.C. (July); Pacific Northwest Arts and Crafts Fair in Bellevue (July); Omak Stampede and Suicide Race (August).

September-December: Ellensburg Rodeo (early September); Lake Chelan Sailing Regatta (September); Western Washington State Fair in Puyallup (September); Autumn Leaf Festival in Leavenworth (late September and early October); Exhibition of Northwest Art in Seattle (November).

55

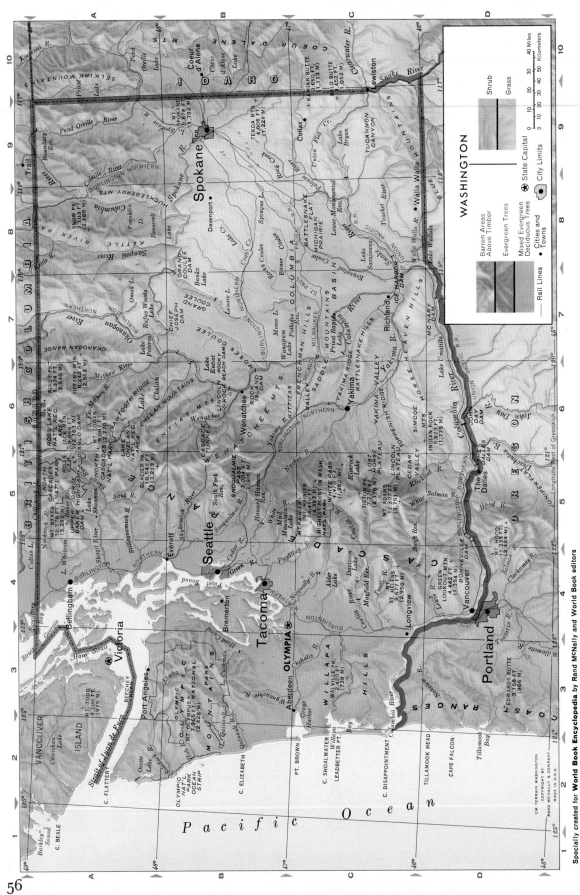

WASHINGTON

Barren Areas
Above Timber

Evergreen Trees

Mixed Evergreen
Deciduous Trees

Cities and
Towns

Rail Lines

Shrub

Grass

State Capital
City Limits

Miles

Kilometers

Pacific Ocean

Specially created for **World Book Encyclopedia** by Rand McNally and World Book editors

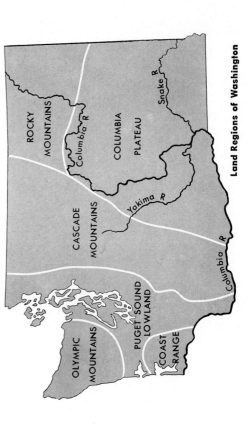

Majestic Mount Rainier, the highest peak in Washington, rises 14,410 feet (4,392 meters) above sea level. Its volcanic cone still gives off gassy fumes, but it has not erupted for hundreds of years.

Washington State Dept. of Commerce

Land Regions of Washington

WASHINGTON/The Land

Land Regions. Washington has six main land regions: (1) the Olympic Mountains, (2) the Coast Range, (3) the Puget Sound Lowland, (4) the Cascade Mountains, (5) the Columbia Plateau, and (6) the Rocky Mountains.

The Olympic Mountains region lies in the northwest corner of the state. It is bordered by the Strait of Juan de Fuca on the north and the Pacific Ocean on the west. Most of the region lies within Olympic National Park. The rugged, snow-capped Olympic Mountains are one of the wildest parts of the United States. Some areas of these mountains have never been explored. The chief industry in the region is logging in the foothills of the mountains.

The Coast Range region covers the southwestern corner of Washington and extends southward into Oregon. The Willapa Hills, which overlook Willapa Bay, are the chief land feature of this region in Washington. Logging and lumber milling are the region's most important economic activities. Many persons also work in fishing and dairying.

The Puget Sound Lowland is a plain that is wedged between the Olympic Mountains on the west and the Cascade Mountains on the east. It extends northward into British Columbia and southward into Oregon. The val-

Bob and Ira Spring
Ray Atkeson, Publix

Bob and Ira Spring

The Cascade Mountains, *right,* raise their rock-ribbed, snowy peaks near Trapper Lake.

Steptoe Butte, *below,* overlooks the fertile Palouse hills region of southeastern Washington.

Grand Coulee Dam, *above,* harnesses the Columbia River in Washington's Columbia Plateau region.

North Head Lighthouse, *left,* guards the rocky Pacific Coast at the mouth of the Columbia River.

Bob and Ira Spring

WASHINGTON

ley of the Chehalis River is also part of the region. The valley extends westward to the Pacific Ocean between the Willapa Hills on the south and the Olympic Mountains on the north.

Puget Sound, a huge bay almost completely enclosed by land, covers the north-central part of the lowland region. The Strait of Juan de Fuca connects Puget Sound with the Pacific Ocean. Narrow, twisting branches of the sound extend far inland. These branches reach south to the cities of Tacoma and Olympia. About three-fourths of Washington's people live on the lowland plain. The plain has about half of the state's cities, and most of its factories and sawmills.

The Cascade Mountains region, east of the Puget Sound Lowland, separates the western section of the state from the eastern section. The Cascade Mountains of Washington are part of a long mountain range that stretches southward from British Columbia into northern California. The snow-covered peaks of several inactive volcanoes rise above the main chain of mountains. One of these long-quiet volcanoes is Mount Rainier, the highest point in the state and one of the highest mountains in the United States. It rises 14,410 feet (4,392 meters) above sea level. Other high peaks include Mount Adams (12,307 feet, or 3,751 meters); Glacier Peak (10,541 feet, or 3,213 meters); and Mount Saint Helens (9,777 feet, or 2,950 meters). All these mountains have glaciers and permanent snowfields on their upper slopes. Farther down the slopes, and on the lower mountains, are magnificent forests. Tall Douglas fir trees grow on the rainy western slopes. Most of the forested area lies within national forests.

The Columbia Plateau covers most of central and southeastern Washington. This great basin lies from 500 to 2,000 feet (150 to 610 meters) or more above sea level, and is surrounded by a rim of higher lands. It makes up part of the largest lava plateau in the world. The basin was formed by lava which flowed out of cracks in the earth's crust thousands of years ago.

Interesting features of the Columbia Plateau are its *coulees* and *scablands*, especially in the Big Bend region. This area lies south and east of a great bend in the Columbia River. Coulees are trenchlike dry canyons with steep walls. They were formed thousands of years ago, when glaciers blocked the Columbia River. Rushing streams of river water and melting ice cut new channels across the lava plateau. After the glacial period ended, the Columbia settled into its present course. The other streams dried up, leaving empty canyons. Grand Coulee and Moses Coulee are the chief dry canyons. Scablands

are areas where patches of hard lava rock lie on the surface of the plateau.

The Wenatchee, Yakima, Snake, Walla Walla, and other irrigated river valleys in the Columbia Plateau region contain fertile cropland. Much of the desert-like Columbia Basin itself is good for growing crops when the land is irrigated. The Yakima Valley in south-central Washington is one of the most productive farm areas in the United States. Farmers there raise beef and dairy cattle, and grow large crops of sugar beets, hops, potatoes, and orchard fruits.

Another important part of the Columbia Plateau is the Palouse country in the southeast. Much of Washington's valuable wheat crop is grown on the gently rolling hills of the Palouse. The deep, fertile soils of this region hold moisture and permit dry farming.

The Blue Mountains in the southeastern corner of Washington extend into Oregon. These mountains are neither as high nor as rugged as the Cascades. Farmers grow grains, hay, and other crops in the larger valleys of this area. The mountain slopes serve as summer pastures for livestock.

The Rocky Mountains cut across the northeastern corner of Washington. The branch of the Rockies in Washington is called the Okanogan Range. The Okanogan Mountains consist of several ridges with valleys in between. The Columbia River and its branch, the Okanogan, are the main rivers in the region. Minerals found in this area include clay, copper, gold, lead, limestone, magnesite, silver, and zinc.

Coastline. Washington's general coastline measures 157 miles (253 kilometers). Its *tidal shoreline* measures 3,026 miles (4,870 kilometers). This measurement includes the shoreline along the Strait of Juan de Fuca, along Puget Sound, and around the islands in Puget Sound. These islands include Bainbridge, Camano, Fidalgo, Vashon, Whidbey, and the more than 170 islands of the San Juan group.

Rivers, Waterfalls, and Lakes. The mighty Columbia River, one of the longest rivers in the United States, flows through Washington for more than 700 miles (1,100 kilometers). It enters the state at the eastern end

of the border with British Columbia. Then it makes a giant southward curve through central Washington. At the Washington-Oregon border it makes a sharp turn to the west and flows to the Pacific Ocean. The river forms most of the boundary between the two states. The Columbia drains more than half of Washington. Many dams on the Columbia and its tributaries control floods and provide water for irrigation and power. The Snake River, which flows into the Columbia in south-central Washington, is the second longest river in the state. Other tributaries of the Columbia River in eastern and central Washington include the Colville, Methow, Okanogan, Pend Oreille, Sanpoil, Spokane, Wenatchee, and Yakima rivers.

Many rivers of western Washington, including the Skagit, Skykomish, and Puyallup, flow from the mountains into Puget Sound. These rivers furnish water for many cities, and provide power for industry. Some of them teem with salmon and other kinds of fishes that travel upstream to lay their eggs. Logging companies use the rivers to float logs to sawmills. Other important rivers include the Chehalis, which flows into the Pacific Ocean at Grays Harbor, and the Cowlitz, which flows into the Columbia River near Longview.

Many of the state's rivers break into falls and rapids in mountainous areas. The chief waterfalls include Cascade, Fairy, Horseshoe, Klickitat, Ladder Creek, Metaline, Nooksack, Palouse, Rainbow, Snoqualmie, Spokane, and White River.

A number of lakes were formed around Puget Sound when glaciers scooped out the land and water filled the hollow places. Some were formed when soil and rock pushed by the glaciers dammed river valleys. The largest and best known of these glacial lakes are Washington, Sammamish, and Whatcom. Other fresh-water lakes include Ozette, Crescent, and Quinault, all on the Olympic Peninsula west of Puget Sound. The Cascade Mountains area has many beautiful lakes. The largest is Lake Chelan, 51 miles (82 kilometers) long, on the eastern slope. Franklin D. Roosevelt Lake, formed by Grand Coulee Dam, covers 130 square miles (337 square kilometers) and is the state's largest lake.

Western Washington has a milder climate than any other region in the United States that is as far north. Westerly winds from the Pacific Ocean help keep the summers pleasantly cool and the winters relatively warm. Seattle's temperature averages about 66° F. (19° C) in July and 41° F. (5° C) in January.

Eastern Washington has warmer summers and colder winters than western Washington. Spokane, near the Idaho border, has an average temperature of 70° F. (21° C) in July and 25° F. (−4° C) in January.

The state's highest temperature, 118° F. (48° C), occurred near Wahluke on July 24, 1928, and at Ice Harbor Dam in southeastern Washington on Aug. 5, 1961. The lowest, −48° F. (−44° C), occurred at Mazama and at Winthrop in the northeast on Dec. 30, 1968.

Moist winds from the Pacific Ocean bring much rain to western Washington. By the time the winds reach eastern Washington, they have lost much moisture. As a result, the east has a much drier climate than the west. *Precipitation* (rain, melted snow, and other forms of moisture) averages over 135 inches (343 centimeters) a year in parts of the Olympic Peninsula. But Washington's central plateau receives only 6 inches (15 centimeters). Much of this area is semidesert.

Snowfall in Washington averages about 5 inches (13 centimeters) a year along the coast. Mount Rainier receives 50 to 75 inches (130 to 191 centimeters) on its lower slopes and over 500 inches (1,300 centimeters) on its higher slopes. In 1970-1971, Paradise Ranger Station on Mount Rainier recorded the heaviest snowfall for one winter in the United States—1,027 inches (2,609 centimeters).

SEASONAL TEMPERATURES

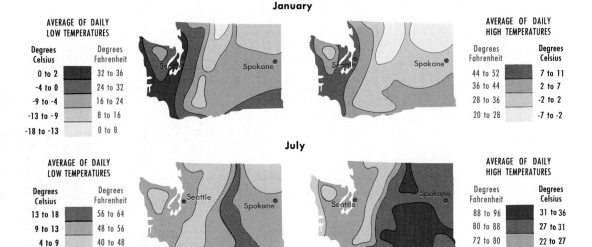

January

AVERAGE OF DAILY LOW TEMPERATURES

Degrees Celsius	Degrees Fahrenheit
0 to 2	32 to 36
-4 to 0	24 to 32
-9 to -4	16 to 24
-13 to -9	8 to 16
-18 to -13	0 to 8

AVERAGE OF DAILY HIGH TEMPERATURES

Degrees Fahrenheit	Degrees Celsius
44 to 52	7 to 11
36 to 44	2 to 7
28 to 36	-2 to 2
20 to 28	-7 to -2

July

AVERAGE OF DAILY LOW TEMPERATURES

Degrees Celsius	Degrees Fahrenheit
13 to 18	56 to 64
9 to 13	48 to 56
4 to 9	40 to 48

AVERAGE OF DAILY HIGH TEMPERATURES

Degrees Fahrenheit	Degrees Celsius
88 to 96	31 to 36
80 to 88	27 to 31
72 to 80	22 to 27
64 to 72	18 to 22

AVERAGE YEARLY PRECIPITATION
(Rain, Melted Snow and Other Moisture)

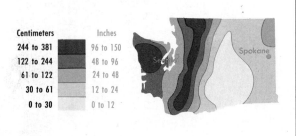

Centimeters	Inches
244 to 381	96 to 150
122 to 244	48 to 96
61 to 122	24 to 48
30 to 61	12 to 24
0 to 30	0 to 12

0   50   100   200 Miles
0   100   200   300 Kilometers

WORLD BOOK maps

AVERAGE MONTHLY WEATHER

	SEATTLE					SPOKANE				
	Temperatures F°		Temperatures C°		Days of Rain or Snow	Temperatures F°		Temperatures C°		Days of Rain or Snow
	High	Low	High	Low		High	Low	High	Low	
JAN.	43	31	6	-1	19	30	20	-1	-7	17
FEB.	48	34	9	1	16	36	23	2	-5	12
MAR.	52	37	11	3	17	46	30	8	-1	13
APR.	58	40	14	4	13	56	37	13	3	7
MAY	65	45	18	7	10	66	44	19	7	9
JUNE	70	50	21	10	11	72	51	22	11	8
JULY	75	53	24	12	6	82	57	28	14	4
AUG.	74	53	23	12	6	81	55	27	13	4
SEPT.	68	49	20	9	8	71	48	22	9	5
OCT.	59	44	15	7	16	58	39	14	4	10
NOV.	50	38	10	3	18	42	30	6	-1	12
DEC.	45	34	7	1	20	34	24	1	-4	16

The Cascade Mountains divide Washington into two major economic regions. The region east of the Cascades is important for agriculture. Farmers in eastern Washington raise large wheat and fruit crops, beef cattle, and many vegetables. Spokane is eastern Washington's chief financial and marketing center.

Most of Washington's industrial centers are in the western lowlands. Seattle, Tacoma, and other port cities are centers for trade, fishing, and shipbuilding. Seattle also has a huge aircraft construction industry. Western Washington is also a dairy farming and bulb-producing region. Lumbering and the processing of wood products are important in many parts of the state.

Millions of tourists visit the state each year. They spend over $1 billion a year there.

Natural Resources. Washington's many natural resources include a plentiful water supply, large timber reserves, and fertile soils.

Water is one of the state's most important resources. Melted snow from the mountains feeds the rivers of western Washington and provides water for industry, electric power, irrigation, and home use. The Columbia River and its tributaries are valuable sources of water in central and eastern Washington. Inlets and bays in the Puget Sound region and along the coast encourage shipping, commercial fishing, and pleasure boating.

Forests cover about 23 million acres (9.3 million hectares) in Washington. About 18 million acres (7.3 million hectares) are of commercial value, with reserves of standing timber estimated at about 325 billion board

Production of Goods in Washington

Total value of goods produced in 1975—$9,386,271,000

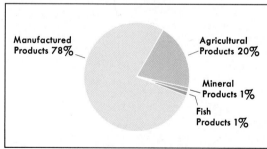

Manufactured Products 78%

Agricultural Products 20%

Mineral Products 1%

Fish Products 1%

Percentages are based on farm income, value added by manufacture, and value of fish and mineral production.
Sources: U.S. government publications, 1976-1977.

Employment in Washington

Total number of persons employed in 1976—1,356,800

	Number of Employees
Wholesale & Retail Trade	306,000
Government	272,900
Manufacturing	246,100
Community, Social, & Personal Services	230,400
Agriculture	89,000
Transportation & Public Utilities	75,100
Construction & Mining	69,300
Finance, Insurance, & Real Estate	68,000

Sources: *Employment and Earnings*, September 1977, U.S. Bureau of Labor Statistics; *Farm Labor*, February 1977, U.S. Department of Agriculture.

feet (767 million cubic meters). In the western part of the state, where the rainfall is heaviest, the western hemlock is the leading timber tree. Douglas fir, Sitka spruce, and western red cedar are also common. The Douglas fir is the chief timber tree in the drier eastern section. Ponderosa (western yellow) pine, western larch, and lodgepole pine also grow there. The eastern forests lie chiefly along the slopes of the Cascades, in the northeastern highlands, and in the Blue Mountains. The most common Washington hardwoods include alder, aspen, cottonwood, and maple.

The state government, the U.S. government, and many private companies work to conserve Washington's valuable timber resources. They use harvesting methods that leave enough trees for natural reseeding. They also grow seedlings in tree nurseries for use in reforestation projects. Tree seeds are scattered from helicopters in areas that are difficult to reach by land. Helicopters and small airplanes are also used to spray insect poisons on forests that are being destroyed by harmful bugs. Two forest-conservation groups originated in Washington. They are the *American Tree Farm System* and the *Keep America Green* movement.

Soils. Washington's best soils for agriculture are the silts and sands of the river valleys and of the irrigated dry lands east of the Cascades. The soils of the Palouse region in southeastern Washington, especially in Whitman County, were built up from fine materials carried by winds from the west. These fertile soils produce large crops of wheat and peas. Most of the high mountain areas have rocky soils.

Minerals. Washington has the only large coal deposits on the Pacific Coast. The state's coal reserves are estimated at about 2 billion short tons (1.8 billion metric tons). The largest coal fields lie in western Washington, especially in Lewis County. Magnesite deposits occur near Chewelah. Gold deposits are found on the eastern slopes of the Cascades and in the Okanogan Mountains. Lead and zinc occur mainly in northeastern Washington. Clay, limestone, and sand and gravel occur in many areas. The state also has deposits of barite, copper, diatomite, gypsum, iron ore, olivine, peat, pumice, silver, soapstone, talc, tungsten, and uranium.

Plants and Animals. Many kinds of plants grow in Washington because of the great variety of climates and elevations. Rare wild flowers bloom in mountain meadows. Colorful lupine, brown-eyed Susan, and goldenrod grow in fields and along roadways. Flowering plants such as the western rhododendron and the western dogwood brighten the forests and hillsides.

Game animals found in Washington include bears and four kinds of deer. These are the elk, the Columbian black-tailed deer, the mule deer, and the western white-tailed deer. Washington also has many small fur-bearing animals such as beavers, martens, minks, muskrats, and western bobcats. Game birds include pheasants, quail, ruffed grouse, sage grouse, wild ducks, and wild geese.

Fishes in the many fresh-water rivers and lakes include grayling, cutthroat trout, rainbow trout, steelhead trout, and whitefish. Enormous sturgeon have been caught in the Columbia and Snake rivers. Salt-water fishes include cod, flounder, halibut, and salmon. Crabs, oysters,

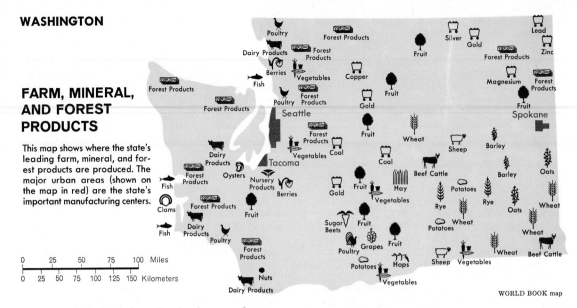

FARM, MINERAL, AND FOREST PRODUCTS

This map shows where the state's leading farm, mineral, and forest products are produced. The major urban areas (shown on the map in red) are the state's important manufacturing centers.

WORLD BOOK map

and several kinds of clams live in the coastal waters.

Washington salmon have an interesting life story. These fish spend most of their lives in the ocean. But when they are old enough to lay eggs, they leave the ocean and swim up rivers. Sometimes they travel long distances, leaping up rapids and waterfalls. When they reach quiet waters far upstream, they lay their eggs and then die. After the young fish hatch, they swim back down the rivers to the ocean. Such salmon "runs" used to take place in many of Washington's rivers and streams. Many of the runs were disturbed by hydroelectric projects. But the state has restored its salmon runs by "planting" rivers with salmon eggs and building "fish ladders" so the fish can swim around dams.

Manufacturing accounts for 78 per cent of the total value of all goods produced in Washington. Products manufactured in the state have a *value added by manufacture* of about $7¼ billion a year. This figure represents the value added to products by Washington's industries, not counting such costs as materials, supplies, and fuels. Washington's chief manufactured products, in order of importance, are (1) transportation equipment, (2) lumber and wood products, and (3) food products.

Transportation Equipment made in Washington has a value added of about $2½ billion a year. Washington is a leading center of the aircraft and space industry. The Boeing Company, with headquarters in Seattle and plants in Auburn, Kent, and Renton, and near Everett, leads the nation in producing commercial airliners. It employs about 50,000 Washingtonians—more than any other manufacturer in the state.

Washington is also a leading shipbuilding center. It has major shipyards at Bremerton, Seattle, and Tacoma. The Puget Sound Naval Shipyard at Bremerton is the largest on the Pacific Coast.

Lumber and Wood Products, not including paper, have a value added of about $1 billion yearly. Washington is a leading lumber producer in the United States. Sawmills and factories in many parts of Washington produce lumber, plywood, shingles, and veneer strips.

Food Products have an annual value added of about $830 million. Food-processing activities include milling

Ray Atkeson, Publix

Sawmills with log-filled ponds, such as this one near Enumclaw, are common in Washington, a leading lumber state.

flour; potato processing; packing fish and meats; canning, freezing, and preserving fruits, vegetables, and berries; and producing butter, cheese, milk, breakfast foods, and bakery goods. The state also refines much beet sugar.

Other Leading Industries. The production of primary metals is the fourth-ranking industrial activity in Washington. Washington leads the states in the production of aluminum. Other leading products, in order of value, are paper products, fabricated metal products, and chemicals. Industries in Washington also make clothing; electric and electronic equipment; nonelectric machinery; petroleum and coal products; printed materials; and stone, clay, and glass products.

Agriculture accounts for about $2 billion yearly, or 20 per cent of the value of goods produced in Washington. Washington has about 29,000 farms. They average about 567 acres (229 hectares) in size.

Farmers produce good crops both by dry farming methods and by irrigation. The chief irrigated regions are in the Columbia Basin and in the valleys of the Okanogan, Snake, Spokane, Walla Walla, Wenatchee, and Yakima rivers. The state has about 13,000 irrigated farms, with an average size of 440 acres (178 hectares). Washington has about 16,000 unirrigated farms. The average size of an unirrigated farm is 669 acres (271 hectares).

Wheat is Washington's most valuable crop. Farmers in eastern Washington raise spring and winter wheat. Washington leads the nation in the production of dry peas. It is also first in the production of hops, used in making beer. The state ranks high in the production of potatoes and sugar beets, grown mainly in Grant, Yakima, and other counties of south-central Washington. Washington is a leading producer of asparagus, dry beans, and green peas, and of barley and other grains. It also produces sweet corn and hay.

Washington grows more apples than any other state. People throughout the country enjoy such famous kinds of Washington apples as the Red Delicious and Golden Delicious. The state ranks high in the production of apricots, cherries, pears, and plums and prunes. Most of the apples and other orchard fruits are grown in central Washington's irrigated valleys. Washington produces important berry crops, especially blueberries, cranberries, raspberries, and strawberries, and ranks high in grape production.

Flower bulbs are also an important Washington crop. The state is one of the world's chief producers of iris and daffodil bulbs. It also grows tulip bulbs and such greenhouse flowers as azaleas, Easter lilies, and poinsettias. The Puyallup, Skagit, and lower Cowlitz river valleys are world-famous sources of bulbs. Washington growers also produce alfalfa seed, mint, and forest products.

Livestock and livestock products account for about a fourth of the value of Washington farm products. Beef cattle, horses, and sheep are raised on large ranches in eastern Washington. Most of the dairy farms are in the western part of the state. Washington farms also produce many *broilers* (chickens 9 to 12 weeks old) and eggs.

Mining. Washington produces about $120 million worth of minerals a year. Coal is the state's most valuable mineral, with an annual production of about 4 million short tons (3.6 million metric tons). Lead, limestone, sand and gravel, and zinc are also important. Other minerals produced in Washington include copper, gold, silver, tungsten, and uranium.

Fishing. Washington has an annual fish catch valued at about $55 million. The state has won fame for its seafoods, especially chinook and sockeye salmon. The Washington fish catch also includes valuable supplies of chum, coho, and pink salmon, clams, cod, crabs, dogfish, flounder, halibut, herring, oysters, rockfish, shrimp, and tuna. Seattle ranks as the chief U.S. market for halibut and salmon caught in Alaskan and Canadian waters.

Electric Power. Washington has more potential water power than any other state. It has developed only about two-fifths of its potential water power. But it leads the states in hydroelectric generating capacity and in yearly hydroelectric power production.

Grand Coulee Dam, the largest concrete dam in the United States, is one of the greatest sources of water power in the world. Other large dams on the Columbia

River include Bonneville, Chief Joseph, John Day, McNary, Priest Rapids, Rock Island, Rocky Reach, The Dalles, and Wanapum. The Snake River also has many dams. Power-producing dams on smaller rivers include Diablo and Ross, on the Upper Skagit; Alder, on the Nisqually; and Mossyrock, on the Cowlitz.

Transportation facilities in Washington help link the United States with Canada, the Orient, and the South Pacific.

Aviation. Washington has about 300 airports and airfields. Twelve airlines serve the state. Seattle-Tacoma International Airport handles passenger and freight service to and from Alaska, Australia, Canada, Denmark, Hawaii, Japan, and New Zealand. Other leading airports are in Spokane, Walla Walla, and Yakima.

Railroads in Washington operate on about 6,000 miles (9,700 kilometers) of track. About 10 rail lines provide freight service. Passenger trains link 10 Washington cities to other cities. In 1883, the Northern Pacific line reached Washington, and in 1887 it was extended across the Cascade Mountains to Tacoma. The Cascade Tunnel, 7.79 miles (12.54 kilometers) long, was completed in 1929. It is the longest railroad tunnel in the Western Hemisphere.

Roads and Highways extend for about 80,000 miles (130,000 kilometers) throughout Washington. About 65,000 miles (105,000 kilometers) are surfaced. Two floating concrete pontoon bridges cross Seattle's Lake Washington. The longest one has a floating portion that is 7,518 feet (2,291 meters) long. The structure is the longest concrete pontoon bridge in the United States. Another long pontoon bridge, the Hood Canal Floating Bridge, spans the Hood Canal. The Tacoma Narrows Bridge, one of the world's longest suspension bridges, crosses a part of Puget Sound.

Shipping and Waterways. Anacortes, Seattle, Tacoma, and several other Puget Sound cities are important seaports. Ocean-going ships enter Puget Sound through the Strait of Juan de Fuca. They bring products from Asia, South America, and other parts of the world. Longview and Vancouver on the Columbia River and Grays Harbor on the Pacific are also important ports.

An artificial waterway, the Lake Washington Ship Canal, cuts across Seattle. It connects Lake Washington and Lake Union with Puget Sound. The Seattle fishing fleet, many pleasure boats, and some ocean vessels travel up the canal to landlocked harbors. A ferry system links the San Juan Islands and the mainland.

Communication. Washington's first newspaper, the *Columbian,* began in Olympia in 1852. Today, Washington has about 200 newspapers, including about 25 dailies. Washington newspapers with the largest circulations are the *Seattle Post-Intelligencer,* the *Seattle Times,* the *Spokane Daily Chronicle, The* (Spokane) *Spokesman-Review,* and the *Tacoma News-Tribune.* Washington publishers also issue about 100 magazines.

Washington's first commercial radio broadcast was made from Everett in 1920 by station KFBL (now KRKO). KING-TV, Washington's first television station, began operating in Seattle in 1948. Today, the state has about 160 radio stations and about 20 television stations.

Indian Days. Many Indians lived in the Washington region before white people came. Tribes of the plateau Indian group lived on the plains and in river valleys east of the Cascades. These included the Cayuse, Colville, Nez Percé, Okanogan, Spokane, and Yakima. The coastal Indians lived west of the Cascade Mountains. These tribes included the Chinook, Clallam, Clatsop, Nisqually, Nooksack, and Puyallup. They lived mainly on salmon and other fish. They carved masks and other items from wood.

Discovery and Exploration. The first white people to see the Pacific Northwest were probably Spanish and English explorers who sailed northward along the coast from California during the 1500's. The Europeans did not land in what is now Washington until the late 1700's. After the mid-1700's, Russian fur traders settled in what is now Alaska. The Spaniards feared that the Russians would move to occupy the region farther south. To prevent this expansion, Spain sent several expeditions to establish Spanish rights to the area.

In 1775, Bruno Heceta and Juan Francisco de la Bodega y Quadra made the first landing on Washington soil, near present-day Point Grenville. They claimed the region for Spain.

The English also sent several explorers to the Pacific Northwest. The first was Captain James Cook, in 1778. He neither touched the coast nor, because of stormy weather, saw much of it. Captain George Vancouver, another English explorer, made a careful survey of Puget Sound and Georgia Gulf between 1792 and 1794. One of his officers, Peter Puget, reached Puget

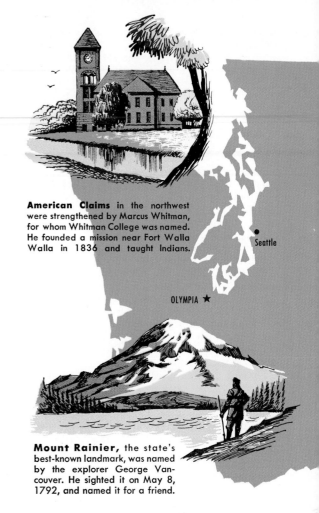

American Claims in the northwest were strengthened by Marcus Whitman, for whom Whitman College was named. He founded a mission near Fort Walla Walla in 1836 and taught Indians.

Seattle

OLYMPIA ★

Mount Rainier, the state's best-known landmark, was named by the explorer George Vancouver. He sighted it on May 8, 1792, and named it for a friend.

Lewis and Clark Reached the Pacific in the autumn of 1805 after crossing the Rockies and descending the Snake and Columbia rivers. President Thomas Jefferson had commissioned them to explore the upper Louisiana Territory.

————— IMPORTANT DATES IN WASHINGTON —————

1775 Bruno Heceta and Juan Francisco de la Bodega y Quadra of Spain made the first landing on Washington soil.

1792 Robert Gray sailed into Grays Harbor and the Columbia River. George Vancouver surveyed the coast of Washington and Puget Sound.

1805 Lewis and Clark reached Washington and the Pacific Ocean.

1810 A British-Canadian fur-trading post was established near present-day Spokane.

1818 Great Britain and the United States agreed to a joint occupation of the Oregon region, including Washington.

1846 A treaty between the United States and Great Britain established Washington's boundary at the 49th parallel.

1853 Congress created the Washington Territory.

1855-1858 Indian wars raged in the Washington Territory.

1883 The Northern Pacific Railroad linked Washington and the East.

1889 Washington became the 42nd state on November 11.

1909 The Alaska-Yukon-Pacific Exposition was held in Seattle.

1917 The Lake Washington Ship Canal opened.

1928 The capitol at Olympia was completed.

1942 Grand Coulee Dam was completed.

1954 A $40,000,000 oil refinery opened at Ferndale.

1962 The "Century 21" World's Fair was held at Seattle.

1964 The Columbia River Treaty of 1961 and related agreements received final approval from the U.S. and Canadian governments.

1974 Expo '74, a world's fair, was held in Spokane.

Sound in 1792. England based its claim to the region on the explorations of Cook and Vancouver.

Captain Robert Gray, an American, headed a fur-trading expedition sent by a Boston company. Gray sailed into the harbor that now bears his name. In 1792, he reached the mouth of the Columbia River. Gray's arrival at the Columbia became a basis for American claims to the region. In 1805, the explorers Meriwether Lewis and William Clark crossed the Rocky Mountains. They reached the Columbia River and followed it to the Pacific Ocean. Their voyage gave the United States a second claim to the Northwest. Between 1807 and 1811, the British strengthened their claim when David Thompson, a Canadian explorer and geographer, traveled down the Columbia to the Pacific.

Settlement. During the early 1800's, British and American fur traders both operated in the region. In 1810, the Canadian North West Company established Spokane House near present-day Spokane for the

"Fifty-Four Forty or Fight" was the cry during the presidential campaign of 1844. But the boundary between Washington and Canada was fixed at latitude 49° by the 1846 Treaty of Oregon.

• Grand Coulee

Spokane •

Hanford •

• Walla Walla

"Biggest Job on Earth." Grand Coulee Dam, begun in 1933 and finished in 1942, ranks as the mightiest piece of masonry built by man. It is made of 10,585,000 cubic yards (8,092,810 cubic meters) of concrete.

"First Atomic City," Hanford, became the site of an atomic-energy plant in 1943. Its large nuclear reactors changed uranium into plutonium, using hydroelectric power from the Columbia River.

Leading Lumber State. Washington's first sawmill, run by water power, was set up in 1826, and the first steam sawmill started operating in 1853. The state has been a leading lumber producer since about 1900.

Fort Okanogan was the first permanent American settlement in the Washington region. It was founded by John Jacob Astor's fur company in 1811.

HISTORIC WASHINGTON

purpose of trading with the Indians. In 1811, a company sent by the American trader John Jacob Astor set up a fur-trading post at Astoria, in present-day Oregon. Astor's group also founded Fort Okanogan, the first permanent American settlement on land that now lies within the state of Washington.

During the War of 1812 between the United States and Great Britain, Astor's company gave up its trading posts. After the war, the two countries could not agree on a boundary line to separate their territories west of the Rocky Mountains. They signed a treaty in 1818 permitting citizens of both countries to trade and settle in the region, which was called the Oregon Country. John McLoughlin of the Hudson's Bay Company, a British trading firm, completed Fort Vancouver (now Vancouver) on the Columbia River in 1825.

During the 1840's, many Americans settled in the Oregon Country. The boundary dispute between the United States and Great Britain reached a climax dur-

ing the presidential campaign of 1844. James K. Polk partially based his campaign on the claim that all the region south of latitude 54° 40′ belonged to the United States (see FIFTY-FOUR FORTY OR FIGHT). In 1846, President Polk signed a treaty with Great Britain which set the boundary line at the 49th parallel, Washington's present northern border. Great Britain kept Vancouver Island, part of which lies south of the 49th parallel.

Territorial Days. A bill creating the Oregon Territory, of which Washington was a part, passed Congress in 1848. General Joseph Lane was appointed governor. In 1853, President Millard Fillmore signed a bill creating the Washington Territory. This region included the present state of Washington, northern Idaho, and western Montana. The capital was established at Olympia. The President appointed Isaac Ingalls Stevens as the first governor of the new territory. Stevens sought treaties with the Indians, in order to put them on reservations and free more territory for white settlers.

WASHINGTON

The coastal Indians signed the treaties. But Stevens' efforts in 1855 to sign treaties with the plateau Indians led to war. Kamiakin, a Yakima Indian chief, led the warring tribes. The war ended in 1858 when the Indians lost a battle near Four Lakes.

In 1859, the Washington Territory was expanded to include the southern parts of what are now the states of Idaho and Wyoming. Washington received its present boundaries in 1863, when the Idaho Territory was established.

Increasing numbers of settlers streamed into Washington after 1860, partly because of the discovery of gold in Idaho, Oregon, and British Columbia. But there were no major gold strikes in Washington. Many who had hoped to find gold in Washington stayed to become farmers or loggers.

Statehood. The completion of a railroad connection with the East in 1883 brought more settlers. President Benjamin Harrison proclaimed the territory as the 42nd state on Nov. 11, 1889. Elisha P. Ferry, former governor of the territory, was elected Washington's first state governor. Olympia remained the capital.

Between 1890 and 1900, parts of the desertlike lands of eastern Washington were reclaimed by irrigation. Large numbers of wheat ranchers and fruit growers came to the state. By 1900, much of the open cattle range had been replaced by wheat fields and fruit orchards. Lumbering, fishing, and mining also increased rapidly, and shipping to the Far East and Alaska became a leading activity. The shipping industry added to the wealth of the ports and railway centers. The state also profited greatly by the Klondike and Alaska gold rush of 1897-1898 (see ALASKA [The Gold Rush]). Seattle served as the chief outfitting center for the prospectors. Washingtonians also made money by handling fish and other Alaskan products.

The Early 1900's. In 1909, the Alaska-Yukon-Pacific Exposition was held in Seattle to celebrate the Alaska gold rush and the growth of the port of Seattle. After the United States entered World War I in 1917, the shipyards of Puget Sound expanded. The state's lumber industry grew, and wheat from the wheat belt of eastern Washington brought high prices. Military centers such as Camp Lewis (now Fort Lewis) were also expanded.

The end of the war brought sharp cutbacks in production. Much unemployment resulted. Organized labor protested with general strikes, including the "Seattle Revolution of 1919," in which about 60,000 workers walked off their jobs. The Great Depression during the 1930's brought even greater reductions in many industries. Food processing remained Washington's only stable industry. Other industries that kept producing on a small scale included metalworking and aircraft construction. These activities, along with construction of Bonneville and Grand Coulee dams, helped the state regain some prosperity in the late 1930's.

The Mid-1900's. During World War II (1939-1945), Washington industries produced aircraft and ships for the armed forces. Expansion occurred in truck and railroad car construction, the wood products industry, and agriculture. In 1943, the government built a nuclear energy center, the Hanford Works, in southeastern Washington. The center helped make the first atomic bombs. In the 1960's, it began to produce electricity. It later became known as the Hanford Project of the U.S. Department of Energy.

Many Washington cities and towns grew as a result of the construction and expansion of military bases. Thousands of people who came to the state to work in defense plants stayed after the war.

During the 1950's and 1960's, the government built a series of dams on the Columbia, Snake, and other rivers. The dams produced electric power and also served such purposes as flood control and irrigation. Six Washington aluminum plants, large users of electricity, began operations during the postwar years. In the 1950's, gas was first pipelined into the state from Canada and the southwestern United States. In 1954, a $40-million oil refinery opened at Ferndale.

Also in the 1950's and 1960's, major agricultural growth took place in the Columbia River Basin as irrigation turned large areas of dry land into rich farmland. Development of the Columbia River led to the growth of inland ports and an increase in river shipping. In 1964, the United States and Canada approved a cooperative plan for hydroelectric and river-control projects on the Columbia and connecting streams.

In 1962, the Seattle World's Fair helped promote tourism, an important industry in the state. The fairgrounds and buildings and the 607-foot (185-meter) Space Needle observation tower remain as a year-round civic and tourist center. Seattle and its suburbs spent $130 million in a nine-year project to clean up polluted Lake Washington and Elliott Bay, two major recreation areas. In 1968, Seattle-area voters approved a $333-million improvement program called "Forward Thrust." Plans included a $118-million expansion of park and recreational facilities.

In the late 1960's, industry and population grew rapidly in Seattle and the Puget Sound Basin. An important reason for this growth was the expansion of the Boeing Company. Boeing, a major military airplane builder in wartime, began to build spacecraft and commercial jets in the 1960's. In 1967, thousands of Boeing employees moved into the Everett area after a huge assembly plant opened there. This plant builds the giant 747 airliners. Businesses developed to serve the Boeing employees and their families.

The Governors of Washington

	Party	Term
Elisha P. Ferry	Republican	1889-1893
John Harte McGraw	Republican	1893-1897
John Rankin Rogers	Democratic-Populist	1897-1901
Henry McBride	Republican	1901-1905
Albert Edward Mead	Republican	1905-1909
Samuel G. Cosgrove	Republican	1909
Marion E. Hay	Republican	1909-1913
Ernest Lister	Democratic	1913-1919
Louis Folwell Hart	Republican	1919-1925
Roland H. Hartley	Republican	1925-1933
Clarence D. Martin	Democratic	1933-1941
Arthur B. Langlie	Republican	1941-1945
Monrad C. Wallgren	Democratic	1945-1949
Arthur B. Langlie	Republican	1949-1957
Albert D. Rossellini	Democratic	1957-1965
Daniel J. Evans	Republican	1965-1977
Dixy Lee Ray	Democratic	1977-

Washington Today is trying to attract new kinds of industry and depend less on federal aerospace and defense contracts. The state's economy is somewhat unstable but is being helped by cheap electric power, by gas brought in through new pipelines, and by increased tourism. To serve vacationers, Washington companies are building ski resorts resembling European ski centers. Many vacationers visited Expo '74, a world's fair held in Spokane in 1974.

Washington's major challenge is to encourage industrial growth and, at the same time, protect its natural resources and recreational areas. In the late 1960's, conservationists blocked construction of an aluminum plant on Guemes Island near Anacortes and an oil refinery on Puget Sound. State pollution control officials and citizen groups are watching other developments to guard against threats to the environment.

By 1990, several nuclear power plants for the production of electricity are scheduled to be built in Washington. Petroleum from new Alaska oil fields is expected to result in more oil refinery construction in the state. Puget Sound will probably become a major deepwater port for the huge new cargo ships being launched by shipbuilders of many nations.

C. BREWSTER COULTER and HOWARD J. CRITCHFIELD

WASHINGTON/*Study Aids*

Related Articles in WORLD BOOK include:

BIOGRAPHIES

Cowles (family)
Handforth, Thomas
Jackson, Henry M.
Joseph, Chief
Landes, Bertha Knight
Puget, Peter
Ray, Dixy Lee
Vancouver, George
Wainwright, Jonathan M.
Whitman, Marcus
Whitman, Narcissa

CITIES

Bremerton
Olympia
Richland
Seattle
Spokane
Tacoma
Vancouver
Walla Walla
Yakima

HISTORY

Chinook Indians
Lewis and Clark Expedition
Nootka Indians
Oregon (Exploration)
Oregon Territory
Western Frontier Life

NATIONAL PARKS AND HISTORIC SITES

Fort Vancouver National
Historic Site
Mount Rainier National Park
North Cascades National Park
Olympic National Park
Whitman Mission
National Historic
Site

PHYSICAL FEATURES

Bonneville Dam
Cape Alava
Cape Flattery
Cascade Range
Cascade Tunnel
Coast Range
Columbia River
Diablo Dam
Fairy Falls
Grand Coulee
Dam
Juan de Fuca,
Strait of
Mount Rainier
Mud Mountain Dam
Olympic Mountains
Puget Sound
Ross Dam
San Juan Islands
Snake River

PRODUCTS

For Washington's rank in production, see:

Aluminum
Apple
Cherry
Electric Power
Forest Products
Grape
Lumber
Pea
Pear
Plum
Potato
Wheat

OTHER RELATED ARTICLES

Pacific Coast States
Pacific Northwest
Puget Sound Naval Shipyard

Outline

I. Government
  A. Constitution
  B. Executive
  C. Legislature
  D. Courts
  E. Local
    Government
  F. Taxation
  G. Politics
II. People
III. Education
  A. Schools
  B. Libraries
  C. Museums

IV. A Visitor's Guide
  A. Places to Visit
  B. Annual Events
V. The Land
  A. Land Regions
  B. Coastline
  C. Rivers, Waterfalls,
    and Lakes
VI. Climate
VII. Economy
  A. Natural Resources
  B. Manufacturing
  C. Agriculture
  D. Mining
  E. Fishing
  F. Electric Power
  G. Transportation
  H. Communication
VIII. History

Questions

On what grounds did both England and the United States claim the region that is now Washington?

Where is the longest railroad tunnel in the United States? Where is the longest concrete pontoon bridge?

Why does less rain fall in eastern Washington than in the western part of the state?

What is Washington's most valuable crop?

In what ways does Washington benefit from the dams in the Columbia River system?

How does the state protect its forest resources?

What is the Space Needle?

In what region do most of Washington's people live?

What is the largest concrete dam in the United States? What are *coulees*? What are *scablands*?

Books for Young Readers

BAILEY, BERNADINE F. *Picture Book of Washington*. Rev. ed. Whitman, 1966.

CARPENTER, ALLAN. *Washington*. Childrens Press, 1966.

KIRK, RUTH. *David, Young Chief of the Quileutes: An American Indian Today*. Harcourt, 1967.

McDONALD, LUCILE S. *Washington's Yesterdays: 1775-1853*. Binfords, 1953. *Search for the Northwest Passage*. 1958.

PELLEGRINI, ANGELO M. *Washington*. Coward, 1967.

Books for Older Readers

AVERY, MARY W. *Washington: A History of the Evergreen State*. Univ. of Washington Press, 1965. *Government of Washington State*. Rev. ed. 1973.

CANTWELL, ROBERT. *The Hidden Northwest*. Lippincott, 1972.

CLARK, NORMAN H. *Washington: A Bicentennial History*. Norton, 1976.

JOHANSEN, DOROTHY O. *Empire of the Columbia: A History of the Pacific Northwest*. 2nd ed. Harper, 1967.

LEE, WILLIAM STORRS, ed. *Washington State: A Literary Chronicle*. Crowell, 1969.

NELSON, GERALD B. *Seattle: The Life and Times of an American City*. Knopf, 1977.

PHILLIPS, JAMES W. *Washington State Place Names*. Univ. of Washington Press, 1971.

The United States Capitol, in Washington, D.C., is the place where Congress makes the nation's laws. Tourists flock to this magnificent building to enjoy its beauty and to see Congress in action.

WASHINGTON, D.C.

WASHINGTON, D.C., is the capital of the United States. It is also one of the country's most beautiful and historic cities and the site of many of its most popular tourist attractions.

As the nation's capital, Washington serves as the headquarters of the federal government. The President of the United States, the members of Congress, the Supreme Court justices, and about 340,000 other government employees work in the Washington area. Decisions made by government leaders in the city affect the lives of people throughout the United States and, sometimes, in other parts of the world. For example, the President suggests laws to Congress and directs U.S. relations with other countries. The members of Congress pass laws every American citizen must obey. The Supreme Court justices decide whether the government's laws and practices are constitutional.

Washington's role as the nation's capital makes it important to the American people in another way. The city is a symbol of their country's unity, history, and democratic tradition.

Every year, millions of persons from all parts of the United States and from other countries visit Washington. They go there to see such important government buildings as the United States Capitol, where Congress meets, and the White House, where the President lives and works. They visit the Washington Monument, Lincoln Memorial, and other famous structures dedicated to American heroes of the past. They also tour the

---- FACTS IN BRIEF ----

Population: *1975 Estimate*—City, 711,518. *1970 Census*—City, 756,668; Metropolitan Area, 2,925,521.

Area: *City*—68 sq. mi. (176 km²). *Metropolitan Area*—2,907 sq. mi. (7,529 km²).

Altitude: 25 feet (7.6 meters) above sea level.

Climate: *Average Temperatures*—January, 37° F. (3° C); July, 78° F. (26° C). *Average Annual Precipitation* (rainfall, melted snow, and other forms of moisture)—50 in. (127 cm). For the monthly weather in Washington, D.C., see MARYLAND (Climate).

Government: Federal District under the authority of Congress. Mayor and city council, elected to four-year terms, help run the government.

Founded: Site chosen, 1791. Became capital, 1800.

The contributors of this article are Eunice S. Grier, a consultant on public policy in Washington, D.C., and Atlee E. Shidler, executive vice-president of the Center for Municipal and Metropolitan Research.

62

city's many museums, which together house the world's largest collection of items from America's past.

Most of Washington's main government buildings, monuments, and museums stand in the west-central part of the city. This area ranks among the nation's most beautiful places. Many of its buildings and monuments are magnificent white marble structures. Scenic parks and gardens, and—in springtime—gorgeous blossoms of Japanese cherry trees, add natural beauty to the man-made splendor of the area.

Outside the west-central area, Washington is much like other big cities. It has large residential areas, including wealthy, middle-class, and poor sections. Suburbs spread out from the city in all directions. Washington faces problems common to all cities, including crime, poverty, traffic jams, and a shortage of good housing. Unlike most cities, Washington has no large industrial areas. This is so because government, rather than manufacturing, is the city's main business.

More than 70 per cent of the people who live in Washington are blacks. No other major American city has so large a percentage of black persons. In Washington's suburbs, however, whites account for more than 90 per cent of the population.

Washington lies in the southeastern United States, between Maryland and Virginia. It is the only American city or town that is not part of a state. It covers the entire area of the District of Columbia, a piece of land under the jurisdiction of the federal government.

Washington is one of the few cities in the world that was designed before it was built. President George Washington chose the city's site in 1791. He hired Pierre Charles L'Enfant, a French engineer, to draw up plans for the city. Washington replaced Philadelphia as the nation's capital in 1800. Congress named it in honor of George Washington. The *D.C.* in the city's name stands for *District of Columbia*.

WORLD BOOK map

Washington, D.C., the capital of the United States, lies between Maryland and Virginia on the east bank of the Potomac River.

Most of Washington's government buildings, famous monuments and museums, and other tourist attractions are located in the west-central part of the city. This area extends from Capitol Hill, which rises near the center of the city, westward to the Potomac River. This section describes the main features of the area. The two-page map provides an overview of it. The last part of the section deals with interesting sights in other parts of Washington and its suburbs. Many of Washington's points of interest also have separate articles in WORLD BOOK. See the list of *Related Articles* at the end of this article.

This section also tells—in general terms—about the activities of the federal government. But for much greater detail, see the article UNITED STATES, GOVERNMENT OF THE, and its list of *Related Articles*.

Capitol Hill

Capitol Hill rises 88 feet (26.8 meters) near the center of Washington. Several huge government buildings stand on the hill. They include the United States Capitol, congressional office buildings, the Library of Congress, the Supreme Court Building, and the conservatory of the United States Botanic Garden. The Folger Shakespeare Library and the Museum of African Art—both private institutions—are also located on Capitol Hill.

United States Capitol is the place where the members of Congress meet to discuss and vote on proposed legislation. The Capitol ranks among Washington's most magnificent buildings. Many tall Corinthian columns and an enormous dome beautify its white marble exterior. A bronze Statue of Freedom 19½ feet (5.94 meters) high stands on top of the dome. The Capitol, including the statue, rises almost 300 feet (91 meters) above the ground. The Capitol has 540 rooms. Many of them contain beautiful paintings, sculptures, and wall carvings that portray events and persons important in American history. Such works of art, along with gorgeous furnishings, give the interior of the Capitol the splendor of a fine museum or a palace.

Many persons visit the Capitol just to enjoy its beauty and its reminders of the country's past. But visitors may also attend sessions of Congress. To do so, however, they must first get a pass from one of the persons who represent them in Congress.

Congressional Office Buildings. Five buildings provide office space for the members of Congress. They are the Dirksen and Russell Senate office buildings, both north of the Capitol; and the Cannon, Longworth, and Rayburn House of Representatives office buildings, south of the Capitol. The members of Congress welcome visits to their offices by people they represent.

Library of Congress is probably the world's largest library. Its collection of more than 70 million items includes books, manuscripts, films, and recordings. The Library of Congress has three huge buildings, all east of the Capitol. The main building is a gray sandstone structure. The Library of Congress Thomas Jefferson Building (formerly called the Annex) is of white marble. The third building, of granite and marble, is called the Library of Congress James Madison Memo-

Milt & Joan Mann

The Capitol's Great Rotunda, or room under its dome, contains many works of art related to American history. These works include paintings of important events and statues of famous people.

Milt & Joan Mann

The Supreme Court Building resembles a Greek temple. In a courtroom inside, the Supreme Court justices make legal decisions that may affect the lives of every American.

rial Building. It is the newest of the library buildings.

The library serves the reference needs of Congress. The public may also use its materials and tour the buildings. The library's many items of special interest to tourists include most of Mathew Brady's Civil War photographs, a Gutenberg Bible printed in the 1450's, and one of the original copies of Abraham Lincoln's Gettysburg Address.

Supreme Court Building also stands east of the Capitol. In this building, the nine justices of the Supreme Court of the United States decide on the constitutionality of laws, government practices, and decisions of lower courts.

The white marble exterior of the Supreme Court Building resembles a Greek temple. The room where the justices hear cases is decorated with long, red drapes, copper gates, and marble columns. Visitors may attend sessions of the court. But seating for Supreme Court sessions is limited, and is available to visitors on a first-come, first-served basis.

United States Botanic Garden is located on the southwest side of Capitol Hill. It exhibits more than 10,000 kinds of plants. The plants include many rare species.

Folger Shakespeare Library, east of the main Library of Congress building, houses the world's most important collection of works by and about William Shakespeare. Only scholars may use its materials. But the library displays rare books and manuscripts for public viewing.

Museum of African Art is located about 2 blocks east of the Supreme Court. It exhibits sculptures and other works of art that reflect black African culture. It also displays works by black American artists.

The National Mall

A long, narrow, parklike area stretches westward from Capitol Hill. Called the *National Mall*, or simply the *Mall*, it provides open space amid west-central Washington's many huge buildings. It is also the location of some of the city's leading tourist attractions.

Several outstanding museums that are part of the Smithsonian Institution stand along the Mall a little west of Capitol Hill. Farther west are the Washington Monument and Lincoln Memorial. A long, narrow body of water called the *Reflecting Pool* lies between these two magnificent structures. Mirrorlike reflections of the monument and memorial can be seen in the pool's water. The Jefferson Memorial lies south of the Washington Monument. The memorial overlooks a lagoon called the *Tidal Basin*. Hundreds of Japanese cherry trees encircle the basin. In springtime, gorgeous pink and white cherry blossoms bloom on the trees. They create a sight of magnificent natural beauty that attracts huge crowds of visitors. The period when the trees are likely to be in bloom is set aside for a festival called the *Cherry Blossom Festival*. Other parts of Washington also have beautiful cherry trees.

Smithsonian Museums. The Smithsonian Institution is a government corporation that operates cultural, educational, and scientific facilities throughout Washington. The facilities include several museums on the Mall that house a total of more than 60 million items. Among the items in the museums are many of the world's greatest paintings, objects of importance to American history, and countless objects from the everyday life of America's past.

The original building of the Smithsonian Institution, called the *Smithsonian Building*, is one of the Mall's most impressive structures. Formerly a museum, it now houses the institution's offices. But the building remains a tourist attraction because it resembles a medieval castle. The names of the Smithsonian museums and some highlights of their collections follow.

Hellmuth, Obata & Kassabaum, Architects

Visitors to the Air and Space Museum view historic airplanes and space vehicles. The museum, a part of the Smithsonian Institution, exhibits the Wright brothers' first airplane, above.

National Air and Space Museum has exhibits that trace the history of flight. Its attractions include the airplane Orville Wright used in making the first successful flight, and the one in which Charles Lindbergh made the first solo flight across the Atlantic Ocean. The exhibits also include spacecraft that carried American astronauts into outer space and rocks that astronauts brought back from the moon.

National Museum of History and Technology displays the flag that inspired Francis Scott Key to write the national anthem. It has large collections of historical automobiles, railroad trains, and industrial machinery. It also houses an enormous collection of everyday objects from the past, including clothing, kitchen utensils, and home furnishings.

National Museum of Natural History exhibits stuffed animals from many parts of the world and skeletons of prehistoric animals. It has lifelike exhibits that show how American Indians and Eskimos lived long ago.

WORLD BOOK photo by Robert Lautman

The Hirshhorn Museum features an outstanding collection of modern American paintings and sculptures. It is a part of the Smithsonian Institution, and its full name is the Hirshhorn Museum and Sculpture Garden.

Dean Brown from Nancy Palmer   Robert H. Glaze, Artstreet   Milt & Joan Mann

Monuments to Three American Presidents are located on the National Mall. The Jefferson Memorial, *left*, stands in a beautiful setting among Japanese cherry trees at the edge of the Tidal Basin. The towering Washington Monument, *center*, ranks as the city's tallest structure. The majestic Lincoln Memorial, *right*, has a famous statue of Lincoln inside.

The museum also features an outstanding gem collection, which includes the famous Hope Diamond.

Smithsonian Arts and Industries Building houses a large collection of items from the 1800's. Its exhibits include locomotives, military weapons, and industrial machinery.

Art Museums. Three of the Smithsonian museums on the Mall are art galleries. The *National Gallery of Art* houses a world-famous collection of paintings and sculptures by Americans and Europeans. The *Hirshhorn Museum and Sculpture Garden* has an outstanding collection of modern American works of art. The *Freer Gallery of Art* features one of the world's finest collections of Oriental art.

The Smithsonian Institution also operates art museums in other parts of Washington. Its Fine Arts and Portrait Galleries Building, at 7th and F streets a few blocks north of the Mall, houses two outstanding museums. They are the *National Collection of Fine Arts*, which surveys American art from colonial days to the present; and the *National Portrait Gallery*, which includes paintings of persons important in American history. The Renwick Gallery, at 17th Street and Pennsylvania Avenue also north of the Mall, features exhibits of American crafts, design, and decorative art.

Washington Monument is a towering, slender, white marble *obelisk* (pillar) dedicated to the memory of George Washington. The tallest structure in Washington, D.C., the monument rises 555 feet 5⅛ inches (169.29 meters). An elevator inside the monument carries visitors to the top. From there, a person can see much of the Washington area.

Lincoln Memorial is a templelike white marble monument that honors Abraham Lincoln. On the outside, 36 Doric columns—one for each state that existed when Lincoln died—support the roof. Inside the monument is a majestic marble statue of Lincoln seated in a chair. Paintings that symbolize Lincoln's accomplishments, and quotations from Lincoln's writings, appear on the interior walls.

Jefferson Memorial honors Thomas Jefferson. It is a circular white marble structure ringed by 26 Ionic columns and topped by a beautiful dome. A bronze statue of Jefferson stands inside. Quotations from Jefferson's writings appear on the walls.

North of the Mall

Many huge government buildings crowd the area north of the Mall. Most of them stand along or near Pennsylvania Avenue. This broad, tree-lined street runs northwestward from Capitol Hill. It connects the Capitol and the White House, and serves as Washington's main parade route.

The White House ranks as the most important government building in the area. Most of the other buildings house offices of the executive branch of the government. The executive branch, headed by the President, is responsible for carrying out government policies. It includes the Executive Office of the President, 11 executive departments, and many government agencies.

Several nongovernment organizations—including the American Red Cross, the Daughters of the American Revolution (DAR), the National Academy of Sciences, and the World Bank—have their headquarters near the government buildings. Also nearby is a major tourist attraction—Ford's Theatre.

White House, at 1600 Pennsylvania Avenue, has served as the home and the office of every United States President except George Washington. Some of the world's most historic decisions have been made in this famous building.

The White House is constructed of white sandstone and has 132 rooms. Five of the rooms are open to the public. They are the Blue Room, East Room, Green Room, Red Room, and State Dining Room. These rooms are famous for their magnificent works of art and furnishings. Visitors are not allowed in the rooms where the President lives and works. But occasionally, the President or a member of his family stops by to greet tourists in the public rooms.

The White House stands on a beautifully landscaped plot that covers 18 acres (7.3 hectares). Lafayette Square lies north of the White House grounds and the Ellipse lies to the south. These parklike areas, together with the White House grounds, are sometimes called the *President's Square*, or *Park*. Blair House, a mansion on the west side of Lafayette Square, serves as a guest-house for high-ranking foreign officials who come to visit the President. President Harry S. Truman lived in Blair House from 1948 to 1952, while the White House was being repaired.

Executive Branch Buildings. The main Executive Office Building stands directly west of the White House. An additional Executive Office Building is located north of the main building. Many of the President's closest advisers work in these buildings. The headquarters of the Department of the Treasury, one of the government's executive departments, lies just east of the White House.

Several huge executive branch buildings stand close together on the south side of Pennsylvania Avenue between the White House and the Capitol. This group of buildings is called the *Federal Triangle* because it forms the shape of a triangle. The Federal Triangle includes the headquarters of the executive departments of Commerce and Justice. It also contains the following federal government agencies: the Federal Trade Commission, Internal Revenue Service, Interstate Commerce Commission, National Archives, and United States Customs Service.

The Department of Labor—an executive department —and the headquarters of the Federal Bureau of Investigation (FBI) lie north of Pennsylvania Avenue between the White House and the Capitol. The FBI headquarters is called the J. Edgar Hoover Building. Two other executive departments—the Department of State and the Department of the Interior—lie several blocks southwest of the White House.

Almost all the executive departments and agencies offer tours of their buildings. Especially popular are the tours of the National Archives and the FBI. The National Archives stores government documents. It displays three of the most important documents for public viewing. These are the original copies of the United States Constitution, the Bill of Rights, and the Declaration of Independence. At the FBI, bureau agents conduct tours that feature highlights of the agency's history and show how the FBI works today. The tours end with a demonstration of agents taking target practice.

Ford's Theatre, the playhouse where Abraham Lincoln was shot, stands about $1\frac{1}{2}$ blocks north of Pennsylvania Avenue, between the White House and Capitol. The theater houses a collection of items related to Lincoln's life and death. *Petersen House*, the house where Lincoln died, is across the street from the theater.

South of the Mall

Originally, almost all the executive branch buildings were located near the White House. But the executive branch has grown tremendously and has spread out to

Robert H. Glaze, Artstreet

The White House has served as the home and office of every United States President with the exception of George Washington. The picture at the left shows the south side of the White House.

Washington, D.C.

This map illustrates west-central Washington, the site of most of the city's main points of interest. Dozens of important buildings and monuments are shown in blue on the map and keyed with a number to the map index, *below*.

1. Blair House   C 1
2. Bureau of Engraving and Printing   D 4
3. Bureau of Indian Affairs   D 2
4. Cannon House Office Building   B 8
5. Civil Service Commission   D 1
6. Corcoran Gallery of Art   D 2
7. Department of Agriculture   D 4
8. Department of Commerce   C 3
9. Department of Housing and Urban Development   C 6
10. Department of Justice   C 4
11. Department of Labor   B 6
12. Department of State   D 1
13. Department of the Interior   D 2
14. Department of the Treasury   C 2
15. Department of Transportation   C 7
16. Dirksen Senate Office Building   A 7
17. Executive Office Buildings   C 1
18. Federal Aviation Administration   C 6
    Federal Bureau of Investigation (see number 32)
19. Federal Reserve System   D 1
20. Federal Trade Commission   B 5
21. Fine Arts and Portrait Galleries Building   B 4
22. Folger Shakespeare Library   A 8
23. Ford's Theatre   B 4
24. Forrestal Building (Department of Energy)   C 5
25. Freer Gallery of Art   C 5
26. General Services Administration   D 1
27. Government Printing Office   A 5

28. Hirshhorn Museum and Sculpture Garden   C 5
    House Office Buildings (see 4, 38, and 49)
29. Hubert H. Humphrey Building (Department of Health, Education, and Welfare)   C 7
30. Internal Revenue Service   C 4
31. Interstate Commerce Commission   C 4
32. J. Edgar Hoover Building (Federal Bureau of Investigation)   C 4
33. Jefferson Memorial   E 5
34. Library of Congress   B 8
35. Library of Congress Thomas Jefferson Building   B 8
36. Library of Congress James Madison Memorial Building   B 8
37. Lincoln Memorial   E 1
38. Longworth House Office Building   B 8
39. Martin Luther King Memorial Library   B 3
40. Museum of African Art   A 8
41. National Aeronautics and Space Administration   C 6
42. National Air and Space Museum   C 6
43. National Archives   C 5
    National Collection of Fine Arts (housed in number 21)
44. National Gallery of Art   B 6
45. National Museum of History and Technology   C 4
46. National Museum of Natural History   C 4
    National Portrait Gallery (housed in number 21)
47. National Visitor Center   A 6
48. Old Post Office Building   C 4

49. Rayburn House Office Building   B 7
50. Renwick Gallery   C 1
51. Russell Senate Office Building   A 7
    Senate Office Buildings (see 16 and 51)
52. Smithsonian Arts and Industries Building   C 5
53. Smithsonian Institution Building (administrative offices)   C 5
    Smithsonian Museums (see 21, 25, 28, 42, 44, 45, 46, 50, and 52)
54. Supreme Court Building   A 8
55. Union Station   A 6
56. United States Botanic Garden   B 7
57. United States Capitol   B 7
58. United States Customs Service   C 4
59. United States Postal Service   D 6
60. Washington Monument   D 3
61. White House   C 2

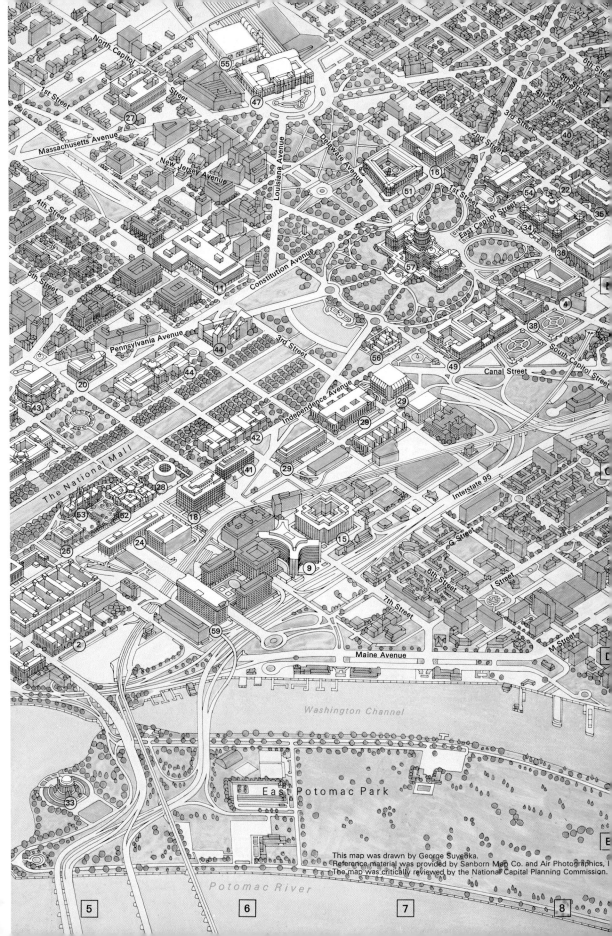

The National Mall

North Capitol

1st Street

Massachusetts Avenue

New Jersey Avenue

4th Street

5th Street

Pennsylvania Avenue

3rd Street

Independence Avenue

Constitution Avenue

Louisiana Avenue

Delaware Avenue

1st Street

2nd Street

3rd Street

East Capitol Street

6th Street

5th Street

3rd Street

South Capitol Street

Canal Street

Interstate 95

G Street

6th Street

I Street

M Street

7th Street

Maine Avenue

Washington Channel

East Potomac Park

Potomac River

This map was drawn by George Suyeoka.
Reference material was provided by Sanborn Map Co. and Air Photographics, l
The map was critically reviewed by the National Capital Planning Commission.

5   6   7   8

55   47   27   16   51   54   22   35 k   40   34   36   4   38   57   44   56   49   20   43   44   42   41   29   29   29   15   28   53   52   18   24   9   25   59   2   33

Jack Rottier, National Parks Service

Ford's Theatre was the scene of the assassination of Abraham Lincoln. The President was sitting in a box seat behind the flags when he was shot. The box overlooks the stage.

other parts of Washington. Several government buildings now stand south of the Mall. They include the buildings of the three newest executive departments—Health, Education, and Welfare; Housing and Urban Development; and Transportation. The Department of Agriculture, another executive department, also lies south of the Mall. In addition, the United States Postal Service, a government agency, is there.

The Bureau of Engraving and Printing ranks as the major tourist attraction south of the Mall. There, government workers engrave and print the country's paper money. Large crowds of visitors flock to the bureau to see these fascinating processes.

Other Points of Interest

The Washington area has dozens of interesting sights in addition to those already described and shown on the two-page map. Some of the most famous ones appear below. Others are included under *The City* section later in this article.

John F. Kennedy Center for the Performing Arts borders the Potomac River northwest of the Lincoln Memorial. Dramatic groups, ballet and opera companies, and orchestras from all parts of the world perform in the modern building. The Kennedy Center also serves as the permanent residence of the American Film Institute and the National Symphony Orchestra. Performances at the center attract large crowds. Thousands of people also visit the center to honor the memory of President Kennedy, to whom it is dedicated.

Watergate is a group of luxurious, modern apartment and office buildings just north of the Kennedy Center. The Watergate Complex became internationally famous in 1972 when campaign workers for President Richard M. Nixon, a Republican, were caught breaking into Democratic political headquarters there. The

Milt and Joan Mann

The Bureau of Engraving and Printing makes the nation's paper money. The employee shown above is inspecting large sheets of newly printed $1 bills.

Dennis Brack, Black Star

John F. Kennedy Center for the Performing Arts features concerts, *above*, as well as ballets, films, operas, and plays. Its activities help make Washington a leading cultural center.

break-in marked the start of a major American political scandal, which led to Nixon's resignation.

National Zoological Park is a zoo about 2 miles (3 kilometers) north of the White House. The zoo contains about 3,000 animals. The animals include two pandas that the Chinese government gave to the United States in 1972.

Pentagon Building, the headquarters of the Department of Defense, ranks as the world's largest office building. It covers 29 acres (11.7 hectares) in Arlington, Va., across the Potomac from Washington.

Arlington National Cemetery, northwest of the Pentagon in Arlington, contains the graves of thousands of persons who served in the United States armed forces. It includes the Tomb of the Unknowns, where three unidentified servicemen who died in action are buried. It also includes the gravesite of President John F. Kennedy.

Marine Corps War Memorial, north of Arlington Cemetery, ranks among Washington's most famous monuments. Often called the *Iwo Jima Statue*, this dramatic bronze sculpture shows five marines and a Navy medical corpsman raising the American flag on the island of Iwo Jima during World War II.

Mount Vernon was the private estate of George Washington. It is located in Fairfax County, Virginia, about 15 miles (24 kilometers) south of the city. The first President's home, many of his belongings, and his grave are there.

Other Museums. Washington has many outstanding museums in addition to the Smithsonian museums and the Museum of African Art. Two of the most famous ones are the Corcoran Gallery of Art and the Phillips Collection. The Corcoran Gallery, about 2 blocks southwest of the White House, displays masterpieces by American painters. The Phillips Collection, at 21st and Q streets about 10 blocks northwest of the White House, houses works by artists from El Greco to the present.

Architectural Styles. Many visitors to Washington enjoy the rich and varied architecture of the city's buildings and monuments. Several structures, including the Capitol, Supreme Court Building, and Lincoln Memorial are built in the classical architectural style of ancient Greece and Rome. Washington Cathedral, an Episcopal church at Massachusetts and Wisconsin avenues in northwestern Washington, features the Gothic style of medieval Europe. The National Shrine of the Immaculate Conception, near 4th Street and Michigan Avenue in northeastern Washington, has elements of two other medieval styles—Byzantine and Romanesque. The *mosque* (Moslem house of worship) of the Islamic Center is a fine example of the Islamic style of architecture. It stands along Massachusetts Avenue near Belmont Road in the northwestern part of the city.

Many buildings in Georgetown, a neighborhood northwest of the White House, provide examples of colonial American architecture. Some of the city's newest office and apartment buildings reflect modern American architecture. But a law limits the height of buildings in the city. As a result, Washington—unlike most other large cities—has no skyscrapers.

Paul S. Conklin

Arlington National Cemetery, in Arlington, Va., includes the gravesite of President John F. Kennedy, *foreground.* Thousands of men and women who served in the armed forces are buried there.

James H. Pickerell

The Marine Corps War Memorial shows servicemen raising the American flag on Iwo Jima during World War II. It stands in Arlington, Va., across the Potomac River from Washington.

Washington, D.C., lies along the east bank of the Potomac River. The city covers 68 square miles (176 square kilometers) and has a population of 711,518. The state of Maryland borders Washington on the north, east, and south. Virginia lies across the Potomac River to the west and south.

Suburban communities of Maryland and Virginia surround Washington. The city and its suburbs form a metropolitan area that covers 2,907 square miles (7,529 square kilometers) and has a population of 2,925,521.

The United States Capitol stands near the center of Washington. Broad streets extend out from the Capitol in all directions like the spokes of a wheel. They include North Capitol Street, which runs north from the Capitol; East Capitol Street, which runs east; and South Capitol Street, which runs south. These three streets, together with the Mall that extends westward from the Capitol, divide Washington into four sections. The sections are *Northwest*, *Northeast*, *Southeast*, and *Southwest*. Each of the sections is named for its direction from the Capitol.

Each address in Washington is followed by one of four abbreviations that tells what section of the city the address is in. The abbreviations and their meanings

Paul S. Conklin

Apartment Buildings line the streets of many Washington neighborhoods. Large numbers of Washington's black residents live in neighborhoods similar to the one above.

are: *NW* (Northwest), *NE* (Northeast), *SE* (Southeast), and *SW* (Southwest).

Northwest Section includes the part of Washington between North Capitol Street and the south end of the Mall. Washington's largest section, it covers almost half the city's area and has almost half of its people. The Northwest section is also Washington's main center of cultural, economic, and government activity.

The southern part of Northwest Washington includes the White House and the many government buildings near it, the Smithsonian museums, and the Washington Monument and Lincoln Memorial. For detailed information on this part of the city, see the *Visitor's Guide* section in this article.

Washington's main shopping district lies in the Northwest section, just to the north of Pennsylvania Avenue between the White House and the Capitol. In this district, department stores and small specialty shops serve the shopping needs of residents and tourists alike.

West of the shopping district, Rock Creek Park winds through Northwest Washington in a north-south direction. The official residence of the Vice-President of the United States is located on the grounds of the Naval Observatory near the park. Dozens of embassies of countries that have diplomatic relations with the United States are also near the park.

Large residential areas lie west and east of the park. Georgetown, an area to the west, ranks among the nation's wealthiest places. It is famous for its beautiful old houses—some dating from the 1700's—and for its small shops that sell antiques and other luxury items. Other residential areas in the Northwest section of the city include high-income, middle-income, and low-income neighborhoods.

Four of the city's largest universities have their campuses in Northwest Washington. These schools are American, George Washington, Georgetown, and Howard universities.

Milt & Joan Mann

Georgetown, a wealthy neighborhood in Northwest Washington, has fine examples of early American architecture. Many of its buildings are 100 to 200 years old, but in excellent condition.

Northeast Section lies between North Capitol and East Capitol streets. It covers about a fourth of the city and has about a fourth of its people. Northeast is chiefly a residential area, and has both middle-class and low-income neighborhoods.

The Museum of African Art and other institutions dedicated to promoting black culture stand near the Capitol in the Northeast section. The campus of Catholic University of America—the national university of the Roman Catholic Church—lies about 3 miles (5 kilometers) north of the Capitol in the section.

The Anacostia River cuts through Northeast Washington east of the Capitol. The National Arboretum and the Kenilworth Aquatic Gardens lie along the river. The arboretum contains trees and shrubs from many parts of the world. The Kenilworth Gardens includes numerous ponds filled with colorful water plants.

Southeast Section is the area between East Capitol and South Capitol streets. It covers about a fourth of the city and has about a fourth of its people. A wealthy residential neighborhood of luxury apartments and restored old houses lies close to the Capitol in the Southeast section. It also extends into the Northeast. Nearby is an old-fashioned market called the *Eastern Market*. Farmers from the area around Washington come to the market to sell such products as fresh fruits and vegetables, cider, eggs, and flowers. Merchants offer bakery products, meat cut to order, and other goods.

The Anacostia River winds through the section farther south. The area south of the river, called *Anacostia*, includes many crowded and run-down sections.

Southwest Section extends from South Capitol Street to the south end of the Mall. Washington's smallest section, it covers about an eighth of the city's land and has only about 4 per cent of its people. Almost all of Southwest Washington has been rebuilt since the 1950's as part of a major urban renewal program. As a result, the section has many relatively new houses and apartment

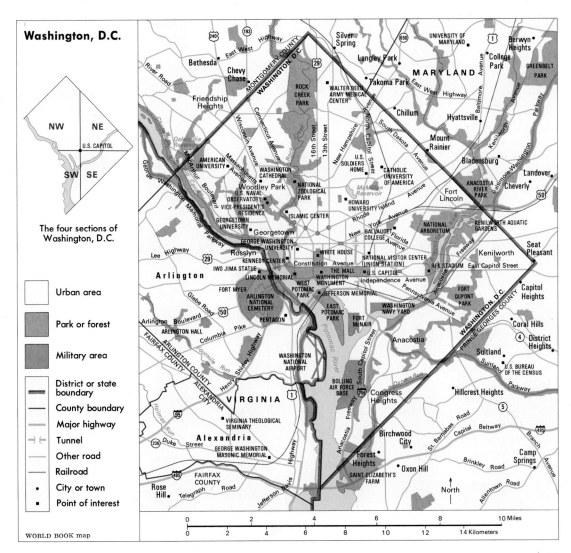

Washington, D.C.

The four sections of Washington, D.C.

Urban area

Park or forest

Military area

District or state boundary

County boundary

Major highway

Tunnel

Other road

Railroad

• City or town

■ Point of interest

WORLD BOOK map

and office buildings. The government's three newest executive departments—Health, Education, and Welfare; Housing and Urban Development; and Transportation—are there.

Metropolitan Area. The Washington metropolitan area, as defined by the federal government, includes the city; Charles, Montgomery, and Prince Georges counties in Maryland; Arlington, Fairfax, Loudoun, and Prince William counties in Virginia; and three Virginia cities that are not part of a county—Alexandria, Fairfax, and Falls Church.

The counties of Washington's metropolitan area include both suburban cities and towns and large open areas of hills, woods, and farms. Most of the suburban cities and towns are under the jurisdiction of the counties in which they are located.

In the Washington area, as in other metropolitan areas, thousands of persons who live in the suburbs work in the city. But during the 1900's, many government agencies have moved from the city to the suburbs. Also, many private businesses have been established in the suburbs. As a result, large numbers of people—from both the city and the suburbs—work in the suburbs. For example, more than 25,000 persons work for the Department of Defense in the Pentagon in Arlington, Va. Other large government agencies in the suburbs include the National Institutes of Health and the Naval Hospital in Bethesda, Md.; the Central Intelligence Agency in McLean, Va.; and the Bureau of the Census in Suitland, Md.

James H. Pickerell

Single-Family Houses line a curving street in the Washington suburb of Bethesda, Md. Thousands of people in the Washington area live in suburbs and commute to jobs in the city.

The Washington metropolitan area includes two of the most famous *new towns* in the United States—Columbia, Md., and Reston, Va. Begun during the early 1960's, these two communities were carefully planned before they were built (see CITY PLANNING [Building New Communities]).

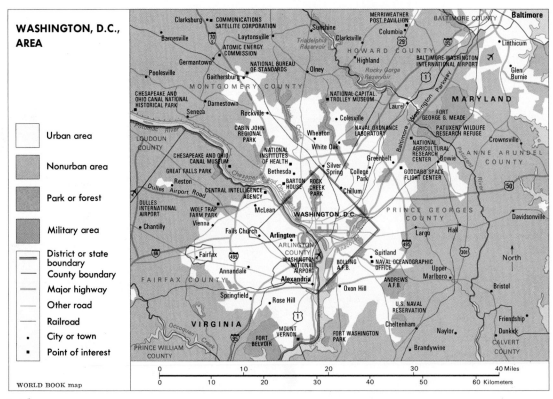

WASHINGTON, D.C., AREA

☐	Urban area
☐	Nonurban area
☐	Park or forest
☐	Military area
—	District or state boundary
—	County boundary
—	Major highway
—	Other road
—	Railroad
•	City or town
▪	Point of interest

WORLD BOOK map

About 71 per cent of Washington's people are blacks. No other major American city has so large a percentage of black persons. Whites make up about 28 per cent of the city's population. The other 1 per cent includes small groups of American Indians and Asians—especially Chinese, Filipinos, and Japanese.

The racial makeup of Washington's suburbs contrasts sharply with that of the city. In the suburbs, about 91 per cent of the people are whites, and only about 8 per cent are blacks. American Indians, Asians, and members of other races account for the other 1 per cent of the suburban population.

About 20,000 persons who live in Washington are citizens of countries other than the United States. Many of these people work for foreign embassies or such international organizations in the city as the Organization of American States and the World Bank. The foreign population includes people from almost every country in the world, and gives the city a *cosmopolitan* (international) flavor.

Ethnic Groups. Washington differs from most big cities in that it has only one large ethnic group—blacks. More than 535,000 black persons live in the city. Blacks make up a majority of the population in each of Washington's four sections. They account for about 91 per cent of the population in Northeast Washington, 87

Robert H. Glaze, Artstreet

Black Washingtonians visit an art exhibit at Howard University, *above.* Washington has a higher percentage of black persons than any other major American city, more than 70 per cent.

per cent in Southeast, 57 per cent in Southwest, and 53 per cent in Northwest.

Thousands of Washington's blacks live in neighborhoods made up almost entirely of people of their own race. The neighborhoods range from poor, to middle-income, to upper-income ones. Many black Washingtonians also live in middle- and upper-income racially integrated areas, both in the city and the suburbs.

About 210,000 white persons live in Washington. In many cities, large numbers of whites of the same ethnic group—such as persons of Irish, Italian, or Polish ancestry—live together in the same neighborhoods. But Washington does not have such ethnic neighborhoods. Its predominantly white neighborhoods are made up of people of many ethnic backgrounds.

Housing. About half of Washington's people live in one- or two-family houses, and about half live in apartment buildings. Only about 28 per cent of Washington's families own their homes. The others rent them. The national average for the percentage of families in cities who own their homes is about 48 per cent.

Washington has some of the nation's most luxurious housing, including the Watergate apartments and the mansions and town houses of Georgetown. It also has much good middle-class housing. However, the city faces a shortage of good housing for low-income, as well as middle-income, families. This housing shortage exists in both the city and the suburbs, and ranks among the Washington area's biggest problems.

Several factors make the housing problem difficult to solve. Each year, some housing units become so run-down that people abandon them, thus reducing the number of usable low-income units. Also, such developments as urban renewal projects sometimes involve replacing housing units with higher income units, or with business or government buildings. In addition, since the 1960's, the cost of housing has risen faster in Washington than in most parts of the country. Rising costs fur-

Paul S. Conklin

Embassy Officials from many nations mix at a party at the Argentine Embassy, *above.* Washington's many embassies give the city a *cosmopolitan* (international) flavor.

ther reduce the amount of housing available to people with low and middle incomes.

Education. The Washington public school system includes about 175 schools with more than 130,000 students. An additional 25,000 students attend about 80 private schools in the city.

The District of Columbia Board of Education governs the public school system. The board consists of 11 members elected by the people to four-year terms. The members appoint a superintendent to administer the system. About 75 per cent of the money needed to run Washington's public schools comes from local taxes, and about 25 per cent from the federal government.

Washington has 13 accredited universities and colleges. The University of the District of Columbia, established in 1975, has three campuses in the city. Howard University is one of the country's largest predominantly black universities. Catholic University of America is the national university of the Roman Catholic Church in the United States.

Social Problems. Washington, like other cities, faces a variety of social problems. Among them are poverty and crime.

Overall, the people of Washington have a high standard of living. But thousands of people in both the city and suburbs do not share in the wealth. About 13 per cent of all the families in the city and about 4 per cent of the families in the suburbs have incomes that classify them as poor by federal government standards. In Washington as elsewhere, poverty affects blacks more than whites. About 15 per cent of all the black families in the metropolitan area are poor, compared to about 4 per cent of all the white families.

Paul S. Conklin

A Soccer Game on the Mall provides recreation for a group of Washington young people, *above*. The Washington Monument rises above the trees in the background.

UNIVERSITIES AND COLLEGES

Washington, D.C., has 13 universities and colleges accredited by the Middle States Association of Colleges and Schools. For enrollments and further information, see UNIVERSITIES AND COLLEGES (table).

Name	Founded
American University	1893
Catholic University of America	1887
District of Columbia, University of the	1975
Dominican House of Studies	1905
Gallaudet College	1864
George Washington University	1821
Georgetown University	1789
Howard University	1867
Mount Vernon College	1968
Oblate College	1958
Southeastern University	1879
Trinity College	1897
Wesley Theological Seminary	1882

Most crime in the Washington area takes place in the city, especially in poor neighborhoods. But in recent years, crime rates have been rising more rapidly in the suburbs than in the city.

Washington's crime problem receives more nationwide publicity than that of any other city with the possible exception of New York City. Whenever a government official is the victim of a crime, the news is carried throughout the country by the news media. As a result of such publicity, many persons believe Washington has the highest, or one of the highest, crime rates in the nation. This is not so, however. More than 60 metropolitan areas have a higher crime rate. Over a dozen metropolitan areas lead Washington in the rate of violent crimes, such as assault and murder.

Cultural Life and Recreation. The museums, government buildings, monuments, libraries, parks, and theaters described under *A Visitor's Guide* help make Washington a leading cultural and recreational center. Residents as well as tourists enjoy these facilities.

Washington also has many cultural and recreational facilities used chiefly by its residents. These include a public library system with about 2 million volumes. The system includes a main library and about 20 branch libraries. The main library is the Martin Luther King Memorial Library at 9th and G streets NW. Washington has many neighborhood museums, including some that specialize in exhibits of black culture. The city's main playhouses—in addition to the Kennedy Center—include the National Theatre at 13th and E streets NW, and the Arena Stage at 6th and M streets SW.

Washington has about 150 parks. The people use the parks for such purposes as picnics, and baseball, touch football, and soccer games. Many Washingtonians enjoy sailing on the Potomac River. Many also enjoy spectator sports. Three professional sports teams perform in the Washington area. The Washington Redskins of the National Football League play in the Robert F. Kennedy, or RFK, Stadium, about 2 miles (3 kilometers) east of the Capitol. The Washington Bullets of the National Basketball Association and the Washington Capitals of the National Hockey League play in the Capital Centre, in Largo, Md.

Washington's economy is based on the activities of the federal government. The government employs more of the Washington area's workers than does any kind of private business. It also generates much of Washington's private economic activity.

The Federal Government provides jobs for about 340,000 persons in Washington and its suburbs, or about a fourth of all the area's workers. The best-known and most important government employees include the President and the President's close advisers, the members of Congress, and the Supreme Court justices. But these key policy-making officials account for only a small portion of Washington's government workers. Hundreds of lower-ranking officials help carry out the day-to-day operations of the government. Thousands of office workers—including accountants, clerks, secretaries, and typists—assist them.

Private Business. The government's attractions make Washington one of the world's leading centers of tourism. Every year, about 20 million tourists visit the city to see the government in action and to enjoy its many interesting and historic sights. The money the tourists spend accounts for Washington's largest source of income other than the government's payroll. It helps support—and provides jobs in—many hotels, motels, restaurants, and other businesses.

Many other economically important businesses and private organizations are located in Washington chiefly because the government is there. They include law offices and research companies that do work for the government. They also include dozens of labor unions and professional organizations that have their headquarters in the city so they can try to influence government policies in the best interests of their members. Such businesses and organizations, as well as the city's tourist-oriented businesses, are called *service industries* because they provide service rather than produce goods. Service industries employ about 25 per cent of the Washington area's workers. The construction industry and wholesale and retail trade also provide many jobs.

Manufacturing—or the production of goods—is far less important in Washington than it is in most large cities. Only about 4 per cent of the area's labor force works in manufacturing industries. Printing and publishing firms employ most of them.

Transportation. Automobiles provide the main means of transportation within Washington and between the city and its suburbs. About 80 per cent of the people who work in the Washington area use cars to get to and from their jobs. The government has built several superhighways to handle the heavy automobile traffic. Even so, huge traffic jams often occur during morning and evening rush hours.

The Washington Metropolitan Transit Authority, a public corporation, provides public transportation in Washington. Called *Metro*, it operates a bus service throughout the city and its suburbs. In 1969, Congress passed legislation providing for a subway system to be operated by Metro. Scheduled for completion by 1984, the subway will extend throughout the city and well into the suburbs.

Three major airports handle Washington's commer-

James H. Pickerell

Government Workers jam Pennsylvania Avenue, *above*, on their way to and from work. The federal government employs about a fourth of all the workers in the Washington area.

cial air traffic. Washington National Airport lies just across the Potomac River in Virginia. Dulles International Airport, also in Virginia, lies about 25 miles (40 kilometers) west of the city. Baltimore-Washington International Airport (formerly Friendship International) is in Maryland, about 30 miles (48 kilometers) northeast of Washington.

The National Visitor Center (formerly Union Station) lies north of the Capitol. Workers at the center advise visitors on what to see in Washington and how to find their way around the city. Adjoining the center is the new Union Station. The station serves passenger trains that run between Washington and other parts of the country. It includes a bus terminal.

Communication. Washington ranks as a leading communication center. Many of the world's major newspapers, magazines, and radio and television networks have permanent correspondents in the city. These reporters provide their readers, listeners, and viewers with firsthand news on government activities.

The government makes Washington one of the nation's chief publishing centers. Its departments and agencies produce pamphlets and books on thousands of subjects. The subjects range from census information to how to solve farm problems and where to go for medical help.

Two national magazines are published in Washington. They are *National Geographic Magazine* and *U.S. News & World Report*.

Washington has two general daily newspapers, the morning *Washington Post* and the afternoon *Washington Star*. Eight television stations and about 20 radio stations serve the Washington area.

WASHINGTON, D.C./*Local Government*

Washington has an unusual local government. As in many cities, the people elect a mayor and a city council to make laws and carry out government functions. But the federal government has final authority in all matters relating to Washington's government.

The mayor serves a four-year term and is responsible for the administration of the government. The mayor appoints the heads of the city's local government departments, such as the police and sanitation departments. The mayor also prepares the city's budget and proposes local laws.

Washington's city council has 13 members. Five of the council's members—including its chairman—are elected in citywide elections. In addition, one council member is elected from each of Washington's eight election districts. All members serve four-year terms.

The city council passes local laws. But Congress also has the power to make laws for the city, including ones that overrule council decisions. The council approves the mayor's budget. But Congress and the Office of Management and Budget section of the Executive Office of the President must approve the budget.

The mayor can *veto* (reject) legislation passed by the city council. The council can *override* (set aside) a veto with a two-thirds majority vote of those voting on the question.

Washington's Flag was adopted in 1938. Its colors and design are based on George Washington's coat of arms.

The City Seal, adopted in 1871, shows Justice placing a wreath on a statue of George Washington.

Washington's city government has an annual budget of more than $1 billion. The city gets about two-thirds of its income from taxes, including property, sales, and local income taxes. The federal government provides most of the rest of the income.

Washington's present system of local government was established by an act of Congress in 1973 and approved by the people in 1974. For 100 years before that time, the people of Washington had almost no voice in their government. The President, rather than the people, chose the city's mayor and council members. See the *History* section of this article for details.

WASHINGTON, D.C./*History*

The first people known to have lived in the Washington area were Piscataway Indians. Whites moved into the area during the late 1600's and established farms and plantations there. In 1749, settlers founded Alexandria, the area's first town, in what was then the colony of Virginia.

Washington Becomes the Capital. Several different cities served as the national capital during the early years of the United States (see UNITED STATES CAPITALS). In 1783, Congress decided that the country should have a permanent center of government. But the states could not agree on a location for it. People assumed that the new capital would become an important commercial and industrial city. As a result, each state wanted it to be located within its borders. Also, both Northerners and Southerners believed the capital should be in their part of the country.

In 1790, Secretary of the Treasury Alexander Hamilton worked out a solution. He proposed that the capital be built on land that belonged to the federal government, rather than to a state. He and others persuaded Northern political leaders to agree to locate the capital in the South. In return, Southern leaders supported certain government policies favored by the North.

Once the disagreements were settled, Congress decided to locate the capital along the Potomac River. It asked President George Washington, who had been raised in the Potomac area, to choose the exact site.

The President's choice, made in 1791, included not only the land now occupied by Washington, but also about 30 square miles (78 square kilometers) of land west of the Potomac. The city's present territory had

belonged to Maryland, and the land west of the river was part of Virginia. The two states turned over the territory to the federal government.

Early Days. George Washington hired Pierre Charles L'Enfant, a French engineer, to create a plan for the physical layout of the city. L'Enfant's plan dealt only

Detail from an engraving by Andrew Ellicott (1792); Library of Congress, Geography and Map Division

Pierre L'Enfant's Plan for the city of Washington showed the location of the Capitol, White House, and Mall. President George Washington hired L'Enfant, a French engineer, to plan the city.

Pennsylvania Avenue in 1827 was a quiet dirt road. The Capitol, *background,* had a different dome and was smaller than it is today. The present Capitol design dates from the 1850's.

View of the Capitol at Washington, D.C., a hand-tinted engraving by C. J. Bentley after a painting by W. H. Bartlett; from *American Scenery,* published in 1840 by George Virtue

with the area between the Anacostia River and Georgetown. But it established the pattern for the entire city. It made the Capitol the center of Washington. The American surveyors Andrew Ellicott and Benjamin Banneker helped work out the plan for the new city.

The federal government moved to Washington from its temporary capital in Philadelphia in 1800. At that time, the entire Washington area had only about 8,000 people. In 1814, during the War of 1812, British soldiers captured Washington. They burned the Capitol, the White House, and other government buildings. Reconstruction of the buildings was completed in 1819.

The Constitution of the United States gave Congress the power to govern Washington. But in 1802, Congress established a local government, including a mayor and a city council, to help run the city. The people of Washington were given the right to elect council members in 1802 and the mayor in 1820, but they were not allowed to vote for members of Congress or the President.

The predictions that Washington would become an important commercial and industrial center did not come true. The city could not compete economically with such long-established cities as Boston, New York, Philadelphia, Baltimore, and Charleston. Lacking economic growth, Washington remained a small city. By the 1840's, it had only about 50,000 people, and only a small part of its present area was built up. As a result, in 1846, Congress returned to Virginia the land that the state had earlier given to the federal government.

Growth and Development. Washington's main periods of growth have been times of crisis, such as wars and depressions. During such times, the role of the federal government has been greatly expanded to help meet the crises. Large numbers of people moved to the city to handle the new jobs that resulted.

The Civil War (1861-1865) was the first crisis that caused Washington to grow. During the war, the city's population soared from about 60,000 to 120,000. The Union stationed thousands of troops in Washington to protect the city from Confederate attacks. Large num-

bers of people flocked to the city to help direct the Union's war effort. In addition, thousands of black slaves who had been freed during the war moved to the city. The enormous population growth led to a severe housing shortage in Washington. In addition, the city's streets, sewer and water systems, and other public facilities could not handle the increased population.

Congress began a major rebuilding and expansion program in Washington after the war. The program solved the city's physical problems. But it indirectly led to an end of the people's right to choose their government leaders. Congress believed that a reorganization of Washington's local government was necessary for a successful rebuilding program. At first, in 1871, it established a territorial government that included a governor appointed by the President, and an elected assembly. Then, in 1874, Congress established a local government made up of three commissioners appointed by the President. Washington became the only American city in which the people did not elect its local officials.

Washington grew gradually for many years after the Civil War. But in 1917, when the United States entered World War I, another period of enormous growth began. Again, the government needed new workers to help direct a war effort. The city's population increased from about 350,000 when the United States entered the war to more than 450,000 in 1918, when the war ended. Shortages developed in housing, office space, schools, and public facilities. The automobile had replaced the horse as the main means of transportation in the city. To accommodate the cars, the Mall was turned into a parking lot. Many new houses, office buildings, and schools went up during the 1920's.

During the Great Depression of the 1930's, jobs became scarce in all parts of the United States except Washington. The federal government became deeply involved in projects designed to end the depression, and thousands of new government jobs became available in the capital. The city's population grew from about 485,000 to 665,000 between 1930 and 1940.

701

Paul S. Conklin

The Watergate Complex, *above,* is a group of modern apartment and office buildings. Built in the 1960's, it is an example of the widespread redevelopment in Washington in recent years.

Recent Developments. Several factors have caused the federal government to grow since the depression. They include the country's participation in World War II from 1941 to 1945, and its struggle against Communism after the war. The government also has taken on many responsibilities in the field of social welfare.

The government's growth has brought about steady growth of the Washington area. The city's population reached a peak of more than 800,000 by 1950. Since then, it has decreased by about 100,000, but the population of the suburbs has soared. Between 1950 and 1970, Washington's metropolitan area population grew faster than that of any other large city. It increased from about 1½ million to almost 3 million.

Almost all the people who moved into the suburbs were whites. Blacks made up a majority of the city's population for the first time in the 1950's. The percentage of blacks in Washington has increased ever since. Blacks began moving into the suburbs in large numbers for the first time in the late 1960's.

In the mid-1900's, many Washingtonians began demanding the right to participate in government. In response, Congress and the states passed a constitutional amendment that allowed the people to vote in presidential elections for the first time in 1964. In 1973, Congress gave the people the right to elect local government officials for the first time in 100 years. Walter E. Washington, appointed as the city's chief administrative officer in 1967, won election as mayor in 1974.

In 1978, Congress approved a constitutional amendment that would allow Washington residents to elect voting delegates to the U.S. House of Representatives and Senate. The amendment must be ratified by 38 states before it becomes part of the Constitution.

EUNICE S. GRIER and ATLEE E. SHIDLER

WASHINGTON, D.C./Study Aids

Related Articles in WORLD BOOK include:

Outline

I. A Visitor's Guide
  A. Capitol Hill
  B. The National Mall
  C. North of the Mall
  D. South of the Mall
  E. Other Points of Interest

II. The City
  A. Northwest Section
  B. Northeast Section
  C. Southeast Section
  D. Southwest Section
  E. Metropolitan Area

III. People
  A. Ethnic Groups
  B. Housing
  C. Education
  D. Social Problems
  E. Cultural Life and
    Recreation

IV. Economy
  A. The Federal Government
  B. Private Business
  C. Transportation
  D. Communication

V. Local Government
VI. History

Questions

How does the federal government influence Washington's economy?

Who planned the physical layout of Washington?

What are some of Washington's tourist attractions?

What are the four sections of Washington? For what are they named?

Why is Washington's local government unusual?

What have been the chief causes of the city's growth?

Why does Washington have no skyscrapers?

What are Washington's chief social problems?

What are some reasons why Washington faces a shortage of low-income housing?

Why did Congress have a difficult time deciding where to locate the capital?

WASHINGTON, BOOKER T. (1856-1915), was the most influential black leader and educator of his time in the United States. He became prominent largely because of his role as founder and head of Tuskegee Institute, a vocational school for blacks in Tuskegee, Ala.

Washington advised two Presidents—Theodore Roosevelt and William Howard Taft—on racial problems and policies. He also influenced the appointment of several blacks to federal office, especially during Roosevelt's Administration. Washington described his rise from slavery to national prominence as an educator in his best-selling autobiography, *Up from Slavery* (1901).

Early Life. Booker Taliaferro Washington was born a slave in Hales Ford, Va., near Roanoke. After the U.S. government freed all slaves in 1865, Washington's family moved to Malden, W. Va. There, Washington worked in coal mines and salt furnaces. From 1872 to 1875, he attended the Hampton Institute, an industrial school for blacks in Hampton, Va. He became a teacher at the institute in 1879. Washington based many of his later educational theories on his training at Hampton.

Educator. In 1881, Washington founded and became principal of Tuskegee Normal and Industrial Institute. He started this school, whose name was later changed to Tuskegee Institute, in an old abandoned church and a shanty. The school taught specific trades, such as carpentry, farming, and mechanics, and it also trained teachers. As the school expanded, Washington spent much of his time raising funds for it. Under Washington's leadership, Tuskegee Institute became famous as a model of industrial education. The Tuskegee Institute National Historic Site, established in 1974, includes Washington's home, student-made college buildings, and the George Washington Carver Museum.

Washington believed that blacks could benefit more from a practical, vocational education rather than a college education. Most blacks lived in poverty in the rural South, and Washington felt they should learn skills, work hard, and acquire property. He believed that the development of work skills would lead to economic prosperity. Washington predicted that blacks would be granted civil and political rights after gaining a strong economic foundation. He explained his educational and social theories in *Up from Slavery* and in other publications.

Racial Leader. In the late 1800's, increasing numbers of blacks became victims of lynchings and *Jim Crow* laws that segregated blacks (see JIM CROW). To reduce racial conflicts, Washington advised blacks to stop demanding equal rights and to simply get along with whites. He also urged whites to give blacks better jobs.

In a speech given in Atlanta, Ga., in 1895, Washington declared: "In all things that are purely social we can be as separate as the fingers, yet one as the hand in all things essential to mutual progress." This speech was often called the *Atlanta Compromise* because Washington accepted inequality and segregation for blacks in exchange for economic advancement. The speech was widely quoted in newspapers and helped make Washington a prominent national figure and black spokesman.

Washington became a shrewd political leader and advised not only Presidents, but also members of Congress and governors, on political appointments for blacks and sympathetic whites. He urged wealthy people to contribute to various black organizations. He also owned or financially supported many black newspapers. In 1900, Washington founded the National Negro Business League to help black business firms.

Throughout his life, Washington tried to please whites in both the North and the South through his public actions and speeches. He never publicly supported black political causes that were unpopular with Southern whites. But he secretly financed lawsuits opposing segregation and upholding the right of blacks to vote and serve on juries.

Opposition to Washington came chiefly from W. E. B. Du Bois, a historian and sociologist. Du Bois criticized Washington's educational and political philosophy and practices. Du Bois supported higher education for talented blacks who could serve as leaders. He feared that the success of Washington's industrial school would limit the development of true higher education for blacks. Du Bois accepted the need for industrial training, but he felt that blacks should also have the opportunity to obtain a college education.

Du Bois attacked Washington's compromising views on political and civil rights. Du Bois felt that blacks must openly strive for their rights. He criticized what he regarded as Washington's surrender of rights and human dignity for economic gain.

In addition, Du Bois attacked some of the ways that Washington used his power. By controlling many black newspapers, for example, Washington made it difficult for differing views to be published. Also, because he was widely acclaimed as the foremost black leader, Washington helped determine what racial policies and practices were "acceptable." Du Bois outlined his criticisms in his book *The Souls of Black Folk* (1903).

Washington remained a powerful leader until his death in 1915. But by 1910, his influence had started to decline as Du Bois and others began new movements. These movements led to the creation of such organizations as the National Association for the Advancement of Colored People (NAACP) and the National Urban League.   RAYMOND W. SMOCK

See also DU BOIS, W. E. B.; BLACK AMERICANS (After Reconstruction); NIAGARA MOVEMENT.

Booker T. Washington National Monument

Booker T. Washington, a black leader and educator, founded Tuskegee Institute and headed the school from 1881 to 1915.

GEORGE WASHINGTON

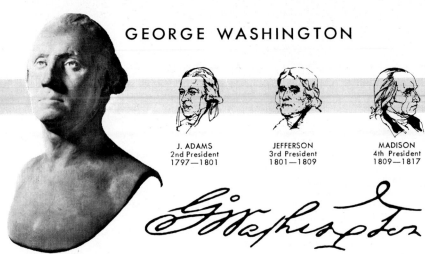

1st PRESIDENT OF THE UNITED STATES 1789-1797

J. ADAMS
2nd President
1797—1801

JEFFERSON
3rd President
1801—1809

MADISON
4th President
1809—1817

Sculpture by Jean Houdon, Library of Congress

WASHINGTON, GEORGE (1732-1799), won a lasting place in American history as the "Father of His Country." For nearly 20 years, he guided his country much as a father cares for a growing child.

In three important ways, Washington helped shape the beginning of the United States. First, he commanded the Continental Army that won American independence from Great Britain in the Revolutionary War. Second, Washington served as president of the convention that wrote the United States Constitution. Third, he was the first man elected President of the United States.

The people of his day loved Washington. His army officers would have made him king if he had let them. From the Revolutionary War on, his birthday was celebrated each year throughout the country.

Washington lived an exciting life in exciting times. As a boy, he explored the wilderness. When he grew older, he helped the British fight the French and Indians. Many times he was nearly killed. As a general, he suffered hardships with his troops in the cold winters at Valley Forge, Pa., and Morristown, N.J. He lost many battles, but led the American army to final victory at Yorktown, Va. After he became President, he successfully solved many problems in turning the plans of the Constitution into a working government.

Washington went to school only until he was about 14 or 15. But he learned to make the most of all his abilities and opportunities. His remarkable patience and his understanding of others helped him win people to his side in times of hardship and discouragement.

There are great differences between the United States of Washington's day and that of today. The new nation was small and weak. It stretched west only to the Mississippi River and had fewer than 4,000,000 people. Most persons made their living by farming. Few children went to school. Few men or women could read or write. Transportation and communication were slow. It took Washington 3 days to travel about 90 miles (140 kilometers) from New York City to Philadelphia, longer than it now takes to fly around the world. There were only 11 states in the Union when Washington became President and 16 when he left office.

Many stories have been told about Washington.

Most are probably not true. So far as we know, he did not chop down his father's cherry tree, then confess by saying: "Father, I cannot tell a lie." He probably never threw a stone across the broad Rappahannock River. But such stories show that people were willing to believe almost anything about his honesty and his great strength. One of Washington's officers, Henry "Light Horse Harry" Lee, summed up the way Americans felt and still feel about Washington:

"First in war, first in peace, and first in the hearts of his countrymen."

Washington the Man

Washington's appearance caused admiration and respect. He was tall, strong, and broad-shouldered. As he grew older, cares lined his face and gave him a somewhat stern look. Perhaps the best description of Washington was written by a friend, George Mercer, in 1760:

"He may be described as being straight as an Indian, measuring 6 feet 2 inches in his stockings, and weighing 175 pounds . . . A large and straight rather than a prominent nose; blue-gray penetrating eyes . . . He has a clear though rather colorless pale skin which burns with the sun . . . dark brown hair which he wears in a queue . . . His mouth is large and generally firmly closed, but which from time to time discloses some defective teeth . . . His movements and gestures are graceful, his walk majestic, and he is a splendid horseman."

Washington set his own strict rules of conduct, but he also enjoyed having a good time. He laughed at jokes, though he seldom told any.

One of the best descriptions of Washington's character was written after his death by his good friend Thomas Jefferson:

"His mind was great and powerful . . . as far as he saw, no judgment was ever sounder. It was slow in operation, being little aided by invention or imagination, but sure in conclusion. . . .

President Washington posed for this portrait by Gilbert Stuart in 1796. It is probably the best known picture of him.

Courtesy Museum of Fine Arts, Boston.
On loan from the Boston Athenaeum.

1732 (Feb. 22) Born in Westmoreland County, Virginia.
1749 Became official surveyor for Culpeper County, Virginia.
1751 Went to Barbados Island, British West Indies.
1753 Carried British ultimatum to French in Ohio River Valley, as a major.
1754 Surrendered Fort Necessity in the French and Indian War, as a colonel.
1755 (July 9) With General Edward Braddock when ambushed by French and Indians.
1755-1758 Commanded Virginia's frontier troops, as a colonel.
1759 (Jan. 6) Married Mrs. Martha Dandridge Custis.
1774 Elected delegate to First Continental Congress.
1775 Elected delegate to Second Continental Congress.
1775 (June 15) Elected Commander in Chief of Continental Army.
1781 (Oct. 19) Victory at Yorktown.
1787 (May 25) Elected President of the Constitutional Convention.
1789 Elected first President of the United States.
1792 Re-elected President of the United States.
1796 (Sept. 19) Published *Farewell Address*, refusing a third term.
1798 (July 4) Commissioned lieutenant general and commander in chief of new United States Army.
1799 (Dec. 14) Died at Mount Vernon at age 67.

Virginia Chamber of Commerce

A Memorial Mansion stands at Washington's birthplace on Pope's Creek in Westmoreland County, Virginia. The original home burned in 1780. This mansion is typical of Washington's time.

"Perhaps the strongest feature in his character was prudence, never acting until every circumstance, every consideration, was maturely weighed; refraining when he saw a doubt, but, when once decided, going through with his purpose whatever obstacles opposed.

"His integrity was most pure, his justice the most inflexible I have ever known . . .

"He was indeed, in every sense of the words, a wise, a good and a great man. . . . On the whole, his character was, in its mass, perfect . . . it may truly be said, that never did nature and fortune combine more perfectly to make a man great . . ."

Early Life (1732-1746)

Family Background. George Washington inherited much more than a good mind and a strong body. Washington belonged to an old colonial family that believed in hard work, in public service, and in worshiping God. The Washington family has been traced back to 1260 in England. The name at that time was de Wessington. It was later spelled Washington. Sulgrave Manor in England is regarded as the home of George Washington's ancestors (see SULGRAVE MANOR).

George's great-grandfather, John Washington (1632-1677), came to live in America by accident. He was mate on a small English ship that went aground in the Potomac River in 1656 or 1657. By the time the ship was repaired, he had decided to marry and settle in Virginia. He started with little money. Within 20 years he owned more than 5,000 acres (2,000 hectares), including the land that later became Mount Vernon. Lawrence Washington (1659-1698), the eldest son of John, was the grandfather of George.

Washington's Parents. George's father, Augustine Washington (1694-1743), was Lawrence's youngest son. After iron ore was discovered on some of his land, he spent most of his time developing an ironworks. He had four children by his first wife, Jane Butler. She died in 1729. In March, 1731, he married Mary Ball (1709?-1789), who became George's mother.

Mary Ball did not have a very happy childhood. Her father and mother both died before she was 13. Although she had a large fortune, she spent all her life worrying about money. After her son George became a man, she wrote him many letters asking for money even though she did not need it.

Augustine and Mary Ball Washington had six children. Besides George, there were: Betty (1733-1797), Samuel (1734-1781), John Augustine (1736-1787), Charles (1738-1799), and Mildred (1739-1740).

Boyhood. George Washington was born on Pope's Creek Farm in Westmoreland County, Virginia, on February 22, 1732 (February 11, on the Old Style Calendar then in use; see CALENDAR). When George was almost 3, his family moved to the large, undeveloped plantation that was later called Mount Vernon. It lay about 50 miles (80 kilometers) up the Potomac River in Virginia and was then called Little Hunting Creek Farm. Here George's only playmates were his younger sister and brothers. No neighbors lived close by. But George had fun exploring the nearby woods and helping out in farm work as well as a small boy could. He saw little of his father, who made many trips to his ironworks, about 30 miles (48 kilometers) away.

In 1738, when George was nearly 7, his father decided to move closer to the ironworks. He bought the 260-acre (105-hectare) Ferry Farm which lay on the Rappahannock River across from Fredericksburg, Va.

Education. George probably began going to school in Fredericksburg soon after the family moved to Ferry Farm. No accurate records have been found that tell who his teachers were. Altogether, he had no more than seven or eight years of school. His favorite subject was arithmetic. He wrote his lessons in ink on heavy paper. His mother then sewed the paper into notebooks.

George studied enough history and geography to know something of the outside world. But he never learned as much about literature, foreign languages, and history as did Thomas Jefferson or James Madison. They had the advantage of much more formal education.

By the time he ended his schoolwork at the age of 14 or 15, George could keep business accounts, write clear

WASHINGTON'S BOYHOOD

Education. Washington had only seven or eight years of formal education. He copied his "Rules of Civility" on sheets of paper that his mother sewed into a notebook. The boy also learned to keep business accounts and to do simple figuring.

Recreation. Washington developed a lifelong love for horses, and often rode on his father's farm. He became an expert dancer and enjoyed the many social activities of a young country gentleman.

Rowing on the Rappahannock River was one of Washington's favorite sports. According to legend, he threw a stone across this broad river. Washington also sailed, fished, and hunted game.

letters, and do simple figuring. During the rest of his life he kept diaries and careful accounts of his expenses.

George's father had probably planned to send him to school in England because there were few schools in Virginia. But Augustine Washington died when George was only 11, and the plans came to nothing. After his father's death, George's mother did not like to have him away from home for long. George was to inherit Ferry Farm when he reached 21. Meanwhile, he, his younger sister and brothers, and the farm were left in the care of his mother.

Plantation Life. Growing up at Ferry Farm, young George helped manage a plantation worked by 20 black slaves. He was observant and hard-working. He learned how to plant and produce tobacco, fruit, grains, and vegetables. He saw how many things a plantation needed to keep operating, such as cloth and iron tools. He also developed his lifelong love for horses.

At the same time, Washington enjoyed the life of a young Virginia country gentleman. He had boyhood romances and wrote love poems. He became an expert dancer. And he enjoyed hunting, fishing, and boating on the river.

Development of Character. As a youth, Washington was sober, quiet, attentive, and dignified. His respect for religion and his dependability made him admired. He experienced the hardships of colonial life on the edge of the wilderness. He learned that life was difficult. This helped make him become strong and patient.

As a schoolboy, Washington copied rules of behavior in an exercise book, perhaps at the suggestion of his mother. Following are some of these rules in his own spelling, capitalization, and punctuation:

> Turn not your Back to others especially in Speaking, Jog not the Table or Desk on which Another reads or writes, lean not upon any one.
> Use no Reproachfull Language against any one neither Curse nor Revile.
> Play not the Peacock, looking every where about you, to See if you be well Deck't, if your Shoes fit well, if your Stockings Sit neatly, and Cloths handsomely.
> While you are talking, Point not with your Finger at him of Whom you Discourse nor Approach too near him to whom you talk especially to his face.
> Be not Curious to Know the Affairs of Others neither approach those that Speak in Private.
> It's unbecoming to Stoop much to ones Meat. Keep your Fingers clean & when foul wipe them on a Corner of your Table Napkin.

George Washington's admiration for his half-brother Lawrence (1718-1752) also influenced his development. Lawrence had been educated in England. He had the polish of a young English gentleman. From 1740 to 1742, Lawrence had gone to Central America as a Virginia militia captain in a brief war between Great Britain and Spain. The militia took no part in the actual fighting. But Lawrence returned to Virginia with many war stories. These tales excited George's imagination. George became a frequent visitor to the fashionable new house that Lawrence had built at Mount Vernon.

Lawrence decided that 14-year-old George should join the British Royal Navy. George wanted to go, but he needed his mother's permission. No matter how much he argued, she would not let him go. She asked

advice of her brother, Joseph Ball. He suggested somewhat jokingly that rather than let George become a sailor, it would be better to apprentice him to a *tinker*, a mender of pots and pans.

Washington the Surveyor (1747-1752)

After teen-aged George Washington gave up hopes of becoming a sailor, he became interested in exploring the frontier. Becoming a surveyor and marking out new farms in the wilderness would give him a chance to leave home to seek adventure. He enjoyed mathematics, and he easily picked up an understanding of fractions and geometry. Then he took his father's old set of surveying instruments out of storage. At 15, he began to earn money as an assistant to local surveyors.

On one of his frequent visits to Mount Vernon, George met Lord Fairfax, the largest property owner in Virginia. Fairfax was a cousin of Lawrence Washington's wife. He owned more than 5 million acres (2 million hectares) of land in northern Virginia. These lands extended to the Allegheny Mountains and included most of the Shenandoah Valley.

First Expedition. Lord Fairfax began planning an expedition to survey his western lands. James Genn, an expert surveyor, was put in charge of the expedition. Sixteen-year-old George Washington was invited to go along. The boy persuaded his mother to let him make his first long trip away from home.

The month-long expedition set out on horseback in March, 1748. Washington learned to sleep in the open and hunt for food. By the time he returned to Mount Vernon, he felt he had grown into a man. He also was now shaving.

Professional Surveyor. In the summer of 1749, Washington helped lay out the newly established town of Alexandria, Va. Later that year he was appointed official surveyor for Culpeper County. In November, Lord Fairfax hired him to make a short surveying trip into the Shenandoah Valley.

Washington lived at Mount Vernon most of that winter. He now supported himself. His surveying work paid

him well. It was one of the few occupations in which a man could expect to be paid in cash. Most other business in Virginia was carried on with payments in tobacco. Washington kept track in his account book of small loans he made to his relatives and friends. He also wrote down winnings and losses at playing cards and billiards.

During 1750, Washington made more and more surveys as settlers moved into the Shenandoah Valley. He carefully saved his money. When he saw a particularly good piece of land, he bought it. By the end of the year he owned nearly 1,500 acres (607 hectares).

Only Foreign Trip. In 1751, George Washington made his only trip away from the shores of America. Lawrence Washington had become seriously ill. He decided to sail to the warm climate of Barbados Island in the British West Indies for his health. He asked George to go along.

The brothers arrived at the island in November. George's diary shows he was interested in comparing farming methods on the island with those of Virginia. Two weeks after arriving, George became ill with smallpox. He carried a few pox scars on his face the rest of his life. A week after recovering, George decided to return to Virginia while Lawrence remained in the tropical sunshine.

George was now 20. He fell in love with 16-year-old Betsy Fauntleroy, the daughter of a Richmond County planter and shipowner. George proposed to her at least twice. Each time he was refused. He sadly wrote that she had given him a "cruel sentence."

In June, 1752, Lawrence Washington suddenly returned home. He died of tuberculosis six weeks later. Lawrence left Mount Vernon to his wife for as long as she lived, then to his daughter. He provided that the estate should go to George if his daughter died with no children of her own. He also left George an equal share of his land with his other three brothers.

Early Military Career (1753-1758)

At the age of 20, George Washington had no experience or training as a soldier. But Lawrence's war stories had interested him in military affairs. He applied to the governor for a commission in the militia. In February, 1753, he was commissioned as a major and put in charge of training militia in southern Virginia. He immediately began reading books on tactics and military affairs.

Messenger to the French. In October, 1753, Washington learned that Robert Dinwiddie, the acting governor of Virginia, planned to send a message to the French military commander in the Ohio River Valley. Dinwiddie intended to warn the French that they must withdraw their troops from the region. The French wanted the Ohio River Valley for fur trading, but the British wanted it for farming. Washington volunteered to carry the message. Dinwiddie gave him the task.

In mid-November, Washington set out into the dangerous wilderness. With him went Christopher Gist, a frontier guide; an interpreter; and four frontiersmen. Washington's party traveled north into western Pennsylvania. Sometimes the men covered as much as 20 miles

Painting by Alonzo Chappel, Chicago Historical Society

(32 kilometers) in a day. They stopped at an Indian village at the site of present-day Pittsburgh, Pa. There, three Indian chiefs agreed to accompany the party to visit the French. The Indians gave George the name *Caunotaucarius*, which meant Towntaker.

Early in December, Washington reached French headquarters at Fort Le Boeuf, just south of present-day Erie, Pa. The French commander rejected Dinwiddie's warning. He said that his orders were to take and hold the Ohio River Valley. He gave Washington a letter to carry back to the British.

Washington experienced many hardships and dangers on the return trip to Virginia. It was late December and bitterly cold. Snow lay deep on the ground. Once an Indian tried to kill Washington. Another time Washington nearly drowned trying to cross the Allegheny River on a raft.

On Jan. 16, 1754, Washington reached Williamsburg and delivered the French reply to Dinwiddie. Washington urged Dinwiddie to build a fort where the Ohio and Allegheny rivers joined (the site of present-day Pittsburgh). He also drew detailed maps of the region. Within five days, Dinwiddie sent a force of frontiersmen to build the fort. The governor had unknowingly taken the first step toward a war that was to spread to many other countries—known in America as the French and Indian War, and in Europe as the Seven Years' War.

First Military Action. The 22-year-old Washington was promoted to lieutenant colonel. He received orders to enlist troops to man the new fort. He found Americans resentful because the British refused to pay them as much as regular British soldiers. Washington himself angrily threatened to resign because his pay was lower than that of a lieutenant colonel in the regular British army. Perhaps for the first time he realized that the British treated American colonists unfairly. It also may have been the first time he thought of himself as an American rather than as an Englishman.

Washington set out with about 160 poorly trained soldiers in April, 1754. He was still 200 miles (320 kilometers) from the fort when he learned the French had captured it. Washington decided to move on toward the fort, which the French had named Fort Duquesne.

On May 28, 1754, Washington captured the first French prisoners of the war. He surprised a group of French troops, killed 10, wounded 1, and took 21 prisoners. Only one of Washington's men was killed. Washington described his feelings in the short fight: "I heard the bullets whistle, and believe me there is something charming in the sound."

Surrender of Fort Necessity. Washington's men built a fort about 60 miles (97 kilometers) south of Fort Duquesne. They completed it in June and named it Fort Necessity. Meanwhile, Washington had been promoted to the rank of colonel.

Early in June, about 180 Virginia militia arrived to reinforce Fort Necessity. Some friendly Indians also joined Washington's forces. But no food arrived. On June 14, just as the last food was being eaten, a company of about 100 British regular army troops arrived. They brought with them some vitally needed supplies.

On July 3, the French attacked Fort Necessity. Washington had only 400 men. A third of the troops were sick, and the rest hungry. The French fired from behind trees and rocks. About 30 of Fort Necessity's defenders were killed and 70 wounded. A rainstorm turned the battlefield into a sea of mud. As night fell, the young colonel had few men, little food, and no dry gunpowder. His position was hopeless. About midnight, Washington agreed to surrender Fort Necessity. The French let him march out of the fort and return to Virginia with his men and guns.

A discouraged Washington returned to Williamsburg two weeks later. The colonists did not blame the young colonel for losing the fort. They praised Washington and his men for their bravery.

In October, Washington again visited Williamsburg. He was shocked when Dinwiddie told him he had orders from London to lower the rank of all colonial officers. Washington wanted a military career, but he angrily resigned, rather than be lowered from the rank of colonel to captain.

Washington had inherited Ferry Farm from his father, but he did not wish to go there to live with his mother. Instead, he decided to rent Mount Vernon from the widow of his brother Lawrence. He agreed to pay a rent of 15,000 pounds (6,800 kilograms) of tobacco a year.

Braddock's Defeat. In March, 1755, Washington received a message from Major General Edward Braddock. The British general invited Washington to help him in a new campaign against the French at Fort Duquesne. Washington agreed to serve without pay as one of Braddock's aides. He believed this was an excellent opportunity to learn military affairs from an experienced general.

Braddock assembled his forces at Fort Cumberland, Md., about 90 miles (140 kilometers) southeast of Fort Duquesne. On June 7, the troops started across the rough country. Washington was upset by the slow march. He wrote in a letter: "They were halting to level every mole hill and to erect bridges over every brook;

Painting by Junius B. Stearns; Bettmann Archive

Gentleman Farmer. Washington managed a large estate called Mount Vernon in Fairfax County, Virginia. He grew wheat and raised fruit trees. Washington was ahead of his time in using such farm methods as crop rotation and prevention of soil erosion.

by which means we were four days getting 12 miles."

During the second week of the march, Washington became seriously ill with a high fever. He was forced to remain behind in camp for nearly three weeks. He warned Braddock to be careful of "the mode of attack which, more than probably, he would experience from the Canadian French and their Indians."

On July 9, the British had nearly reached Fort Duquesne. Braddock ordered his long column to march forward. Wearing bright red uniforms, the British soldiers looked as though they were parading before the king. Washington was not yet well, but he had rejoined the army and rode his horse with pillows tied to the saddle. Braddock was confident that the French would wait at their fort for his attack. What happened next was later described by Washington:

"We were attacked (very unexpectedly I must own) by about 300 French and Indians. Our numbers consisted of about 1,300 well armed men, chiefly regulars, who were immediately struck with such a deadly panic that nothing but confusion and disobedience of orders prevailed amongst them.

". . . the English soldiers . . . broke and ran as sheep before the hounds . . . The general (Braddock) was wounded behind in the shoulder and into the breast, of which he died three days after . . .

"I luckily escaped without a wound, though I had four bullets through my coat and two horses shot under me . . ."

With Braddock's defeat and death, Washington was released from service. He rode home to Mount Vernon. Shortly after, in a letter to one of his brothers, he summed up his military career thus far:

"I was employed to go a journey in the winter (when I believe few or none would have undertaken it) and what did I get by it? My expenses borne! I then was appointed with trifling pay to conduct a handful of men to the Ohio. What did I get by this? Why, after putting myself to a considerable expense by equipping and providing necessaries for the campaign, I went out, was soundly beaten, lost them all—came in, and had my commission taken from me, or in other words, my command reduced, under pretense of an order from home . . . I have been on the losing order ever since I entered the service . . ."

Frontier Commander. The French encouraged the Indians to attack English settlers. In August, 1755, Dinwiddie persuaded Washington to accept a new commission as colonel. Washington would take command of Virginia's colonial troops to defend the colony's 350-mile (563-kilometer) western frontier.

Many of the Virginians recruited by Washington and his officers were homeless men. A British officer described them as "an extremely bad collection of broken inn-keepers, horse jockeys, and Indian traders."

Washington constantly urged that a new attack be made on Fort Duquesne. The British finally decided in 1758 to attack Fort Duquesne again. An advance British force of 800 men again was ambushed by the French and Indians. More than 300 British soldiers were killed. When the main army, including Washington, finally reached the fort in late November, the French had burned it and retreated toward Canada.

Washington returned to Virginia to hang up his sword. He was now the most famous American-born soldier. Perhaps the most important thing he had learned was that the British army could be beaten.

The Peaceful Years (1759-1773)

At the age of 26, Washington turned to seek happiness as a country gentleman and to build a fortune. During the next 16 years, he became known as a skilled farmer, an intelligent businessman, a popular legislator, a conscientious warden of the Church of England, and a wise county court judge.

Marriage. On Jan. 6, 1759, Washington married Mrs.

74d

THE PEACEFUL YEARS

Mount Vernon, Washington's home, overlooks the Potomac River. Thousands of tourists visit the estate every year. The home has been preserved as it looked during Washington's lifetime.

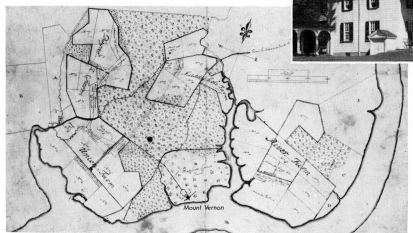

Louis C. Williams

Five Farms made up the Mount Vernon estate. They were Dogue Run Farm, Muddy Hole Farm, Union Farm, River Farm, and Mansion House Farm. They were shown on a map, *left*, drawn by Washington. A star shows where his home stood on Mansion House Farm.

The Huntington Library, San Marino, Calif.

Martha Dandridge Custis (see WASHINGTON, MARTHA CUSTIS). She was a widow, eight months older than George. The marriage probably took place at New Kent County, Virginia, at the bride's plantation home, which was called the *White House.* Her first husband had left a fortune of about 17,000 acres (6,880 hectares) of land and $100,000. This was divided equally among the widow and her two children, John "Jackie" Parke Custis (1754-1781) and Martha "Patsy" Parke Custis (1756-1773). Washington became a loving stepfather to the children and gave them many gifts. He and Martha had no children of their own.

Legislator. After a six-week honeymoon at the White House, Washington took his new family to Williamsburg. There he served for the first time in the colonial legislature. He had been elected to the House of Burgesses in 1758, while still on the frontier. Although he had not personally campaigned, he had paid bills for his friends to entertain voters during the campaign.

During the next 15 years, Washington was re-elected time after time to the legislature. He seldom made speeches and did not put any important bills before the legislature. More important, he learned the process of representative government. He saw the difficulties in getting a law passed. The experience gave him patience in later years when he had to deal with Congress during the Revolutionary War and as President. He also became acquainted with Thomas Jefferson, Patrick Henry, and other Virginia leaders.

Farmer and Landowner. Washington brought his wife and children to Mount Vernon in April, 1759. He found it badly run down by the neglect of his overseers. In 1761, Washington inherited Mount Vernon because his half-brother Lawrence's widow and daughter had both died. He began to buy farms that lay around the estate. He also bought western lands for future development. In 1770, Washington made a trip west as far as the present town of Gallipolis, O., searching for

good land to buy. By 1773, he owned about 40,000 acres (16,000 hectares). He also controlled the large Custis estate of his wife and her children. He rented much of his land to tenant farmers.

Washington was a careful businessman. He did his own bookkeeping and recorded every penny of expense or profit. His ledgers tell us when he bought gifts for his family, and what prices he received for his crops.

As a large landowner, Washington had to supervise many different activities. He wanted to learn more about farming, so he bought the latest books on the subject. When he discovered he could not grow the best grade of tobacco at Mount Vernon, he switched to raising wheat. He saw the profit in making flour, so he built his own flour mills. Large schools of fish swam in the Potomac River, and Mount Vernon became known for the barrels of salted fish it produced. Washington experimented with tree grafting to improve his fruit orchards. His weavers made cloth for the Negro slaves. He hired out his carpenters, bricklayers, and blacksmiths to other plantation owners.

Social Life at Mount Vernon and nearby plantations was gay and lighthearted. The men shot ducks, fished, and hunted wild game. The greatest social events were the fox hunts. On weekends when hunts were planned, Mount Vernon housed many guests and their servants. Barbecues, dinners, dancing, and games made the hours pass quickly and pleasantly.

The Coming Revolution (1774-1775)

The American colonists in the late 1760's and early 1770's grew angrier and angrier at the taxes placed on them by Great Britain. As a legislator and as a leading landowner, Washington was deeply concerned as relations with Great Britain became worse. During this time his knowledge of colonial affairs increased under the guidance of his neighbor, George Mason, a leading statesman of the time (see MASON, GEORGE).

WASHINGTON THE SOLDIER

First Commander in Chief. Washington led the first American army. He accepted no pay for his services. After the Revolutionary War, he submitted a record of his expenses.

Washington's Monument, a sculpture by Kirk Brown and J. Q. A. Ward; U.S. Military Academy, West Point, N.Y. (U.S. Army)

Lord Botetourt, the British governor, dismissed the Virginia legislature in 1769 because the representatives had protested the taxation imposed by the British Townshend Acts. Washington met with other legislators in a Williamsburg tavern. He presented a plan prepared by Mason for an association to boycott imports of British goods. The plan was quickly adopted.

Washington became one of the first American leaders to consider using force to "maintain the liberty." He wrote Mason in April, 1769: ". . . That no man should scruple, or hesitate a moment to use arms in defense of so valuable a blessing, on which all the good and evil of life depends, is clearly my opinion; yet Arms, I would beg leave to add, should be the last . . . resort."

In 1774, the British closed the port of Boston as punishment for the Boston Tea Party. Virginia legislators who protested were dismissed by Governor Lord Dunmore. Again the representatives met as private citizens. They elected seven delegates, including Washington, to attend the First Continental Congress in Philadelphia. Washington wrote: ". . . shall we supinely sit and see one province after another fall a prey to despotism?"

First Continental Congress. The Continental Congress met in September, 1774. There, Washington had his first chance to meet and talk with leaders of other colonies. The members were impressed with his judgment and military knowledge. Washington made no speeches and he was not appointed to any committees. But he worked to have trade with Great Britain stopped by all the colonies. The trade boycott was approved by the Congress. Then Congress adjourned.

In March, 1775, representatives from each Virginia county met in a church in Richmond, Va. Washington and the others thrilled to Patrick Henry's famous speech in which he cried: "Give me liberty or give me death!" The representatives again elected Washington to attend the Second Continental Congress in Philadelphia. See CONTINENTAL CONGRESS.

Elected Commander in Chief. By the time Washington left Mount Vernon to attend the Second Continental Congress, the Battles of Lexington and Concord already had been fought in Massachusetts. The Congress opened on May 10, 1775. For six weeks the delegates debated and studied the problems facing the colonies. The majority, including Washington, wanted to avoid war. At the same time, they feared they could not avoid it.

To express his desire for action, Washington began wearing his red and blue uniform of the French and Indian War. He was appointed to one military committee after another. He was asked to prepare a defense of New York City, to study ways to obtain gunpowder, to make plans for an army, and to write army regulations.

Then, on June 14, Congress called on Pennsylvania, Maryland, and Virginia to send troops to aid Boston, which had been placed under British military rule. John Adams, who in later years would be Washington's Vice-President and successor as President, rose to discuss the need of electing a commander in chief. Adams praised Washington highly and said his popularity would help unite the colonies. Many New England delegates believed a northerner should be made commander in chief. But the following day Washington was elected unanimously.

Washington had not sought the position. He particularly wanted to make everyone understand he did not want the $500 monthly pay that had been voted. He said he would keep track of his expenses, and would accept nothing else for his services. His acceptance speech, on June 16, was presented with modesty. "I beg it may be remembered by every gentleman in the room," Washington said, "that I this day declare with the utmost sincerity, I do not think myself equal to the command I am honored with."

"First in War" (1775-1783)

"These are the times that try men's souls," Thomas Paine wrote during the Revolutionary War. "The summer soldier and the sunshine patriot will in this crisis shrink from the service of his country . . ."

During the eight years of war, Washington's soul was tried many times both by "summer soldiers," who did not care to fight in winter, and by "sunshine patriots," who were friendly to the American cause only when things went well. Only his strong will to win made it possible for Washington to overcome his many discouragements.

The following sections describe the most important problems that Washington overcame to win the Revolutionary War. For an account of the main battles, see the article REVOLUTIONARY WAR IN AMERICA.

Symbol of Independence. To most Americans of his time, Washington became the chief symbol of what they were fighting for. The colonists had been brought up to

The Metropolitan Museum of Art, New York. Gift of John S. Kennedy, 1897.

Crossing the Delaware River, Washington led a surprise attack on the Hessians at Trenton, N.J., in December, 1776. He won a great victory. This famous painting by Emanuel Leutze incorrectly shows an American flag that was not adopted until 1777.

respect the British king. They did not easily accept the idea of independence. The Congress that approved the Declaration of Independence on July 4, 1776, was not elected by the people, but by the legislatures of the states. And the legislatures were elected only by property owners. As a result, some people who did not own property and had no vote viewed independence with suspicion. Thousands of *Loyalists*, as British sympathizers were called, refused to help the fight for independence in any way.

Although many people did not especially wish for independence and did not trust Congress, they came to believe in Washington. They sympathized with him for the misery he shared with his soldiers. They cheered his courage in carrying on the fight.

"Washington retreats like a general and acts like a hero," the *Pennsylvania Journal* said in 1777. "Had he lived in the days of idolatry, he had been worshiped as a god." That same year, the Marquis de Lafayette wrote to Washington: ". . . if you were lost for America, there is nobody who could keep the Army and Revolution for six months."

Discouragement. Praise did not keep Washington from feeling discouraged. Often he believed he could not hold out long enough to win. Following are several comments he wrote throughout the war.

1776—"Such is my situation that if I were to wish the bitterest curse to an enemy on this side of the grave, I should put him in my stead with my feelings . . ."

1779—". . . there is every appearance that the Army will infallibly disband in a fortnight."

1781—". . . it is vain to think that an Army can be kept together much longer, under such a variety of sufferings as ours has experienced."

The Army. Throughout the war, Washington seldom commanded more than 10,000 troops at any one time.

He described his soldiers as "raw militia, badly officered, and with no government." There were two kinds of troops: (1) soldiers of the Continental Army, organized by Congress, and (2) militia, organized by the states.

Washington had trouble keeping soldiers in the Continental Army. At the beginning of the war, Congress let soldiers enlist for only a few months. Toward the end of the war, Washington convinced Congress that enlistments had to be longer. When their enlistments were up, the soldiers of the Continental Army went home. Sometimes a thousand men marched off at once.

Washington often had to plan battles for certain dates, because if he waited longer the soldiers' enlistments would be up. For example, Washington attacked the Hessian (German) troops at Trenton, N.J., on the day after Christmas in 1776 for this reason. His army had shrunk to only about 5,000 men and the enlistments of most of his soldiers would be up at the end of December. The victory at Trenton inspired many of his soldiers to re-enlist.

From time to time, Washington asked the states to call out their militia to help in a particular battle. The militia included storekeepers, farmers, and other private citizens. They were poorly trained and did not like being called from their homes to fight. The militia complained so much that troops of the Continental Army called them "long faces." Washington's army was defeated many times because the militia turned and ran when they saw redcoated British soldiers.

Desertion by his soldiers was another one of Washington's major problems. Many soldiers enlisted only to collect bonuses offered by Congress. At some times, as many men deserted each day as were enlisted. Washington authorized harsh punishment for deserters. He had some hanged. Dangerous mutinies also occurred.

"We are, during the winter, dreaming of independence and peace, without using the means to become so," Washington wrote in 1780. "In the spring, when our recruits are with the Army in training, we have just discovered the necessity of calling for them, and by the fall, after a distressed and inglorious campaign for want of them, we begin to get a few men, which come in just in time enough to eat our provisions . . ."

From the time Washington took command to the end of the war, he had few capable generals. Congress appointed the generals without asking Washington's advice. The states appointed officers in the militia. Most officers were chosen for political reasons. Some generals, such as Charles Lee and Horatio Gates, believed they should have been chosen commander in chief. They sometimes failed to obey Washington's orders in an effort to make him look like a poor general. One foreign-born general, Thomas Conway, organized a conspiracy known as the *Conway cabal* to make Major General Horatio Gates commander in chief (see CABAL). Washington sometimes hesitated to give orders to generals older than himself. In planning a battle or campaign, he usually called for a council of his generals and accepted the opinion of the majority.

Shortage of Supplies. Washington's troops lacked food, clothing, ammunition, and other supplies throughout the war. If the British had attacked the Americans around Boston in 1775, Washington could have issued only enough gunpowder for nine shots to each soldier. He had to give up Philadelphia to the British in 1777 because he could not risk losing the few supplies he had. The army repeatedly ran out of meat and bread. Sometimes hundreds of troops had to march barefoot in the snow because they had no shoes.

"The want of clothing, added to the misery of the season," Washington wrote in the winter of 1777-1778 at Valley Forge, Pa., "has occasioned (the soldiers) to suffer such hardships as will not be credited but by those who have been spectators."

In the winter of 1779-1780 at Morristown, N.J., Major General Nathanael Greene described Washington's army: "Poor fellows! They exhibit a picture truly distressing—more than half naked and two thirds starved. A country overflowing with plenty are now suffering an Army, employed for the defense of everything that is dear and valuable, to perish for want of food."

Winning the War. From the beginning of the war, Washington knew the powerful British navy gave the enemy a great advantage. The ships of the British could carry their army anywhere along the American coast. Washington's tiny, ragged army could not possibly defend every American port.

On the other hand, Washington knew from his experience in the French and Indian War that the British army moved slowly on land. He also knew it could be beaten. He proved that he could stay one jump ahead of the slow-moving British by quick retreats. Meanwhile, Washington waited and prayed for the French to send a large fleet of warships to America. He hoped then to trap the British while the French navy prevented them from escaping.

Washington's prayers came true at Yorktown, Va.

There, on Sept. 28, 1781, he surrounded Lord Cornwallis' army. The French fleet prevented the British from escaping by ship. Washington began attacking on October 6. On October 19, Cornwallis and 8,000 men surrendered.

Turning Down a Crown. After Cornwallis surrendered, the British lost interest in continuing the war. Peace talks dragged on in Paris for many months.

In May, 1782, Colonel Lewis Nicola sent a document to Washington on behalf of his officers. It complained of injustices the army had suffered from Congress. It suggested that the army set up a monarchy with Washington as king. Washington replied that he read the idea "with abhorrence." He ordered Nicola to "banish these thoughts from your mind."

In November, 1783, word finally arrived that the Treaty of Paris had been signed two months earlier. The last British soldiers went aboard ships at New York City on November 25. That same day Washington led his troops into the city. About a week later, on December 4, he said goodby to his officers in a meeting at Fraunces Tavern (see FRAUNCES TAVERN).

On his way home to Virginia, he stopped at Annapolis, Md., where Congress was meeting. He returned his commission as commander in chief, saying: ". . . I resign with satisfaction the appointment I accepted with diffidence."

"First in Peace" (1784-1789)

Washington, now 51 years old, reached Mount Vernon in time to spend Christmas, 1783, with Martha. The war had aged him. He now wore glasses. As he had told his officers: "I have grown gray in your service and now find myself growing blind."

For the next five years, Washington lived the life of a Virginia planter. Many guests and visitors dropped in at Mount Vernon. His entertainment expenses were large. In 1787, he wrote: "My estate for the last eleven years has not been able to make both ends meet."

Washington believed strongly in the future development of the West. This made him search for more land to buy. In 1784, he made a 680-mile (1,090-kilometer) trip on horseback through the wilderness to visit his land holdings southwest of Pittsburgh. He helped promote two companies interested in building canals along the Potomac and James rivers. He took part in plans to drain the Dismal Swamp in southern Virginia.

Washington also widened his interest in farming. In many ways his farm methods were ahead of the times. He began breeding mules. He introduced rotation of crops to his farms. He began using waste materials from his fishing industry as fertilizer. He also took steps to prevent soil erosion.

Constitutional Convention. In 1786, Washington wrote: "We are fast verging to anarchy and confusion." In Massachusetts, open revolt broke out (see SHAYS' REBELLION). Finally, the states agreed to call a meeting in 1787 to consider revising the weak Articles of Confederation (see ARTICLES OF CONFEDERATION). Washington was elected unanimously to head the Virginia delegates. A huge welcome greeted Washington when he arrived in Philadelphia in May. All the bells in the city were rung. The Constitutional Convention opened on May 25. The delegates elected Washington president of the convention.

Debate on the proposed constitution went on

Virginia Museum of Fine Arts, Gift of
Col. and Mrs. Edgar W. Garbisch

WASHINGTON
IN GOVERNMENT

Constitutional Convention. Washington presided over the convention that wrote the United States Constitution in 1787. He spoke little during this historic meeting, but his presence helped bring about an agreement.

First Inauguration. Washington took the oath as first President on the balcony of Federal Hall in New York City. His second inauguration took place in Philadelphia. He was the only President to be inaugurated in two cities.

Brown Bros.

throughout the hot summer. Washington wrote: "I see no end to my staying here. To please all is impossible . . ." As president, Washington took little part in the debates, but helped hold the convention together. The convention finally reached agreement in September. See CONSTITUTION OF THE UNITED STATES.

Elected President. By the summer of 1788, enough states had approved the Constitution so the government could be organized. Throughout the country, people linked Washington's name directly to the new Constitution. They took it for granted that he would be chosen as the first President. But Washington had many doubts as to whether he should accept the position. He wrote: ". . . If I should receive the appointment, and if I should be prevailed upon to accept it, the acceptance would be attended with more diffidence and reluctance than I ever experienced before in my life."

In February, 1789, members of the first Electoral College met in their own states and voted (see ELECTORAL COLLEGE). At that time, each elector voted for two persons. The candidate with the most votes became President, and the runner-up became Vice-President. Washington was elected President with 69 votes—the largest number possible—from the 69 electors. John Adams was elected Vice-President with 34 votes.

First Administration (1789-1793)

Washington's journey from Mount Vernon to New York City was the parade of a national hero. Every town and city along the way held a celebration.

Inauguration Day was April 30, 1789. The 57-year-old Washington rode in a cream-colored coach to Federal Hall at Broad and Wall streets. Washington walked upstairs to the Senate Chamber, then out onto a balcony. Thousands watched as Washington raised his right hand and placed his left hand on an open Bible. Solemnly he repeated the presidential oath of office given by Robert R. Livingston of New York. Washington added the words, "So help me God!" and kissed the Bible. Cannons fired a 13-gun salute. Then President Washington walked back to the Senate Chamber and delivered his inaugural address.

Life in the Executive Mansion. The house of Samuel Osgood on Cherry Street in New York City was the first Executive Mansion. In February, 1790, Washington moved to a larger house on Broadway. When Congress later made Philadelphia the capital, the Washingtons moved into the home there of financier Robert Morris. It was the finest house in the city.

The Washingtons entertained a great deal. They had a large staff of servants and slaves. The President held two afternoon receptions each week so he could meet the hundreds of persons who wanted to see him. Every Friday night, Mrs. Washington held a formal reception. These affairs ended at 9 P.M. because, she said, the President "always retires at 9 in the evening." Each year on his birthday Washington gave a ball at which dancing lasted until well after midnight.

Martha Washington's two young grandchildren, Eleanor Parke Custis and George Washington Parke Custis, came to live with the Washingtons in 1789. Their father, John Custis, had died during the Revolutionary War and their mother had remarried.

Martha Washington was described in a letter by Abigail Adams, wife of the Vice-President: "She is plain in her dress, but that plainness is the best of every article . . . Her hair is white, her teeth beautiful, her person rather short . . . Her manners are modest and unassuming, dignified and feminine . . ."

The Washingtons made many trips home to Mount Vernon during the next eight years. The President sometimes stayed there as long as three months when Congress was not in session.

New Precedents of Government. "I walk on untrodden ground," Washington said as he began his new responsibilities. "There is scarcely any part of my conduct that may not hereafter be drawn into precedent."

Washington believed strongly in the constitutional provision that the executive, legislative, and judicial branches of the government should be kept as separate as possible. He thought the President should not try to influence the kinds of laws Congress passed. But he believed that if he disapproved of a bill, he should let Congress know by vetoing it. He regarded the duties of his office largely as administering the laws of Congress and supervising relations with other countries.

The Union included only 11 states when Washington became President. In November, 1789, North Carolina accepted the Constitution, and in 1790 Rhode Island joined the Union. Vermont was admitted in 1791, and Kentucky in 1792.

On July 4, 1789, Washington received the first important bill passed by the new Congress. It provided income to run the government by setting taxes on imports. He signed it with no comment.

By September, Congress had established three executive departments to help run the government: the Department of Foreign Affairs (now Department of State), and the Departments of War and the Treasury. Congress provided for an Attorney General and a continuation of the Post Office. Congress also adopted the Bill of Rights amendments to the Constitution, and established a system of federal courts.

Cabinet. In September, Washington began making important appointments. He chose men whom he knew and could trust:

Chief Justice of the United States—John Jay, who had been Secretary of Foreign Affairs under the Articles of Confederation.

Secretary of State—Thomas Jefferson, who had served with Washington for five years in the Virginia legislature.

Secretary of War—Henry Knox, Washington's chief of artillery during the Revolutionary War.

Secretary of the Treasury—Alexander Hamilton, who had been one of Washington's military aides.

Attorney General—Edmund Randolph, former governor of Virginia and a member of the Constitutional Convention. Randolph had been Washington's friend for years.

During his first administration, Washington relied heavily on the advice of Hamilton and James Madison, a Congressman from Virginia. At first, Washington did not call his department heads together as a group. Instead, he asked them to give him written opinions or

--- VICE-PRESIDENT AND CABINET ---

Vice-President..............*John Adams

Secretary of State...........*Thomas Jefferson
           *Edmund Randolph (1794)
           Timothy Pickering (1795)

Secretary of the Treasury.....*Alexander Hamilton
           Oliver Wolcott, Jr. (1795)

Secretary of War............*Henry Knox
           *Timothy Pickering (1795)
           *James McHenry (1796)

Attorney General............*Edmund Randolph
           William Bradford (1794)
           Charles Lee (1795)
       *Has a separate biography in WORLD BOOK.

THE WORLD OF

WORLD EVENTS

1789-1799 The French Revolution ended absolute monarchy in France.
1791 The British Parliament passed the Canada Constitution Act.
1794 Aga Mohammed founded the Kajar dynasty in Persia (now Iran).
1795 Austria, Prussia, and Russia partitioned Poland among themselves.
1797 The French Army under Napoleon drove the Austrians from Italy.

★   ★   ★   ★   ★   ★   ★

UNITED STATES EVENTS

North Carolina became a state in 1789, Rhode Island in 1790, Vermont in 1791, Kentucky in 1792, and Tennessee in 1796. U.S. population was 4,900,000 in 1797, when Washington retired.

The United States Flag had 13 stars when Washington became President in 1789.

1789 (June 1) Washington signed the first act of Congress, concerning the administration of oaths.
1789 Congress established the Department of Foreign Affairs (now the Department of State).
1790 Washington approved plans for a U.S. Capitol.
1790 (Feb. 1) The Supreme Court held its first session.
1791 The Cabinet held its first recorded meeting.
1791 Congress chartered the Bank of the United States.
1791 Congress established the District of Columbia.
1792 Congress established a national mint.
1792 Rival national political parties began developing in the United States.
1793 (April 22) Washington issued the Neutrality Proclamation to keep the United States out of the war between France and Great Britain.
1793 (Sept. 18) Washington laid the cornerstone of the U.S. Capitol in Washington, D.C.

1795 Washington signed the unpopular Jay Treaty to maintain trade with Great Britain.

PRESIDENT WASHINGTON

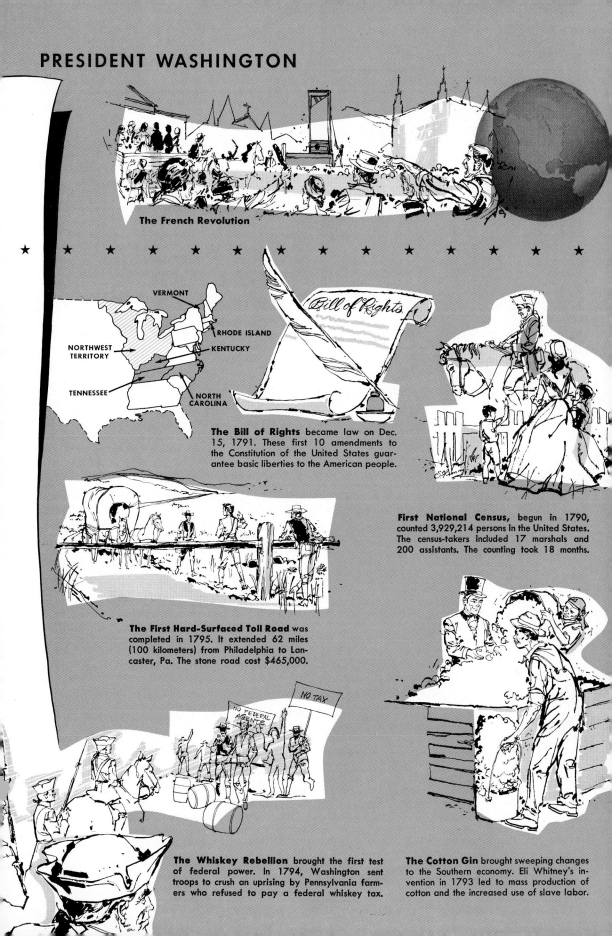

The French Revolution

VERMONT

RHODE ISLAND

NORTHWEST TERRITORY

KENTUCKY

TENNESSEE

NORTH CAROLINA

The Bill of Rights became law on Dec. 15, 1791. These first 10 amendments to the Constitution of the United States guarantee basic liberties to the American people.

First National Census, begun in 1790, counted 3,929,214 persons in the United States. The census-takers included 17 marshals and 200 assistants. The counting took 18 months.

The First Hard-Surfaced Toll Road was completed in 1795. It extended 62 miles (100 kilometers) from Philadelphia to Lancaster, Pa. The stone road cost $465,000.

NO TAX

NO FEDERAL AGENTS

The Whiskey Rebellion brought the first test of federal power. In 1794, Washington sent troops to crush an uprising by Pennsylvania farmers who refused to pay a federal whiskey tax.

The Cotton Gin brought sweeping changes to the Southern economy. Eli Whitney's invention in 1793 led to mass production of cotton and the increased use of slave labor.

A Marble Statue of Washington by Jean Houdon stands in the Virginia Capitol in Richmond. It is the only statue for which Washington posed.

in a strong national government, took Hamilton's side and signed the law.

First Veto by Washington of Congressional legislation was made in April, 1792. The first census of the United States had shown that the population was 3,929,214, including 697,000 slaves. Congress then passed a bill in March to raise the number of U.S. representatives from 67 to 120. Washington believed the bill was unconstitutional because some states would have greater representation in proportion to population than other states. Many persons thought the bill favored Northern states over Southern states. Congress failed to override Washington's veto, and then revised the bill to provide for a House of 103 members.

Rise of Political Parties. Washington was disturbed as he saw that Jefferson and Hamilton were disagreeing more and more with each other. Men and newspapers who supported Hamilton's views of a stronger and stronger national government called themselves *Federalists* (see FEDERALIST PARTY). The Federalists became the party of the Northern states and of banking and manufacturing interests. Those who favored Jefferson's ideas of a strict interpretation of the Constitution in defending states' rights called themselves *Anti-Federalists*, or *Democratic-Republicans* (see DEMOCRATIC-REPUBLICAN PARTY). The Democratic-Republicans mainly represented the Southern states and the farmers.

Washington attempted to favor neither party. He tried to bring Hamilton and Jefferson into agreement and tried to discourage the growth of political parties.

Re-Election. In 1792, Washington began to make plans for retirement. In May he asked Madison to help him prepare a farewell address. Madison did so, but urged Washington to accept re-election. Hamilton, Knox, Jefferson, and Randolph each asked Washington to continue as President. Perhaps one of the strongest arguments came from Jefferson, who wrote: "Your being at the helm will be more than an answer to every argument which can be used to alarm and lead the people in any quarter into violence or secession. North and South will hang together if they have you to hang on."

Members of the Electoral College cast their votes in December, 1792. Their ballots were counted on Feb. 13, 1793, and Washington again was elected President with the largest number of votes possible—132. Adams received 77 votes and was again the runner-up and Vice-President.

Second Administration (1793-1797)

Washington's second inauguration took place in Congress Hall in Philadelphia on March 4, 1793. The 61-year-old Washington faced greater problems during his second administration than during his first.

Neutrality Proclamation. Word came in April, 1793, that a general war had begun in Europe. England, Spain, Austria, and Prussia were all fighting against the new French republic. Although the United States had signed an alliance with the French king in 1778, Wash-

to talk with him individually. Washington allowed his department heads to act independently. He did not try to prevent Hamilton, Jefferson, or the others from influencing Congress. Toward the end of his first administration, he began calling the group together for meetings. In 1793, Madison first used the term *cabinet* to refer to the group (see CABINET).

Finances. Washington's new government had millions of dollars in debts which the Congress of the Articles of Confederation had been unable to pay. Hamilton drew up a plan to straighten out the finances. There was much argument, but finally the plan passed in July, 1790. The law provided that the national government would assume the wartime debts of the states. It also called for borrowing $12 million from other countries and for paying interest on the public debts.

New National Capital. Congress approved a bill in July to transfer the government to Philadelphia until 1800. After that, the capital would be moved to a federal district to be located on the Potomac River. The President took up residence in Philadelphia in November, 1790. During the next several years, Washington devoted much time to the plans for the new national capital, which came to bear his name.

Constitutional Debate. Hamilton obtained passage in 1791 of a bill setting up the First Bank of the United States (see BANK OF THE UNITED STATES). Washington had to decide whether the government had powers under the Constitution to charter such a corporation. Jefferson and Randolph believed that the bill was unconstitutional. They said such powers were not mentioned in the Constitution. Hamilton argued that the government could use all powers except those denied by the Constitution. Washington, who believed

WASHINGTON

Washington Cutting Down a Cherry Tree was a legend invented by the writer and clergyman Mason Locke "Parson" Weems. Grant Wood painted this scene.

Courtesy Mrs. Adelaide Marquand, Cambridge, Mass.

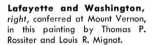
Washington and Lee University.
Photo courtesy *American Heritage,*
The Magazine of History

As a Colonel of Militia, *above,* Washington led Virginia troops against Indians when he was only 23 years old. Charles W. Peale painted this portrait in 1772.

Lafayette and Washington, *right,* conferred at Mount Vernon, in this painting by Thomas P. Rossiter and Louis R. Mignot.

The Metropolitan Museum of Art, New York, Bequest of William Nelson, 1905.

The Winter at Valley Forge was one of the darkest chapters for the Continental Army in the Revolutionary War. In this painting by William T. Trego, Washington watches his tattered troops pass in review. His great courage held his men together.

Valley Forge Historical Society

ington wanted to "maintain a strict neutrality." Jefferson, who favored the recent French Revolution, did not want to issue a neutrality statement. Hamilton believed neutrality was necessary. Washington ordered Attorney General Randolph to write up a statement. On April 22, the President signed the Neutrality Proclamation which called for "conduct friendly and impartial" to all the warring nations. It also forbade American ships from carrying war supplies to the fighting countries.

Relations with France. The United States' decision to stay out of the European war pleased the English, but it angered the French. Leaders of the French Revolution believed the United States should stand by its alliance of 1778 with King Louis XVI. But the revolutionaries had beheaded the king who made the alliance. This posed a delicate point in international law, and Washington had no precedents to guide him. He finally decided to be cool and formal in receiving Edmond Genêt, the new minister appointed by the French republic.

Genêt seemed determined to draw Americans into the war on the side of France. He tried secretly to win Democratic-Republicans to the French cause during the spring and summer of 1793. This upset Washington. The President's patience gave out when Genêt tried to outfit warships in American ports and send them to sea against the British. After a stormy Cabinet meeting in July, 1793, Washington asked France to recall Genêt because he endangered American neutrality. Genêt was stripped of his power, but was allowed to stay in the United States. The neutrality crisis of 1793 passed, and the United States remained at peace.

Whiskey Rebellion. In 1794, Washington proved that the government could enforce federal laws in the states. Farmers in four counties in western Pennsylvania had refused to pay federal taxes on manufacturing whiskey. They armed themselves and attacked federal officials. Washington raised 15,000 troops and sent them to western Pennsylvania. By November, 1794, the rebellion had been crushed and the ringleaders arrested.

Relations with Britain. Washington worried as relations with Great Britain grew worse. British warships stopped American ships carrying food supplies to France and seized their cargoes. They sometimes took seamen off the American ships and forced them into the British navy. British troops refused to give up western frontier forts they were supposed to have surrendered under terms of the treaty of 1783. The British also were stirring up Indian fighting on the western frontier. In an effort to settle problems with Britain, Washington sent Chief Justice John Jay to London in 1794.

In March, 1795, Washington received a copy of a treaty Jay had signed on Nov. 19, 1794. Earlier copies had been lost in the mail. Most of the treaty had to do with regulation of trade between America and Britain. It also called for British troops to give up the frontier forts in 1796. But it contained no agreement that British ships would stop waylaying American ships and taking seamen. See JAY TREATY.

Washington called a special session of the Senate in June to study the treaty. Federalists supported the Jay Treaty because it insured continuing trade with Britain. The Democratic-Republicans violently opposed the treaty because they believed it would harm France. The Federalists controlled the Senate, so the treaty was ratified by a vote of 20 to 10, except for one section. This section opened trade with the British West Indies to United States ships, but it also severely restricted this trade. Washington could not make up his mind whether or not to sign the treaty. He went home to Mount Vernon to think about it.

At Mount Vernon, the President received word of riots in many cities protesting the Jay Treaty. A mob in New York City stoned Hamilton. A Philadelphia mob broke windows at the British embassy.

Cabinet Scandal. Washington returned to Philadelphia on Aug. 11, 1795. He learned that the British had captured a French diplomatic message which seemed to indicate that Edmund Randolph, who was now secretary of state, was a traitor. Washington read a translation of the French message. He believed that Randolph might have sold secrets to the French.

Without saying anything to Randolph about his suspicions, Washington called a Cabinet meeting to discuss the Jay Treaty. At the meeting, Randolph argued against signing the treaty as long as Britain continued to seize American ships. Washington became convinced Randolph was in the pay of France, and so he signed the treaty.

As soon as the Jay Treaty had been delivered to the British embassy, Washington called in Randolph and showed him the captured French message. Randolph denied his guilt, but resigned. He swore he would prove his innocence. Randolph later published a book in which he declared that he had never betrayed his country.

Washington now suffered the bitterest criticism of his career. He was accused by Democratic-Republican newspapers of falling victim to a Federalist plot in signing the Jay Treaty. It was even suggested that he should be impeached because he had overdrawn his $25,000 salary. Washington's feelings were badly hurt.

Public opinion of Washington began to improve when he was able to announce a few months later that a treaty had been negotiated with Spain opening up the Mississippi River to trade. Agreement also had been reached with the pirates of the Barbary States to release American prisoners and to let American ships alone for a payment of $800,000 ransom, plus $24,000 tribute each year. Peace treaties also had been signed with Indian tribes on the frontier.

Farewell Address. Washington, who believed the office of President should be above political attack, had become tired of public office. The new House of Representatives had a large Democratic-Republican majority and was unfriendly to Washington. He also felt himself growing old.

In May, 1796, Washington dusted off the draft of his *Farewell Address* that he and James Madison had worked on four years earlier. He sent it to Jay and to Hamilton for their suggestions. Finally, in September, the much edited address, all in Washington's handwriting, was ready. He gave it to the editor of the *American Daily Advertiser*, a Philadelphia newspaper, which published it on September 19.

In the election campaign that followed, Washington favored John Adams, the Federalist candidate for President. But Washington did not take an active part in the

★ ★

QUOTATIONS FROM THE FAREWELL ADDRESS

Washington published his 6,000-word *Farewell Address* in a Philadelphia newspaper on Sept. 19, 1796. It contained, as he said, "the disinterested warnings of a parting friend" to the American people. Some of its highlights follow:

Unity. "The Unity of Government which constitutes you one people . . . is a main Pillar in the Edifice of your real independence . . ."

The Constitution. ". . . The basis of our political systems is the right of the people to make and to alter their constitutions of government. But the Constitution which at any time exists, 'till changed by an explicit and authentic act of the whole People, is sacredly obligatory upon all."

Political Parties. ". . . the common and continual mischiefs of the spirit of party . . . agitates the Community with ill founded jealousies and false alarms, kindles the animosity of one part against another, foments occasionally riot and insurrection."

Checks and Balances in Government. ". . . the habits of thinking in a free Country should inspire caution in those entrusted with its administration, to confine themselves within their respective Constitutional spheres; avoiding in the exercise of the Powers of one department to encroach upon another . . . "

Religion and Morality. ". . . reason and experience both forbid us to expect that national morality can prevail in exclusion of religious principle."

Education. "Promote . . . institutions for the general diffusion of knowledge . . . it is essential that public opinion should be enlightened."

Public Debt and Taxes. "As a very important source of strength and security, cherish public credit . . . timely disbursements to prepare for danger frequently prevent much greater disbursements to repel it . . . no taxes can be devised which are not more or less inconvenient and unpleasant . . ."

International Relations. "Observe good faith and justice towards all Nations. Cultivate peace and harmony with all . . . nothing is more essential than that permanent, inveterate antipathies against particular Nations and passionate attachments for others should be excluded . . .

"The Great rule of conduct for us, in regard to foreign Nations is in extending our commercial relations to have with them as little political connection as possible. So far as we have already formed engagements let them be fulfilled, with perfect good faith. Here let us stop . . .

" 'Tis our true policy to steer clear of permanent Alliances, with any portion of the foreign world . . . Taking care always to keep ourselves, by suitable establishments, on a respectable defensive posture, we may safely trust to temporary alliances for extraordinary emergencies . . ."

★ ★

campaigning. The Democratic-Republican candidate was Thomas Jefferson. When the Electoral College met, it gave 71 votes to Adams and 68 to Jefferson. Under the existing constitutional provision, Adams became President and Jefferson Vice-President.

At the inauguration in March, 1797, Adams sensed Washington's relief at retirement. Adams wrote to his wife: "He seemed to me to enjoy a triumph over me. Methought I heard him say, 'Ay! I am fairly out and you fairly in! See which of us will be the happiest!' "

"First in the Hearts of His Countrymen" (1797-1799)

Washington was 65. He happily went home to Mount Vernon. Friends said he looked even older. But he did not lose touch with public affairs. Almost every day visitors dropped in to see him. On July 31, 1797, he wrote: "Unless someone pops in unexpectedly—Mrs. Washington and myself will do what has not been done within the last twenty years by us—that is to set down to dinner by ourselves."

He described his daily routine in a letter:

"I begin . . . with the sun . . . if my hirelings are not in their places at that time I send them messages expressive of my sorrow for their indisposition . . . breakfast—a little after seven o'clock . . . This over, I mount my horse and ride round the farms . . . The usual time of sitting at table, a walk, and tea, brings me within the dawn of candlelight . . . I resolve that . . . I will retire to my writing table and acknowledge the letters I have received; but when the lights are brought, I feel tired, and disinclined to engage in this work."

Managing the several farms which made up the more than 8,000 acres (3,200 hectares) of Mount Vernon took much of his time. He made frequent trips to watch construction in the new city of Washington, D.C., which then was called the Federal City.

Recall to Duty. While Washington enjoyed his retirement, relations between the United States and France grew worse. The government decided to raise an army for defense. President Adams asked Washington's help. On July 4, 1798, Washington was commissioned as "Lieutenant General and Commander in Chief of the armies raised or to be raised."

He went to Philadelphia for a few weeks in November to help plan the new army. He had dinner one night in Debtor's Prison with financier Robert Morris, in whose Philadelphia home he had lived while President. Morris had been sent to prison because he could not pay his debts.

During his last year of life, Washington wrote many letters to the various men he chose as generals for the new army. Federalist leaders asked if he would consider running for a third term. He said no. Washington also was saddened by the deaths of friends and relatives. Patrick Henry died on June 6, 1799, and Washington's last living brother, Charles Washington, died on Sept. 20, 1799.

Death. On December 12, Washington wrote his last letter. It was to Alexander Hamilton. In it he discussed the importance of establishing a national military academy. After finishing the letter, Washington went for his daily horseback ride around Mount Vernon. The day was cold, with snow turning into rain and sleet. Washington returned after about five hours and sat down to dinner without changing his damp clothes. The next day he awoke with a sore throat. He went for a walk. Then he made his last entry in his diary, noting down the weather: "Morning Snowing and abt. 3 inches deep . . . Mer. 28 at Night." These were his last written words.

Between 2 and 3 A.M. on Dec. 14, 1799, Washington awakened Martha. He had difficulty speaking and was

National Gallery of Art, Washington, D.C., Andrew W. Mellon Collection

The Washingtons had no children of their own. They reared his two step-grandchildren. This painting by Edward Savage shows, *left to right*, George Washington Parke Custis, Washington, Eleanor Parke Custis, and Mrs. Martha Washington.

Martha Washington was a 27-year-old widow when she married the future President in 1759. John Wollaston painted this portrait of her about 1757.

quite ill. But he would not let her send for a doctor until dawn. James Craik, who had been his friend and doctor since he was a young man, hurried to Mount Vernon. By the time he arrived, Washington already had called in an overseer and had about a cup of blood drained from his veins. Craik examined Washington and said the illness was "inflammatory quinsy." Craik bled Washington again. Present-day doctors believe the illness was a streptococcal infection of the throat.

Two more doctors arrived in the afternoon. Again Washington was bled. Late in the afternoon he could hardly speak, but told the doctors: "You had better not take any more trouble about me, but let me go off quietly. I cannot last long."

About 10 P.M. on December 14, Washington whispered: "I am just going. Have me decently buried, and do not let my body be put in the vault in less than two days after I am dead. Do you understand me?" His secretary answered: "Yes, sir." Washington said: " 'Tis well." He felt for his own pulse. Then he died.

On Dec. 18, Washington was given a military funeral. His body was laid to rest in the family tomb at Mount Vernon. Throughout the world people were saddened by his death. In France, Napoleon Bonaparte ordered 10 days of mourning. In the United States, thousands of people wore mourning clothes for months.

No other American has been honored more than Washington. The nation's capital, Washington, D.C., was named for him. There, the giant Washington Monument stands. The state of Washington is the only state named after a President. Many counties, cities, towns, streets, bridges, lakes, parks, and schools bear his name. Washington's portrait appears on postage stamps, on the $1 bill, and on the quarter. He is the only person whose birthday is a federal holiday.

After the siege of Boston in 1776, the Massachusetts legislature in a resolution had said: ". . . may future generations, in the peaceful enjoyment of that freedom, the exercise of which your sword shall have established, raise the richest and most lasting monuments to the name of Washington." The legislators foresaw the place he would hold forever in the hearts of Americans.

In 1976, the U.S. Congress granted Washington the nation's highest military title, General of the Armies of the United States. Washington's title at the end of the Revolutionary War in America was lieutenant general, then the highest rank. But through the years, Washington had been outranked by many American military officers. Critically reviewed by SAUL K. PADOVER, MARY WELLS ASHWORTH, and JOHN ALEXANDER CARROLL

Outline

Questions

Why is Washington called the "Father of His Country"?

When did Washington first notice that the British treated Americans as second-class citizens?

How did Washington react to his first sound of bullets in war?

What was Washington referring to when he said: "I went out, was soundly beaten, lost them all . . ."?

How did Washington acquire Mount Vernon?

When and why did Washington make his only trip outside of America?

Why did Washington's presidential receptions usually end at 9 P.M.?

As a farmer, how was Washington ahead of his time?

How did Washington show the Second Continental Congress that he was ready to defy Great Britain?

Who praised Washington as "First in war, first in peace, and first in the hearts of his countrymen"?

Reading and Study Guide

See *Washington, George,* in the RESEARCH GUIDE/INDEX, Volume 22, for a *Reading and Study Guide.*

Books to Read

CUNLIFFE, MARCUS F. *George Washington and the Making of a Nation.* Harper, 1966. For young readers.

FLEXNER, JAMES T. *George Washington.* Little, Brown, 1965-1972. *Washington: The Indispensable Man.* 1974.

FOSTER, GENEVIEVE. *George Washington's World.* Scribner, 1941. Washington's place in world history. For young readers.

FREEMAN, DOUGLAS S. *George Washington.* 7 vols. Scribner, 1948-1957. Winner of a Pulitzer prize.

WASHINGTON, LAWRENCE. See WASHINGTON, GEORGE (Development of Character; Only Foreign Trip).

WASHINGTON, MARTHA CUSTIS (1731-1802), was the wife of George Washington. When he took office as the first President in 1789, she became America's first First Lady.

Martha Washington was born on June 2, 1731, near Williamsburg, Va. Her father, Colonel John Dandridge, was a wealthy landowner. Martha had no formal schooling. Until she married Washington, she had never traveled beyond Virginia. At the age of 17, she married Daniel Parke Custis, a wealthy Virginia planter who was 13 years older than she. They had four children, two of whom died in childhood. The other two died before Washington became President. The death of Custis in 1757 made her one of the richest women in Virginia.

No one knows when Martha Custis first met George Washington. They may have met at a neighbor's home in Williamsburg early in 1758. Washington was then a colonel in the militia. She was eight months older than he. They were married on Jan. 6, 1759.

Washington called his wife by her childhood nickname, "Patsy." During the Revolutionary War, she traveled long distances to share his hardships. Mrs. Washington joined him at his camp at Valley Forge, Pa., during the winter of 1777-1778. She also spent the harsh winters of 1778-1779 and 1779-1780 with him in camp at Morristown, N.J. She organized a women's sewing circle and mended clothes for the troops.

As First Lady, Mrs. Washington managed the President's home with dignity and grace. But she did not enjoy being First Lady. She said she felt like a "state prisoner." Many persons called her "Lady Washington." But Mrs. Washington dressed so plainly that people often mistook her for the family maid.

After Washington's death in 1799, she continued to live at Mount Vernon, their estate. Shortly before she died on May 22, 1802, she burned the letters Washington had written her. Mrs. Washington was buried at Mount Vernon. Critically reviewed by MARY WELLS ASHWORTH

See also WASHINGTON, GEORGE.

WASHINGTON, MOUNT. See MOUNT WASHINGTON.

WASHINGTON, TREATY OF, was a treaty signed in 1871 by the United States and Great Britain in Washington, D.C. The treaty settled a number of disputes between the two countries. It provided that the *Alabama* Claims be referred to a special court for arbitration (see ALABAMA [ship]). The court met at Geneva, Switzerland. The settlement of the claims came to be known as the Geneva Arbitration. U.S. Secretary of State Hamilton Fish negotiated the treaty. The treaty also ended quarrels about fishing rights in Canadian waters.

The treaty set down three rules for the court to follow in settling the *Alabama* Claims. (1) It provided that a neutral country should guard against the arming of any vessels within its jurisdiction which might be intended for the use of a country at war. (2) It provided that a neutral country should close its ports to any belligerent which tried to use them as bases for naval operations. (3) It placed on a neutral country the responsibility of guarding against any violations of the first two provisions of the treaty.

WASHINGTON, UNIVERSITY OF

The Washington Treaty granted the U.S. fishing industry the continued use of the waters off the coasts of Quebec, Nova Scotia, New Brunswick, and Prince Edward Island. The British also gained similar fishing rights along the U.S. coast north of the 39th parallel.

The treaty also referred the United States claim to the San Juan, or Haro, Islands, off Puget Sound, to the German emperor for arbitration. His decision upheld the United States claim.   JOHN DONALD HICKS

WASHINGTON, UNIVERSITY OF, is a coeducational state-supported institution in Seattle. It has colleges of architecture and urban planning, arts and sciences, education, engineering, fisheries, forest resources, and pharmacy. It also has a graduate school and schools of business administration, dentistry, law, librarianship, medicine, nursing, public affairs, public health and community medicine, and social work. The university grants bachelor's, master's, and doctor's degrees.

The University of Washington is the oldest state university on the West Coast. It was founded in 1861 in what is now downtown Seattle. The school moved to its present location along Lake Washington in 1895. For the university's enrollment, see UNIVERSITIES AND COLLEGES (table).

See also SEATTLE (picture).

WASHINGTON AND LEE UNIVERSITY is a privately controlled institution for men in Lexington, Va. It has an undergraduate college of liberal arts and a school of commerce, economics, and politics. The university also has a coeducational graduate school of law.

Established in 1749 as Augusta Academy, the school was chartered as Liberty Hall Academy in 1782, when it began granting college degrees. The school was renamed Washington Academy in 1798, after George Washington gave it a gift of stock valued at $50,000. It received its present name in 1871. The name honors both Washington and Robert E. Lee, who was president of the school from 1865 until his death in 1870. Lee and his family are buried in the chapel he built on the campus. For the enrollment of the university, see UNIVERSITIES AND COLLEGES (table). ROBERT E. R. HUNTLEY

WASHINGTON CATHEDRAL, also called THE NATIONAL CATHEDRAL, is an Episcopal church in Washington, D.C. Its official name is THE CATHEDRAL CHURCH OF SAINT PETER AND SAINT PAUL.

The building is laid out in the form of a cross, 525 feet (160 meters) long and 275 feet (84 meters) wide at its widest point. It is Gothic in style, with pointed arches and vaulted ceilings. The cathedral is noted for its rich carvings and beautiful stained-glass windows. Stones from historic buildings and shrines in all parts of the world were used in building it. The *Gloria* tower of the cathedral contains a large carillon with 53 bells and a 10-bell English peal.

Work on the cathedral began in 1907, and services have been held in some of its chapels since 1912. President Woodrow Wilson and Admiral George Dewey are among the well-known persons buried in the cathedral.   ALAN GOWANS

WASHINGTON CONFERENCE ON LIMITATION OF ARMAMENTS. See DISARMAMENT.

WASHINGTON ELM was a great elm tree in Cambridge, Mass. Under it, in 1775, George Washington took command of the American army. The tree was named the Washington Elm. It stood for about 150 years. The passage of time and storms gradually wore it down until little more than a stump remained. What was left of the tree was cut up and distributed among interested groups and the various states. A monument now stands where the tree once stood.   JOHN R. ALDEN

WASHINGTON MONUMENT is a great obelisk built in honor of George Washington. It stands in Washington, D.C., near the Potomac River, about halfway between the Capitol and the Lincoln Memorial.

The monument has the shape of the obelisks of ancient Egypt, but it is several times larger than they were. It is 555 feet $5\frac{1}{8}$ inches (169.29 meters) high, and measures 55 feet $1\frac{1}{8}$ inches (16.79 meters) along each of its four sides at the bottom. The sides slant gradually inward as they rise to the base of the *pyramidion* (small pyramid) which tops the pillar. At this point, each side of the pillar is 34 feet $5\frac{1}{2}$ inches (10.50 meters) long. The pyramidion rises 55 feet (16.8 meters). The walls of the monument are 15 feet (4.6 meters) thick at the bottom and 18 inches (46 centimeters) thick at the top. They are covered with white marble from Maryland. The stones covering the pyramidion are 7 inches (18 centimeters) thick. A cap of cast aluminum protects the tip of the pyramidion.

Inside, the monument is hollow. The inner walls are set with 189 carved memorial stones, many of historic interest. The stones were presented by individuals, societies, cities, states, and other countries. Visitors must take an elevator to the top of the monument. To descend, they can either take the elevator or walk down the 898 steps leading from the top. The view of Washington, D.C., is impressive. More than a million persons visit the Washington Monument each year.

Some persons planned a memorial to Washington while he was still alive, but he objected to the expense. In 1833, the Washington National Monument Society began raising funds for a monument. A design by Robert Mills had already been accepted in part. The government approved the project, and the cornerstone was laid on July 4, 1848, with the same trowel that Washington had used to lay the cornerstone of the Capitol in 1793. But engineers found the ground too soft to support the monument, so they moved the site to the north.

Many persons donated stones for the monument. Pope Pius IX sent a marble block from the Temple of Concord in Rome. One night in 1854, a group believed to be Know-Nothings, or members of the American party, stole this block (see KNOW-NOTHINGS). This act shocked the public, and contributions almost stopped. In 1855, Congress agreed to give some financial aid to the project. But Know-Nothings broke into the society's offices and claimed possession of the monument. In 1876, Congress voted to finish the project at government expense. Work began on Aug. 17, 1880. It was completed on Dec. 6, 1884. The monument was dedicated on Feb. 21, 1885, and opened to the public on Oct. 9, 1888. Its total cost was $1,187,710.31. The monument is maintained as a national memorial by the National Park Service.   JAMES J. CULLINANE

See also WASHINGTON, D.C. (color picture).

WASHINGTON NAVAL CONFERENCE OF 1921. See DISARMAMENT.

WASHINGTON STATE UNIVERSITY is a coeducational, state-controlled institution in Pullman, Wash. It has colleges of agriculture, economics and business, education, engineering, home economics, pharmacy, sciences and arts, and veterinary medicine. Washington State also has a graduate school. The university was founded in 1890. For the enrollment of Washington State University, see UNIVERSITIES AND COLLEGES (table).   GLENN TERRELL

WASHINGTON UNIVERSITY is a privately controlled coeducational school in St. Louis, Mo. The university has a college of liberal arts, a graduate school of arts and sciences, and schools of architecture, business and public administration, dentistry, engineering, fine arts, law, medicine, and social work. It also maintains the Sever Institute of Technology. The school was chartered in 1853 as Eliot Seminary, and received its present name in 1857. For enrollment, see UNIVERSITIES AND COLLEGES (table).   FRANCIS X. O'BRIEN

WASHINGTON'S BIRTHDAY is celebrated as a federal holiday on the third Monday in February. It honors the first President of the United States. George Washington was born on Feb. 22, 1732, according to the calendar we now use. But according to the Old Style Calendar then in use, his birth date was February 11. People first celebrated the anniversary of Washington's birth in the late 1700's, some on the 11th and some on the 22nd.

WASHITA BATTLEFIELD. See OKLAHOMA (Places to Visit).

WASHITA RIVER. See OUACHITA RIVER.

WASP. The wasps are among the most interesting and intelligent insects on earth. They are stinging insects, and related to the bees and the ants.

Some wasps live in colonies, like ants and honeybees. The colony is made up of different types of wasps—queens, males, and workers—and each type has different work to do. Those wasps that live together and cooperate with one another are called *social* wasps. Social wasps include the hornets and yellow jackets. Other kinds do not live in communities, but build separate nests. These are known as *solitary* wasps. All the social wasps fold their wings once lengthwise like parts of a fan when they are at rest. Solitary wasps hold their wings flat or at an angle when at rest.

Most wasps are helpful to humanity. They sometimes damage fruit, but they also destroy large numbers of harmful insects and caterpillars. Wasps do far more good than harm.

Most wasps have slender bodies and four wings. Different wasps have bodies of different colors. Most often they are steel blue, black, yellow, or reddish. The abdomen usually is marked with crosswise bands or rings. The insect's mouth parts are fitted for chewing hard things and lapping up liquids. Some kinds of solitary wasps have a narrow stalk joining the front and back parts of the body (thorax and abdomen). Wasps can give painful stings, but they sting only when they are bothered or frightened. Only female and worker wasps have the sting, which is a thin, pointed drill hidden in the rear tip of the abdomen.

Social Wasps. These wasps are the papermakers of the insect world. They build their nests of wasp paper, which is a mixture of old wood and tough plant fibers. Wasps chew this material to a pulp, using much saliva.

Then they form it into feltlike masses. It is then real paper, made of cellulose, just like the paper on which these words are printed. It is said that the Chinese invented paper after watching wasps make it.

The completed wasp nest is made of rows of cells, like those of a bee honeycomb. One group of wasps, the *Polistes*, builds a nest of a single comb, without any protecting cover. But the hornets and their relatives, called *Vespa*, build round or pear-shaped nests with several stories of combs. The outside covering is made of many layers of paper, and will shed water.

Social wasps build their nests in all sorts of places. Single combs can be found in a snug shelter under a porch roof or rafter. Others are in the open, attached to the limbs of trees, bushes, or even weeds. The single-comb nest hangs attached by a short stalk, much like an upside-down mushroom.

There are two types of American hornets and yellow jackets. One has a long face; the other has a short one. The long-faced wasps hang their nests from trees, bushes, roofs, bridge timbers, and overhanging rocks. The short-faced kind builds in the ground or in stumps.

Unlike a bee colony in a hive, a wasp colony lasts only through the summer. Most wasps store no food, and in the fall all the members die except a crop of young queens. These are the wasps which will be the mothers of new colonies. One spring day a queen comes out of the nook or crevice where she has slept through the winter, and begins to build a new home. First she makes a few cells shaped like cones, and surrounds them with a wall made of two or three layers of paper. In each cell she lays an egg. The larvae which hatch from the eggs are plump, soft grubs. The queen tends them carefully. Every day for about two weeks, she chews up the bodies of insects and brings them to the grubs for food. At last the larvae spin tough cocoons around themselves. Then they go through a change called *pupation*, and in about ten days they come out of the cocoon as full-grown wasps. They are all workers. After that, the queen does nothing except to lay eggs. These eggs all hatch into worker wasps, until in late summer the queen lays some which develop into males and young queens.

Meanwhile, the workers care for the young and make the nest larger. They tear paper away from the inside of the nest wall and add new layers to the outside. A

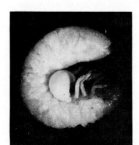

Julian J. Chisholm II

The Korean Digger Larva, *above center,* feeds on the Japanese beetle grub and kills it.

The Digger Wasp was brought into the United States to help control the destructive Japanese beetle.

Julian J. Chisholm II

Polistes Wasps build a co-operative single comb nest, *above*. They lay their eggs in the open rows of paper cells.

USDA

The Mud Dauber Wasp builds its nest in the shape of a mud ball, *above*. Saliva mixed with mud forms the mortar for it.

Cornelia Clarke

Some Mud Wasps build their nests in the shape of organ pipes, *above*. The female lays her eggs in the long tunnels.

L. W. Brownell

A Cross Section of the mud dauber's nest, *above*, shows the tiny, tube-shaped cells where the larvae hatch and grow.

Cornelia Clarke

carry material back and forth. When the nest is finished, the wasp flies out to catch insects for her hungry larvae. Wasps eat caterpillars, spiders, beetles, flies, ants, or other insects. The larva of each type of wasp has a certain insect it prefers. The adults eat nectar and fruit juices, but the young must have spiders or insects, and they like their food alive. The mother wasp usually does not kill her prey, but stings and paralyzes it.

After she stings and paralyzes her victim, the wasp drags it into the nest. Then she goes out for more. When she has collected a large enough supply, she lays an egg on one of the bodies, and seals up the nest. The larva hatches in a few days and finds an ample supply of fresh food. The larva feeds on the insects until grown and then spins its silken cocoon. When the wasp is in the cocoon it is called a *pupa*. It may remain a pupa only two or three weeks, but often it stays that way through the winter. At the end of the pupal stage the full-grown wasp gnaws its way out of the nest.

Scientific Classification. Wasps are insects of the order *Hymenoptera*. The best known of the superfamilies are *Vespoidea* and *Sphecoidea*. *Vespoidea* includes all the social species, some of the parasitic kinds, most of the mason and carpenter wasps, and a few diggers. *Sphecoidea* includes most of the diggers and mud daubers. The hornets, yellow jackets, and *Polistes* are in the family *Vespidae* in the *Vespoidea*. The short-faced hornets of the genus *Vespa* belong to the subgenus *Vespula*. The long-faced kind are *Dolichovespula*.   DALE W. JENKINS

Related Articles in WORLD BOOK include:

Bee	Hornet	Sawfly
Fig (Growing Figs)	Ichneumon Fly	Yellow Jacket

WASSAIL. See CHRISTMAS (In Great Britain).

WASSERMANN, *VAHS er mahn*, **AUGUST VON** (1866-1925), a German physician and bacteriologist, is best known for developing the *Wassermann Test*, a blood test for diagnosing syphilis. A distinguished pupil of Robert Koch and Paul Ehrlich, he performed important research in cancer and tuberculosis.

Wassermann was appointed to a professorship at the University of Berlin in 1901. In 1906, he assumed charge of experimental therapeutics and serum research at the Royal Institute for Infectious Diseases at Berlin. He became director of the Kaiser Wilhelm Institute at Dahlem, Germany, in 1913. He was born at Bamberg, Bavaria, and studied at Erlangen, Munich, Vienna, and Strasbourg universities.   HENRY J. L. MARRIOTT

WASTE DISPOSAL is the process of getting rid of human waste products. People produce *gaseous waste*, such as carbon monoxide from cars; *liquid waste*, such as sewage; and *solid waste*. The almost countless kinds of solid waste include paper and plastic products, glass bottles, aluminum and steel cans, garbage, and junked automobiles. Solid waste is also called *refuse*. If not disposed of properly, it looks ugly, smells foul, and attracts insects, rats, and other animals that spread disease.

This article deals with the disposal of solid waste. For information on gaseous waste, see the WORLD BOOK article on ENVIRONMENTAL POLLUTION. See also the SEWAGE article for information on the disposal of waste matter from sinks and toilets.

People produce millions of tons of solid wastes each year, and the production is increasing rapidly. They also produce more and more wastes that are difficult to handle. For example, tin and steel cans that rust and become part of the soil are being replaced by aluminum

nest of wasps may finally contain thousands of insects —males, females, workers, and young. Worker wasps have wings. Sometimes, when they are well fed, they can lay eggs.

Solitary Wasps. The solitary wasps do not live together in colonies, but in some ways they are even more interesting than the social wasps. They have learned to do so many remarkable things that they seem to think instead of acting by instinct. The social wasps are paper-makers. The solitary wasps are masons, carpenters, and excavators, or diggers. The solitary wasps in one group make homes in the nests of other insects. One amazing thing about most solitary wasps is that they work and sacrifice for their offspring, but they never see them.

There are both potters and stoneworkers among the mason wasps. Some of the potters make mortar out of mud and saliva, and shape dainty mud nests that look like urns. They often fasten two or three little jugs upon one twig. The "mud daubers" work up mud with the saliva, and build their nests in the form of little tube-shaped cells. They plaster these nests on the underside of a porch roof or some other protected place. The stone-workers mix pebbles with the mortar. They build their nests on surfaces of rocks in the open. Carpenter wasps tunnel into the wood of trees or old posts, or bore into the stems of herbs. There are also earth-miner and digger wasps. These wasps dig tunnels running down into the ground.

There are no separate workers among the solitary wasps. The female builds the nest and gathers the food. She uses her strong *mandibles* (jaws) to bore, dig, and cans that stay in their original state for years. Paper packaging that decays and burns easily is being replaced by plastic packaging that decays slowly and gives off gases when burned.

Solid waste from homes, office buildings, and restaurants is called *municipal solid waste*. This article discusses how to dispose of such waste.

Solid waste also comes from industries and farms. For information on these two sources of waste, see the WORLD BOOK article on ENVIRONMENTAL POLLUTION.

Methods of Waste Disposal. Most United States cities and towns have a waste-collecting department or a private firm that gathers refuse from homes and other buildings. Workers haul the refuse away in trucks. Communities use two chief methods to dispose of municipal solid waste: (1) land disposal and (2) incineration.

Land Disposal involves hauling the refuse to an area owned by a community or by a private firm. In the United States, such areas range from unsanitary *open dumps* to properly operated *sanitary landfills*.

Open dumps are a poor method of waste disposal because they cause environmental problems. For example, they can ruin the appearance of an area and provide a home for rats and other animals that spread disease. If garbage is exposed, it rots and smells foul. Most dumps allow some burning, which causes smoke and foul-smelling air. In addition, rain water can drain through refuse and carry harmful substances to streams.

Properly operated sanitary landfills cause little damage to the environment. At such sanitary landfills, the wastes are packed firmly together by tractors and covered with earth each day. The cover of earth prevents insects and rodents from getting into the refuse. Operators of these sites forbid burning. In time, sanitary landfill sites become filled up. Many communities then cover the site for a final time and use the area for tennis courts or other recreational purposes.

Many communities do not operate their sanitary landfills properly. For example, a community may allow burning at the site, or it may cover the site with earth only occasionally. Concern for the environment has caused many communities and states to establish strict laws to control land disposal sites. Many federal agencies work with state boards of health to help communities improve their land disposal methods.

Incineration burns waste products. Incinerators vary in design according to the type of wastes they burn. Many large cities use incinerators because they do not have enough vacant areas for land disposal sites nearby. Large numbers of municipal incinerators lack adequate air pollution control devices. Burning in many of these plants releases gases and solid particles that may harm human health, damage property, and kill plants.

Some homes have small household incinerators or backyard burners that burn trash and garbage produced by the occupants. Many communities prohibit open backyard burning at residences.

Uses of Solid Waste. Many substances in refuse have value. They include glass, wood fiber from paper products, and metal. Scientists have developed ways of recycling many wastes so they can be used again. Extensive recycling of waste materials would significantly reduce the amount of waste that must be burned or buried. See RECYCLING.

The heat from the burning of wastes can also be used.

In some communities, the heat from municipal incinerators is used to produce steam. The steam drives engines that produce electric power.   HARVEY WILKE

See also ENERGY SUPPLY (Solid Wastes); GARBAGE DISPOSER.

WASTEWATER. See SEWAGE.

WAT TYLER'S REBELLION, also called the PEASANTS' REVOLT, was an uprising by English farm laborers in 1381. The peasants objected to the harsh conditions under which they lived, such as forced labor and heavy taxation. An unfair new tax touched off the uprising. During eight days, blacksmith Wat Tyler dominated the movement. It was supported by many small landholders, tradespeople, and skilled workers.

Riots broke out in many parts of England. Mobs destroyed private property and killed many wealthy persons. On June 12, 1381, Tyler and Jack Straw gathered together more than 100,000 angry peasants from Kent and Essex and led them in a march on London. The leaders demanded to see King Richard II. The king was only 14 years old. Richard faced the angry mob alone, because his royal advisers had deserted him. But he could not quiet the rioters, and finally agreed to listen to their demands at Mile-End on June 14.

The rebels demanded an end to serfdom, and a low rental payment on freed lands. They also called for a repeal of oppressive labor laws. The young king agreed to their terms, and most of the mob disbanded. However, Tyler remained with about 30,000 supporters to gain further advantages for his people. He grew bold and demanding. His attitude led to his being killed by the mayor of London. Meanwhile, troops came to support the king, and drove the rebels away. The promises of the king were put aside and the oppression of the peasants continued. However, Wat Tyler's Rebellion inspired other popular movements for freedom and equality in England.   ROBERT S. HOYT

WATAUGA ASSOCIATION was a group of early American settlers. In 1772, they drew up one of the first written constitutions in North America. In 1769, a party of settlers established a colony on the banks of the Watauga River in what is now the state of Tennessee. They thought their settlement fell within the boundaries of the colony of Virginia. But in 1771, the Watauga settlers discovered that their territory lay within the limits of the colony of North Carolina. North Carolina refused to give legal protection to the settlers. The Watauga pioneers decided to keep order by organizing their own government. The leaders of the movement were John Sevier and James Robertson (1742-1814). Robertson was one of the founders of Nashville, Tenn. (originally Fort Nashborough), in the Cumberland Valley.

In 1772, the Watauga group became the first American-born settlers to form a free and independent community. They drew up a document which they called the *Articles of the Watauga Association*. The Articles provided for an executive council, a legislature, a sheriff, and an attorney. In 1776, the Watauga community, known as the Washington District, sent representatives to the assembly of North Carolina. Later, it became part of the state of Tennessee.   JOHN R. ALDEN

WATCH. See NAVY, UNITED STATES (A Typical Day).

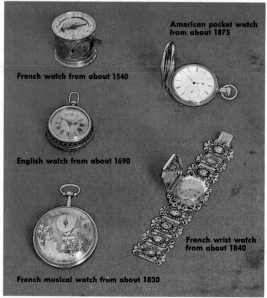

American pocket watch from about 1875

French watch from about 1540

English watch from about 1690

French wrist watch from about 1840

French musical watch from about 1830

Time Museum, Rockford, Ill. (WORLD BOOK photo)

Some Early Watches are shown above. The French watch from about 1540 has only an hour hand. The English watch has a hairspring. The French musical watch tells time by playing a melody. The French wrist watch has a gold and enamel bracelet. The American pocket watch is enclosed in a hinged gold case.

WATCH is a small, portable clock. People use watches to tell time and also wear or carry them as personal accessories. More than 50 million watches are sold in the United States annually.

Some of the first watches were used during the 1500's by town watchmen in Europe. A watchman carried a small clock on a strap to time his rounds of duty. These rounds were called *watches*. Through the years, the small clocks also became known as watches.

Kinds of Watches

Most modern watches are wrist watches. But some watches are designed to be carried in pockets, and others can be mounted in decorative pins, rings, or necklaces. Watches range from plain models costing less than $10 to ones that are decorated with precious stones and cost more than $50,000. Some watches, called *dial watches*, have mechanical hands that show the time by pointing to numbers on a dial. Other watches are called *electronic display watches*. Most electronic display watches are *digital watches*, which show the time in lighted digits.

Many watches give information in addition to the passing of hours and minutes. Most also show the passage of seconds. Many show the day of the week, the date, and the year. Some watches sound an alarm at any desired time. Various electronic display watches have tiny calculators for solving mathematical problems.

How Watches Work

Every watch has two main parts, the *case* and the *works*, or *movement*, inside the case. The works shows the time, provides power to run the watch, and regulates the speed of the watch. Watches differ according to

how their works perform these functions. This article divides watches into two groups, *dial* and *electronic display*, based on how they show the time.

Dial Watches use the traditional method of showing time by hands on the watch face. There are two kinds of dial watches, *mechanical watches* and *electric watches*.

Mechanical Watches are powered by a coiled spring called a *mainspring*. In many watches, the mainspring is wound by turning a screw that extends outside the watch case. Other watches, called *self-winding watches*, contain a weight mechanism that winds the mainspring automatically when the watch is moved about. As the watch runs, the mainspring unwinds. Its motion turns several tiny gear wheels that are connected in a series called the *train*. A watch's hands are attached to individual gear wheels that turn at specific speeds. The speed of each wheel is partially determined by a mechanism called the *escapement*.

The escapement includes an *escape wheel*, a *balance wheel*, a *balance spring*, and an *escape lever*. The escape wheel is connected to the train and turns when the watch runs. It also transmits energy to the balance wheel, which is the timekeeping device in the watch. The balance spring, also called the *hairspring*, makes the balance wheel *oscillate* (swing back and forth) at a specific frequency. Most balance wheels oscillate 5 times a second. Each forward swing of the balance wheel moves the escape lever. Two hooks called *pallets* —one at each end of the lever—catch on the escape wheel. This action stops the escape wheel and makes the ticking sound in the watch. When the balance wheel swings back, the lever shifts and allows the escape wheel to turn slightly. This process regulates the speeds of the escape wheel and the wheels in the train.

Many mechanical watches have more than 100 parts. In the best watches, the parts are finished by hand to assure accuracy and durability. In addition, the pallets and various other parts are made from tiny, hard jewels, such as natural or synthetic rubies, to reduce friction. Most good watches contain from 17 to 23 jewels.

Watches called *pin-lever watches* make up about 70 per cent of the watches sold in the United States. These watches have metal pins instead of pallets on the escape lever. Pin-lever watches contain no jewels, and their parts are not hand finished. They are inexpensive, but they wear out sooner than do finer watches.

Electric Watches get their power from a tiny battery. Electric watches with a balance wheel were first sold in the United States in the late 1950's. A battery-powered watch introduced in the 1960's contains a tuning fork instead of a balance wheel. Electricity from the battery activates the tuning fork, which vibrates 360 times a second. This vibrating motion makes the train move. An *indexing mechanism* translates the number of vibrations into the correct speeds for the gear wheels. Watches with a tuning fork make a humming sound. They are accurate to within 60 seconds a month.

Another battery-powered watch, called the *quartz-based watch*, was introduced in the early 1970's. This watch has a vibrating bar of quartz crystal instead of a tuning fork. Quartz-based watches also contain an electronic integrated circuit that is printed on a tiny piece of material called a *chip* (see ELECTRONICS [picture: Devices Used in Microelectronics]). The circuit translates the vibrations of the crystal into seconds, min-

A Mechanical Watch has hands that show the time on a dial face. In the photo at the far right, the back of the case of a mechanical watch has been removed to show some of the works. The winding knob winds the mainspring, which powers the watch. The balance wheel regulates the watch's speed, and the sweep-seconds wheel turns the second hand.

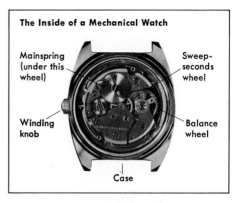

The Inside of a Mechanical Watch

Mainspring (under this wheel) — Sweep-seconds wheel — Winding knob — Balance wheel — Case

An Electronic Display Watch shows the time in digits or with hands that are formed electronically. The photo at the far right shows the inside of a digital watch from the back. Energy from the battery makes the quartz crystal vibrate. The integrated circuit translates the number of vibrations into time information for display on the face of the watch.

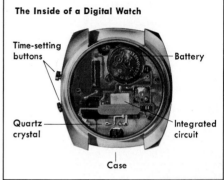

The Inside of a Digital Watch

Time-setting buttons — Battery — Quartz crystal — Integrated circuit — Case

Westclox, a Talley Industries Company (WORLD BOOK photos)

utes, hours, and calendar dates. Then the circuit activates a motor that moves the watch hands at the correct speeds. Most quartz crystals vibrate 32,768 times a second, and quartz-based watches are accurate to within 60 seconds a year.

Electronic Display Watches are quartz based and work much the same way as quartz-based dial watches. However, electronic display watches have no moving parts. Their circuits translate the time information directly into an electronic display on the watch face. There are two main kinds of displays, *liquid crystal displays* (LCD's) and *light-emitting diode displays* (LED's).

Liquid Crystal Displays use digits formed from a liquid crystal substance that reflects the light around it. In some LCD watches, the liquid forms hands, instead of digits, to indicate the time. A liquid crystal display requires little power from the battery and therefore appears continuously. But the display cannot be seen clearly in dim light. Some LCD watches have a light that can be turned on to illuminate the face. Others use tritium, a radioactive substance that produces a greenish glow, to light the background. Tritium makes the display visible even in complete darkness.

Light-Emitting Diode Displays have digits shaped from electronic devices called *diodes*, which give off light. The diodes can be seen easily in poor light but are not clear in bright light. Diodes also require more power than do LCD's. To save power, LED watches show the time only when the wearer turns on the display.

History

The first watches may have been made in Italy during the 1400's. But Peter Henlein, a German locksmith, has traditionally been credited with making the first watch. In the early 1500's, Henlein invented a mainspring to power clocks. Until then, clocks had been driven by falling weights and had to stand upright for the weights to operate. Mainsprings enabled clockmakers to produce small, portable clocks. Watchmaking soon spread to England, France, and Switzerland.

The earliest watches were heavy and inaccurate. They weighed so much that they had to be suspended from a cord or chain and worn around the neck or hanging from a belt. Early watches had only an hour hand, and their cases were spherical or drum-shaped. Unusual shapes, including skulls and crosses, became popular during the mid-1600's.

Many watches had a minute hand by the late 1600's, but a hand for the seconds did not become common until the 1900's. The balance spring and escape lever mechanisms had been developed by the late 1700's.

During the late 1600's, watches became small and light enough to fit into a pocket of a jacket or vest. These *pocket watches* were the most popular style of watch for more than 200 years. Wrist watches became common in the late 1800's, but they were designed for women only. During World War I (1914-1918), soldiers realized that wrist watches were more convenient than pocket watches. As a result, wrist watches soon became accepted as masculine accessories. Electric dial watches were introduced in the 1950's, and electronic display watches appeared in the 1970's.   WILLIAM GOWEN

See also CHRONOMETER; CLOCK; SWITZERLAND (Manufacturing).

WATCH TOWER BIBLE AND TRACT SOCIETY. See JEHOVAH'S WITNESSES.

WATER

Lawrence Smith, Joe Munroe: Photo Researchers

WATER is the most common substance on earth. It covers more than 70 per cent of the earth's surface. It fills the oceans, rivers, and lakes, and is in the ground and in the air we breathe. Water is everywhere.

Without water, there can be no life. Every living thing—plants, animals, and man—must have water to live. In fact, every living thing consists mostly of water. Your body is about two-thirds water. A chicken is about three-fourths water, and a pineapple is about four-fifths water. Most scientists believe that life itself began in water—in the salty water of the sea. The salty taste of our blood, sweat, and tears suggests that this might be true.

Ever since the world began, water has been shaping the earth. Rain hammers at the land and washes the soil into rivers. The oceans pound against the shores, chiseling cliffs and carrying away land. Rivers knife through rock, carve steep canyons, and build up land where they empty into the sea. Glaciers plow valleys and cut down mountains.

Luna B. Leopold, the contributor of this article, is senior research hydrologist of the U.S. Geological Survey.

Water helps keep the earth's climate from getting too hot or too cold. Land absorbs and releases heat from the sun quickly. But the oceans absorb and release the sun's heat slowly. So breezes from the oceans bring warmth to the land in winter and coolness in summer.

Throughout history, water has been man's slave—and his master. Great civilizations have risen where water supplies were plentiful. They have fallen when these supplies failed. Men have killed one another for a muddy water hole. They have worshiped rain gods, and prayed for life-giving rain. Often, when rains have failed to come, crops have withered and starvation has spread across a land. Sometimes the rains have fallen too heavily and too suddenly. Then rivers have overflowed their banks, drowning everything and everyone in their paths.

Today, more than ever, water is both slave and master to man. We use water in our homes for cleaning, cooking, bathing, and carrying away wastes. We use water to irrigate dry farmlands so we can grow more food. Our factories use more water than any other material. We use the water in rushing rivers and thundering waterfalls to produce electricity.

Inland Steel Co.; George Holton, Benschneider, Photo Researchers; WORLD BOOK photo

Our demand for water is constantly increasing. Every year, there are more people in the world. Factories turn out more and more products, and need more and more water. We live in a world of water. But almost all of it —about 97 per cent—is in the oceans. This water is too salty to be used for drinking, farming, and manufacturing. Only about 3 per cent of the world's water is *fresh* (unsalty). Most of this water is not easily available to man because it is locked in glaciers and icecaps. By 1980, the world demand for fresh water will be twice what it was in the 1960's. But there will still be enough to meet man's needs.

There is as much water on earth today as there ever was—or ever will be. Almost every drop of water we use finds its way to the oceans. There, it is evaporated by the sun. It then falls back to the earth as rain. Water is used and reused over and over again. It is never used up.

Although the world as a whole has plenty of fresh water, some regions have a water shortage. Rain does not fall evenly over the earth. Some regions are always too dry, and others too wet. A region that usually gets enough rain may suddenly have a serious dry spell, and another region may be flooded with too much rain.

Some regions have a water shortage because the people have managed their supply poorly. People settle where water is plentiful—near lakes and rivers. Cities grow, and factories spring up. The cities and factories dump their wastes into the lakes and rivers, turning them into sewers. Then the people look for new sources of water. Shortages also occur because some cities do not make full use of their supply. They have plenty of water, but they do not have enough storage tanks and distribution pipes to meet the people's needs.

As man's demand for water grows and grows, he will have to make better and better use of his supply. The more he learns about water, the better he will be able to meet this challenge.

This article tells broadly about water. It discusses water's importance to civilization and to life itself. It describes the nature of water. For a discussion of man's water problems and how he uses and abuses his water supply, see WATER POLLUTION. Separate WORLD BOOK articles, including CLIMATE, CONSERVATION, LAKE, OCEAN, RAIN, and RIVER, provide further details about the broad subject of water.

Every plant, animal, and human being needs water to stay alive. This is because all the life processes—from taking in food to getting rid of wastes—require water. But man depends on water for more than just to stay alive. We also need it for our way of life. We need water in our homes—to brush our teeth, cook food, and wash dishes. We need water in our factories—to manufacture almost everything from automobiles to zippers. We need water for irrigation—to raise crops in regions that do not get enough rain.

Water in Living Things. Every *organism* (living thing) consists mostly of water. Your body is about 65 per cent water. So is that of a mouse. An elephant and an ear of corn are about 70 per cent water. A potato and an earthworm are about 80 per cent water. A tomato is about 95 per cent water.

All living things need a lot of water to carry out their life processes. Plants, animals, and human beings must take in *nutrients* (food substances). Watery solutions help dissolve these nutrients and carry them to all parts of an organism. Through chemical reactions, the organism turns the nutrients into energy, or into materials it needs to grow or to repair itself. These chemical reactions can take place only in a watery solution. Finally, the organism needs water to carry away waste products.

Every living thing must keep its water supply near normal, or it will die. A man can live without food for more than a month, but he can live without water for only about a week. If his body loses more than 20 per cent of its normal water content, he will die painfully. A man must take in about 2½ quarts (2.4 liters) of water a day. It can be in the form of the water or beverages he drinks, or the water in the food he eats.

Water in Our Homes. In our homes, we use far more water than the amount we need simply to stay alive. We require water for cleaning, cooking, bathing, and carrying away wastes. For many people, such water is a luxury. Millions of homes in Asia, Africa, and South America have no running water. The people must haul water up by hand from the village well, or carry it in jars from pools and rivers far from their homes.

The United States has more homes with kitchen faucets and flush toilets than any other country. Every American uses an average of about 70 gallons (260 liters) of water a day in his home. It takes about 3 gallons (11 liters) of water to flush a toilet. It takes 30 to 40 gallons (110 to 150 liters) to take a bath, and each minute under a shower takes at least 5 gallons (19 liters). It takes up to 10 gallons (38 liters) of water to wash the dishes, and up to 30 gallons (110 liters) to run an automatic washing machine.

Water for Irrigation. Most of the plants that man raises need great quantities of water. For example, it takes 115 gallons (435 liters) of water to grow enough wheat to bake a loaf of bread. Man raises most of his crops in areas that have plenty of rain. But to raise enough food for his needs, man must also irrigate dry areas. The rainfall that crops use to grow is not considered a water use, because the water does not come from a country's supply. Irrigation is a water use because the water is drawn from rivers, lakes, or wells.

The water a nation uses for irrigation is important to its water supply because irrigation is a *consumptive use* of water. Plants take in water through their roots. They then pass it out through their leaves into the air as a gas called *water vapor*. Winds carry away the vapor, and the liquid water is gone. On the other hand, the use of water in our homes is a *nonconsumptive use*. Nearly all the water is carried by sewer pipes back to rivers, and can be used again.

The United States uses about 110 billion gallons (416 billion liters) of water a day for irrigation. This is enough water to fill a lake 5 miles (8 kilometers) long, 1 mile (1.6 kilometers) wide, and 100 feet (30 meters) deep. About 41 per cent of all the water used in the United States is for irrigation. For a discussion of irrigation systems, see the article IRRIGATION.

Water for Industry. Industry uses more water than any other material. It takes about 270 tons of water to make a ton of steel and about 250 tons of water to make a ton of paper. Manufacturers use about 10 gallons of water to refine 1 gallon (3.8 liters) of gasoline or to brew 1 gallon of beer. Factories in the United States draw about 140 billion gallons (530 billion liters) of water every day from wells, rivers, or lakes. This total is about 52 per cent of all water used in the country. Many factories also buy water from city water systems.

Industry uses water in many ways. It uses water for cleaning fruits and vegetables before canning and freezing them. It uses water as a raw material in soft drinks, canned foods, and many other products. It uses water to air-condition and clean factories. But most of the water used by industry is for cooling. For example, water cools the steam used in producing electric power from fuel. It cools the hot gases produced in refining oil, and the hot steel made by steel mills.

Although industry uses a lot of water, only about 2 per cent of it is consumed. Most of the water used for cooling is piped back to the rivers or lakes from which it is taken. The water consumed by industry is the water added to soft drinks and other products, and the small amount of water that turns to vapor in the cooling processes.

Water for Power. Man also uses water to produce electric power to light his homes and to run his factories. Electric power stations burn coal or other fuel to turn water into steam. The steam supplies the energy to run machines that produce electricity. Hydroelectric power stations use the energy of falling water from waterfalls and dams to produce electricity. See WATER POWER; ELECTRIC POWER.

Water for Transportation and Recreation. After man learned to build crude small boats, he began using rivers and lakes to carry himself and his goods. Later, he built larger boats and sailed the ocean in search of new lands and new trade routes. Today, man still depends on water transportation to carry such heavy and bulky products as machinery, coal, grain, and oil. See TRANSPORTATION.

Man builds most of his recreation areas along lakes, rivers, and seas. People enjoy water sports, such as swimming, fishing, and sailing, and the beauty of a quiet lake, a thundering waterfall, or a roaring surf.

U.S. WATER BUDGET

On the average, 4,200,000,000,000 gallons (15,900,000,000,000 liters) of precipitation falls on the United States every day. About 70 per cent of this moisture returns directly to the air by evaporation, or is used by plants where it falls. People use about 6 per cent of the precipitation.

Precipitation returned to the air by evaporation or used where it falls by plants 70%

Industrial use 3.12%

Irrigation use 2.46%

City use 0.42%

Precipitation returned unused to the sea 24%

WORLD BOOK diagram by Murrie-White & Associates, Inc.

Ford Motor Co.

Automobile Manufacturing

KVP Sutherland Paper Co.

Papermaking

Grant Heilman

Irrigation

WORLD BOOK photo by E. F. Hoppe

Washing and Bathing

Chicago Fire Dept.

Fire Fighting

The waters of the earth move continuously from the oceans, to the air, to the land, and back to the oceans again. The sun's heat evaporates water from the oceans. The water rises as invisible vapor, and falls back to the earth as rain, snow, or some other form of moisture. This moisture is called *precipitation* (pronounced *prih SIP uh TAY shuhn*). Most precipitation drops back directly into the oceans. The remainder falls on the rest of the earth. In time, this water also returns to the sea, and the cycle starts again. This unending circulation of the earth's waters is called the *water cycle* or *hydrologic cycle*.

Because of nature's water cycle, there is as much water on earth today as there ever was—or ever will be. Water changes only from one form to another, and moves from one place to another. The water you bathed in last night might have flowed in Russia's Volga River last month. Or perhaps Alexander the Great drank it more than 2,000 years ago.

The Waters of the Earth. The earth has a tremendous amount of water, but almost all of it is in the oceans. The oceans cover about 70 per cent of the earth's surface. They contain about 97 per cent of all the water on earth, and are the source of most precipitation that falls to earth. Ocean water is too salty to be used for drinking, agriculture, or industry. But the salt is left behind during evaporation, and the precipitation that falls to earth is sweet, unsalty water.

Only about 3 per cent of the water on earth is fresh water—and most of it is not easily available to man. It includes water locked in glaciers and icecaps, more than 2 per cent of the earth's water. About half of 1 per cent of the earth's water is beneath the earth's surface. Rivers and lakes contain only about one-fiftieth of 1 per cent of the earth's water.

Water in the Air. At one time or another, all the water on earth enters the air, or atmosphere, as water vapor. This vapor becomes the life-giving rain that falls to the earth. Yet, the atmosphere contains only one-thousandth of 1 per cent of the earth's water.

Moisture in the air comes mostly from evaporation. The sun's heat sucks up water from land, lakes, rivers, and, especially, the oceans. About 85 per cent of the vapor in the air comes from the oceans. Plants also add moisture. After plants have drawn water from the ground through their roots, they pass it out through their leaves as vapor in a process called *transpiration*. For example, a birch tree gives off about 70 gallons (260 liters) of water a day. Corn gives off about 4,000 gallons per acre (37,000 liters per hectare) daily. See EVAPORATION; TRANSPIRATION.

THE WATER CYCLE

This diagram traces the never-ending circulation of the earth's water as it makes its long journey from the oceans, to the air, to the land, and back to the oceans again.

WORLD BOOK diagram by George Suyeoka

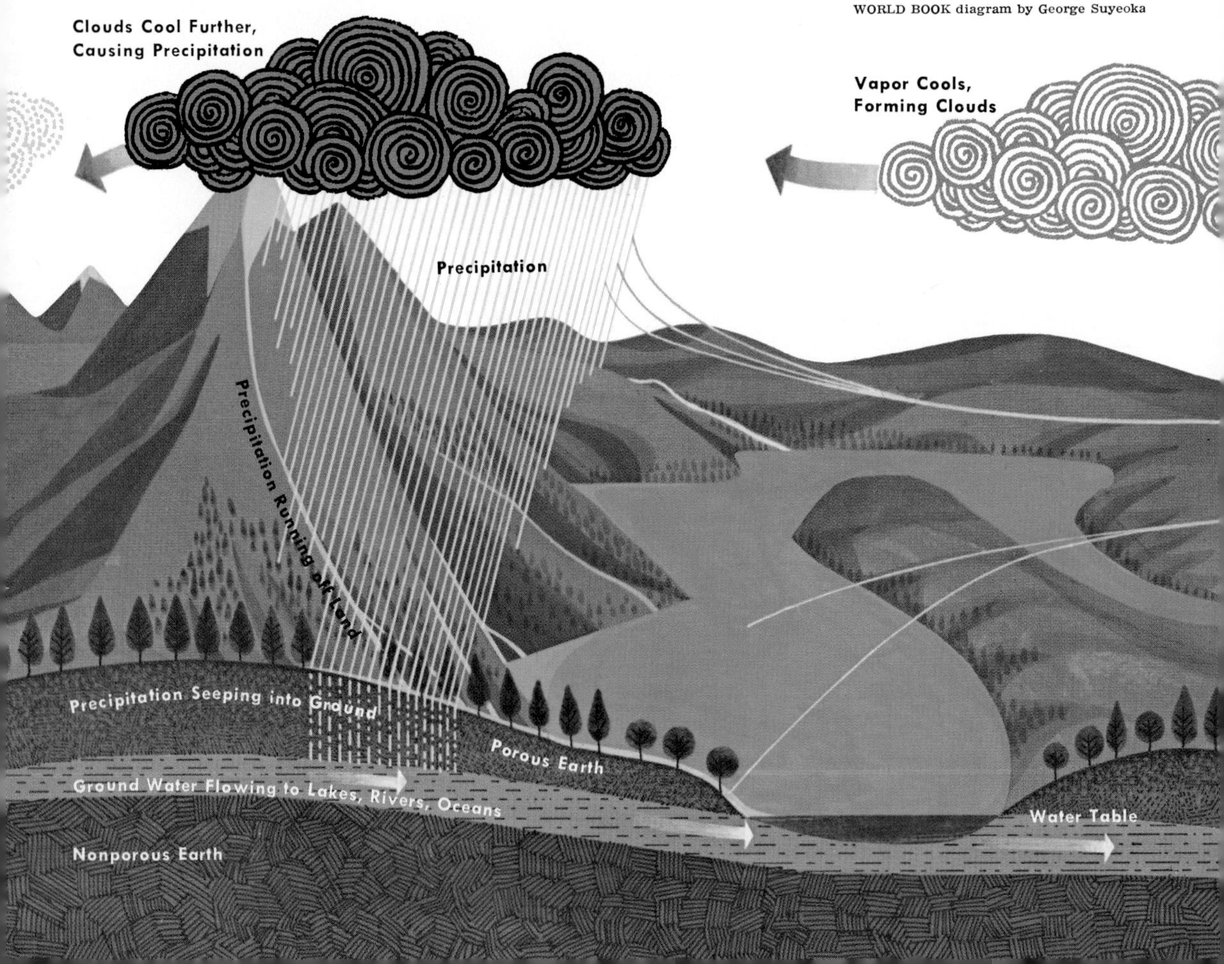

Clouds Cool Further, Causing Precipitation

Vapor Cools, Forming Clouds

Precipitation

Precipitation Running off Land

Precipitation Seeping into Ground

Porous Earth

Ground Water Flowing to Lakes, Rivers, Oceans

Water Table

Nonporous Earth

Precipitation. Vapor is carried by the air moving over the earth. The moisture-filled air cools wherever it is forced up by colder air or by mountains or hills. As the air cools, the vapor *condenses* into droplets of liquid water, forming clouds. The droplets fall to the earth as rain. If the vapor is chilled enough, it condenses in ice crystals, and falls as snow.

About 75 per cent of the precipitation falls back directly on the oceans. Some of the rest evaporates immediately—from the surface of the ground, from rooftops, from puddles in the streets. Some of it runs off the land to rivers. From the rivers, it flows back to the sea. The rest of the precipitation soaks into the earth and becomes part of the *ground water* supply. Ground water moves slowly through the ground to the rivers and returns to the sea. This movement of ground water to rivers keeps the rivers flowing during periods without rain. See Rain; Snow; Weather; Ground Water.

How Water Shapes the Earth. Water changes the face of the earth as it moves through the great water cycle. It wears down mountains, carves valleys, cuts deep canyons, builds deltas, and straightens coastlines.

During precipitation, some water falls on highlands and mountains. The force of gravity pulls the water downhill. As the water flows to lower levels, it *erodes* (wears away) the soil and rocks. In this way, after many thousands of years, mountains are worn down. The water that runs off the land during precipitation cuts small channels. The small channels drain into larger channels. The larger channels drain into still larger ones, until finally the water empties into the main stream that runs to the sea. The water carries to the sea the materials it has eroded from the land. See River.

Some of the precipitation that falls is captured in mountain glaciers. As the glaciers slide down mountainsides, they cut the mountains into sharp and jagged peaks. See Glacier.

The ocean also changes the face of the land. As waves pound against the shore, they cut away land and leave steep cliffs. Much of the material the waves wear away from the land is carried far out to sea. Some piles up near shore in sand bars. For more information on how water shapes the earth, see Earth (How the Earth Changes); Erosion; Ocean (The Changing Shoreline).

How Water Began. The question of how water began on earth is part of the question of how the earth itself began. Many scientists believe the earth was formed from materials that came from the hot sun. These materials included the elements that make up water. As the earth cooled and grew solid, water was trapped in rocks in the earth's crust. The water was gradually released, and the ocean basins filled with water. Other scientists have other ideas about how the earth and water began. For a discussion of these ideas, see the articles Earth (How the Earth Began) and Ocean (How the Oceans Began).

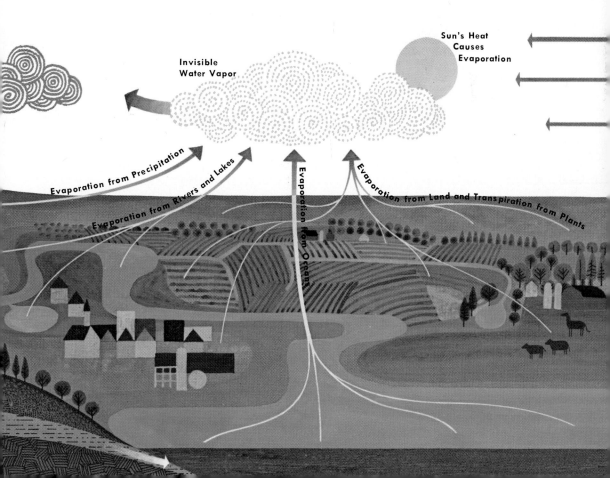

Sun's Heat Causes Evaporation

Invisible Water Vapor

Evaporation from Precipitation

Evaporation from Rivers and Lakes

Evaporation from Ocean

Evaporation from Land and Transpiration from Plants

Shortages of fresh water have troubled man throughout history. Today, they trouble him more than ever because his demand for water is growing rapidly. Many people fear that the world does not have enough water to meet man's needs. Yet the world has—and always will have—the same amount of water it has always had. All the water we use passes through the great water cycle and can be used again and again.

The total amount of water on earth is enough for man's needs. But water is distributed unevenly. Some regions suffer a constant *drought* (lack of rain). Other regions generally have plenty of water, but they may be struck by drought. In addition, man has created many water problems by mismanaging his supply.

World Distribution of Water. The earth has an enormous amount of water—about 326 million cubic miles (1.4 billion cubic kilometers) of it. In a cubic mile, there are more than a million million—1,000,000,000,000—gallons, or 3.8 million million liters. But 97 per cent of this water is in the salty oceans, and more than 2 per cent is in glaciers and icecaps. The rest totals less than 1 per cent. Most of this water is underground, and the remainder includes the water in lakes, rivers, springs, pools, and ponds. It also includes rain and snow, and the vapor in the air.

A country's water supply is determined by its precipitation. In regions with plenty of precipitation year after year, there is plenty of water in lakes, rivers, and underground reservoirs.

The earth as a whole receives plentiful rain. If this rain fell evenly, all the land would receive about 26 inches (66 centimeters) a year. But the rain is distributed unevenly. For example, over 400 inches (1,000 centimeters) drenches northeastern India every year. But northern Chile may not get rain for years.

Generally, the world's most heavily populated areas receive enough rain for their needs. These areas include most of Europe, Southeast Asia, the Eastern United States, India, much of China, and northwestern Russia. But about half the earth's land does not get enough rain. These dry areas include most of Asia, central Australia, most of northern Africa, and the Middle East.

The United States has plenty of water. It averages about 30 inches (76 centimeters) of rain annually. This total is large, but it is distributed unevenly. Over 135 inches (343 centimeters) soaks parts of western Washington each year, but Nevada averages only about 7 inches (18 centimeters). Most states east of the Mississippi get 30 to 50 inches (76 to 130 centimeters) of precipitation a year—more than enough to grow crops. But large regions in the West get less than 10 inches (25 centimeters). There, only a little grass and shrubs can grow without irrigation.

Canada's annual precipitation is also distributed unevenly. In the southeast, it ranges from 30 inches (76 centimeters) in central Ontario to 55 inches (140 centimeters) in eastern Nova Scotia. From 14 to 20 inches (36 to 51 centimeters) of precipitation falls in most of the Prairie Provinces. Parts of the west coast get over 100 inches (250 centimeters).

Water Shortages. Many regions of the world have a constant water shortage because they never get enough rain. But even a region that normally has enough rain may suddenly have a dry year or several dry years. The climates in regions that receive only light rainfall are especially changeable. Such regions can have a series of destructive dry years. In the 1930's, one of the worst droughts in United States history struck the Southwest, an already dry region. Winds whipped the dry soil into gigantic dust storms, and most of the region became known as the *Dust Bowl*. Hundreds of farm families had to leave their homes. See Dust Bowl.

Periods of low rainfall alternate with periods of high rainfall from year to year and from place to place. During the 1960's, for example, drought struck the Northeastern United States, and parts of China, Brazil, Nicaragua, Portugal, and other countries. Meanwhile, floodwaters spilled over the land in the Midwestern and Western United States, and in parts of Italy, Mexico, Honduras, and other countries.

Many regions have water shortages because the people have not prepared for a period of less than normal rainfall. These shortages could have been prevented if the people had built pipelines, storage tanks, and other facilities to carry them through a drought.

The United States is especially rich in water. But every year, a number of U.S. communities must ration their water. As a result, many people fear that the country is running out of water. The United States as a whole has as much water today as the land had when Christopher Columbus sailed to the New World. But rainfall patterns change. In addition, the demand for water is increasing faster in the United States than in any other country. More and more Americans want air conditioners, garbage disposers, automatic washers, and an extra bathroom. Industry also demands more water as production rises. When drought strikes a water-hungry U.S. community, the effects can be severe—especially if the people are not prepared.

During the 1960's, rainfall in the Northeastern United States fell below normal for several years. Many cities had to restrict the use of water. New York City suffered especially, because it is so heavily populated. To save water, people turned off their air conditioners and let their lawns wither. Restaurants tried not to serve water to customers. The city was declared a disaster area. New York City's troubles came about because the city did not have enough storage tanks, distribution lines, and other facilities for a long period of light rainfall.

Water Conservation. Throughout history, man has attempted to increase his water supply by trying to "make rain." He has prayed to rain gods and performed rain dances (see Rain Dance). He has sprayed the clouds with chemicals to make them release their moisture (see Rain Making). Man also has always looked to the sea as a source of water (see the section *Fresh Water from the Sea*). But often, man does not need more water. He only needs to manage the supply better.

Many water problems in the United States have arisen because the country has had a plentiful and easily available water supply. Water has been cheap, and people have been careless and wasteful. They have dumped untreated sewage and other wastes into rivers

THE UNEQUAL DISTRIBUTION OF PRECIPITATION

■ Always Enough Rain ■ Usually Not Enough Rain
■ Usually Enough Rain ■ Never Enough Rain

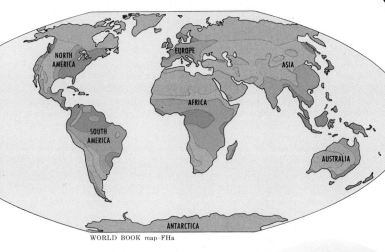

WORLD BOOK map-FHa

Carl Frank, Photo Researchers

Too Much Rain falls in many tropical regions every year, producing steaming jungles.

Charbonnier, Photo Researchers

Too Little Rain falls on about half the earth's land, producing deserts and near-deserts.

Sudden Downpours can drench regions that seldom get enough rain, causing landslides.

Wide World

Drought can strike regions that usually get enough rain, baking the moist earth dry.

Rene Burri, Magnum

and lakes, spoiling the water (see WATER POLLUTION). In most U.S. cities, people pay about 45 cents per 1,000 gallons (12 cents per 1,000 liters) of water. In New York City, which has had severe water shortages, water is free to many people. Many landlords pay a fixed fee, and a tenant can let the water run as long as he likes. Neither he nor the landlord pays a penny extra.

The supply of cheap, easily available water is shrinking in the United States. The development of new supplies will become more and more costly. It will then be cheaper to reuse water from old supplies. For example, steel companies use great quantities of water for cooling. As costs rise, they may use a small amount of water over and over in a circulating cooling system.

Sewage can be treated and turned into usable water. Such water is used today, and will be used more in the future. Many Texas communities water their lawns with treated sewage water. In Santee, Calif., people swim and fish in lakes of purified sewage water.

Personal Responsibility. A country's problems are caused by the attitudes and habits of all the people. People must care if lakes and rivers are spoiled with wastes, or if water is wasted. Water can be conserved only if many people become interested in learning about water problems. A person should begin by learning where his city gets its water, and how it is treated, used, and disposed of. He should find out how his city plans to meet future water demands. After he learns about his city's water situation, he can better understand his country's water problems. Such understanding by many people will help the nation develop a good water conservation program.

99

When you turn on a faucet, you expect clean, pure water to flow out. You also expect your city to have plenty of water for its industries, for fighting fires, and for cleaning streets. The job of supplying a modern city with water is tremendous. First of all, there must be sources of plentiful water to meet the demands of a growing city. Then, the water must be purified. Next, it must be piped into every house, office building, factory, and hotel in the city. Finally, the used water must be piped away.

About 21,000 cities and towns in the United States have a public water supply system. These systems serve about 175 million persons, or about 80 per cent of the U.S. population.

Sources of Supply. Cities can draw fresh water from only two sources: (1) rivers and lakes, or (2) the ground. Most U.S. cities, especially those with fewer than 5,000 persons, get their water from underground supplies. Most larger cities get theirs from rivers or lakes. Nationwide, most Americans are served by rivers and lakes.

Rivers and Lakes. Most cities that depend on rivers for their water are located on small rivers—simply because most rivers are small. The amount of water in a river can vary from time to time, depending on rainfall. During a dry spell, a river's water level may fall sharply, especially if it is a small river. Then, a city may not have enough water. For this reason, many cities that de-pend on small rivers store water during rainy periods so they will always have a good supply. Some cities build a dam on the river and store water behind it in a reservoir. Others store water in a water tower or in a pond. See RESERVOIR.

A city that draws its water from a lake has a natural storage reservoir in the lake itself. Lakes are fed by rivers and by waters moving through the ground. During wet spells, lakes store some of the extra water they receive. This extra water helps keep lake levels from dropping below normal during dry periods.

Ground Water. Many cities are not near rivers or lakes large enough for their needs. These cities use water that is stored underground. This water comes from rain that soaks into the ground. As it trickles downward, it fills the spaces between grains of sand and cracks and pores in rocks. In time, the water reaches a layer of rock or other material that is watertight. The water collects above the watertight layer, and the ground becomes *saturated* (soaked). This saturated zone is called an *aquifer*. The top of the zone is called the *water table*. Cities obtain underground water by drilling wells below the water table and pumping up the water. See GROUND WATER; WELL.

Uses of City Water Supplies. Public waterworks supply U.S. cities with a total of about 25 billion gallons (95 billion liters) of water a day. They provide each per-

How Chicago Treats Its Water
This diagram traces the eight-hour course of water as it flows through the Central Water Filtration Plant. The water enters intake cribs (1) about 2½ miles (4 kilometers) out in Lake Michigan, and flows through tunnels (2) under the lake into the plant's intake basin (3). Water can also enter the plant directly through a shore intake (4). Screens (5) keep out fish, plants, and trash. Pumps (6) lift the water about 20 feet (6 meters) above the lake level, so that it flows by gravity through the filtration processes. Alum, chlorine, lime, fluoride, and other chemicals are added (7), and then thoroughly mixed

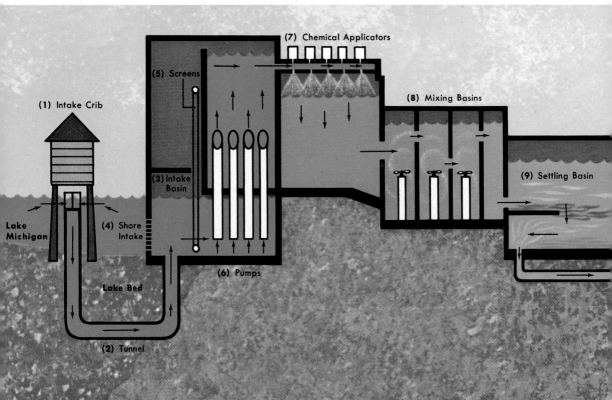

(7) Chemical Applicators

(5) Screens

(8) Mixing Basins

(1) Intake Crib

(3) Intake Basin

(9) Settling Basin

Lake Michigan

(4) Shore Intake

(6) Pumps

Lake Bed

(2) Tunnel

Chicago's Central Water Filtration Plant is the world's largest water treatment plant. It serves almost 3 million persons in Chicago and nearby suburbs, and can produce nearly 1¾ billion gallons (6.6 billion liters) of water a day. The plant is on a 61-acre (25-hectare) man-made peninsula in Lake Michigan.

Bob Brandt

with the water in mixing basins (8). Bacteria, silt, and other impurities stick to the alum, which sinks to the bottom of settling basins (9). The water then trickles through sand and gravel filters (10), which screen out any remaining impurities. The filtered water collects in clear wells (11), and then flows to reservoirs (12), where it receives a final treatment with chlorine and other chemicals. The purified water passes through tunnels (13) to pumping stations (14). The pumping stations send the water through underground mains to homes, factories, and other buildings.

WORLD BOOK diagram by Murrie-White & Associates, Inc.; courtesy Department of Water and Sewers, City of Chicago

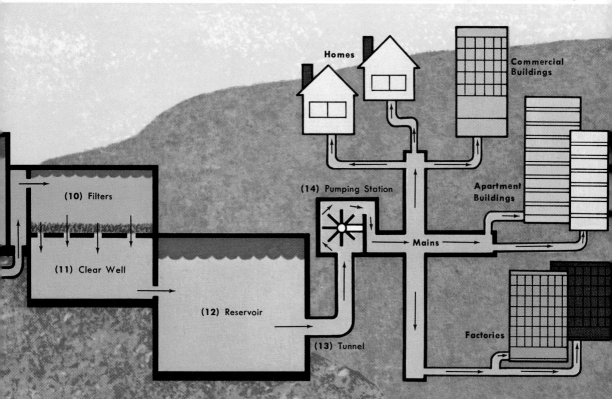

son with the average of 70 gallons (260 liters) a day that he uses in his home. Factories and such businesses as hotels and restaurants also use about 70 gallons of water a day for each person in a city. In addition, city water systems provide water for fighting fires, cleaning streets, and sprinkling park lawns. On the average, these uses total about 10 gallons (38 liters) a day for each city dweller.

Another "use" of a city's water is waste. In many cities, homeowners pay a flat fee, no matter how much water they use. They do not have meters that measure the water they use. If their faucets leak, the water is wasted. Water is also wasted through leaks in a city's underground pipes. Generally, water lost through leakage is at least 20 per cent of a city's water use. Chicago loses about 150 million gallons (568 million liters) of water daily through leakage—about five times as much as all the city's downtown buildings use.

Purifying and Treating Water. People want drinking water that is free of bacteria, sparkling clear, and without an objectionable taste or odor. Water in its natural state seldom has these qualities. So after water is drawn from a source, it is piped into a treatment plant. The plant may put the water through one or several processes, depending on the quality of the untreated water, and on a city's standards. Many cities use three basic processes: (1) coagulation and settling, (2) filtration, and (3) disinfection.

Coagulation and Settling. The *raw* (untreated) water flows into the treatment plant and is mixed with chemicals. Some of these chemicals are *coagulants*. The most widely used coagulant is a fine powder called *aluminum sulfate* or *alum*. In the water, the alum forms tiny jelly-like globs called *flocs*. Bacteria, mud, and other impurities stick to the flocs. The water then passes into a *settling basin*, where the flocs settle to the bottom. Coagulation and settling remove most impurities.

Filtration. The water is then passed through a filter. The filter consists of a bed of sand usually about $2\frac{1}{2}$ feet (76 centimeters) deep on top of a bed of gravel about 1 foot (30 centimeters) deep. As the water trickles down through the filter, any remaining particles are screened out. The water then flows to huge reservoirs for a final treatment that kills bacteria.

Disinfection kills disease-carrying bacteria. Most plants sterilize water by adding a substance called *chlorine*. Chlorine may be added before coagulation and settling, or after filtration. Some plants add it at both times. Most cities chlorinate their water, even if they do not treat it in any other way. See CHLORINE.

Other Processes are also used to remove unpleasant tastes or smells, or to give water special qualities. *Aeration* improves taste and odor. In this process, water is usually sprayed or trickled through the air. The oxygen in the air takes away the bad taste and odor. Many communities have water containing minerals that make it *hard*. Hard water requires lots of soap to make a lather. It also forms deposits on pipes and other equipment. Several processes can be used to *soften* the water (see WATER SOFTENING). Some cities add *lime* to their water to help prevent pipes from rusting. *Activated carbon* helps get rid of fishy odors. Many communities add a substance called *fluoride* to their water to help reduce tooth decay (see FLUORIDATION).

Distributing Water. The treated water flows to a pumping station, where it is pumped into large cast

A SMALL TOWN WATER SYSTEM

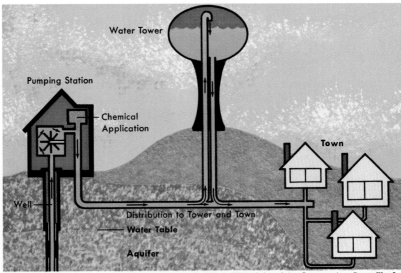

Chicago Bridge & Iron Company

Water Tower

Pumping Station

Chemical Application

Town

Well

Distribution to Tower and Town

Water Table

Aquifer

WORLD BOOK diagram by Murrie-White & Associates, Inc.; courtesy SyncroFlo, Inc.

Most small U.S. towns get water by drilling wells and pumping up underground water. The water is chemically treated, and then pumped to consumers. Most towns also pump water into tall water towers, *left*. These tanks provide storage, and help keep water pressure high at all times. When water is released from the tanks, the force of gravity distributes it through the piping system.

HOW NEW YORK CITY GETS ITS WATER

Almost all of New York City's water comes from storage reservoirs 25 to 125 miles (40 to 201 kilometers) away. These reservoirs are formed by damming rivers. The water flows by gravity through aqueducts to distribution reservoirs in and near the city. The number after each reservoir shows capacity in billions of gallons. One billion gallons equal 3.8 billion liters.

Labels on map:

NEW YORK
MASSACHUSETTS
Schoharie Reservoir (20)
Shandaken Tunnel
Cannonsville Reservoir (97)
Pepacton Reservoir (144)
Esopus Creek
East Delaware Tunnel
Ashokan Reservoir (131)
West Delaware Tunnel
Neversink Reservoir (36)
Rondout Reservoir (50)
Neversink Tunnel
Delaware River
Hudson River
Delaware Aqueduct
PENNSYLVANIA
CONNECTICUT
Catskill Aqueduct
Hudson River Pumping Station
West Branch Reservoir (13)
Croton Falls Reservoir (30)
New Croton Reservoir (24)
Cross River Reservoir (11)
New Croton Aqueduct
Kensico Reservoir (31)
Old Croton Aqueduct
Long Island Sound
NEW JERSEY
Hill View Reservoir (1)
Jerome Park Reservoir (¾)
LONG ISLAND
Central Park Reservoir (1)
NEW YORK CITY
Silver Lake Reservoir (½)
STATEN ISLAND
Richmond Tunnel
Atlantic Ocean

WORLD BOOK map by George Suyeoka

iron pipes called *mains*. The mains run beneath the streets. They carry water to every fire hydrant, and connect with smaller pipes that lead to every home, office building, and restaurant. The pumping station sends the water into the mains under enough pressure to carry it to every faucet. This pressure is usually so high that you cannot hold back the water by putting your finger under a fully opened faucet.

Sometimes the demand for water may be too great for the pressure a pumping station can supply. Then, water may only trickle from the faucets. This can happen on a hot summer day when everyone in the neighborhood is watering his lawn, filling the backyard pool, or taking a shower. The pressure may also fall when a large amount of water is used to fight a big fire. Most cities pump water into storage tanks to help keep their water pressure high at all times. The tanks are built on hills, or they are tall water towers. When water is released from these tanks, gravity pulls the water downward, giving it the pressure to rush through the mains.

Disposing of Used Water. Most of the water in our homes is used to carry away wastes. This water, and the wastes it carries, is called *sewage*. Factories also use water to wash away such industrial wastes as acids and greases. In most U.S. cities, a piping system under the streets carries away the sewage from homes, factories, hotels, and other buildings. This system is called a *sewerage system*.

Sewage has a bad odor. But more important, it contains disease-producing bacteria. Most cities have treatment plants that clean sewage water and kill the bacteria in it. The purified water can then be dumped safely into a river or lake. To learn how sewage is purified, see SEWAGE.

About 89 per cent of the sewage in the United States undergoes some type of sewage treatment. The remaining 11 per cent of the sewage is dumped untreated into rivers. This dumping of untreated sewage causes serious problems for the cities downstream that take their water from the same rivers.

About 97 per cent of the water on earth is in the salty oceans. In their thirst for water, people have looked longingly throughout history at this endless supply. Today, more than ever, many people believe that desalting ocean water holds the answer to the ever-increasing demand for fresh water.

The salt in seawater is mostly common table salt. A person can safely drink water that contains less than $\frac{1}{2}$ pound of salt to 100 pounds of water, or 0.5 kilogram to every 100 kilograms. But seawater has about 7 times this amount of salt. A person who drinks only seawater will die of thirst because the kidneys cannot get rid of all the salt. The person's body will *dehydrate* (dry out) as it tries to wash out the excess salt. Nor can people use seawater in agriculture or industry. It kills most crops, and quickly rusts most machinery.

People have found many ways to *desalinate* (remove the salt from) seawater. Desalination offers hope of relieving water shortages near seacoasts. But desalination does not hold the answer to all the water problems people face. Even if the oceans contained fresh water, people would still have such problems as pollution and flood control.

In the United States, the federal government and many private companies conduct desalination research. The government's program is carried out chiefly by the Office of Water Research and Technology. It operates desalination testing plants at Roswell, N. Mex., and Wrightsville Beach, N.C. In 1967, a municipally owned desalination plant began providing fresh water for Key West, Fla. The world's largest desalination plant is being built at Yuma, Ariz. This plant, scheduled to begin operation in the early 1980's, will be managed by the U.S. Bureau of Reclamation.

There are three main desalination processes: (1) distillation, (2) electrodialysis, and (3) freezing. Distillation and freezing remove the water from the salt. Electrodialysis takes the salt from the water.

Distillation is the oldest and most common method of turning seawater into fresh water. Most ocean ships use it to obtain drinking water. Seawater can be distilled simply by boiling it in a teapot, and piping the steam into a cool bottle. The steam rises, leaving the salt behind. As the steam cools in the bottle, it condenses into sweet water.

Every day, the sun evaporates millions of tons of water from the ocean's surface. The water vapor then condenses and falls back to earth as fresh water. For centuries, people have copied nature and used the sun's heat to distill seawater. Two thousand years ago, Julius Caesar used solar distillation in Egypt to obtain drinking water for his soldiers. Today, the people of Guam, the Galapagos Islands, and other places still use the sun's heat to distill seawater.

Solar distillation can be done simply by filling a shallow basin with seawater and covering it with a transparent plastic dome, or a sloping sheet of glass. The salt water turns to vapor under the sun's heat. The vapor rises until it hits the underside of the dome or glass, where it condenses. The fresh water runs down into collecting troughs. This type of distillation produces little water. In one day, such a basin in a sunny climate can produce only about 6,500 gallons of water per acre (60,800 liters per hectare) of the basin's area.

Most modern desalting plants use a process called *multistage flash distillation*. This is a type of the age-old method of boiling and condensation. In flash distillation, hot seawater flows into a large chamber in which the pressure is low. The low pressure causes some of the water to *flash* (turn quickly) into steam. The steam is condensed into salt-free water. The seawater passes through several distillation chambers. Often, the final water is so pure that it is tasteless, and some salt must be tossed back in to give it flavor. The desalting plants at the Guantánamo Navy base and Key West, Fla., use this process. They each produce over 2 million gallons (8 million liters) of fresh water a day.

Another distilling process called *forced-circulation vapor-compression* is used by the United States government's Roswell, N.Mex., desalting plant. This plant can produce 1 million gallons (4 million liters) of water a day.

Electrodialysis is used chiefly to desalt *brackish* (slightly salty) ground water. Electrodialysis is based on

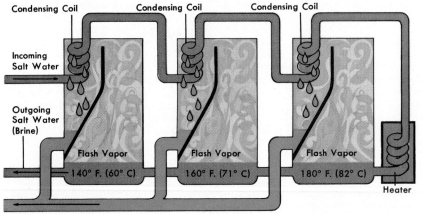

Condensing Coil   Condensing Coil   Condensing Coil

Incoming Salt Water

Outgoing Salt Water (Brine)

Flash Vapor — 140° F. (60° C)   Flash Vapor 160° F. (71° C)   Flash Vapor 180° F. (82° C)

Heater

Outgoing Fresh Water

Flash Distillation is the most widely used desalting process. Incoming seawater is heated and then released into a low-pressure chamber. This causes part of the water to flash into steam, even though its temperature is below 212° F. (100° C). The steam condenses into fresh water on a condensing coil, which is cooled by incoming seawater. The remaining seawater passes through similar chambers, each at a successively lower pressure.

the fact that when salt is dissolved in water, it breaks up into *ions* (electrically charged particles) of sodium and chloride. Sodium ions carry a positive charge, and chloride ions carry a negative charge.

The process uses a large chamber divided into many compartments by thin plastic sheets called *membranes*. Two types of membranes are used, and they are placed alternately. One type allows only positive ions to pass through it. The other lets only negative ions through. One of the end compartments contains a positive *electrode* (electrical pole). The other end compartment contains a negative electrode.

When an electric current is sent through the water, the negative ions are drawn through the membranes permeable to negative ions toward the positive electrode. The positive ions are drawn through the membranes permeable to positive ions toward the negative electrode. Thus, the salt in every other compartment is drawn off, leaving fresh water.

The U.S. government's plant in Webster, S.Dak., uses the electrodialysis process. This plant produces about 250,000 gallons (946,000 liters) of water daily from the region's brackish ground water.

Freezing. Ice is pure water. When seawater freezes, the ice crystals produced are pure water in solid form. The salt is separated and trapped between the ice crystals. There are several freezing processes. The main problem lies in separating the ice crystals from the salt. This is usually done by washing off the salt with fresh water. The ice is then melted and becomes fresh liquid water.

The U.S. government's plant in Wrightsville Beach, N.C., uses a freezing process. It can produce about 200,000 gallons (760,000 liters) of water a day.

Other Desalting Processes are also being studied. One of the most promising is *reverse osmosis*. In normal osmosis, a less concentrated liquid flows into a more concentrated one. Thus, if salt water and fresh water are separated in a chamber by a semipermeable membrane, the fresh water will flow through the membrane into the salt water. However, if enough pressure is placed on the salt water, this normal flow can be reversed. Fresh water will then be squeezed from the salt water as it passes through the membrane, leaving the salt behind. The reverse osmosis desalting process works in this way.

The Future of Desalting. All methods of desalination require large amounts of energy. Producing energy is expensive, whether it comes from hydroelectric, fuel-burning, or nuclear power plants. In the United States, it costs about $1 to produce 1,000 gallons (3,800 liters) of fresh water from seawater. In comparison, U.S. cities pay an average of only about 30 cents for 1,000 gallons taken and distributed from fresh sources.

Desalination can relieve water shortages chiefly in dry regions along seacoasts. But it offers little hope of ending shortages in cities far from a seacoast or in mountains. The cost of bringing the water to such cities could be greater than the cost of desalting.

In places where only seawater is available, the high cost of desalination is less important. For this reason, more than 200 desalting plants have been built throughout the world—from Australia to California, and from Greenland to South America. Most of these plants are small. Many of them serve military posts in isolated regions, oil-drilling crews in deserts, island resorts, or industrial plants.

The world's desalting plants produce a total of about 50 million gallons (189 million liters) a day, a small fraction of the world's daily demand for water. The world's largest plant is at Ash Shuwaykh, in the Arab country of Kuwait. It produces more than 6 million gallons (23 million liters) of water a day.

Much government and private research is centered on building large nuclear-powered dual purpose desalination plants to lower the cost of desalting. These plants would be able to produce electricity as well as desalted water.

Electrodialysis is based on the fact that when salt dissolves in water, it breaks up into negatively and positively charged ions. This diagram, showing three compartments of an electrodialysis unit, illustrates how the ions are drawn from the middle one.

Freezing. In the process shown here, seawater enters a vacuum freezing chamber. Part of the water flashes into vapor, and part turns into an icy slush. The salt is washed off the ice in a separation unit. The ice melts and the vapor condenses in a melter.

WORLD BOOK diagrams by Murrie-White & Associates, Inc.

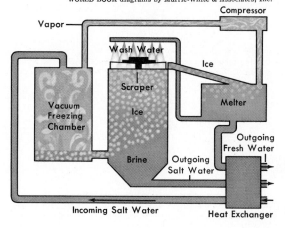

Positive Electrode
Negative Electrode
Incoming Salt Water
Positively Charged Sodium Ions
Negatively Charged Chloride Ions
Membrane
Outgoing Salt Water (Brine)
Outgoing Fresh Water

Compressor
Vapor
Wash Water
Ice
Scraper
Vacuum Freezing Chamber
Ice
Melter
Brine
Outgoing Salt Water
Outgoing Fresh Water
Incoming Salt Water
Heat Exchanger

Water is not only the most common substance on earth, it is also one of the most unusual. No other substance can do all the things that water can do. Water is an exception to many of nature's rules because of its unusual *properties* (qualities).

The Chemistry of Water. Water consists of tiny particles called *molecules*. A drop of water contains many millions of molecules. Each molecule, in turn, consists of even smaller particles called *atoms*. Water molecules consist of atoms of hydrogen and oxygen. Hydrogen and oxygen by themselves are gases. But when two atoms of hydrogen combine with one atom of oxygen, they form the chemical compound H_2O—water.

Even the purest water contains substances besides ordinary hydrogen and oxygen. For example, water contains very tiny portions of *deuterium*, a hydrogen atom that weighs more than the ordinary hydrogen atom. Water formed by a combination of deuterium and oxygen is called *heavy water* (see HEAVY WATER; DEUTERIUM). Water is actually a combination of several different substances, but these substances make up only a small fraction of it.

The Properties of Water. Water can be a solid, a liquid, or a gas. No other substance appears in these three forms within the earth's normal range of temperature. The molecules that make up water are always moving, and the form water takes depends on how fast they move. The molecules in solid water (ice) are far apart and almost motionless. The molecules in liquid water are close together and move about freely. The molecules in water vapor, a gas, move about violently and bump into one another.

Ice. Most substances contract as they grow colder.

The Water Molecule

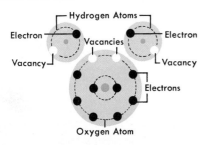

A water molecule consists of two hydrogen atoms and one oxygen atom. Each hydrogen atom has room for another electron around its nucleus. The oxygen atom has room for two more electrons.

Water Molecule

The two hydrogen atoms and one oxygen atom fill their empty spaces by sharing electrons. The resulting water molecule is an extremely tight structure because its atoms share their electrons.

But when water reaches 32° F. (0° C) and freezes into ice, it expands. For this reason, ice floats on liquid water. If water contracted upon freezing, any volume of ice would be heavier than an equal volume of liquid water. Ice would then sink. If ice sank, the earth would become a lifeless arctic desert. Each winter, more and more ice would pile up on the bottom of lakes, rivers, and oceans. In summer, the sun's heat could not reach deep enough to melt the ice. Water life would die. The hydrologic cycle would slow down. In time, all of the water on the earth would turn to solid ice, except perhaps for a thin layer of water over the ice during the summer.

Liquid. Water is a liquid at temperatures found in most places on the earth. No other common substance is liquid at ordinary temperatures. In fact, the temperatures at which water is a liquid are unusual. Water is a liquid between 32° F. (0° C), its freezing point, and 212° F. (100° C), its boiling point. But substances with a structure like that of water are not liquid in this temperature range. These substances include gases with the formulas H_2Te, H_2Se, and H_2S. As their formulas show, they are closely related to water (H_2O). Each has two atoms of hydrogen, plus an atom of the elements tellurium, selenium, or sulfur. If water behaved like these close relatives, it would be a liquid between about −148° F. (−100° C) and −130° F. (−90° C). In that case, there would be no liquid water on earth since the earth's temperatures are far higher than −130° F.

Water weighs about 62.4 pounds per cubic foot (1 kilogram per liter). Scientists compare the weight of other substances with the weight of water in order to find the *specific gravity* of the substance (see GRAVITY, SPECIFIC).

Vapor. If an uncovered glass of water stands in a room for a few days, the water will gradually disappear. This is because the water molecules are moving constantly. Those at the surface break free of those below and enter the air as vapor. The higher the temperature of the water, the faster it evaporates, because the molecules move faster.

Water can also be turned into vapor by boiling it, and creating *steam*. It takes an enormous amount of heat to produce steam. Water boils at 212° F. (100° C). But when water reaches the boiling point, it does not immediately turn into steam. First there is a pause, during which the water absorbs additional heat without any rise in the temperature. This heat is called *latent heat*. More than five times as much heat is required to turn boiling water into steam as to bring freezing water to a boil. Thus, steam holds a great amount of latent heat energy. People use this energy to run machinery.

Water vapor in the air also holds a tremendous amount of latent heat energy. This energy is released when the vapor cools and condenses, and falls as rain. The high latent heat of water is related to water's remarkable heat capacity.

Heat Capacity is the ability of a substance to absorb heat without becoming much warmer itself. Water has a greater heat capacity than any other substance except ammonia. To illustrate water's unusual heat capacity, imagine a pound of water, a pound of gold, and a pound of iron—all at −459.67° F. (−273.15° C). This is *absolute zero*, the temperature at which a substance supposedly contains no heat at all. If all three substances were heated and each absorbed the same amount of energy, the gold would melt at 2016° F. (1102° C). But the ice would still be at −300° F. (−184° C). When the iron began to melt at 2370° F. (1299° C), the ice would finally have reached 32° F. (0° C).

Surface Tension is the ability of a substance to stick to itself and pull itself together. Water's surface tension is extremely high. A dripping faucet shows how water sticks to itself. As the water drips, each drop clings to the faucet, stretches, lets go, and then snaps into a tiny ball. Water molecules cling together so tightly that water can support objects heavier than itself. For example, a needle or a razor blade can float on water. Insects can walk on water. Water can also stick to other substances. For example, water sticks to cloth, glass, and soil. By sticking to these substances, it wets them. See SURFACE TENSION.

Capillarity is the ability of a liquid to climb up a surface against the pull of gravity. You can see water's climbing ability in a glass of water. The water is higher around the edges, where it touches the glass. The capillarity of water helps it circulate through soil, and up through the roots and stems of plants. It also helps circulate blood, which is mostly water, throughout our bodies. See CAPILLARITY.

Dissolving Ability. Water can dissolve almost any substance. It dissolves the hardest rocks as it runs over the land and seeps through the ground. In time, it carries the dissolved materials to the oceans. Water also dissolves the nutrients that all living things need. It dissolves and carries the nutrients in soil to plants, and to the cells within plants. Water also dissolves the food that human beings and animals eat, and carries it to the cells.

How Water Is Held Together. Water's unusual properties depend on the forces that hold it together. These forces are (1) chemical bonds and (2) hydrogen bonds.

Chemical Bonds are the forces that hold the two hydrogen atoms and the one oxygen atom together in a water molecule. Each hydrogen atom has one electron whirling in orbit around its nucleus. But each of these atoms has room for two electrons. The oxygen atom has six electrons in its outer orbit, but it has room for eight. The hydrogen and oxygen atoms each fill their empty spaces by sharing their electrons. The two electrons from the two hydrogen atoms enter the orbit of the oxygen atom. At the same time, two electrons from the oxygen atom fill the empty spaces in the two hydrogen atoms. The resulting water molecule is an extremely tight structure.

Hydrogen Bonds are the forces that link water molecules together. Water molecules have a lopsided shape because the two hydrogen atoms bulge from one end of the oxygen atom. The hydrogen end of the water molecule has a positive electric charge. At the opposite end, the molecule has a negative charge. Water molecules link together because opposite charges attract. The positive ends of water molecules attach to the negative ends of other water molecules, whose positive ends attach to the negative ends of still other water molecules.

Experiments Showing Some Properties of Water

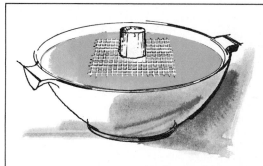

Surface Tension. Carefully place a piece of window screen on the surface of a bowl of water. The screen is much heavier than water, but it will float because water molecules cling together tightly. A cork can even be added.

Dissolving Ability. Fill two large glasses with an equal amount of water and place a dozen sugar cubes in one of them. The level of water in both glasses will remain about the same because water dissolves the sugar completely.

WORLD BOOK illustrations by Murrie-White & Associates, Inc.

Capillarity. Put one end of a piece of absorbent string into a pan of water. Let the other end hang over the edge below the water's level. Water will climb up the string against the pull of gravity and drip off the tip.

Water and Civilization.

Water and Civilization. Water has been vital to the development and survival of civilization. The first great civilizations arose in the valleys of great rivers—in the Nile Valley of Egypt, the Tigris-Euphrates Valley of Mesopotamia, the Indus Valley of Pakistan, and the Hwang Ho Valley of China. All these civilizations built large irrigation systems, made the land productive, and prospered. See CIVILIZATION.

Civilizations crumbled when water supplies failed or were poorly managed. Many historians believe the Sumerian civilization of Mesopotamia fell because of poor irrigation practices. Salt in irrigation water is left behind during evaporation, and tends to build up in the soil. This can be avoided by washing the salt away with extra water. But if the land is not well drained, it becomes water-logged. The ancient Sumerians failed to achieve a balance between salt accumulation and drainage. The salt and excess water harmed their crops. Farm production gradually declined, and food shortages developed. With the collapse of agriculture, the Sumerian civilization fell.

The ancient Romans built aqueducts, canals, and reservoirs throughout their empire. They turned regions along the coast of northern Africa into prosperous civilizations. After the Romans left, their water projects were abandoned. Today, these places are desert.

The Challenge of Today, as in ancient times, is for people to make the best use of water. But the challenge is greater than ever before because more and more water is needed as industry and population grow. The earth has enough water to meet the growing demand, but the water is distributed unevenly. Also, people waste and pollute water and manage it poorly in other ways.

People are beginning to realize how precious water is, and how necessary it is to understand water problems in order to solve them. During the late 1960's and the 1970's, the U.S. government and individual state governments set up various antipollution programs. In addition, the federal government and private companies worked to improve desalination processes.

Nations have begun to cooperate with one another in trying to solve water problems. In 1965, the First International Symposium on Water Desalination was held in Washington, D.C. At this conference, representatives from more than 60 countries shared their knowledge of desalting techniques. Since 1965, about 70 nations have taken part in the International Hydrological Decade, a program directed by the United Nations to promote scientific research on water resources. A United Nations Water Conference was held in 1977 to help plan more efficient ways of using and conserving the world's water supply.   LUNA B. LEOPOLD

WATER / Study Aids

Related Articles in WORLD BOOK include:

FORMS OF WATER

Artesian Well	Hail	Sleet
Cloud	Heavy Water	Snow
Dew	Humidity	Spring
Fog	Ice	Steam
Frost	Iceberg	Waterfall
Geyser	Liquid	Waterspout
Glacier	Mineral Water	Well
Ground Water	Rain	Whirlpool

PURIFICATION AND DISTRIBUTION OF WATER

Aqueduct	Filter	Pump	Sewage
Chlorine	Fluoridation	Reservoir	Water Meter
Dam	Plumbing	Sanitation	Water Softening

OTHER RELATED ARTICLES

Boiling Point	Hydrography	Rainmaking
Canal	Hydrology	River
Capillarity	Hydrolysis	Salt
Climate	Hydrophonics	Surface Tension
Deuterium	Hydrosphere	Transpiration
Electric Power	Irrigation	Transportation
Erosion	Lake	Water Pollution
Eutrophication	Life	Water Power
Evaporation	Ocean	Water Wheel
Flood	Osmosis	Weather
Hydraulics		

Outline

I. Water in Our Daily Lives
    A. Water in Living Things
    B. Water in Our Homes
    C. Water for Irrigation
    D. Water for Industry
    E. Water for Power
    F. Water for Transportation and Recreation

II. Nature's Water Cycle
    A. The Waters of the Earth
    B. Water in the Air
    C. Precipitation
    D. How Water Shapes the Earth
    E. How Water Began

III. The Water Supply Problem
    A. World Distribution of Water
    B. Water Shortages
    C. Water Conservation
    D. Personal Responsibility

IV. City Water Systems
    A. Sources of Supply
    B. Uses of City Water Supplies
    C. Purifying and Treating Water
    D. Distributing Water
    E. Disposing of Used Water

V. Fresh Water from the Sea
    A. Distillation
    B. Electrodialysis
    C. Freezing
    D. Other Desalting Processes
    E. The Future of Desalting

VI. What Water Is and How It Behaves
    A. The Chemistry of Water
    B. The Properties of Water
    C. How Water Is Held Together

VII. Water and the Course of History

Questions

What are some of the ways in which people use water?
Why do all living things need water to live?
What are some reasons for water shortages?
Why would people die if they drank only seawater?
What are some ways in which water shapes the earth?
How much of the earth is covered with water?
Why would the earth become a lifeless arctic desert if ice did not float?
What is the *water,* or *hydrologic, cycle?*

Reading and Study Guide

See *Water* in the RESEARCH GUIDE/INDEX, Volume 22, for a *Reading and Study Guide.*

WATER BAROMETER. See BAROMETER.

WATER BEECH. See IRONWOOD.

WATER BEETLE is the name given to many separate families of beetles that live in the water. Typical water beetles are the *whirligigs*, the *diving beetles*, the *crawling water beetles*, and the *water scavenger beetles*. Some of these insects live in the water all their lives. Others live in or near the water only in the *larval* (young) stage.

Whirligigs whirl on the top of the water. They have *antennae* (short feelers), long-clawed front legs, paddle-shaped hind legs, and compound eyes. These eyes are divided into two pairs, a lower pair and an upper pair. Diving beetles have long, threadlike antennae. Their hind legs are flat and fringed, and used for swimming. Water scavenger beetles have short, stubby antennae. Like the diving beetle, they eat small fish and larvae of insects. All water beetles are well suited to life in aquariums.

Scientific Classification. Water beetles are in the order *Coleoptera*. The crawling water beetles belong to the family *Haliplidae;* the diving beetles to *Dytiscidae;* and the whirligig to *Gyrinidae*. The giant water scavenger is in the family *Hydrophilidae*. It is genus *Hydrous*, species *H. triangularis*. H. H. ROSS

See also BEETLE (picture: A Giant Water Beetle).

WATER BIRD. For examples, see BIRD (color pictures: Water Birds; Wild Ducks and Wild Geese) and also the lists of Water Birds and Oceanic Birds in the Related Articles section.

WATER BOA. See ANACONDA (snake).

WATER BOATMAN. See WATER BUG.

WATER BUFFALO. Several kinds of wild oxen may be called water buffaloes. Some have been domesticated, and are among the most useful of all farm animals. The water buffalo of India is one of the largest of wild cattle. The *bulls* (males) are often 5 to 6$\frac{1}{2}$ feet (1.5 to 2 meters) tall, and their horns may spread 12 feet (3.7 meters) from tip to tip, measured along the curve. The horns sweep out and back to form almost a circle, and are three-sided. The Indian buffalo's hide is bluish black, and is easy to see through its thin hair. Wild Indian buffaloes graze in herds of about 50 animals. Both wild and domesticated buffaloes have a keen sense of smell.

They like to wallow in the mud and water a large

Cornelia Clarke

The Water Scavenger Beetle has swimming legs fringed with bristles. It is shown from above, *left*, and below, *right*.

part of the day. They are fierce when wild, and a water buffalo is said to be a match for a large lion or tiger. The Indian buffalo has long been used in the rice fields of Asia, and makes rice farming possible on a large scale. This powerful animal can plow knee deep in mud. It has been imported to many other parts of the world— Egypt, Spain, Italy, Hungary, southern Soviet regions, southern Asia, the East Indies, and the Philippines.

Buffalo hide is tough and thick, and makes good leather. The milk of the cow is nourishing, with more fat than the milk of domestic cows. It is used in India for making a liquid butter.

The *carabao* is a smaller water buffalo of the Philippines. It is also important in farming. A native wild buffalo on Mindoro Island is called the *tamarau*. Africa is the home of two types of wild buffalo that are not actually water buffaloes. These are the big Cape buffalo, which has flattened horns, and the smaller Congo buffalo of central Africa.

Scientific Classification. Water buffaloes are in the subfamily *Bovinae* of the bovid family, *Bovidae*. The Indian water buffalo is a member of the genus *Bubalus*, species *B. bubalis*. DONALD F. HOFFMEISTER

See also BUFFALO; CARABAO; CHINA (picture: Chinese Farmers Lack Modern Tools).

WATER BUG is the general name given to insects which spend all or part of their lives in the water. The most familiar of the water bugs are the *water boatmen*, the *back swimmers*, the *giant water bugs*, and the *water striders*. The large Oriental cockroach is also sometimes called the *water bug*.

Both water boatmen and back swimmers have long, flattened, fringed hind legs. These legs serve as oars and cause the insects to move through the water. Water boatmen eat algae and bottom scum, and back swimmers eat smaller animals which live in the water. These insects come to the surface for air from time to time. During the winter they lie inactive in the mud at the bottom of the water. The water boatmen lay their eggs and attach them to the stems of plants. Back swimmers often lay their eggs within the stems of plants. They receive their name because of their habit of swimming through the water while lying on their backs.

The large bug often seen flying around electric lights in hot weather is a water bug. It leaves its home in the water for short periods in the air, to look for a mate or for a new pool. Water striders have long spiderlike legs.

Ylla, Rapho-Guillumette

Powerful Water Buffaloes will work in bogs and flooded fields where other work animals cannot find footing. Rice farmers in Southeast Asia use them in their rice paddies because water buffaloes enjoy mud and water.

WATER CHINQUAPIN

Cornelia Clarke
Water Boatman

Ralph Buchsbaum
Giant Water Bug

They do not swim through the water but stride about on the surface film. Many water bugs can cause painful bites.

Scientific Classification. Water bugs belong to the class *Insecta* and order *Hemiptera*. The water boatmen belong to the family *Corixidae*, the back swimmers to the family *Notonectidae*, the giant water bugs to the family *Belostomatidae*, and the water striders to the family *Hydrobatidae*, or *Gerridae*.   R. E. BLACKWELDER

WATER CHINQUAPIN. See LOTUS.

WATER CLOCK, or CLEPSYDRA (*KLEP sih druh*), is an instrument for recording time by measuring water escaping from a vessel. Its invention is generally accredited to Plato about 400 B.C. People used it long before modern clocks were invented. It consisted of a glass jar, with a scale of markings on its side. These were so arranged that, as the water ran out, the water left in the jar marked the time. Various improvements were made in the device, such as having a floating figure point to the hour. Another design caused the dripping water to turn a small wheel which was connected with the hands on the face of a dial. The water clock was used in Rome as early as 159 B.C. It was used in Athens to regulate the length of speeches in the law courts.   ARTHUR B. SINKLER

WATER COLOR is one of the most popular forms of painting. It has some drawbacks for the artist. The paints dry so quickly that correction or alteration is difficult. Most water colors have soft, pastel tones that do not lend themselves to rich, deep coloring. As a result, most artists use water colors for dry, delicate, sketchy effects. The paints are most suitable when the artist wants to put a great deal of light into a picture. The artist can do this with water colors by allowing the white paper to show through.

Young children enjoy using water colors. The paints are inexpensive, and children using them can learn to handle paints and brushes. But many art teachers recommend that children start with crayons, chalk, and tempera before they use water colors.

Water color paints are made from *pigments* (coloring matter) that are ground to a powder and mixed with water and gum size or some other binding material. The paints are usually made in the form of small cakes. The artist rubs a damp brush lightly over one of the cakes and then applies it to the paper.

Many great artists have found water colors a challenge to their ability. Some of the world's finest paintings are water colors. These paints were used in ancient times, but first gained wide popularity in the 1800's in England.   THOMAS MUNRO

For more detailed information and pictures, see PAINTING (Water Color Painting). See also GOUACHE; TEMPERA.

WATER CRESS. See CRESS.

WATER CYCLE. See WATER (color picture: The Water Cycle).

WATER DOG. See MUD PUPPY.

WATER DUST. See RAIN (How Rain Falls).

WATER FLEA is a tiny fresh-water shellfish about $\frac{1}{10}$ inch (2.5 millimeters) long. It is not an insect. Biologists call it *Daphnia* (*DAF nih uh*). It skips and jumps through water like a flea, using its feelers as oars. These feelers are the *antennae*. The water flea has a transparent *carapace* (body covering) that surrounds most of its body. Because the action of the water flea's heart and other organs can be seen directly, the animal is often used in scientific experiments on the effects of drugs. The head of the water flea narrows into a long snout, which bears a pair of compound eyes. The animal also has five pair of leg parts called *appendages*. These appendages move continually, and their motion helps the animal breathe. They also sweep in food and water. Water fleas are sold as food for tropical fish. In the summer, millions of these tiny creatures swarm in ponds and marshes.

Scientific Classification. Water fleas belong to the class *Crustacea*, and to the order *Cladocera*. They form the genus *Daphnia*.   R. E. BLACKWELDER

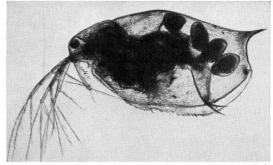

H. Bade
The Water Flea's Transparent Body Aids Science.

WATER FRAME. See ARKWRIGHT, SIR RICHARD.

WATER GAP. See GAP; APPALACHIAN MOUNTAINS.

WATER GAS. See GAS (How Gas Is Manufactured).

WATER GLASS, or SOLUBLE GLASS (chemical formula Na_2SiO_3), is a jellylike compound of sodium, silicon, and oxygen. Its chemical name is sodium metasilicate. Pure water glass is colorless, and readily dissolves in water. It is insoluble in alcohol and acids.

The solution is used to preserve eggs. It makes the shells airtight by filling their pores. The solution is also used in soaps, in preserving wood, and in fireproofing wood, cloth, and paper. Water glass will also waterproof walls. Industry uses it as an adhesive in manufacturing fiberboard shipping cases, greaseproof boxes, and similar containers. It is also used in cement manufacture, and for hardening concrete. Water glass is used in the purification of fats and oils, in refining petroleum, and in the manufacture of silica gel.   GEORGE L. BUSH

WATER HEN. See GALLINULE.

WATER HYACINTH is a plant that grows chiefly in the tropical regions of the world. It floats on lakes, rivers, and swamps and grows to a height of about 2 feet (61 centimeters) above the water. A water hyacinth has as many as 38 purple flowers grouped around the top of the stem.

Diseases and insects control the growth of water hyacinths in South America, where the plants first grew. But in the Southern United States and other regions where people have introduced the plant, there are no natural controls on its growth. In those regions, water hyacinths are a serious environmental problem because they grow so fast. The plants may double in number every 10 days. They form floating mats that can cover entire water surfaces and destroy the plant and animal life below. Plants need sunlight to live, and fish must have oxygen. The thick growth of water hyacinths blocks the sunlight and causes the oxygen content of the water to decrease. In addition, boats cannot travel on waterways that are choked with water hyacinths.

Many scientists are exploring possible uses of water hyacinths. In the early 1970's, researchers began the experimental use of the plants to clean up polluted streams. Water hyacinths can absorb many chemicals—including sewage and industrial wastes—from the water in which the plants grow. Thus, polluted water might be purified by passing it through a series of tanks that contain water hyacinths. Other investigators are studying the possibility of making cattle feed from dried water hyacinths.

Scientific Classification. The water hyacinth belongs to the pickerelweed family, Pontederiaceae. It is *Eichhornia crassipes.*   GEORGE K. REID

WATER-LEVEL GAUGE. See GAUGE.

WATER LILY, or POND LILY, is the popular name for various beautiful water plants that grow in both temperate and hot climates. The American water lily is related to the lotus. These plants send their long, stout leaf and flower stalks up from the mud bottom of clear,

WATER METER

shallow water. Their narrow to round green leaves grow submerged or are seen floating on the surface of the water. The flowers are usually raised above the water on long flower stalks. The white-flowered water lily is the most common. The flowers may be as large as 1 foot (30 centimeters) across. Some water lilies bloom during the day and others during the night. The water lily is the flower for the month of July.

Scientific Classification. Water lilies belong to the water lily family, *Nymphaeaceae.* The native white water lily of the eastern United States is classified as genus *Nymphia,* species *N. odorata.*   THEODOR JUST

See also FLOWER (color picture: Flowers That Grow in Wet Places).

WATER METER is a device that measures the amount of water that flows through a pipe or a large channel. The most widely known type of water meter turns numbers on a register that operates like an *odometer* (mileage recorder) of an automobile. This type is used by water companies to measure the water used in homes, factories, and business establishments.

In mild climates, such a home water meter is installed in a small box outside a house on the *service line* (pipe)

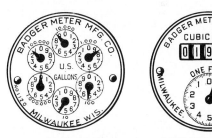

Reading a Water Meter. Start with the circle of the highest denomination on which 1 or more is shown. Set down the figure and those on the other circles in order. The meter on the left shows 188,540 gallons and the one on the right 1,959 cubic feet.

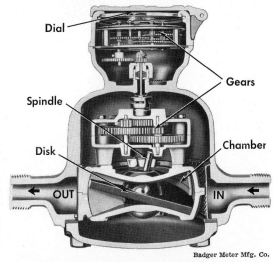

Badger Meter Mfg. Co.

How a Water Meter Works. Water fills the meter and surrounds a chamber containing a disk and spindle. When water flows out of the chamber, the disk nods back and forth, measuring the flow. This makes the spindle turn the gears that work the dial.

Agricultural Research Service, USDA

Water Hyacinths are an environmental problem in the Southern United States. The plants have plugged up this canal in Florida.

leading to the street. In cold climates, the meter is installed inside a house—usually in the basement—to protect it from freeze-ups during winter. The meter is often connected to a register mounted outside the house so that the meter reader does not have to go inside to make readings.

The measuring chamber of a residential-type water meter usually contains a disk. Incoming water causes the disk to wobble. The amount of water that flows through the chamber determines how much the disk moves. The motion of the disk turns the numbers on the register. Many water meters use a magnetic coupling to transfer the disk's motion to the register. The register records the flow of water in cubic feet, gallons, or liters.

Other types of meters, used in filtration plants, pumping stations, and industries, continuously register the flow of water on a chart-recording instrument.

The *venturi* meter and the *orifice* meter restrict the passage through which the water moves. They are used to measure the difference in water pressure to determine the amount of the flow.

The *magnetic flow meter* uses two electrodes mounted flush in the walls of a pipe, outside of which have been mounted powerful magnets. *Ions* (electrically charged atoms or groups of atoms) carried in the water pass through the magnetic field and generate voltage used by the magnetic flow meter to measure the water flow.

Electronic meters measure water flow by measuring changes in the wave length of the sounds made by moving water. A variety of other devices are used to measure the flow of water in open channels, such as sewers and rivers. Critically reviewed by the CHICAGO WATER BUREAU

WATER MOCCASIN is a poisonous snake that lives in the Southeastern United States. It is also called *moccasin snake* and *cottonmouth*. Water moccasins live in the area south of a line running from Cape Charles, Va., to the middle of the Alabama-Georgia boundary, then to southern Illinois, and from there to the point where the Pecos River and the Rio Grande meet in Texas. Water moccasins rarely appear above this line.

The water moccasin is a pit viper, like the rattlesnake. It has a hollow, or pit, in the side of its head, in front of the eye and below its level. Several harmless water snakes have a broad head like the moccasin, but they all lack the pit.

The Water Moccasin is one of the few poisonous snakes in North America. The moccasin, also called the cottonmouth, lives in southern swamps and bayous.

New York Zoological Society

Most water moccasins are about $3\frac{1}{2}$ feet (107 centimeters) long, though some grow 5 feet (1.5 meters) long. They usually have broad dark-olive bands across their bodies. Water moccasins feed on frogs, fish, and other small backboned animals. The young are born alive.

The moccasins like to stay in watery places, on the wooded banks of rivers, in large streams, and on lake shores. This habit makes it easier for people to avoid the water moccasin. The bite of the water moccasin is highly dangerous, and may be fatal. See SNAKEBITE.

This snake is called a cottonmouth because it is supposed to have a whiter mouth than other snakes, but the difference in appearance is not great.

Scientific Classification. The water moccasin belongs to the family Viperidae. It is genus *Agkistrodon*, species *A. piscivorus*.　　　　　　　　　　　　　CLIFFORD H. POPE

See also SNAKE (color picture); VIPER.
WATER OF CRYSTALLIZATION. See HYDRATE.
WATER OF HYDRATION. See HYDRATE.
WATER ON THE KNEE. See KNEE.
WATER OUZEL, *OO z'l*, is a small thrushlike bird of western North America which dives and dips under water. It is also called the *dipper*. It lives in mountain regions and is an active little bird, fearlessly diving into mountain streams for water insects. The water ouzel sometimes builds its nest of moss in a sheltered crack of rock behind waterfalls.

The bird has slate-gray feathers on its back and lighter feathers on the breast. It has short wings, and carries its short tail upward. The female lays three to five white eggs. Relatives of the water ouzel live in Mexico, Central and South America, and Europe.

Eric Hosking
Water Ouzel, or Dipper

Scientific Classification. The water ouzel belongs to the family *Cinclidae*. It is classified as genus *Cinclus*, species *C. mexicanus unicolor*.

WATER PIG. See CAPYBARA.
WATER PIPIT. See PIPIT.
WATER PLANT, or AQUATIC PLANT, is the name which refers to any special group of plants that live wholly or partly in water. The term *aquatic* as ordinarily used refers to the higher, more complex plants that grow in water, and does not include the algae, which are simpler in structure.

Aquatic seed plants may be rooted in the mud and have their leaves and blossoms above the surface of the water, or they may be wholly beneath the surface of the water. Submerged water plants are frequently equipped with air bladders, or have large air pores in their stems and leaves. Some of the best-known water plants are the several varieties of seaweed; the water lily, which is common on lakes and ponds; water cress, which spreads so rapidly that it sometimes blocks the channels of streams; and the cattail, or bulrush.　　WILLIAM C. BEAVER

Related Articles in WORLD BOOK include:

Bladderwort	Duckweed	Pondweed
Bulrush	Lotus	Rush
Cattail	Papyrus	Seaweed
Cress	Plant (Aquatic	Water Hyacinth
Diatom	Regions; pictures)	Water Lily

WATER POLLUTION occurs when man dumps wastes into rivers, lakes, oceans, and other bodies of water. Small amounts of wastes cause little harm because natural processes change them into harmless substances. But too much waste upsets these natural processes, and the water becomes polluted. Waste materials that pollute water include human and animal wastes, chemicals, metals, and oil.

Polluted water may look dirty, smell bad, and contain germs or chemicals that can cause disease. The impurities must be removed before such water can be used for drinking, cooking, or washing, or for cleaning or laundering. Even some industries must clean the water used in their manufacturing processes. In the United States, large areas of some rivers and lakes—including the Great Lakes—and the coastal waters have become dangerously polluted. Boating, fishing, and swimming have been forbidden in those areas.

Cities and towns with the most people and factories have the most water pollution. But farming, mining, and other activities cause water pollution in rural areas as well.

Water pollution has become a serious problem in many countries, including Canada, Germany, Japan, Russia, and the United States. Governments have passed laws limiting the amount and kinds of wastes that can be dumped into water. Cities and towns have built sewage treatment plants to control water pollution. Industry has spent millions of dollars on research and equipment to reduce it. But in the 1970's, the problem remained far from solved.

Sources

There are three chief sources of water pollution: (1) industrial wastes, (2) sewage, and (3) agricultural chemicals and wastes. Pollutants from these sources either reduce the amount of oxygen in the water or poison the water—or do both. By the year 2020, the United States will probably produce nearly three times as much sewage as it did in 1970. In addition, industrial wastes are increasing several times as fast as sewage.

Industrial Wastes. United States industries discharge three to four times as many pollutants into waste water as do all the sewerage systems in the country. These pollutants include many chemicals. In addition, industries use large quantities of water to cool equipment. Heat from the equipment makes the water hot. When it is discharged into a stream, it may cause *thermal pollution* that can harm animal and plant life. In the early 1970's, four industries—organic chemicals, paper, petroleum, and steel—discharged more than half of all the industrial wastes. Other industries that dumped large

HOW EUTROPHICATION AFFECTS A LAKE

Eutrophication, the process by which waste materials add nutrients to water, changes the balance of life there. The diagram at the left shows a lake with few waste nutrients added. Algae grow, using nutrients already in the lake, and provide food for fish. As the fish and algae die, their remains become organic wastes. Bacteria, using oxygen from the water, convert these wastes into nutrients and the cycle repeats. Nutrients and organic wastes added by man unbalance the cycle, as shown by the diagram at the right. Nutrients increase the growth of algae. As the algae die, they add to the wastes in the lake. Bacteria now use so much oxygen converting wastes into nutrients that few fish survive.

Balanced Cycle

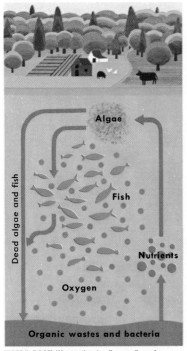

Unbalanced Cycle

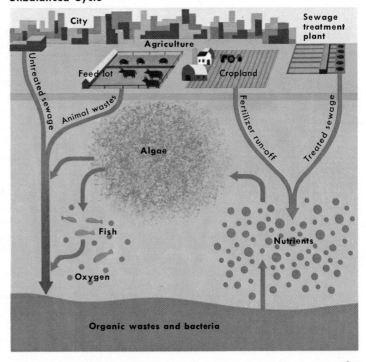

WORLD BOOK illustration by George Suyeoka

amounts of wastes included the food, plastics, rubber, and textile industries.

Sewage consists of human wastes, garbage, and water that has been used for laundering or bathing. Over 78 per cent of the sewage in the United States goes through treatment plants that turn it into less polluting substances. The treatment plants discharge these substances into lakes and rivers or dispose of them on land. About 11 per cent of the sewage is treated in *septic tanks* and disposed of on land (see SEWAGE [Rural Sewerage Systems]). The remaining 11 per cent of the sewage in the United States goes untreated into waterways.

Agricultural Chemicals and Wastes. Rain water flowing from farmland into streams carries chemical fertilizers and pesticides that have been put into the land. As a result of modern methods of raising livestock, animal wastes also cause water pollution. Cattle, hogs, sheep, and poultry that are raised on feed lots do not distribute their wastes over widespread pastureland. Instead, most of their wastes go into nearby streams.

Effects

Water polluted with human and animal wastes can spread typhoid fever and other diseases. In the United States, community water supplies are disinfected to kill disease-causing germs. However, disinfection does not remove chemicals and metals, such as arsenic, lead, and mercury. In the early 1970's, these substances were seldom found in sufficient amounts in drinking water to cause immediate harm. But scientists were concerned about the possible harmful effects of drinking small quantities of these substances for many years.

Pollution prevents people from using and enjoying water for recreation. For example, odors and floating slime make boating and swimming unpleasant, and the risk of disease makes polluted water unsafe. Oil spilled from ships or offshore oil wells may float to shore. The oil can cause serious pollution and kill water birds and other wildlife. In addition, water pollution affects fishing, both commercial and sport. Fish have been killed by oil or a lack of oxygen in the water. Industrial wastes, such as polychlorinated biphenyls (PCB's), also harm fish. Fish and shellfish from some waters cannot be eaten because they contain PCB's, mercury, and other chemicals in amounts dangerous to humans.

Water pollution also upsets various natural processes that constantly take place in water. These processes, which involve the use of the oxygen in water, work to make wastes harmless. In one process, *aerobic bacteria* break down wastes into simpler substances. Some of these substances serve as *nutrients* (food) for plants.

The aerobic bacteria use up oxygen in the water when breaking down the wastes. Scientists can find out how much waste the water contains by measuring how much oxygen the bacteria use in breaking it down. This measurement is called the *biochemical oxygen demand* (BOD) of the water. If the water contains too much waste, the bacteria will use up most of the oxygen in it. Some valuable species of game fish—such as sturgeon, whitefish, and several kinds of pike—will be unable to live in the water. Fish that need less oxygen replace them. These include carp and catfish. If all the oxygen is used up, another kind of bacteria, called *anaerobic*

bacteria, begin to break down the waste without using oxygen. This process darkens the water and produces bad odors, and fish can no longer live in the water.

Too much nutrient material in water may add to pollution by a process called *eutrophication* or *nutrient enrichment*. Many nutrients result from the natural decay of wastes. But large amounts of additional nutrients come from fertilizers washing off farmland, or from treated sewage. All the nutrients fertilize tiny water plants called *algae*. Greater and greater numbers of algae grow as a result of the additional nutrients. As the increased number of algae grow, an increased number also die. They become waste, and oxygen is used up as bacteria cause them to decay. During eutrophication, the lake changes into a marsh because of algae and other plants.

Thermal pollution can reduce the amount of oxygen that dissolves in water. The high temperature of the water also can kill some kinds of plants and animals.

Control

Most U.S. cities and towns use sewage treatment to control wastes dumped into water. In the early 1970's, some industries began using a method called *pretreatment of wastes* to reduce the amount of wastes in water.

Sewage Treatment. The most efficient sewage treatment plants use three separate processes—*primary treatment, secondary treatment,* and *advanced treatment.* But few sewage treatment plants use all three processes. As a result, much treated sewage still contains nutrients and chemicals. See SEWAGE (Urban Sewerage Systems).

Pollution control also involves disposal of waste materials after they leave a treatment plant. If dumped into water, these materials can cause eutrophication.

Pretreatment of Wastes. Industries can reduce pollution by treating wastes to remove harmful chemicals before dumping the wastes into water. Industrial wastes can also be reduced by using manufacturing processes that recover and reuse polluting chemicals.

Drinking Water Standards. In 1974, the U.S. Congress passed the Safe Drinking Water Act to help protect the nation's public water supply against pollution. This act authorized the Environmental Protection Agency (EPA) to establish uniform quality standards for about 240,000 public water systems throughout the United States. The standards were designed to reduce the amount of harmful bacteria, chemicals, and metals in drinking water. The EPA, together with the state governments, began enforcing its standards in 1977.

In 1978, the EPA proposed rules to limit the amount of chloroform and other related organic chemicals called *trihalomethane* (THM) in the drinking water of large cities. These chemicals are formed at treatment plants when chlorine is added to drinking water to kill disease-causing bacteria. Extended exposure to high levels of THM's, especially chloroform, is thought to increase the risk of cancer.   JACOB I. BREGMAN

Related Articles in WORLD BOOK include:

Algae	Ocean (A Vast
Environmental Pollution	Dumping Ground)
Environmental	Phosphate
Protection Agency	Sanitation
Eutrophication	Sewage

See also *Environmental Pollution* in the RESEARCH GUIDE/INDEX, Volume 22, for a *Reading and Study Guide*.

Water Polo is a rough sport played in a pool. Two teams try to score by throwing or pushing a ball into their opponent's goal. This picture shows a player, *lower left,* preparing to pass the ball to a teammate for a shot. The opposing goalie, *upper left,* will try to keep the ball from going into his team's goal.

Stan Pantovic, Focus on Sports Inc.

WATER POLO is a sport similar to hockey or soccer. Two teams in a pool try to score by throwing or pushing a hollow rubber ball into the opponent's goal. Water polo is one of the roughest sports because the players sometimes hold an opponent's head under the water, though such action is against the rules.

Men's water polo is played in an area that measures from 66 to 98 feet (20 to 30 meters) long and 26 to 66 feet (8 to 20 meters) wide. Women's matches are played in an area no larger than 82 by 56 feet (25 by 17 meters). The goals are 10 feet (3 meters) wide and usually 3 feet (.9 meters) above the water.

A team consists of a goalie and six field players. The goalie can handle the ball with both hands, but the field players may use only one hand at a time. Players move the ball by passing it or swimming with it. Each time a team gets the ball, it has 35 seconds to try to score. If it does not shoot the ball at the goal within that time, the other team gets the ball.

If a player commits a minor foul, the other team is given three seconds to pass the ball without opposition. When a major foul is committed, the player must leave the game—without a substitute—for 45 seconds or until a goal is scored. An even more serious foul results in a *penalty throw,* in which an opposing player shoots at the goal with only the goalie defending it.

Men's games are 20 minutes long and are divided into 5-minute quarters. Women's matches last 24 minutes and are divided into 6-minute quarters. Water polo originated in England in the 1870's. Burton W. Shaw, Jr.

WATER POWER is a valuable source of energy. When such fuels as coal, oil, and even nuclear fuels are burned up as a source of energy, they cannot be reused. But water used as a source of energy is not used up. The earth's constant flow of water can be harnessed to produce useful mechanical and electric power.

Wheels mounted on a frame over a river were the first devices used to harness water power. Blades around the outside of the wheels dipped into the river, and the flowing water striking the blades caused the wheels to turn. The ancient Romans connected water wheels to grinding stones and used the power to mill grain.

During the Industrial Revolution, large water wheels were used to run machinery in factories. The power was not completely reliable, however. Floodwaters created more power than was needed, and droughts left the fac-

tories without power. By the end of the 1800's, the steam engine had replaced water power in most factories.

The first water-powered plant for generating electricity was built in Appleton, Wis., in 1882. This *hydroelectric plant* established water power as an important source of electricity. Hydroelectric power is now used all over the world. Many hydroelectric plants are combined with *thermal power plants* (those using fuel). With this combination, the thermal plant can supply power if the hydroelectric plant is affected by drought. Hydroelectric plants are especially useful for producing electricity during periods when it is in great demand, because they can be turned on and off rapidly.

The Mechanics of Water Power. Water cannot create power unless it is flowing from a higher place to a lower place as in a river, a waterfall, or a dam. People use the effects of *gravity* (the attraction the earth exerts on an object) pulling the water downward when they harness water for power. For example, in the customary system of measurement, a cubic foot of water weighs 62.4 pounds. The pull of gravity then creates a pressure of 6,240 pounds per square foot at the base of a body of water 100 feet tall. If this water were released from a nozzle at the bottom of its source, the stream of water would travel at a speed of about 80 feet per second. The force of this stream striking the blades of a water wheel would cause the wheel to turn, producing useful mechanical energy.

In the customary system, power is measured in *horsepower.* One horsepower is the work required to raise 550 pounds one foot in one second. In the metric system, power is measured in kilowatts. One horsepower equals 1.34 kilowatts. The horsepower of a waterfall is estimated by multiplying the flow of the water in cubic feet per second by the height of the fall in feet. This product is then multiplied by 0.113 (which is equal to 62.4, the weight of a cubic foot of water, divided by 550, the standard weight used in measuring horsepower). The *potential* (greatest possible) power of a waterfall 50 feet high with a flow of 500 feet per second would be $50 \times 500 \times 0.113$, or 2,825 horsepower. But a mechanical system must be used to make useful energy out of the power of the waterfall, and no mechanical system can make use of all potential power. The power which the mechanical system develops is found by multiplying

A **Water-Skier** practices on shore, *above*, before testing his skill in the water. Skimming over the water, a skier holds on to a tow line extending from a speeding motorboat, *right*.

the potential power of the fall by the percentage of the potential power which the system uses.

World Water Power Production. The potential water power of the world is about $2\frac{1}{4}$ billion kilowatts, or about 3 billion horsepower. This is a very general estimate, because the flow of many large rivers has not been measured. Of this potential, about 329 million kilowatts, or about 441 million horsepower, is developed.

The United States has about a fifth of the world's developed power. But the 60 million kilowatts, or 80 million horsepower, which is developed is only about 32 per cent of the country's potential. Canada, Australia, and Europe have most of the rest of the developed power. The potential of Asia, Africa, and South America is just beginning to be developed.

The world's largest hydroelectric power plant, on the Yenisey River near Krasnoyarsk, Russia, has a capacity of more than 6 million kilowatts. One of the newest water power plants is at the Rance Estuary in France. It uses the rising and falling tide of the Atlantic Ocean to generate electricity.   RAY K. LINSLEY

Related Articles. See the sections on Electric Power in state articles, such as ARIZONA (Electric Power). See also:

Conservation	Electric Power	Reservoir
Dam	Irrigation	Turbine

WATER PRESSURE. See HYDRAULICS.

WATER PURIFICATION. See WATER (City Water Systems); KUWAIT (Land).

WATER-SKIING is a popular outdoor sport in which persons skim swiftly over the surface of the water on skis. It resembles snow skiing, because water-skiers wear similar, though wider, skis of varying lengths. The water-skier holds on to a towrope attached to a motorboat and is pulled across the surface of the water. Outboard boats of 25 horsepower (19 kilowatts) and over, and inboard boats of 50 horsepower (37 kilowatts) or more, are the kinds most often used for water-skiing. The towrope is usually about 75 feet (23 meters) long

and may be made of manila hemp, cotton, or other material. Water-skiing equipment can be rented at most waterside resorts. The American Water Ski Association and other groups offer booklets for the beginner and the advanced skier.   GUY W. HUGHES

WATER SOFTENING is a method of removing from water the minerals that make it hard. Hard water does not dissolve soap readily. It forms scale in pipes, boilers, and other equipment in which it is used. The principal methods of softening water are the lime-soda process and the ion-exchange process.

In the *lime-soda process*, soda ash and lime are added to the water in amounts determined by chemical tests. These chemicals combine with the calcium and magnesium in the water to make insoluble compounds that settle to the bottom of the water tank.

In the *ion-exchange process*, the water filters through minerals called *zeolites* (see ZEOLITE). As the water passes through the filter, the sodium ions in the zeolite are exchanged for the calcium and magnesium ions in the water, and the water is softened. After household softeners become exhausted, a strong solution of *sodium chloride* (salt) is passed through the filter to replace the sodium that has been lost. The use of two exchange materials makes it possible to remove both metal and acid ions from water.   C. FRED GURNHAM

WATER SPORTS include all sports that are played under, on, or above the water. Some are traditional, like swimming, fishing, diving, and boating. Others were developed in the 1800's and 1900's.

Among more recent water sports are aquaplaning, skin diving, spearfishing, surfing, water polo, and water-skiing. The Olympic Games program includes swimming, diving, and other water sports (see OLYMPIC GAMES). All water sports mentioned here have separate articles in WORLD BOOK.   SAM J. GRELLER

WATER STRIDER. See WATER BUG.

WATER SUPPLY. See WATER.

WATER TABLE. See DRAINAGE; GROUND WATER.

WATER TURBINE. See TURBINE (Water Turbines).

WATER TURKEY. See DARTER (bird).

WATER VAPOR. See EVAPORATION.

WATER-VASCULAR SYSTEM. See ECHINODERM.

WATER WHEEL changes the energy of falling water into mechanical energy which can be used for running machinery. The best source of water power in nature is found in waterfalls and rapids in rivers. The water is directed into the wheel through a chute. The wheel is mounted on an axle, which is connected by belts or gearing with the machinery it is to operate.

There are two main types of water wheels, vertical and horizontal. The vertical wheels include the overshot and the undershot.

The overshot water wheel has many scooplike buckets around its edge. Water is delivered to the top of the wheel. The weight of the water falling into the buckets causes the wheel to turn. An overshot water wheel may have an efficiency of up to 80 per cent. That is, it may turn as much as 80 per cent of the energy of the water fed to it into mechanical energy.

The undershot water wheel is built so the water strikes against blades at the bottom of the wheel. The power of the wheel depends on the speed of the water as it strikes the blades. The undershot wheel has such a low efficiency that it is rarely used.

Most modern water wheels are horizontal. A horizontal wheel rotates on a vertical shaft. It is driven by the force of the water striking the blades on one side of the wheel. Horizontal wheels are highly efficient if properly designed for the conditions of their use.

Historians believe the water wheel was developed in the 100's B.C. It was used mainly to grind corn. Later it was used for many kinds of mechanical operations. It was a major source of power until the development of the steam engine in the 1700's.   RAY K. LINSLEY

See also WATER POWER; TURBINE (Water Turbines).

Ewing Galloway

This Old Overshot Water Wheel in West Virginia is still in use more than 150 years after it was first put into service.

WATER WITCH. See GREBE.

WATER WONDERLAND. See MICHIGAN.

WATERBUCK. See ANTELOPE (Kinds).

WATERBURY, Conn. (pop. 108,033; met. area 216,-808), is called the *Brass Center of the World*. It lies on the Naugatuck River, 25 miles (40 kilometers) north of Long Island Sound (see CONNECTICUT [political map]).

Waterbury ranks first among the cities of the United States in the manufacture of brass and copper goods, brass casting, sheet and rolled brass, and other brassware products. Waterbury mills make the "blanks" for United States nickels and the coins for many South American countries. Other products include buttons, clocks, and foundry and machine-shop products.

People from nearby Farmington bought the Waterbury area from Indians in 1674. They established a frontier outpost called *Mattatuck*. The name became Waterbury when the town was incorporated in 1686. The manufacture of brass goods began in 1802. Waterbury received its city charter in 1853. It has a mayor-council type of government.   ALBERT E. VAN DUSEN

WATERFALL is any sudden descent of a stream from a higher to a lower level. In wearing down its channel, a river uncovers certain layers of rock that are softer than others. If the hard rock is farther upstream than the soft, the channel below is worn more rapidly, and a waterfall results. Sometimes the hard ledge forms the edge of a vertical cliff, over which the water plunges.

If the volume of water is small, the fall may be called a *cascade*. If the volume of water is large, a fall of this sort is called a *cataract*. Niagara Falls is such a cataract. Other noted cataracts are Victoria Falls on the Zambezi River in Africa, the Falls of the Iguaçu near the Paraná River in South America, and Churchill Falls of the Churchill River in Labrador. Usually, however, the term *cataract* is applied to a series of rapids or falls caused by the flow of the stream over a rapidly sloping rocky bed. Examples of these are the cataracts of the Nile and the Orinoco rivers. Cataracts which have small, gradual falls are termed *rapids*. Some of the most noted rapids in North America are those at Sault Sainte Marie, at the outlet of Lake Superior, and the rapids in the Saint Lawrence River.

Small waterfalls or cascades are often of great height. Such are the Upper Yosemite Falls in California, 1,430 feet (436 meters) high; the Sutherland, New Zealand, 1,904 feet (580 meters); and the Staubbach of the Alps, 984 feet (300 meters). Some lower waterfalls are noted for their beauty. These include Montmorency Falls, near Quebec; Multnomah Falls, near the Columbia River, Oregon; numerous cascades in the Rocky and Selkirk mountains; and the Upper and Lower falls in Yellowstone National Park.

Falls usually occur in mountainous countries. But sometimes they are caused by the descent of streams to a flood plain. The line along which several rivers flowing into the same body of water descend to this lower level is called the *fall line*. The fall line of those rivers south of Chesapeake Bay which flow into the Atlantic Ocean is marked by the location of manufacturing cities whose sites were chosen because they were near water power, which later became even more valuable as hydroelectric power. Examples of these industrial centers are Rich-

Famous Waterfalls

Each waterfall is drawn to scale, and is shown as it appears in its natural setting. In cases where a series of falls have the same name and are sometimes considered to be one fall, only the highest is shown. Heights are given for both the highest fall in the series and for the total drop.

1,000 feet
(305 meters)

Waterfalls of North America

500 feet
(152 meters)

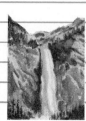

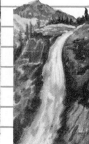

Niagara
New York
182 feet
(55 meters)
Ontario
173 feet
(53 meters)

Yellowstone Lower Falls
Wyoming
308 feet
(94 meters)

Vernal
California
317 feet
(97 meters)

Yosemite Lower Falls
California
320 feet
(98 meters)

Illilouette
California
370 feet
(113 meters)

Multnomah
Oregon
542 feet
(165 meters)
Total—620 feet
(189 meters)

Nevada
California
594 feet
(181 meters)

2,000 feet
(610 meters)

1,500 feet
(457 meters)

Other Waterfalls of the World

1,000 feet
(305 meters)

500 feet
(152 meters)

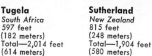
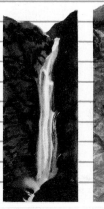
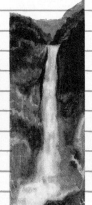

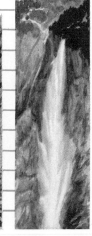

Victoria
On Rhodesia-Zambia border
355 feet
108 meters)

Tugela
South Africa
597 feet
(182 meters)
Total—2,014 feet
(614 meters)

Sutherland
New Zealand
815 feet
(248 meters)
Total—1,904 feet
(580 meters)

Jog
India
830 feet
(253 meters)

Great Falls
Guyana
840 feet
(256 meters)

Vettisfoss
Norway
900 feet
(274 meters)

Staubbach
Switzerland
984 feet
(300 meters)

rce: National Geographic Society.

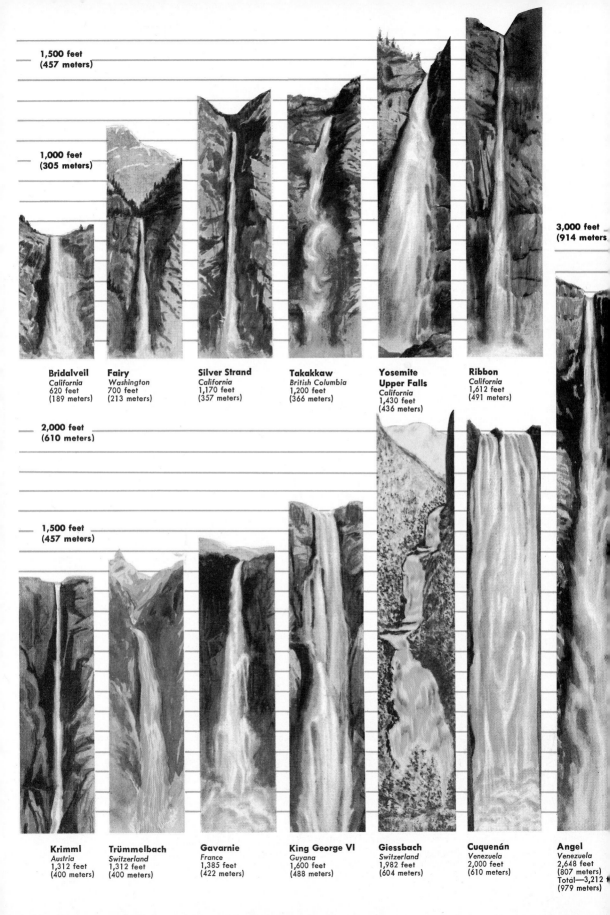

1,500 feet
(457 meters)

1,000 feet
(305 meters)

3,000 feet
(914 meters)

Bridalveil
California
620 feet
(189 meters)

Fairy
Washington
700 feet
(213 meters)

Silver Strand
California
1,170 feet
(357 meters)

Takakkaw
British Columbia
1,200 feet
(366 meters)

**Yosemite
Upper Falls**
California
1,430 feet
(436 meters)

Ribbon
California
1,612 feet
(491 meters)

2,000 feet
(610 meters)

1,500 feet
(457 meters)

Krimml
Austria
1,312 feet
(400 meters)

Trümmelbach
Switzerland
1,312 feet
(400 meters)

Gavarnie
France
1,385 feet
(422 meters)

King George VI
Guyana
1,600 feet
(488 meters)

Giessbach
Switzerland
1,982 feet
(604 meters)

Cuquenán
Venezuela
2,000 feet
(610 meters)

Angel
Venezuela
2,648 feet
(807 meters)
Total—3,212
(979 meters)

mond, Va., Raleigh, N.C., Augusta and Columbus, Ga., and Columbia, S.C.   SAMUEL N. DICKEN

Related Articles in WORLD BOOK include:

WATERFORD GLASS. See GLASSWARE.

WATERGATE was the name of the biggest political scandal in United States history. It included various illegal activities designed to help President Richard M. Nixon win re-election in 1972. Watergate resulted in Nixon's resignation from the presidency in 1974.

Watergate differed from most previous political scandals because personal greed apparently did not play an important role. Instead, Watergate represented an attack on one of the chief features of a democracy—free and open elections.

The Watergate activities included burglary, wiretapping, violations of campaign financing laws, and sabotage and the attempted use of government agencies to harm political opponents. The scandal also involved a cover-up of many of those actions. About 40 persons were charged with crimes in the scandal and with related crimes. Most of these persons were convicted by juries or pleaded guilty.

Watergate involved more high-level government officials than any previous political scandal. It led to the conviction on criminal charges in 1975 of former Attorney General John N. Mitchell and two of Nixon's top aides, John D. Ehrlichman and H. R. Haldeman. Also in 1975, former Secretary of Commerce Maurice H. Stans, a leader of Nixon's re-election campaign, pleaded guilty to Watergate criminal charges and was fined $5,000. The Watergate scandal also had resulted in the resignation of Attorney General Richard G. Kleindienst in 1973.

The Break-In and Cover-Up. The scandal took its name from the Watergate complex of apartment and office buildings in Washington, D.C. On June 17, 1972, police arrested five men for breaking into the Democratic Party's national headquarters there. One of the burglars was the security coordinator of the Committee for the Re-election of the President (CRP). The five men, along with another CRP aide and a White House consultant, were indicted for a number of crimes, including burglary and wiretapping. In January, 1973, five of the seven pleaded guilty, and the other two were found guilty by a jury.

Nixon's press secretary had declared repeatedly that the scandal involved no member of the White House staff. But the press found evidence that White House aides had helped finance sabotage and spying operations against candidates for the 1972 Democratic presidential nomination. Newspaper reporters Carl Bernstein and Bob Woodward of *The Washington Post* led the investigation.

Early in 1973, evidence was uncovered that tied several top White House aides to plans for the Watergate break-in or to concealment of evidence that implicated members of the Nixon Administration. The evidence indicated that White House officials had tried to involve the Central Intelligence Agency and the Federal Bureau of Investigation in the cover-up. These officials falsely claimed that national security was involved.

On April 30, 1973, Nixon stated that he had no part in either planning the Watergate break-in or covering it up. He promised that the Department of Justice would appoint a special prosecutor to handle the case. In May, Archibald Cox, a Harvard Law School professor, was named to that position. Also in May, the Senate Select Committee on Presidential Campaign Activities began hearings on Watergate. Senator Sam J. Ervin, Jr., of North Carolina headed the committee. Former Presidential Counsel John W. Dean III became the chief witness against Nixon in the hearings. Dean admitted that he had played a major role in a White House cover-up and charged that Nixon knew of his activities. Dean also revealed Administration plans to use the Internal Revenue Service and other government agencies to punish opponents whom the White House had placed on so-called enemies lists. Dean was later sentenced to a prison term of 1 to 4 years. After serving four months, his sentence was reduced to that time and he was released.

The Tape Controversy. In July, the Senate committee learned that Nixon had secretly made tape recordings of conversations in his White House offices since 1971. The committee and Cox believed the tapes could answer key questions raised in their investigations. They asked Nixon to supply them with certain tapes, but he refused to do so. Nixon argued that, as President, he had a constitutional right to keep the tapes confidential. In August, Cox and the committee sued Nixon to obtain the tapes. U.S. District Court Judge John J. Sirica decided to review the tapes himself and ordered Nixon to give them to him. Nixon appealed the order, but a U.S. court of appeals supported Sirica.

In October, Nixon offered to provide summaries of the tapes. But Cox declared that summaries would be unacceptable as evidence in court and rejected the offer. Nixon ordered Attorney General Elliot L. Richardson to fire Cox, but Richardson refused to do so and resigned. Deputy Attorney General William D. Ruckelshaus also resigned after being ordered to dismiss Cox. Nixon then named Solicitor General Robert H. Bork acting attorney general, and Bork fired Cox. Leon Jaworski, a noted Texas attorney, later succeeded Cox.

The President's actions angered many Americans. In October, a number of members of the House of Representatives began steps to impeach him. Later in 1973, Nixon agreed to supply the tapes to Sirica. Then it was discovered that three key conversations were missing. The White House said that the tape-recording system failed to work properly during two of the talks and that the third had been accidentally erased.

In April, 1974, Jaworski served Nixon with a *subpoena* (legal request) to obtain tape recordings and documents relating to 64 White House conversations. Jaworski said the materials contained evidence in the cover-up case. At the end of April, Nixon released 1,308 pages of edited transcripts of White House conversations. He said they told the full Watergate story.

Jaworski, however, insisted on receiving the original tapes and documents that he had requested. Nixon again claimed he had a constitutional right to protect confidential documents. Jaworski then sued the President in federal court. In July, the Supreme Court of the United States ordered Nixon to give Jaworski the materials. The Supreme Court ruled unanimously that a President cannot withhold evidence in a criminal case.

The Cover-Up Trial. In March 1974, seven former officials of Nixon's Administration or his 1972 re-election committee were indicted on charges of conspiracy in covering up the Watergate break-in. Among the former officials indicted were Domestic Council Chief Ehrlichman, White House Chief of Staff Haldeman, and Attorney General Mitchell.

The cover-up trial lasted from October 1974, to January 1975. Ehrlichman, Haldeman, and Mitchell were each convicted of conspiracy, obstruction of justice, and perjury, and sentenced to a prison term of from $2\frac{1}{2}$ to 8 years. The sentences were later reduced to terms of 1 to 4 years.

The Resignation of Nixon. The President suffered another major setback in July 1974, when the House Judiciary Committee recommended that he be impeached. The committee adopted three articles of impeachment for consideration by the full House of Representatives. The first article accused Nixon of obstructing justice in the scandal. The other two articles accused him of abusing presidential powers and illegally withholding evidence from the judiciary committee.

Nixon's chief defenders continued to argue that the President had committed no impeachable offense. But on August 5, Nixon released additional transcripts of taped White House conversations. The transcripts convinced most Americans that Nixon had authorized the Watergate cover-up at least as early as June 23, 1972—six days after the break-in. Nixon immediately lost almost all his remaining support in Congress. He resigned on August 9, and Vice-President Gerald R. Ford took office as President that day. On September 8, Ford pardoned Nixon for all federal crimes that Nixon might have committed while serving as President.

Other Effects of Watergate. In 1974, Congress approved reforms in the financing of federal election campaigns. Some reforms limit the amount of money contributors may give to candidates for President, Vice-President, and Congress. Other reforms require detailed reporting of both contributions and expenses. Many state legislatures limited contributions and spending in state election campaigns and adopted codes of ethics for government employees.   HARRY M. ROSENFELD

See also TELEVISION (picture: Government Hearings).

WATERLOO, Iowa (pop. 73,064; met. area pop. 132,916), is a meat-packing and farm-machinery manufacturing center in northeastern Iowa. It lies on the Cedar River about 90 miles (140 kilometers) northeast of Des Moines. Some of the best livestock in the world are exhibited each fall at the National Dairy Cattle Congress in Waterloo. The first settlers, who arrived in 1845, called the place Prairie Rapids. The town was renamed Waterloo in 1851 and incorporated as a city in 1868. It has a mayor-council government.   WILLIAM J. PETERSEN

WATERLOO, BATTLE OF, fought on June 18, 1815, was the final battle of the French military genius, Napoleon Bonaparte. It put an end to his political am-

bitions to rule Europe. His defeat was so crushing that, when a person suffers a disastrous reverse, we say the person has "met his (or her) Waterloo."

Napoleon Returns to France. After abdicating in 1814, Napoleon was exiled to the island of Elba, off the coast of Italy. He spent less than a year there before he decided to return to rule France. He saw that the allies at the Congress of Vienna seemed unable to settle their differences, and he hoped to take advantage of this split to regain power.

But the allies joined forces against Napoleon as soon as they heard of his return to France. Napoleon marched north into Belgium to meet this threat. The Duke of Wellington commanded the allied forces of Belgium, Great Britain, Hanover, and The Netherlands. Neither commander had good intelligence services. Napoleon was not in good health at the time, and failed to display his earlier energy and military grasp.

The Battle took place at Waterloo, a small town near Brussels. The two armies were about equal in size. Napoleon had about 74,000 troops, and superior cavalry and artillery. Wellington had about 67,000 troops. He placed them in a strong defensive position. The French started a fierce attack against the allied lines on June 18. Wellington's troops resisted the French assaults.

Napoleon might have won at Waterloo if he had attacked earlier in the day. But he waited until noon because of a heavy rain the night before. This delay permitted Marshal Gebhard von Blücher to arrive with his Prussian troops to reinforce Wellington. The battle was a draw until the arrival of Blücher's forces. These forces helped turn the battle against the French.

Napoleon made one last effort to win the battle. He flung his best troops, the famous "Old Guard," against the enemy's lines. Three battalions of the Guard fought bravely, but were overwhelmed. The French then retreated from a fierce bayonet counterattack.

Both sides lost many killed and wounded in the battle. The French suffered about 40,000 casualties, and the allies about 23,000. After this defeat, Napoleon failed to gather a new army. He had no choice left but to abdicate a second time.   ROBERT B. HOLTMAN

See also BLÜCHER, GEBHARD L. VON; NAPOLEON I; WELLINGTON, DUKE OF.

WATERLOO, UNIVERSITY OF, is a private, coeducational university in Waterloo, Ont. It is supported mainly by student fees and government grants. The university has divisions of arts, engineering, environmental studies, human kinetics and leisure studies, mathematics, and science. It grants bachelor's, master's, and doctor's degrees. Four church-owned colleges in Waterloo are associated with the university. The school was established in 1957. For enrollment, see CANADA (table: Universities and Colleges).

Critically reviewed by the UNIVERSITY OF WATERLOO

WATERMARK is an identifying mark pressed into paper as it is formed by a papermaking machine. Usually, it is the mark left by wires bent into the watermark pattern and attached to the *dandy roll* of a Fourdrinier machine (see PAPER [diagram: How Paper Is Made]). As the wire pattern comes into contact with the layer of wet pulp, a translucent impression is made, which can be seen when the finished paper is held in

WATERMELON

front of a light. Watermarked paper is often used for documents, to prevent counterfeiting.   JOHN B. CALKIN

WATERMELON is a vine plant that produces large green fruits with delicious red (sometimes yellow) pulp. The plant is related to the pumpkin, squash, muskmelon, and cucumber. The fruit is 93 per cent water, and has a sweet, refreshing taste.

The fruit has a hard *rind* (outer shell) that encloses the pulp. This pulp colors as the fruit ripens. The seeds found in the pulp may be white, brown, or black. The vines may branch out 12 to 15 feet (4 to 5 meters). The

Leading Watermelon-Growing States

Tons of watermelons grown in 1976

Florida	495,000 short tons (449,100 metric tons)
Texas	225,000 short tons (204,100 metric tons)
Georgia	121,000 short tons (109,800 metric tons)
California	98,000 short tons (88,900 metric tons)
South Carolina	59,000 short tons (53,500 metric tons)

Source: *Vegetables—Fresh Market, 1976 Annual Summary*, U.S. Department of Agriculture.

few fruits they produce are large, averaging from 20 to 35 pounds (9 to 16 kilograms), and weighing as much as 60 pounds (27 kilograms). They may be round, oblong, or oval. Their color varies from plain dark green to striped green, to almost white.

Scientists have produced many varieties of watermelons. Bantam-size watermelons that weigh 5 to 10 pounds (2.3 to 4.5 kilograms) and giant watermelons weighing over 100 pounds (45 kilograms) have been developed. Seedless watermelons are available.

The watermelon is a warm-season crop, but it grows as far north as Canada. The seeds should not be planted until the heat of summer has come. Watermelons grow best in sandy, moist soils. The vine has many blooms, but only a few of the blossoms produce melons. The vines are so long that the plants must be spaced 8 to 10 feet (2.4 to 3 meters) apart. For best flavor, the fruit should not be picked until fully ripe. The fruits ripen in 80 to 90 days, depending on the variety. Most varieties are ripe when the rind gets very hard and the melon sounds hollow when tapped. The skin of a recently developed midget watermelon turns golden when it is ripe.

Watermelons first grew in Africa, and spread to southern Asia in early times. The people of North America have long used the watermelon as a type of luxury food. Watermelons were plentiful in Massachusetts Colony as early as 1629. In 1673, Father Marquette noted the abundance of watermelons along the Wisconsin and Mississippi rivers. Watermelons were raised by the Indian tribes along the Colorado River during the late

1700's. Today, watermelons are produced chiefly in the Southern States.

Scientific Classification. Watermelons belong to the gourd family, *Cucurbitaceae*. They are genus *Citrullus*, species *C. vulgaris*.   ERVIN L. DENISEN

WATERPROOF MATCH. See MATCH (History).

WATERPROOFING is a way of treating cloth, leather, wood, or other materials so that they will shed water. Many different chemical solutions are used in waterproofing. Nearly all of them work by forming a protective coating over the material to be waterproofed.

Materials which have pores are often soaked in solutions of rubber, linseed oil, paraffin, or some other substance which is itself waterproof. The waterproof solution fills the pores. Silicone is widely used to waterproof clothing and building materials (see SILICONE).

The textile industry uses the most advanced methods of waterproofing. The fibers of cloth may be coated either before or after they are woven. Water-repellent solutions in spray containers are sold for home use.

In 1823, Charles Macintosh of England invented a waterproof fabric made of cloth and rubber. A raincoat made of his protective material came to be commonly known as a *mackintosh*. The Japanese have waterproofed paper umbrellas for centuries by dipping the paper in a simple chemical solution.   ELIZABETH CHESLEY BAITY

WATERS, ETHEL (1896-1977), a black actress and singer, overcame many hardships to become a leading performer on the American stage and screen. She sang in the musicals *Lew Leslie's Blackbirds* (1930), *As Thousands Cheer* (1933), and *Cabin in the Sky* (1940).

Her great dramatic hits were *Mamba's Daughters* (1939) and *Member of the Wedding* (1950). She starred in the motion pictures *Cabin in the Sky* (1943) and *Pinky* (1949).

Waters wrote two autobiographies, *His Eye Is on the Sparrow* (1951) and *To Me It's Wonderful* (1972). She was born in Chester, Pa.   MARY VIRGINIA HEINLEIN

WATERSHED. See DIVIDE.

WATERSPOUT is a whirling cloud mass over a lake or ocean. It is a rotating column that consists of air and watery mist. Lake water or seawater may be

WORLD BOOK photo by Robert N. Becker

A Waterspout's Whirling Column is spectacular but dangerous. This waterspout was sighted over the Gulf of Mexico.

drawn up at the base of the column. Some waterspouts cause strong winds and may damage ships, but others are harmless.

Most waterspouts occur in tropical regions. The severe type forms under unstable weather conditions. A center of low pressure develops, and winds begin to whirl around it. Many harmful waterspouts develop from clouds that bring thunderstorms. Such waterspouts begin to form in the clouds and develop downward. A harmless waterspout forms when the wind is weak and weather conditions are fairly stable. It receives its energy from the surface of the water.　WAYNE M. WENDLAND

WATERTON-GLACIER INTERNATIONAL PEACE PARK is on the United States-Canadian boundary line between Montana and Alberta. It covers over 1 million acres (400,000 hectares) on the United States side, and over 130,000 acres (52,600 hectares) in Canada. The park unites Glacier National Park in Montana with Waterton Lakes National Park in Alberta. See also GLACIER NATIONAL PARK; ALBERTA (color picture: Town of Waterton Park).　NICHOLAS HELBURN

WATERTON LAKES NATIONAL PARK. See CANADA (National Parks); NATIONAL PARK SYSTEM (picture).

WATERWAY is a water route suitable for boat and barge traffic. Nature provides many waterways, such as lakes and rivers, while others are artificially created. The most famous artificially created waterways include the Erie Canal, Panama Canal, St. Lawrence Seaway, and Suez Canal. See also CANAL; INLAND WATERWAY, with their lists of Related Articles.

WATIE, STAND (1806-1871), became the only Indian brigadier general in the Confederate Army. Born near Rome, Ga., he moved to Oklahoma with the Cherokee Indians in 1838 and became a tribal leader. Watie entered the army when the Cherokee allied with the Confederacy in 1861. He led a regiment of Cherokee volunteers called the Cherokee Mounted Rifles. In 1864, he was made a brigadier general. Watie was one of the last Confederate officers to surrender. After the war, he farmed in Oklahoma.　W. EUGENE HOLLON

WATKINS GLEN. See FINGER LAKES; NEW YORK (Places to Visit [State Parks; picture]).

WATSON, DOCTOR. See DETECTIVE STORY (History); HOLMES, SHERLOCK.

WATSON, HOMER (1856-1936), was a Canadian landscape painter. His works show the beauty and majesty of Canadian woods, fields, and streams. Watson was the first president of the Canadian Art Club, and was president of the Royal Canadian Academy from 1918 to 1922. He was born in Doon, Ont. He studied landscape painting for a time in Great Britain and the United States. Some of his landscapes are in Windsor Castle.　WILLIAM R. WILLOUGHBY

WATSON, JAMES DEWEY (1928-　), is an American biologist. He shared the 1962 Nobel prize for physiology or medicine with biologist Francis H. C. Crick and biophysicist Maurice H. F. Wilkins, both of Great Britain. Watson and Crick, on the basis of research by Wilkins, devised a model of the molecular structure of *deoxyribonucleic acid* (DNA). DNA serves to carry genetic information from one generation to the next.

The so-called *Watson-Crick* model looks like a twisted ladder. The sequence of certain chemicals on successive "rungs" of DNA forms a code that determines such things as size, structure, and function in an organism.

Watson published his findings when he was 25 years old. Born in Chicago, he studied at the University of Chicago and Indiana University. In 1961, he became professor of biology at Harvard University.　IRWIN H. HERSKOWITZ

See also BIOLOGY (picture); CELL (The 1900's; picture: A Model of DNA); NUCLEIC ACID.

WATSON, JOHN BROADUS (1878-1958), an American psychologist, became best known as the leader of a revolutionary movement in psychology called *behaviorism*. His early work in biology, medicine, and the behavior of lower organisms led him to question the existence of the mental processes which psychologists claimed to be studying. He undertook to account for the behavior of both man and animals in purely physiological and physical terms. He discussed this behavior in his *Psychology from the Standpoint of a Behaviorist* (1919).

Watson also rejected the notion of innate abilities. He claimed that in the proper environment a healthy child would acquire any given talent or skill. He studied the emotional behavior of children and expressed strong views on child care. For example, he cautioned parents against the possible ill effects of strong displays of affection. Although his extreme views are not widely held today, he was an important "ice-breaking" influence in psychology, particularly in the United States.

Watson was born in Greenville, S.C. He received a Ph.D. degree in psychology at the University of Chicago. He later worked at Johns Hopkins University. In 1920, he retired from his scientific career to enter the field of advertising.　B. F. SKINNER

See also PSYCHOLOGY (Behaviorism).

WATSON, THOMAS AUGUSTUS. See BELL, ALEXANDER GRAHAM; TELEPHONE (History).

WATSON, THOMAS EDWARD (1856-1922), was an American political leader. Elected to the United States House of Representatives as a Democrat in 1890, he joined the new Populist party, which represented the farmers (see POPULISM). The Populists nominated Watson for Vice-President of the United States in 1896 and for President in 1904. As a newspaper editor and author in Atlanta and New York City, he agitated for radical reforms. He later became a Democrat again, and was elected to the Senate in 1920. Watson was born near Thomson, Ga.　NELSON M. BLAKE

WATSON, THOMAS JOHN (1874-1956), was a famous American industrialist. He worked for the National Cash Register Company (now NCR Corporation) for 15 years. Then in 1914, he was made president of a company which became International Business Machines Corporation in 1924. Under his leadership from 1914 to 1956, it became an international organization. He was born in Campbell, N.Y.　W. H. BAUGHN

WATSON-CRICK MODEL. See WATSON, JAMES D.

WATSON-WATT, SIR ROBERT ALEXANDER (1892-1973), a Scottish electronics engineer and inventor, helped develop radar. He patented in 1935 a radar device that could detect and follow a flying airplane. He invented a crude form of radio direction finder in 1919 while associated with the British weather bureau. He described the finder as "useful for meteorological purposes such as the location of atmospheric discharges." He received his patent while doing radio research with the Department of Scientific and Industrial Research

WATT

and with the National Physical Laboratory.

Watson-Watt was born in Brechin, Scotland, and graduated from University College at St. Andrew's University. He was knighted in 1942. He received many other honors, including the Hughes medal of the Royal Society, the United States Medal of Merit, and many honorary degrees. G. Gamow

WATT, *waht,* is a unit used to measure *power* (rate of producing or using energy). It is most often used to measure electric power. An electric device uses 1 watt when 1 volt of electric potential drives 1 ampere of electric current through it. The number at the top of a light bulb shows its power requirement in watts. A light bulb operating at 100 volts and using 2 amperes consumes 200 watts (100 × 2 amperes). Electric power is often measured in *kilowatts* (1,000 watts).

The watt is used to measure mechanical power in the metric system. A machine produces a power of 1 watt if it uses 1 joule of energy in 1 second. The unit was named for the Scottish engineer and inventor, James Watt. Benjamin J. Dasher

See also Ampere; Kilowatt; Joule; Watt, James.

WATT, JAMES (1736-1819), was a Scottish engineer whose improved engine design first made steam power practicable. Crude steam engines were used before Watt's time, but they burned large amounts of coal and produced little power. Their *lateral* (back-and-forth) motion restricted their use to operating pumps. Watt's invention of the "separate condenser" made steam engines more efficient, and his later improvements made possible their wide application.

Watt, the son of a shopkeeper and carpenter, was born in Greenock on Jan. 19, 1736. When he was 18, he went to Glasgow and then to London to learn the trade of a mathematical instrument maker. In 1757, he became instrument maker at the University of Glasgow.

The Steam Engine. In 1763, Watt received a model of a Newcomen steam engine to repair. Although he made it work, he was not satisfied with how it operated and set about to improve it. He obtained advice from students and professors at the university, and discovered the principle of the separate condenser. He patented his discovery in 1769.

In the old engines, steam filled the cylinder space

Bundy Tubing Co.
James Watt Used Steam Coils to heat his office in 1784. This was the first practical use of steam for heating.

under the piston. The steam was then condensed, leaving a vacuum into which the piston was pushed by atmospheric pressure. This meant alternately heating and chilling the cylinder. Watt reasoned that because steam was an elastic vapor, it would fill any container into which it was admitted. If the steam-filled cylinder opened into a separate, chilled container, steam would continually move into the container and condense there, producing the vacuum in the cylinder without having to chill it (see Condenser, Steam).

Watt spent several years trying to develop an operating engine of the new design. He also worked as a surveyor and construction engineer during this period. In 1774, he obtained the support of Matthew Boulton, an energetic Birmingham manufacturer. Boulton persuaded Parliament to renew Watt's patent for 25 years. The two then organized a company to rent the design of the new engine and to supervise its construction and operation. The firm succeeded.

Watt developed crank movements so the engine could turn wheels. He also invented an "expansive, double-acting" engine, a throttle valve, a governor for regulating engine speed, and many other devices. He did scientific research in chemistry and metallurgy, and was one of the first persons to suggest that water is a compound, not an element. He retired as a wealthy man in 1800. The power unit, the watt, is named in his honor (see Watt). Robert E. Schofield

See also Industrial Revolution (The Steam Engine); Steam Engine (History); Invention (picture: James Watt's Steam Engine).

WATT-HOUR METER. See Electric Meter.

WATTEAU, *wah TOH,* **ANTOINE** (1684-1721), a French painter, introduced the style of delicately romantic art that became popular in France during the 1700's. In 1717, he painted his most celebrated picture, *The Embarkation for Cythera,* which hangs in the Louvre in Paris. The picture gained Watteau membership in the French Academy. It appears in color in the Painting article. Antoine Watteau's art is notable for its small scale, exquisite coloring, and charming design. In his softly lighted glades and parks, realistic young men and women wander, talking or making love. These pictures suggest a hauntingly melancholy world where people live the dreams that real life denies them. The costumes have the glow and shine of real cloth, and the bodies are alive and solid, but the parks and hills seem insubstantial and dreamlike. This sentimental attitude toward life represented a reaction to the stiff formality of the age of Louis XIV. Pictures such as Watteau painted became immensely popular in an escapist society moving toward the French Revolution of 1789. *Gilles* and *The Mezzetin* represent some of his best work. Watteau's drawings established his reputation as a master in that field.

He was born Jean Antoine Watteau in Valenciennes, Flanders, and came to Paris as a young man in 1702. Watteau worked under several masters, including Claude Gillot and Claude Audran. Pierre Crozat, a wealthy collector of pictures, took the young painter into his household and gave him commissions, after which Watteau's fortunes improved. Joseph C. Sloane

WATTERSON, HENRY (1840-1921), an American newspaper editor, won the 1918 Pulitzer prize for edi-

118

torial writing. He was associated in 1868 in the consolidation of Louisville's newspapers into the *Courier-Journal*, and was its outspoken editor for 50 years. He hated slavery and thought secession wrong, but out of loyalty to the South served in the Confederate Army during the Civil War. Watterson left the *Courier-Journal* in 1919 because that paper supported the League of Nations. He was born in Washington, D.C. ALVIN E. AUSTIN

WATTLE, a shrub or tree. See ACACIA.

WATTMETER is an instrument used to measure electric power. There are several kinds of wattmeters. The one most commonly used is called an *electrodynamic* wattmeter. The electrodynamic wattmeter has two coils of wire. A *fixed* coil is arranged to receive the current of the circuit to be measured. A *movable* coil, supported by jeweled pivots that permit it to turn, is arranged to receive a current proportional to the voltage. When the circuit is energized, the magnetic fields produced by the currents make the movable coil try to turn so that its axis is parallel to the axis of the fixed coil. Springs stop it in a position that depends on the power in the circuit. A pointer shows the power in watts on a scale. BENJAMIN J. DASHER

Simpson Electric Co.

A Wattmeter

WATTS. See BLACK AMERICANS (Unrest in the Cities); LOS ANGELES (South-Central Los Angeles; picture).

WATTS, ISAAC (1674-1748), an English clergyman, wrote 761 hymns and psalms, 29 treatises on theology, volumes of sermons, and many books on ethics, psychology, and teaching. His best hymns are notable for simplicity of poetic structure, apt use of figures of speech, and emotional vitality.

Many of Watts's finest hymns still appear in nearly every English hymnal. He wrote "Joy to the World," "O God, Our Help in Ages Past," "When I Survey the Wondrous Cross," and "There Is a Land of Pure Delight."

Watts was born in Southampton, England. He became pastor of London's Mark Lane Independent Chapel in 1702. Watts was considered one of the great preachers of his time. ARTHUR L. RICH

WATUSI. See BURUNDI (People; History); RWANDA (People; History).

WAUGH, *waw,* is the family name of two brothers who became noted English writers.

Alec Waugh (1898-   ) is a popular novelist, poet, and travel writer. He has been praised for his absorbing and entertaining stories. Waugh created a sensation with his first novel, *The Loom of Youth* (1917), a satirical exposé of the fashionable Sherbourne School that he had attended. Waugh has traveled widely and has written both fiction and nonfiction based on his adventures and observations. *The Early Years of Alec Waugh* (1962) is an autobiography. Alexander Raban Waugh was born in London.

Evelyn Waugh (1903-1966) was best known for his humorous and satirical novels. Most of his early novels appear to be light, satiric portraits of England's wealthy and fashionable younger generation. But in these works are serious criticisms of modern civilization. Such novels include *Decline and Fall* (1928), *Vile Bodies* (1930), *Black Mischief* (1932), and *A Handful of Dust* (1934). In *Scoop* (1938), Waugh satirized journalism and broadcasting. In *The Loved One* (1948), he mocked funeral practices in the United States.

Waugh became intensely religious after being converted to Roman Catholicism in 1930. His work after his conversion shows an increasing concern with religious and historical questions. *Brideshead Revisited* (1945) deals with the roles of fate and religious faith in the lives of a wealthy Roman Catholic family. Waugh wrote three related novels that examine the nature of war and of the struggle between good and evil. The trilogy consists of *Men at Arms* (1952), *Officers and Gentlemen* (1955), and *Unconditional Surrender* (1961; U.S. title, *The End of the Battle*). Evelyn Arthur St. John Waugh was born in London. DARCY O'BRIEN

WAVE BAND is a group of radio frequencies used for one purpose, such as commercial, ship-to-shore, amateur, airplane, or police broadcasting. Wave band also refers to a smaller group of frequencies set aside for a single broadcaster called a *station*.

Engineers set each radio transmitter so that its *carrier wave* remains at a certain frequency. But because sounds *modulate* (change) the frequency slightly, each station uses a band of frequencies to prevent interference with other stations. Most stations allow a margin of five kilohertz on either side of their carrier wave. Two stations using the same frequency must be far apart. Otherwise they interfere with one another (see INTERFERENCE). In the United States, the Federal Communications Commission assigns frequencies.

Ordinary broadcasting uses a low-frequency band that ranges from approximately 500 to 1,500 kilohertz. Amateur radio operators, frequency modulation (FM), and television use high-frequency wave bands, or short waves. PALMER H. CRAIG

Related Articles in WORLD BOOK include:

Frequency Modulation	Television (Transmitting)
Radio (How Radio Works)	Ultrahigh Frequency Wave
Short Wave	Very High Frequency Wave

WAVE MECHANICS. See PHYSICS (Relativity and Quanta); ATOM (Modern Theories).

WAVE THEORY. See LIGHT (Man's Understanding of Light).

WAVELENGTH. See ELECTROMAGNETIC WAVES; LIGHT (The Nature of Light); WAVES.

WAVELL, *WAY vul,* **ARCHIBALD PERCIVAL** (1883-1950), VISCOUNT WAVELL OF CYRENAICA AND TRIPOLITANIA, was a British soldier and statesman. He was born near his father's army post in Essex, and attended Winchester College and the Royal Military College at Sandhurst. During World War I (1914-1918), Wavell served in France and in the Middle East. At the beginning of World War II (1939-1945), he took command of all British army forces in the Middle East. Wavell successfully defended Egypt against an Italian invasion in 1940. In 1941 he became commander in chief of British forces in India. From 1943 to 1947, he served as viceroy of India. CHARLES LOCH MOWAT

WAVERLEY NOVELS. See SCOTT, SIR WALTER.

WAVES

WAVES are motions that carry energy, but not matter, from one place to another. A simple experiment will show how waves carry energy but not matter. First have two boys hold the ends of a rope. When one boy moves his end of the rope up and down sharply, energy passes from one section to the next as a wave. Each part of the rope is set into motion as the wave passes, but the rope itself does not move forward with the wave. The boy holding the other end will feel the energy carried by the wave move his hand.

Next, have one boy throw a baseball to the other. The catcher feels some of the energy used in throwing the ball. But unlike the wave, the matter—that is, the ball—moves forward, and carries the energy with it.

Waves on a rope or water are familiar examples of waves, but many other waves move around us all the time. For example, the sound of people speaking travels to our ears as waves. Radio and television programs travel to our homes as waves.

L. Wallace Dean, the contributor of this article, is a project engineer with Pratt and Whitney Aircraft and a specialist in fluid waves.

Many kinds of waves travel on or in a material. Scientists call the substance through which the waves travel the wave *medium*. For waves on a rope, the rope is the medium. Ocean waves travel on the surface of the water and *seismic* (earthquake) waves travel through the earth. Some waves do not need to travel through a material medium. For example, the electromagnetic waves that carry light, radio, and television signals can travel through a vacuum. The medium for these waves is an electric and magnetic *field* (area containing lines of force).

Characteristics of Waves

Waves are caused when something disturbs a medium. A rock dropped into a still pond sets water waves in motion. The rock is called the *source* of the waves. When you move the free end of a rope, you become the source of the waves on the rope. If you move the rope high and low, you will make large waves. Scientists call the top part of any wave the *crest* and the bottom part the *trough*. The height of a crest above the level of the rope when no waves are moving on it is called the *amplitude* of the wave. Amplitude can also be meas-

THE SHAPE OF A WAVE

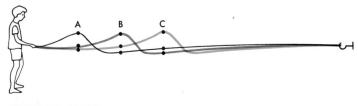

Many Waves Resemble Hills and Valleys. Scientists have various terms to describe waves, *left*. They call the hills *crests* and the valleys *troughs*. The *amplitude* is a measure of how much the medium carrying the wave rises or falls from its usual position. *Wave length* is the distance between comparable points on two waves next to each other.

TRANSVERSE WAVE

Transverse Waves cause individual particles of the medium to move up and down while the wave moves forward. As a single wave moves down the rope away from the boy, *left*, the crest passes from point A to point B and then to point C. But the three points themselves do not move along the rope.

STANDING WAVE

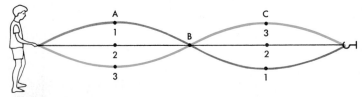

Standing Waves do not move along the medium. Instead, they vibrate in a certain whole number of loops. To make two loops, the boy makes a wave with a wave length equal to the length of the rope. Then he holds his end still. Points A and C on the loops move, but point B—between them—does not move.

LONGITUDINAL WAVE

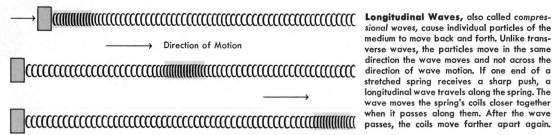

Direction of Motion

Longitudinal Waves, also called *compressional waves*, cause individual particles of the medium to move back and forth. Unlike transverse waves, the particles move in the same direction the wave moves and not across the direction of wave motion. If one end of a stretched spring receives a sharp push, a longitudinal wave travels along the spring. The wave moves the spring's coils closer together when it passes along them. After the wave passes, the coils move farther apart again.

A WORLD BOOK SCIENCE PROJECT

EXPERIMENTING WITH WAVES

The purpose of this project is to learn about the behavior of waves by studying water waves in a ripple tank. Wave behavior such as reflection, diffraction, and interference is shown in the photos taken of a homemade ripple tank. Experiment with various objects in the tank to see how they affect the motion of the waves.

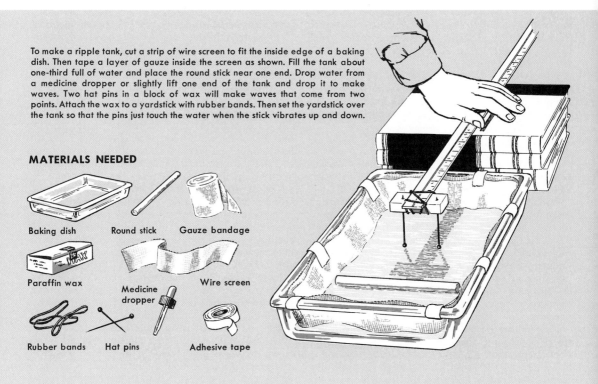

To make a ripple tank, cut a strip of wire screen to fit the inside edge of a baking dish. Then tape a layer of gauze inside the screen as shown. Fill the tank about one-third full of water and place the round stick near one end. Drop water from a medicine dropper or slightly lift one end of the tank and drop it to make waves. Two hat pins in a block of wax will make waves that come from two points. Attach the wax to a yardstick with rubber bands. Then set the yardstick over the tank so that the pins just touch the water when the stick vibrates up and down.

MATERIALS NEEDED

Baking dish   Round stick   Gauze bandage

Paraffin wax

Medicine dropper   Wire screen

Rubber bands   Hat pins   Adhesive tape

WAVE PATTERNS IN A RIPPLE TANK

Reflected Waves form curved arches near the barrier that reflected them. The original waves form nearly complete circles near the top of the picture.

Curved Diffracted Waves in the top half of the picture, *below,* resulted when parts of parallel waves passed through the small slit in the barrier.

Interfering Waves cancel each other along the faint gray lines coming from the center. They strengthen themselves where the bright dashed lines occur.

WORLD BOOK Photos

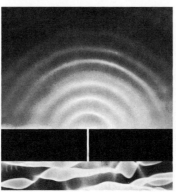

WAVES

ured from the bottom of the trough to the still rope.

By moving the free end of the rope up and down faster, you make more waves on the rope. You have increased the *frequency* of the waves because more waves pass any point in one second. But no matter how fast or how high you make the rope move, you cannot make the waves travel faster. The speed of a wave does not depend on either its amplitude or its frequency. The speed of the wave depends only on the stiffness and *density* (mass of a unit of volume) of the medium (see DENSITY). For example, a tightly stretched rope will have a higher wave speed than a slack rope. Waves will also travel faster on a light, less dense rope that is stretched the same amount as a heavy rope.

When you increase the frequency of the waves, you also shorten the distance between the crests or troughs. Scientists call this distance the *wave length*. You can find the wave length by dividing the frequency into the wave speed.

Wave Motion

When a wave moves along a medium, there are really two motions to watch. One is the motion of the wave and the other is the motion of the medium itself.

Transverse Waves cause the medium to move up and down while the wave travels along it. Waves that move this way are called transverse waves, because the motion of the medium is perpendicular to the motion of the waves. Rope waves are transverse. Other examples of transverse waves include electromagnetic waves such as light, and water waves. If the rope moves vertically or horizontally, the waves have a vertical or horizontal *polarization*. That is, the medium vibrates in only one direction. Only transverse waves can have polarization.

Longitudinal Waves, also called *compressional waves*, travel in the same direction that the medium moves. For example, these waves are made in a stretched spring by compressing a few coils at one end and then releasing them. Sound waves and some earthquake waves are longitudinal waves.

Traveling and Standing Waves. In the previous examples with waves on a rope, the waves have traveled from one end of the rope to the other. These waves are *traveling waves*. However, under certain conditions, waves may be trapped in a piece of rope or other medium. For example, if a string is held at both ends and plucked, the energy in the waves cannot leave the string at either end. This creates patterns called *standing waves*. The size of the space in which the waves are confined determines the wave length the waves can have. Standing waves can exist on a surface such as a drumhead, or within an enclosed space, such as a room. The possible wave lengths are still determined by the size of the medium.

How Waves Behave

So far, only individual waves in a single medium have been discussed. But waves behave differently when they move from one medium to another, when some part of the waves are stopped, or when other waves are also present in the medium.

Reflection and Refraction. When waves leave one medium and enter another, some of the energy in the waves is reflected and some is *refracted* (transmitted) into the new medium. The amount of energy that is reflected and refracted depends on the angle at which the *incident* (incoming) waves strike the new medium. The larger the angle between the path of the waves and an imaginary line perpendicular to the surface of the new medium, the more the waves will be reflected.

The amount of reflection and refraction also depends on certain properties of the two mediums. For example, reflection and refraction of sound waves depends on the density of the two mediums and the speed of sound in them. If the two properties are nearly the same, most of the sound will be refracted into the new medium. If they are different, most of the sound will be reflected. Air is much less dense than the ground and carries sound much more slowly. Consequently, most of the energy in sound waves is reflected from the ground.

Diffraction. An expanding ring of waves moves away from a stone dropped into a still pond. As the ring becomes larger, any short part of the *wave front* (the outside edge of the ring) becomes a nearly straight line. But if the wave front passes through a small slit in a barrier, the wave coming out on the other side will not form a straight line. Instead, it will spread out from the slit in a curved line.

The changing of the straight wave front into a curved wave is called *diffraction*. Diffraction occurs because each point on the wave front is a source of a tiny curved wave called a *wavelet*. The wavelets along the front combine to make the straight wave. But the slit lets only a few wavelets pass through. The wavelets on either side are cut off and the front is no longer straight.

Interference. Where the crests of two waves with the same frequency pass a given point at the same time, the waves are in *phase*. But, if the crest of one wave passes the point at the same time as the trough of the other, one wave is half a wave length ahead of the other. Scientists measure the difference in phase between two waves in degrees. They multiply the number of degrees in a circle (360) by the fraction of the wave length between the two waves. In this case, the waves are 180° out of phase.

Waves of the same frequency make each other stronger where they are in phase and cancel each other where they are 180° out of phase. Scientists say the two sources *interfere* with each other. The waves will travel away stronger in some directions and weaker in others.

Wave Theory. The ideas that apply to light, sound, and other waves also apply to the tiny parts of atoms. Scientists have discovered that electrons, neutrons, and protons, which are usually thought of as particles, sometimes behave like waves. Their waves are called *matter waves*. The wave theory of atomic particles has given scientists a greater understanding of the structure of atoms and their nuclei. See PHYSICS (Relativity and Quanta); QUANTUM MECHANICS.   L. WALLACE DEAN

WAVES. See Navy, UNITED STATES (Women in the Navy).

WAX is a fatty substance that is widely used as a protective coating for various surfaces. It resists air, water, and chemical change. Most wax is solid at room temperature, but it becomes soft when heated. The word *wax* comes from the Anglo-Saxon word *weax*, meaning *beeswax*.

Manufacturers produce three chief kinds of wax: (1) mineral, (2) animal, and (3) vegetable. Most manufacturers blend two or more types of wax to give their product the desired qualities.

Mineral Wax. Most wax comes from petroleum. Manufacturers chill and filter oil and then use various chemical processes to separate the wax from it. There are three major kinds of petroleum wax: (1) *paraffin wax*, (2) *microcrystalline wax*, and (3) *petrolatum*. These waxes differ in color, hardness, and melting point.

Petroleum wax resists moisture and chemicals and has no odor or taste. It serves as a waterproof coating for such paper products as milk cartons and waxed paper. Petroleum wax also is used in making polishes for automobiles, floors, and furniture. It does not conduct electricity, and so it can serve as an electric insulator. Manufacturers use wax molds in casting jewelry and machinery parts. Most candles are made from paraffin wax. Microcrystalline wax is used mostly in making paper for packaging. Petrolatum, also called *petroleum jelly*, is used in making cosmetics and medicines.

Other mineral waxes include *montan wax*, which comes from coal; *ozokerite*, made from shale; and *peat wax*, made from peat. *Synthetic* (artificially created) wax is made from *ethylene glycol*, a chemical obtained from petroleum. These waxes are usually blended with petroleum wax.

Animal Wax is used alone or is blended with petroleum wax in making candles, polishes, and other products. Bees produce *beeswax* in building honeycombs. *Wool wax* comes from a greasy coating on unprocessed wool. *Lanolin*, a form of wool wax, is used in making cosmetics. *Spermaceti*, obtained from the oil of the sperm whale, is used in making creams and salves.

Vegetable Wax. Many plants have a natural wax coating that protects them from heat and moisture. *Carnauba wax*, the hardest and most widely used vegetable wax, coats the leaves of the carnauba palm tree. It remains solid in hot weather and is an important ingredient in automobile wax and other polishes. Other vegetable waxes include *bayberry wax*, *candelilla wax*, *Japan wax*, and *sugar cane wax*.   RICHARD F. BLEWITT

Related Articles in WORLD BOOK include:

Beeswax	Microcrystalline Wax	Petrolatum
Candle	Painting (Encaustic	Polish
Candleberry	Painting)	Sealing Wax
Carnauba Wax	Paraffin	Spermaceti

WAX MYRTLE is a large evergreen shrub or small tree found along the eastern coast of the United States, and as far west as Texas. It grows as high as 40 feet (12 meters), and has gray flowers. The 2- to 3-inch (5- to 8-centimeter) leaves are alternate along the branches. The wax myrtle is grown as an ornamental shrub and does best in damp soil.

Scientific Classification. Wax myrtles belong to the sweet gale family, *Myricaceae*. They are classified as genus *Myrica*, species *M. cerifera*.   WILLIAM M. HARLOW

WAXBERRY. See CANDLEBERRY.

WAXWING is a silky-feathered, grayish-brown bird larger than a sparrow, with a conspicuous crest or topknot. It has a band of yellow across the end of its tail, and red, waxlike drops on its wing feathers.

The *cedar waxwing* is the best known of these birds. It lives in most parts of North America, as far north as central Canada and Labrador. These birds eat berries and fruits, and insects. They build bulky nests, usually in a fruit or shade tree. Many cedar waxwings are found on the islands of Lake Superior and around the lakes of Ontario and northern Minnesota in the summer. The birds cannot sing, but are able to utter a few high hissing notes. The female lays three to five eggs which are a pale bluish or purplish gray, speckled with black, brown, or purple. See BIRD (picture: Other Bird Favorites).

The *Bohemian waxwing* is a slightly larger bird. It has yellow marks on its wings and reddish-brown undertail feathers. It lives in the northern latitudes of the world. In the winter, the Bohemian waxwing appears in the

F. J. Alsop III, Bruce Coleman Inc.

Cedar Waxwings live in most parts of North America. They build bulky nests and eat berries, fruits, and insects.

James R. Simon, Van Cleve photography

The Bohemian Waxwing lives in forests near the Arctic, but many of these birds fly hundreds of miles south in winter.

northwestern and central northern United States and northern Europe. The *Siberian waxwing* lives in southeastern Siberia and Japan.

Scientific Classification. Waxwings belong to the waxwing family, *Bombycillidae.* The cedar waxwing is genus *Bombycilla,* species *B. cedrorum;* the Bohemian, *B. garrulus,* and the Siberian, *B. japonica.*   LEONARD W. WING

WAYBILL. See BILL OF LADING.

WAYLAND BAPTIST COLLEGE. See UNIVERSITIES AND COLLEGES (table).

WAYNE, ANTHONY (1745-1796), was an American officer in the Revolutionary War. He became known as "Mad Anthony" Wayne because of his reckless courage. He was the hero of the recapture of Stony Point, N.Y., a British post on the Hudson River, in 1779. Wayne commanded the attack, which was considered one of the most daring of the war.

He was born on Jan. 1, 1745, in Chester County, Pennsylvania. He studied at an academy in Philadelphia where he qualified as a surveyor. A Philadelphia land company sent him to Nova Scotia in 1765 to supervise the surveying and settlement of land. He returned to Pennsylvania and served in the colonial assembly. When the war began in 1775, he raised a regiment for the Canadian campaign, and later served in the garrison at Ticonderoga. In 1777, Wayne became a brigadier general and joined Washington's army to command the Pennsylvania line. He led a division at Brandywine, commanded the right wing at Germantown, and spent the winter with Washington at Valley Forge. He led the advance attack at Monmouth the next year. In 1781, Wayne served with the Marquis de Lafayette against General Cornwallis, and took part in the siege of Yorktown. Cornwallis' surrender at Yorktown helped bring the Revolutionary War to an end.

In 1783, Wayne became a brevet major general, but he retired the same year. He represented Georgia in Congress in 1791, but the seat was declared vacant because of election irregularities. He returned to the army in 1791 as a major general and commander in chief. He fought against the Indians in Ohio in 1794, defeating them at the Battle of Fallen Timbers. Wayne made a treaty with the Indians in 1795 which secured a great

tract of land for the United States. He died at Presque Isle (now Erie, Pa.) the next year.   JOHN R. ALDEN

See also INDIAN WARS (picture: "Mad Anthony").

WAYNE, JOHN (1907-1979), an American motion picture actor, became famous for his he-man roles. He starred in such western films as *Red River* (1948) and in other action movies, including *Sands of Iwo Jima* (1950) and *The Quiet Man* (1952). He won an Academy Award for his performance in *True Grit* (1969). Wayne made more than 175 movies.

Wayne, whose real name was Marion Michael Morrison, was born in Winterset, Iowa. He made his film debut in 1928 after working as a prop boy. He failed in a leading role in *The Big Trail* (1930) and then worked mostly in low-budget westerns until the late 1930's. *Stagecoach* (1939) and *The Long Voyage Home* (1940) established him as a star. Wayne's other motion pictures include *She Wore a Yellow Ribbon* (1949), *The Searchers* (1956), and *The Comancheros* (1961).   HARVEY R. DENEROFF

Warner Bros. Inc.
John Wayne

WAYNE STATE COLLEGE. See UNIVERSITIES AND COLLEGES (table).

WAYNE STATE UNIVERSITY. See UNIVERSITIES AND COLLEGES (table).

W.C.T.U. See WOMAN'S CHRISTIAN TEMPERANCE UNION.

WEA INDIANS. See MIAMI INDIANS.

WEAKFISH, or SQUETEAGUE, *SKWEE teeg*, is a saltwater food fish of the croaker family. Its name comes from the fact that its mouth is tender and easily torn. The fish reaches a length of 1 to 2 feet (30 to 61 centimeters) or more. Although *sea trout* is one of its common names, it is not even closely related to the trout. The squeteague lives along the eastern and Gulf coasts of the United States from Massachusetts to Texas. The four kinds are the *common squeteague,* the *spotted squeteague,* the *silver squeteague,* and the *sand squeteague.* Most weak-

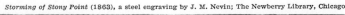

Storming of Stony Point (1863), a steel engraving by J. M. Nevin; The Newberry Library, Chicago

Pastel on paper (about 1796) by James Sharples, Sr.; Independence National Historical Park Collection, Philadelphia

"Mad Anthony" Wayne, *above,* led a daring attack in which American troops defeated the British at Stony Point, N.Y., in 1779, *left,* during the Revolutionary War.

fish weigh less than 15 pounds (7 kilograms), but some weigh up to 30 pounds (14 kilograms).

Scientific Classification. Squeteagues, or sea trout, belong to the drum family, *Sciaenidae*. The common squeteague is genus *Cynoscion*, species *C. regalis;* the silver is *C. nothus;* and the spotted is *C. nebulosus*.   CARL L. HUBBS

WEAPON, *WEHP un.* Weapons have played an important part in the history of humanity. They have helped people conquer vast areas of wilderness and defend their homes and families from enemies. Nations use weapons to carry on wars. They continue to develop new weapons that kill more and more people. Many people believe nuclear weapons are the greatest threat to humanity because of their destructive power.

Related Articles. See FIREARM with its list of *Related Articles*. See also the following:

EXPLOSIVES

Atomic Bomb	Fragmentation	PETN
Bomb	Fuse	Plastic Bomb
Bullet	Grenade	RDX
Cartridge	Guncotton	Shrapnel
Cordite	Gunpowder	TNT
Depth Charge	Hydrogen Bomb	Torpedo
Detonator	Nitroglycerin	

OTHER WEAPONS

Ax	Crossbow	Guided	Sling
Bayonet	Dagger	Missile	Spear
Blowgun	Flail	Knife	Sword
Boomerang	Flame	Mace	Toma-
Bowie Knife	Thrower	Machete	hawk
Catapult		Rocket	Ulu

OTHER RELATED ARTICLES

Ammunition	Chemical-Biological-	Magazine
Archery	Radiological	Ordnance
Arrowhead	Warfare	Powder Horn
Arsenal	Disarmament	Prehistoric People
Ballistics	Fire Control	(Weapons)
	Greek Fire	Shot Tower

WEASEL is a small furry animal with a long slender body and short legs. Most weasels have brown or reddish-brown fur on the back and sides and white or yellow fur on the underside. Some weasels have black and white fur similar to that of skunks. In winter, the fur of weasels that live in cold climates changes to white. This valuable white fur is called *ermine*.

Weasels are native to every continent except Australia and Antarctica. A common North American species, the *long-tailed weasel*, grows from 12 to 18 inches (30 to 46 centimeters) long, including the tail. It weighs up to 12 ounces (340 grams). The *short-tailed weasel* is from 8 to 13 inches (20 to 33 centimeters) long and weighs up to 5 ounces (140 grams). The *least weasel* of North America, one of the world's smallest flesh-eating animals, grows about 8 inches (20 centimeters) long and weighs about 2 ounces (57 grams). The weasel family includes badgers, ferrets, otters, and skunks.

Weasels have a sharp sense of smell and keen sight and are excellent hunters. They move quickly and catch animals their own size or larger for food. Weasels kill mice, squirrels, and other rodents. They cut the victim's spinal column with one or two strong, swift bites at the base of the skull. Weasels also eat earthworms, frogs, lizards, rabbits, shrews, snakes, and small birds. Weasels raid farms and often kill more chickens than they need for food. As a result, many farmers dislike weasels even though they destroy farmyard pests.

John Gerard, NAS

The Long-tailed Weasel lives throughout most of North America and northwestern South America. It has yellowish-white underparts and a reddish-brown back.

A. W. Ambler, NAS

The Grison is a large weasel that lives in Central and South America. It grows as long as 21 inches (53 centimeters). Its black legs and underparts contrast with its brown or gray back.

The weasel's slim body and short legs enable it to hunt in the narrow openings of stone walls, under logs and rocks, and in rodent burrows. A weasel can follow a mouse to the end of the mouse's burrow and can squeeze through knotholes into chicken coops. Weasels are chiefly ground animals, but some climb trees. The weasel's chief enemy is the great horned owl. Weasels, like skunks, discharge a foul-smelling liquid called *musk* when threatened or attacked.

Weasels live in a variety of environments. They make their dens in rock piles, under tree stumps, or in abandoned rodent burrows. They sometimes store food in these dens and make nests from the fur and feathers of past meals. Weasels are more active at night than during the day and remain active in winter. Most female weasels have four to eight young at a time.

Scientific Classification. Weasels belong to the weasel family, *Mustelidae*. The long-tailed weasel is genus *Mustela*, species *M. frenata*. JOHN H. KAUFMANN and ARLEEN KAUFMANN

Related Articles in WORLD BOOK include:

Badger	Marten	Polecat	Skunk
Ermine	Mink	Ratel	Tayra
Ferret	Otter	Sable	Wolverine

WEATHER includes all the daily changes in temperature, wind, moisture, and air pressure. It affects everyone. Today's weather may make us feel hot or cold. We may get soaking wet in a sudden shower, or have to struggle through deep snow. Bright sunshine may make the day cheerful and happy. Dark, dull clouds may make us sad and unhappy. Too much rain can cause floods. Too little rain may kill farm crops.

We cannot change the weather very much at present, but we can adjust ourselves to it. We put on raincoats when it rains, and boots when it snows. We heat our homes in cold weather and cool them in hot weather.

Weather plays an important part in many human activities. Farmers need good weather so that their crops will grow and ripen. Storms or sudden frosts can destroy valuable crops. This raises the prices we pay for food at our neighborhood stores. Weather even affects sales in department stores. Fewer persons shop in rainy or snowy weather. Transportation and communication also suffer in bad weather. Snow may make trains late. Fog often prevents airplanes from taking off. Icy highways slow automobile and truck traffic. Storms can break telephone and electric-power lines. Ships at sea often have to change their courses to avoid bad weather. In wartime, weather plays an important part in planning military operations. During World War II, a storm over the English Channel delayed the Allied invasion of France for a day.

Weather forecasting helps us fit our plans to future weather. We can hear weather forecasts on the radio,

"Will It Snow Tomorrow?" and other questions about weather conditions are answered in the weather reports on radio and television and in newspapers. TV forecasters show simplified versions of weather maps prepared by the National Weather Service.

watch them on television, and read them in the newspaper. *Meteorologists*, the scientists who study weather, gather information about weather conditions and predict what the weather will be tomorrow, next week, or even next month. The weatherman's forecasts may save thousands of lives and millions of dollars in property. Forecasters warn fruitgrowers of early frosts and give them time to set out smudge pots. Ranchers who learn of storms in advance have a chance to shelter their cattle. Weathermen track destructive hurricanes and tell people when to expect floods. They also help families plan picnics, vacations, and other activities.

Weather is not the same as climate. *Climate* is a summary of weather conditions in a certain region for a period of many years. Climate is based on average temperatures, average amounts of rain and snow, and averages of sunshine, wind, and humidity. See CLIMATE.

Weather Forecasting

Weather forecasts depend on observations made at weather stations throughout the world. Forecasters analyze the information and base their predictions on the patterns that highs, lows, and other weather elements usually follow. But weather systems do not always act in the same way, and no two weather situations are

WIND

PRECIPITATION

TEMPERATURE

Wide World; Yugoslav Info. Center; Gendreau

ed States National Weather Service forecast centers throughout the country. The National Weather Service exchanges weather reports with the Canadian Meteorological Service. It also receives about 2,500 weather reports every day from other countries. It sends out about the same number of reports on American weather conditions. All weather observations are transmitted to the National Meteorological Center near Washington, D.C. See WEATHER SERVICE, NATIONAL.

Analysis. As weather information pours into the analysis center, experts called *plotters* decode the messages. They record the observations from each weather observer on maps, using numbers and symbols. *Analysts* draw *isobars*, or lines connecting places that have the same air pressure. Then they draw *isotherms*, or lines connecting places with the same temperature. Other lines show the locations of cold and warm fronts between air masses. These analyzed maps are copied and sent over facsimile networks (see FACSIMILE). Facsimile recorders reproduce the maps at hundreds of weather stations throughout the United States.

Forecast centers that receive weather observations by teletype also plot weather maps. But smaller National Weather Service offices do not. They prepare their forecasts from the maps sent out by the analysis center.

In order to predict the weather, a forecaster first studies the analyzed maps. Like blueprints, these maps give him a three-dimensional picture of the weather systems. He knows how these systems—highs, lows, air masses, and fronts—normally develop and move. He can quickly predict what to expect. But weather systems do not always behave normally. So the forecaster compares the new maps with earlier ones. He learns how the motion and development of the systems differ from their normal behavior. If past maps show that the present weather system is not moving normally, the forecaster must determine whether it probably will con-

exactly alike. Weather processes are much too complicated, too rapidly changing, and too different in places near each other for perfect forecasting. A forecast for a short time ahead may be highly accurate. But for longer and longer times ahead, the forecast is less and less accurate. A forecast made for a month ahead may be little more than a guess.

Observations. A weatherman can forecast future weather only if he knows present and past conditions. But if a forecaster knows the conditions only for his own area, he cannot forecast weather for more than a few hours ahead. For a longer forecast, he must know the present and recent weather over a much larger region. Weather conditions affecting the United States and Canada as you read this article began a week ago over the oceans and other countries. Generally, the farther ahead a forecaster predicts weather, the larger the area for which he must know the present weather.

Observers record the weather conditions at weather stations in all parts of the United States. They report air pressure, temperature, humidity, wind speed and direction, cloud forms, amounts of rain and snow, and such obstructions to visibility as fog, haze, and smoke. Airplane pilots report the weather by radio. Radar operators observe and report clouds and precipitation more than 200 miles (320 kilometers) away (see RADAR [Weather]). Crew members on ships at sea report the weather conditions in various parts of the ocean. All these observers code their information in condensed form and transmit it by radio and teletype to Unit-

--- **WEATHER TERMS** ---

Air Mass is a large body of air that has about the same weather conditions throughout it. Air masses may be warm or cold, dry or humid.

Front is a long, narrow band of changing weather between two kinds of air masses.

High, or **Anticyclone,** is a large area of high pressure. In the Northern Hemisphere, winds blow clockwise in a high. They blow counterclockwise in the Southern Hemisphere.

Humidity is the amount of moisture, or water vapor, in the air.

Low, or **Cyclone,** is a large area of low pressure. Winds in a low rotate counterclockwise in the Northern Hemisphere and clockwise in the Southern Hemisphere.

Precipitation is water droplets or ice crystals that fall to earth as rain, snow, sleet, or hail.

Pressure is the force produced by the weight of air pressing down on the earth.

Temperature measures the degree of heat in the air.

Tornado is the smallest, most violent kind of destructive storm. The dark, funnel-shaped cloud that extends to the ground is usually only about 300 yards (270 meters) across. Its twisting winds may whirl 300 miles (480 kilometers) per hour.

Wind is the movement of masses of air. Winds are named by the direction *from* which they blow. For example, a south wind blows from south to north.

An Observer at a weather station records information about weather conditions. He relays this information to the National Meteorological Center for use in making forecasts.

Weather Radar shows storms within several hundred miles of a radar station. The operator follows the storms and provides information that helps forecasters predict their path.

tinue to move in the same way, or will begin to move in a more nearly normal manner.

Finally, the forecaster examines the details of the maps. He notices little things that may seem unimportant, such as a slight increase of cloudiness or a small change in the shape of a front. These details may indicate important trends, such as increasing precipitation or a new area of falling pressure.

Now the forecaster draws a number of *prognostic* charts that show his predictions of the weather. The prognostic charts prepared in the analysis center are transmitted immediately by facsimile to the local National Weather Service offices. Local weathermen interpret these maps for their areas and send forecasts to newspapers and radio and television stations.

The electronic computer has taken some of the burden of decision from the forecaster. Since May, 1955, computers have been used to help make some of the weather forecasts. They can predict certain basic elements of future weather. Computers can even analyze weather maps. As meteorologists learn more about the patterns of weather and their variations, computers can make even better forecasts.

Kinds of Forecasts. Weathermen use different methods to make forecasts for various lengths of time. The differences consist mainly in the kind of maps used and the details given in the forecasts.

Short-Range Forecasts (up to one or two days ahead) are based mainly on daily weather charts. Local forecasters in National Weather Service offices throughout the United States prepare and distribute them to the public. They revise them as they get new information.

Extended Forecasts are made by the National Weather Service's long-range forecast center in Washington. These forecasts cover periods of 5 days and 30 days. Forecasters prepare 5-day forecasts based on charts showing the average conditions over a 5-day period. They prepare new 5-day forecasts three times every week. Twice each month, on about the 1st and the 15th, the forecast center releases 30-day forecasts giving the average weather conditions expected for the next 30 days. They base these forecasts on 30-day average charts. The longer the period covered by the forecasts, the fewer details they include. A forecaster may predict rain for tomorrow afternoon, but he will be less certain about the time rain may fall five days from now. A 30-day forecast predicts whether the amount of rainfall over the whole period will be above or below normal.

The Story of a Storm

One of the important services performed by weather forecasters is tracking major storms and predicting where they will strike. Here is the story of the birth, life, and death of a typical storm that demonstrates how weather forecasters work.

Birth of a Storm. A small area of thunderstorms, the first sign that a major storm is forming, appears on a September day over the Atlantic Ocean west of the Cape Verde Islands. During the next two or three days, the area of thunderstorms increases and the air pressure slowly falls. Then a definite center of low pressure forms, and winds begin to whirl around it. A tropical cyclone is born. While winds carry the new storm westward, it grows in size and strength.

Tracking a Storm. No one has yet seen the storm. But forecasters in the National Weather Service's Hurricane Warning Service at Miami, Fla., become suspicious. Their charts show a *trough* (low-pressure area) in the middle of the tropical Atlantic. They know hurricanes often "hide" in such troughs. They keep close watch, hoping a ship in the area will radio a weather report. Fortunately, a weather satellite passing over the area transmits a picture showing the spiral cloud bands of a hurricane. Finally, a ship's observer reports unusually low air pressure, strong winds, and squalls. The forecasters feel sure that the storm is a hurricane. They

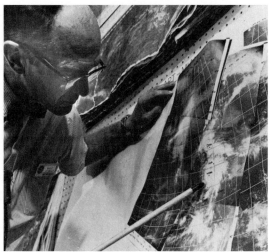

National Oceanic and Atmospheric Administration

Worldwide Weather Patterns appear in photographs taken by space satellites. Forecasters study these patterns to discover weather systems that might affect nearby weather conditions.

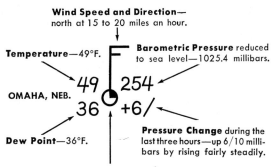

Wind Speed and Direction—
north at 15 to 20 miles an hour.

Temperature—49°F.

Barometric Pressure reduced to sea level—1025.4 millibars.

OMAHA, NEB.

49   254

36   +6/

Dew Point—36°F.

Pressure Change during the last three hours—up 6/10 millibars by rising fairly steadily.

Cloud Cover—about one-fourth of the sky covered by clouds.

Weather Information from individual weather stations is recorded on weather maps as numbers and symbols. Computers at the National Meteorological Center draw the maps after receiving data from many stations and other sources.

National Oceanic and Atmospheric Administration

consult the year's list of names, and christen it "Hannah." Meteorologists periodically make up alphabetical lists of women's names, which are given to hurricanes as they appear. The letter "H" for "Hannah" tells that this is the eighth hurricane of the year.

United States Air Force and Navy pilots, called *hurricane hunters,* fly out to examine the storm and track its position. They look at the ocean waves, the spiral bands of clouds, and the central *eye.* The eye is a region of relative calm and nearly clear skies in the center of the storm. It is about 20 miles (32 kilometers) in diameter. Pilots drop *radiosondes* into the storm. These instruments measure temperature, air pressure, and humidity. They are carried by balloons or dropped by parachutes. Those dropped by parachute are also called *dropsondes.* Pilots estimate wind strength, and report their observations to the hurricane warning center.

Forecasters analyze the reports from the hurricane hunters, and learn that Hannah's center is about 800 miles (1,300 kilometers) east of Puerto Rico. The storm is moving westward at 15 miles (24 kilometers) per hour. Its winds are rotating 100 miles (160 kilometers) per hour around the calm eye. If the hurricane stays on its course, it will reach Puerto Rico in two days. The forecasters issue a *hurricane watch* announcement to the islanders. This announcement tells them that a hurricane is near and that they should be ready to protect themselves if a *hurricane warning* is issued.

During the next two days, Hannah's course veers toward the west-northwest, so Puerto Rico does not receive the worst part of the storm. Now the forecasters must predict if and when Hannah will strike the mainland of the United States.

The storm is beginning to follow the typical curving path toward north and then toward northeast. It might cross the coast anywhere from Florida northward. Or it could curve far to the northeast and miss the mainland entirely. The forecasters study their maps of surface and

National Oceanic and Atmospheric Administration

Weather Forecasters analyze weather maps. They note the position of main weather systems and refer to older maps to learn how the systems are moving. Then they make their forecasts.

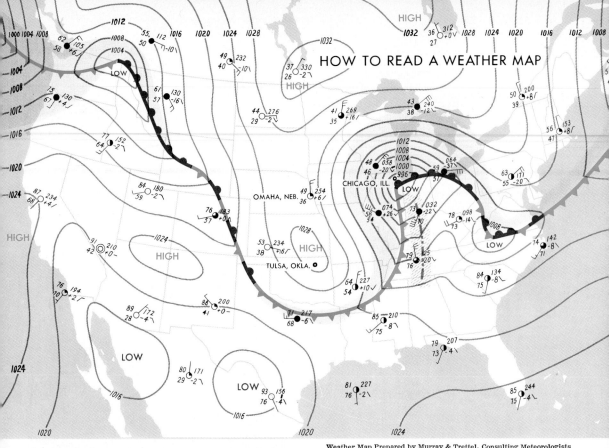

HOW TO READ A WEATHER MAP

Weather Map Prepared by Murray & Trettel, Consulting Meteorologists

A Weather Map pictures weather conditions in various parts of the country. This map of a mid-April day shows cloudy weather in the East, rain in the Middle West, and clear skies in the Southwest. The squall line centers on an area that has gusty winds and frequent rain. Wavy isobars connect places that have the same air pressure, as indicated by the numbers on the lines.

WEATHER MAP SYMBOLS

Cold Front	Warm Front	Stationary Front	Squall Line	Isobar	Precipitation

Cloud Cover is the portion of the sky covered by clouds.

Clear	One Quarter	One Half	Three Quarters	Completely Overcast

Wind. The "feathers" show speed in mph. The end of the arrow with the "feathers" points in the direction from which the wind is blowing.

Calm	1-4	5-8	9-14	15-20	21-25
26-31	32-37	38-43	44-49	50-54	55-60	61-66	67-71	72-77

THE EFFECT OF AIR PRESSURE ON THE WEATHER

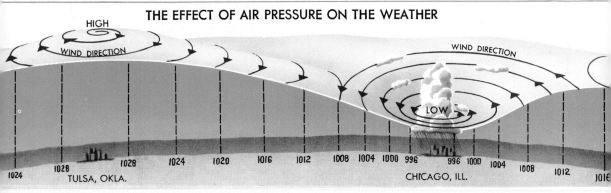

The Ocean of Air that presses down on the earth affects the weather. Air pressure varies from place to place. A *high*, or area of high pressure, resembles a mountain of air. It rises above surrounding air masses. It is heavier than the air around it. Winds in a high spiral *outward* and *downward*, causing clouds to evaporate. Highs usually bring fair weather. A *low*, or area of low pressure, resembles a valley. It weighs less than surrounding air masses. Winds in a low spiral *inward*, and force the air in the center to rise. As the air rises, it cools, and may condense to form clouds, fog, or rain. Lows often bring wet, stormy weather.

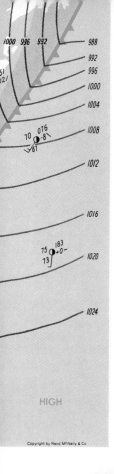

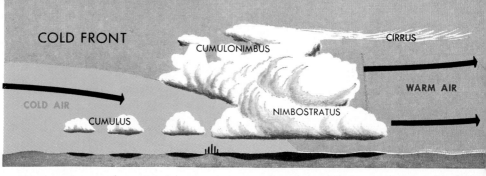

COLD FRONT

CIRRUS

CUMULONIMBUS

WARM AIR

COLD AIR

NIMBOSTRATUS

CUMULUS

A Cold Front forms when a cold air mass forces its way underneath a warmer air mass, and pushes the warm air upward. As the front moves along in the direction shown by the black arrows, cold air replaces warmer air. A narrow zone of clouds forms at the front, and violent rainstorms often rage along it.

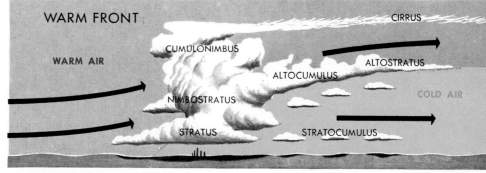

WARM FRONT

CIRRUS

WARM AIR

CUMULONIMBUS

ALTOSTRATUS

ALTOCUMULUS

NIMBOSTRATUS

COLD AIR

STRATUS

STRATOCUMULUS

A Warm Front forms when a mass of warm air overtakes, and moves on top of, a mass of colder air. Warm air replaces the colder air as the front moves in the direction shown by the black arrows. Clouds, steady rain or snow, and sometimes thunderstorms, form within a fairly wide zone ahead of a warm front.

TORNADO

Funnel-Shaped Cloud of a tornado contains winds that whirl at over 300 miles (480 kilometers) per hour.

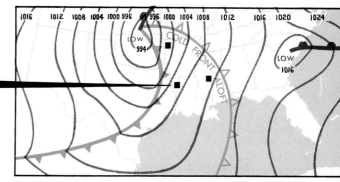

Tornadoes usually form along a cold front. As the front moves, some cold air may jut forward from the front and rise above the warm, moist air. The cold air aloft and the warm air combine to form a whirling tornado funnel.

HURRICANE

Destructive Power of a Hurricane is increased by huge waves that lash coastal areas as it passes.

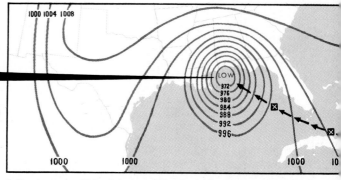

A Hurricane has high winds that whirl around a low-pressure center. Hurricanes that affect the United States start in the tropical parts of the North Atlantic Ocean. They usually travel northward in a curving path.

upper air. They decide that air movement will steer Hannah toward the coast of North Carolina. But they cannot be sure, so they issue a hurricane watch for the coast from Florida to Virginia.

Meanwhile, hurricane hunters make regular flights into the storm to record its position, course, and intensity. They find that it is beginning to move northwest at 20 miles (32 kilometers) per hour. The next day, its center is about 500 miles (800 kilometers) south of Cape Hatteras and it is moving directly north at 22 miles (35 kilometers) per hour. The forecasters warn residents along the coast from South Carolina to Delaware. They tell them to move inland, away from the low coastal areas where the storm's winds will build up a high tide. Shortly before the storm hits the coast, they issue hurricane warnings to areas in Hannah's path.

Effects of a Storm. Finally, hurricane Hannah rips into the coastal area with winds of 100 miles (160 kilometers) per hour. The storm uproots trees and telephone poles, leaving many towns without light or communication. It tears the roofs off houses and breaks windows. The rains that accompany the hurricane bring floods to small rivers and creeks. The storm raises the tide so that it carries some boats inland and dumps them on dry land. The tide drowns a number of coastal dwellers who have not left their homes for higher land. The water ruins homes and belongings.

Leaving behind wreckage, water, and fallen trees, the storm curves to the northeast. It moves into the busy shipping lanes of the North Atlantic. In a final burst of fury, Hannah tosses up waves as high as 50 feet (15 meters), producing seasickness and injuries for passengers on battered ships. Then the storm moves into an area of low pressure near Iceland, and loses its identity.

What Makes Up Weather?

Weather changes constantly. One day may be dry and sunny, and the next day cloudy and rainy. The main elements that make up the weather are: (1) temperature, (2) wind, (3) moisture, and (4) air pressure.

Temperature affects the weather more than anything else. The sun sends huge amounts of energy into space. Some of this energy, or sunshine, reaches the earth. The atmosphere, the clouds, and the surface of the earth reflect some of it back into space. The rest is absorbed by the atmosphere and earth and changed into heat. This heat warms the earth and the atmosphere.

The atmosphere traps sunshine much as a greenhouse does. Sunshine is radiation in the form of *short waves*. Short waves pass easily through the glass panes of a greenhouse. Plants in the greenhouse absorb some of the sunshine and change it into heat. The plants then radiate the heat in the form of *long waves*. Long waves cannot pass easily through the glass panes, so they remain in the greenhouse and keep it warm. The atmosphere acts as do the glass panes in the greenhouse. It lets in short-wave sunshine, but traps the long heat waves. See RADIATION (How Radiation Affects Life on Earth).

Thermometers measure the temperature of the air. To find the correct air temperature, place a thermometer in a shady spot. A thermometer placed in the sun will show a higher temperature than the actual temperature of the air. Direct sun heats the glass and mercury in the

thermometer more than it heats the air. See TEMPERATURE; THERMOMETER.

Wind is the movement of air over the surface of the earth. Winds rank as an important factor in weather conditions. A soft breeze may make a summer day more pleasant. A violent windstorm may bring injuries and destruction to people and property in its path. Wind is also important because it moves the other elements of weather from one place to another. A wind from the north may bring low temperatures. A sea breeze carries cool, moist air over the land. Weather vanes and anemometers supply accurate information on the direction and speed of the wind. These devices usually record the information automatically. See WIND; WIND CHILL.

Weather vanes are instruments that indicate the direction of the wind. Winds receive their names from the direction *from* which they blow. The arrow on a weather vane points to the direction from which the wind is blowing. See WEATHER VANE.

Meteorologists use *anemometers* to find the speed of the wind. An anemometer has long spokes with cups attached to them. The wind makes the cups whirl around. The speed at which the cups move indicates the wind speed. In the United States, wind speed is stated in miles per hour, or in *knots* (one knot equals 1.15 miles, or 1.85 kilometers, per hour). See ANEMOMETER.

Moisture affects the weather in several ways. It may fall to earth as *precipitation*—rain, snow, hail, or sleet. Or it may remain in the atmosphere as *humidity*, or water vapor. Water vapor may condense to form tiny droplets of water or ice crystals that do not fall to earth. If the droplets or crystals condense high above the earth, they form clouds. If they are near the surface of the earth, they form fog. See CLOUD; FOG; RAIN; SNOW.

Meteorologists use several kinds of *hygrometers* to measure the amount of water vapor in the air. One kind, called a *psychrometer*, consists of two thermometers set on a support so they can be whirled in the air. The bulb of one thermometer is covered with a wet cloth. It is called a *wet-bulb* thermometer. The other is a *dry-bulb* thermometer. When the two are whirled in the air for a few minutes, water evaporates from the wet cloth and cools the wet-bulb thermometer. The amount of evaporation depends on the amount of moisture in the air. In dry air, more evaporation takes place. The difference between the temperatures of the two thermometers measures moisture in the air. Humidity is calculated from this difference. See HUMIDITY; HYGROMETER.

Meteorologists use an instrument called a *rain gauge* to measure rainfall. The inches or centimeters of rainfall can be calculated by measuring the amount that drops into a long tube inside the gauge. Snowfall may also be measured with a rain gauge. Snow that falls into the tube may be melted and measured as rain. Or it may be weighed. Then meteorologists calculate the inches or centimeters of melted snow. Some snow is heavier than other snow. A 6-inch (15-centimeter) layer of moist snow or a 30-inch (76-centimeter) layer of dry snow equals about 1 inch (2.5 centimeters) of rain. See RAIN GAUGE.

Air Pressure, or the weight of air pushing on the earth, varies from time to time and from place to place. Meteorologists do not know all the reasons for these differences in air pressure around the earth. But they do know that variations in temperature cause some of the pressure differences. Warm air weighs less than cold air.

It exerts less pressure on the earth and creates an area of low pressure. Cold air, which is heavier, creates an area of high pressure. See AIR (Weight and Pressure).

Weathermen call large low-pressure areas *lows* or *cyclones*. Large areas of high pressure are called *highs* or *anticyclones*. Air generally moves from a high-pressure area into a low-pressure area. In the same way, winds blow out of a high and into a low.

Highs usually bring fair weather. The air in the center settles downward, and is compressed. This compression heats the air and evaporates clouds. Lows generally bring cloudy or stormy weather. Air currents in lows move upward, and the air cools. Clouds often form in the cooling air.

Barometers show the air pressure. A *mercury barometer* is a long glass tube with its open end in a cup of mercury. As the air pressure changes, so does the height to which the mercury rises in the tube. The scale on a barometer may be marked in inches, in millimeters, or in *millibars*, a special scale for measuring pressure. A millibar is $\frac{1}{1,000}$ of a *bar*, which is a pressure of 29.53 inches (75.01 centimeters) of mercury at sea level. To obtain an accurate measurement, the reading on a barometer must be corrected for variations in altitude, temperature, and gravity differences at different latitudes.

Aneroid barometers record changes in pressure by using an airtight box. Most of the air is removed from the box. The metal surfaces of the box move in or out as air pressure increases or decreases. These changes control a pointer on a dial. Aneroid barometer readings do not need corrections for temperature and gravity differences. See BAROMETER.

Weather Patterns

Weather conditions move from one place to another. A storm that starts in Canada can bring snow and freezing temperatures to the Midwestern United States. A hurricane that develops in the Caribbean Sea can destroy homes on the New England coast. As meteorologists learn more about the patterns and movement of weather, they can improve their forecasts.

Temperature Patterns. The angle at which the sun's rays strike the earth affects the temperature in different areas. Sunshine strikes the earth at almost a right angle (90°) near the equator, and at acute angles in polar regions. This causes the difference in temperature between the equator and the poles.

The changing angle of the sun's rays also causes the changing seasons. In winter, the sun is low in the sky. Sunshine must pass through more atmosphere when the sun is low. Much of it is absorbed or scattered back to space, never reaching the earth's surface. The sunshine that does reach the earth is spread over a larger area. It cannot heat the earth as well as sunshine that strikes at almost a right angle. In summer or at lower latitudes, the sunshine strikes the earth at higher angles. The energy of the sun's rays is not absorbed, scattered, or spread out as much. See SEASON.

A flashlight can help you understand how the angle of the sun's rays affects the amount of energy the earth receives. If you shine a flashlight beam straight down on a piece of paper, the light will be concentrated in a circle. If you hold it at an angle, the light will spread out and not be so strong.

A ruler and a jar of water can show you how the

angle of the sun's rays affects the amount of atmosphere they pass through. First, put the ruler straight down in the water and note how much of the ruler becomes wet. Then, put the ruler in the water at an angle. You will see that the water will reach higher up on the ruler. This shows that the slanting ruler has passed through more water.

Air Movement. The earth would become hotter and hotter if the atmosphere could not get rid of stored-up heat. Winds carry excess heat from the equator to the cold polar regions.

The warm air at the equator weighs less than the cooler air farther north or south. Because of this, a permanent low-pressure area forms around the earth near the equator. This area is called the *equatorial low*. The cold air at the poles sinks to the earth, creating areas of *polar highs*. The heavier air from the polar highs moves toward the equator. It pushes underneath the warm air, and forces it upward into the upper atmosphere. There, the warm air moves toward the poles. This movement of air from the poles to the equator and back again goes on continuously. Cold air becomes warm as it reaches the equator. It is then forced upward by more cold air, and begins moving toward the poles.

However, air masses do not move directly north or directly south. The rotation of the earth creates a force called the *Coriolis force*. This force pushes air currents to the right of the direction they are moving in the Northern Hemisphere, and to the left in the Southern Hemisphere. By experimenting with a globe, you can see how the Coriolis force causes the winds to change directions. Spin the globe in the same direction as the earth turns (to the right). While the globe spins, draw a chalk line directly down from the North Pole toward the South Pole. When you stop the globe, you will not see a straight line. You will see a curve that comes toward the equator and crosses it at an angle. The chalk line looks as if it had been drawn from the northeast toward the southwest. See CORIOLIS FORCE.

Because of the Coriolis force, the heavy air at the earth's surface pushing toward the equatorial low does not blow directly from the north in the Northern Hemisphere. It blows from the northeast. In the Southern Hemisphere it blows from the southeast. These northeast and southeast winds are called *trade winds* (see TRADE WIND).

Scientists do not clearly understand why the exchange of air between the equator and the poles is not so simple as they might expect. The air mass traveling in the upper atmosphere from the equator toward the poles begins to sink near 30° latitude. As the air drops, it spreads out. Some of it returns toward the equator. The rest moves along the earth's surface toward the poles. This subtropical region (near 30° latitude) has a belt of high pressure around the earth.

The air that drops to earth and continues moving toward the poles begins to change its direction. In the Northern Hemisphere, the rotation of the earth changes it from a south wind to a southwest or nearly westerly wind. The winds in this region are called *prevailing westerlies* (see PREVAILING WESTERLY). Farther north, these polebound air masses meet the cold, heavy air of the polar region. The warm, light westerlies rise above

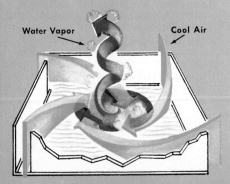

A HOMEMADE HURRICANE

The purpose of this project is to show how hurricanes form and to demonstrate how the winds of a hurricane spin in different directions in the Northern and Southern Hemispheres.

CAUTION: This project involves working with electricity, which can cause burns, shock, or fire. If you are not familiar with the precautions for working with electricity, you must have a knowledgeable person help you.

MATERIALS AND ASSEMBLY

You can buy all the materials you need for this project at a hardware store. To build the hurricane generator, first assemble the wooden boxes that serve as the top and bottom. Then attach the corner metal angles to the bottom box, insert three glass walls and a Masonite wall, and attach the upper box and stovepipe. Paint the inside of the top box white to reflect light and heat. Paint the rest of the hurricane generator black.

The Hurricane Generator. A real hurricane begins when the sun heats the ocean, producing a rising cloud of warm, moist air. In the hurricane generator, a cloud of water vapor is formed by heating water in a pan. Cool air enters at the sides of the generator, forcing the cloud to twist upward like a real hurricane.

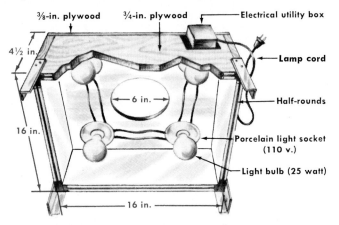

The Upper Box is built of ¾-inch plywood side pieces and a ⅜-inch plywood top piece. Cut a 6-inch hole in the top for the stovepipe. Cut a 1-inch hole in one side and screw the electrical box over the hole. Fasten half-rounds on the inside and outside edges of the bottom of the box. The half-rounds serve as guides for sliding the pieces of glass and the Masonite.

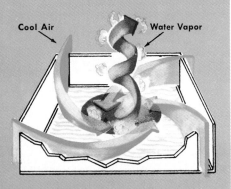

The Direction of Spin is controlled by sliding the glass panels to the left or right. A Northern Hemisphere hurricane, *above*, twists counterclockwise. A Southern Hemisphere hurricane, *below*, twists upward in a clockwise way.

The Lower Box is also built of ¾-inch and ⅜-inch plywood. Cut an 8½-inch hole in the top so that a standard 9-inch pie pan fits snugly just below its rim. A close fit is necessary to prevent air from entering around the pan. Drill seven ½-inch ventilating holes near the top of any two facing sides. Fasten seven half-rounds to the edges of the top of the box. One side should have only an inside half-round so that the Masonite wall can be pulled out easily. You can make legs by nailing strap iron pieces across each corner. Drill a ⅜-inch hole in each piece and use ⅜-inch bolts as legs.

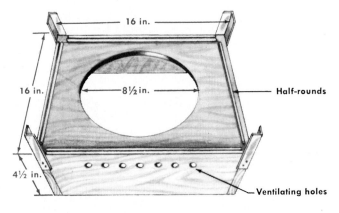

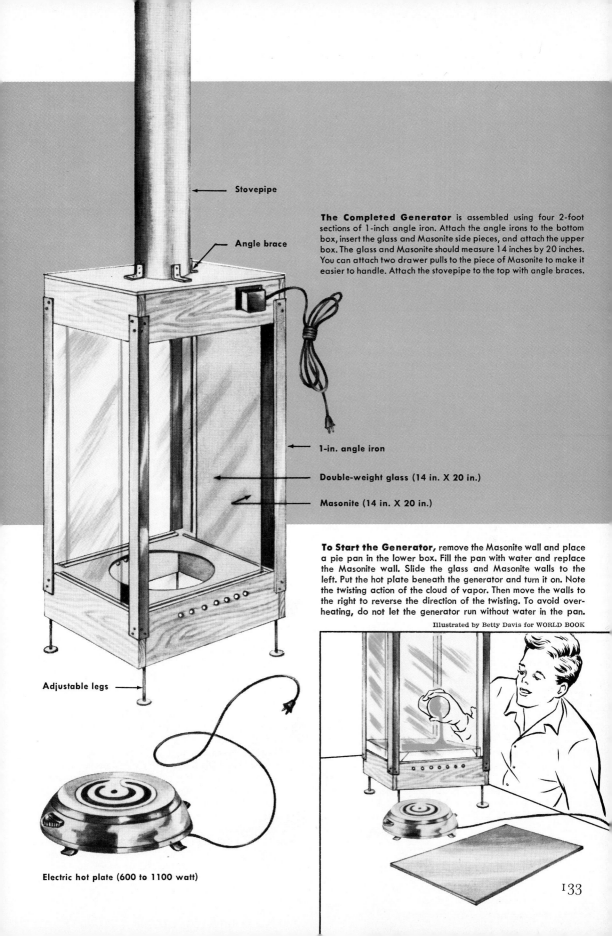

Stovepipe

Angle brace

The Completed Generator is assembled using four 2-foot sections of 1-inch angle iron. Attach the angle irons to the bottom box, insert the glass and Masonite side pieces, and attach the upper box. The glass and Masonite should measure 14 inches by 20 inches. You can attach two drawer pulls to the piece of Masonite to make it easier to handle. Attach the stovepipe to the top with angle braces.

1-in. angle iron

Double-weight glass (14 in. X 20 in.)

Masonite (14 in. X 20 in.)

To Start the Generator, remove the Masonite wall and place a pie pan in the lower box. Fill the pan with water and replace the Masonite wall. Slide the glass and Masonite walls to the left. Put the hot plate beneath the generator and turn it on. Note the twisting action of the cloud of vapor. Then move the walls to the right to reverse the direction of the twisting. To avoid overheating, do not let the generator run without water in the pan.

Illustrated by Betty Davis for WORLD BOOK

Adjustable legs

Electric hot plate (600 to 1100 watt)

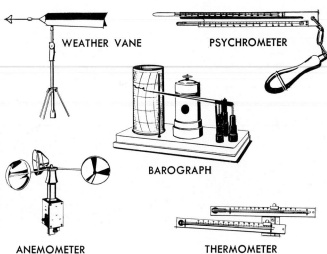

WEATHER VANE   PSYCHROMETER

BAROGRAPH

ANEMOMETER   THERMOMETER

Students Learn to Use Weather Instruments to find out the exact weather conditions. Then they can try to make weather predictions for the next few days.

Weather Instruments. A *weather vane* shows the wind's direction, and an *anemometer* shows its speed. A *psychrometer* measures the dampness of the air, and a *barograph* records its pressure. A *thermometer* indicates temperature.

the polar air. The boundary between the warm and cold air mass is called the *polar front*. The westerlies are quite strong about 6 or 7 miles (10 or 11 kilometers) above the ground over the polar front. They form bands of air called *jet streams* that move from west to east. The streams are over 100 miles (160 kilometers) wide and they travel up to 300 miles (480 kilometers) an hour. The main stream passes over the United States at about 40° latitude. But its path varies greatly. The jet stream may bring storms and floods to areas below it.

The warm air that has traveled from the equator loses much of its heat in the polar region. Then it sinks and joins the cold polar air mass that pushes against fresh, warm air arriving from the subtropics.

Geography. The movements of air masses do not settle into a simple, constant pattern. Many factors act together in complex ways to keep the forces that control weather constantly out of balance.

Differences in Heating Land and Water. The sun heats land faster than it heats water. But water holds more heat, and holds it longer. So land and water areas that lie next to each other may have different temperatures. Breezes from oceans or large lakes modify the weather in areas that they reach. They cool the land in summer and warm it in winter. For example, a breeze from Lake Michigan in summer may lower the temperature in Chicago as much as 15 degrees Fahrenheit (8.3 degrees Celsius). Warm ocean currents may flow toward the poles and bring warm winds to lands at high latitudes. For example, the Japan Current brings warm weather to Alaska. Other places at that latitude are colder. See CLIMATE (Differences in Land and Water Temperatures); OCEAN (How the Ocean Moves).

Position of the Sun. The sun shines directly above the equator only two days a year. The position of the equatorial low and other pressure areas depends on the direction of the sun's rays. But the direction of the sun's rays changes throughout the year. The pressure areas

are constantly moving as the path of the sun moves.

Uneven Surface of the Earth. Mountain ranges and other geographic features may alter the temperature and direction of the prevailing winds. Mountains along a coast may block ocean breezes from inland areas. For example, the mountains of western Oregon and Washington block rain-bearing winds from the Pacific Ocean. The western parts of these states are wet, but the eastern parts are relatively dry. Altitude also affects weather. Cities on mountains or plateaus usually have cooler temperatures than the surrounding lower areas.

Fronts are narrow bands of changing weather between two different air masses. Most weather changes take place along fronts. When a cold air mass pushes a warmer air mass out of the way, it forms a *cold front*. When the warm air mass pushes against the cold air mass, it forms a *warm front*. If the battle goes neither way, it becomes a *stationary front*. A front formed when a cold front overtakes a warm front is called an *occluded front*. Weather forecasters expect overcast skies and continuous rain or snow ahead of a warm front. Showers or squalls usually form along a cold front.

Most weather changes in North America occur along the polar front. In this region, the cold, dry polar air mass battles with the warm, moist air mass from the high-pressure belt of the subtropics. Many storms result from these differences in temperature and humidity between air masses. See STORM.

Where Our Weather Comes From. In winter, lows called *extra-tropical cyclones* enter North America along the Pacific Coast. These cyclones form in the middle latitudes, usually on the polar front. They may cover an area 600 miles (970 kilometers) wide. The lows are carried along on the prevailing westerly winds, and bring moist air and rain or snow to the Western States and the Rocky Mountains. They generally turn southeast over the middle part of the United States, then northeast in the Appalachian region or Atlantic states. Southwest

PREDICTING TOMORROW'S WEATHER

Careful observation of cloud formations, wind direction, and barometer readings will help you predict what the coming weather will be like. The diagrams below show four typical weather situations, and indicate what kinds of weather they foretell.

Continued Fair Weather. When scattered cumulus clouds dot the sky, the barometer remains steady or rises, and the wind blows gently from the west or northwest, fair weather will probably continue.

BAROMETER RISING

WIND DIRECTION

Rainstorm Approaching. Alto-cumulus clouds gathering on the horizon, winds blowing from the south or southwest, and a falling barometer usually indicate an approaching storm.

BAROMETER FALLING

WIND DIRECTION

Continued Rain or Snow. When dull-gray alto-stratus clouds darken the whole sky, the wind blows from a southeasterly direction, and the barometer drops, rain or snow will probably continue to fall.

BAROMETER FALLING

WIND DIRECTION

Falling Temperatures. A clear night sky, a light wind blowing from the north or the northwest, and a steadily rising barometer usually indicate a coming drop in temperature.

BAROMETER RISING STEADILY

WIND DIRECTION

Birds Do Not Roost Before a Storm as many people believe. There is no scientific basis for this superstition.

A Cricket can act as a thermometer. Crickets chirp faster as the temperature rises. On warm days, adding 37 to the number of chirps in 15 seconds will about equal the Fahrenheit temperature.

Aching Corns and other pains are not reliable guides for predicting bad weather, although changes in air pressure and moisture may possibly cause pain at sensitive spots.

winter. Those that come from the northern Pacific are only moderately cold.

In spring and autumn, the movement of weather is much the same. But the prevailing west winds are weaker than in winter. The weather changes are not so rapid or severe. In summer, the atmosphere over the United States is usually quiet or moving slowly. The weather becomes warm or hot. Local storms and thundershowers cause most of the rainfall. Air from the tropics moves over the Southern States during the summer, bringing weather from the Gulf of Mexico and the Caribbean Sea.

History of Weather Forecasting

Early Days. Benjamin Franklin was one of the first persons to realize that storms moved across the land in a regular way. He found that most storms along the Atlantic Coast moved in a northeasterly pattern. But at that time (the late 1700's) this knowledge could not be used to forecast storms. The storms moved faster than the mails. By the time weather observations arrived in a city, the storm had come and gone.

After 1844, when Samuel Morse perfected the telegraph, weather reports could reach an area before the

winds bring moist Gulf and Atlantic air to the area east of the Rockies, causing rain in the Southern States and rain or snow in the Northern States.

Most lows are followed by highs. The highs usually bring clear skies and colder winds from points farther north. The weather often changes quickly in the fronts between these warm and cold air masses. Highs that move south from northern Canada bring severe cold in

---

UNUSUAL FACTS ABOUT THE WEATHER

Driest Place on earth is Arica, Chile. A 59-year average annual rainfall was 3/100 inch (0.76 millimeter). No rain fell in Arica for a 14-year period.

Heaviest Rainfall recorded in 24 hours was 73.62 inches (186.99 centimeters), at Cilaos on the island of Reunion on March 15-16, 1952. The most rain in one year was at Cherrapunji, India, where 1,041.78 inches (2,646.12 centimeters) fell from August 1860 to July 1861. The wettest place is Mount Waialeale, on the island of Kauai in Hawaii, with an average annual rainfall of 460 inches (1,168 centimeters).

Heaviest Snowfall recorded in North America in 24 hours—76 inches (193 centimeters)—fell at Silver Lake, Colo., on April 14-15, 1921. The most snow recorded in North America in one winter—1,122 inches (2,850 centimeters)—fell at Rainier Paradise Ranger Station in Washington in 1971-1972.

Highest Air Pressure at sea level was recorded at Agata, Siberia, on Dec. 31, 1968, when the barometric pressure reached 32.01 inches (81.31 centimeters).

Highest Temperature recorded was 136.4° F. (58.0° C), at Al Aziziyah, Libya, on Sept. 13, 1922. The highest temperature recorded in the Western Hemisphere was 134° F. (57° C), in Death Valley, Calif., on July 10, 1913.

Largest Hailstone in the U.S. fell on Coffeyville, Kans., on Sept. 3, 1970. It measured $17\frac{1}{2}$ inches (44.5 centimeters) in circumference and weighed 1 pound 11 ounces (0.77 kilogram).

Lowest Air Pressure at sea level was estimated at 25.90 inches (65.79 centimeters), during a typhoon in the Philippine Sea on Sept. 24, 1958.

Lowest Temperature observed on the earth's surface was −126.9° F. (−88.28° C), at Vostok, Antarctica, on Aug. 24, 1960. The record low in the U.S. was −79.8° F. (−62.1° C), at Prospect Creek, Alaska, on Jan. 23, 1971.

Strongest Winds measured on the earth's surface were recorded at Mount Washington, N.H., on April 12, 1934. For five minutes the wind blew at 188 mph (303 kph). One gust reached 231 mph (372 kph).

Sources: National Oceanic and Atmospheric Administration; *Weather Extremes Around the World, 1974,* Geographic Sciences Laboratory, U.S. Army Engineer Topographic Laboratories.

WEATHER SUPERSTITIONS

The Ground Hog is supposed to leave its den at noon, February 2. Tradition says that if it sees its shadow, cold weather will continue for six more weeks. This belief has no basis in fact.

The Migration of Birds does not forecast whether cold winter weather will arrive early or late. Birds may fly south early or late in the season for many different reasons.

weather did. In 1849, Joseph Henry, secretary of the Smithsonian Institution, received and analyzed the first weather reports sent by telegraph. The French astronomer Urbain Leverrier (1811-1877) first used the telegraph in a practical way to forecast weather conditions. He showed that a central office, receiving weather reports by telegraph from many places, could forecast storms. In 1854, Napoleon III, the French emperor, instructed Leverrier to organize a weather-forecasting system for France. By the late 1800's, the United States and many countries in Europe had set up systems of daily observations and forecasts. In 1870, the U.S. Congress set up a national weather service as part of the Army Signal Corps. In 1890, the service was changed to a civilian organization known as the Weather Bureau.

Scientific Advances. Since the 1880's, meteorologists have learned much about the behavior of weather elements and storms. By the early 1900's, weather forecasts were accurate enough to be useful. At that time, two men proposed new ideas that completely changed the methods of weather forecasting.

The Norwegian meteorologist Vilhelm Bjerknes (1862-1951) observed that air above the earth can be thought of as masses with different properties. Separating these masses, he found zones of rapidly changing conditions. He called these zones *fronts*. Bjerknes, his son Jakob, and other Norwegian meteorologists, analyzed the conditions and movements of these masses and fronts. Their theories greatly improved the accuracy of weather forecasting.

The British meteorologist Lewis Fry Richardson (1881-1953) thought that the principles of mathematics could be used to help forecast weather. He used the laws of motion and heat to make calculations from weather observations. From these calculations, he showed how weather forecasts could be made. His basic concept was correct, but his idea was not practical in the early 1900's. The calculations took so long that the weather had come and gone before the forecast was finished. There were too few observations available to make accurate forecasts, and Richardson's equations were not in the right form to predict weather accurately.

For many years, scientists thought that Richardson's idea had no practical value. Then, in the late 1940's,

Certain Kinds of Flies tend to bite excessively before a storm. Some scientists believe this behavior is caused by changes in barometric pressure and increased humidity in the air.

electronic computers were developed. They could do the needed calculations quickly enough to be useful. By this time, the number of weather stations and the frequency of observations had increased. At the end of World War II, a group of American meteorologists, led by the mathematician John von Neumann (1903-1957), found a way to write the laws of physics so that meteorologists could use them to make forecasts.

During World War II, pilots flying over Japan found the winds at certain high altitudes extremely strong. Carl-Gustaf Rossby (1898-1957), a Swedish-American meteorologist, investigated these winds after the war. The winds, called *jet streams*, have great importance to aviation because they affect the speeds of high-altitude flights. Meteorologists believe that the jet stream helps form, intensify, and direct highs, lows, hurricanes, and other weather conditions on the earth. Forecasters pay close attention to the location, strength, and movement of jet streams.

Information about conditions in the upper atmosphere helps meteorologists forecast accurately. They receive most of this information from instrument-carrying balloons. In 1959, the United States sent into orbit the first satellite specifically designed to gather, record, and transmit weather information back to earth.

Much of the information gathered during the International Geophysical Year (IGY) in 1957 and 1958 increased weather knowledge. Antarctic bases established

WEATHER REPORTS FROM SPACE

Tiros I, the "Weather Eye," was the first satellite designed to photograph weather. The U.S. launched it April 1, 1960.

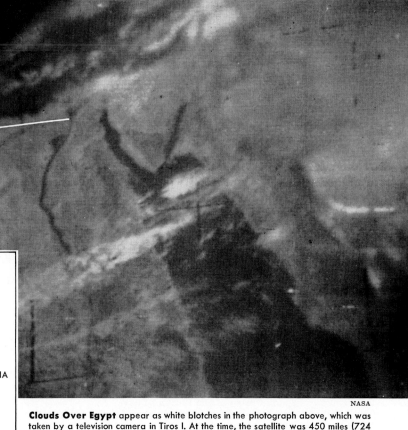

NASA

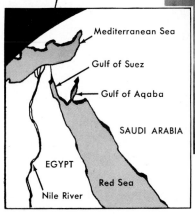

Mediterranean Sea

Gulf of Suez

Gulf of Aqaba

SAUDI ARABIA

EGYPT

Red Sea

Nile River

Clouds Over Egypt appear as white blotches in the photograph above, which was taken by a television camera in Tiros I. At the time, the satellite was 450 miles (724 kilometers) above the earth. Pictures of cloud cover help in understanding and forecasting weather. Map, *left*, shows area of photograph.

during the IGY made it possible for weathermen to obtain information for making the first complete world weather map.

On April 1, 1960, the United States launched the first artificial satellite equipped to provide photographs of the earth's weather conditions. Known as Tiros I, its two television cameras transmitted both broad and detailed pictures of the earth's cloud cover. During the early 1960's, Tiros I and other weather satellites continued to provide valuable information about weather conditions in many parts of the world. The National Aeronautics and Space Administration (NASA) cooperated with the United States Weather Bureau (now the National Weather Service) in launching and using U.S. weather satellites. In 1963, the United States and Russia agreed to exchange weather information from satellites. The two countries set up a research exchange line kept open 24 hours a day and began exchanging photographs of cloud formations.

In 1963, the World Meteorological Organization, a specialized agency of the United Nations, approved a plan for mapping the weather around the globe. The plan, known as a *World Weather Watch*, called for artificial satellites and thousands of land and sea stations

to gather weather information. Three world centers would use this information to make long-range weather forecasts.

Attempts to Control the Weather. Many ancient and primitive societies tried to find ways to control the weather. They wanted rain to make their crops grow, or they wanted to stop the rain to prevent floods. Some tribes made offerings or sacrifices to their gods. Others held dances to pray for rain. More civilized people tried to control the weather by shooting off cannons or by setting off other explosions. In farm areas, some men called themselves "rainmakers" and earned their living by promising to make rain during droughts.

Cloud seeding is the modern, scientific approach to rainmaking. An airplane may drop dry ice, salt particles, water spray, or other substances into a cloud in order to "seed" it. Or silver iodide "seeds" may be released from the ground and carried into the cloud by the wind. If conditions are favorable, tiny droplets of water from the cloud collect around each "seed" and fall to the earth as rain or snow. But cloud seeding is not successful unless the clouds are almost ready to produce rain. See RAINMAKING.

Cloud seeding is usually used to make rain when

there is a drought. But cloud seeding methods have also been used to get rid of fog and to prevent fruit trees and other crops from being damaged by wind and hail. By seeding the clouds before they reach an area with valuable crops, experts can sometimes reduce the strength of a storm and save crops from harm.

Scientists have experimented with controlling the weather in several other ways. These include sending an electric current through a cloud, and seeding clouds with chemicals other than silver iodide.

Meteorologists in all parts of the world study cloud seeding and other ways of controlling the weather. They hope to learn how to alter the paths of hurricanes, control the evaporation from the seas, thaw out frozen areas near the North and South poles, and change wind patterns over the land.   JAMES E. MILLER

Related Articles in WORLD BOOK include:

ELEMENTS OF WEATHER

Blizzard	Fog	Norther	Squall
Chinook	Frost	Prevailing	Storm
Cloud	Hail	Westerly	Temperature
Cloudburst	Harmattan	Rain	Thunder
Cyclone	Humidity	Rainbow	Tornado
Dew	Hurricane	Sandstorm	Trade Wind
Drought	Ice	Simoom	Typhoon
Dust	Jet Stream	Sirocco	Waterspout
Dust Storm	Lightning	Sleet	Whirlwind
Evaporation	Mistral	Snow	Wind
Foehn	Monsoon		

WEATHER INSTRUMENTS

Anemometer	Radiosonde	Thermograph
Barometer	Rain Gauge	Thermometer
Hygrometer	Thermocouple	Weather Vane
Kite		

OTHER RELATED ARTICLES

Air	Doldrums	Rainmaking
Air Conditioning	Flag (color pic-	Season
Airport (Watching	ture: Flags	Spring
the Weather)	That Talk)	Summer
Autumn	Horse Latitudes	Sunspot
Balloon	Indian Summer	Troposphere
(Scientific Uses)	Isobar	Weather Service,
Boating	Isotherm	National
(picture: Warn-	Meteorology	Winter
ing Signals)	Radar (In Weather	World Meteoro-
Calms, Regions of	Observation and	logical Or-
Climate	Forecasting)	ganization

Outline

I. Weather Forecasting
  A. Observations
  B. Analysis
  C. Kinds of Forecasts
II. The Story of a Storm
  A. Birth of a Storm
  B. Tracking a Storm   C. Effects of a Storm
III. What Makes Up Weather?
  A. Temperature   C. Moisture
  B. Wind   D. Air Pressure
IV. Weather Patterns
  A. Temperature Patterns D. Fronts
  B. Air Movement   E. Where Our Weather
  C. Geography   Comes From
V. History of Weather Forecasting

Questions

What are the four main elements of weather?
How does the earth's rotation affect wind direction?
Why must weather forecasters know the weather in distant areas?

How does the Coriolis force affect the direction of weather in the United States?
How do weather forecasters track a hurricane?
How are computers used in weather forecasting?
Why are weather forecasts not always accurate?
How does the earth's surface affect weather?
What is the difference between weather and climate?
How does temperature affect air pressure?
What is an anemometer? A hygrometer? A rain gauge?

WEATHER BALLOON. See BALLOON.

WEATHER BUREAU. See WEATHER SERVICE, NATIONAL.

WEATHER FORECASTING. See WEATHER.

WEATHER SATELLITE. See WEATHER (Scientific Advances; pictures).

WEATHER SERVICE, NATIONAL, provides forecasts, observations, and records of the weather in the United States and its territories. It is a part of the National Oceanic and Atmospheric Administration of the U.S. Department of Commerce. The service issues forecasts and reports, and provides special services. It sends out warnings of hurricanes, tornadoes, and other dangerous storms. It measures rainfall and river levels to forecast navigation, flood, and water-supply conditions, and issues special weather information for farmers and airplane pilots. It keeps records of the climate of the United States and other countries, and studies ways to improve weather forecasting.

The agency has its central office in Washington, D.C., and regional offices in New York City; Kansas City, Mo.; Fort Worth, Texas; Salt Lake City, Utah; Honolulu, Hawaii; and Anchorage, Alaska. About 300 weather stations in the United States and its possessions have full-time staffs. These stations take observations every three or six hours. The National Weather Service has more than 12,000 substations that gather information on climate.

The Severe Local Storm Center at Kansas City, Mo., watches the entire nation for conditions that may produce tornadoes or other severe local storms. The National Hurricane Center in Miami, Fla., provides forecasts and warnings of tropical storms threatening the East and Gulf coasts of the United States.

Several federal agencies work with the Weather Service. For example, the Coast Guard gathers weather information from merchant ships. The Federal Aviation Administration helps the service gather weather information at airport stations and supply weather reports to pilots.

Weather reports pour into the Weather Service's National Meteorological Center near Washington, D.C. There, the Analysis and Forecast, Computation, and Extended Forecast branches analyze the reports. They make forecasts with the aid of high-speed computers and distribute them to local offices. The Weather Service also exchanges reports with other nations.

Weather advice, forecasts, reports, and warnings are given to the public by means of newspapers, radio, telephone, and television. Many Weather Service offices are connected to radio stations, and the local forecasters speak directly to the public.

The public weather service of the United States began in 1870 as part of the Army Signal Corps. In 1890, Congress organized the Weather Bureau under

WEATHER VANE

the Department of Agriculture. The President transferred the bureau to the Department of Commerce in 1940. In 1965, Congress made the Weather Bureau part of the Environmental Science Services Administration, a branch of the Department of Commerce. The bureau was renamed the National Weather Service in 1970, when it became part of the National Oceanic and Atmospheric Administration.

Critically reviewed by the NATIONAL WEATHER SERVICE

See also WEATHER (Weather Forecasting; History).

WEATHER VANE is a device that turns freely on an upright rod and points in the direction from which wind comes. It is also called a *wind vane* or *weathercock*. The weather vane is one of the oldest weather instruments and is often ornamental in shape.

The part of the vane which turns into the wind is usually shaped like an arrow. The other end is wide,

Whitehall Metal Studios

A Weather Vane shows the direction from which the wind comes. The crowing rooster on the arrow gave it the name *weathercock.*

so it will catch the smallest breeze. The breeze turns the arrow until it catches both sides of the wide end equally. Thus, the arrow always points into the wind. Below the arrow is a round plate on which the directions are marked. Vanes used by weather bureaus have electrical connections that record wind direction in a room far from the vane itself. JOHN V. FINCH

WEATHERING. See EARTH (How the Earth Changes); SOIL (How Soil Is Formed).

WEAVER, ROBERT CLIFTON (1907-   ), served as secretary of the Department of Housing and Urban Development under President Lyndon B. Johnson from 1966 to 1969. As head of the new department, he became the first black Cabinet member in United States history.

Weaver was born in Washington, D.C. He received B.S., M.A., and Ph.D. degrees from Harvard University. He began his government career in 1933 as adviser on black affairs in the Department of the Interior. Weaver was named New York Deputy State Housing Commissioner in 1954. Appointed State Rent Administrator in 1955, he became the first black to

attain New York state cabinet rank. From 1961 to 1966 he served as administrator of the federal Housing and Home Finance Agency. Weaver also served as chairman of the National Association for the Advancement of Colored People (NAACP). He received the Spingarn Medal in 1962. In 1969, he became president of Bernard Baruch College in New York City. CARL T. ROWAN

WEAVERBIRD is a small bird that usually weaves a hanging nest. There are about 275 kinds of weaverbirds. They live in most parts of the world. The familiar *house* or *English sparrow* found in the United States is a weaverbird. Weaverbirds eat seeds and grain. They chatter continually. Most females and young weaverbirds are plainly colored. But the males are generally brightly colored during the mating season.

The *sociable weaver* of South Africa builds an umbrella-shaped community roof of sticks and grass in a tree. The roof is often as large as an African hut. The underside of the roof is divided into compartments, each occupied by a pair of birds. As many as 95 individual nests have been counted under one roof. The female lays three or four speckled, purple-gray eggs.

The *Java sparrow* weaves a grass nest with a side opening. The female lays six or more white eggs. The *baya*, which lives in India and Sri Lanka, builds a flask-shaped nest with a long, tubular-shaped entrance.

Scientific Classification. Weaverbirds belong to the weaver finch family, *Ploceidae.* The sociable weaver is genus *Philetaerus,* species *P. socius.* The house sparrow is *Passer domesticus.* LEONARD W. WING

See also BIRD (Building the Nest; color picture: Birds of Other Lands); ENGLISH SPARROW.

Karl H. Maslowski, National Audubon Society

Many Kinds of Weaverbirds, including this masked weaverbird, build hanging nests by weaving grass and twigs together.

140

The Craft of Weaving has been practiced throughout the world for thousands of years. These Tunisian girls are hand-weaving a colorful wool rug with traditional patterns on a large floor loom in their home.

WEAVING is the process of making cloth by crossing two sets of threads over and under each other. Many fabrics and most blankets, clothing, and rugs are woven. Weavers may use thread spun from such natural fibers as cotton, silk, and wool. Strong man-made fibers, including nylon and Orlon, are also popular.

Narrow strips of almost any flexible material can also be woven. People learned to weave thousands of years ago with grasses, leafstalks, palm leaves, and thin strips of wood. Today, craftsmen throughout the world still use such fibers to weave baskets, hats, and other articles. Weaving also plays an important part in the manufacture of such products as screens, metal fences, and rubber tire cord.

Weaving ranks as a major industry in Japan, Russia, the United States, and many other countries. In the United States, the value of factory-woven goods totals more than $3½ billion yearly. Weaving is also a popular craft. Artists exhibit and sell decorative woven items at art fairs, galleries, and museums. Many people design and weave colorful fabrics as a hobby.

Types of Weaves

Weavers use three basic kinds of weaves: (1) the *plain weave*, or *tabby weave;* (2) the *twill weave;* and (3)

the *satin weave.* More complex types of weaves are known as *fancy weaves.* All weaves consist of two sets of threads. One set, called the *warp,* stretches lengthwise on a loom or frame. To make cloth, the weaver repeatedly draws a set of crosswise threads called the *weft* over and under the warp. The weft is sometimes called the *woof* or the *filling.*

The Plain Weave, or **Tabby Weave,** is the simplest and most common type of weave. In the odd-numbered rows of this weave, a weft thread passes under the first warp thread, over the second, and so on. In the even-numbered rows, the weft passes over the first warp, under the second, and so on. This close weave produces a strong, flat-textured cloth that wears well. Plain-woven fabrics include gingham, muslin, and percale.

The *basket weave,* a variation of the plain weave, has a bulkier texture that resembles the weaves of a basket. The weft is drawn under two or more warp threads, then over the same number of threads, and so on. This method adds fullness to the weave.

The Twill Weave produces sturdy cloth that has raised diagonal lines. Each weft thread crosses two, three, or four warp threads at a time, creating extra width. This added width makes a decorative fabric that holds its shape despite repeated wear. Each row of

Some Kinds of Weaves

The Plain, or **Tabby, Weave** is the simplest type of weave. A *weft* (crosswise thread) passes under one *warp* (lengthwise thread), over the next, and so on.

The Twill Weave forms diagonal lines in fabric. The weft crosses several warps at once. Each row's pattern begins slightly left or right of that of the previous row.

The Satin Weave produces such luxurious fabrics as rayon, satin, and silk. Each weft spans up to 12 warps in creating a smooth, glossy finish.

weft threads follows the same pattern. But each row's pattern begins slightly to the right or left of the pattern in the previous row. This technique puts a series of diagonal lines in the fabric. The weaver may create unusual patterns by changing the direction of the weave and adding various colored threads.

Common twill fabrics include flannel, gabardine, and serge. The twill weave produces strong, tightly-woven cloth used to make coats, work clothes, and men's suits.

The Satin Weave makes soft, luxurious fabrics, such as damask, sateen, and satin. The wefts of a satin weave can cover as many as 12 warps. The threads may interlace at such wide intervals that the diagonal line of the weave cannot be seen without a magnifying glass. Satin-weave cloth may snag easily. It is used to make such products as draperies and formal clothes.

Fancy Weaves produce a variety of designs and textures in fabric. A *pile weave* has cut or looped weft yarns that extend above the fabric surface and provide a furry texture. Pile weaves include corduroy, terrycloth, velvet, and most carpet fabrics. A *double weave* binds two layers of cloth together for added strength and warmth. Blankets, coats, drapes, and upholstery fabrics may be double woven. A *gauze weave* is a loose, open weave that makes a sheer, lightweight fabric. The warp threads are arranged in pairs and twisted around the weft threads. Gauze-woven cotton, rayon, and silk make attractive curtains and lightweight clothing.

Weaving on a Loom

How a Loom Works. Almost all looms have the same basic features and weave fabric in much the same way. On most looms, cloth is woven on a metal or wooden frame located at the front of the loom and parallel to the floor.

The weaver must thread the loom before weaving. A set of warp threads is wound onto a cylinder called the *warp beam* at the back of the loom. Each warp

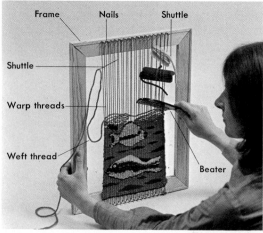

Frame   Nails   Shuttle

Shuttle

Warp threads

Weft thread

Beater

WORLD BOOK photo

A Simple Hand Loom can be made from a wooden picture frame. Nails hammered into the top and bottom of the frame hold the warp in place. This photograph shows a weaver using a comb as the beater. A needle and two pieces of cardboard serve as shuttles.

thread is then passed through one of two or more vertical frames called *harnesses*. The number of harnesses depends on the complexity of the weave. In the harnesses, each warp is threaded through a narrow opening in one of many strings or wires called *heddles*. The heddles hold the individual threads in place and prevent tangling. The warp threads then stretch over the weaving frame.

Next, the weaver winds the weft thread around a spool called the *bobbin*. The bobbin is held in an oblong metal or wood container called the *shuttle*. The shuttle serves as a needle that draws the weft thread over and under the warp. The weaving process begins when the weaver lifts the harness that holds the odd-numbered threads. This action creates a space called the *shed* through which the shuttle and weft then pass. Finally, the weaver lowers the first harness and pushes the newly woven row into place with a device called the *beater*, or *reed*. The beater is in a frame located in front of, and parallel to, the harnesses. It has comblike "teeth" made of steel wires that push each weft row compactly into place to tighten the weave.

To weave the next row, the weaver raises the second harness and passes the shuttle through the shed. The weaving of each row involves the same process. The finished cloth is wound around a bar called the *apron beam*, or *cloth beam*, at the front of the loom.

Kinds of Looms. There are two basic types of looms, hand looms and power looms. A hand loom is any loom that is not power driven, such as a *table loom* or a *floor loom*.

A table loom is a compact, portable device that stands on a table or some other flat surface. Table looms of various sizes can weave cloth that measures from 8 to 36 inches (20 to 91 centimeters) wide. Table looms generally have from 2 to 8 harnesses, which the weaver controls by raising and lowering levers by hand. A table loom threads easily and costs less than most other kinds of looms. But weaving on a hand loom can be tiring because the weaver must put down the shuttle and operate the harnesses manually after every row.

Floor looms are large and stationary and measure from 20 inches (51 centimeters) to 5 feet (1.5 meters) wide. The weaver raises and lowers the harnesses of a floor loom by pressing foot pedals called *treadles*. This action frees the weaver's hands to pass the shuttle rhythmically through the sheds. Such rhythm adds speed and enjoyment to the weaving process.

Power looms produce millions of yards of textiles on factory assembly lines yearly. Looms run by steam, electricity, or water power have shuttles that refill automatically and can move as fast as 60 miles (97 kilometers) an hour. The beaters and harnesses on power looms move faster than the eye can follow.

Weaving Without a Loom

Artists and hobbyists have developed many ways to weave without a mechanical loom. In *paper weaving*, for example, strips of colored construction paper serve as the warps and wefts. The weaver interlaces the strips by hand to make place mats, wallhangings, and other decorative objects.

In *finger weaving*, or *Indian braiding*, several pieces of cord tied together at one end serve as the warp. A

Dan River Inc.

Many Modern Commercial Looms can weave as much as 7 yards (6.4 meters) of cotton cloth an hour.

longer cord, also attached to the warp, is threaded over and under the lengthwise pieces to make belts and sashes. Some artists weave reeds, yarn, and other materials through flexible wire screens. The weaver can then bend the decorated wire into sculptural forms.

A loom made from a piece of cardboard can be used to weave yarn place mats, potholders, and purses. Evenly spaced notches cut at the top and bottom of the cardboard hold the warps in place. The weaver slips a stick under alternate warp threads to create a shed and passes a threaded needle through the shed.

History

Thousands of years ago, people discovered how to weave baskets from grasses. Historians do not know when the process of weaving cloth developed. But civilizations in central Europe, the Middle East, and Pakistan probably had learned to weave textiles by 2500 B.C. Ancient wall-paintings illustrate weaving techniques mastered by the Egyptians as early as 5000 B.C.

The Chinese learned to weave sometime between 2500 and 1200 B.C. They became famous for spinning silk thread that was woven into exquisite brocade and damask fabrics in Persia (now Iran) and Syria.

The Pueblo and other Indian tribes of what is now the Southwestern United States began to weave cotton textiles during the A.D. 700's. The two-bar loom mounted in a frame was used in Europe by the 1200's. By the 1400's, the art of weaving had become highly developed in Europe. For example, skilled weavers in the city of Arras, in what is now France, produced beautiful tapestries that decorated castles and cathedrals.

The greatest improvements in machinery for weaving came during the Industrial Revolution, a period of rapid industrial growth in Europe during the 1700's and early 1800's. In 1785, an English inventor named Edmund Cartwright developed the first power loom (see CARTWRIGHT, EDMUND). The French inventor Joseph M. Jacquard developed the Jacquard loom in 1801. It uses punched cards and other attachments that guide the threads in weaving complex patterns.

Today, many textile firms use high-speed looms that have many tiny shuttles called *darts* instead of a single large shuttle. The darts pick up weft yarns that lie beside the loom and pass them through the shed faster than other kinds of shuttles.   DONA Z. MEILACH

Related Articles in WORLD BOOK include:

Basket Weaving	Jacquard, Joseph M.
Beadwork	Northern Ireland
Colonial Life in America	(picture)
(picture: Spinning and	Rugs and Carpets
Weaving)	Spinning Jenny
Indian, American (pictures)	Syria (picture)
Industrial Revolution	Tapestry
(The Textile Industry)	Textile

WEB. See SPIDER.

WEBB is the family name of two noted British reformers, husband and wife. Sidney and Beatrice Webb helped lead the British socialist movement in the late 1800's and early 1900's. They were influential Fabian Socialists, and helped form British Labour Party policies (see FABIAN SOCIETY). Their writings led to reforms that aided the poor, strengthened trade unions, and improved public education. Their books include *The History of Trade Unionism* (1894) and *Soviet Communism: A New Civilization?* (1935).

Sidney James Webb (1859-1947), BARON PASSFIELD, joined the Fabian Society in 1885. He helped found the London School of Economics and Political Science in 1895. He served in the House of Commons from 1922 to 1928, and went to the House of Lords in 1929. Webb served as president of the Board of Trade in 1924 and colonial secretary in 1929. He was born in London.

Beatrice Potter Webb (1858-1943) was born near Gloucester, the daughter of a rich industrialist. She became a social worker in London in 1887. The Webbs were married in 1892.   VERNON F. SNOW

WEBB INSTITUTE OF NAVAL ARCHITECTURE is a private coeducational engineering college in Glen Cove, N.Y. It is the only college which devotes its curriculum to naval architecture and marine engineering. All students have free-tuition scholarships for the four-year course. Admission is by competitive examination. Webb Institute was founded in 1889. For enrollment, see UNIVERSITIES AND COLLEGES (table).   W. A. BROCKETT

WEBB-KENYON ACT. See PROHIBITION.

WEBER, *VAY buhr,* is a unit used to measure magnetic flux in a magnetic field. The concentration of flux determines the strength of a magnetic field. A strong magnetic field may have a strength of two or more webers per square meter. The weber was named for the German physicist Wilhelm Weber. It equals 100 million smaller units called *maxwells.*   SAMUEL SEELY

WEBER, CARL MARIA VON (1786-1826), was the first important composer of German romantic opera. This kind of opera is based on conflict between a mortal and a supernatural being.

Weber's most popular romantic opera is *Der Freischütz* (*The Free-Shooter,* 1821). This opera tells about a pact that a hunter makes with the devil to get magic bullets that will strike anything he chooses. An important romantic feature of *Der Freischütz* is its atmospheric settings. A major scene takes place in a frightening wild rocky place called the "Wolf's Glen." The rest of the story is set in a friendlier region inhabited by hunters and farmers. Weber's other operas include *Euryanthe* (1823) and *Oberon* (1826). His other works include the piano piece *Invitation to the Dance* (1819). Weber was born in Eutin, near Lübeck.   ROBERT BAILEY

WEBER, *VAY ber,* **MAX** (1864-1920), was a German sociologist and economist. His theories and writings helped establish the foundations of modern sociology. Weber considered *bureaucracy* to be the most important feature of modern society. Bureaucracy is a method of organization based on specialization of duties, action according to rules, and a stable order of authority. Weber also developed an *ideal type* method for studying society. This method studies the basic elements of social institutions and how they relate to each other.

In *The Protestant Ethic and the Spirit of Capitalism* (1904-1905), Weber developed a theory that certain Protestant religious beliefs promoted capitalism. He argued that the Calvinist belief in working hard and avoiding luxury promoted the expansion of business enterprise. According to Weber, the Calvinist doctrine of business success as a sign of spiritual salvation justified the desire for profits. Weber also wrote on other religions and their relationship to the social system.

Weber was born in Erfurt, Germany. He studied at the universities of Berlin, Göttingen, and Heidelberg. Other important works by Weber which have been translated into English include *From Max Weber: Essays in Sociology* and *The Theory of Social and Economic Organization.*   DANIEL R. FUSFELD

WEBER, *WEB ur,* **MAX** (1881-1961), was a pioneer modern painter in America. He is best known for the abstract works he painted between 1912 and 1919, and for his later paintings of figures with expressive gestures and the appearance of motion. Several of his pictures deal with Jewish themes, reflecting his background.

Weber was born in Western Russia and moved with his family to New York City when he was ten. He came under the influence of modern artists while painting and studying in Paris from 1905 to 1908. Until the late 1920's, many critics considered his work too extreme. Then Weber's paintings began to receive favorable criticism. In 1930, the Museum of Modern Art in New York City presented a one-man show of Weber's works. It marked the first time the museum devoted a one-man show to a living American artist.   GEORGE EHRLICH

WEBERN, *VAY buhrn,* **ANTON** (1883-1945), was an Austrian composer. Webern, Alban Berg, and their teacher, Arnold Schönberg, were the most important members of the modern Viennese school. This group of composers produced their most influential work from 1910 to the mid-1930's.

Webern's earliest compositions show the impact of Schönberg's style (see SCHÖNBERG, ARNOLD). These works include *Passacaglia* (1908) and *Five Movements for String Quartet* (1909). *String Trio* (1927), *Symphony* (1928), and other Webern compositions of the 1920's influenced composers of the period following the end of World War II in 1945. More than half of Webern's music consists of choral works and songs for individual voices. His major choral works include *Das Augenlicht* (1935), *First Cantata* (1939), and *Second Cantata* (1943). Webern's cantatas are his longest and most lyrical works. Most of his music lasts less than 10 minutes.

Webern was born in Vienna. The Nazis banned his work in 1938 after taking over Austria.   MILOŠ VELIMIROVIĆ

WEBSTER, DANIEL (1782-1852), was the best-known American orator, and one of the ablest lawyers and statesmen of his time. He gained his greatest fame as the champion of a strong national government. For years after his death, schoolboys memorized thrilling lines from his speeches. Such words as "Liberty *and* Union, now and forever, one and inseparable!" inspired many Northern soldiers during the Civil War.

Early Career. Webster was born on Jan. 18, 1782, in Salisbury (now Franklin), N.H., and was graduated from Dartmouth College (see NEW HAMPSHIRE [color picture: Daniel Webster's Birthplace]). He studied law in Boston, and then became a successful lawyer in Portsmouth, N.H. At the beginning of his career, Webster did not favor a strong national government. Instead, he stood for the rights of the states.

Portsmouth was a thriving seaport until President Thomas Jefferson's embargo and the War of 1812 destroyed most of its overseas trade. Siding with the local shipowners, Webster opposed trade restrictions and war. As a Federalist in the United States House of Representatives from 1813 to 1817, he objected to war taxes, and helped defeat a bill for drafting soldiers. He said that state governments should "interpose" to protect their citizens from the national government.

Webster moved to Boston in 1816. New spinning and weaving mills were springing up along New England streams where there was water power. In much of the Northeast, manufacturing came to be more important than shipping. The manufacturers desired a strong national government that could aid business.

As a friend and attorney of northeastern businessmen, Webster changed his views on national power and states' rights. In the Dartmouth College case, he argued against New Hampshire's claim to control the college and won the verdict of the Supreme Court of the United States (see DARTMOUTH COLLEGE CASE). In another famous case, he held that it was constitutional for the federal government to charter a national bank. Representing Massachusetts in the United States House of Representatives from 1823 to 1827, he insisted that a protective tariff was unconstitutional. But after his election to the United States Senate in 1827, he became the country's most eloquent tariff advocate.

The U.S. Senator. The so-called "Tariff of Abominations," passed in 1828, led John C. Calhoun of South Carolina to develop the theory that a state could "nullify" federal laws, and refuse to obey them (see NULLIFICATION). Senator Robert Y. Hayne of South Carolina made a brilliant defense of nullification in 1830, and Webster answered him with a famous speech declaring that the Constitution had created a single, unified nation (see HAYNE, ROBERT YOUNG). Two years later, when South Carolina tried to put nullification into effect, Webster gave powerful support to President Andrew Jackson in resisting the attempt.

But Webster disagreed with Jackson on other issues, especially on the question of the Bank of the United States. When Jackson vetoed a bill for rechartering the bank, Webster did his best to save the institution, but failed (see BANK OF THE UNITED STATES).

During his last years in the Senate, Webster opposed adding Texas to the Union, and also opposed the war with Mexico. He feared that the country might break up over a quarrel over territories in the West.

Daniel Webster, standing, *right*, with his arm raised, addressed the United States Senate in the great debate on the Constitution and Union in 1850. Webster urged acceptance of the Compromise of 1850 to help preserve the Union.

Culver

Most Northerners wished to keep slavery from spreading into the new territories, but Southerners were ready to separate from the Union if the spread of slavery was prevented. In a "Union-saving" speech, Webster favored the Compromise of 1850, and helped get it passed (see COMPROMISE OF 1850). Some Northerners denounced him because he was willing to give Southerners part of what they wanted.

Secretary of State. Webster served as secretary of state under Presidents William Henry Harrison and John Tyler, and then under President Millard Fillmore. Under Tyler, he negotiated the Webster-Ashburton Treaty which settled the Maine boundary dispute and avoided a war with Great Britain (see WEBSTER-ASHBURTON TREATY). Under Fillmore, he befriended the Hungarian patriot Lajos Kossuth and spoke for Hungarian independence (see KOSSUTH, LAJOS).

The Man. After the founding of the Whig Party in the 1830's, Webster became one of its top leaders, along with his great rival, Henry Clay. His Whig friends thought he deserved to be President, and he ran as one of the party's three candidates in 1836. His later failures to become President made him bitter at the end of his life. In 1957, Webster was one of the first men elected to the United States Senate Hall of Fame. A statue of him represents New Hampshire in Statuary Hall in the United States Capitol.

Personally, Webster was a handsome, imposing man with deep-set, penetrating eyes, craggy brows, dark complexion, and a rich voice.   RICHARD N. CURRENT

WEBSTER, JOHN (1580?-1625?), an English playwright, is noted for two tragedies, *The White Devil* (completed about 1612) and *The Duchess of Malfi* (completed about 1613). Essentially, both plays deal with the common Elizabethan subject of revenge. But their power lies in the complexity of the characters' motives for acting as they do, the physical horror of the situations, and poetic dialogue which is second only to that of William Shakespeare. The plays show the world as corrupt and immoral. However, Webster used dramatic action to express the concern of all great tragic writers in the restoration of moral order.

Webster was born in London, but little is known of his life. He wrote or collaborated in writing more than a dozen plays and entertainments and his works were apparently popular with audiences.   ALAN S. DOWNER

WEBSTER, MARGARET (1905-1972), an actress and director, became famous for her exciting productions of Shakespeare's plays. In 1938, she achieved overnight success in New York City with her direction of *Richard II*. She also directed *Hamlet* and *Henry IV*, and acted in *The Sea Gull, Family Portrait, Alice in Wonderland,* and *John Gabriel Borkman*. She acted with the Old Vic and other English theatrical companies. She was born in New York City, the daughter of British parents. Her mother was the English actress Dame May Whitty.   MARY VIRGINIA HEINLEIN

WEBSTER, NOAH (1758-1843), was an American educator and journalist who won fame for compiling *Webster's Dictionary*. This work was the finest English dictionary of its time. The most recently revised form of the dictionary is *Webster's Third New International Dictionary*.

Webster was born in the village of West Hartford, Conn., on Oct. 16, 1758. He was descended from John Webster, governor of Connecticut in 1656, and from William Bradford, who governed Plymouth Colony for more than 30 years. Webster graduated from Yale College. He then studied law and was admitted to the bar at Hartford. But Webster practiced law for only a short time.

Noah Webster

Brown Bros.

While teaching school at Goshen, N.Y., in the 1780's, he compiled an elementary spelling book. He then compiled a grammar, and, finally, a reader for school children. Millions of copies of the speller were sold well into the 1900's, and they helped to standardize spelling and pronunciation in the United States.

WEBSTER-ASHBURTON TREATY

Webster campaigned for the first American copyright laws. He became an active member of the Federalist party, and wrote many political pamphlets. In 1787, he became the editor of two Federalist newspapers. After 1803, he devoted most of his time to dictionary work.

In 1806, Webster published his first dictionary. He thought of it as a preliminary effort. His great dictionary, *An American Dictionary of the English Language*, appeared in two volumes in 1828. This work, which was enlarged for an edition in 1840, included 12,000 words and 40,000 definitions that had never before appeared in a dictionary. After his death, Webster's heirs sold the dictionary rights to the G. and C. Merriam Co. of Springfield, Mass. G. E. BENTLEY

See also DICTIONARY (History).

WEBSTER-ASHBURTON TREATY was an agreement signed by representatives of the United States and Great Britain. It settled a number of annoying disputes between the two countries.

Secretary of State Daniel Webster signed it for the United States and Lord Ashburton for Great Britain at Washington, D.C., in August, 1842.

The most important dispute settled was the fixing of the boundary line between Canada and the state of Maine. The United States received more than half of the disputed area of 12,000 square miles (31,100 square kilometers). The treaty settled other disputes of a minor nature, and a clause of the treaty provided for the mutual extradition of criminals.

The negotiations also provided opportunity for the peaceful discussion of problems arising from British efforts to suppress the African slave trade. The Webster-Ashburton Treaty was one of the many instances in which the United States and Great Britain settled disputes without going to war. JOHN DONALD HICKS

WEBSTER COLLEGE. See UNIVERSITIES AND COLLEGES (table).

WEDDING. See MARRIAGE.

WEDDING ANNIVERSARY. It is customary for married couples to celebrate their wedding anniversaries. A certain type of gift is appropriate for each anniversary. For example, gold or goldlike gifts are given to a couple married for 50 years.

Invitations to anniversary celebrations may be as formal as wedding invitations or very simple. Guests are not expected to bring gifts, but many do. Few couples observe each anniversary. But many couples celebrate their 10th, 25th, and 50th wedding anniversaries.

Certain anniversaries and the gifts appropriate for them are listed in the table below. AMY VANDERBILT

WEDDING RING. See RING; EGYPT (Village Life); MARRIAGE (Wedding Ceremonies and Customs).

WEDEKIND, *VEY deh kint,* **FRANK** (1864-1918), was a German playwright who savagely attacked the smugness, hypocrisy, and corruption he saw in middle-class morality. His characters are overdrawn and sometimes grotesque symbols of the individual's sexual freedom and physical vitality. They scorn the conformity of the middle class. The plays *Earth Spirit* (1894), *Pandora's Box* (1894), and *The Marquis von Keith* (1900) are variations on Wedekind's view of society.

An earlier play, *Spring's Awakening* (1890-1891), established Wedekind's reputation as a controversial playwright. In this play, Wedekind says the torments of youth are caused by the cruelty and narrow-mindedness of the adult world.

Wedekind was born in Hannover and grew up in Switzerland. In 1912, he formed a theater company that toured Germany performing his plays. PETER GONTRUM

WEDGE. See GOLF (The Equipment).

WEDGE is a device that has two or more sloping surfaces that taper either to a sharp edge or to a point. Wedges are used to split or pierce materials, and to adjust the positions of heavy objects. Knives, chisels, axes, pins, needles, and nails are wedges.

A wedge must overcome the resistance of friction as well as the resistance of the material it is being used on. The total resistance may be high enough to require heavy blows from a hammer to drive the wedge forward. The greater the angle between the surfaces of a wedge, the greater the force needed to advance it. If the wedge angle is too great, it is impossible to drive the wedge into the material. The limiting angle varies from 90° to 180°, depending on the amount of friction acting on the wedge surfaces.

See also MACHINE (picture: Six Simple Machines).

WEDGWOOD, JOSIAH (1730-1795), was the outstanding leader in the pottery industry during the greatest period of British pottery making. He became a master potter at 29, and was successful in his own business. Three years later, in partnership with Thomas Bentley, a London merchant, he started the Etruria factory at Hanley. There he perfected the clays, glazes, and processes that made Wedgwood ware famous (see WEDGWOOD WARE).

Wedgwood improved upon the known processes of his time, and invented and perfected new ones. Wedgwood was born in Burslem, Staffordshire, a district rich in pottery clays. EUGENE F. BUNKER, JR.

WEDGWOOD WARE is a high-grade chinaware first made by England's most famous potter, Josiah Wedgwood. His experiments resulted in the creation of

---

WEDDING ANNIVERSARY GIFTS

First	Paper, plastics, furniture	Twelfth	Linen, silk, nylon
Second	Cotton, china	Thirteenth	Lace
Third	Leather, any leatherlike article	Fourteenth	Ivory, agate
Fourth	Linen, silk, rayon, nylon, other synthetic silks	Fifteenth	Crystal, glass
		Twentieth	China or occasional furniture
Fifth	Wood and decorative accessories for the home	Twenty-fifth	Silver
		Thirtieth	Pearls or personal gifts
Sixth	Iron	Thirty-fifth	Coral, jade
Seventh	Wool, copper, brass	Fortieth	Rubies, garnets
Eighth	Bronze, electrical appliances	Forty-fifth	Sapphires, tourmalines
Ninth	Pottery, china, glass or crystal	Fiftieth	Gold
Tenth	Tin, aluminum	Fifty-fifth	Emeralds, turquoise
Eleventh	Steel	Sixtieth, Seventy-fifth	Diamonds, diamondlike stones, gold

WORLD BOOK photo

Wedgwood Ware ranks among the finest pottery in the world. Examples of this excellent English ware include the plate with a grape design and the jasper vase shown above. The vase has the white figures and colored background typical of most jasper.

Queen's Ware, in 1762, in honor of Queen Charlotte, wife of George III. Later, other classes of Wedgwood ware became important. They included Egyptian black, or *basalts*, used for medallion portraits, vases, busts, seals, and similar objects; red ware, or *Rosso antico*, used for cameo reliefs; *white semiporcelain*, or fine stoneware, with a lustrous, smooth surface; and *jasper*, the final product of the great potter.

For jasper, Josiah Wedgwood used white, various tints of blue, lilac, pink, sage green, olive green, yellow, and black. Objects made of this ware include medallions, cameos, statuettes, pedestals, flowerpots, and vases. Figures in relief, or with a raised design, represented classical art, and adorned many objects made from jasper. Famous artists made the designs. White cameo reliefs on a blue background have been used in many inexpensive copies.   EUGENE F. BUNKER, JR.

See also WEDGWOOD, JOSIAH.

WEDNESDAY, *WENZ dih,* is the English name for the fourth day of the week. This day gets its name from Woden, or Odin, the chief god in Teutonic mythology, to whom it was sacred. At the beginning of the Christian Era, the Germans called it Woden's-day. Its name later changed to *Wednesday*. The first to name the days of the week after gods in mythology were the ancient Romans. They called the fourth day of the week after the god Mercury. From this name, the French called Wednesday *mercredi*.   GRACE HUMPHREY

See also ASH WEDNESDAY; ODIN; WEEK.

WEED is a plant that is troublesome and worthless where it is growing. Plants that are considered weeds in one place may be useful plants in another. For example,

corn growing in a bluegrass lawn is a weed. But corn growing in a cultivated cornfield is a useful crop. Many plants such as poison ivy are called weeds wherever they grow, because they have no known use.

Weed damage in the United States alone costs farmers over $2½ billion each year. American farmers spend another $2½ billion a year to kill weeds. Weeds damage crops because they take light, water, and food that the crops need. They also shelter insects and diseases that may damage valuable crops. Some weeds, such as poison ivy, are poisonous to human beings and livestock. Hay fever is caused by the pollen of ragweed and other such weeds.

Weeds must be cleared from along highways, railroad tracks, and telephone and electric lines so that they do not interfere with communication lines and with highway safety. Weeds also are an unsightly nuisance. They take away from the beauty of flower beds and lawns.

However, weeds are not completely useless. Some serve as food for livestock and wildlife. Some weeds are used by human beings as food and in making medicines.

Kinds of Weeds

Weeds are usually classified as *common* or *noxious*. Common weeds are those that are fairly easy to kill. They usually spread seed which starts new plants. Common weeds usually can be cleared from a field if they are killed before they release the new seeds. Pigweed and many narrow-leaved grasses are examples.

Noxious weeds are more difficult to control. Many weed control methods do not kill them. Most noxious weeds are *perennial plants*. That is, they grow year after year without producing seeds. Many of them spread by stems that grow underground or along the top of the soil. Quack grass and many broadleaf plants, including Canada thistle, are noxious weeds.

Weed Control

Weeds can be pulled out of the ground, cut off above the ground, or killed by breaking up the soil with a hoe. Most farmers use machinery called *cultivators* to break up the soil so that weeds cannot grow. Rice farmers flood fields with water to kill weeds. Farmers may also drain land to kill weeds that grow well in water. Weeds may be burned, or they may be smothered by covering them with hay or a sheet of plastic.

Weeds can also be prevented from growing by planting crops that grow more easily and are "stronger" than the weeds. A "strong" crop will crowd out weeds, taking over all the growing space and leaving no room for them to grow. However, most crops will not do this.

Herbicides, chemical preparations that are sometimes called *weedkillers*, have been widely used since World War II. They are one of the most inexpensive ways to control weeds, because they can be sprayed on crops with relatively little manpower or labor.

Most herbicides are *selective*. That is, they can kill weeds but will not harm the crop, even though they are sprayed on both plants. For example, a selective herbicide can kill a pigweed growing in a cotton field, but it will not harm the cotton. Herbicides must be carefully chosen, however, so that they kill only the weeds and do not damage the crop. *Soil sterilants* are herbicides that are not selective. They kill all plants and keep anything from growing in the soil. They are often used along fences, highways, driveways, and other such areas where plants are not wanted.

Kinds of Herbicides. Many kinds of herbicides are made to kill weeds. They can be made in the form of tiny particles, as gas, or as liquid. They are sprayed on crops or mixed in the soil. Most of them contain carbon, hydrogen, and oxygen and are called *organic* herbicides.

An organic herbicide called 2,4-D was one of the first major herbicides. It kills such broadleaf weeds as pigweed or cocklebur that grow in corn, pastures, and other grass crops. Other important herbicides include simazine, diuron, and trifluralin.

More than one kind of herbicide can be used on a crop. For example, a farmer may put a herbicide on his corn crop that kills unwanted grasses and another that kills broadleaf weeds.

Most herbicides can be used at almost any time in a crop's growing season without damaging the crop. They may be mixed into the soil before the crop is planted, or applied after the crop has been planted. Other kinds are applied after the crop appears above the surface of the soil. Some herbicides are poisonous to animals and human beings. They should be stored where small children and animals cannot get them. However, most are not highly poisonous.   PAUL W. SANTELMANN

Related Articles in WORLD BOOK include:

Amaranth	Horsetail	Ragweed
Beggarweed	Indian Mallow	Saint John's-Wort
Bindweed	Jimson Weed	Smartweed
Brome Grass	Knotgrass	Solanum
Burdock	Lamb's-Quarters	Sorrel
Canada Thistle	Locoweed	Sow Thistle
Cinquefoil	Lupine	Spurge Family
Cocklebur	Milkweed	Stickseed
Compass Plant	Mullein	Teasel
Dandelion	Nettle	Thistle
Dock	Parsnip	Toadflax
Dodder	Pigweed	Tumbleweed
Glasswort	Plantain	Viper's Bugloss
Goldenrod	Poison Ivy	Water Hyacinth
Grass	Poison Oak	Wild Carrot
Gromwell	Pokeweed	Witchweed
Hemlock	Purslane	

WEED, THURLOW (1797-1882), was an American journalist and political leader. He became one of the leaders of the Whig and Republican parties, and was largely responsible for the election of two Whig presidents, William Henry Harrison and Zachary Taylor. His support of William H. Seward, U.S. secretary of state, led to Weed's appointment as a commissioner to England and France at the outset of the Civil War. Weed was born at Cairo, N.Y. In 1830 he established the Albany (N.Y.) *Evening Journal.*   JOHN ELDRIDGE DREWRY

WEEDKILLER. See WEED.

WEEK is a division of time which includes seven days. We do not know exactly how this man-made division of time came into being, but the ancient Hebrews were among the first to use it. The book of Genesis in the Bible says that the world was created in six days and the seventh day, or Sabbath, was a day of rest and worship.

The ancient Egyptians named each day of the week

for one of the planets. They considered the seventh day merely as a day of rest and play. Among the later Romans, the seven days of the week were named after the sun, moon, and five planets which were then known. Each day was considered sacred to the Roman god who was associated with that planet. The days were known as Sun's-day, Moon's-day, Mars'-day, and so on. This system was used about the beginning of the Christian Era. The English names for the days *Tuesday, Wednesday, Thursday,* and *Friday* were derived from the names of Norse gods.   PAUL SOLLENBERGER

See also separate articles in WORLD BOOK on each day of the week.

WEEKS, SINCLAIR (1893-1972), an American businessman, served as secretary of commerce from 1953 to 1958 under President Dwight D. Eisenhower.

Weeks served in the Army in World War I, then began his business career as a bank clerk. In 1928, he became vice-president of Reed and Barton Corporation, silversmiths. He later served as board chairman. Weeks also served as Republican national committee treasurer from 1941 to 1944, and national finance committee chairman from 1949 to 1953. Weeks was born in West Newton, Mass. He was graduated from Harvard University in 1914.   CARL T. ROWAN

WEEMS, MASON LOCKE (1759-1825), was an American writer, clergyman, and bookseller. An Episcopal priest, he was often called "Parson" Weems. He wrote the first popular biography of George Washington, *The Life and Memorable Actions of George Washington* (about 1800). It includes many tales which Weems apparently invented, notably the one about the young Washington chopping down a cherry tree. Weems also wrote biographies of other leading Americans, as well as several moral tracts. Weems was born in Anne Arundel County, Maryland.   ARVID SHULENBERGER

WEEMS, P.V.H. See NAVIGATION (Important Dates).

WEEVIL, *WEE v'l,* is the name of many kinds of beetles with a long snout. They are among the worst insect pests that attack farm crops. The cotton boll weevil, commonly called the *boll weevil,* probably causes more loss than any other insect in the United States. The name weevil is also given to the *grubs*

E. O. Essig
Rice Weevil

USDA
Alfalfa Weevil

(larvae) of these beetles. Grubs usually do the damage.

Adult weevils are sometimes so small that they are hard to see. They have long snouts that may be longer than the rest of the body. These insects lay their eggs in the stalk, seed, or fruit of the plant. The grub then feeds on these plant parts, causing great damage.

Besides the boll weevil, there are other kinds that attack grain, fruit, clover, and alfalfa. The *granary weevil* is harmful to wheat. It lays its eggs on the wheat after it is stored, and the grubs burrow into the grain. The *rice weevil* destroys rice and other cereals in the same way. The *alfalfa weevil* first appeared in Salt Lake City about 1904. It has spread rapidly, and causes great loss in alfalfa-growing regions every year. This insect is less than $\frac{1}{4}$ inch (6 millimeters) long, and is tawny red. It came to the United States from Europe and Asia. In its native home it has many insect enemies which eat the weevil and its eggs, and keep it in check. The United States Department of Agriculture has imported large numbers of weevil enemies. It has spread them among the weevils to keep down the damage to alfalfa.

There are also many kinds of fruit weevils. The *plum curculio* is the most important of the group that attacks plums and cherries. The larvae of these insects feed on the fruit, which falls off or becomes wormy.

Scientific Classification. Weevils belong to the weevil or snout-beetle family, *Curculionidae*.   R. E. BLACKWELDER

See also BOLL WEEVIL; GRAIN WEEVIL.

WEFT. See WEAVING (Types of Weaves).

WEHRMACHT. See WORLD WAR II (Mobilization).

WEIDENREICH, *VY dun ryk,* **FRANZ** (1873-1948), was a German-American physical anthropologist. He gained fame for his studies of the fossils representing *Sinanthropus pekinesis* (Peking man), and for demonstrating the relationship of this early man to Java man and other *Pithecanthropus* forms. He wrote *Apes, Giants, and Man* (1946), an important book on fossil man. Weidenreich was born in Edenkoben, Germany.   DAVID B. STOUT

WEIGHING SCALE. See SCALE, WEIGHING.

WEIGHT is the gravitational force put forth on an object by the planet on which the object is located. The weight of any object depends on (1) the distance from the object to the center of the planet and (2) the *mass* (amount of matter) of the object.

An object's weight is largest if the object is on the surface of the planet. The weight becomes smaller if the object is moved away from the planet. The object has no weight in space where the gravitational force acting on it is too weak to be measured.

The weight of an object also depends on the mass of the planet. If the mass of a planet is smaller than that of the earth, the gravitational force there is smaller. For example, a man who weighs 200 pounds (91 kilograms) on the earth would weigh only 32 pounds (15 kilograms) on the moon. He would weigh 76 pounds (34 kilograms) on Mars, 178 pounds (81 kilograms) on Venus, and 529 pounds (240 kilograms) on Jupiter.

Common units used to measure weight are the *ounce* and the *pound*. The metric system uses the *gram* and the *kilogram*.   VERA KISTIAKOWSKY

See also GRAVITATION; WEIGHTS AND MEASURES; SCALE, WEIGHING.

WEIGHT, ATOMIC. See ATOM (Atomic Weight).

WEIGHT, MOLECULAR. See MOLECULE.

WEIGHT, TABLES OF. For boys and girls, see GROWTH.

WEIGHT CONTROL is the process of losing or avoiding excessive body fat. It is based on the relationship between the amount of food you eat and the amount of exercise you get. The less you eat and the more you exercise, the less fat you will have. Weight control has great medical importance because being *obese* (too fat) can lead to severe health problems. Serious emotional and social problems may also result from obesity.

Overweight people may not be obese, though the word *overweight* is often used when *obese* is meant. Being overweight simply means weighing more than the average for a certain height.

Some people weigh less than average for their height because they have small bones and muscles. Others are underweight because they have less fat. In either case, being underweight is not unhealthy. But people may be underweight as the result of a disease—cancer, diabetes, or tuberculosis, for example. In some children, underweight may be the first sign of growth failure. An underweight person should consult a doctor. If no illness is found, there is no reason to worry.

Jean Mayer, the contributor of this article, is President of Tufts University and the author of Overweight: Causes, Cost, and Control. *He formerly was Professor of Nutrition at Harvard University.*

An overweight person who is not too fat does not need to lose weight for health reasons. The person would do better simply to stay physically fit with such exercise as walking or taking part in sports.

A simple way of determining whether you are too fat is to look at yourself nude in a mirror. If you think you look obese, you probably are.

Dangers of Obesity

Obese people are more likely than thin people to get certain diseases. The treatment of these diseases among the obese is also less likely to succeed. Such diseases include appendicitis, cirrhosis, diabetes, and diseases of the heart and blood vessels, especially coronary heart disease. A fat patient with one of these diseases has a better chance of recovery if he or she reduces.

Obese people have more falls and other accidents than thin people because they are slower and clumsier. Their recovery from injury is often difficult because surgery performed on them is dangerous. Obesity cuts down freedom of movement, especially in the elderly, and thus can lower general health because of lack of exercise. The decreased freedom of movement in obese patients with arthritis also makes treatment difficult.

In many parts of the world, obese people may be rejected in various ways. Fat people are often treated unkindly by others, including their classmates in school. They generally have less social success than other people, and may find it harder to get jobs.

Causes of Obesity

Overeating. You will gain or lose weight as a result of eating more or fewer calories than you need. A calorie is a unit used to measure the heat energy that the body gets from a certain amount of food. If you eat more calories than you use, they will turn into body fat. If you eat fewer than you use, your body will convert its

WEIGHT CONTROL

own fat into energy. During any period of days or weeks, if you eat 3,500 more calories than you use, you will gain 1 pound (0.5 kilogram). You will lose a pound if you eat 3,500 fewer calories than you use. Some countries that use the metric system measure the heat energy obtained from food in *joules* instead of calories. About 4,182 joules equal one calorie.

A surplus of calories is necessary for growth in children and pregnant women. But they will gain body fat if they eat too many calories. See CALORIE.

The amount of food you eat plays a much more important role in weight control than the kinds of food. People who are overweight, of normal weight, or underweight may all eat the same kinds of food. Their weight difference results from the amount of food they eat in relation to the amount of energy they use.

Certain centers in the brain control appetite, hunger, and *satiety*, the group of sensations that cause you to stop eating when your appetite and hunger have been satisfied. These brain centers normally make people eat an amount of food that provides enough energy for their needs. The *feeding centers* cause people to want to eat. The *satiety centers* act as a brake on the feeding centers and make people want to stop eating.

The feeding and satiety centers are extremely complicated mechanisms. Their operation may be disturbed by a number of causes, including emotional pressures and inherited physical characteristics. For example, emotional pressures such as great disappointment cause some people to stop all physical activity. At such times, these people eat more than they usually do —and gain weight. Other people who are under pressure move around more and eat much less—and lose weight.

Some scientists believe that overfeeding infants causes them to develop too many fat cells. They claim that these cells store fat so readily that such persons are likely to be obese for the rest of their lives.

Physical Inactivity can lead to obesity among all age groups. It does so especially among children and teen-agers, who are the most active groups. Most obese young people do not eat more than those of normal weight. In fact, most of them eat less. But they are so inactive that, even with a moderate appetite, they eat more than they need—and accumulate excess fat.

Exercise uses up many calories, and the more vigorous the activity, the more calories are used. A 150-pound (68-kilogram) person walking at an average speed of 3½ miles (5.6 kilometers) per hour will use up 502 calories—the number of calories in a malted milk shake—in 97 minutes. He will use up the same number of calories in 61 minutes by riding a bicycle, or in 26 minutes by running.

The number of calories used is proportional to weight. If you weigh 75 pounds, for example, you will use up half as many calories as a 150-pound person by doing the same exercise for the same length of time.

An active person's appetite will increase if he becomes very active. If he becomes inactive, however, his appetite will not necessarily decrease. Appetite does not go below a minimum level even if activity drops.

Heredity. Scientists have learned much about the relationship between heredity and obesity in animals, especially mice. This relationship is based on *genes*, the basic units in cells that determine inherited characteristics. Scientists have discovered that some mice have a gene that causes the satiety center not to operate. Other genes in some mice cause their bodies to overproduce certain chemical substances called *hormones*. As a result of these hormones, the mice make body fat too easily or use it up with difficulty. Still other genes cause some mice to become obese more quickly than others when physically inactive or when given a diet high in fat. See GENE; HORMONE.

In man, the action of genes is not so well known as in animals. But there is evidence that some people are more likely to become obese than others because of their genes. For example, studies of high school students

ENERGY EQUIVALENTS OF FOOD CALORIES

This table shows the calories in some foods, and the minutes it would take a 150-pound (68-kilogram) person to use them up in various ways. A person half that weight would need twice as long.

Food	Calories	Minutes of Lying Down	Minutes of Walking	Minutes of Bicycle Riding	Minutes of Swimming	Minutes of Running
Apple, large	101	78	19	12	9	5
Beans, green, 1 serving	27	21	5	3	2	1
Bread and butter	78	60	15	10	7	4
Cake, 1/12, 2-layer	356	274	68	43	32	18
Carrot, raw	42	32	8	5	4	2
Chicken, TV dinner	542	417	104	66	48	28
Egg, fried	110	85	21	13	10	6
Ham, 2 slices	167	128	32	20	15	9
Hamburger	350	269	67	43	31	18
Ice cream, 1 serving	193	148	37	24	17	10
Malted milk shake	502	386	97	61	45	26
Milk, 1 glass	166	128	32	20	15	9
Pancake with syrup	124	95	24	15	11	6
Peas, green, 1 serving	56	43	11	7	5	3
Pie, apple, 1/6	377	290	73	46	34	19
Pizza, cheese, 1/8	180	138	35	22	16	9
Pork chop, loin	314	242	60	38	28	16
Shrimp, French-fried	180	138	35	22	16	9
Spaghetti, 1 serving	396	305	76	48	35	20
Steak, T-bone	235	181	45	29	21	12
Strawberry shortcake	400	308	77	49	36	21

Adapted from Frank Konishi's "Food Energy Equivalents of Various Activities," *Journal of the American Dietetic Association*, March, 1965.

show that only about 8 per cent of the children of thin parents were obese. Among families where one parent was obese, 70 per cent of the children were fat. Among families with both parents obese, 80 per cent of the children were fat. Adopted children do not show this relationship to their adoptive parents.

The role of genes in obesity is also indicated by the fact that certain inherited body types are more likely to become fat than others. People with broad hands and short, stubby fingers are more likely to be obese than people with narrow hands and long fingers.

A child with obese parents is not doomed to obesity. To become obese, the child still would have to eat more calories than are needed.

Diseases and Other Causes. Obesity may result from a number of diseases. Some ailments of the endocrine glands cause these glands to release too much of a hormone into the blood stream. The excess hormone disturbs the feeding and satiety centers of the brain. Obesity also can result from damage to these brain centers caused by infection, injury, or a tumor.

How to Control Obesity

You should consult a physician and have a medical checkup before starting an extensive weight reduction program. It is also useful to have the advice of a dietitian. An obese person may need psychological help as well, especially if the person is young and has been teased and made to feel guilty, hopeless, or worthless. The first step in psychological treatment is to remove these feelings and to treat the obesity as a medical problem.

Diet. Any reducing diet must provide fewer calories. If a man needs 3,000 calories a day to maintain his weight with his habits of life, he should eat only 2,000 calories a day to lose 2 pounds (0.9 kilogram) a week. It is generally dangerous to lose weight any faster.

The foods in a reducing diet must be well-balanced. That is, they must provide enough of all the nutrients needed for good health. There is no evidence that extreme diets—for example, "low carbohydrate" or "low protein" diets, or diets based on single foods—have any advantage over a well-balanced diet. (For information on well-balanced diets and their importance to good health, see NUTRITION.) A reducing diet should also be good tasting and easy to buy and to cook.

A weight reducer should study charts that give the number of calories in various foods. Many people believe that such foods as baked potatoes and bread have many more calories than they do. They also underestimate the calories in such foods as steak.

The distribution of calories among meals and snacks is up to the individual. Some people do not get too hungry if they divide their calories among four or five light meals or snacks a day. Others can follow a diet better if they eat three meals a day and have no snacks.

Exercise. A person going on a reducing diet should get more exercise. But an obese person—even one who is otherwise healthy—should not suddenly start a program of prolonged, heavy exercise. The strain on the heart would be dangerous. An exercise program should be developed gradually. One good way to start is to take walks every day, increasing their duration. More demanding exercises can be added as the person becomes thinner and fitter.   JEAN MAYER

See also DIET; NUTRITION.

Bruce Klemens

A Powerful Weight Lifter strains to raise a heavy metal bar bell above his head in a lift called the *clean and jerk.*

WEIGHT LIFTING is a sport that is also frequently used to develop the body and to help athletes prepare for competition in other sports. In weight-lifting contests, participants lift heavy *bar bells.* They compete in classes with other lifters of about the same weight.

There are two chief kinds of weight-lifting competition—*Olympic lifts* and *power lifts.* Olympic lifts consist of the *snatch* and the *clean and jerk.* These are the two lifts used in the Olympic Games. They are also the most common lifts in Amateur Athletic Union (AAU) competition. In the snatch, the lifter, using both hands, grips the bar bell resting in front of him on the floor. Then with one motion, he lifts the bar bell over his head and locks his arms. In the clean and jerk, the lifter first raises the bar bell from the floor to shoulder level. Then he jerks the bar bell to arm's length over his head. In both lifts, the competitor must hold the bar bell steadily over his head until a referee's signal permits him to lower it.

There are three power lifts. In order of performance, they are (1) bench press; (2) deep knee bend, or squat; and (3) dead lift. In the bench press, the lifter lies on his back on a bench. The bar bell rests on his chest. He raises the bar bell above him until his arms are extended, and then lowers it back to his chest. In the deep knee bend, the lifter stands in an upright position and holds the bar bell at shoulder height. He then drops to a squatting position, stops, and rises to an upright position again. In the dead lift, the bar bell rests on the floor in front of the lifter. He bends down, lifts the weight with one motion until he is in a standing position, and then lowers it.

A referee and two judges decide if an Olympic lift or a power lift is valid. Each competitor is allowed three attempts at each lift. If he completes a lift successfully, additional weight is added for the next attempt. The competitor with the highest total weight from all lifts wins the event.   THOMAS KIRK CURETON, JR.

See also OLYMPIC GAMES (table).

WEIGHTLESSNESS. See SPACE TRAVEL (Living in Space); ASTRONAUT (Training the Astronauts).

WEIGHTS AND MEASURES

WEIGHTS AND MEASURES are the standards used to find the size of things. People in the United States and a few other countries use standards that belong to the *customary*, or *English, system of measurement*. This system was developed in England from older measurement standards, beginning about the 1200's. People in nearly all other countries—including England—now use a system of measurement called the *metric system*. The metric system was created in France in the 1790's. During the 1970's, strong efforts were made in the United States to convert to the metric system. For a complete discussion of metric measurement, see the WORLD BOOK article on the METRIC SYSTEM.

Weights and measures form one of the most important parts of our life today. Many weights and measures have

METRIC CONVERSION TABLE

This table can help you change measurements into or out of metric units. To use it, look up the unit you know in the left-hand column and multiply it by the number given. Your answer will be approximately the number of units shown in the right-hand column.

WHEN YOU KNOW:	MULTIPLY BY:	TO FIND:
Length and Distance		
inches (in.)	25	millimeters
feet (ft.)	30	centimeters
yards (yd.)	0.9	meters
miles (mi.)	1.6	kilometers
millimeters (mm)	0.04	inches
centimeters (cm)	0.4	inches
meters (m)	1.1	yards
kilometers (km)	0.6	miles
Surface or Area		
square inches (sq. in.)	6.5	square centimeters
square feet (sq. ft.)	0.09	square meters
square yards (sq. yd.)	0.8	square meters
square miles (sq. mi.)	2.6	square kilometers
acres	0.4	hectares
square centimeters (cm²)	0.16	square inches
square meters (m²)	1.2	square yards
square kilometers (km²)	0.4	square miles
hectares (ha)	2.5	acres
Volume and Capacity (Liquid)		
fluid ounces (fl. oz.)	30	milliliters
pints (pt.), U.S.	0.47	liters
pints (pt.), imperial	0.568	liters
quarts (qt.), U.S.	0.95	liters
quarts (qt.), imperial	1.137	liters
gallons (gal.), U.S.	3.8	liters
gallons (gal.), imperial	4.546	liters
milliliters (ml)	0.034	fluid ounces
liters (l)	2.1	pints, U.S.
liters (l)	1.76	pints, imperial
liters (l)	1.06	quarts, U.S.
liters (l)	0.88	quarts, imperial
liters (l)	0.26	gallons, U.S.
liters (l)	0.22	gallons, imperial
Weight and Mass		
ounces (oz.)	28	grams
pounds (lb.)	0.45	kilograms
short tons	0.9	metric tons
grams (g)	0.035	ounces
kilograms (kg)	2.2	pounds
metric tons (t)	1.1	short tons
Temperature		
degrees Fahrenheit (° F.)	5/9 (after subtracting 32)	degrees Celsius
degrees Celsius (° C)	9/5 (then add 32)	degrees Fahrenheit

——— MISCELLANEOUS WEIGHTS AND MEASURES ———

Angstrom is a unit once used with the metric system to measure small distances. It equals 0.0000001 of a millimeter (0.0000000039 inch).

Assay Ton, used for testing ore, equals 29.167 grams (1.029 ounces).

Bolt, used in measuring cloth, equals 120 feet (36.6 meters).

Butt, formerly used for liquids, equals 126 gallons (477 liters).

Carat, used to weigh precious stones and pearls, equals 200 milligrams (0.007 ounce).

Catty, used to measure tea and other materials, weighs about 1⅓ pounds (0.6 kilogram).

Chaldron, a capacity measure, equals 36 imperial bushels (1.31 cubic meters).

Cubit, in the customary system, is 18 inches (46 centimeters). It is based on the length of the forearm.

Ell, used in measuring cloth, equals 45 inches (114 centimeters).

Firkin, used to measure lard or butter, equals either about 9 imperial gallons (40.9 liters) or about 56 pounds (25 kilograms).

Fortnight is a period of 14 days.

Hand, used to measure the height of horses, from the ground to the withers, equals 4 inches (10 centimeters).

Hogshead, used to measure liquids, equals 63 gallons (238 liters).

Kilderkin, used to measure liquids, equals 18 imperial gallons (82 liters).

Knot is a speed of 1 nautical mile (1.1508 statute miles or 1.852 kilometers) per hour.

Light-Year, the distance light travels in a year. It is about 5.88 trillion miles (9.46 trillion kilometers).

Line, used to measure buttons, is $1/40$ inch (0.6 millimeter).

Load, of earth or gravel, equals 1 cubic yard (0.76 cubic meter).

Mole is a metric base unit for the amount of a substance. It equals 602,257,000,000,000,000,000,000 atoms, molecules, or whatever other elemental particles are being measured.

Nail, used in measuring cloth, equals 2.25 inches (5.72 centimeters).

Palm equals 3 or 4 inches (8 or 10 centimeters).

Perch, used for masonry, equals 24.75 cubic feet (0.7 cubic meter).

Perch, a measure of length in the customary system, equals 1 rod (5.03 meters).

Pin, used to measure liquids, equals 4½ gallons (17 liters).

Pipe, used to measure liquids, equals 126 gallons (477 liters).

Pole, a measure of length in the customary system, equals 1 rod (5.03 meters).

Puncheon, used to measure liquids, equals 84 gallons (318 liters).

Quarter, used to measure grain, equals 25 pounds (11 kilograms).

Rood, used to measure land, equals ¼ acre (0.1 hectare).

Score is a group of 20.

Skein, used to measure yarn, equals 360 feet (110 meters).

Square, used to measure floor or roofing material, is an area of 100 square feet (9.3 square meters).

Tierce, used to measure liquids, equals 42 gallons (159 liters).

Tun, used to measure liquids, equals 252 gallons (954 liters).

Vara, used to measure land, equals 33⅓ inches (84.6 centimeters) in Texas; 33 inches (84 centimeters) in California; and from 32 to 43 inches (81 to 109 centimeters) in Spain, Portugal, and Latin-American countries.

Daniel V. De Simone, the contributor of this article, is Deputy Director of the Office of Technology Assessment, an agency of the United States Congress. He directed the U.S. Metric Study conducted by the government from 1968 to 1971.

had a fascinating history. For a complete discussion of the history of measurement, see MEASUREMENT.

The tables in this article show how to convert from customary to metric units and from metric to customary units. Suppose you want to change customary units to metric units. Multiply the number of customary units—inches, feet, pounds, and so on—by the number of metric units in *one* of the customary unit. For example, to change 22 miles to kilometers, multiply 22, the number of miles, by 1.6093, the number of kilometers that

make up one mile: 22 × 1.6093 = 35.4046. So 22 customary-unit miles equal 35.4046 metric-unit kilometers.

DANIEL V. DE SIMONE

Related Articles. See MEASUREMENT with its list of Related Articles. See also the following articles:

Apothecaries' Weight
Avoirdupois
International Bureau of
 Weights and Measures
Metric System

National Bureau of
 Standards
Time
Troy Weight
Weight

LENGTH AND DISTANCE

Lengths and distances are measured from one point to another, usually along a straight line. Length usually refers to the measurement of an object. Distance usually refers to the measurement of the space between two places. The customary and metric units for length and distance are listed in the tables below. The tables also show the nautical units used to measure distances at sea, and the chain units used to survey land.

Customary				Metric		Metric			Customary	
1 inch (in.)			=	2.54	cm	1 nano-				
1 foot (ft.)	=	12 in.	=	30.48	cm	meter (nm)		=	0.00000003937	in.
1 yard (yd.)	=	3 ft.	=	0.9144	m	1 micron (μ)	= 1,000 nm	=	0.00003937	in.
1 rod (rd.)	=	5½ yd.	=	5.0292	m	1 milli-				
1 furlong (fur.)	=	40 rd., or ⅛ mi.	=	201.168	m	meter (mm)	= 1,000 μ	=	0.03937	in.
1 statute,						1 centi-				
or land,						meter (cm)	=	10 mm =	0.3937	in.
mile (mi.)	=	5,280 ft.,	=	1.6093	km	1 deci-				
		or 0.86897624				meter (dm)	=	10 cm =	3.937	in.
		nautical mi.				1 meter (m)	=	10 dm =	39.37	in.
1 statute						1 deka-				
league	=	15,840 ft.,	=	4.8280	km	meter (dam)	=	10 m =	393.7	in.
		or 3 statute mi.,				1 hecto-				
		or 2.6069287				meter (hm)	=	10 dam =	328.0833	ft.
		nautical mi.				1 kilometer (km)	=	10 hm =	0.62137	mi.

Nautical

					Customary		Metric	
1 span			=		9	in.	= 22.8	cm
1 fathom (fm.)	=	8 spans	=		6	ft.	= 1.83	m
1 cable's length	=	120 fathoms	=		720	ft.	= 219.46	m
1 nautical mile, or								
1 International Nautical Mile (INM)			=		6,076.11549	ft.,	= 1.852	km
					or 1.150779 statute mi.			
1 nautical league	=	3 nautical mi.	=		18,228.346	ft.,	= 5.556	km
					or 3.452338 statute mi.			

Surveyor's, or Gunter's, Chain

					Customary		Metric	
1 link (li.)			=		7.92	in.	= 20.12	cm
1 chain (ch.)	=	100 li.	=		66	ft.	= 20.12	m
1 furlong (fur.)	=	10 ch.	=		660	ft.	= 201.168	m
1 statute mile (mi.)	=	8 fur.	=		5,280	ft.	= 1.6093	km

Engineer's Chain

					Customary		Metric	
1 link (li.)			=		1	ft.	= 30.48	cm
1 chain (ch.)	=	100 li.	=		100	ft.	= 30.48	m
1 mile (mi.)	=	52.8 ch.	=		5,280	ft.	= 1.6093	km

WEIGHTS AND MEASURES

SURFACE OR AREA

An area of land or the surface of an object is measured in square units. These units result from multiplying the length of the area or object by its width. The square units of both the customary and metric systems are based on units of length and distance. A small 2, placed to the right and above the abbreviation of a metric unit, indicates a square unit.

Customary					Metric	Metric				Customary	
1 square inch (sq. in.)			=		6.4516 cm^2	1 square millimeter (mm^2)		=		0.002	sq. in.
1 square foot (sq. ft.)	=	144	sq. in.	=	0.0929 m^2	1 square centimeter (cm^2)	= 100 mm^2	=		0.155	sq. in.
1 square yard (sq. yd.)	=	9	sq. ft.	=	0.8361 m^2	1 square decimeter (dm^2)	= 100 cm^2	=		15.5	sq. in.
1 square rod (sq. rd.)	=	30¼	sq. yd.	=	25.293 m^2	1 square meter (m^2)	= 100 dm^2	=	1,550		sq. in.
1 acre		= 160	sq. rd.	=	0.4047 ha	1 square dekameter (dam^2)	= 100 m^2	=		119.6	sq. yd.
1 square mile (sq. mi.)	=	640	acres	=	258.9988 ha,	1 square hectometer (hm^2)	= 100 dam^2	=		2.4711	acres
					or 2.590 km^2	1 square kilometer (km^2)	= 100 hm^2	=		247.105	acres,
									or	0.3861	sq. mi.

Metric Land Measurement

Metric				Customary	
1 centiare (ca)			=	1,550	sq. in.
1 are (a)	=	100 ca	=	119.6	sq. yd.
1 hectare (ha)	=	100 a	=	2.4711	acres
1 square kilometer (km^2)	=	100 ha	=	247.105	acres,
			or	0.3861	sq. mi.

Surveyor's Land Measurement

				Customary			Metric
1 square link (sq. li.)			=	62.73	sq. in.	=	404.686 cm^2
1 square pole (sq. p.)	=	625 sq. li.	=	30.25	sq. yd.	=	25.293 m^2
1 square chain (sq. ch.)	=	16 sq. p.	=	484	sq. yd.	=	404.686 m^2
1 acre	=	10 sq. ch.	=	4,840	sq. yd.	=	4,046.856 m^2
1 section (sec.)	=	640 acres	=	1	sq. mi.	=	2.590 km^2
1 township (tp.)	=	36 sec.	=	36	sq. mi.	=	93.240 km^2

VOLUME AND CAPACITY

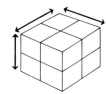

Volume refers to the amount of space occupied by an object. Capacity is the amount of a substance that a container can hold. Volume and capacity are both measured in cubic units. Cubic units combine length, width, and depth. But the names of many common cubic units, such as liter and quart, do not include the word *cubic*. A small 3, placed to the right and above the abbreviation of a metric unit, indicates a cubed unit.

Volume Measurement

Customary				Metric
1 cubic inch (cu. in.)			=	16.387 cm^3
1 cubic foot (cu. ft.)	=	1,728 cu. in.	=	0.0283 m^3
1 cubic yard (cu. yd.)	=	27 cu. ft.	=	0.7646 m^3

Metric			Customary	
1 cubic milli- meter (mm^3)			= 0.00006	cu. in.
1 cubic centi- meter (cm^3)	=	1,000 mm^3	= 0.0610	cu. in.
1 cubic deci- meter (dm^3)	=	1,000 cm^3	= 0.0353	cu. ft.
1 cubic meter (m^3)	=	1,000 dm^3	= 1.308	cu. yd.
1 cubic deka- meter (dam^3)	=	1,000 m^3	= 1,308	cu. yd.
1 cubic hecto- meter (hm^3)	=	1,000 dam^3	= 1,308,000	cu. yd.

Metric Capacity Measure

Metric			Customary	
1 milliliter (ml)		=	0.0610	cu. in.
1 centiliter (cl)	= 10 ml	=	0.6103	cu. in.
1 deciliter (dl)	= 10 cl	=	6.1025	cu. in.
1 liter (l)	= 10 dl	=	61.025	cu. in.,
		or	1.057	liquid qt.,
		or	0.908	dry qt.
1 dekaliter (dal)	= 10 l	=	610.25	cu. in.
1 hectoliter (hl)	= 10 dal	=	6,102.55	cu. in.
1 kiloliter (kl)	= 10 hl	=	35.316	cu. ft.,
		or	264.179	gal.,
		or	28.38	bu.

Household Capacity Measurement

Customary				Metric
1 teaspoon		=	⅙ fl. oz.	= 4.9 ml
1 table- spoon	= 3 teaspoons	=	½ fl. oz.	= 14.8 ml
1 cup	= 16 tablespoons	=	8 fl. oz.	= 236.6 ml
1 pint	= 2 cups	=	16 fl. oz.	= 473.2 ml
1 quart	= 2 pints	=	32 fl. oz.	= 946.3 ml
1 gallon	= 4 quarts	=	128 fl. oz.	= 3.785 l

Customary Liquid Capacity Measurement

		Customary				Metric
1 gill (gi.)			=	7.219 cu. in.	=	0.1183 l
1 pint (pt.)	= 4	gi.	=	28.875 cu. in.	=	0.4732 l
1 quart (qt.)	= 2	pt.	=	57.75 cu. in.	=	0.9463 l
1 gallon (gal.)	= 4	qt.	= 231	cu. in.	=	3.7854 l
1 barrel (bbl.), liquids	= 31.5	gal.	=	4.21 cu. ft.	=	119.24 l
1 barrel (bbl.), petroleum	= 42	gal.	=	5.61 cu. ft.	=	158.98 l

	Imperial		Customary		Metric
1 imperial pint	= 1.201 U.S. pt.	=	34.6775 cu. in.	=	0.568 l
1 imperial quart	= 1.201 U.S. qt.	=	69.354 cu. in.	=	1.13652 l
1 imperial gallon	= 1.201 U.S. gal.	=	277.42 cu. in.	=	4.54609 l

Customary Dry Capacity Measurement

		Customary		Metric	
1 pint (pt.)		=	33.600 cu. in.	= 550.61	cm³
1 quart (qt.)	= 2 pt.	=	67.20 cu. in.	= 1,101.22	cm³
1 peck (pk.)	= 8 qt.	=	537.61 cu. in.	= 8,809.77	cm³
1 bushel (bu.)	= 4 pk.	=	2,150.42 cu. in.	= 0.035239	m³
1 barrel (bbl.)		=	4.08 cu. ft.	= 0.115627	m³

	Imperial	Customary		Metric	
1 imperial pint	= 1.032 U.S. pt.	=	34.6775 cu. in.	= 568.26092	cm³
1 imperial quart	= 1.032 U.S. qt.	=	69.354 cu. in.	= 1,136.52	cm³
1 imperial bushel	= 1.032 U.S. bu.	=	2,219.36 cu. in.	= 0.03637	m³

Apothecaries' Fluid Measurement

		Customary	Metric
1 minim or drop (min. or ℳ)		= 0.002083 fl. oz.	= 0.0616 ml
1 fluid dram (fl. dr. or f℥)	= 60 min.	= 0.125 fl. oz.	= 3.6966 ml
1 fluid ounce (fl. oz. or f℥)	= 8 fl. dr.	= 1 fl. oz.	= 0.0296 l
1 pint (O.)	= 16 fl. oz.	= 16 fl. oz.	= 0.4732 l
1 gallon (C.)	= 8 O.	= 128 fl. oz.	= 3.7853 l

Shipping Capacity Measurement

		Customary	Metric
1 barrel bulk		= 5 cu. ft.	= 0.1416 m³
1 shipping ton, or 1 measurement ton, or 1 freight ton,	= 8 barrels bulk	= 40 cu. ft.	= 1.1327 m³
1 displacement ton		= 35 cu. ft.	= 0.9911 m³
1 register ton		= 100 cu. ft.	= 2.8317 m³

WEIGHT AND MASS

The customary system measures the weight of various materials. Avoirdupois weight measures ordinary materials. Apothecaries' weight once measured drugs and medicines. Troy weight measures precious metals and gems. The metric system measures *mass* (amount of material something contains). An object's mass does not change, but its weight decreases with altitude. These two measurement units are equal at sea level on the earth, and the comparisons in this table are based on that location.

Avoirdupois Weight

				Metric
1 grain (gr.)	=			0.0648 g
1 dram (dr.)	=	27.34375	gr. =	1.7718 g
1 ounce (oz.)	=	16	dr. =	28.3495 g
1 pound (lb.)	=	16	oz. =	453.5924 g, or 0.4536 kg
1 hundred-weight (cwt.)	=	100	lb. =	45.3592 kg
1 short ton	= 2,000		lb. =	907.18 kg, or 0.9072 t

Special British Units

		Customary		Metric
1 stone (st.)	=	14	lb. =	6.35 kg
1 hundred-weight (cwt.)	=	112	lb. =	50.80 kg
1 long ton	= 2,240		lb. =	1,016.05 kg, or 1.0160 t

Metric Weight

				Avoirdupois
1 milligram (mg)			=	0.0154 gr.
1 centigram (cg)	=	10 mg	=	0.1543 gr.
1 decigram (dg)	=	10 cg	=	1.5432 gr.
1 gram (g)	=	10 dg	=	15.4324 gr.
1 dekagram (dag)	=	10 g	=	0.3527 oz.
1 hectogram (hg)	=	10 dag	=	3.5274 oz.
1 kilogram (kg)	=	10 hg	=	2.2046 lb.
1 metric ton (t)	=	1,000 kg	= 2,204.62	lb.

WEIGHTS AND MEASURES

Apothecaries' Weight

				Avoirdupois		Metric	
1 grain (gr.)			=	0.002286 oz.	=	0.0648	g
1 scruple (s. ap. or ℈)	=	20 gr.	=	0.04571 oz.	=	1.296	g
1 dram (dr. ap. or ʒ)	=	3 s. ap.	=	0.1371 oz.	=	3.888	g
1 ounce (oz. ap. or ℥)	=	8 dr. ap.	=	1.0971 oz.	=	31.1035	g
1 pound (lb. ap. or ℔)	=	12 oz. ap.	=	13.1657 oz.	=	373.24	g, or 0.3732 kg

Troy Weight

				Avoirdupois		Metric	
1 grain (gr.)			=	0.002286 oz.	=	0.0648	g
1 pennyweight (dwt.)	=	24 gr.	=	0.054857 oz.	=	1.56	g
1 ounce (oz. t.)	=	20 dwt.	=	1.0971 oz.	=	31.1035	g
1 pound (lb. t.)	=	12 oz. t.	=	13.1657 oz.	=	373.24	g, or 0.3732 kg

TIME

Both the customary and metric systems use the same units to measure time. The shortest unit of time in the customary system is the second. But the metric system has four units of time shorter than the second.

1 picosecond (ps)			=	0.000000000001	s
1 nanosecond (ns)			=	0.000000001	s
1 microsecond (µs)	=	1,000 ns	=	0.000001	s
1 millisecond (ms)	=	1,000 µs	=	0.001	s
1 second (s)	=	1,000 ms	=	$\frac{1}{3,600}$	hr.
1 minute (min.)	=	60 s	=	$\frac{1}{60}$	hr.
1 hour (hr.)	=	60 min.			
1 day (da.)	=	24 hr.			
1 week (wk.)	=	7 da.			
1 common lunar year (yr.)	=	354 da.			
1 common solar year	=	365 da.			
1 leap year	=	366 da.			
1 decade	=	10 yr.			
1 century	=	100 yr.			
1 millennium	=	1,000 yr.			

TEMPERATURE

The customary system measures temperature in Fahrenheit degrees. The metric system measures temperatures in Celsius degrees. The two temperature scales are shown below, with the freezing and boiling points of water indicated on both.

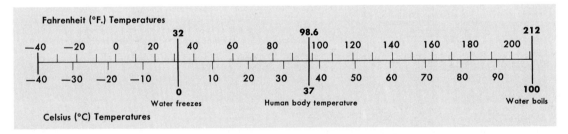

OTHER MEASURES

The tables below and on the next page show other common measurement units. All these measurements are based on the customary system except for the metric wood measurement and the circular and angular measurement in radians.

Wood Measurement

		Customary		Metric	
1 board foot (bd. ft.)	=	144 cu. in. (1 ft. x 1 ft. x 1 in.)	=	.00236	m³
1 cord foot (cd. ft.)	=	16 cu. ft. (4 ft. x 4 ft. x 1 ft.)	=	0.4531	m³
1 cord (cd.)	=	8 cd. ft. (4 ft. x 4 ft. x 8 ft.)	=	3.625	m³

Circular and Angular Measurement

Degrees				Radians		
1 second ('')		= $^1/_{1,296,000}$ circle		0.017454 radians (rad.) =		1°
1 minute (')	= 60 seconds	= $^1/_{21,600}$ circle		1 radian		= 57.2958°
1 degree (°)	= 60 minutes	= $^1/_{360}$ circle		2π radians		= 360°
1 quadrant,					**Mils**	
or 1 right angle	= 90 degrees	= ¼ circle		**1** mil =		0.056250°
1 circumference	= 4 quadrants =	1 circle		**17.778** mils =		1°
				6,400 mils = 360°		

Counting Measure					
	1 dozen (doz.)			=	12 units
	1 gross (gr.)	=	12 doz.	=	144 units
	1 great gross	=	12 gr.	=	1,728 units

Paper Measure			
	1 quire (qr.)	=	24 or 25 sheets
	1 ream (rm.)	=	20 quires
	1 perfect ream	=	516 sheets
	1 bundle (bdl.)	=	2 reams
	1 bale	=	5 bundles

Printing Measure			Customary	Metric
	1 point		= approx. $^1/_{72}$ or 0.013837 in.	= 0.3514598 mm
	1 pica	= 12 points	= approx. ⅙ or 0.166044 in.	= 4.2175176 mm

WEILL, *vyl,* **KURT** (1900-1950), was a German composer of music for the stage. His *The Threepenny Opera* (1928) is a jazz version of John Gay's *The Beggar's Opera* (1728). Born in Dessau, Weill studied music from the age of 14. He conducted opera and concerts in Westphalia, and achieved success with his own opera, *The Protagonist* (1926). Weill left Germany in 1933, and settled in the United States in 1935. There he wrote musicals and motion-picture scores. HALSEY STEVENS

WEIMAR REPUBLIC. See GERMANY (The Weimar Republic).

WEIMARANER is a hunting dog that originated in Weimar, Germany, in the 1800's. It is related to the German short-haired pointer. The Weimaraner's silver-gray or fawn-gray coat, and eyes, nose, and lips of matching color, give the dog a striking appearance. The dog has short fur, hound's ears, and a tail cropped to be about 6 inches (15 centimeters) long when the dog is full grown. The Weimaraner weighs 55 to 85 pounds (25 to 39 kilograms) and is about 24 inches (61 centimeters) high. It has an unusually keen sense of smell and has been used for many purposes. It is best known as a game bird hunter. The dog is sometimes called the *gray ghost* because of its color and its silent movements when hunting. It has a pleasant disposition and has made many obedience records. MAXWELL RIDDLE

See also DOG (picture: Sporting Dogs).

WEINBERGER, CASPAR WILLARD (1917-), served as secretary of the Department of Health, Education, and Welfare (HEW) from 1973 to 1975. As secretary, Weinberger supervised such HEW agencies as the Food and Drug Administration, the Office of Education, and the Social Security Administration.

Weinberger was born in San Francisco and graduated from Harvard University in 1938. He earned a law degree from the Harvard Law School in 1941. Weinberger entered politics in 1952, when he won election to the California Assembly. In 1968, he became California state finance director. President Richard M. Nixon named Weinberger chairman of the Federal Trade Commission in 1970. In 1972, Nixon appointed him director of the Office of Management and Budget. Weinberger served in that post until his appointment to head HEW. CHARLES BARTLETT

WEISGARD, LEONARD (1916-), is an American artist and illustrator of books for children. He won the Caldecott medal in 1947 for his illustrations in the book *The Little Island* by Golden MacDonald. These illustrations are examples of Weisgard's frequently lavish use of color.

Weisgard was born in New Haven, Conn., and studied art at Pratt Institute, in Brooklyn. Among the books he illustrated are several by Margaret Wise Brown, including *The Golden Egg Book* (1947) and the *"Noisy Books."* Weisgard also wrote and illustrated *Silly Willy Nilly* (1953), *Treasures to See* (1956), *Mr. Peaceable Paints* (1957), and *The Athenians in the Classical Period* (1963). RUTH HILL VIGUERS

WEISMANN, *VICE mahn,* **AUGUST** (1834-1914), a German biologist, is known chiefly for his theories of heredity and evolution. He stressed the independence from the rest of the body of the *germ plasm,* his name for the factors of inheritance in the sex cells. He denied that acquired characteristics can be inherited. He located the germ plasm in the chromosomes, a prediction that was proved correct early in the 1900's. Weismann upheld the theory of natural selection and was one of the first German scientists to support the British scientist Charles Darwin.

In Weismann's later years, he devoted himself chiefly to theoretical studies, and wrote extensively on heredity and evolution. His major work, *The Germ Plasm,* appeared in 1892. Weismann was born in Frankfurt, now part of West Germany. MORDECAI L. GABRIEL

WEISSMULLER, JOHNNY. See OLYMPIC GAMES (The Modern Games).

WEIZMANN, *VYTS mahn,* **CHAIM,** *KY ihm* (1874-1952), served as the first president of Israel from 1949 until his death. From 1920 to 1931 and from 1935 to 1948, he headed the World Zionist Organization, which worked to establish a national homeland for Jews in Palestine. He headed the Jewish delegation to the Paris Peace Conference in 1919, and worked there to have the League of Nations assign administration of Palestine to Great Britain. In 1917, Britain had issued the Balfour Declaration, which supported the idea of a Jewish national homeland in Palestine (see BALFOUR DECLARATION; PALESTINE [World War I and the Balfour Declaration]).

Weizmann was born in Motol, Russia, and educated in Germany and Switzerland. He taught chemistry at Manchester University in England from 1904 to 1914. During World War I, Weizmann discovered an improved method of making acetone and butyl alcohol for explosives. This discovery aided Britain's war effort.   ELLIS RIVKIN

WELCH, ROBERT. See JOHN BIRCH SOCIETY.

WELDING is a method of permanently joining two pieces of metal, usually by means of heat. The heat partially melts the metal surfaces and combines the two pieces into a single piece of metal. After the metal cools and hardens, the welded joint is as strong as any other part of the metal. Manufacturers use welding to make a wide variety of products, including automobiles, home appliances, and furniture. Construction companies use it in bridges, buildings, and other structures.

Equipment and Materials

A welder works with a small gas torch or electric welding tool or with a large automatic welding machine. Welding processes differ, but most use a *filler metal* that strengthens a welded joint. The welder usually adds the filler metal in the form of a *welding rod* or a *consumable electrode* attached to the welding tool. The heat of the welding process melts the rod or electrode, which mixes with the melted base metal and fills in the joint.

In most welding processes, the heated metals must be shielded to prevent absorption of nitrogen and oxygen from the air. If the metals absorbed these gases, the

Arc Welding joins metals by means of the heat produced by an electric arc. In shielded metal-arc welding, the arc forms between a flux-covered electrode and the metals to be welded.

WORLD BOOK diagram

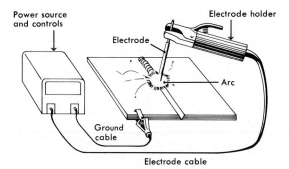

weld would be weak and brittle. Shielding is provided by (1) spraying an inactive gas such as argon, carbon dioxide, or helium on the metals during welding, or (2) applying a nonmetallic *flux* to the metal before welding. Some processes use flux-covered welding rods or flux-covered electrodes. The heat of welding melts the flux, which covers and protects the metals.

Welding Processes

There are about 40 welding processes. The four most important ones are (1) arc welding, (2) resistance welding, (3) gas welding, and (4) brazing.

Arc Welding joins metals by using heat produced by an electric arc. The welder uses an electrode holder, an electrode or welding rod, and a generator that produces an electric current. The most common methods of arc welding include the following.

Shielded Metal-Arc Welding forms an electric arc between the metal and a flux-covered electrode. The heat of the electric arc melts the metal, the electrode, and the flux.

Submerged Arc Welding. In this method, the arc is covered by powdered flux dropped from a container attached to the welding tool. The arc forms between the metal and a consumable wire electrode that adds filler metal to the weld. The wire electrode is fed continuously from a coil through the welding tool to the arc.

Gas Metal-Arc Welding also has the arc between the metal and a bare wire electrode. Instead of flux, a jet of shielding gas is sprayed over the weld to protect it from the air.

Gas Tungsten-Arc Welding is similar to the gas metal-arc method. It uses a tungsten electrode, which does not melt in the heat of the welding process. A separate welding rod must be used if filler metal is needed for the joint.

Plasma Arc Welding. For this method, a gas, such as argon, is electrically heated until it forms an ionized gas called a *plasma.* A jet of plasma is sprayed on the metals to be welded, and a filler metal is supplied separately. The plasma itself provides shielding that protects the weld from the air. A plasma arc produces extremely high temperatures and can be used to weld metals that are difficult to weld by any other process.

Resistance Welding joins metals by means of the heat produced by resistance to the flow of an electric current. This process does not use filler metal or flux. The metals are clamped together, and electrodes apply pressure on opposite sides. An electric current passing through the electrodes meets resistance when it flows across the metals. The resulting heat melts the metals and welds them together.

There are two main methods of resistance welding. In *resistance-spot welding,* rod-shaped electrodes form spot welds along the surface of the metals. In *resistance-seam welding,* electrodes in the form of rollers create a continuous seam or *bead* across the metals.

Gas Welding uses the heat of a gas torch to join two metal parts. The most common welding gas is acetylene mixed with oxygen (see ACETYLENE). If the job requires a filler metal, the welder holds a welding rod in one hand and directs the torch flame at it over the joint. A flux may be applied to the metal beforehand.

Power source and controls

Electrode holder

Electrode

Arc

Ground cable

Electrode cable

Linde Division/Union Carbide Corp.

A Welder wears gloves and a mask with a special lens that protects the eyes from the intense light of the welding process.

Brazing joins two exceptionally close-fitting parts by means of a melted filler metal, such as brass, bronze, or a silver alloy. The powdered filler metal and a special flux are placed on the two parts and heated in an oven or with a gas torch. The filler metal melts and flows into the joint where it spreads into, and alloys with, the surfaces of the parts. The heat applied in brazing is not high enough to melt the parts.

Other Welding Processes use electron beams, lasers, and ultrasonic waves to produce the necessary energy to join metals. These processes require complex, specialized equipment. EDWARD A. FENTON

See also LASER (In Industry).

WELF. See GUELPHS AND GHIBELLINES.

WELFARE is the term used for government and private programs that provide food, money, and other necessities for needy people. There are two basic types of welfare programs, *social insurance* and *public assistance*.

Social insurance pays benefits to people—and their families—who have worked and have paid certain special taxes in the past. Most people receive such benefits at some time in their life. Social-insurance programs include the social security system in the United States and the Canada Pension Plan.

Public assistance provides benefits based on a person's need, regardless of how much the individual has earned or paid in taxes. Such programs include Aid to Families with Dependent Children (AFDC) and the Canada Assistance Plan.

The Social Security Act of 1935 provides the legal basis of most U.S. welfare programs, both social insurance and public assistance. Social insurance pays about $147 billion yearly in pensions, in survivors' benefits, and in medical and hospital payments. National, state, and local public-assistance programs pay about $49 billion annually.

Many people use the term *social security* to mean any kind of social insurance, and *welfare* to mean public assistance. Another term for public assistance is *relief*.

Welfare in the United States

Social-Insurance programs in the United States include (1) Social Security, (2) Unemployment Insurance, (3) Workers' Compensation, and (4) Medicare. Social Security pays benefits to retired or disabled workers and their dependents, and to the survivors of workers

who have died. Unemployment Insurance makes payments to workers who have lost their job. Workers' Compensation provides cash payments and medical care for workers injured on the job, and death benefits for the dependents of persons who die from injuries suffered at work. Medicare provides free hospital insurance and low-cost medical insurance for the aged and disabled.

Public-Assistance programs in the United States include (1) Aid to Families with Dependent Children, (2) Supplemental Security Income for the Aged, Blind, and Disabled, (3) General Assistance, (4) Medicaid, (5) food stamps, and (6) veterans' benefits. Private charities also provide some relief.

Aid to Families with Dependent Children (AFDC) provides financial aid primarily to needy families that have no father present. In more than half the states, families with a father present may qualify for AFDC under certain conditions. In most families that qualify for AFDC, the father is dead, missing, or unable to support the family.

Each state runs its own AFDC program. The state estimates the minimum income needed to support families of different sizes. If a family's income falls below this level, and if the family has no other means of support, the family receives AFDC. Many of the states do not pay enough to bring families up to the state's own minimum income levels. The federal government provides from 50 to 80 per cent of the cost of each state's program, depending on the economic condition of the state.

Supplemental Security Income for the Aged, Blind, and Disabled (SSI) guarantees a minimum income for persons who are at least 65 years old, and for the blind and disabled. The federal government administers and finances SSI. Some states provide a higher minimum-income level than that set by the federal government. These states supplement the federal payment.

General Assistance (GA) is the term for various state and local programs that help needy persons who do not qualify for AFDC or SSI. In most cases, welfare agencies use GA to provide temporary emergency aid. The federal government does not finance general-assistance programs, and not all states have them.

Public Assistance in the United States*

Program	Total Annual Payment	Average Number of Persons Receiving Aid Each Month	Average Monthly Payment per Person
Medicaid	$14,703,606,130	9,133,000	$129.97
Aid to Families with Dependent Children	10,726,866,000	10,668,568	83.79
Supplemental Security Income for the Aged, Blind, and Disabled	6,498,336,000	4,296,000	131.47†
Food Stamps	5,165,208,676	16,043,861	26.83
General Assistance	1,218,778,000	807,544	125.77

*Figures are for fiscal year 1978 (October 1, 1977-September 30, 1978); Medicaid figures are for fiscal year 1976 (July 1, 1975-June 30, 1976).
†Based on last month of fiscal year.
Sources: U.S. Department of Agriculture; U.S. Department of Health, Education, and Welfare.

WELFARE

Medicaid provides health care for many people who cannot pay for it. Under Medicaid, each state pays physicians, dentists, and hospitals for services to individuals who receive public assistance. Half of the states provide Medicaid for persons who are *medically indigent*. Such people may be aged, disabled, or members of a family with dependent children. They are not on welfare. However, their income is so low that a large medical bill could force them to apply for public assistance.

Food Stamps are issued by the U.S. Department of Agriculture. They are given to needy persons, such as low-wage workers, unemployed persons, and families living on social-security or public assistance payments. These people exchange the stamps for food at cooperating grocery stores. The number of stamps issued depends on family size and income.

Veterans' Benefits. The Veterans Administration operates a program of benefits for former members of the United States armed forces. See VETERANS ADMINISTRATION.

Private Charities often meet emergency needs because they can act more quickly than government agencies can. Private charities in the United States include the Red Cross and the Salvation Army.

Criticism of the Welfare System. Much criticism of the U.S. welfare system has resulted from certain beliefs about persons who receive public assistance. For example, many people believe that those on welfare could work if they chose to do so. Actually, able-bodied men make up only about 1 per cent of the welfare rolls. Most welfare clients in the United States are children; old, blind, or disabled people; or mothers with small children.

Many people also believe that AFDC mothers deliberately have many children so they can increase their monthly benefits. But statistics show that two-thirds of all AFDC families have three or fewer children. Some people also think that most welfare clients are black. But blacks make up only about 40 per cent of the people who receive public assistance. In addition, poverty is heavily concentrated among blacks, so it is not surprising that they are likely to need aid.

Much criticism has been directed at the AFDC program in general. In some cases, AFDC provides almost as much as an unskilled laborer could earn. As a result, the program has encouraged many fathers to leave their families and has discouraged many mothers from seeking work. The Work Incentive Program was created to provide training and help such people find jobs. The program has not succeeded in reducing the welfare rolls, however. In addition, AFDC has become extremely costly for industrial states to which large numbers of poor people go in search of a job. Many states have been accused of trying to save money by paying low benefits or by treating welfare applicants harshly. State and local welfare departments also spend much time investigating cases in an attempt to weed out "welfare chiselers." Critics charge that this process humiliates many honest but poor people.

Many experts have proposed replacing the nation's system of public assistance with a program called the *negative income tax* or *guaranteed annual income*. Under this plan, any family with an income below a certain level would receive cash payments from the government. Such programs already in effect include Supplemental Security Income for the Aged, Blind, and Disabled and Canada's Guaranteed Income Supplement.

Welfare in Canada

Social-Insurance programs in Canada include (1) the Canada Pension Plan, (2) Old-Age Security, (3) Guaranteed Income Supplement, (4) unemployment insurance, (5) family and youth allowances, and (6) medical and hospital insurance.

The Canada Pension Plan provides monthly benefits for retired or disabled workers and for the families of workers who have died. The plan operates on contributions from both workers and employers. The federal government administers the plan in all the provinces except Quebec. Quebec operates a separate program called the Quebec Pension Plan.

Old-Age Security pays a monthly pension to persons of 65 or older who have lived in Canada at least 10 years. They do not have to stop working to qualify.

Guaranteed Income Supplement provides additional income for persons who receive an old-age security pension and have little or no other income.

Unemployment Insurance provides income for workers whose earnings stop because of unemployment, including unemployment due to illness or pregnancy. Workers and employers both contribute to this program. Unemployment insurance covers nearly all Canadian workers.

Family and Youth Allowances. All families with children receive cash grants from the federal government. The government pays a *family allowance* for every child 15 years old or younger and a *youth allowance* for each child of 16 or 17 who remains in school.

Medical and Hospital Insurance. Each province operates an insurance program that pays for most medical and hospital services. The federal government pays about half the cost of these programs. The insured person and the province pay the remainder of the cost according to a system determined by the provincial government.

Public Assistance. The Canada Assistance Plan provides nearly all the public assistance in Canada. This plan gives cash assistance to the poor, including needy mothers and aged, disabled, or unemployed persons. The provinces administer the program, and the national and provincial governments each pay half its cost.

Welfare in Europe

All European countries provide many services to promote the health and welfare of their citizens. The programs in Great Britain, Norway, and Sweden are so complete that those nations are sometimes called *welfare states*. They furnish free medical and hospital care, family allowances, pensions for retired workers, and many other services. For more information on these programs, see the *Social Welfare* section of the articles on GREAT BRITAIN, NORWAY, and SWEDEN.

History

In Early Times, the responsibility for taking care of the poor usually fell on families and neighbors. Governments seldom stepped in to relieve poverty.

During the Middle Ages, the church assumed much responsibility for helping the poor. Religious groups operated hospitals, orphanages, and poorhouses. Merchant and craft guilds also aided the poor, especially members and their families in need.

The 1600's to the 1800's. In 1601, the English Parliament passed the Act for the Relief of the Poor. This act, known as the *Elizabethan Poor Law*, made the local government units called *parishes* responsible for their own poor. The law provided for taxing parishioners to support the needy in each parish.

Most localities maintained poorhouses, also called *almshouses* or *workhouses*, which not only housed poor people, but also put them to work. One goal of these institutions was to get enough work out of the residents to pay for the cost of supporting them. Few poorhouses succeeded in paying for themselves. The conditions in most of them were dreadful enough to discourage the poor from seeking help.

In the United States, early welfare laws resembled those of Great Britain. By the early 1900's, many states required cities and counties to aid the aged, the blind, and fatherless children. Some state governments helped pay the costs of this aid.

The federal government did not become active in assisting the poor until the Great Depression of the 1930's. The Federal Emergency Relief Administration (FERA), established in 1933, gave funds to the states to relieve the hardships caused by unemployment. The FERA required each state to have an agency that either took charge of a state welfare program or supervised local programs.

In 1935, Congress approved the social security system, which replaced the FERA. The Social Security Act has been amended many times, but it still provides the framework for federal welfare programs in the United States.   BRUNO STEIN

Related Articles in WORLD BOOK include:

Aid to Families with	Poverty
Dependent Children	Social Security
Food Stamp Program	Social Work
Medicaid	Unemployment Insurance
Medicare	Veterans Administration
Pension	Workers' Compensation

WELFARE ORGANIZATIONS. See CARE; CATHOLIC CONFERENCE, UNITED STATES; FAMILY SERVICE ASSOCIATION OF AMERICA; JEWISH WELFARE BOARD, NATIONAL; PUBLIC WELFARE ASSOCIATION, AMERICAN; SERVICE CLUB.

WELFARE STATE is a term sometimes applied to a country in which the government assumes major responsibility for the social welfare of its people.

WELFARE WORK. See SOCIAL WORK.

The Depth of a Water Well depends on the level of the water table. A well must be deep enough to reach water in dry weather.

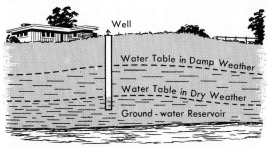

WELL is a hole in the earth from which a fluid is withdrawn. Water wells are the most common type. Oil and natural-gas wells are also common. Mining companies also use wells to remove salt and sulfur from deep in the ground. They pump down steam or hot water to remove these materials.

Water Wells. The underground water that flows into wells is called *ground water* (see GROUND WATER). This water comes from rain that soaks into the ground and slowly moves down to the *ground water reservoir*, an area of soil and rock saturated with water. The top of this zone is the *water table*, the level at which water stands in a well that is not being pumped.

In damp places, the water table may lie just below the surface. It is easily reached by digging. A dug well is usually lined with bricks, stone, or porous concrete, to keep the sides from caving in. In drier places, the water table may be hundreds of feet or meters down. It may then be necessary to drill the well and sink pipes. Power-driven pumps usually are used to draw the water out of deep wells.

In some areas, underground water moving down from the slopes of hills and mountains becomes trapped under watertight layers of clay or shale. Wells drilled through these layers in valleys and plains run into water under pressure. In such wells, called *flowing artesian wells*, the pressure may be strong enough to make water flow without pumping. See ARTESIAN WELL.

Many persons still depend on wells for their water supply, especially in rural areas. Many cities also get

A Properly Built Well has brick sides that reach to the water table. Below this, a lining of loose stones and gravel allows water to seep in. A tight cover keeps out contaminated surface water.

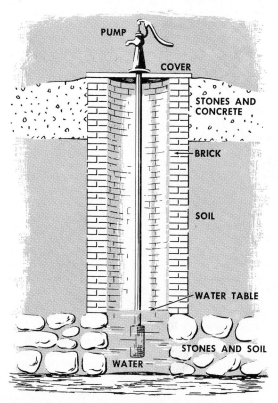

their water from wells. Underground water is usually pure, because the soil makes a good filter. It generally contains dissolved minerals. A well that taps water with a high mineral content is called a *mineral well*.

Water wells should be located so that they do not collect poisons or disease germs. A well should be at least 100 feet (30 meters) from a cesspool, and should never be located so that sewage drains toward it. Water from a well sunk through limestone may be dangerous because water runs through crevices and caves in limestone without being filtered. It is also important that surface water does not drain into a well.

Oil and Natural-Gas Wells. Oil and natural gas are lighter than water. Because of this, they would normally float upward and escape from the ground. But oil and gas become trapped beneath thick beds of rock in areas called *pools*. Wells penetrate deep into the earth to reach these pools and bring the oil and gas to the surface. *Wildcat wells* are drilled in search of new pools. A *production well* is drilled into a proven field.

Drilling oil and gas wells is a highly developed science. The workers who drill deep wells must have many years of training and experience. The cost of a deep oil well may be several hundred thousand dollars. See GAS (From Well to User; picture); PETROLEUM (Drilling an Oil Well).

Locating Wells also requires a high degree of training. Geologists and engineers must be able to find where large amounts of oil or water lie, and determine at what rate they can take these materials out of the ground, and how much they can remove without damaging the natural resources.

Today, scientists and engineers use modern equipment such as seismographs to locate underground deposits (see SEISMOGRAPH). But at one time, and sometimes even today, people have used a kind of magic in an attempt to locate water. For example, some people used a forked branch in order to locate water. If such a branch, called a *divining rod*, is gripped firmly on the two forks and bent outward, the main stem will move up or down, unless the holder exerts effort to prevent this. A slight relaxation permits the main stem to point down. Some persons believe that when this happens, the stem is pointing to a water source. Persons using this device are sometimes successful, but only because they have a common-sense idea of where water is usually found. RAY K. LINSLEY

WELLAND SHIP CANAL is one of Canada's greatest engineering projects. It forms a navigable waterway 27 miles (43 kilometers) long between Lake Erie and Lake Ontario. The only natural connection between these two lakes is the Niagara River. But falls and rapids make the river useless as a commercial waterway.

The Welland Canal extends from Port Colborne to Port Weller, just east of Port Dalhousie. A ship up to 700 feet (210 meters) long can sail on the canal. Lake Erie is about 325 feet (99 meters) higher than Lake Ontario, so ships must be raised and lowered by locks. This is done by a series of eight locks.

The project to connect Lake Erie and Lake Ontario was completed in 1829. The original canal was built by a private company, and cost about $7,700,000. A small ditch was dug from Port Dalhousie on Lake Ontario to

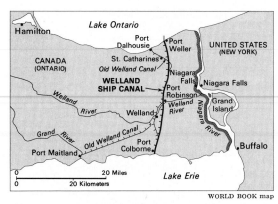

Location of the Welland Ship Canal

Port Robinson on the Welland River. Ships sailed down the creek to the Niagara River, and then went up Lake Erie. In a short time, the shipping industry was looking for a larger waterway to handle ships of much greater length than could be sailed on the first canal. The project was taken over by the government of Upper Canada, which is now Ontario. It was greatly enlarged in 1871, at a cost of $21,749,000.

In 1912, the Canadian government began added improvements which resulted in the Welland Canal of today. The canal opened on Aug. 6, 1932. It cost $130 million. Only the St. Lawrence Seaway cost more to build. A reforestation project has been developed along the canal route to protect vessels from crosswinds. Loading docks service cities and factories along this route. The canal carries about 67 million short tons (61 million metric tons) of freight a year. It can be used by the largest bulk carriers on the Great Lakes.

Ships can sail through the new canal in 8 hours or less, compared to the 16 hours required over the old waterway. The Welland Canal forms an important part of the Saint Lawrence Seaway.

In 1973, workers completed a $110-million project to straighten and widen about 8 miles (13 kilometers) of the canal. The project also included the construction of several tunnels and bridges. D. M. L. FARR

See also CANADA, HISTORY OF (color picture); SAINT LAWRENCE SEAWAY.

WELLER, THOMAS HUCKLE (1915-   ), a research biologist, shared the 1954 Nobel prize for physiology or medicine with John F. Enders and Frederick C. Robbins (see ENDERS, JOHN F.; ROBBINS, F. C.).

The men grew poliomyelitis viruses on tissues of human embryos outside the body (see POLIOMYELITIS). Weller also isolated and grew chicken pox, mumps, and shingles viruses. He was born in Ann Arbor, Mich. He became head of Harvard University's public health department in 1954. HENRY H. FERTIG

WELLES, *welz,* **GIDEON** (1802-1878), was secretary of the Navy in the Cabinet of President Abraham Lincoln. Originally a Democrat, he joined the Republican Party when it was organized. Lincoln appointed him secretary of the Navy at the beginning of the Civil War. Under his management, the Union Navy set up a blockade along the Confederate coast, and formed a fleet of gunboats and ironclad vessels on the Mississippi River. Welles remained in the Cabinet of President Andrew

Johnson, and vigorously upheld the President's Reconstruction policy.

Welles was born in Glastonbury, Conn. From 1826 to 1836, he edited the *Hartford* (Conn.) *Times*. He later served as chief of the Bureau of Provisions and Clothing of the U.S. Navy Department.　　　W. B. HESSELTINE

Brown Bros.

Gideon Welles

United Press Int.

Orson Welles

WELLES, ORSON (1915-　　), is an actor and motion-picture director. In 1938, he directed a radio broadcast that described a fictional invasion of New Jersey by men from Mars. The broadcast was so realistic that thousands of alarmed listeners in the Eastern United States flooded authorities with calls. On the strength of this sensation, Welles was hired to write, direct, and act in his own films in Hollywood.

Welles' first film, *Citizen Kane* (1941), was a thinly disguised, largely critical portrait of publisher William Randolph Hearst. It was an immediate critical success. Welles' next films, *The Magnificent Ambersons* (1942) and *Journey into Fear* (1943), failed at the box office. Since that time, Welles has acted in many films. But he has written and directed only a few, notably *The Lady from Shanghai* (1948), *The Trial* (1963), and *Falstaff* (1966). Some critics have accused Welles of flamboyance and emotional shallowness. But his artistic independence inspired many young film makers. Welles was born in Kenosha, Wis.　　　RICHARD GRIFFITH

See also MOTION PICTURE (Orson Welles).

WELLESLEY COLLEGE is a privately controlled liberal arts school for women in Wellesley, Mass. It grants bachelor's and master's degrees. Wellesley is noted for its art and library collections and its science laboratories. Henry Fowle Durant founded Wellesley College in 1870. It opened in 1875. For enrollment, see UNIVERSITIES AND COLLEGES (table).　　　RUTH M. ADAMS

WELLINGTON (pop. 327,414) is the capital and second largest city of New Zealand. It ranks as one of the country's chief seaports and manufacturing centers. Wellington lies along the harbor of Port Nicholson, on the southern coast of the North Island. For location, see NEW ZEALAND (map). Wellington's central city area has a population of 139,566. The central city and the surrounding area make up one of the most highly populated regions of New Zealand.

The port of Wellington handles foreign trade and also shipping and transportation between the North Island and the South Island, the largest islands of New Zealand. Factories in the Wellington area assemble automobiles and manufacture chemicals, clothing, electrical machinery, processed foods, and other products.

Wellington is the home of Victoria University of Wellington. Other places of interest include the parliament buildings, two cathedrals, and the Dominion Museum and National Art Gallery.

British settlers founded Wellington in 1840. The capital was moved there from Auckland in 1865 because of Wellington's central location.　　　GORDON R. LEWTHWAITE

See also NEW ZEALAND (picture: Parliament House).

WELLINGTON, DUKE OF (1769-1852), ARTHUR WELLESLEY, was a British soldier and statesman who was known as *The Iron Duke*. He became famous as the general who overcame the armies of Napoleon in Spain and Portugal, and defeated Napoleon at the Battle of Waterloo. Later, he became a leader of the Tory Party and served as prime minister.

Young Soldier. Wellington was born in Dublin, Ireland, the fourth son of Garrett Wellesley, earl of Mornington. He was educated at Eton College and at a military college in France. At 18, he entered the army.

Wellington rose rapidly and by 1796 had reached the rank of colonel. He first saw combat in 1794 in the campaign in Flanders, and made a reputation as a brave soldier. In 1796, his regiment was sent to India, where his brother was governor general. Wellington became a major general before he was 35, and in 1803 he was given command of the British forces in the Mahratta War. He soon defeated the Mahratta chiefs and firmly established British power in India.

Peninsular War. In 1805, Wellington returned to England, and was elected the next year to Parliament. Two years later he was appointed chief secretary of Ireland. While there, he worked for new laws that would establish fair rents for tenants. He also laid the foundation for organization of the Irish police.

In 1808, Spain revolted against Napoleon, and the British sent troops there to help the Spanish. Wellington was promoted to lieutenant general and took command of one of the British divisions fighting in the peninsula of Spain and Portugal. Three weeks after he landed in Portugal, he defeated the French in the Battle of Vimeiro and forced them to leave Portugal.

Victory in Spain. In 1809, Wellington became commander of all British forces in the Peninsular War. He received little help from the inefficient armies and governments of Spain and Portugal. But his small army won victory after victory. Slowly, he drove the French forces from the peninsula. In April, 1814, Wellington won the Battle of Toulouse, and the British troops were able to enter France. Napoleon quit his throne, and the war ended. Wellington returned to England in triumph, and was given the title of duke of Wellington.

Victory at Waterloo. In July, 1814, Wellington was appointed ambassador to France. The following year, he represented Great Britain at the Congress of Vienna, although the Con-

Ewing Galloway

Duke of Wellington

159

gress had completed most of its work before he arrived (see VIENNA, CONGRESS OF). He was at Vienna when the Congress heard of Napoleon's escape from Elba and return to France. Wellington signed the declaration that named Napoleon "the enemy and disturber of the peace of the world," and took command of the allied forces in The Netherlands. At the Battle of Waterloo, Wellington fought Napoleon himself for the first time. In this battle, Wellington rode at the head of his troops and, with Prince Gebhard Blücher's Prussian army, completely crushed Napoleon's power (see BLÜCHER, GEBHARD L. VON). After that, Wellington commanded the army that occupied France for a short time. See WATERLOO, BATTLE OF.

Political Career. In 1818 Wellington returned to England and held various government and diplomatic posts. He became commander in chief of the army in 1827, but resigned in 1828 to become prime minister.

Wellington belonged to the Tory Party, but he angered many in his party by pushing through a Catholic emancipation act that gave the vote to Roman Catholics and removed political liabilities from them. The British demanded parliamentary reform, and Wellington's opposition to a reform bill made his government unpopular. In 1830, he was forced to resign.

The Tory Party returned to power in 1834, but Wellington refused to become prime minister again. Seven years later, he became a member of Sir Robert Peel's cabinet and again served as commander in chief of the army. He retired in 1846. Although his opposition to reform made him unpopular at times, Wellington was respected as a national hero and was buried in Saint Paul's Cathedral.   CHARLES F. MULLETT

WELLMAN, WALTER. See AIRSHIP (U.S. Airships).

WELLS, H. G. (1866-1946), was a famous English novelist, historian, science writer, and author of science-fiction stories. Wells's novel *Tono-Bungay* (1909) best reveals his varied talents. The novel, a story of the dishonest promotion of a patent medicine, contains social criticism tinged with satire. In it, Wells described trips in airplanes and submarines at a time when such journeys seemed like science fiction.

Herbert George Wells was born in Bromley, Kent. He drew on his lower-middle-class background in some of his finest novels, including *Kipps* (1905) and *The History of Mr. Polly* (1909). His training as a scientist is reflected in his imaginative science-fiction stories. *The Time Machine* (1895) describes the adventures of a man who can transport himself into the future. Wells wrote about an invasion from Mars in *The War of the Worlds* (1898) and described a fictional utopia in *The Shape of Things to Come* (1933).

Wells supported social reform in the novel *The New Machiavelli* (1911), in the nonfiction study *The Work, Wealth and Happiness of Mankind* (1932), and in other books. He wrote

Culver

H. G. Wells

The Outline of History (1920), a story of the development of the human race. The book shows Wells's knowledge of biology and his liberal attitude in politics. With his son Geoffrey and Sir Julian Huxley, Wells wrote *The Science of Life* (1929-1930), a four-volume discussion of the principles of biology. Wells told his life story in *Experiment in Autobiography* (1934).   HARRY T. MOORE

WELLS, HEBER M. See UTAH (Territorial Days and Statehood).

WELLS, HENRY. See WELLS, FARGO & COMPANY.

WELLS, HORACE. See DENTISTRY (History).

WELLS-BARNETT, IDA BELL (1862-1931), was an American journalist and reformer. She was known chiefly for her campaign against the lynching of blacks during the late 1800's and early 1900's (see LYNCHING). Many blacks were lynched without even a trial after being accused of a crime, and others were lynched for no apparent reason at all. Wells-Barnett worked to expose such killings and to establish laws against lynching.

Ida Wells was born a slave in Holly Springs, Miss. She moved to Memphis in 1884. In 1889, she became part-owner and a reporter for *Free Speech*, a Memphis newspaper. In 1892, after three of her friends were hanged in Memphis, she began to investigate lynchings and other violence against blacks. Her work led to the establishment of many antilynching organizations.

She moved to Chicago in 1894 and the next year married Ferdinand L. Barnett, a lawyer and journalist. In 1909, Wells-Barnett helped found the National Association for the Advancement of Colored People (NAACP). She also took part in the campaign to give women the right to vote.   OTEY M. SCRUGGS

WELLS, FARGO & COMPANY was an early American express organization. Henry Wells and William G. Fargo founded the company in 1852. They planned an express service from San Francisco to New York City, with the American Express Company serving as eastern representative. In 1866, Benjamin Holladay sold his overland mail and stagecoach business to Wells, Fargo & Company, which soon became the most powerful firm in the Far West.

Wells, Fargo & Company carried passengers, freight, and mail. It specialized in shipping gold and silver from western mines. It also developed a banking business on the Pacific Coast.

The firm lost heavily after the completion of the Central-Union Pacific in 1869. Wells, Fargo & Company merged with the six other major express companies in 1918 to form the American Railway Express Company.   W. TURRENTINE JACKSON

See also FARGO, WILLIAM GEORGE.

WELSBACH, *VELS bahk,* **BARON VON** (1858-1929), CARL AUER, was an Austrian chemist and pioneer in artificial lighting. He is noted chiefly as the inventor of a gaslight called the *Welsbach mantle*. He also invented the osmium filament for electric lamps and isolated the elements neodymium and praseodymium.

Welsbach was born in Vienna, and studied chemistry at Heidelberg University. Later, he attended the University of Vienna.   K. L. KAUFMAN

See also NEODYMIUM; PRASEODYMIUM.

WELSH. See WALES (People).

WELSH CORGI. See CARDIGAN WELSH CORGI; PEMBROKE WELSH CORGI.

WELSH LANGUAGE AND LITERATURE. See WALES (Language; The Arts).

WELSH SPRINGER SPANIEL looks like its relative, the English springer. It is a little smaller, and its coat is always red and white. As a sporting dog, the Welsh springer has a keen sense of smell, and will work well even in bad weather and rough brush. It can retrieve game on land or in the water. But unless the Welsh springer spaniel is trained well while it is young, it may be headstrong and independent. MAXWELL RIDDLE

WORLD BOOK photo by E. F. Hoppe
The Welsh Springer Spaniel Has a Keen Sense of Smell.

WELSH TERRIER is one of the oldest English breeds of dogs. It has been known in Wales for several hundred years. It is closely related to the original black and tan terrier of England. The Welsh looks like a small-sized Airedale, with its wiry coat of deep red and jet black markings. It has a long head and powerful jaws. This terrier weighs about 20 pounds (9 kilograms). See also DOG (color picture: Terriers). JOSEPHINE Z. RINE

WELTERWEIGHT. See BOXING (The Classes).

WELTY, EUDORA (1909-   ), is an American short-story writer and novelist known for her searching studies of small-town life in the South. She has lived in Mississippi most of her life, and her affection for the South can be seen in her work.

Welty's style combines delicacy with shrewd, robust humor. The mixture of realism and fantasy in some of her stories gives them an almost mythical quality. Her major themes extend beyond the South—loneliness, the pain of growing up, and the need for people to understand themselves and their neighbors.

Welty's short stories appear in several collections, including *A Curtain of Green* (1941), *The Wide Net* (1943), and *The Bride of the Innisfallen* (1955). Her longer fiction consists of two novelettes and three novels. The novelettes are *The Robber Bridegroom* (1942) and *The Ponder Heart* (1954). Her novels include *Delta Wedding* (1946), *Losing Battles* (1970), and *The Optimist's Daughter* (1972). She received the 1973 Pulitzer prize for *The Optimist's Daughter*. Eudora Welty was born in Jackson, Miss. JOHN B. VICKERY

WELWITSCHIA, *wel WICH ih uh,* is a peculiar plant which grows in the sandy deserts of the southwestern coasts of Africa. It was named for Friedrich Welwitsch,

Field Museum of Natural History
The Welwitschia Plant of Southwestern Africa has two long leaves, each of which is usually split by the wind.

an Austrian botanist of the 1800's. Its short, woody trunk rises from a large taproot and spreads like a table top to a width of 5 to 6 feet (1.5 to 1.8 meters). The plant resembles a giant, flattened mushroom. It is also called *Tumboa.*

A single pair of green leaves spills over the top. They are 2 to 3 feet (61 to 91 centimeters) wide and often twice as long. The leaves are woody, and grow from the base. They live as long as the plant does. Hot winds blow the leaves about and split them into long, slender, ribbonlike shreds.

Every year, stiff, jointed, stemlike growths from 6 to 12 inches (15 to 30 centimeters) long develop at the point where the leaves join the trunk. These growths bear small, erect flower spikes called *cone clusters.* The male cones are small, but the bright scarlet female cones are about as large as a fir cone. They are pollinated by insects. The plants live 100 years or more.

Scientific Classification. Welwitschia belongs to the gnetum family, *Gnetaceae.* It is genus *Welwitschia,* species *W. mirabilis.* EDMUND C. JAEGER

WEN is a growth, or cyst, in the skin. It forms when the secretion of a sebaceous gland collects inside the gland. It is also known as a sebaceous cyst. Round or oval lumps, from the size of a pea to a walnut, may slowly appear, usually on the scalp, face, or shoulder. They might appear on any part of the body but the sole of the foot and the palm. Wens are soft and painless. They hold a yellowish-white matter, which may have a rancid odor. Any lump or growth in the skin should be seen by a doctor as soon as possible. HYMAN S. RUBINSTEIN

WENCHOW, *WUN JOH,* or YUNGKIA, *YOONG jih AH* (pop. 250,000), is a busy seaport and the most important city in the Chekiang Province of China. It stands on the Wu River, 40 miles (64 kilometers) from the East China Sea and 240 miles (386 kilometers) southwest of Shanghai. For location, see CHINA (political map).

The city is an important marketing center for farm products and raw materials from the interior, and a major shipping port for timber and bamboo. Manufactures include leather goods, straw mats, and umbrellas. The city was opened to foreign trade in 1876 and was a center of the tea trade.   THEODORE H. E. CHEN

WENHAM, FRANCIS H. See HELICOPTER (Early Experiments).

WENTWORTH, BENNING (1696-1770), served as royal governor of New Hampshire from 1741 to 1767. He is chiefly remembered for making land grants in what is now Vermont, an area then claimed both by New York and New Hampshire. In each town grant, he took 500 acres (200 hectares) for himself. Bennington, Vt., is named after him. Wentworth was born in Portsmouth, N.H., and was graduated from Harvard. He helped make New Hampshire independent of Massachusetts.   BRADFORD SMITH

WENTWORTH, THOMAS. See STRAFFORD, EARL OF.

WENTWORTH, WILLIAM. See AUSTRALIA (Exploration).

WEREWOLF, according to superstition, is a person who changes into a wolf. Werewolves appear in many old stories. In some tales, they turn themselves into wolves. They may do this by putting on a wolf skin, by drinking water from a wolf's footprint, or by rubbing a magic ointment on their bodies. In other stories, people are transformed by someone else's magic power.

The werewolves in most stories try to eat people. The people in the stories who are threatened by werewolves use various methods to bring them back to human form. These methods include saying the werewolf's real name, hitting the werewolf three times on the forehead, and making the sign of the cross. According to the stories, one way to find out a werewolf's identity is to wound it and later look for a human with similar wounds.

Stories about werewolves have been most common in Europe. Tales from other parts of the world tell of people who turn into various other kinds of animals. These animals include tigers, in Burma and India; foxes, in China and Japan; leopards, in western Africa; and jaguars, among South American Indians.

The technical word for werewolf is *lycanthrope*. This word comes from *Lycaon*, the name of a king in Greek mythology who was turned into a wolf by the god Zeus. *Lycanthropy* is a form of mental illness in which a person imagines himself to be a wolf.   ALAN DUNDES

WERFEL, *VAIR ful*, **FRANZ** (1890-1945), was an Austrian novelist, playwright, and poet. His novel, *The Song of Bernadette* (1941), became a successful motion picture. His first prose work, *Not the Murderer* (1920), introduced the expressionistic movement in the German novel. Werfel also wrote the play *Jacobowsky and the Colonel* (1944); and the novels *The Pure in Heart* (1929), and *The Forty Days of Musa Dagh* (1933). He was born in Prague. His earliest works were poems criticizing the militaristic philosophy of the early 1900's. He came to the United States to live in 1940. GOTTFRIED F. MERKEL

WERGELAND, *VER guh lahn*, **HENRIK ARNOLD** (1808-1845), was a Norwegian patriot and author. He helped arouse Norwegian national feeling by urging his countrymen to seek independence from Sweden and to develop their own intellectual and cultural life. Many Norwegians consider him a national hero.

Wergeland wrote poetry, drama, and prose, but his poems are his greatest works. They include *Creation, Man, and Messiah* (1830); *Jan van Huysum's Flower Piece*

(1840); *The Jew* (1842); *The Jewess* (1844), and *The English Pilot* (1844). Wergeland was born in Kristiansand, Norway, the son of a clergyman.   EINAR HAUGEN

WERNER, ABRAHAM GOTTLOB (1749?-1817), a German geologist, formulated a theory on the origin of the earth that was widely accepted in his time. Werner believed all rocks of the earth were formed from a giant ocean. Scientists accepted this incorrect theory for many years because Werner was the leading geologist of the late 1700's and early 1800's. He also introduced a system of identifying and classifying rocks and established new methods of describing minerals.

Werner taught at the Freiberg School of Mines in Freiberg from 1775 until his death. Students came from throughout Europe to hear him explain complex ideas in a simple way. His lectures helped geology gain respect as an important area of study.   R. H. DOTT, JR.

See also GEOLOGY (The Rock Dispute).

WERNER, ALFRED. See NOBEL PRIZES (table [1913]).

WERTHEIMER, MAX. See PSYCHOLOGY (Gestalt).

WESER RIVER, *VAY zer*, is an important German waterway. Its main headwater, the Werra, rises on the southwestern slopes of the Thüringian Forest in central Germany. The Weser winds 500 miles (800 kilometers) to its mouth at the North Sea near Bremerhaven. For location, see GERMANY (physical map). In 1894, its channel was deepened from the mouth to Bremen, 46 miles (74 kilometers) to the south, so that large ships could sail to Bremen.   FRANK O. AHNERT

WESLEY is the family name of three prominent British clergymen, a father and two sons.

Samuel Wesley (1662-1735) was a minister of the Church of England. In 1695, he was appointed rector of Epworth parish, near Lincoln. A devout and serious pastor, he suffered from the opposition of his parishioners and from indebtedness. He wrote several books, including *History of the New Testament Attempted in Verse* (1701) and the massive *Dissertation on Job* (1736).

Wesley was born in Dorset, the son of a dissenter from the Church of England. He was educated as a dissenter, but was converted to the Church of England later.

John Wesley (1703-1791), son of Samuel Wesley, became a leader of the Evangelical Revival and founder of the Methodist Church in Great Britain and America. He was born in Epworth, and raised strictly. Almost as soon as the children could walk, they learned the alphabet and began to read the Bible. When John was five, the rectory burned down, and he was the last person rescued. After that, he thought of himself as "a brand plucked from the burning" by God.

Education. John Wesley attended Charterhouse School in London, and Oxford University. For two years, he helped his father as curate of Epworth. During this time, John's brother Charles started the Holy Club, a small group of students who met at Oxford for Bible study and prayer. When John returned to Oxford, he joined in the group's activi-

Detail of painting (1766) by Nathaniel Hone; National Portrait Gallery, London

John Wesley

ties, and soon became the leader. This attempt to lead a Christian life through *method* (discipline) was an important step in his spiritual growth, and led more worldly students to call the group "Methodists."

Georgia and Conversion. Between 1735 and 1738, Wesley went as a chaplain on a mission to the colony of Georgia. He hoped to convert the Indians and to save his own soul. Although he believed that he failed in both purposes, he learned much about people and faith. Wesley was impressed by the calm courage of Moravian missionaries on his ship during a great storm.

After long searching, Wesley was given "saving faith" on May 24, 1738, during a Moravian meeting in Aldersgate Street, London. His "heart was strangely warmed" as he listened to a reading of Martin Luther's preface to the Epistle to Romans, a book of the New Testament. A short time later, he preached a sermon on salvation by faith, a theme he emphasized for 50 years.

Organization of Methodist Societies. Wesley settled down to a long career of preaching in England, Ireland, and Scotland. Between 1739 and 1744, he showed his amazing skill at organization by forming the societies that eventually became the Methodist Church. When authorities who disapproved of his new methods and different preaching closed the pulpits of Anglican churches to him, he followed the lead of George Whitefield and preached in the open fields and on street corners (see WHITEFIELD, GEORGE).

Wesley trained a group of lay preachers who traveled endlessly. In 1742, he applied the plan of class meetings. Under this plan, classes of 12 met weekly for prayer, Bible study, religious discussion, and mutual help in Christian living. In 1744, Wesley met with a few other Methodist ministers in the first organized conference.

Rise of the Methodist Church. As long as he lived, Wesley remained loyal to the Church of England, of which he was an ordained minister. At the time of the American Revolutionary War, however, he formally recognized his differences with the Anglican Church by ordaining two preachers and appointing Thomas Coke and Francis Asbury joint superintendents of work in America. This was the beginning of a separate Methodist Episcopal Church.

Wesley continued to travel, mostly on horseback, visiting his societies and preaching, sometimes four or five times a day. He probably traveled over 250,000 miles (402,000 kilometers). When he died, the church had about 175,000 members and 630 lay preachers. Wesley wrote many works, some of which, especially his *Journal* (1735-1790), have become classics.

Charles Wesley (1707-1788), a younger son of Samuel Wesley, was the famous hymn writer of Methodism. He perhaps wrote more than 6,000 hymns. These hymns made him famous among evangelical Protestants, who still sing them. His more familiar hymns include "O for a Thousand Tongues," "Jesus, Lover of My Soul," and "Love Divine, All Loves Excelling."

Wesley was born in Epworth, and studied at Westminster School in London and at Oxford University. At Oxford, he led in the formation of the Holy Club. He was ordained in 1735 and sailed with his brother John to Georgia.

On May 21, 1738, after a reading of Martin Luther's commentary on the Epistle to the Galatians, a book of the New Testament, Charles Wesley was "born again"

into new Christian faith. For 17 years, he was a traveling minister among the Wesleyan societies. Although he differed with his brother on some points, they always remained loyal to each other.   F. A. NORWOOD

See also ASBURY, FRANCIS; CHRISTMAS (Carols [Hark! The Herald Angels Sing!]); HYMN; METHODISTS.

WESLEYAN CHURCH is a religious denomination that was founded in 1968. It was formed by the merger of the Wesleyan Methodist Church and the Pilgrim Holiness Church. The Wesleyan Methodist Church had been established in 1843, and the Pilgrim Holiness Church in 1897. Many beliefs of the Wesleyan Church are based on doctrines set forth by the Dutch theologian Jacobus Arminius and the English minister John Wesley.

The Wesleyan Church conducts missionary work in Africa, Asia, Australia, Latin America, the Pacific Islands, and several nations in the Caribbean region. In the United States, it operates five colleges, two academies, and a children's home. The church has headquarters in Marion, Ind.

Critically reviewed by the WESLEYAN CHURCH

See also ARMINIUS, JACOBUS; WESLEY (family).

WESLEYAN COLLEGE. See UNIVERSITIES AND COLLEGES (table).

WESLEYAN UNIVERSITY. See UNIVERSITIES AND COLLEGES (table).

WESSEX. See ENGLAND (The Anglo-Saxon Period).

WEST, in international relations. See COLD WAR.

WEST, BENJAMIN (1738-1820), was an American painter who became famous for his large pictures of historical subjects. Many critics today agree with the painter Gilbert Stuart, who scorned West's "ten-acre pictures." But West influenced painters of his day, and taught many of the finest early American painters. His students included John Singleton Copley, Ralph Earl, Samuel F. B. Morse, Charles Willson Peale, Rembrandt Peale, Gilbert Stuart, and John Trumbull.

West was born in Springfield, Pa. He taught himself how to paint. West went to Italy when he was 21, and studied and copied the Roman sculptures and Renaissance and baroque paintings there for three years. West settled permanently in London in 1763. In the early 1770's, he gained fame for his paintings *The Death of General Wolfe* and *Penn's Treaty with the Indians.* In 1772, King George III of England made West his official painter of history. In 1792, West became the second president of the Royal Academy of Arts, which he had helped establish in 1768.   EDWARD H. DWIGHT

See also WOLFE, JAMES (picture); UNITED STATES, HISTORY OF THE (picture: Early Colonists); MONROE, JAMES (picture: Elizabeth Kortright Monroe).

WEST, JERRY (1938-), became one of the greatest all-around players in basketball history. West, a guard for the Los Angeles Lakers of the National Basketball Association (NBA),

Los Angeles Lakers

Jerry West

won fame for his scoring ability and for his ball-handling and defensive skills. West became head coach of the Lakers in 1976.

West played in the NBA from 1960 to 1974. When he retired as an active player, West ranked third in the NBA in regular-season scoring, with 25,192 points. West also became the first NBA player to score more than 4,000 points in play-off competition.

Jerome Allen West was born in Cabin Creek, W. Va., near Charleston. He won all-American honors at the University of West Virginia.   BILL GLEASON

WEST, JESSAMYN (1907-   ), is an American author. Her first and most famous book is *The Friendly Persuasion* (1945). In a series of sketches, it describes the rural life of a Quaker family in the mid-1800's.

Miss West is a Quaker, and Quaker ideals of brotherhood can be found throughout her work. She writes on a variety of subjects. Her second novel, *The Witch Diggers* (1951), is a symbolic story set on a poor farm in southern Indiana. *Cress Delahanty* (1953) describes a young girl midway between childhood and maturity. *Except for Thee and Me* (1969) is another novel about characters who appeared in *The Friendly Persuasion*. A selection of her stories was published as *Crimson Ramblers of the World, Farewell* (1971).

Jessamyn West was born in Indiana. In addition to novels, stories, and essays, she has written several screenplays, including the script for the film *Friendly Persuasion* (1956).   JOHN CROSSETT

WEST, NATHANAEL (1903?-1940), was an American novelist noted for his brilliant but bitter view of modern American life. He published only four short novels during a brief career that ended when he was killed in an automobile accident. *Miss Lonelyhearts* (1933) is a grim satire about a newspaperman who writes a column advising people on their problems. *The Day of the Locust* (1939) is a fantastic and sometimes nightmarish satire of life in Hollywood, where West wrote movie scripts in the 1930's.

West was born Nathan Wallenstein Weinstein in New York City. He wrote his first novel, *The Dream Life of Balso Snell*, in the mid-1920's. It was published in 1931. West also wrote *A Cool Million* (1934). West's reputation rose after his death.   ROBERT A. CORRIGAN

WEST, DAME REBECCA (1892-   ), is a British author. Her nonfiction writings cover a variety of subjects. She wrote *The Meaning of Treason* (1949) and *A Train of Powder* (1955), political and psychological studies of why people betray their countries. She expanded and revised *The Meaning of Treason* in 1964, under the title *The New Meaning of Treason*. In *Black Lamb and Grey Falcon* (1942), she wrote a penetrating analysis of the political history of Yugoslavia and the other Balkan countries.

Dame Rebecca's first book of literary criticism, *Henry James* (1916), de-

Baron
Dame Rebecca West

scribes the importance of James in shaping the modern novel. Her novels show the influence of James in their emphasis on the psychological motives behind the characters' actions. Her novels include *The Thinking Reed* (1936) and *The Birds Fall Down* (1966).

Dame Rebecca was born Cicily Isabel Fairfield in County Kerry, Ireland. She became interested in women's rights and took the pen name of Rebecca West from the strong-willed heroine of Henrik Ibsen's play *Rosmersholm*. She was made Dame Commander in the Order of the British Empire in 1959.   JOHN ESPEY

WEST, THE. In American history, the *frontier* (unsettled area) usually lay to the west of settled regions. For this reason, the terms *west* and *frontier* came to have the same meaning. To the first colonists, the frontier lay beyond the Appalachian Mountains. Later, pioneers who lived in the Midwest considered the plains and mountains farther west to be the frontier. Today, the West usually means the last frontier—the plains and the mountain region that white settlers occupied after the Civil War.   WALKER D. WYMAN

See also PIONEER LIFE IN AMERICA; WESTERN FRONTIER LIFE; WESTWARD MOVEMENT.

WEST BENGAL. See BENGAL.

WEST BERLIN. See BERLIN.

WEST COAST UNIVERSITY. See UNIVERSITIES AND COLLEGES (table).

WEST FLORIDA, UNIVERSITY OF. See UNIVERSITIES AND COLLEGES (table).

WEST GEORGIA COLLEGE. See UNIVERSITIES AND COLLEGES (table).

WEST GERMANY. See GERMANY.

WEST HIGHLAND WHITE TERRIER is the only all-white breed of Scottish terriers. The breed was developed from the white puppies that appeared occasionally in litters of cairn, Scottish, and Skye terriers. It has bright eyes and carries its tail high and its ears straight up. It has a wiry coat about 2 inches (5 centimeters) long. The dog weighs from 13 to 19 pounds (6 to 9 kilograms).   JOSEPHINE Z. RINE

WEST INDIA COMPANY, DUTCH. See DUTCH WEST INDIA COMPANY.

West Highland White Terriers Are Faithful Pets.
WORLD BOOK photo by E. F. Hoppe

West Indies

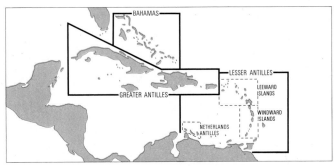

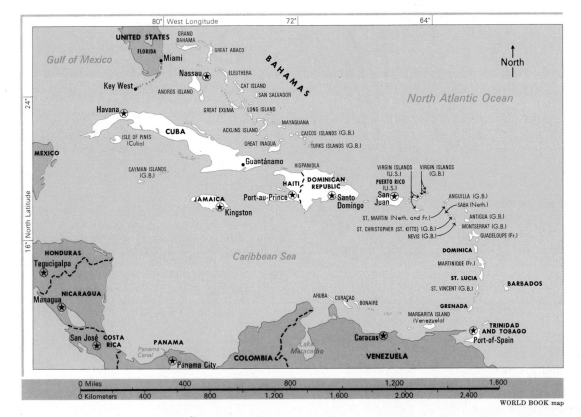

WORLD BOOK map

WEST INDIES are a long chain of islands that separates the Caribbean Sea from the rest of the Atlantic Ocean. The islands stretch in a 2,000-mile (3,200-kilometer) curve from an area near the southern tip of Florida and the eastern tip of the Yucatán Peninsula in Mexico to the coast of Venezuela. The West Indies cover a land area of 92,052 square miles (238,416 square kilometers), and have a population of about 28,054,000. Cuba is the largest island. Sometimes the term *Antilles* is used for all the islands except the Bahamas.

The West Indies consist of three major groups of islands: (1) the Bahamas in the north, (2) the Greater Antilles near the center, and (3) the Lesser Antilles to the southeast. The Lesser Antilles are divided into the Leeward Islands and the Windward Islands.

The Bahamas, Barbados, Cuba, Dominica, the Dominican Republic, Grenada, Haiti, Jamaica, St. Lucia, and Trinidad and Tobago are independent countries in the West Indies. Other islands or groups of islands are territorial possessions of the United States and several European countries. The United States governs some of the Virgin Islands as a territory. Puerto Rico is a commonwealth of the United States. British possessions include the rest of the Virgin Islands; the Caicos Islands; the Cayman Islands; the Turks Islands; and Montserrat. Antigua, St. Christopher (St. Kitts)-Nevis-Anguilla, and St. Vincent are states in association with Great Britain. The Netherlands controls two groups of islands called the Netherlands Antilles. Martinique and Guadeloupe are overseas departments of France.

The Land and Its Resources. The West Indies are the peaks of an underwater mountain chain often called the Caribbean Andes. This chain linked North and South America during prehistoric times. Most of the

165

islands are of volcanic origin, but some are formed of coral and sand. There are many mountains and inactive volcanoes in the West Indies. The islands differ in size, scenery, and natural resources. But they have the same tropical climate and similar forms of plant life.

Their mild winters make them one of the world's most popular resort areas. Temperatures average between 70° and 85° F. (21° and 29° C) along the coasts. But they often fall as low as 40° F. (4° C) in the mountainous interior of some of the larger islands. The rainy season, between August and October, brings from 60 to 70 inches (150 to 180 centimeters) of rain each year throughout most of the West Indies. Violent hurricanes often strike the West Indies during this time.

The soil is the most important natural resource in most of the islands. Many islands have thick forests and lush tropical vegetation. Agricultural products grow abundantly. But agriculture is usually limited to the plains and valleys in the mountainous islands. Hardwoods such as cedrela, ebony, and mahogany are the chief forest products. Jamaica's bauxite and the natural asphalt and petroleum of Trinidad and Tobago are the largest mineral resources. The islands have some chromium, copper, iron, manganese, and nickel.

The People. The people of the West Indies represent many races and nationalities. Most of the people are of Negro or mixed-Negro ancestry. But there are also people of Chinese, Danish, Dutch, East Indian, English, French, Portuguese, Spanish, and Carib Indian heritage. Most of the people speak either English, French, or Spanish. Many of them use colorful local dialects.

Most of the people live on farms and in small villages. Living standards on many of the islands are poor because the workers receive low wages. Those who live in the cities dress much like people who live in United States and Canadian cities. In rural areas of the West Indies, the men usually wear blue denim work clothes and most of the women wear cotton dresses.

TEN LARGEST CITIES OF THE WEST INDIES

Name	Location	Population
Havana	Cuba	1,755,360
Santo Domingo	Dominican Republic	654,757
San Juan	Puerto Rico	452,749
Port-au-Prince	Haiti	386,250
Santiago de Cuba	Cuba	275,970
Camagüey	Cuba	196,854
Bayamón	Puerto Rico	147,552
Holguín	Cuba	131,508
Santa Clara	Cuba	131,504
Guantánamo	Cuba	130,061

Most of the people are Roman Catholics. Other major religions in the islands include Baptist, Episcopal, Methodist, and Seventh-day Adventist.

Work of the People. Most West Indians work on farms and plantations. Sugar cane is the most important crop. Farm workers on nearly all of the islands harvest large crops of sugar cane. Cuba is one of the leading sugar cane growers in the world. Fruit, including bananas, oranges, and grapefruit, is also an important crop. Tobacco is one of the leading crops in Cuba, the Dominican Republic, Haiti, and Puerto Rico. Other crops include cacao, coffee, cotton, molasses, sisal, and vegetables. Raising livestock is important in the Bahamas, the Dominican Republic, Trinidad and Tobago, and the Virgin Islands.

Agricultural production has had a strong effect on the industrial development of the West Indies. Many industries refine products grown in the islands. Sugar-refining is the leading industry. It produces such items as sugar, molasses, and rum. Mining is an important industry in Jamaica and Trinidad and Tobago. Jamaica has large deposits of bauxite, an ore used in the manufacture of aluminum. Trinidad and Tobago has large deposits of natural asphalt and petroleum. Fishing is an important industry in the Bahamas and

Roberto Cole, Puerto Rico News Service

West Indies Industry has developed greatly since the 1940's, including Puerto Rico's clothing and textile factories. This clothing factory, *left*, is in Guayama, Puerto Rico.

Fritz Henle, Photo Researchers

Charlotte Amalie, capital of the United States Virgin Islands, is on St. Thomas Island. Like many cities in the West Indies, it has a fine harbor and good accommodations for tourists.

Mardi Gras in Haiti is a time for costumes. Carnivals are held throughout the islands before the start of Lent.

Vories Fisher

Fishing Is an Important Industry and sport in the West Indies. These men on Grenada are using a *seine* (weighted net).

Grenada Tourist Board

WEST INDIES

Jamaica. Other industries in the West Indies produce furniture, handicrafts, leather, matches, shoes, soap, textiles, and tobacco products. Exports from the West Indies include bauxite, cigarettes, cigars, cocoa beans, coffee, cotton, molasses, petroleum products, rum, sugar, and tropical fruit. Imports include food, drugs, automobiles, machinery, chemicals, and clothing. The tourist industry is important to the economy of the West Indies.

History. Christopher Columbus arrived in the West Indies and claimed them for Spain in 1492. He called them *Indies* because he thought that they were part of the Indies islands of Asia. Arawak and Carib Indians lived there when Columbus came. The Spanish established colonies in the islands in the 1500's. Most of the Indians died from disease and overwork under Spanish rule. The Spaniards gained great wealth from sugar and tobacco grown in the West Indies. They imported large numbers of Negro slaves from West Africa to the islands to work on their sugar and tobacco plantations.

Other European nations soon challenged Spain's monopoly in the West Indies. Bold seamen such as Francis Drake and John Hawkins of England helped to weaken Spanish power in the West Indies by attacking Spanish ships, seizing valuable cargo, and disrupting trade. During the 1600's, the Danes, Dutch, English, and French established colonies in the West Indies. The British-held islands became known as the British West Indies.

During the 1800's, revolutions weakened colonial control in some of the larger islands. Several independent nations were established, including Haiti and the Dominican Republic. In the late 1800's, a revolution in Cuba helped to bring the United States into the Spanish-American War. Cuba became independent after that war, and the United States won possession of Puerto Rico. In 1917, the United States bought the Virgin Islands from Denmark.

During the 1900's, many dictators gained power in the independent countries. Between 1930 and 1961, Rafael Trujillo ruled in the Dominican Republic. Several dictators, including Paul E. Magloire and François Duvalier controlled Haiti in the mid-1900's. From 1924 to 1959, dictators such as Gerardo Machado and Fulgencio Batista ruled Cuba. In 1959, Fidel Castro ousted Batista, and established a dictatorship.

A number of the British-held islands established the West Indies Federation in 1958. But the federation was dissolved in 1962 after Jamaica and Trinidad and Tobago withdrew and became independent. Antigua, Dominica, Grenada, St. Christopher-Nevis-Anguilla, and St. Lucia became states associated with Great Britain in 1967. In 1969, St. Vincent also became a state associated with Great Britain.

Anguilla declared its independence from St. Christopher-Nevis in 1967 and from Britain in 1969. Britain sent troops to restore British rule in Anguilla in 1969. By late 1969, all British troops had been withdrawn. In 1976, Anguilla became—in effect—a separate British dependency with its own government. But technically, the island remained part of St. Christopher-Nevis-Anguilla. The Bahamas became independent in 1973. Grenada gained independence in 1974. Dominica be-

came independent in 1978, and St. Lucia gained independence in 1979. W. L. BURN

Related Articles in WORLD BOOK include:

Bahamas	Jamaica	Turks and
Barbados	Leeward Islands	Caicos
Cuba	Martinique	Islands
Dominica	Netherlands Antilles	Virgin
Dominican Republic	Puerto Rico	Islands
French West Indies	Saint Lucia	Windward
Grenada	Trinidad and	Islands
Guadeloupe	Tobago	
Haiti		

WEST INDIES ASSOCIATED STATES are three island states in the Caribbean Sea. They are Antigua; St. Christopher (St. Kitts)-Nevis-Anguilla; and St. Vincent. Once British colonies, the states became individually associated with Great Britain in the 1960's. Antigua and St. Christopher (St. Kitts)-Nevis-Anguilla did so in 1967, and St. Vincent in 1969. The British government is responsible for the foreign affairs and defense of each state, but the states are self-governing in all other matters. Each state may end its association with Great Britain at any time.

The three states lie in the eastern part of the Caribbean Sea, north of Venezuela. For location, see WEST INDIES (map).

The governments of the three states are similar. Queen Elizabeth II is head of state, and appoints a governor to represent her in each state. A premier directs each state's government, with the assistance of a Cabinet. Each state has an elected legislature. The states share a regional supreme court. The island of Anguilla is only technically a part of the state of St. Christopher-Nevis-Anguilla. In practice, the island operates under its own government, separate from that of the state.

Most people in the associated states are of African or mixed African and European descent. English is the official language in each state. Most of the people of the states belong to the Church of England.

Antigua consists of Antigua, Barbuda, and Redonda islands. Antigua island has an area of 108 square miles (280 square kilometers). Barbuda, 25 miles (40 kilometers) north of Antigua, covers 62 square miles (161 square kilometers). Redonda, southwest of Antigua, covers only $\frac{1}{2}$ square mile (1.3 square kilometers). Antigua and Barbuda are flat, coral limestone islands. Most of the state's 75,000 people live on Antigua. No one lives on Redonda. The economy is based on cotton and sugar production and tourism. About half of the working people work in the cotton and sugar industries. St. John's, a city on Antigua Island with over 24,000 persons, is the capital.

St. Christopher (St. Kitts)-Nevis-Anguilla consists of four islands: St. Christopher (also called St. Kitts), Nevis, Anguilla, and Sombrero. About 46,000 of the state's 67,000 people live on 65-square-mile (168-square-kilometer) St. Christopher. Central St. Christopher is mountainous and has green forests. Sugar is its main crop. The sugar industry has a 36-mile (58-kilometer) railroad. Nevis, 2 miles (3 kilometers) south of St. Christopher, is a cone-shaped island that covers 36 square miles (93 square kilometers). Most of its 15,000 people raise cotton and other crops. Anguilla lies 65 miles (105 kilometers) northwest of St. Christopher. It covers 35 square miles (91 square kilometers). Most of its 5,500 people raise livestock, mine salt, and fish. Sombrero covers only about 2 square miles (5 square kilometers). Basseterre, a city on St. Christopher with about 16,000 persons, is the capital.

St. Vincent consists of the island of St. Vincent and a number of tiny islands of the Grenadine chain (see GRENADINES). It has an area of 150 square miles (388 square kilometers). A backbone of thickly wooded mountains runs the length of the island of St. Vincent. The highest point is Soufrière (4,048 feet, or 1,234 meters), a volcano at the northern end of the island. Most of the state's 128,000 people live on St. Vincent island and work as farmers. Bananas are the chief crop and export. Copra, spices, and arrowroot, a plant used in making starch, are also exported. St. Vincent also produces valuable sea-island cotton. Kingstown, a city on St. Vincent island with about 22,000 persons, is the capital.

History. The Arawak Indians were the first people to live on these islands, but the Carib Indians drove them out. Christopher Columbus probably reached the islands between 1493 and 1498. Great Britain and France fought over them in the 1500's and 1600's. All were British colonies by the early 1800's.

The islands were part of the West Indies Federation from 1958 until it was dissolved in 1962 when Jamaica and Trinidad and Tobago became independent. Efforts to form another federation were unsuccessful.

In 1966, representatives of Great Britain and the islands agreed to end the islands' colonial status. Antigua, Dominica, Grenada, St. Christopher-Nevis-Anguilla, and St. Lucia became states associated with Britain early in 1967, and St. Vincent did so in 1969.

Anguilla *seceded* (withdrew) from statehood with St. Christopher and Nevis and declared its independence in the spring of 1967. The secession was declared ended after a meeting of representatives of Anguilla, St. Christopher, Great Britain, and the four Commonwealth countries. But the people of Anguilla rejected the declaration. In 1969, Anguilla's leader announced that the island had voted to sever its ties with Britain. British troops then landed on Anguilla, but all had been withdrawn by late 1969. In 1976, Britain granted a constitution to Anguilla. In effect, the constitution made Anguilla a separate British dependency. However, the island technically remained part of St. Christopher-Nevis-Anguilla. The people of Anguilla accepted this new arrangement. In 1974, Grenada withdrew from the West Indies Associated States and became an independent nation. Dominica withdrew and became an independent nation in 1978, and St. Lucia did so in 1979. GUSTAVO A. ANTONINI

WEST INDIES FEDERATION was a state composed of several British-held islands or groups of islands in the West Indies. It was formed in 1958 as a member of the Commonwealth of Nations and was dissolved in 1962. The federation included: (1) Antigua; (2) Barbados; (3) Dominica; (4) Grenada; (5) Jamaica; (6) Montserrat; (7) St. Christopher (St. Kitts)-Nevis-Anguilla; (8) St. Lucia; (9) St. Vincent; and (10) Trinidad and Tobago. For the location of the islands, see WEST INDIES (map).

Government included a two-house legislature. A governor general, representing the British Crown, nominated the 19-member Senate on the advice of the governor of each island unit. The people elected the 45 members of the House of Representatives. A prime minister served as the federation's chief executive.

History. The islands were known as the British West Indies during the 1800's. The idea of a general federation developed after the British made a federal group out of the Leeward Islands in 1871. The British Caribbean Act of 1956 allowed the British Crown to establish a federation. In 1957, the British Cabinet issued an order establishing the new state. The West Indies Federation was formally established on Jan. 3, 1958.

In 1961, a constitutional conference decided that the federation would become independent on May 31, 1962. But Jamaica voted to secede from the federation when it became independent. Trinidad and Tobago also withdrew from the federation when it became independent. Due to these withdrawals, Great Britain dissolved the federation on Feb. 6, 1962. W. L. BURN

WEST PALM BEACH, Fla. (pop. 57,375), a resort and commercial center, lies across Lake Worth from Palm

© Ed Tancig, Southern Stock Photos

West Palm Beach lies in southeastern Florida. Modern apartment buildings line Royal Palm Way, above, near Lake Worth.

Beach and the Atlantic (see FLORIDA [political map]). The city, together with Boca Raton, forms a metropolitan area with a population of 348,993. West Palm Beach is the farm and retail trade center of five southern Florida counties. It produces air-conditioning equipment, aircraft engines, chemical and machine products, electronics systems, and prefabricated buildings. Palm Beach Atlantic College is in West Palm Beach. The city was founded in 1893, and incorporated in 1894. It has a council-manager government and is the seat of Palm Beach County. KATHRYN ABBEY HANNA

WEST POINT, N.Y., a U.S. military reservation, has served as the site of the U.S. Military Academy since 1802. For location, see NEW YORK (political map). The reservation stands on a plateau above the west bank of the Hudson River, and covers about 16,000 acres (6,470 hectares). It also includes Constitution Island, in the river, site of several Revolutionary War forts. See also UNITED STATES MILITARY ACADEMY.

Brickyards—Buckhannon, West Virginia by Fred L. Messersmith from the WORLD BOOK Collection

Deserted Brickyards in Central West Virginia

Automatic Coal Loader

WEST VIRGINIA

THE MOUNTAIN STATE

WEST VIRGINIA, in the Appalachian Highlands, has some of the most rugged land in the United States. The state has no large areas of level ground, except for strips of valley land along the larger rivers. Mountain chains cover the eastern section. Steep hills and narrow valleys make up the region west of the mountains. The extreme ruggedness of the land gives West Virginia its nickname, the *Mountain State.*

The state's rough land has sometimes caused difficulties for West Virginians. Much of the ground is too steep and rocky for farming. Highways, railroads, and airports are hard to build. Floods from mountain streams often threaten valley settlements. But West Virginia's beautiful mountain scenery and mineral springs attract many visitors. Forests of valuable hardwood trees grow on the slopes, and vast mineral deposits lie under the ground.

West Virginia ranks second only to Kentucky in U.S. coal production. Coal deposits lie under about half the land, and mining towns dot the hills and valleys. West Virginia industries are based on coal and other important mineral resources found in the state. These resources include clay, limestone, natural gas, petroleum, salt, and sand.

Industrial cities line the banks of the broad Ohio River, which forms West Virginia's western border. Wheeling, Weirton, and other northern river cities produce iron and steel. Chemical plants operate in the Ohio, Kanawha, and Potomac river valleys. Charleston, West Virginia's capital, lies in the Kanawha Valley. The Charleston area is a manufacturing center for chemicals and metal products.

West Virginia was part of Virginia until the Civil War. Virginia joined the Confederate States in 1861. But the people of the western counties remained loyal to the Union and formed their own government. West Virginia became a separate state in 1863. The hardy independence of West Virginians is reflected in the state's motto, *Mountaineers Are Always Free.*

For the relationship of West Virginia to other states in its region, see the article on SOUTHERN STATES.

The contributors of this article are Harry G. Hoffmann, former Editor of the Charleston Gazette; *James Gay Jones, Emeritus Professor of History at Glenville State College; and Richard S. Little, Associate Professor of Geography at West Virginia University.*

West Virginia (blue) ranks 41st in size among all the states, and 12th in size among the Southern States (gray).

FACTS IN BRIEF

Capital: Charleston.

Government: *Congress*—U.S. senators, 2; U.S. representatives, 4. *Electoral Votes*—6. *State Legislature*—senators, 34; delegates, 100. *Counties*—55.

Area: 24,181 sq. mi. (62,628 km²), including 111 sq. mi. (287 km²) of inland water; 41st in size among the states. *Greatest Distances*—east-west, 265 mi. (426 km); north-south, 237 mi. (381 km).

Elevation: *Highest*—Spruce Knob in Pendleton County, 4,862 ft. (1,482 m) above sea level. *Lowest*—240 ft. (73 m) above sea level along the Potomac River in Jefferson County.

Population: *Estimated 1975 Population*—1,803,000. *1970 Census*—1,744,237; 34th among the states; distribution, 61 per cent rural, 39 per cent urban; density, 72 persons per sq. mi. (28 per km²).

Chief Products: *Agriculture*—milk, beef cattle, apples, broilers, eggs, turkeys. *Manufacturing*—chemicals; primary metals; stone, clay, and glass products; fabricated metal products; nonelectric machinery. *Mining*—coal, natural gas, petroleum, natural gas liquids, sand and gravel.

Statehood: June 20, 1863, the 35th state.

State Abbreviations: W. Va. (traditional); WV (postal).

State Motto: *Montani Semper Liberi* (Mountaineers Are Always Free).

State Songs: "The West Virginia Hills." Words by Ellen King; music by H. E. Engle. "This is My West Virginia." Words and music by Iris Bell. "West Virginia, My Home Sweet Home." Words and music by Julian G. Hearne, Jr.

Constitution. West Virginia adopted its first constitution in 1863, when it became the 35th state in the Union. The state is now governed by its second constitution, adopted in 1872. The constitution has been amended more than 35 times. Constitutional amendments may be proposed in either house of the state legislature. They must be approved by a two-thirds majority of both houses, and then by a majority of the voters. The constitution may also be revised by a constitutional convention. Before a constitutional convention can be called, it must be approved by a majority of the legislators and the voters.

Executive. The governor of West Virginia is elected to a four-year term and may serve any number of terms, but not more than two terms in succession. The governor receives a yearly salary of $50,000. The heads of many state administrative departments are appointed by the governor. For a list of all the governors of West Virginia, see the *History* section of this article.

Other top state officials include the secretary of state, auditor, treasurer, attorney general, and commissioner of agriculture. They are elected to four-year terms.

Legislature of West Virginia consists of a senate and a house of delegates. The voters of each of the state's 17 senatorial districts elect two senators to four-year terms. The house of delegates has 100 members. They serve two-year terms. Each of the state's 36 delegate districts elects from 1 to 13 delegates, depending on population.

The legislature meets every year. Regular sessions begin on the second Wednesday of January, except in the year after an election for governor is held. Then, the regular session starts on the second Wednesday of February. The governor may call special sessions.

Courts. The highest court in West Virginia is the supreme court of appeals. It has five judges elected to

12-year terms. The court chooses a president from among its members. The state has 29 judicial districts. Each district has a circuit court headed by a judge elected to an eight-year term. The first circuit court, of Brooke, Hancock, and Ohio counties, has two judges. Some counties have *inferior courts*. These courts include intermediate, criminal, common pleas, domestic relations, and juvenile courts. The lowest courts are justice-of-the-peace courts. Justices of the peace are elected to four-year terms.

Local Government. Each of West Virginia's 55 counties elects a circuit clerk, a county clerk, and three county commissioners. These officials serve six-year terms. Other elected county officials include a surveyor, prosecuting attorney, sheriff, and assessor. They serve four-year terms.

A 1936 amendment to the state constitution gives West Virginia cities with populations of over 2,000 the right to adopt or change their own charters. This right is called *home rule*. Only 10 West Virginia cities have taken advantage of the home rule law. Most of these cities have a council-manager form of government. Most of the state's other cities have a mayor-council government. West Virginia's home-rule cities are not so independent as the home-rule cities of some other states. This is because West Virginia courts continue to uphold the right of the state legislature to control many city affairs.

Taxation. Over 30 per cent of the state government's income comes from business, occupation, and sales taxes. The federal government provides another 30 per cent in the form of grants and other programs. Other sources of state revenue include horse racing fees, profits from the state's liquor sales, and taxes on corporate and personal incomes, cigarettes, gasoline, insurance, licenses, and transportation carriers.

West Virginia Dept. of Commerce

The Governor's Mansion, *left,* is north of the Capitol grounds. The two-story, red brick building has six huge white columns that support a portico high above the main entrance. Inside the mansion, *above,* is a spacious main entrance hall. The hall is noted for a pair of beautiful polished mahogany staircases.

The State Seal

Symbols of West Virginia. On the front of the seal, the rock and the ivy represent stability and continuity. The rock bears the inscription "June 20, 1863," the date on which West Virginia became a state. The farmer and miner symbolize the state's industries. On the back of the seal, West Virginia's industries are represented in a landscape showing a farmhouse, derrick, and factory, some livestock, and a wooded mountain. The seal was adopted in 1863. An adaptation of the front of the seal appears on the state flag, which was adopted in 1929.

Bird and flower illustrations, courtesy of Eli Lilly and Company

Politics. Since 1864, West Virginia has divided its vote about equally between Republicans and Democrats in state and national elections. From 1896 to 1928, the Republicans won every state election except one. The Democrats won control of the state in 1932 and held it until 1956. Since then, about the same number of Democratic and Republican candidates have won the governorship. Democrats have usually won control of the state legislature.

Since the early 1930's, West Virginia voters have greatly favored Democratic presidential candidates over Republican presidential candidates. For West Virginia's voting record in presidential elections, see ELECTORAL COLLEGE (table).

The State Flag

The State Bird
Cardinal

The State Flower
Rhododendron

West Virginia Dept. of Commerce

The State Capitol, in Charleston, stands on the north bank of the Kanawha River. The gold-embossed dome is topped by a golden eagle on a bronze shaft. Charleston has been the capital since 1885. Other capitals were Wheeling (1863-1870), Charleston (1870-1875), and Wheeling (1875-1885).

The State Tree
Sugar Maple

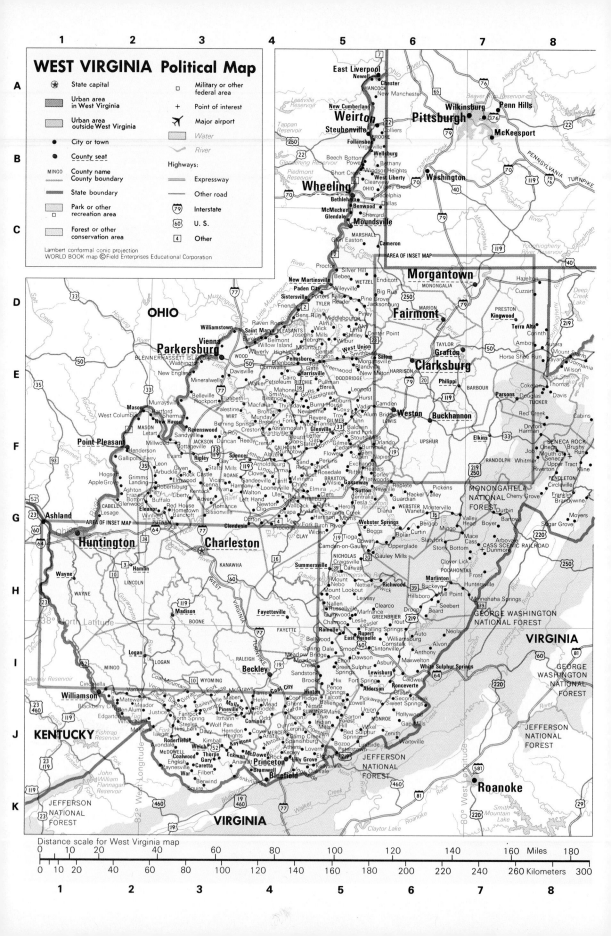

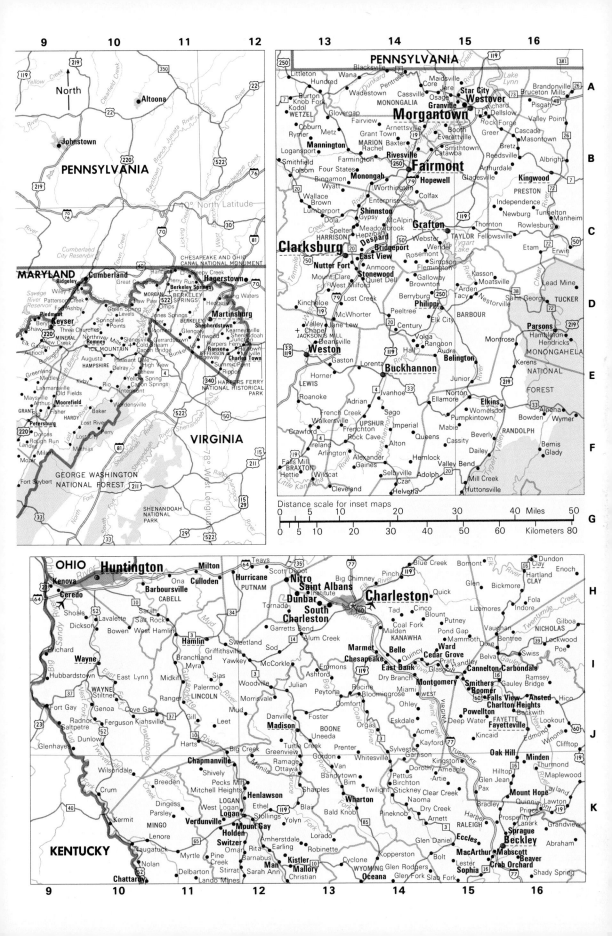

WEST VIRGINIA MAP INDEX

Population

1,803,000 Estimate..1975
1,744,237 ..Census..1970
1,860,421 ....."....1960
2,005,552 ....."....1950
1,901,974 ....."....1940
1,729,205 ....."....1930
1,463,701 ....."....1920
1,221,119 ....."....1910
958,800 ....."....1900
762,794 ....."....1890
618,457 ....."....1880
442,014 ....."....1870
376,688 ....."....1860
302,313 ....."....1850
224,537 ....."....1840
176,924 ....."....1830
136,808 ....."....1820
105,469 ....."....1810
78,592 ....."....1800
55,873 ....."....1790

Metropolitan Areas

Charleston 257,140
Huntington-Ashland (Ky.) 286,935 (144,499 in W.Va.; 56,868 in O.; 85,568 in Ky.)
Parkersburg-Marietta (O.) .148,132 (90,972 in W. Va.; 57,160 in O.)
Weirton-Steubenville (O.) ....165,627 (96,193 in O.; 69,434 in W.Va.)
Wheeling ....182,712 (101,795 in W.Va.; 80,917 in O.)

Counties

Barbour ...14,030..E 7
Berkeley ...36,356..D 11
Boone .....25,118..H 3
Braxton ...12,666..F 5
Brooke ....29,685..B 5
Cabell ....106,918..G 2
Calhoun ....7,046..F 4
Clay ....9,330..G 4
Doddridge ..6,389..E 5
Fayette ....49,332..I 4
Gilmer ......7,782..F 5
Grant ......8,607..E 9
Greenbrier .32,090..H 5
Hampshire .11,710..E 10
Hancock ...39,749..A 5
Hardy ......8,855..F 9
Harrison ..73,028..E 6
Jackson ....20,903..F 3
Jefferson ..21,280..E 11
Kanawha .229,515..H 3
Lewis .....17,847..F 6
Lincoln ....18,912..H 2
Logan .....46,269..I 2
Marion ....61,356..D 6
Marshall ...37,598..C 5
Mason .....24,306..F 2
McDowell ..50,666..J 2
Mercer ....63,206..J 4
Mineral ....23,109..D 9
Mingo .....32,780..I 2
Monongalia 63,714..D 6
Monroe ....11,272..J 5
Morgan .....8,547..D 10
Nicholas ...22,552..H 5
Ohio ....64,197..B 5
Pendleton ..7,031..F 8
Pleasants ..7,274..D 4
Pocahontas .8,870..H 6
Preston ....25,455..D 7
Putnam ....27,625..G 2
Raleigh ....70,080..I 4
Randolph ..24,596..F 7
Ritchie ....10,145..E 4
Roane .....14,111..F 4
Summers ..13,213..J 4
Taylor .....13,878..E 6
Tucker ......7,447..E 8
Tyler ....9,929..D 5
Upshur ....19,092..F 6
Wayne .....37,581..H 1
Webster ....9,809..G 6
Wetzel ....20,314..D 5
Wirt ....4,154..F 3
Wood .....86,818..E 3
Wyoming ..30,095..I 3

Cities, Towns, and Villages

Abraham ....K 16
Acme ....J 14
Adolph ....F 15
Adrian ....E 14
Advent ....G 3
Albright ......319..B 16
Alderson ...1,278..I 5
Alexander ....F 14
Alma ....D 5
Alpena ....E 16
Altizer ....F 4
Alton ....F 14
Alum Creek ....I 13
Alvon ....I 6
Amboy ....E 8
Ameagle ....K 15
Amherstdale [-Robinette] ....1,602..K 13
Anawalt .....801..J 3
Anmoore .....944..C 14
Annamoriah ....F 4
Ansted .....1,511..I 16
Anthony ....I 6
Antioch ....E 9
Apple Grove ....G 2
Arbovale ....G 7
Arbuckle ....F 2
Arden ....D 15
Arista ....J 4
Arlington ....F 13
Arnett ....K 14
Arnoldsburg ....F 4
Arthur ....E 9
Arthurdale ....B 16
Asbury ....I 5
Ashford ....I 13
Ashton ....G 2
Athens ....967..J 4
Auburn ......115..E 5
Audra ....E 15
Augusta ....E 10
Aurora ....E 8
Auto ....I 6
Avondale ....J 3
Baileysville ....J 3
Baker ....E 10
Bald Knob ....K 13
Baldwin ....F 5
Ballengee ....J 5
Bancroft .....446..G 3
Bandytown ....K 13
Barboursville 2,279..H 10
Barnabus ....K 12
Barrackville* 1,596..D 6
Bartow ....G 7
Baxter ....B 14
Bayard ....475..E 8
Beard ....H 6
Beatrice ....E 4
Beaver .....1,711..K 16
Bebee ....D 5
Beckley ....19,884.°I 4
Beckwith ....J 16
Beech Bottom 544..B 5
Belington ...1,567..E 15
Belle ......1,786..I 14
Belleville ....E 3
Bellwood ....I 5
Belmont ......802..D 4
Belva ....I 15
Bemis ....F 16
Bens Run ....D 4
Bentree ....I 15
Benwood ...2,737..C 5
Berea ....E 5
Bergoo ....G 6
Berkeley Springs ....944.°D 11
Berryburg ....D 15
Berwind ....K 3
Beryl ....D 9
Bethany ......602..B 5
Bethlehem ..2,461..C 5
Beverly ......470..F 15
Bickmore ....H 16
Big Chimney ....H 14
Big Creek ....J 12
Big Otter ....G 4
Big Run ....D 5
Bigbend ....F 4
Bim ....K 13
Bingamon ....B 13
Birch River ....G 5
Birchton ....K 14
Blackberry City ....J 2
Blacksville ...264..A 14
Blair ....K 13
Blandville ....E 5
Bloomery ....D 10
Bloomingrose ....I 13
Blount ....H 14
Blue Creek ....H 14
Bluefield ..15,921..K 4
Boggs ....G 5
Bolair ....G 6
Bolivar* .....943..E 12
Bolt ....K 15
Bomont ....H 15
Boomer .....1,261..I 15
Booth ....B 15
Bowden ....F 16
Bowen ....I 10
Boyer ....G 7
Bozoo ....J 5
Bradley ....K 16
Bradshaw* .1,048..J 3
Bramwell ...1,125..J 4
Branchland ....I 11
Brandonville ..82..A 16
Brandywine ....G 8
Breeden ....K 11
Brenton ....J 3
Bretz ....B 16
Bridgeport ..4,777..C 14
Brohard ....F 4
Brooks ....I 5
Brown ....C 13
Brownton ....D 14
Bruceton Mills 209..A 16
Brushy Run ....F 8
Buckeye ....H 6
Buckhannon 7,261.°F 6
Buffalo ....831..G 2
Bunker Hill ....E 11
Burlington ....E 9
Burning Springs ...F 4
Burnsville ....591..F 5
Burnt House ......E 5
Burton ....A 13
Cabins ....F 9
Cairo ....412..E 4
Caldwell ....I 6
Camden ....E 5
Camden-on-Gauley .....243..G 5
Cameron ....1,537..C 5
Camp Creek ....J 4
Cannelton-Carbondale ......I 15
Canvas ....H 5
Capon Bridge 211..E 10
Capon Springs .....E 10
Caretta ....J 3
Cascade ....B 16
Cass ....173..G 7
Cassity ....F 15
Cassville ....A 14
Catawba ....B 15
Cedar Grove 1,275..I 14
Cedarville ....F 5
Center Point ......D 5
Central Station ....E 5
Centralia ....G 5
Century ....D 14
Ceredo .....1,583..H 9
Chapmanville ......1,175..J 12
Charles Town .....3,023.°E 12
Charleston .71,505.°G 3
Charmco ....H 5
Chattaroy ..1,145..K 10
Cherry Grove ....G 8
Cherry Run ....D 11
Chesapeake .2,428..I 14
Chester .....3,614..A 6
Chloe ....F 4
Christian ....K 12
Cinco ....H 14
Cinderella ....I 2
Circleville ....G 8
Clarksburg .24,864.°E 6
Clay ....479.°H 16
Clear Creek ....K 15
Clear Fork ....J 3
Clearco ....H 5
Clearview .....512..B 5
Clem ....G 5
Clendenin ..1,438..G 4
Cleveland ....G 13
Clifftop ....J 16
Clintonville ....I 5
Clio ....G 4
Clover ....F 4
Clover Lick ....H 7
Coal City ...1,089..I 4
Coal Fork ....H 14
Coal Mountain .....I 3
Coalwood ....J 3
Coburn ....B 13
Coketon ....E 8
Cold Stream ....E 10
Colfax ....B 14
Colliers ....B 6
Colored Hill* .....1,031..J 4
Comfort ....J 14
Cool Ridge ....J 4
Copen ....F 5
Core ....A 14
Corinth ....D 8
Corley ....F 5
Cornstalk ....I 6
Cornwallis ....E 4
Corrinne ....1,090..J 4
Corton ....G 4
Cottageville ....F 3
Cove Gap ....J 11
Covel ....J 4
Cowen ....467..G 5
Coxs Mills ....E 5
Crab Orchard ..1,758..K 15
Craigsville ....H 5
Crawford ....F 13
Cremo ....F 4
Creston ....F 4
Crum ....K 10
Culloden ...1,033..H 11
Curtin ....G 6
Cuzzart ....D 8
Cyclone ....K 13
Czar ....G 14
Dailey ....F 15
Dallas ....C 6
Danville .....580..J 13
Davis ....868..E 8
Davisville ....E 3
Davy ....993..J 3
Dawson ....I 5
Deansville ....E 13
Deep Water ....J 15
Delbarton ....903..K 11
Dellslow ....A 15
Delray ....E 10
Despard ....1,400..C 14
Diana ....G 6
Dickson ....I 10
Dingess ....K 11
Dixie ....I 15
Dola ....C 13
Dorcas ....F 9
Dorothy ....K 14
Douglas ....E 8
Droop ....H 6
Dry Branch ....I 14
Dry Creek ....K 14
Dryfork ....F 8
Duck ....G 5
Dunbar .....9,151..H 13
Duncan ....F 3
Dundon ....H 16
Dunlow ....J 10
Dunmore ....G 7
Dunns ....J 4
Durbin ....347..G 7
Earling ....K 12
East Bank ..1,025..I 14
East Lynn ....I 10
East Rainelle ....I 5
East View ..1,618..C 13
Eccles ......1,105..K 15
Eckman ....J 3
Edgarton ....J 2
Edmond ....J 16
Eleanor ....1,035..G 2
Elgood ....J 5
Elizabeth ....821.°E 4
Elk City ....D 15
Elk Garden ..291.°D 9
Elkins ......8,287.°F 7
Elkview* ...1,486..G 3
Ellamore ....E 15
Ellenboro .....267..E 4
Ellison ....J 4
Elmira ....G 5
Elmwood ....F 3
Elton ....I 5
Emmons ....I 13
Endicott ....D 5
English ....J 3
Enoch ....H 16
Enterprise ....C 14
Erwin ....C 16
Eskdale ....J 14
Etam ....C 16
Ethel ....K 12
Eureka ....D 4
Evans ....F 3
Everettville ....B 15
Exchange ....F 5
Fairmont ..26,093.°D 6
Fairview .....640..A 14
Falling Springs .....255..I 6
Falling Waters ....D 12
Falls View-Charlton Heights .I 15
Falls Mill ....F 12
Fanrock ....J 3
Farmington ...595..B 14
Fayetteville .1,712.°H 4
Fellowsville ....C 16
Fenwick ....H 5
Ferguson ....J 10
Filbert ....J 3
Fisher ....E 9
Five Forks ....F 4
Flat Top* ....J 4
Flatwoods ....220..F 5
Flemington ...458..C 14
Floe ....G 4
Flower ....F 5
Fola ....H 16
Follansbee ..3,883..B 5
Folsom ....B 13
Forest Hill ....J 5
Fort Ashby ....D 10
Fort Gay .....792..J 9
Fort Seybert ....G 9
Fort Spring ....I 6
Foster ....J 13
Four States ....B 13
Franklin .....695.°G 8
Fraziers Bottom ....G 2
French Creek ....F 14
Frenchton ....F 13
Friendly .....190..D 4
Frost ....H 7
Gaines ....F 13
Gallipolis Ferry ....F 2
Galloway ....D 14
Gandeeville ....F 4
Gap Mills ....J 6
Garretts Bend .....I 12
Garrison ....J 14
Gary ....J 3
Gassaway ...1,253..G 5
Gaston ....E 13
Gauley Bridge .....I 16
Gauley Mills ......G 5
Gay ....F 3
Gem ....F 5
Genoa ....I 10
Gerrardstown ......D 11
Ghent ....J 4
Gilbert ....778..J 2
Gilboa ....H 16
Gill ....J 11
Gilmer ....F 5
Given ....F 3
Glace ....I 6
Gladesville ....B 15
Glady ....F 16
Glasgow ......904..I 14
Glen ....H 15
Glen Daniel ....K 15
Glen Easton ....C 5
Glen Jean [-Hilltop] 1,510..K 16
Glen Rodgers .....K 14
Glenalum ....J 2
Glendale ...2,150..C 5
Glenfork ....K 14
Glengary ....D 11
Glenhayes ....J 9
Glenville ...2,183.°F 5
Glenwood ....G 2
Glovergap ....A 13
Goffs ....E 4
Gordon ....J 13
Gormania ....E 8
Grafton ....6,433.°E 7
Graham Heights* .1,008..D 6
Grandview ....K 16
Grant Town ..946..B 14
Grantsville ...795.°F 4
Granville ...1,027..A 15
Great Cacapon .....D 11
Green Spring ......D 10
Green Sulphur Springs ....I 5
Greenland ....E 9
Greenview ....J 13
Greenwood ....E 5
Greer ....B 16
Griffithsville ....I 12
Grimms Landing ...F 2
Guardian ....G 6
Guyan ....J 3
Gypsy ....C 13
Hacker Valley .....G 6
Hall ....E 14
Hallburg ....G 4
Halltown ....E 12
Hambleton ....328..D 16
Hamlin .....1,024.°H 2
Hancock ....D 11
Handley ....I 15
Harman ......142..F 8
Harmony ....F 3
Harper ....K 15
Harpers Ferry 423..E 12
Harrison ....G 5
Harrisville ..1,464.°E 4
Hartford .....527..F 2
Hartland ....H 16
Harts ....J 11
Hazelgreen ....E 4
Hazelton ....D 8
Heaters ....F 5
Hebron ....E 4
Hedgesville ...274..D 11
Helen ....I 4
Helvetia ....G 14
Hemlock ....F 14
Henderson ....496..F 2
Hendricks ....317..E 16
Henlawson ....K 12
Hepzibah ....C 13
Herndon Heights ...J 4
Herold ....G 5
Hettie ....F 13
Hico ....J 16
High View ....E 10
Highland ....E 4
Hillsboro .....267..H 6
Hilltop, see Glen Jean [-Hilltop]
Hinton .....4,503.°I 5
Hix ....I 5
Hogsett ....F 2
Holden .....2,325..K 11
Hollywood ....J 6
Hometown ....G 3
Hopewell ....B 14
Horner ....E 13
Horse Shoe Run ...E 8
Hubbardstown .....I 9
Hundred .....475..A 13
Huntersville ....H 7
Huntington 74,315.°G 1
Hurricane ..3,491..H 12
Hurst ....E 5
Huttonsville ..167..G 15
Iaeger ....822..J 3

°County seat
*Does not appear on map; key shows general location.

Source: Latest census figures (1970). Places without population figures are unincorporated areas and are not listed in census reports.

© Gary T. Truman

The Mountain State Art and Craft Fair in Ripley features modern artwork and traditional West Virginia crafts. This blacksmith is demonstrating the use of hammer and tongs.

© 1977 William C. Blizzard, Uniphoto

Skill at Handicrafts is part of the heritage of many West Virginians. This Charleston woman sells wooden barrels and other objects that she has decorated with hand-painted designs.

WEST VIRGINIA/*People*

The 1970 United States census reported that West Virginia had 1,744,237 persons. The population of the state had decreased 6 per cent from the 1960 census figure, 1,860,421. Many persons who left West Virginia moved to northern and western states to find jobs. The U.S. Bureau of the Census estimated that by 1975 the state's population was about 1,803,000.

Almost two-thirds of the people of West Virginia live in rural areas. The state has about 170 cities, towns, and villages with populations of less than 2,500. Many are coal-mining towns and trading centers for farm areas. West Virginia's large cities lie in river valleys, where the land is least hilly. They are centers for the chemical, iron, and steel industries. Huntington, Charleston, and Wheeling are the largest cities. See the separate articles on West Virginia cities listed in the *Related Articles* at the end of this article.

The areas around Charleston, Huntington, Parkersburg, Weirton, and Wheeling are Standard Metropolitan Statistical Areas (see METROPOLITAN AREA). For the populations of these metropolitan areas, see the *Index* to the political map of West Virginia.

Almost all West Virginians were born in the United States. Many of their ancestors came from Germany, Great Britain, Hungary, Ireland, Italy, and Poland. Many immigrants came to West Virginia in the late 1800's and early 1900's to work in the coal mines.

Methodists and Baptists are the largest religious groups in West Virginia. Other religious bodies with large memberships in the state include Episcopalians, Presbyterians, and Roman Catholics.

POPULATION

This map shows the *population density* of West Virginia, and how it varies in different parts of the state. Population density is the average number of persons who live in a given area.

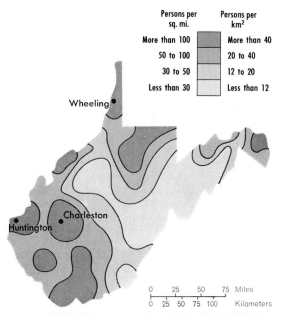

Persons per sq. mi.		Persons per km²
More than 100		More than 40
50 to 100		20 to 40
30 to 50		12 to 20
Less than 30		Less than 12

Wheeling

Charleston

Huntington

0	25	50	75	Miles
0	25	50	75	100	Kilometers

WORLD BOOK map

176

West Virginia University's Medical Center, near Morgantown, was completed in 1961. Four columns, depicting the history of medicine, guard the entrance to the main building.

Marshall University

Marshall University, in Huntington, was established in 1837. Its buildings include the James E. Morrow Library, above.

WEST VIRGINIA/*Education*

Schools. Pioneer children in the West Virginia region attended classes in log cabins that served as both schools and churches. Parents paid the teachers in cash, in farm products, and with "bed and board." In 1796, the Virginia legislature passed a law providing for free district schools in counties that wished to establish them. But few schools were set up, because most county officials believed parents should pay only to educate their own children. In 1810, the legislature created a literary fund for the education of poor children.

West Virginia established a free school system in 1863, after joining the Union. The state constitution of 1872 provided tax funds to support the schools. Until 1875, children in rural schools were not divided into different grades. Alexander L. Wade, school superintendent of Monongalia County, worked out a system of teaching subjects of various grade levels to children of different ages.

Today, a state superintendent of schools, appointed by the state board of education, supervises the public school system. The counties receive state funds to maintain minimum educational standards and to buy textbooks for children whose parents cannot afford them. Children between the ages of 7 and 16 must attend school. For information on the number of students and teachers in West Virginia, see EDUCATION (table).

Libraries. A subscription library was operating in Wheeling as early as 1809. Members of this library contributed money to buy books, which they could use without charge. Public libraries did not become common until after 1900. West Virginia established a state library commission in 1929 to help regulate and expand library services in the state.

Today, about 130 public library systems serve the people. Bookmobiles provide service for areas that lack libraries. The West Virginia University Library has the largest collection in the state. Large public libraries include those at Charleston, Clarksburg, Huntington, Parkersburg, and Wheeling.

Museums. The West Virginia State Museum in Charleston has collections that feature West Virginia history. This museum also has several industrial exhibits. The Sunrise Foundation in Charleston has an art gallery, museum, and planetarium. Other museums in West Virginia include the Hawks Nest Museum at Hawks Nest State Park in Fayette County, the Oglebay Park Mansion Museum in Wheeling, the Marshall University Geology Museum in Huntington, the Huntington Galleries, and the Parkersburg Art Center.

─────── **UNIVERSITIES AND COLLEGES** ───────

West Virginia has 18 universities and colleges accredited by the North Central Association of Colleges and Schools. For enrollments and further information, see UNIVERSITIES AND COLLEGES (table).

Name	Location	Founded
Alderson-Broaddus College	Philippi	1871
Bethany College	Bethany	1840
Bluefield State College	Bluefield	1895
Concord College	Athens	1872
Davis and Elkins College	Elkins	1904
Fairmont State College	Fairmont	1867
Glenville State College	Glenville	1872
Marshall University	Huntington	1837
Morris Harvey College	Charleston	1888
Salem College	Salem	1888
Shepherd College	Shepherdstown	1871
West Liberty State College	West Liberty	1837
West Virginia College of Graduate Studies	Institute	1972
West Virginia Institute of Technology	Montgomery	1895
West Virginia State College	Institute	1891
West Virginia University	Morgantown	1867
West Virginia Wesleyan College	Buckhannon	1890
Wheeling College	Wheeling	1954

Blackwater Falls State Park

Dennis K. Scott, Alpha

Beautiful scenery, mineral springs, and a variety of wildlife attract tourists, campers, hunters, and fishermen to the mountains of West Virginia. Long trails and bridle paths wind through mountain parks and forests. Ski slopes near Davis, Morgantown, and Wheeling are open during the winter, usually from December to March. Glass factories and other West Virginia plants offer tours and lectures. At Beckley, visitors can take a trip through the underground passageway of an exhibition mine. Exhibits there show the development of coal mining.

June Folk Festival in Glenville

West Virginia Department of Commerce

William C. Blizzard, Alpha
Pheasant Hunting in West Virginia

PLACES TO VISIT

Following are brief descriptions of some of West Virginia's many interesting places to visit.

Berkeley Springs, a health resort city in Morgan County, was long called *Bath* after the famous resort city in Great Britain. George Washington noticed the health-giving qualities of the springs when he surveyed the land for Lord Fairfax. In 1756, Fairfax granted the site of the town to the Virginia Colony. Lord Fairfax bathed apart from the other health seekers in a rock-lined hollow now called the *Fairfax Bathtub.*

Blennerhassett Island, in the Ohio River near Parkersburg, was the site of a mansion built by Harman Blennerhassett about 1800. Blennerhassett, with Aaron Burr and others, was suspected of planning an independent government in the southwestern United States.

Cass, in Pocahontas County, has a state-owned scenic railroad powered by a steam locomotive. The train runs through beautiful mountain country on the tracks of a former logging railroad.

Charles Town, the county seat of Jefferson County, was founded in 1786 by Charles Washington, younger brother of George Washington. A jury at the *Jefferson County Courthouse* found John Brown guilty of murder and treason after his 1859 raid on Harpers Ferry. Three stone markers designate the site of the *John Brown Gallows.* Several historic homes stand in the area around Charles Town. George Washington designed *Harewood,* built about 1770, for his brother Samuel. Dolley Payne Todd and James Madison were married in this house in 1794. Charles Washington built *Mordington,* or "Happy Retreat," about 1774. Bushrod Washington, grand-nephew of the President, built *Claymont Court* in 1820.

Jackson's Mill, near Weston, was the family farm where General Thomas J. "Stonewall" Jackson spent his boyhood. In 1921 this area became the first state 4-H Club camp to be established in the United States.

National Radio Astronomy Observatory, in Green Bank, is a center for the study of radio waves from space.

Jack Zehrt, FPG

Harpers Ferry National Historical Park

During the summer, visitors may inspect radio telescopes that measure the waves, and view a film about the observatory's work.

Seneca Rock, in Pendleton County, towers 1,000 feet (300 meters) above the valley below. This landmark has many colorful layers of rock.

National Forests and Historical Parks. Monongahela National Forest lies entirely within the state of West Virginia. It is located in the eastern part of the state. Parts of George Washington and Jefferson national forests extend into West Virginia from Virginia. See NATIONAL FOREST (table).

The town of Harpers Ferry is famous in Civil War history. Harpers Ferry National Historical Park lies on the boundary between West Virginia and Maryland. The Chesapeake and Ohio Canal National Historical Park, which also extends over the West Virginia-Maryland border, is nearby.

State Parks and Forests. West Virginia has about 30 state parks and nine state forests. Among the best known state parks is Blackwater Falls, near Davis. There, sparkling water tumbles 63 feet (19 meters) over a rocky ledge. For information on the parks and forests of West Virginia, write to Chief, Division of State Parks and Recreation, Department of Natural Resources, State Office Building, Charleston, W.Va. 25305.

ANNUAL EVENTS

The Mountain State Forest Festival, held early in October at Elkins, is among the most colorful annual events in West Virginia. Most of the festival takes place on the campus of Davis and Elkins College. It includes a horse show, riding tournaments, wood-chopping and sawing contests, and archery and shooting exhibitions. Other annual events in West Virginia include the following.

January-May: Alpine Festival in Davis (March); White Water Weekend in Petersburg (late March and early April); House and Garden Tour in Martinsburg (April); Wildflower Pilgrimage at Blackwater Falls State Park (May); Strawberry Festival in Buckhannon (May).

June-August: Folk Festival in Glenville (June); Mountain State Art and Craft Fair in Ripley (July); *Honey in the Rock* and *Hatfields and McCoys*, two plays about West Virginia history, at Grandview State Park (June through Sunday before Labor Day); Poultry Festival in Moorefield (July or August); Cherry River Festival in Richwood (August); West Virginia State Fair in Lewisburg (August); Appalachian Arts and Crafts Festival in Beckley (late August and early September).

September-December: West Virginia Water Festival in Hinton (September); New Martinsville Saddle Club Show, Town & Country Days, and Inboard Regatta in New Martinsville (September); Preston County Buckwheat Festival in Kingwood (September); Annual Black Walnut Festival in Spencer (October); Annual Chrysanthemum Show in Wheeling (November).

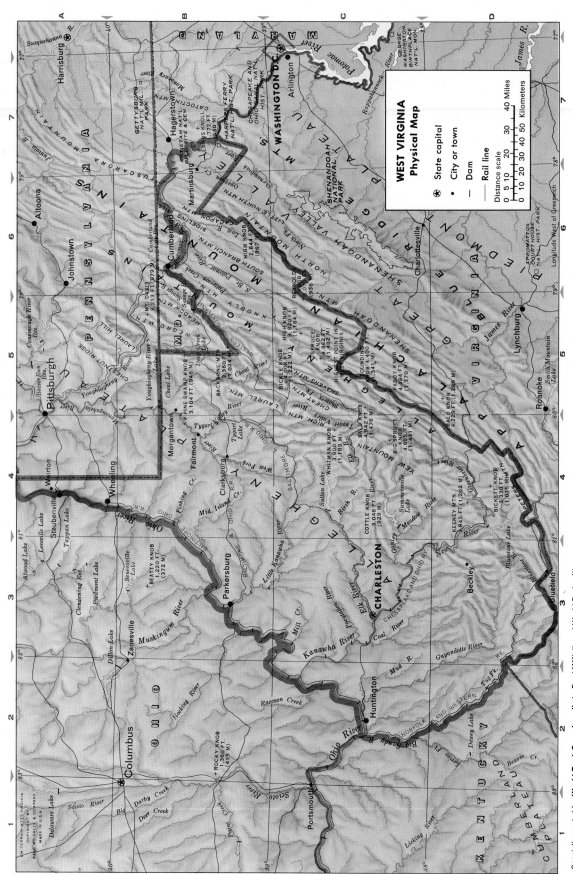

WEST VIRGINIA
Physical Map

⊛ State capital
• City or town
• Dam
— Rail line

Distance scale

Specially created for **World Book Encyclopedia** by Rand McNally and World Book editors

Land Regions. In most places, West Virginia's boundaries follow the courses of rivers or the peaks of mountain chains. For this reason, the state has crooked boundaries. A narrow strip of West Virginia called the *Northern Panhandle* extends northward between Ohio and Pennsylvania. Another extension of West Virginia runs northward and eastward between Maryland and Virginia. It is called the *Eastern Panhandle*.

West Virginia has no large areas of level ground. Mountains cover the eastern third of the state. Spruce Knob, the highest point in West Virginia, rises 4,862 feet (1,482 meters) above sea level near the eastern border. The widest valleys lie near the Ohio River in the west, and in a small part of the Eastern Panhandle between the Allegheny and Blue Ridge mountains. The rest of the state has steep hills and narrow valleys.

West Virginia has three main land regions: (1) the Appalachian Ridge and Valley Region, (2) the Appalachian Plateau, and (3) the Blue Ridge.

The Appalachian Ridge and Valley Region covers a wide strip of West Virginia along the state's eastern border. The Allegheny Mountains of this region belong to the Appalachian Mountain system. They form part of a series of long ridges and valleys that run from northeast to southwest across several eastern states. These mountains are made of folded layers of *sedimentary rock* (rock formed from deposits laid down by ancient rivers and seas). Erosion has worn down the softer layers, forming long parallel ridges of harder rock with valleys in between. Most streams and rivers run along the

valleys between the ridges. A few streams cross the ridges in *water gaps* (breaks in the ridges). Water gaps occur where weak rock was worn away, or where streams cut through hard rock as nature lifted and folded it. Caves and underground streams are common throughout the region. Forests cover the mountainsides.

The western border of the region lies along the *Allegheny Front*. The Allegheny Front occurs where the sharply folded rock layers of the Appalachian Ridge and Valley Region meet the more gently folded layers of the Appalachian Plateau. The front appears in some places as a high, rugged *escarpment* (slope). In southern West Virginia, it becomes lost in the roughness of the southern Allegheny Mountains.

The Appalachian Plateau covers the entire state west of the Appalachian Ridge and Valley Region. The plateau has a rugged surface. Streams have carved narrow valleys, leaving flat-topped uplands and rounded hills. The slopes are steep, especially in the west. Many peaks in the northeastern part of the region rise more than 4,000 feet (1,200 meters) above sea level.

Most of West Virginia's coal, salt, petroleum, and natural gas deposits are found in the Appalachian Plateau. Nearly all the state's larger cities lie in the wider river valleys of this region.

The Blue Ridge, a mountain range that forms part of the Appalachian system, touches the easternmost tip of West Virginia's Eastern Panhandle. The Blue Ridge Mountains are made of *igneous rock* (rock formed by the cooling of hot, melted material) and *metamorphic rock*

── Map Index ──

Land Regions of West Virginia

William C. Blizzard, Alpha

Kanawha River Valley at Winfield, surrounded by rolling hills, is typical of the land that forms the Appalachian Plateau.

Alpha Photo Assoc.

Turkey Farm nestles between sharply rising mountains of the Appalachian Ridge and Valley Region.

Bradley Smith, Photo Researchers

Apple Harvest in the Shenandoah Valley of far eastern West Virginia produces large crops.

(rock changed by heat and pressure). Apple and peach orchards grow on the slopes and in the fertile river valleys of this region.

Rivers and Lakes. The Ohio River flows along the western boundary of West Virginia for over 275 miles (442 kilometers). It provides a route to the Mississippi River and the Gulf of Mexico. The major rivers of the Appalachian Plateau flow northwestward into the Ohio. The Kanawha River is the Ohio's largest tributary in West Virginia. The Kanawha and its branches, which include the Elk, Gauley, and New rivers, drain a large portion of the state. The Big Sandy, Guyandotte, and Little Kanawha rivers also flow into the Ohio.

The Monongahela River begins near the northern border of West Virginia. It flows northward through Pennsylvania and helps form the Ohio River at Pittsburgh. The Monongahela and its branches, including the Cheat, Tygart, and West Fork rivers, form the main drainage system of north-central West Virginia. A separate system drains the Eastern Panhandle. The Shenandoah and other rivers in that region flow northward and eastward into the Potomac River.

West Virginia has no large natural lakes. Dams and reservoirs have been built to hold back water during flood seasons and to release it during periods of low flow. The reservoirs serve as lakes for fishing and recreation.

Charleston Regional Chamber of Commerce and Development

The Kanawha River flows past Morris Harvey College, *foreground*, and the central business district of Charleston, W. Va. The river drains much of the land of western West Virginia.

WEST VIRGINIA/Climate

West Virginia has warm summers and moderately cold winters. The valleys are usually warmer than the mountains. Maximum summer temperatures average over 85° F. (29° C), but in the mountains, they are from 5 to 10 degrees Fahrenheit (3 to 6 degrees Celsius) cooler. Minimum winter temperatures average about 25° F. (−4° C) in the central and northeastern mountains, and nearly 30° F. (−1° C) in the south and southwest. The state's highest recorded temperature, 112° F. (44° C), occurred at Moorefield on Aug. 4, 1930, and at Martinsburg on July 10, 1936. The record low, −37° F. (−38° C), was set at Lewisburg on Dec. 30, 1917.

Rainfall is plentiful in all parts of the state. It is heaviest in the southern mountains, and lightest in the upper Potomac River valley in the east. The ample rainfall benefits agriculture and industry, but it also creates problems. Summer thunderstorms sometimes cause flash floods that damage property in valley settlements. Heavy winter and spring floods occur in the lower river valleys. Thick fogs often cover the valleys.

The southwest has the lightest snowfall—less than 20 inches (51 centimeters) a year. The mountains sometimes get as much as 100 inches (250 centimeters).

Dennis Scott, Alpha

Autumn Foliage covers the craggy heights of Seneca Rock in Pendleton County. The colorful layers of rock tower 1,000 feet (300 meters) above the valley.

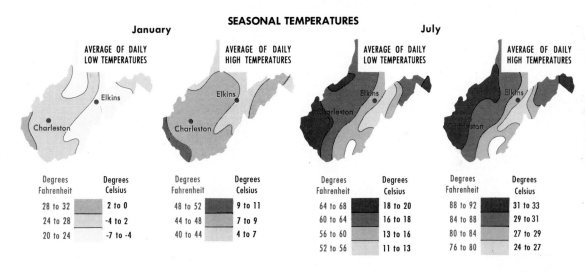

SEASONAL TEMPERATURES

January

AVERAGE OF DAILY LOW TEMPERATURES

Degrees Fahrenheit	Degrees Celsius
28 to 32	2 to 0
24 to 28	-4 to 2
20 to 24	-7 to -4

AVERAGE OF DAILY HIGH TEMPERATURES

Degrees Fahrenheit	Degrees Celsius
48 to 52	9 to 11
44 to 48	7 to 9
40 to 44	4 to 7

July

AVERAGE OF DAILY LOW TEMPERATURES

Degrees Fahrenheit	Degrees Celsius
64 to 68	18 to 20
60 to 64	16 to 18
56 to 60	13 to 16
52 to 56	11 to 13

AVERAGE OF DAILY HIGH TEMPERATURES

Degrees Fahrenheit	Degrees Celsius
88 to 92	31 to 33
84 to 88	29 to 31
80 to 84	27 to 29
76 to 80	24 to 27

AVERAGE YEARLY PRECIPITATION
(Rain, Melted Snow and Other Moisture)

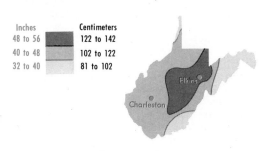

Inches	Centimeters
48 to 56	122 to 142
40 to 48	102 to 122
32 to 40	81 to 102

0   50   100 Miles
0   100   Kilometers

AVERAGE MONTHLY WEATHER

	CHARLESTON					ELKINS			
	Temperatures				Days of Rain or Snow	Temperatures				Days of Rain or Snow
	F° High	F° Low	C° High	C° Low		F° High	F° Low	C° High	C° Low	
JAN.	46	27	8	-3	18	43	22	6	-6	18
FEB.	49	28	9	-2	14	44	21	7	-6	16
MAR.	57	33	14	1	16	52	27	11	-3	17
APR.	68	42	20	6	15	63	36	17	2	15
MAY	77	50	25	10	14	72	45	22	7	14
JUNE	85	60	29	16	11	79	54	26	12	15
JULY	87	64	31	18	12	83	57	28	14	14
AUG.	86	62	30	17	10	81	56	27	13	12
SEPT.	81	56	27	13	9	76	50	24	10	10
OCT.	71	44	22	7	9	65	38	18	3	11
NOV.	57	35	14	2	11	52	29	11	-2	13
DEC.	48	29	9	-2	13	43	22	6	-6	16

The economy of West Virginia is heavily influenced by the nature of the land, especially the hilliness. A plentiful supply of cheap fuel, water, and raw materials near great population centers favors manufacturing. But manufacturing is generally limited to valley areas with fairly level land and available transportation. Farming is also limited to these areas, or to patches of level or gently sloping ground in the hills. Mining and forestry are the chief economic activities in the upland and mountainous areas that cover much of the state.

Natural Resources. Few areas of similar size have so great a variety of resources as West Virginia. These resources include mineral deposits, many kinds of timber, scenic recreational areas, and abundant rainfall.

Minerals are West Virginia's most valuable natural resources. Deposits of *bituminous* (soft) coal lie under about half the state. The coal deposits are in a broad belt that covers all the central counties and almost all the western counties. Fields of natural gas and petroleum-bearing sands are found in the western half of the state. Brine and rock salt come from the Ohio and Kanawha river valleys. Limestone is found in the mountains along the eastern border. Sand used in glass-making comes from several north-central counties and from Morgan County in the Eastern Panhandle. Other West Virginia minerals include clay, sandstone, and shale.

Forests cover about 12 million acres (4.8 million hectares) of West Virginia. Most of the virgin forests have been cut. But second-growth woodlands, many of them on farms, provide large quantities of commercial timber. The most important trees are such hardwoods as cherry, oak, and tulip trees. Evergreen trees, including hemlock, red spruce, and white pine, grow on mountain ridges and plateaus, and in river gorges.

More than enough new timber grows each year to replace the timber that is cut. State nurseries provide seedlings for reforestation.

Plants and Animals. The river valleys of West Virginia bloom with wild flowers from early spring to late fall. Bloodroot and hepaticas blossom beneath dogwood, redbud, white-blossomed hawthorn, and wild crab-apple trees. Azaleas and rhododendrons bloom in late spring and early summer. In autumn, the fields glow with asters, black-eyed Susans, and goldenrod.

White-tailed deer and black bears live in the mountains. Small woodland animals include gray and red foxes, minks, opossums, and raccoons. Many kinds of fish, including bass, trout, and walleyed pike, are found in the rivers and streams.

Soils. The blackest, most fertile soils are in the river valleys. Some of the sandy soils that cover the rest of the state contain natural lime that makes the land especially good for grain crops and fruit trees.

Mining. West Virginia ranks high among the states in the value of mineral production. Mining accounts for 51 per cent of the value of goods produced in West Virginia, or about $3½ billion a year. Bituminous coal ranks as the most important mining product in the state.

Coal. West Virginia has ranked high among the nation's leading producers of bituminous coal since 1931.

Production of Goods in West Virginia

Total value of goods produced in 1975—$6,623,782,000

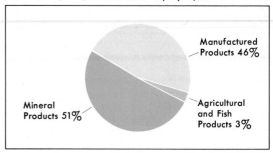

Manufactured Products 46%

Mineral Products 51%

Agricultural and Fish Products 3%

Percentages are based on farm income, value added by manufacture, and value of fish and mineral production. Fish products are less than 1 per cent.

Sources: U.S. government publications, 1976-1977.

Employment in West Virginia

Total number of persons employed in 1976—635,000

	Number of Employees
Manufacturing	124,000
Wholesale & Retail Trade	117,100
Government	109,200
Community, Social, & Personal Services	84,100
Mining	68,500
Agriculture	40,800
Transportation & Public Utilities	39,200
Construction	33,600
Finance, Insurance, & Real Estate	18,500

Sources: *Employment and Earnings*, September 1977, U.S. Bureau of Labor Statistics; *Farm Labor*, February 1977, U.S. Dept. of Agriculture.

Production averages about 109 million short tons (99 million metric tons) a year. McDowell and Monongalia counties lead in coal production.

Certain kinds of coal from southern West Virginia are popular because they contribute relatively little air pollution when they burn. These coals also have excellent heating and steam-producing qualities, and they are rich in such by-products as coal tar, creosote, and pitch.

Natural Gas and Petroleum. Gas fields lie nearly everywhere under the Appalachian Plateau. Gas production in West Virginia totals about 154 billion cubic feet (4 billion cubic meters) yearly. West Virginia also produces about 2½ million barrels of petroleum annually. Empty reservoirs from which natural gas has been taken serve as storage places for gas from Texas and Louisiana. Pipelines carry the gas to West Virginia, where it is stored in the reservoirs for use locally and in the northeastern states.

Stone. West Virginia produces about 11 million short tons (10 million metric tons) of stone a year. Manufacturers use limestone to make cement, chemicals, and flux for steel mills. Glass manufacturers grind sandstone into fine sand for use in high-quality glass.

Sand, Gravel, and Clay. About 5 million short tons (4.5 million metric tons) of sand and gravel are produced in West Virginia annually. Construction com-

FARM, MINERAL, AND FOREST PRODUCTS

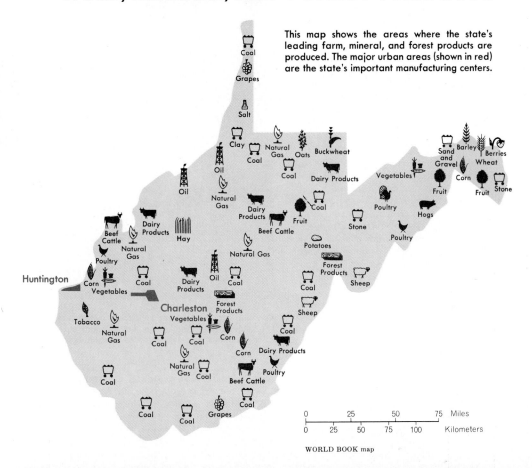

This map shows the areas where the state's leading farm, mineral, and forest products are produced. The major urban areas (shown in red) are the state's important manufacturing centers.

Coal
Grapes
Salt
Clay
Natural Gas
Oats
Buckwheat
Coal
Coal
Dairy Products
Vegetables
Sand and Gravel
Barley
Wheat
Berries
Oil
Corn
Oil
Fruit
Fruit
Stone
Natural Gas
Dairy Products
Fruit
Coal
Poultry
Hogs
Beef Cattle
Stone
Beef Cattle
Dairy Products
Hay
Poultry
Natural Gas
Poultry
Natural Gas
Potatoes
Huntington
Corn
Coal
Dairy Products
Oil
Coal
Forest Products
Sheep
Vegetables
Coal
Charleston
Vegetables
Forest Products
Sheep
Tobacco
Corn
Natural Gas
Coal
Coal
Corn
Dairy Products
Coal
Natural Gas
Coal
Beef Cattle
Poultry
Coal
Coal
Grapes
Coal

```
0        25        50        75   Miles
0    25    50    75    100   Kilometers
```

WORLD BOOK map

© Gary T. Truman

The Chemical Industry is West Virginia's chief manufacturing industry. This huge chemical plant in the Kanawha River Valley uses natural gas, oil, and other resources from the region.

panies use most of this material. A mountain near Berkeley Springs contains sand that is 98 per cent silica and excellent for making glass. Miners remove about 278,000 short tons (252,200 metric tons) of clay each year from pits in the state.

Salt. The state produces about 1 million short tons (900,000 metric tons) of salt a year. In 1943, chemical companies began to develop a huge underground bed of pure rock salt in the upper Ohio Valley. This deposit has an area of about 6,000 square miles (15,500 square kilometers) and has an average thickness of 100 feet (30 meters). The salt is removed by forcing water into the bed to dissolve the salt, and then pumping out the brine.

Manufacturing employs more West Virginia workers than any other activity. It accounts for 46 per cent of the value of goods produced in the state. Products manufactured in West Virginia have a *value added by manufacture* of about $3 billion a year. This figure represents the value added to products by West Virginia industries, not counting such costs as materials, supplies, and fuels.

Chemical Industry is West Virginia's most important manufacturing industry. It earns a greater income than any other industry in the state. Chemical products made in West Virginia have a value added of about $1 billion yearly. The chemical industry operates chiefly in the Kanawha and Ohio river valleys. It uses coal, natural gas, oil, and salt found in the region. Factories in Charleston, Huntington, Parkersburg, and Wheeling make dyes, detergents, paints, plastics, synthetic rubber, and salt cake (sodium sulfate).

Primary Metals Industry adds about $585 million a year to the value of West Virginia products. It centers in the Northern Panhandle. Huge furnaces and mills line the banks of the Ohio River near Wheeling and Weirton. Almost all the iron ore comes from mines in Minnesota and Michigan. Freighters bring the ore to ports along Lake Erie. From there, trains carry it to West Virginia. Weirton produces galvanized sheet steel, and Wheeling produces structural steel. A huge chrome-plating plant also operates in Weirton. Huntington has a large nickel plant, and Ravenswood produces aluminum.

Stone, Clay, and Glass Products made in West Virginia have a value added of about $375 million a year. The state is famous for its glassware and pottery. Leading glass-producing communities in West Virginia include Charleston, Fairmont, and Huntington. Clarksburg and Parkersburg manufacture millions of glass marbles every year. Table glassware comes from Clarksburg, Huntington, Milton, Morgantown, Moundsville, Weston, and Williamstown. Other glass products produced in the state include blown glass, bottles, crystalware, plate glass, stained glass, and structural glass, such as glass bricks.

Most of the pottery plants are in Hancock County, although a few operate elsewhere along the Ohio River. They produce such products as chinaware, firebrick, paving brick, porcelain, and tile.

Other Leading Industries in West Virginia produce electric and electronic equipment, fabricated metal

Devaney, Publix

Coal Mining is one of West Virginia's chief industries. In these tall buildings, called *tipples,* the coal is loaded into railroad cars after it has been washed and sorted in a preparation plant.

products, food products, nonelectric machinery, printed materials, and transportation equipment. Charleston has one of the largest hand-tools plants in the world. It also has factories that produce mining and farming equipment. Parkersburg has factories that produce oil-well machinery. Railroad-car and foundry works are centered around Huntington. Huntington also produces industrial controls and household appliances. Bluefield plants make electrical parts for engines. Several plants in Fairmont and Logan also produce electrical equipment.

Agriculture accounts for 3 per cent of the value of goods produced in West Virginia, or about $165 million a year. West Virginia has about 17,000 farms. They average 207 acres (84 hectares) in size.

Livestock, poultry, and dairy products provide the greatest source of farm income. Beef cattle and milk are the most valuable sources. Many West Virginia farmers have prize herds of purebred beef cattle. Many farmers also raise *broilers* (chickens between 9 and 12 weeks old), hogs, and sheep. Because the winters are fairly mild, stock can usually graze most of the year.

West Virginia fruit growers raise large crops of apples and peaches. They also grow cherries, grapes, pears, and plums. Orchard crops come mainly from the Eastern Panhandle. Farmers in almost all parts of the state raise blackberries.

The easternmost part of West Virginia lies in the Shenandoah Valley, one of the best apple-growing regions in the United States. Farmers in West Virginia were the first to grow Grimes Golden and Golden Delicious apples. Apple growers from West Virginia, Virginia, Maryland, and Pennsylvania maintain a marketing organization in Martinsburg, where large plants produce canned apples and cider.

Glassmaking uses two of West Virginia's natural resources, silica-rich sand and natural gas. This craftsman etches a drinking glass.

Steelmaking is the leading activity of West Virginia's primary-metals industry, which centers in the Northern Panhandle. Much of the state's steel comes from a plant in Weirton, above.

Corn has been one of West Virginia's most important field crops since pioneer days. The largest harvests come from level valley lands near the Ohio and Potomac rivers. Other crops grown in these areas include barley, potatoes, oats, and wheat. Farmers in many counties raise hay. Large crops of tobacco grow in West Virginia's lower Ohio Valley.

Electric Power. West Virginia's many rivers and streams could furnish a vast amount of water power. But only a few hydroelectric projects have been built to use this power. Most electric power comes from steam-generating plants.

Transportation. West Virginia's rugged land surface has made transportation difficult. Early settlers used trails that followed the streams and rivers through the mountains. Later, steamboats operated on the larger rivers. During the 1800's, the state began to improve its waterways and built new highways and railroads. But many backwoods areas remained isolated until their first paved roads were built in the early 1900's.

West Virginia has about 36,000 miles (57,900 kilometers) of roads and highways, about three-fourths of which are surfaced. The West Virginia Turnpike runs 88 miles (142 kilometers) between Charleston and Princeton. West Virginia has had more road-building problems than any other state east of the Rocky Mountains. Construction crews must cut across rugged mountains and bridge many streams.

Railroads operate on about 4,000 miles (6,400 kilometers) of track in West Virginia. About 15 rail lines provide freight service, and passenger trains link about 10 West Virginia cities to other cities. The first railroad to reach the state, the Baltimore & Ohio, entered Harpers Ferry in 1836. By 1852, it had reached Wheeling, by way of Cumberland, Md. Crews built 11 tunnels and

113 bridges between Cumberland and Wheeling, a distance of about 200 miles (320 kilometers). Railroads helped West Virginia develop its mineral and forest resources.

West Virginia has about 500 miles (800 kilometers) of navigable waterways. Ships and barges on the Ohio, Monongahela, and Kanawha rivers carry about 185 million short tons (168 million metric tons) of goods a year. These goods include chemicals, coal, lumber, oil, sand, steel, and other bulky products.

During the 1930's, the federal government built a series of locks and dams on the Ohio River and its branches. These improved the rivers of West Virginia for barge traffic. The United States Army Corps of Engineers has continued to develop the state's waterways.

Aviation developed slowly because it is difficult to build runways on the state's rolling surface. West Virginia now has about 50 airports. Four major airlines serve the state. Charleston is the chief center of West Virginia's network of scheduled air routes.

Communication. The state's first newspaper, the *Potomak Guardian and Berkeley Advertiser*, appeared in Shepherdstown in 1790. The state now has about 115 newspapers, approximately 35 of which are dailies. The *Intelligencer*, founded in 1852 in Wheeling, is still being published. Other dailies include the *Bluefield Daily Telegraph*, the *Charleston Gazette*, the *Charleston Daily Mail*, the *Huntington Herald-Dispatch*, the *Parkersburg News*, and the *Wheeling News-Register*.

The state's first radio station, WSAZ, began broadcasting from Huntington in 1923. WSAZ-TV, the first television station, started operations in Huntington in 1949. Today, West Virginia has about 100 radio stations and 12 television stations.

Indian Days. The earliest Indians of the region were Mound Builders (see MOUND BUILDERS). Hundreds of their burial mounds may still be seen in the Ohio and Kanawha river valleys. These Indians had disappeared long before the first white men arrived in the 1670's.

White explorers found several Indian tribes using the region as hunting grounds. These tribes included the Cherokee, Conoy, Delaware, Shawnee, and Susquehanna. None of them claimed the rugged area as a permanent home. The Indians hunted game and gathered salt from pools of brine during the summer. They moved back to their homes in the east and north as winter approached. They often fought wars for control of the hunting grounds and brine pools. See INDIAN, AMERICAN (Table of Tribes).

Exploration. The area that became West Virginia formed part of the Virginia Colony. King James I granted the colony to the London Company, a group of British merchants and investors, in 1606. The boundaries reached from present-day South Carolina north to Pennsylvania, and extended westward and northwestward indefinitely. The German explorer John Lederer and his companions were probably the first white men to see the region that became West Virginia. Lederer's expedition reached the crest of the Blue Ridge, probably in 1669. In 1671, Thomas Batts and Robert Fallam led another expedition into the region in search of fur-hunting areas and transportation routes. Other exploring parties visited the region during the next few years.

Early Settlement. The first settler in the region was Morgan Morgan of Delaware, who built a cabin at Bunker Hill, probably in 1726. Germans seeking greater religious freedom came from Pennsylvania in 1727. They established a settlement called New Mecklenburg (now Shepherdstown). Other settlements were soon founded, many of them by Scotch-Irish from Northern Ireland. Most of these pioneer farmers settled in the Eastern Panhandle, in the Ohio Valley, and along the Greenbrier and New rivers.

The Indians often attacked the settlers, who were taking over their hunting grounds. The pioneers built a number of forts and blockhouses, many of which formed the beginnings of towns and cities. They included Fort Henry (now Wheeling), Fort Lee (Charleston), and Fort Randolph (Point Pleasant). George Washington led an unsuccessful raid against the French and Indians in 1754, during the French and Indian War (see FRENCH AND INDIAN WARS). The French and Indians almost wiped out the forces of General Edward Braddock in 1755.

The explorer John P. Salley discovered coal on the Coal River near Racine in 1742. But the deposits were not developed until railroads began expanding in the mid-1800's. The lumber industry began after 1755, when people started to use water-powered sawmills to produce lumber.

In 1763, King George III refused to let the colonists in America take any land west of the Alleghenies until treaties could be made with the Indians for peaceful settlement. The Scotch-Irish ignored the order. The Germans and the Dutch paid no attention to the order because they could not even read it.

HISTORIC WEST VIRGINIA

Point Pleasant

Point Pleasant

The First Natural-Gas Well in the country was accidentally discovered by James Wilson while he was water-drilling at Charleston in 1815.

Coal Was Discovered near Racine by John Peter Salley in 1742. West Virginia ranks as a leading coal-producing state.

Settlers pushed over the mountains into the forbidden green valleys in greater and greater numbers. They notched trees with their axes to mark their land claims. By treaties signed in 1768, the Cherokee and Iroquois gave up all claim to the lands they had used as hunting grounds between the Allegheny Mountains and the Ohio River. By 1775, about 30,000 settlers lived there.

Demands for Separation. The Allegheny Mountains separated Virginia's western settlers from the seat of government at Williamsburg in the east. People in the west developed a social and economic life quite different from that of the eastern settlements. Plantation owners in the east specialized in tobacco and trade. Western farmers relied on livestock and food crops. Fewer persons lived in the west, and they led more solitary lives than did the aristocratic easterners.

Settlers in the west began to demand their own government as early as 1776, when they sent petitions to the Continental Congress. The Revolutionary War

Fort Henry

Wheeling •

During the Civil War, Confederate troops often raided West Virginia from positions in the Shenandoah Valley. The town of Romney changed hands 56 times.

Berkeley Springs was one of George Washington's favorite health resorts. Lord Fairfax gave these springs to the state in 1756.

Berkeley Springs •

Romney • Ice Mountain • Halltown
Uvilla • • Harpers Ferry
Charles Town •

The Battle of Point Pleasant in 1774 is called "the first battle of the Revolutionary War" by some historians. Settlers defeated Indians to gain control of the Northwest Territory. In the Revolutionary War's "final" battle in 1782, Indians and British attacked Ft. Henry at Wheeling.

John Brown's Raid on the federal arsenal at Harpers Ferry in 1859 was an unsuccessful attempt to cause a Negro rebellion.

CHARLESTON
★

Racine
•

George Washington surveyed land along the south branch of the Potomac River in 1748.

Ice Mountain has ice at its base even on hot summer days. Cold air sweeping through underground passages forms the ice.

The First Rural Free Delivery began in 1896 on mail routes from Charles Town, Halltown, and Uvilla, W. Va.

IMPORTANT DATES IN WEST VIRGINIA

1669? John Lederer and his companions became the first white men to see the West Virginia region.

1726? Morgan Morgan, the state's first settler, built a cabin at Bunker Hill in Berkeley County.

1727 Germans from Pennsylvania established a settlement at New Mecklenburg (now Shepherdstown).

1742 John P. Salley discovered coal on the Coal River.

1754-1755 The French and Indians defeated troops led by George Washington and General Edward Braddock.

1776 People in western Virginia sent petitions to the Continental Congress asking for a separate government.

1815 Gas was discovered near Charleston.

1836 The first railroad reached the state at Harpers Ferry.

1859 John Brown and his followers raided the federal arsenal at Harpers Ferry.

1861 The counties of western Virginia refused to secede with Virginia. These counties organized a separate government that supported the Union.

1863 West Virginia became the 35th state on June 20.

1872 The people ratified the present state constitution.

1915 The Supreme Court of the United States ruled that West Virginia owed Virginia $12,393,929.50 as part of the state debt at the time of separation.

1920-1921 Miners fought with mine guards, police, and federal troops in a dispute over organizing unions.

1939 West Virginia made the final payment of its debt to Virginia.

1943 Geologists found vast salt deposits in the northwestern counties.

1946 Major chemical industries began operating in the Ohio River Valley.

1959 The National Radio Astronomy Observatory began operating at Green Bank.

1965 The state abolished capital punishment.

1968 Explosions and fire in a West Virginia coal mine took 78 lives. The disaster led to new mine safety laws.

1972 The worst flood in West Virginia history killed more than 100 persons near Man.

halted this attempt. The western settlers contributed their full share of men and supplies to the war. Indian armies led by British officers invaded the region three times between 1777 and 1782, but were driven out.

Industries began to develop during the Revolutionary War. In 1794, Peter Tarr built the first iron furnace west of the Alleghenies in the Northern Panhandle. In 1808, the Kanawha Valley began producing large quantities of salt.

Sectional Strife. During the early 1800's, the differences between eastern and western Virginia became even greater. Trade in the east moved to the Atlantic Ocean, while commerce in the west used waterways that flowed toward the Mississippi River. The landowning, slaveholding aristocracy of eastern Virginia represented the larger part of the population. The easterners controlled state affairs. They opposed public improvements that the western farmers and industrialists wanted. Bitter disputes developed over slavery, taxation, use of public funds, education, and other issues.

Further discoveries of mineral resources continued the economic development of the western section. Natural gas was discovered in 1815 near Charleston. In 1841, William Tompkins, a salt-maker in the Kanawha Valley, first used natural gas as a fuel for manufacturing. An oil well drilled at Burning Springs in 1860 began a stampede for oil. Burning Springs became a thriving village with hundreds of shacks and tents.

Civil War and Statehood. Disputes over slavery reached a climax in 1859 when John Brown and his followers seized the federal arsenal at Harpers Ferry (see BROWN, JOHN). Virginia had to choose sides when Confederate troops in South Carolina fired on Fort Sumter on April 12, 1861. On April 17, a state convention voted for secession. But a majority of the people in the western counties supported the Union. These counties declared their independence and formed a government they called the Restored Government of Virginia.

In August, 1861, the western counties approved the formation of a new state named *Kanawha*. This Indian word is believed to mean *place of the white stone*, referring to the salt deposits in the region. The westerners prepared a state constitution in November, 1861. In it, they changed the name of the proposed state to West Virginia. The people adopted the constitution in April, 1862. Congress admitted West Virginia to the Union on June 20, 1863, as the 35th state. At that time, West Virginia had a population of about 380,000, including about 15,000 slaves. Arthur I. Boreman became the first governor. Wheeling became the state capital.

The new state furnished about 30,000 men to the Union armies. More than 8,000 men joined the Confederate armies. Battles raged in many parts of West Virginia during the first year of the war. After a series of defeats in 1861, Confederate forces stopped trying to capture land west of the Alleghenies. But they often raided the state for food, for grain, and especially for salt, which was scarce in the South. Small Confederate detachments also invaded West Virginia in an unsuccessful attempt to destroy the Baltimore and Ohio Railroad. This line connected the West and Washington, D.C.

Virginia asked West Virginia to reunite with it after the war ended in 1865, but West Virginia refused to do so. Virginia then insisted that West Virginia pay part of the state debt at the time of separation. Legal battles continued over this issue until 1915, when the Supreme Court of the United States ruled that West Virginia owed Virginia $12,393,929.50. West Virginia made its final payment on the debt in 1939.

A West Virginia law denied voting rights to about 15,000 men who had fought for the Confederacy or helped it in other ways. But the legislature repealed this law in 1871. A new constitution was adopted in 1872. The state capital was moved to Charleston in 1870. It was moved back to Wheeling in 1875, but was returned to Charleston in 1885.

The development of railroads speeded industrial expansion during the years after the Civil War. Railroads and branch lines built during the late 1800's opened up valuable mineral and timber resources in the interior of the state. Coal production increased greatly to meet the needs of the railroads and new industries.

Experiments conducted in Pennsylvania in 1874 showed that natural gas could be used to produce industrial power on a large scale. Many industries came to West Virginia in the late 1800's to take advantage of this fuel. The lumber industry grew rapidly after 1881, when steam power replaced water power for sawmills.

Labor Troubles. Between 1860 and 1920, West Virginia mining companies hired great numbers of immigrants. Wages were low and working conditions were poor. Coal miners tried to organize unions so they could make strong demands for better working conditions. The mining companies defeated most of these attempts. A few unions were organized during the 1870's, but working conditions improved only slightly. A single mine explosion in 1907 killed 361 miners.

The United Mine Workers of America began to organize workers in West Virginia in 1890. Miners at

THE GOVERNORS OF WEST VIRGINIA

		Party	Term
1.	Arthur I. Boreman	Republican	1863-1869
2.	Daniel D. T. Farnsworth	Republican	1869
3.	William E. Stevenson	Republican	1869-1871
4.	John J. Jacob	Democratic	1871-1877
5.	Henry M. Mathews	Democratic	1877-1881
6.	Jacob B. Jackson	Democratic	1881-1885
7.	Emanuel W. Wilson	Democratic	1885-1890
8.	Aretas B. Fleming	Democratic	1890-1893
9.	William A. MacCorkle	Democratic	1893-1897
10.	George W. Atkinson	Republican	1897-1901
11.	Albert B. White	Republican	1901-1905
12.	William M. O. Dawson	Republican	1905-1909
13.	William E. Glasscock	Republican	1909-1913
14.	Henry D. Hatfield	Republican	1913-1917
15.	John J. Cornwell	Democratic	1917-1921
16.	Ephraim F. Morgan	Republican	1921-1925
17.	Howard M. Gore	Republican	1925-1929
18.	William G. Conley	Republican	1929-1933
19.	Herman G. Kump	Democratic	1933-1937
20.	Homer A. Holt	Democratic	1937-1941
21.	Matthew M. Neely	Democratic	1941-1945
22.	Clarence W. Meadows	Democratic	1945-1949
23.	Okey L. Patteson	Democratic	1949-1953
24.	William C. Marland	Democratic	1953-1957
25.	Cecil H. Underwood	Republican	1957-1961
26.	William Wallace Barron	Democratic	1961-1965
27.	Hulett C. Smith	Democratic	1965-1969
28.	Arch A. Moore	Republican	1969-1977
29.	John D. Rockefeller IV	Democratic	1977-

Paint Creek and at Cabin Creek went on strike in April, 1912. Mineowners refused to talk with the workers. Twelve miners and four mine guards were killed in battles. Peace was restored only after Governor William E. Glasscock sent state militia to the area. In 1913, Governor Henry D. Hatfield proposed that the owners guarantee the miners a nine-hour workday and the right to organize. The miners and owners agreed to this plan, and the strike ended on April 28, 1913.

Labor disputes quieted down after the United States entered World War I in 1917. The state provided raw materials and manufactured products for the war effort. Trouble flared up again after the war. In 1919, hundreds of union miners gathered near Charleston to march on Logan County to organize the miners there. Governor John J. Cornwell stopped the march by promising to investigate the union miners' complaints.

In May, 1920, mineowners at Matewan, in Mingo County, locked union miners out of their jobs. The firms hired detectives to put the miners out of their company-owned homes. Fighting broke out, and the miners and city police routed the company detectives. Miners and mine guards in Mingo County fought again in August. Governor Cornwell requested federal troops, and President Woodrow Wilson sent 500 soldiers. The union then threatened a statewide strike unless the soldiers were withdrawn. Cornwell gave in, but fresh riots brought the troops back and the governor declared martial law.

The riots quieted during the winter, but broke out again early in 1921. Union miners marched on the city of Logan to organize the miners there. Mine guards met the miners with armed airplanes and machine guns. A four-day battle followed near Blair. The arrival of federal troops and a squadron of bombers forced the miners to retreat. Later, the state indicted 543 miners for taking part in the march. Twenty-two of them were tried for treason against West Virginia. A jury found them innocent. Many men left the union because of the miners' defeat. Almost 45,000 men were in the union in 1920; by 1932 only about 100 members remained.

After the National Recovery Administration (NRA) was established in 1933, many mine workers rejoined the union. Under the terms of the NRA, the mining companies raised wages, shortened work hours, and generally improved working conditions.

During the 1920's and 1930's, the federal government built many locks and dams on the Ohio, Monongahela, and Kanawha rivers. These projects improved the rivers for barge traffic. In 1932, the state dedicated its present Capitol in Charleston.

The Mid-1900's. World War II (1939-1945) speeded industrial growth in West Virginia. Mines and factories produced coal, steel, chemicals, and other war supplies. The discovery of huge salt deposits in 1943 attracted major chemical industries to the Ohio River Valley in 1946. Employment reached record levels.

During the 1950's, West Virginia entered a period of economic adjustment. Defense industries no longer needed so many of the state's products. The demand for coal dropped as railroads shifted from coal-burning to diesel engines. More and more families began to use oil and gas as heating fuels. To meet this competition, the coal industry began to use more machines to do the work of coal miners. The machines lowered the price of coal, but many jobless workers left the state to seek other employment. Between 1950 and 1960, West Virginia lost 7 per cent of its population, mostly younger people. Many of the older people who stayed behind received public welfare aid and government surplus food.

The chemical and textile industries in the Ohio and Kanawha river valleys continued to grow, and glass and metal production also increased. In 1959, the National Radio Astronomy Observatory opened at Green Bank.

The 1960 presidential campaign brought Senator John F. Kennedy to West Virginia and focused national attention on the state's economic problems. Under Presidents Kennedy and Lyndon B. Johnson, federal aid was increased for West Virginia and other sections of the 11 Appalachian Mountain states. In 1965, Congress approved an aid-to-Appalachia program. It provided funds for building roads, developing water resources and pasturelands, restoring forests, and retraining workers. Also in 1965, West Virginia abolished capital punishment. In 1967, the state legislature passed laws to control water and air pollution and strip mining.

Labor troubles continued in the 1960's. In 1969, retired coal miners marched on the West Virginia Capitol in a successful demand for increased benefits. Also in 1969, a public employee strike resulted in the mass firing of 2,600 state highway workers.

During the 1960's, floods and coal mine disasters took many lives and caused widespread property damage. In 1968, coal mine explosions and a fire at Farmington trapped and killed 78 miners. After the tragedy, Congress passed stronger laws regulating mine safety and working conditions. These laws included provisions for benefits to miners disabled by *pneumoconiosis*, a coal dust disease known as "black lung."

In 1972, the collapse of a dam on Buffalo Creek near Man caused the worst flood in West Virginia history. The flood killed more than 100 persons.

West Virginia Today is showing signs of solid economic growth. It was one of the poorest states during the early 1960's. The state ranked 45th in *per capita* (per person) income and had an unemployment rate of about 15 per cent.

During the 1970's, West Virginia jumped ahead of about 10 more states in per capita income. In addition, its unemployment rate was almost the same as the national average, about 7 per cent.

New coal mines have been opened in an effort to strengthen the state's industry. Thousands of skilled workers are needed to operate mining machines. Coal companies are finding new markets, both at home and abroad. They are also developing new methods of shipment.

The growth of manufacturing industries and tourism offer hope for raising economic levels in West Virginia. Tax benefits offered by the state legislature to attract new industries have helped create new jobs and reverse a population decline. Thousands of new jobs have been provided by new factories and plant expansions. The state is also completing more than 850 miles (1,370 kilometers) of new interstate and state highways. These roads have helped the state by opening new areas to industry and tourism.

HARRY G. HOFFMANN, JAMES GAY JONES, and RICHARD S. LITTLE

WEST VIRGINIA / Study Aids

Outline

I. **Government**
    A. Constitution   D. Courts   F. Taxation
    B. Executive   E. Local   G. Politics
    C. Legislature   Government
II. **People**
III. **Education**
    A. Schools   B. Libraries   C. Museums
IV. **A Visitor's Guide**
    A. Places to Visit   B. Annual Events
V. **The Land**
    A. Land Regions
    B. Rivers and Lakes
VI. **Climate**
VII. **Economy**
    A. Natural Resources   E. Electric Power
    B. Mining   F. Transportation
    C. Manufacturing   G. Communication
    D. Agriculture
VIII. **History**

Questions

What were three reasons that led West Virginia to separate from Virginia?

Where do West Virginia's iron and steel industries get their iron ore supplies?

What two well-known varieties of apples were first grown in West Virginia?

How did the development of railroads affect West Virginia's economy?

Why did Governor John J. Cornwell call for federal troops in 1920?

What growing West Virginia industries offer hope for improving the state's economy?

How does West Virginia rank among the states in coal production?

Where are most West Virginia manufacturing industries located? Why?

Why did many workers move to West Virginia between 1860 and 1920? Why did the state's population decrease between 1950 and 1960?

What is the most important field crop in West Virginia?

Books for Young Readers

BAILEY, BERNADINE. *Picture Book of West Virginia.* Rev. ed. Whitman, 1970.

CARPENTER, ALLAN. *West Virginia.* Childrens Press, 1968.

CURRY, JANE LOUISE. *The Daybreakers.* Harcourt, 1970. *The Watchers.* Atheneum, 1975. Both books are fiction.

SUTTON, FELIX. *West Virginia.* Coward, 1968.

WERSTEIN, IRVING. *Labor's Defiant Lady: The Story of Mother Jones.* Crowell, 1969. Fiction.

Books for Older Readers

AMBLER, CHARLES H., and SUMMERS, F. P. *West Virginia, the Mountain State.* 2nd ed. Prentice-Hall, 1958.

COMETTI, ELIZABETH, and SUMMERS, F. P., eds. *The Thirty-Fifth State: A Documentary History of West Virginia.* McClain, 1966.

MUSICK, RUTH ANN. *The Telltale Lilac Bush, and Other West Virginia Ghost Tales.* Univ. Press of Kentucky, 1965.

NUGENT, TOM. *Death at Buffalo Creek: The 1972 West Virginia Flood Disaster.* Norton, 1973.

RICE, OTIS K. *The Allegheny Frontier: West Virginia Beginnings, 1730-1830.* Univ. Press of Kentucky, 1970. *West Virginia: The State and Its People.* McClain, 1972.

WILLIAMS, JOHN A. *West Virginia: A Bicentennial History.* Norton, 1976. *West Virginia and the Captains of Industry.* West Virginia Univ. Library Press, 1976.

WEST VIRGINIA INSTITUTE OF TECHNOLOGY. See UNIVERSITIES AND COLLEGES (table).

WEST VIRGINIA STATE COLLEGE. See UNIVERSITIES AND COLLEGES (table).

WEST VIRGINIA UNIVERSITY is a state-controlled coeducational institution in Morgantown, W.Va. It has colleges of agriculture and forestry, arts and sciences, business and economics, engineering, human resources and education, law, and mineral and energy resources. There are also schools of dentistry, journalism, medicine, nursing, pharmacy, physical education, and social work; a graduate school; and centers for the creative arts and for extension and continuing education. Courses lead to bachelor's, master's, and doctor's degrees. The university was founded in 1867. For enrollment, see UNIVERSITIES AND COLLEGES (table).

Critically reviewed by WEST VIRGINIA UNIVERSITY

WESTCOTT, EDWARD NOYES (1846-1898), wrote *David Harum,* which was published shortly after his death. Westcott was born in Syracuse, N.Y., and became a banker and broker. He wrote *David Harum* while dying of tuberculosis. It was an immediate best seller. The actor William H. Crane dramatized it, and acted in the play. Will Rogers and Evelyn Venable took roles in the motion picture made from the book. Westcott also composed some songs. EDWARD WAGENKNECHT

WESTERGAARD, HARALD MALCOLM (1888-1950), a distinguished American civil engineer and mathematician, became noted for his applications of mathematical analysis in the solution of engineering problems. He developed methods for the design of dams and of pavements for roads, bridges, and airports. Westergaard was born in Copenhagen, Denmark, and came to the United States in 1914. ROBERT W. ABBETT

WESTERLY WIND. See PREVAILING WESTERLY.

WESTERMARCK, EDWARD ALEXANDER (1862-1939), was a Finnish anthropologist. Before reaching the age of 30, he wrote and published his major work, *The*

History of Human Marriage (1891). He served as a professor at the University of London from 1907 to 1930. During this period, Westermarck wrote several works on marriage, the history and development of morals, and customs in Morocco. Westermarck was born in Helsinki.   DAVID B. STOUT

WESTERN AUSTRALIA is the largest state in the Commonwealth of Australia. This vast region covers the western third of the continent. Perth is its capital.

Location, Size, and Surface Features. The state covers 975,100 square miles (2,525,500 square kilometers) in the western part of Australia (see AUSTRALIA [political map]). Mountain ranges include the Hamersley Range in the northwest, the Darling Range along the southwestern coast, and the Stirling Range farther south. The Ashburton, Fitzroy, Gascoyne, and Murchison rivers flow across the western part of the state. Much of the inland area is a wasteland. The Great Sandy Desert lies in the north, and the Great Victoria Desert covers part of the southeast. The Gibson Desert lies between them (see AUSTRALIAN DESERT). The state's central part is a plain over 1,000 feet (300 meters) above sea level.

Natural Resources. Gold is the most important mineral in the state. The chief gold fields lie in the Kalgoorlie district, 365 miles (587 kilometers) east of Perth. Other minerals include arsenic, asbestos, coal, iron ore, petroleum, silver, and tin. The state's most fertile regions are in the southwest near Perth. Great forests of *eucalyptus* (gum) trees also grow in the southwest.

Climate. Temperatures in central Western Australia range from 80° to 90° F. (27° to 32° C) in January and average about 60° F. (16° C) in July. January temperatures north of the central area also average 80° to 90° F., and July temperatures range around 70° F. (21° C). Temperatures in the south vary from 70° to 80° F. (21° to 27° C) in January to 60° F. (16° C) in July. Less than 10 inches (25 centimeters) of rain falls annually in the central area. From 10 to 20 inches (25 to 51 centimeters) falls north and south of this region. Most coastal areas get 20 to 40 inches (51 to 100 centimeters).

The People and Their Work. Western Australia has a population of 1,144,857. About 26,000 persons are *Aborigines* (descendants of the first inhabitants of Australia). About two-thirds of the people live and work in the Perth area. Most others work in the gold fields, timberlands, or farmlands. Workers raise barley, oats, potatoes, and wheat. Other occupations include dairying, iron ore mining, and stock raising. Perth is the only large city, and Kalgoorlie is the chief mining town.

Transportation. Rail and air lines link the state with the rest of the country. The state owns over 3,650 miles (5,874 kilometers) of railroads. One of the world's longest stretches of track without branches or rail connections extends about 1,000 miles (1,600 kilometers) from Kalgoorlie to Port Augusta, South Australia. There are about 93,000 miles (150,000 kilometers) of roads.

Education. All children must attend school until they reach the age of 14. The University of Western Australia is near Perth.

Government. The British Crown appoints a governor for the state. A premier heads the government, assisted by a Cabinet of Ministers. The 50 members of the Legislative Assembly, elected by popular vote, serve three years. The 30 members of the Legislative Council,

elected by homeowners or occupants, serve six years.

History. In 1616, the Dutch explorer Dirck Hartog became the first European to sight the coast of Western Australia. A military settlement was made at King George Sound in 1826. But full colonization did not begin until 1829. That year, Captain James Stirling founded the Swan River settlement and the towns of Perth and Fremantle. In 1901, Western Australia became one of the six original states of the Australian Commonwealth.   C. M. H. CLARK

See also PERTH; KALGOORLIE.

WESTERN BAPTIST BIBLE COLLEGE. See UNIVERSITIES AND COLLEGES (table).

WESTERN CHURCH was a name given to the Roman Catholic Church after the Great Schism of the 800's to distinguish it from the Eastern Orthodox Church. See also ROMAN CATHOLIC CHURCH.

WESTERN CONNECTICUT STATE COLLEGE. See UNIVERSITIES AND COLLEGES (table).

WESTERN CONSERVATIVE BAPTIST SEMINARY. See UNIVERSITIES AND COLLEGES (table).

WESTERN ELECTRIC COMPANY is the world's largest manufacturer of communications equipment. The company is owned by the Bell Telephone System. Most of its manufactured products are used by the Bell system. Western Electric also produces missile guidance systems, radar units, and other electronic equipment for the U.S. government. Its subsidiary, Teletype Corporation, manufactures teletypewriter equipment. Western Electric maintains major manufacturing plants in several cities, including Allentown, Pa.; Baltimore; Chicago; Columbus, Ohio; Indianapolis; Kearny, N.J.; North Andover, Mass.; Oklahoma City; and Omaha. For sales, assets, and number of employees, see MANUFACTURING (table: 100 Leading U.S. Manufacturers).

Three men founded the Western Electric Manufacturing Company in 1869. They were Elisha Gray, an inventor; Enos Barton, a former Western Union telegrapher; and Anson Stager, vice-president of the Western Union Telegraph Company. After the invention of the telephone in 1876, the company began to manufacture telephones. The Bell Company acquired control of Western Electric in 1882, in order to have a reliable source of uniform equipment. The new company expanded its operations, and became known as Western Electric Company. In 1925, the Western Electric Research Force was incorporated into a single research organization called Bell Telephone Laboratories. This is owned jointly by Western Electric and the American Telephone and Telegraph Company, the parent organization of the Bell Telephone System (see AMERICAN TELEPHONE AND TELEGRAPH COMPANY). Headquarters of Western Electric are at 195 Broadway, New York, N.Y. 10007.   DAVID F. ROBINSON

WESTERN EUROPEAN UNION (WEU) is a defense alliance to which Great Britain, France, Italy, Belgium, The Netherlands, Luxembourg, and West Germany belong. Agreements signed in October, 1954, formed WEU, and it was formally organized in May, 1955. All countries in the union are also members of NATO. The members of WEU discuss and act upon problems of control and production of armaments and on cultural and economic matters.   CHARLES P. SCHLEICHER

Famous Names of the West included John Stetson, maker of wide-brimmed hats, and Sam Colt, whose pistol was "the gun that won the West."

Montgomery Ward

Colt's Patent Fire Arms Manufacturing Company, Inc.

A Western Saddle had a curved *horn* in front, which held the cowboy's lariat.

Barbed Wire provided farmers with cheap fencing, and helped put an end to the open range.

The Steel Plow, ideal for sticky prairie soil, became "the plow that broke the Plains."

WESTERN FRONTIER LIFE marks one of the most exciting chapters in American history. The settlement of the West represented the dreams of gold-hungry prospectors, and of homesteaders whose back-breaking labor transformed barren plains into fields of grain. It is the story of cowboys and the open range. It is the drama of Indians and outlaws, of the trains and stagecoaches they attacked, and of the citizens who brought order to the frontier. It is a living tradition that symbolizes to men and women everywhere the American achievement of taming a wild and beautiful land.

The far western frontier appeared about 1850, and vanished about 1890. Adventurous settlers had crossed the Appalachian Mountains during the 1700's and pushed through the Cumberland Gap in the 1770's. They built homes along the Mississippi River a few

years later. Traders and scouts reached the Pacific Coast in the early 1800's. But the area west of the Mississippi—"the last frontier"—did not attract many settlers until after 1850. The final period of western settlement lasted from 1850 to 1890. For the complete story of western expansion in the United States, see WESTWARD MOVEMENT.

The western frontier produced many colorful figures. Some, such as Jesse James and Billy the Kid, symbolize outlaws who "died with their boots on." Others, such as Wyatt Earp and "Wild Bill" Hickok, gained fame as fearless defenders of law and order. "Buffalo Bill" Cody —scout, Indian fighter, and showman—probably did more than anyone else to create interest in the old West. Other men, though less well-known, did more to develop the area itself. Charles Goodnight, a fiery rancher and cattle breeder, helped bring order to the Texas range. Granville Stuart of Montana, who had been an illiterate prospector, became United States minister to Paraguay and Uruguay. Adolph Sutro, a German immigrant, built a vast tunnel through Nevada's Comstock Lode, and later served as mayor of San Francisco.

The West promised to satisfy the needs and dreams of thousands of Americans who sought new homes, wealth, or perhaps only adventure. Some found happiness in green valleys or among tall mountains. Others died horrible deaths, riddled by bullets or scalped by Indians. Ambition, energy, and sometimes greed lay behind the development of the western frontier. The westward rush brought great personal achievements, but it also produced crime and violence. Life on the western frontier seems colorful when we look back on it today. But the people who settled there found it difficult and dangerous—and even dull at times.

Building the Frontier

For many years, the land on the western side of the Mississippi River formed the frontier of American settlement. Only a few thousand settlers had moved to Texas and California in the early 1800's. Land was still plentiful in the East, and treaties with the Indians forbade white settlements in many areas of the West. But, after 1850, many causes led to westward expansion. During the Civil War, the Union government encouraged mining, because the valuable ores helped pay for the war. The Homestead Act of 1862 provided cheap farm land for new settlers. So did gifts of huge tracts of land to the railroads. At the same time, thousands of Europeans wanted to come to America. Revolutionary movements had failed in many countries. Poor harvests caused famines in Ireland. The Scandinavian nations had become overpopulated. Government agents increased their persecution of the Jews in Russia, Poland, and other areas of Central Europe.

The land between the Missouri River and the Pacific Coast forms two great belts, running roughly north and south. The grasslands of the Great Plains stretch west from the Missouri River to the Rocky Mountains. Beyond the plains, from the Rocky Mountains to the Pacific Coast, lies a belt of land with many mountain ranges and several valleys. Because the Far West had many different land regions and climates, it developed on several frontiers, not just one.

The rush to the west affected both belts of land, but it touched the Great Plains only briefly at first. Here appeared what the novelist Hamlin Garland called "the land of the straddlebug." *Locators*, or land salesmen, picked the best farms on the grassy plains. They marked their claims with *straddlebugs*, three boards fastened together like tepee poles. But when *homesteaders*, or farmers, arrived later with their families, they often found themselves in trouble. They had little protection against the Plains Indians. When they rode horses, they could not use the long rifles they had carried in the woods. Even more serious, the Great Plains lacked water, and crops often withered and died. The plains also lacked trees, and farmers had difficulty finding wood for shelter, fuel, and fences. The surge into this territory slowed down. At the same time, adventurous settlers moved into the western belt, beyond the Rockies.

The Search for Gold and Silver attracted thousands of miners to the western mountains. About 100,000 adventurers had hurried to California in the gold rush of 1849. They mined in the Sierra Nevada mountains east of Sacramento. However, gold in this area had become difficult to mine by the middle 1850's. So the prospectors moved eastward looking for *strikes*, or discoveries.

Several areas became important mining centers during the period from 1858 to 1875. The first was in the Rocky Mountains west of Denver. It drew a great rush of fortune seekers, who vowed to reach "Pikes Peak or Bust." Central City and Leadville grew up almost overnight in Colorado. A second area centered around Virginia City in western Nevada, and encouraged further discoveries in the desert valleys and mountains. Both these areas began as gold fields. But black sand in Colorado and blue clay in Nevada clogged the simple machines the early miners used. The mines did not become profitable until mining companies found that the sands and clays contained rich silver deposits.

A third mining region, in Idaho, Montana, and Washington, led to the settlement of such towns as Lewiston, Ida.; Helena, Mont.; and Walla Walla, Wash. The last great gold rush in the United States took place in the Black Hills of South Dakota in 1874 and 1875. Deadwood, founded in 1876, gained fame as one of the last frontier mining camps.

East Meets West. The swarm of miners into the West showed the need for better transportation. Thousands of new settlers ran short of supplies. Prospectors could mine gold with pick, shovel, and pan, but silver-mining companies needed heavy machinery to dig the ore, and some means of shipping it to smelters. Such needs encouraged companies to build transcontinental railroad networks. Two companies began the first of these railroad systems in the early 1860's, starting from both east and west. From the east came the Union Pacific, with Irish laborers who established such towns as Cheyenne and Laramie, Wyo. The Central Pacific line, from the west, had thousands of Chinese in its road gangs. The two sets of tracks met at Promontory, near Ogden, Utah, in 1869. Other lines soon followed, including the Southern Pacific and the Atchison, Topeka, and Santa Fe. See RAILROAD (History; picture: The Meeting of Two Railroads).

With the railroads to supply them, white men had little fear of waterless deserts or hostile Indians. The growth of railroads almost led to the extermination of the bison, or American buffalo. Millions of these animals had roamed throughout the West, but hunters soon killed most of them. The hunters killed for sport or for buffalo hides, but seldom for meat.

The Cattle Boom. With the railroads came the period of "the cattle kingdom" on the Great Plains. Ranching started in southern Texas, where farmers raised Mexican Longhorn cattle. The ranchers branded the cattle to show ownership, and guarded them on horseback as they roamed the range. By the end of the Civil War, the number of cattle had increased, and people in the North had money to buy beef.

The era of "the long drive" began when the ranchers saw that they could ship cattle east if they could get

Early Settlers in the Far West
crossed the plains to Oregon or California. Their high Conestoga wagons
had already become museum pieces
by the time of the last frontier.

Tom Hollyman, courtesy *Holiday*, © 1955 Curtis Publishing Co.

A Stagecoach Roars Across the Desert with Indian
attackers in close pursuit. In *Downing the Nigh Leader*,
Frederic Remington caught the drama and excitement that
symbolize "the Wild West" to people throughout the world.

Sunday Morning in the Mines by Charles Nahl. Permanent
Collection E. B. Crocker Art Gallery, Sacramento, California

In the Gold Fields, some
miners spent Sunday reading
the Bible or washing their
clothes. Others wrestled or
took part in horse racing.

Railroads helped tame the
West. The train *at right* ran
out of Virginia City, Nev., on
the Virginia & Truckee line.

The Western Pacific Railroad Company

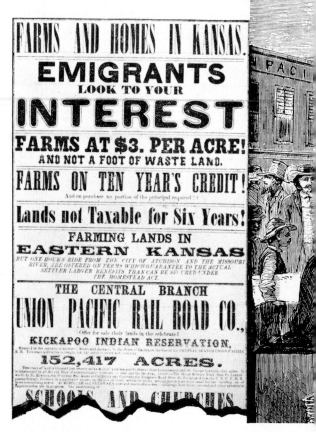

the animals to the railroads. A favorite route led along the Chisholm Trail, which ran from the Mexican border through Austin and Waco, Tex., to Abilene, Kan. Farther west, the Western Trail led to Dodge City, Kan. Millions of cattle plodded along these trails, sometimes as many as 4,000 in a single drive.

The open range did not last long. By 1885, overstocking had ruined many ranchers. They had bought more cattle than the land could support. Fierce blizzards in the winter of 1886-1887 spelled the end for many more. Sheep raisers began moving into the Plains. Their herds cropped the grass so short that cattle could not graze the land. Farmers built fences on the open range, limiting the amount of pastureland. Ranchers tried to keep out *nesters*, or permanent settlers, in a series of *range wars*. But the open range had disappeared, and the cattle boom came to an end.

Homesteading on the Plains. New developments in the 1870's made it possible for eager settlers to farm the grasslands. Barbed wire, invented in 1873, provided the first cheap substitute for wood fences. Windmills solved the problem of bringing up water that lay far underground. Agricultural experts worked out methods of farming that would work in the dry climate (see DRY FARMING). With improved machinery, farmers could cultivate large areas. The railroads offered cheap land to homesteaders. Thousands of settlers moved into Kansas, Nebraska, and the Dakotas. The government opened a large section of Indian Territory in 1889, and the Oklahoma Territory was born (see INDIAN TERRITORY). So much of the Far West had filled up by 1890 that the Bureau of the Census declared in a report that a definite frontier no longer existed.

Life on the Frontier

The People of the western frontier formed a varied mixture. Americans streamed west from the East Coast, the Middle West, and the South. Some who had committed crimes went west because they wanted to get as far away from the law as possible. Others found life boring in the East, and wanted to try something new and different. Professional people and merchants cared for the needs of growing communities. Land speculators hoped to make quick fortunes. But most settlers were farmers, laborers, unskilled mechanics, miners, and former soldiers. They wanted to get rich in a hurry, and were willing to risk their lives to do it.

Large numbers of blacks moved to the frontier to escape the prejudice they had experienced in the East and South. Thousands of black homesteaders settled in California, Kansas, Nebraska, and Texas during the second half of the 1800's. Some of the best-known cowboys of that period were blacks. One, a ranch hand named Nat Love, gained fame for horsemanship and other skills on cattle drives. Bose Ikard, a former slave, was foreman of one of the largest ranches in Texas. Black soldiers in the U.S. Army fought Indians on the frontier. See BLACK AMERICANS (After Reconstruction).

Many other groups also lived in the Far West. Mexicans and Californians had settled in the Southwest and California since the 1700's. Indians furnished cheap labor. Basques from France and Spain worked as sheepherders (see BASQUES). Scandinavians and other Europeans bought farms on the Great Plains. Miners came from England and Wales to join the search for precious metals. Chinese came to build the railroads, then drifted to mining camps where they ran laundries, restaurants, and small shops.

Most frontier people fell into two classes, *solid folk* and *boomers*. The solid folk settled down if they liked the life, or went home if they did not. Boomers were always heading for a new boom town. They seldom stayed long enough to make much money, and squandered their earnings in high living. Even among the steady people, few persons came to stay, as settlers had stayed on the land east of the Missouri River. Most of them wanted to get rich and go home.

The frontier was a man's world, and favored the jack-of-all-trades. Wyatt Earp served as a marshal, sheriff, buffalo hunter, stagecoach driver, and prospector. Hank Monk, a famous stagecoach driver, also mined, and rode the pony express. George Jackson, credited with discovering gold in the Rockies, had been a sheepherder, prospector, farm hand, miner, and roustabout, and later became a businessman.

Food on the frontier was usually simple. Flour served as the basic food, because it was nourishing and did not spoil. The people used it in sourdough biscuits and bread, and in *flapjacks*, or pancakes. Other important

foods included dried beans; game, such as bison, deer, elk, antelope, and wild fowl; and preserved meats such as bacon, salt pork, and *jerky*, or dried meat. Cattlemen could always eat beef, and sheep raisers had mutton. Frontiersmen rarely ate fresh fruit and vegetables or dairy products. Even cowboys did not milk cows.

People on the frontier had no need for fancy cooking—the men were too busy, and women were scarce. Meat with biscuits or flapjacks provided a feast. Old Len Martin of Carson City, Nev., declared while stewing a chicken that there was no sense "picking a chicken too darned close—anybody that don't like the feathers can skim 'em off."

Clothing had to be practical, and most men wore the same plain garments day after day. They wore cowhide boots; *levis*, or blue jeans; a wool shirt; a jacket or vest; and a felt hat. Some had socks. A man often wore a red bandanna handkerchief around his neck to protect himself from the dust and cold. Women wore sunbonnets and simple calico and gingham dresses. Cowboys wore leather *chaps* to protect their legs from brush. Cowboy hats, called *sombreros*, had a wide brim to shield the eyes, and a deep crown so that the hat would not blow off. Some men bought deerskin clothes from the Indians. Wealthy men and women bought clothes from New York City, London, or Paris.

Many frontiersmen, particularly outlaws and law-enforcement officers, carried weapons. Especially popular were Winchester rifles; Colt revolvers, including the famous six-shooter; and bowie knives (see REVOLVER [picture]; BOWIE KNIFE).

Amusements on the frontier varied with the area and the type of settler. Homesteading families on the plains met for square dances, holiday celebrations, and house-raising or corn-husking bees. Many miners and cowboys spent most of their leisure time drinking and gambling in the saloons that sprang up in every town. Dance halls called *hurdy-gurdies* attracted many people, although men often had to dance with each other, because women were scarce. Informal rodeos featured expert horsemanship and other cowboy skills (see RODEO). Throughout the West, people enjoyed horse races, shooting contests, and wrestling and boxing matches. In larger towns, settlers welcomed traveling dramatic groups and vaudeville shows. They applauded such famous performers as Edwin Booth, Laura Keene, and Helena Modjeska.

Religion came to the western frontier even before most white settlers arrived. In the early 1800's, Catholic and Protestant missionaries such as Father Pierre De Smet and Marcus Whitman had pushed into the Far West to convert the Indians (see DE SMET, PIERRE JEAN; WHITMAN, MARCUS). But new settlements often grew up far from the missions, and people had to rely on traveling preachers called *circuit riders* to perform religious services. These men rode about constantly. When they arrived in a town, they preached sermons and conducted marriages, baptisms, and other services for people who had sometimes waited many weeks. Among farm families on the plains, circuit riders set up Sunday schools and held summer camp meetings. See CAMP MEETING; CIRCUIT RIDER.

WESTERN FRONTIER LIFE

Frontier Towns sprang up almost overnight. An early arrival in Bovard, Nev., told how he passed through the town in the morning and noticed four or five tents. When he returned in the afternoon, Main Street was 1 mile (1.6 kilometers) long and business was booming in a string of tent saloons. Some towns, such as Butte, Mont., started as shipping points for ore. Others, including Wichita, Kan., boomed as cattle transport centers. Many, such as Tombstone, Ariz., grew up around mines. Transportation centers usually grew and prospered. But most mining camps became ghost towns of rubble and sagebrush after the ores had been worked out or metal prices fell.

Most frontier towns provided few comforts. A miner often slept outdoors in summer, and built a dugout or crude shack in the winter. He might have a tent or make a shelter out of rocks, empty bottles, or packing cases. Two early settlers in Treasure City, Nev., collected all the rocks they could find for shelter against the winter. The next spring, they discovered that the walls were high-grade silver ore worth $75,000!

House furnishings were simple and often homemade. Miners needed blasting powder more than fine dishes. They papered their shacks with newspapers to make them warmer. Today, visitors can sometimes still read about events in a ghost town on the walls of its crumbling buildings. A few wealthy persons shipped in furniture, tableware, and wallpaper at great expense. If a town became fairly permanent, the people built board sidewalks on each side of the dirt streets, lined with poles and stakes for hitching posts. Square false fronts made small buildings look impressive.

Life in frontier towns was difficult. People often lacked conveniences, and even necessities. Usually the only water available in mining camps was warm and dirty. Sometimes men hauled water a great distance and sold it for several dollars a barrel. In many areas on the plains, no trees grew.

Because of such shortages, western towns often grew in groups, such as the one built around Virginia City, Nev. The rich silver and gold mines of the Comstock Lode centered around Virginia City, but the town had no wood or water. Other towns grew up nearby to supply these needs. Empire became a smelter town on the Carson River; Washoe, near the Sierra Nevadas, supplied fuel; and Reno grew up where the local railroad joined the main line of the Central Pacific.

During the 20-year period between 1860 and 1880, the Comstock Lode yielded more than $300 million worth of ore. Because of this great wealth, all the comforts of the day soon appeared in Virginia City. At first, supplies came in by muleback, a few at a time. When a road was built, slow freight wagons brought supplies. Finally, a railroad served the town with several trains a day. By 1876, Virginia City had 23,000 persons, 20 laundries, 54 dry-goods stores, 6 churches, and 150 saloons. The vice-president of the express company built a four-story French-style mansion. An opera house and several theaters presented Italian light operas, vaudeville, lectures, and even Shakespeare's plays. The miners' union had a library. A local newspaper, the *Territorial Enterprise*, employed a young reporter who began writing under the name of Mark Twain. At any time, a man might find silver ore in his basement and be worth $1 million the next day. His neighbors had to be careful that they and their children did not fall into his new mine.

Life in the Country resembled that in the towns, except that settlers found it harder to obtain supplies. Prospectors roamed about with supplies loaded on a burro or two, but they had to return to a mining camp when they ran short. Country life on the frontier usually meant living on a ranch or a farm.

Ranches usually lay in mountain valleys watered by melting snow, or in broad uplands that had some moisture. Most ranches consisted only of a few simple buildings and some *corrals* (cattle pens) surrounded by high, strong fences made of stakes and poles. The grassland of the open range provided pastures. The *Texas house*, two log cabins joined by a roofed space, developed into the ranch-style house of today. The rancher used one cabin for cooking and eating, and the other for sleeping. As the ranch grew, the rancher might build a house for his family, a cookshack, and a bunkhouse for the *hands* (cowboys).

Cattlemen let their herds graze on the open range, so they needed few buildings and no fences. But they did need cowboys to turn the cattle out to graze in spring, and move them to rich mountain pastures. Cowboys constantly guarded the herds against mountain lions and bands of rustlers. In the fall, all the ranchers in an area held a *roundup* to gather in the cattle. Cowboys had already marked the grown cattle by branding them or cropping their ears. Men from each ranch sorted out these cattle by their markings. New calves followed their mothers. Then the cowboys cropped the ears of the calves or branded them with the owner's mark.

Cowboys also drove herds to *cow towns* to be shipped east on the railroads. On the *long drive*, cattle moved in long lines, with riders ahead, behind, and on both sides. A *chuck wagon* carried food for the cowboys, and a *wrangler* took care of extra horses. When all went well, the cattle moved slowly but steadily. But they sometimes *stampeded* when they were afraid to swim a river, or were frightened by Indians or rustlers. After several weeks, the drive plodded into a cow town such as Abilene or Dodge City, where cowboys loaded the cattle into freight cars. For a description of cowboys and their work, see COWBOY; RANCHING.

Farms, unlike ranches, depended on the soil, not the grass. Farmers plowed the grass under and raised grain, mainly wheat. Grasshoppers, hot winds, and prairie fires often made life hard for settlers on the plains. So did the ranchers, who resented the barbed-wire fences that destroyed the open range. Bloody fights developed in the range wars, or barbed-wire wars, that followed. Farmers fenced in watering places or blocked trails, then cattlemen cut the wires. Barbed wire finally won, and farms spread farther and farther out over the rich grasslands of the Great Plains.

Life on the plains resembled that of pioneers east of the Missouri River. But there was a basic difference. While the farmer in Ohio might have too many trees, the farmer on the plains usually had no wood at all. The western farmer's land has often been called *the sod-house frontier*, because so many men built houses of dirt and sod. A farmer plowed furrows of sod and cut

Virginia City bustled with activity in the 1860's. The town perched 6,500 feet (1,980 meters) high in the Sierra Nevada, close to Mt. Davidson, site of the fabulous Comstock Lode.

Library of Congress; Nevada Historical Society

A Teamster Who "Struck It Rich" built this mansion near Virginia City. Sandy Bowers later went "ter Yoorup" to spend his fortune.

them crosswise into blocks about 1 foot (30 centimeters) square. He piled rows of sod blocks on top of each other to make walls, and covered them with a thatch roof. Sometimes he brought wood with him and built a frame to support the roof, or found a little wood nearby. A sod house remained warm in winter and cool in summer, but it had many disadvantages. Dirt sifted down on the food, crumbled from the walls, and rose from the clay floor. Rats and mice lived in the thatch, and snakes and gophers often dug tunnels through the walls or floor. For fuel, the farmer used twigs, grass, corncobs, peat, and buffalo *chips*, or manure. Later, settlers often improved their *soddies* by whitewashing the walls and hauling in lumber for doors and ceilings.

Transportation and Communication

Transportation varied with the area and the means at hand. Until the railroads appeared, travel was always slow and uncomfortable, and often dangerous. Roads were few and bad, and schedules were irregular.

Most people traveled by stagecoach. A group of passengers could defend themselves more easily against Indians or bandits than a person alone. One famous line, the Butterfield Overland Express, ran four coaches weekly between St. Louis and San Francisco. The coaches bumped along day and night, covering about 100 miles (160 kilometers) in 24 hours. The passengers, grimy with dust in summer and shivering with cold in winter, tried to sleep on the hard seats. Crude wood or adobe "stations" every 10 miles (16 kilometers) or so provided food for both passengers and horses. Travelers

faced the constant danger of robbery and Indian attack. Traveling alone was even more dangerous, but people in a hurry rode horseback. Settlers moving with their families traveled in wagons.

Wagon trains served as the best means of hauling freight before railroads were built. They usually included about 25 heavy, high-wheeled wagons, each pulled by a team of 6 to 20 oxen or mules. Men called *bullwhackers* or *mule skinners* drove the wagons and guarded the freight. The wagons lumbered along at 1 or 2 miles (1.6 or 3.2 kilometers) per hour, or about 100 miles (160 kilometers) in a seven-day week, because "there was no Sunday west of Omaha." The wagons hauled ore from mines and brought in mining machinery and blasting powder. They carried the food and water that made life possible in desert camps. If blizzards stopped them, the price of flour might soar to $100 a sack. Famous freight lines included Ben Holladay's Central Overland California and Pikes Peak Express Company, and the Wells, Fargo line (see WELLS, FARGO & COMPANY). Frontiersmen also used burros to carry goods. Some even used camels, imported from Asia because they could live on the desert (see CAMEL).

Communication. News traveled slowly, most of it by stagecoach. A letter took months to go from California to the Middle West, and snows in the mountains cut off almost all communication in winter.

The pony express carried the mail between St. Joseph, Mo., and Sacramento, Calif., a distance of almost 2,000 miles (3,200 kilometers). As Mark Twain described it, "There were about eighty pony-riders in the

Jesse James, according to an old ballad, "killed many a man, and robbed the Glendale train." He and his gang terrorized Missouri for several years. The scene above, by Thomas Hart Benton, is a section of a mural in the state Capitol at Jefferson City.

saddle all the time, night and day, stretching in a long, scattering procession . . . forty flying eastward and forty toward the west." At first, it cost $5 to send ½ ounce (14 grams) of mail by pony express, so that this volume of THE WORLD BOOK ENCYCLOPEDIA, for example, would have cost more than $450 to send. Pony-express riders changed horses every 10 to 15 miles (16 to 24 kilometers), and new riders took over every 75 miles (121 kilometers). The pony express covered about 250 miles (402 kilometers) a day, so that mail traveled from St. Joseph to Sacramento in eight or nine days. This remarkable system began in April, 1860, but lasted only about 18 months. It was discontinued after the telegraph reached California in October, 1861. See PONY EXPRESS.

Law and Order

Farm families on the frontier lived quietly, but crime flourished in the mining camps and *cow towns*. These isolated settlements often had great wealth in precious metals, and attracted many men who came only to cheat and steal. Other men meant well, but wanted to have a good time. Drinking and gambling sometimes led to fighting and killing. The *Wild West* had little difficulty living up to its nickname.

Crime often resulted from the temptations of gold and silver. A miner who had *struck it rich* usually celebrated by getting drunk. Then he might be stabbed and robbed, or cheated in a poker game by a *cardsharp* who used a marked deck of cards. Gold and silver also tempted bandits, who followed shipments on their way to California or to the East. They picked a deserted spot in which to attack a wagon or stagecoach. Criminals also included *claim jumpers*, who illegally took over mine

claims that belonged to someone else. *Confidence men* (swindlers) often sold worthless stocks. Many dealt in "salted" mines, selling worthless holes after putting in small amounts of good ore.

Horses, cattle, and sheep also provided a temptation for lawbreakers. The animals roamed great areas, and could be moved under their own power. Rustlers stole cattle from the range, drove them to a *shebang* (hideout), and altered their brands. One valley in the Pahranagat Range of southeastern Nevada became a refuge for rustlers who roamed through Utah, Arizona, Nevada, and Idaho. A rider passing through the valley could count as many as 350 different brands on cattle stolen from as many ranches. One story tells of a sheriff who returned from such a robbers' roost looking triumphant. "Get your man?" somebody asked. "No," the sheriff replied, "but I rode plumb through the place without getting shot."

Disturbances also arose from the constant feuding between cattlemen and the sheep owners and farmers. The Lincoln County War inflamed New Mexico in 1878. Army troops and Governor Lew Wallace finally quieted the rival cattlemen. See NEW MEXICO (Territorial Days). In 1892, cattlemen in Johnson County, Wyoming, imported a trainload of gunmen to terrorize farmers. The army finally ended this Johnson County Cattle War after several killings on both sides. See WYOMING (The Johnson County War).

The *desperadoes* (outlaws) usually worked together in gangs, such as those led by Henry Plummer, the Younger brothers, "the Dalton boys," and Frank and Jesse James. They robbed banks, trains, and stagecoaches throughout large areas. Sam Bass once stole $60,000 in gold from a single Union Pacific train traveling through Nebraska. Billy the Kid was said to have killed 21 men. Some of the most famous desperadoes were honest and kindly until drink or anger aroused them. Then they became killers. But even among lawbreakers, the code of the West demanded that men give each other a chance to defend themselves. A gunman who shot from behind or attacked an unarmed man was considered a coward. Outlaws who obeyed this code had many friends and admirers in spite of their crimes. They came to symbolize the independence and vitality of the West, and many legends grew up around them. Sooner or later most of them were shot or hanged.

Law Enforcement. When Americans settled unorganized territory in the Far West, they brought with them federal, state, and local laws from their former homes. Even miners often adopted simple codes. But these laws did not always help new communities. Often they did not take into account new and different situations, such as cattle rustling. Even when laws suited a community, enforcement proved difficult because of the great distances between settlements. For example, the sheriff at Pioche, Nev., was responsible for law and order as far away as the mining camp of El Dorado, 300 miles (480 kilometers) distant. If the sheriff did capture a murderer, there was often no jail to keep him in. And the outlaw's friends might kill innocent citizens to free him. Every man had to be ready to "shoot it out." Judge Roy Bean, "the law west of the Pecos," held court in his saloon in Langtry, Tex., with the aid of a single law book and a six-shooter.

But law-abiding people lived in all parts of the frontier, and sooner or later they established order. The West often found law officers as fearless as the outlaws themselves. Many served as federal marshals. Tom Smith, the marshal of Abilene, Kan., did not drink or swear, but he shocked a tough cow town into behaving by knocking out armed men with his bare fists. Other

famous marshals included Wyatt Earp, "Bat" Masterson, Ben Thompson, and "Wild Bill" Hickok, who succeeded Smith. The Texas Rangers also helped maintain law and order (see TEXAS RANGERS).

The citizens themselves provided another answer to the problem of law enforcement. They banded together in groups of *vigilantes* to capture and punish criminals. Sometimes these groups killed innocent men in their haste, but most victims deserved the punishment they received. See VIGILANTE.

Indian Fighting disturbed the frontier for many years. The federal government had reserved large areas of western land for Indian use throughout the 1800's, but land-hungry white settlers constantly moved into these sections. Agents of the Indian Bureau tried to protect the Indians and to enforce regulations for both Indians and whites. But most frontier troops, stationed in about 100 posts throughout the West, agreed with the claim many westerners made that "the only good Indians are dead Indians." In 1864, an army force killed nearly 300 peaceful Indians near Sand Creek, Colorado. Such events, and the revenge they inspired, aroused the whole frontier. For the story of Indian wars in the West, see INDIAN WARS.

An American Tradition

The frontier is gone now. Most of its mining camps have become empty ghost towns. Other settlements of the wild West have grown into peaceful communities. Denver, Cheyenne, Boise, and Salt Lake City now stand where settlers once pitched their tents. But western frontier life left behind a great American tradition because of its dramatic appeal. Even before "Buffalo Bill" Cody organized his "Wild West Show" in 1883, the western frontier had captured the interest of people in all parts

IV, *Texas Longhorns*, by Tom Lea, collection of the Dallas Museum of Fine Arts

Arizona Highways

Cowboys changed horses often, and kept a "pool" of extras, called a *remuda*. Ross Santee's sketch shows a *wrangler*, who looked after them.

Texas Longhorn Cattle, hardy and fierce, were descended from wild cattle brought to America by the Spanish. Ranch owners branded them or notched their ears to identify them.

of the world. Books, stories, paintings, songs, plays, and motion pictures about the old West still pour forth in a seemingly endless stream. Almost 450 works have appeared about Billy the Kid alone—including poems, novels, plays, ballets, and motion pictures. The West has also produced its own folklore heroes. Febold Feboldson performed amazing feats on the sod-house frontier of the Great Plains. Pecos Bill taught the cowboys all they knew, and even showed broncos how to buck. See FEBOLD FEBOLDSON; PECOS BILL.

Many works of poor quality have strayed far from the truth, presenting only the most sensational parts of frontier life. But other works have artistic merit, and give a true picture of those who settled the West.

Literature. Most of the early writing about the West came from men who had taken part in its development. Mark Twain's *Roughing It* became a frontier classic. Bret Harte's short stories and Joaquin Miller's poems found admirers in Europe as well as the United States. One of the most important novels about the West, Owen Wister's *The Virginian*, did much to stimulate interest in the subject. Andy Adams, a cowboy, gave a truer picture of range life in *The Log of a Cowboy*. One of Emerson Hough's many novels, *The Covered Wagon*, became a popular motion picture. Hamlin Garland, with *A Son of the Middle Border*, and O. E. Rölvaag, with *Giants in the Earth*, immortalized the sod-house frontier. Zane Grey wrote more than 50 colorful western novels. Later books include Walter Van Tilburg Clark's *The Oxbow Incident*, Conrad Richter's *The Sea of Grass*, and A. B. Guthrie's *The Big Sky*.

Music of the West, like literature, has been mainly popular, rather than serious. Famous cowboy songs include "The Chisholm Trail," "The Lone Prairie," and "Streets of Laredo." Many of these ballads grew out of English or Spanish folk songs that the cowboys sang to quiet the cattle, or to help fill the long, lonely, empty hours. Serious music with western themes includes Giacomo Puccini's opera *The Girl of the Golden West*, Aaron Copland's ballets *Billy the Kid* and *Rodeo*, Ferde Grofé's *Grand Canyon Suite*, and Hershey Kay's ballet *Western Symphony*. One of the most popular of all American musical plays, *Oklahoma!*, by Richard Rodgers and Oscar Hammerstein II, tells how the cowboys clashed with the "hoe hands," or farmers.

Art. The color of the western landscape and the vigor of running horses, stampeding cattle, and rugged men have appealed to many artists. Frederic Remington, probably the most famous, painted and drew over 2,700 pictures of the West. Remington learned life on the frontier at first hand, and preserved it in realistic paintings, sketches, and statues. Others who have painted the West include Charles Marion Russell and N. C. Wyeth. Many artists, including Thomas Hart Benton and Georgia O'Keeffe, have used western backgrounds. Will James, Tom Lea, Ross Santee, and others have illustrated their own books on the West.

Entertainment. Motion pictures and television have made western frontier life familiar to people everywhere. With cowboys and soldiers fighting outlaws and Indians, the "western" offers endless opportunities for battles and thrilling chases through mountains and deserts. *The Squaw Man* of 1914, one of the first full-length films

made in Hollywood, began a trend that continues today. William S. Hart, a typical two-gun cowboy, became a national hero. Other motion-picture cowboy idols have included Harry Carey, Buck Jones, Tom Mix, Roy Rogers, and William Boyd, who made the first "Hopalong Cassidy" film in 1934. Many "westerns" provide poor entertainment, but some have been fine motion pictures. Among these, such films as *Stagecoach* and *High Noon* achieved a high level. On the stage, Will Rogers gained fame as "the cowboy philosopher." Radio and television present hundreds of western dramas every year. Rodeos, especially in the Western States, feature daring cowboys who ride bucking broncos and wild cattle. Thousands of persons spend vacations on dude ranches, dressing like cowboys in settings that try to recapture a bygone era.   CHARLTON LAIRD

Related Articles. See the articles on the various Western States, such as MONTANA. See also the following articles:

FAMOUS WESTERNERS

Bass, Sam	Calamity Jane	Hickok, "Wild
Bean, Judge Roy	Deadwood Dick	Bill," James B.
Billy the Kid	Earp, Wyatt B. S.	James, Jesse W.
Buffalo Bill	Fargo, William G.	Oakley, Annie

OTHER RELATED ARTICLES

Boom Town	Pioneer Life	Turner,
Circuit Rider	in America	Frederick J.
Comstock Lode	Pony Express	Vigilante
Cowboy	Ranching	Wells, Fargo &
Ghost Town	Rodeo	Company
Homestead Act	Texas Rangers	Westward
Indian Wars	Trails of Early	Movement
	Days	

Outline

I. **Building the Frontier**
  A. The Search for Gold and Silver
  B. East Meets West
  C. The Cattle Boom
  D. Homesteading on the Plains
II. **Life on the Frontier**
  A. The People   E. Religion
  B. Food   F. Frontier Towns
  C. Clothing   G. Life in the Country
  D. Amusements
III. **Transportation and Communication**
  A. Transportation   B. Communication
IV. **Law and Order**
  A. Crime   C. Indian Fighting
  B. Law Enforcement
V. **An American Tradition**
  A. Literature   C. Art
  B. Music   D. Entertainment

Questions

Why was there so much crime on the western frontier? How did settlers enforce the law?

Why were traveling preachers called *circuit riders?*

What ended the period of the open range?

How did the first transcontinental railroad affect the development of the western frontier?

Why was the western farmer's land often called "the sod-house frontier"?

What caused flour to become worth $100 a sack?

Why did some people import camels?

Why did some western towns grow up in groups?

What forms of entertainment have made western frontier life more popular than ever?

Why was the pony express discontinued?

WESTERN HEMISPHERE. See HEMISPHERE.

WESTERN ISLES. See HEBRIDES.

WESTERN MEADOW LARK is the state bird of five states: Kansas, Montana, Nebraska, North Dakota, and Oregon. See also MEADOW LARK.

WESTERN ONTARIO, UNIVERSITY OF, is a private, coeducational university in London, Ont. It is supported mainly by the provincial government. The university has divisions of arts and science, business administration, dentistry, education, engineering, graduate studies, law, library and information science, medicine, music, and nursing. Brescia College (Roman Catholic), Huron College (Anglican Church of Canada), and King's College (Roman Catholic) are affiliated with the university. Students at these colleges earn University of Western Ontario degrees. The university was founded in 1878. For enrollment, see CANADA (table: Universities and Colleges). LAWRENCE T. MOORE

WESTERN RESERVE. In 1662, King Charles II of England granted the colony of Connecticut a charter. This charter gave Connecticut title to lands which stretched westward from the Atlantic Ocean to the Pacific. In 1786, Connecticut gave to the new United States government the great stretch of western land which it held under its original charter. But Connecticut kept a strip of land bordering Lake Erie in Ohio. This strip was called the *Western Reserve.* It extended westward about 120 miles (193 kilometers) from the northwestern boundary of Pennsylvania, and covered 3,667,000 acres (1,483,982 hectares). In 1795, the Connecticut Land Company bought most of it for $1,200,000. In 1800, Connecticut and the U.S. government agreed to attach the land as a county to the Ohio territory. See also CLEVELAND. RICHARD HOFSTADTER

WESTERN SAHARA, formerly *Spanish Sahara,* is an area on the northwest coast of Africa. It lies between Morocco, Algeria, Mauritania, and the Atlantic Ocean. For the location of Western Sahara, see AFRICA (political map). The area belonged to Spain in the early 1500's and again from 1860 to 1976. Today, it is claimed by Morocco and Mauritania. But Algeria and some of the people who live in Western Sahara oppose the claims of Morocco and Mauritania.

About 165,000 people live in the area. Most of them are Arabs or Berbers. The majority of the people are nomads who move about constantly, seeking water and grass for their herds of camels, goats, and sheep. Some of the people fish for a living along the Atlantic coast.

Western Sahara covers 102,703 square miles (266,000 square kilometers). Most of the land is barren, rocky desert which receives little rainfall. Vegetation is scanty except for patches of coarse grass and low bushes near the coast. But the land yields large quantities of valuable chemicals called *phosphates.* Phosphates are used as fertilizers and in the manufacture of some detergents.

Spain claimed the area in 1509. Morocco ruled it from 1524 until Spain regained control in 1860. Spain made the area one of its provinces—called the Province of Spanish Sahara—in 1958.

In 1976, Spain gave up its control of Spanish Sahara and ceded it to Morocco and Mauritania. The area

came to be called Western Sahara. Morocco claimed the northern part of the former Spanish province, and Mauritania claimed the southern part. Algeria and an organization of people of Western Sahara called the Polisario Front opposed the claims of Morocco and Mauritania, and demanded independence for the area. Fighting broke out in the area between the opposing sides. JAMES W. FERNANDEZ

WESTERN SAMOA is an island country in the Pacific Ocean. It lies about 1,700 miles (2,740 kilometers) northeast of New Zealand. American Samoa, a United States territory, lies east of Western Samoa (see AMERICAN SAMOA). Western Samoa, one of the smallest countries in the world, consists of two main islands, Upolu and Savai'i, and several smaller islands. All the islands combined occupy less area than Rhode Island, the smallest state in the United States.

Samoans are tall, brown-skinned Polynesians, the same group as the original people of Hawaii. Most Samoans live by raising their own food on small plots of ground and have little cash income. By some standards, Western Samoa is a poor, or developing, country. However, the people are healthy and have all the food and clothing they need.

Polynesians have lived in Western Samoa for at least 2,000 years. The first Europeans landed there in the 1700's, and Germany took control in 1900. During World War I, New Zealand occupied the islands. It ruled them until Western Samoa gained independence in 1962. One of Western Samoa's most distinguished

Peter N. D. Pirie, the contributor of this article, is Professor of Geography at the University of Hawaii and has done research in Western Samoa.

Western Samoa

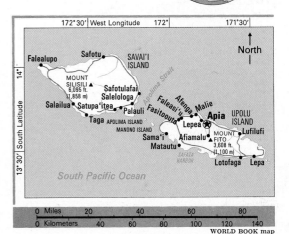

⊛ Capital

• Other City or Town

— Road

▲ MOUNTAIN

～ River

New Zealand National Publicity Studios

Most Western Samoan Houses have thatched roofs and open sides because of the country's warm, pleasant climate.

Authenticated News Int.

Polynesians, such as the men and women shown above, make up about 90 per cent of the population of Western Samoa.

residents was the noted writer Robert Louis Stevenson, who lived there several years. He died there and was buried near Apia in 1894.

Western Samoa's official name in Samoan is SAMOA I SISIFO. Apia, a city with more than 30,000 persons, is the capital and only city (see APIA).

Government. Western Samoa's head of state, Malietoa Tanumafili II, holds office for life. When he dies, the Legislative Assembly will elect a head of state every five years from one of Samoa's two royal families.

The 47 members of the Legislative Assembly serve three-year terms. Forty-five members are elected by *matai* (heads of Samoan family groups) and two are elected by people—chiefly Europeans—who do not belong to matai. The 45 assembly members elected by the matai elect the prime minister. The prime minister selects a cabinet from among these assembly members.

───────── **FACTS IN BRIEF** ─────────

Capital: Apia.
Official Languages: Samoan and English.
Form of Government: Parliamentary.
Area: 1,097 sq. mi. (2,842 km²). *Greatest Distances*—east-west, on each of the two main islands, 47 mi. (76 km); north-south, 15 mi. (24 km) on Upolu, 27 mi. (43 km) on Savai'i. *Coastline* (total for both islands)—about 230 mi. (370 km).
Elevation: *Highest*—Mount Silisili (on Savai'i), 6,095 ft. (1,858 m). *Lowest*—sea level.
Population: *Estimated 1980 Population*—157,000; distribution, 70 per cent rural, 30 per cent urban; density, 142 persons per sq. mi. (55 persons per km²). *1971 Census*—151,275. *Estimated 1985 Population*—165,000.
Chief Products: *Agriculture*—bananas, cacao, coconuts.
Flag: The flag has a red field with a blue canton in the upper left-hand corner. Five white stars on the canton symbolize the Southern Cross constellation. The red, white, and blue colors stand for loyalty, purity, and patriotism. Adopted in 1962. See FLAG (picture: Flags of Asia and the Pacific).
Money: *Basic Unit*—Tala.

The prime minister and cabinet actually run the government. Laws passed by the assembly do not go into effect until the head of state approves them. A *pulenu'u* (head chief) is appointed to represent the government in each village. There are no political parties.

People. Most Samoans are of full Polynesian descent. About 10 per cent of the people are of mixed Samoan and European descent. A few Europeans, Chinese, and persons from other Pacific islands live in Western Samoa. The people speak *Samoan*, a Polynesian dialect. The better-educated people also speak English.

Samoans live simply, much as their ancestors did. Samoan life centers around the family. The people live with their relatives in family groups called *aiga*. The aiga elects a matai who serves as head of the family. Some of the young people resent the matai power, but the system is still strong.

The people live in open-sided *fale* (houses) that have a thatched roof supported by poles. They let down palm leaf blinds when it rains. Most Samoan men and some women wear only a *lava-lava*, a piece of cloth wrapped around the waist like a skirt. Some wear a blouse or shirt with their lava-lava. Most of the women wear dresses, or a skirt and blouse.

Samoans greatly enjoy dancing. They also love to play their own version of cricket, a game they learned from the English missionaries. They play cricket with teams that may have from 10 to 300 players, compared to 11 players in a normal cricket game.

Almost all Samoans are Christians. The most important religious groups in the country are the Congregational, Methodist, and Roman Catholic.

Western Samoa provides good medical care and the people are generally healthy. Most districts have government hospitals that provide free care.

Most Samoans can read and write Samoan. About half of them can read and write English. Education is free, but not compulsory. The government operates elementary schools in most villages, and also has a few high schools. Some lessons are given by radio in all government schools. Many children attend mission schools. Western Samoa has four colleges. Some students go overseas for further schooling.

Land. The islands of Western Samoa were formed by erupting volcanoes. A volcano on Savai'i is still active. It last erupted from 1905 to 1911, covering part of the island with lava rock that is still bare. The islands are fringed with coral reefs.

The island shores are lined with tall, graceful coconut palm trees. The rocky, reddish-brown soil near the coasts is fertile enough to produce bananas; *taro*, a plant with an edible underground stem; and *cacao*, a tree whose seeds are used to make chocolate and cocoa. Further inland, heavy rains have *leached* the soil (dissolved the minerals and washed them away). Few food crops can grow there. Tropical rain forests cover the high volcanic peaks at the center of the islands.

The climate is tropical and humid, but the southeast trade winds make it mild. Temperatures seldom rise above 85° F. (29° C) or fall below 75° F. (24° C). Rainfall ranges from about 70 inches (180 centimeters) a year on the northwest coast to over 150 inches (381 centimeters) in the southeast. The most pleasant months are from May to September, when the temperatures and rainfall are lowest.

Economy is based on agriculture, and about 70 per cent of the people are farmers. The chief food crops are bananas, coconuts, tropical fruit called *breadfruit*, and taro. The people also raise pigs and chickens and catch fish for food. They export some bananas, cacao, and *copra* (dried coconut meat).

The annual average income in Samoa, including government allowances, is about $75. This is very low by world standards, but most Samoans have little need for money. They raise most of their own food, build their own houses, and make most of their own clothing.

Some of the people work for the government, for traders in Apia, or for the missions. People of mixed Samoan and European descent run many of the businesses. Western Samoa has few industries. It imports some manufactured goods, processed foods, and petroleum products from New Zealand, Australia, Great Britain, Japan, the United States, and West Germany.

Most villages are linked by roads, and small boats travel regularly between the islands. The Western Samoan airline flies to American Samoa, Tonga, and Fiji. Ocean-going ships dock at Apia, the only port.

History. People have lived in Samoa for at least 2,000 years, probably coming there from Fiji and the New Hebrides. The Samoans drove out invaders from the Tonga Islands and began forming their own nation about 1,000 years ago. Many chiefs ruled the people until a woman, Salamasina, united them in the 1500's.

Jacob Roggeveen, a Dutch explorer, was the first European to reach Samoa. He discovered the islands in 1722. But few Europeans visited Samoa until the first mission was established in Savai'i in 1830. Once the Samoans accepted the missionaries, whaling and trading ships began making regular stops in the islands.

Two royal families ruled different parts of Samoa during the mid-1800's, and they fought among themselves over who would be king. Germany, Great Britain, and the United States supported rival groups. In 1899,

the three countries agreed that Germany and the United States would divide the islands, and Germany took control of Western Samoa in 1900. Germany improved farm production and also expanded the economy.

In 1914, a military force from New Zealand occupied German Samoa. After World War I, the League of Nations gave New Zealand a *mandate* (order) to govern Western Samoa.

New Zealand's rule began disastrously. An influenza epidemic struck Western Samoa in 1918 and about one-fifth of the people died. The New Zealand government became more and more unpopular in the 1920's. In 1926, Samoans began refusing to obey the laws or cooperate with the government. They continued their civil disobedience activities until 1936, when New Zealand officials met some of their demands.

After World War II, the United Nations made Western Samoa a trust territory and asked New Zealand to begin preparing the islands for independence. In 1957, members of the Legislative Assembly were elected for the first time and Samoan members controlled the assembly. A Cabinet headed by a Samoan prime minister gained executive powers in 1959. In 1961, the people voted to accept a new constitution. Western Samoa became independent on Jan. 1, 1962. It joined the Commonwealth of Nations in 1970. PETER N. D. PIRIE

WESTERN UNION TELEGRAPH COMPANY owns and operates a commercial telegraph system and many other communication services in the United States. In 1861, the company completed the first transcontinental telegraph line in the United States. This line made it possible for coast-to-coast messages to be received almost instantly. It also helped end the pony express (see PONY EXPRESS).

In 1851, a group of men in Rochester, N.Y., organized the New York and Mississippi Valley Printing Telegraph Company. The name of the firm was changed to Western Union Telegraph Company in 1856. The firm grew rapidly during the late 1800's and built a national telegraph system. By 1900, it operated two transatlantic cables and more than 1 million miles (1.6 million kilometers) of telegraph wire.

Through the years, Western Union has modernized its equipment and introduced new communication services. In 1945, for example, it started to send messages via radio beams relayed by a network of transmitting towers. Prior to this development, messages were sent by means of electrical impulses transmitted through telegraph wires. In 1970, the company introduced the Mailgram message service, which combines the facilities of Western Union and the U.S. Postal Service to deliver messages.

In 1974, Western Union began operating the first domestic satellite communications system in the United States. This system, called *Westar*, consists of two orbiting satellites and six transmitting stations on the earth. The system handles telephone calls and television programs in addition to telegraph transmissions. Western Union's headquarters are at 1 Lake Street, Upper Saddle River, N.J. 07458.

Critically reviewed by the WESTERN UNION TELEGRAPH COMPANY

See also TELEGRAPH.

WESTERN WALL. See WAILING WALL.

WESTINGHOUSE, GEORGE

George Westinghouse
Brown Bros.

WESTINGHOUSE, GEORGE (1846-1914), an American inventor and manufacturer, invented the air brake for railroad trains. He introduced alternating current for electric power transmission. He invented a system of pipes to conduct natural gas into homes safely. He also invented the gas meter.

Westinghouse was born on Oct. 6, 1846, in Central Bridge, N.Y. As a boy, he worked in his father's machine shop. At 15 he invented a rotary engine. He served in the Union army and navy during the Civil War.

By 1866, he had already perfected two inventions, a device for replacing derailed railroad cars and a railroad frog, which made it possible for a train to pass from one track to another. Westinghouse perfected the air brake in 1868. The brake was immediately successful, and he organized a company to produce it. He patented hundreds of inventions and organized over 50 companies. He was president of 30 corporations, including the Westinghouse Electric Company. W. H. BAUGHN

See also BRAKE.

WESTINGHOUSE ELECTRIC CORPORATION is one of the world's largest producers of machines and equipment that control, distribute, generate, and use electric power. It produces about 8,000 products that range from light bulbs to computers and nuclear reactors. The company sells its products throughout the world.

For electric utilities and industry, Westinghouse builds steam and gas turbines, transformers, motors, and electrical control equipment of many kinds. It also develops entire electrical systems for industry and the armed services. Its construction and consumer products include air-conditioning, lighting, and X-ray equipment.

The corporation has designed and built nuclear reactors and equipment for many nuclear-powered generating stations throughout the United States and overseas. Nuclear reactors produced by Westinghouse provide power for most of the U.S. Navy's nuclear-powered ships.

Main Westinghouse offices are in Pittsburgh. The company owns and operates many radio and television stations. It was founded by George Westinghouse in 1886. For the sales, assets, and number of employees, see MANUFACTURING (table: 100 Leading U.S. Manufacturers).

Critically reviewed by the WESTINGHOUSE ELECTRIC CORPORATION

WESTMINSTER, the government district of London. See LONDON (Greater London; picture).

WESTMINSTER, STATUTE OF. See CANADA, GOVERNMENT OF (International Relations).

WESTMINSTER ABBEY is a great national church that stands near the Houses of Parliament in London. This church is world-famous and is one of the most beautiful in England. Its official name is the Collegiate Church of Saint Peter. Its name of Abbey comes from the fact that it once served as the church of an ancient monastery.

Westminster Abbey marked the scene of many great events in English history. All the English rulers from the time of William the Conqueror, except Edward V and Edward VIII, were crowned there. In the chapel of Edward the Confessor stands the old Coronation Chair that dates from 1300. See CORONATION.

Burial in Westminster Abbey is one of the greatest honors England can give. Many kings and queens are buried in the chapel of Henry VII. Political leaders and other important people of England are buried in other parts of the Abbey. The bodies of many of England's greatest poets lie in the Poets' Corner.

The Coronation Chair in Westminster Abbey was built to enclose the *Stone of Scone*, which Edward I seized from Scotland in 1296.
Pix

Westminster Abbey in London is a shrine of the British Commonwealth and the burial place of Britain's honored dead.
Pix

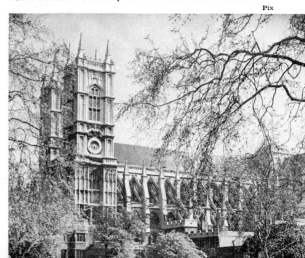

Westminster Abbey became the seat of a bishop in 1539. This act made the Abbey a cathedral. However, only this one bishop has ever served there. A dean has headed the Abbey from the time of Queen Elizabeth I to the present day.

Edward the Confessor built a church on the site of the Abbey between about 1042 and 1065. But the main part of the Abbey was begun in 1245 by Henry III. He made the Abbey one of the best examples of French Gothic architecture in England (see GOTHIC ART). In the 1500's, Henry VII added the chapel that bears his name. The towers were completed in 1740.

The floor plan of Westminster Abbey is in the shape of a Latin cross. The church is 513 feet (156 meters) long. The *transepts* (crossarms) extend 203 feet (62 meters). The *nave* (main hall) is 38 feet (12 meters) wide and 102 feet (31 meters) high. The twin towers on the west are 225 feet (69 meters) high. The square central tower barely rises above the roof.

Cloisters surrounding the Abbey date from the 1200's and 1300's. The chapter house was built in the 1200's. West of the main cloisters is the famous Jerusalem Chamber, dating from the 1300's. Air raids in World War II damaged parts of the Abbey. A program designed to completely restore Westminster Abbey and maintain it began in 1953.   ALAN GOWANS

WESTMINSTER CHOIR is one of the most famous choral organizations in the United States. It was founded in 1921 by John Finley Williamson in connection with the Westminster Choir School (now College) in Princeton, N.J.

WESTMINSTER CHOIR COLLEGE. See UNIVERSITIES AND COLLEGES (table).

WESTMINSTER COLLEGE. See UNIVERSITIES AND COLLEGES (table).

WESTMINSTER HALL is a building connected with the House of Parliament in London. Originally, it was the great hall of the Palace of Westminster, where the rulers of England held court for almost 500 years. Many great events in English history took place in the hall. Sir Thomas More, Lady Jane Grey, the Earl of Strafford, and Warren Hastings stood trial there. Charles I was condemned to death there. William II built the hall in 1097. Westminster Hall is 240 feet (73 meters) long, 68 feet (21 meters) wide, and 89½ feet (27 meters) high.   TALBOT HAMLIN

WESTMINSTER KENNEL CLUB SHOW. See DOG (Dog Shows).

WESTMINSTER SCHOOL is one of the oldest public schools of England. Henry VIII founded it in 1540 as part of Westminster Abbey. Its official name is SAINT PETER'S COLLEGE.

WESTMONT COLLEGE. See UNIVERSITIES AND COLLEGES (table).

WESTMORELAND, WILLIAM CHILDS (1914-   ), commanded United States forces in the Vietnam War from 1964 to 1968. He directed U.S. operations in a war that had no battle lines (see Vietnam WAR). He became Army chief of staff when he returned from Vietnam and remained in that position until he retired in 1972. Westmoreland sought the Republican nomination for governor of South Carolina in 1974, but he lost the party's primary election.

General Westmoreland was born in Spartanburg County, South Carolina. He graduated from the U.S. Military Academy in 1936. From 1942 to 1944, during World War II, he fought as an army artillery officer in Tunisia, Sicily, France, Belgium, and Germany. As chief of staff of the Ninth Infantry Division, he fought in Germany in 1944 and 1945. Westmoreland commanded a combat team and made two parachute jumps in battle during the Korean War. From 1960 to 1963, he was superintendent of the U.S. Military Academy. In January, 1964, Westmoreland went to Vietnam as deputy commander of United States forces there.

WESTMOUNT, Quebec (pop. 22,153), is a residential suburb of Montreal. It was incorporated as a village in 1874 and became a city in 1908. It has a council-manager form of government.

WESTON, EDWARD (1850-1936), an inventor and manufacturer, was noted for pioneering in the development of electric meters. He began manufacturing meters in 1882, and founded the Weston Electric Instrument Company in 1888.

Born near Wolverhampton, England, Weston moved to the United States in 1870. He entered the electroplating business, and developed an electroplating generator, an arc-lighting system, and an incandescent lighting system.   ROBERT P. MULTHAUF

WESTON, EDWARD (1886-1958), was an American photographer. He produced dramatic pictures of people, landscapes, and such simple objects as seashells, seaweed, and rocks. Many of Weston's photographs emphasize the forms and textures of objects and scenes from nature.

Weston was born in Highland Park, Ill. Early in his career, he won many awards for his photographs in the hazy, out-of-focus style that had become popular in the late 1800's. In the 1920's, however, Weston adopted the technique of *straight photography*, a style featuring focused, detailed photographs that portray subjects simply and directly. In 1932, he helped form a group of progressive photographers who promoted straight photography.

In 1937, Weston became the first photographer to win a Guggenheim Fellowship, a grant given to scholars, scientists, and artists to advance their work. His close-up photograph called "Halved Cabbage" appears in the PHOTOGRAPHY article.   CHARLES HAGEN

WESTOVER AIR FORCE BASE, Mass., is a United States Air Force site for training Air Force reservists flying tactical airlift planes. The base covers over 4,900 acres (1,980 hectares), and lies about 3 miles (5 kilometers) north of Chicopee Falls, Mass. The base was established in 1940. It was named for Major General Oscar Westover, chief of the Air Corps, who was killed in an airplane crash in 1938.   RICHARD M. SKINNER

WESTPHALIA, *wehst FAYL yuh,* is a former Prussian province of western Germany. *Westphalia,* or *Westfalen* in German, means *western plain.* It lies just east of The Netherlands. For location, see GERMANY (political map). Westphalia once belonged to the Duchy of Saxony. In the late 1100's, the name *Westphalia* was given to a region ruled by the Archbishop of Cologne. Prussia gained control of the area at the Congress of Vienna (1814-1815). In 1946, Westphalia became part of the state of North Rhine-Westphalia.   JAMES K. POLLOCK

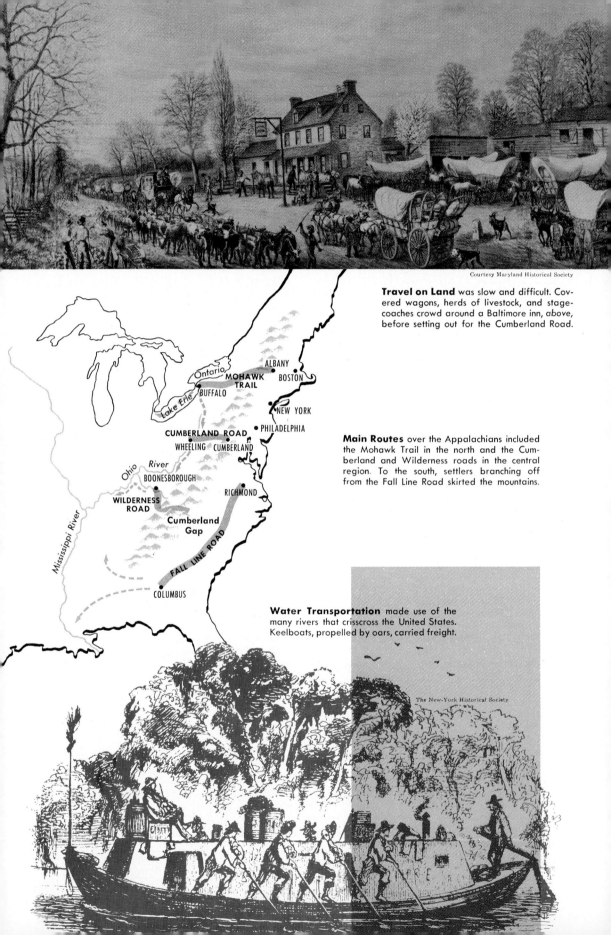

Travel on Land was slow and difficult. Covered wagons, herds of livestock, and stagecoaches crowd around a Baltimore inn, *above*, before setting out for the Cumberland Road.

Main Routes over the Appalachians included the Mohawk Trail in the north and the Cumberland and Wilderness roads in the central region. To the south, settlers branching off from the Fall Line Road skirted the mountains.

Water Transportation made use of the many rivers that crisscross the United States. Keelboats, propelled by oars, carried freight.

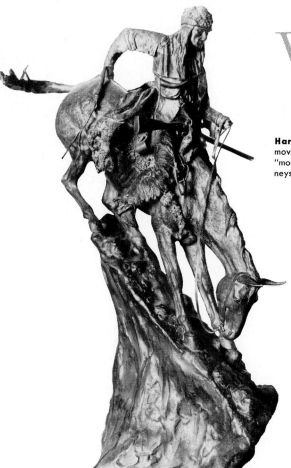

WESTWARD MOVEMENT

Hardy Explorers, Trappers, and Traders led the movement westward. Frederic Remington's sculpture of a "mountain man" dramatizes the dangerous, lonely journeys of these men who loved the "wide-open spaces."

lonely prairies, and long stretches of waterless desert.

The men, women, and children of the westward movement struggled across the continent on foot and on horseback through the Cumberland Gap. They rode on canal barges through the Erie Canal and floated on rafts down the broad Ohio. Some went on steamboats down the Mississippi and up the Missouri. Others loaded all their household goods into covered wagons and followed the Santa Fe and Oregon trails.

The westward movement took place in several stages. The first frontiers along the Atlantic Coast had become settled by 1763. The pioneers then began to move across the Appalachian Mountains in the period up to 1815. After the War of 1812, pioneers flocked west and south to settle the land around the Great Lakes, along the Gulf of Mexico, and in the Mississippi Valley. From 1840 to 1860, the settlers moved into Utah, California, and the Oregon country. During and after the Civil War, cattlemen, miners, and farmers settled the Rocky Mountain region and the Great Plains. Finally, in 1890, the Superintendent of the Census announced that a frontier no longer separated the settled and unsettled parts of the United States.

For descriptions of the life of the people during this period, see the separate articles on COLONIAL LIFE IN AMERICA, PIONEER LIFE, and WESTERN FRONTIER LIFE.

The First Frontiers

The Original Settlements. America's first frontier was really a frontier of Europe. Pioneers created it in the early 1600's as they built their villages along the Atlantic Coast: Jamestown in Virginia, St. Mary's in Maryland, Plymouth and Boston in Massachusetts, and New Amsterdam in New York. As each feeble outpost grew, it served as a gateway to the interior. From Jamestown and St. Mary's, new settlers from England moved out along the river valleys of the James, the Rappahannock, and the Potomac, where the soils were deep and rich. Then they pushed into the higher land that lay between the valleys. From Plymouth, Boston, and New Amsterdam, settlers spread along the coast, turning forests into fields and marshes into pastures. Then they, too, moved on, conquering the river bottoms in the Connecticut, Merrimac, and Hudson valleys. By 1670, pioneers had settled in the coastal lowlands as far as the *fall line*, where waterfalls or rapids stopped navigation.

The Appalachian Highland. Now the advance into a new frontier began. Just west of the fall line lay the hilly

WESTWARD MOVEMENT carried the settlers of North America across the entire continent. For more than 200 years, daring pioneers pushed the frontier westward. Hardy men and women blazed trails, cleared land, and set up new settlements from the Appalachian Mountains to the Pacific Ocean. They made it possible for others who followed to turn the vast wilderness into prosperous lands of farms and cities. The lure of the West drew people like a magnet, even though the westward movement halted for short periods of time.

No matter what their origin, or why they sought new homes, most of the people caught up in the westward movement were courageous, hard-working, and helpful to their neighbors. Out of the experiences of the westward movement, an American national character developed, with traits and institutions found nowhere else in the world.

The daring pioneers dreamed of a better world in which they and their families could live. They had the courage to turn their backs on the comforts of civilization and set out into the little-known West to make their dreams come true. They had to fight off attacks by Indians and shoot wild animals for food. Nature itself slowed their progress with thick forests, high mountains,

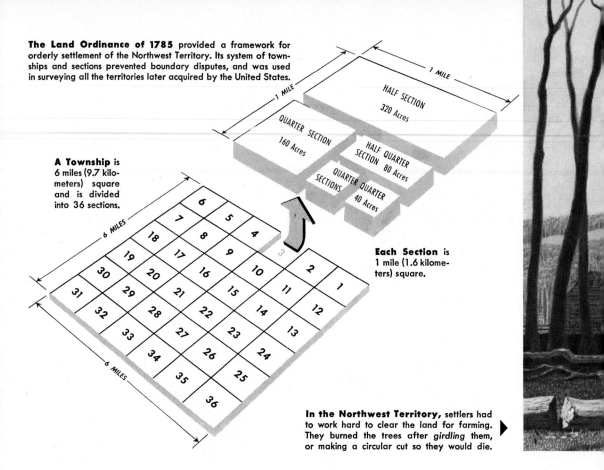

The Land Ordinance of 1785 provided a framework for orderly settlement of the Northwest Territory. Its system of townships and sections prevented boundary disputes, and was used in surveying all the territories later acquired by the United States.

1 MILE

HALF SECTION
320 Acres

QUARTER SECTION
160 Acres

HALF QUARTER SECTION 80 Acres

QUARTER QUARTER
SECTIONS 40 Acres

1 MILE

A Township is 6 miles (9.7 kilometers) square and is divided into 36 sections.

6 MILES

6 MILES

6 MILES

6	5	4	3	2	1
7	8	9	10	11	12
18	17	16	15	14	13
19	20	21	22	23	24
30	29	28	27	26	25
31	32	33	34	35	36

Each Section is 1 mile (1.6 kilometers) square.

In the Northwest Territory, settlers had to work hard to clear the land for farming. They burned the trees after *girdling* them, or making a circular cut so they would die.

uplands at the base of the Appalachian Mountains. Settlers began a new pattern when they occupied this area, often called "the Old West." Some pioneers moved into the area from the coastal plains, following the old pattern of looking for better lands. But others were Scotch-Irish and German farmers who fled famine and persecution in Europe by the tens of thousands during the early 1700's. Most of them landed in the new colony of Pennsylvania, where William Penn welcomed oppressed persons of every race and creed. These new farmers could not afford expensive lands near the coast, so they moved into the interior of Pennsylvania. Their descendants still live in this region. When these lands became occupied, newcomers turned to the north or south along the Great Valley of the Appalachians, which promised greater opportunity than the rugged mountains lying just to the west. Through the years, their tidy settlements filled the Shenandoah Valley of Virginia, then extended into the mountain valleys of the Carolinas. Other settlers turned northward into the Hudson and Mohawk valleys of New York. By the 1760's, these communities stretched in a long line that bordered the western frontier of the thirteen colonies.

The pattern of life in "the Old West" reflected the frontier surroundings the people faced. The rugged pioneers in this back-country area were separated from many contacts with Europe that continued along the seaboard. They built log cabins instead of frame houses, and wore deerskins rather than imported fabrics. They felt more at home in the deep forests than on the streets of Philadelphia or Boston. They copied large "Palatine

barns" from the Germans, and developed a German weapon into the efficient *Kentucky rifle*, one of the most important tools in conquering the wilderness. The Scotch-Irish contributed Presbyterian *circuit riders*, or wandering preachers (see CIRCUIT RIDER).

Regional Conflicts. The differences between the frontier and the East led to quarrels that burst into open conflict just before the Revolutionary War. Neither side trusted the other. Easterners regarded frontier people as wild savages who could not handle their own affairs. Westerners felt that the wealthy people in the east wanted to keep them from governing themselves, and meant to tax them out of existence. These conflicts almost led to bloodshed in Pennsylvania in 1764. Pioneers gathered at Paxton and other western towns to march on the capital at Philadelphia. Benjamin Franklin turned "the Paxton Boys" back before they reached the capital. Then trouble flamed in the Carolinas, where pioneers formed a society called "The Regulation." Members vowed to stop paying taxes until they were sure that the money would be spent properly. Colonial officials branded the "Regulators" as outlaws and sent troops to subdue them. The "rebels" lost the Battle of Saluda River in South Carolina in 1769 and the Battle of Alamance in North Carolina in 1771. Many of them fled farther west to escape punishment.

Across the Mountains, 1763-1815

Some of the thirteen original colonies claimed land to the west of the Appalachian Mountains. But the French actually controlled most of this territory until

after the British won the French and Indian Wars (see FRENCH AND INDIAN WARS). Then the way was open for settlers to push into the heart of North America. But before the rush could begin, pioneers had to get around British restrictions. Great Britain hoped to prevent Indian wars by rigidly regulating the course and speed of the westward movement. For this purpose, the British government issued the Proclamation of 1763 (see FRANKLIN, STATE OF [map]). It decreed that no settlers could move into the lands beyond a line drawn through the mountains. But pressure from impatient settlers and land speculators forced this line steadily westward. The treaties of Hard Labor and Fort Stanwix opened the back country of Virginia (now West Virginia), New York, and Pennsylvania in 1768.

New Settlements. The bold frontiersmen paid little attention to official borders. As long as good lands lay ahead, nothing could hold them back. Between 1763 and 1776, frontiersmen pushed forward in three areas. One area was western Pennsylvania and what is now West Virginia. Settlers transformed Fort Pitt into Pittsburgh, and built their cabins in the nearby river valleys. In eastern Tennessee, James Robertson and John Sevier helped build bustling communities along the Holston, Watauga, and Clinch rivers (see WATAUGA ASSOCIATION). The third area was the Bluegrass country of Kentucky—the land of Daniel Boone. In 1775, Boone blazed the Wilderness Road through the Cumberland Gap and led a band of settlers westward to build their cabins at Boonesborough (see WILDERNESS ROAD). Other settlers established St. Asaph's Station, Leestown,

and other outposts. All that year, the wilderness rang with the sound of axes and the crash of falling trees.

When the Revolutionary War broke out in 1775, Indian raiders, often encouraged by the British, drove most of the pioneers back east of the mountains. In 1778, George Rogers Clark led an expedition into Illinois territory to attack British outposts that were stirring up trouble. His successful exploits were important in obtaining the vast Northwest Territory for the United States (see NORTHWEST TERRITORY; REVOLUTIONARY WAR IN AMERICA [Clark's Campaign]). As soon as the fighting ended, settlers surged westward again. By the time American independence was recognized in 1783, western Pennsylvania teemed with settlers, and some 25,000 persons lived in Kentucky. Eastern Tennessee bustled with activity.

Solving Frontier Problems. The rapid growth of new settlements created many difficulties. The newly formed government of the United States had to find some way to sell land, provide government for the West, and get the Indians to withdraw peacefully. The first two problems were solved brilliantly.

The Ordinance of 1785 provided for surveys of the Northwest Territory into townships 6 miles (9.7 kilometers) square. Townships were divided into sections of 1 square mile, or 640 acres (259 hectares). The sections were sold at auction at a minimum price of $1 an acre. This system freed settlers from conflicts over land titles.

The Northwest Ordinance, or Ordinance of 1787, set up government for the new area. This ordinance assured

203

In the 1760's, settlers had pushed westward into the Appalachian highlands. Some had gone beyond the mountains, in spite of a law against it.

By 1783, communities had grown up as far west as the Mississippi. The newly independent nation had to find ways of protecting and governing these outlying territories.

During the Early 1800's, land-hungry pioneers staked out claims in the fertile areas beyond the Mississippi River. Traders, trappers, and explorers ventured even farther west.

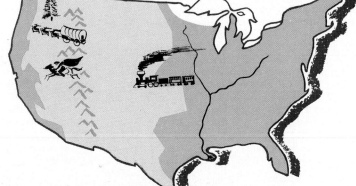

As Early as 1850, Americans had reached the Pacific Coast. During the next 40 years, miners, ranchers, and farmers filled up the sparsely settled regions of the Great Plains.

IMPORTANT DATES IN THE WESTWARD MOVEMENT

1775 Daniel Boone opened the Wilderness Road, which aided the settlement of Kentucky.

1778-1779 George Rogers Clark's campaign won the Northwest Territory for the United States.

1785 The Land Ordinance provided an orderly system for surveying and selling government lands.

1787 The Northwest Ordinance provided for government and encouraged education in the Northwest Territory.

1794 Victory over the Indians and a treaty with Great Britain brought peace to the Northwest Territory.

1795 Pinckney's Treaty with Spain opened the mouth of the Mississippi River to American navigation.

1803 The Louisiana Purchase opened a vast area beyond the Mississippi River to American settlers.

1804-1805 Lewis and Clark explored the northern part of the Louisiana Territory.

1825 The Erie Canal opened, providing improved transportation westward.

1845 The United States annexed Texas.

1846 A treaty with Great Britain added the Oregon country to the United States.

1846-1848 War with Mexico resulted in the acquisition of California and the Southwest.

1848 The discovery of gold in California inspired the gold rush.

1862 The Homestead Act promised free land to settlers in the West.

1869 The first transcontinental rail system was completed.

1890 Settlement of the main areas of the western United States brought an end to the frontier.

The Museum of Science and Industry, Chicago

Pioneers East of the Mississippi often walked all the way in order to spare their livestock. They usually found fuel, water, and plentiful game along the trail. Joshua Shaw, an early pioneer, drew these sketches of the men and women with whom he traveled in the 1820's.

Bettmann Archive

Crossing the Plains, settlers faced severe hardships. New graves and abandoned wagons marked many of the trails leading west. But most people pressed onward in spite of fuel and water shortages, bad weather, and hostile Indians.

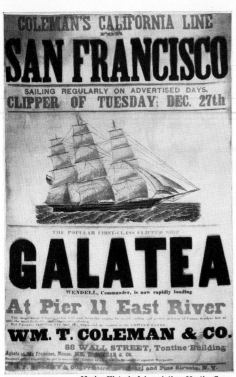

Marine Historical Association, Mystic, Conn.

The Smithsonian Institution

"Gold Fever" Infected Almost Everyone. San Francisco Harbor in the winter of 1852-1853 presented an odd sight. Hundreds of ships had been left to rot while their crews went off to "strike it rich" in the gold fields.

The Gold Rush carried thousands of Americans westward after the precious metal was discovered in 1848. A clipper ship could make the trip from New York City to California, sailing around Cape Horn, in about 115 days.

pioneers that they would not lose their right to self-government when they moved to the frontier. See NORTHWEST ORDINANCE.

Removal of the Indians proved more difficult. European governments used the Indians as pawns in their efforts to harass the weak new United States. British agents encouraged Indians in the Northwest Territory to go on the warpath in the early 1790's. The Indians defeated two expeditions before General Anthony Wayne led a third party that routed them in the Battle of Fallen Timbers in 1794 (see INDIAN WARS [Other Midwestern Conflicts]). A year later, Wayne forced the Indians to sign the Treaty of Greenville, in which they surrendered the southern half of Ohio to the United States. In 1794, the British signed the Jay Treaty, giving up their Northwest posts (see JAY TREATY). Pinckney's Treaty of 1795 settled a conflict with Spain in the Southwest. This treaty gave westerners the right to send their products down the Mississippi River for export.

These military and diplomatic triumphs brought peace to the frontier after 1795 and launched one of the greatest westward migrations in history. During two months in 1795, more than 25,000 people crossed the Cumberland River into western Tennessee. The tide of newcomers became so great that Kentucky achieved statehood in 1792 and Tennessee in 1796. Far to the north, New Englanders flooded into western New York after the Iroquois Indians were forced out. Other settlers pushed into the Ohio lands opened by the Treaty of Greenville. They bought land from the government or from the Ohio Company, a New England land-speculating firm that had obtained title to much of the Muskingum Valley (see OHIO COMPANY). Marietta, Ohio, founded in 1788, became the first seat of government in the Northwest Territory. Ohio became a state in 1803,

and the stream of settlers flowed steadily westward.

New Indian wars halted the westward-flowing tide in 1808 and 1809. Led by the Shawnee chief Tecumseh, the Indians struck back against the frontiersmen who were seizing their hunting grounds in the Midwest (see TECUMSEH). The Indian warfare soon merged into a larger struggle, the War of 1812. This war gave the westerners an opportunity to win two important victories over the Indians. Tecumseh was killed in the first, the Battle of the Thames, in 1813. In the second, the Battle of Horseshoe Bend, in 1814, a militia force under General Andrew Jackson defeated the Creek Indians of Georgia. The Indians then surrendered most of their lands east of Alabama without further struggle.

Settling the Midwest and South, 1815-1840

The "Great Migration" to the frontier that began after the War of 1812 was more spectacular than all those that had gone before. Within five years after the war ended in 1815, about 1,250,000 persons had built new homes in the level lands near the Great Lakes or on the Gulf Plains bordering the Gulf of Mexico.

The Old Northwest. In the years just after the War of 1812, thousands of newcomers established small farms in the Northwest Territory, called *the Old Northwest.* Most of these people came from the South, where the growth of plantations had driven them out. By 1830, their settlements filled southern Indiana and Illinois, and they were overrunning Missouri beyond the Mississippi River. After that time, most newcomers came from the Northeast and settled around the Great Lakes. By 1836, Detroit had grown into a sizable community, with many schools and churches, a theater, a museum, and a public garden. The opening of the Erie Canal in 1825 gave settlers a convenient and inexpensive way

Prospectors at Their "Diggings" looked for gold in and near streams. A day's "washing" might yield as much as $500. But hundreds of them returned home with little to show for their labor.

William A. Croft, *Pioneers in the Settlement of America*, 1876

to move west. At the same time, the canal started the "rural decay" of New England. Farmers on the hilly fields of New England and New York found they could not compete with farmers on the fertile plains around the Great Lakes. Many of them sold out or simply abandoned their farms, and moved west. Others moved to the growing cities nearby. By 1840 almost all the Old Northwest had been carved into states. See ERIE CANAL.

The Gulf Plains and Florida. During this period, pioneers were also moving into the newly acquired territory of Florida. Another stream of settlers began pouring into the land bordering the Gulf of Mexico, known as *the Old Southwest*. These pioneers came almost entirely from the Southeast, and all had one ambition—to find good fields where they could grow cotton. Western Georgia was occupied first. Then, as the government uprooted Indian tribes from Alabama and Mississippi, these states were quickly overrun. The area around Natchez, Miss., had 75,000 persons by 1820. Small farmers led the rush, as they had in the Old Northwest. Following them came planters who brought slaves and money in the hope of buying good cotton land. Their plantations soon blanketed the best soil of the entire Gulf Plains region. The small farmers were doomed to poorer lands. By 1840, settlers had occupied the entire area, and pioneers were already pushing beyond the Mississippi to begin the conquest of the Far West. Behind them, they left the roaring life of river-boat gamblers, outlaws, and adventurers who moved between Natchez and New Orleans.

Beyond the Mississippi, 1803-1840

Exploration. When President Thomas Jefferson bought Louisiana from France in 1803, he focused American attention on the territory beyond the Missis-

sippi River (see LOUISIANA PURCHASE). Jefferson was curious about the vast area he had purchased in one of the greatest real-estate bargains in history. He sent a number of exploring expeditions westward. Most important was the Lewis and Clark expedition. Between 1804 and 1805, Meriwether Lewis and William Clark followed the Missouri River to its source, crossed the continental divide, and reached the Pacific Ocean at the mouth of the Columbia River. Zebulon M. Pike, who set out in 1806 to explore southern Louisiana, was less successful. A Mexican army captured his expedition near the headwaters of the Rio Grande River in Mexico and held the party for several months. The War of 1812 stopped exploration until 1820, when Major Stephen H. Long investigated the lands near the Red and Arkansas rivers. He called the whole Great Plains region "the Great American Desert," and branded it unfit for occupation.

Far to the north, Canadian explorers also pushed westward. Sir Alexander Mackenzie, Simon Fraser, and David Thompson led expeditions to the Pacific Coast in the late 1700's and early 1800's. In 1812, Scottish immigrants under Lord Selkirk founded the Red River Colony in Manitoba. But Canada's west did not attract heavy settlement for many years.

The true explorers of the West were traders and fur trappers, not government or company agents. In 1821, adventurous traders opened the Santa Fe route between New Mexico and Missouri. Fur trappers were even more important than traders in the conquest of the West. These far-roaming "mountain men" began trapping beavers and other animals in the Rocky Mountain country in the mid-1820's. Some trading companies sent exploring parties to search for untrapped streams. Jedediah Smith, who led two expeditions to the Pacific

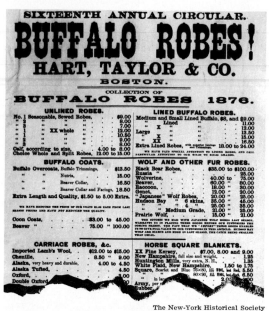

SIXTEENTH ANNUAL CIRCULAR.
BUFFALO ROBES!
HART, TAYLOR & CO.
BOSTON.
COLLECTION OF
BUFFALO ROBES 1876.

UNLINED ROBES.		LINED BUFFALO ROBES.	
No. 1 Seasonable, Sewed Robes,	$9.00	Medium and Small Lined Buffalo, $8, and $9.00	
" 2 " " "	8.00	Lined	11.00
" 3 " " "	7.00	" "	11.00
" 1 XX whole "	12.00	Large X " "	13.50
" 2 " " "	10.50	" I " "	13.50
" 3 " " "	9.00	" XX " "	15.00
" 0 " " "	8.00	" " "	16.50
Calf, according to size,	4.00 to 8.00	Extra Lined Robes, with superior linings 18.00 to 24.00	
Choice Whole and Split Robes,	12.00 to 15.00	WE HAVE PAID SPECIAL ATTENTION TO LINING ROBES, AND CALL PARTICULAR ATTENTION TO OUR $10.00 TO $16.00 GRADES.	

BUFFALO COATS.		WOLF AND OTHER FUR ROBES.	
Buffalo Overcoats, Buffalo Trimmings,	$13.50	Black Bear Robes,	$35.00 to $100.00
" " Nutria,	15.00	Russia,	25.00
" " Beaver Collar,	16.50	Wolverine,	40.00 to 75.00
" " Beaver Collar and Facings,	18.50	Beaver,	60.00 to 90.00
Extra Length and Quality, $1.50 to 5.00 Extra.		Raccoon,	18.00 to 30.00
		Genet,	12.00 to 20.00
WE HAVE REDUCED THE PRICE OF OUR COATS $1.50 EACH FROM LAST SEASON PRICES AND HAVE NOT REDUCED THE QUALITY.		"Japanese" Wolf Robes,	30.00 to 35.00
		Hudson Bay " 6 skins,	35.00 to 45.00
Coon Coats,	$3.00 to 45.00	" " Medium Grade,	25.00 to 35.00
Beaver "	75.00 " 100.00	Prairie Wolf,	21.00 to 25.00
		" " 15.00 to 21.00	
		THE SUCCESS WE HAD WITH JAPANESE WOLF ROBES LAST SEASON, WARRANTS US IN PLACING THESE GOODS BEFORE OUR CUSTOMERS THE COMING SEASON. THE FACT THAT WE "IMPORT" THESE GOODS ENABLES US TO GIVE FULL VALUE TO OUR CUSTOMERS IN THIS ARTICLE. HUDSON BAY WOLF ARE BLACK AND HIGH AS LAST SEASON. THE LINED ROBES ARE SMALLER THAN USUAL.	

CARRIAGE ROBES, &c.		HORSE SQUARE BLANKETS.	
Imported Lamb's Wool,	$12.00 to $15.00	XX Fine Kersey,	$7.00, 8.00 and 9.00
Chenille,	8.50 " 9.00	New Hampshire, full size and weight,	1.25
Alaska, very heavy and durable,	4.00 to 4.50	Huntington Mills, very extra, N. H.,	1.35
Alaska Tufted,	4.50	White Plaid, New Hampshire,	1.50 to 1.75
Oxford,	3.00	Square, Scarlet and Blue 76x80, ill. wool, ea bed, 5.50	
Double Oxford,		" " 80x90, ill. wool, ea bed, 6.50	
		" in large " 2.00 " 9.00	
		Army, per "	
		Rubber,	

The New-York Historical Society

An 1876 Handbill advertises buffalo robes and other items for sale. Millions of buffalo were slaughtered for food, fur, or "sport" by hunters and settlers in the late 1800's.

Coast, probably saw more unexplored territory than any other Americans except Lewis and Clark. By the beginning of the 1840's, most of the beaver had been killed. But, at the same time, the mountain men had investigated almost every nook and cranny of the Far West. They spread word of the riches in the area.

The news came at a time when restless pioneers were already looking for new lands. The farming frontier at this time stopped just beyond the first states west of the Mississippi River. This area had filled up rapidly. Missouri achieved statehood in 1821, and Arkansas in 1836. Iowa received thousands of settlers after Indian lands there were opened in 1833. Beyond these states lay the Great Plains, still known at the time as "the Great American Desert." This giant grassland lacked timber for fuel, fences, and homes. The dry climate did not look promising for growing crops. The area also included a number of Indian reservations, where the government had only recently settled many tribes. There seemed to be no way to get past this barrier, yet pioneers were eager to be on the move.

The Southwest. Some pioneers went southward. Beginning in 1822, great caravans of covered wagons plodded across the plains to Santa Fe, loaded with goods to be traded for Mexican gold and silver. The Santa Fe traders learned how to travel on the plains, and taught later pioneers how to travel. They also speeded expansion into the Southwest by reporting that Mexico had only a weak hold on the region. See SANTA FE TRAIL.

But Texas attracted most of the permanent settlers. This Mexican province was opened to Americans in the 1820's, largely through the efforts of Stephen F. Austin. By 1830, around 20,000 settlers had moved into the area. Conflicts with Mexican officials followed when American pioneers began to outnumber the Mexicans.

These conflicts grew into a revolution in 1835. The Texans under Sam Houston won the Battle of San Jacinto in 1836, and the Republic of Texas was born.

Settling the Far West, 1840-1860

Pioneers soon heard of rich valleys lying far to the west—the Sacramento and San Joaquin valleys of California and the Willamette and Puget Sound valleys of the Oregon Country. The news came from fur traders, from merchants who carried on a thriving sea trade with Spanish missions in California, and from missionaries, who had begun their work in Oregon as early as 1834.

The first major caravans of covered wagons creaked over the Oregon and California trails in 1843. For many years after that, hundreds of eager adventurers gathered at Independence, Mo., every spring to organize caravans. They pushed westward along the Platte River, over the Rocky Mountains through South Pass, and northward to the Snake River. There, some followed the Snake and Columbia rivers to the Oregon Country. Others turned southward across the dusty deserts of Utah and Nevada to the Sierra Nevada mountains. They scaled the mountains, suffering incredible hardships, and arrived at Sutter's Fort (now Sacramento) in California. By 1840, about 5,000 Americans lived in the Oregon Country, and nearly 1,000 in California. See OREGON TRAIL.

This movement had important results. For many years, Great Britain had contested American claims to the Oregon Country. Its Hudson's Bay Company controlled the region. But the trading company feared the newcomers and hurriedly pulled out. Britain surrendered most of the area south of the 49th parallel to the United States in the Oregon Treaty of 1846. That same year, American pioneers in California launched the Bear Flag Rebellion against their Mexican rulers. This outbreak soon became part of the Mexican War. The Treaty of Guadalupe Hidalgo ended the war. It gave the United States not only California but also the entire Southwest. The United States now stretched from sea to sea, with vast new lands open for settlement.

Utah. The first settlers to arrive were not profit-seeking adventurers, but a band of devoted men and women hunting an isolated spot where they could worship their God as they pleased. The Mormons had been persecuted in New York, Ohio, Missouri, and Illinois before they followed Brigham Young westward. The migration that brought them to the shores of Utah's Great Salt Lake in 1847 was one of the best organized in history. Their conquest of the desert was just as well planned. The Mormons used cooperative techniques unique in frontier history. They fenced fields, built irrigation ditches, and laid out Salt Lake City. In a remarkably short time, they established a prosperous community. See MORMONS (History).

California. The early trickle of migration into the Far West swelled to a torrent when a worker at a sawmill near Sacramento discovered gold in the American River early in 1848. At first, the rush attracted only Californians, Mexicans, and Oregonians. But when President James K. Polk discussed the discovery in his message to Congress in December, 1848, gold fever swept the nation. More than 100,000 "Forty-Niners" poured into California. In their camps—given such picturesque names as Poker Flat, Hangtown, and

The End of the Frontier in 1890 brought to a close the era of western expansion. Civilization, in the form of telegraph wires, had come even to the desert. In Henry Farny's painting, a bewildered Indian listens to *The Song of the Talking Wire.*

Skunk Gulch—rooms rented for $1,000 a month, and eggs cost $10 a dozen. Relatively few miners actually found gold, but many others settled down as farmers and shopkeepers. California became a state in 1850.

The Last Frontiers, 1860-1890

Much of the West remained unsettled even after the frontier reached the Pacific Ocean. But during the Civil War, pioneers settled in the mountain and basin region between the Rocky Mountains and the Sierras. After the war, cattle ranchers and farmers occupied the Great Plains. New railroads helped bring an end to the frontier. In the United States, the Union Pacific and Central Pacific lines met in 1869 to form the first transcontinental rail system. The Canadian Pacific Railway (now CP Rail) first crossed Canada in 1885.

Mining Towns. Most of the pioneers who conquered the mountains and deserts of the Far West were disappointed Forty-Niners. They moved eastward from California in the years after 1855, prospecting for precious metals everywhere. Some spread out over the Southwest, hoping to "strike it rich" in Arizona and Nevada. Others turned northward to find "pay dirt" in Idaho, Montana, and British Columbia. Still more searched for gold in the Rockies and in the Black Hills region of South Dakota. Wherever the miners went, farmers and merchants followed.

Ranches and Homesteads. By the middle 1860's, the Great Plains country was the only region in the United States that remained unsettled. Soon after the Civil War, Texas cattle ranchers began driving their herds northward to the railroads that crossed Kansas and Nebraska, so that the cattle could be shipped eastward. Almost overnight, the whole region became a giant pasture. But the day of "the cattle kingdom" was brief. The Homestead Act of 1862 encouraged farmers to move in from the East. As they followed the railroads westward, they took over the land, fenced it in, and barred the roving cattle herds. By 1890, the frontier was no more. Some areas, such as Oklahoma, had land rushes after this date, but the pioneers had conquered the West.

Some adventurers went beyond the country's boundaries in search of new lands and opportunities. Many went to Alaska in the Klondike Gold Rush of 1897.

Others looked for wealth in Hawaii, Puerto Rico, or the Philippines. But there was no rush comparable to the great migrations of the 1800's. Instead, more than 1 million Americans homesteaded in the Prairie Provinces of Canada. Here, about 1920, frontier expansion on the American continent came to a close.

Causes and Effects

Why People Went West. Opportunity drew people westward to the rich farm and pasture lands beyond settled areas. Some left their homes in the East when their farm lands wore thin. Others wanted elbowroom that they could not have in what they thought were crowded Eastern communities. In the middle 1700's, a Connecticut farmer wrote that "many are inclined to Remove to new Places . . . that they may have more Room, thinking that we live too thick." Still others moved westward because they were driven by a desire for adventure or a change of scene.

Patterns of Settlement. The westward movement followed a set pattern. Whenever times were good and attractive lands lay ahead, there was a rush to the frontier. Occasionally the movement halted when the pioneers met some obstacle. This might be a mountain barrier or natural condition unfamiliar to them, such as the prairies of Indiana and Illinois or the Great Plains farther west. More often, Indian uprisings checked their march. Each time the settlers advanced, they took more land from these "First Americans." The Indians were finally driven to the warpath to protect their hunting grounds (see INDIAN WARS). While fighting raged, migration slowed down. As soon as the frontier became peaceful again, a new rush westward began.

Growth of Communities. The constant movement westward meant that for more than 200 years society was being created again and again on the frontier. The pioneers soon found that many of the ideas and habits they brought with them did not work in the wilderness. The pioneers did not need a complicated government and many government services. They did not need social classes or cultural interests such as theaters and libraries. They needed most of their energy to battle nature on their farms. So frontier communities found easier ways of doing things. Groups of settlers governed themselves. Each family made all the things it needed, or else did without them. Barn dances and corn-husking bees replaced more elaborate entertainment. Children learned little more from books than how to read, write, and work simple arithmetic problems.

Gradually, as newcomers arrived, society began to grow more complicated. Established governments developed. People began to specialize in one kind of work. Schools and literary societies blossomed. Social classes began to appear. Eventually the frontier communities became fully developed, but they differed from those in the East.

Each community developed separately, in its own area. The people who settled it, and the area they settled, both affected the growth of the community. As a result, pioneers developed an "American" way of life that was different from what they had known before.

Contributions of the Frontier. Certain traits and ways of life became so rooted in the national character that they lasted long after the frontier itself had disappeared. Pioneers constantly had to invent new gadgets and techniques to solve unfamiliar problems. People in the United States are still noted for their inventiveness and their willingness to experiment. The early settlers were strongly individualistic, and "rugged individualism" is still a national trait. The pioneers developed a deep faith in democracy. A person's ability to overcome the problems of the frontier mattered more than family position. As the people faced common hardships in the untamed West, they developed the idea that they were all more or less equal. The American faith in democratic principles owes a great deal to this frontier heritage.

The westward movement influenced United States history in other ways. It stimulated nationalism. Settlers in western communities came from many backgrounds. It was easier for them to become "Americans," with a new pride in a new country, than to remain loyal to the various homelands they had left behind them. Western expansion also promoted a strong central government. The frontier presented complex problems, such as building roads and controlling the Indians. These problems could be solved only by a federal government.

Europe, too, felt the influence of the westward movement. Many Europeans were attracted to the United States by accounts they read of life in the new west, and by the efforts of railroad lines and steamship companies to encourage immigration.

People Who Led the Way

The Frontier Process is easier to understand if we do not consider the frontier as a line separating the settled and unsettled portions of the continent. The frontier was really a series of westward-moving areas. Each area represented a different stage in the growth of American civilization. In the zone farthest from settlements, fur trappers and traders roamed. These adventurers made no attempt to tame the wilderness. They explored it and prepared the way for others. Miners also ventured beyond the farming frontier whenever someone discovered deposits of gold, silver, or lead. Next came the cattle ranchers, seeking pastures where their herds could roam freely without being restricted by farmers' fences. We think today of cowboys tending great herds of cattle

only in the Far West. But bellowing herds were a familiar sight in the Virginia back country of the 1600's and on the prairies of Illinois in the early 1800's.

The trappers, miners, and cattle ranchers were usually followed by pioneer farmers. Many of these farmers were restless drifters who used the land but did not own it. These *squatters* built crude log cabins and cleared a few fields. They might acquire title to the land through *squatter's rights* (see SQUATTER'S RIGHTS). Some pulled out as more people moved in. They usually sold their property to farmers who had some money and ambition, and wanted to settle down. Such a newcomer cleared more fields, built a permanent home, hacked out split-rail fences, and worked on roads to connect the farm with nearby markets. Then merchants, millers, doctors, lawyers, and many other people arrived and provided all the services of a fully developed community.

As the frontier moved westward, it left behind a settled area. This in turn contributed to the stream of settlers already moving into the newer "West" beyond.

Leaders and Promoters. The way westward was pioneered by thousands of unknown people. But, now and then, born leaders shaped the course of the movement. Daniel Boone, Jim Bridger, and others found happiness only in solitude. They were less concerned with finding new homes for other people than in escaping the restraints of society. Some leaders wanted to build a better place for others to live in. Brigham Young led the Mormons to the shores of Great Salt Lake because he believed they could live their own lives there. Still others obeyed their God or their consciences as they braved the wilderness. Thomas Hooker heard such a call when he gathered his Cambridge congregation for the march to the Connecticut Valley in 1636. So did Father De Smet, Jason Lee, and Marcus Whitman when they ventured into the western wilderness 200 years later to convert the Indians to Christianity.

But the vast majority of frontier leaders were practical men who wanted only to improve their lives by moving to a land of greater opportunity. John Sevier and James Robertson had such ambitions as they paved the way into Tennessee just before the Revolutionary War. So did Rufus Putnam when he created the Ohio Company, and John Bidwell when he formed the first wagon train for the cross-country march to California. The people who led the way westward were drawn from every background and driven by almost every ambition. They had only one thing in common—a bold faith in their own ability to conquer the wilderness and find what they were seeking.   RAY ALLEN BILLINGTON

Related Articles. See the History sections of the various state articles, such as TEXAS (History). See also:

LEADERS OF THE WESTWARD MOVEMENT

Austin	Lee, Jason
Boone, Daniel	Lewis, Meriwether
Bridger, James	Long, Stephen Harriman
Carson, Kit	Mackenzie, Sir Alexander
Chouteau	McLoughlin, John
Clark, George Rogers	Pike, Zebulon Montgomery
Clark, William	Putnam, Rufus
Colter, John	Sevier, John
Crockett, David	Smith, Jedediah Strong
Fargo, William	Sublette, William Lewis
Frémont, John Charles	Thompson, David
Gist, Christopher	Whitman, Marcus
Houston, Samuel	Young, Brigham

Outline

I. The First Frontiers
II. Across the Mountains, 1763-1815
III. Settling the Midwest and South, 1815-1840
IV. Beyond the Mississippi, 1803-1840
V. Settling the Far West, 1840-1860
VI. The Last Frontiers, 1860-1890
VII. Causes and Effects
VIII. People Who Led the Way

Questions

Who were "the mountain men"?
What were the Ordinances of 1785 and 1787?
What American qualities arose on the frontier?
How did the War of 1812 affect westward migration?
What routes did caravans follow to Oregon and California?
Why was the Erie Canal important to both the East and the West?
Why did pioneers at first avoid settling the Plains?
What types of people were the first to move West?
What event in 1848 led to the rapid development of California?
Why did men like Daniel Boone go west?

WET MILLING. See CORN (Milling).

WETLAND is an area of land where the water level remains near or above the surface of the ground for most of the year. Wetlands support a variety of plant and animal life and occur throughout the world.

There are several kinds of wetlands. The major types include *bogs, fens, marshes,* and *swamps*. Bogs and fens are found primarily in northern climates. Bogs are characterized by acidic soils and the heavy growth of mosses, particularly sphagnum moss. Grasses and sedges characterize fens, where the soil is neither highly acidic nor basic. Both bogs and fens contain large amounts of partially decayed plant life called *peat*. Some bogs and fens have trees and shrubs, but woody plants are absent from others. Marshes and swamps generally occur in warmer climates. Marshes are dominated by grasses, reeds, rushes, sedges, and other nonwoody plants. Swamps, on the other hand, include many trees and shrubs.

A number of shorebirds and waterfowl make their homes in wetlands. These areas also provide food and shelter for such mammals as mink, moose, and muskrats. The wet areas are valuable ecologically in other ways as well. For example, they help control floods because they hold back water. In addition, wetlands store large amounts of water for long periods.

Many people consider wetlands to be waste areas. For this reason, more than 35 per cent of the wetlands in the United States had been drained and destroyed by the 1970's. Since the early 1970's, however, there has been an increasing awareness of the ecological value of wetlands. In the United States, various programs have been undertaken to preserve remaining wetlands, especially coastal salt marshes.   ROBERT LEO SMITH

See also BOG; MARSH; PEAT; PEAT MOSS; SWAMP.

WETTIN. See WINDSOR (family); SAXONY.

WEU. See WESTERN EUROPEAN UNION.

WEYDEN, ROGIER VAN DER. See VAN DER WEYDEN, ROGIER.

WEYERHAEUSER, FREDERICK (1834-1914), was the leading American lumberman of his time. He came to the United States from Germany at the age of 18. In 1856, he went to work for a lumber firm in Rock Island, Ill. Four years later, Weyerhaeuser and his brother-in-law, Frederick Denkmann, bought the mill. In 1870, they joined 16 other lumber firms and formed the Mississippi River Logging Company.

The new company floated rafts of logs down northern tributaries to the Mississippi. There, the logs were cut into lumber, which the firm sold in the Midwest. Through the years, Weyerhaeuser and his associates bought more and more woodland in the Midwest. In 1900, they incorporated the Weyerhaeuser Timber Company to purchase large areas of timberland in the Pacific Northwest. Weyerhaeuser became president of the firm. He was born in Niedersaulheim, near Mainz, in what is now West Germany.   BARRY W. POULSON

WEYGAND, *VAY GAHN,* **MAXIME** (1867-1965), a French soldier, served as chief of staff to Marshal Ferdinand Foch during World War I. In 1920 and 1921, he was military adviser to the Polish government during the Russo-Polish War, and helped the Poles defeat the Russian Bolsheviks. He was chief of the French General Staff from 1930 to 1935.

During the German invasion of France in World War II, Weygand was brought from the Middle East to command the French army. But he could not prevent the French defeat. He served the Vichy government, first as minister of war and later as commissioner in North Africa. He would not join with the Allied invasion forces in 1942, but was suspected by the Germans. They later recalled him and held him prisoner until 1945. After the war, Weygand was charged with collaborating with the Germans, but in 1948 a French court found him not guilty. He was born in Brussels, Belgium, and entered the French army in 1888.   ERNEST JOHN KNAPTON

See also WORLD WAR II (Retreat to Dunkerque).

WEYLER Y NICOLAU, *WAY ler ee nee koh LAH oo,* **VALERIANO** (1838-1930), MARQUIS OF TENERIFE, a Spanish general, was appointed governor of Cuba in 1896. His cruel methods aroused such a storm of protest in the United States that the Spanish government recalled him in 1897. Weyler put down revolts in Cuba in 1868, fought in Spain against Spanish rebels known as *Carlists,* and served as minister of war. Weyler was born on the island of Majorca.   J. CARY DAVIS

WEYMOUTH, Mass. (pop. 54,610), is on an inlet of Massachusetts Bay, about 12 miles (19 kilometers) southeast of Boston (see MASSACHUSETTS [political map]). Industries in Weymouth produce shoes, fertilizer, and electrical equipment. The Abigail Adams House, birthplace of the wife of President John Adams, stands in Weymouth. The town was founded in 1622, and incorporated in 1635. Weymouth claims it originated the New England town meeting form of government (see TOWN MEETING).   MICHAEL G. MENSOIAN

WFL. See FOOTBALL (Professional Football).

WHA. See HOCKEY (Professional Leagues).

A Mother Whale and Her Calf remain close together for at least a year. This baby humpback whale is resting on its mother's back as she swims along just beneath the surface of the water.

WHALE

WHALE is a huge sea animal that looks much like a fish. But whales are not fish. They belong instead to the group of animals called *mammals*. Other mammals include chimpanzees, dogs, and human beings. Like these mammals, whales have a highly developed brain and so are among the most intelligent of all animals.

Most whales are enormous creatures. One kind, the blue whale, is the largest animal that has ever lived. Blue whales may grow up to 100 feet (30 meters) long and weigh more than 100 short tons (91 metric tons). However, some kinds of whales are much smaller. Belugas and narwhals, for example, grow only 10 to 15 feet (3 to 5 meters) long.

Whales have the same basic shape as fish, but they differ from fish in many ways. The most visible difference is the tail. Fish have *vertical* (up and down) tail fins, but whales have sideways tail fins. Fish breathe by means of gills, which absorb dissolved oxygen from

water. Whales, on the other hand, have lungs and must come to the surface from time to time to breathe. But they can hold their breath for long periods. One kind of whale, the sperm whale, can hold its breath up to 75 minutes.

Like other mammals, whales give birth to live young and feed them with milk produced by the mother's body. Most fish, however, lay eggs and do not feed their offspring. Whales are also *warm-blooded*—that is, their body temperature remains about the same regardless of the temperature of their surroundings. Almost all fish are *cold-blooded*. Their body temperature changes with changes in the temperature of the water.

Down through the ages, whales have gradually lost some of the characteristics of mammals. For example, hair covers the bodies of most mammals. But whales have only a few stiff hairs on the head. Most mammals also have four legs. A whale has no hind legs. The only traces of them that remain are two tiny hipbones. In addition, the front legs have developed into flippers, which help a whale steer and keep its balance.

People have hunted whales since prehistoric times. In early days, people killed whales for their meat and for whale oil, which they used as a fuel for lamps and for cooking. Today, whale oil is used in a great variety

H. Dean Fisher, the contributor of this article, is Professor of Zoology at the University of British Columbia.

of products, including cosmetics, soaps, and varnishes. People in Japan and some other countries still eat whale meat.

During the 1900's, whaling fleets have killed huge numbers of whales and so have seriously endangered the survival of some kinds of whales. For this reason, the International Whaling Commission limits the number of whales that may be killed each year. It also completely prohibits the killing of certain kinds of whales. The United States government forbids the import of whale products into the United States.

Whales belong to a group of mammals called *cetaceans* (pronounced *see TAY shuhnz*). This name comes from a Latin word meaning *large sea animal*. Cetaceans also include dolphins and porpoises. Scientists have identified at least 75 kinds of cetaceans. They divide the various kinds into two major groups—*baleen whales*, which do not have teeth, and *toothed whales*, which have teeth. This article discusses the chief kinds of whales in each group. It also describes the bodies of whales and the life of whales. Finally, it traces the history of whaling and looks at the future of whales.

Kinds of Baleen Whales

Baleen whales have no teeth. Instead, they have hundreds of thin plates in the mouth. A whale uses these plates to strain out food from the water. The plates are called *baleen* or *whalebone* and consist of the same material as human fingernails. The baleen hangs from the whale's upper jaw. The inside edges of the plates have brushlike fibers that filter out the food. Baleen whales feed mainly on *plankton*—drifting masses of tiny plants and animals.

There are 10 kinds of baleen whales. Scientists divide them into three groups: (1) right whales; (2) gray whales; and (3) rorquals.

Right Whales have a thick, solid body and an unusually large head. The head of most right whales makes up about a third of the total body length. Right whales swim slowly, averaging about 3 miles (4.8 kilometers) per hour. They feed by swimming into a mass of plankton with their mouths open. Water flows through the baleen, and the plankton becomes entangled in the baleen fibers. There are three main kinds of right whales: (1) bowhead whales; (2) black right whales; and (3) pygmy right whales.

Bowhead Whales, also called *Greenland whales*, have the longest baleen of all baleen whales. They have a highly arched mouth suited to the huge baleen, which may grow as long as 13 feet (4 meters). Bowhead whales

William A. Watkins, Woods Hole Oceanographic Institution

A Baleen Whale has no teeth. Instead, it has hundreds of thin plates, called *baleen*, in the mouth. The whale uses these plates to filter out food from the water. Baleen whales form one of the two major groups of whales. Toothed whales make up the other group.

are black with white areas on the tail and the tip of the lower jaw. They measure up to 60 feet (18 meters) long and live only in the Arctic Ocean.

Black Right Whales usually are called simply *right whales*. Compared with bowhead whales, they have shorter baleen and a less highly arched mouth. They are black, and some have white areas on the belly. Right whales live in all the oceans and may grow up to 60 feet (18 meters) long. They have a calluslike area called a *bonnet* on the snout.

Pygmy Right Whales, the smallest of all baleen whales, grow no longer than 20 feet (6 meters). They live south of the equator and are seldom seen by people.

Gray Whales live in the North Pacific Ocean. In spite of their name, they may be black or dark gray. Their skin is dotted with white blotches, some of which are shellfish called *barnacles*. Gray whales have a series of low humps on the lower back. The animals may measure up to 50 feet (15 meters) long. Gray whales eat small animals that live on the sandy ocean bottom. The whales scoop up the sand and use their baleen to strain out the animals. They also feed on plankton and small fish.

Rorquals are baleen whales that have long grooves on the throat and chest. These grooves may number from 10 to 100 and are 1 to 2 inches (2.5 to 5 centimeters) deep. They enable a rorqual to open its mouth extremely wide and gulp enormous quantities of food and water. As the whale closes its mouth, its tongue forces the water out of the mouth through the baleen. The food becomes trapped inside the baleen and is swallowed by the whale. All rorquals have a *dorsal*, or back, fin, and so they are sometimes called *finback whales*. Most of them have a long, streamlined shape and can swim faster than other whales.

There are six kinds of rorquals. They are (1) blue whales; (2) Bryde's (pronounced *BROO dahs*) whales; (3) fin whales; (4) humpback whales; (5) Minke whales; and (6) sei (*say*) whales.

Blue Whales are the largest animals that have ever lived. They may grow up to 100 feet (30 meters) long

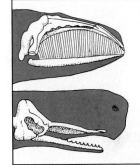

WORLD BOOK illustration by Marion Pahl

Baleen consists of thin plates that hang from the upper jaw of baleen whales. Baleen is made of the same type of material as human fingernails.

Peglike Teeth grow from the lower jaw of nearly all species of toothed whales. Some species have teeth in the upper jaw as well.

Some Kinds of Whales

The illustrations on this page and the following page show some of the major kinds of baleen and toothed whales. Baleen whales include nearly all the extremely large types of whales. Among toothed whales, only the sperm whale can compare in size with baleen whales. Unlike baleen whales, the various kinds of toothed whales differ greatly in both size and appearance.

Baleen Whales

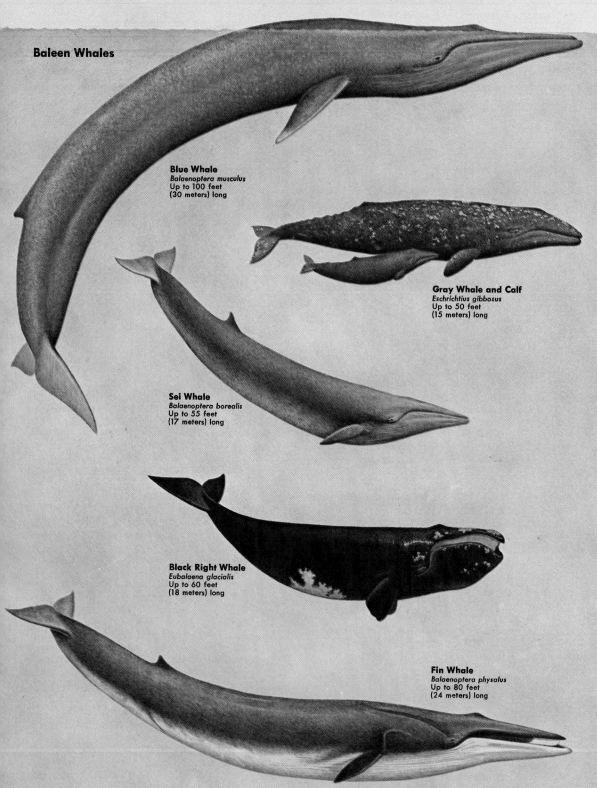

Blue Whale
Balaenoptera musculus
Up to 100 feet
(30 meters) long

Gray Whale and Calf
Eschrichtius gibbosus
Up to 50 feet
(15 meters) long

Sei Whale
Balaenoptera borealis
Up to 55 feet
(17 meters) long

Black Right Whale
Eubalaena glacialis
Up to 60 feet
(18 meters) long

Fin Whale
Balaenoptera physalus
Up to 80 feet
(24 meters) long

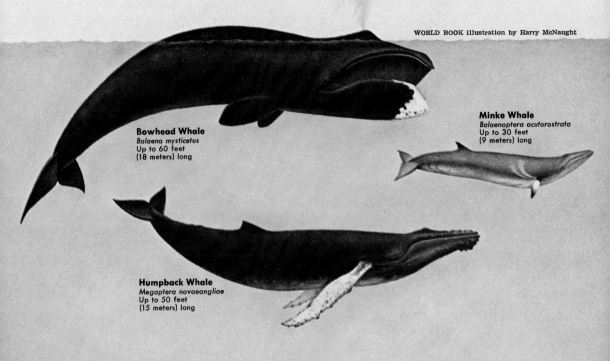

WORLD BOOK illustration by Harry McNaught

Bowhead Whale
Balaena mysticetus
Up to 60 feet
(18 meters) long

Minke Whale
Balaenoptera acutorostrata
Up to 30 feet
(9 meters) long

Humpback Whale
Megaptera novaeangliae
Up to 50 feet
(15 meters) long

Toothed Whales

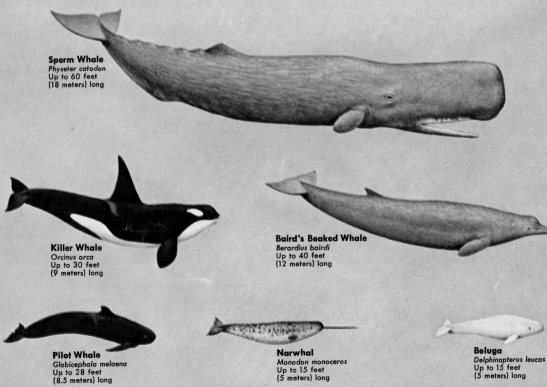

Sperm Whale
Physeter catodon
Up to 60 feet
(18 meters) long

Killer Whale
Orcinus orca
Up to 30 feet
(9 meters) long

Baird's Beaked Whale
Berardius bairdi
Up to 40 feet
(12 meters) long

Pilot Whale
Globicephala melaena
Up to 28 feet
(8.5 meters) long

Narwhal
Monodon monoceros
Up to 15 feet
(5 meters) long

Beluga
Delphinapterus leucas
Up to 15 feet
(5 meters) long

214a

and weigh more than 100 short tons (91 metric tons). They are dull blue. But some of them have growths of tiny yellowish, or sulfur-colored, plants called *diatoms* on the belly. For this reason, blue whales are sometimes called *sulfur-bottom whales*. Blue whales live in all the oceans but are rare. They feed almost entirely on small shrimplike animals called *krill*, which are part of the plankton.

Bryde's Whales live only in tropical and subtropical seas. They are bluish-gray with a white belly and may reach 45 feet (14 meters) in length. Unlike other rorquals, Bryde's whales eat mainly small fish and *squid*, an octopuslike animal.

Fin Whales are black on top and whitish below. They have cream-colored baleen in the front of the mouth and bluish-gray in the back. The lower jaw is white on the right side and black on the left. Fin whales grow up to 80 feet (24 meters) long and live in all the oceans. Fin whales that live south of the equator eat krill, but those in the Northern Hemisphere also eat anchovies, herring, and other small fish.

Humpback Whales grow no longer than 50 feet (15 meters) and are chubby compared with other rorquals. The humpback whale's most outstanding feature is its exceptionally long flippers, which may be a third as long as its body. The body is black on top and white underneath. Wartlike knobs cover the head and flippers. In spite of its name, the humpback whale has no hump on its back. Humpback whales live in all the oceans and often swim in coastal waters. They feed chiefly on krill but also eat small fish.

Minke Whales, the smallest of the rorquals, measure no more than 30 feet (9 meters) long. They are blue-gray on top and white below. Minke whales dwell in all the seas. Those that live in the Southern Hemisphere feed on krill, but those in the Northern Hemisphere eat mainly small fish.

Sei Whales look much like small fin whales, except that the lower jaw is black on both sides. They may grow up to 55 feet (17 meters) long. Sei whales live in all the oceans, but the greatest numbers dwell in the

Bruce Coleman Inc.

Toothed Whales use their teeth only to capture prey, not to chew it. All toothed whales swallow their food whole.

waters around Antarctica. They feed on krill and other plankton animals.

Kinds of Toothed Whales

Unlike baleen whales, toothed whales have teeth. There are about 65 kinds of toothed whales. They differ greatly in size, in shape, and in the number of teeth they have. Some toothed whales eat fish, and others eat such animals as cuttlefish and squid.

Scientists divide the various kinds of toothed whales into five groups: (1) sperm whales; (2) beaked whales; (3) belugas and narwhals; (4) dolphins and porpoises; and (5) river dolphins. Most people do not consider dolphins and porpoises to be whales. But scientists classify them as toothed whales because they have the same basic body features as other toothed whales.

Sperm Whales, also called *cachalots* (*KASH uh lahts*), are by far the largest toothed whales. They grow up to 60 feet (18 meters) long and range in color from blue-gray to black. Sperm whales have an enormous, square-shaped head. It makes up about a third of the total body length. The lower jaw is long and extremely thin. It has 16 to 30 peglike teeth on each side. The upper jaw has no visible teeth.

Almost all sperm whales live only in tropical and *temperate* (mild) waters, though a few males spend the summer in polar seas. Sperm whales dive to great depths in search of their food, which consists mainly of cuttlefish and squid. They also eat certain fishes, such as barracuda and sharks. The sperm whale has a small relative, the pygmy sperm whale, which grows only about 12 feet (3.7 meters) long.

Beaked Whales have a beaklike snout and only two or four teeth in the lower jaw. They have no upper teeth. Some kinds of beaked whales grow only about 15 feet (5 meters) long, and others reach 40 feet (12 meters). Beaked whales live in all the oceans and feed mainly on squid and fish.

Belugas and Narwhals measure 10 to 15 feet (3 to 5 meters) long. Narwhals and most belugas live in the Arctic, but some belugas are found farther south. Belugas and narwhals eat mostly fish and squid. Belugas are milk-white when fully grown and are often called *white whales*. They have 32 to 40 teeth. Narwhals are grayish on top and whitish underneath and have dark spots over the entire body. They have only two teeth. The teeth of female narwhals remain buried in the upper jaw. Among most males, the left tooth develops into a spiral tusk up to 9 feet (2.7 meters) long.

Dolphins and Porpoises live in all the oceans. Most porpoises grow 4 to 6 feet (1.2 to 1.8 meters) long, making them the smallest cetaceans. Dolphins range from about 7 to 30 feet (2.1 to 9 meters) long. The largest dolphins include killer whales and pilot whales. For more information on dolphins and porpoises, see DOLPHIN; KILLER WHALE; PILOT WHALE; PORPOISE.

River Dolphins, unlike other cetaceans, do not live in the sea. They live in the muddy waters of such rivers as the Amazon in South America and the Ganges in India. They measure about 8 feet (2.4 meters) and have a long beak and poorly developed eyesight.

The Bodies of Whales

Several features of the whale body suggest that whales are closely related to hoofed mammals, particu-

The Body of a Female Fin Whale

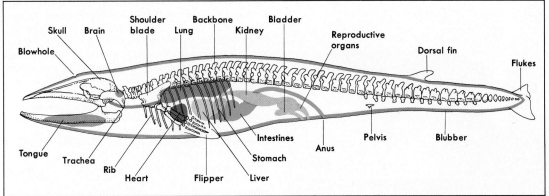

WORLD BOOK illustration by Marion Pahl

larly split-hoofed mammals, such as cattle and deer. Scientists believe that whales developed from primitive meat-eating mammals. The oldest whale fossil yet discovered dates from about 45 million years ago. However, scientists think that whales probably began to develop as early as 70 million years ago.

Whales basically have the same body features as other mammals. But whales also have many special characteristics suited to living in water. In addition, living in water enables them to reach enormous sizes. A land animal can grow only so big before its bones and muscles can no longer support its body weight. However, the *buoyancy* (lift) of water helps support a whale's body and makes it possible for whales to grow far larger than any land animal.

Body Shape. Whales have a highly streamlined shape, which enables them to swim with a minimum of resistance. Their shape resembles that of fish. But a whale's powerful tail fins, called *flukes*, are horizontal instead of vertical like the tail fins of a fish. A whale propels itself through the water by moving its flukes up and down. Most fish swim by swinging their tail fins from side to side.

The ancestors of whales lived on land and had four legs. But after these animals moved into the sea, their body features gradually changed. Over millions of years, the front legs developed into flippers and the hind legs disappeared. A whale uses its flippers to help in steering and in keeping its balance.

Skeleton. A whale's backbone, ribcage, and shoulder blades resemble those of other mammals. The absence of hind legs, however, distinguishes the whale skeleton from that of most other mammals. Two small bones buried in the hip muscles are all that remain of the whale's hind legs.

Almost all mammals have seven neck vertebrae. But in whales, these vertebrae are greatly compressed into a short length or joined together into one bone. This feature keeps the head from moving about as a whale swims. It also contributes to the whale's streamlined shape by joining the head directly to the body.

Skin and Blubber. Whales have smooth, rubbery skin that slips easily through the water. Most mammals are covered with hair, which holds warm air next to the body. Whales, however, do not have a coat of hair to provide them with insulation. A few bristles on the head are all the hair that whales have.

Beneath the skin, whales have a layer of fat called *blubber*, which keeps them warm. Actually, rorquals have more difficulty getting rid of excess heat than keeping warm. Their blubber, therefore, never grows more than about 6 inches (15 centimeters) thick. In contrast, right whales may have a layer of blubber up to 20 inches (50 centimeters) thick. If food is scarce, whales can live off their blubber for a long period. Blubber is lighter than water, and so it also increases the buoyancy of whales.

Respiratory System. Like all other mammals, whales have lungs. They must therefore come to the surface regularly to breathe. Baleen whales usually breathe every 5 to 15 minutes, but they can go as long as 40 minutes without breathing. A sperm whale can hold its breath up to 75 minutes.

Whales can go for long periods without breathing for several reasons. Their muscles store much more oxygen than do the muscles of other mammals. Human

WORLD BOOK illustration by Marion Pahl

A Rapid Forward Roll enables a whale to surface, breathe, and begin a new dive in one continuous motion. This movement gives the whale only about two seconds to exhale and inhale. Many kinds of whales throw their *flukes* (tail fins) clear of the water when beginning a deep dive.

WHALE

Jen and Des Bartlett, Bruce Coleman Inc.

Impressive Leaps from the water are performed by some species of whales. Scientists call this behavior *breaching*. The playful right whale shown above is breaching off the coast of Argentina.

beings, for example, store only about 13 per cent of their oxygen supply in the muscles, compared with about 41 per cent for whales. During a dive, a whale's body greatly reduces the blood flow to the muscles but keeps a normal flow to the heart and brain. The heartbeat also slows, which helps save oxygen. After a dive, a whale must take several breaths to recharge its tissues with oxygen before diving again.

When a whale comes up to breathe, it rolls forward as it breaks the surface. This movement gives the whale only about two seconds to blow out and breathe in up to 2,100 quarts (2,000 liters) of air. Whales breathe through nostrils, called *blowholes*, at the top of the head. Toothed whales have one blowhole, but baleen whales have two. Powerful muscles and valves open the blowholes wide for whales to breathe, and then the openings snap tightly shut.

When a whale exhales, it produces a cloud called a *blow* or *spout*. The blow consists chiefly of water vapor. It may also include mucus and oil droplets. Experts can identify the species of a whale by the height and shape of its blow. Blows range in height from about 6 feet (1.8 meters) in humpback whales to 25 feet (8 meters) in sperm whales. Right whales have a double V-shaped blow, and rorquals have a pear-shaped one. Sperm whales blow forward and to the left.

Senses. Whales have no sense of smell, and most species have poor eyesight. Studies indicate that some kinds of toothed whales may have a limited sense of taste, but most whales cannot taste. However, all whales have well-developed senses of touch and hearing. Their keen hearing provides them with most of their information about their surroundings. They can hear an extremely wide range of sounds, including low- and high-pitched sounds far beyond the range of human hearing. Unlike people, whales can also tell from what direction a sound is coming underwater.

Toothed whales produce sounds within the *nasal sac system*, a series of air-filled pouches around the blowhole. The whales locate underwater objects by listening for the echoes produced when objects reflect the sounds. From the echoes, they determine the distance to an object and the direction in which it lies. This method of navigation is called *echolocation*. Biologists do not know for sure whether baleen whales echolocate, but some experts believe that they do.

The Life of Whales

Reproduction. Most kinds of whales mate during a specific season. The male, called a *bull*, and the female, called a *cow*, engage in playful courting as part of the mating process. During the courting, the whales may stroke each other with their flippers. Humpback and right whales may also make spectacular leaps from the water. Humpback whales sometimes hug each other with their long, curved flippers.

The pregnancy period varies from species to species, but in most kinds of whales it lasts 10 to 12 months. A

Paul Thomas, Black Star

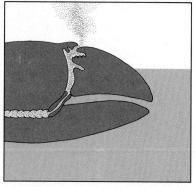

A Visible Cloud called a *spout* is produced when a whale exhales through its *blowhole*, or nostril, *left*. Toothed whales have one blowhole. Baleen whales have two.

A Whale's Short, Wide Nasal Passage, *below*, helps the whale breathe quickly.

WORLD BOOK Illustration by Marion Pahl

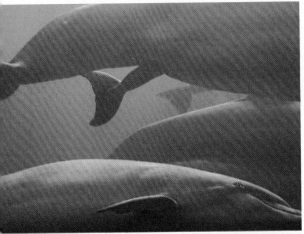

The Birth of a Whale, such as that of a bottle-nosed dolphin shown above, occurs tailfirst. In many cases, other female whales help the mother while she gives birth.

A Newborn Whale begins swimming immediately, but it depends on its mother for food and protection. As soon as the baby is born, the mother helps it to the surface to take its first breath.

female sperm whale, however, carries her baby 16 months. In almost all cases, a whale has only one baby, called a *calf*, at a time. Twins rarely occur. One or more females may help the mother during birth. Whales are already giant animals at birth. Newborn blue whales, for example, average about 2 short tons (1.8 metric tons) in weight and 23 feet (7 meters) in length. As soon as the baby is born, the mother nudges it to the surface to take its first breath.

The mother whale is highly protective of her baby and stays close to it for at least a year. Like all other mammals, whales nurse their young. The female has special breast muscles that pump milk into the baby's mouth. Whale milk is highly concentrated and much richer in fat, protein, and minerals than the milk of other mammals. This rich food helps the calves grow amazingly fast. Baby blue whales gain about 200 pounds (91 kilograms) per day. Young blue and fin whales nurse up to seven months. Other whales nurse for nearly a year.

Group Life. Toothed whales appear to be more socially organized than baleen whales. Bottle-nosed whales and many species of dolphins swim in herds of 100 to 1,000. Sperm whales form several kinds of smaller groups. A "harem" school consists of one adult male and several females and their young. Females with young calves form "nursery" groups. "Bachelor" schools are composed of playful young males.

Some types of baleen whales, such as blue and sei whales, live mostly in family groups. Such a family consists of a male, a female, and one or two offspring. Baleen whales sometimes gather in large groups to feed. Humpback whales migrate in groups—mothers and their young first, males and nonpregnant females next, and pregnant females last.

Whales communicate with one another by making a wide variety of sounds called *phonations*. Whales can easily hear these sounds over great distances. Microphones have picked up the deep moans of bowhead whales at a distance of 50 miles (80 kilometers). The best-known whale sounds are the songs of humpback whales. Each song consists of a series of sounds that lasts 7 to 30 minutes and is then repeated. All songs produced by a particular whale are basically alike, but the songs of different individuals vary greatly. Scientists do not yet know what information whales communicate through phonations.

Migrations. Most kinds of baleen whales migrate between polar and tropical regions. The cold waters of the Arctic and Antarctic have the richest concentrations of plankton. The whales spend the summer in these areas, feeding and storing up large reserves of blubber. As winter approaches, the polar waters freeze over and the whales move to warmer seas near the equator. There they mate and the females that are already pregnant give birth. The warm waters provide a comfortable environment for the babies, which lack a thick layer of blubber to keep them warm.

In the tropics, adult whales live mostly off their blubber because food is scarce. Mother whales convert part of their blubber into milk for the babies. By late spring, the young whales are large enough to move with the group to the polar feeding area.

Two kinds of baleen whales do not migrate. Bryde's whales live in the tropics the year around, and bowhead whales never leave the Arctic. Most species of toothed whales also do not migrate. Belugas and narwhals stay in Arctic waters. Among sperm whales, the adult females, the young, and most adult males live only in tropical or temperate seas. A few males spend the summer in polar waters.

Life Span. The life span of whales ranges from 15 years for the common porpoise to 40 or more years for baleen whales. Human hunters account for many whale deaths. But aside from people, whales have almost no natural enemies. Killer whales, which are dolphins, occasionally attack young whales, small dolphins, and weak or diseased baleen whales. However, most whales that escape the hunter's harpoon probably live to old age and die of natural causes.

Some whales die after stranding themselves on a beach. In some cases, a whale swims ashore alone. In other instances, an entire school of whales becomes stranded. Only toothed whales beach themselves in

215

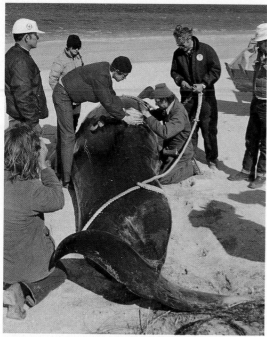

Larry Smith, Black Star

Scientists Examine a Beached Whale that died after stranding itself ashore. Studies of beached whales and of whales killed by whalers provide most of our knowledge about whale anatomy.

groups. People often return beached whales to the sea, but most rescued whales immediately swim back onto the beach. Stranded whales cannot live long. Out of water, the whales may overheat, become crushed by their own weight, or drown when the tide covers their blowholes.

Scientists do not know for certain what causes beachings, but they have proposed a number of explanations. Some suggest that parasites in the whales' ears or brains interfere with the animals' ability to echolocate. Others suggest that gently sloping beaches reflect sounds over the heads of the whales. As a result, the whales are not warned that they are swimming onto a beach. Still other scientists think that a variety of these and other causes may be responsible for beachings.

The Early Days of Whaling

The First Whalers. People began to hunt whales in prehistoric times. At first, they simply killed and ate whales that had stranded on beaches. People who lived in what is now Norway were probably the first whalers to seek out and kill whales in the sea. Norwegian rock carvings about 4,000 years old show a variety of whaling scenes. The earliest written record of Norwegian whaling dates from about A.D. 890. However, this record does not reveal what methods the whalers used or the types of whales they hunted.

The Basque People of southern France and northern Spain established the first large whaling industry. During the 900's, the Basques began to hunt baleen whales in the Bay of Biscay, which lies west of France and north of Spain. They first hunted near the shore from small open boats. The whalers maneuvered their boat close enough to a whale so that one of them could

harpoon it. A rope connected the harpoon to the boat. In time, the whale became exhausted. The whalers then killed it with sharp lances and towed the body to shore for processing.

During the 1200's, the Basques began to equip large sailing ships for whaling voyages. Each ship carried several small whaleboats from which the whalers set out to kill whales. After killing a whale, the whalers brought it alongside the ship. Then with long-handled knives, they peeled off the blubber in strips as the body turned over and over in the water. The ship's crew used ropes to lift the blubber onto the ship. The whalers then removed the baleen from the whale and discarded the rest of the body.

The whalers stored blubber and baleen on the ship until they had a full load. The ship then returned to shore, where the blubber was cooked to make oil. The Basques burned whale oil in lamps and used baleen in such articles as corsets, dress hoops, and whips.

The Basques chiefly hunted one type of whale, which became known as the *right whale*. The Basques considered it the right, or correct, whale to hunt because it swims slowly, floats when dead, and has great quantities of baleen. After right whales became scarce in the Bay of Biscay, the Basque whalers ventured farther out to sea. During the 1500's, their voyages even carried them as far as the coast of Newfoundland.

The Growth of European Whaling. Many European nations began whaling during the 1600's. Dutch and English explorers reported that the Arctic waters were filled with whales. These reports attracted whalers from many countries, including Denmark, England, Germany, and The Netherlands. Bowhead whales were especially plentiful around Svalbard, a group of islands north of Norway. Svalbard became the main center of Arctic whaling. The Dutch and the English in particular developed profitable whaling industries there. At first, they employed Basques to kill and cut up the whales, but soon the Dutch and the English learned to do these jobs themselves. By 1720, whalers had killed all the whales around Svalbard and moved on to other areas of the Arctic.

American Whaling. The first American whalers were Indians, who hunted from shore in much the same way as the early Basques. During the early 1600's, the American colonists began to hunt right whales off the Atlantic coast. The colonists used baleen from these whales in making such products as corsets, fishing rods, and umbrellas. In 1712, a ship hunting for right whales was carried far from land by a storm. The ship came upon a school of sperm whales, killed one, and brought it back to port. This chance event began the sperm-whaling industry in America.

Shore-based whaling for right whales declined during the 1700's, but sperm whaling developed into a major industry by the end of the century. Nantucket and New Bedford, Mass., became the chief American whaling ports. By 1770, Americans were hunting sperm whales throughout the Atlantic Ocean. American sperm whaling expanded into the South Pacific Ocean about 1790.

Whalers obtained three valuable substances from sperm whales. The most important was *sperm oil*, which came from the head and the blubber. People used the oil as a fuel for lamps and as a lubricant. Whalers also took another type of oil called *spermaceti* from the sperm whale's head. This oil became the chief ingredient in candles. The third substance, called *ambergris*, came from the intestines of sperm whales. It was used as a base for expensive perfumes. Whalers found ambergris in only a few of the whales they killed. Nevertheless, the substance brought them much income because perfume manufacturers paid extremely high prices for it.

American whalers used basically the same methods as European whalers. However, the Americans cooked the blubber on board ship instead of storing it and carrying it back to land for processing. They extracted the oil by *trying out* (cooking) the blubber in large iron pots called *try pots*. Unlike blubber, the oil did not spoil during long voyages through the tropics. It also required much less storage space than blubber.

The American sperm-whaling industry had its greatest prosperity from about 1820 to 1850. During this period, it employed more than 70,000 persons and killed about 10,000 whales annually. The whaling fleet consisted of over 730 ships, which sailed all the oceans. Much whaling took place in the Pacific Ocean, and San Francisco became a major whaling port. By this time, many voyages lasted as long as four to five years. Whaling ships sent their whale oil home by cargo ship from time to time and continued whaling.

The decline of American sperm whaling began with the California gold rush in 1849. Many crew members of whaling ships deserted to seek their fortunes prospecting for gold. But the American Civil War (1861-1865) dealt the most severe blow to the whaling industry. During the war, Southern ships sank many whaling vessels. Whaling began to revive after the war, but the birth of the U.S. petroleum industry posed a new threat. Petroleum products soon replaced sperm oil as a fuel for lamps and spermaceti as a base for candles. American sperm whaling declined throughout the late 1800's and early 1900's. After 1925, all that remained of the industry were a few shore-based whaling operations along the Pacific coast.

Modern Whaling

Hunting Techniques. During the 1860's, a Norwegian whaling captain named Svend Foyn invented a new type of harpoon and a gun to fire it. His harpoon was tipped with a bomb that would explode inside the whale and cause death much sooner than an ordinary harpoon. Foyn mounted the harpoon gun on the bow of another of his inventions—a steam-powered whaling boat. This *catcher boat* could travel much faster than the sailing ships and small open boats that whalers had used previously. Foyn's boat and harpoon enabled whalers to hunt rorquals, whose great speed and power had formerly protected them from whalers.

About 1900, whalers began to hunt rorquals in the waters surrounding Antarctica. The number of rorquals was enormous, and the modern hunting methods proved to be highly effective. As a result, more whales were killed during the first 40 years of the 1900's than in the preceding four centuries. The number of whales killed worldwide peaked in 1962, when whalers killed more than 66,000. Excessive killing, however, greatly reduced the world's whale population and jeopardized the survival of some species. The whale catch thus declined sharply in the late 1960's and the 1970's. In 1975, about 29,000 whales were killed.

Today, only Japan and Russia have large whaling industries. Japanese and Russian whalers use diesel-powered catcher boats and an updated version of Foyn's harpoon. Fleets of catcher boats operate from huge vessels called *factory ships*. A factory ship carries up to 12 catcher boats and a crew of about 400. It is equipped to process a wide variety of whale products.

Detail of *Panorama of a Whaling Voyage Round the World* (about 1847), a painting by Benjamin Russell and Caleb P. Purrington; New Bedford Whaling Museum, New Bedford, Mass.

American Whaling flourished throughout the first half of the 1800's. The scene above shows hunters killing right whales off the northwest coast of North America in the 1840's.

Paolo Curto, Bruce Coleman Inc.

Harpoon Guns, such as the one shown above, fire explosive harpoons that kill whales within minutes in most cases.

Matt Herron, Black Star

Modern Whaling Vessels enable whalers to kill and process whales efficiently and quickly. The Russian *factory ship* on the left is towing in a dead whale to be processed on board. *Catcher boats,* such as the one on the right, chase down and kill the whales.

A factory ship and its fleet of catcher boats can roam over great distances. Spotters in airplanes or helicopters help the whalers in their search for whales. In addition, the ships have sonar to trace whales underwater. These advanced techniques enable the crew of a catcher boat to track down and kill any whale that they spot. After harpooning a whale, the whalers pump air into its body cavity to keep it afloat. They also mark each whale that they kill with a radar reflector and with a flag bearing the number of their boat. Later, the catcher boats or special *buoy boats* tow the dead whales to the factory ship.

Processing Whale Products. The crew of the factory ship attaches an iron claw to the flukes of a whale and hauls it up onto the deck. There, workers called *flensers* use long knives to cut slits along the whale's body. They then peel off the blubber, cut it up, and drop the pieces through holes in the deck. The blubber falls into cookers, which remove the oil.

After the blubber has been peeled off, workers called *lemmers* cut up the rest of the body. They cut the meat that will be sold as human food into large chunks and freeze it. The bones, the rest of the meat, and some internal organs are cooked to make such products as cattle feed and fertilizer.

In some countries, manufacturers make such products as cosmetics, margarine, soap, and varnish from whale oil. Sperm oil is also used in numerous products, but especially in lubricants and automatic transmission fluid. Many kinds of cosmetics contain spermaceti. People in Japan and some other countries eat the meat of baleen whales.

The Future of Whales

Many of the larger kinds of whales face an uncertain future. Whalers have killed so many blue, bowhead, humpback, and right whales that those species are threatened with extinction. Overhunting has also greatly reduced the number of fin and sei whales.

In 1946, the major whaling countries formed the International Whaling Commission (IWC) to protect whales from overhunting and to regulate the whaling industry. For many years, the IWC set unrealistically high *quotas* (limits) on the number of whales that could be killed. Today, the commission sets greatly reduced quotas and completely forbids the hunting of blue, bowhead, gray, humpback, and right whales. The IWC also prohibits the killing of fin whales in the Southern Hemisphere and sei whales in the North Atlantic. In addition, the commission requires nations to exchange observers to report on one another's whaling.

Karen E. Moore, Woods Hole Oceanographic Institution

Removing the Blubber from a whale is called *flensing.* Most flensing is done aboard factory ships, but some whales are processed on land at whaling stations like the one above.

Effective control of whaling remains difficult because the IWC has no power to enforce its regulations. A member nation can refuse to follow any rule set by the commission. Some whaling countries, particularly in South America, refuse to join the IWC.

The United States vigorously opposes whaling. In 1971, the federal government ordered an end to U.S. whaling and outlawed the import of whale products.

During the 1970's, many people in the United States, Canada, and some European countries began to protest the continuation of whaling. In 1974, antiwhaling groups agreed to *boycott* (refuse to buy) products from Japan and Russia until those countries stop whaling. The boycott and other forms of public pressure have helped influence Japan, Russia, and some other whaling nations to abide by the IWC's regulations.

Most biologists believe that all species of whales have been saved for the present. However, complete protection of endangered species must continue for a long time to allow them to recover from years of extreme overhunting. Even with protection, some species may not be able to recover. For example, the right whale has been fully protected since 1935, but it has not yet made a significant comeback.

Every year, the number of people in the world increases about 2 per cent, and so the demand for food rises constantly. This fact may threaten the survival of whales. If the population does not level off, people may have to compete with whales for food in the sea. Some nations have already begun experimental fishing for krill, the main food of whales in Antarctic waters.

Scientific Classification. Whales belong to the order Cetacea, which is divided into two suborders. Toothed whales form the suborder Odontoceti. Baleen whales make up the suborder Mysticeti.　　H. DEAN FISHER

Related Articles in WORLD BOOK include:

Ambergris	Dolphin
Antarctica (Seals	Killer Whale
and Whales)	Krill
Beluga	Mammal
Blubber	Narwhal
Cetacean	Northwest Territories
Colonial Life in	(picture: Small
America (picture:	White Whales)
Colonial Whaling)	Pilot Whale

Joanne Kalish, The Sea Library from Tom Stack & Assoc.

Antiwhaling Groups campaigned in the 1970's to end whaling. Protestors, such as those shown here, urged people not to buy any goods from the two major whaling nations, Japan and Russia.

WHARTON, JOSEPH

Porpoise	Sperm Whale
Rorqual	Spermaceti

Outline

I. Kinds of Baleen Whales
  A. Right Whales   C. Rorquals
  B. Gray Whales

II. Kinds of Toothed Whales
  A. Sperm Whales   D. Dolphins and
  B. Beaked Whales   Porpoises
  C. Belugas and Narwhals E. River Dolphins

III. The Bodies of Whales
  A. Body Shape   D. Respiratory System
  B. Skeleton   E. Senses
  C. Skin and Blubber

IV. The Life of Whales
  A. Reproduction   C. Migrations
  B. Group Life   D. Life Span

V. The Early Days of Whaling
  A. The First Whalers C. The Growth of Euro-
  B. The Basque People   pean Whaling
                      D. American Whaling

VI. Modern Whaling
  A. Hunting Techniques
  B. Processing Whale Products

VII. The Future of Whales

Questions

Why can whales grow far larger than any land animal?
What are the two major groups of whales?
In what ways do whales differ from fish?
How do whales communicate with one another?
What functions does blubber serve for a whale?
What people established the first large whaling industry?
Why do beached whales die?
What events led to the decline of American whaling?
How does the International Whaling Commission try to protect whales from overhunting?
What are some uses of whale products?

Reading and Study Guide

See *Whale* in the RESEARCH GUIDE/INDEX, Volume 22, for a *Reading and Study Guide*.

WHALE SHARK. See SHARK (Kinds of Sharks; picture).

WHALES, BAY OF. See AMUNDSEN, ROALD.

WHARF. See HARBOR.

WHARTON, EDITH NEWBOLD JONES (1862-1937), an American novelist, was noted for her stories about society life. In them, she pictured the dignity and good taste of the old social order and contrasted it with the "dog-eat-dog" characteristics she ascribed to the new society. Her most representative novels deal with the social and psychological conflicts of wealthy society in New York City. These novels include *The Age of Innocence* (1920), for which she won the 1921 Pulitzer prize for fiction. *The House of Mirth* (1905) satirized the dominant social class as a class without genuine gaiety or wealth of spirit.

Wharton published her first short stories in *The Great Inclination* (1899). Her novel *The Valley of Decision* (1902) is set in Italy in the 1700's, and *Ethan Frome* (1911) takes place in rural New England. Her other works include *Summer* (1917), *A Son at the Front* (1923), *The Mother's Recompense* (1925), and *Here and Beyond* (1926), a collection of short stories. She was born in New York City.　　HARRY H. CLARK

WHARTON, JOSEPH. See IRON AND STEEL (Famous People in Iron and Steel).

Fields of Wheat cover more of the world's farmland than any other food crop. Farmers harvest wheat with a combine, such as the one at the left, which cuts and threshes the grain in one operation. The photograph at the right shows the ripe wheat before harvesting.

WHEAT

WHEAT is the world's most important grain crop. Wheat *kernels* (seeds) are ground into flour to make bread and other products. These wheat products are the main food of hundreds of millions of people throughout the world. As a result, wheat covers more of the earth's surface than any other food crop. The world's farmers grow about 13 billion bushels of wheat a year. This amount of wheat would fill a freight train stretching about $2\frac{1}{4}$ times around the world.

Wheat is a grass-type plant. It belongs to the group of grains called *cereals* (see GRAIN). Other important cereals are rice, oats, corn, barley, and rye. Wheat is a common food in North and South America, Europe, Africa, Australia, and much of Asia.

At harvesttime in the great wheat-producing regions, the rippling fields of grain stretch across the land like a golden ocean. Giant machines knife through these fields of grain, cutting and threshing the wheat.

Different kinds of wheat grow successfully in hot, cold, or dry climates. Scientists are always developing new varieties of wheat that will resist cold, plant disease, and insects, and also will increase the yield.

The Wheat Plant

Appearance. Especially when it is young, wheat looks like grass. The wheat plant is a bright green color.

Allen D. Tillman, the contributor of this article, is a scientist for the Rockefeller Foundation at Gadjah Mada University in Yogyakarta, Indonesia.

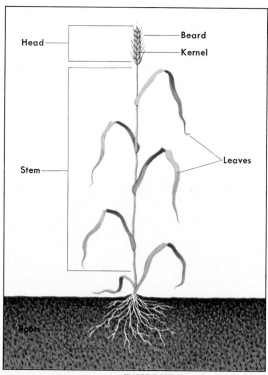

Head — Beard
— Kernel

Leaves

Stem

Roots

WORLD BOOK diagram by James Teason

The Wheat Plant grows up to 5 feet (1.5 meters) high and turns golden brown when ripe. The head of the plant holds an average of 50 kernels of grain. Many varieties of wheat have a *beard* of coarse, prickly hairs on the husks of the kernels.

It may grow up to 5 feet (1.5 meters) tall, and it turns golden-brown when it is ripe. Most of the root system of the wheat plant is in the upper 15 to 20 inches (38 to 51 centimeters) of the soil. In loose ground, the roots may extend down farther. The leaves are long and slender. The wheat *head* that holds the kernels is at the top of the main center stem. Many varieties of wheat have coarse, prickly hairs called *beards* on the husk of the wheat kernel. A healthy plant produces an average of fifty kernels of wheat. The clusters of kernels cling tightly to the stem until they are fully ripe. The grains of wheat are white, red, or yellow. In a few regions, purple wheat is grown.

The Wheat Kernel is $\frac{1}{8}$ to $\frac{1}{4}$ inch (3 to 6 millimeters) long. It is divided into three main parts. These are the germ, the bran, and the endosperm. The *germ* is the part where growth starts after the seed is planted. It makes up a small part of the kernel. The *bran*, or "coat," is made up of several layers that protect the kernel. It is much like the shell of a nut. The bran makes up about 15 per cent of the kernel and is used primarily in making livestock feed. The *endosperm* makes up the largest part of the kernel, about 83 to 85 per cent. It is used in making bread and other bakery goods. The endosperm contains a protein called *gluten* that makes dough rise in the presence of yeast (see GLUTEN). The husk of the kernel is called *chaff*.

How Wheat Is Used

In most Western countries, wheat appears in some form at almost every meal. About three-fourths of all the flour milled is used by commercial bakers to make bread, rolls, buns, cookies, cakes, pies, and other goods.

Wheat Flour. About 543 million bushels of wheat are *milled* (ground) into 24 billion pounds (10.9 billion kilograms) of flour in the United States each year. Each person in the United States uses an average of about 107 pounds (49 kilograms) of wheat a year.

To produce *whole wheat* flour, millers grind the entire kernel of wheat. Such flour thus contains nutrients found in all three parts—the bran, endosperm, and germ. To produce *white flour*, millers remove the bran and germ and use only the endosperm. Some vitamins and minerals are therefore lost. The processing of white flour removes additional nutrients. In the United States and many other countries, bakers or millers add vitamins and minerals to most white flour to improve its food value. Such flour is called *enriched flour*. Products made from enriched flour or whole wheat flour provide important amounts of iron, protein, starch, and the B vitamins niacin, riboflavin, and thiamine. When milk is added to flour, it further improves the flour's food value. Nevertheless, many nutritionists believe that additional substances should be added to further improve flour and foods made from flour.

Breakfast Foods. Some wheat is used in making breakfast foods. These breakfast foods are of two general types. *Ready-to-eat* wheat breakfast foods include puffed wheat, wheat flakes, shredded wheat biscuits, and bran flakes. *Cooked* wheat breakfast foods include wheat meal, whole-wheat meal, cracked wheat, rolled wheat, malted cereals, farina, and similar products.

Macaroni Products. Coarse particles of wheat are mixed into a paste and forced through machines to make macaroni and spaghetti. Wheat paste is rolled

into sheets and cut into strips for noodles. See MACARONI.

Animal Feed. The bran layer and some other parts of the kernel that remain after white flour is milled are used as livestock and poultry feed. Actually, these products contain higher levels of protein, minerals, and vitamins than does the endosperm. Wheat grains not suitable for milling are also fed to animals.

Other Products. Wheat germ and wheat-germ oil are taken from the *embryo* (germ) of the wheat kernel. These products are used in some breakfast foods, and are sometimes added to specialty breads and other foods. Wheat germ contains vitamin E and the B vitamins riboflavin and niacin. Glutamic acid is another by-product of wheat. A well-known product made from glutamic acid is *monosodium glutamate*. This saltlike substance has little flavor of its own, but it brings out the flavor of other foods.

Cross Section of a Kernel of Wheat

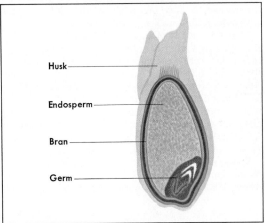

WORLD BOOK diagram by James Teason

Food Value of Whole-Grain Wheat

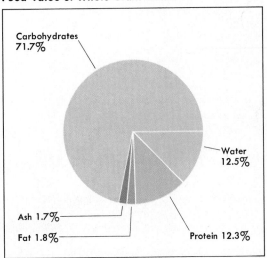

Carbohydrates 71.7%

Water 12.5%

Ash 1.7%

Fat 1.8%

Protein 12.3%

Source: *Composition of Foods—Raw, Processed, Prepared*, Agriculture Handbook No. 8, Agricultural Research Service, U.S. Department of Agriculture, 1975.

WHEAT

Wheat may also be used to produce alcohol for synthetic rubber or munitions. Flour paste, the filler for insect-destroying preparations, and certain coffee substitutes require wheat. Strawboard used in boxes and straw for fertilizer and other uses are products made from the stem of the wheat plant.

The Search for New Uses. Wheat has become so important in the United States that there are many milling laboratories and agricultural experiment stations devoted to research on this grain. Milling and baking companies and allied industries maintain testing kitchens to develop new uses for wheat products.

Plant breeders and research workers are hard at work, not only on crossbreeding wheat for superior qualities, but also on developing new kinds of cereals.

Kinds of Wheat

There are two general groups of wheat, *winter wheat* and *spring wheat*. The kind planted depends primarily on the climate. Winter wheats are used in mild climates. Spring wheats are found in areas where the winters are extremely cold. Each major wheat group includes varieties of both hard and soft wheat.

Winter Wheat is planted in the fall and harvested the following spring or summer. Winter wheat gets a start before cold weather begins. Growth stops during the winter, then begins again in the spring. If winter wheat is planted in the spring, it ordinarily will not *head* (produce a crop). Winter wheat needs fairly low temperatures so that it can develop properly during early growth. Among important varieties of winter wheat grown in the United States are *Triumph*, *Wichita*, *Pawnee*, *Cheyenne*, *Comanche*, *Knox*, and *Seneca*.

Spring Wheat is planted in the spring and ripens the same summer, usually a few weeks after the winter wheat. If spring wheat is planted in the fall, it will not live through the winter except in mild climates or during unusually warm winters. Among important varieties of spring wheat grown in the United States are *Selkirk*, *Lee*, *Thatcher*, *Conley*, *Rescue*, *Rushmore*, and *Centana*.

Species of Wheat. All the wheat grown throughout the world belongs to one of fourteen species. Seven of these species are grown in the United States, but only three are of special importance. These are common, club, and durum wheats.

Common wheat is bread wheat. It is closely related to club wheat. It probably originated in Turkey and southern Russia. The most important common wheat states are Texas, Kansas, Nebraska, Oklahoma, Colorado, North and South Dakota, Montana, and Minnesota. *Club* wheats are grown only in the Pacific Coast states. Elgin and Hymar are the leading

SPECIES OF WHEAT

Common Name	Latin Name	Common Name	Latin Name
Club	*Triticum compactum*	English	*T. turgidum*
		Shot	*T. sphaerococcum*
Common	*T. aestivum*	Spelt	*T. spelta*
Durum	*T. durum*	Wild Einkorn	*T. aegilopoides*
Einkorn	*T. monococcum*		
Emmer	*T. dicoccum*	Wild Emmer	*T. dicoccoides*
Macha	*T. macha*		
Persian	*T. persicum*	Timopheevi	*T. timopheevi*
Polish	*T. polonicum*		

club wheats. *Durum* is a hard, tough wheat. It is similar to Polish and English wheats, but is much more important commercially. Spaghetti and macaroni makers use Stewart and mindum varieties of durum wheat, because they hold together well while cooking. In North America, durum wheat grows in North Dakota, South Dakota, Montana, and Minnesota, and in parts of Canada.

Varieties of Wheat. Each species of wheat is divided into many varieties. About 30,000 varieties of wheat are

Varieties of Wheat Grown in the United States include, *from left to right,* Triumph, two types of Selkirk, and Conley. Triumph is planted in the fall and harvested the following spring or summer. Selkirk and Conley are planted in the spring and harvested during the summer.

Plowing the Field is the first step in preparing the soil for planting wheat. The plow turns and loosens the earth to aid in planting. Plowing also makes it easier for the seeds to sprout and grow.

grown in various parts of the world. More than 200 of these grow in the United States. Each is different from the others in some way. Experts study these varieties in milling laboratories and agricultural experiment stations. They analyze these wheats and crossbreed them to get the best qualities of each. Wheat from other countries is brought to the United States for experiments. The U.S. Department of Agriculture has collected nearly 15,000 varieties of wheat.

The varieties of wheat are named in various ways. Sometimes a wheat is named for the person or people who developed it. Examples are *Dicklow* and *Dawson*. Sometimes a wheat gets its name from the experiment station where it was developed. *Kanred*, the name of a hard, red winter wheat, was selected by the Kansas Experimental Station. Indian names such as Pawnee and Comanche are now being used to avoid the idea of geographical limitations implied by state names.

Hybrid Wheats are developed by crossbreeding varieties of wheat. For example, one variety may be especially valuable because it will resist rust and other diseases. Another variety may be particularly good for its breadbaking qualities. The plant breeder crosses the two in an attempt to get a good, rust-resistant bread wheat.

Growing and Harvesting Wheat

A good wheat crop depends on several things. The soil and the weather must be right. The seed must be good, and free from disease. The grain must be harvested at the right time.

Climate and Soil. The best soils for growing wheat are the silt and clay loams. The soil should contain much *humus* (decayed vegetable or animal matter) to provide food for the plant. Wheat will grow at the equator or at the Arctic circle. It will grow at sea level or at an altitude of 10,000 feet (3,000 meters) or more. But fairly dry and mild regions are best for wheat farming.

Crop Rotation. In some places, farmers grow wheat in rotation with other crops. For example, farmers plant corn, oats, clover, timothy, or soybeans one year

and wheat the next year. They sometimes plant wheat every other year and keep the soil *fallow* (idle) to store moisture in the years in between the wheat crops. See DRY FARMING.

Preparing the Ground. Farmers prepare the ground well in advance of planting so that moisture and useful organic matter can collect in the soil. The first step is plowing. The plow turns the soil, leaving a *furrow* (trench). A tractor pulls a single plow or a number of plows joined together. Then the farmer uses a *disk harrow* to break up large chunks of earth that remain after plowing. The sharp, round blades of the disk harrow cut the lumps of earth. Large tractors may pull several disk harrows at once. Fertilizers are usually added to the soil before the wheat is planted. However, a fertilizer called *nitrogen* may be added after the wheat is up and growing.

Planting. After the ground is ready, the farmer plants the wheat, using from $\frac{3}{4}$ bushel to 2 bushels of seed per acre (1.9 to 4.9 bushels per hectare). This amount will produce a yield of from 10 to 50 bushels of wheat per acre (25 to 124 bushels per hectare), depending on the weather and soil.

Most wheat farmers use a piece of farm machinery called a *drill* to plant the seed. The drill drops seeds directly into the furrows, and then covers them with earth. With a large power drill, one person can plant over 100 acres (40 hectares) of wheat in a day.

Care During Growth. After the wheat seed is in the ground there is not a great deal the farmer can do for the crop. While the wheat is growing, busy farmers usually find time to repair and service their equipment in preparation for the harvesting season. They hope for favorable weather, and for freedom from plant disease and from harmful insects. Sometimes the farmer sprays chemicals on fast-growing weeds to kill them and keep them from robbing the wheat plants of nourishment.

Effects of Weather. Winter wheat is planted early enough in the fall to get a good start before winter. The kernels absorb moisture and then they sprout. Cold

223

Planting Wheat requires from ¾ bushel to 2 bushels of seeds per acre (1.9 to 4.9 bushels per hectare). A machine called a *drill*, *left*, drops the seeds into the ground and covers them with soil.

Grant Heilman

weather halts their growth. Snow actually serves as a blanket to keep the cold from the winter wheat. The farmer who plants wheat in the fall fears extremely cold winters with little snow. When spring arrives, winter wheat plants awaken and begin to grow again.

Wheat planted in the spring has a much shorter growing period and faces fewer weather hazards. Either extremely wet weather or very dry weather will destroy both spring and winter wheat. Other weather hazards include hail, high winds, and dust storms.

Harvesting Wheat. Once wheat is ready, it must be harvested as soon as possible before bad weather can ruin the crop. Wheat is ready for harvest when it is dry and hard. Farmers can test it by breaking the wheat head from the stalk, and chewing to feel the break of the kernels on their teeth. They also can take it to a grain elevator for a moisture test. On most farms, machines called *combines* do the harvesting. These implements are combinations of reaping and threshing machines. They cut, thresh, and clean the wheat. Before the development of the combine, harvesting machines cut the wheat. Then threshing machines separated the chaff and stems from the kernels of grain. See COMBINE; REAPER; THRESHING MACHINE.

The Enemies of Wheat

Nature subjects wheat to many attacks. Among the enemies of wheat are insects, and diseases such as rust and smut. Some wheat varieties are resistant to some of these enemies. Other varieties are not.

Rust is one of the most destructive of wheat diseases. It produces small rust-colored spots on the leaves, stems, and heads of wheat. These spots later turn brown. There are two important kinds of rust—*stem* rust and *leaf* rust. Stem rust is more destructive. It attacks the plants at any time after the heads appear. The rust uses most of the food and water needed by the wheat plant, so the kernels of wheat dry up. There is not much that the grower can do to prevent rust except to destroy plants

such as barberry that harbor the rust that later spreads to the wheat. Scientists keep developing varieties of wheat that resist rust. See RUST.

Smut. Another serious disease which attacks the wheat kernels is smut. The two main kinds in this country are *covered smut* and *loose smut*. When the wheat kernels are infected with covered smut, the inside of the kernel becomes a powdery black ball filled with smut spores. The wheat kernels then are known as *smut balls*.

When these smut balls break, they have a foul, fishy odor. When they break during threshing, the smut spreads and may infect thousands of healthy kernels. If infected kernels are used for seed, the next crop is damaged also. The disease can be controlled best by seed treatment before planting, and by planting varieties of wheat which are resistant to smut.

Wheat plants infected with loose smut have both kernels and chaff replaced with the black smut spores. Only the central stem of the wheat remains. The spores are carried by the wind to other plants. Loose smut is difficult to treat. Smut spores flow into the young wheat flowers and grow into the young kernels. A dust preparation will not kill loose smut, but the smut can be killed by putting the grain in water heated to a temperature of 129° F. (54° C). A slightly higher temperature will kill the wheat and a lower one will not kill the smut. See SMUT.

Other Diseases. There are several other wheat diseases caused by fungi, including *scab*, *take-all*, *flag smut*, *leaf spot*, and *glume blotch*. These diseases usually do not cause wide-spread damage. *Black chaff*, a disease caused by bacteria, and *mosaic*, a disease caused by a virus, are of less importance. See MOSAIC DISEASE.

Insects. The Hessian fly causes great damage to wheat. This fly is about the size of a mosquito. It lays eggs on the leaves of the wheat plant. The *maggots* (young flies) that hatch from the eggs crawl between the leaf and the stem and suck the juice of the plant. Small stems may be killed at once, and stronger stems may be weakened so much that they break before harvest. Planting winter wheat after the fall brood of flies has hatched helps to avoid heavy crop damage. Scientists have developed several varieties of wheat that are resistant to the Hessian fly. See HESSIAN FLY.

Grasshoppers and locusts cause a great deal of wheat damage in some areas. See GRASSHOPPER; LOCUST.

Other insect enemies are wheat jointworms, sawflies, chinch bugs, army worms, wireworms, and green bugs. See ARMY WORM; CHINCH BUG; GRAIN WEEVIL.

Weeds are another enemy of wheat. Weeds use the water and nourishment from the soil which are needed by the wheat plant. Morning-glories damage wheat fields, especially in the Pacific Northwest. Weeds can be killed by dusting or spraying with poison. Sometimes this dusting is done by airplane. Planes can dust or spray large areas in a short time. Ground equipment is used whenever it is impractical to use airplanes.

Main Wheat Regions of the World

In the United States, the many varieties of wheat are planted at different times of the year and in different areas. In the southern Great Plains—Oklahoma, Texas, Kansas, Colorado, and Nebraska—hard red winter wheats are grown. Farmers of the northern Great Plains —North Dakota, South Dakota, Montana, and Minnesota—plant hard red spring wheat. The winters are often too severe for winter wheat in this region.

In the eastern United States, in the valleys of the Ohio and Potomac Rivers, wheat is often grown in rotation with other crops. Soft red winter wheat is planted widely in these areas. Wheat is also grown in the Columbia River Basin, and in the "dry farm" uplands of Washington, Oregon, and Idaho. This region has rolling land and deep, fertile soils that hold water well. Most of the rain falls during the winter months.

Leading Wheat-Growing States and Provinces

Bushels of wheat grown each year*

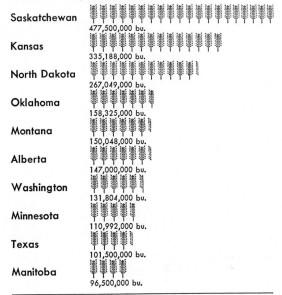

Saskatchewan — 477,500,000 bu.
Kansas — 335,188,000 bu.
North Dakota — 267,049,000 bu.
Oklahoma — 158,325,000 bu.
Montana — 150,048,000 bu.
Alberta — 147,000,000 bu.
Washington — 131,804,000 bu.
Minnesota — 110,992,000 bu.
Texas — 101,500,000 bu.
Manitoba — 96,500,000 bu.

*One bushel equals 60 pounds (27 kilograms).
Based on a 4-year average, 1975-1978.
Sources: U.S. Department of Agriculture; Statistics Canada.

In this region, wheat usually is planted every other year to take advantage of the rainfall for two years. Hard or soft varieties of white wheat are popular in this region. Considerable wheat also grows in New York and Michigan.

The durum wheat used in making macaroni products grows in northern Minnesota, Montana, North

Wheat-Producing Areas in North America

Wheat is grown in large quantities in the United States and Canada. Spring wheat is raised in the northern Great Plains states and in the Prairie Provinces. Severe winters prevent planting in both these regions in the fall. The winter wheat belt extends from the southern Great Plains states through the eastern United States.

Spring wheat
- Major producing area
- Other producing area

Winter wheat
- Major producing area
- Other producing area

WORLD BOOK map

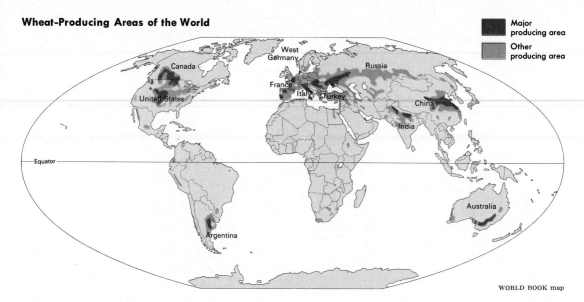

Major producing area

Other producing area

WORLD BOOK map

Dakota, and South Dakota. The rainfall there is light. In such dry sections, the land often is plowed in the summer and planted the next spring. This practice is called *summer fallowing.*

In Canada, the spring wheat region extends through the provinces of Manitoba, Saskatchewan, and Alberta. Rainfall is light and summer fallowing is common. Durum wheat grows well in Canada.

In Other Countries. Russia ranks as the leading wheat-producing country in the world. But Russia does not grow enough wheat for its own needs. The United States is second among the wheat-producing countries.

Leading Wheat-Growing Countries

Bushels of wheat grown in 1978*

Country	Bushels
Russia	4,225,526,000 bu.
United States	1,777,991,000 bu.
China	1,616,723,000 bu.
India	1,139,055,000 bu.
Canada	761,770,000 bu.
France	749,571,000 bu.
Australia	532,784,000 bu.
Turkey	488,691,000 bu.
Italy	328,856,000 bu.
Pakistan	298,653,000 bu.

*One bushel equals 60 pounds (27 kilograms).
Source: U.S. Department of Agriculture.

The soil in south Russia is suitable for wheat. This black-soil belt extends over 1,500 miles (2,410 kilometers) from the Ural Mountains on the northeast into the Danube River Basin on the southwest. This level prairie land has a deep, fertile soil. The climate is similar to that of the Great Plains area of the United States, though the winters are much colder and there is less rainfall. Wheat has grown in Russia for hundreds of years. Many tough, drought-resistant kinds have been developed there. Wheat also is a major crop in Argentina, Australia, China, France, Germany, Great Britain, India, Italy, Pakistan, Poland, Romania, and Turkey.

In South America, the chief wheat-producing region is the fertile, level prairie extending from the Atlantic Ocean to the foothills of the Andes Mountains. This region includes parts of Argentina and Uruguay. The climate is mild, but frosts sometimes cause damage. Large grain farms are scattered among cattle ranches.

Southeastern Australia, northwestern India, Pakistan, and northeastern China all produce much wheat. Australia exports a large part of its crop.

Marketing Wheat

Transportation. Years ago, transporting wheat was not a great problem, because only small amounts of grain were moved. Farmers stored their grain and took it to the mill to be ground when they needed flour. Usually, the miller kept part of the farmer's wheat as payment for the grinding. The miller could then use the wheat to buy other goods. When cities grew large, the transportation of wheat became a problem. Wagons, river boats, railroads, and ships were used to keep pace with the growing demand for the food and other products made from wheat.

Today, large trucks usually carry grain to near-by country elevators for storage. The grain is held there for shipment to a milling company or to large terminal elevators or storage bins. At the terminal elevators, the kernels are poured through great spouts into freight cars. On the Great Lakes, ships carry wheat to the mills.

Storage. When wheat is trucked to grain-storage elevators, a machine lifts and tips each truck so the

How Wheat is Handled in a Country Elevator After wheat has been harvested, it is brought to a country elevator. The elevator has machinery for cleaning and storing wheat and other kinds of grain. Elevators also test grain and grade it for quality according to U.S. government standards. Grain is bought and sold on the basis of its grade.

Grant Heilman

Delivering the Wheat. Trucks carry wheat from farms to the elevator, *above*. It is stored in the elevator until it is taken to milling companies or to larger elevators at major shipping points.

Milt and Joan Mann

Unloading the Wheat. A truck empties the wheat into a pit below the elevator. There, the grain is picked up by a conveyor belt that carries it to the top of the elevator.

Milt and Joan Mann

Storing the Wheat. After the wheat reaches the top of the elevator, the conveyor belt deposits it in the various storage bins by pouring the grain through a chute, *above*.

Milt and Joan Mann

Testing the Wheat. The elevator supervisor uses the instrument shown above to measure the amount of moisture in the wheat deposited in each of the storage bins.

wheat runs into a pit below. Then small metal buckets on cups attached to a moving belt scoop up the wheat. The belt carries the grain to the top of the elevator and dumps it inside the tall, round bin. See GRAIN ELEVATOR.

Most storage elevators are near highways, railroads, or waterways. There are about 15,000 of these elevators in the United States. Wheat in small, country elevators often is sold to larger storage centers. Some of the largest grain elevators are in Chicago; Minneapolis; Kansas City, Mo.; Portland, Ore.; Buffalo; Enid, Okla.; Superior, Wis.; and St. Louis. From the elevators, the wheat is sold to flour mills or for export to other countries.

The country elevators do more than store grain. They often run grading tests. Wheat is graded for quality according to government standards, and the grain is bought and sold on this basis. The elevators provide equipment for drying and cleaning the grain. They also furnish the farmer with marketing information.

Selling. In the United States, country elevators usually are the first buyers of the farmer's wheat, although some grain is bought direct by the miller. Much of the wheat later is bought and sold through a *grain exchange*. A grain exchange is a place where people who want to buy grain meet those who want to sell it. The exchange itself does not buy or sell. One of the largest grain exchanges is the Chicago Board of Trade. It has nearly 1,500 members. These members may include farmers, and representatives of elevators, flour-milling companies, brewers, meat packers, and exporters. At the exchange, customers may see samples of the grain they buy. At the Chicago Board of Trade,

At a Grain Exchange, *above,* brokers buy and sell wheat and other crops. The brokers represent farmers, grain elevator operators, milling and processing companies, and exporters.

A Terminal Elevator, such as the one shown above, receives wheat from country elevators. The wheat is stored for use by millers or to await shipment by barge, ship, or railroad.

buyers purchase wheat that is already in storage. They also make contracts to buy grain to be delivered in the future. This kind of buying and selling is called the *futures market.* The exchange has rules to govern the futures contracts. Millers and other buyers need a constant supply of wheat and the assurance of steady prices. Often, buyers will buy and sell wheat for future delivery. This system, called *hedging,* gives protection against price changes. See COMMODITY EXCHANGE.

International Marketing Problems. Nations that grow more wheat than their own people need sell the extra grain to other countries. In years of high yield, the wheat-growing nations often raise more grain than

HARVESTTIME AROUND THE WORLD

Harvesting the world's wheat crop takes place all year. Each month, wheat is gathered and threshed somewhere in the world, as shown below.

January: Argentina, Australia, Chile, and New Zealand.
February: India.
March: India and upper Egypt.
April: Algeria, lower Egypt, India, Iran, Mexico, Morocco, and Tunisia.
May: Arizona, southern California, Texas, China, Japan, and Spain.
June: China, southern France, Greece, Italy, Portugal, Spain, Turkey, and the United States south of about 40° north latitude.
July: Bulgaria, southern England, France, Germany, Hungary, Romania, Russia, northern United States, and Yugoslavia.
August: Belgium, Canada, Denmark, northern England, The Netherlands, central Russia, and northern United States.
September and October: Parts of Canada, northern Russia, Scandinavian countries, and Scotland.
November: Argentina, Peru, and South Africa.
December: Argentina and Australia.

they can use at home or sell abroad. Then they store the wheat. In some years, the stored wheat supply in the United States and other important wheat-producing countries is greater than the next crop expected. This situation can cause an international problem. First one nation and then another cuts the price of wheat to get rid of its surplus. Finally, the price falls far below the cost of producing the wheat. Such radical drops in price can completely ruin a wheat farmer. On the other hand, the nations that import wheat can be harmed during periods of short supply. During these times, the price of wheat may become so high that some nations that depend on wheat are not able to afford the amounts they need.

Government Wheat Programs. From the early 1930's until the early 1970's, many wheat farmers in the United States participated in federal price support programs. Farm policies under these programs included providing payments to farmers who agreed to take a certain percentage of their cropland out of production. The aim of the programs was to control wheat prices by keeping wheat supplies in line with domestic and foreign demand.

In the early 1970's, severe grain shortages developed throughout the world. Serious droughts in 1972 in Russia, China, Argentina, and Australia significantly reduced the wheat supply. The price of wheat increased tremendously because of the short supply and increasing demand for the grain. Other agricultural products were also in short supply, and this situation led to higher food prices throughout the world.

In 1972, Russia purchased almost one-fourth of the wheat produced in the United States that year. This transaction became highly controversial. Many American farmers believed that large U.S. grain companies had made excessive profits on the sale. Many consumers charged that the sale had left the United States with inadequate wheat supplies and was partly to blame for rising food prices.

In 1973, the government greatly revised its price support policies on wheat and certain other farm crops. The Agriculture and Consumer Protection Act of 1973 ended many price support measures that had been in effect, including measures limiting the amount of land a farmer could plant. Under the new program, farmers were encouraged to produce as much wheat as possible. The government hoped this action would reduce world grain shortages and lower food prices.

The law set a target price for wheat and guaranteed that the government would pay farmers if wheat prices fell below the target price. The target price was much higher than prices farmers had been guaranteed in the past, but lower than current market prices. The plan significantly reduced government support of wheat. By 1977, however, the nation had a large wheat surplus. As a result, the government again set limits on the amount of land on which farmers could plant wheat. The target price program was also continued with provisions for adjusting the price depending on supply and demand.

History

The development and progress of civilization can be linked to the history of wheat. People once roamed constantly across the forests and plains in search of food. Then they discovered they could grow wheat and other grains. This food could be stored to eat during the winter, and seed could be planted in the spring. People at last could settle down in one place, and be sure of having enough food. They could build homes and plan ahead.

With the improvement in agriculture and processing methods, people in some lands grew enough grain to feed people in other countries. In this way, trade began. Thriving cities replaced tiny villages.

Nations have waged war to gain control of wheat-producing lands. It is often pointed out that wars usually start after a harvest. In World War I, Germany was defeated when its enemies cut off its food supply—an important part of which was wheat.

Origin of Wheat. No one is certain when and where wheat first was used as a food. But when it was first used, it probably was chewed, as many farm children chew it now during harvest time. Scientists believe that wheat was first cultivated in Asia between the Tigris and Euphrates rivers. This land was then called Mesopotamia. It is now known as Iraq. In 1948, the American archaeologist Robert J. Braidwood found kernels of wheat in Iraq that date from about 6,700 B.C. The two kinds of wheat Braidwood found are similar in many ways to wheat that grows today. Scientists studying ancient civilizations have found tools for grinding wheat, and the ovens in which it was cooked. Ancient people later discovered that yeast would make a dough mixture rise to produce bread.

The Bible often mentions the production, uses, storage, and diseases of wheat. Thus, we know this grain was an important food in Palestine and Egypt. Theophrastus, a Greek philosopher who lived about 300 B.C., wrote about the many kinds of wheat grown in the countries bordering the Mediterranean Sea. Wheat was grown in China long before the time of Christ.

In Colonial America. Columbus brought wheat to the Western Hemisphere when he returned to the West Indies in 1493. Cortés took wheat from Spain to Mexico in 1519. Missionaries carried it from there into what are now Arizona and California.

Bartholomew Gosnold planted wheat at Buzzards Bay, Mass., in 1602. As early as 1618, colonists grew wheat at Jamestown, Va. The Pilgrims planted wheat when they settled at Plymouth Colony, Mass., but it did not grow as well as the corn the Indians planted along the Atlantic Coast. During the late 1700's, pioneers settling in western New York and the Ohio Valley had better luck with their wheat crops.

Early Days in the United States. Wheat became one of the important products shipped from west to east when canals were built in the eastern United States. In the Pacific Northwest, wheat was grown at a trading post in Fort Vancouver, Wash., as early as 1825. By 1860, Indiana and Illinois were the leading wheat-producing states. However, wheat acreage increased rapidly in Minnesota and the Dakotas, as immigrants from Europe came to these areas. Red Fife, a spring wheat from Canada, grew especially well in these states.

Wheat acreage expanded in Kansas and Oklahoma after 1873, when Mennonite immigrants from Russia settled there. They brought with them a new variety of wheat called Turkey Red. This wheat was brought to Halstead, Kan., from the Crimea in Southern Russia by a man named Bernhard Warkentin. This variety of wheat was far better than those in use, and soon spread throughout Kansas. For the next sixty years, practically all the wheat produced in Kansas and the Southwest was Turkey Red, or some closely related variety.

Development of Modern Tools. Before the 1800's, methods of harvesting and threshing were crude. For about 4,000 years, the *sickle* was the most common tool used. The sickle is a knife with a curved metal blade attached to a short wooden handle. The farmer walked through the wheat fields swinging the hooked blade to cut the stalks of wheat close to the ground. Then the wheat had to be gathered into bundles.

The *scythe* was an improvement. It had a longer sharp blade, fastened to a longer wooden handle. The work went faster. Then the *cradle* was invented. The cradle had a wooden framework with long curved fingers set parallel to the blade. When the stalks of wheat were cut, they fell together on the frame. As the farmer swung the cradle back for another stroke, the cut wheat dropped away so that it could be tied in bundles easily. But the cradle was a heavy implement to handle.

One of the earliest methods of threshing was to drive livestock over a plot of hard ground to trample the grain and loosen it. Then a tool called the *flail* was invented. The flail is a stick with a series of flat strips loosely hinged together by leather to the handle. The wheat was beaten on the ground with the flail to separate the kernels from their dry hulls—much like breaking the shells on peanuts. Then the wheat and hulls were tossed into the air. The wind blew away the light straw and dry bits of chaff clinging to the kernels of wheat. This process was called *winnowing*.

WHEAT

Cyrus McCormick invented the *reaper* in the 1830's, partly because the heavy cradle was so hard to handle. Cyrus was trying to help his father, who had attempted unsuccessfully to build a machine to cut wheat. It took Cyrus some time to get all the parts of the reaper perfected. But, in 1831, when he was 22 years old, he tried out his invention. The machine worked. With various improvements, it has been used since. With the reaper, one person could do the work of many. See Mc-CORMICK, CYRUS HALL.

Wisconsin State Historical Society (International Harvester)

Cutting Wheat with a Cradle, *above,* was the most efficient way of harvesting until the invention of the reaper in 1831. A farmer could cut about 2 acres (0.8 hectare) a day with a cradle.

About 1830, the first *threshing machines* were used. John and Hiram Pitts of Winthrop, Me., in 1834 patented a threshing machine. The wheat was fed into the machine, which pounded and broke away the kernels from the hull and straw. The wheat kernels poured out from one side of the machine. The straw and chaff were blown out separately. With a threshing machine, a few workers could do in a few hours the work once done by many people in several days.

The *self-binder* was an important improvement added to the reaper. Sylvanus D. Locke of Janesville, Wis., developed the first practical self-binder in 1871. A belt caught the cut grain, gathered it, and tied it with wire into bundles, or *sheaves*. The binder made it easier to gather the wheat for threshing. The sheaves were arranged in small stacks or shocks, piled so the water would drain in case of rain, and left to ripen before threshing.

A hundred years ago, it took more than 64 hours to prepare the soil for planting, plant the seed, and cut and thresh 1 acre (0.4 hectare) of wheat. Now the same amount of work takes less than three hours. In 1939, it took 47 hours to produce 100 bushels of wheat, while today it takes 31 hours. This means farmers today have more time to learn new methods of agriculture and improve their farms. They have more time to be with their families and to enjoy life than when they spent all the daylight hours in the fields.

Wheat Breeding. Many of the most important developments in the history of wheat during the 1900's have resulted from the scientific breeding of wheat. Agricultural scientists collect and study different types of wheat and use plant *genetics* (the study of heredity) to produce new and better strains of wheat. All heredi-

The Library of Congress

A Steam-Powered Threshing Machine, *above,* was used by wheat farmers of the late 1800's and early 1900's. The machine separated the kernels from the stalks and blew the husks from the kernels. Threshers were so expensive that a group of farmers bought and shared one machine.

International Harvester

The Self-Binder was developed in 1871. This machine not only cut wheat but also gathered it and tied it into bundles for threshing. Self-binders were replaced by combines in the 1930's.

Grasshopper	Locust	Rust
Hessian Fly	Mosaic Disease	Smut

GROWING AND HARVESTING WHEAT

Agriculture	North Dakota (picture:
Alberta (picture)	North Dakota's Sunny
Combine	Weather)
Dry Farming	Oklahoma (pictures)
Farm and Farming	Reaper
Grain Elevator	Saskatchewan (picture)
Kansas (pictures)	Threshing Machine
McCormick, Cyrus Hall	

PRODUCTS FROM WHEAT

Bran	Flour	Macaroni
Bread	Gluten	Starch

OTHER RELATED ARTICLES

Borlaug, Norman E.	Europe (picture:
Commodity Exchange	The Old and
Cooperative	the New)
Dust Bowl	Grain

Outline

I. The Wheat Plant
  A. Appearance
  B. The Wheat Kernel

II. How Wheat Is Used
  A. Wheat Flour   E. Other Products
  B. Breakfast Foods   F. The Search for New
  C. Macaroni Products   Uses
  D. Animal Feed

III. Kinds of Wheat
  A. Winter Wheat
  B. Spring Wheat
  C. Species of Wheat
  D. Varieties of Wheat
  E. Hybrid Wheats

IV. Growing and Harvesting Wheat
  A. Climate and Soil   D. Planting
  B. Crop Rotation   E. Care During Growth
  C. Preparing the   F. Effects of Weather
     Ground   G. Harvesting Wheat

V. The Enemies of Wheat
  A. Rust   D. Insects
  B. Smut   E. Weeds
  C. Other Diseases

VI. Main Wheat Regions of the World
  A. In the United States
  B. In Canada
  C. In Other Countries

VII. Marketing Wheat
  A. Transportation   D. International Mar-
  B. Storage   keting Problems
  C. Selling   E. Government
                       Wheat Programs

VIII. History

Questions

How long a freight train would it take to hold all the wheat grown in the world in one year?

How many kernels of wheat does the average plant have?

What are some of the weather hazards of wheat growing?

What are the four leading wheat-growing states in the United States? The four leading wheat-growing countries of the world?

What are the two chief diseases that damage wheat?

Where do scientists think that wheat was first grown?

How much time does a farmer spend to grow 1 acre (0.4 hectare) of wheat compared to 100 years ago? What has caused this change?

What are the chief uses of wheat?

tary characteristics of plants are determined by tiny cell particles called *genes*. The scientist controls the hereditary process by combining genes of different wheat types, by changing the genes, and by using many other methods. For further information on how plant characteristics are inherited, see the WORLD BOOK articles on HEREDITY; CELL; and GENE.

The chief aim of this research is to increase the yield of wheat per acre or hectare of land. To produce high-yield varieties, scientists seek strains that resist disease and insects, and that react favorably with fertilizers and other soil nutrients. They may produce wheat that matures early in order to allow the grain to escape sudden climatic changes, such as early frosts. Breeders also seek to develop wheat plants with strong stalks. These types are less likely to be blown over by strong winds or rains before they are fully developed.

During the 1960's, scientists achieved remarkable success in breeding certain cereal grains, especially wheat. They produced wheat varieties that yield huge amounts of grain when used with proper fertilizers. The varieties have short, strong stalks, which enable the plants to stand upright under the great weight of the higher yield.

Because of these new varieties, wheat production in such countries as India, Pakistan, the Philippines, Sri Lanka, and Thailand has greatly increased. With normal weather conditions, farmers in these nations can produce two to four times as much wheat as they had been able to produce earlier on the same land. The worldwide effort to increase the yield of wheat and other grains in underdeveloped countries is sometimes called the *Green Revolution*. In 1970, Norman E. Borlaug, an American agricultural scientist, was awarded the Nobel peace prize for his wheat research that led to the development of the high-yield varieties. See GREEN REVOLUTION; BORLAUG, NORMAN E.

Scientific Classification. Wheat is in the grass family, *Gramineae*. It makes up the genus *Triticum*. ALLEN D. TILLMAN

Related Articles in WORLD BOOK include:

ENEMIES OF WHEAT

Army Worm	Chinch Bug	Grain Weevil

WHEAT GERM

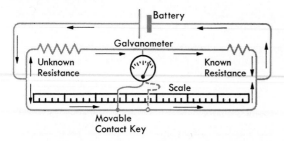

The Slide-Wire Wheatstone Bridge is balanced by moving a contact key along a wire. The portion of wire to the left of the key is R_3, that to the right, R_4. The unknown resistance equals the known resistance times the ratio R_3/R_4. This ratio is found by dividing the lengths of R_3 and R_4 as measured on the scale.

WHEAT GERM. See WHEAT (Other Products).

WHEAT STATE. See KANSAS.

WHEATLEY, PHILLIS (1753?-1784), was the first important black American poet. She was born in Africa and was taken to Boston on a slave ship at the age of about 8. John Wheatley, a Boston tailor, bought her at an auction and made her a servant for his wife.

The Wheatleys taught Phillis to read and write. They also encouraged her to study geography, history, and Latin. Phillis started to write poetry when she was about 14, and her poems soon began to be published. A book of her verse called *Poems on Various Subjects, Religious and Moral* was published in London in 1773.

Wheatley was deeply religious, and some of her poems express her happiness about being brought from Africa into a Christian society. She also wrote about issues of her time, especially in "To the Right Honorable William, Earl of Dartmouth" (1772). In this poem, she contrasted the American Colonies' demand for independence from Great Britain with her status as a slave. CLARK GRIFFITH

Dictionary of American Portraits
Phillis Wheatley

WHEATSTONE, SIR CHARLES (1802-1875), was a British physicist and inventor. He became best known for his work on electrical measuring devices, including "Wheatstone's bridge" which he did not invent but improved, and for his work in electrical telegraphy (see TELEGRAPH [Development]; WHEATSTONE BRIDGE).

Wheatstone experimented on the speed of electricity in wires, and suggested that electricity be used to send messages. With W. F. Cooke, he patented an electrical telegraph in 1837, about the same time that Samuel Morse developed his telegraph in the United States. Wheatstone's device was widely used in Great Britain. He also invented a cryptographic machine and studied arc spectra analysis of metals.

Wheatstone was born in Gloucester. He became professor of experimental philosophy at King's College, London, in 1834. ROBERT E. SCHOFIELD

WHEATSTONE BRIDGE is a device that measures the electrical resistance of a conductor. A Wheatstone bridge consists of two resistances known as the *bridge arms*. The resistances of these bridge arms are known. The bridge also has a third resistance that is adjustable so that the resistance can be changed. These three resistances are connected in an electrical circuit with the unknown resistance. A battery and a galvanometer are also connected in the circuit. The adjustable resistor is then varied until the galvanometer shows no flow of current in the circuit. At this point the bridge is said to be *balanced*. The value of the unknown resistance (R_1) can then be computed from the known values of the bridge arms (R_3, R_4) and the adjustable resistance (R_2) as follows:

$$R_1 = \frac{R_2 R_3}{R_4}$$

See also GALVANOMETER. PALMER H. CRAIG

WHEEL. The discovery of the wheel about 5,000 years ago marked one of the most important steps in the development of civilization. The first important use of the wheel was in transportation. Wheeled carts were easier and faster to pull than sledges. They also permitted people to make better use of the work of horses and other animals. In more recent times, the wheel has found another important use in mechanics in controlling the flow of power. Without the wheel, today's civilization would be impossible. See also WHEEL AND AXLE; TRANSPORTATION (The Wheel). ALLEN S. HALL, JR.

WHEEL AND AXLE, *ACK s'l,* is a mechanical device used in lifting loads. The simplest wheel and axle has a cylinder and a large wheel, fastened together and turning on the same axis. The wheel and axle is a first-class lever (see LEVER). The center of the axle (the cylinder) corresponds to the fulcrum. The radius of the axle corresponds to the load arm. The radius of the wheel corresponds to the force, or effort, arm to which force is applied. Sometimes a crank is used instead of a wheel.

The Advantage of a Wheel and Axle is that it can lift heavy weights for us with only little effort on our part. The following law gives the ratio between the two: *The force applied multiplied by the radius of the wheel equals the load multiplied by the radius of the axle.* To reduce this to a formula, let F stand for force; R for the radius of the wheel; L for the load; and r for the radius of the axle.

$$F \times R = L \times r, \text{ or } \frac{L}{F} = \frac{R}{r}$$

The mechanical advantage of a machine is always the ratio of the load (L) to the force (F) (see MACHINE [Mechanical Advantage]). Let us use an example in which the radius of the wheel (R) is 10 inches, the radius of the axle (r) is 1 inch, and the load (L) is 20 pounds. If there were no friction, the formula would be expressed as $\frac{20}{F} = \frac{10}{1}$. Since $10F = 20$, the force needed would be the same as that normally used to lift a mere 2 pounds. The mechanical advantage, the ratio of L to F, would be $\frac{20}{2}$, or 10.

Uses of the Wheel and Axle. In the ordinary windlass used for raising water from a well, a crank replaces the wheel. The hand applies the effort to the crank. The weight of the bucket of water is the load. In a grindstone, the radius of the wheel is usually longer than the crank handle, because speed is needed as well

The Wheel ranks as one of man's most important inventions. No one knows when or how the first wheel was developed. The earliest known wheeled vehicles were shown on tablets made in Sumer about 3500 B.C., *above*. The people of this ancient Mesopotamian region built chariots to carry their armies. Ancient people also put wheels on devices used for irrigation and pottery making.

Wagon

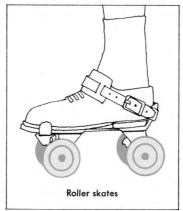

Roller skates

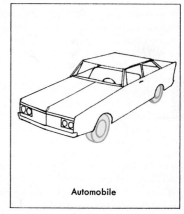

Automobile

Wheels Provide Motion by reducing the friction between a surface and an object moving on it. Countless objects move on wheels. Children pull wheeled wagons, skate on wheels, and play with simple wheeled toys. Complex vehicles would not work without many kinds of wheels. For example, the wheels on an automobile include front and rear wheels, gears, and a steering wheel.

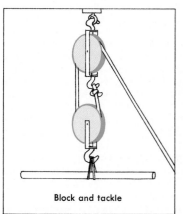

Block and tackle

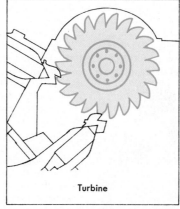

Turbine

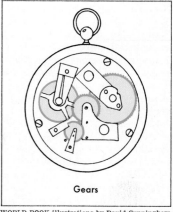

Gears

Many Kinds of Machines depend on the rotary motion provided by wheels. A block and tackle has wheels with ropes passing over them. These pulleys make it easy to lift heavy loads. Huge spinning turbines convert moving water or other fluids into energy. Gears are wheels that connect with one another. This action transfers power from one part of a precision instrument to another.

as force. Sometimes teeth or cogs may be placed around the edge of the wheel, as in a cogwheel, or on the sprocket wheel of a bicycle.   S. Y. LEE

See also RATCHET; WINDLASS; WORK.

WHEEL LOCK. See HARQUEBUS; MUSKET; PISTOL (Early Pistols).

WHEELBARROW is a device for moving loads too heavy to lift by hand. It consists of a tub or box mounted on a wheel with two handles that extend under the body and join on the axle of the wheel. The wheelbarrow is an application of the principle of the lever, and is the kind known as a second-class lever (see LEVER). The longer the handles of a wheelbarrow, the less force required to lift a given load. Wheelbarrows now usually have rubber tires, and may be made of wood or light metals such as aluminum.   ALLEN S. HALL, JR.

WHEELER, BURTON KENDALL (1882-1975), an American statesman, served in the United States Senate as a Montana Democrat from 1923 until 1947. In 1924, he ran unsuccessfully for Vice-President on the Progressive Party ticket (see PROGRESSIVE PARTY). He helped expose the scandals during the presidential administration of Warren G. Harding. Wheeler was an extreme isolationist before World War II. In 1962, he published his autobiography, *Yankee from the West.* He was born in Hudson, Mass.   HARVEY WISH

WHEELER, EARLE GILMORE (1908-1975), a general in the U.S. Army, was Chairman of the Joint Chiefs of Staff from 1964 to 1970. He served as chief of staff for the U.S. Army from 1962 until his appointment as chairman by President Lyndon B. Johnson. Wheeler was with the 63rd Division during campaigns in Europe in World War II. He also held high staff positions in Europe with United States and North Atlantic Treaty Organization (NATO) forces after the war. Wheeler was born in Washington, D.C., and was graduated from the U.S. Military Academy.   MAURICE MATLOFF

WHEELER, JOSEPH (1836-1906), was an American soldier. He served in campaigns against the Indians, before he joined the Confederate Army in 1861. During the Civil War, he made a brilliant record as a cavalry general at the Battle of Shiloh and in campaigns in Tennessee and Georgia. After the war, Wheeler practiced law in Alabama, and served several terms as a Democratic U.S. congressman between 1881 and 1900. He also commanded American forces during the Spanish-American War and in the Philippine Insurrection of 1900. He was born near Augusta, Ga., and was graduated from the U.S. Military Academy. A statue of Wheeler represents Alabama in Statuary Hall.   ARTHUR A. EKIRCH, JR.

WHEELER, SCHUYLER S. See ELECTRIC FAN.

WHEELER, WILLIAM ALMON (1819-1887), served as Vice-President of the United States from 1877 to 1881 under President Rutherford B. Hayes. He also served as a Republican from New York in the U.S. House of Repre-

Brown Bros.
William A. Wheeler

sentatives from 1861 to 1863 and from 1869 to 1877. As a congressman, he devised the Wheeler Adjustment in 1874 to settle a disputed election in Louisiana.

Wheeler showed that he had strict principles by opposing the Salary Grab Act of 1873. Congress, however, voted itself the disputed pay increase. Wheeler refused to profit from the additional income. He bought government bonds, and then had the bonds canceled.

Wheeler was born in Malone, N.Y. He was a successful lawyer and businessman.   IRVING G. WILLIAMS

WHEELER DAM. See MUSCLE SHOALS.

WHEELER-HOWARD INDIAN REORGANIZATION ACT. See INDIAN, AMERICAN (Indians Today).

WHEELING, W.Va. (pop. 48,188; met. area pop. 182,-712), an industrial city on the Ohio River, lies about 60 miles (97 kilometers) southwest of Pittsburgh, Pa. (see WEST VIRGINIA [political map]). The city has an area of about 16 square miles (41 square kilometers). It includes Wheeling Island in the Ohio River. Wheeling is the seat of Ohio County. The Wheeling metropolitan area includes Belmont County in Ohio.

Description. Wheeling lies on a level plain, which rises to steep hills, along the Ohio River. A scenic plaza was built in the heart of the business district. Several bridges connect Wheeling Island with the rest of the city. Wheeling Downs, which features dog races and horse races, occupies one end of the island. Wheeling has two principal parks and several neighborhood parks. Oglebay Park, a 1,400-acre (567-hectare) recreational area, lies outside the city.

Wheeling has about 40 public schools. Other educational institutions include Linsly Military Institute, a preparatory school for boys; Mount de Chantal Academy for Girls; and Wheeling College, established by the Roman Catholic Church in 1954. West Liberty State College is located near Wheeling.

Industry. Wheeling lies near West Virginia's great coal- and natural-gas-producing region, and these minerals furnish power for many of the city's industries. About 400 mills and plants operate in Wheeling. The most important manufactures include iron and steel, aluminum, bronze, tin plate, metal stampings, plastics, glass, ceramics, tile, chemical products, and textiles and garments. The city is also a coal shipping center.

History. Colonel Ebenezer Zane and his brothers founded Wheeling in the winter of 1769-1770. They came from the south branch of the Potomac Valley in Virginia to settle a claim at the present site of the city. Other settlers soon joined them, and in 1774 they erected Fort Fincastle. In 1776, they changed the fort's name to Fort Henry in honor of Patrick Henry. The town of Wheeling was laid out in 1793, incorporated in 1806, and first chartered as a city in 1836. The National Road, now U.S. Highway 40, reached the Ohio River at Wheeling in 1818.

For many years, the city served as a center of trade in the upper Ohio Valley. In 1852, it became the first city on the Ohio River below Pittsburgh to be reached by a railroad from the east. During the Civil War, Wheeling was the headquarters of Virginians who opposed secession from the Union. Union supporters organized the state of West Virginia in Wheeling on June 20, 1863, and the city served as the state capital from 1863 to 1870 and from 1875 to 1885. Wheeling has a city-manager form of government.   FESTUS PAUL SUMMERS

(1798-1873), an American businessman, devoted most of his life to developing transportation and communication in South America. In 1823 his ship was wrecked near Buenos Aires, and he decided to settle in South America. He was appointed U.S. Consul at Guayaquil, Ecuador, in 1824. He later moved to Valparaíso, Chile, and in 1840 established a steamship line to serve the western coast of South America. Wheelwright discovered coal and copper deposits in Chile and built the first railroad in South America, from the mines to the coast. He built other railroads in Chile and Argentina, and developed the port of La Plata. He also built the continent's first telegraph line. He was born in Newburyport, Mass. JOHN B. McFERRIN

WHELK is a large sea snail with a sturdy spiral shell. There are many *species* (kinds) of whelks. Most species are edible. The *waved whelk* lives in 6 to 500 feet (1.8 to 150 meters) of water off the coasts of northern Europe and of the northeastern coast of North America. It grows up to 3 inches (8 centimeters) long. The *knobbed whelk* of the U.S. Atlantic coast reaches 8 inches (20 centimeters) in length. See also SHELL (picture).

Scientific Classification. Waved whelks are in the family *Buccinidae*. They are genus *Buccinum*, species *B. undatum*. Knobbed whelks are in the family *Melongenidae*. They are *Busycon carica*. R. TUCKER ABBOTT

WHETSTONE is any abrasive stone, natural or artificial, that is used for grinding and sharpening. Artificial abrasives, such as silicon carbide and aluminum oxide, are most often used. At one time a fine-grained variety of quartz, called *novaculite*, was used for grindstones. Its uniform hard grains made it capable of grinding quickly and withstanding wear. FREDERICK H. POUGH

WHEY. See CHEESE (How Cheese Is Made; History).

WHIG PARTY, *hwihg*, was a name applied to political parties in England, Scotland, and America. *Whig* is a short form of the word *whiggamore*, a Scotch word once used to describe persons from western Scotland who opposed King Charles I of England in 1648.

In the late 1600's, Scottish and English opponents of the growing power of royalty were called Whigs. The Whig party maintained a strong position in English politics until the 1850's, when the Whig progressives adopted the term Liberal. See GREAT BRITAIN (History).

In the American Colonies, the Whigs were those people who resented British control, and favored independence from Great Britain. The term was probably first used in New York City about 1768. The Whigs supported the American Revolutionary War. British loyalists, called *Tories*, opposed the Whigs in the struggle (see TORY PARTY). The terms *Whig* and *Tory* fell into disuse after the colonies won their independence.

The Whig Party of the 1800's began to take shape about 1832. Political groups that opposed Andrew Jackson and his theories started to combine and unify themselves into a political party. These groups included the National Republicans, certain conservative factions of the Democratic-Republican party, and some former members of the Anti-Masonic party. Some of the political leaders of the Whig party included such well-known National Republicans as Henry Clay, John Quincy Adams, and Daniel Webster. Soon many wealthy Southern cotton planters joined in protest against the democratic, leveling doctrines of the Jacksonians. In the north and east, many factory owners also joined the

group because it supported a protective tariff. First as the National Republicans and later under the name of Whigs, these groups advocated new and broader activities for both state and national governments.

The First Program of the Whigs followed Henry Clay's "American System." It included a proposal for a high protective tariff to encourage the growth of American industry. Clay wanted to distribute to the states money received from the sale of federal lands, so that they would construct new transportation systems of canals and highways. Clay argued that Western and Southern farmers and Eastern manufacturers formed a natural and interdependent economic unit that would furnish markets for each other, if they were connected with good transportation facilities.

When Jackson and his followers came out against the United States Bank, Clay immediately supported it. The Whigs soon adopted an advanced financial program calling for federal control of the banking system in the interest of sound currency. They also wanted to insure a supply of credit adequate to meet the increasing demands from expanding commercial interests in the East and from the moving frontier in the West. Clay opposed Jackson with this program in the presidential election of 1832, but was defeated. In 1836 the Whig party nominated William Henry Harrison, Hugh White, and Daniel Webster for the presidency. But the Democratic candidate, Martin Van Buren, won easily.

In the 1840's, many able men joined the party. They included Horace Greeley, editor of the New York *Tribune;* William H. Seward of New York; and Edward Everett, the Whigs' most brilliant orator.

The Whigs nominated William Harrison as their presidential candidate in 1840. He won the election, but died after serving only one month in office. Vice-President John Tyler followed Harrison as President. Tyler had received the nomination for Vice-President mainly to attract the Southern votes. Actually, Tyler was not a Whig, and opposed the Whig program. His opposition as President weakened the Whig strength.

In 1844 the Whigs renominated Henry Clay for the presidency, but he lost a second time. One reason for his defeat lay in his refusal to take a position on slavery. This cost Clay many Northern Whig votes. In the election of 1844, the Whigs for the first time presented a real political program. It included a high tariff, regulated currency, and a single term for the presidency.

Decline of the Whigs. The Whigs managed to win the presidency with the popular Zachary Taylor in 1848. Four years later they tried to repeat the victory with General Winfield Scott. But the Democratic candidate, Franklin Pierce, defeated him. In 1856 a Whig convention backed Millard Fillmore, the unsuccessful Know-Nothing candidate for the presidency.

The Whig party had already begun to break into sectional groups over the question of slavery. The Kansas-Nebraska Bill of 1854 split the party still further. Most Northern Whigs joined the new Republican party. Many Southern Whigs returned to the Democratic party. The remaining Whigs became a part of the Constitutional Union party by 1860. DONALD R. McCOY

See also the separate articles for the various Whig leaders mentioned in this article, such as CLAY, HENRY.

WHIN. See FURZE.

WHIPPET is a swift, lean, muscular dog that looks like a small greyhound. It was bred from the Italian greyhound and the terrier.

A whippet weighs from 18 to 23 pounds (8 to 10 kilograms) and stands 18 to 22 inches (46 to 56 centimeters) high. It may be black, red, white, fawn, or brindle. It has a narrow, pointed head, muscular neck, long back, and long, tapering tail. Whippets are popular with sportsmen for hunting rabbits and for racing. They can run as fast as 35 miles (56 kilometers) per hour.   OLGA DAKAN

See also DOG (color picture: Hounds).

WHIPPING POST is a post to which persons are tied when being whipped as a form of punishment. Such beatings once took place in public. Most villages in England and the American Colonies had whipping posts in their public squares. The posts were often set up with another punishment device called the *stocks* (see STOCKS).

Today, few persons are sentenced to be whipped. Fines and prison terms have replaced physical beating as forms of punishment in most countries. British law allowed whipping until 1948. Whipping is still a legal punishment in some countries including Canada, South Africa, and Sri Lanka. Delaware is the only state that permits whipping. The whipping penalty was last inflicted in Delaware in 1952. In 1964, a Delaware court imposed a whipping sentence, but the governor refused to let it be carried out.   MARVIN E. WOLFGANG

WHIPPLE, GEORGE H. See MINOT, GEORGE.

WHIPPLE, WILLIAM (1730-1785), was a New Hampshire signer of the Declaration of Independence. He served as a delegate to the provincial congress in 1775, and to the Continental Congress in 1775-1776, and 1778. He fought as a brigadier general in the Revolutionary War. Whipple served in the state assembly from 1780 to 1784, and as financial receiver for New Hampshire from 1782 to 1784. He was an associate justice of the superior court from 1782 until his death. Whipple was born in Kittery, Me.   RICHARD B. MORRIS

WHIPPOORWILL is a North American bird named for its odd, whistling call, which sounds like "whip-poor-will, whip-poor-will." The whippoorwill lives in the eastern, central, and southern United States, as far

A. A. Francesconi, National Audubon Society

The Whippoorwill's Spotted, Brown Feathers blend with its woodland surroundings and protect the bird from enemies.

north as southeastern Canada and as far south as Mexico and Honduras. It spends the winter along the Gulf Coast, in Mexico, and in Central America.

The whippoorwill is about 10 inches (25 centimeters) long. Its spotted, brown feathers make the bird hard to see in the heavily wooded areas in which it lives. During the day, the whippoorwill usually rests on the ground or perches lengthwise on a log. It flies mostly at night. Soft feathers help the whippoorwill fly silently. The bird uses its wide mouth rimmed with long bristles to catch flying insects. The female lays her two eggs among the leaves on the ground. The white eggs are delicately marked with lilac and brown. The whippoorwill and its relatives, the *chuck-will's widow* and the *poor-will*, often help farmers. They eat insects which harm crops.

Scientific Classification. The whippoorwill belongs to the goatsucker family, *Caprimulgidae*. It is genus *Caprimulgus*, species *C. vociferus*.   ALBERT WOLFSON

See also BIRD (color picture: Birds' Eggs).

WHIRLIGIG. See WATER BEETLE.

WHIRLPOOL is a mass of water which spins around and around rapidly and with great force. A whirlpool may form in water for several reasons. It may occur when the water current strikes against a bank which has a peculiar form. It may also occur when opposing currents meet, and it may be caused by the action of the wind. Rocks or tides may get in the way of an ocean current. Whirlpools often form as a result.

There are several well-known whirlpools. One of these is the whirlpool in the gorge below the falls of the Niagara River. This whirlpool was caused by the wearing away of a side basin out of the line of the river's course. The Maelstrom, which is off the coast of Norway, is formed by rocks and tides which oppose the current. The Charybdis, between Sicily and Italy, is formed by winds which act against the tidal currents. During storms the whirlpools become violent and dangerous to ships.   ELDRED D. WILSON

See also MAELSTROM; NIAGARA FALLS AND NIAGARA RIVER (The Whirlpool).

WHIRLWIND is a circular whirling column of air. It is caused by the rising of an overheated layer of air near the ground. Whirlwinds occur most frequently in the deserts, where the sun heats the air near the dry ground to a high temperature. The motion of the air as it rises can often be seen, because it may carry sand and dust 1,000 feet (300 meters) or more above the earth. Over tropical oceans, some *waterspouts* form in much the same way. See also WATERSPOUT.   REID A. BRYSON

WHISKEY is a strong alcoholic beverage distilled from grain and malt. Whiskey is made in three steps: (1) mashing, (2) fermenting, and (3) distilling. First, whiskey makers soak the grain in hot water to make a mash. Then they add malt to change the starch of the grain into sugar. Next, they add yeast to the mash and allow the mixture to ferment. Fermentation changes the sugar into alcohol. Finally, they distill the mash to concentrate the alcohol to not more than 80 per cent (160 proof). This is known as *straight whiskey*. The whiskey makers add distilled water to lower the alcoholic content to from 40 to 50 per cent (80 to 100 proof). Then they store the whiskey in barrels to age.

Blended whiskey is a mixture containing not less than 20 per cent straight whiskey with pure alcohol and water. *Bonded whiskey* is any type that contains not less than 50 per cent alcohol (100 proof) and has been aged at least four years in oak barrels.

Bourbon whiskey is made from mash in which corn is the chief ingredient. *Rye whiskey* has rye grains as its chief mash ingredient. *Sour-mash whiskey* is made by using a mash which has already been fermented to make ordinary whiskey. *Canadian whiskey* is a distinctive product of Canada. This whiskey, which contains no distilled spirits less than two years old, is light in color and body. *Scotch whisky* and *Irish whiskey* are made chiefly from barley malt.

The manufacture and the sale of whiskey are prohibited by law in parts of some states in the United States.   J. BERNARD ROBB

WHISKEY REBELLION of 1794 was brought about by a federal tax in 1791 on United States whiskey makers. The Whiskey Rebellion was led by angry farmers in western Pennsylvania. These farmers found it profitable to turn much of their corn and rye crop into whiskey. They could ship whiskey to markets more easily and profitably than they could ship the bulky grain, because early roads and transportation facilities were poor.

The federal tax law permitted government agents to enter homes and collect money from small whiskey producers. Farmers throughout the Union immediately protested against this. In 1792, the Congress of the United States removed the tax from the smallest stills. This change satisfied Virginia and North Carolina farmers, but whiskey makers in Pennsylvania still refused to pay the tax.

In the summer of 1794, the federal government ordered certain Pennsylvania ringleaders arrested. A series of bitter fights between United States marshals and the rebel farmers resulted. Several persons were killed or wounded before President George Washington sent in troops to stop the rebellion. Two rebel leaders were convicted of treason, but Washington later pardoned them. The Whiskey Rebellion was an early "testing ground" on the use of federal power to enforce a federal law within a state.   RICHARD HOFSTADTER

WHISKEY RING was an association of whiskey manufacturers and high government officials that was active during the 1870's in the United States. The conspirators banded together to cheat the United States government of taxes imposed on distilled liquors. The Whiskey Ring was one of the great political scandals of the Ulysses S. Grant administration.

The association was formed in Saint Louis, Mo., and soon spread to other cities in the United States. Many distillers were forced to join the ring in order to save their businesses. The illegal profits were divided among the conspiring government officials, some of whom held important positions. One of them was the chief clerk in the Department of the Treasury. Another, General Orville E. Babcock, was the private secretary of President Grant.

The Treasury Department soon realized that it was losing millions of dollars in liquor revenue. It tried to trace the loss, but investigation was difficult. The thieves had friends in the Treasury Department who warned them of government activities. But Secretary of the Treasury Benjamin H. Bristow finally found evidence against the lawbreakers in 1875. Many persons

were convicted, but the leaders escaped with light punishment.   JOHN DONALD HICKS

WHISKY-JACK. See JAY.

WHIST, *hwist,* is an old English card game from which bridge developed. Like bridge, it is played with a pack of 52 cards, divided into four suits—clubs, diamonds, hearts, and spades (see BRIDGE). The ace is the highest card, and the deuce is the lowest card.

Usually, four persons play whist. Partners sit facing each other. The cards are shuffled, *cut* (divided), and dealt one at a time. The dealer turns the last card face-up. The suit turned up is called the *trump suit.* Any card in the trump suit is higher than any card in the other three suits. For example, the deuce of trump is higher than the aces of the other suits.

The player on the dealer's left lays down a card. The play moves clockwise and each player lays down a card. Each player must play a card of the suit that was led. If a player cannot follow suit, he or she may play a card of another suit or a trump card. If trump have not been played, the highest card played in the suit that was led wins the four cards, called the *trick.* If trump have been played, the highest trump card wins the trick. The player who wins the trick leads the first card in the next trick. The object is to win as many tricks as possible.

After all the cards have been played, the score is added. Each trick taken above six tricks is worth one point. Taking all 13 tricks is called a *slam.* The first team to score seven points wins the game. LILLIAN FRANKEL

WHISTLE is a device that makes a sound when air or steam is blown through it. Most whistles consist of a tube with a sharp edge or lip. The air or steam is blown in one end of the tube and goes into a swirling motion when it strikes the lip. This motion first compresses and then expands the air, causing a sound.

Steam whistles are seldom used today. Steam locomotives used steam whistles. But today's diesel locomotives use various types of air horns, some of which sound like steam whistles. Police officers and sports officials blow small air whistles.   PAUL J. SCHEIPS

WHISTLER, JAMES ABBOTT McNEILL (1834-1903), was an American artist. He spent most of his life in Europe. Whistler's paintings, his love of publicity, his clever wit, and his quarrelsome nature made him an international celebrity.

Whistler's best-known painting is *Arrangement in Gray and Black: Portrait of the Artist's Mother* (1872), commonly called *Whistler's Mother* (see MOTHER [picture]). The flattened forms and unsymmetrical composition of this painting are characteristic of Whistler's style. He was influenced by Japanese artists who used similar techniques in their woodcuts.

Whistler named many of his paintings for types of musical compositions, such as nocturnes and symphonies. He believed that paintings, like music, should be abstract. He also felt that the forms in a painting are more important than the subject.

The English art critic John Ruskin criticized one of Whistler's most abstract paintings, *Nocturne in Black and Gold—The Falling Rocket* (about 1874). Ruskin declared that Whistler had flung "a pot of paint in the public's face." Whistler sued Ruskin for libel and defended his theories on art in court. He won the case but received less than a penny in damages. The cost of the lawsuit forced Whistler into bankruptcy. Nevertheless, he enjoyed the publicity that the case brought him. Whistler included excerpts from his defense in a book of his collected writings, *The Gentle Art of Making Enemies* (1890).

In addition to his paintings, Whistler became well known for his prints and interior decorations. Nearly all the prints are etchings or lithographs. Whistler created about 440 etchings, including many illustrations of Venice and the River Thames (see ETCHING [picture: An Etching by James Whistler]). The most famous example of Whistler's interior decoration is the Peacock Room, which he designed for a house in London. The room is now in the Freer Gallery in Washington, D.C.

Whistler was born in Lowell, Mass. In 1843, he moved with his family to St. Petersburg (now Leningrad), Russia, where his father directed the construction of a railroad. He returned to the United States in 1849. In 1851, Whistler entered the U.S. Military Academy at West Point. He was expelled during his junior year because of low grades in chemistry. From November, 1854, to February, 1855, Whistler worked as a chartmaker for the United States Coast and Geodetic Survey. He showed little interest in the job but received fine training in the technique of etching. In 1855, Whistler went to Paris to study art. He moved to London in 1859 and died there.   ANN LEE MORGAN

Old Battersea Bridge: Nocturne—Blue and Gold (1865), an oil painting on canvas; The Tate Gallery, London

Whistler's Paintings show how the artist used a few related colors to establish delicate relationships between tone and form.

WHITE. See COLOR.

WHITE is the family name of two popular American journalists, father and son.

William Allen White (1868-1944) was a country editor who became known as the *Sage of Emporia*. He made his small-town newspaper, the *Emporia* (Kans.) *Gazette*, one of the most famous papers in the world. In 1923, he won the Pulitzer prize for editorial writing. He also was awarded a Pulitzer prize in 1947, after his death, for his autobiography.

White was born in Emporia, Kans., and was educated at Emporia College and at the University of Kansas. In 1890, he left college and took a job on the El Dorado (Kans.) *Republican*. After various newspaper jobs in Kansas, he returned to Emporia in 1895 and became owner and editor of the *Gazette*. A year later, White wrote an editorial entitled "What's the Matter with Kansas?" This made him famous overnight. The Republican Party reprinted the article and used it in the campaign to elect William McKinley as President of the United States. From that time on, White's editorials played an important part in the political affairs of the country.

William Lindsay White (1900-1973), the son of William Allen White, won fame during World War II as a war correspondent and an author of books about the war. He was born in Emporia, and graduated from Harvard University. After college, he worked with his father on the *Gazette*. In 1935, White joined the staff of the *Washington Post*, and two years later left to work for *Fortune* magazine. In 1940, White became a member of the staff of the *Reader's Digest*.   JOHN ELDRIDGE DREWRY

WHITE, ALFRED HOLMES (1873-1953), pioneered in the development of engineering as a profession in the United States. He was associated with the University of Michigan. His books, *Technical Gas and Fuel Analysis* (1913) and *Engineering Materials* (1939), became important texts. His work with the American Institute of Engineers, and the Society for the Promotion of Engineering Education set the standards for the American engineering education program. White was born in Peoria, Ill.   HERBERT S. RHINESMITH

WHITE, BYRON RAYMOND (1917-   ), became an associate justice of the Supreme Court of the United States in 1962. President John F. Kennedy appointed him to succeed Justice Charles E. Whittaker, who had retired. White was deputy attorney general at the time.

During the early 1970's, White and Justice Potter Stewart frequently held the court's *swing votes*. A swing vote can decide the outcome of a case in which the vote is almost evenly divided between conservatives and liberals. During those years, the court had four conservative justices appointed by President Richard M. Nixon and three liberal justices appointed by previous Presidents. Many court decisions followed a conservative or liberal viewpoint, depending on how Stewart and White voted.

White was born in Fort Collins, Colo. He graduated from the University of Colorado in 1938 and from Yale Law School in 1946. He won national fame and the nickname "Whizzer" as an all-American halfback at Colorado. He later played professional football to help finance his law studies.

After law school, White served as a law clerk to Chief Justice Fred M. Vinson. He joined a Denver law firm in 1947 and became a partner in 1950. He was appointed deputy attorney general in 1961.   OWEN M. FISS

See also SUPREME COURT OF THE U.S. (picture).

WHITE, E. B. (1899-   ), is an American author. He is known chiefly as an essay writer, but he also writes poetry and children's books. His essays, which deal with both serious and light subjects, have a clear, witty style. White writes in an informal, personal manner.

White has written three children's books. *Stuart Little* (1945) tells of a mouse with human parents, and *Charlotte's Web* (1952) concerns a girl, a pig, and a spider. *The Trumpet of the Swan* (1970) tells about a swan without a voice. In these books, which deal with friendship and love, the animals talk and act like human beings. Several collections of White's writings have been published, including *One Man's Meat* (1942), *The Second Tree from the Corner* (1954), and *The Points of My Compass* (1962).

Elwyn Brooks White was born in Mount Vernon, N.Y. He started writing for *The New Yorker* magazine in 1925 and strongly influenced its literary style. Many of his works tell of his life in Maine, where he lives. In 1963, White received the Presidential Medal of Freedom.   MARCUS KLEIN

WHITE, EDWARD DOUGLASS (1845-1921), served as chief justice of the United States from 1910 to 1921. In 1894, he was appointed an associate justice of the Supreme Court of the United States. White became best known for his dissent in the case declaring the national income tax unconstitutional, and for his antitrust decisions requiring the dissolution of the Standard Oil and American Tobacco companies. He was born in Lafourche Parish, La. A statue of White represents Louisiana in the United States Capitol in Washington, D.C.   JERRE S. WILLIAMS

WHITE, EDWARD HIGGINS, II (1930-1967), in 1965 became the first United States astronaut to leave his craft while in outer space. The space walk lasted 21 minutes and took place during a four-day flight made by White and James A. McDivitt. White and astronauts Virgil Grissom and Roger Chaffee died on Jan. 27, 1967, when a flash fire swept through their Apollo spacecraft. The fire occurred during a test at Cape Kennedy (now Cape Canaveral), Fla.

White was born on Nov. 14, 1930, in San Antonio, Tex. He graduated from the U.S. Military Academy in 1952 and went into the Air Force. In 1959, he earned a master's degree in aeronautical engineering from the University of Michigan.   WILLIAM J. CROMIE

WHITE, HUGH LAWSON (1773-1840), an American statesman and jurist, was a candidate for President of the United States in 1836. In that year, Martin Van Buren ran as Andrew Jackson's hand-picked successor on the Democratic ticket. The Whigs hoped to defeat Van Buren by running Daniel Webster, William Henry Harrison, and White. The plan failed, and White carried only two states, Georgia and Tennessee.

White was born in Iredell County, North Carolina. He moved to Tennessee, where he practiced law and became a judge, state senator, and U.S. attorney. He was a U.S. senator from 1825 to 1840.   RICHARD N. CURRENT

WHITE, JOHN. See LOST COLONY.

WHITE, PATRICK (1912-   ), an Australian novelist, won the 1973 Nobel prize for literature. He became the first Australian writer to receive this award.

White writes in a complex, flowery style. He often uses the *stream of consciousness* technique, which describes in detail the thoughts that flow through the mind of the characters.

The major characters in White's novels are emotionally isolated from other people. In his first novel, *Happy Valley* (1939), White wrote an ironic account of life in a dreary Australian village. He gained international recognition with his fourth novel, *The Tree of Man* (1955), which tells the story of an Australian family. *Voss* (1957), a historical novel, describes an explorer's expedition across Australia in the mid-1800's. White's other novels include *The Aunt's Story* (1948), *Riders in the Chariot* (1961), and *The Eye of the Storm* (1973). He also has written plays, poetry, and short stories. Patrick Victor Martindale White was born in London, England.   THOMAS A. ERHARD

WHITE, PAUL DUDLEY (1886-1973), an American physician, was regarded as one of the world's great authorities on heart diseases. He served as president of the American Heart Association from 1942 to 1944, and became president of the International Society of Cardiology in 1954. He headed many committees and foreign missions, and was a consultant of governments. He acted as a consultant to President Dwight D. Eisenhower. White was born in Boston.   NOAH D. FABRICANT

WHITE, PEREGRINE (1620-1703), was the first English child born in New England, on the *Mayflower* in Cape Cod Bay. His father, William, died soon afterwards. His mother, Susanna White, then married Edward Winslow, becoming both the first mother and the first bride in Plymouth. Peregrine became a captain of militia and settled in Marshfield.   BRADFORD SMITH

WHITE, STANFORD (1853-1906), was a prominent American architect. He had a marked talent as a draftsman and decorator. In 1880, White became a partner in the New York firm of McKim, Mead & White. He designed much of the decorative detail of the Villard Houses, the Madison Square Garden built in 1890, the Century Club, and the old Herald Building, all in New York City. White's murder by Harry K. Thaw created a national sensation. White was born in New York City.   HUGH MORRISON

WHITE, WALTER FRANCIS (1893-1955), an American writer, devoted his life to helping the Negro. Although White did not look like a Negro, he chose to regard himself as one. And in his books, *Fire in the Flint* (1924), *Flight* (1926), *Rope and Faggot* (1929), *Rising Wind* (1945), and *A Man Called White* (1948), he dealt with the problems and hopes of nonwhite people.

White was born in Atlanta, Ga., and graduated from Atlanta University. He served as secretary of the National Association for the Advancement of Colored People from 1931 until his death. White received the Spingarn medal in 1937 for his work in promoting Negro rights.   EDWIN H. CADY

WHITE ANT. See TERMITE.
WHITE BLOOD CELL. See BLOOD.
WHITE-CHEEKED GOOSE. See CANADA GOOSE.
WHITE-FOOTED MOUSE. See MOUSE (Deer Mice).
WHITE GOLD. See GOLD (Jewelry); PLATINUM.
WHITE HEART. See DUTCHMAN'S-BREECHES.
WHITE HEATH. See BRIER.

The North Portico of the White House Faces Pennsylvania Avenue in Washington, D.C.

WHITE HOUSE is the official residence of the President of the United States. The President lives and works in the world-famous mansion in Washington, D.C. The White House contains the living quarters for the Chief Executive's family and the offices in which the President and his staff conduct official business of the United States. Some of the most important decisions in history have been made there.

The 132-room White House stands in the middle of a beautifully landscaped 18-acre (7-hectare) plot at 1600 Pennsylvania Avenue (see WASHINGTON, D.C. [map]). The building was popularly known as the *White House* in the 1800's. However, its official name was first the *President's House* and then the *Executive Mansion* until 1901. That year, President Theodore Roosevelt authorized *White House* as the official title.

The White House is one of the most popular tourist attractions in the United States. Every year, more than 1½ million visitors go through parts of the mansion that are open to the public. Certain rooms in the White House are open to the public Tuesday through Saturday between 10 A.M. and noon. Tourists may take special tours by obtaining passes from their Senators or Representatives. The building is closed to the public on Sundays, Mondays, and holidays.

Outside the White House

The Main Building is 175 feet (53 meters) long and 85 feet (26 meters) high. A wide curved *portico* (porch) with Ionic columns two stories high stands on the south side of the mansion. A square portico on the north side serves as the main entrance. Two long, low galleries extend

from the east and west sides of the main building. The terraced roof covering them forms a promenade on the first floor level. Facilities for the White House press corps are under the west terrace, and a theater is under the east terrace.

The East and West Wings stand at the end of the terraces. The west (executive) wing contains the offices of the President and his staff, and the Cabinet room. The east wing contains the offices of the social secretary's staff and the President's military aides.

The South Lawn, often called the President's Park, contains many trees and shrubs planted by former occupants of the White House. For example, the south portico is shaded by magnificent magnolia trees planted by President Andrew Jackson.

Inside the White House

Public Rooms. Tourists enter the White House through the east wing. Most visitors are shown only five rooms on the first floor of the mansion, but these rooms represent the elegance and beauty of the entire interior.

The State Dining Room at the west end of the main building can accommodate as many as 140 dinner guests at one time. It was remodeled in 1902.

The Red Room is furnished in the style of the period from 1810 to 1830. The walls are hung with gold-bordered red silk.

The Blue Room is the main reception room for guests of the President. Its furnishings represent the period from 1817 to 1825. President James Monroe, who occupied the White House during these years, ordered much of the furniture now in this oval room.

famous rooms in the
WHITE HOUSE

Second Floor

Treaty Room   Lincoln Bedroom   Queen's Room

Entrance Hall   Main Hallway

First Floor

State Dining Room   Red Room   Blue Room   Green Room   East Room

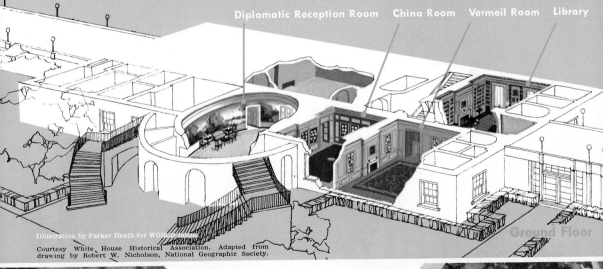

Diplomatic Reception Room   China Room   Vermeil Room   Library

Ground Floor

Illustration by Parker Heath for WORLD BOOK
Courtesy White House Historical Association. Adapted from drawing by Robert W. Nicholson, National Geographic Society.

Lorenzo S. Winslow, Architect

This Model Shows the Original Main Building and the Two Wings Added Later

East Wing

President's Office

Executive Wing

Main Building

Movie Theater for Family

White House Press Facilities

The Diplomatic Reception Room, *above,* serves as the entrance to the White House for official functions. The wallpaper in this oval room was printed in France in 1834. It shows scenes of the American outdoors.

The Library, *left,* is decorated chiefly in the style of the early 1800's. The crystal chandelier once belonged to the family of American novelist James Fenimore Cooper. The style of the carpet was popular in France during the 1800's.

The State Dining Room, *below,* is the scene of the President's official banquets. Its tables can accommodate 140 guests for a state dinner.

All photographs by the National Geographic Society, courtesy of the White House Historical Association

The Red Room, *left,* is furnished in the American Empire style, popular between 1810 and 1830. The walls are hung with red silk edged with gold trim. The Red Room serves as a parlor.

All photographs by the National Geographic Society, courtesy of the White House Historical Association

The Green Room, *above,* is decorated in the style popular between 1800 and 1814. A light green silk material covers the walls. The Green Room, like the Red Room, is a parlor.

The Blue Room, *left,* is an oval drawing room. It serves as the main reception room for guests of the President. President James Monroe ordered many of the furnishings in the room.

WHITE HOUSE

The Green Room has been restored in the style of the years between 1800 and 1814. Its walls are covered with a light green silk moire. Its furniture is in the style of Duncan Phyfe, a noted American furniture maker of the late 1700's and early 1800's.

The East Room is the largest room in the White House, 79 feet (24 meters) long and 36¾ feet (11.2 meters) wide. Guests are often entertained in the East Room after formal dinners. It is at the end of the first floor. The East Room was remodeled in 1902.

Private Rooms. The President, his family, their guests, and the President's staff use many other rooms every day. The ground floor contains the Diplomatic Reception Room, used as the entrance for formal functions; the kitchen; the library; the map room; and offices of the White House physician and curator.

The second floor contains the private living quarters of the President and his family. The Lincoln Bedroom, the Treaty Room, and the Queen's Room are also on the second floor. The third floor contains guest rooms, staff quarters, and storage rooms.

History of the White House

The Original Building was begun in 1792. It was designed by James Hoban, an Irish-born architect. Hoban's design was selected in a competition sponsored by the federal government. It showed a simple Georgian mansion in the classical Palladian style of Europe in the 1700's.

President and Mrs. John Adams became the first occupants of the White House in 1800. But it was not yet

1807

1814

The White House changed appearance several times during the 1800's. It was almost completely rebuilt following a fire in 1814. The photograph of the White House about 1860 was taken by Mathew Brady, the famous Civil War photographer. It may be the first photograph of the White House.

From the Book *The White House* by Amy La Follette Jensen, Published by McGraw-Hill Book Co., Inc.; Brady-Handy Collection

1848

1860

completed, and they suffered many inconveniences. Mrs. Adams used the East Room to dry the family laundry.

The White House became more comfortable and beautiful during the administration of Thomas Jefferson. With the assistance of architect Benjamin H. Latrobe, Jefferson carried out many of the original White House plans, and added terraces at the east and west ends of the building.

A New Building. British forces burned the mansion in 1814, during the War of 1812. President James Madison and his wife, Dolley, were forced to flee. The White House was rebuilt and President and Mrs. James Monroe moved into it in 1817. The north and south porticos were added in the 1820's.

President Theodore Roosevelt had the building repaired in 1902. He rebuilt the east terrace, added the executive wing on the west terrace, and attempted to furnish the White House in a consistent style.

Franklin D. Roosevelt enlarged the west wing. The east wing was also rebuilt and enlarged, and an indoor swimming pool was added there.

Rebuilding and Redecorating. The White House underwent extensive repairs during the presidency of Harry S. Truman between 1945 and 1953. Workmen used concrete and steel to strengthen the dangerously weakened structure of the mansion. The third floor was converted into a full third story, and a second-story balcony was added to the south portico for the President's private use. The basement was expanded, and the total number of rooms was increased from 125 to 132.

But the historic rooms familiar to the American public remained basically unchanged until the administration of John F. Kennedy. In 1961, Mrs. Kennedy appointed a Fine Arts Committee to restore the White House interior to its original appearance in the late 1700's and early 1800's. The White House Historical Association was chartered in 1961 to publish guide books on the mansion and to acquire historic furnishings for the White House. A library committee was formed to stock the White House library with books representing American thought throughout the history of the United States.

Persons interested in obtaining further information about the White House may write to the White House Historical Association, 726 Jackson Place NW, Washington, D.C. 20025.   CLEMENT E. CONGER

Related Articles. See the section on Life in the White House in articles on the Presidents. Other related articles in WORLD BOOK include:

Blair House	Secret Service,
Easter (picture)	United States
President of the United States	White House
(In the White House)	Hostesses

WHITE HOUSE CONFERENCES are national meetings of businessmen, clergymen, physicians, social workers, teachers, and other community leaders of the United States. The President calls the conferences to discuss important issues facing the American people. Several Presidents of the 1900's have called such meetings. Issues discussed have included child care, conservation, drug abuse, education, highway safety, national resources for the future, and national security.

The first White House conference, called by President Theodore Roosevelt in 1908, met to consider conservation of natural resources. Many later conferences have dealt with problems involving young people. In 1919, a conference called by President Woodrow Wilson discussed child welfare standards. White House conferences called by Presidents Herbert Hoover, Franklin D. Roosevelt, and Harry S. Truman also centered on children.

The first White House conference to deal with educational problems met in 1955 at the request of President Dwight D. Eisenhower. President Lyndon B. Johnson also called a conference on education in 1965. White House conferences called by President Richard M. Nixon discussed children, in 1970; the aged, nutrition, and youth, in 1971; and the industrial world of the future, in 1972. President Gerald R. Ford called a conference on domestic and economic affairs in 1975. Ford also called a conference on the handicapped. It took place in 1977, after Jimmy Carter became President. In 1978, a conference called by Carter discussed the nation's economic growth. A conference on libraries was scheduled to be held in 1979.   DWIGHT W. ALLEN

WHITE HOUSE HOSTESSES are the women who receive and entertain the President's guests at the White House, in place of the President's wife. Thomas Jefferson was the first President to come to the White House without a wife. Dolley Madison, the wife of Secretary of State James Madison, acted as Jefferson's hostess.

Andrew Jackson's hostess was his wife's niece, Emily Donelson; and for Martin Van Buren, his daughter-in-law, Angelica Singleton Van Buren. The wife of William Henry Harrison was too ill to travel to Washington, D.C. She sent their daughter-in-law, Jane Irwin Harrison, as hostess. John Tyler's wife died shortly after he became President. His daughter-in-law, Priscilla Cooper Tyler, and later his daughter Letitia Tyler Semple, officiated until he remarried in 1844.

Zachary Taylor's wife refused to attend social affairs. Her daughter, Betty Bliss, presided for her. Millard Fillmore's daughter, Mary Abigail, served in place of her invalid mother. Harriet Lane, niece of James Buchanan, a bachelor, served as his hostess. Martha Johnson Patterson, the daughter of Andrew Johnson, presided in place of his invalid wife. Hostess for Chester Arthur was his sister Mary Arthur McElroy. Rose Cleveland, Grover Cleveland's sister, was his hostess until he married in 1886. After the death of Woodrow Wilson's first wife, his daughter Margaret officiated until he remarried in 1915.   HELEN E. MARSHALL

See also the section on Life in the White House in articles on those Presidents mentioned above.

WHITE LEAD is a pigment once widely used to make white paint. A synthetic called *titanium dioxide* has replaced white lead in most house paints, partly because the synthetic performs better. Titanium dioxide is also safer to use than white lead. Children may develop lead poisoning after eating chips of dried paint that contain white lead. For this reason, the United States government restricts the lead content in household paint (see LEAD POISONING).

White lead may be produced by placing layers of sheet lead in earthen pots that contain a weak solution of acetic acid. The pots are buried in spent tanbark, which ferments, producing heat and carbon dioxide. The heat turns the acetic acid to vapor. This and the carbon dioxide act on the lead to produce white lead. The powder is then ground in linseed oil. The chemical formula of white lead is $2PbCO_3 \cdot Pb(OH)_2$.

New England Council
Profile Mountain Is in the White Mountains.

WHITE MAGIC. See MAGIC (Kinds of Magic).

WHITE MATTER. See BRAIN (Gray and White Matter); NERVOUS SYSTEM (The Axon).

WHITE MOUNTAIN, BATTLE OF. See THIRTY YEARS' WAR (The Bohemian Period).

WHITE MOUNTAINS are part of the Appalachian Mountain system. They stretch in a southwestern direction from Maine into New Hampshire. The White Mountains received their name because their rocky summits appear white when they reflect sunlight. For location, see NEW HAMPSHIRE (physical map).

The White Mountains cover about 1,000 square miles (2,590 square kilometers). Few people live in the area because of the rugged terrain and lack of good farmland. The mountains include a number of ranges. The Presidential Range in New Hampshire is the most important. Chief mountains in this range bear the names of early U.S. Presidents. Mount Washington (6,288 feet, or 1,917 meters) is the highest peak in New Hampshire. Sixty-eight other peaks in the mountains are over 3,900 feet (1,190 meters).

Deep canyons called "notches" cut through the White Mountains. The best known of these are the Carter, Crawford, Dixville, Franconia, Kinsman, and Pinkham. The famous "Old Man of the Mountain" is a feature of Profile Mountain in Franconia Notch. Wind and rain have carved a natural profile of a man's face on this cliff. Nathaniel Hawthorne immortalized the profile in his story "The Great Stone Face."

Since 1911, much of the White Mountains area has been included in a national forest. State forests have helped preserve two of the notches. Crawford was established in 1911, and Franconia in 1925.

A nonprofit organization, called Mt. Washington Observatory, Inc., keeps daily records of temperature, wind velocity, and radioactive "fallout" in the mountains. On Apr. 12, 1934, the observatory recorded a wind of 231 miles (372 kilometers) per hour, the highest wind velocity ever recorded on earth. Since 1955, Mount Washington has been a testing site for cloud seeding to produce rainfall.   J. DUANE SQUIRES

See also MOUNT WASHINGTON; NEW HAMPSHIRE (pictures).

WHITE PAPER is a British government report or policy statement on an important subject. It is a common name for *command papers* (documents technically submitted to the House of Commons on "command of the Crown"). The British called these documents *white papers* because many were prepared hastily and submitted without the traditional blue cover which was used for important documents. The U.S. government does not use the term officially. But certain U.S. documents are popularly referred to as "white papers."

WHITE PLAINS, BATTLE OF, was one of the early battles of the Revolutionary War. It was fought near White Plains, N.Y., on Oct. 28, 1776. British troops under General Sir William Howe attacked General George Washington's positions and forced him to retreat.

WHITE RIVER rises in the Boston Mountains in northwestern Arkansas. It flows northeast into Missouri, where the waters are dammed at Table Rock and Lake Taneycomo dams. The river then re-enters Arkansas. It joins the Mississippi River near Rosedale, Miss. Near its mouth, a channel joins it to the Arkansas River. White River is about 690 miles (1,110 kilometers) long and is navigable to some extent below Batesville, Ark. It is also dammed by Beaver and Bull Shoals dams in Arkansas. For its location, see ARKANSAS (physical map). WALTER L. BROWN

WHITE RUSSIAN SOVIET SOCIALIST REPUBLIC. See BYELORUSSIA.

WHITE SANDS MISSILE RANGE, N. Mex., is the largest all-land rocket testing range in the United States. The U.S. Army operates it for all the armed services to test and develop rockets and guided missiles. The range covers 2,226,013 acres (900,835 hectares) in south-central New Mexico. It extends 120 miles (193 kilometers) from north to south, and 40 miles (64 kilometers) from east to west. Its headquarters lie 50 miles (80 kilometers) southwest of Alamogordo, N.Mex. Major commands there include the Army's missile test center, electronic research and developmental activity, and the Navy's ordnance missile test facility. The Air Force missile development center lies on the east side of the range (see HOLLOMAN AIR FORCE BASE). The Army established the White Sands Proving Ground in 1945 and renamed it in 1958. SAMUEL J. ZISKIND

WHITE SANDS NATIONAL MONUMENT is in southern New Mexico. It contains great deposits of windblown gypsum sand. In bright light, the sands resemble a vast snowfield. The monument was established in 1933. For its area, see NATIONAL PARK SYSTEM (table: National Monuments). See also NEW MEXICO (picture).

WHITE SEA, called *Beloye More* in Russia, is an arm of the Arctic Ocean. It reaches into the northern part of Russia. For location, see RUSSIA (physical map). The Onega, Dvina, and Mezen' rivers flow into the White Sea. Onega and Archangel are the largest cities on this sea. The sea is icebound from September until June, but shipping is heavy in summer. The Dvina, Volga, and Dnepr rivers link the sea to the Caspian and Black seas. The Norwegian explorer Ottar discovered the White Sea in the A.D. 800's. JOHN D. ISAACS

WHITE SEA-BALTIC CANAL. See CANAL (table).

WHITE SHARK. See SHARK (Kinds of Sharks).

WHITE SULPHUR SPRINGS, W. Va. (pop. 2,869), named for its mineral springs, is a famous health resort. It lies about 120 miles (193 kilometers) east of Charles-

ton, the state capital. For location, see WEST VIRGINIA (political map). The city has a mayor-council government.

Settlers first came to the region about 1750. Fashionable people of the Old South visited the springs as early as 1779. After the resort became famous, its *President's Cottage* served as the summer home of Presidents Martin Van Buren, John Tyler, and Millard Fillmore. During the Civil War, soldiers fought the Battle of Dry Creek near the resort. FESTUS P. SUMMERS

WHITE WALNUT. See BUTTERNUT.

WHITE WHALE. See BELUGA.

WHITE WOMAN OF THE GENESEE. See JEMISON, MARY.

WHITEAKER, JOHN. See OREGON (History).

WHITEFIELD, *HWIHT feeld,* **GEORGE** (1714-1770), was an Anglican preacher and evangelist. In Great Britain, Whitefield played an important part in the founding of Methodism. In the American Colonies, he became a leader of a series of religious revival movements called the Great Awakening (see GREAT AWAKENING).

Whitefield was born in Gloucester, England. While studying at Oxford University in the early 1730's, he was influenced by Charles and John Wesley, the founders of Methodism. Whitefield experienced a religious conversion in 1735 that he claimed changed his life. He was ordained an Anglican deacon in 1736 and became known for his bold, dramatic, and severely critical preaching. Some Anglican ministers accused him of disrupting their congregations and refused to let him preach in their churches. Whitefield began to preach outdoors and attracted large crowds. His success influenced John Wesley to begin outdoor preaching, which became typical of the Methodists.

Between 1738 and 1770, Whitefield visited America seven times. There he angered some ministers who resented his attacks on various colonial religious groups. These ministers also denied their pulpits to Whitefield, so he again turned to outdoor preaching, with great success. L. C. RUDOLPH

WHITEFISH is the name of a group of fishes that live in fresh water, particularly the lakes and streams of the northern regions of North America, Europe, and Asia. The whitefishes are related to the salmon family. They are among the most important food fishes found in fresh water. The *lake whitefish* of the northern American lakes is the most valuable of the whitefishes. The lake whitefish has a long body, a cone-shaped snout, and a forked tail. The mouth is toothless and its upper jaw projects beyond the lower jaw. The average whitefish weighs 4 pounds (1.8 kilograms). It feeds on insects and shellfish and usually lives in deep water.

The so-called "herring" of the Great Lakes is a member of the whitefish family. It is also a fine food fish, and is more abundant than the lake whitefish. Another excellent food fish is the *mountain whitefish*. It lives in many western mountain streams. The *Menominee whitefish* is a commercially valuable fish that lives in the lakes of New England and the Adirondacks, in the Great Lakes, and in Alaskan waters.

Many steps are taken to protect the lake whitefish in the waters of the Great Lakes. This fish lays millions of eggs, but these eggs are eaten by yellow perch, crawfish, wild birds, and other creatures. Federal and state fishery departments grow the fish in hatcheries and plant them in lakes to keep up their numbers. The fish are mostly caught by the use of gill and trap nets.

Scientific Classification. Whitefish belong to the whitefish family, *Coregonidae*. The lake whitefish is genus *Coregonus*, species *C. clupeiformis*. The lake herring is *Leucichthys artedi;* mountain whitefish, *Prosopium williamsoni;* Menominee whitefish, *P. quadrilaterale*. CARL L. HUBBS

See also FISH (picture: Fish of Temperate Waters).

WHITEHEAD, ALFRED NORTH (1861-1947), was an English mathematician and philosopher. His writings did much to narrow the gap between philosophy and science. Whitehead's works reflect his firsthand knowledge of science, his philosophical insight, and his imaginative writing style. He insisted that scientific knowledge, though precise, is incomplete. It must be supplemented, he said, by philosophical principles and by the insights of poets.

Whitehead was born in Ramsgate. He taught at Cambridge University and London University until 1924, when he joined the faculty of Harvard University. Whitehead's writings on mathematics, logic, and the theory of knowledge laid the groundwork for his philosophical classic, *Process and Reality* (1929). This book explains that process and growth are the fundamental ideas which lead us to understand God, nature, and our own experiences. Whitehead also wrote *Principia Mathematica* (with Bertrand Russell, 1910-1913) and *Science and the Modern World* (1925). JOHN E. SMITH

WHITEHEAD, ROBERT. See GYROSCOPE (History).

WHITEHEAD, WILLIAM. See POET LAUREATE.

WHITEHORSE, Yukon Territory (pop. 13,311), is the territory's capital and chief distribution and communication center. Whitehorse lies on the Yukon River, 111 miles (179 kilometers) north of Skagway, Alaska. It is the northern terminal of the White Pass and Yukon Railway. It is located on the Alaska Highway. The city has regional headquarters of the Royal Canadian Mounted Police and several federal government departments. Mining products are shipped from Whitehorse to outside markets. Lake trout and grayling swim in neighboring streams and lakes. The region has bears, moose, and other game animals. For location, see YUKON TERRITORY (map).

Airlines link Whitehorse with cities in Canada and the United States. A dam built above Whitehorse Rapids in 1959 to furnish power has created a lake in Miles Canyon. Many gold seekers came past Whitehorse in the rush of 1897-1898. W. D. MACBRIDE

WHITEMAN, PAUL (1890-1967), was a famous American orchestra conductor. He was often called the "King of Jazz." In 1919, Whiteman introduced the first "symphonic jazz." Later he conducted the first performances of such compositions as George Gershwin's *Rhapsody in Blue* (1924) and Ferde Grofé's *Grand Canyon Suite* (1931), both of which show jazz influences. Whiteman was born in Denver, Colo., and played first viola in the Denver Symphony Orchestra while still in his teens. Not long after World War I, he formed his own orchestra and toured the United States and Europe. In the 1930's, Whiteman became a popular conductor on radio programs. In 1943, he became musical director of the Blue Network, which later became the American Broadcasting Company. DAVID EWEN

WHITEWASH is a white mixture made from whiting, glue, water, common salt, rice flour, and unslaked lime.

It is used instead of paint to put a coating on basement walls, the walls of lighthouses, fences, and other spots where a clear white is desired and where paint is too expensive to be practical. Whitewash is applied with a brush. A heavy coating over rough mortar plaster closes the pores against moisture and dirt. JOHN R. KOCH

WHITING. See CHALK.

WHITING, a fish. See HAKE.

WHITLAM, GOUGH (1916-), served as prime minister of Australia from 1972 to 1975. In November 1975, Sir John Kerr, the governor general of Australia, removed Whitlam from office. Kerr took this action after a dispute between Whitlam—head of Australia's Labor Party—and the leaders of the country's Liberal and Country parties threatened to stop the operations of the government. Liberal and Country party leaders charged members of Whitlam's government with improper conduct in financial matters. They demanded that Whitlam call for new elections. When Whitlam refused, they blocked the approval of funds needed to run the government. Kerr then dismissed Whitlam and named a new prime minister. Whitlam's Labor Party lost elections held in December 1975 and in 1977. Whitlam retired from politics in 1978.

Wide World

Gough Whitlam

Edward Gough Whitlam was born in Kew, a suburb of Melbourne. He graduated from the University of Sydney. Whitlam won election to the Australian House of Representatives in 1952, and became leader of the country's Labor Party in 1967. As prime minister, Whitlam ended Australia's participation in the Vietnam War. He also ended policies that placed racial restrictions on immigration to Australia, and worked to restore land rights to the Aborigines—the original inhabitants of Australia. C. M. H. CLARK

WHITLOW, *HWIT loh*, is a painful, inflamed condition of the fingers, and sometimes of the toes. It is one form of the infection known as *felon*. A whitlow generally forms dark tissue around and under the nail. Usually, it is caused by septic material that has entered through a small wound or pin prick. One type of whitlow is at the surface, and another is deep. The deep kind generally requires an incision, sometimes to the bone. Treatment includes the use of hot packs and the draining of pus. PAUL R. CANNON

WHITMAN, MARCUS (1802-1847), was an American pioneer, doctor, and missionary among the Indians. Appointed as a Presbyterian missionary physician to Oregon by the American Board for Foreign Missions, he visited the Pacific Northwest with Samuel Parker in 1835. He returned there in 1836, with his wife, the Reverend Henry Spalding and his wife, and W. H. Gray. They established two missions, one near the site of the present city of Walla Walla, Wash.

They drove their wagon as far as Fort Boise, and thus were credited with opening that part of the

Visual Education Service

Marcus Whitman

wagon road to Oregon. In the winter of 1842, Whitman rode to the East to gain further missionary support, and to try to encourage emigration to Oregon. He also hoped to interest the government in settling the area.

The new settlers of 1847 brought with them an epidemic of measles that caused the death of many Indian children. The missionaries' medicine did not help them. In 1847, a band of Cayuse Indians, who probably believed their children were poisoned, attacked the mission. They killed Whitman, his wife, and 12 other persons, and burned all the buildings. Whitman was born in Rushville, N.Y. He practiced medicine for eight years before becoming a missionary. THOMAS D. CLARK

See also WHITMAN, NARCISSA; WHITMAN MISSION NATIONAL HISTORIC SITE.

WHITMAN, NARCISSA (1808-1847), was a missionary teacher to the Indians of the Pacific Northwest. Born in Prattsburg, N.Y., she married the missionary Marcus Whitman in 1836. She was one of the first two white women to journey overland to the Northwest. The couple began a mission among the Cayuse Indians at Waiilatpu, in what is now Washington. Indians massacred the Whitmans and 12 other persons on Nov. 29, 1847. See also WHITMAN, MARCUS. EARLE E. CAIRNS

WHITMAN, WALT (1819-1892), was an American poet who wrote *Leaves of Grass*. This collection of poems is considered one of the world's major literary works.

Whitman's poems sing the praises of the United States and of democracy. The poet's love of America grew from his faith that Americans might reach new worldly and spiritual heights. Whitman wrote: "The chief reason for the being of the United States of America is to bring about the common good will of all mankind, the solidarity of the world."

Whitman began working on *Leaves of Grass* in 1848. The collection's form and content were so unusual that no commercial publisher would publish it. In 1855, he published the first edition of the collection at his own expense. The edition contained only 12 poems. In the preface, Whitman said: "The United States themselves are essentially the greatest poem." Between 1855 and his death, Whitman published several revised and enlarged editions of his book. He believed that *Leaves of Grass* had grown with his own emotional and intellectual development.

His Work. The beginning student of Whitman will find it easiest to study the poems separately. He should try to understand each poem's imagery, symbolism, literary structure, and unity of theme.

"Song of Myself," the longest poem in *Leaves of Grass*,

Ewing Galloway

Walt Whitman received literary acclaim from English writers long before American critics recognized him as a great poet.

is considered Whitman's greatest. It is a lyric poem told through the joyful experiences of the narrator, simply called "I," who chants the poem's 52 sections. Sometimes "I" is the poet himself—"Walt Whitman, an American." In other passages, "I" speaks for the human race, the universe, or a specific character being dramatized. Like all Whitman's major poems, "Song of Myself" contains symbols. For example, in the poem he describes grass as a symbol of life—"the babe of vegetation," "the handkerchief of the Lord."

"Out of the Cradle Endlessly Rocking" tells of a little boy observing a mockingbird. The bird is mourning its mate, which was lost in a storm at sea. The bird's song teaches the boy the meaning of death and makes him decide to become a poet. The theme is that death is part of the cycle of birth, life, death, and rebirth.

Whitman wrote "When Lilacs Last in the Dooryard Bloom'd" on the death of Abraham Lincoln. Lincoln died in April, a time of rebirth in nature. As his coffin is transported from Washington, D.C., to Springfield, Ill., it passes the young wheat, "every grain from its shroud in the dark-brown fields uprisen." Whitman says that each spring the blooming lilac will remind him not only of the death of Lincoln, but also of the eternal return to life. The evening star Venus symbolizes Lincoln, who has "droop'd in the western sky."

In "Passage to India," Whitman says that poets will teach men to use modern achievements in transportation and communication to unite the Eastern and Western worlds. And eventually poets will lead men's souls back to God.

A group of Civil War poems called "Drum Taps" describes battlefield scenes and Whitman's emotions during wartime. "O Captain! My Captain!," another poem on Lincoln's death, is Whitman's most popular poem, but differs from his others in rhyme and rhythm. A group of poems called "Children of Adam" defends the sacredness of sex. The "Calamus" poems praise companionship.

Whitman wrote in a form similar to *thought-rhythm*, or *parallelism*. This form is found in Old Testament poetry. It is also found in sacred books of India, such as the *Bhagavad-Gita*, which Whitman knew in translation. The rhythm of his lines suggests the rise and fall of the sea he loved so much. This structure is better suited to expressing emotion than to logical discussion.

In general, Whitman's poetry is idealistic and romantic while his prose is realistic. His best prose is in a book of essays, mostly autobiographical, called *Specimen Days* (1882). Whitman's essay "Democratic Vistas" (1871) deals with his theory of democracy and with the creation of a democratic literature.

His Life. Walter Whitman was born in West Hills, Long Island, New York, and grew up in Brooklyn. He worked as a printer and journalist in the New York City area. He wrote articles on political questions, civic affairs, and the arts. Whitman loved mixing in crowds. He attended debates, the theater, concerts, lectures, and political meetings. He often rode on stagecoaches and ferries just to talk with people.

During the Civil War, Whitman was a volunteer assistant in the military hospitals in Washington, D.C. After the war, he worked in several government departments until he suffered a stroke in 1873. He spent the rest of his life in Camden, N.J., where he continued to write poems and articles. See CAMDEN.

Whitman believed that the vitality and variety of his life reflected the vitality and variety of American democracy during his time. Most critics have accepted this view of the man and his poems. However, some insist Whitman was not a prophetic spokesman, but simply a powerful and unusual lyric poet. GAY WILSON ALLEN

WHITMAN MISSION NATIONAL HISTORIC SITE is in southeastern Washington. It includes the site of an Indian mission and school established in 1836 by Marcus Whitman and his wife. The mission was a landmark on the Oregon Trail, and the school was the first mission school in the Pacific Northwest. It was made a national monument in 1936 and became a national historic site in 1963. For area, see NATIONAL PARK SYSTEM (table: National Historic Sites).

WHITNEY, ELI (1765-1825), an American inventor, has two claims to fame. His cotton gin made cotton-growing profitable, and helped make the United States the largest cotton producer in the world. His method of making guns by machinery marked the beginning of mass production in the United States.

Early Life. Whitney was born on Dec. 8, 1765, in Westborough, Mass., the son of a farmer. Even as a boy, he showed mechanical aptitude. He made a violin when he was 12. During the Revolutionary War, when

Brown Bros.
Eli Whitney

he was still in his teens, he had his own business, making handwrought nails. After the war, times were hard. Whitney did not have the money to go to college. He taught school for five years, at $7.00 a month, entered Yale College at 23, and graduated in 1792.

He then went to Georgia to teach and study law. When he got there, he found another man had the job. Catherine Littlefield Greene, General Nathanael Greene's widow, invited him to be her guest while he studied law. Whitney wanted to be "worth his keep" and began fixing things around the house. His mechanical talent must have impressed her. One night, some guests were talking of green seed cotton. They could not grow it profitably because of the time needed to clean it. Mrs. Greene said, "Mr. Whitney can make a machine to clean it." By April 1793, he had built the cotton gin, which could clean cotton as fast as 50 persons working by hand.

His Inventions. Whitney applied for a patent on his machine. With the backing of a partner, Phineas Miller, he began making gins in New Haven, Conn. Then trouble began. It took almost a year to get the patent. Whitney could not make gins fast enough to meet the demand; and then the factory burned. Soon others were making and using imitations of his machine. Whitney sued them. After long years of court trials, he won. The courts declared he had the sole right to his patent. But the life of the patent had almost run out. He pleaded for a renewal, but Congress refused to grant it.

In 1798, Whitney built another factory near New Haven and began to make muskets by a new method. Until then, each gun had been handmade by skilled workers, and no two guns were alike. Whitney invented tools and machines so that unskilled workers could turn out absolutely uniform parts. Setting up the machinery took time. The government grew impatient and asked for the guns. Whitney amazed government representatives by assembling guns from pieces chosen at random from piles of parts. Eventually, his arms factory made him rich. But his role as the father of mass production is almost unknown. JEAN LEE LATHAM

See also COTTON GIN; MASS PRODUCTION. For a *Reading and Study Guide*, see *Whitney, Eli*, in the RESEARCH GUIDE/INDEX, Volume 22.

WHITNEY, MOUNT. See MOUNT WHITNEY.

WHITSUNDAY. See PENTECOST.

WHITTAKER, CHARLES EVANS (1901-1973), was a justice of the Supreme Court of the United States from 1957 to 1962, when he resigned because of poor health. President Dwight D. Eisenhower nominated him as a United States District Judge in 1954, and two years later he became a judge of the U.S. Court of Appeals, Eighth Circuit. Whittaker was born in Doniphan County, Kansas. As a youth, he trapped animals and sold their pelts to earn $700 for his law studies. MERLO J. PUSEY

WHITTAKER, JAMES WARREN (1929-   ), became the first American to reach the summit of Mount Everest. He reached the top of the world's highest peak on May 1, 1963, with Sherpa guide Nawang Gombu. They were the first of three U.S. teams to scale the 29,028-foot (8,848-meter) peak in a single month. Whittaker was born in Seattle, Wash. He was a mountain guide in the United States before the Everest expedition.

WHITTIER, JOHN GREENLEAF

WHITTIER, JOHN GREENLEAF (1807-1892), was an American poet. His best-known poems fall into two groups—those attacking slavery, and those praising the charms of New England country life. Whittier's simple, direct, and sentimental style has made his poems popular with both young readers and adults.

Whittier was born in Haverhill, Mass. His parents were Quaker farmers. Whittier's poetry shows the influence of his Quaker religion and rural New England background, and he is often called the "Quaker poet." The Scottish poet Robert Burns also influenced him. Like Burns, Whittier wrote many ballads on rural themes. But Whittier's poetry lacks the wit of Burns's work.

Brown Bros.
John Greenleaf Whittier

From 1833 to 1863, Whittier was active in politics and the antislavery movement. He called for the abolition of slavery in newspaper articles and while serving in the Massachusetts legislature in 1835. The abolitionist cause also dominated his poetry. In "The Moral Warfare" (1838) and "Massachusetts to Virginia" (1843), he attacked the injustices of slavery. He also condemned what he considered the hypocrisy of a nation that was founded on ideals of freedom but allowed slavery.

Whittier's finest political poem is "Ichabod" (1850), a lyric. It criticizes Senator Daniel Webster of Massachusetts for his role in the passage of the Compromise of 1850. Whittier objected to the compromise because it required that runaway slaves be returned to their owners. But Whittier used a dignified, restrained tone that makes "Ichabod" seem less an attack on Webster than an expression of sympathy for him.

In two ballads, "Skipper Ireson's Ride" (1857) and "Telling the Bees" (1858), Whittier showed his interest in the people, customs, legends, and settings of New England. These features appear in his masterpiece, "Snow-Bound" (1866). This long poem tells of a family marooned in their farmhouse during a blizzard. Whittier's affectionate descriptions of Quaker life, combined with his simple style and organization, made "Snow-Bound" extremely popular. CLARK GRIFFITH

See also FRIETCHIE, BARBARA; LIBERTY PARTY.

WHITTINGTON, DICK (1358?-1423), was an English merchant. According to legend, he was apprenticed to a London merchant who was about to send cargo to sell to a foreign port. When told he could send one of his own possessions, Whittington chose his cat. It proved to be the most valuable item in the cargo. The king of Barbary, whose land had many rats, bought it for a large sum.

In the meantime, Whittington had run away. The captain returned with Whittington's money, but was unable to find him. As Whittington ran through Newgate, he thought he heard the Bow Bells ringing and saying, "Turn again, Whittington, Lord Mayor of London." He returned and learned of his good

fortune. Later, he was Lord Mayor of London three times. Richard Whittington was probably born in Gloucestershire. KNOX WILSON

WHITTLE, SIR FRANK (1907-   ), became one of the leading pioneers in the development of the turbojet engine. His company, Powerjets, Limited, produced the Whittle engine. This engine powered Britain's first jet plane in 1941. It became the model for the first U.S. turbojets (see JET PROPULSION [Jets Put to Use]).

Whittle was born in Coventry, England, the son of an inventor. He entered Leamington College on a scholarship at the age of 11, and joined the Royal Air Force when he was 16. Whittle distinguished himself in a mechanics course and was assigned to officers' flight training. He became interested in light turbine engines and received his first patent in 1930 after the Air Ministry rejected his jet engine proposals.

Whittle's basic patents lapsed in 1935 because he did not have enough money to pay patent fees. Later that year, a group of engineers became interested in his work and, with the government and Whittle, formed Powerjets, Ltd., to produce engines. Whittle was knighted in 1948. ROBERT B. HOTZ

WHITTLING. See CARVING (Carving as a Hobby); WOOD CARVING.

WHITWORTH, SIR JOSEPH (1803-1887), was a British mechanical engineer and inventor. He invented measuring machines and found a method of milling and testing plane surfaces. He introduced a system of standard measures, gauges, and screw threads. His experiments in ordnance established principles of gun design that were adopted by all major countries except his own. Whitworth was born in Stockport, England. He founded a company that became a leader in tool design and manufacture. ROBERT E. SCHOFIELD

WHO. See WORLD HEALTH ORGANIZATION.

WHOLE WHEAT. See BREAD; WHEAT (Wheat Flour).

WHOLESALER. See DISTRIBUTION; SALESMANSHIP (Mass Production).

WHOOPER. See WHOOPING CRANE.

WHOOPING COUGH, *HOOP ing*, is a highly contagious disease that affects children more often than adults. Doctors often call the disease *pertussis*. It is more serious than most persons think. Whooping cough kills many persons every year by bringing on bronchitis, pneumonia, hemorrhage, or convulsions.

A person can catch whooping cough at any age, but an adult has a better chance to recover than a child. The fatality rate for all ages together is 1 per cent but rises 10 to 25 per cent for children under four years of age. Two-thirds of all deaths occur in children under one year of age. One attack almost always makes the patient immune. Jules Bordet, a Belgian bacteriologist, discovered the germ that causes the disease.

Early Symptoms of whooping cough are a slight fever and a dry cough. After a few days, the symptoms grow worse, particularly at night. The coughing comes in spells, or paroxysms, and usually causes vomiting. Any child who shows these signs should be kept away from other children. About a week later, most children coming down with the disease begin to give the whoop —a long drawing-in of the breath that sounds like a high crow. A doctor can recognize the disease earlier, in other ways.

There are four or five coughing spells a day even in

mild cases. More frequent attacks come from overeating, crying, excitement, or too violent exercise. The climax occurs about the end of the fourth week. Then the spells gradually grow fewer and less severe. Sometimes, especially in cold weather, the whoop goes on for two or three months. Any fever after the climax should be reported at once to the doctor.

Treatment. Parents must be careful to keep a child who has whooping cough away from other children. The disease spreads rapidly through the spray of droplets from the mouth and nose. This spray can travel up to 5 feet (1.5 meters) from ordinary talking and up to 18 feet (5.5 meters) by coughing. During coughing attacks, the discharges from nose and mouth should be caught in a piece of cloth. The cloth should then be burned. Patients should have their own dishes, silver, washcloths, and towels. They must also have nourishing food and a well-ventilated sleeping room.

A rabbit serum and one made from human blood can be used in treating children. Severely ill patients may need oxygen. For specific treatment or prevention of complications, there are three antibiotic drugs: *chloramphenicol*, *Aureomycin*, and *Terramycin*. These may be given by mouth or by injection (see ANTIBIOTIC). Special care should be given to the diet. A patient should be isolated from others for about three weeks.

A vaccine that makes a person immune in 60 to 75 per cent of cases has been developed. All infants should be immunized with the vaccine. AUSTIN SMITH

WHOOPING CRANE is one of the rarest birds of North America. It is a symbol of wildlife conservation. Whooping cranes, also called *whoopers*, are named for their loud, buglelike call.

Whooping cranes are the tallest birds in North America. They stand about 5 feet (1.5 meters) tall and have long legs and a long neck. The adults are white, with black-tipped wings and a patch of bare, red skin on their heads. Whoopers less than a year old are rust colored. See CRANE (picture).

Wild whooping cranes breed in marshy areas of the Northwest Territories of Canada. They make nests of piles of grasses or other plants. The female usually lays two eggs, but only one chick survives in most cases. Whoopers migrate to the coast of Texas for the winter. Their food in winter includes clams, crabs, and crayfish, but scientists know little about what they eat the rest of the year.

Whoopers once nested between Louisiana and Canada. They began to die out during the 1800's, when increasing numbers of settlers disturbed their habitats. By 1941, only 15 whoopers remained. Ecologists are working to save the species, but progress has been slow. By the mid-1970's, there were more than 60 of the birds.

Wild whooping cranes are protected by law. Their breeding and wintering grounds are protected, and the birds are closely watched during their migrations. Conservation laws also prohibit shooting whoopers.

In a further effort to save the species, scientists remove one egg from some of the nests of wild whoopers. In one program involving these eggs, scientists have established a captive flock of whoopers. They hope to release offspring from this flock to increase the wild population. In a second program, which began in 1975, ecologists transfer some whooper eggs to the nests of sandhill cranes in Idaho. The sandhill cranes hatch and raise the young whooping cranes. Scientists hope the transplanted chicks will eventually establish a new flock of wild whoopers.

Scientific Classification. Whooping cranes belong to the crane family, Gruidae. They are species *Grus americana*. ERIC G. BOLEN

WHORTLEBERRY. See HUCKLEBERRY.

WHYMPER, EDWARD. See MATTERHORN.

WICHITA, *WIHCH uh taw* (pop. 276,554; met. area pop. 389,352), is the largest city in Kansas. It serves as a major manufacturing center and as the distribution center for a large farm region that produces dairy products, grain, and livestock. Wichita is called the *Air Capital of the World* because it manufactures about two-thirds of all the small planes in the world.

Wichita lies in south-central Kansas where the Little Arkansas and Arkansas rivers meet. For location, see KANSAS (political map). White settlers first came to the area to trade with the Wichita Indians. The city's name came from that tribe.

The City covers about 98 square miles (254 square kilometers) and is the county seat of Sedgwick County. About a fifth of Wichita lies west of the Arkansas River. The city's main business and industrial districts are in the area east of the river.

Century II, a cultural-convention center completed in 1969, covers 5 acres (2 hectares) in the heart of down-

Wichita Area Chamber of Commerce

Wichita is the largest city in Kansas. The domed Century II cultural-convention center, *above*, in downtown Wichita includes a concert hall, exhibition halls, and a theater.

WICHITA

town Wichita. This $15-million project includes an auditorium, a concert hall, convention and exhibition halls, and a theater. The A. Price Woodard, Jr., Memorial Park, with its fountains, trees, waterfalls, and an outdoor amphitheater, lies between Century II and the river. Wichita's old city hall, completed in 1892, still stands in the downtown area. Its unusual architectural design and towers attract many tourists.

More than 98 per cent of Wichita's people were born in the United States. They are descendants of people representing many nationalities. Blacks form about 9 per cent of the population. Wichita's largest religious groups include Baptists, Methodists, and Roman Catholics.

Economy. Wichita ranks as the largest manufacturing center in Kansas. The more than 500 manufacturing plants in the Wichita metropolitan area employ nearly 60,000 persons. The production of small aircraft is the major industry. Wichita also ranks as the petroleum capital of Kansas. Oil fields lie just outside the city, and many major oil companies and independent oil firms have offices or refineries in Wichita. Other industries produce chemicals, camping and recreational equipment, metal products, and plastics.

Wichita ranks high among the nation's cities as a meat processor. Its stockyards can handle about 40,000 animals daily. The city lies in a rich, wheat-growing area, and Wichita's flour mills grind more wheat than any other Kansas city.

Railroad passenger and freight trains serve the city, and truck lines also operate there. Wichita Municipal Airport is about 7 miles (11 kilometers) from the downtown area of the city.

Wichita has two daily newspapers, the *Beacon* and the *Eagle*. Three television stations and 11 radio stations broadcast from the area.

Education and Cultural Life. Wichita's public school system includes about 100 elementary schools and 7 high schools. The city also has about 20 parochial and private schools.

Wichita State University is the third largest college in the state. The university is known for its Institute of Logopedics, the world's largest center for helping persons with speech and hearing handicaps. Friends University and Kansas Newman College (formerly Sacred Heart College) are also in Wichita. The city's public library system consists of a central library and seven branches.

The Wichita Symphony Orchestra performs at the Century II Concert Hall. The Wichita Community Theatre presents four plays every season.

Historic Wichita Cow Town, which consists of about 40 restored buildings, traces the city's history from 1868 to 1880. The Wichita Historical Museum also offers exhibits on local history. The city has two art museums—the Wichita Art Association and the Wichita Art Museum. The Wichita Art Museum houses the famous Roland P. Murdock Collection, one of the nation's largest collections of American art.

Wichita's public park system includes 65 parks and covers a total of 2,546 acres (1,030 hectares). Pawnee Prairie, the largest park in the city, covers 700 acres (280 hectares) and includes a golf course. The Sedgwick County Zoo lies on the northwest border of the city.

Government. Wichita has a council-manager form of government. The voters elect five commissioners to four-year terms, and the commissioners choose one of their group as mayor. The mayor presides at commission meetings, but has the same duties as the other commissioners. The five commissioners appoint a city manager, who serves as the administrative head of the city government. The city manager appoints the heads of the various city departments, but the appointees are subject to the approval of the commissioners. Property taxes provide most of Wichita's income.

History. The Wichita Indians once lived in what is now the Wichita area. Whites first settled there in 1866 and traded with the Indians. In 1870, the whites incorporated their settlement as a town. The Santa Fe Railroad began to serve Wichita in 1872, and the town soon became an important shipping point for cattle. Cowboys drove Texas Longhorn cattle along the Chisholm Trail, fattened them on Kansas grass, and then shipped them from Wichita to distant markets.

During the late 1880's, Wichita became known for its cowboys, dance halls, gambling, and saloons. Wyatt Earp, the famous frontier lawman, served as a peace officer in the town from 1875 to 1876. Although Wichita gained attention for lawlessness, the people also built churches, a library, schools, and some industry, including a brick plant and a meat-packing plant.

Wichita received a city charter in 1886. The population of the community grew from 4,911 in 1880 to 23,853 in 1890. Much of this growth resulted from land speculation.

The discovery of oil in the Wichita area during the early 1900's brought further growth. The city's population rose from 24,671 in 1900 to 111,110 in 1930. In 1919, Wichita's first airplane manufacturing company built its factory. Wichita soon became the nation's aircraft production center. The city won fame for its pioneers in the industry, including Walter H. Beech, Clyde V. Cessna, and Lloyd C. Stearman.

The prospering aircraft and oil industries helped Wichita avoid hard times during the 1930's. The rest of the Kansas region suffered those years from dust storms and the Great Depression.

During World War II (1939-1945), Wichita's three airplane factories produced more military aircraft than any other U.S. city. After the war, Wichita continued to rank among the leading producers of jet bombers for the Air Force. In 1951, McConnell Air Force Base opened in Wichita. Aircraft production soared again during the Korean War (1950-1953).

The city grew during the early 1960's, when another aircraft corporation built a plant there. This plant helped Wichita become the world's largest producer of small aircraft.

The city's aircraft industry suffered after the demand for small planes dropped sharply in the late 1960's and early 1970's. The reduced demands resulted from a slowdown in the entire United States economy. From 10,000 to 15,000 aircraft workers lost their jobs in 1970 and 1971. The industry began to flourish again during the mid-1970's.

Important developments in Wichita during the 1970's included construction of a new 14-story City Hall, completed in 1975, and the Mid-America All

Indian Center, which opened in 1976. Construction of a coliseum began in 1976.   CHARLES G. PEARSON

For the monthly weather in Wichita, see KANSAS (Climate). See also KANSAS (pictures).

WICHITA FALLS, Tex. (pop. 96,265; met. area pop. 128,642), is headquarters for the oil industry in north-central Texas. It lies along the Wichita River (see TEXAS [political map]). Wichita Falls is the home of Midwestern State University, Wichita Falls State Hospital, and Sheppard Air Force Base.

Wichita Falls has oil-well equipment factories. Other leading industries produce electronic equipment, medical products, foundry products, air-conditioning equipment, and various processed foods.

Wichita Falls was established in 1882 as a station on the Fort Worth and Denver City Railroad. It was incorporated as a city in 1889. The city adopted a council-manager government in 1928. Wichita Falls lies in an area that has been struck by many tornadoes. In 1979, a tornado killed 46 persons and caused over $200 million in property damage in the city. Wichita Falls is the seat of Wichita County.   H. BAILEY CARROLL

WICHITA STATE UNIVERSITY is a state coeducational university in Wichita, Kans. It offers degrees in business administration and industry, education, engineering (including aeronautical), fine arts, and liberal arts and sciences. The university has a graduate program and an adult education program.

Wichita State University was founded in 1895 as Fairmount College. It became a municipal university in 1926. In 1964, it came under the control of the Kansas Board of Regents. For enrollment, see UNIVERSITIES AND COLLEGES (table).   EMORY LINDQUIST

WICKERSHAM, GEORGE WOODWARD (1858-1936), an American lawyer, served as attorney general from 1909 to 1913 in the Cabinet of President William Howard Taft. He was interested in constitutional reform in New York state, and in international arbitration. In later years, he served as chairman of the National Commission on Law Observance and Enforcement. This commission was created in 1929 by President Herbert Hoover to study the problem of enforcing the national prohibition laws. Wickersham was born in Pittsburgh, Pa. He studied at Lehigh University.   H. G. REUSCHLEIN

WICLIF, JOHN. See WYCLIFFE, JOHN.

WIDENER LIBRARY. See CAMBRIDGE (Mass.).

WIDGEON. See WIGEON.

WIECHERT, ERNST. See GERMAN LITERATURE (German Literature after 1945).

WIECK, FRIEDRICH. See SCHUMANN, CLARA; SCHUMANN, ROBERT.

WIELAND, *VEE lahnt,* **HEINRICH OTTO** (1877-1957), a German chemist, developed basic theories of the mechanism by which living cells produce energy by oxidation. His work on the structure of the bile acids and poisons produced by toads led to discoveries of the nature of hormones, vitamins, and other natural products. Wieland won the 1927 Nobel prize for chemistry. Wieland was born in Pforzheim.   HENRY M. LEICESTER

WIEN, the official name for Vienna. See VIENNA.

WIENER. See SAUSAGE.

WIENER, *WEE nur,* **NORBERT** (1894-1964), a mathematician and logician, had an important role in developing high-speed electronic computers. He adopted the word *cybernetics,* and used it as the title of a book he published in 1948. He did mathematical work at the Aberdeen (Md.) Proving Ground during World War I, and helped develop high-speed electronic computers during World War II. Wiener's nontechnical books include *The Human Use of Human Beings* (1950), *Ex-Prodigy* (1953), and *I Am a Mathematician* (1958). He won the National Medal of Science in 1964.

Wiener was born in Columbia, Mo. He graduated from Tufts University at 14, and received a Ph.D. from Harvard at 18. He taught at the Massachusetts Institute of Technology from 1919 to 1960.   PHILLIP S. JONES

See also CYBERNETICS.

WIENIAWSKI, *vyeh NYAHF skee,* **HENRI** (1835-1880), one of the most celebrated violinists of the 1800's, has often been called the *Chopin of the violin.* His style reveals a full-blooded romantic temperament. He was also a composer. His works give the performer great opportunity for brilliant display. He composed *Légende, Concerto No. 2 in D minor* for violin and orchestra, *Souvenir de Moscou,* and a fantasy on *Faust.* Wieniawski was born in Lublin, Poland.   HANS ROSENWALD

WIESBADEN, *VEES bah dun* (pop. 260,600), is a resort city 6 miles (10 kilometers) northeast of Mainz in West Germany. It lies in a valley on the southern slope of the Taunus Mountains (see GERMANY [political map]). In 1945, it became the capital of the newly created state of Hesse. Many mineral springs in and around Wiesbaden attract visitors. The tourist trade is the chief source of income. The springs in this area were known to the Romans, and many relics of the Roman period have been discovered there. The city's Latin name was *Aquae Mattiacum,* meaning *water of the Mattiaci* (a German tribe). Its German name, *Wiesbaden,* means *baths on the meadows.*   JAMES K. POLLOCK

WIESE, *VEE zuh,* **KURT** (1887-   ), an American artist and writer, illustrated more than 100 books. He began to draw while a World War I prisoner of the Japanese. He wrote and illustrated *The Chinese Ink Stick* (1929), *Liang and Lo* (1930), *You Can Write Chinese* (1945), and *The Thief in the Attic* (1965). His animal pictures for Felix Salten's *Bambi* (1932) were memorable. He was born in Minden, Germany. NORMAN L. RICE

WIFE. See FAMILY; MARRIAGE.

WIG is a false covering of hair for the head. The name comes from the word *periwig.* The custom of wearing wigs dates back to ancient times. Egyptian mummies have been found with them. The ancient Greeks and Romans wore them. In the 1700's, the French made wigs fashionable. Wigs then became large and heavy, and expensive. Usually they were powdered white. Wigs were worn by nobles, courtiers, ministers, judges, doctors, and professional people. English judges began wearing wigs in the days of Queen Anne and still wear them today. Wigs were fashionable in colonial America and became popular in the 1960's and 1970's. They are also worn by persons who are bald. Quality wigs are made of the best grade of human hair. Wigmakers also make *toupees* (small hairpieces used to cover bald spots).   MARY EVANS

See also HAIRDRESSING (with pictures); CLOTHING (The 1700's; picture: Men Began Wearing Periwigs); COLONIAL LIFE IN AMERICA (Clothing); LONDON (picture: London Lawyers).

WIGEON

WIGEON, *WIJ un,* or WIDGEON, is a duck found in North America and in Europe. Hunters locate the *American wigeon* (baldpate) by its distinctive call, *whew, whew, whew* (see BALDPATE).

The *European wigeon* lives in the northern part of Europe, and occasionally in the United States. Both species are about 19 inches (48 centimeters) long. The female lays 7 to 12 creamy-white eggs in ground nests near water.

Scientific Classification. Wigeons are in the duck family, *Anatidae.* The American is genus *Anas,* species *A. americana.* The European is *A. penelope.*   JOSEPH J. HICKEY

WIGGIN, KATE DOUGLAS (1856-1923), was an American writer and educator. She wrote *The Birds' Christmas Carol* (1888), her first successful story, and *Rebecca of Sunnybrook Farm* (1903), one of the most popular children's books of its time. She and her sister, Nora Archibald Smith, published several collections of folk tales, fairy stories, and fables.

Kate Douglas Wiggin was born in Philadelphia. She went to Santa Barbara, Calif., to teach at the age of 17. In 1878, she organized in San Francisco the first free kindergarten west of the Rocky Mountains. In 1880, she founded the California Kindergarten Training School. She published her autobiography, *My Garden of Memory,* in 1923.   EVELYN RAY SICKELS

Courtesy of Houghton Mifflin Co.
Kate Douglas Wiggin

WIGGLESWORTH, MICHAEL (1631-1705), was a Puritan pastor, doctor, and poet of colonial New England. He is best known for his somber poem *The Day of Doom: or, A Poetical Description of the Great and Last Judgment* (1662). Wigglesworth believed that many people were disobeying God and that God judged both individuals and nations. He wrote *The Day of Doom* as a warning to the New England colonists. His crude but dramatic ballad presented theology to the colonists in a form they could easily read and memorize. *The Day of Doom* became a best seller.

Wigglesworth was born in England and moved to America with his parents at the age of 7. He attended Harvard College, where he became a respected student and teacher. In 1656, he settled in Malden, Mass., and served as minister and physician.   L. C. RUDOLPH

WIGHT, *wite,* **ISLE OF,** lies off the southern coast of England (see ENGLAND [map]). A strait called *The Solent* separates the island from the mainland county of Hampshire. The island covers 147 square miles (381 square kilometers), and has a population of 108,480.

The Isle of Wight is famous for its mild climate and its scenery, which attracts tourists. The island's administrative center is Newport. Cowes, its leading port, is known for its yacht races. The chief industries are farming and sheep raising.   FREDERICK G. MARCHAM

WIGHTMAN, HAZEL HOTCHKISS. See TENNIS (Tennis Tournaments; table: U.S. Championships).

WIGMAN, MARY. See DANCING (Modern Dance).

WIGNER, *WIG nuhr,* **EUGENE PAUL** (1902-   ), is an American physicist. He worked with Enrico Fermi when Fermi produced the first nuclear chain reaction in 1942. Wigner developed many practical uses for nuclear energy. He won the Atomic Energy Commission's Enrico Fermi award in 1958, and shared the 1959 Atoms for Peace award with Leo Szilard. He shared the 1963 Nobel prize in physics with J. Hans Jensen and Maria Goeppert-Mayer. Wigner was born in Budapest, Hungary, and became a U.S. citizen in 1937. He became a professor of mathematical physics at Princeton University in 1938.   AARON J. IHDE

See also SZILARD, LEO.

WIGWAGGING is a method of signaling with one flag. Semaphore requires two flags (see SEMAPHORE). The three motions used in wigwagging represent a dot, a dash, and the end of a word or paragraph. Messages are sent by using combinations of these motions. Wigwagging is seldom used today.   PAUL J. SCHEIPS

WIGWAM is the name for a kind of dwelling used by the Algonkian-speaking Indians of the eastern woodlands. In the East, the foundation was usually made of light poles tied together with bark, forming an oval-shaped dome. The covering was layers of bark or perhaps reed mats, laid on like shingles. Other wigwams had a rectangular frame and gabled roof. Some northern Algonkians used a cone-shaped tent.   RUTH M. UNDERHILL

See also INDIAN, AMERICAN (picture: Indian Ways of Life [Eastern Woodlands]).

WILBERFORCE is the family name of two noted Englishmen, the father a statesman and the son a clergyman.

William Wilberforce (1759-1833) was a leader in the fight to abolish the slave trade and slavery in the British Empire. In 1780, he entered Parliament and became a leading Tory, noted for his eloquence. In 1786, Thomas Clarkson asked him to join in attacking slavery in the West Indies. The reformers decided to attack the slave trade first. Wilberforce, supported by William Pitt, led the first campaign in Parliament in 1789. The bill to end the slave trade passed the House of Commons in 1792, but failed in the House of Lords. When such a bill became law in 1807, Wilberforce turned against slavery itself. He retired from Parliament in 1825, but continued to support emancipation. Wilberforce was born in Hull and studied at Cambridge University.

Samuel Wilberforce (1805-1873), the third son of William Wilberforce, gave new vitality to the Church of England. As bishop of Oxford and then of Winchester, he held key positions during the crisis created by the conversion of John Henry Newman to the Roman Catholic Church. Wilberforce stood outside the Tractarian (Oxford) Movement (see OXFORD MOVEMENT). But he advocated strengthening the Church of England ritual and tradition. He was in great demand as a speaker. Wilberforce was born in London.   LOUIS FILLER

WILBERFORCE UNIVERSITY is a coeducational liberal arts university in Wilberforce, Ohio. It is operated by the African Methodist Episcopal Church. The university has divisions of business and economics, education, humanities, natural science, and social science. Courses lead to the bachelor's degree. All Wilberforce students alternate periods of study on the campus with periods of work at approved off-campus jobs. Wilberforce was founded in 1856 and is the oldest predominantly black university in the United States. For enrollment, see UNIVERSITIES AND COLLEGES (table).

Critically reviewed by WILBERFORCE UNIVERSITY

WILBUR, RICHARD (1921-   ), is an American poet. His volume *Things of This World* won the 1957 Pulitzer prize for poetry. He was co-winner of the 1970 Bollingen prize for poetry. Wilbur often uses myth and philosophy to illuminate ordinary experience. His poems see the dark side of human failure redeemed by a respect for intelligence, artistry, and "the things of this world." From his first published work, *The Beautiful Changes* (1947), to *Advice to a Prophet* (1961), Wilbur tried to show how the mind and the senses can combine to enrich our understanding of the world. Wilbur's poems are usually written in a formal style, have a musical quality, and are witty and mentally stimulating.

Wilbur was born in New York City. He wrote a children's book, *Loudmouse* (1963), and skillfully translated *The Misanthrope*, *The School for Wives*, and *Tartuffe*, three satirical comedies by the great French playwright Molière.   MONA VAN DUYN

WILD ANIMAL. See ANIMAL; WILDLIFE CONSERVATION.

WILD ASS. See DONKEY.

WILD BARLEY is a troublesome weed related to the grass family. It grows in various parts of the North American continent. The plant has a slender, rounded stem that grows about 2 feet (61 centimeters) tall. The spikes of the flowers develop a bristly beard around them. Because this beard somewhat resembles a squirrel's tail, the name *squirreltail* has been given to wild barley. Wild barley is a pest because it grows rapidly and kills off other plants. Also, the seeds of wild barley cling to the wool of sheep and irritate their hides. When animals eat the leaves and flowers of the plant, the leaves and flowers sometimes stick in their throats and cause them to choke. A fungus that grows on wild barley produces the poisonous drug ergot (see ERGOT).

Scientific Classification. Wild barley belongs to the grass family, *Gramineae*. It is classified as genus *Hordeum*, species *H. jubatum*.   FRANK THONE

WILD BOAR. See BOAR, WILD.

WILD CANARY. See GOLDFINCH.

WILD CARROT, or QUEEN ANNE'S LACE, is a carrot that grows wild. The cultivated carrot that people eat has a European and Asiatic origin. In North America, many carrot plants grow wild as common weeds. The name *Queen Anne's lace* was given the plants because of their lacy clusters of small white or yellowish flowers. The wild carrot is either an annual or a biennial. It grows to 3 feet (91 centimeters) tall. Its roots resemble the domestic carrot, but they should not be eaten.

Scientific Classification. Wild carrots belong to the parsley family, *Umbelliferae*. They are genus *Daucus*, species *D. carota*.   THEODOR JUST

WILD CELERY. See EELGRASS.

WILD FLOWER. See FLOWER (Wild Flowers; Studying Wild Flowers; color pictures).

WILD FLOWER PRESERVATION SOCIETY OF AMERICA is a nonprofit educational organization that attempts to save American wild flowers from destruction. Its headquarters are at the New York Botanical Gardens, New York, N.Y. 10458.

WILD GINGER. See GINGER.

WILD MORNING-GLORY. See BINDWEED.

WILD PINK is a wild, perennial herb of eastern North America. It has notched petals and small rose or white flowers about an inch wide. The plant grows as high as 9 inches (23 centimeters). It blooms from April to June. The erect stem is tufted with sticky hairs. Wild pink is sometimes grown in gardens. It is easy to grow from seeds, divisions, or cuttings.

Scientific Classification. Wild pink belongs to the pink family, *Caryophyllaceae*. It is classified as genus *Silene*, species *S. caroliniana*.   THEODOR JUST

WILD RICE is an aquatic grass that grows from 4 to 8 feet (1.2 to 2.4 meters) high. It is not related to rice (see RICE). Wild rice is not cultivated, but grows naturally in the shallow lakes of Minnesota, Wisconsin, and central Canada. The grain has large amounts of vitamin B. Indians harvested wild rice by bending the heads of the plant over the edge of a boat. They beat the grains loose with two sticks.

Scientific Classification. Wild rice belongs to the grass family, *Gramineae*. It is classified as genus *Zizania*, species *Z. aquatica*.   RICHARD A. HAVENS

WILD ROSE. See EGLANTINE; FLOWER (color picture: Flowers of Roadside, Field, and Prairie); ROSE.

WILD WEST. See WESTERN FRONTIER LIFE.

WILD WEST SHOW. See BUFFALO BILL.

WILDCAT is a name generally given to small, wild members of the cat family. The true wildcat lives in Europe. It is an extremely vicious animal, larger and stronger than the domestic cat. It has yellowish fur and black streaks around the body, legs, and tail.

In North America, several species of lynx are called wildcats. The lynxes have longer bodies, longer legs, and shorter tails than domesticated cats. They prowl at night. Their ears have tufts of fur on them, and their coats vary in color and thickness. The northern species of lynx has a long, clear-gray coat. The southwestern species, often called a *bobcat*, has short, yellowish-brown fur, covered with dark spots and other markings.

The Egyptian cat, a tropical species of wildcats, is

The Wild Carrot is well known to wild flower lovers as Queen Anne's lace. Flower clusters are brilliant and showy.

believed to be an ancestor of the common house cat.

Scientific Classification. Wildcats belong to the cat family, *Felidae*. The European species is classified as genus *Felis*, species *F. silvestris*. Bobcats are genus *Lynx*, species *L. rufus*.   HAROLD E. ANTHONY

See also BOBCAT; CAT (The Cat in History); LYNX; SERVAL.

WILDCAT BANK was the name for unstable banking institutions that issued paper money called *wildcat currency*. They operated under state charters, particularly in the South, during the early and middle 1800's. They became especially numerous and irresponsible after President Andrew Jackson's successful struggle against the Second Bank of the United States.

The Bank of the United States used its influence to restrain state banks from issuing more paper money, or *wildcat currency*, than their assets would justify. When Jackson succeeded in withdrawing government deposits from the Bank of the United States, his victory so crippled the Bank that it could no longer restrain the state banks. Many banks, especially in the South and West, then issued unreasonably large amounts of paper money, and lent it freely on the flimsiest security.

As a result, this caused a money inflation, followed by a period of wild speculation in Western land. The situation finally alarmed Jackson, who then issued his famous "Specie Circular," ordering government agents to accept nothing but gold and silver in payment for public lands. In consequence, many of the wildcat banks were unable to meet the demands made on them and failed abruptly. These bank failures contributed to the serious financial panic in 1837.   JOHN DONALD HICKS

See also JACKSON, ANDREW (The Money Surplus).

WILDCATTING. See GAS (Exploring for Gas).

WILDE, OSCAR (1854-1900), was an author, playwright, and wit. He preached the importance of style in both life and art and attacked Victorian narrowmindedness and complacency.

Wilde was born in Dublin, Ireland. His full name was OSCAR FINGAL O'FLAHERTIE WILLS WILDE. At 20, Wilde left Ireland to study at Oxford University where he distinguished himself as a scholar and wit. He soon became a well-known public figure, but the period of his true achievement did not begin until he published *The Happy Prince and Other Tales* in 1888. In these fairy tales and fables, Wilde found a literary form well-suited to his talents. Wilde's only novel, the ingenious *Picture of Dorian Gray* (1890), is an enlarged moral fable. It describes a man whose portrait ages and grows ugly as a reflection of his moral corruption while his actual appearance remains the same. The book seems to show the destructive side of a devotion to pleasure and beauty similar to Wilde's own.

Wilde's plays taken together are his most important works. *Lady Windermere's Fan* (1892), *A Woman of No Importance* (1893),

Brown Bros.
Oscar Wilde

and *An Ideal Husband* (1895) combine then current fashionable drama of social intrigue with witty high comedy. In each play, Wilde brings together an intolerant young idealist and a person who has committed a social sin in the past. They meet in a society where appearances are everything. The effect is always to educate the idealist to his own weaknesses and to show the need for tolerance and forgiveness.

In *The Importance of Being Earnest* (1895), his masterpiece, Wilde departed from his standard formula by combining high comedy with farce. Thematically, Wilde unites his own concern with style with society's concern with appearances. He ridicules social hypocrisy and the Puritan idea of earnestness and sincerity. The result is a satirical fantasy on surfaces in which apparently trivial matters such as a name are treated with extravagant seriousness. Wilde also wrote *Salomé* in French (1893), a one-act Biblical tragedy.

In 1895, Wilde was at the peak of his career and had three hit plays running at the same time. But in that year he was accused of having homosexual relations with Lord Alfred Douglas by Douglas' father, the marquis of Queensbury. As a result, Wilde became involved in a hopeless legal dispute and he was sentenced to two years in prison at hard labor. From his prison experiences came his best poem, *The Ballad of Reading Gaol* (1898), and a remarkable autobiographical document sometimes called *De Profundis*.

Wilde left England after his release. Ruined in health, finances, and creative energy, but with his wit intact, he died in France three years later.   MARTIN MEISEL

WILDEBEEST. See GNU.

WILDER, BILLY (1906-   ), is a leading motion-picture director, producer, and writer. His movies combine technical skill, keen dialogue, and a rather cynical realism about human behavior. Wilder often works with other writers on his scripts. Wilder's films vary in tone. They include the grim *Double Indemnity* (1944), *The Lost Weekend* (1945), and *Sunset Boulevard* (1950); the serio-comic *The Apartment* (1960); the satirical *One, Two, Three* (1961), *The Fortune Cookie* (1966), and *Some Like It Hot* (1959); and the sophisticated *Sabrina* (1954), and *Love in the Afternoon* (1957). Wilder won Academy Awards for his directing of *The Lost Weekend* and *The Apartment* and shared three awards for best screenplay.

Wilder was born Samuel Wilder in Vienna, Austria. He came to the United States in 1934 and became a U.S. citizen in 1940.   HOWARD THOMPSON

WILDER, LAURA INGALLS (1867-1957), was an American author of books for children. She is best known for her series of nine novels called the "Little House" books. Wilder based most of the series on her experiences growing up in the pioneer Midwest in the late 1800's. The series has been praised as a colorful literary saga of the spirit of American frontier life. The stories show the importance of a closely knit family, and are filled with humor and tenderness.

Laura Ingalls was born in Pepin, Wis. She lived a rugged pioneer life with her family as they moved from place to place. She described her childhood in the first "Little House" book, *Little House in the Big Woods* (1932). She married Almanzo Wilder, who came from an old established family in northern New York. *Farmer Boy* (1933) is the story of his childhood. *These Happy Golden Years* (1943) unites the families with the marriage of Laura and Almanzo.

The other books in the series are *Little House on the Prairie* (1935), *On the Banks of Plum Creek* (1937), *By the Shores of Silver Lake* (1939), *The Long Winter* (1940), *Little Town on the Prairie* (1941), and *The First Four Years* (published in 1971, after the author's death).

The Laura Ingalls Wilder Award was established in 1954 by the Children's Library Association. Laura

Harper & Bros.
Laura Ingalls Wilder

Ingalls Wilder herself received the first award for her lasting contribution to children's literature. The award is given every five years to an author or artist whose work in the field of children's books and literature is outstanding for several years.   GEORGE E. BUTLER

WILDER, THORNTON NIVEN (1897-1975), was an American playwright and novelist. He won Pulitzer prizes in both fields—in 1928 for his novel *The Bridge of San Luis Rey* (1927) and in 1938 and 1943 for the plays *Our Town* (1938) and *The Skin of Our Teeth* (1942).

The Bridge of San Luis Rey examines the relationship between character, fate, and chance. With deep psychological and philosophical insights, the book tells the story of five persons who die when a footbridge in Peru collapses. Wilder describes in precise and skillful prose how the lives of these persons led them to the bridge.

The novel *The Ides of March* (1948) is a fascinating re-creation of the ancient world. It tells the story of the Roman poet Catullus and his love affair with Clodia. The story also involves the dictator Julius Caesar and the orator Cicero. Wilder's other novels include *The Cabala* (1926), *Heaven's My Destination* (1934), *The Eighth Day* (1967), and *Theophilus North* (1973).

In *Our Town*, Wilder pioneered in breaking customary notions of time and space in the theater. The play tells the stories of several generations of a New England town at almost the same time. *The Skin of Our Teeth* is broadly humorous, yet sensitive and profound. It surveys man's capacity to survive everything, even his own folly. Wilder revised his play *The Merchant of Yonkers* (1938) under the title *The Matchmaker* (1955). The musical *Hello, Dolly!* (1964) is based on it.

Wilder was born in Madison, Wis. He grew up in China and traveled much of his life.   JOHN CROSSETT

WILDERNESS, BATTLE OF THE. See CIVIL WAR ("If It Takes All Summer").

WILDERNESS ROAD was an important pioneer road. In March 1775, 30 axmen led by Daniel Boone began to cut a trail. Their route began at the Block House in Virginia, passed through the Powell River Valley, crossed the Cumberland Mountains through Cumberland Gap, and ended in central Kentucky. Boone and his followers built a settlement called *Boonesborough* at the trail's end near present-day Lexington. Another branch of the Wilderness Road led to Harrodsburg.

The road was the only usable route through the mountains to Kentucky. It was a rocky trail menaced by unfriendly Indians. By 1800, about 200,000 settlers had traveled the road.   W. TURRENTINE JACKSON

See also TRAILS OF EARLY DAYS (map).

WILDLIFE CONSERVATION

WILDLIFE CONSERVATION includes all human efforts to preserve wild animals and plants and save them from extinction. It involves the protection and wise management of wild species and their environment. Some species have been killed off by natural causes, but the greatest danger to wildlife results from human activities. Thus, people themselves created the need for wildlife conservation.

Throughout history, wildlife has suffered because of human beings and their activities. The invention of increasingly efficient weapons, such as the bow and arrow and, later, the rifle and shotgun, enabled people to kill game with growing ease. Hunters have killed off some kinds of animals and have greatly reduced the numbers of others. People also have cleared forests, drained swamps, and dammed rivers to clear the way for agriculture and industry. These activities have limited the space available for many kinds of wildlife. In addition, human pollution of the environment has affected a number of wild species.

Various species had become extinct even before people appeared on the earth. In the past, however, other species developed and replaced those that died off, and the total variety of life did not diminish. Today, human activities kill off species with no hope for their replacement, and so the variety of life decreases.

Since about 1600, many kinds of wildlife have become extinct. In North America, such species include the Carolina parakeet, the passenger pigeon, the California grizzly bear, the Florida black wolf, the Franklinia tree of Georgia, and a birch that once grew in Virginia.

Beginning in the late 1800's, growing concern for the world's vanishing wildlife has led to increased conservation action. The governments of many nations have passed protective laws and set aside national parks and other reserves for wildlife. Such efforts have saved the American bison, the pronghorn, the California big tree, and many of the rare plants found on such islands as the Hawaiian and Galapagos islands.

However, several hundred species of animals and thousands of species of plants still face the danger of extinction. Such animals include the Asiatic lion, the Bengal tiger, the blue whale, the orang-utan, the mountain gorilla, the whooping crane, the California condor, the ivory-billed woodpecker, and all the Asian rhinoceroses. Plants facing extinction include the black cabbage tree, the Ozark chestnut, the St. Helena redwood, several kinds of California manzanitas, and the frankincense tree of the Ethiopia-Somalia region of Africa.

Values of Wildlife Conservation

If people ignore the need for wildlife conservation, today's endangered species will soon become extinct. Many other species will also face extinction. If this happens, human beings will lose much of great value that cannot be replaced. Wildlife is important to people for four main reasons: (1) beauty, (2) economic value, (3) scientific value, and (4) survival value.

Beauty. Every kind of animal and plant differs from every other kind and thus contributes in a special way to the beauty of nature. Most people feel that such beauty enriches their life. It also heightens the enjoy-

WILDLIFE CONSERVATION

ment of camping and other forms of outdoor recreation.

Economic Value. Wild species of animals and plants provide many valuable substances, such as wood and other plant products, fibers, meat and other foods, and skins and furs. The financial value of wild species is of major importance in the economies of many nations.

Scientific Value. The study of wildlife provides valuable knowledge about various life processes. Such study has helped scientists understand how the human body functions and why people behave as they do. Scientists have also gained medical knowledge and discovered important medical products by studying wildlife. In addition, by observing the effect of environmental pollution on wild animals, scientists have learned how pollution affects human life.

Survival Value. Every species of wildlife plays a role in helping maintain the balanced, living systems of the earth. These systems must continue to function if life is to survive. Thus, the loss of any species can threaten the survival of all life, including human beings.

Classifications of Scarce Wildlife

Wildlife biologists use three main classifications for animals and plants that face possible extinction: (1) endangered, (2) threatened, and (3) rare.

Endangered Species face the most serious threat of extinction. They require direct human protection for survival. The California condor is endangered because only about 50 birds of this species still exist. They must be completely protected from human interference, or the species will die out.

Threatened Species are generally abundant in some areas, but they face serious dangers nevertheless. These dangers may result from unfavorable changes in the environment. They also may be due to extensive hunting, fishing, or trapping, or even to collecting by hobbyists. The gray wolf, a threatened species, is still plentiful in some places. But its overall numbers throughout the world are being steadily reduced by hunting, trapping, and poisoning.

Rare Species have small populations. They live in protected environments, and their numbers are not decreasing. The Torrey pine tree is classified as rare. It grows only in two small areas of southern California, but human actions do not threaten or endanger its survival.

Methods of Wildlife Conservation

The method used to protect wildlife depends on the source of the danger to the threatened species. In many cases, wildlife can be helped by ensuring that their environment provides enough food, water, and shelter. This method, called *habitat management*, involves such action as soil conservation, good forestry practices, and water management.

Many species of wildlife have been threatened by human destruction of their habitat. For example, poor farming practices may destroy land, or the spread of cities and industries may pave over former wildlife habitats. Pollution may poison the air, water, plants, and animals in the habitat. To save wildlife habitats, people must set aside areas in which wild animals and plants can survive.

An animal threatened by too much hunting can be protected by laws that forbid or regulate such killing. Laws can also protect plants endangered by over-collection. If an entire habitat requires protection, the area may be made a national park or wildlife refuge. In some cases, the predatory animals that kill an endangered species must be controlled until the endangered animal has built up in numbers. On the other hand, a species may become too numerous. It could threaten its own survival—or the survival of other species—by eating too much of the food supply. This problem has occurred with elk and hippopotamuses in national parks. The numbers of such a species must then be reduced, either by controlled hunting or by restoring its natural enemies where they have become scarce.

If a species can no longer survive in its natural environment, it may be raised in captivity and then released into a protected area. This method saved the Hawaiian goose, and conservationists hope to save the whooping crane the same way. Some kinds of animals valued by sport hunters, such as quail and rabbits, are raised on *game farms* for later release into hunting areas. A species threatened by disease may be helped by sanitation measures in its habitat. Rare plants can be maintained in botanical gardens, or their seeds can be saved in seed banks for future replanting.

The success of wildlife conservation depends on a knowledge of the *ecology* of a species. In other words, it requires an understanding of the way in which a species lives, and how it relates to everything, both living and nonliving, in its environment. See ECOLOGY.

History

Early Efforts. The first wildlife conservation probably occurred among prehistoric peoples. These peoples may have limited their hunting to preserve the supply of wild animals they needed for food. Rulers of ancient civilizations set up the first game reserves—as their personal hunting grounds—and medieval European kings continued this practice. These kings also forbade hunting by anyone other than a member of the ruling class. But such action resulted from a ruler's love of hunting as a sport, rather than any awareness of the need for conservation. Certain forests were protected for religious reasons, and others were preserved for their value in providing timber to build ships.

During the 1600's and 1700's, the British colonies in America passed laws to protect wildlife. But most of the colonists ignored these laws. Effective wildlife conservation in the United States began during the late 1800's. Congress established Yellowstone National Park, the world's first national park, in 1872. In 1903, President Theodore Roosevelt established Pelican Island, in Florida, as the nation's first federal wildlife refuge. Also during the late 1800's, many states began to pass—and enforce—game laws. Beginning in the 1890's, millions of acres of forests were protected by the national forest system.

Congress set up the National Park System in 1916 under the direction of the National Park Service, an agency of the Department of the Interior. In 1940, the government created the Fish and Wildlife Service in the same department to strengthen the wildlife conservation program. The service manages the federal wildlife refuges, which in 1966 were organized into the National

Wildlife Refuge System. Many private wildlife conservation organizations, including the National Audubon Society and the National Wildlife Federation, have been founded in the United States since 1900.

Wildlife protection has a long history in Europe. In Italy, for example, what is now Gran Paradiso National Park has been a wildlife sanctuary since 1856. Canada created its first national park, Banff National Park, in 1887. Australia set up its first national park in 1879. In 1898, the Sabi Game Reserve (now Kruger National Park) was established in what is now South Africa. This reserve was the beginning of the extensive network of national parks and game reserves that covers Africa. The first Asian and South American national parks were created during the early 1900's. Governments have also established wildlife refuge systems and have passed laws for the protection of wildlife.

International Cooperation in wildlife conservation began on a worldwide scale after the birth of the United Nations (UN) in 1945. The Food and Agriculture Organization of the United Nations (FAO) and the United Nations Educational, Scientific and Cultural Organization (UNESCO), set up wildlife conservation programs. In 1948, UNESCO helped establish the International Union for the Conservation of Nature and Natural Resources (IUCN) to support worldwide conservation. As part of this international program, the IUCN started to gather information on the world's endangered species. It publishes this data in its *Red Data Book*. In 1961, the IUCN helped set up the World Wildlife Fund to raise money for wildlife conservation programs.

Wildlife Conservation Today. There are more than 1,200 national parks, wildlife reserves, and similar protected areas throughout the world. In addition, most countries have laws that protect wildlife. In the United States, the National Park System has about 300 protected areas, and the National Wildlife Refuge System includes more than 350 refuges.

State and federal laws also protect wild animals and plants in the United States. For example, the Endangered Species Act of 1973 protects rare wildlife from being hunted, collected, or otherwise threatened. Among other things, the act prohibits federal projects, such as the construction of dams, that would destroy an area where an endangered species lives. In 1978, the act was amended to permit the exemption of certain federal projects.

But in spite of the many conservation efforts, the future remains uncertain for the world's wildlife. The continued growth of the human population, the destruction of wildlife habitats, and the spread of environmental pollution present an increasing threat to the survival of wild species. RAYMOND F. DASMANN

Related Articles in WORLD BOOK include:

Audubon Society, National
Balance of Nature
Bird (How We Protect Birds)
Conservation (Wildlife Conservation)
Extinct Animal
Fish and Wildlife Service
Fishing Industry (Conservation)
Game
Izaak Walton League of America
Leopold, Aldo
National Wildlife Federation

See also *Wildlife Conservation* in the RESEARCH GUIDE/INDEX, Volume 22, for a *Reading and Study Guide*.

WILEY, HARVEY. See PURE FOOD AND DRUG LAWS (History).

WILFRID, THOMAS. See CLAVILUX.

WILFRID LAURIER UNIVERSITY in Waterloo, Ont., is a coeducational school supported by the province. It offers courses in arts, science, business administration, social work, and theology. The university grants bachelor's and master's degrees. It was founded in 1911. For enrollment, see CANADA (table: Universities and Colleges). Critically reviewed by WILFRID LAURIER UNIVERSITY

WILHELM, *VIHL hehlm*, in English, WILLIAM, was the name of two German emperors.

Wilhelm I (1797-1888) became king of Prussia and the first emperor of modern Germany. During the revolution of 1848, Wilhelm became unpopular because he opposed constitutional reform. He was forced to leave the country, but he soon came back and put down an uprising in Baden.

In 1858, Wilhelm became regent for his brother, Frederick William IV, who was suffering from mental disorders. He was proclaimed king of Prussia and given the title Wilhelm I in 1861. He supported the policies of his prime minister, Otto von Bismarck, who brought about three wars in the process of unifying Germany (see BISMARCK). During the Franco-Prussian War in 1871, Wilhelm became *Kaiser* (emperor) of a united Germany (see FRANCO-PRUSSIAN WAR; GERMANY [The Unification of Germany]).

Wilhelm was born in Berlin, the second son of Frederick William III, king of Prussia. He was trained as a soldier from his early youth, and he fought in the war of 1814 and 1815 against Napoleon I. See also PRUSSIA.

Bettmann Archive

Wilhelm I   **Wilhelm II**

Wilhelm II (1859-1941) was the last emperor of Germany. The Hohenzollern dynasty, which had ruled Prussia since 1701, ended with him (see HOHENZOLLERN). Wilhelm was the Kaiser of World War I (1914-1918). Although he received blame for the war, historians now believe that Russia and Austria were equally guilty.

Wilhelm, the grandson of Wilhelm I, was born in Berlin. He was the oldest son of Emperor Frederick III and Princess Victoria, daughter of Queen Victoria of England. George V of England and Nicholas II of Russia, who fought against him during World War I, were his cousins. His education emphasized military training, and made him friendly to the aristocratic military class. Wilhelm had a paralyzed left arm. He hid this weakness and ruled as the most powerful figure in Germany.

WILHELMINA

Wilhelm came to the throne in 1888 after the 100-day reign of his father (see FREDERICK [III] of Prussia). Bismarck was still chancellor and prime minister, but Wilhelm dismissed him in 1890. Under Wilhelm's reign, Germany became prosperous. He encouraged manufacturing and trade. He gained colonies in Africa and in the Pacific Ocean, and he built up the army and the navy until they were among the world's greatest. His program of colonial, naval, and foreign trade expansion brought Germany into conflict with Britain.

In 1890, Wilhelm broke the old Prussian alliance with Russia. This diplomatic blunder forced Germany in 1914 to fight a two-front war and led that nation to ultimate defeat (see GERMANY [History]). Early in November 1918, several revolts broke out and the German Navy mutinied. On November 7, the prime minister demanded that Wilhelm give up his throne. Wilhelm abdicated two days later. He fled to The Netherlands, which was neutral. For more than 20 years he lived in comfortable exile at Doorn.   GABRIEL A. ALMOND

WILHELMINA, *WIL hel ME nuh* (1880-1962), became queen of The Netherlands in 1890 when her father, William III, died. Her mother, Queen Emma, ruled as regent until 1898. In 1901 Wilhelmina married Henry, duke of Mecklenburg-Schwerin.

When the Germans invaded The Netherlands in 1940, they tried to capture Wilhelmina. But she escaped to London and directed The Netherlands forces against both Germany and Japan. After the war, her people joyfully welcomed her home. She celebrated her Golden Jubilee in August, 1948, and then gave up her throne to her daughter, Juliana (see JULIANA). She became the princess of The Netherlands. She was born at The Hague, The Netherlands.   JANE K. MILLER

WILKES, CHARLES (1798-1877), was an American rear admiral in the Civil War. He won fame for his explorations in the Antarctic, and for seizing the Confederate envoys, James Mason and John Slidell. His removal of the envoys from the British mail packet *Trent* near Cuba in November 1861, caused the "Trent Affair." It threatened to involve the United States in war with England (see TRENT AFFAIR).

Wilkes was born on April 3, 1798, in New York City. In 1838, he commanded an expedition in the Pacific Ocean. He sighted land on Jan. 30, 1840, and called it the *Antarctic Continent.* Wilkes was the first person to recognize Antarctica as a separate continent and not just a field of ice. The land he sighted was named Wilkes Land 72 years later.   RICHARD S. WEST, JR.

WILKES-BARRE, *WILKS bar uh,* Pa. (pop. 58,856), is a manufacturing and trading center in eastern Pennsylvania. It lies in the Wyoming Valley on the east bank of the Susquehanna River, about 100 miles (160 kilometers) northwest of Philadelphia (see PENNSYLVANIA [political map]). Wilkes-Barre and nearby Hazleton and Scranton form a metropolitan area with 621,858 persons. The city is the home of King's and Wilkes colleges. Wilkes-Barre manufactures such products as aircraft and missile parts, electronic equipment, pencils, shoes and apparel, and rubber products.

Connecticut colonists made the first settlement on the site of Wilkes-Barre in 1769. The settlement was twice destroyed by fire and rebuilt. Wilkes-Barre be-

came a city in 1871. In 1972, a tropical storm struck Wilkes-Barre and caused about $65 million in damages. The city has a council-manager government and is the seat of Luzerne County.   S. K. STEVENS

WILKINS, SIR HUBERT (1888-1958), was an Australian explorer, scientist, aviator, and photographer. He became famous for his air explorations in the Arctic and Antarctic.

U.S. Army
Sir Hubert Wilkins

Wilkins learned to live in the Arctic while on an expedition under explorer Vilhjalmur Stefansson from 1913 to 1916. Wilkins led a natural history expedition into northwestern Australia for the British Museum between 1923 and 1925. In 1928, after two unsuccessful attempts, he and Carl Ben Eielson became the first to fly an airplane across the Arctic Ocean from Point Barrow, Alaska, to Spitsbergen in the Arctic Ocean, a distance of 2,200 miles (3,540 kilometers). King George V of Britain knighted Wilkins that year.

Later in 1928, Wilkins led an Antarctic expedition, and made the first Antarctic airplane flights while surveying the Palmer Peninsula. In 1931, he tried, but failed, to reach the North Pole by submarine. He managed explorer Lincoln Ellsworth's Antarctic expeditions from 1933 to 1936, and served as a United States government adviser from 1942 to 1958.

George Hubert Wilkins was born in Mount Bryan East, in the state of South Australia. JOHN EDWARDS CASWELL

WILKINS, MARY ELEANOR. See FREEMAN, MARY ELEANOR WILKINS.

WILKINS, MAURICE HUGH FREDERICK (1916-   ), is a British biophysicist. He shared the 1962 Nobel prize for physiology or medicine with biologists James D. Watson of the United States and Francis H. C. Crick of Great Britain. Wilkins performed X-ray studies on *deoxyribonucleic acid* (DNA), the substance that transmits genetic information from one generation to the next. This work led Watson and Crick to create a model of the molecular structure of DNA. See NUCLEIC ACID.

Wilkins worked on the World War II Manhattan Project that developed the atomic bomb. He turned to biophysics research after the war. Working at King's College in London, Wilkins became an authority on the structure of nucleic acids. Wilkins was born in Pongaroa, New Zealand.   IRWIN H. HERSKOWITZ

WILKINS, ROY (1901-   ), is a noted black American leader and is often called "Mr. Civil Rights." He served as executive secretary of the National Association for the Advancement of Colored People (NAACP) from 1955 to 1977. He helped direct the fight for equal

NAACP
Roy Wilkins

rights and opportunities for blacks. In 1964, he won the Spingarn medal for his work in civil rights.

Wilkins was born in St. Louis, Mo., the grandson of a slave. He graduated from the University of Minnesota. Wilkins worked for a black newspaper, the *Kansas City Call*, before he joined the NAACP in 1931. Wilkins edited the NAACP magazine *The Crisis* from 1934 to 1949.   CARL T. ROWAN

WILKINSON, GEOFFREY. See NOBEL PRIZES (table: Nobel Prizes for Chemistry—1973).

WILL, in law, is a document that disposes of a person's property and becomes effective after the person's death. The person who makes the will is called the *testator*, if a man, and the *testatrix*, if a woman.

The persons named in the will to whom the testator's property is to be distributed are usually called the *distributees*. Personal property left by will is called a *bequest*, or a *legacy*. Real estate left by will is called a *devise*.

It is important to have a will prepared by a lawyer in order to be sure that it effectively disposes of property and that it may not be successfully contested by persons who disagree with its terms. If the testator owns more than a certain amount of property when he dies, the government of the state where he lives and the United States government will collect an estate tax. Unless the will has been carefully drawn by a lawyer, this estate tax may be unnecessarily large and the distributees may not receive as much as the testator had intended them to receive.

Administration. A testator may dispose of his property in any way he chooses, so long as the disposal is not contrary to law. The will usually names some person as an *executor*. The executor has the duty of seeing that the wishes of the testator are carried out. If no executor has been named, the court which has jurisdiction over estates may appoint an *administrator*, whose duties are the same as those of an executor. The general rule is that all executors, even close relatives, must give a money pledge called a *bond* or *surety* for the faithful performance of their duties. If an executor does not faithfully carry out the provisions of the will, the bond is forfeited. Usually, the giving of a bond may be waived if the will so provides.

Estate Plan. It is desirable that persons who own considerable property have an estate plan in which the will is only a part. An estate plan is prepared by a specially skilled lawyer, often after consultation with the testator's family, his insurance agent, his accountant, and his business associates. Its purpose is to make the provisions of the will consistent with the testator's insurance policies, the circumstances of his business, the wills of other members of his family, and the state and federal tax laws. A properly drawn estate plan may save many thousands of dollars that otherwise would have to be paid in estate taxes.

Codicil is an addition made after the will has been prepared. It changes or modifies the will in some way. A will may be altered or destroyed by the testator at any time. Such alteration will be legal provided that the testator is of sound mind and that proof is available to show that the alteration was not caused by undue influence from parties interested in the change. In addition, the codicil must be made according to the formalities required by state law just as the will must be. If the will must be witnessed by two persons, or by

three persons, then the codicil must be witnessed by the same number.

State Laws. The formalities required by state law differ widely. Each U.S. state and each province of Canada has laws governing wills. Some laws require that a will be witnessed. Others do not. The number of witnesses required may vary. Some states say that persons in a confidential or close blood relationship with the testator are not competent as witnesses. Others say they may serve as witnesses, but may not receive any benefit from the will if they do.

A number of states accept the so-called *holographic* will, or one prepared in the testator's own handwriting and unwitnessed. But such a will, invalid in many states, often leads to litigation even in states where it may be valid. Many states allow a person, under certain circumstances, to make a *nuncupative*, or oral, will. But these circumstances may vary. A person may die *intestate*, or without a valid will. The person's property then descends according to state law. This distribution may be contrary to the individual's intentions. A will should be prepared by a lawyer to ensure that it is valid and reflects the testator's intention. WILLIAM TUCKER DEAN

See also CODICIL; EXECUTOR; LEGACY; PROBATE.

WILL, in psychology, is the name given to a person's ability to act purposefully. When you turn on the light to see what is in a room, you may be said to have *willed* the action. This type of act is called *voluntary*. But when you blink your eyes spontaneously at a flash of light, this act is not willed, and is called *involuntary*.

Psychologists often think of the will as a special capacity by which the individual translates desires and ideas into action. Thus, if you desire to improve your grades in school, your will can keep you at your books even though you might be tempted to go swimming.

Many present-day psychologists prefer to use the term *will*, not to refer to a capacity of the mind, but as a name for several factors within a person. These are the factors which go into the process of making a decision. Prominent among these factors are our habits, interests, and desires. We often find a conflict within ourselves because we want a variety of things. For example, we would like to have good grades as well as a swim. We are loyal to a variety of ideals—to personal integrity as well as to friendship. We may be undecided and feel frustrated by our various needs. The need we feel to make up our minds often comes out of such indecision. The achievements of many of history's greatest persons started as their reaction to a feeling of frustration.

There need not be a clash, however, between the two views of the will, because they bring out different aspects. Taken as a distinct power, the will signifies our basic and our enduring tendency to obtain what perfects and satisfies our whole nature. But the will does not act in isolation. It works in and through our particular habits, interests, and attitudes. They enable the will to follow an intelligent and effective plan. And, in turn, our inclinations and interests have to be brought to some decision and integrated with our basic needs and desires. This is done through the will's acts of choice. Suppose you wish to change one of your attitudes, such as that of envying certain persons. This change must occur through effort to allow other attitudes toward these persons to dominate your feelings.

We might say that a person is what he strives for. He can often be understood best through his wishes and his ambitions. His will power expresses his determination to achieve a certain goal. A person's will power can often make the difference between success and failure. HADLEY CANTRIL

See also FREE WILL.

WILL-O'-THE-WISP is a ghostly, bluish light sometimes seen over marshes and graveyards. Scientists believe it is caused by the natural burning of *methane* (marsh gas) produced by decaying plants. Will-o'-the-wisp is also called *jack-o'-lantern*, *foxfire*, and *ignis fatuus*, a Latin term that means *foolish fire*.

Will-o'-the-wisp often seems to move away or vanish when approached. It was once thought to be a spirit that enjoyed misleading travelers. People who followed such a light would suddenly find themselves hopelessly lost in a swamp. In several English legends, the hero turns one of his garments inside out in order to magically end the power of will-o'-the-wisp. Other traditions speak of will-o'-the-wisp as the soul of a dead person. ALAN DUNDES

See also METHANE.

WILLAMETTE RIVER, *wih LAM et*, rises in the Cascade and Coast mountains of west-central Oregon. It flows northward for about 190 miles (306 kilometers), and empties into the Columbia River. For location, see OREGON (physical map). The Willamette Valley is the richest farming area in Oregon. Ocean-going ships can sail up the river for 12 miles (19 kilometers) to Portland, Oregon's largest city. A canal around Willamette Falls allows small boats to go up the river to Harrisburg, about 90 miles (140 kilometers) south of Portland. RICHARD M. HIGHSMITH, JR.

WILLARD, ARCHIBALD M. See SPIRIT OF '76.

WILLARD, EMMA HART (1787-1870), became known as the first American woman publicly to support higher education for women. Her efforts advanced that movement in the United States. She also wrote a volume of poems which included "Rocked in the Cradle of the Deep" (1830).

Mrs. Willard was born in Berlin, Conn., and started teaching school there at the age of 16. In 1809 she married John Willard, who helped her establish a girls' boarding school at Middlebury, Vt. Later, she founded a girls' seminary at Waterford, N.Y. It was later moved to Troy, N.Y., where it became famous as the Emma Willard School.

Wayne Davis
Emma Willard

She strongly supported the establishment of public schools, and educated hundreds of teachers in her schools for girls. CLAUDE A. EGGERTSEN

WILLARD, FRANCES ELIZABETH CAROLINE (1839-1898), was an American educator and social reformer. She organized the temperance movement on the plan by which it attained national prohibition (see PROHIBI-TION; TEMPERANCE). She served as president of the Woman's Christian Temperance Union (W.C.T.U.) from 1879 until her death, and made the W.C.T.U. a national organization (see WOMAN'S CHRISTIAN TEMPERANCE UNION). In 1883, Miss Willard founded a world temperance union. She was also a strong advocate of woman suffrage.

Miss Willard was born on Sept. 28, 1839, at Churchville, N.Y. She served as president of the Evanston (Ill.) College for Ladies. When it merged with Northwestern University, she became the dean of the Woman's College.

A statue of Frances Willard represents the state of Illinois in Statuary Hall in the United States Capitol in Washington, D.C. LOUIS FILLER

Brown Bros.
Frances E. Willard

WILLEMITE. See ZINC.

WILLEMSTAD, *VIL um staht* (pop. 43,547; met. area pop. 94,133), capital of the Netherlands Antilles, lies on the southwest coast of Curaçao Island (see VENEZUELA [color map]). It has one of the finest harbors in the West Indies. A free port, it is a warehousing and shopping center for the southeastern Caribbean.

WILLET is a large shore bird of North and South America. The willet is often called the *duck snipe*, and has 10 or more other common names. The *eastern willet* breeds along the Atlantic Coast between Virginia and the Bahama Islands, and migrates in winter as far south as Peru. It is rarely seen in Europe. The *western willet* ranges from Manitoba to Texas, and migrates south to the area around the Caribbean Sea in winter.

The willet measures about 16 inches (41 centimeters) long, and appears gray or white-colored below, and dark gray above. Its extended wings display striking black and white markings. Its long bill is straight and slender. The bird nests in a clump of weeds or grass in marshes close to the shore. The female lays four greenish-white or brownish-olive eggs that are speckled brown and purple.

Scientific Classification. The eastern willet belongs to the sandpiper family, *Scolopacidae*. It is genus *Catoptrophorus*, species *C. semipalmatus semipalmatus*. The western willet is *C. semipalmatus inornatus*. HERBERT FRIEDMANN

WILLIAM was the name of four kings of England.

William I, the Conqueror (1027?-1087), was the first Norman king of England. He was born at Falaise, France. He was the son of Robert I, duke of Normandy, and inherited Normandy at about the age of 8 in 1035. During his youth, there were many disorders. In 1047, William put down a great rebellion at the battle of Val-ès-dunes, which he won with the aid of his lord, King Henry of France. From that time on, William ruled Normandy with an iron hand.

In 1051, King Edward the Confessor of England promised William succession to the English throne as his nearest adult heir. Edward probably sent the promise to William through an English archbishop who passed through Normandy on his way to Rome. In 1064, Edward's brother-in-law Harold was shipwrecked on the Norman coast and taken prisoner. Harold promised to support William's claim to the throne in return for freedom. But Harold won the throne in 1066 through a deathbed grant by Edward and election by the nobles (see HAROLD [II] of England).

William immediately invaded England. His expedition had the pope's blessings, because William was expected to depose the Anglo-Saxon archbishop of Canterbury and introduce ecclesiastical reforms. Before William could sail, the king of Norway invaded northern England. King Harold hurried north and defeated the Norwegian invaders at Stamford Bridge. William landed before Harold could return to defend the coast. The Normans destroyed the Anglo-Saxon army and killed Harold at the Battle of Hastings (see HASTINGS, BATTLE OF; NORMAN CONQUEST).

On Christmas Day, 1066, William was crowned king. William then suppressed local rebellions. He took lands from those who resisted him, and gave them to his followers to hold in return for their military service to him. To emphasize the legitimacy of his crown, William confirmed the laws of Edward the Confessor and retained all the powers of the Anglo-Saxon monarchy. He levied *Danegeld*, the only national tax on landed property in all of Europe at that time. At Salisbury in 1086, he made all the landholders, even the vassals of his barons, swear allegiance directly to him as king.

William was devout, firm in purpose, and unchanging in gaining his ends. His greatest monument is *Domesday Book*, an exhaustive survey of the land, the principal landholders, the farm population, and the material and financial resources of his realm (see DOMESDAY BOOK).

See also FLAG (color picture: Historical Flags of the World [Early English Flags]).

William II (1057?-1100), son of William I, became king in 1087. He was called Rufus, meaning *red*, because of his ruddy complexion. Lustful for power and completely illiterate, he ruled with violence rather than strength. The clergy denounced his brutality and his infringements on church rights.

In 1088, several powerful Norman barons revolted against William. He put down the revolt and strengthened his position. Later, he gained control of Normandy by financing the crusading ventures of his brother Robert, Duke of Normandy. He also invaded Scotland and brought it under his control in 1097.

William's reign was marked by a bitter quarrel with the Roman Catholic Church. William kept the see of Canterbury vacant after the archbishop died in 1089, in order to collect its revenues for himself. When he fell seriously ill in 1093, he welcomed the election of Anselm as archbishop to atone for his sins. But when he recovered his health, he forced Anselm into exile. An arrow shot by a fellow hunter killed William while he was hunting. The clergy refused to give him a church funeral. ROBERT S. HOYT

William III (1650-1702), known as WILLIAM OF ORANGE, was king of England, Scotland, and Ireland. He was born in The Hague, the son of the Prince of Orange and Mary, the daughter of Charles I of England. He gained fame by his opposition to King Louis XIV of France.

When Louis invaded The Netherlands in 1672, the Dutch chose William as their leader. William was defeated time and again, but continued to fight. Once he was forced to open the dikes and flood the land. This stopped the French for a while, and William had time to build up an alliance against them. In 1677, he married his cousin Mary. Her father, James, Duke of York, later became James II of England.

William hoped to gain England's support. He became friendly with those opposed to King James II, who was a Roman Catholic. When James' son was baptized a Catholic, the Protestants turned to William and Mary. Both were related to the royal family, and both were Protestant. The leaders of the political parties invited them to rule England. Although they were to rule jointly, William insisted on making the decisions.

William landed in England with an army of 14,000 men in 1688. No blood was shed in this "Glorious Revolution," and James escaped to France. William and Mary became rulers of England in 1689, after they promised to obey the terms of the Declaration of Rights (later called the Bill of Rights). In 1690, William defeated James and a French and Irish army at the Battle of the Boyne, in Ireland. The Protestants of Ulster, Ireland, backed William, and are still called *Orangemen* today.

William was one of the ablest kings of England, but he was not popular. The people did not understand his ways, and he did not understand the English political system. He let Parliament limit his power in order to gain its support against France. He proved to be a good soldier and a clever diplomat in the struggle with France over Louis XIV's attempt to annex the Spanish Empire. He made alliances in 1701 with nearly all Europe against Louis, but he died soon after the War of the Spanish Succession began.

See also BILL OF RIGHTS (English Bill of Rights).

William IV (1765-1837) was the son of King George III and Charlotte of Mecklenburg-Strelitz. He succeeded his older brother George IV, and ruled from 1830 to his death. Three of England's greatest reforms were passed during his reign. They were the Reform Bill of 1832, the abolition of slavery in England's colonies, and factory reform (see GREAT BRITAIN [The Era of Reform]). WILLARD M. WALLACE

WILLIAM, of Germany. See WILHELM.

WILLIAM I (1772-1843) was the first king of the present-day kingdom of The Netherlands. He was the son of William V, Prince of Orange, the last Netherlands governor, or *stadthouder*, who lost his throne to the French in 1795. William I joined the Prussian Army against Napoleon I, and in 1806 lost the German duchy of Nassau. He regained Nassau in 1815, but then he traded it for the duchy of Luxembourg at the Congress of Vienna.

The Congress made William king of the new state of The Netherlands, including Belgium and Luxembourg. In 1830, Belgium demanded its independence, which was recognized in 1839. Because of trouble within the country, William gave up The Netherlands throne in 1840, in favor of his son William II. JANE K. MILLER

WILLIAM I, PRINCE OF ORANGE (1533-1584), was the father of the Dutch Republic. He was called *William the Silent* because of his cautious nature.

William was born in Dillenburg, near Wetzlar, Germany. His parents were Lutherans, but William became a Roman Catholic to please Emperor Charles V, who had taken a liking to him. He put William in command of troops on the French frontier in 1555.

In 1556, Charles gave the throne to his son Philip II. Philip tried to increase control of the Low Countries (Belgium and The Netherlands). When he also tried to stamp out the Protestant religion there, William joined the Protestant Church. He led a rebellion against Spain in 1568. Although William tried hard to unite all the Low Countries in the revolt, he did not succeed. In 1579, the seven northern provinces formed a league which later became the Dutch Republic. In 1581, Philip put a price on William's head, and three years later a half-insane assassin killed him.   JANE K. MILLER

See also NETHERLANDS (picture: William I).

WILLIAM AND MARY, COLLEGE OF, is a coeducational, state-supported college of liberal arts and sciences in Williamsburg, Va. It is the second oldest college in the United States. The college was founded in 1693 by King William III and Queen Mary II of England. Its buildings include the Sir Christopher Wren, built in 1695; the Brafferton, built in 1723; and the President's house, built in 1732. Courses lead to bachelor's, master's, and doctor's degrees.

Christopher Newport College, a branch of William and Mary, is in Newport News, Va. The college grants bachelor's degrees in liberal arts programs. Richard Bland College, in Petersburg, Va., is a two-year branch campus of William and Mary.

The Marshall-Wythe School of Law offers the degree of Master of Law and Taxation, the first of its kind in the United States. The college lists many famous Americans among its former students. These include Thomas Jefferson, James Monroe, John Tyler, and John Marshall. George Washington received his surveyor's license from William and Mary in 1749. He served as its chancellor from 1788 until his death in 1799.

Phi Beta Kappa, an honorary scholastic society, was founded at William and Mary in 1776 (see PHI BETA KAPPA). The honor system was also founded there in 1779. The college was the first in the United States to have an elective system of study (1779), a school of modern language (1779), and a school of modern history (1803). For enrollment, see UNIVERSITIES AND COLLEGES (table).   Critically reviewed by the
COLLEGE OF WILLIAM AND MARY

WILLIAM OF OCKHAM (1284?-1347?), or OCCAM, was an English philosopher and theologian. He was the most influential scholastic thinker of the 1300's (see SCHOLASTICISM). His attitudes toward knowledge, logic, and scientific inquiry played a major part in the transition from medieval to modern thought.

Ockham believed that the primary form of knowledge came from experience gained through the senses. He based scientific knowledge on such experience and on self-evident truths—and on logical propositions resulting from those two sources.

In his writings, Ockham stressed the Aristotelian principle that "entities must not be multiplied beyond what is necessary." This principle became known as *Ockham's Razor*. In philosophy, according to Ockham's Razor, a problem should be stated in its basic and simplest terms. In science, the simplest theory that fits the facts of a problem is the one that should be selected.

Ockham was born in southern England. He joined the Franciscans and eventually became prominent in that religious order. Ockham studied at Oxford University and then taught theology. In 1324, Pope John XXII summoned him to Avignon, France, to answer charges of *heresy* (teaching false doctrine). Ockham remained in Avignon for four years. In 1328, he fled from Avignon to the protection of Louis of Bavaria, who was the Holy Roman emperor and an enemy of the pope. Ockham lived in Munich, Germany, from 1330 until his death.   WILLIAM J. COURTENAY

WILLIAM THE CONQUEROR. See WILLIAM (I) of England.

WILLIAM THE SILENT. See WILLIAM I, PRINCE OF ORANGE.

WILLIAMS, DANIEL HALE (1856-1931), an American doctor, pioneered in surgery on the human heart. In 1893, he became the first surgeon to repair a tear in the *pericardium* (sac around the heart). Williams, a black, helped improve medical opportunities for members of his race. In 1891, he founded Provident Hospital in Chicago, the country's first interracial hospital and training school for black nurses and interns. Later, he established a nursing school for blacks at Freedman's Hospital in Washington, D.C. Williams also established surgical clinics at Meharry Medical College, Nashville, Tenn.

Williams was born in Hollidaysburg, Pa. He graduated from Chicago Medical College in 1883 and began his Chicago practice. He was the only black original member of the American College of Surgeons, which was founded in 1913.   JOHN A. BARBOUR

WILLIAMS, EMLYN (1905-   ), achieved fame as a playwright, actor, and platform reader. He wrote more than 20 plays and performed over 150 stage and film roles. He based his play *The Corn Is Green* (1938) on his experiences as a poor boy in Wales. Williams was born in Mostyn, Wales.   RICHARD MOODY

WILLIAMS, GEORGE. See YOUNG MEN'S CHRISTIAN ASSOCIATION.

WILLIAMS, HANK (1923-1953), was a country and western singer and composer. His songs helped country music spread from the rural South and Southwest to other regions of the United States. Williams' best-known songs include "Cold, Cold Heart" (1951), "Jambalaya" (1952), and "Your Cheatin' Heart" (1953).

Hiram Williams was born in Georgiana, Ala. He taught himself to play the guitar when he was 8 years old. At the age of 13, Williams formed his own band, the Drifting Cowboys. The band began to perform on radio the next year.

In 1947, Williams moved to Nashville, Tenn., the recording and broadcasting center of country music. There he achieved his greatest popularity through recordings and radio performances, particularly on the "Grand Ole Opry" program. Williams died of a heart ailment at the age of 29 while traveling to a performance.   BURT KORALL

WILLIAMS, JAMES M. See PETROLEUM (The Birth of the Oil Industry).

WILLIAMS, RALPH VAUGHAN. See VAUGHAN WILLIAMS, RALPH.

WILLIAMS, ROGER (1603?-1683), was a clergyman, a founder of the colony of Rhode Island, and a great

Chicago Historical Society

Roger Williams won the friendship and trust of the Indians who lived in what is now Rhode Island.

apostle of religious and political liberty. He advocated complete religious freedom as a right of the people, rather than mere religious toleration that could be denied at the government's will. Williams exercised influence and set an example which contributed greatly to the separation of church and state in the colony of Rhode Island and later, in the United States. The government he fashioned for the colony became an important part of the democratic tradition which was later expressed in the United States Constitution.

Early Years. Williams was born in London, the son of a shopkeeper. He was educated at Cambridge University. He became a student of Sir Edward Coke, the great English judge, and served briefly as chaplain to a wealthy family. But he was a religious nonconformist at the time that King Charles I and Archbishop William Laud were persecuting those who dissented from the Church of England.

Williams sailed for New England, and came to Boston on Feb. 5, 1631. When he arrived in America, he refused an invitation to become minister of the Boston church because he believed the church was dishonest in not publicly acknowledging its separation from the Church of England. In 1633, however, he became minister of the church at Salem.

By this time Williams had the reputation of being a troublesome person. He asserted that the royal charter did not justify taking land which belonged to the Indians, and he declared that people should not be punished for religious differences. To escape being sent back to England by officials of Massachusetts Bay Colony, he fled into the wilderness in January, 1636. He secured land from the Indians beyond the borders of Massachusetts, and founded Providence, later the capital of Rhode Island.

Settles in Rhode Island. Williams established a government based on the consent of the settlers. It provided for frequent elections, a flexible constitution, and local home rule. In order to safeguard this government for the colony, he went to England first in 1643 to secure a charter, and then in 1651 to save it from others who tried to infringe on his grant. His most famous work,

The Bloudy Tenent of Persecution (1644), was published during the first visit and influenced the course of the English Civil War. He wrote it as part of a long dispute with John Cotton, a Puritan leader of Massachusetts Bay Colony (see COTTON, JOHN). From 1654 to 1657, Williams was president of the Rhode Island colony.

Williams earned his living by farming and trading with the Indians. He was a warm friend of the Indians, and compiled a dictionary of their language. He went on missionary journeys among them, and their trust in him helped preserve the peace for all New England.

For a brief period after his banishment, Williams was a Baptist. For most of his life he was an intensely religious man, but without a church he could call his own. In his 70's, Williams served as a soldier in King Philip's War, and when he died he was buried with military honors. Rhode Island placed a statue of him in Statuary Hall.   WINTHROP S. HUDSON

See also BAPTISTS; RHODE ISLAND (History).

WILLIAMS, TED (1918-   ), became one of the greatest hitters in baseball history. He batted .406 in 1941, the first time any batter had reached .400 since 1930. He won his sixth American League batting title in 1958 and, when he retired in 1960, his lifetime batting average was .344. Theodore Samuel Williams was born in San Diego, Calif. He started playing with the Boston Red Sox in 1939. He was a Marine Corps pilot in World War II and the Korean War. He was elected to the National Baseball Hall of Fame in 1966. From 1969 to 1972, he was manager of the Washington Senators (now the Texas Rangers).   ED FITZGERALD

WILLIAMS, TENNESSEE (1911-   ), is an American playwright whose dramas portray the loneliness and isolation of man. He has been criticized for his use of violence and sexual abnormality, but his dominant tone is one of tenderness and compassion. The language in his plays is occasionally coarse in the naturalistic tradition, but it is generally poetic.

Williams is best known for two plays. In *The Glass Menagerie* (1945), a narrator, Tom Wingfield, relates his memories of his sister, Laura, and mother, Amanda. Laura, a cripple, lives in the make-believe world

261

Alex Gotfryd ©
Tennessee Williams

of the glass animals in her toy menagerie. Amanda withdraws into delusions about her girlhood. *A Streetcar Named Desire* (1947) concerns Blanche DuBois, an aging Southern belle who lives in a world of illusion. She is confronted with harsh reality when she goes to live with her sister Stella. After being raped by Stella's husband, Stanley Kowalski, Blanche becomes insane. The play won a Pulitzer prize in 1948.

Williams' play *Cat on a Hot Tin Roof* (1955) won a Pulitzer prize in 1955. His other plays include *The Rose Tattoo* (1951), *Camino Real* (1953), *Sweet Bird of Youth* (1959), and *The Night of the Iguana* (1961).

Williams was born Thomas Lanier Williams in Columbus, Miss. He chose Tennessee as a pen name. Williams also wrote poetry and fiction.   MARDI VALGEMAE

WILLIAMS, WILLIAM (1731-1811), was a signer of the Declaration of Independence. He was a delegate to the Continental Congress from 1776 to 1778, and a delegate to the Congress of the Confederation in 1783 and 1784. He helped frame the Articles of Confederation. He also served in the Connecticut convention that ratified the United States Constitution in 1787. He was born in Lebanon, Conn.   RICHARD B. MORRIS

WILLIAMS, WILLIAM CARLOS (1883-1963), was an American poet. Of all modern American poets, he is probably the closest in spirit and technique to Walt Whitman. Like Whitman, Williams tried to reveal the essential worth of every object and every experience. Like Whitman, he favored a kind of free verse based on what he called the "variable foot." The meter was determined by the nature of the subject matter rather than the requirements of conventional literary form.

Williams was born in Rutherford, N.J. He received his M.D. from the University of Pennsylvania Medical School in 1906 and specialized in the care of children in Rutherford for over 40 years. It was medicine, Williams observed in his *Autobiography* (1951), that "gained me entrance to . . . the secret gardens of the self. . . . I was permitted by my medical badge to follow the poor, defeated body into those gulfs and grottos."

Williams felt poetry should "see the thing itself without forethought and without afterthought but with great intensity of perception." His concentration on the individuality of his subject matter produced a hard, clear poetry quite different from the indirect, intellectual work of his close friend Ezra Pound and the imaginative richness of another friend, Wallace Stevens.

Williams' *Pictures from Breughel* won the 1963 Pulitzer prize for poetry. *Paterson* (1946-1958), a long major poem, is designed to provide a complex picture of the history and people of an American city. His *Selected Essays* were published in 1954. *Many Loves*, a collection of his plays, appeared in 1961.   ELMER BORKLUND

WILLIAMS COLLEGE. See UNIVERSITIES AND COLLEGES (table).

WILLIAMSBURG, Va. (pop. 9,069), is a historic city that lies on a peninsula between the James and York rivers (see VIRGINIA [political map]). Today, Williamsburg is a famous tourist attraction because it looks much as it did in colonial times. More than 80 of the city's original buildings, including many homes, have been restored to their appearance of the 1700's.

Williamsburg was the capital of the Virginia Colony from 1699 to 1776 and of the Commonwealth of Virginia from 1776 to 1780. During colonial times, the city ranked with Boston, New York City, and Philadelphia as a cultural, political, and social center.

Many principles of self-government were established in Williamsburg. In 1765, the famous statesman Patrick Henry delivered a noted speech against the Stamp Act in the Williamsburg Capitol. There, the colonists adopted the Virginia Declaration of Rights in 1776. This document included the guarantees of liberty that became models for the Bill of Rights, the first 10 amendments to the United States Constitution.

Early Days. English colonists established the Williamsburg settlement in 1633. They chose the site because it had fewer mosquitoes and better soil drainage for crops than did the area around Jamestown, Va., the first permanent English settlement in America. The colonists called their community Middle Plantation because it lay in the middle of the peninsula. The settlers built a fence of stakes 6 miles (10 kilometers) long across the peninsula for protection against the Indians. The College of William and Mary, the second oldest in the United States, was founded in Middle Plantation in 1693.

In 1699, the colonists renamed their settlement Williamsburg in honor of King William III of England. Also in 1699, the capital of the Virginia Colony was moved to Williamsburg after a fire destroyed Jamestown. Williamsburg received a city charter in 1722.

Williamsburg ranked as the most important city in the Virginia Colony. Twice each year, plantation owners and their families gathered in Williamsburg to attend sessions of the General Court, Virginia's highest court. On these occasions, called *publick times*, Virginians also conducted business and attended auctions, balls, fairs, horse races, and other social events. The colony's first newspaper, the *Virginia Gazette*, was published in Williamsburg in 1736. In 1773, the first public mental institution in the English colonies was opened in the city.

The Virginia Colony became one of the first colonies to vote for independence from England. It passed the Virginia Resolution for American Independence in Williamsburg in May, 1776. In 1780, during the Revolutionary War, the Virginians moved their capital from Williamsburg to Richmond. The westward shift of Virginia's population made the more central location desirable. The people also feared that English warships might attack Williamsburg from the James River.

Williamsburg declined in importance and population after the Revolutionary War. Its economy came to depend largely on the College of William and Mary. The city changed little during the 1800's and early 1900's.

Restoration. In 1926, the philanthropist John D. Rockefeller, Jr., became interested in restoring and

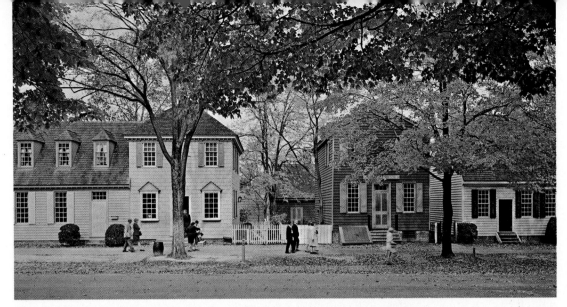

Duke of Gloucester Street is lined with restored homes that show how Williamsburg looked during the 1700's. The street is in the city's large historic section, called Colonial Williamsburg.

The Interiors of Several Restored Homes in Colonial Williamsburg are open to visitors.

A Blacksmith Shop is one of the 15 craft shops in Williamsburg. The master blacksmith works at an anvil while his helper fans a fire in the forge.

WORLD BOOK map

WILLIAMSBURG

VIRGINIA

Williamsburg

Williamsburg lies between the James and York rivers in eastern Virginia. The map at the right shows the city's restored area in yellow and the major points of interest.

☐ Restored area
■ Important building
☐ Other building

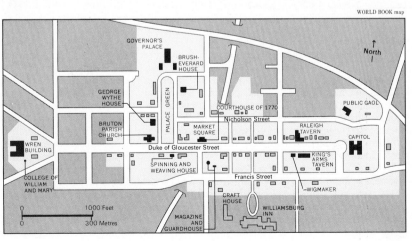

263

Colonial Williamsburg

The Governor's Palace is one of Williamsburg's chief attractions. Visitors may ride to the palace in a horse-drawn carriage.

preserving the colonial appearance of Williamsburg. The idea came from a Williamsburg minister, W.A.R. Goodwin. Rockefeller provided the money that set up the Colonial Williamsburg Foundation. By the 1970's, the foundation had restored more than 80 colonial buildings and had rebuilt more than 50 major buildings on their original sites.

Today, the historic area of Williamsburg covers more than 170 acres (69 hectares). Eleven major historic buildings and many colonial shops are open to the public daily. Guides in colonial costume escort visitors through the buildings and demonstrate such colonial skills as barrelmaking, cabinetmaking, and candle dipping. The furnishings of the homes, public buildings, and shops make up one of the finest collections of American and English antiques in the United States.

Williamsburg Today attracts more than a million visitors a year. Among the tourist attractions near Williamsburg is Carter's Grove, a plantation mansion built in the mid-1700's. Colonial National Historical Park includes much of Jamestown Island, several historic Yorktown homes, the Yorktown battlefield, and a scenic parkway that connects these sites. Jamestown, Williamsburg, and Yorktown form what is often called the "historic triangle" of Virginia.

Williamsburg covers about 5 square miles (13 square kilometers), almost three times its area in colonial times. Many modern housing developments surround the city. Williamsburg has a council-manager form of government. The people elect the five members of the council to two-year terms. A city manager, hired by the coun-

cil, supervises public services. Williamsburg is the seat of James City County.   WILL MOLINEUX

See also COLONIAL LIFE IN AMERICA (pictures); VIRGINIA (color picture).

WILLIAMSON, HUGH (1735-1819), was one of the North Carolina signers of the United States Constitution. He also worked for its ratification, and later served in Congress from 1790 to 1793. Then he moved to New York and devoted the rest of his life to literary and scientific work. Williamson was born in West Nottingham, Pa. His profession was medicine, but he was also a professor of mathematics and a merchant. He was a friend of Benjamin Franklin, and joined him in many experiments in electricity.   KENNETH R. ROSSMAN

WILLIAMSPORT, Pa. (pop. 37,918; met. area pop. 113,296), is an industrial and trade center in north-central Pennsylvania. It lies on the West Branch of the Susquehanna River (see PENNSYLVANIA [political map]). The city's industries produce aircraft engines and parts, chemicals, foods, leather goods, metals and metal products, paper, parts for electrical equipment, and textiles. Until the 1870's, Williamsport was the sawed-lumber center of the country. It is the home of Lycoming College and of the international headquarters of Little League baseball.

Williamsport was first settled in 1756. It was incorporated as a city in 1866. Williamsport has a mayor-council form of government. The city is the seat of Lycoming County.   S. K. STEVENS

WILLINGDON, MARQUIS OF (1866-1941), FREEMAN FREEMAN-THOMAS, was a British colonial official who served as governor general of Canada from 1926 to 1931. He then became viceroy and governor general of India. In 1936, he was made Lord Warden of the Cinque Ports and chancellor of the Order of St. Michael and St. George. Earlier, he was governor of Bombay and Madras. He headed the Boxer Indemnity Committee delegation that visited Canada in 1926.   LUCIEN BRAULT

WILLIS, WILLIAM. See RAFT.

WILLKIE, WENDELL LEWIS (1892-1944), was the Republican candidate for President of the United States in 1940 when Franklin D. Roosevelt ran for a third term. Willkie was defeated, but he polled over 22 million votes. His running mate for the Vice-Presidency was Senator Charles L. McNary of Oregon.

His political career was one of the most unusual in American history. Most of his life he had been a loyal member of the Democratic Party, but he became a Republican in the middle 1930's. He rose to political prominence without the aid of a regular political machine, and most of Willkie's advisers were political amateurs. The chant "We want Willkie" from the galleries at the 1940 Republican National Convention forced many unwilling Republican leaders to give Willkie the party nomination for President of the United States.

His Life. Willkie was born on Feb. 18, 1892, in Elwood, Ind. His first name was originally Lewis

Harris & Ewing

Wendell L. Willkie

and his middle name Wendell. But when he enlisted in the army during World War I, the army mistakenly reversed them and he accepted the change. He studied law at Indiana University.

In 1929, he became legal adviser to the Commonwealth and Southern Electric Utilities Company. Four years later, he was elected the company's president. He fought a long legal battle against the Tennessee Valley Authority. But when in 1939 the Supreme Court of the United States refused to consider the question of the constitutionality of the authority's activities, he sold the properties of the Tennessee Electric Power Company, a subsidiary of Commonwealth and Southern, to the TVA for $78 million.

His Public Career. Willkie became prominent for his opposition to the New Deal of President Roosevelt. He favored many of its social reforms, but opposed its business regulations. He favored removing controls and changing the tax system to encourage business expansion. He largely agreed with Roosevelt's foreign policy.

After the United States entered World War II, Willkie rallied his followers in a program of national unity. Roosevelt sent him on a number of visits to other countries as his unofficial envoy. After Willkie returned from an airplane trip around the world in 1942, he wrote the book *One World* (1943). In it, he outlined his ideas for international cooperation. Willkie entered the Wisconsin primary in 1944 as a candidate for the Republican nomination for President. He was defeated and retired from politics. HARVEY WISH

See also ROOSEVELT, FRANKLIN D. (Election of 1940).

WILLOW is a large group of graceful trees and shrubs that usually have slender branches and narrow leaves. There are about 300 *species* (kinds) of willows, and about 100 of them are native to North America. The smallest willow is a tiny shrub about 1 inch (2.5 centimeters) high that grows in arctic regions and above the timberline on mountains. The largest willows grow more than 120 feet (37 meters) high.

The twigs of the willow are soft, slender, and bend easily. Because of this, the wood is used to make baskets and furniture. Willow wood also produces a high grade of charcoal that once was used to make gunpowder. The bitter bark yields *tannin*, a substance that is used to tan leather.

Willows usually grow near water. Sometimes they are planted in damp regions so that their roots take up water and dry the soil. The roots interlace to form a tough network that holds the soil together and prevents soil erosion. Willows also are planted to provide shade and to protect fields from winds.

Most willows have long, narrow leaves that taper to a point and have finely toothed edges. Some willows have small, oval-shaped leaves.

In early spring, willows produce upright clusters of tiny, yellowish-green flowers. These flower clusters are called *catkins* because in some types of willows they resemble a cat's tail. The female flower develops a flask-shaped pod that splits open and releases tiny seeds with white, silky hairs.

The *black willow* is an important tree in the Eastern United States. Most willow lumber comes from the black willow. The wood is used mainly for boxes, crates, furniture, cabinetwork, caskets, and for artificial limbs. The black willow has rough, dark bark.

Gerard, National Audubon Society

The Drooping Branches of the Weeping Willow add beauty and charm to parks, and the strong roots prevent soil erosion.

Wicker furniture and baskets are usually made from young shoots of the shrubby *basket willow*. The basket willow grows in New York, Michigan, and Europe.

The *white willow* is a popular decorative tree. The underside of its leaves appears white and silky. The *crack willow* gets its name from the fact that its brittle twigs break off in high winds. The *weeping willow*, native to China, has graceful, drooping branches. The *pussy willow* develops furry catkins, and its twigs are often used as decorations.

Scientific Classification. Willows belong to the willow family, *Salicaceae*. They are genus *Salix*. The black willow is *S. nigra;* basket willow is *S. viminalis;* weeping willow is *S. babylonica;* white willow is *S. alba;* crack willow is *S. fragilis;* pussy willow is *S. discolor.* E. L. LITTLE, JR.

See also CATKIN; OSIER; PUSSY WILLOW; TREE (Familiar Broadleaf and Needleleaf Trees [picture]).

WILLOW HERB. See FIREWEED.

WILLOW PTARMIGAN. See PTARMIGAN; BIRD (picture: Color Protects Them).

WILLS, HELEN NEWINGTON (1906-   ), won more major tennis championships than any other woman in the world. She won the United States women's title seven times and the British championship at Wimbledon eight times. She was noted for her ability to hit the ball harder than any woman she faced and for poise that earned her the name "Little Miss Poker Face." She won her first U.S. women's tournament in 1923, and retired after winning at Wimbledon in 1938. She was born at Centerville, Calif. Her name during part of her playing career was Helen Wills Moody. PAT HARMON

See also TENNIS (picture; tables).

WILLS, WILLIAM. See AUSTRALIA (Exploration; map).

WILLSON, T. L. See CALCIUM CARBIDE.

WILLSTÄTTER, RICHARD. See NOBEL PRIZES (table: Nobel Prizes for Chemistry—1915).

WILLYS, JOHN NORTH (1874-1935), was an American automobile manufacturer. He purchased the Overland Automobile Company in 1907 and from it organized the Willys-Overland Company. The company's sales increased from 50 automobiles the first year to more than 300,000 about 20 years later. The company made the Overland, Willys-Knight, and Whippet.

By 1917, Willys' holdings included the car company and airplane, truck, and plow companies. But he lost control of his giant corporation in 1920. He reorganized the firm, and regained control in 1924. Willys was born in Canandaigua, N.Y. He was U.S. ambassador to Poland from 1930 to 1932.   SMITH HEMPSTONE OLIVER

WILMINGTON, Del. (pop. 80,386; met. area pop. 499,493), is the largest city and the chief manufacturing center of the state. Wilmington is called the *Chemical Capital of the World* because the city's metropolitan area is the home of several leading chemical firms. They include the Du Pont Company, one of the world's largest manufacturers of chemical products. The city lies in northeast Delaware, where the Brandywine and Christina rivers join the Delaware River. For the location of Wilmington, see DELAWARE (political map).

In 1638, a group of Swedes arrived in what is now the Wilmington area. They planned to set up a fur-trading and shipping center. The colonists chose the site because it had a natural wharf on what they named the Christina River. They built Fort Christina, the first permanent settlement in Delaware.

Description. Wilmington, the county seat of New Castle County, covers 16 square miles (41 square kilometers). Many tourists visit the Fort Christina Monument, Old Swedes Church, and Old Town Hall, which includes a historical museum. The Delaware Center for the Performing Arts presents concerts, plays, and other productions. Two museums are near Wilmington. The Hagley Museum features exhibits of industries of the 1800's. The Henry Francis du Pont Winterthur Museum has a collection of Early American furniture. Wilmington College is also near the city.

Wilmington has about 20 manufacturing plants. The chemical companies employ about a third of the workers of the area. Other products include automobiles and dyed fabrics. The city is a center for exporting and importing automobiles, and many ocean-going ships dock there. Delaware Bay links the Delaware River and the Atlantic Ocean.

History. Leni-Lenape Indians lived in what is now the Wilmington area before the white settlers arrived. Swedish colonists built Fort Christina there in 1638, but Dutch forces seized it in 1655. The English captured the settlement in 1664 and, in 1739, they named it Wilmington in honor of the Earl of Wilmington.

In 1802, Éleuthère Irénée du Pont, a French chemist, built some gunpowder mills near Wilmington. These mills grew into the Du Pont Company. Many other firms also established offices in Wilmington during the 1800's and 1900's.

Wilmington started several construction projects in the 1970's. A six-block downtown mall was completed in 1976, and a civic center was scheduled for completion in 1977. The mall includes Old Town Hall, five houses built in the 1700's, a performing-arts center, and stores and office buildings. Wilmington has a mayor-council form of government.   JAMES E. O'BRIEN

For the monthly weather in Wilmington, see DELAWARE (Climate). See also DELAWARE (A Visitor's Guide; pictures).

WILMINGTON COLLEGE. See UNIVERSITIES AND COLLEGES (table).

WILMOT, DAVID (1814-1868), a Pennsylvania Democrat, served in the United States House of Representatives from 1845 to 1851. In 1846, he sponsored the Wilmot Proviso, an amendment that would have forbidden slavery in territory that the United States gained from the Mexican War (see WILMOT PROVISO). He helped found the Republican Party in 1854, and was elected to the United States Senate in 1861 as a Republican. Wilmot was born in Bethany, Pa.   S. K. STEVENS

WILMOT PROVISO, *pruh VY zoh.* President James K. Polk asked Congress in August 1846, to appropriate $2 million to negotiate a peace with Mexico, then at war with the United States. The President hoped to purchase new territory for the United States from Mexico. David Wilmot, a Democratic representative from Pennsylvania, offered an amendment to the bill in the House of Representatives. This amendment, called the *Wilmot Proviso,* declared that slavery should be forbidden in any territory obtained by the United States with the $2 million.

The House of Representatives approved the amendment on Feb. 15, 1847. But the Senate, where Southern representation was stronger, refused to pass it. For several years, the proviso was offered unsuccessfully as an amendment to many bills. It became the basis for bitter debate over the issue of slavery in the territories. The issue was settled in 1862, when Congress banned slavery in any United States territory. NORMAN A. GRAEBNER

WILSHIRE BOULEVARD. See LOS ANGELES (Central Los Angeles).

WILSON, N.C. (pop. 29,347), is the largest bright-leaf tobacco market in the Western Hemisphere. Every year, the city markets from 50 million to 90 million pounds (23 to 41 million kilograms) of tobacco, worth from $30 million to $54 million. Wilson lies in the upper coastal plain of the state, in the heart of the bright-leaf tobacco belt. For location, see NORTH CAROLINA (political map).

Wilson is the home of Atlantic Christian College. It has a council-manager government.   HUGH T. LEFLER

WILSON, ALLEN B. See SEWING MACHINE (History).

WILSON, ANGUS (1913-   ), is a British author of novels and satirical short stories. His books deal with the deceptions that occur in human relationships, both public and private. Wilson uses masses of detail to create a realistic atmosphere.

The heroes of Wilson's novels *Hemlock and After* (1952), *Anglo-Saxon Attitudes* (1956), and *The Middle Age of Mrs. Eliot* (1958) are all middle-aged or elderly. They lead lives of frustration and confusion and are bogged down in everyday detail. Wilson enlivens these dreary characters with brilliant, witty dialogue and sharp observations on society. Twenty-five of Wilson's short stories were collected in *Death Dance* (1969). He also wrote *The World of Charles Dickens* (1970). Angus Frank Johnstone-Wilson was born in Bexhill-on-Sea, England.   FREDERICK R. KARL

WILSON, CHARLES THOMSON REES (1869-1959), a British physicist, invented the Wilson cloud chamber in 1912 (see WILSON CLOUD CHAMBER). This device made the tracks of high-speed atomic and nuclear particles visible by means of trails of water droplets condensed on the ions produced along their paths. Wilson shared the 1927 Nobel Prize in physics for his invention.

Wilson also did research on atmospheric electricity and on the absorption of penetrating radiation. He was born in Glencorse, Scotland.　　　　G. GAMOW

WILSON, EDMUND (1895-1972), an American author, wrote about a wide variety of subjects. He became known for important works in such fields as Biblical studies, history, literature, and political science.

Wilson's many books reflect his broad interests. He learned Russian so he could conduct research on two of his books, *Travels in Two Democracies* (1936) and, later, *A Window on Russia* (1972). Wilson also mastered Hebrew to conduct research for *Scrolls from the Dead Sea* (1955). Some of his books reflect his broad knowledge of cultural, social, and historical subjects. They include *To the Finland Station* (1940), *Apologies to the Iroquois* (1960), and *Patriotic Gore: Studies in the Literature of the American Civil War* (1962).

Wilson's first work of literary criticism, *Axel's Castle* (1931), is a study of the symbolist movement in literature. *The Triple Thinkers* (1938), *The Boys in the Back Room* (1941), and *The Wound and the Bow* (1941) examine the writings of noted European and American authors. Wilson also wrote a number of essays and reviews for magazines. Many were collected in *Classics and Commercials* (1950), *The Shores of Light* (1952), and *American Earthquake: A Documentary of the 20's and 30's* (1958). Wilson wrote one novel, *I Thought of Daisy* (1929).

Wilson was born in Red Bank, N.J., and graduated from Princeton University in 1916. He served as managing editor of *Vanity Fair* magazine from 1920 to 1921 and as associate editor of the *New Republic* from 1926 to 1931. Many of his essays and reviews first appeared in *The New Yorker* magazine. At his death, Wilson left over 2,000 pages of notes. The first volume of the notes was published as *The Twenties* (1975).　　DEAN DONER

WILSON, ETHEL (1890-　　), is a Canadian author. Most of her novels and short stories are gentle, sympathetic treatments of people from humble backgrounds. Most of her novels are set in or around Vancouver, B.C. She describes the city, its people, and the surrounding countryside with wit and understanding. Her first novel, *Hetty Dorval* (1947), describes the relationship between a young girl and a mysterious older woman. Her other novels include *The Innocent Traveller* (1949), *Swamp Angel* (1954), and *Love and Salt Water* (1956).

Wilson was born in Port Elizabeth, South Africa, and was raised in England and Vancouver. She taught school in Vancouver and, in 1937, began to write short stories for magazines. These stories were collected in *Mrs. Golightly and Other Stories* (1961).　　CLAUDE T. BISSELL

WILSON, SIR HAROLD (1916-　　), served as prime minister of Great Britain from 1964 to 1970 and from 1974 to 1976. He was also the leader of Britain's Labour Party from 1963 to 1976.

Wilson served as prime minister during times of great economic difficulty in Britain. The country faced such problems as inflation, strikes, low industrial production, and a deficit in its balance of payments. To try to solve these economic problems, Wilson's government took such steps as devaluing the British pound, raising taxes, and putting a ceiling on prices and wages. For more details, see GREAT BRITAIN (Economic Problems; History).

James Harold Wilson was born in Huddersfield, Yorkshire, England. He graduated from Oxford University in 1937 and taught economics there for two years. During World War II (1939-1945), Wilson served as an economist for the government. He was first elected to Parliament in 1945. Also, in 1945, Wilson became parliamentary secretary for the Ministry of Works. In 1947, he was named secretary of overseas trade. Later in 1947, he became president of the Board of Trade. He resigned in 1951. In 1954, he became a member of the Labour Party's parliamentary committee. Wilson became the party's leader in 1963. The party won the parliamentary election in 1964, and Wilson became prime minister. He replaced Sir Alexander Douglas-Home of the Conservative Party. The Labour Party lost the 1970 election, and Conservative leader Edward Heath replaced Wilson. In 1974, the Labour Party regained power, and Wilson became prime minister again. Wilson retired in 1976. He was knighted by Queen Elizabeth II that year.　　RICHARD ROSE

Camera Press-Pix from Publix
Sir Harold Wilson

WILSON, HENRY (1812-1875), served as Vice-President of the United States from 1873 to 1875 under President Ulysses S. Grant. He was a Republican U.S. senator from Massachusetts from 1855 to 1873.

Wilson helped found the Republican Party. He served in both houses of the Massachusetts legislature, but was defeated when he ran for governor in 1853. Wilson was chairman of the Senate Military Affairs Committee during the Civil War, and a "Radical Republican" during Reconstruction (see RECONSTRUCTION). Wilson was implicated in the Credit Mobilier scandal of 1872 (see CREDIT MOBILIER OF AMERICA).

Wilson was born Jeremiah Jones Colbaith in Farmington, N.H., but later changed his name. He had little formal schooling, but he was an avid reader. Wilson moved to Natick, Mass., in 1833, and became a shoe manufacturer. He was called the *Natick Cobbler*. Wilson wrote the *History of the Rise and Fall of the Slave Power in America*.　　IRVING G. WILLIAMS

See also VICE-PRESIDENT OF THE UNITED STATES (picture).

WILSON, JAMES (1742-1798), was a Pennsylvania signer of the Declaration of Independence and the United States Constitution. In 1774, he wrote a widely circulated pamphlet in which he rejected the British Parliament's legislative authority over the American colonies. Later, he became active in the movement to increase the power of the United States government, and played an important role in the Constitutional Convention of 1787. He was a leader of the forces in the Pennsylvania convention that favored ratifying the Constitution. He was an associate justice of the Supreme Court of the United States from 1789 to 1798. Born and educated in Scotland, Wilson came to America in 1765.　　RICHARD B. MORRIS

WOODROW WILSON

T. ROOSEVELT
26th President
1901 — 1909

TAFT
27th President
1909 — 1913

WILSON, WOODROW (1856-1924), led the United States through World War I and gained lasting fame as a champion of world peace and democracy. Wilson was one of the most remarkable men in American history. Before reaching the height of popularity as a world statesman, he had achieved success in two other careers. First, as a scholar, teacher, and university president, he greatly influenced the course of education. Then, as a political leader, he brought successful legislative reforms to state and national government. Wilson would have won a place in history even if he had been active in only one of his three careers.

Wilson was first of all a scholar. Even his physical appearance was like the popular idea of a scholar. He was thin, of medium height, and wore glasses. His high forehead, firm mouth, and jutting jaw all gave signs of thoughtfulness and strength. He was also a strong leader as a teacher, university president, and statesman. He was by nature somewhat headstrong and ready to fight. He was often unforgiving toward persons who disagreed with him. In his letters, Wilson often said he was not able to establish close friendships. But in truth, he had a great capacity for warm friendship. His energy, magnetic personality, and high ideals won for him the loyalty of many friends and political supporters.

Historians consider Wilson one of the three or four most successful Presidents. They agree that, as a spokesman for humanity in a world crisis, he stood for integrity, purity of purpose, and responsibility. Not even Wilson's enemies suggested he was weak or stupid. They knew he was honest, and that not even friendship could turn him aside from what he thought was right.

A minority of the voters elected Wilson to the presidency in 1912. That year the Republicans split their votes between President William Howard Taft and former President Theodore Roosevelt. In 1916, the people reelected Wilson, partly because "He kept us out of

Arthur S. Link, contributor of this article, is Shelby Cullom Davis Professor of American History at Princeton University and editor of The Papers of Woodrow Wilson.

war." Three months later, German submarines began unrestricted attacks on American ships. Wilson went before Congress and called for war. After the war ended in 1918, the President fought for a peace treaty that included a League of Nations. Wilson saw his dream of U.S. leadership of the League crumble in 1920 when Warren G. Harding was elected President. Harding opposed American membership in the new organization.

In many ways, the Wilson era separated an old America from the modern nation of today. In 1910, when Wilson was elected governor of New Jersey, a majority of Americans lived on farms or in rural regions. By 1920, toward the end of Wilson's presidency, farmers had become a minority group in the United States. In 1910, Americans drove fewer than 500,000 automobiles. By 1920, more than 8 million cars, many of them Model T Fords, crowded the highways. Throughout this brief period of 10 years, the speeding-up in the nation's way of life could be seen in many ways. The electrical industry grew rapidly, skyscrapers rose in large cities, machinery revolutionized farm life, and good roads began to crisscross the country.

The period also brought great social changes. From 1910 to about 1914, Americans lived largely in a world of unchanging moral values and romantic ideals. These were reflected in the popularity of such books as Zane Grey's *Riders of the Purple Sage* and Jean Webster's *Daddy Long Legs*. New currents began to stir the mainstream of American culture about 1914. One was the development of motion pictures, which became popular during Wilson's administration. Another was the increasing popularity of jazz music, which first appeared on phonograph records in 1917. World War I revolutionized social life in America. It began a wave of far-reaching social changes, including the prohibition of liquor, giving women the right to vote, and the migration of blacks from the South to the North.

Early Years

Childhood. Woodrow Wilson was probably born on Dec. 29, 1856, at Staunton, Va. Confusion exists over the date because the family Bible shows it as "$12\frac{3}{4}$ o'clock" at night on December 28. Wilson's mother said he was born "about midnight on the 28th." Wilson

--- **IMPORTANT DATES IN WILSON'S LIFE** ---

1856 (Dec. 29) Born at Staunton, Va.
1885 (June 24) Married Ellen Louise Axson.
1902 (June 9) Named president of Princeton University.
1910 (Nov. 8) Elected governor of New Jersey.
1912 (Nov. 5) Elected President of the United States.
1914 (Aug. 6) Mrs. Ellen Wilson died.
1915 (Dec. 18) Married Mrs. Edith Bolling Galt.
1916 (Nov. 7) Reelected President.
1919 (Sept. 26-Oct. 2) Suffered collapse and stroke.
1920 (Dec. 10) Awarded Nobel prize for peace.
1924 (Feb. 3) Died in Washington, D.C.

Painting by F. Graham Cootes in the White House Collection

HARDING
29th President
1921 — 1923

COOLIDGE
30th President
1923 — 1929

28TH PRESIDENT

OF THE

UNITED STATES

1913-1921

himself used December 28. He was the third of the four children of Joseph Ruggles Wilson and Janet "Jessie" Woodrow Wilson. The Wilsons named their second son Thomas Woodrow for his maternal grandfather. As a child, he was called "Tommy," but he dropped the name Thomas soon after being graduated from college.

Wilson's father, a Presbyterian minister, had grown up in Ohio. James Wilson, his grandfather, was a Scotch-Irish immigrant who had become a well-known Ohio newspaperman and legislator. Wilson's mother was born in Carlisle, England, near Scotland. Her Scottish father, also a Presbyterian minister, brought his family to the United States when Janet was 9.

An atmosphere of religious piety and scholarly interests dominated Wilson's early years. From the time of his birth, he lived among people who were deeply religious, believed in Presbyterian doctrines, and stressed the importance of education. Before Wilson was 2, his family moved to Augusta, Ga., where his father became pastor of a church. Between the ages of 4 and 8, Wilson lived in an atmosphere colored by the

Civil War. His earliest memory was of a passer-by shouting in great excitement that Abraham Lincoln had been elected President and that war would follow. Years later, Wilson wrote about General William Sherman's famous march through Georgia saying, "I am painfully familiar with the details of that awful march." During the war, Joseph Wilson, a strong Southern sympathizer, turned his church into a hospital for wounded Confederate soldiers.

Education. Wilson did not begin school until he was 9, mainly because the war had closed many schools. But his father taught the boy much at home. On weekdays, the minister would take him to visit a corn mill, a cotton gin, or some other plant. During the war, they visited ammunition factories and iron foundries. After these trips, Wilson always had to discuss what he had seen, because his father believed the exact expression of ideas was necessary for clear understanding. At home, the Wilsons read the Bible together every day, and gathered to sing hymns on Sunday evenings.

In 1870, Wilson's father became a professor in the

269

Wilson's Birthplace, *above,* stands in Staunton, Va. It is now a historic site.
Wilson Had Three Daughters by his first wife. *Left to right* are Margaret, Mrs. Ellen Wilson, Eleanor, Jessie, and Wilson.

Presbyterian theological seminary at Columbia, S.C. Three years later, when Wilson was 17, he entered Davidson College at Davidson, N.C. The school still suffered from the effects of the war. Davidson students had to carry their own water and firewood, as well as perform other chores. Wilson did well, and he enjoyed his freshman year at Davidson. But he withdrew at the end of the year because he wanted to attend Princeton University (then called College of New Jersey) at Princeton, N.J. His father was offered a post in a large church in Wilmington, N.C., and could now afford to send his son to Princeton. Wilson stayed home for a year to learn shorthand and to further prepare himself for his studies.

In September, 1875, Wilson enrolled in the college at Princeton. While a student, Wilson practiced public speaking, became a leader in debating, and read the lives of great American and British statesmen. During his senior year, he served as managing editor of the college newspaper, the *Princetonian.* In 1879, Wilson was graduated 38th in a class of 106. He planned a career in public life.

In October, Wilson entered the University of Virginia Law School at Charlottesville, Va. He felt that law would provide the best path to the career he desired. Wilson took an active part in the university's debating societies. He withdrew from school in 1880 because of ill health.

Beginning Career

Lawyer. In 1882, Wilson established a law office in Atlanta, Ga. He attracted few clients, and spent much of his time reading, writing newspaper articles, and studying political problems. By the spring of 1883, Wilson realized that he was not suited to be a lawyer. He decided to become a college teacher, and began graduate study in history and political science at Johns Hopkins University in Baltimore, Md.

Graduate Student. At Johns Hopkins, Wilson came into contact with brilliant, thoughtful men. He worked hard to improve his writing style and to master history and political science. In 1885, Wilson published his first book, *Congressional Government, A Study in American Politics.* Educators, lawmakers, and students praised

his analysis of the federal government and of American legislative practices. Wilson later presented this study as his doctoral thesis, and Johns Hopkins awarded him the Ph.D. degree in June, 1886.

Wilson's Family. In 1883, Wilson made a business trip to Rome, Ga. There he met and fell in love with Ellen Louise Axson (May 15, 1860-Aug. 6, 1914), the daughter of a Presbyterian minister. They were married on June 24, 1885.

Mrs. Wilson became the most influential person in her husband's life. She appreciated his talents and greatness, and sympathized with his ideals. Mrs. Wilson had many literary and artistic interests. But she devoted most of her time to making a comfortable home where her husband could relax from the cares of his work.

The Wilsons had three daughters: Margaret Wilson (1886-1944), Jessie Woodrow Wilson (1887-1933), and Eleanor Randolph Wilson (1889-1967). Wilson was tender and affectionate, and enjoyed nothing more than rollicking with his children or telling them stories at the dinner table. Like his father, Wilson spent many evenings reading Scott, Dickens, or Wordsworth aloud to his family. He often played charades with his daughters, and once dressed up in a velvet curtain, feather scarf, and one of his wife's hats to look like an old lady.

Teacher. In the autumn of 1885, Wilson began a three-year period as associate professor of history at Bryn Mawr College, a woman's school in Bryn Mawr, Pa. He then became professor of history and political economy at Wesleyan University in Middletown, Conn. Wilson also coached football at Wesleyan, and developed one of the school's greatest teams. He told his players: "Go in to win. Don't admit defeat before you start." In 1889, Wilson published *The State,* one of the first textbooks in comparative government. This book is considered his most important scholarly work. In 1890, Princeton University invited him to become professor of jurisprudence and political economy.

University President

At Princeton, Wilson's reputation as a scholar and teacher grew steadily. He worked constantly to express

his thoughts precisely in writing. He also became a popular and distinguished lecturer. On June 9, 1902, the Princeton trustees unanimously elected Wilson president of the university. Never before had anyone but a clergyman held this position.

As soon as Wilson took office, he announced his intention to change Princeton from "a place where there are youngsters doing tasks to a place where there are men thinking." But his belief that "the object of a university is simply and entirely intellectual" found little support among students devoted largely to social events and athletics.

Wilson helped to reorganize the university's undergraduate course program. He introduced a new method of teaching which he called the *Preceptorial System*. He believed that this system, using individual instruction by tutors, would bring students and teachers into a closer relationship. He also believed it would help students organize scattered information from their undergraduate programs and from general reading.

Wilson's educational reforms won high praise from the few who understood them. But what brought the president of Princeton to public attention was his fight to reform the eating-clubs. These organizations somewhat resembled the fraternities of other schools. Some of the clubs had restricted their memberships and become exclusive. Wilson felt that the clubs were undemocratic and detracted from the intellectual life of Princeton. He wanted to replace them by rebuilding the university with separate colleges, each arranged in a quadrangle around a central court. Each college would have its own dormitories, eating hall, master, and tutors. Wilson felt this arrangement, which became known as the *Quad Plan*, would stimulate the intellectual life of the university.

At first, many Princeton students, including members of the clubs, approved Wilson's idea. But the alumni disliked the plan because they enjoyed coming back to their clubs at reunions and football games. Bitter feelings were aroused. Finally, the board of trustees asked Wilson to withdraw his proposal. Twenty years later, Harvard and Yale both adopted a form of Wilson's Quad Plan. In this, Wilson proved himself an educator ahead of his time.

Wilson suffered a second defeat in the development of plans for Princeton's graduate school. He tried to integrate this school with the undergraduate college. He believed such a move would make the graduate school more responsive to his authority and establish it as the center of intellectual life on the campus. Andrew West, Dean of the Graduate College, opposed Wilson's plan. The two men even battled over the location of a proposed new building for the graduate school. The bitter fight ended in defeat when a graduate died and left a sum thought to be several million dollars to the graduate school on condition that West remain in charge.

Wilson's struggles at Princeton attracted wide public notice. Newspapers reported the argument over the Quad Plan as a fight by Wilson for democracy and against snobbery. He was pictured as a man who favored the common people against the rich and powerful. Such a picture distorted Wilson's main objectives, but it made him politically appealing.

Governor of New Jersey

James Smith, Jr., the Democratic party boss in New Jersey, began to think of Wilson as a possible candidate for governor. The party's record was so bad that it needed a candidate whose honesty was above question. At this same time, Colonel George B. M. Harvey, a party leader and the editor of *Harper's Weekly*, also became interested in Wilson. Smith and Harvey together could almost control the nomination for governor, and they offered it to Wilson.

They timed their offer well. Because of his disappointments at Princeton, Wilson was ready to change careers. As a scholar in the field of government, he knew the facts of machine politics. He suspected that Smith planned to use him for some purpose of his own. But Wilson wanted to run for governor as the first step toward the White House, and Smith badly needed Wilson. The two men agreed, therefore, not to attempt to control each other.

On Oct. 20, 1910, Wilson resigned from Princeton to campaign for governor. The power and eloquence of his campaign speeches stirred voters throughout the state. He was elected by the largest majority received by a Democrat in New Jersey up to that time.

Political Reformer. Wilson at once made it clear that he wanted nothing to do with the political practices of the Democratic machine headed by Smith. Smith, who had previously served in the U.S. Senate, decided to run for that office again. At that time, Senators were elected by the state legislatures. If no candidate received a majority of the votes in each house of a legislature, both houses met in joint session to elect a Senator. Wilson's victory had given the Democrats a majority in the joint session of the New Jersey legislature. When Smith refused to withdraw, Wilson endorsed a rival candidate who won. A reporter wrote that Wilson had "licked the gang to a frazzle."

Meanwhile, Wilson was pushing a series of reforms through the legislature. These laws changed New Jersey from one of the most conservative states into one of the most progressive. During its first session, the legislature enacted the most important proposals of Wilson's campaign. It passed a primary-election law, a corrupt-practices act, a public-utilities act, and an employers' liability law. At Wilson's urging, it also passed various school-reform laws, and enacted a law permitting cities to adopt the commission form of government. Wilson did not hesitate to break long-established customs in his political fights. He hired a superintendent of schools from outside the state. He frequently asked the advice of members of the legislature, and

U&U

turned up unexpectedly at some of their private meetings. He sometimes appealed directly to the people, over the heads of legislators and officials.

Presidential Candidate. Wilson's reforms in New Jersey brought him national attention at an opportune time. The progressive wing of the Democratic party was seeking a presidential candidate to replace William Jennings Bryan, who had been defeated three times. By 1911, Wilson had clearly become a candidate for the nomination. He started speaking on national issues throughout the country, and progressive Democrats began to support him. Most importantly, Wilson won the confidence of Bryan, the party's official leader.

The Democratic national convention met at Baltimore in June, 1912. Champ Clark of Missouri, Speaker of the House of Representatives, received a majority of the delegates' votes on the 10th ballot. Not since 1844 had a candidate who gained a majority failed to go on and receive the two-thirds vote then necessary for nomination. But Wilson's followers stayed with him. On the 14th ballot, Bryan swung his support to Wilson. The old progressive rose dramatically in the crowded convention hall to explain his vote. He pointed out that Charles Francis Murphy, the boss of New York City's Tammany Hall machine, had thrown his support to Clark. He said he could never vote for Clark as long as the Speaker had Tammany's support. From this point on (although not because of Bryan's change of vote), Wilson gained slowly until the 46th ballot, when he won the nomination. The convention nominated Governor Thomas R. Marshall of Indiana for Vice-President.

Wilson's nomination meant almost certain election, because the Republican party was badly split. Conservative Republicans had renominated President William Howard Taft. Progressive Republicans then formed a new Progressive party that nominated former President Theodore Roosevelt. In a series of campaign speeches, later published as *The New Freedom*, Wilson stirred the public with his understanding of national problems.

The popular vote, overwhelmingly for Wilson and Roosevelt, was a clear endorsement of a liberal reform program. Wilson received 435 electoral votes; Roosevelt, 88; and Taft, 8.

Wilson's First Administration (1913-1917)

Inauguration. During his inauguration on March 4, 1913, Wilson noticed that a wide space had been cleared in front of the speaker's platform. He motioned to the police holding back the crowd and ordered: "Let the people come forward." His supporters said the phrase expressed the spirit of his administration.

In his inaugural address, the President accepted the challenge of the November landslide that had also swept a Democratic Congress into office. "No one can mistake the purpose for which the nation now seeks to use the Democratic party," he declared. "It seeks to use it to interpret a change in its plans and point of view." Among the laws that needed to be changed, Wilson named those governing tariffs, industry, and the banking system.

Wilson was the last President to ride to his inauguration in a horse-drawn carriage. Neither he nor his wife

Boarding a Ship for Europe after World War I, Wilson led the U.S. delegation to the Paris Peace Conference. The President hoped to get Allied approval of his Fourteen Points.

National Archives

liked large social affairs, so the Wilsons did not give an inaugural ball. On March 15, only 11 days after his inauguration, Wilson held the first regular presidential press conference. He felt that the people were entitled to reports on the progress of his administration.

Legislative Program. Wilson called Congress into special session on April 7, 1913, to consider a new tariff bill. For the first time since the presidency of John Adams, the President personally delivered his legislative requests to Congress. In October, after some debate, Congress passed Wilson's first important reform measure, the Underwood Tariff Act. This law lowered rates on imports, and removed all tariffs from wool, sugar, iron ore, steel rails, and many other items. After signing the bill, Wilson remarked: "I have had the accomplishment of something like this at heart ever since I was a boy."

On June 23, as Congress debated the tariff bill, Wilson presented his program for reform of the banking and currency laws. He spoke of this reform as "the second step in setting the business of this country free." Representative Carter Glass of Virginia introduced a bill to establish a central banking system. It was designed to provide a new currency and to help the flow of capital through 12 reserve banks, under the direction of a Federal Reserve Board. Congress debated the bill hotly for six months. In December, it passed the Federal Reserve Act basically in the form the President had recommended. Amendments also provided for

--- **WILSON'S FIRST ELECTION** ---

Place of Nominating Convention	Baltimore
Ballot on Which Nominated	46th
Progressive Opponent	Theodore Roosevelt
Republican Opponent	William Howard Taft
Electoral Vote	435 (Wilson) to:
	88 (Roosevelt)
	8 (Taft)
Popular Vote	6,293,454 (Wilson) to:
	4,119,538 (Roosevelt)
	3,484,980 (Taft)
Age at Inauguration	56

Landing in France, Wilson met U.S. troops, above. In Paris, he conferred with David Lloyd George of Britain, Vittorio Orlando of Italy, and Georges Clemenceau of France, *right.* These leaders formed the Allied "Big Four."

exclusive governmental control of the Federal Reserve Board and for short-term agricultural credit through the new reserve banks. This act is regarded as the most effective banking and currency bill in the nation's history. See FEDERAL RESERVE SYSTEM.

Wilson also asked for a series of other reforms. In 1914, Congress established the Federal Trade Commission to investigate and stop unfair trade practices (see FEDERAL TRADE COMMISSION). That same year, it passed the Clayton Antitrust Act which increased the power of the federal government to police unfair practices of big business. In 1916, Wilson led Congress in adopting a series of reform measures. The Adamson Act established the eight-hour working day for railroad employees. The Child Labor Act, which limited children's work hours, began a new program of federal regulation of industry. Heavy taxes were placed on wealth. A tariff commission was established to "take the tariff out of politics." Other programs were started to improve rural education and rural roads.

Foreign Affairs demanded much of the President's attention. He persuaded Congress to repeal the Panama Tolls Act, which had allowed American ships to use the Panama Canal toll-free when sailing between U.S. coastal ports. Wilson believed this law violated a treaty with Great Britain. The President also refused to approve a bankers' loan to China, and put himself on record against "dollar diplomacy." Wilson insisted that his party live up to its campaign promise of preparing the Philippines for independence. In 1916, Congress passed the Jones Bill, which greatly increased Philippine self-government and made many reforms in the administration of the islands.

Crisis in Mexico. Relations between the United States and Mexico were frequently troubled during Wilson's first administration. In 1913, the President told Congress that there could be no peace in Mexico while Victoriano Huerta ruled as dictator. Wilson declared that the United States "can have no sympathy with those who seek to seize the powers of government to advance their own personal interests or ambition." Wilson tried unsuccessfully to negotiate for Huerta's

retirement. Then the President permitted the dictator's enemies, who had begun a revolution, to obtain arms in the United States. Wilson let the Mexican groups fight it out for a while. But when Huerta's forces arrested 14 American sailors who had gone ashore at Tampico, Mexico, the President struck hard. He refused to accept Huerta's apology, and demanded that Huerta publicly salute the American flag in Tampico. When Huerta refused, Wilson in April, 1914, ordered American forces to occupy the Mexican port of Veracruz. Eighteen Americans were killed in the action.

At this point, Wilson accepted an offer of the ABC powers (Argentina, Brazil, and Chile) to arbitrate the dispute. A peaceful settlement was worked out. Huerta fled from Mexico, and Venustiano Carranza, the leader of the anti-Huerta rebels, became acting president of Mexico. Pancho Villa, one of Carranza's chief generals, then quarreled with his leader and led a revolution against him. Carranza's soldiers drove Villa into northern Mexico, where he began raiding American settlements across the Rio Grande. Many Ameri-

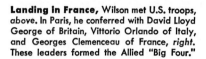

--------- **VICE-PRESIDENT AND CABINET** ---------

Vice-President	*Thomas R. Marshall
Secretary of State	*William Jennings Bryan
	*Robert Lansing (1915)
	Bainbridge Colby (1920)
Secretary of the Treasury	William Gibbs McAdoo
	*Carter Glass (1918)
	David F. Houston (1920)
Secretary of War	Lindley M. Garrison
	Newton D. Baker (1916)
Attorney General	James C. McReynolds
	Thomas W. Gregory (1914)
	*A. Mitchell Palmer (1919)
Postmaster General	Albert S. Burleson
Secretary of the Navy	Josephus Daniels
Secretary of the Interior	Franklin K. Lane
	John B. Payne (1920)
Secretary of Agriculture	David F. Houston
	Edwin T. Meredith (1920)
Secretary of Commerce	William C. Redfield
	Joshua W. Alexander (1919)
Secretary of Labor	William B. Wilson

*Has a separate biography in WORLD BOOK.

United Press Int.

Wide World

Wilson's Second Wife was Mrs. Edith Galt, widow of a Washington, D.C., jeweler. They had no children.

Wilson's Campaign to gain support for the League of Nations ended in his collapse. He suffered a stroke and was an invalid for the rest of his life.

cans called for war, but Wilson would not yield to their pressure. "Watchful waiting" became his policy. He sent troops under General John J. Pershing to patrol the border. Then, in 1916, he ordered Pershing to pursue Villa deep into Mexico. Carranza warned that he would resist any further invasion. Fighting did occur, and only a series of dramatic events in the late spring of 1916 averted open war. In 1917, Wilson officially recognized the Mexican government that had been established by a new constitution. But relations were never cordial with Mexico during the rest of the Wilson era. See MEXICO (The Revolution of 1910; The Constitution of 1917).

Caribbean Problems. Both Wilson and Secretary of State William Jennings Bryan spoke out against taking more land for the United States by the use of force. But their policies toward many small nations of Latin America and the Caribbean area did not differ much

─── **HIGHLIGHTS OF WILSON'S ADMINISTRATION** ───

1913 Wilson signed a bill creating an independent Department of Labor.
1913 Amendment 17 to the Constitution, providing for the election of U.S. Senators by popular vote instead of by state legislatures, became law.
1913 Congress passed the Underwood Tariff Act and established the Federal Reserve System.
1914 Congress passed the Clayton Antitrust Act and created the Federal Trade Commission.
1914 Wilson emphasized U.S. neutrality, following the outbreak of World War I in Europe.
1917 Congress approved the purchase of the Virgin Islands from Denmark.
1917 (April 6) Congress declared war against Germany.
1918 (Jan. 8) Wilson set forth the Fourteen Points.
1918 (Oct. 6—Nov. 11) Wilson negotiated the armistice with Germany.
1919 (Jan. 18—June 28) Wilson helped draft the Versailles Treaty at the Paris Peace Conference.
1919 Amendment 18 to the Constitution, banning the manufacture, sale, and transportation of alcoholic beverages, became law.
1919 Congress rejected the Versailles Treaty and American membership in the League of Nations.
1920 Amendment 19 to the Constitution, giving women the right to vote, became law.

from those of previous Presidents. In 1914, Wilson and Bryan took over most of the control of revolution-torn Nicaragua. They sent troops in 1915 to occupy Haiti. A year later, the Dominican Republic was placed under American military government.

World War I Begins. In August, 1914, the outbreak of World War I stunned people everywhere. Most Americans joined in a single cry: "Let's stay out of it." Wilson proclaimed the neutrality of the United States. He said the nation "must be neutral in fact as well as in name . . . we must be impartial in thought as well as in action."

But neutrality became easier to think about than to maintain. On May 7, 1915, a German submarine torpedoed and sank the British passenger liner *Lusitania*, killing 128 Americans. This incident enraged some Americans, but Wilson remained calm. He began negotiations with the Germans and got them to order their submarines not to attack neutral or passenger ships. Angry men and women called Wilson "a human icicle" who did nothing to avenge the loss of American lives. But most Americans approved the President's fight for peace and neutrality.

Life in the White House. With the help of her three daughters, Mrs. Wilson put her greatest efforts into making the White House as much like a private home as possible. She had little interest in entertaining, and often sat silently through dinner parties. She devoted herself to welfare work and to small groups interested in literature and art.

Then family life in the White House changed radically. Within an eight-month period, from November, 1913, to July, 1914, two of the President's daughters were married, and Mrs. Wilson became ill. After a short illness, the President's wife died on Aug. 6, 1914. Wilson was so saddened by her death that he nearly lost his will to live. Wilson's unmarried daughter, Margaret, and his first cousin, Helen Woodrow Bones, became hostesses for the President.

Remarriage. In March, 1915, Wilson met Mrs. Edith Bolling Galt (Oct. 15, 1872-Dec. 28, 1961), widow of a Washington jeweler. He fell in love with the charming

272

Mrs. Galt almost at once, and sent long letters and flowers to her every day. They were married in Mrs. Galt's home in Washington on Dec. 18, 1915.

The second Mrs. Wilson was an intelligent and strong-minded woman. Wilson again found the happiness and security he had known with his first wife.

Election of 1916. In June, 1916, the Democrats renominated Wilson and Marshall. The Republicans had healed the split in their party, and chose a ticket of Supreme Court Justice Charles Evans Hughes and former Vice-President Charles W. Fairbanks. The war in Europe overshadowed all other issues in the campaign. Democrats sought votes for Wilson with the slogan, "He kept us out of war." Wilson himself appealed to those who favored peace, but he also stressed the reforms his administration had accomplished.

On election night, the outcome was confused because of delays in receiving the election returns. Wilson went to bed believing Hughes had won. Many newspapers carried stories of Wilson's "defeat." But the final count in California gave the state to Wilson by 4,000 votes. This insured his re-election.

Wilson's Second Administration (1917-1921)

Declaration of War. During the next three months, Wilson devoted all his efforts to halting the fighting in Europe. But in February, 1917, the Germans began unlimited submarine warfare against all merchant shipping, including American ships. The President immediately broke off diplomatic relations with Germany. Later that month, British agents uncovered a German plot to start a war between Mexico and the United States. German submarines began to attack American ships without warning in March, and enraged Americans demanded war.

Wilson decided the United States could no longer remain neutral. On the evening of April 2, the President drove to the Capitol with an escort of cavalry. As he stepped before a joint session of Congress, his face was tense and white. He spoke in a voice heavy with feeling. He said actions by Germany were "in fact nothing less than war against the government and people of the United States." Thunderous applause greeted the President's words. He asked Congress to declare war against Germany, declaring that "the world must be made safe for democracy."

Four days later, on April 6, 1917, Congress passed a joint resolution declaring war on Germany. For a complete discussion of the United States in the war, see WORLD WAR I (The Fourth Year; The Final Year).

War Leader. The President proved himself as great a leader in war as he had been in peace. His many speeches in support of the American and Allied cause stirred free men everywhere. Wilson stated the great

---

———— WILSON'S SECOND ELECTION ————

Place of Nominating Convention...St. Louis

Ballot on Which Nominated.......1st

Republican Opponent............Charles Evans Hughes

Electoral Vote....................277 (Wilson) to 254 (Hughes)

Popular Vote....................9,129,606 (Wilson) to 8,538,221 (Hughes)

Age at Second Inauguration......60

---

issues of the war, and defined the aims for which the democracies fought. He also pointed out the necessity of making a better world after the war. The American people rallied with great loyalty and patriotism. A crusading spirit, almost hysterical in its intensity, swept the nation. People sang "I'm a Yankee Doodle Dandy," "Over There," and other popular war songs. Well-known film stars, such as Mary Pickford, Douglas Fairbanks, and Charlie Chaplin, drew huge crowds to purchase Liberty bonds at rallies.

The Fourteen Points. Wilson delivered his most important speech on Jan. 8, 1918. In this address to Congress, he named Fourteen Points to be used as a guide for a peace settlement. Five points established general ideals. Eight points dealt with immediate political and territorial problems. The fourteenth point called for an association of nations to help keep world peace. The Fourteen Points are summarized below.

1. Open covenants of peace openly arrived at, with no secret international agreements in the future.
2. Freedom of the seas outside territorial waters in peace and in war, except in case of international action to enforce international treaties.
3. Removal of all possible economic barriers and establishment of equal trade conditions among nations.
4. Reduction of national armaments to the lowest point consistent with domestic safety.
5. Free, open-minded, and absolutely impartial adjustment of all colonial claims.
6. Evacuation of German troops from all Russian territory, an opportunity for Russia independently to determine its own political development and national policy, and a welcome for Russia into the society of free nations.
7. Evacuation of German troops from Belgium and the rebuilding of that nation.
8. Evacuation of German troops from all French territory and the return of Alsace-Lorraine to France.
9. Readjustment of Italian frontiers along the clearly recognizable lines of nationality.
10. Limited self-government for the peoples of Austria-Hungary.
11. Evacuation of German troops from Romania, Serbia, and Montenegro, and independence guaranteed for the Balkan countries.
12. Independence for Turkey, but an opportunity to develop self-government for other nationalities under Turkish rule, and guarantees that the Dardanelles be permanently opened as a free passage to ships of all nations.
13. Independence for Poland.
14. "A general association of nations must be formed under specific covenants for the purpose of affording mutual guarantees of political independence and territorial integrity to great and small states alike."

Wilson's speech did much to undermine German morale during the final months of the war. It also gave the Germans a basis upon which to appeal for peace. On Nov. 9, 1918, only 10 months after the President had stated his Fourteen Points, Kaiser Wilhelm II gave up control of the German government. Two days later, an armistice negotiated by Wilson was proclaimed.

The Peace Settlement. After the armistice had been signed, Wilson decided to lead the United States delegation to the peace conference at Paris. He wanted to make certain that his Fourteen Points would be carried out. The President also thought the United States should be represented by its political leader, as were

Great Britain, France, and the other powers. Wilson appointed a peace delegation that included no member of the U.S. Senate and no influential Republicans. He was criticized for this, and later it helped cause the Senate to reject the treaty agreed upon at Paris.

Wilson knew the United States would be the only country represented at the peace table that wanted nothing for itself. He also believed he would be the only representative of the great powers who really cared about establishing an association of nations to prevent war. The President was determined to use his power and prestige to have the final peace settlement include a plan for a League of Nations.

Wilson was the first President to cross the Atlantic Ocean while in office. He landed at Brest, France, on Dec. 13, 1918, and the next morning rode through the streets of Paris. Never had the people of Paris given a king or emperor such a joyous reception. Banners welcomed "Wilson le Juste." From France, Wilson went to England where he stayed at Buckingham Palace. In Rome, he met with Pope Benedict XV, and became the first President to talk with a pope while in office. Everywhere he went in Europe, great crowds cheered him as the hope of humanity.

At the Paris Peace Conference, held from January to June, Wilson obtained only part of the treaty provisions he wanted. In order to win support for the League and other provisions in the Fourteen Points, he compromised on several major issues. Wilson's concessions weakened his moral position in the eyes of the world, although they insured establishment of the League of Nations. See WORLD WAR I (Peace Aims; The Peace Treaties); LEAGUE OF NATIONS; VERSAILLES, TREATY OF.

Opposition to the League. In February, 1919, Wilson returned to the United States briefly to discuss the League and the peace treaty with the Senate. The Constitution required two-thirds approval by the Senate for the United States to adopt the treaty which included the League. The President also hoped to quiet rising criticism throughout the country. Wilson's position was no longer strong politically. He had asked for the election of Democrats to Congress in 1918 as an indication of personal trust. But the voters had chosen more Republicans than Democrats.

Wilson soon discovered that he could not win Senate ratification of the League without some amendments to satisfy his critics at home. He went back to Paris in March, 1919, and the conference delegates accepted several of these provisions. Wilson returned to the United States early in July with the text of the treaty. He found public debate on the peace terms in full swing, with mounting congressional opposition to the treaty and the League of Nations.

American opinion on the treaty was split into three groups. The isolationists, led by Senators William E. Borah, Hiram W. Johnson, and James A. Reed, stood firmly against any League. They argued that the United States should not interfere in "European affairs." The second group consisted of Wilson and his followers, who urged that the treaty be ratified with no important changes or compromises. The men in the largest group, led by Senator Henry Cabot Lodge, took a middle ground between Wilson and the isolationists. They were ready to ratify the treaty with important changes. Some of these men, including Lodge, demand-

WORLD EVENTS

1914 World War I began in Europe.

1915 A German submarine sank the *Lusitania*.

1918 Wilson proposed his Fourteen Points.

1919 The Allies and Germany signed the Treaty of Versailles, which officially ended World War I.

1920 The League of Nations was established.

The United States Flag had 48 stars throughout Wilson's term of office.

U.S. population was 108,600,000 in 1921, when Wilson retired from the presidency. There were 48 states in the Union.

ed changes that would reduce or eliminate America's obligations to the League.

Wilson's Collapse. The President decided to take his case for the League to the American people—the method that had worked successfully for him in the past. On September 4, Wilson began a speaking tour through the Midwest and the Far West. His doctor had advised him against the trip, because his strenuous labors over the past several years had weakened his health. On September 25, Wilson spoke at Pueblo, Colo., urging approval of the League. That night, as his train sped toward Wichita, Kans., Wilson collapsed from fatigue and nervous tension. He canceled the remainder of his tour and returned to Washington. On October 2, the President suffered a paralytic stroke.

Wilson was an invalid for the rest of his life, but he did not give up the presidency. The Constitution did not then state clearly who inherits executive power when a President becomes severely ill but does not die or resign. After October, Wilson left his bed only for simple recreation or for purely formal tasks. These greatly taxed his strength, and his wife guided his hand when he signed official documents. Wilson did not call a meeting of the Cabinet until April 13, 1920. Before that, the Cabinet met unofficially and carried on much of the routine work of government during Wilson's long illness.

PRESIDENT WILSON

The Panama Canal connecting the Atlantic and Pacific oceans opened on July 12, 1920. Work on the canal began in 1906.

World War I began in 1914. The four-year conflict between the Allies and Central Powers cost more than 37,000,000 military casualties. The United States entered the war in 1917.

First Airmail Route was established in 1918 between New York City, Philadelphia, and Washington, D.C. In 1919, two British fliers made the first nonstop transatlantic flight.

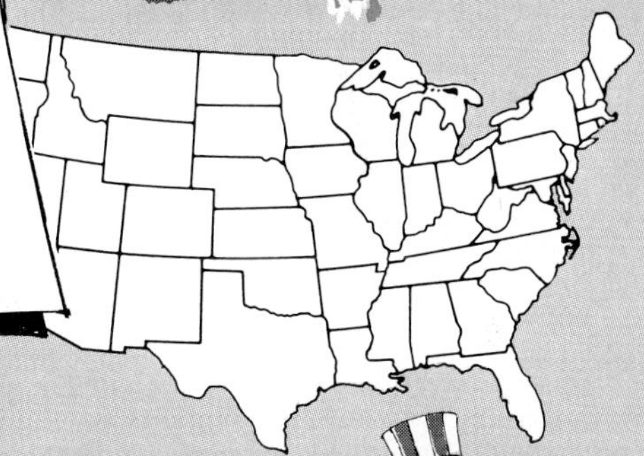

Federal Reserve System, created in 1913, set up a central banking system for the United States.

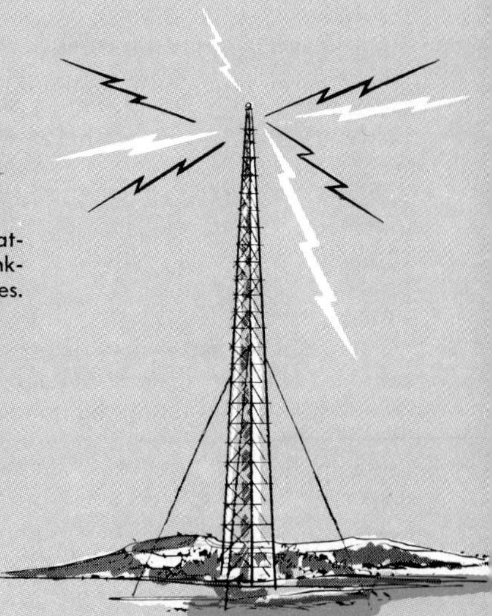

Amendment 18 1919

Amendment 17 1913

Amendment 19 1920

The Virgin Islands were purchased by the United States from Denmark in 1917 for $25,000,000.

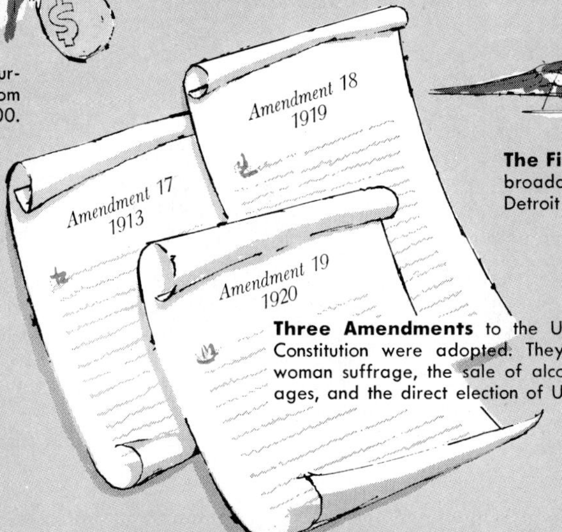

The First Commercial Radio broadcasts were made from Detroit and Pittsburgh in 1920.

Three Amendments to the United States Constitution were adopted. They dealt with woman suffrage, the sale of alcoholic beverages, and the direct election of U.S. Senators.

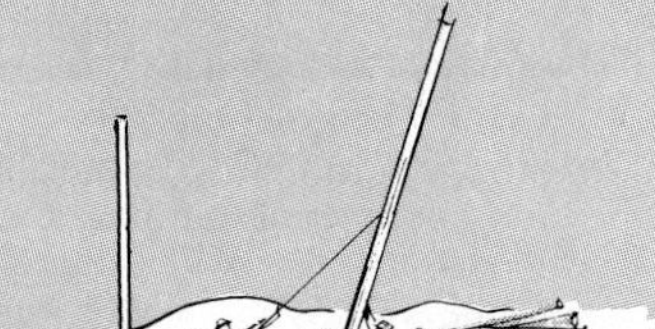

The First Telephone Line linking New York City and San Francisco began operating in 1915.

From his sickbed, the President helplessly watched the losing fight for his treaty. Senator Lodge, chairman of the Senate Foreign Relations Committee, presented the treaty for vote in November 1919. He and his committee had added 14 reservations. The most important one declared that the United States assumed no obligation to support the League of Nations unless Congress specifically approved by joint resolution. Claiming that this reservation would destroy the League, Wilson instructed Senate Democrats to vote against approval of the treaty containing the Lodge reservations. As a result, the treaty failed to win two-thirds approval. The treaty came up for vote again in March 1920, but once more it failed.

Wilson insisted that the treaty and the League should be the chief issue of the 1920 presidential campaign. The Democratic platform endorsed the League, and the Republican platform opposed it. In the election, Warren G. Harding, the Republican nominee, overwhelmingly defeated James M. Cox, his Democratic opponent. As far as the United States was concerned, the League of Nations was dead.

On Dec. 10, 1920, Wilson was awarded the 1919 Nobel peace prize for his work in founding the League of Nations and seeking a fair peace agreement.

Last Years

For almost three years after his term ended in March 1921, Wilson lived in quiet retirement in Washington. He formed a law partnership with Bainbridge Colby, his third Secretary of State. Although Wilson had regained partial use of his arms and legs, his physical condition did not permit any actual work. He saw an occasional motion picture or play, listened to books and magazines read aloud to him, and sometimes invited friends for lunch.

Wilson was confident that future events would prove him correct regarding the League and the peace terms. In his last public speech, to a group of friends outside his home on Armistice Day, 1923, Wilson declared: "I cannot refrain from saying it: I am not one of those who have the least anxiety about the triumph of the principles I have stood for. I have seen fools resist Providence before and I have seen their destruction, as will come upon these again—utter destruction and contempt. That we shall prevail is as sure as that God reigns."

Wilson continued to bear the crushing blows of defeat with dignity and calm. But he told his friends he was "tired of swimming upstream." On Feb. 3, 1924, he died in his sleep. Two days later, Wilson was buried in Washington Cathedral. He is the only President interred in Washington, D.C.   Arthur S. Link

Related Articles in World Book include:

Bryan (William Jennings)
Fourteen Points
House, Edward Mandell
League of Nations
Marshall, Thomas Riley
Nobel Prizes (picture)
President of the U.S.

Roosevelt, Theodore
  (Later Years)
South Carolina (picture)
Versailles, Treaty of
World War I (The Fourth
  Year; The Final Year)

Outline

I. **Early Years**
  A. Childhood   B. Education

II. **Beginning Career**
  A. Lawyer
  B. Graduate Student
  C. Wilson's Family
  D. Teacher
III. **University President**
IV. **Governor of New Jersey**
  A. Political Reformer   B. Presidential Candidate
V. **Wilson's First Administration (1913-1917)**
  A. Inauguration   E. Caribbean Problems
  B. Legislative   F. World War I Begins
     Program   G. Life in the White House
  C. Foreign Affairs   H. Remarriage
  D. Crisis in Mexico   I. Election of 1916
VI. **Wilson's Second Administration (1917-1921)**
  A. Declaration   D. The Peace Settlement
     of War   E. Opposition to the
  B. War Leader   League
  C. The Fourteen Points F. Wilson's Collapse
VII. **Last Years**

Questions

Why was Wilson's election to the presidency in 1912 almost certain following his nomination?

What were Wilson's main educational reforms at Princeton University?

What brought Wilson to national attention as a presidential prospect?

What were the most important achievements in domestic affairs during his first administration?

What was one of Wilson's most valuable techniques for winning legislation that he wanted?

Why was Wilson's family life so important to him?

Why did Wilson personally attend the Paris Peace Conference in 1919?

Why do historians regard Wilson as one of the nation's greatest Presidents?

What were his three main careers?

In what connection did Wilson make the statement: "Let the people come forward"?

Reading and Study Guide

See *Wilson, Woodrow*, in the Research Guide/Index, Volume 22, for a *Reading and Study Guide.*

Books to Read

Archer, Jules. *World Citizen: Woodrow Wilson.* Simon & Schuster, 1967. For younger readers.
Bailey, Thomas A. *Woodrow Wilson and the Great Betrayal.* Quadrangle, 1963. Originally published in 1945.
Jacobs, David. *An American Conscience: Woodrow Wilson's Search for World Peace.* Harper, 1973. For younger readers.
Link, Arthur S. *Wilson.* 5 vols. Princeton, 1947-1965. These volumes cover the years 1856 to 1917.

WILSON CLOUD CHAMBER is a device that enables scientists to determine the path of atomic particles. Charles T. R. Wilson, a British physicist, invented the instrument. Wilson noticed that water vapor condenses on dust to form raindrops. He wondered whether water vapor also condenses on a thing as small as an atomic particle. He found that it does. Wilson perfected the cloud chamber about 1912.

A simple cloud chamber consists of a glass flask with a rubber bulb attached to one end. The bulb and about two-thirds of the flask are filled with water. As the water in the flask evaporates, the air space becomes saturated with water vapor. A radioactive material, such as radium, in the air space gives off atomic particles. As those particles which are electrically charged pass through the air space, they knock electrons off some of the gas molecules in the air. The gas molecules that lose electrons are called *ions*. If the rubber bulb is slowly compressed and then suddenly released, the air and the water vapor become cooler. Some of the cool vapor condenses on the ions to form drops of water. These drops show the path taken by the charged particles. Scientists call the path *tracks.*

Electrically charged particles can be identified by the path they make. *Alpha particles* (helium nuclei) make a straight, dense path. *Beta particles* (electrons) make a light, irregular path that is difficult to trace. The paths disappear quickly, so physicists study them in photographs.

Scientists can use other devices to show atomic particle paths. The *bubble chamber,* developed in the 1950's, shows paths as a string of tiny bubbles in a superheated liquid. A *spark chamber,* developed in the early 1960's, shows paths as tiny sparks.   PALMER H. CRAIG

See also ATOM; BUBBLE CHAMBER; RADIOACTIVITY (Kinds of Radiation); SPARK CHAMBER; WILSON, CHARLES T. R.

WILSON COLLEGE. See UNIVERSITIES AND COLLEGES (table).

WILSON DAM. See MUSCLE SHOALS; TENNESSEE VALLEY AUTHORITY (map); ALABAMA (picture).

WILT, in plants, is a condition in which the leaves and stems droop and die. It is usually a symptom of plant

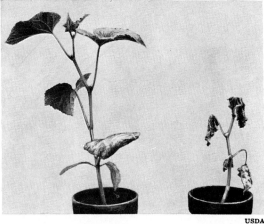

USDA

Wilt Caused by a Fungus has attacked the cucumber plant at the right. At the left is a normal, healthy cucumber vine.

diseases which cause the cells to collapse. A plant wilts if it needs water. Disease bacteria that cause wilting stop up the channels that carry water in the plant. Many fungi that attack plants may cause wilting, sometimes by secreting poisons into the plant tissues.

Many root diseases bring about wilting. *Fusarium* is a fungus that wilts asters, potatoes, tomatoes, cotton, flax, and other plants. *Sclerotinia,* another fungus, wilts many garden vegetables. Dutch elm disease, or *Graphium wilt,* also is caused by a fungus. This disease kills many elm trees every year.

Control of wilt depends on the disease that causes it. Generally, one should destroy the diseased plants, and disinfect the soil. Some of the newer varieties of plants produced by scientists resist wilt.   WILLIAM F. HANNA

See also DUTCH ELM DISEASE.

WILTON. See RUGS AND CARPETS (Weaving).

WIMBLEDON. See TENNIS.

WIMPLE. See CLOTHING (The Middle Ages).

WIMSEY, LORD PETER. See SAYERS, DOROTHY.

WINANT, JOHN GILBERT (1889-1947), was United States ambassador to Great Britain from 1941 to 1946. Winant served as a Republican in the New Hampshire House of Representatives from 1917 to 1921, and again from 1923 to 1925. He served as a state senator from 1921 to 1923, and as governor from 1925 to 1927, and 1931 to 1935. Winant supported social security, the abolition of child labor, old-age insurance, and a shorter work week. In 1935, he became the first chairman of the U.S. Social Security Board. He was named director of the International Labor Organization in 1938. Winant represented the United States on the European Advisory Commission from 1943 to 1946. In 1946, he represented the United States on the Economic and Social Council of the United Nations. Winant was born in New York City.   J. DUANE SQUIRES

WINCH is a crank used to give rotary motion to a machine. It is also the name of a device with a crank attached to a drum around which rope is wound. The rope is attached to a heavy object. By turning the crank, a person can *winch* (move) the object to a desired position or height.

See also DERRICKS AND CRANES.

WINCHELL, WALTER (1897-1972), an American newspaperman and commentator, became important for making the gossip column a regular newspaper feature. Critics accused him of unethical snooping, but his column became widely read and imitated. In his column, Winchell used a type of jargon that has been widely copied. He coined colorful words and phrases, such as "lohengrined" and "middle-aisled" for "married."

Winchell was born in New York City. He played in vaudeville before beginning to write for *The Vaudeville News* in 1920. He became nationally known in 1929 through his syndicated column about Broadway. He also appeared on radio and television. He retired in 1969.   PAUL MOLLOY

WINCHESTER (pop. 31,070) was the chief town of England in Anglo-Saxon times. It is a religious and educational center. Winchester lies on the River Itchen in southern England (see ENGLAND [map]).

Both Alfred the Great and the Danish King Canute were buried at Winchester. After the Normans conquered England in 1066, Winchester continued to rival London as a trade and political center. William of Wykeham completed Winchester's famous cathedral in the 1300's. This cathedral, which is 556 feet (169 meters) long, is the longest church in England. William also founded Winchester College, one of the leading English public schools.   FRANCIS H. HERRICK

WINCHESTER COLLEGE at Winchester, England, is one of the oldest and most prominent public schools in the country. William of Wykeham, bishop of Winchester, founded it in 1382, and it was opened in 1394. The motto of the school is "Manners Makyth Man." The college was originally established for 70 poor scholars, but greater numbers were gradually admitted. It flourished until the 1700's, when a decline began. William Stanley Goddard, who became headmaster in 1796, saved the school by his reforms. Winchester College was one of the first public schools to introduce courses in science and mathematics.   R. W. MORRIS

WIND

WIND is air moving across the earth's surface. Wind may blow so slowly and gently that it can hardly be felt. Or it may blow so fast and hard that it smashes buildings and pushes over large trees. Strong winds can whip up great ocean waves that damage ships and flood land. Wind can blow away soil from farmland so crops cannot grow. Sharp grains of dust carried by wind wear away rock and change the features of land.

Wind is also a part of weather. A hot, moist day may suddenly turn cool if a wind blows from a cool area. Clouds, rain, and lightning may form where the cool air meets the hot, moist air. Later, another wind may blow the clouds away and allow the sun to warm the land again. Wind can carry a storm great distances.

Winds are named according to the direction *from* which they blow. For example, an *east* wind blows from east to west. A *north* wind blows from north to south.

Causes of Wind

Wind is caused by the uneven heating of the *atmosphere* (the air around the earth) by energy from the sun. The sun heats the surface of the earth unevenly. Air above hot areas expands and rises. Air from cooler areas then flows in to take the place of the heated air. This process is called *circulation*. Two kinds of circulation produce wind: (1) *general circulation* extending around the earth, and (2) smaller *secondary circulation*. Winds that occur only in one place are called *local winds*.

General Circulation occurs over large sections of the earth's surface. It produces *prevailing winds*. Near the equator, heated air rises to about 60,000 feet (18,000 meters). Surface air moving in to replace the rising air produces two belts of prevailing winds. These belts lie between the equator and about 30° north and south latitude. The winds there are called *trade winds* because sailors once relied on them in sailing trading ships.

The trade winds do not blow straight toward the equator. Instead, they blow somewhat from east to west. The westward part of their motion is caused by the spinning of the earth. The earth and the air around it rotate eastward together. Each point on the earth's surface travels around a complete circle in 24 hours. Points near the equator travel around larger circles than points near 30° north or south latitude, because the earth is larger at the equator. So, the points near the equator travel faster. As air moves toward the equator, it reaches faster-moving points on the earth's surface. Because these surface points are moving eastward faster than the air, a person standing on the earth feels a wind blowing westward against him.

There are no prevailing winds near the equator and up to about 700 miles (1,100 kilometers) on either side of it, because the air rises there instead of moving across the earth. This calm belt is called the *doldrums*.

Some of the air that rises at the equator returns to the earth's surface at about 30° north and south latitude. Air moving downward there produces no wind. These areas are called the *horse latitudes*, possibly because many horses died on sailing ships that were stalled by the lack of wind there. The name may also have come from a Spanish sailing term that called the winds there unpredictable, supposedly like a female horse.

Two other kinds of prevailing winds result from the general circulation in the atmosphere. The *prevailing westerlies* blow somewhat from west to east in two belts between latitudes of about 30° and 60° north and south of the equator. These winds result from surface air moving away from the equator and reaching slower-moving points nearer the poles. Prevailing westerlies carry weather eastward across the northern United States and southern Canada. The *polar easterlies* blow somewhat from east to west in two belts between the poles and about 60° north and south latitude. Surface air moving away from the poles moves westward across faster-moving points nearer the equator.

Secondary Circulation is the motion of air around relatively small regions of high and low pressure in the

The contributor of this article is James E. Miller, Head of the Department of Meteorology and Oceanography at Polytechnic Institute of New York.

GENERAL CIRCULATION OF AIR AROUND THE EARTH

Prevailing winds result from the general circulation of air around the earth, shown at the *right*. In this drawing, the circulation has been greatly simplified. At the equator, air is heated by the sun and rises, as shown by the blue arrows. In the upper atmosphere, this air flows away from the equator. When the air returns to the earth's surface, it flows across the surface, as shown by the black arrows. This moving surface air produces the six belts of prevailing winds around the earth. The turning of the earth causes the prevailing winds to blow toward the east in belts where the air moves away from the equator. In belts where the air moves toward the equator, the prevailing winds blow toward the west.

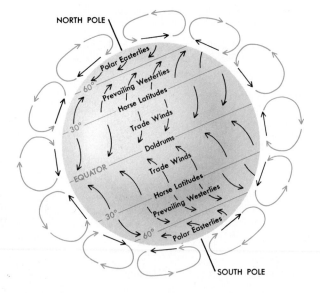

atmosphere. These regions form within the larger general circulation. Air flows toward low-pressure regions called *lows* or *cyclones*. Air flows away from high-pressure regions called *highs* or *anticyclones*. As in the general circulation, air moving toward the equator moves in a generally westerly direction and air moving away from the equator moves in an easterly direction. As a result, secondary circulation in the Northern Hemisphere is clockwise around a high and counterclockwise around a low. These directions are reversed in the Southern Hemisphere.

Secondary circulations move with the prevailing winds. As they pass a given spot on the earth, the wind direction changes. For example, a low moving eastward across Chicago produces winds that shift from southwest to northwest.

Local Winds arise only in specific areas on the earth. Local winds that result from the heating of land during summer and the cooling of land during winter are called *monsoons*. They blow from the ocean during summer and toward the ocean during winter. Monsoons control the climate in Asia, producing wet summers and dry winters. A warm, dry, local wind that blows down the side of a mountain is called a *chinook* in the western United States and a *foehn* in Europe. These and other local winds are discussed in articles listed in the *Related Articles* at the end of this article.

Measuring Wind

Two features of wind, its speed and its direction, are used in describing and forecasting weather.

Wind Speed is measured with an instrument called an *anemometer*. Several kinds of anemometers are used today. The most common kind has three or four cups attached to spokes on a rotating shaft. The spokes turn the shaft as the wind blows. The wind speed is indicated by the speed of the spinning shaft.

In the United States, wind speeds are stated in miles per hour or in *knots* (nautical miles per hour). But in many other countries, they are stated in kilometers per hour.

Wind Direction is measured with an instrument called a *weather vane*. A weather vane has a broad, flat blade attached to a spoke pivoted at one end. Wind blowing

on the blade turns the spoke so that the blade lines up in the wind direction. The wind direction may be indicated by an arrow fastened to the spoke, or by an electric meter remotely controlled by the weather vane.

Wind directions are often indicated by using the 360 degrees of a circle. On this circle, north is indicated by 0°. An east wind blows from 90°, a south wind blows from 180°, and a west wind blows from 270°. Winds at various altitudes often differ in speed and direction. For example, smoke from a chimney may be blown northward while clouds higher in the sky are blown eastward.

Winds high above the earth's surface are measured by sending up helium-filled balloons. A balloon moves with the same speed and direction as the wind. Its motion is measured either by sight or by radar.

The Beaufort Wind Scale is a series of numbers, ranging from 0 to 17, used to indicate wind speeds. The scale was devised in 1805 by British Rear Admiral Sir Francis Beaufort. Beaufort defined the numbers in terms of the effect of various winds on sailing vessels. For example, in a standard version published in 1874, the number 2 indicated a wind defined as "That in which a well-conditioned man-of-war, with all sail set, and clean full, would go in smooth water from 1 to 2 knots." Wind indicated by the number 12 was defined as "That which no canvas could withstand."

Today, the Beaufort scale is defined in terms of wind speeds measured 10 meters (about 33 feet) above the ground. The scale is sometimes used to estimate wind speeds.   JAMES E. MILLER

Related Articles in WORLD BOOK include:

LOCAL WINDS

Chinook	Mistral	Simoom
Foehn	Monsoon	Sirocco
Harmattan	Norther	Whirlwind

OTHER RELATED ARTICLES

Air	Dune	Storm
Anemometer	Erosion	Tornado
Calms, Regions of	Horse Latitudes	Trade Wind
Climate	Hurricane	Waterspout
Cloud	Jet Stream	Weather
Cyclone	Prevailing Westerly	Weather Vane
Doldrums	Squall	Wind Chill

BEAUFORT WIND SCALE

Beaufort number	Name	Miles per hour	Kilometers per hour	Effect on land
0	Calm	less than 1	less than 1	Calm; smoke rises vertically.
1	Light Air	1-3	1-5	Weather vanes inactive; smoke drifts with air.
2	Light Breeze	4-7	6-11	Weather vanes active; wind felt on face; leaves rustle.
3	Gentle Breeze	8-12	12-19	Leaves and small twigs move; light flags extend.
4	Moderate Breeze	13-18	20-28	Small branches sway; dust and loose paper blow about.
5	Fresh Breeze	19-24	29-38	Small trees sway; waves break on inland waters.
6	Strong Breeze	25-31	39-49	Large branches sway; umbrellas difficult to use.
7	Moderate Gale	32-38	50-61	Whole trees sway; difficult to walk against wind.
8	Fresh Gale	39-46	62-74	Twigs broken off trees; walking against wind very difficult.
9	Strong Gale	47-54	75-88	Slight damage to buildings; shingles blown off roof.
10	Whole Gale	55-63	89-102	Trees uprooted; considerable damage to buildings.
11	Storm	64-73	103-117	Widespread damage; very rare occurrence.
12-17	Hurricane	74 and above	more than 117	Violent destruction.

WIND CAVE NATIONAL PARK

WIND CAVE NATIONAL PARK is a park in the rolling hills of southwestern South Dakota which surrounds one of the most unusual caves in the United States. Strong currents of wind that blow alternately in and out of the mouth of the cave suggested its name. In the cave, the wind is quiet, and the temperature remains a cool 47° F. (8° C). The cave was formed as water slowly dissolved away layers of limestone.

Wind Cave has a series of strange boxwork and frostwork formations which are not found elsewhere in the United States. The boxwork formations are calcite crystal structures, which vary from bright yellow through pink and rich browns to deep blue. The frostwork is made up of many tiny white crystals along the ceilings and walls. Electric lights in the cave make the boxwork shine with soft glowing color, and the frostwork gleam like millions of bright jewels.

Tom Bingham, a Black Hills pioneer, is credited with discovering the cave in 1881. While deer hunting, he heard a strange whistling sound which came from a clump of brush. He searched and found an opening in the rock, about 10 inches (25 centimeters) in diameter, from which a strong draft came. This opening is a few steps from the present entrance to the cave, which was built later.

The land around Wind Cave was made a national park in 1903. The park is located about 10 miles (16 kilometers) north of Hot Springs, S.Dak. For the area of the park, see NATIONAL PARK SYSTEM (table: National Parks). The surface area is a wildlife preserve for buffalo, deer, prairie dogs, pronghorn, and other animals.   JAMES J. CULLINANE

WIND CHILL is an estimate of how cold the wind makes a person feel in cold weather. The faster the wind blows, the faster the body loses heat. Therefore, the feeling of cold increases as the speed of the wind increases. For example, when the temperature is 10° F. and the wind is blowing at a speed of 10 mph, the wind chill temperature is equal to −9° F. This means that with a 10 mph wind at 10° F. people lose as much heat and feel as cold as they do when the temperature is −9° F. and the wind is calm.

EQUIVALENT WIND CHILL TEMPERATURES

Wind (mph)	Thermometer reading (° F.)							
calm	30	20	10	0	−10	−20	−30	−40
5	27	16	7	−6	−15	−26	−35	−47
10	16	2	−9	−22	−31	−45	−58	−70
20	3	−9	−24	−40	−52	−68	−81	−96

Wind chill is not an exact measurement of cold because temperature and wind are not the only conditions that make people feel cold. Someone who is thin or whose clothes are damp will lose more heat and feel colder than another person. But wind chill temperatures can give a better idea of how cold it feels than a thermometer reading alone. Wind chill measurements were developed from experiments performed in Antarctica in 1939. The table above is part of a larger table published by the U.S. National Weather Service. That agency reports wind speeds in miles per hour and temperatures in degrees Fahrenheit.   RALPH F. GOLDMAN

WIND EROSION. See DUST STORM; EROSION.

WIND GAP. See GAP.

WIND INSTRUMENT. See MUSIC (Musical Instruments); SOUND (Musical Sounds).

WIND RIVER RANGE. See WYOMING (Land Regions).

WIND TUNNEL is used to test the action of air against an airplane, an automobile, a jet engine, a guided missile, or some other object. Wind is blown through the tunnel at different speeds. Air pressure and air temperature also can be controlled. Scale models of airplane and engine parts are tested in wind tunnels before production begins.

Wind tunnels are built in many shapes and for different purposes. Some are big enough to test full-sized experimental airplanes. Others can test only small models. Tunnels in which the speed of the wind is less than the speed of sound are called *subsonic* tunnels. Those with speeds faster than sound are *supersonic*. Tunnels that use air speeds five or more times faster than sound are called *hypersonic*. In some tunnels, temperature can be made very low, in order to represent conditions at high altitudes. These tunnels are used to investigate icing on aircraft. In others, temperature is made very high to represent conditions met by a guided missile in its flight through the earth's atmosphere. The stability and control of airplanes are tested in *free-flight* tunnels. In these, an operator outside the tunnel controls the plane as it flies freely inside. There also are *spin* tunnels to test the tail spinning of aircraft. *Gust* tunnels test the action of gusts of wind on airplanes. Large electric fans make the wind in most subsonic tunnels. Air compressors, like those used in paint sprayers, make the wind in supersonic tunnels.

Supports that extend into the test section of the tunnel hold the model. The supports are fastened to balances, which are outside the test section. These balances record the action of the wind on the model. Instruments measure pressures at many places on the model. In supersonic tunnels, special optical instruments are used to see the changes in density of air as it flows around the model.   H. S. STILLWELL

See also AERODYNAMICS; AIRPLANE (Design and Testing); WRIGHT BROTHERS.

WIND VANE. See WEATHER VANE.

WINDERMERE, *WIN der meer,* is the largest lake in England. This beautiful body of water lies in the county of Cumbria, in northwestern England. It forms part of the famous English Lake District (see GREAT BRITAIN [map]). The scenery surrounding Windermere inspired English poets William Wordsworth, Robert Southey, and Samuel Coleridge. Wooded hills rise as much as 1,000 feet (300 meters) high around the lake. The small islands in the center of the lake form a picturesque group. Windermere covers 5.69 square miles (14.7 square kilometers), and is from 30 to 200 feet (9 to 61 meters) deep, or deeper. Its greatest width is 1 mile (1.6 kilometers), and it is about 10½ miles (16.9 kilometers) long. The River Leven flows from Windermere into Morecambe Bay.   JOHN W. WEBB

WINDFLOWER. See ANEMONE; WOOD ANEMONE.

WINDHOEK, *VINT hook* (pop. 64,095), is the capital of South West Africa. Windhoek lies on a plateau near the center of the country. For location, see SOUTH AFRICA (color map). The city is connected by railroad with Walvis Bay on the Atlantic Coast, and with cities in South Africa.   HIBBERD V. B. KLINE, JR.

WINDHOVER. See KESTREL.

WINDLASS, *WIND lus,* is a simple machine used to lift weights and pull loads. It was once commonly used to hoist water from wells. The windlass is a form of the wheel and axle which raises a heavy load by the application of a small amount of force. The simple windlass consists of a cylinder which can be turned by a crank. A rope or chain is wound around this cylinder. A bucket fastened to the end of the rope or chain was lowered into a well and raised again by turning the crank. Modern forms of the windlass include drums and cables of cranes and elevators, and capstans used on docks and on ships. Most modern windlasses are turned by machines rather than by hand. ALLEN S. HALL, JR.

See also WHEEL AND AXLE.

WINDMILL is a machine that is a member of the class known as prime movers. It uses the energy of the wind to produce power.

Windmills are generally used to pump water and to drive electric generators for lighting and for charging storage batteries on farms. A mill used to pump water has a wheel of blades set at a common angle and mounted on a horizontal shaft. The wheel is held with its face toward the wind by a vane, or rudder. The wind strikes the blades of the windmill at an angle and forces the wheel to revolve. The mill gets the full force of the wind by being mounted on a tower, at least 20 feet (6 meters) high, above surrounding obstructions.

Windmills now are usually built of steel. The old-fashioned, picturesque Dutch windmill with its four long arms carrying cloth sails is seldom seen on American farms, and it is gradually disappearing from the countryside of The Netherlands.

Within limits, the power of windmills increases with the diameter of the wheel. But there is a practical limit in diameter over which there is little gain in power on account of the increased weight. In tests, a steel wheel

Windmills Use the Power of the Wind to Pump Water.

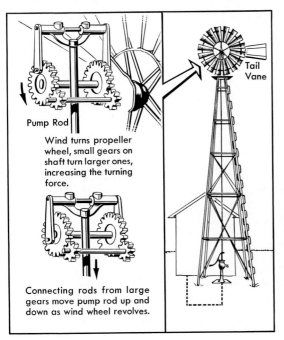

Pump Rod

Wind turns propeller wheel, small gears on shaft turn larger ones, increasing the turning force.

Tail Vane

Connecting rods from large gears move pump rod up and down as wind wheel revolves.

8 feet (2.4 meters) in diameter developed 0.53 horsepower (395 watts) in a 20-mile (32-kilometer) wind. One 10 feet (3 meters) in diameter produced 1.06 horsepower (790 watts) in the same wind.

Wind-electric plants have a propeller-type wheel, with two or three blades, which turns at a high speed. The wheel is usually mounted on a mast held up by guy cables. The wheel is connected to an electric generator through gears. The sizes of wind-electric plants range from those that produce 100 watts to those that produce 2,000 watts. A. D. LONGHOUSE

See also RUISDAEL, JACOB VAN (picture); TURBINE (Early Days).

WINDMILL POINT. See SOUTH CAROLINA (Places to Visit [Forts]).

WINDOW was at first merely an opening to provide light and air in a building. Only crude shutters and lattices covered the first windows. Later, linen, oiled paper, and sometimes mica or gypsum were used for windowpanes, in addition to wooden shutters. Glass panes were first used in windows during ancient Roman times.

When the great Gothic cathedrals of Europe were built in the Middle Ages, beautiful colored glass was used in their famous windows. Their rose windows became famous. The windows were rich with tracery; and the glass, in small pieces, was set in lead strips (see TRACERY). Such windows may be seen today in many cathedrals of France and England. Some of the best are in the Cathedral of Chartres.

Small-paned glass windows began to be used in palaces in the 1200's, and were common in large houses from the 1500's on. In England these windows were often very large. However, in smaller city houses and in farmhouses, glass windows were uncommon until the 1700's.

Architects now plan most buildings, whether they are homes, office buildings, or factories, so that windows will let in the most daylight possible. Sometimes they use walls made of glass blocks. Many new homes have extra-large *picture windows* in one or more rooms. *Jalousie windows,* shaped and operated like Venetian blinds, became popular in the 1950's. They have slats of clear or frosted glass that keep out rain without shutting off outside air.

The disadvantage of having many large windows in a building is that they permit a great amount of heat to be lost during cold weather. But this heat loss is reduced to a minimum by windows having two panes of glass separated by an insulating air space. Methods of opening and closing windows and of ventilating rooms are constantly being improved.

The design and location of windows has become very important in architecture. Windows are placed to let in sunlight in winter and to prevent its entrance on hot summer days, as well as to give the most beautiful view. Most modern decorators avoid using heavy drapes and curtains. A feeling of much extra space in a room can be produced by walls of clear glass giving a view of distant scenery or a garden. TALBOT HAMLIN

See also GLASS; STAINED GLASS; VENETIAN BLIND.

WINDOW DISPLAY. See ADVERTISING (Other Ways of Advertising).

WINDPIPE is the tube that carries air from the *pharynx* (an air passage from the nose and mouth) to the lungs. Scientists call it the *trachea*. A human windpipe is about 4½ inches (11 centimeters) long and 1 inch (2.5 centimeters) in diameter. It is held open by a series of C-shaped pieces of cartilage. These cartilages form the hard ridges on the neck just below the "Adam's apple."

The bump called the Adam's apple is the *larynx* (voice box). It is at the top of the windpipe. Air passing over the vocal cords of the larynx causes the cords to vibrate and produce sounds.

The lower end of the windpipe divides into two *bronchi* (tubes), which lead to the lungs. The right tube is straighter than the left one. Foreign objects that enter the windpipe usually lodge on the right side. The *epiglottis*, a leaf-shaped structure, normally forms a lid that prevents swallowed food from entering the windpipe. WILLIAM V. MAYER

Related Articles. See the Trans-Vision three-dimensional color picture with HUMAN BODY. See also:

Cartilage	Larynx	Pharynx
Cilia	Lung	Throat

WINDSOR, *WIHN zuhr*, is the name of the present royal family of Great Britain. In 1960, Queen Elizabeth II announced that future generations, except for princes and princesses, will bear the surname *Mountbatten-Windsor* in honor of her husband Philip Mountbatten. The name *Windsor*, adopted in 1917, was taken from Windsor Castle, a royal residence. The new name was chosen to replace *Saxe-Coburg-Gotha*, abandoned during World War I because of its German origin.

The first British king of the line preceding the Windsors was George I of Hanover. The family name of Hanover originated from the Electorate of Hanover, in Germany, which the British kings also ruled. The last Hanoverian king was William IV, Victoria's uncle. The laws of Hanover did not permit a woman ruler, and when Victoria became Queen of Great Britain, the Electorate of Hanover passed from the British royal family to Ernest Augustus, brother of William IV.

Saxe-Coburg was a duchy in Saxony held by the Wettin family. One of the daughters of Duke Francis,

ruler of the duchy, married the Duke of Kent, son of George III of England. She was Victoria's mother.

In 1826 the Saxon lands were redivided. Ernest, son of Duke Francis, exchanged Saalfeld for Gotha and founded the house of Saxe-Coburg-Gotha. Ernest had two sons, Ernest II and Albert, who were first cousins of Victoria. Albert married Victoria in 1840. Victoria's children took their father's name, and Edward VII, her son, was the first English king to bear the name of Saxe-Coburg-Gotha. His son George V was the first to use the name of Windsor. CHARLES LOCH MOWAT

See also EDWARD (VII; VIII); ELIZABETH II; GEORGE, of England; VICTORIA; WINDSOR CASTLE.

WINDSOR, Ont. (pop. 196,526; met. area pop. 247,-582), is the southernmost city of Canada. It is the chief port of entry between Canada and the United States. Windsor lies on the southwest bank of the Detroit River, opposite Detroit (see ONTARIO [political map]). The city's location on one of the world's busiest inland waterways makes it a major transportation center. Windsor leads all other Canadian cities in the production of automobiles and automotive products.

About 1750, French explorers established the first permanent white settlement in what is now the Windsor area. English settlers came to the area during the 1790's. In 1836, the people named their community for Windsor, England.

Description. Windsor covers 49 square miles (127 square kilometers). It is the home of the St. Clair College of Applied Arts and Technology and the University of Windsor. The city's attractions include the Art Gallery of Windsor, the Hiram Walker Historical Museum, and Memorial Convention Hall. The Windsor Light Opera Association and the Windsor Symphony perform in the Cleary Auditorium. Windsor has 47 acres (19 hectares) of riverfront parks.

Economy. Windsor's leading industry is the manufacture of transportation equipment, chiefly automobiles and automotive parts. This industry employs more than 27 per cent of the city's workers. Windsor produces about 25 per cent of Canada's automotive products and is sometimes called the *City That Put Canada on Wheels*. Many of Windsor's people work in Detroit office buildings and automobile plants. These workers commute

Walter Jackson, Windsor Star

The City Hall is a landmark of Windsor, Ont., the southernmost city of Canada. Windsor leads all Canadian cities in the production of automobiles and automotive products.

via the bridge and a tunnel that connect the two cities.

Other leading Windsor industries include chemicals, food and beverages, and metal products. The city's docks can handle oceangoing ships.

Government and History. Windsor has a council-manager government. The city council consists of a mayor and eight aldermen, all of whom are elected to two-year terms. The council appoints a city manager.

Huron and Iroquois Indians lived in what is now the Windsor area before French explorers claimed it in the mid-1600's. The French government gave land to people who established a village there in the mid-1700's. English settlers arrived in the 1790's. A log ferryboat connected the village with Detroit, and in 1812 the people named their community The Ferry. They later changed its name to Richmond. In 1836, a dispute arose over whether to call it The Ferry, Richmond, or South Detroit. The people compromised by renaming it Windsor, the name of a borough near Richmond, England.

Windsor received a city charter in 1892. The Ford Motor Company produced the first Canadian-made Ford there in 1904. Two other U.S. automakers, the Chrysler and General Motors corporations, established plants in the city in 1920. Windsor annexed the towns of East Windsor, Sandwich, and Walkerville in 1935. The city's population reached 100,000 that year. During the mid-1960's, Windsor annexed all or part of four other communities—Ojibway, Riverside, Sandwich East, and Sandwich West.

Windsor's $3-million Main Library opened in 1973. Several expansion projects were also completed during the 1970's. They involved such institutions as Metropolitan General Hospital, the St. Clair College of Applied Arts and Technology, and the University of Windsor.　　　　　　　　　　　　CARL MORGAN

WINDSOR, DUCHESS OF. See EDWARD (VIII).
WINDSOR, DUKE OF. See EDWARD (VIII).
WINDSOR, UNIVERSITY OF, is a private, coeducational university in Windsor, Ont. It is supported by the provincial and federal governments. The university grants bachelor's, master's, and doctor's degrees. It offers courses in arts, business administration, education, engineering, human kinetics, law, nursing, sciences, and social sciences. Assumption University, Canterbury College, Holy Redeemer College, and Iona College are associated with the university. The University of Windsor received its charter in 1963. Degrees were formerly granted by Assumption University, which was founded in 1857. For enrollment, see CANADA (table: Universities and Colleges).

Critically reviewed by the UNIVERSITY OF WINDSOR

WINDSOR CASTLE is the chief residence of the rulers of Great Britain. It stands in Windsor, about 21 miles (34 kilometers) west of London. William the Conqueror chose the site and built a castle there. Edward III tore this castle down and began the present structure. Later kings added to the castle until it now covers about 24 acres (10 hectares). It stands in the Little Park, which joins the Great Park south of Windsor. Queen Victoria and her husband are buried in the Little Park.

The most important feature of the castle is the round *keep* (tower) which dates from the time of Edward III. It is 80 feet (24 meters) high, and can be seen from far away. Four other towers also rise from the walls of the castle.

The section west of the central tower is called the Lower Ward. It contains Saint George's Chapel, begun by Edward IV and finished by Henry VIII. In the

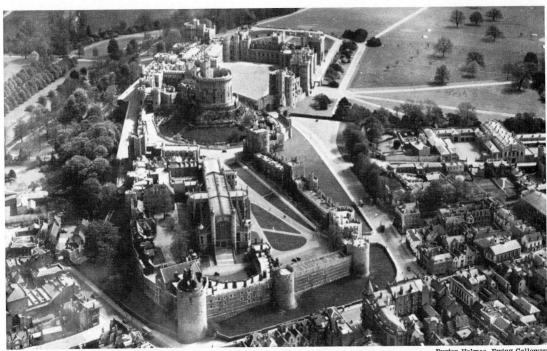

Burton Holmes, Ewing Galloway

Windsor Castle Covers About 24 Acres (10 Hectares) Near London.

chapel vault lie the bodies of Henry VIII, Charles I, William IV, George V, George VI, and other English rulers. The beautiful Albert Memorial Chapel also stands in the Lower Ward. Henry III began this chapel, Henry VII rebuilt it, and Queen Victoria completed it in memory of her husband. King Edward VII was buried there in 1910. The Upper Ward, to the east, contains the royal apartments and great state rooms. These were built chiefly during the 1800's.   G. HOLMES PERKINS

WINDWARD ISLANDS are a group of islands that lie in the southeastern West Indies. They stretch around the eastern end of the Caribbean Sea to South America (see WEST INDIES [map]). The islands are so named because they are exposed to northeast trade winds. The Windward group includes Grenada and St. Lucia, both of which are independent nations; St. Vincent, a state associated with Great Britain; Martinique, a French possession; and the Grenadines, a small cluster of islands, part of which are governed by Grenada and part by St. Vincent.

The Windward Islands cover about 950 square miles (2,460 square kilometers), and have a population of about 718,000. Most of the people on the islands are blacks. English is the official language on all of the islands except Martinique, where French is spoken. The chief products of the islands include arrowroot, bananas, cacao, cotton, nutmeg, sugar, and sugar cane.

Arawak Indians were the first known inhabitants of the Windward Islands. Europeans settled there in the early 1600's. Between 1763 and 1814, the islands, except for Martinique, became British colonies. Grenada became independent in 1974, and St. Lucia gained independence in 1979.   W. L. BURN

WINE is a moderately alcoholic beverage made from the juice of fresh, ripe grapes. Wine can also be made from the juice of many fruits and plants, including apples, cherries, and dandelions. But the word *wine* most often refers to the beverage made from grapes.

Throughout history, people have used wine to complement meals and to celebrate joyful occasions. They also have used it in cooking various dishes. The early Greeks used wine as a medicine, and today many physicians believe wine can aid digestion and help relieve tension. Wine also plays an important part in the religious services of many faiths.

Wine experts classify wine in many ways. Some group wines by the country that makes them. Others list wines by *generic* and *varietal* names. But most people who produce and use wines divide them into six main classes, according to when the wines are generally served.

Where Wine Comes From. Most nations produce some wine. The countries most famous for their wine include France, Germany, Italy, and the United States.

Wines from France rank among the finest in the world because of their quality and variety. The most important wine regions of France are Bordeaux, Burgundy, and Champagne. The Bordeaux region, which surrounds the city of Bordeaux in southwestern France, produces chiefly red and white wines. A red Bordeaux is also called a claret.

The Burgundy region, in east-central France, also makes red and white wines. The best of the red Burgundy vineyards extend from Dijon to an area south-

Robert Tixador, Agence Top

Wine is made from the juice of crushed grapes. Many European winemakers use a mechanical press such as the one pictured above to crush the grapes. The juice runs out the bottom of the press.

west of Beaune, a distance of about 30 miles (48 kilometers). South of this strip of land, called the Côte d'Or (Slope of Gold), winemakers produce a popular red Burgundy called Beaujolais. Leading white Burgundies include Chablis, Montrachet, and Pouilly-Fuissé. The Champagne region, in northern France, first produced the well-known bubbling wine of the same name.

Wines from Germany include white wines that have been imitated in many other countries. Two of these wines are Moselle, or Mosel, wines and Rhine wines. These wines come from the valleys of the Rhine and Moselle rivers in western Germany.

Wines from Italy. Grapevines grow throughout Italy, but the best wines come from a northern region called the Piedmont. Wines from this region include Asti Spumante, Barbaresco, and Barolo. Chianti, probably the most familiar Italian wine, comes from the Tuscany region in western Italy.

Wines from the United States may be divided into two groups: California wines and Eastern American wines. Over 85 per cent of the wine made in the United States comes from California.

California wines resemble wines from the principal European wine regions because they are made from the same varieties of grapes. These grapes belong to the species *Vitis vinifera* and are called European grapes. The finest California wines come from the coastal counties near San Francisco Bay. Washington and Oregon also produce wine made from vinifera grapes.

Eastern American wines are made from native American grapes, chiefly those of the species *Vitis labrusca*. New York ranks as the chief producer of Eastern American wines, but many other states also make them.

Wines from Other Countries include port, which was first produced in northern Portugal. Madeira wines originated on the Portuguese island of that name. The first sherry and Malaga wines came from Spain.

The United States government sets various standards

Grape Juice Becomes Wine through the process of fermentation, which takes place in a large vat. Carbon dioxide escapes from the juice, causing a bubbling action, *above*.

Wine Institute

Wine Is Aged in Storage Casks after it has fermented. Aging may take months or years, depending on the wine. A worker uses a device called a *wine thief* to take the wine from a cask to test it, *above*.

David Moore, Colorific

for labeling wines that are claimed to be from a specific country, state, or grape-growing region. For example, at least 75 per cent of the wine in a bottle of French wine must be produced in France. But at least 85 per cent of the wine in a bottle of French Bordeaux must be made from grapes grown in that region.

Generic and Varietal Names. Wines may also be classified by a generic name or by a varietal name. A generic name refers to the region in Europe where wines of that general type were first produced. Generic names include Burgundy and Chablis. A wine that has a generic name does not necessarily resemble the wine from the region for which it was named. For this reason, wine producers in the United States and some other countries use varietal names for their best wines.

A varietal name refers to the name of the principal grape used to make the wine. Such wines—called *varietals*—include Cabernet Sauvignon, Chardonnay, Chenin Blanc, and Pinot Noir. U.S. government regulations require that at least 51 per cent of the wine in a bottle of varietal wine must come from the grape for which the wine is named.

The Six Main Classes of Wine are (1) appetizer wines, (2) red table wines, (3) *rosé* (pink) table wines, (4) white table wines, (5) dessert wines, and (6) sparkling wines. Wine producers base these classifications on commonly accepted ideas of when the wines are served. However, personal taste plays an important part in the enjoyment of wine, and so the classifications are usually considered only a guide.

Appetizer Wines stimulate the appetite and are usually served alone, or with appetizers, before the main course of a meal. Their alcoholic content ranges from about 15 to 20 per cent. The leading appetizer wines, sherry and vermouth, vary in taste from sweet to *dry* (nonsweet). Most people prefer the drier kinds because sweet wines may interfere with the taste of the food to follow. Wines called *pop wines* may also be drunk alone or with

appetizers. They have an alcoholic content of about 8 or 9 per cent and resemble soft drinks in taste.

Red Table Wines. Most of these wines have a hearty flavor that complements such main-course dishes as red meats, game, spaghetti, and various highly seasoned foods. These wines, like all table wines, have an alcoholic content of from about 8 to 15 per cent. Popular red wines with generic names include Burgundy, Claret, and Chianti. Well-known varietals include Cabernet Sauvignon, Pinot Noir, and Zinfandel. Red table wines are served unchilled.

Rosé Table Wines are considered all-purpose wines. They share some characteristics of both red and white table wines, and can be used with any kind of food. Rosés are served chilled, as are white wines. The best rosés are made from the grenache grape.

White Table Wines are generally served with such delicately flavored foods as chicken and fish. These wines range in color from pale to deep gold and vary in taste from sweet to extremely dry. Popular white wines with generic names include Chablis, Rhine wine, and Sauterne. Important varietals include Catawba, Chardonnay, Chenin Blanc, Delaware, and Semillon.

Dessert Wines are sweet, rich wines that are often served alone or with desserts. They have an alcoholic content of from 15 to over 20 per cent and are usually served unchilled. Madeira, muscatel, port, and sweet sherry rank as the favorite dessert wines.

Sparkling Wines bubble and sparkle because they contain carbon dioxide gas. They may be served with any food and are most often used to celebrate festive occasions. Sparkling wines have an alcoholic content of from 10 to 14 per cent and are served chilled. Champagne ranks as the most famous of these wines. Others include pink champagne, sparkling Burgundy, and sparkling rosé. See CHAMPAGNE.

How Wine Is Made. The grape harvest, called the *vintage*, takes place each year in late summer or in fall.

283

Leading Wine-Producing States and Provinces

Wine production in 1976

State/Province	Production
California	●●●●●●●●●●●●●●●●●●●●●●●●●●●●
	449,081,000 gallons (1,699,957,000 liters)
New York	●●(
	42,223,000 gallons (159,831,000 liters)
Illinois	◖
	8,346,000 gallons (31,593,000 liters)
Ontario	(
	7,264,000 gallons (27,497,000 liters)
British Columbia	(
	4,367,000 gallons (16,531,000 liters)
Virginia	(
	2,235,000 gallons (8,460,000 liters)
Georgia	(
	1,879,000 gallons (7,113,000 liters)
Washington	(
	1,544,000 gallons (5,845,000 liters)
Michigan	(
	1,363,000 gallons (5,160,000 liters)
New Jersey	(
	1,311,000 gallons (4,963,000 liters)

Source: U.S. Department of the Treasury; Statistics Canada.

Leading Wine-Producing Countries

Wine production each year*

France	●●●●●●●●●●●●●●●●●●●●●●●●●●●
	1,994,000,000 gallons (7,548,100,000 liters)
Italy	●●●●●●●●●●●●●●●●●●●●●●●●●
	1,905,000,000 gallons (7,211,200,000 liters)
Spain	●●●●●●●●●●(
	906,110,000 gallons (3,430,000,000 liters)
Russia	●●●●●●●●
	707,981,000 gallons (2,680,000,000 liters)
Argentina	●●●●●●●(
	644,580,000 gallons (2,440,000,000 liters)
United States	●●●●●
	404,183,000 gallons (1,529,999,000 liters)
Portugal	●●●(
	280,022,000 gallons (1,059,999,000 liters)
West Germany	●●(
	224,546,000 gallons (849,999,100 liters)
Romania	●●(
	190,204,000 gallons (720,000,500 liters)
Yugoslavia	●●
	169,070,000 gallons (639,999,600 liters)

*Based on a four-year average, 1973-1976.
Source: FAO.

Many wine producers, especially those in Europe, label most of their table wines by the year of the vintage. In some years, a favorable climate in Europe produces superior grapes, and these grapes may produce superior wines. For this reason, wine experts often use a wine's vintage year as one way of judging the wine's quality.

During the harvest, workers carefully pick the grapes and deliver them to a winery, where the fruit is crushed mechanically. In some countries, people crush the grapes by walking on them. The crushed grapes and their *must* (juice) are then pumped into tanks, where a process called *fermentation* occurs. Fermentation turns grape juice into wine.

During fermentation, yeast converts sugar in the grape juice into alcohol and carbon dioxide gas. To make a red wine, the winemaker puts the grape skins into the fermenting tanks with the must. The pigment from the skins gives the wine its color. To make a rosé, the skins remain in the tanks only a short time. For white wines, the must is fermented without the grape skins.

Complete fermentation produces a dry wine. To make a sweet wine, the winemaker interrupts the fermentation. For dessert or sweet appetizer wines, the winemaker usually does this by adding grape brandy. This step accounts for the greater alcoholic strength of these wines as compared with table wines. Sparkling wines undergo a second fermentation, which produces their bubbles.

After fermentation, the wine is aged in storage casks to develop its flavor and *bouquet* (fragrance). Aging may take months or even years, depending on the kind of wine and the grape variety. Wine must be transferred from cask to cask during the aging process to get rid of solid matter that has settled in the containers. After the wine has aged, it is filtered and then bottled. Bottled wine stored for long periods is kept in a dark, moderately cool place to prevent spoilage. Table and spar-

kling wines are placed on their side so the corks stay moist and thus airtight.

Many wines are actually a blend of two or more wines. A winemaker blends wines to produce a more uniform product. Blending may take place after fermentation or aging, or during crushing by mixing different grapes.

History. No one knows when wine was first made. Prehistoric human beings grew grapes, and may have used wine because grape juice turns naturally into the beverage. The earliest references to wine include those found in the picture writing of the ancient Egyptians and Babylonians who lived about 5,000 years ago. The Chinese made wine some time before 2000 B.C. The Bible tells of winemaking in Palestine, and the ancient Greeks and Romans wrote extensively of wine.

Wine spread along with civilization from the Near East to Europe. Historians believe winemaking had begun throughout Western Europe by the 50's B.C. During the period from A.D. 500 to 1400, Europe became the wine center of the world. The Roman Catholic Church, the most influential force in Europe during the period, also encouraged winemaking because of wine's role in the Mass and in various church activities.

During the late 1500's, Spanish adventurers brought European grapevines to Mexico. By the late 1700's, Franciscan missionaries had carried the European species north into what is now California.

Wild grapes had grown in what is now the eastern United States long before white people first arrived. The American colonists tried for about 200 years to cultivate the wild grapes, but they failed to do so. They also imported vines cultivated in Europe, but the vines could not withstand the climate. The colonists finally succeeded in cultivating wild grapes of the species *Vitis labrusca* in the late 1700's. BERN C. RAMEY

See also GRAPE; EUROPE (picture: Grapes).

WINFRID. See BONIFACE, SAINT; CHRISTMAS (The Christmas Tree).

WING. See AIRPLANE (The Wing); AERODYNAMICS; BEE (Wings); BIRD (How Birds Fly); INSECT (Wings).

WINGATE'S RAIDERS were British commandos who fought behind Japanese lines in Burma during World War II. British Major General Orde Charles Wingate organized the group in 1941 and led it. He built his fighting force from Burmese and British troops. Wingate's Raiders relieved Japanese pressure on China and probably prevented a Japanese invasion of India.

The Raiders cut railroad lines, blew up bridges and highways, exploded ammunition dumps, and destroyed military installations. In 1944, they supported the Burma advance led by the American General Joseph W. Stilwell. Wingate died in an airplane crash in April 1944, but his Raiders continued their fight against the Japanese.　　　　FREDERIC S. MARQUARDT

See also COMMANDO.

WINGED BULL is an imaginary creature of Assyrian sculpture. It has the head of a man and body of a bull, and wings on its shoulders. These figures first appeared about 1000 B.C. They were placed in pairs at the entrance to a palace to frighten away evil spirits. Some stand 17 feet (5 meters) high. They have five legs, so that from the side they appear to be walking, while from the front they appear to stand still. The Persians later erected similar figures at their palace gates. See also ASSYRIA (picture: A Winged Bull).　FLORENCE HOPE

WINGED LION is an imaginary creature found mainly in the art of Babylonia and Assyria. It is represented as a figure with the head of a man, the wings of an eagle, and the body of a lion. Winged lions, like winged bulls, often stood in pairs at the entrance gate of a king's palace. They were supposed to frighten away enemies or evil spirits. The sculptors carved the lions with five legs. From the side they appear to be walking, but from the front they seem to be standing still.　FLORENCE HOPE

WINGED VICTORY, or **NIKE,** *NI kee,* OF SAMO-THRACE, *SAM oh thrays,* is a beautiful Greek statue that stands in the Louvre Museum in Paris. The Winged Victory was found in 1863 on the island of Samothrace in the Aegean Sea. The statue was in many fragments. Later they were pieced together, but the figure remained headless and armless. In 1950, its right hand was found and reunited with the statue. The statue was set up by the Greeks to honor Nike, goddess of victory and messenger of Zeus and Athena. No one knows who made the statue, or when. Some scholars place its date around 300 B.C., while others believe it to be a work of the 100's B.C. It is one of the finest examples of the sculpture of the Hellenistic period.　　　　　　FLORENCE HOPE

WINKELRIED, *VING kul reet,* **ARNOLD VON,** is the legendary national hero of Switzerland. He was supposed to have brought victory to the Swiss in the battle of Sempach against the Austrians in 1386. According to legend, the Swiss were beginning to retreat when Winkelried, a Swiss soldier, dashed boldly into the Austrian ranks and seized with his bare hands as many enemy spears as he could reach. As he fell, pierced by the spears, he created a gap in the Austrian ranks. The Swiss rushed through the opening, and won the battle in hand-to-hand fighting.　　　　ARTHUR M. SELVI

WINKLE, RIP VAN. See RIP VAN WINKLE.

WINNEBAGO, LAKE. See LAKE WINNEBAGO.

WINNEBAGO INDIANS, *WIN ee BAY goh,* were an eastern woodland tribe related to the Sioux. Tribal traditions say that at one time their home was near the Missouri River, but that they were forced east and settled near Green Bay in Wisconsin.

The language of the Winnebago resembled that of the Sioux in many ways (see SIOUX INDIANS). They hunted buffalo, caught fish, and raised corn and squash. They built long lodges with arched roofs and arbors over the entrances. Chiefs, who were sometimes women, inherited their rank. Important tribal ceremonies included the Medicine Dance, organized around a secret society, and the Winter Feast, a war ceremony.

The Winnebago were nearly destroyed by the Illinois sometime before 1670. But small groups continued to live along Lake Winnebago and elsewhere in southern Wisconsin and northern Illinois. They were friendly to most nearby tribes, and to the French. During the Revolutionary War and the War of 1812, the Winnebago sided with Great Britain. Some Winnebago lived in a village, now called Prophetstown, on the Rock River in Illinois. The town was named after their leader, Wabokieshiek (White Cloud), who was called the Prophet. The Winnebago ceded their lands in Wisconsin and Illinois to the federal government in the 1830's. They were moved to Minnesota, then to South Dakota, and finally to Nebraska. Some of the Winnebago refused to leave Wisconsin and Minnesota, and they still live there.　　　　　　　　WAYNE C. TEMPLE

WINNEMUCCA, *WIHN uh MUHK uh,* **SARAH** (1844?-1891), was an American Indian who won fame for her criticism of the government's mistreatment of her people. Winnemucca, a member of the Paiute tribe, began to speak out against the government as early as 1870. She later established two schools for Indian children.

Winnemucca, called *Thoc-me-tony* (Shell Flower) by the Paiutes, was born near Humboldt Lake in what is now Nevada. During the late 1860's and the 1870's, she served as an interpreter, guide, and scout for various government officials. In the 1870's, she protested such abuses of the Paiutes as seizure of their lands and an Army attack on a Paiute settlement.

In 1880, Winnemucca met on her people's behalf with President Rutherford B. Hayes. The next year, she lectured in Boston and other Eastern cities on the government's mistreatment of the Paiutes. She also wrote a book called *Life Among the Paiutes: Their Claims and Wrongs* (1883). In 1881, Winnemucca opened a school for Indian children at Vancouver Barracks, an Army post in the Washington Territory (now Washington). She later founded a school for Paiute children near Lovelock, Nev.　　　　W. ROGER BUFFALOHEAD

WINNETKA PLAN is a teaching plan designed to provide individualized instruction. It was developed in the public elementary and junior high schools of Winnetka, Ill., after World War I. It influenced widely the growth of the progressive education movement. According to the plan, teachers deal with each pupil individually so that pupils can develop their own particular abilities at their own rate of speed. Pupils work alone in their regular studies, but take part in many group activities in which their achievements are not measured.

WINNIE-THE-POOH. See MILNE, A. A.

The Winnipeg Art Gallery (Ernest Mayer)

The Winnipeg Art Gallery, *left,* helps make the city a leading cultural center of Canada. Winnipeg is the capital of Manitoba and ranks as Canada's third largest city, behind Toronto and Montreal.

WINNIPEG, *WIHN uh pehg,* is the capital of Manitoba, and Canada's third largest city. Only Montreal and Toronto are larger. Winnipeg is Canada's main grain market and one of the nation's leading centers of culture, finance, industry, and trade. About half of Manitoba's people live in the city.

Winnipeg lies about 60 miles (97 kilometers) north of the Canadian-United States border and almost midway between the Atlantic and Pacific oceans. The city's central location makes it the chief transportation center linking eastern and western Canada. Winnipeg is also the principal distribution point for goods traveling west from eastern Canada. The city has the nickname *Gateway to the West.* It was named after Lake Winnipeg, about 40 miles (64 kilometers) to the north. The word *Winnipeg* comes from the Cree Indian words *win nipee,* meaning *muddy water.*

The City covers 218 square miles (565 square kilometers). It lies at the junction of the Red and Assiniboine rivers. Main Street, once an important settlers' trail, is Winnipeg's chief north-south street. Portage Avenue, the beginning of the old overland route to Edmonton, Alta., is the main east-west street. The 34-story Richardson Building, Winnipeg's tallest structure, rises at Main and Portage. The city's chief public buildings are in the nearby Civic Centre. The Manitoba Legislative Building stands in the center of the Mall, a park on the north bank of the Assiniboine River (see MANITOBA [color picture: Legislative Building]).

Winnipeg's metropolitan area, often called *Greater Winnipeg,* covers 269 square miles (697 square kilometers). More than half of Manitoba's people live in this area. Greater Winnipeg ranks as Canada's fifth largest metropolitan area in population.

The People. More than 80 per cent of Winnipeg's people were born in Canada, and about half have British ancestors. The city also has people of Dutch, French, German, Italian, Polish, Scandinavian, or Ukrainian descent.

A large number of Indians and *métis* (persons of mixed Indian and white ancestry) live in Winnipeg. Most of the people in these groups moved to the city from rural areas. Many have little or no education or employment skill and find it hard to get jobs. They live in the city's poorest sections. The Indian and Métis Friendship Centre provides a place for advice, companionship, and recreation. But the low standard of living of many Indians and métis remains a major problem in Winnipeg.

About 60 per cent of the city's people are Protestants. Approximately half of this group belong to the United Church of Canada. Roman Catholics make up about 30 per cent of the population.

Economy. Greater Winnipeg ranks as one of Canada's leading manufacturing centers. About a fifth of the workers in the metropolitan area are employed in manufacturing. Greater Winnipeg's more than 1,000

───────── **FACTS IN BRIEF** ─────────

Population: 560,874. *Metropolitan Area Population*—578,217.

Area: 218 sq. mi. (565 km²). *Metropolitan Area*—269 sq. mi. (697 km²).

Altitude: 760 ft. (232 m) above sea level.

Climate: *Average Temperature*—January, 0° F. (−18° C); July, 68° F. (20° C). *Average Annual Precipitation* (rainfall, melted snow, and other forms of moisture)—23 inches (58 centimeters). For the monthly weather in Winnipeg, see MANITOBA (Climate).

Government: Mayor-council. *Terms*—3 years for the mayor and 50 councillors.

Founded: 1870. Incorporated as a city in 1873.

factories produce goods worth more than $1 billion yearly. The chief products include buses, cement, clothing, farm machinery, furniture, metal products, processed foods, and rockets and airplane parts.

Winnipeg lies in a rich wheat-growing region, and the Winnipeg Grain Exchange is Canada's major grain market. The Canadian Wheat Board and many grain companies have their main offices in Winnipeg. Canada's largest stockyard is in the St. Boniface district of the city. The Winnipeg Stock Exchange helps make the city a major financial center.

The city's location also makes it an important transportation center. Canada's two transcontinental railroads have their western headquarters in Winnipeg, and a U.S. railroad serves the city. The Trans-Canada Highway and Manitoba's main highways pass through Winnipeg. Winnipeg International Airport is one of Canada's busiest airports.

Winnipeg is Canada's largest and most important trading point between Toronto and Vancouver, B.C. But the rapid development of such cities as Calgary and Edmonton in Alberta has lessened Winnipeg's importance as a distribution point. The city is trying to meet this problem by seeking more industry. Winnipeg's older industries are working to modernize their plants and to expand their markets.

Education. Winnipeg's public school system has about 180 elementary schools and 55 high schools, with a total enrollment of approximately 115,000. The city also has about 30 parochial and private schools. Property taxes provide the chief source of income for the public schools. But rapidly rising school costs have become a heavy burden for many property owners. To ease this problem, the provincial government has taken over a larger share of the school expenses.

The University of Manitoba, founded in Winnipeg in 1877, has more than 14,000 students. The University

of Winnipeg is located in the city's downtown area.

Cultural Life. Winnipeg is one of the chief cultural centers of Canada. The world-famous Royal Winnipeg Ballet and the Winnipeg Symphony Orchestra perform in Concert Hall. The hall is part of the downtown Manitoba Centennial Arts Centre, which also includes the Manitoba Theatre Centre, the Museum of Man and Nature, and a planetarium. The Winnipeg Art Gallery attracts thousands of visitors yearly.

The Winnipeg Public Library operates Winnipeg Centennial Library and seven branches. The city's two daily newspapers are the *Free Press* and the *Tribune*. Twelve radio stations and five television stations serve Winnipeg, including one French-language radio station and one French-language television station.

Winnipeg has about 300 parks, squares, and athletic fields. Assiniboine Park, covering 375 acres (152 hectares), is the largest park. It includes beautiful gardens and a zoo with more than 750 animals and birds. The Winnipeg Blue Bombers of the Canadian Football League play their home games in Winnipeg Stadium. The Winnipeg Jets of the National Hockey League compete in the Winnipeg Arena.

Ross House, western Canada's first post office, is in downtown Winnipeg. It opened in 1855. Lower Fort Garry, north of Winnipeg, is the only stone fur-trading post still standing in North America (see MANITOBA [color picture: Lower Fort Garry]).

Government. Winnipeg has a mayor-council government. The people in each of Winnipeg's 29 *wards* (voting areas) elect one councillor to the city council. The councillors serve three-year terms. They also elect a mayor to a three-year term as administrative head of the government. A five-member board of commissioners, including a chief commissioner, supervises various

CITY OF WINNIPEG

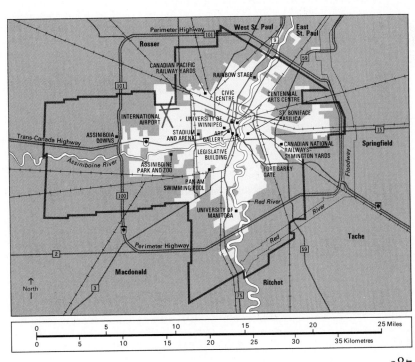

Winnipeg, a major transportation center, lies in southern Manitoba at the junction of the Red and Assiniboine rivers. The map shows the city and its major points of interest.

——— City boundary

☐ Built-up area

▨ Nonbuilt-up area

═══ Main road

——— Other road

┼┼┼ Rail line

• Point of interest

WORLD BOOK map

departments of the government. Property taxes provide about two-thirds of Winnipeg's income.

History. The Assiniboin and Cree Indians lived in the Winnipeg area before the first whites arrived. In 1738, Sieur de la Vérendrye, a French-Canadian fur trader, became the first white person to reach the site of what is now Winnipeg. He built Fort Rouge at the junction of the Red and Assiniboine rivers and traded for furs with the Indians. See LA VÉRENDRYE, SIEUR DE.

During the early 1800's, the Winnipeg area became the center of fur-trade rivalry between the North West Company and the Hudson's Bay Company. In 1812, Scottish and Irish farmers established the area's first permanent settlement along the Red River (see MANITOBA [The Red River Colony]). The Hudson's Bay Company absorbed its chief rival in 1821. That year, the company enlarged Fort Gibraltar, a post at the site of present-day Winnipeg, and renamed it Fort Garry. The company rebuilt the fort in 1835 and called it Upper Fort Garry. A trading post north of Winnipeg was known as Lower Fort Garry. Upper Fort Garry became the center of the Red River settlement.

In 1870, Manitoba entered the Dominion of Canada. The Red River settlement was renamed Winnipeg that same year, and it became the capital of the new province. It was incorporated as a city in 1873. By then, it had about 1,900 people. In 1878, Manitoba's first railroad linked Winnipeg and St. Paul, Minn. The Canadian Pacific Railway (now CP Rail) connected Winnipeg with eastern Canada in 1881. The government's offer of free land in western Canada helped Winnipeg's population reach 16,694 by 1884.

During the early 1900's, large numbers of Europeans settled in Winnipeg. Industry grew rapidly in the city during this period, and Winnipeg became the manufacturing center of western Canada. By 1914, the city's population had climbed to 203,000. The opening of the Panama Canal in 1914 slowed Winnipeg's expansion. Companies in eastern Canada could now send their products to the West cheaper by ship through the canal than by railroad. Winnipeg's economy continued to suffer during the Great Depression of the 1930's.

During World War II (1939-1945), sharp increases in the demand for livestock, lumber, metals, and wheat brought prosperity back to Winnipeg. Between 1946 and 1950, about 200 industries began in Winnipeg. The city's population fell during the 1960's, partly because of a trend toward suburban living. In 1960, Winnipeg was Canada's fourth largest city. By 1967, it ranked eighth.

In 1960, the Manitoba legislature established the Metropolitan Corporation of Greater Winnipeg to administer a number of services for Winnipeg and 11 of its suburbs. These services included planning and zoning, public transportation, and water supply. Each municipality in the corporation also had its own governing council to administer local affairs.

During the 1960's, officials of the metropolitan agency and those of the local councils often challenged each other's jurisdiction over various matters. Partly because of these disputes, the Manitoba legislature in 1971 combined Winnipeg and the suburbs into one municipality, the city of Winnipeg. The merger took effect on Jan. 1,

1972, and increased Winnipeg's area from 31 to 218 square miles (80 to 565 square kilometers). It also made Winnipeg the third largest city in Canada.

A downtown building boom that began in the late 1960's continued into the 1970's. Tall apartment and office buildings and hotels replaced many old structures. New construction included the Winnipeg Convention Centre, which opened in 1975, and a system of enclosed walkways above the streets.　　PETER McLINTOCK

WINNIPEG, LAKE. See LAKE WINNIPEG.

WINNIPEG, UNIVERSITY OF, is a coeducational university in Winnipeg, Man. It is associated with the United Church of Canada, but receives most of its funds from the province. The university offers programs in arts, education, science, and theology, and grants bachelor's, master's, and doctor's degrees. The school was founded in 1871 as Manitoba College. In 1926, it merged with Wesley College (founded 1877) and, as United College, was affiliated with the University of Manitoba until 1967. For enrollment, see CANADA (table: Universities and Colleges).

Critically reviewed by the UNIVERSITY OF WINNIPEG

WINNIPEG RIVER is part of the Saskatchewan-Nelson river system that empties into Hudson Bay. The river is 140 miles (225 kilometers) long. It rises in western Ontario and flows west in a winding course, draining the Lake of the Woods. It empties into Lake Winnipeg, near the city of Winnipeg. The river supplies power for Winnipeg. During pioneer days, the Winnipeg River was on the fur-trade route to the Northwest. For location, see MANITOBA (physical map).　　D. M. L. FARR

WINNIPEGOSIS, LAKE. See LAKE WINNIPEGOSIS.

WINNIPESAUKEE, LAKE. See LAKE WINNIPESAUKEE.

WINSLOW, EDWARD (1595-1655), a founder of Plymouth Colony, joined the Pilgrims in Leiden, The Netherlands, and came to Plymouth on the *Mayflower*. He and Susanna White became the first to marry in the new colony. He arranged the first treaty with Massasoit, and explored and traded with the Indians. Winslow served as an assistant for 20 years and governor of the colony for three. Winslow left Plymouth in 1646 and served in Oliver Cromwell's government in England. He was born in Droitwich, England.　　BRADFORD SMITH

WINSLOW, JOHN A. See ALABAMA (the ship).

WINSOR, JUSTIN (1831-1897), was an American historian and librarian. His first ambition was to be an author, and he wrote many books and articles. Winsor became interested in libraries after his appointment in 1866 as a Boston Public Library trustee. He became librarian at the Boston Public Library in 1868, and at Harvard College in 1877. Winsor promoted the development of libraries throughout the country, and served as first president of the American Library Association. He was born in Boston. He edited the eight-volume *Narrative and Critical History of America*.　　R. B. DOWNS

WINSOR DAM, sometimes called QUABBIN DAM, is a water-supply project on the Swift River in western Massachusetts. It is 295 feet (90 meters) high, with a top length of 2,640 feet (805 meters). An earth dam, it contains 4 million cubic yards (3.1 million cubic meters) of materials. It was completed in 1940. Winsor Dam and Quabbin Dike, built in 1937, form Quabbin Reservoir. The reservoir provides the main water supply for Boston and stores 1,265,000 acre-feet (1,560,400,000 cubic meters) of water.　　T. W. MERMEL

WINSTON-SALEM, N.C. (pop. 133,683), has one of the largest tobacco-manufacturing plants in the world and one of the largest leaf-tobacco markets. The city lies in northwestern North Carolina, about 30 miles (48 kilometers) from the Blue Ridge Mountains (see NORTH CAROLINA [political map]). With Greensboro and High Point, it forms a metropolitan area with 724,129 persons. Winston-Salem plants produce men's and boys' underwear, hosiery, electronic equipment, and tobacco products. Salem College, Wake Forest University, and several other schools are in the city.

A group of Moravians founded Salem in 1766. Winston was founded in 1849. Winston and Salem consolidated in 1913. The city has a council-manager form of government. HUGH T. LEFLER

WINTER is the coldest season of the year. The Northern Hemisphere, the northern half of the earth, has winter weather during December, January, February, and early March. In the Southern Hemisphere, winter weather begins in late June and lasts until early September. For dates of the first day of winter and information about the position of the earth and sun during winter, see SEASON.

During winter, the polar region is especially cold because the sun does not rise there for weeks or months at a time. Cold, dry air moves south from this region, bringing cold weather. Storms move from west to east along the southern edge of the cold air. In the United States, winter storms produce large snowfalls in some areas. The most snow falls in the western mountains and in much of the northern region east of the Rocky Mountains. Many winter storms bring rain to warmer southern areas. The lowest winter temperatures usually occur in the middle of all continents. JOHN E. KUTZBACH

See also DECEMBER; JANUARY; FEBRUARY; MARCH.

WINTER SPORTS. See CURLING; HOCKEY; ICE SKATING; ICEBOATING; SKIING; TOBOGGANING.

WINTERBERRY is a shrub related to the holly. Many winterberries grow on swampy land in the eastern United States. The shrub is sometimes called *black alder*, or *deciduous holly*. It grows 6 to 12 feet (2 to 4 meters) tall. Its bright red berries appear in November.

Scientific Classification. The winterberry belongs to the holly family, *Aquifoliaceae*. It is classified as genus *Ilex*, species *I. verticillata*. J. J. LEVISON

WINTERGREEN is a hardy woodland plant that bears white flowers. It grows in almost all parts of the Northern Hemisphere and received its name because its leaves remain green all winter. The name also applies to other plants of this type. The wintergreen is a low-

Keystone
Flowers and Berries of the Wintergreen

growing shrub with creeping, or subterranean, stems. Its glossy oval leaves cluster at the top of short, erect reddish branches. Its attractive flowers are shaped like urns. They cannot be seen easily because the plant's leaves hide them. The plant also produces a bright red berry. Wintergreen provides a pleasant-smelling, pleasant-tasting oil. Wintergreen oil serves as a flavoring for candy, medicine, chewing gum, and tooth powder.

Scientific Classification. Wintergreen belongs to the heath family, *Ericaceae*. It is genus *Gaultheria*, species *G. procumbens*. HAROLD NORMAN MOLDENKE

WINTHROP is the family name of three American colonial leaders, father, son, and grandson.

John Winthrop (1588-1649) was a Puritan governor of the Massachusetts Bay Colony. He was born in Edwardstone, Suffolk, England, of well-to-do country people. In 1602, he went to Cambridge University. He married at 17, practiced law, and became devoutly religious. In 1629, he became governor of the Massachusetts Bay Company, and in 1630, he sailed to Salem on the *Arbella*. About a thousand settlers followed him. Taking over the government from John Endecott, Winthrop soon settled Boston. He helped establish a Congregational church, and led the colony through the first hard winter. He was governor almost continuously until his death.

Winthrop's principles were high, and he tended to be aristocratic. In any community, he said, "the best part is always the least, and of that part the wiser part is always the lesser." Yet he knew how to be lenient, as when he "cured" a thief of stealing from his woodpile during a cold winter by telling him to help himself. He took part in all the major affairs of the colony, such as forming the New England Confederation. A statue of him represents Massachusetts in the U.S. Capitol.

John Winthrop, Jr. (1606-1676), was a colonial governor of Connecticut. He came to America in 1631. In 1633, he founded the town of Ipswich, Mass. He represented Massachusetts Bay Colony in England in 1634. He returned to govern a new colony in Saybrook, Conn. In 1646, Winthrop founded what is now New London, Conn., and later he served as governor of Connecticut. He was born in Groton, England.

John Winthrop III (1638-1707), son of John Winthrop, Jr., served in Richard Cromwell's parliamentary army in England. He returned home to fight the Dutch and Indians, and was rescued by Indian friends when Governor Leisler of New York tried to execute him for failing to capture Montreal in 1690. During the last 10 years of his life, Winthrop served as governor of Connecticut. He was born in Ipswich, Mass. BRADFORD SMITH

WIPO. See WORLD INTELLECTUAL PROPERTY ORGANIZATION.

WIRE is a long, thin, flexible metal rod that has a uniform cross section. Only *ductile* metals, or metals that can be drawn out, can be used for making wire. The chief ductile metals are copper, steel, brass, tungsten, gold, silver, and aluminum.

How Wire Is Made. From early ages until the 1300's, wire was made by hammering metal into plates. These plates were then cut into strips and rounded by beating. Then crude methods of "drawing" wire were introduced. Machine-drawn wire was first made in England in the mid-1800's. Today, all wire is machine-made. Steel or

289

How Wire Is Made

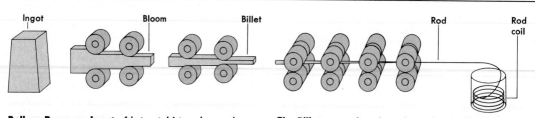

Ingot   Bloom   Billet   Rod   Rod coil

Rollers Press an Ingot of hot metal into a longer shape called a *bloom*. Further rolling of the bloom produces a bar called a *billet*, which measures 2 inches (5 centimeters) square.

The Billet passes through another series of rollers and comes out as a *rod* about ¼ inch (6 millimeters) in diameter. Machines cast the rod into a coil for easy handling.

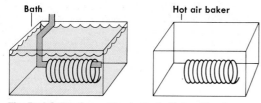

Bath   Hot air baker

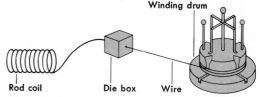

Winding drum

Rod coil   Die box   Wire

The Rod Coil is cleansed in a bath of sulfuric acid and water. Then it is coated with lime. A hot air baker dries the lime coating, which will act as a carrier for a lubricant.

The Rod is lubricated and drawn through a die box onto a winding drum. As it passes through the funnel-like die, the rod becomes longer and thinner until it is wire.

WORLD BOOK diagrams by Steven Liska

iron *billets*, 2-inch (5-centimeter) square blocks of metal, are heated and run through rollers that press them into smaller, longer shapes. They come out as long rods about ¼ inch (6 millimeters) in diameter. The hot rods are cast into coils and cleansed in sulfuric acid and water.

Pulling the rods through a series of tungsten carbide dies draws them out thin to form wire. The die has a funnel-like shape with a round opening smaller than the rod. The rod, which is pointed at one end by hammering, may be run into the die as thread runs through the eye of a needle. As soon as the pointed end passes through the die, it is seized with a pair of pincers and drawn far enough to be attached to an upright drum. The drum rotates, pulling the wire through the die. The wire winds on the drum. Fine wire may be drawn through a series of dies. Drawn wire tends to harden, and so it is softened and made less brittle by being heated in a furnace. For drawing the finest kinds of wire, extremely hard dies made of diamonds are used.

Sizes of Wire. The size of wire differs according to its gauge, or diameter. *American*, or *Brown and Sharpe*, is the standard gauge used in the United States for copper and other nonferrous wire. This gauge varies from No. 000000, which equals 0.58 inch (15 millimeters) in diameter, to No. 51, which is 0.000878 inch (0.022301 millimeter). A number of other U.S. standards are used. Sometimes the *imperial* gauge of England is used. France and Germany use gauges based on the millimeter. The *steel wire gauge* is the standard gauge for steel wire in the United States. Wire may be square, oval, flat, or triangular, but most wire is round.

Uses of Wire. Manufacturers make telegraph, telephone, and electric-power wires of copper, which is unusually ductile and one of the best conductors of electricity. The extremely thin wires used in telescopes are made of platinum. These have been drawn out to a thinness of $\frac{1}{50,000}$ inch (0.0005 millimeter). People

find other uses for wire in making nails, fences, watch springs, screens, and strings for musical and scientific instruments. Wire is also used in making automobile springs, bolts, fasteners, nuts, paper clips, screws, and staples. Magnet wire is used in generators and motors. Wire netting, gauze, and cloth are woven from wire. Wire ropes and cables consist of a number of single wires twisted together. The Golden Gate Bridge in San Francisco, and other large suspension bridges, are supported by steel-wire cables. Each cable consists of many separate wires that have been bunched together for flexibility and strength. Wire ropes are used in mining and oil drilling.   LAURENCE W. COLLINS, JR.

Related Articles in WORLD BOOK include:
Annealing	Ductility
Barbed Wire	Galvanized Iron and Steel
Copper (Copper Wire)	Wire Glass

WIRE GLASS consists of sheets of glass from ¼ to ¾ inch (6 to 19 millimeters) thick that contain a wire mesh embedded during the manufacturing process. The wire mesh strengthens the glass and holds it in place after breakage occurs. It has been used widely for windows and doors. The invention of wire glass is attributed to two men, Frank Shuman of Philadelphia and Leon Appert of France. They achieved practically the same result by different processes. The *Appert process* consists of rolling one sheet of glass and laying the meshed wire on it, then rolling another sheet of glass on the top and pressing the wire and the sheets of glass into one solid sheet. The *Shuman process* consists of rolling one sheet of glass, into which the wire netting is pressed and rolled. Wire glass can also be made by placing the wire on a casting table and holding it in position while glass is poured around it. One surface of wire glass is always smooth, and the other may be figured with various designs to diffuse light and obscure vision. Wire glass is usually ¼ inch (6 millimeters) thick.   C. J. PHILLIPS

WIRE-HAIRED FOX TERRIER. See FOX TERRIER.

WIRE-HAIRED POINTING GRIFFON is a hunting dog that originated in France and The Netherlands in the late 1800's. A good retriever, it shows where game is by pointing its body toward the game. It has a rough, steel-gray coat, with splashes of chestnut. The dog

WORLD BOOK photo by E. F. Hoppe
The Wire-Haired Pointing Griffon Is a Hunting Dog.

works deliberately, locating game by scent on the wind. Owners usually *dock* (cut off) about two-thirds of the tail. The dog stands 19 to 23 inches (48 to 58 centimeters) high at the shoulder and weighs from 50 to 60 pounds (23 to 27 kilograms).   MAXWELL RIDDLE

WIRE RECORDER. See TAPE RECORDER (History).

WIRELESS. See RADIO (History; picture: Guglielmo Marconi).

WIREPHOTO. See TELEPHOTO.

WIRETAPPING usually means the interception of telephone conversations by a listening device connected to the telephone wire or placed nearby. The message may be heard live, or it may be recorded or transmitted to another location.

Wiretapping is sometimes used as part of an investigative procedure called *audio surveillance*. The term *wiretapping* sometimes refers to the use of any electrical or electronic device to eavesdrop on private conversations. However, the interception of nontelephone conversations is usually called *bugging*.

Sophisticated methods and devices permit eavesdropping in almost any situation. Some types of microphones may be attached to a wall or a door so that conversations can be overheard through the partition. Directional microphones may be beamed or focused to pick up conversations from as far as 100 feet (30 meters). Even greater distances can be overcome by concealed miniature microphones and transmitters that send messages to a radio receiver.

In most countries, the right of people to speak freely in their homes and businesses and in public places—without fear of eavesdroppers—is considered extremely important. Many nations, states, and provinces have passed laws restricting or prohibiting various types of electronic surveillance. But much illegal eavesdropping continues, both by individuals and by governments.

In the United States, the problem of wiretapping and bugging has become a confusing and controversial legal

issue. Most Americans agree that wiretapping and bugging by private individuals should not be permitted. But there is much disagreement about (1) the constitutionality of electronic surveillance by law enforcement agencies and (2) methods of controlling government eavesdropping if it is permitted.

The wiretapping controversy began in 1928, when the Supreme Court of the United States ruled that wiretapping did not violate the Fourth Amendment to the Constitution. This amendment sets forth restrictions on search and seizure.

In 1934, Congress passed the Federal Communications Act, which prohibits the interception and public disclosure of any wire or radio communication. On the basis of this law, the Supreme Court ruled in 1937 that evidence obtained by wiretapping cannot be used in a federal court. Following this ruling, federal officials argued that the 1934 law did not prohibit wiretapping by the government so long as the evidence was not used in court. Since 1940, U.S. Presidents have claimed constitutional power to order wiretaps in matters of national security.

In 1968, Congress passed a law permitting federal, state, and local government agencies to use wiretapping and bugging devices in certain crime investigations. Before undertaking such surveillance, an agency would have to obtain a court order. The law stated that nothing in it was intended to limit the President's constitutional authority to order wiretapping without court warrants in national security cases.

In the late 1960's and early 1970's, the executive branch broadly interpreted the national security provisions of the 1968 law. It conducted electronic surveillance without court approval on a number of domestic radicals it considered subversive. In 1972, the Supreme Court ruled that such surveillance without a court warrant was unconstitutional.   JOSEPH D. NICOL

See also WARRANT.

WIREWORM is the name given to the hard-skinned grubs, or larvae, of click beetles. They received their

USDA
The Wireworm Causes Great Damage to Farm Crops.

name because they look somewhat like a piece of wire. These grubs usually live in the earth or in decaying wood for two or three years. They often do great damage to crops by eating the roots of plants. Wireworms appear yellowish or brownish in color and measure from $\frac{1}{4}$ to $\frac{1}{2}$ inch (6 to 13 millimeters) long. They have three pairs of legs. Sometimes the farmers rotate the crops to help reduce the number of wireworms. Or they may apply insecticides to the soil, either as pure granules or in liquid fertilizer. See also CLICK BEETLE.

Scientific Classification. Wireworms are in the beetle order, *Coleoptera*. They form the click beetle family, *Elateridae*.   H. H. ROSS

WIRT, WILLIAM ALBERT. See INDIANA (Schools).

WISCONSIN

The Badger State

Harmann Studio
Sailboats in a Harbor in Door County

─────────── FACTS IN BRIEF ───────────

Capital: Madison.
Government: *Congress*—U.S. senators, 2; U.S. representatives, 9. *Electoral Votes*—11. *State Legislature*—senators, 33; representatives, 99. *Counties*—72.
Area: 56,154 sq. mi. (145,438 km²), including 1,690 sq. mi. (4,377 km²) of inland water but excluding 10,062 sq. mi. (26,060 km²) of Lakes Michigan and Superior; 26th in size among the states. *Greatest Distances*—north-south, 320 mi. (515 km); east-west, 295 mi. (475 km). *Shoreline*—673 mi. (1,083 km).
Elevation: *Highest*—Timms Hill, 1,952 ft. (595 m) above sea level, in Price County. *Lowest*—581 ft. (177 m) above sea level, along the western shore of Lake Michigan.
Population: *Estimated 1975 Population*—4,607,000. *1970 Census*—4,417,933; 16th among the states; distribution, 66 per cent urban, 34 per cent rural; density, 79 persons per sq. mi. (31 persons per km²).
Chief Products: *Agriculture*—milk, beef cattle, hogs, corn, potatoes. *Manufacturing*—nonelectric machinery, food products, fabricated metal products, transportation equipment, paper products, electric and electronic equipment, primary metals, printed materials, chemicals. *Mining*—sand and gravel, stone, iron ore.
Statehood: May 29, 1848, the 30th state.
State Abbreviations: Wis. (traditional); WI (postal).
State Motto: *Forward.*
State Song: "On, Wisconsin!" Words by J. S. Hubbard and Charles D. Rosa; music by William T. Purdy.

WISCONSIN is a Midwestern state that has long been famous for its dairy products. Thousands of herds of milk cows graze on the rich, green pastures of the rolling Wisconsin countryside. They make Wisconsin the nation's leading milk producer. The state also produces about 40 per cent of the country's cheese and about 20 per cent of its butter. This tremendous output of dairy products has earned Wisconsin the title of *America's Dairyland.* But manufacturing, not agriculture, is Wisconsin's chief industry. The value of goods manufactured in Wisconsin is five times as great as the state's farming income.

Wisconsin is one of the leading states in the manufacture of engines, turbines, and other nonelectric machinery. The state is a leader in canning peas, sweet corn, and other vegetables, as well as in processing many dairy products. Wisconsin brews more beer than any other state. It also produces great amounts of fabricated metal products, including cutlery, hardware, metal cans, and metal forgings and stampings. Wisconsin ranks among the top states in automobile production. The thick forests that cover almost half the state help provide the basis for another important industry—papermaking. Wisconsin ranks high among the states in the value of paper production. It is also an important producer of electric and electronic equipment, such as electric motors and household appliances.

The natural beauty and recreational resources of Wisconsin attract millions of vacationers every year. Wisconsin has more than 8,000 lakes to delight swimmers, fishing enthusiasts, and boaters. Hikers and horseback riders follow paths through the deep, cool north woods of Wisconsin. Hunters shoot game animals in the forests and fields. In winter, sports fans enjoy skiing and tobogganing down the snow-covered hills, and ice-boating on the frozen lakes.

Wisconsin has won fame as one of the nation's most progressive states. An important reform movement called *Progressivism* started in Wisconsin during the early 1900's. The state began many educational, social, political, and economic reforms that were later adopted by other states and the federal government. Many of these reforms were sponsored by the La Follettes, one of the most famous families in American political history.

Wisconsin led the way to direct primary elections, regulation of public utilities and railroads, pensions for mothers and teachers, minimum-wage laws, and worker's compensation. Wisconsin also was the first state to end the death penalty for crime.

The first schools for training rural teachers were established in Wisconsin. The state also set up the first vocational schools. The University of Wisconsin was one of the first universities to offer correspondence

Near La Crosse by Carl Verburgt from the WORLD BOOK Collection

Grainfield in Southwestern Wisconsin

courses. The nation's first kindergarten began in Wisconsin. Wisconsin established the first library for state legislators.

Wisconsin has been a leader in the development of farmers' institutes and cooperatives, dairy farmers' associations, and cheese-making federations. The Republican Party was founded in Wisconsin. One of the nation's first hydroelectric plants was installed in Wisconsin. Wisconsin was the first state to adopt the number system for marking highways. It passed the first law requiring safety belts in all new automobiles bought in the state.

Wisconsin is an Indian word. There are several possible meanings of the word, including *gathering of the waters*, *wild rice country*, and *home land*. Wisconsin has been nicknamed the *Badger State*, and its people are known as *Badgers*. This nickname was first used for Wisconsin lead miners in the 1820's. Some of these miners lived in caves that they dug out of the hillsides. They reminded people of badgers burrowing holes in the ground.

Madison is the capital of Wisconsin, and Milwaukee is the largest city. For the relationship of Wisconsin to other states in its region, see the article on the MIDWESTERN STATES.

Wisconsin (blue) ranks 26th in size among all the states, and 10th in size among the Midwestern States (gray).

The contributors of this article are Robert W. Finley, Professor of Geography Emeritus in the University of Wisconsin Center System and University Extension; Eric Edwin Lampard, author of The Rise of the Dairy Industry in Wisconsin; *and Elliott Maraniss, Executive Editor of* The Capital Times *of Madison.*

Constitution. Wisconsin is still governed under its original Constitution, adopted in 1848. Only six other states are governed under older constitutions. An amendment to Wisconsin's Constitution may be proposed in either house of the state Legislature. The amendment then must be approved by a majority of each house in two successive legislative sessions. Next, it must be approved by a majority of the persons who vote on the amendment. The Constitution may also be amended by a constitutional convention. A proposal to call such a convention must be approved by a majority of the Legislature and by a majority of the persons voting on the proposal.

Executive. The governor of Wisconsin holds office for a four-year term and can serve an unlimited number of terms. The governor receives a yearly salary of $59,304. For a list of all the governors of Wisconsin, see the *History* section of this article.

The lieutenant governor, secretary of state, attorney general, treasurer, and state superintendent of public instruction are also elected to four-year terms. The governor appoints about 30 full-time state officers and a number of part-time officers who serve as members of state boards and commissions.

Legislature consists of a Senate of 33 members and an Assembly of 99 members. Voters in each of Wisconsin's 33 senatorial districts elect one senator to a four-year term. One representative from each of 99 districts is elected to the Assembly. Representatives serve two-year terms.

Regular legislative sessions meet every year and begin on the first Tuesday after January 15. There is no time limit on the sessions. The governor may call special sessions of the Legislature. Such sessions also have no time limit.

Courts. The highest court in Wisconsin is the state Supreme Court. It has seven justices, elected to 10-year terms. The justice who has been on the court for the longest time serves as the chief justice. Other Wisconsin courts include appellate, circuit, and county courts. The people elect the judges of these courts to six-year terms. All Wisconsin judges are elected on *nonpartisan ballots* (ballots without political party labels). In 1966, Wisconsin abolished the office of justice of the peace.

Local Government. Wisconsin has 72 counties. A board of elected supervisors governs each county in the state. The supervisors select one of their members as head of the board. Other county officials in Wisconsin include the sheriff, treasurer, surveyor, coroner, and district attorney.

Wisconsin law allows cities and villages to operate under the mayor, manager, or commissioner form of government. A few cities and villages have the manager form. All the rest have the mayor-council form.

Taxation. Taxes and licenses bring in about three-fifths of the state government's income. Much of the rest comes from federal grants and other U.S. government programs. Individual and corporation income taxes provide about half of the state's tax revenue. A general sales tax is another leading source of income in Wisconsin. Motor-fuel taxes and motor-vehicle license fees are used for highway construction and maintenance. Hunting and fishing license fees are used for conservation programs.

Politics. Wisconsin voters are divided about evenly between the Democratic and Republican parties. A

Milwaukee Journal photo

The Executive Residence is in Maple Bluff. The 20-room stone mansion was built in the 1920's as a private home. The state bought it in 1949.

The State Seal

Symbols of Wisconsin. On the state seal, a sailor and a miner hold a shield with symbols representing Wisconsin's agriculture, mining, manufacturing, and navigation. The horn of plenty stands for prosperity, and the pyramid of pig lead symbolizes the state's mineral wealth. The badger represents Wisconsin's nickname—the *Badger State.* The seal, adopted in 1851, appears in the center of the state flag. The flag was adopted in 1913.

The State Flag

Bird and flower illustrations, courtesy of Eli Lilly and Company

majority of the voters in Milwaukee, Madison, and other urban centers are Democrats. Republican strength lies mainly in Wisconsin's rural areas.

Throughout most of its history, Wisconsin has strongly favored the Republican Party. In fact, the party was founded in a Ripon schoolhouse in 1854. Three times as many Republicans as Democrats have served as governor of the state. Republicans also dominated the state legislature and Wisconsin's congressional delegations until the late 1950's. Then the state began sending more Democrats than Republicans to Congress. Since 1958, Democrats have also won the governorship and gained control of the Assembly in the state legislature several times.

In presidential elections, Wisconsin has supported the Republican candidate about twice as often as the Democratic candidate. In the 1924 presidential election, Wisconsin cast its votes for a native son, Senator Robert M. La Follette, Sr., who ran unsuccessfully as a Progressive. For the state's voting record in presidential elections since 1848, see ELECTORAL COLLEGE (table).

The State Bird
Robin

The State Flower
Wood Violet

The State Capitol is in Madison, which has been Wisconsin's capital since 1848. Territorial capitals were Belmont (1836); Burlington, now in Iowa (1837-1838); and Madison (1838-1848).
Ellis Sawyer, FPG

The State Tree
Sugar Maple

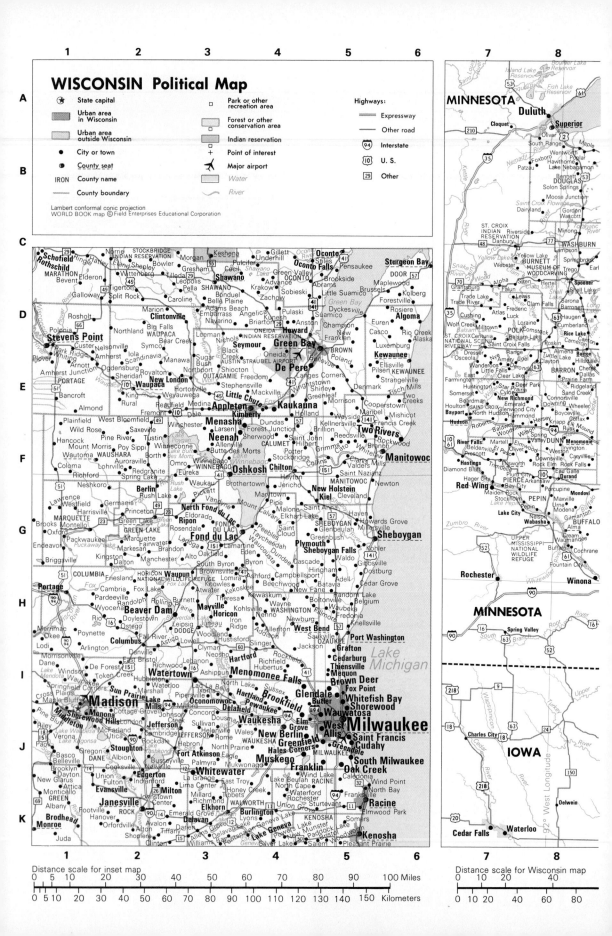

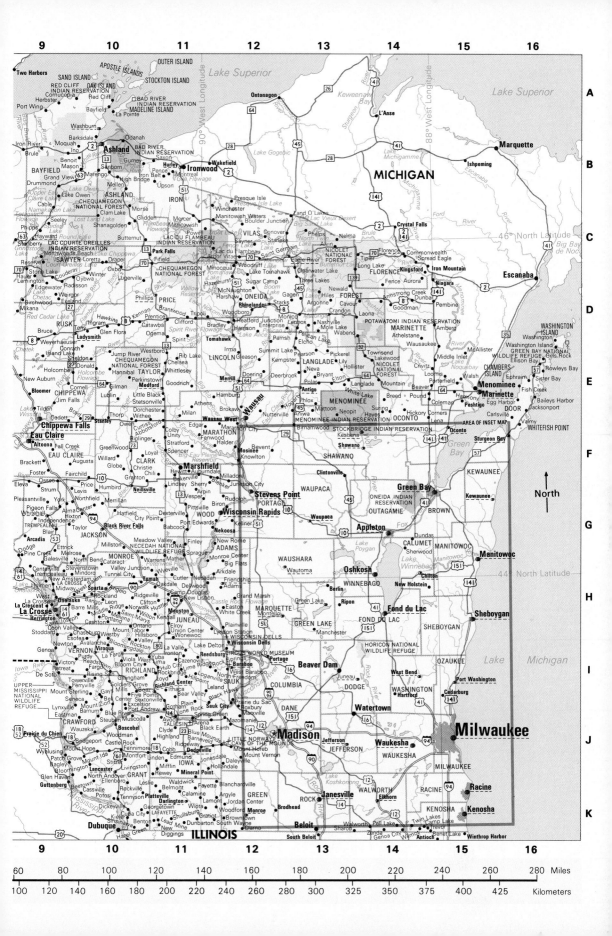

WISCONSIN MAP INDEX

Population

4,607,000 Estimate..1975
4,417,933 ..Census..1970
3,951,777 ....."....1960
3,434,575 ....."....1950
3,137,587 ....."....1940
2,939,006 ....."....1930
2,632,067 ....."....1920
2,333,860 ....."....1910
2,069,042 ....."....1900
1,693,330 ....."....1890
1,315,497 ....."....1880
1,054,670 ....."....1870
775,881 ....."....1860
305,391 ....."....1850
30,945 ....."....1840

Metropolitan Areas

Appleton-
Oshkosh 276,948
Eau Claire 114,936
Green Bay 158,244
Kenosha 117,917
La Crosse 80,468
Madison 290,272
Milwaukee 1,403,884
Minneapolis-St. Paul
(Minn.) 1,965,391
(1,931,037 in Minn.;
34,354 in Wis.)
Racine 170,838
Superior-Duluth
(Minn.) 265,350
(220,693 in Minn.;
44,657 in Wis.)

Counties

Adams ......9,234..G 12
Ashland ...16,743..B 10
Barron ....33,955..E 8
Bayfield ...11,683..B 9
Brown ....158,244..G 15
Buffalo ....13,743..G 8
Burnett .....9,276..C 8
Calumet ....27,604..G 14
Chippewa ..47,717..E 9
Clark ......30,361..F 10
Columbia ..40,150..I 12
Crawford ..15,252..J 9
Dane .....290,272..J 12
Dodge .....69,004..I 13
Door .....20,106..E 16
Douglas ...44,657..B 8
Dunn ......28,991..F 8
Eau Claire .72,237..F 9
Florence ....3,298..C 14
Fond
du Lac ..84,567..H 14
Forest ......8,265..D 13
Grant ......48,398..K 10
Green ......26,714..K 12
Green Lake 16,878..H 13
Iowa ....19,306..J 11
Iron ....6,533..B 11
Jackson ....15,325..G 10
Jefferson ...60,060..J 13
Juneau .....18,455..H 11
Kenosha ..117,917..K 15
Kewaunee ..18,961..F 15
La Crosse ..80,468..H 9
Lafayette ..17,456..K 11
Langlade ...19,220..E 13
Lincoln ....23,499..E 12
Manitowoc .82,294..G 15
Marathon ..97,457..F 11
Marinette ..35,810..D 14
Marquette ...8,865..H 12
Menominee ..2,607..E 13
Milwau-
kee ...1,054,249..J 15
Monroe ....31,610..H 10
Oconto ....25,553..F 14
Oneida ....24,427..D 12
Outagamie 119,398..G 14
Ozaukee ...54,461..I 15
Pepin ....7,319..G 8
Pierce .....26,652..F 7
Polk ....26,666..D 7
Portage ....47,541..G 12
Price ....14,520..D 11
Racine ....170,838..K 15
Richland ...17,079..I 10
Rock ......131,970..K 13
Rusk ....14,238..D 9
St. Croix ..34,354..E 7
Sauk ....39,057..I 12
Sawyer .....9,670..C 9
Shawano ..32,650..F 13
Sheboygan .96,660..H 15
Taylor ......16,958..E 10
Trempea-
leau .....23,344..G 9
Vernon ....24,557..I 10
Vilas ......10,958..C 12
Walworth ..63,444..K 14
Washburn ..10,601..C 8
Washington 63,839..I 14
Waukesha .231,335..J 14
Waupaca ..37,780..G 13
Waushara .14,795..G 13
Winnebago 129,946..H 14
Wood ......65,362..G 11

Cities and Villages

Abbotsford ..1,375..F 11
Abrams ....D 4
Adams ......1,440..H 12
Adell ....380..H 5
Afton ....K 2
Albany ....975..K 1
Albion ....J 2
Algoma .....4,023..D 6
Allens Grove ....K 3
Allenton ....H 4
Allouez* ...13,753..G 15
Alma ....956.°G 8
Alma Center .495..G 10
Almena ......423..D 8
Almond ......440..E 1
Alpha ....D 7
Alto ....G 3
Altoona ....4,164..F 9
Amberg ....D 15
Amery ......2,126..E 7
Amherst ......585..E 1
Amherst
Junction ...141..E 1
Angelo ....H 10
Aniwa ....233..E 13
Anston ....D 4
Antigo ......9,005.°E 13
Appleton ..56,377.°G 14
Arbor Vitae ....C 12
Arcadia .....2,159..G 9
Arena ....377..J 11
Argonne ....D 13
Argyle ....673..K 12
Arkansaw ....F 8
Arlington .....379..I 1
Armstrong Creek ...D 14
Arnott ....E 1
Arpin ....G 11
Ashford ....H 4
Ashippun ....I 3
Ashland ....9,615.°B 10
Ashwau-
benon* .....9,323..G 15
Athelstane ....D 14
Athens ....856..E 11
Auburndale ...468..F 11
Augusta .....1,405..F 9
Auroraville ....F 2
Avalon ....K 2
Avoca ....421..J 11
Babcock ....G 11
Bagley ....271..J 9
Baileys
Harbor ....E 16
Bakerville ....F 11
Baldwin .....1,399..E 7
Balsam Lake .648.°D 7
Bancroft ....E 1
Bangor ....974..H 10
Baraboo ....7,931.°I 12
Barneveld ....528..J 11
Barron ......2,337.°D 8
Barronett ....D 8
Basco ....J 1
Batavia ....H 5
Bay City .....317..F 7
Bayfield ....874..A 10
Bayside* .....4,461..J 15
Bear Creek ....520..D 3
Beaver Dam 14,265..I 13
Beechwood ....H 4
Beetown ....K 10
Beldenville ....F 7
Belgium ....809..H 5
Bell Center ....110..I 10
Belleville .....1,063..J 1
Belmont ....688..K 11
Beloit ....35,957..K 13
Beloit West* 1,903..K 13
Benton ....873..K 11
Berlin ....5,338..H 13
Bevent ....F 12
Big Bend* ..1,148..J 14
Big Falls .....112..D 2
Birchwood ....394..D 9
Birnamwood ..632..F 13
Biron ....725..G 12
Black Creek ..921..E 3
Black Earth 1,114..J 12
Black River
Falls .....3,273.°G 10
Blair ....1,036..G 9
Blanchardville 794..K 12
Blenker ....F 11
Bloom City ....I 10
Bloomer .....3,143..E 9
Bloomingdale ....I 10
Bloomington ..719..J 10
Blue Mounds .261..J 12
Blue River ....369..J 10
Boardman ....E 7
Boaz ....126..I 10
Bohners
Lake* ....1,417..K 14
Boltonville ....H 4
Bonduel ....995..D 3
Boscobel ....2,510..J 10
Boulder Junction ...C 12
Bowler ....272..C 2
Boyceville .....772..E 8
Boyd ....574..F 10
Brackett ....F 9
Branch ....F 5
Brandon ......872..G 3
Briggsville ....G 1
Brill ....D 8
Brillion .....2,588..F 4
Bristol ....K 5
Brodhead ...2,515..K 12
Brokaw ....312..E 12
Brookfield .33,371..J 4
Brooklyn .....565..J 1
Brooks ....G 1
Brothertown ....F 4
Brown Deer 12,582..I 5
Browns
Lake* ....1,669..K 14
Brownsville ...374..H 3
Browntown ...297..K 12
Bruce ....799..D 9
Brule ....B 9
Brussels ....D 6
Buffalo ....671..G 8
Burlington ..7,479..K 4
Burnett ....H 3
Butler ......2,261..I 4
Butte des
Morts .....1,111..F 3
Butternut .....453..C 10
Byron ....G 4
Cable ....281..C 9
Cadott ....977..F 9
Calamine ....K 11
Caledonia ....J 5
Cambria ......631..H 2
Cambridge ....689..J 2
Cameron .....893..D 8
Camp Douglas 547..H 11
Camp Lake .1,898..K 15
Camp-
bellsport ..1,681..H 4
Canton ....D 9
Caroline ....D 2
Cascade ......603..G 5
Casco ....481..D 6
Cashton ......824..H 10
Cassville ....1,343..K 10
Cataract ....H 10
Catawba .....215..D 10
Cato ....F 5
Cavour ....D 14
Cazenovia ....335..I 11
Cecil ....369..C 3
Cedar Grove .1,276..H 5
Cedarburg ...7,697..I 15
Centerville ....H 9
Centuria .....632..D 7
Chaseburg ....224..I 9
Chelsea ....E 11
Chenequa* ....642..J 14
Chenequa
North* ....1,106..J 14
Chetek ......1,630..E 9
Chili ....F 11
Chilton .....3,030.°H 14
Chippewa
Falls ....13,810.°F 9
Clarks Mills ....F 5
Clarno ....K 12
Clayton ....306..E 8
Clear Lake ....721..E 8
Clearwater Lake ....C 13
Cleveland .....761..G 5
Clifton ....H 11
Clinton ......1,333..K 2
Clintonville .4,600..F 13
Clyman ....327..I 3
Cobb ....410..J 11
Cochrane .....506..G 8
Colby ....1,178..F 11
Coleman ......683..E 15
Colfax ....1,026..E 8
Collins ....F 5
Coloma ....336..F 1
Columbus ...3,789..I 2
Combined
Locks* ....2,771..G 14
Commonwealth .....C 14
Como* ......1,132..K 14
Comstock ....D 8
Concord ....J 3
Connorsville ....E 8
Conover ....C 12
Conrath ......114..E 10
Cooksville ....J 1
Coon Valley ..596..H 10
Cooperstown ....E 5
Cornell ......1,555..E 9
Cornucopia ....A 9
Cottage Grove .478..J 2
Couderay .....123..D 9
Crandon ....1,765.°D 13
Crivitz ....E 15
Cross Plains 1,478..I 1
Cuba City ...1,993..K 11
Cudahy ....22,078..J 5
Cumberland .1,839..D 8
Curtiss ....135..F 11
Cushing ....D 7
Custer ....D 1
Cylon ....E 7
Dale ....E 3
Daleyville ....J 12
Dallas ....359..E 8
Dalton ....G 2
Danbury ....C 7
Dane ....486..I 1
Darien ....839..K 3
Darlington ..2,351.°K 11
Dayton ....J 1
Deer Park ....217..E 7
Deerfield* ...1,067..J 13
De Forest ...1,911..I 1
Delafield ....3,182..J 4
Delavan ....5,526..K 3
Delavan
Lake .....2,124..K 3
Denmark ....1,364..E 5
De Pere ...14,626..E 4
De Soto ......494..I 9
Diamond Bluff ....F 7
Dickeyville ..1,057..K 10
Dodge ....G 9
Dodgeville ..3,255.°J 11
Dorchester ....491..E 11
Dousman .....451..J 3
Downing ......215..E 8
Downsville ....F 8
Doylestown ...265..H 2
Dresser ....636..E 7
Drummond ....B 9
Dunbar ....D 14
Dundee ....H 4
Durand .....2,103.°F 8
Dyckesville ....D 5
Eagle ....745..J 3
Eagle River .1,326.°C 13
Earl ....C 8
East Troy ....1,711..K 4
Eastman ......319..J 10
Easton ....H 12
Eau Claire 47,697.°F 9
Eau Claire
Southeast* 2,316..F 9
Eau Galle ....F 8
Eden ....376..G 4
Edgar ....928..F 11
Edgerton ...4,118..J 2
Edmund ....J 11
Egg Harbor ..184..E 16
Eland ....229..C 2
Elcho ....D 13
Elderon ....185..D 1
Eldorado ....G 3
Eleva ....574..F 9
Elk Mound ...471..F 8
Elkhart Lake .787..G 5
Elkhorn ......3,992.°K 14
Ellison Bay ....E 16
Ellisville ....E 5
Ellsworth ...1,983.°F 7
Elm Grove ..7,201..J 4
Elmwood ......737..F 8
Elmwood Park 456..K 5
El Paso ....F 7
Elroy ....1,513..H 11
Elton ....E 13
Embarrass ....472..D 3
Emerald ....E 8
Emerald Grove .....K 2
Endeavor .....328..G 1
Enterprise ....D 12
Ephraim ......236..E 16
Ettrick ....463..G 9
Eureka ....F 3
Evansville ..2,992..K 1
Excelsior ....J 10
Exeland ......189..D 9
Fairchild .....537..F 10
Fairwater .....373..G 2
Fall Creek ....914..F 9
Fall River ....633..H 2
Falun ....D 7
Fence ....D 14
Fennimore ..1,861..J 11
Fenwood ......147..F 11
Ferryville .....183..I 9
Fifield ....C 11
Fish Creek ....E 16
Florence ....°C 14
Fond du
Lac ......35,515.°H 14
Fontana on
Geneva
Lake .....1,464..K 3
Footville ......698..K 1
Forest Junction .....F 4
Forestville ....349..D 6
Fort Atkin-
son ....9,164..J 3
Foster ....F 9
Fountain
City ......1,017..G 8
Fox Lake ...1,242..H 2
Fox Point ...7,939..I 5
Francis Creek 494..F 5
Franklin ...12,247..J 5
Franksville ....K 5
Frederic ....1,058..D 7
Fredonia ....1,045..H 5
Freedom ....E 4
Fremont ....598..E 2
Friendship ....641.°H 12
Friesland .....301..H 2
Fulton ....J 2
Galesville ...1,162..H 9
Galloway ....D 1
Gays Mills ...623..I 10
Genoa ....304..I 9
Genoa City .1,085..K 14
Germania ....G 1
German-
town* ....8,219..J 14
Gibbsville ....G 5
Gillett ......1,288..C 4
Gills Rock ....E 16
Gilman ....328..E 10
Gilmanton ....G 8
Gleason ....E 12
Glen Flora .....69..D 10
Glen Haven ....K 9
Glenbeulah ...496..G 5
Glendale ...13,426..I 5
Glenwood City 822..E 8
Glidden ....C 10
Goodman ....D 14
Gordon ....C 8
Gotham ....J 11
Grafton .....7,169..I 5
Grand Marsh ......H 12
Grand View ....B 9
Granton ......288..F 11
Grantsburg ...930.°D 7
Gratiot ....249..K 11
Green Bay .88,304.°G 15
Green Lake .1,109.°H 13
Green Valley ....C 4
Greenbush ....G 4
Greendale ..15,089..J 5
Greenfield .24,424..J 5
Greenleaf ....E 4
Greenwood ...1,036..F 10
Gresham .....448..C 3
Grimms ....F 5
Gurney ....B 10
Hager City ....F 7
Hales
Corners ...7,771..J 5
Hallie* .....1,223..F 9
Hamburg ....E 11
Hammond .....768..E 7
Hancock ......404..F 1
Hannibal ....E 10
Hanover ....K 2
Harrisville ....G 1
Hartford ....6,499..I 14
Hartland ....2,763..I 4
Hatfield ....G 10
Hatley ....315..C 1
Haugen ....246..D 8
Hawkins ......385..D 10
Hayton ....F 4
Hayward ....1,653.°C 9
Hazel Green ..982..K 11
Hazelhurst ....D 12
Heafford Junction ..D 12
Hebron ....J 3
Helenville ....J 3
Herbster ....A 9
Hersey ....E 8
Hewitt ....211..F 11
Highland .....785..J 11
Hilbert ....896..F 4
Hiles ....D 13
Hillpoint ....I 11
Hillsboro ....1,231..I 11
Hillsdale ....E 8
Hingham ....H 5
Hixton ....300..G 10
Holcombe ....E 9
Holland ....E 4
Hollandale ...256..J 11
Hollister ....E 13
Holmen .....2,153..H 9
Honey Creek ....K 4
Horicon ....3,356..H 3
Hortonville .1,524..E 3
Houlton ....E 7
Howard ......4,911..D 4
Howards Grove
[-Millers-
ville] ....998..G 5
Hubertus ....I 4
Hudson .....5,322.°E 7
Humbird ....G 10
Hurley ......2,418.°B 11
Hustisford ....789..I 3
Hustler ....190..H 11
Hutchins* ....409..F 13
Independ-
ence .....1,036..G 9
Indianford ....K 2
Ingram ....109..D 10
Iola ....900..E 2
Irma ....E 12
Iron Belt ....B 11
Iron Ridge ....480..H 3
Iron River ....B 9
Ironton ....195..I 11
Irvington ....F 8
Ithaca ....I 11
Ixonia ....I 3
Jackson ......1,355..I 4
Jacksonport ....E 16
Janesville ..46,426.°K 13
Jefferson ...5,429.°J 13
Jericho ....F 4
Jim Falls ....E 9
Johnson Creek 790..J 3
Johnstown Center ..K 2
Juda ....K 1
Jump River ....E 10
Junction City .396..F 12
Juneau .....2,043.°I 14
Kaukauna .11,308..E 4
Kekoskee ....233..H 3
Kellner ....G 12
Kellnersville ..260..E 5
Kendall ......468..H 11
Kennan ....167..D 10
Kenosha ...78,805.°K 15
Keshena ....F 14
Kewaskum ..1,926..H 4
Kewaunee ...2,901.°G 15
Kiel ....2,848..G 5
Kieler ....K 10
Kimberly ....6,131..E 4
King ....E 2
Kingston ......343..G 2
Knapp ....369..F 8
Knellsville ....H 5
Knowles ....H 3

Kohler .....1,738..G 5
Krakow ....D 4
Lac La Belle ..227..I 3
La Crosse ..48,864.°H 9
Ladysmith ..3,674.°D 9
La Farge .....748..I 10
Lake Beulah ....J 4
Lake Delton .1,059..I 12
Lake Geneva 4,890..K 4
Lake Mills ..3,556..J 2
Lake Nebagamon ....523..B 8
Lake Tomahawk ...D 12
Lake Wazeecha* 1,285..G 12
Lake Wissota* ..1,419..E 9
Lakewood ....E 14
Lamartine ....G 3
Lancaster ...3,756.°J 10
Land O' Lakes .....C 13
Langlade ....E 13
Lannon* ....1,056..J 15
Laona ....D 14
La Pointe ....A 10
Larsen ....F 3
La Valle .....411..I 11
Lead Mine ....K 11
Lebanon ....I 3
Lena ....569..F 15
Leopolis ....D 2
Lewis ....D 7
Lily ....E 13
Lima Center ....K 3
Lime Ridge ...203..I 11
Linden ....408..J 11
Little Chute .5,522..E 4
Little Suamico .....D 5
Livingston ....503..J 11
Lodi ....1,831..I 1
Loganville ....199..I 11
Lohrville .....195..F 2
Lomira .....1,084..H 3
London ....J 2
Lone Rock ....597..J 11
Long Lake ....C 14
Loretta ....C 10
Lowell ....322..I 3
Loyal ....1,126..F 10
Lublin ....143..E 10
Luck ....848..D 7
Luxemburg ...853..D 5
Lyndon Station .....533..H 11
Lynxville .....149..J 10
Lyons ....K 4
Mackville ....E 4
Madison ..168,671.°J 12
Maiden Rock .172..F 7
Manawa ....1,105..E 2
Manchester ....H 13
Manitowish Waters .C 11
Manitowoc .33,430.°G 15
Maple Bluff .1,974..I 1
Maplewood ....D 6
Marathon City ......1,214..F 12
Marengo ....B 10
Maribel ....316..E 5
Marinette ..12,157.°E 15
Marion .....1,218..D 2
Markesan ...1,377..G 2
Marquette ......161..G 2
Marshall ....1,043..I 2
Marshfield .15,619..F 11
Martell ....F 7
Marytown ....G 4
Mason ....119..B 10
Mather ....G 11
Mattoon ....377..E 13
Mauston ....3,466.°H 11
Mayville ....4,139..H 3
Mazomanie ..1,217..J 12
McFarland .2,386..J 1
Medford ....3,454.°E 11
Medina ....E 3
Mellen ......1,168..B 10
Melrose ....505..G 10
Melvina ....116..H 10
Menasha ...14,836..F 3
Menomonee Falls ....31,697..I 4
Menomonie 11,275.°F 8
Mequon ....12,150..I 5
Mercer ....C 11
Merrill .....9,502.°E 12
Merrillan .....612..G 10
Merrimac .....376..H 1
Merton* ......646..J 14
Middleton ..8,246..I 1
Midway ....H 9
Mifflin ....J 11
Mikana ....D 9
Milan ....E 11
Milford ....I 2
Milladore ....229..F 12
Millersville, see Howards Grove [-Millersville]
Millston ....G 10
Milltown .....634..D 7
Milton .....3,699..K 2
Milwaukee 669,022.°J 15
Mindoro ....H 9
Mineral Point .....2,305..J 11
Minocqua ....C 12
Minong ....420..C 8
Mishicot .....938..E 6
Modena ....G 8
Mole Lake ....D 13
Mondovi ....2,338..F 8
Monico ....D 13
Monona ....10,420..J 1
Monroe ....8,654.°K 12
Monroe Center .....H 11
Montello ....1,082.°H 12
Montfort ......518..J 10
Monticello ....870..K 1
Montreal .....877..B 11
Morrison ....E 5
Morrisonville ....I 1
Mosinee .....2,395..F 12
Mount Calvary 942..G 4
Mount Hope ..176..J 10
Mount Horeb 2,402..J 12
Mount Ida ....J 10
Mount Morris ......F 2
Mount Sterling 181..I 10
Mountain ....E 14
Mukwonago 2,367..J 4
Muscoda ....1,099..J 11
Muskego ...11,573..J 4
Nashotah* ....410..J 14
Navarino ....D 3
Necedah ....740..H 11
Neenah ....22,902..F 3
Neillsville ...2,750.°G 10
Nekoosa .....2,409..G 11
Nelson ....G 8
Nelsonville ....152..E 1
Neopit ....1,122..E 13
Neosho ....400..I 3
Neshkoro ......385..F 2
New Amsterdam ...H 9
New Auburn ....368..E 9
New Berlin 26,910..J 4
New Diggings ......K 11
New Fane ....H 4
New Glarus .1,454..J 1
New Holstein 3,012..H 15
New Lisbon .1,361..H 11
New London 5,801..E 3
New Munster ....K 4
New Richmond .....3,707..E 7
Newald ....D 13
Newburg ......562..H 5
Newville ....J 2
Niagara ....2,347..D 15
Nichols ....207..D 3
Norrie ....C 1
North Bay ...263..K 5
North Bend ....H 9
North Cape ....K 4
North Fond du Lac ....3,286..G 3
North Freedom ....596..I 12
North Hudson ....1,547..E 7
North Lake ....J 4
North Prairie .669..J 4
Northwoods Beach ....C 9
Norwalk ....432..H 10
Oak Creek .13,928..J 5
Oakdale ....H 11
Oakfield ....918..G 3
Oconomowoc 8,741..I 3
Oconomowoc Lake* ....599..J 14
Oconomowoc Lake South* ....1,473..J 14
Oconto ....4,667.°F 15
Oconto Falls 2,465..C 4
Odanah ....B 10
Ogdensburg ...206..E 2
Ogema ....D 11
Ojibwa ....D 9
Okauchee* ..3,134..J 14
Okee ....I 1
Oliver ....210..B 8
Omro ....2,341..F 3
Onalaska ....4,909..H 9
Oneida ....E 4
Ontario ....392..H 10
Oostburg ....1,309..H 5
Oregon ....2,553..J 1
Orfordville ....888..K 1
Osceola ......1,152..E 7
Oshkosh ...53,082.°H 14
Osseo ....1,356..F 9
Owen ....1,031..F 10
Oxford ....453..G 1
Packwaukee ....G 1
Paddock Lake .....1,470..K 4
Palmyra ....1,524..J 3
Paoli ....J 1
Pardeeville ..1,507..H 1
Park Falls ..2,953..C 11
Park Ridge ...817..D 1
Patch Grove ..187..J 10
Patzau ....B 8
Peebles ....G 4
Pelican Lake ....D 13
Pell Lake ..1,284..K 14
Pella ....D 3
Pembine ....D 15
Pence ....B 11
Pensaukee ....C 5
Pepin ....747..G 8
Perkinstown ....E 10
Perry Go Place* ....5,912..K 13
Peshtigo ....2,836..E 15
Pewaukee ...3,271..J 4
Pewaukee West* ....3,401..J 14
Phelps ....C 13
Phillips ....1,511.°D 11
Phlox ....E 13
Pickerel ....E 13
Pickett ....G 3
Pigeon Falls ..198..G 9
Pine Bluff ....J 1
Pine Creek ....G 9
Pine River ....F 2
Pipe ....G 4
Pittsville .....708..G 11
Plain ....688..J 11
Plainfield .....642..F 1
Platteville ...9,599..K 11
Pleasant Prairie ...K 5
Plover ......2,743..E 1
Plum City ....451..F 8
Plymouth ...5,810..G 5
Poland ....E 5
Polar ....E 13
Polonia ....D 1
Poplar ....455..B 8
Port Edwards ..2,126..G 12
Port Washington ....8,752.°I 15
Port Wing ....A 9
Portage ......7,821.°I 12
Poskin ....D 8
Potosi ....713..K 10
Potter ....F 4
Pound ....284..E 15
Powers Lake ....K 4
Poy Sippi ....F 2
Poynette ....1,118..H 1
Prairie du Chien .....5,540.°J 9
Prairie du Sac ....1,902..J 12
Prairie Farm .426..E 8
Prentice ......519..D 11
Prescott .....2,331..F 7
Presque Isle ....C 12
Princeton ...1,446..G 2
Pulaski .....1,717..D 4
Pulcifer ....C 4
Racine ....95,162.°K 15
Radisson ......206..D 9
Randolph ...1,582..H 2
Random Lake ......1,068..H 5
Readfield ....E 3
Readstown ....395..I 10
Red Cliff ....A 10
Redgranite ...645..F 2
Reedsburg ...4,585..I 11
Reedsville ....994..F 5
Reeseville* ...566..J 13
Reserve ....C 9
Retreat ....I 9
Rewey ....232..K 11
Rhinelander 8,218.°D 12
Rib Lake .....782..E 11
Rice Lake ...7,278..D 8
Richfield ....I 4
Richland Center ....5,086.°I 11
Richwood ....I 3
Ridgeland .....266..E 8
Ridgeway .....463..J 11
Ringle ....C 1
Rio ....792..H 1
Rio Creek ....D 6
Riplinger ....F 11
Ripon ......7,053..H 13
River Falls .7,238..F 7
River Hills* 1,561..I 15
Roberts ....631..E 7
Rochester .....546..K 4
Rock Elm ....F 8
Rock Falls ....F 8
Rock Springs .432..I 11
Rockbridge ....I 11
Rockdale .....172..J 2
Rockfield ....I 4
Rockland .....289..H 10
Rockwood ....F 5
Rolling Prairie ....H 3
Rome ....J 3
Rosendale ....464..G 3
Rosholt ....466..D 1
Rothschild ..3,141..C 1
Roxbury ....J 12
Royalton ....E 2
Rudolph ....349..G 12
Rural ....E 2
Rusk ....F 8
St. Anna ....G 4
St. Cloud .....550..G 4
St. Croix Falls .....1,425..D 7
St. Francis .9,951..J 5
St. Germain ....C 12
St. Joseph ....H 10
St. Nazianz ..718..F 5
Salem ....K 4
Sanborn ....B 10
Sand Creek ....E 8
Sarona ....D 8
Sauk City ..2,385..J 12
Saukville ....2,012..H 5
Saxeville ....F 2
Saxon ....B 11
Sayner ....C 12
Scandinavia ..268..E 2
Schofield ...2,577..C 1
Seneca ....J 10
Sextonville ....J 11
Seymour ....2,194..D 4
Sharon ......1,216..K 13
Shawano ....6,488.°F 14
Sheboygan .48,484.°H 15
Sheboygan Falls .....4,771..G 5
Sheboygan South* ...1,920..H 15
Sheboygan West* ....1,361..H 15
Sheldon ....218..E 10
Shell Lake ...928.°D 8
Sherry ....F 11
Sherwood ......350..F 4
Shiocton ....830..E 3
Shopiere ....K 2
Shorewood .15,576..J 5
Shorewood Hills .....2,206..J 1
Shullsburg ..1,376..K 11
Silver Lake .1,283..K 4
Sinsinawa ....K 10
Siren ....811..D 7
Sister Bay ....483..E 16
Slinger .....1,022..I 4
Sobieski ....D 4
Soldiers Grove ......514..I 10
Solon Springs 598..B 8
Somers ....K 5
Somerset .....778..E 7
South Byron ....H 3
South Milwaukee ..23,297..J 5
South Range ....B 8
South Wayne .436..K 12
Sparta ......6,258.°H 10
Spencer ......1,181..F 11
Spooner ....2,444..D 8
Spread Eagle ....C 14
Spring Green 1,199..J 11
Spring Lake ....F 2
Spring Valley ......995..F 8
Springbrook ....C 9
Stanley ......2,049..F 10
Star Prairie ..362..E 7
Stephensville ......E 3
Stetsonville ....305..E 11
Steuben ......179..J 10
Stevens Point ....23,479.°G 12
Stiles ....C 4
Stitzer ....J 10
Stockbridge ...582..F 4
Stockholm .....99..G 7
Stoddard .....750..I 9
Stone Lake ....C 9
Stoughton ...6,096..J 2
Stratford ....1,239..F 11
Strum ....738..G 9
Sturgeon Bay 7,202.°F 16
Sturtevant ..3,376..K 5
Suamico ....D 4
Sugar Camp ....C 12
Sullivan ....467..J 3
Summit Lake ....E 13
Sun Prairie ..9,935..I 2
Superior ...32,237.°A 8
Superior* ....476..B 8
Suring ....499..E 14
Sussex ......2,758..I 4
Symco ....D 2
Taycheedah ....G 4
Taylor ....322..G 9
Tennyson .....402..K 10
Theresa ....611..H 3
Thiensville ..3,182..I 5
Thorp ....1,469..F 10
Three Lakes ....D 13
Tiffany ....K 2
Tigerton ....742..D 2
Tilleda ....C 2
Tipler ....C 14
Tisch Mills ....E 6
Token Creek ....I 1
Tomah ......6,621..H 10
Tomahawk ..3,419..D 12
Tony ....144..D 10
Townsend ....E 14
Trego ....C 8
Trempealeau ..743..H 9
Trevor ....K 15
Troy Center* ......K 14
Tunnel City ....H 10
Turtle Lake ..637..E 8
Tustin ....F 2
Twin Lakes .2,790..K 14
Two Rivers .13,243..F 6
Underhill ....C 4
Union Center .205..I 11
Union Grove 2,703..K 5
Unity ....363..F 11
Upson ....B 11
Valders ....821..F 5
Valley Junction ....H 11
Valmy ....F 16
Vandyne ....G 3
Verona .....2,334..J 1
Vesper ....355..G 11
Victory ....I 9
Viola ....659..I 10
Viroqua ....3,739.°I 10
Wabeno ....D 14
Waldo ....408..G 5
Waldwick ....K 11
Wales ....1,075..J 4
Walworth ...1,637..K 14
Warrens ....263..G 10
Wascott ....C 8
Washburn ..1,957.°B 10
Washington Island ....E 16
Waterford ...1,922..K 4
Waterloo ....2,253..I 2
Watertown .15,683..J 14
Waubeka ....H 5
Waukau ....F 3
Waukesha .39,695.°J 14
Waumandee ....G 8
Waunakee ...2,181..I 1
Waupaca ....4,342.°G 13
Waupun ....7,946..H 3
Wausau ...32,806.°F 12
Wausau West ......6,399..F 12
Wausaukee ....557..E 15
Wautoma ...1,624.°H 13
Wauwatosa 58,676..J 5
Wauzeka ......437..J 10
Wayne ....H 4
Wayside ....E 5
Webster ....502..C 7
Wentworth ....B 8
West Allis .71,649..J 5
West Baraboo .563..I 12
West Bend .16,555.°I 14
West La Crosse ....H 9
West Lima ....I 10
West Milwaukee* ..3,799..J 15
West Salem .2,180..H 9
Westboro ....E 11
Westby ....1,568..I 10
Westfield ....884..G 1
Weston* .....3,375..E 12
Weyauwega .1,377..E 2
Weyerhaeuser .285..D 9
Wheeler ....212..E 8
White Creek ....H 12
White Lake ...309..E 13
Whitefish Bay ......17,402..I 5
Whitehall ..1,486.°G 9
Whitelaw ......557..F 5
Whitewater 12,038..J 3
Whiting .....1,782..E 1
Wild Rose .....585..F 1
Willard ....F 10
Williams Bay ......1,554..K 3
Wilmot ....K 14
Wilson ....130..F 8
Wilton ....500..H 10
Winchester ....C 11
Winchester ....F 3
Wind Lake ....J 4
Wind Point .1,251..K 5
Windsor ....I 1
Winnebago ....F 3
Winneconne .1,611..F 3
Winter ....309..D 10
Wiota ....K 11
Wisconsin Dells .....2,419..I 12
Wisconsin Rapids ..18,134.°G 12
Withee ....480..F 10
Wittenberg ....895..C 2
Wonewoc ....835..I 11
Woodford ....K 12
Woodland ....H 3
Woodman ....102..J 10
Woodruff ....C 12
Woodville ....522..F 7
Woodworth ....K 5
Wrightstown 1,020..E 4
Wyalusing ....J 9
Wyeville ....203..H 11
Wyocena ......809..H 1
Yuba ....79..I 11
Zachow ....D 4
Zenda ....K 14

*Does not appear on the map; key shows general location.
°County seat.

Sources: Latest census figures (1970 and special censuses). Places without population figures are unincorporated areas and are not listed in census reports.

WISCONSIN /People

The 1970 United States census reported that Wisconsin had 4,417,933 persons. The population had increased 12 per cent over the 1960 figure, 3,951,777. The U.S. Bureau of the Census estimated that by 1975 the state's population had reached about 4,607,000.

About two-thirds of the people live in urban areas. Almost a third live in the metropolitan area of Milwaukee. The state has nine Standard Metropolitan Statistical Areas (see METROPOLITAN AREA). In addition, the Minneapolis-St. Paul, Minn. metropolitan area extends into Wisconsin. For the populations of these metropolitan areas, see the *Index* to the Wisconsin political map.

Milwaukee, Wisconsin's largest city, is a leading center of German-American culture in the United States. Milwaukee began as a fur-trading center. It is now known for its manufacturing, its brewing industry, its harbor on Lake Michigan, its fine restaurants, and its spirit of *gemütlichkeit* (a German word meaning *good fellowship*). The leading industry of Milwaukee is the manufacture of electrical equipment. The port of Milwaukee handles almost 7 million short tons (6.4 million metric tons) of freight each year.

Madison, the state capital, is Wisconsin's second largest city. It has one of the nation's most beautiful capitols. The granite dome of the Wisconsin Capitol towers 286 feet (87 meters) above Madison. Three lakes lie within the city and help make Madison one of the loveliest capital cities in the country. The oldest campus of the University of Wisconsin is in Madison.

Racine, Kenosha, and Green Bay, other large Wisconsin cities, are important manufacturing and shipping centers. Superior has one of the largest iron-ore docks in the world, and one of the largest grain elevators in the United States. See the articles on Wisconsin cities in the *Related Articles* at the end of this article.

About 97 of every 100 Wisconsinites were born in the United States. Most of those who were born in other lands came from Germany, Italy, Poland, Russia, and Yugoslavia. Church membership in Wisconsin is about evenly divided between the Protestant and Roman Catholic faiths. The largest Protestant groups include the Lutheran, United Church of Christ, United Methodist, and United Presbyterian.

Worker in a Wisconsin Paper Factory inspects huge sheets of paper. Wisconsin is a leading state in paper production.

Consolidated Papers, Inc.

Harmann Studios

Cheese Maker chops the curd before pressing it into molds. Wisconsin produces about 40 per cent of the nation's cheese.

Harmann Studios

Commercial Fishermen catch smelts as the fish spawn in spring. Fishing in Wisconsin's many lakes is also popular with sportsmen.

POPULATION

This map shows the *population density* of Wisconsin, and how it varies in different parts of the state. Population density means the average number of persons who live in a given area.

Persons per sq. mi.	Persons per km²
More than 150	More than 58
50 to 150	20 to 58
25 to 50	10 to 20
Less than 25	Less than 10

0   50   100 Miles
0   50 - 100   150 Kilometers

WORLD BOOK map

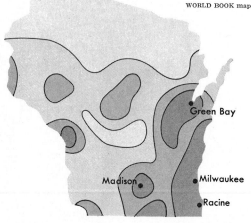

Green Bay

Madison

Milwaukee

Racine

Schools. Michael Frank, a newspaper editor in Southport (now Kenosha), led the movement for free schools in Wisconsin. In 1845, Southport established Wisconsin's first public school. The state Constitution, adopted in 1848, provided for a school fund to be used for free schooling of all children between the ages of 4 and 20. In 1856, Mrs. Carl Schurz opened the nation's first kindergarten in Watertown.

A 1911 Wisconsin law required all cities and towns with populations of 5,000 or more to establish vocational schools. This was the first law of its kind in the United States. Today, the Milwaukee Vocational School ranks as one of the largest trade schools in the United States. In 1891, the University of Wisconsin established one of the first correspondence schools in the nation.

Wisconsin's public schools are directed by the superintendent of public instruction, who is elected to a four-year term. Children aged 6 to 16 must attend school. For information on the number of students and teachers in Wisconsin, see EDUCATION (table).

Libraries. Wisconsin has about 350 public libraries, many of which make up the 13 regional library systems in the state. Wisconsin also has about 80 college and university libraries, and 330 other special libraries serving industry, institutions, and government. The State

Library, also known as the Law Library, was founded in Madison in 1836. State support for free public libraries began in 1872. A reference library for legislators is in the state Capitol. It was founded in 1901, and was the first library of its kind in the nation.

Today, the State Department of Public Instruction is responsible for the promotion and development of library service in the state. The largest libraries in the state are the Milwaukee Public Library and the University of Wisconsin Library in Madison. Each has more than two million books. The State Historical Society Library in Madison has one of the nation's largest collections of books, newspapers, and manuscripts on United States history.

Museums. The Milwaukee Public Museum owns a collection of prehistoric Indian tools, weapons, and other items. The Dard Hunter Paper Museum at the Institute of Paper Chemistry in Appleton traces the history of papermaking from its beginning in A.D. 105. Stonefield Village in Cassville has a museum that exhibits early farm tools. It has model shops of the village blacksmith, harness maker, and cobbler. The State Historical Society of Wisconsin in Madison has displays dealing with life in Wisconsin during the state's early days. The Milwaukee Art Center features sculptures, paintings, and etchings.

─────────────── UNIVERSITIES AND COLLEGES ───────────────

Wisconsin has 24 universities and colleges accredited by the North Central Association of Colleges and Schools. For enrollments and further information, see UNIVERSITIES AND COLLEGES (table).

Name	Location	Founded	Name	Location	Founded
Alverno College	Milwaukee	1887	Milwaukee School of Engineering	Milwaukee	1916
Beloit College	Beloit	1846	Mount Mary College	Milwaukee	1850
Cardinal Stritch College	Milwaukee	1937	Mount Senario College	Ladysmith	1962
Carroll College	Waukesha	1840	Northland College	Ashland	1892
Carthage College	Kenosha	1847	Ripon College	Ripon	1851
Edgewood College	Madison	1927	St. Francis de Sales College	Milwaukee	1856
Holy Redeemer College	Waterford	1968	St. Francis Seminary School of		
Lakeland College	Sheboygan	1862	Pastoral Ministry	Milwaukee	1856
Lawrence University	*	*	St. Norbert College	De Pere	1898
Marian College of Fond du Lac	Fond du Lac	1936	Silver Lake College		
Marquette University	Milwaukee	1864	of the Holy Family	Manitowoc	1935
Medical College of Wisconsin	Milwaukee	1913	Viterbo College	La Crosse	1931
Milton College	Milton	1867	Wisconsin, University of	*	*

*For campuses and founding dates, see UNIVERSITIES AND COLLEGES (table).

First U.S. Kindergarten, shown in a reconstruction, was founded by Mrs. Carl Schurz in Watertown in 1856 for the children of German immigrants.
Watertown Historical Society

WISCONSIN/A Visitor's Guide

Wisconsin's natural beauty has made the state a favorite playground of the nation. Tourists spend hundreds of millions of dollars in the state every year. Vacationists enjoy Wisconsin's sparkling lakes, rolling hills, quiet valleys, deep forests, and cool, pine-scented breezes. Hikers follow twisting trails through dark, beautiful woods. The thousands of lakes attract swimmers and boating enthusiasts. People fish for bass, muskies, salmon, and trout. Hunters bag bear, deer, rabbits, and game birds. Wisconsin winters are ideal for skating, skiing, snowmobiling, and tobogganing.

Goat Cart Ride at the Circus World Museum in Baraboo
William R. Wilson

William R. Wilson
Boating on the Wisconsin River near Wisconsin Dells

PLACES TO VISIT

Following are brief descriptions of some of Wisconsin's many interesting places to visit.

Apostle Islands, offshore from Bayfield, offer "deep-sea" fishing for huge lake trout. Anglers come from all parts of the country to try their luck.

Cave of the Mounds, between Mount Horeb and Blue Mounds, has hundreds of colorful stone formations. They hang from the ceiling and rise from the floor in the cavern's 14 rooms.

Circus World Museum, in Baraboo, has a large collection of equipment used by U.S. circuses. Displays include items used by the Ringling brothers, who started their world-famous circus in Baraboo in 1884. A small circus show is held in the summer.

House on the Rock is a 22-room home 11 miles (18 kilometers) north of Dodgeville. It sits atop a huge rock that rises 450 feet (137 meters). The house has six fireplaces, seven pools, and many antiques.

Little Norway, near Mount Horeb, was built in 1926. It resembles a tiny Norwegian village of the early 1800's. The 160-acre (65-hectare) tract has several picturesque houses. Rooms in the houses have Scandinavian-style furnishings. Isak Dahle, a Chicago businessman, hired Norwegian craftworkers to build the village.

Old World Wisconsin, near Eagle, is an outdoor museum that contains a number of houses and other structures built by Wisconsin immigrants of the 1800's.

Taliesin, near Spring Green, was the 200-acre (81-hectare) country estate of the architect Frank Lloyd Wright. During the summer months, visitors may tour the school Wright built to teach young architects.

Wisconsin Dells, in Adams, Columbia, Juneau, and Sauk counties, is one of the state's most beautiful regions. The Wisconsin River has cut a channel 7 miles (11 kilometers) long and 100 feet (30 meters) deep through soft sandstone. Weird formations have been carved out of the rock. They have such names as Devil's Elbow, Grand Piano, and Fat Man's Misery.

Parklands. The Ice Age National Scientific Reserve consists of several separate areas in southern and northwestern Wisconsin. The reserve is designed to preserve the features left on the land by the glaciers that once covered these parts of Wisconsin. The state also has a number of recreation areas managed by the National Park Service. For information on these areas, see the map and tables in the WORLD BOOK article on NATIONAL PARK SYSTEM.

National Forests. Wisconsin has two national forests, both established in 1933. Chequamegon National Forest lies in north-central Wisconsin. It has more than 170 lakes within its borders. Nicolet National Forest, in northeastern Wisconsin, has over 260 lakes. Both national forests offer hunting, fishing, and skiing. For the areas and chief features of these national forests, see NATIONAL FOREST (table).

State Parks and Forests. Wisconsin has 57 state parks and 9 state forests. It began developing its state park system in 1900. For information on the state parks and forests of Wisconsin, write to Wisconsin Department of Natural Resources, Box 7921, Madison, Wis. 53707.

Cave of the Mounds, Inc.

Cave of the Mounds near Blue Mounds

William R. Wilson

Annual Wilhelm Tell Drama in New Glarus

Taliesin, Frank Lloyd Wright's Home near Spring Green

Taliesin Associated Architects

Little Norway, a Village near Mount Horeb

William R. Wilson

ANNUAL EVENTS

A popular annual event in Wisconsin is the crowning of "Alice in Dairyland." The crowning is held in a different Wisconsin city each year during June, which is Dairy Month in the state. At that time, a Wisconsin girl is selected to reign for one year as the symbol of the state's main agricultural activity. During the year, she makes public appearances throughout the United States.

Many communities in Wisconsin stage curling matches during the winter months, and others hold snowmobile derbies. Winnebago Indians perform colorful ceremonial dances at the Wisconsin Dells every evening from late June to September 10.

Other annual events in Wisconsin include the following.

January-March: Ski-jumping tournaments in Middleton and Westby (January and February); World Championship Snowmobile Derby in Eagle River (January).

April-June: Syttende Mai Norwegian Festival in Stoughton and Westby (May); Fyr Bal Fest in Ephraim (June); Heidi Festival in New Glarus (June).

July-September: Summerfest in Milwaukee (July); Sports car races at Road America near Elkhart Lake (July); Holland Festival in Cedar Grove (July); Lumberjack World Championship in Hayward (July); Cherry Harvest in Door County (July); Scandinavian Festival on Washington Island (August); Wisconsin State Fair in Milwaukee (August); Musky Jamboree in Boulder Junction (August).

October-December: World Dairy Exposition in Madison (October); Fall Festival in Sister Bay (October); Holiday Folk Fair in Milwaukee (November).

Wisconsin is a land of rolling hills, ridges, fertile plains and valleys, and beautiful lakes. A series of glaciers that began about a million years ago traveled over most of present-day Wisconsin. The glaciers scraped hilltops, filled in valleys, and changed most of the surface. As the ice melted and the glaciers wasted away, they left thick deposits of earth materials. These deposits blocked drainage of the water, causing lakes, marshes, and streams with falls and rapids. Glaciers do not appear to have touched southwestern Wisconsin. Much of this area is rough, with steep-sided ridges and deep valleys.

Land Regions. Wisconsin has five major land regions. They are (1) the Lake Superior Lowland, (2) the Superior Upland, or Northern Highland, (3) the Central Plain, (4) the Western Upland, and (5) the Great Lakes Plains, or Eastern Ridges and Lowlands.

The Lake Superior Lowland is a flat plain that slopes gently upward toward the south from Lake Superior. The plain ends from 5 to 20 miles (8 to 32 kilometers) inland at a steep cliff.

The Superior Upland covers most of northern Wisconsin. It slopes gradually downward toward the south. The region is a favorite vacationland because of its heavily forested hills and hundreds of small lakes. Timms Hill, the state's highest point, rises 1,952 feet (595 meters) above sea level in Price County.

The Central Plain curves across the central part of the state. Glaciers covered the eastern and northwestern parts of this region. Much of the southern portion was not touched by glaciers. In this southern portion, the Wisconsin River has carved the scenic gorge called the Wisconsin Dells.

The Western Upland is one of the most attractive parts of Wisconsin. Steep slopes and winding ridges, untouched by glaciers, rise in the southwestern part of the region. Limestone and sandstone bluffs of breathtaking beauty stand along the Mississippi River.

The Great Lakes Plains region extends from the Green Bay area southward to Illinois. Gently rolling plains of glacial material partly cover limestone ridges that run from north to south. This region is the richest agricultural section of Wisconsin. It has the state's largest areas of high-grade soil, and its longest growing season.

Shoreline of Wisconsin extends 381 miles (613 kilometers) along Lake Michigan and 292 miles (470 kilometers) along Lake Superior. Bluffs and sandy beaches line the Lake Michigan shore. Lake Superior's shoreline also has sandy beaches, but fewer rugged bluffs. Wisconsin's largest ports include Ashland, Green Bay, Manitowoc, Milwaukee, and Superior.

Rivers, Waterfalls, and Lakes. An east-west *divide* cuts across northern Wisconsin. This ridge of land separates short rivers that enter Lake Superior—such as the Bad, Montreal, and Nemadji rivers—from the longer rivers that flow southward—such as the Flambeau and St. Croix. A north-south divide runs down the eastern third of the state. West of this divide, the rivers flow into the Mississippi. These rivers include the Black, Chippewa, La Crosse, St. Croix, and Wisconsin. Streams east of the divide empty into Lake Michigan directly or through Green Bay. These rivers include the Fox, Menominee, Milwaukee, Oconto, and Peshtigo.

Wisconsin has hundreds of waterfalls. The highest is Big Manitou Falls in Pattison State Park, in the ex-

Land Regions of Wisconsin

LAKE SUPERIOR LOWLANDS
St. Croix R.
SUPERIOR UPLAND
Wisconsin R.
CENTRAL
Black R.
PLAIN
Mississippi R.
WESTERN
UPLAND
GREAT LAKES PLAINS

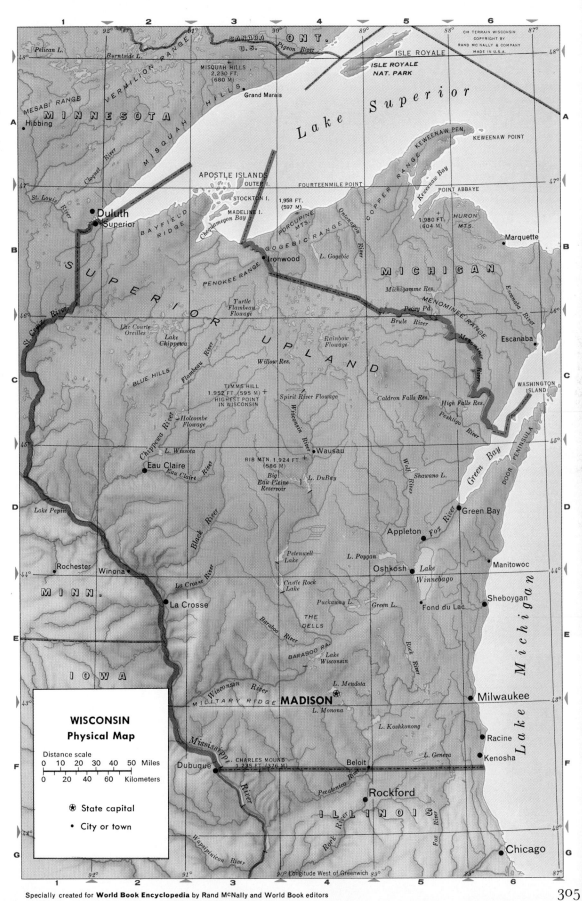

WISCONSIN

Physical Map

Distance scale

| 0 | 10 | 20 | 30 | 40 | 50 | Miles |

| 0 | 20 | 40 | 60 | Kilometers |

⊛ State capital

• City or town

Specially created for **World Book Encyclopedia** by Rand McNally and World Book editors

305

WISCONSIN

treme northwest. The falls, located on the Black River, drop more than 165 feet (50 meters).

Wisconsin has over 8,000 lakes. Lake Winnebago, the state's largest lake, covers 215 square miles (557 square kilometers). Green Lake, more than 237 feet (72 meters) deep, is the deepest lake. Other large natural lakes include Butte des Morts, Geneva, Koshkonong, Mendota, Pepin, Poygan, Puckaway, and Shawano. The chief man-made lakes include Beaver Dam, Castle Rock, Chippewa, Du Bay, Flambeau, Petenwell, Wisconsin, and Wissota.

George P. Koshallek, Jr., *Milwaukee Journal*

Clarence P. Schmidt, *Milwaukee Journal*

Kettle Lakes Dot Wisconsin, *above.* Glaciers once covered part of the Central Plain region. After they retreated, blocks of buried ice that were left behind melted and formed these lakes.

Holstein Dairy Cattle graze in hilly pastures in southern Wisconsin, *below.* The Great Lakes Plains region is Wisconsin's richest dairy-farm land. It has the state's longest crop-growing season.

J. C. Allen and Son

Dundee Mountain, *left,* in Kettle Moraine State Forest is one of the many interesting geological formations in the Great Lakes Plains region. The mountain was created by a glacier.

Thomas P. Lake

Sparkling Water races over Little Falls on the Flambeau River. Lakes and rivers in the Superior Upland region attract thousands of vacationers to Wisconsin every year.

WISONSIN / Climate

Wisconsin usually has warm summers and long, severe winters. Lake Michigan and Lake Superior make summers somewhat cooler and winters slightly milder along the shores. Average January temperatures range from 12° F. (−11° C) in the northwest to 22° F. (−6° C) in the southeast. Danbury recorded the state's lowest temperature, −54° F. (−48° C), on Jan. 24, 1922. Average July temperatures range from 69° F. (21° C) in the north to 73° F. (23° C) in the south. Wisconsin Dells set the state's record high, 114° F. (46° C), on July 13, 1936. Annual *precipitation* (rain, melted snow, and other forms of moisture) averages about 30 inches (76 centimeters). Annual snowfall averages from over 100 inches (250 centimeters) in northern Iron County to about 30 inches (76 centimeters) in southern Wisconsin.

Hagedorn Studios

Warm Summer Sun brings many visitors to the beaches in Peninsula State Park. The park covers part of the western shore of Door County peninsula, one of Wisconsin's popular resort areas.

SEASONAL TEMPERATURES

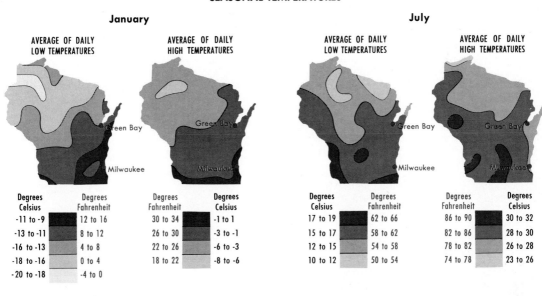

January

AVERAGE OF DAILY LOW TEMPERATURES

AVERAGE OF DAILY HIGH TEMPERATURES

Degrees Celsius	Degrees Fahrenheit
-11 to -9	12 to 16
-13 to -11	8 to 12
-16 to -13	4 to 8
-18 to -16	0 to 4
-20 to -18	-4 to 0

Degrees Fahrenheit	Degrees Celsius
30 to 34	-1 to 1
26 to 30	-3 to -1
22 to 26	-6 to -3
18 to 22	-8 to -6

July

AVERAGE OF DAILY LOW TEMPERATURES

AVERAGE OF DAILY HIGH TEMPERATURES

Degrees Celsius	Degrees Fahrenheit
17 to 19	62 to 66
15 to 17	58 to 62
12 to 15	54 to 58
10 to 12	50 to 54

Degrees Fahrenheit	Degrees Celsius
86 to 90	30 to 32
82 to 86	28 to 30
78 to 82	26 to 28
74 to 78	23 to 26

AVERAGE YEARLY PRECIPITATION
(Rain, Melted Snow and Other Moisture)

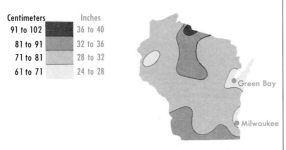

Centimeters	Inches
91 to 102	36 to 40
81 to 91	32 to 36
71 to 81	28 to 32
61 to 71	24 to 28

```
0    50   100        200 Miles
0      100   200   300 Kilometers
```

WORLD BOOK maps

AVERAGE MONTHLY WEATHER

	MILWAUKEE					GREEN BAY			
	Temperatures				Days of	Temperatures				Days of
	F°		C°		Rain or	F°		C°		Rain or
	High	Low	High	Low	Snow	High	Low	High	Low	Snow
JAN.	29	15	-2	-9	10	25	8	-4	-13	10
FEB.	32	17	0	-8	9	26	9	-3	-13	9
MAR.	41	26	5	-3	11	37	20	3	-7	11
APR.	53	36	12	2	11	52	32	11	0	11
MAY	64	45	18	7	13	65	44	18	7	12
JUNE	75	55	24	13	11	75	54	24	12	11
JULY	81	61	27	16	9	81	59	27	15	10
AUG.	79	61	26	16	9	79	57	26	14	10
SEPT.	72	53	22	12	8	70	50	21	10	9
OCT.	60	42	16	6	8	58	39	14	4	8
NOV.	45	30	7	-1	10	41	26	5	-3	9
DEC.	33	19	1	-7	10	27	13	-3	-11	11

Natural Resources of Wisconsin include rich soil, plentiful water, minerals, vast forests, and abundant plant and animal life.

Soil. Southeastern, southern, and western Wisconsin are the state's best agricultural areas. These areas have mostly gray-brown forest soils. They also have scattered sections of dark prairie soils. In northern Wisconsin, soils are less fertile and often contain too much acid.

Water. Wisconsin has 1,690 square miles (4,377 square kilometers) of inland water in addition to its outlying waters of Lake Michigan and Lake Superior. These two Great Lakes and the Mississippi River provide inexpensive transportation. Wisconsin's thousands of lakes help make the state a popular vacationland. Rainfall is abundant, and little of the state's vast water resources is needed for irrigation.

Minerals. Almost every Wisconsin county has sand and gravel. Stone, including dolomite and granite, is also valuable. Dolomite is found mainly in the southern part of the state and granite in the central and northern sections. Iron ore is found in Jackson County, and there are large deposits also in Ashland and Iron counties. Deposits of lead and zinc are found in Grant, Iowa, and Lafayette counties. Sulfide deposits containing large amounts of copper and zinc are in Forest, Oneida, and Rusk counties. The sulfide deposits at Crandon in Forest County are believed to include one of the five largest supplies of zinc ever discovered in North America. Other minerals include basalt, clay, peat, quartzite, sandstone and silica sand, and shale.

Forests cover almost half the state. Hardwood trees make up about 80 per cent of the forests. Most of the woodlands in Wisconsin have second-growth trees. The most valuable hardwoods include ash, aspen, basswood, elm, maple, oak, and yellow birch. Softwoods include balsam fir, hemlock, pine, spruce, tamarack, and white cedar.

Other Plant Life. Blueberries, huckleberries, Juneberries, wild black currants, and other shrubs grow in parts of northern and central Wisconsin. Pink trailing arbutus blossoms over rocks and under trees in early spring. More than 20 kinds of violets bloom in all sections. In autumn, the Wisconsin countryside is a blaze of color. The red and gold tree leaves blend with brilliant asters, fireweeds, and goldenrods.

Animal Life. In Wisconsin's deep forests, hunters trail bears, coyotes, deer, and foxes. Fur trappers snare beavers and muskrats. Badgers, Wisconsin's state animal, gophers, and prairie mice scurry through the underbrush. Other animals include chipmunks, porcupines, raccoons, and woodchucks.

Wisconsin is a delight for fishing enthusiasts. The northern lakes and streams abound with such game fish as bass, muskellunge, pickerel, pike, sturgeon, and trout. The muskellunge is the state fish.

Hunters shoot duck, geese, jacksnipes, partridges, pheasants, ruffed grouse, and woodcocks. Loons and other waterfowl breed on the northern lakes. The marshes shelter bitterns, black terns, and coots. Other birds found in Wisconsin include chickadees, nuthatches, snipes, swallows, warblers, and wrens. The robin is Wisconsin's state bird.

Manufacturing accounts for 82 per cent of the value of all goods produced in Wisconsin. Goods manufactured in the state have a *value added by manufacture* of about $13 billion yearly. This figure represents the value created in products by Wisconsin's industries, not counting such costs as materials, supplies, and fuel. Wisconsin's chief manufactured products, in order of importance, are: (1) nonelectric machinery, (2) food products, (3) fabricated metal products, (4) transportation equipment, and (5) paper products.

Nonelectric Machinery produced in Wisconsin has a value added of about $3 billion yearly. Wisconsin ranks high among the states in the manufacture of nonelectric machinery. This machinery includes engines and turbines, farm machinery, power cranes and other construction equipment, machine tools, and metalworking machinery. Most of the factories are in the Milwaukee area and in other southeastern cities.

Food Products have a value added of about $2 billion annually. Wisconsin produces more milk than any other state. Its cheese factories make about 40 per cent of the cheese produced in the United States. Wisconsin also ranks high among the states in the production of butter, ice cream, and evaporated and dried milk. Plants that process dairy products are located throughout most of the state. Cudahy, Green Bay, and Madison have large meat-packing plants. Factories in Clyman, Green Bay,

Production of Goods in Wisconsin

Total value of goods produced in 1975—$15,885,660,000

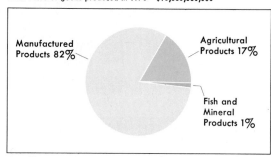

Manufactured Products 82%

Agricultural Products 17%

Fish and Mineral Products 1%

Percentages are based on farm income, value added by manufacture, and value of fish and mineral production. Fish products are less than 1 per cent.

Sources: U.S. government publications, 1976-1977.

Employment in Wisconsin

Total number of persons employed in 1976—1,922,300

	Number of Employees
Manufacturing	512,300
Wholesale & Retail Trade	389,500
Community, Social, & Personal Services	306,400
Government	288,600
Agriculture	198,000
Transportation & Public Utilities	82,200
Finance, Insurance, & Real Estate	77,200
Construction & Mining	68,100

Sources: *Employment and Earnings,* September 1977, U.S. Bureau of Labor Statistics; *Farm Labor,* February 1977, U.S. Dept. of Agriculture.

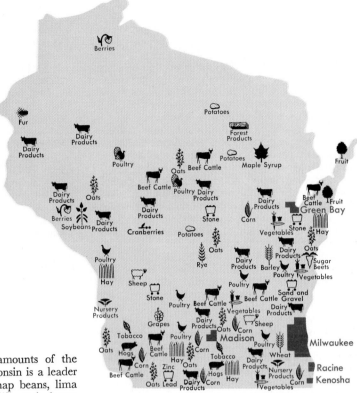

FARM, MINERAL, AND FOREST PRODUCTS

This map shows where the state's leading farm, mineral, and forest products are produced. The major urban areas (shown on the map in red) are the state's important manufacturing centers.

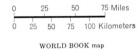

WORLD BOOK map

Lomira, and other cities can huge amounts of the state's vegetable and fruit crops. Wisconsin is a leader in canning peas, sweet corn, beets, snap beans, lima beans, cranberries, and sour cherries. Wisconsin brews more beer than any other state. The largest breweries are in Milwaukee, which has been nicknamed the *Beer Capital* of the United States.

Fabricated Metal Products have a value added of about $1,290,000,000 a year. The chief products include cutlery and hardware, metal cans, and metal forgings and stampings. The leading production centers include Manitowoc, Milwaukee, and Racine.

Transportation Equipment has a value added of about $1,230,000,000 yearly. The industry's chief products are automobiles, truck and bus bodies, and ships and boats. Wisconsin is a leader among the states in automobile manufacturing. The state's major transportation equipment centers are Kenosha, Milwaukee, Racine, and Winnebago counties. The cities of Janesville and Kenosha are centers for automobile production.

Paper Products have a value added of about $1,220,-000,000 yearly. The leading paper-producing areas are in the lower Fox River Valley and the upper Wisconsin River Valley. Wisconsin mills produce about 6 per cent of the nation's paper supply. Wisconsin ranks among the leading states in the value of paper and paperboard production. Mills in the state also manufacture paper boxes, tissue paper, heavy wrapping paper, cardboard, and other items.

Other Leading Industries. The production of electric and electronic equipment is the state's sixth-ranking industry. The largest factories that manufacture electric and electronic equipment are in Milwaukee and other cities along Lake Michigan. Electric equipment produced in Wisconsin includes household appliances and electric motors. Industries in the state also make

chemicals and related products, lumber and wood products, primary metals, printed materials, rubber and plastics products, and stone, clay, and glass products.

Agriculture. Wisconsin's farm income totals about $2¾ billion yearly. This is 17 per cent of the value of all goods produced in the state. Wisconsin has about 89,000 farms. They average about 197 acres (80 hectares) in size. Wisconsin farms cover a total of about 18 million acres (7 million hectares).

Dairying is the most important type of farming in Wisconsin. The dairy industry started about 1870. It was encouraged through the efforts of many people, especially William Dempster Hoard. Hoard helped organize the Wisconsin Dairymen's Association in 1872. The association did much to improve and promote Wisconsin dairy products. Later, it urged farmers to work together and to market their products cooperatively. Today, more than 500 farm cooperatives have headquarters in Wisconsin (see COOPERATIVE).

Dairy Products provide the chief source of farm income. They account for about $1½ billion yearly. Since about 1912, Wisconsin has led the nation in the value of dairy products. The state has about 2½ million dairy cattle. They produce about 2 billion gallons (7.6 billion liters) of milk yearly.

Meat Animals account for about $480 million annually in farm income. Most of the beef cattle and hogs raised in Wisconsin are sent to meat-packing plants in Cudahy, Green Bay, Madison, and Milwaukee.

Field Crops. Farmers in all regions of the state raise hay for livestock feed. Corn is fed to hogs, and oats, hay,

306c

and corn are fed to cattle. Other field crops raised by Wisconsin farmers include barley, soybeans, tobacco, and wheat.

Vegetables and Fruits. Wisconsin leads the states in the production of beets, green peas, snap beans, and sweet corn. It is also a chief producer of cabbages, carrots, and lima beans. Other vegetables produced in Wisconsin include cucumbers, lettuce, onions, and potatoes. Cherries and apples thrive in Door County. Wisconsin farmers also raise raspberries, strawberries, and other small fruits. Wisconsin grows more cranberries than any other state.

Other Farm Products include poultry and eggs. Some Wisconsin farmers keep honeybees. Wisconsin is one of the nation's leading producers of honey. Farmers also sell beeswax for use in making candles, lipstick, and other items. Wisconsin has many mink ranches and raises more minks than any other state.

Mining. Wisconsin was one of the major lead-producing states in the mid-1800's. Today, the principal product from the lead mines is zinc, with some lead as a by-product. Iron ore is mined in Jackson County. Sand, gravel, and stone for construction are Wisconsin's most valuable mineral products.

Electric Power. Coal and other fuels produce 62 per cent of the state's electric power. Nuclear power plants generate 33 per cent, and hydroelectric power plants produce the rest. Wisconsin's largest power plants have been built along Lake Michigan and the Mississippi River. One of the first hydroelectric power plants in the United States was built in Appleton on the Fox River in 1882.

Transportation. Many of Wisconsin's first settlers traveled up the Mississippi River in flat-bottomed boats called *bateaux.* Later settlers came by steamboat up the Mississippi, by ship on Lake Michigan, and overland by wagon. Mississippi River traffic declined with the growth of railroads. Great Lakes transportation increased following the opening of the St. Lawrence Seaway in 1959.

The first railroad in Wisconsin was opened in 1851. It ran between Milwaukee and Waukesha, a distance of about 20 miles (32 kilometers). Today, about 6,000 miles (9,700 kilometers) of railway track cross the state. Twelve railroads provide freight service. Passenger trains serve about 10 Wisconsin cities. Wisconsin has about 300 airports. Airlines serve Green Bay, Madison, Milwaukee, and other large cities.

Wisconsin has over 100,000 miles (160,000 kilometers) of roads and highways. About 95 per cent are surfaced. In 1917, Wisconsin became the first state to adopt the number system for highways. Other states soon adopted the system.

Milwaukee, a major Great Lakes port, exports dairy products, flour, grain, iron and steel scrap, machinery, and other products. Ocean-going ships also dock at Green Bay, Kenosha, Manitowoc, Sheboygan, and Superior. Green Bay, Milwaukee, and Superior receive and distribute much of the coal used in Wisconsin and Minnesota. A car ferry service operates across Lake Michigan between the Wisconsin cities of Kewaunee, Manitowoc, and Milwaukee, and the Michigan cities of Frankfort, Ludington, and Muskegon. A canal located at Sturgeon Bay links Green Bay and Lake Michigan.

Communication. Wisconsin's first newspaper, the *Green-Bay Intelligencer,* was founded in 1833. Today, Wisconsin publishers issue about 275 newspapers, of which almost 40 are dailies. Daily newspapers with the largest circulations include the *Green Bay Press Gazette,* the *Milwaukee Journal,* the *Milwaukee Sentinel,* and the *Wisconsin State Journal* of Madison. Wisconsin publishers also issue about 185 periodicals.

In 1853, the Wisconsin Press Association was founded. It was the nation's first state news service. The association, now the Wisconsin Newspaper Association, collects and distributes news among member newspapers. It has a membership of about 240 weekly papers and 37 dailies.

The history of radio in Wisconsin dates from 1909. That year, University of Wisconsin scientists conducted wireless experiments. The university station was licensed as 9XM in 1916, and became WHA in 1922. The state's first television station, WTMJ-TV, started broadcasting from Milwaukee in 1947. Wisconsin now has about 225 radio stations and about 20 television stations.

WISCONSIN /History

Indian Days. The Winnebago, Dakota, and Menominee Indians lived in the Wisconsin region when the first white explorers came in the early 1600's. These Indians were skilled craftworkers. They lived in lodges made of bark, saplings, and rushes. They fished and hunted, and grew corn, beans, and squash. The Winnebago lived in the area between Green Bay and Lake Winnebago. The Dakota lived in the northwest. The Menominee lived west and north of Green Bay.

Many other tribes moved into the Wisconsin area during the later 1600's. Some had been driven from their eastern homes by white people. Others fled into the region to escape the warring Iroquois nation. The Chippewa came from the northeast and settled along the southern shore of Lake Superior. Other tribes came from the Michigan region. The Sauk settled west of Green Bay, the Fox along the Fox River, and the Ottawa along the southern shore of Lake Superior. The Kickapoo made their home in the south-central area, and the Huron in the northwestern section. Bands of Miami and Illinois Indians spread along the upper Fox River. The Potawatomi camped in what is now Door County. See INDIAN, AMERICAN (Table of Tribes).

Exploration and Settlement. In 1634, the French explorer Jean Nicolet became the first white person to set foot in the Wisconsin area. He landed on the shore of Green Bay while seeking a water route to China. Nicolet stepped ashore wearing a colorful robe and firing two pistols. He was disappointed when Winnebago Indians, not Chinese officials, greeted him. Nicolet returned to

HISTORIC WISCONSIN

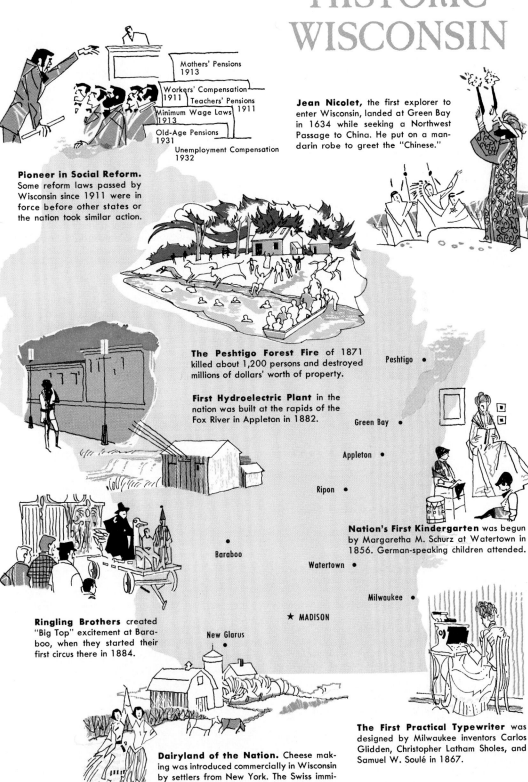

Mothers' Pensions 1913

Workers' Compensation 1911

Teachers' Pensions 1911

Minimum Wage Laws 1913

Old-Age Pensions 1931

Unemployment Compensation 1932

Pioneer in Social Reform. Some reform laws passed by Wisconsin since 1911 were in force before other states or the nation took similar action.

Jean Nicolet, the first explorer to enter Wisconsin, landed at Green Bay in 1634 while seeking a Northwest Passage to China. He put on a mandarin robe to greet the "Chinese."

The Peshtigo Forest Fire of 1871 killed about 1,200 persons and destroyed millions of dollars' worth of property.

First Hydroelectric Plant in the nation was built at the rapids of the Fox River in Appleton in 1882.

Peshtigo •

Green Bay •

Appleton •

Ripon •

Baraboo •

Watertown •

Milwaukee •

★ MADISON

New Glarus •

Nation's First Kindergarten was begun by Margaretha M. Schurz at Watertown in 1856. German-speaking children attended.

Ringling Brothers created "Big Top" excitement at Baraboo, when they started their first circus there in 1884.

Dairyland of the Nation. Cheese making was introduced commercially in Wisconsin by settlers from New York. The Swiss immigrants who settled New Glarus in 1845 also helped develop the Wisconsin dairy industry.

The First Practical Typewriter was designed by Milwaukee inventors Carlos Glidden, Christopher Latham Sholes, and Samuel W. Soulé in 1867.

New France (Quebec), and reported that America was far vaster than anyone had imagined.

About 25 years later, Pierre Esprit Radisson and Médard Chouart, Sieur des Groseilliers, explored the Wisconsin area while searching for furs. The first missionary to the Wisconsin Indians, Father René Ménard, arrived about 1660. He established a Roman Catholic mission near present-day Ashland. Father Claude Jean Allouez came to Wisconsin about 1665 and set up several missions. With the help of Father Louis André, he established a center for missionary work on the site of present-day De Pere. Other French explorers and missionaries who visited the area included Louis Joliet, Father Jacques Marquette, and Robert Cavelier, Sieur de la Salle.

Struggle for Control. From the time of Nicolet's visit, the French had friendly relations with most of the Wisconsin Indian tribes. But in 1712, a long war broke out between the French and the Fox Indians. Both wanted control of the Fox and Wisconsin rivers, the region's chief water route. After many bloody battles, the French finally defeated the Fox in 1740. But the long war had weakened France's defenses in the region. France also lost the friendship of many former Indian allies.

In 1754, the French and Indian War began. This war was fought between Great Britain and France over rival claims in America. Britain won the war. Under the terms of the 1763 Treaty of Paris, France lost Canada and almost all its possessions east of the Mississippi

River. Control of the Wisconsin region thus passed to the British. See FRENCH AND INDIAN WARS (The French and Indian War).

English fur traders took over the fur-trading posts of the French. In 1774, the British passed the Quebec Act. Under this act, Wisconsin became part of the province of Quebec. The Quebec Act was one of the causes of the revolt by the American colonies against Britain in 1775. The 1783 Treaty of Paris ended the American Revolutionary War. Under the treaty, Britain gave up all its territory east of the Mississippi and south of the Great Lakes. The Wisconsin region then became part of the United States.

Territorial Days. Wisconsin formed part of the Indiana Territory from 1800 to 1809, part of the Illinois Territory from 1809 to 1818, and part of the Michigan Territory from 1818 to 1836. Settlement of southwestern Wisconsin began during the 1820's. This region had rich deposits of lead ore. In the 1820's, the demand for lead for use in making paint and shot rose sharply. Lead miners from nearby states and territories poured into the region, and the population boomed. Some of the miners lived in shelters they dug out of the hillsides. These miners were nicknamed *Badgers*, which, in time, became the nickname of all Wisconsinites.

The Indians made their last stand in Wisconsin against white people in the Black Hawk War of 1832. The Sauk Indians of northwestern Illinois had been pushed across the Mississippi River into Iowa by the arrival of white settlers. Black Hawk, a Sauk leader, wanted to return to his homeland and grow corn. In April, 1832, he led a thousand Indians back across the Mississippi. The white settlers panicked, and volunteer militiamen and regular troops were called out. Black Hawk's Indians retreated into Wisconsin, where several bloody battles were fought. When the war ended in August, only about 150 Indians were left.

On April 20, 1836, Congress created the Wisconsin Territory. The territorial legislature met temporarily in Belmont and later in Burlington (now in Iowa). The first meeting in Madison, the capital of the territory and later of the state, took place in 1838. The Wisconsin Territory included parts of present-day Minnesota, Iowa, and North and South Dakota. President Andrew Jackson appointed Henry Dodge as the first territorial governor. Congress created the Iowa Territory in 1838. Wisconsin's western boundary then became the Mississippi River, with a northward extension to Lake of the Woods in present-day Minnesota. About a third of the present state of Minnesota remained part of Wisconsin until 1848.

Statehood. Wisconsin joined the Union as the 30th state on May 29, 1848. Its boundaries were set as they are today. The people had already approved a constitution. They elected Nelson Dewey, a Democrat, as the first governor. In 1840, 30,945 white persons lived in Wisconsin. By 1850, the population had soared to 305,391. Newcomers came from other parts of the United States and from other countries. All saw opportunities for a better life in frontier Wisconsin.

In 1854, Wisconsin citizens became aroused over the introduction of the Kansas-Nebraska Bill in Congress. This bill was designed to allow the new territories of Kansas and Nebraska to decide for themselves whether they wished to permit slavery. Most Wisconsinites op-

---

———— IMPORTANT DATES IN WISCONSIN ————

1634 Jean Nicolet, a French explorer, landed on the Green Bay shore.

c. 1670 Fathers Claude Jean Allouez and Louis André founded a missionary center at De Pere.

1673 Louis Joliet and Father Jacques Marquette traveled through the Wisconsin region.

1740 The French defeated the Fox Indians.

1763 England received the Wisconsin region from France under terms of the Treaty of Paris.

1783 Wisconsin became part of the United States.

1836 Congress created the Wisconsin Territory.

1848 Wisconsin became the 30th state on May 29.

1871 About 1,200 persons were killed in a forest fire that destroyed Peshtigo and nearby villages and spread into Michigan.

1872 William D. Hoard and others organized the Wisconsin Dairymen's Association.

1901 Robert M. La Follette, Sr., became governor, and the Progressive era began.

1911 The state legislature set up a teachers' pension, established a commission to settle labor disputes, and passed other progressive legislation.

1924 Robert M. La Follette, Sr., was defeated as the Progressive party candidate for U.S. President.

1932 Wisconsin passed the first state unemployment-compensation act.

1958 Wisconsin voters elected their first Democratic governor, Gaylord Nelson, since 1932.

1964 Wisconsin became the first state to have its legislative districts reapportioned by its supreme court.

1971 The state legislature created a state university system—the University of Wisconsin System.

posed slavery and did not want it extended to new territories. A group of Wisconsinites held a protest meeting against the bill in Ripon in February, 1854. This meeting contributed to the development of the Republican party. See KANSAS-NEBRASKA ACT.

The Republican party quickly became a powerful force in the North. Wisconsin's first Republican governor, Coles Bashford, took office in 1856. For the next hundred years, except for brief periods, the Republicans controlled the state government.

During the Civil War (1861-1865), Wisconsin generals at various times commanded the Iron Brigade, one of the Union's outstanding fighting groups. The brigade consisted largely of Wisconsin regiments.

In 1871, Wisconsin was struck by the worst natural disaster in its history—the great Peshtigo forest fire. The summer and fall of 1871 were extremely dry, and many small fires broke out at various places in northeastern Wisconsin. Then, on the night of October 8, northeastern Wisconsin erupted in flame. The fire wiped out the town of Peshtigo and several villages. The fire also spread into Michigan. About 1,200 persons were killed —900 more than the number of persons killed in the Great Chicago Fire, which occurred that same night. The fire destroyed more than $5 million worth of property.

The Progressive Era. During the 1890's, a split developed in the Republican party in Wisconsin. The party had been controlled by political bosses who represented lumber and railroad interests. Robert M. La Follette, Sr., a Madison lawyer and former U.S. Congressman, began to lead a movement to overthrow the rule by bosses.

La Follette won the Wisconsin governorship in 1900.

He was re-elected in 1902 and 1904. Under "Battling Bob," the state made important social, political, and economic reforms. La Follette's program was called *Progressivism.* La Follette set up a "brain trust" of University of Wisconsin professors and experts on government to advise him on state problems. The brain trust was part of the "Wisconsin Idea." This was the theory that the state should be served by its best minds and its best experts in legislation and administration. Measures adopted under La Follette included an inheritance tax, a railroad property tax, regulation of railroad rates and service, and a direct primary law (see PRIMARY ELECTION). La Follette entered the U.S. Senate in 1906 and served there until 1925. See LA FOLLETTE (Robert Marion La Follette, Sr.).

In 1911, Wisconsin established a commission to settle labor disputes and to enforce labor laws. That same year, the legislature set up a teachers' pension. It also passed a workers' compensation law and model laws for the incorporation of cooperatives. Minimum-wage laws for women and minors, and pensions for mothers were adopted in 1913. In 1921, Wisconsin granted full civil and property rights to women.

In 1924, La Follette ran for President as the Progressive party candidate. President Calvin Coolidge, a Republican, won the election. La Follette received the electoral votes of only one state—Wisconsin. But he got almost 5 million popular votes. La Follette died in 1925, and his eldest son, Robert, Jr., was elected to fill his Senate seat. Young La Follette served in the Senate for 21 years.

Wisconsin's First Capitol, *left,* was in Belmont. The territorial legislature met in this building for a 46-day session in 1836 to decide on a permanent capital.

State Historical Society of Wisconsin

State Historical Society of Wisconsin

The Treaty of Butte des Morts was signed on this site in Winnebago County on Aug. 11, 1827. The treaty adjusted the boundaries of the territories of the Chippewa, Menominee, and Winnebago Indians in Wisconsin.

The 1930's.

In 1930, Philip F. La Follette, the youngest son of Robert M. La Follette, Sr., was elected governor. La Follette, a Republican, lost the governorship in 1932. But he was re-elected in 1934 and 1936 as a Progressive. Much of the legislation enacted under La Follette sought to relieve the suffering caused by the Great Depression of the 1930's. In 1932, under his administration, the first state unemployment-compensation act was passed.

In the spring of 1938, La Follette tried to organize a new national third party, the National Progressives of America. But he won little support. The voters rejected La Follette in 1938 and elected Julius P. Heil, a Republican, to the governorship. Heil worked to cut government costs. He did away with many agencies that La Follette had set up. Heil was re-elected in 1940.

The Mid-1900's.

After World War II (1939-1945), Wisconsin agriculture, long the state's top-ranking industry, began to decline in importance to the economy. At the same time, the importance of manufacturing increased. Heavy beef imports from other countries, in addition to low milk prices, hurt agriculture in the state. Changes in the American diet, with emphasis on low-calorie foods, lowered the demand for dairy products. Between 1951 and 1969, the number of Wisconsin dairy farms fell from about 132,000 to 63,000. A number of cheese factories, creameries, and other processing plants closed. Many small farms merged, and the use of farm machinery increased. All these changes reduced the need for farmworkers in Wisconsin, and the population began to shift from farms to cities.

In politics, La Follette Progressivism declined. After 21 years in the U.S. Senate, Robert M. La Follette, Jr., lost the 1946 primary election to Republican Joseph R. McCarthy. McCarthy won election to the Senate that year and later became one of the most controversial figures in American politics.

After 26 years of Republican or Progressive control of the state government, Democrat Gaylord A. Nelson won the governorship in 1958. He was re-elected in 1960. In 1962, Nelson ran for the U.S. Senate and defeated Republican Alexander Wiley, who had been a senator since 1939. Nelson won re-election in 1968.

In 1962, Wisconsin voters elected another Democratic governor, John W. Reynolds. But in 1964, they chose Republican Warren P. Knowles. Knowles was re-elected in 1966 and 1968. Also in 1964, the voters elected Bronson La Follette, grandson of Robert M. La Follette, Sr., as state attorney general.

During the 1960's, Governors Nelson and Reynolds battled with the Republican-controlled legislature over *reapportionment* (redivision) of the state's legislative and congressional districts. The Wisconsin Constitution requires that the districts be redrawn every 10 years, if necessary, to provide fair representation. Both Nelson and Reynolds vetoed reapportionment bills passed by the legislature. They said the bills did not make the districts equal in terms of population. In 1963, the legislature passed a bill that reapportioned the state's 10 congressional districts. Reynolds signed this bill, but he and the legislature could not agree on a bill for the legislative districts. Finally, in 1964, the Wisconsin Supreme Court drew up a reapportionment plan. This was the first time any state supreme court had reapportioned a state legislature. The court's plan went into effect with the 1964 elections.

In 1969, the state assembly cut Governor Knowles's recommended welfare program for urban areas. A group of protesters occupied the assembly chamber for 11 hours until police removed them.

The need for money to pay for education, public welfare, and other programs resulted in state tax increases during the 1960's. The state legislature also passed a law, in 1961, that established the first sales tax in Wisconsin's history. In 1963, the legislature increased the number of items covered by the sales tax.

During the mid-1900's, Wisconsin expanded its educational facilities. Between 1956 and 1970, the University of Wisconsin opened 15 branches throughout the state. In 1971, the state legislature merged the university and Wisconsin State University to form a state university system called the University of Wisconsin System.

Wisconsin Today.

Wisconsin faces increasing costs in the 1970's for education, welfare, control of water pollution, and the purchase of land for recreational purposes. The state is also concerned with the problems of the cities, especially poverty in Milwaukee.

Officials of the University of Wisconsin tightened their control over student activities in the 1970's. In 1969, following several student disorders on the Madi-

---

THE GOVERNORS OF WISCONSIN

	Party	Term
Nelson Dewey	Democratic	1848-1852
Leonard J. Farwell	Whig	1852-1854
William A. Barstow	Democratic	1854-1856
Arthur MacArthur	Democratic	1856
Coles Bashford	Republican	1856-1858
Alexander W. Randall	Republican	1858-1862
Louis P. Harvey	Republican	1862
Edward Salomon	Republican	1862-1864
James T. Lewis	Republican	1864-1866
Lucius Fairchild	Republican	1866-1872
Cadwallader C. Washburn	Republican	1872-1874
William R. Taylor	Democratic	1874-1876
Harrison Ludington	Republican	1876-1878
William E. Smith	Republican	1878-1882
Jeremiah McLain Rusk	Republican	1882-1889
William D. Hoard	Republican	1889-1891
George W. Peck	Democratic	1891-1895
William H. Upham	Republican	1895-1897
Edward Scofield	Republican	1897-1901
Robert M. La Follette, Sr.	Republican	1901-1906
James O. Davidson	Republican	1906-1911
Francis E. McGovern	Republican	1911-1915
Emanuel L. Philipp	Republican	1915-1921
John J. Blaine	Republican	1921-1927
Fred R. Zimmerman	Republican	1927-1929
Walter J. Kohler, Sr.	Republican	1929-1931
Philip F. La Follette	Republican	1931-1933
Albert G. Schmedeman	Democratic	1933-1935
Philip F. La Follette	Progressive	1935-1939
Julius P. Heil	Republican	1939-1943
Walter S. Goodland	Republican	1943-1947
Oscar Rennebohm	Republican	1947-1951
Walter J. Kohler, Jr.	Republican	1951-1957
Vernon W. Thomson	Republican	1957-1959
Gaylord A. Nelson	Democratic	1959-1963
John W. Reynolds	Democratic	1963-1965
Warren P. Knowles	Republican	1965-1971
Patrick J. Lucey	Democratic	1971-1977
Martin J. Schreiber	Democratic	1977-1979
Lee S. Dreyfus	Republican	1979-

son campus, the state legislature passed laws to control such disturbances. These laws established fines and imprisonment for campus misconduct.

Manufacturing, with the help of the Wisconsin Development Authority, continues to expand in the state. But agriculture remains vital to the economy of Wisconsin. Although dairying still provides the most agricultural income, livestock and livestock products are becoming the basis of the state's agriculture. Farms in Wisconsin continue to decrease in number and increase in size.

The Democratic Party continued to gain strength in Wisconsin during the 1970's. Wisconsin reelected both of its Democratic U.S. senators, William Proxmire in 1970 and 1976 and Gaylord A. Nelson in 1974. Democrat Patrick J. Lucey won the governorship in 1970 and was reelected in 1974. But a Republican, Lee S. Dreyfus, was elected governor in 1978.   ROBERT W. FINLEY,
ERIC EDWIN LAMPARD, and ELLIOTT MARANISS

WISCONSIN/Study Aids

Related Articles in WORLD BOOK include:

BIOGRAPHIES

Allis, Edward P.	McCarthy, Joseph R.
Andrews, Roy Chapman	Meyer, Albert Cardinal
Babcock, Stephen M.	Mitscher, Marc A.
Berger, Victor L.	Nicolet, Jean
Ferber, Edna	Proxmire, William
Gale, Zona	Schurz (family)
Jolliet, Louis	Turner, Frederick J.
La Follette (family)	Vandenberg, Hoyt S.
Laird, Melvin R.	Welles, Orson
Lunt, Alfred	Wilder, Thornton N.
Marquette, Jacques	Wright, Frank Lloyd

CITIES

Green Bay	Milwaukee	Sheboygan
Kenosha	Oshkosh	Superior
La Crosse	Racine	Wauwatosa
Madison		

HISTORY

Northwest Territory	Westward Movement
Republican Party	Winnebago Indians

PHYSICAL FEATURES

Great Lakes	Mississippi River
Green Bay	Rock River
Lake Winnebago	Wisconsin River

PRODUCTS

For Wisconsin's rank among the states, see:

Alfalfa	Cheese	Oats
Automobile	Corn	Paper
Building Stone	Honey	Pea
Butter	Leather	Potato
Cattle	Milk	

OTHER RELATED ARTICLES

Cooperative	Midwestern States

Outline

I. Government
 A. Constitution   E. Local Government
 B. Executive   F. Taxation
 C. Legislature   G. Politics
 D. Courts
II. People
III. Education
 A. Schools   C. Museums
 B. Libraries
IV. A Visitor's Guide
 A. Places to Visit   B. Annual Events
V. The Land
 A. Land Regions   C. Rivers, Waterfalls, and Lakes
 B. Shoreline
VI. Climate
VII. Economy
 A. Natural Resources   B. Manufacturing

 C. Agriculture   F. Transportation
 D. Mining   G. Communication
 E. Electric Power
VIII. History

Questions

What was the greatest natural disaster in Wisconsin's history?

How many state constitutions has Wisconsin had?

How long has Wisconsin led the nation in the production of dairy products?

How did Wisconsin get the nickname the *Badger State*?

In what Wisconsin city was the Republican Party founded?

What was the "Wisconsin Idea"?

What are Devil's Elbow and Fat Man's Misery?

Why was Jean Nicolet disappointed when he landed on the Green Bay shore in 1634?

Who is "Alice in Dairyland"?

What are some of the reforms Wisconsin began that other states later adopted?

Books for Young Readers

ARCHER, MARION F. *There Is a Happy Land*. Whitman, 1963. Fiction.

BRINK, CAROL R. *Caddie Woodlawn*. Macmillan, 1935. Fiction.

BUTLER, BEVERLY. *Feather in the Wind*. Dodd, 1965. Fiction.

CARPENTER, ALLAN. *Wisconsin*. Childrens Press, 1964.

DERLETH, AUGUST W. *Wisconsin*. Coward-McCann, 1967.

FRADIN, DENNIS B. *Wisconsin in Words and Pictures*. Childrens Press, 1977.

HENDERSON, MARGARET G., and others. *It Happened Here: Stories of Wisconsin*. State Historical Society of Wisconsin, 1949.

NORTH, STERLING. *Rascal: A Memoir of a Better Era*. Dutton, 1963.

WILDER, LAURA I. *Little House in the Big Woods*. Harper, 1932. Fiction. The author's early life in Wisconsin.

Books for Older Readers

BARNOUW, VICTOR. *Wisconsin Chippewa Myths and Tales and Their Relation to Chippewa Life*. Univ. of Wisconsin Press, 1977.

CURRENT, RICHARD N. *The History of Wisconsin*. Vol. Two: *The Civil War Era, 1848-1873*. State Historical Society of Wisconsin, 1976. *Wisconsin: A Bicentennial History*. Norton, 1977.

GARD, ROBERT E. *This Is Wisconsin*. Wisconsin House, 1969.

NESBIT, ROBERT C. *Wisconsin: A History*. Univ. of Wisconsin Press, 1973.

SMITH, ALICE E. *The History of Wisconsin*. Vol. One: *From Exploration to Statehood*. State Historical Society of Wisconsin, 1973.

THELEN, DAVID P. *Robert M. La Follette and the Insurgent Spirit*. Little, Brown, 1976.

University of Wisconsin

Bascom Hall, on the University of Wisconsin-Madison campus, is one of the campus's oldest buildings.

WISCONSIN, UNIVERSITY OF, is a coeducational state-supported educational system. Its official name is the University of Wisconsin System. It consists of 13 universities, 14 two-year campuses, and a statewide extension system. The Wisconsin State universities and the University of Wisconsin merged to form the system in 1971. The system's administrative offices are in Madison. Each of the universities in the system is called the University of Wisconsin (UW) and has its location or its campus name as part of its title.

UW-Madison has colleges of agricultural and life sciences, engineering, and letters and science; and schools of allied health professions, business, education, family resources and consumer sciences, law, medicine, nursing, and pharmacy. It grants bachelor's, master's, and doctor's degrees.

UW-Eau Claire has schools of arts and sciences, business, education, and nursing. It grants bachelor's and master's degrees.

UW-Green Bay has colleges of community sciences, creative communication, environmental sciences, and human biology. It grants bachelor's degrees.

UW-La Crosse has a college of education and a college of arts, letters, and sciences. It also has schools of business administration; health and human services; and health, recreation, and physical education. It grants bachelor's and master's degrees.

UW-Milwaukee has colleges of applied science and engineering, and of letters and science. It has schools of allied health professions, architecture, business administration, education, fine arts, library science, nursing, and social welfare. It grants bachelor's, master's, and doctor's degrees.

UW-Oshkosh has colleges of business administration, education, letters and science, and nursing. It grants bachelor's and master's degrees.

UW-Parkside, located between Kenosha and Racine, has a college of science and society, and a school of modern industry. It grants bachelor's degrees.

UW-Platteville has colleges of agriculture, arts and sciences, business and industry, education, and engineering. It grants bachelor's and master's degrees.

UW-River Falls has colleges of agriculture, arts and sciences, and education. It grants bachelor's and master's degrees.

UW-Stevens Point has colleges of fine arts, letters and science, natural resources, and professional studies. It grants bachelor's and master's degrees.

UW-Stout at Menomonie has schools of education, home economics, industry and technology, and liberal studies. It grants bachelor's and master's degrees.

UW-Superior has colleges of business and economics, education, fine and applied arts, and letters and science. It grants bachelor's and master's degrees.

UW-Whitewater has colleges of the arts, business and economics, education, and letters and science. It grants bachelor's and master's degrees.

For enrollments, see UNIVERSITIES AND COLLEGES (table). Critically reviewed by the UNIVERSITY OF WISCONSIN

WISCONSIN DELLS. See DALLES; WISCONSIN (Places to Visit); WISCONSIN RIVER.

WISCONSIN RIVER is a beautiful stream that rises in Lac Vieux Desert on the Michigan-Wisconsin boundary. It flows south to Portage, Wis., and then turns westward. The Wisconsin empties into the Mississippi River below Prairie du Chien. It is about 430 miles (692 kilometers) long. The river was an important waterway in pioneer days, but its commercial use has declined. Portage, Merrill, Wausau, Wisconsin Rapids, and Stevens Point are among the cities on its banks.

Near the town of Wisconsin Dells, the Wisconsin River forms one of the most scenic spots in North America. Here the stream has cut its way through the sandstone rock to a depth of about 150 feet (46 meters). It forms canyon walls cut in unusual shapes.   JAMES I. CLARK

WISDOM TOOTH. See TEETH (Permanent Teeth).

WISE, ISAAC MAYER (1819-1900), a prominent American rabbi, is generally considered the pioneer of Reform Judaism in America. He founded the Hebrew Union College in Cincinnati for the training of rabbis, and was its president from the time of its organization in 1875 until his death. Wise also helped organize the Union of American Hebrew Congregations in 1873, and the Central Conference of American Rabbis in 1889. He served as president of the Conference for 11 years. He was born at Steingrub, Bohemia, and came to the United States in 1846.   CLIFTON E. OLMSTEAD

WISE, JOHN (1652-1725), was a Congregational minister of colonial Massachusetts. He vigorously opposed actions by both church and government that he believed would deprive colonists of their rights and privileges.

In 1687, Wise led a protest against what he felt was an unfair tax levied by Sir Edmund Andros, the English colonial governor. In the early 1700's, Wise opposed an attempt by some Massachusetts clergymen, led by Increase and Cotton Mather, to organize themselves into associations. These associations would have taken over many functions previously controlled by individual churches. Wise argued that the associations would reduce the ability of local church members to direct their own affairs. His opposition led to the plan's defeat.

Wise was born in Roxbury, Mass. From 1680 until his death, he served as minister of a Congregational church in Ipswich, Mass.   L. C. RUDOLPH

WISE, STEPHEN SAMUEL (1874-1949), was one of the best-known American Jewish leaders. He became noted for his liberalism and his wide activities in political and social life. He was born in Budapest, Hungary, and came to the United States in 1875. He was educated at the College of the City of New York and Columbia University. In 1907, Wise founded the Free Synagogue in New York City, and served as its rabbi until his death. In 1922, he founded the Jewish Institute of Religion and served as its first president. He also helped organize the American Jewish Congress.

Wise was a champion of Zionism, and established the first section of the Federation of American Zionists (see ZIONISM). He wrote many books, including *How to Face Life* (1917) and *Child Versus Parent* (1922). He also edited the magazine *Opinion*.   CLIFTON E. OLMSTEAD

WISHART, GEORGE. See KNOX, JOHN.

WISSLER, CLARK (1870-1947), an American anthropologist, was noted for his studies of the American Indians. He spent most of his career as a staff member of the American Museum of Natural History, and was also a professor at Yale University. In addition to many specialized writings on American Indians, his books include *The American Indian* (1917) and *Indians of the United States* (1940). Wissler was born in Wayne County, Indiana, and studied at Indiana and Columbia universities.   DAVID B. STOUT

WISTAR, CASPAR. See GLASS (Early American Glass); GLASSWARE (Wistarberg Glass).

WISTER, OWEN (1860-1938), was an American novelist. He became noted for *The Virginian* (1902) and other stories of Western life as seen by a Philadelphian and Harvard graduate. Wister wrote biographies of Ulysses S. Grant, George Washington, and his friend, Theodore Roosevelt. Other works include *Red Men and White* (1896), *Philosophy 4* (1903), and *Lady Baltimore* (1906). Wister was born in Philadelphia.   HARRY H. CLARK

WISTERIA, *wihs TIHR ee uh*, is the name of a group of thick-growing vines that bear great clusters of flowers and belong to the pea family. The wisteria that is most often seen growing around homes in the United States is a native of China. One of the showiest climbing plants, it has graceful clusters of bluish-lavender blossoms that resemble pea blossoms. They droop from a heavy screen of foliage. The flower clusters of the wisteria are 1 to 2 feet (30 to 61 centimeters) long. One kind of wisteria is said to have branches that reach out 300 feet (91 meters) from each side of the central woody stalk. Another is said to have covered nearly 1,000 square feet (93 square meters) of wall space. Wisteria is an easy plant to grow in deep soil with plenty of mois-

ture. Wisteria pods and seeds contain a poison that can cause severe stomach upset if eaten.

Scientific Classification. Wisteria belongs to the pea family, *Leguminosae*. The Chinese wisteria is genus *Wisteria*, species *W. sinensis*.   ALFRED C. HOTTES

WITAN. See WITENAGEMOT.

WITCH. See WITCHCRAFT.

WITCH BALLS. See GLASSWARE (Nailsea Glass).

WITCH HAZEL is a shrub or small tree used to make a soothing lotion. The witch hazel grows in the eastern United States and Canada. Its jointed, twisting branches point in all directions. The forked twigs have been used for divining rods, and the name witch hazel comes from this use by superstitious people. It is sometimes called *tobaccowood, spotted alder,* or *winterbloom.*

After the leaves have died, in October or November, the witch hazel bears its flowers. They grow in feathery, golden clusters. The fruits do not ripen until the next year. Then the seeds shoot from their small woody capsules to a distance of several yards or meters.

Witch hazel lotion, or *hamamelin,* is a tonic and healing astringent, applied on the skin or taken internally. It is made by distilling the bark and leaves in alcohol. Doctors prescribe it for bruises, sprains, piles, ulcers, hemorrhage, and skin troubles.

Scientific Classification. Witch hazel makes up the witch hazel family, *Hamamelidaceae*. It is genus *Hamamelis*, species *H. virginiana*.   THEODORE W. BRETZ

J. Horace McFarland
Witch Hazel Has Showy Flowers After Its Leaves Die.

WITCH OF ENDOR lived in a town by that name (now called 'En-Dor) in Palestine. The Bible tells us that Saul, the first king of the Hebrews, consulted her before the battle with the Philistines in which he was killed (I Sam. 28:7).

WITCHCRAFT is the use of supposed magic powers, generally to harm people or to damage their property. A witch is a person believed to have received such powers from evil spirits. From earliest times, people in all parts of the world have believed in witches. According to some scholars, more than half the people in the world today think witches can influence their lives.

Through the centuries, witchcraft as practiced in countries with a European tradition and culture has differed from witchcraft elsewhere. European witchcraft is anti-Christian and involves an association with the devil. For example, a person wanting to be a witch

J. Horace McFarland
Wisteria Flowers grow in long, graceful clusters which make the wisteria one of the most attractive vining plants. The flowers resemble pea blossoms. Climbing wisteria vines grow to great heights on outdoor walls.

Woodcut by Francesco Guazzo from *Compendium Maleficarum*, The Newberry Library, Chicago

WORLD BOOK illustration

The Devil Holds Court at the initiation of several witches, *left*, in this artist's portrayal of a witch's rejection of God and dedication to Satan. The star with a goat's face, *above*, a symbol used in witchcraft, represents Satan.

might sell his or her soul to the devil in exchange for magic powers.

On the other hand, witchcraft in Africa and the West Indies and among the Indians of North America does not involve the devil. Most of the time, such non-European witchcraft seeks to harm people. But it may also be used to help people. For example, a person in love may ask a witch for a love *potion* (drink) to give the loved one. Drinking the potion will supposedly make the loved one return the giver's love.

The word *witch* comes from the Anglo-Saxon word *wicca*, meaning *wise one* or *magician*. Originally, a witch was either a man or a woman who supposedly had supernatural powers. But through the years, only women came to be considered witches. Men with similar powers were called *sorcerers*, *warlocks*, or *wizards*.

The Powers of Witches

People who believe in witchcraft think a witch can harm her victim in various ways. By giving him a magic potion, for example, she can make him fall in love against his will. In another form of witchcraft, the witch makes a small wax or wooden image of her victim. She may put something from the victim's body into the image, such as fingernail clippings or a lock of hair. She then destroys the image by cutting it with a knife, burning it, or sticking pins into it. The victim supposedly suffers severe pain or even death.

Sometimes a witch casts a spell by reciting a magic formula. The spell makes her victim suffer. The witch usually mutters the victim's name while she casts the spell. In some societies, people use false names so that witches can have no power over them.

People once blamed witches for any unexplained misfortune, such as illness, a sudden death, or a crop failure. Many persons accused witches of marrying demons and bearing monster children. Witches might make cows go dry by stealing their milk or cast a spell on a churn to prevent butter from forming. People also thought witches could raise storms, ruin crops, and turn people into beasts. In addition, witches could ride through the air on a broom, and make themselves invisible. In ancient times, many people believed that witches and

warlocks assembled on October 31 to worship their master, the devil. Today, children dress up as witches and goblins on this date to celebrate Halloween (see HALLOWEEN).

Witchcraft has led to many widely believed superstitions. For example, many people in southern Europe and the Near East fear a power called the *evil eye*. This power enables witches to cause harm or bring bad luck to others by merely looking at them. According to another superstition, a black cat brings bad luck if it crosses a person's path. This superstition came from the belief that every witch had a personal demon called a *familiar*. Many familiars, which lived with and served their witches, existed in the form of a black cat or some other animal.

History

Ancient Times. A number of witches appear in ancient Greek and Latin literature. In Homer's epic poem, the *Odyssey*, the witch Circe had the power to turn men into animals. Medea, another famous witch, used magic spells to help the Greek hero Jason obtain the Golden Fleece. See CIRCE; MEDEA.

The Old Testament includes several references to witches and witchcraft. For example, the commandment "Thou shalt not suffer a witch to live" appears in Exodus (22:18). Hundreds of years later, witch-hunters accepted such Biblical statements as proof that witches existed. They also used the statements to justify the persecution of persons accused of witchcraft.

From the 1400's Through the 1700's. Some scholars regard witchcraft as an extremely old system of organized religious worship. They trace it back to pre-Christian times in many parts of Europe. From the 1400's through the 1700's, church authorities tried to stamp out witchcraft. But people in many parts of the world continued to practice witchcraft as a religion.

Church persecution of witches occurred in England, France, Germany, Italy, Scotland, and Spain. In 1430, Joan of Arc, the French national heroine, was condemned to death as a witch by the English. They burned her at the stake in 1431. From 1484 to 1782, according to some historians, the Christian church put to

The Witches' Sabbath (1823), an oil painting by Francisco Goya; The Prado, Madrid, Spain (MAS)

Witches Assemble at a Witches' Sabbath to Worship Their Master, the Devil.

death about 300,000 women for witchcraft. Many of these women suffered such terrible torture that they confessed to being witches simply to avoid further torment.

People used many kinds of tests to determine whether a woman was a witch. For example, they looked for moles, scars, or other marks on the woman's body where a pin could be stuck without causing pain. Such *devil's marks* were said to be places where the devil had touched the accused woman. Devil's marks also included birthmarks. In another test, people tied the suspected woman's arms and legs and threw her into deep water. If she floated, she was considered guilty of being a witch. If she sank, she was innocent.

During the 1600's and 1700's, an almost hysterical fear of witchcraft swept most of Europe. Thousands of persons were tried and executed as witches. The courts allowed gossip and rumor to be used as evidence. Many children testified against their own parents.

The American colonists brought the belief in witchcraft from England. Suspected witches suffered persecution in Connecticut, Massachusetts, and Virginia. The most famous witch hunt in American history occurred in Salem, Mass. Many historians believe that Cotton Mather, a colonial preacher, did much to stir up public feeling against the supposed evil deeds of witches. In 1692, the Massachusetts colonists executed 20 persons as witches and imprisoned 150 others. See MATHER; SALEM (Mass.).

Witchcraft Today. Belief in witchcraft exists in many societies today. Such societies include those of the Hopi and Navajo Indians of the southwestern United States, the Maori of New Zealand, and many peoples of southern Africa. In the West Indies and elsewhere, the beliefs and practices of *voodoo* closely resemble those of witchcraft (see VOODOO). Certain groups believe an individual may inherit witch powers from a parent. Such persons do not have to deal with evil spirits to become witches.

Witchcraft may serve as a means of social control among the members of a community. For example, a person who becomes too rich or powerful may be accused by neighbors of using witchcraft. The fear of being called a witch could keep such a person from acquiring too much wealth or power.

During the mid-1900's, a new interest in witchcraft occurred in Europe and the United States. As a result, witchcraft as an organized religion has attracted large

numbers of believers. These people meet regularly in local *covens* (groups of 13 or fewer members). Witchcraft festivals called Witches' Sabbaths take place four times a year, one in each season. The most important festival occurs on Halloween.

Books, motion pictures, and television shows have done much to lessen the fear of witches and witchcraft. Today, many witches are portrayed as attractive, slightly unusual persons whose supernatural activities do harm to no one. ALAN DUNDES

See also EVIL EYE; HECATE; HYPNOTISM (In Early Practice); MAGIC; SEWALL, SAMUEL.

WITCHWEED is a plant that grows as a parasite on the roots of corn and some kinds of grass. It was first identified in the United States in 1955. It has small, narrow leaves and red or yellow flowers. The tiny seeds of the witchweed are spread by the wind and live many years.

Scientific Classification. The witchweed belongs to the figwort family, *Scrophulariaceae*. It is classified as genus *Striga*, species *S. asiatica*. ARTHUR CRONQUIST

WITENAGEMOT, *WIT uh nuh guh MOHT,* means *a meeting of the witan* (or *wise men*) of Anglo-Saxon England. The witan were royal counsellors, including bishops, abbots, earls, and the *thanes*, or followers, who held household offices or important positions in local government. The king could summon any thane he wished to attend.

The king consulted his witan before taking important steps, such as issuing laws, granting lands, making war or peace, appointing bishops or earls, or granting privileges to churches or monasteries. The witan also functioned as a royal court, giving judgment in important lawsuits. The witan could assume extraordinary powers, such as dethroning a king or choosing a new king in a disputed succession. The Norman conquerors of England in 1066 replaced the witenagemot with the *curia regis* (king's court). ROBERT S. HOYT

WITHDRAWAL ILLNESS. See DRUG ADDICTION; SEDATIVE.

WITHERITE. See BARIUM.

WITHERSPOON, JOHN (1723-1794), was a leader in American political, religious, and educational life. He served in the Continental Congress and signed the Declaration of Independence. Witherspoon was born in Scotland. He was a Presbyterian minister before coming to America in 1768 to become president of the College of New Jersey (now Princeton University). After the

WITHHOLDING TAX

Revolutionary War, he continued his duties as college president.   RICHARD B. MORRIS

WITHHOLDING TAX. See RUML, BEARDSLEY; INCOME TAX.

WITNESS is a person who gives testimony before a court or in a judicial proceeding. Such testimony is given under oath, or, if the witness's religion forbids an oath, under affirmation. A witness may also be a person who signs a legal instrument, such as a will or deed, that another person executes in the witness's presence.

A court witness is ordered to appear in court by a *subpoena*, which compels the person to attend and to give evidence. A person who fails to appear is liable to punishment for contempt of court. A witness who testifies untruthfully is guilty of the crime of *perjury*, and can be severely punished. Witnesses may legally refuse to testify against themselves or their spouses.

The question of who is fit to serve as a witness is regulated by *rules of evidence*. The law regards certain persons as unfit to give legal testimony. Insane persons and persons unable to understand the nature of a binding oath are included in this class.   HUNTINGTON CAIRNS

See also OATH; PERJURY; SUBPOENA.

WITTGENSTEIN, *VIHT gehn SHTYN*, **LUDWIG** (1889-1951), was one of the most important philosophers of the 1900's. His ideas greatly influenced two philosophical movements called *positivism* and *ordinary language philosophy*.

Wittgenstein believed that most philosophical problems result because philosophers think most words are names. For example, philosophers have asked, "What is time?" and they have been puzzled because they could not find anything named *time*. Wittgenstein said this is the wrong way to find out what time is. All that is necessary is to determine how the word *time* is used in a sentence. In the sentence, "It is time to go home," we know what *time* means, and so its meaning is not a problem. The word *time* has no meaning except for its use in such a sentence. Wittgenstein claimed that this way of viewing language "dissolves" the traditional problems of philosophy. His approach to language has greatly influenced scholars in many fields.

Wittgenstein was born in Vienna, Austria. He studied at Cambridge University in England and later taught there. He gained recognition for his books *Tractatus Logico-Philosophicus* (1921) and *Philosophical Investigations* (published in 1953, after his death).   W. T. JONES

WIZARD. See WITCHCRAFT.

WIZARD OF MENLO PARK. See EDISON, THOMAS A.

WIZARD OF OZ. See BAUM, LYMAN FRANK.

W. K. KELLOGG FOUNDATION. See KELLOGG FOUNDATION, W. K.

WODEHOUSE, *WOOD hows,* **P. G.** (1881-1975), was a famous novelist and short-story writer. His books became popular for their rich and outlandish humor and for their carica-

Bettmann Archive

P. G. Wodehouse

tures of English types. Several of his characters, especially Bertie Wooster, Jeeves, and Psmith, have become famous. His works include *Leave It to Psmith* (1923), *The Inimitable Jeeves* (1924), *The Code of the Woosters* (1938), *French Leave* (1959), *Carry on, Jeeves* (1961), and *Stiff Upper Lip, Jeeves* (1963). Pelham Grenville Wodehouse was born in Guildford, England, and studied at Dulwich College. Later he wrote a humorous column for a London newspaper. Wodehouse became an American citizen in 1955. He was knighted by Queen Elizabeth II in 1975.   R. W. STALLMAN

WODEN. See ODIN.

WÖHLER, *VUH ler,* **FRIEDRICH** (1800-1882), a German chemist, in 1828 became the first person to make an organic substance (in this case urea) from inorganic chemicals. His experiments destroyed the belief that organic substances could be formed only in the living bodies of plants or animals.

Wöhler isolated the element beryllium, and was the first person to measure the specific gravity of aluminum (see ALUMINUM [The First Aluminum]). His method of preparing phosphorus was similar to that still used after World War I. Wöhler's studies on cyanates and uric acid were of fundamental importance to science.

Wöhler was born at Eschersheim, near Frankfurt, West Germany. In 1825, he became a chemistry instructor at the Polytechnic School in Berlin. Wöhler later became professor of chemistry at the University of Göttingen.   K. L. KAUFMAN

See also CHEMISTRY (picture: Famous Chemists).

WOJCIECHOWSKA, MAIA (1927-   ), won the 1965 Newbery medal for her children's book *Shadow of a Bull* (1964). She also wrote *Market Day for 'Ti Andre* (1952). She was born in Warsaw, Poland, but became a United States citizen in 1951. She studied in Europe and at Immaculate Heart College in Los Angeles.

WOLCOTT is the family name of three Connecticut patriots who were active in early American politics.

Roger Wolcott (1679-1767) was colonial governor of Connecticut from 1750 to 1754. He was second in command at the Battle of Louisbourg in 1745. Wolcott wrote *Poetical Meditations* (1725), the first poetry book published in Connecticut. He was born in Windsor, Conn.

Oliver Wolcott (1726-1797), the son of Roger Wolcott, was a Connecticut signer of the Declaration of Independence. He served in the Continental Congress from 1775 to 1778 and again in 1780 and 1781. Wolcott was a member of the Congress of the Confederation from 1781 to 1784. He commanded 14 Revolutionary War regiments that helped defend New York in 1776. He was governor of Connecticut from 1796 until his death. Wolcott was born in Windsor, and graduated from Yale College.

Oliver Wolcott, Jr. (1760-1833), the son of Oliver Wolcott, succeeded Alexander Hamilton as Secretary of the Treasury in 1795. He resigned in 1800 after he and Hamilton became involved in a political attack against President John Adams. Wolcott was governor of Connecticut from 1817 to 1827. He was born in Litchfield, and graduated from Yale.   RICHARD B. MORRIS

WOLF is one of the largest members of the dog family. Wolves are expert hunters and prey chiefly on large hoofed animals, such as caribou, deer, elk, and moose. Many people fear wolves. They believe wolves attack human beings, and the animal's eerie howl frightens

The Timber Wolf lives in forests of northern Asia, Europe, and North America. Most timber wolves have fur that is brown or gray or a mixture of those colors, but some have jet black coats.

Young Wolves learn some hunting skills by scuffling with one another. They begin to hunt with the pack when they are about 6 months old. This family of wolves includes a black pup.

them. But wolves avoid people as much as possible.

Almost all wolves belong to a species called the *gray wolf*. There are two chief types of gray wolves, the *timber wolf* and the *tundra wolf*. The timber wolf lives in wooded, subarctic regions. The tundra wolf makes its home on the treeless plains of the Arctic. Some zoologists believe there is a separate species of wolves called the *red wolf*. This animal lives in Louisiana and Texas but is nearly extinct.

Wolves can live in almost any kind of climate, though they are seldom found in deserts or tropical forests. In ancient times, they roamed throughout the northern half of the world. But wherever large numbers of people settled, they destroyed wolves. As a result, these animals have disappeared from many areas. Today, most wolves live in sparsely populated northern regions, such as Alaska, Minnesota, Canada, China, and Russia. Small numbers of wolves still inhabit wilderness areas of Greece, India, Mexico, Spain, and other countries.

The Body of a Wolf

Wolves look much like large German shepherd dogs. But a wolf has longer legs, bigger feet, a wider head, and a long bushy tail. Most adult male wolves weigh from 75 to 120 pounds (34 to 54 kilograms). They measure from 5 to $6\frac{1}{2}$ feet (1.5 to 2 meters) long, including the tail, and are about $2\frac{1}{2}$ feet (76 centimeters) tall at the shoulder. Female wolves are smaller than the males.

The fur of a wolf varies in color from pure white on the Arctic plains to jet black in the subarctic forests. Most wolves have gray fur. Wolves of the northern and Arctic regions grow long, thick winter coats that protect them from the bitter cold.

A wolf has excellent vision, a keen sense of smell, and fine hearing. These three senses help the animal locate prey. A wolf can see and smell a deer more than a mile (1.6 kilometers) away.

A wolf has 42 teeth, including four fangs at the front of the mouth that are used to wound, grab, and kill prey. The fangs may measure up to 2 inches (5 centimeters) long from root to tip. The small front teeth are used to nibble and pull at skin. The sharp side teeth cut easily through tough muscle. The flat back teeth crush thick bone so it can be swallowed.

The wolf has a large stomach and can eat as much as 20 pounds (9 kilograms) of food at one time. However, a wolf can go without food for two weeks or longer.

The Life of a Wolf

Wolves live in family groups called *packs*. Most packs have about 8 members, but some may have more than 20. Zoologists believe the members of a pack remain together because they have strong affection for one another. Some wolves leave the pack and become *lone wolves*. A lone wolf travels alone until it finds a mate. These two wolves may have pups and form their own pack.

Habits. Each wolf pack has a social order called a *dominance hierarchy*. Every member of the pack has a certain rank in the hierarchy. High-ranking members, called *dominant wolves*, dominate low-ranking members, known as *subordinate wolves*. A dominant wolf and a subordinate wolf show their rank almost every time they meet. The dominant wolf stands erect, holds its tail aloft, and points its ears up and forward. It may show its teeth and growl. The subordinate wolf crouches, holds its tail between its legs, and turns down its ears. Instead of growling, it whines.

A pack lives within a specific area called a *territory*. Studies indicate that the size of the territory depends mainly on the availability of prey. If prey is scarce, the territory may cover more than 200 square miles (520 square kilometers). If prey is plentiful, the area may be as small as 30 square miles (77 kilometers).

Wolves claim a territory by marking it with their scent. The leader of the pack urinates on rocks, trees, and other objects along the boundaries of the area. Other wolves then know where the territory is located. A pack does not allow other wolves to hunt in its territory. If wolves from another pack trespass, they may be attacked.

Young. Wolves mate during the winter. The female carries her young inside her body for about 65 days. She then gives birth to 1 to 11 pups in a sheltered area called a *den*. The den may be in a cave, a hollow log, an abandoned beaver lodge, or underground.

Wolf pups weigh about 1 pound (0.5 kilogram) at birth and are blind, deaf, and helpless. At first, they live only on the mother's milk. When they are about

3 weeks old, they begin to eat meat and to leave the den for short periods. Adult wolves provide the pups with meat. An adult eats a large amount of meat after killing an animal. To get some of this meat, the pups lick the mouth of the adult wolf. The adult coughs up the meat, and the pups eat it.

Wolf pups leave the den permanently when they are about 2 months old. They move to an unsheltered area called a *rendezvous site* and remain there during the summer while the adults hunt and bring back food. In the fall, the pups and the adults begin to hunt together as a pack.

How Wolves Hunt. Wolves eat almost any animal they can catch. Many of the animals they hunt, such as caribou and elk, are faster and stronger than wolves. Therefore, wolves must be quick, tireless, and clever to catch them.

Wolves hunt at any time of the day or night. When the members of a pack gather to begin a hunt, they greet each other with howls. Their howling may become very loud, and it warns other wolves to stay out of the pack's territory.

Wolves roam through their territory until they find prey. They move in on an animal by traveling toward it in the opposite direction that the wind is blowing. This method prevents the animal from smelling the wolves. The wolves quietly inch closer to their prey, perhaps in single file. Then they break into a run, and the chase begins.

Wolves hunt and chase many more animals than they can catch. If wolves can catch their prey, they attack the rump or sides of the animal. They try to wound the animal and make it bleed until it weakens. Then they grab the victim by the throat or snout. Wolves can usually kill a large animal in only a few minutes. But the entire hunt may take several hours. The wolves may give up the chase if the animal is very strong, such as a healthy moose. They also may abandon the hunt if the animal is exceptionally fast.

Sick, injured, or aged animals that lag behind their herds make easy targets for wolves. The wolf helps strengthen the herds of its prey by killing such animals. An old or unhealthy animal can be a burden to its herd. For example, an aged caribou eats food that other members of the herd need to raise their young. A sick elk may infect other members of the herd. By eliminating such animals, wolves perform an important natural function.

Wolves and People

Many people despise the wolf because it kills other animals. Wolves provoke farmers and ranchers by destroying sheep, cows, and other livestock. Many hunters dislike the wolf because it kills game animals, such as antelope and deer. These hunters mistakenly think that wolves wipe out game in certain areas.

Folklore also has contributed to the wolf's bad reputation. In many old sayings, the animal is a symbol of badness or evil. For example, "to keep the wolf from the door" means to prevent hunger or poverty. "A wolf in sheep's clothing" describes a person who acts friendly but has evil intentions. Fables and other folk tales pass on the misleading notion that wolves attack people. In the story of Little Red Riding Hood, a wolf threatens to eat a little girl.

Hatred and fear of wolves have led people to destroy large numbers of them. In the United States, organized hunts have killed thousands of wolves. *Bounties* (rewards) have been offered for their pelts. In the late 1970's, from 5,000 to 15,000 wolves lived in Alaska. There were only about 1,200 wolves elsewhere in the United States, most of them in Minnesota. The U.S. government has classified the wolf as an endangered species in every state except Alaska and Minnesota. It is classified as a threatened species in Minnesota.

Scientific Classification. Wolves belong to the family Canidae. The gray wolf is *Canis lupus*. The red wolf is *C. rufus*. 　　　　　　　　　　　　　　L. DAVID MECH

WOLF, HUGO. See MUSIC (The Later 1800's).

WOLF, TASMANIAN. See TASMANIAN WOLF.

WOLF CREEK DAM is a flood-control and power project on the Cumberland River near Jamestown, Ky. The combination concrete and earth dam is 258 feet (79 meters) high, with a top length of 5,736 feet (1,748

Rolf O. Peterson

A Wolf Pack closes in on a moose fleeing through the snow. However, the wolves may not be able to kill their prey after cornering it. Many large animals are too strong for even a group of hungry wolves to kill.

meters). It can control a volume of 11,568,900 cubic yards (8,845,059 cubic meters) of water. It was built under the direction of the United States Army Corps of Engineers. The Wolf Creek Reservoir is 101 miles (163 kilometers) long, and covers an area of 63,530 acres (25,710 hectares). See also DAM.

WOLF FISH live in the North Atlantic and the North Pacific. The wolf fish gets its name from its terrifying appearance. This savage fish will try to attack anyone who captures it. It has powerful jaws and its bite can be extremely painful. It is reddish or grayish and has no pelvic fins. The Atlantic wolf fish grows about 3 feet (91 centimeters) long. The North Pacific wolf fish, called the *wolf eel*, may reach 8 feet (2.4 meters). The fish spawns large eggs that cluster in a ball.

WORLD BOOK illustration by Tom Dolan
The Atlantic Wolf Fish Feeds on Shellfish.

The wolf fish uses its broad, strong front teeth to crush the shells of the animals it eats. Its flesh tastes much like that of the cod. It is a favorite food fish in Iceland. Its strong, durable skin makes a good leather used for pouches, book bindings, and other articles.

Scientific Classification. The Atlantic wolf fish is in the family *Anarhichadidae.* It is genus *Anarhichas,* species *A. lupus.* The wolf eel belongs to the family *Anarhichthyidae.* It is classified as genus *Anarrhichthys,* species *A. ocellatus.*   LEONARD P. SCHULTZ

WOLFE, JAMES (1727-1759), was the British general whose success in the battle of Quebec in 1759 won Canada for the British Empire. His victory against the French came after several discouraging failures, due in part to his poor judgment. His greatness as a general has sometimes been exaggerated because of his dramatic death at the moment of victory.

Before the attack on Quebec, Wolfe moved his troops up the Saint Lawrence River to a landing well above the city. The troops moved down the river during the night of Sept. 12-13, 1759, to a point much nearer Quebec. They landed there, and then climbed a steep bluff on the north side of the river to the plains outside the city walls. When General Montcalm, the French commander, discovered the British in the morning, he decided to fight on the site Wolfe had chosen.

The battle lasted less than 15 minutes. Wolfe was wounded twice, but continued in command until a third bullet struck him in the lungs. Wolfe died just as the French troops were breaking. General Montcalm was also mortally wounded, and lived only a few hours longer (see MONTCALM, MARQUIS DE; QUEBEC, BATTLE OF).

Wolfe was born in the County of Kent, England. He joined the army when he was 14, and served in Flanders and Scotland. He was a brigadier in the French and Indian War, which began in 1754. He served under Lord Jeffery Amherst in the Battle of Louisbourg in 1758 (see AMHERST, LORD JEFFERY; LOUISBOURG).

Wolfe returned to England after that battle. William Pitt, who was then directing England's foreign affairs, chose Wolfe to command the expedition against Quebec. Wolfe's success there, at the cost of his life, permitted the British to seize Montreal in the following year and to complete the conquest of Canada (see CANADA, HISTORY OF [The British Conquest]). W. B. WILLCOX

WOLFE, THOMAS CLAYTON (1900-1938), was an American author who won fame for his autobiographical novels. Wolfe claimed that all great art was necessarily autobiographical. The story of his childhood and youth assumes a symbolic significance in his novels. The reader traces the experiences of a sensitive, worthwhile person who is Thomas Wolfe. The reader also becomes aware of an equally important theme —the development of the artist in America.

Pinchot
Thomas Wolfe

Wolfe was born in Asheville, N.C. He graduated from the University of North Carolina in 1920 and then entered the Harvard University graduate school. He wrote two plays while at Harvard, but considered them failures and turned to writing novels. Wolfe received his M.A. from Harvard in 1924. He taught English at New York University between 1924 and 1930.

Maxwell E. Perkins, an editor at Scribner's publishers, was the most important influence in Wolfe's career. Wolfe wrote long, rambling works, and Perkins helped him cut and organize the material. Wolfe's first novel was *Look Homeward, Angel* (1929). It was followed by a sequel, *Of Time and the River* (1935). After Wolfe's death, Edward Aswell, an editor at Harper publishers, edited and directed the publication of his two other novels— *The Web and the Rock* (1939) and *You Can't Go Home Again* (1940). The character of Eugene Gant in the first two novels is modeled on Wolfe as a young man. The other novels also draw on Wolfe's personal experiences. The main character in these two novels is called George Webber.

Wolfe's writing has been criticized for its apparent lack of discipline and artistic control. Some critics believe that each novel is a torrent of undigested details and that Perkins' editing is responsible for whatever form the novels have. Wolfe seemed to support this view in *The Story of a Novel* (1936), in which he critically examined his own writings. However, later critics have stressed that Wolfe was more than a reporter. They note that he chose details and emphasized elements that make each episode in his novels a dramatic unit. Although Wolfe has been frequently criticized for excesses in language, at his best he wrote a powerful prose that is often close to poetry. *The Notebooks of Thomas Wolfe* (1970) describes Wolfe's struggle to become a mature writer. OLGA W. VICKERY

WOLFF, CASPAR FRIEDRICH. See HEREDITY (From Harvey to Darwin).

WOLFHOUND is the name of a family of dogs made up of three breeds—the *Irish wolfhound*, the *Russian wolfhound*, and the *Scottish deerhound*. The Irish dog is the largest of all dogs, although not the heaviest. It was the companion of kings in ancient Ireland, and is still used for hunting.

The Russian wolfhound resembles the greyhound except for its long, luxuriant coat. This breed of wolfhound was developed by the Russian czars. The czars used these dogs to chase after and destroy wolves.

The Scottish deerhound descended from the staghound and other large breeds once used for stalking

deer. It is a large, striking dog, though smaller than the Irish wolfhound. OLGA DAKAN

See also BORZOI; DOG (color picture: Hounds); IRISH WOLFHOUND; SCOTTISH DEERHOUND.

WOLFRAM. See TUNGSTEN.

WOLFRAM VON ESCHENBACH (1170?-1220?) was a German knight and poet. His rhymed poem *Parzival* is considered a masterpiece of medieval literature.

Parzival is about a courageous boy who finds his way through ignorance and guilt to manhood and wisdom. During years of wandering, Parzival grows in purity and humility until finally God judges him worthy of the Grail, a holy stone that transmits God's will by means of a mysterious inscription. Wolfram based his poem on a French romance by Chrétien de Troyes. Richard Wagner based his opera *Parsifal* on Wolfram's masterpiece. Wolfram also wrote short poems and two unfinished verse epics— *Titurel* and *Willehalm*.

Little is known of Wolfram's life. He was born into a noble family in Bavaria and probably served as a knight under powerful lords. JAMES F. POAG

WOLFRAMITE is one of the two most important ores of tungsten. It consists of iron, manganese, oxygen, and tungsten, and its chemical symbol is $(Fe,Mn) WO_4$. Tungsten is a chemical element that is important in making electronic equipment and industrial tools (see TUNGSTEN). The other chief tungsten ore is scheelite.

Wolframite is a black to brownish mineral that occurs in crystals. It is often found with quartz and in veins of granite. Australia, Bolivia, China, Korea, and Russia have major wolframite deposits. E. WM. HEINRICH

WOLLASTON LAKE covers 906 square miles (2,347 square kilometers) in northeastern Saskatchewan, Canada. The lake is 70 miles (110 kilometers) long and 25 miles (40 kilometers) across at its widest point. Its waters flow into both the Mackenzie and Churchill rivers. The lake is named for William Hyde Wollaston (1766-1828), a famous English chemist.

WOLLSTONECRAFT, MARY. See GODWIN (Mary Wollstonecraft).

WOLSELEY, *WOOLZ lih*, **GARNET JOSEPH** (1833-1913), VISCOUNT WOLSELEY, was a British soldier. He fought in the second Burmese War, the Crimean War, the Indian Mutiny in 1857, and in China. In 1870 he put down the Red River Rebellion in Canada, and in

WORLD BOOK photo
The Irish Wolfhound Belongs to the Wolfhound Family.

1882, the revolt of Arabi Pasha in Egypt (see RED RIVER REBELLION). Wolseley served as chief of the army from 1895 to 1899. He was born in Ireland, and joined the British Army at the age of 19. JAMES L. GODFREY

WOLSEY, *WOOL zih,* **THOMAS CARDINAL** (1475?-1530), was an English statesman and a cardinal of the Roman Catholic Church. He was the most powerful person in England for many years.

Wolsey was born at Ipswich, where his father was a butcher. He was educated at Magdalen College, Oxford University. Several years after his graduation, he was elected a fellow of the college. In 1498, he was ordained a priest, and became rector of Limington, in Somerset. He later became chaplain to the archbishop of Canterbury, and then chaplain to the English governor of Calais. Wolsey's Oxford friends and his own driving ambition helped his rapid rise to political power. By 1507 he had become chaplain to King Henry VII. The king often used Wolsey in diplomatic missions, and rewarded him in 1509 by making him dean of Lincoln.

When Henry VIII became king in 1509, Wolsey's affairs prospered. He became canon of Windsor in 1511 and received high church positions. He also became a member of the Privy Council in 1511, and soon was the controlling figure in all matters of state. In 1514, he was made bishop of Lincoln, and then archbishop of York. Pope Leo X made him a cardinal in 1515. Wolsey loved display and wealth. He lived in royal splendor and reveled in his power. His ambition was to become pope.

Cardinal Wolsey spent his great abilities as a statesman and administrator mainly in managing England's foreign affairs for Henry VIII. Despite the many enemies his greed and ambition earned him, he held Henry VIII's confidence until Henry decided to divorce his wife, Catherine of Aragon, and marry Anne Boleyn (see HENRY VIII). Wolsey disapproved of this, and was slow in arranging the divorce. The delay angered the king, and made Wolsey an enemy of Anne Boleyn and her friends.

His fall was sudden and complete. Stripped of office and property, he was permitted to remain archbishop of York. But shortly afterward, he was accused of treason and ordered to London. In great distress, he set out for the capital. He fell ill and died on the way. "If I had served God," the cardinal said remorsefully, "as diligently as I have done the king, He would not have given me over in my grey hairs." PAUL M. KENDALL

Oil painting (about 1600) by Sampson Strong; Christ Church College, Oxford, England

Thomas Cardinal Wolsey was the most powerful religious and political leader in England during the early 1500's.

WOLVERINE, *WOOL vur EEN,* is a fur-bearing animal which lives in the northern woods of Europe, Asia, and North America. Europeans call it the *glutton.* It is related to badgers, skunks, and otters. The animal has a heavy build and short legs. It is about $2\frac{1}{2}$ feet (76 centimeters) long. It looks somewhat like a bear. The animal has dark, shaggy hair with tan markings. The wolverine is one of the most powerful animals for its size.

The wolverines of North America once roamed from northern Canada to the northern United States. They could steal bait from hunters' traps with great cunning. They seemed to kill for the love of killing, and destroyed more animals than they could eat. They are rare today because they have been hunted ruthlessly.

Scientific Classification. The wolverine belongs to the weasel family, *Mustelidae.* It is classified as genus *Gulo,* species *G. gulo.* HAROLD E. ANTHONY

WOLVERINE STATE. See MICHIGAN.

James R. Simon, Van Cleve Photography

The Wolverine lives in North America, northern Europe, and Asia. It is one of the most powerful animals of its size.

WORLD BOOK photo

A Woman may devote herself to being a wife and mother, *above*. Or she may choose to work outside the home or combine these roles. Women have worked in such professions as teaching, *above right*, for over a hundred years. Other fields, including stock-broking, *right*, have been open to women for a much shorter time.

Tana Hoban, DPI

WORLD BOOK photo

WOMAN has played many roles in various societies throughout history. She has been a wife, a mother, a farmer, a laborer, a business executive, a teacher, or a volunteer worker. Most women have combined two or more of these roles.

Through the centuries, almost every society has developed definite ideas of what activities are proper for women. Some societies have given women honor. Others have considered women less important than men. Some of these ideas have disappeared or have changed greatly, but others have changed little or not at all.

Today, women in many countries make at least some of the decisions about what they will do with their lives. In the United States, Canada, and most European nations, a woman can choose whether she wants a career, whether she wants to marry, and whether she wants to raise children. In many countries throughout the world, women are increasingly challenging society's traditional image of what a woman may choose to be.

Physical Characteristics and Woman's Roles

Most societies have related their ideas about women to beliefs about their physical characteristics. Some of these beliefs have little or no scientific basis. But they have been accepted for so many years that few people question them.

Cynthia Fuchs Epstein, the contributor of this article, is Professor of Sociology at Queens College of the City University of New York. She is the author of Woman's Place: Options and Limits of Professional Careers.

Motherhood has played a major part in determining woman's place in society. In almost all societies, people have believed that woman's ability to bear children makes it every woman's duty to do so. Many women have chosen the job of caring for their family as a demanding and rewarding career. But there is no adequate scientific evidence that women have a *maternal instinct*—that is, a natural desire to bear and care for children. Many sociologists maintain that the so-called maternal instinct results from society's teaching girls that they should get married and raise children.

From earliest times, motherhood has helped bring about a division of tasks between men and women. In most societies, women remain home while pregnant or nursing their babies. This may be why they have traditionally done most of the jobs connected with the home. Men, on the other hand, have taken jobs near or far from home. In a primitive society, such a division of labor might not suggest inequality. But in a more advanced society, the tradition of women staying home and men going to work gives men economic superiority. A woman who stays home must depend on someone else to earn money for the necessities of life.

Size and Strength. Distinctions between the roles of men and women have also developed because most women are smaller and less powerful than most men. Such physical differences have led to men holding the most physically demanding and dangerous jobs. However, some differences in strength might result from society's traditional belief that boys should develop their muscles but girls should not.

Eventually, the division of tasks that may have been

determined by physical differences and motherhood became based almost exclusively on the sex of an individual. All societies have not classified male and female work in the same way, but most cultures have observed strict divisions between the two. Most societies have considered it improper for men to do women's work or for women to do men's work. In almost all societies, for example, women have the major responsibility for child rearing. In many societies, even unmarried women and older women who have stopped bearing children are given jobs close to the home.

Science and technology have eliminated many of the reasons for work differences between the sexes. For example, women can easily operate machines that do much of the heavy work once assigned only to men. Various methods of birth control enable women to limit the number of children they bear, to determine when to bear them, or to avoid bearing any. Many women practice birth control so they can take part in activities outside the home. Women in developed societies live about a third of their lives past their child-bearing years. Mothers may therefore enter—or resume—careers after raising their children.

Temperament and Emotions have traditionally been attributed to biological differences between men and women. In many societies, people believe that women are naturally more emotional than men, particularly during menstruation and the *menopause*, the time in life when menstruation ends. But scientists have found little evidence that woman's emotional makeup differs significantly from man's. Research shows that a woman's feelings depend strongly on what she has been taught. Many women are taught that they can expect to become emotionally upset during menstruation and the menopause. These women experience such upsets more frequently than do women who have been taught that menstruation and the menopause are normal parts of life.

Many people believe that a person's sex determines his or her intelligence, creativity, and ability to make decisions. But, though boys and girls may develop physically at different rates, no major differences in intelligence exist between men and women. Neither is there scientific evidence that a person's sex affects the ability to do creative work or make decisions. Many societies label women as naturally indecisive, one of the main reasons that men hold the majority of jobs requiring important decisions.

Western cultures consider gentleness, meekness, and motherliness as feminine traits, and aggressiveness and bravery as masculine characteristics. Some people believe that hormones create such definite masculine and feminine personality traits. These traits supposedly appear at *puberty*, a period that marks the end of childhood and the beginning of physical maturity. Scientists have tested this theory by injecting female rats with male hormones and male rats with female hormones. The females became aggressive, and the males became gentle. But male and female behavior varies so widely among different animal species that such tests cannot be considered proof of the effects of human hormones. For example, some female spiders and the female mantid eat their mates.

The American anthropologist Margaret Mead indicated that culture, more than biological features, determines masculine and feminine personality traits. She studied three tribes that lived on islands in the Pacific Ocean. In one tribe, both men and women had a gentle, quiet nature. In the second tribe, both men and women behaved aggressively. In the third tribe, the women took the dominant and impersonal role, and the men were gentle and tender.

Research shows that men and women have the same range of emotional characteristics. Social scientists believe that societies may harm individuals by insisting that they conform to a certain cultural pattern of masculine and feminine behavior. In Western societies, for example, a tender, sensitive boy may be mocked as a sissy, and a noisy, adventurous girl may be scolded for being unladylike. Such *stereotypes* (fixed images) of masculinity and femininity have barred many men and women from jobs and other activities that they enjoy and for which they are qualified.

Woman's Roles Through the Ages

In Ancient Societies, most women married and began raising children soon after reaching puberty. They remained at home, received no formal education, and had little economic or social power. Exceptions included the women judges who are mentioned in the Bible and the women of ancient Egypt and Sparta. Both Egyptian and Spartan women could own and inherit property. In addition, Egyptian women could work outside the home, and Spartan women could receive a formal education.

In ancient Rome, the law gave husbands control over their wives. But Roman women had more legal and social freedom than did most women in Europe for the next several centuries. They were highly respected, managed household affairs, and moved freely through the city to attend public functions.

In India, women owned property and took part in public debates thousands of years before the birth of Christ. But about 200 B.C., Hinduism developed laws that gave women an inferior status to men. Most Hindu parents arranged for their daughters to be married before reaching puberty and taught them to always obey their husbands. Later, other religions, including Christianity, adopted practices that gave men a status superior to that of women.

In Medieval and Early Modern Societies, religion remained an important factor in determining woman's position. As Christianity spread through Europe, women lost much of the freedom they had had under Roman law. The Roman Catholic Church followed Old Testament law and early German tradition regarding male domination. A European nobleman of the Middle Ages could end his marriage if his wife did not bear at least one son. Most women received no formal education. Noblewomen learned to sew, spin, weave, and direct household servants. Peasant men and women had fairly equal legal and social rights, though the men were dominant.

The Reformation, the religious movement of the 1500's that gave rise to Protestantism, removed some church restrictions on marriage and divorce. But Protestant leaders also regarded women as being completely under the control of their fathers or husbands.

Islam, the religion of the Muslims, spread through the Middle East, northern Africa, and parts of Europe and Asia from the 700's to the 1200's. Like Christianity and Hinduism, Islam taught women to obey their husbands. Men were allowed to have more than one wife. Muslim women began wearing veils over their face, and many men secluded their women in harems (see HAREM). But Muslim women did have the right to own property and to divorce their husbands.

Before the 1800's, most women worked only in and around the home. In England, a number of women worked in trade, and some were partners with their husbands. Men approved such work only if it did not take women out of the home. The few women who did work outside the home did not have the right to spend their own wages.

Until the 1800's, few women had any voice in politics or economics except through their husbands. Most European countries forbade wives to own property or to enter a profession. According to English common law, a husband controlled his wife and any property she had owned before their marriage (see COMMON LAW).

In Industrialized Societies. During the 1700's and early 1800's, the Industrial Revolution brought great changes in the lives of people in many countries (see INDUSTRIAL REVOLUTION). A shortage of men resulted in large numbers of women beginning to work outside the home. English and American textile mills of the early 1800's were among the first factories to employ women. Later, other kinds of factories in industrialized nations started to hire women, partly because not enough men were available.

At first, the labor shortage assured women of fairly good working conditions—though they worked long hours and earned less than men. Unmarried working women gained some independence from their families because they could spend their earnings or save for an education. But many single women lived under strict supervision in dormitories operated by their employers. Married women had no legal right to do as they wished with their own earnings.

By the 1830's, many thousands of women worked in the textile mills of such industrialized regions as England and the New England States. In time, industry developed better machines, and large factories began to replace small shops. At the same time, more people left farming and sought factory work. As a result, working conditions became worse and wages dropped. But many unmarried women and widows continued to work in factories because they had little chance of finding other jobs.

Women's Rights Movements began to develop during the first half of the 1800's, when social and political revolutions were occurring in many nations. Various groups in Europe and the United States debated woman's role in business, the family, politics, and society.

Some of the first organized attempts to improve woman's status took place in the United States. These actions occurred in the areas of educational, social, and political reform. In 1835, Oberlin College in Oberlin, Ohio, became the first U.S. coeducational college. In 1841, Oberlin became the first college in the country to award degrees to women. During the next several decades, coeducation developed rapidly in the United States, with much support from state universities.

As women gained more education and greater opportunities to work outside the home, they began to demand other rights as well. During the 1840's, married women in New York led a campaign to revise state property laws. In 1848, the New York legislature passed a bill giving married women the right to own real estate in their own name.

In 1848, two reformers—Lucretia Mott and Elizabeth Cady Stanton—called a Woman's Rights Convention in Seneca Falls, N.Y. From then on, until the Civil War began in 1861, national women's rights conventions met almost every year. The delegates discussed the rights of women regarding divorce, guardianship of children, property control, voting, and other matters. During the Civil War, from 1861 to 1865, most women reformers, both North and South, abandoned the movement and gave their full support to war activities.

In 1868 and 1870, the 14th and 15th amendments to the U.S. Constitution guaranteed *suffrage* (the right to vote) to all men, but not to any women. Thereafter, the women's rights movement directed most of its efforts at gaining suffrage. Several groups split away from the movement because they thought other social and political reforms deserved equal effort. A constitutional amendment granting women full suffrage was introduced during every session of Congress from 1878 to 1920, when it passed as the 19th Amendment.

During the late 1800's and early 1900's, woman suffrage became an important issue in many countries. In 1893, New Zealand became the first nation to grant all women full voting rights. Australia and the Scandinavian countries did so in the early 1900's. Russia gave women the vote in 1917 when the newly formed Soviet government declared equality of the sexes. The next year, Canada granted women the same voting rights as men in national elections. British women campaigned more than 40 years before receiving full voting rights in 1928. See WOMAN SUFFRAGE.

Educational and employment reforms slowly increased the rights of European and American women during the last half of the 1800's and in the early 1900's. British women fought for education and the right to choose a profession. In 1848, Queen's College for Women opened in London. Other women's colleges followed, but women could not go to college with men. In 1884, Oxford University began admitting women to examinations for a bachelor's degree. But Oxford did not admit women as full-time students until 1920.

In the late 1800's, British women began finding jobs outside the home and factory. In 1870, the government started to employ women for typing and other clerical work. But many positions remained closed to women. Women could study medicine but had to take their qualifying examinations outside England until 1875, when the Royal College of Surgeons began to admit women. Nor could women doctors work in British hospitals until 1877, when a London hospital opened to them. British women could not become lawyers until 1919.

In the United States, women had first graduated from medical school and started practicing medicine in 1849, though they met much opposition. In 1869, Iowa licensed the first woman lawyer in the United States. But not until 1920 did all the states allow women to practice law under the same provisions as men. In the United States, as in most other Western countries, women teachers did not become common before 1850.

In Great Britain before 1870, married women who worked could not spend their own earnings, though divorcees and unmarried women could. In 1881, French law gave married female factory workers the right to open a bank account without their husband's consent. Other French working wives received that right in 1907.

Wartime Changes. During World War I (1914-1918) and World War II (1939-1945), women in the warring countries took over many traditionally male jobs to free men for combat. Thousands of women served in the U.S., Canadian, and British armed forces. In the United States, about 18 million women worked in war plants during World War II. Many industries sponsored child-care centers so that mothers could be free to work. The U.S. government established a policy of equal pay for equal work in industries with government contracts. Many labor unions also adopted this policy. But little discussion took place about equal employment and advancement opportunities for men and women. After both world wars, most women returned to their old jobs or to their homes. Until the 1960's, few women campaigned actively to extend women's rights.

Woman's Roles Today

In the 1970's, more women went to college and held a wider variety of jobs than ever before. Women in many countries could, if they wished, live independently and control their own earnings and property. Women can vote and run for public office in almost all countries that have elections. In 1971, the male voters of Liechtenstein defeated a proposal to give women the vote. All other European nations have woman suffrage.

The United Nations has a Commission on the Status of Women. Many nations have agreed to follow the

Mary Ellen Mark, Woodfin Camp, Inc.

Women's Liberation Demonstrations became common in the United States and Canada during the 1960's and 1970's. Women of all ages joined in a demand for equal rights.

commission's policies on divorce, education, property rights, suffrage, and other issues related to women's rights. One commission document provides that no marriage should take place unless both the man and woman freely consent. This policy protects women from marriages arranged against their will. But the commission does not have the power to enforce its policies.

In the United States and Canada. Women make up about 40 per cent of the labor force in the United States. In Canada, about 37 per cent of the workers are women. In both the United States and Canada, about 40 per cent of the college graduates are women.

Despite the high percentage of working women in both the United States and Canada, few hold executive or managerial positions. In the early 1970's, more than a third of the U.S. working women held clerical jobs, such as secretary, file clerk, or telephone operator. Less than 7 per cent of the working men held similar jobs. In general, women received only about 60 per cent of the pay men received for the same job.

In the United States, women make up about 7 per cent of the physicians, 3 per cent of the lawyers, and less than 1 per cent of the engineers. In Canada, about 9 per cent of the physicians, 2 per cent of the lawyers, and less than 1 per cent of the engineers are women. These low figures result partly from the attitude that such professions are unsuitable for women. But today, more women than ever before graduate from professional schools and go on to careers in traditionally male fields.

Although women in both countries may run for public office, no woman has been President of the United States or Prime Minister of Canada. The United States has had only five women governors. Neither nation has had many women in its national legislature.

Laws passed in the United States and Canada during the 1960's and early 1970's aimed at ensuring equal treatment of men and women. The Canadian Bill of Rights, passed in 1960, states that no individual may be denied any rights because of his or her sex. All of Canada's 10 provinces and the Northwest Territories passed laws in the 1950's and 1960's providing for equal pay for equal work by men and women.

In the United States, the Civil Rights Act of 1964 prohibits job discrimination on the basis of sex. In 1971, the Supreme Court ruled that unequal treatment based only on sex violates the 14th Amendment to the U.S. Constitution. This amendment provides all citizens with equal protection under the law.

In March, 1972, the Senate approved the so-called Women's Equal Rights Amendment. This amendment states, "Equality of rights under the law shall not be denied or abridged by the United States or any state on account of sex." The House of Representatives had approved it in 1971.

Legal experts believe the amendment, if passed, would make several state and local laws unconstitutional. For example, it would outlaw limits on the jobs women may hold and the hours they may work. The amendment would prohibit limitations on women's right to do business on an equal basis with men. It would ban laws that treat women more harshly than men for certain crimes, such as adultery or drunkenness. It also would end the favorable treatment women had automatically received in alimony, child custody, and child support cases. For example, in most divorce proceedings, the mother has received custody of the children, and the father has been forced to provide money to support them. Under the amendment, each case would be decided individually without regard to sex.

Women's rights groups had demanded such an amendment for 49 years, but many people thought the 14th Amendment made it unnecessary. By mid-1979, 35 states had ratified the Equal Rights Amendment. An amendment becomes law when 38 states approve it.

The Women's Liberation Movement. Many women's groups protest what they consider unequal treatment of men and women. Such groups became prominent in the 1960's and 1970's. The activities of these groups came to be known as the Women's Liberation Movement.

In 1963, an American woman named Betty Friedan published *The Feminine Mystique.* In this book, she attacked society for having long treated women as second-class citizens. She helped form the National Organization for Women (NOW) in 1966. This organization has grown into the largest group in the women's movement. NOW has been active in demanding reform of educational policies, which it claims teach girls to aim only for "women's jobs." Such jobs include nursing, office work, and teaching. Other women's liberation groups in the United States include the National Women's Political Caucus and the Women's Equity Action League. In Canada, the movement developed among female members of the Student Union for Peace Action. This group first organized for nuclear disarmament and later protested the Vietnam War (1957-1975).

Women's liberation groups work for strict enforcement of laws and regulations that promote women's equality. Most of these groups call for better child-care facilities that would free mothers for work outside the home. Some groups demand that abortion be legalized without restriction so that every woman can decide for herself whether to bear a child. Many women's liberation groups insist that the abbreviation "Ms.," rather than "Miss" or "Mrs.," should be used before women's names. They believe there is no reason to have different titles for married and unmarried women.

Some women's liberation groups think that women will achieve equality only through basic changes in society. These groups say men should help with housework and child care to free women for outside work. They believe such sharing of tasks would result in relationships between men and women based on mutual interests, respect, and affection, rather than on men's economic and physical dominance.

In Other Countries, changing laws and customs are giving women a greater voice in political and social matters. In 1960, Sirimavo Bandaranaike of Sri Lanka became the first female prime minister in the world. She held office until 1977. Indira Gandhi served as prime minister of India from 1966 to 1977, and Golda Meir was prime minister of Israel from 1969 to 1974. Isabel Perón served as president of Argentina from 1974 to 1976. Margaret Thatcher became prime minister of Great Britain in 1979.

In Africa, more women are being educated than ever before. About 40 per cent of Kenya's high school pupils

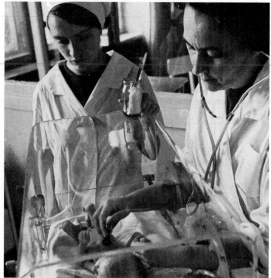

Sovfoto

Russian Women, such as these children's doctors, make up about three-fourths of their nation's physicians. Women in Russia also have prominent roles in economics, engineering, and law.

are women, and the number of educated women is rising in other African countries. Some women occupy important government positions, such as supreme court judge in Ghana and chief minister in the Congo.

In the 1960's and 1970's, many women left their villages to seek education or work in the cities. But most African women still live in villages and devote their lives to child raising and housework. Many men have more than one wife. In many areas, a man must pay a woman's parents a *bride price* before he can marry her.

In Western Europe, women make up a large portion of the labor force, but few hold high-paying jobs. Although almost half the women in Sweden work, they make up only about 11 per cent of their country's lawyers, 19 per cent of the physicians, and 15 per cent of the schoolteachers. In West Germany, about 30 per cent of the women work, but they hold only a low percentage of the best jobs. In Great Britain, only about 6 per cent of the top positions are held by women.

As elsewhere, many women in Western Europe are demanding increased rights. They have demonstrated for liberalized divorce laws, the widespread availability of birth control information, and enforcement of existing laws providing equal pay for equal work.

In South America, most women accept traditional roles of housekeeping and raising families. But many who live in the major cities or have had some high school education seek jobs outside the home. Most Latin-American nations recognize the principle of equal pay for equal work, and most have women's bureaus connected with their department of labor. These bureaus teach women about their rights as workers and provide technical training to help women get better jobs. The Organization of American States, an association of North and South American countries, has a commission that aids the women's bureaus of member states.

In Russia, women and men receive equal pay for equal work. But men still hold most top government and management positions. Most Russian women work outside the home. But they also do almost all the housework and shopping. The Russian government provides nurseries where working mothers can leave their preschool children.

Women make up about half the labor force of Russia. About 75 per cent of the nation's physicians, almost half its judges, and a third of its engineers and lawyers are women. Women make up about 70 per cent of the teachers and 60 per cent of the economists. About a third of the members of the Supreme Soviet, Russia's parliament, are women, but few women are on the Central Committee of the Communist Party.

In China, as in Russia and other Communist countries, society considers women equal to men and expects them to work just as hard. Women drive trucks and bulldozers, work on street construction crews, and fly military planes. Women make up more than half the labor force of China's textile industry and from 30 to 40 per cent of the farm and commune workers. Most of the nation's teachers are women. Working mothers leave their children in child-care centers or with elderly relatives. Many Chinese women hold important positions on local government bodies, but few serve on the Central Committee of the Communist Party. Although two women have served on the Party's 21-member Politburo, none sits on the Politburo's 5-member standing committee, which rules China.

In Japan, a growing number of married women work outside the home. Women make up about a third of the nation's work force, but more than 60 per cent of this group work in family-owned businesses. Women earn an average of less than half as much pay as men.

Many Japanese women belong to organizations that work to improve the status of women. During the late 1960's and early 1970's, these women's groups often marched and picketed to protest high food prices, the lack of child-care facilities, and other conditions.

In India, women have equal legal rights, including the right to vote and the right to own property. Political parties encourage women to run for political office. During the 1960's and early 1970's, increasing numbers of educated working women emerged in India. Over 10 million women have professional or technical jobs. But most of them came from the top levels of Indian society. About 19 per cent of all Indian women can read and write compared with 40 per cent of the men.

In Arab Lands, women's roles are changing slowly. Women in some areas of Bahrain, Kuwait, and Saudi Arabia see few men outside their immediate families. Some restaurants and hotels in these areas separate men and women. But many young husbands and wives attend social events together, and the tradition of keeping women in harems has almost disappeared.

For centuries, Arab custom required women to veil their faces. Turkey banned the veil in the 1920's, and Iran abolished it in 1935. Today, few women wear veils in Egypt, Iraq, Lebanon, and Syria. Saudi Arabian law still requires veils, but many women choose veils of thin fabric that does not conceal the face.

Arab families arrange most marriages, and most girls marry in their teens. But many women attend high school and continue their education in college, a correspondence school, or a foreign institution. Women make up about a fourth of all students in Arab universities. A small but growing percentage of women work outside the home, especially in such professions as teaching.   CYNTHIA FUCHS EPSTEIN

Related Articles in WORLD BOOK include:

LEADERS IN WOMEN'S RIGHTS MOVEMENT

See the biographies listed at the end of WOMAN SUFFRAGE. See also:

Adams, Abigail S.	Lease, Mary E.
Beecher (Catharine)	Mill (Harriet Taylor)
Blackwell, Antoinette B.	Murphy, Emily G.
Bloomer, Amelia J.	O'Reilly, Leonora
Bly, Nellie	Sanger, Margaret
Dickinson, Anna E.	Steinem, Gloria
Friedan, Betty	Terrell, Mary C.
Gilman, Charlotte P.	Truth, Sojourner
Goldman, Emma	Walker, Mary E.
Grimké (family)	Wells-Barnett, Ida Bell
Howe (Julia Ward)	Willard, Emma H.

OTHER RELATED ARTICLES

Abortion	Feminism	Planned
Alimony	Marriage	Parenthood
Birth Control	Menopause	Pregnancy
Childbirth	Menstruation	Sparta (Way of Life)
Divorce	National Organiza-	Woman Suffrage
Equal Rights	tion for Women	Women's Bureau
Amendment	Pioneer Life	Wyoming (Terri-
Family	in America	torial Progress)

Outline

I. **Physical Characteristics and Woman's Roles**
   A. Motherhood   C. Temperament and
   B. Size and Strength   Emotions
II. **Woman's Roles Through the Ages**
   A. In Ancient Societies
   B. In Medieval and Early Modern Societies
   C. In Industrialized Societies
III. **Woman's Roles Today**
   A. In the United States and Canada
   B. In Other Countries

Questions

What subjects did the women's rights conventions of the 1800's discuss?

What special rights did ancient Egyptian and Spartan women have?

How did the two world wars change woman's position in society?

How did factory work change the lives of unmarried women?

What professions include large percentages of women in Russia?

How do cultural stereotypes harm both sexes?

What role has religion played in determining woman's status in society?

What helped cause the divisions between men's and women's work, dating back to earliest times?

How does the Civil Rights Act of 1964 affect women?

How is the role of Arab women changing?

Reading and Study Guide

See *Women* in the RESEARCH GUIDE/INDEX, Volume 22, for a *Reading and Study Guide.*

WOMAN SUFFRAGE is the right of women to vote. Today, women in nearly all countries have the same voting rights as men. But they did not begin to gain such rights until the early 1900's, and they had to overcome strong opposition to get them. The men and

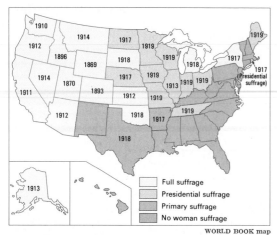

Full suffrage
Presidential suffrage
Primary suffrage
No woman suffrage

WORLD BOOK map

Woman Suffrage existed in three forms before it became law throughout the United States in 1920—voting in all elections, voting only in presidential elections, or voting only in primary elections. The dates shown are the years in which these states granted women the right to vote.

women who supported the drive for woman suffrage were called *suffragists*.

In the United States

During colonial times, the right to vote was limited to adult males who owned property. Many people thought property owners had the strongest interest in good government and so were best qualified to make decisions. Most women could not vote, though some colonies gave the vote to widows who owned property.

By the mid-1700's, many colonial leaders were beginning to think that all citizens should have a voice in government. They expressed this belief in such slogans as "No Taxation Without Representation" and "Government by the Consent of the Governed."

After the United States became an independent nation, the Constitution gave the states the right to decide who could vote. One by one, the states abolished property requirements and, by 1830, all white male adults could vote. Only New Jersey gave women the right to vote, but in 1807, that state also limited voting rights to men.

Beginnings of the Movement. Changing social conditions for women in the early 1800's, combined with the idea of equality, led to the birth of the woman suffrage movement. For example, women began to receive more education and to take part in reform movements, which involved them in politics. As a result, they started to ask why they were not also allowed to vote.

One of the first public appeals for woman suffrage came in 1848. Two reformers, Lucretia Mott and Elizabeth Cady Stanton, called a women's rights convention in Seneca Falls, N.Y., where Stanton lived. The men and women at the convention adopted a Declaration of Sentiments that called for women to have equal rights in education, property, voting, and other matters. The declaration, which used the Declaration of Independence as a model, said, "We hold these truths to be self-evident: that all men and women are created equal...."

Suffrage quickly became the chief goal of the women's rights movement. Leaders of the movement be-

lieved that if women had the vote, they could use it to gain other rights. But the suffragists faced strong opposition. Opponents of woman suffrage believed women were less intelligent and less able to make political decisions than men. They argued that men could represent their wives better than the wives could represent themselves. Some people feared that women's participation in politics would lead to the end of family life.

Growth of the Movement. The drive for woman suffrage gained strength after the passage of the 15th Amendment to the Constitution, which gave the vote to black men but not to any women. In 1869, suffragists formed two national organizations to work for the right to vote. One was the National Woman Suffrage Association, and the other was the American Woman Suffrage Association.

The National Woman Suffrage Association, led by Stanton and another suffragist named Susan B. Anthony, was the more radical of the two organizations. Its chief goal was an amendment to the Constitution giving women the vote. In 1872, Anthony and a group of women voted in the presidential election in Rochester, N.Y. She was arrested and fined for voting illegally. At her trial, which attracted nationwide attention, she made a stirring speech that ended with the slogan "Resistance to Tyranny Is Obedience to God."

The American Woman Suffrage Association, led by the suffragist Lucy Stone and her husband, Henry Blackwell, was more conservative. Its main goal was to induce individual states to give the vote to women. The two organizations united in 1890 to form the National American Woman Suffrage Association. The Woman's Christian Temperance Union and other organizations also made woman suffrage a goal.

During the early 1900's, a new generation of leaders brought a fresh spirit to the woman suffrage movement. Some of them, including Carrie Chapman Catt and Maud Wood Park, were skilled organizers who received much of their support from middle-class women. These leaders stressed organizing in every congressional district and lobbying in the nation's capital. Other leaders, including Lucy Burns, Alice Paul, and Stanton's daughter Harriot E. Blatch, appealed to young people, radicals, and working-class women. This group of leaders devoted most of their efforts to marches, picketing, and other active forms of protest. Paul and her followers even chained themselves to the White House fence. The suffragists were often arrested and sent to jail, where many of them went on hunger strikes.

Action by Individual States. In 1869, the Territory of Wyoming gave women the right to vote. The Utah Territory did so a year later. Wyoming entered the Union in 1890 and became the first state with woman suffrage. Colorado adopted it in 1893, and Idaho in 1896. By 1920, 15 states—most of them in the West—had granted full voting privileges to women. Twelve other states allowed women to vote in presidential elections, and two let them vote in primary elections.

The 19th Amendment. A woman suffrage amendment was first introduced in Congress in 1878. It failed to pass but was reintroduced in every session of Congress for the next 40 years.

During World War I (1914-1918), the contributions of women to the war effort increased support for a suffrage amendment. In 1918, the House of Representatives held another vote on the issue. Spectators packed the galleries, and several congressmen came to vote despite illness. One was brought in on a stretcher. Representative Frederick C. Hicks of New York left his wife's deathbed—at her request—to vote for the amendment. The House approved the amendment, but the Senate defeated it. In 1919, the Senate finally passed the amendment and sent it to the states for approval.

By 1920, the required number of states had ratified what became the 19th Amendment to the Constitution. The amendment says, "The right of citizens of the United States to vote shall not be denied or abridged by the United States or by any state on account of sex."

In Other Countries

In 1893, New Zealand became the first nation to grant women full voting rights. In 1902, Australia gave women the right to vote in national elections. Other countries that enacted woman suffrage during the early 1900's included Canada, Finland, Germany, Great Britain, and Sweden. In the mid-1900's, China, France, India, Italy, Japan, and other nations gave women the vote. By the late 1970's, only eight nations—most of them in the Middle East—still denied women the right to vote. They were Bahrain, Kuwait, Liechtenstein, Oman, Qatar, Saudi Arabia, the United Arab Emirates, and Yemen (Sana).   ANNE FIROR SCOTT

Related Articles in WORLD BOOK include:

Anthony, Susan B.	Pankhurst, Emmeline G.
Blatch, Harriot E. S.	Paul, Alice
Catt, Carrie Chapman	Rose, Ernestine P.
Davis, Paulina Wright	Shaw, Anna Howard
Duniway, Abigail J. S.	Spencer, Anna G.
Kelley, Florence	Stanton, Elizabeth Cady
League of Women Voters	Stone, Lucy
Lockwood, Belva A. B.	Thomas, Martha Carey
McClung, Nellie	Willard, Frances E. C.
Morris, Esther H.	Woodhull, Victoria C.
Mott, Lucretia C.	

WOMAN'S CHRISTIAN TEMPERANCE UNION is an international organization of women who believe in personal total abstinence from all alcoholic beverages, and who work for the abolition of the liquor traffic. The Youth Temperance Council (high school and college), the Loyal Temperance Legion (grade-school age), and the eight departments of work promote the organization's broad program. The program includes scientific narcotics education, good citizenship, child welfare, and world peace. The W.C.T.U. has played an active part in getting laws passed which provide that young people in the public schools be taught the scientific facts about what alcohol is and what it does.

The organization has branches in all the states of the Union, and in Puerto Rico and the Virgin Islands. It was founded in 1874. The W.C.T.U. grew out of the Women's Temperance Crusade of 1873. During this campaign, women church members went into saloons, sang hymns, prayed, and asked the saloonkeepers to stop selling liquor. The Temperance Crusade swept over 23 states, and resulted in the closing of thousands of places that sold liquor throughout the nation.

A group of Crusaders attending the Chautauqua Sunday School Assembly in 1874 issued the call which resulted in the organization of the National Woman's Christian Temperance Union in November 1874 at Cleveland, Ohio. Its first president was Annie Witten-

myer, and the second was the noted educator and reformer, Frances E. Willard.

The organization grew rapidly, and its influence increased with its growth. It worked through schools, churches, and other organized groups. Finally the Eighteenth Amendment to the Constitution of the United States (passed in 1919) prohibited the manufacture, import, export, and sale of alcoholic beverages. This amendment remained in force between 1920 and 1933, when the Twenty-first Amendment replaced it.

In 1883, Willard founded the first international organization for women, called the World's Woman's Christian Temperance Union. It is made up of women's temperance groups in 72 countries and has about 1 million members. The W.C.T.U. has national headquarters at 1730 Chicago Avenue, Evanston, Ill. 60201.

Critically reviewed by the WOMAN'S CHRISTIAN TEMPERANCE UNION

See also AMERICAN COUNCIL ON ALCOHOL PROBLEMS; PROHIBITION; WILLARD, FRANCES E.

WOMAN'S RELIEF CORPS, NATIONAL, is the oldest woman's patriotic organization in the United States. In July 1883, it was voted the official auxiliary of the Grand Army of the Republic, an organization of veterans of the Union Army in the Civil War. It has about 50,000 members, and is the only existing patriotic organization that was founded solely on the basis of loyal womanhood, regardless of kinship. Headquarters are at 629 S. Seventh Street, Springfield, Ill. 62703.

The aims of the Woman's Relief Corps were to aid and memorialize the Grand Army of the Republic, and to perpetuate the memory of its dead. The organization also works to assist veterans of all wars of the United States. Members try to promote universal liberty, equal rights, and love of country.   EULA M. NELSON

WOMBAT is a thickset, burrowing animal, about 3 feet (91 centimeters) long. It is a *marsupial* (a mammal that carries its young in a pouch). Wombats live on the island of Tasmania and in southern Australia. Their fur is yellow-black to gray-brown. Wombats dig burrows. They leave their burrows only at night to feed on roots, vegetables, and leaves. Wombats make good pets.

Scientific Classification. Wombats belong to the wombat family, *Phascolomidae*. The common wombat is classified as genus *Phascolomis*.   FRANK B. GOLLEY

New York Zoological Society

The Wombat Uses Its Heavy Claws to Dig Burrows.

WOMEN'S AMERICAN ORT is the largest affiliate of the worldwide *Organization for Rehabilitation through Training*, or *ORT*. Women's American ORT has about 125,000 members in the United States. The worldwide ORT is a nonprofit agency founded in 1880 to free underprivileged and uprooted Jewish people from dependence upon charity by teaching them skills and trades. It maintains over 700 installations in 22 countries on 5 continents. About 75,000 persons a year use its high school credit courses, its short-term apprenticeship and adult-training courses, or its junior colleges. Courses are geared to the labor needs of the countries in which the schools are located. The ORT program is financed by governments, local communities, the American Jewish Joint Distribution Committee, and by affiliated ORT groups. Headquarters are at 1250 Broadway, New York, N.Y. 10001. Critically reviewed by WOMEN'S AMERICAN ORT

WOMEN'S BUREAU is an agency of the United States Department of Labor. It develops policies and programs to improve the welfare and status of women as jobholders, homemakers, and citizens. The bureau is chiefly a fact-finding, service, and promotional agency and does not administer any laws.

The Women's Bureau develops programs to improve job opportunities for women and girls, especially in fields that have not traditionally been open to them. It encourages improved vocational counseling, better job-training programs, and continuing education for women. It supports the expansion of children's daycare centers and other home-related services. The bureau also promotes legislation to improve the economic, political, and social status of women and to eliminate sex discrimination. It conducts various studies and publishes its findings.

The bureau provides information and assistance to individuals; employers; labor unions; schools; employment agencies; federal, state, and local government agencies; and the United Nations. The Women's Bureau was established in 1920. It succeeded the Woman-in-Industry Service, which began in 1918. Critically reviewed by the WOMEN'S BUREAU

WOMEN'S CLUBS, GENERAL FEDERATION OF, is an international organization of about 11 million women who belong to women's clubs in about 55 countries. This total includes more than 700,000 members in more than 14,000 clubs in the United States.

The General Federation of Women's Clubs was founded in 1890. In that year, Sorosis of New York, one of the oldest clubs in the United States, invited delegates from other clubs to a general convention. This meeting set up the framework for the general federation. The international headquarters of the General Federation of Women's Clubs are at 1734 N Street NW, Washington, D.C. 20036. GRACE D. NICHOLAS

WOMEN'S EQUAL RIGHTS AMENDMENT. See EQUAL RIGHTS AMENDMENT.

WOMEN'S INTERNATIONAL BOWLING CONGRESS (WIBC) regulates women's organized bowling competition. It has more than 4 million members and ranks as the largest women's sports organization in the world. Its members include both amateur and professional bowlers.

The WIBC establishes and enforces rules for leagues and tournaments, gives awards for outstanding achievements, and promotes interest in bowling. It conducts the annual WIBC Championship Tournament and the Queens Tournament, an event for only the top women bowlers.

The WIBC was founded in 1916. It has headquarters at 5301 S. 76th Street, Greendale, Wis. 53129. The WIBC shares a headquarters building with the American Bowling Congress (ABC), which governs men's organized bowling. The building also houses the National Bowling Museum and Hall of Fame. Critically reviewed by the WOMEN'S INTERNATIONAL BOWLING CONGRESS

WOMEN'S LIBERATION MOVEMENT. See WOMAN (In the United States and Canada).

WOMEN'S TRADE UNION LEAGUE OF AMERICA, NATIONAL, was a federation of women interested in the American labor movement. It was officially discontinued in 1950. The organization acted as an information clearing house for labor unions, individuals, and groups. It was founded in Boston in 1903.

At one time, the Trade Union League had more than a million members. Its chief aim was to organize women workers into trade unions. ELISABETH CHRISTMAN

WONDER, STEVIE (1950-   ), is an American singer, composer, and musician known for the originality and force of his music. Wonder is generally considered a rock singer, but many of his songs show characteristics of traditional popular music.

Wonder's real name is Stevland Morris. He was born in Saginaw, Mich., and has been blind all his life. Wonder recorded his first major success, "Fingertips" (1963), when he was 12 years old. His early records were lively, rhythmic songs.

Wonder's musical style became more complex after he reached adulthood. He created powerful rock compositions, such as "Superstition" (1972) and "Higher Ground" (1973), in which he played the synthesizer and other electronic instruments. Wonder also sang and composed lyrical melodies, including "All in Love Is Fair" (1973) and "You Are the Sunshine of

Tony Korody, Sygma
Stevie Wonder

My Life" (1973). He has written songs about serious subjects as well, such as his religious beliefs and social issues concerning blacks. JERRY M. DEAN

WONDER DRUG. See ANTIBIOTIC.

WONDERS OF THE WORLD. See SEVEN WONDERS OF THE WORLD.

WONSAN, *WUHN sahn* (pop. 350,000), is an eastern coastal city in North Korea that is important for its naval base. A narrow peninsula shelters the city's deep, natural harbor. For location, see KOREA (map).

Wonsan serves as a commercial center for the surrounding agricultural and gold-mining area. The city's chief exports include fish, rice, and soybeans. From 1910 to 1945, during the period that Japan ruled Korea, Wonsan served as a major port for the export of Korean farm products to Japan. WILLIAM E. HENTHORN

WOOD is a tough substance under the bark of trees, shrubs, and certain other plants. The physical properties of wood, plus its chemical composition, make it one of the most valuable natural resources. Wood is used in making thousands of products, including baseball bats, furniture, lumber, musical instruments, railroad ties, cellophane, charcoal, and paper.

Wood's physical properties make it especially useful for construction work. It is tough, strong, and easy to handle. Wood also insulates well, does not rust, and resists high heat better than steel. However, wood shrinks and swells, depending on how much moisture it loses or absorbs.

Every piece of wood has a distinctive—and different—pattern called the *figure*. The figure is a highly desirable feature of wood used for furniture, cabinets, and other fine wood products.

This article discusses the physical and chemical properties of wood. For additional information on wood and its many uses, see the WORLD BOOK articles on FOREST PRODUCTS, LUMBER, and TREE.

Kinds of Wood. There are two general kinds of wood, *softwood* and *hardwood*. These terms refer to the type of tree from which wood comes. They do not indicate the hardness of wood.

Softwood comes from cone-bearing trees, called *conifers*. Most conifers have needlelike, evergreen leaves. Common softwoods include Douglas fir, hemlock, pine, and redwood. These woods can be easily sawed, planed, chiseled, and bored, and so they are good for construction purposes. Softwoods also supply most of the pulpwood used to make cellophane and paper products.

Hardwood comes from broad-leaved trees. Most of these trees are *deciduous*—that is, they lose their leaves every autumn. Birch, elm, mahogany, maple, and oak are common hardwoods. The rich and distinctive figures of these woods add to the beauty of furniture, cabinets, paneling, and floors.

The Composition of Wood. Wood consists of tiny, tube-shaped cells that form layers of permanent tissue around a plant stem. The walls of wood cells contain three chief substances—*cellulose, lignin,* and *hemicellulose.* Cellulose makes up about half of wood by weight and gives wood its strength and structure. Lignin holds the fibers of wood together. Hemicellulose resembles both cellulose and lignin. Wood also contains substances called *extractives.* They include fats, gums, oils, and coloring matter.

The proportion of cellulose, lignin, hemicellulose, and extractives varies among different kinds of wood. The cellular structure also differs. These variations make some wood heavy and some light, some stiff and some flexible, and some plain and some colorful.

Manufacturers obtain several useful chemicals and by-products from wood. For example, cellulose is used in making explosives, fabrics, paints, paper, and many other products. Lignin has a variety of uses, especially in making animal feeds, plastics, and artificial vanilla. The extractives of certain woods provide oils, pitch, turpentine, and tar. Hemicellulose has few uses.

Wood Figures are determined chiefly by the growth process of the tree. They result from combinations of color, luster, texture, and grain.

Some Types of Wood   Wood is classified as *softwood* or *hardwood.* Softwoods can be easily sawed, planed, or bored, and so they are used chiefly for structural work. Hardwoods have beautiful grain patterns and are widely used for furniture, floors, and paneling. Some of the most popular hardwoods are shown below.

Chester B. Stem, Inc. (WORLD BOOK photos)

Beech   Birch   Cherry   Elm

Hickory   Mahogany   Maple   Oak

Red Gum   Rosewood   Sycamore   Walnut

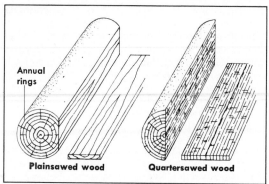

Wood Patterns are determined partly by the way logs are cut. Plainsawed wood is cut along the edges of a tree's annual rings, and quartersawed wood is cut through the rings.

The color comes mainly from extractives. Uneven distribution of the extractives produces a *pigment figure*, found especially in ebony, rosewood, and walnut. Luster is the way wood reflects light. Many woods, including birch and pearwood, require a coat of varnish or another clear finish to bring out their luster. The texture of wood results from the structure of the cells. For example, beech, satinwood, and sycamore have small, closely spaced cells, which produce a fine texture. The grain depends on the arrangement and direction of the cells. The grains of ash, birch, mahogany, and walnut give these woods a wavy *fiddleback figure*. Maple trees have a *bird's eye figure*, which looks like a knot.

The figure is also determined by the way wood is sawed. There are two ways of cutting wood, *plainsawing* and *quartersawing*. Plainsawing produces oval and curved figures. These patterns increase the beauty of such woods as cedar, cherry, and walnut. Quartersawing gives wood a striped appearance. Mahogany, oak, and sycamore have rich figures when quartersawed.

In some woods, the figure depends on the part of the tree from which the wood is cut. For example, tree stumps and wartlike outgrowths called *burls* have attractive patterns. The most popular stumpwood is American walnut. Cherry and walnut have highly prized burls. HARRY E. TROXELL

Related Articles. For more information on the uses of wood, see FOREST PRODUCTS, LUMBER, and TREE with their lists of *Related Articles*. See also the following articles:

Cellulose	Plywood	Veneer
Furniture	Stain	Wallboard
Lignin	Varnish	Woodworking

WOOD, GRANT (1892-1942), an American painter, portrayed scenes of Midwestern rural life as well as simplified, childlike versions of American history. His earlier works were unusual in combining photographic realism with satirical intent, as in the painting *Daughters of the Revolution*. His *American Gothic*, painted in 1930, brought him immediate fame. This painting appears in color in the PAINTING article. Wood was one of the first of the "regionalist" painters in the United States, along with such men as Thomas Hart Benton and John Steuart Curry (see BENTON, THOMAS H.; CURRY, JOHN S.).

Wood was born near Anamosa, Iowa, and was always connected with that state. He studied, and later taught, at the University of Iowa. MILTON W. BROWN

See also WASHINGTON, GEORGE (color picture).

University of Iowa; *Art Digest*
Grant Wood

WOOD, JETHRO (1774-1834), a Quaker farmer, produced an improved cast-iron plow with removable pieces at points of greatest wear. His moldboard design remains almost unchanged in plows made since then (see PLOW [The Moldboard Plow Bottom]). Wood found that people accepted his improvements. Despite a patent issued in 1819, infringers used Wood's design. He exhausted his money and energy in lawsuits, but never enjoyed material benefits from his work. He was born in Dartmouth, Mass. RICHARD D. HUMPHREY

WOOD, LEONARD (1860-1927), was an American soldier and colonial administrator. As military governor of Cuba from 1899 to 1902, he prepared the island for independence. He built roads and schools, and helped stamp out yellow fever by cleaning up swamps and mosquito-ridden areas, making Cuba a more healthful place in which to live.

Wood was born in Winchester, N.H. After graduating from Harvard Medical School, he joined the Army Medical Corps. He commanded the *Rough Riders*, a famous volunteer regiment in which Theodore Roosevelt also served, during the Spanish-American War (see ROUGH RIDERS). Wood commanded the United States forces in the Philippines from 1906 to 1909, and served as chief of staff from 1910 to 1914. He urged military preparedness during World War I. In 1920, a movement among Republicans to nominate Wood for the presidency failed. He served as governor general of the Philippines from 1921 until his death. NELSON M. BLAKE

WOOD, ROBERT ELKINGTON (1879-1969), an American industrialist and soldier, helped make Sears, Roebuck and Company one of the world's largest general merchandising firms. Wood joined Sears as a vice-president. He persuaded the mail-order firm to enter the retail field. He became president in 1928 and chairman of the board in 1939. He retired in 1954, but continued as a board member until 1968, when he became honorary board chairman.

Wood was born in Kansas City, Mo. He graduated from the United States Military Academy in 1900. During World War I (1914-1918), he held the rank of brigadier general and served as commander of the quartermaster corps. W. H. BAUGHN

WOOD, ROBERT WILLIAMS (1868-1955), was an American physicist. His principal interest was in spectrum analysis of metallic vapor (see LIGHT [The Visible Spectrum]). His experiments contributed to the development of new theories about the structure of matter. He pioneered in the development of color photography. Wood was born in Concord, Mass. He graduated from Harvard University. RICHARD D. HUMPHREY

WOOD ALCOHOL. See METHANOL.

WOOD ANEMONE, *uh NEM oh nee*, is an attractive perennial plant grown chiefly in rock gardens. The wood anemone, often called the *windflower*, grows in Europe, Siberia, and in the eastern part of the United States. The root of the wood anemone is a tuber, which is thick and fleshy like a potato. The plant has a single whorl of leaves near the base of the stem. Its white flowers appear cup-shaped and grow singly. The plant grows best in moist, sandy soil. It is reproduced by seeds or root cuttings.

Scientific Classification. The wood anemone belongs to the crowfoot family, *Ranunculaceae*. It is genus *Anemone*. The American species is *A. quinquefolia*, and the European species is *A. nemorosa*.   THEODOR JUST

See also ANEMONE.

WOOD-BLOCK PRINT. See BLOCK PRINTING; HOKUSAI KATSUSHIKA (picture); JAPANESE PRINT.

WOOD BUFFALO NATIONAL PARK. See CANADA (National Parks).

WOOD CARVING. For at least 5,000 years, people have carved ornaments, figures, or useful objects from wood. Wood carvings may decorate the surface of an object, such as a door panel or a chest. The wood carver may also make separate objects to stand alone. This is called carving in the round.

How the Wood Carver Works. The easiest woods for the wood carver to cut and finish are basswood, white pine, black walnut, and mahogany. Other good woods for carving include oak, beech, holly, sycamore, and redwood. The wood should be well seasoned and have a smooth texture and color. A master carver often uses wood burls or knotted wood which produce a beautiful surface pattern when properly finished.

Tools Needed. Wood carving need not require many tools. One or two very sharp knives and a sharp chisel will do for the beginner. A penknife makes the best tool for carving small objects. For larger pieces, a jackknife or hunting knife is needed. The blades must be of good steel, and must be kept as sharp as a razor.

How to Cut the Wood. The beginner should practice carving strokes on a piece of soft wood about $\frac{1}{4}$ to $\frac{3}{8}$ inch (6 to 10 millimeters) thick. An outline of a simple design should be drawn on the face of the wood. Then the figure can be carved out, stroke by stroke. The second piece may be of thicker wood, with the edges rounded

off. Then a simple figure may be carved in full. To do this, select or cut a block of wood in the size needed. Draw a separate view of the figure in outline on each side. First, carve out the front and back, and then do the sides. Simple lines cut with single strokes are best. The sharp edges of the stroke are left to help show the planes of the figure.

History of Wood Carving. Wood carving is one of the oldest arts. Wood carvings have been found in Egypt which were made about 5,000 years ago. The Bible also mentions its use. Historical accounts tell of Greek wood carvings from very early times. The wood carvers of the Middle Ages helped to decorate many cathedrals.

Many artists of the Renaissance carved in wood as well as in stone. One of the greatest wood carvers was Grinling Gibbons (1648-1720), who carved the stalls of Saint Paul's Cathedral in London.

After the middle of the 1800's, wood carving attracted less interest. But, in Switzerland, Austria, and southern Germany, many craftworkers still carve wood as a regular occupation. Fine wood carving is also done by some artists in America, as well as in Europe. Artists in the Far East have long done fine carving. Many persons carve wood as a hobby.   WILLIAM M. MILLIKEN

See also CARVING; FURNITURE; INDIAN, AMERICAN (Arts and Crafts); NEW ZEALAND (picture); SCULPTURE (The Sculptor at Work).

WOOD DUCK is a colorful bird that lives in the woods of southern Canada and throughout the United States. The male is the most colorful of North American ducks. Its upper feathers glitter with green, blue, and purple. Underneath, it is red, yellow, and white. Females are brown above and yellowish below. Both males and females have large crests. The birds measure about 20 inches (51 centimeters) long, and have short necks and long tails.

Wood ducks spend much time in ponds and streams near woods. They go into the woods for nuts and insects. They nest in hollow trees, sometimes 40 feet (12 meters) from the ground, and usually in the woods away from water. The female lays 8 to 15 creamy-white eggs.

The Metropolitan Museum of Art, New York

The Art of Wood Carving is thousands of years old. An Egyptian figure, *far left*, was carved of cedar nearly 4,000 years ago. The Chinese figure, *center*, dates from the Ming dynasty. The figure of a girl, *left*, is a modern prizewinning ebony carving.

WOOD IBIS

Wood ducks nearly died out, but in recent years seem to be coming back.

Scientific Classification. The wood duck is a member of the surface duck family, *Anatidae*. It is classified as genus *Aix*, species *A. sponsa*.   JOSEPH J. HICKEY

See also BIRD (color picture: Wild Ducks); DUCK (with pictures).

WOOD IBIS. See STORK.

WOOD LOUSE, or SOW BUG, is a small flat animal with seven pairs of legs. It is a crustacean, related to the crab and the lobster. It lives in the bark of trees, old wood, or under stones, and can roll itself up into a ball. A form that lives in the sea, the *gribble*, is destructive to the timber of piers and ships.

Scientific Classification. The common wood louse belongs to the family *Oniscidae*. It is genus *Oniscus*, species *O. asellus*. The gribble is *Limnoria lignorum*.

See also CRUSTACEAN.

WOOD MEASURE. See WEIGHTS AND MEASURES.

WOOD NYMPH. See BUTTERFLY (Kinds of Butterflies; color picture: Common Butterflies).

WOOD NYMPH, in mythology. See DRYAD; NYMPH.

WOOD PEWEE is a small bird related to the flycatcher. It nests in the summer in Canada and the eastern United States, and spends the winters in Central and South America. It is also called the *Eastern pewee*. The *Western pewee* resembles it, but has a different song.

The wood pewee looks somewhat like the phoebe, but has a grayer brown coloring, and white bars on its wings. Its plaintive call sounds somewhat like *pee a wee*. The pewee sings at the first sign of daybreak, and also in the early evening when shadows begin to fall.

The wood pewee builds one of the daintiest nests. It weaves various plant fibers together tightly and covers the outside with lichens. The bird places its nest on a horizontal limb of a tree. The female lays two to four eggs, colored a creamy-white and speckled with brown. The wood pewee is useful to human beings because it eats many insect pests.

Scientific Classification. The wood pewee belongs to the flycatcher family, *Tyrannidae*. It is classified as genus *Contopus*, species *C. virens*.   ARTHUR A. ALLEN

WOOD PULP. See PAPER; FOREST PRODUCTS; LUMBER (introduction); TREE (Wood Products).

WOOD RAT. See PACK RAT.

WOOD SORREL. See OXALIS; SHAMROCK.

WOOD SPIRIT. See METHANOL.

WOOD THRUSH. See BIRD (color picture: Favorite Songbirds); THRUSH.

WOOD TICK. See TICK; ROCKY MOUNTAIN SPOTTED FEVER with picture.

WOODBINE. See HONEYSUCKLE; VIRGINIA CREEPER.

WOODCHUCK, or GROUND HOG, is an animal that belongs to the squirrel family. Woodchucks are a kind of marmot (see MARMOT). They live in Canada, and in the eastern and midwestern parts of the United States. According to an old superstition, a person can tell when spring will come by watching what a woodchuck does on Ground-Hog Day (see GROUND-HOG DAY).

Several subspecies of woodchucks live in North America. The *common ground hog* of Canada and the eastern United States is typical of the group. It is about 2 feet (61 centimeters) long, including its bushy tail, and has a broad, flat head. The animal's coarse fur is gray on the upper parts of its body and yellowish-orange on the under parts.

Woodchucks build complex burrows that contain several compartments. They dig their burrows with the sharp claws of their front feet, and scrape the dirt out of the hole with their hind feet.

When a woodchuck goes to look for food, it first sits up on its haunches at the entrance to its burrow. It looks and listens for any sign of danger. This habit makes the woodchuck an easy target for hunters. Woodchucks eat such plants as alfalfa and clover. They are considered pests because they destroy farm crops.

Woodchucks *hibernate* (sleep through the winter). They eat large amounts of food in the fall. The extra food is changed to fat in their bodies, and the woodchucks live on this fat during their winter sleep. Female

Wide World

The Woodchuck, or ground hog, makes its home in a burrow that it digs with the sharp claws on its front and hind feet.

Olin Sewall Pettingill, Jr.

The Wood Pewee Sings at Daybreak and at Twilight.

woodchucks give birth to four or five young in the spring.

Scientific Classification. The woodchuck belongs to the squirrel family, *Sciuridae*. It is genus *Marmota*, species *M. monax*.   DANIEL BRANT

WOODCOCK is the name of several species of birds in the snipe family. These birds live in moist woods and sheltered bogs in many parts of the world. The *American woodcock* lives in the eastern United States and southern Canada. It is about 11 inches (28 centimeters) long, and has a heavy body. It has short legs and tail, and a long bill with a sensitive tip. The woodcock uses its bill to search for earthworms in the mud.

The American woodcock flies south to Missouri, New Jersey, and the Gulf Coast in winter. It comes north again in spring, appearing by the first of March. It lives on the ground in the woods, and makes nests of dry leaves. The female lays four tannish and reddish-brown eggs. Woodcocks are wood brown with black bars. These colors make the bird blend with its background in the thickets and help protect it from enemies.

On spring evenings, the cock performs its courtship flight for the hen. As it circles high in the air, it makes whistling sounds with its wing feathers and utters various voice calls. After the young hatch, a parent woodcock may carry them between its thighs during flight.

Scientific Classification. Woodcocks belong to the family *Scolopacidae*. The American woodcock is genus *Philohela*, species *P. minor*.   ALFRED M. BAILEY

See also BIRD (color picture: Game Birds).

WOODCOCK, LEONARD (1911-   ), is an American labor leader and diplomat. He served as president of the United Automobile Workers (UAW), one of the largest labor unions in the United States, from 1970 to 1977. In 1979, Woodcock became U.S. ambassador to China.

Woodcock was a Detroit factory worker before he became a union organizer of the Congress of Industrial Organizations (CIO) in 1938. He joined the UAW staff in 1940. From 1947 to 1955, Woodcock held many leadership posts in the union. In 1955, he became a UAW vice-president and the union's chief negotiator with the General Motors Corporation. In the early 1970's, Woodcock led a drive to establish national health insurance in the United States. He served on the U.S. Pay Board in 1971 and 1972. In 1977, President Jimmy Carter appointed Woodcock chief of the U.S.

Liaison Office in Peking, China. Woodcock was named ambassador to China in 1979, after the United States and China established full diplomatic ties. He was born in Providence, R.I.   ABRAHAM J. SIEGEL

WOODCUT is a picture or design made from a block of wood. The block itself is also called a woodcut. Since the 1400's, artists have produced woodcuts that rank among the masterpieces of printmaking.

Artists make most woodcuts from pine blocks. The artist removes portions of the surface, using chisels, gouges, and knives. The cutaway sections appear white in the final print, and the uncut parts produce the desired image. The artist coats the uncut parts with ink and places a sheet of paper over the block. The paper is then rubbed with the back of a spoon or with some similar implement. The rubbing transfers the inked image onto the paper. To make colored woodcuts, the artist generally uses colored ink and a number of separate blocks, one for each color. Each block has a portion of the picture. The artist must cut the blocks so they appear in exactly the correct *registration* (relationship to each other) in the completed woodcut.

Woodcuts were first used in Europe during the Middle Ages to print patterns on textiles. Beginning in the 1400's, artists made woodcuts to portray religious subjects, to decorate and illustrate books, and to make playing cards. During the late 1400's and early 1500's, the German artist Albrecht Dürer created woodcuts that achieved new heights of expression and technical skill. For examples of early woodcuts, see BATHS AND BATHING, BOOKPLATE, CARD GAME, LITERATURE FOR CHILDREN (picture: *The New England Primer*), and SWITZERLAND (picture: The Battle of Sempach).

During the 1700's and 1800's, Japanese artists produced many outstanding woodcuts. These prints greatly influenced such European artists as Edgar Degas, Edouard Manet, Henri de Toulouse-Lautrec, and Vincent van Gogh. The Europeans admired the Japanese woodcuts for their bold, flat shapes of brilliant color; delicate flowing lines; and superb composition. For examples of Japanese woodcuts, see JAPANESE PRINT, DRAMA (Asian Drama), and HOKUSAI KATSUSHIKA.

During the 1900's, expressionist artists created many fine woodcuts (see EXPRESSIONISM). These artists in-

WORLD BOOK photos

Making a Woodcut. An artist creates a picture by cutting away portions of a block of wood with sharp tools, *left*. To make a print of the picture, the uncut surfaces of the block are coated with ink, *center*, and a sheet of paper is placed over the block. The paper is then rubbed with the back of a spoon or some similar object. The rubbing transfers the inked image onto the paper, *right*.

WOODEN, JOHN

cluded Ernst Ludwig Kirchner of Germany and Edvard Munch of Norway.   ANDREW J. STASIK, JR.

See also DÜRER, ALBRECHT; ILLUSTRATION (Printed Illustrations); WARD, LYND K.

WOODEN, JOHN (1910-   ), was one of the greatest coaches in college basketball history. He coached the University of California at Los Angeles (UCLA) to a record 10 National Collegiate Athletic Association (NCAA) championships from 1964 to 1975. In that period, his teams won 335 games and lost 22. His teams won a record seven straight NCAA championships from 1967 to 1973. From 1971 to 1974, UCLA won 88 consecutive games, a college basketball record. He coached many all-Americans, including Kareem Abdul-Jabbar, Gail Goodrich, Bill Walton, and Sidney Wicks.

John Robert Wooden was born in Martinsville, Ind., and graduated from Purdue University. He won all-America honors as a guard on the Purdue basketball team in 1930, 1931, and 1932. Wooden became basketball coach at UCLA in 1948 and retired in 1975. He is the only man to be elected to the Naismith Memorial Basketball Hall of Fame as both a player and a coach.   NICK CURRAN

WOODEN HORSE. See TROJAN WAR.

WOODEN SHOE is a type of footwear worn chiefly by persons who live in the moist lowlands of The Netherlands. These shoes, called *klompen* by the Dutch, keep feet drier and warmer than other types. Persons in parts of France and Belgium also wear wooden shoes. People rarely wear wooden shoes indoors.

WOODHENGE. See STONEHENGE.

WOODHULL, VICTORIA CLAFLIN (1838-1927), was the first woman to run for President of the United States. In 1872, she ran as the candidate of the newly formed Equal Rights Party. Women's voting rights organizations admired Woodhull's stand in favor of allowing women to vote. But they refused to support her candidacy because she also spoke out for the right of women to have love affairs, whether married or not.

In 1870, Victoria Woodhull and her sister Tennessee Claflin established the first stock brokerage firm ever owned by women, near Wall Street in New York City. That same year, they founded a weekly newspaper. Both ventures did very well for several years.

Victoria Woodhull was born in Homer, Ohio, near Utica. She received little formal education. She and her sister moved to England in 1877.   MIRIAM SCHNEIR

Bettmann Archive
Victoria C. Woodhull

WOODMEN OF AMERICA, MODERN, is a fraternal benefit society. The society's principal services center in a youth development program. The society grants death, disability, orphan, and other benefits without extra cost to its premium-paying members. Modern Woodmen of America was founded in Lyons, Iowa, on Jan. 5, 1883. It has about 450,000 members. Headquarters are at 1701 First Avenue, Rock Island, Ill. 61201.
                    Critically reviewed by MODERN WOODMEN OF AMERICA

WOODPECKER is a bird that uses its strong, chisel-like bill to bore holes in trees in search of insects. Woodpeckers live in all parts of the world except Australia and Madagascar. Most have their toes so arranged that they can cling to trees and branches, and climb up and down the trunks. Two of these toes are pointed forward and two are pointed backward. They use their stiff tail as a support while they cling to a trunk. Woodpeckers have long tongues, usually with barbed, horny tips and coated with sticky saliva. They thrust out these tongues to spear insects and draw them out of hiding places. Woodpeckers also eat berries, fruits, and nuts.

The Mating Call. Woodpeckers have harsh voices. Their mating call is a rapid drumming, performed by striking the bill on a dead limb or other resounding surface. Their feathers are usually barred or spotted black and white, or brown and black. The male may have red or yellow markings on the head.

The birds make holes in the trunks of trees for their nests, and leave fine chips of wood on the bottom to cushion the white eggs. The young are hatched featherless. Woodpeckers rarely are seen in groups, except in the fall. The sapsucker is the only woodpecker that sometimes harms trees.

Types of Woodpeckers. One of the woodpeckers, called the *ivory-billed woodpecker*, is one of the rarest birds in North America. It is a large, wild, shy bird with a high, scarlet crest. It lives in the forests of the southeastern United States. The *pileated woodpecker* is another North American bird. It is smaller than the ivory-billed, and is still common in the forests. The *yellow-bellied sapsucker* and the *flicker* are also North American woodpeckers. The *redheaded woodpecker* has red, white, and bluish-black feathers. The *hairy woodpecker* and the *downy woodpecker* both live throughout the year in the Northern States and Canada. The small downy woodpecker is the most common. The *acorn woodpecker* lives on the Pacific Coast of North America.

The *green woodpecker* is a brightly colored bird of Europe. The *great-spotted woodpecker* looks like the hairy woodpecker. It lives in Europe and Asia Minor. The *ground woodpecker* lives in South Africa. It feeds on the ground and digs its nest in clay banks.

Scientific Classification. Woodpeckers are in the woodpecker family, *Picidae*. The ivory-billed is genus *Campephilus*, species *C. principalis;* the pileated is *Dryocopus pileatus;* and the redheaded is *Melanerpes erythrocephalus*. The hairy woodpecker is genus *Dendrocopos*, species *D. villosus;* and the downy is *D. pubescens*.   ARTHUR A. ALLEN

See also BIRD (color pictures: Birds That Help Us, Bird Nests); FLICKER; SAPSUCKER; WRYNECK.

WOODS, LAKE OF THE. See LAKE OF THE WOODS.

WOODS HOLE OCEANOGRAPHIC INSTITUTION is a research and study center for marine science on Cape Cod, at Woods Hole, Mass. It was founded in 1930. The institution has a land laboratory and several research ships that explore in the North Atlantic and inshore. They collect information on the ocean and its animal and plant life. The institution also works with the International Commission for the Northwest Atlantic Fisheries. This commission was established in 1951 by the United States and four other countries to preserve the North Atlantic fishing industry.   JAN HAHN

WOOD'S METAL. See ALLOY (Other Alloys).

WOODSON, CARTER GOODWIN (1875-1950), is widely regarded as the leading writer on black history of his time. A black American, Woodson devoted his life to bringing the achievements of his race to the world's attention. His founding of the Association for the Study of Negro Life and History (now the Association for the Study of Afro-American Life and History) in 1915 has been called the start of the black history movement. The association began publishing the scholarly *Journal of Negro History* in 1916. The best known of Woodson's 16 books is *Negro in Our History* (1922). Many scholars consider it one of the finest full-length works on black history.

Woodson was born in New Canton, Va. His parents were former slaves. Woodson received a Ph.D. degree in history from Harvard University. He won the Spingarn medal in 1926.   RICHARD BARDOLPH

See also BLACK HISTORY WEEK.

WOODSWORTH, JAMES SHAVER (1874-1942), was a Methodist minister and one of Canada's leading social reformers of the 1900's. He recommended many of the social welfare programs that Canada has adopted since World War II ended in 1945. These welfare programs include old age pensions and unemployment relief.

Woodsworth was born near Toronto, Ont. In the early 1900's, he became known for his dedication to helping needy farmers and workers. Woodsworth strongly opposed violence, and during World War I (1914-1918), he spoke out against Canada's military draft. He participated in the Winnipeg general strike of 1919, in which about 30,000 workers in Winnipeg, Man., struck for various rights. In 1921, Woodsworth won election to the Canadian Parliament as a member of the Manitoba Independent Labour Party. He served there until his death.

In 1933, Woodsworth helped found the Co-operative Commonwealth Federation, Canada's former socialist party. He led the party (now the New Democratic Party) until 1940. Woodsworth was the only member of the House of Commons who voted against Canada's entry into World War II in 1939.   RICHARD ALLEN

WOODWARD, ROBERT BURNS. See NOBEL PRIZES (table: Nobel Prizes for Chemistry—1965).

WOODWIND INSTRUMENT. See MUSIC (Musical Instruments [Woodwind Instruments]; illustration); ORCHESTRA (The Musicians; illustration).

The Male Pileated Woodpecker, *left,* is often mistaken for the ivory-billed woodpecker. It is found in eastern North America and in parts of the Northwest. Both sexes have a high crest on the head.

M. Vinciguerra, N.A.S.

Ivory-Billed Woodpecker
Campephilus principalis
Once found in southeastern United States, now almost extinct
Body length: 20 inches (51 centimeters)

Green Woodpecker
Picus canus
Found in Eurasian forests
Body length: 12 inches (30 centimeters)

WORLD BOOK illustration by Marion Pahl

Hairy Woodpecker
Dendrocopos villosus
Found in North America
Body length: 10 inches (25 centimeters)

WORLD BOOK illustrations by Guy Coheleach

THE WOODPECKER'S TONGUE

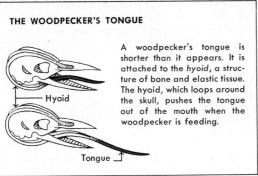

A woodpecker's tongue is shorter than it appears. It is attached to the *hyoid,* a structure of bone and elastic tissue. The hyoid, which loops around the skull, pushes the tongue out of the mouth when the woodpecker is feeding.

Hyoid

Tongue

A Home Woodworking Shop equipped with a set of basic tools can provide a hobbyist with many hours of enjoyment.

WOODWORKING is the forming and shaping of wood to make useful and decorative objects. It is one of the oldest crafts and ranks as a popular hobby and an important industry.

A skilled woodworker with a well-equipped home workshop can build items as simple as a birdhouse or as complicated as decorative furniture. Tools for a workshop can be purchased at hardware and department stores. Lumber stores and hobby shops sell a wide variety of wood.

The construction industry employs carpenters who construct the wooden framework of buildings. Other kinds of woodworkers include *finish carpenters* and *cabinetmakers*. Finish carpenters do the inside trim work around windows, cabinets, and other features that must fit exactly. Cabinetmakers design, shape, and assemble furniture and such items as built-in cabinets and stairways.

This article discusses woodworking as a hobby. For information on woodworking in industry, see the WORLD BOOK article on CARPENTRY.

The history of woodworking goes back to about 8,000 B.C., when people first used an ax as a woodworking tool. During the Middle Ages, woodworkers and other craftworkers formed organizations called *guilds*. These organizations served as models for the labor unions of today.

In 1873, electric power was used to drive machine tools for the first time. Through the years came the development of the power tools commonly used for woodworking today. The first practical hand drill was patented in 1917. By 1925, woodworkers could buy electric portable saws for their home workshop. Today, power tools can be used in any woodworking operation, but many people enjoy shaping wood with hand tools instead.

Steps in Woodworking

Woodworking projects, together with plans for their construction, can be found in books, magazines, and manuals in bookstores and public libraries. This article includes plans for building a desk rack to hold a set of WORLD BOOK. There are five main steps in woodworking: (1) planning and design, (2) cutting, (3) boring, (4) fastening, and (5) sanding and finishing.

Planning and Design. Careful planning can prevent mistakes and save time and materials. A scale drawing of the object being built should be made before starting any woodworking project. This drawing includes the exact measurements of the object. The craftworker marks the measurements on the wood with a pencil and lists all the steps to be followed in the project.

A woodworking *tape* and *rule* are used to measure dimensions. A *square* can also be used for measuring and for making straight lines and angles. Various *gauges* make marks and parallel lines for the woodworker to follow when cutting joints and attaching hinges.

The parts of the finished object will fit together properly if the drawing has been prepared correctly and if measuring and construction have been done accurately. A well-designed object is both attractive and the right size for its purpose. For example, a birdhouse must have an entrance large enough for the kinds of birds that will use it.

Cutting wood to the right size and shape can be done with a variety of hand and power tools, including *saws*, *chisels*, and *planes*. The largest and most familiar handsaws are the *crosscut saw* and the *ripsaw*. Crosscut saws cut across the grain of the wood, and ripsaws cut with the grain.

Power tools can perform a job far more quickly, easily, and accurately than hand tools. For example, a *circular saw* has a toothed disk that spins at great speed. Different disks can be attached for a variety of cutting operations, such as crosscutting and ripping. A circular saw can also cut joints to connect sections of wood.

A common hand tool for cutting joints is the *backsaw*, which has a thin rectangular blade for fine work. The blade has a metal bar along its back to make it stiff.

Chisels, which can cut deeply into the surface of wood, can be used for making joints or for trimming and carving. A *portable electric router* has attachments called *bits* that can be used to trim or shape wood and to make joints and decorative cuts.

A hand tool called a *coping saw* consists of a metal frame that holds a narrow blade used for cutting curves in wood. *Jigsaws* and *saber saws*, power tools that cut curves, have a thin blade that moves up and down at great speed.

Mechanical planes, called *jointers*, and hand planes

Basic Tools for Woodworking   Hobbyists use many of the woodworking tools pictured below in home workshops. Although power tools can be used in any woodworking operation, many people prefer to shape wood with hand tools.

WORLD BOOK illustrations by Dick Keller

Measuring Tools

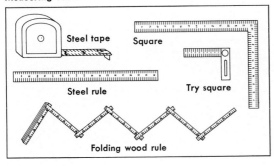

Steel tape   Square

Steel rule   Try square

Folding wood rule

Boring Tools

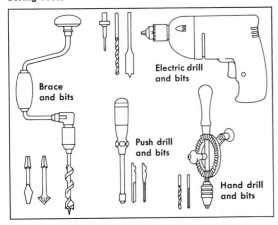

Electric drill and bits

Brace and bits

Push drill and bits

Hand drill and bits

Cutting Tools

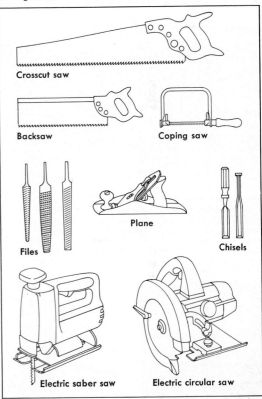

Crosscut saw

Backsaw   Coping saw

Files   Plane   Chisels

Electric saber saw   Electric circular saw

Fastening Tools

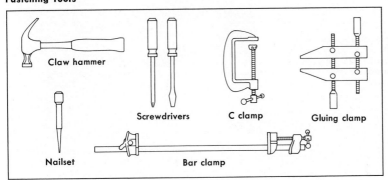

Claw hammer

Screwdrivers   C clamp   Gluing clamp

Nailset   Bar clamp

Sanding Tools

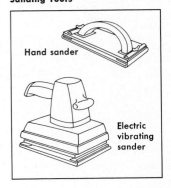

Hand sander

Electric vibrating sander

332a

How to Build a WORLD BOOK Desk Rack

Materials
1- by 3-in. board, 55 in. long
1- by 10-in. board, 17 in. long
8 flat-head wood screws
size 12, 2 in. long

Tools
Pencil
Rule
Square
Screwdriver

Crosscut saw
Coping saw
Drill and bits
Sandpaper

Making the supports and end pieces

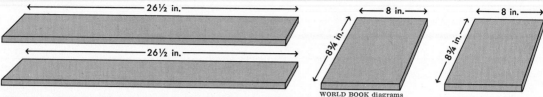

WORLD BOOK diagrams

With a crosscut saw, cut the 1- by 3-inch board into two 26½-inch lengths. These sections will serve as the back and bottom supports of the WORLD BOOK desk rack. Next, use the crosscut saw to cut the 1- by 10-inch board into two sections. Each section should measure 8 inches wide and 8¾ inches high. These sections will be the end pieces of the desk rack.

Marking the end pieces

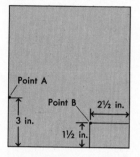

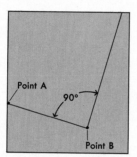

With a pencil, mark points A and B on each end piece according to the measurements given in the diagram at the left above. Draw a line from A to B. Place a square along the line and extend the line upward to form a 90° (right) angle, as shown in the diagram at the right above.

Locating the supports

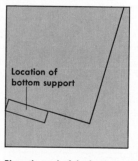

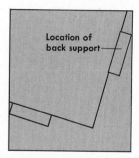

Place the end of the bottom support against the line that connects points A and B, as shown in the diagram at the left above. Draw lines around the edge of the support. Place the end of the back support against the other line, as shown in the diagram at the right above. Draw lines around the support's edge.

Drilling the holes

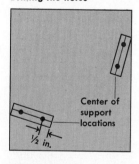

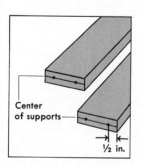

Draw a line through the center of each of the rectangles you have marked on the end pieces, as shown in the diagram at the far left. On the lines, mark the locations of the screw holes ½ inch from the ends of the rectangles. Drill holes slightly larger than the screws you will use. Next, draw lines through the center of each of the ends of the supports, as shown in the diagram at the left. Mark the lines with the locations of the screw holes, as shown, and drill holes smaller than the screws you will use.

Cutting the feet

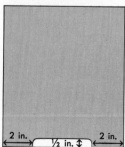

Before assembling, use a coping saw to cut out the feet of the end pieces, as shown in the diagram at the left.

WORLD BOOK photo

To Complete the Desk Rack, first sand all edges, rough surfaces, and tool marks. After assembling the pieces, you may finish the rack by staining and varnishing it or by painting it.

332b

have sharp blades that smooth and shape wood. A *wood-turning lathe* shapes wood into rounded forms by rapidly spinning it against a cutting edge held by the operator. A *file* shapes wood in places where a sharper cutting tool does not fit. Files can also be used to sharpen tools.

Boring enables a woodworker to connect sections of wood with *screws*, *metal plates*, *hinges*, and *joints*. *Braces* and *hand drills* have bits to make holes of different sizes for various purposes. For example, one kind of bit bores holes for *dowel joints*. These joints connect two sections of wood with a wooden peg that fits tightly into holes drilled in each section. *Portable electric drills* and *drill presses* also use bits to bore holes. These machines have attachments for sanding and other uses as well.

Fastening. Sections of wood are fastened together with metal fasteners, such as *screws* and *nails*, and with *adhesives*. Tools for fastening include *screwdrivers* and *hammers*. Screwdrivers insert screws that connect sections of wood and hold hinges and metal plates. Hammers drive in nails and other types of metal fasteners.

Gluing is one of the oldest methods of fastening sections of wood, and a variety of adhesives are used in woodworking. *Polyvinyl resin emulsion glue*, or white glue, can be applied directly from the bottle. It should not be used if it will come in contact with water or high temperatures. *Urea-formaldehyde resin glue* and *resorcinol formaldehyde resin glue* both must be mixed by the user. Urea glue can resist cold water for short periods, but it cannot withstand high temperatures. Resorcinol glue is waterproof and heat resistant.

After gluing, wood should be put into *clamps* for as long as 12 hours. The length of time depends on the temperature, the kind of wood, and the type of glue. Clamping holds the wood in place and spreads the glue into the pores.

Sanding and Finishing. Sanding removes tool marks and makes wood surfaces smooth for finishing. Sanding should not begin until the wood has been cut to its final size. Most *sandpaper* manufactured for use by hand has rough particles of the minerals *flint* or *garnet*. *Aluminum oxide* is a common sanding material used in such machines as a *portable belt sander* or a *vibrating sander*. Portable belt sanders work better than vibrating sanders on large wood surfaces.

Woodworkers use a variety of *finishes* to protect wood and to bring out the beauty of the grain. A *stain* is a dye that colors wood without hiding the pattern and feel of the grain. *Paint* covers the grain of the wood and provides a color of its own. *Varnish*, such as *lacquer* and *shellac*, gives wood a hard, glossy finish. *Wax* protects varnish and has a smooth, shiny finish when polished. *Enamel* is a varnish paint.

Tool Care and Safety

Tools are made to be safe when used correctly. They can be preserved—and accidents can be prevented—by using the right tools for the job and keeping them clean and sharp. A woodworker must use extra pressure with a dull tool, and injury could result if the tool slips. Many tools can be sharpened on the rough surface of an *oilstone*. A broken or damaged tool does not work properly and should not be used.

Whenever possible, wood should be held in a vise or by clamps, so that both hands are free to handle the

tool being used. Floors should be kept clean of such substances as sawdust and finishing materials, which are slippery and also could catch fire. Safety glasses should be worn during cutting and boring operations to protect the eyes from flying particles of wood. Loose clothing and jewelry that could get caught in a machine should not be worn in a woodworking area.

A craftsman can prevent accidents by holding a portable power tool until all the moving parts have stopped. A machine should never be left running unless the operator is present, and it should be disconnected when not in use. The hazard of electric shock can be reduced by connecting *ground wires* to machines that have not been previously grounded.

Wood for Woodworking

Woodworkers classify wood as *hardwood* or *softwood*, depending on the type of tree from which it comes. Most hardwood trees are *deciduous*—that is, they lose their leaves every autumn. Most softwood trees, called *conifers*, have narrow, pointed leaves and stay green the year around. However, this classification system does not indicate the hardness of wood because various softwoods are harder than some hardwoods.

Hardwoods have beautiful grain patterns and can be used to make fine furniture. Some hardwoods have large pores and must be treated with a paste or liquid called *filler* before being covered with a finish. Wood to be finished with paint does not need a fancy grain to be attractive because the paint covers the pattern. Hardwoods used in woodworking include birch, mahogany, maple, oak, and walnut.

Most softwoods can easily be sawed, planed, chiseled, or bored. They are used mainly for structural work, but such softwoods as Douglas fir, ponderosa pine, red cedar, and white pine can be used for woodworking and furniture.

Hardwood or softwood can also be used to make a type of manufactured board called *plywood*. Plywood consists of an odd number of thin layers of wood glued together. It is lightweight and strong and can be purchased in many sizes and wood patterns.   W. Carlisle Anderson

See also Plywood; Saw; Wood; Wood Carving.

WOODWORTH, ROBERT SESSIONS (1869-1962), was an American psychologist known for his work in experimental psychology. Woodworth also worked in the fields of learning, physiological psychology, psychophysics, and testing. He believed that the study of individual behavior should concentrate on physical as well as mental activities.

Woodworth was born in Belchertown, Mass. He graduated from Amherst College in 1891 and entered Harvard University in 1895. At Harvard he studied with the famous psychologist William James and received an M.A. in 1897. In 1899, Woodworth earned a Ph.D. from Columbia University and joined the Columbia faculty. In 1903, Woodworth studied physiology in Liverpool, England with Sir Charles S. Sherrington. He returned to the United States in the same year, and rejoined the faculty at Columbia. Woodworth taught there until 1958.   Robert G. Weyant

WOODY NIGHTSHADE. See Bittersweet.

WOOF. See Weaving.

Sheep Shearers use power clippers to remove a fleece. An expert shearer can clip 200 or more sheep a day. In most parts of the world, sheep are sheared once a year.

Grant Heilman

WOOL is a fiber that comes from the fleece of sheep and some other animals. It is made into durable fabrics used in manufacturing blankets, clothing, rugs, and other items. Wool fabrics clean easily, and they resist wrinkles and hold their shape well. Wool also absorbs moisture and insulates against both cold and heat. All these features make wool popular for coats, sweaters, gloves, socks, and other clothing.

Wool fibers are nearly cylindrical in shape. Overlapping scales on the surface make the fibers mat and interlock under heat, moisture, and pressure. This property of wool fibers is called *felting*. Felting increases the strength and durability of wool fabrics. It also enables wool to be made into felt. See FIBER (picture: Wool Fibers).

The Wool Products Labeling Act of 1939 established guidelines in the United States for defining and labeling wool products. This law defines wool as the fiber from the fleece of sheep. It also includes such fibers as alpaca, from alpacas; camel's hair; cashmere, from Cashmere goats; mohair, from Angora goats; and vicuña, from vicuñas.

Worldwide production of raw wool totals about $5\frac{3}{4}$ billion pounds (2.6 billion kilograms) annually. The leading wool-producing nations are Australia, Russia, New Zealand, Argentina, and South Africa, in that order. Every state in the United States except Hawaii produces some wool. Texas is the leading producer, followed by Wyoming, California, Colorado, and South Dakota, in that order. The United States uses more wool than it produces, and so it imports some wool.

Sources of Wool. Almost all wool comes from sheep. These animals—and their wool—are classified into five groups, depending on the quality of the fleece. The five classes of wool, listed here in order of quality, are (1) fine wool, (2) crossbred wool, (3) medium wool, (4) long wool, and (5) coarse wool, or carpet wool.

Fine-Wooled Sheep include the Merino and other breeds with Merino ancestry, such as the Debouillet and the Rambouillet. These sheep produce the finest wool, which is used in making high-quality clothing.

Crossbred-Wooled Sheep, such as the Columbia and Corriedale, are crossbreeds of fine- and long-wooled breeds. Their wool is used for rugged clothing.

Leading Wool-Producing States

Wool clipped from sheep in 1977

Texas	21,000,000 lbs. (9,525,440 kg)
Wyoming	10,880,000 lbs. (4,935,090 kg)
California	9,925,000 lbs. (4,501,900 kg)
Colorado	8,809,000 lbs. (3,995,700 kg)
South Dakota	6,236,000 lbs. (2,828,600 kg)
Utah	5,453,000 lbs. (2,473,400 kg)
Idaho	5,281,000 lbs. (2,395,400 kg)
New Mexico	4,656,000 lbs. (2,111,900 kg)
Montana	4,462,000 lbs. (2,023,900 kg)
Oregon	3,401,000 lbs. (1,542,700 kg)

Source: *Wool and Mohair*, March 1978, U.S. Dept. of Agriculture.

Leading Wool-Producing Countries

Wool clipped from sheep in 1977

Australia	1,549,000,000 lbs. (702,610,000 kg)
Russia	1,010,000,000 lbs. (458,100,000 kg)
New Zealand	666,898,000 lbs. (302,499,900 kg)
Argentina	368,172,000 lbs. (167,000,000 kg)
South Africa	243,611,000 lbs. (110,500,100 kg)
Uruguay	138,009,000 lbs. (62,599,830 kg)
China	136,687,000 lbs. (62,000,180 kg)
Turkey	120,152,000 lbs. (54,500,030 kg)
United States	110,231,000 lbs. (49,999,940 kg)
Great Britain	103,397,000 lbs. (46,900,090 kg)

Source: *Production Yearbook, 1977*, FAO.

Medium-Wooled Sheep provide wool used in making industrial and upholstery fabrics. Cheviot, Dorset, Hampshire, Oxford, Shropshire, Southdown, and Suffolk sheep are in this group.

Long-Wooled Sheep include the Cotswold, Leicester, Lincoln, and Romney. They produce wool used for carpets and industrial fabrics.

Coarse-Wooled Sheep include the Karakul and Scottish Blackface. The wool of these animals is used mostly for carpets and handicraft yarns.

Types of Wool are determined by the quality of a sheep's fleece. The quality depends on the age and physical condition of the animal and by the climate in which it lives. The fleece of a healthy sheep is covered by an oily substance called *yolk*. Yolk consists of wool grease and *suint* (dried perspiration). It protects the sheep from rain and keeps the fleece from becoming matted.

Young sheep produce the best wool. The softest and finest wool, called *lamb's wool*, comes from 6- to 12-month-old sheep. *Hog wool*, also called *hogget wool*, is the first fleece sheared from a sheep that is 12 to 14 months old. After a sheep has been sheared for the first time, its wool is called *wether wool*.

Lower quality wool comes from dead or diseased sheep. Sheep that have been slaughtered for their meat provide *pulled wool*, sometimes called *skin wool* or *slipe wool*. *Dead wool* is taken from sheep that have died of disease or have been killed by other animals. Aged sheep have matted and tangled fleeces that provide *cotty wool*. Fleeces soiled by manure or dirt are called *tag locks* in the United States and *stain pieces* in England and Australia.

The United States Federal Trade Commission, which administers the Wool Products Labeling Act, classifies wool into three different kinds of categories. *Virgin wool*, or *new wool*, has never been spun into yarn or made into felt. Some fabrics are made of fibers that have been reclaimed from previously spun or woven wool. *Reprocessed wool* comes from wool products that have never been used by a consumer. *Reused wool* comes from products that have been used. Reprocessed and reused wool are sometimes called *shoddy*.

Processing of Wool involves four major steps: (1) shearing, (2) sorting and grading, (3) making yarn, and (4) making fabric.

Shearing. Most sheep shearers use power shears, and experts can clip 200 or more animals a day. They remove the fleece in one piece so the various parts can be easily identified for sorting and grading. Different parts of a fleece vary in quality. For example, the best wool comes from the shoulders and sides of the sheep.

In most parts of the world, sheep are sheared once a year, in spring or early summer. But in some regions, the fleeces may be cut off twice yearly.

Sorting and Grading. Workers remove any stained, damaged, or inferior wool from each fleece and sort the rest of the wool according to the quality of the fibers. Wool fibers are judged not only on the basis of their strength, but also by their (1) *fineness* (diameter), (2) length, (3) *crimp* (waviness), and (4) color.

In the United States, the fineness of wool fibers is determined by comparing them to the fineness of Merino wool. In England, fineness depends on the number of fibers per inch. In Australia, the diameter of the fibers is generally measured in units called *microns*. A micron equals a millionth of a meter (.000039 inch).

Fiber length is important in determining what processes will be used to make yarn and fabric. *Carding length fibers*, also called *clothing length fibers*, measure less than 1½ inches (3.8 centimeters) long. *French combing length fibers* range from 1½ to 2½ inches (3.8 to 6.4 centi-

Making Wool Yarn involves several steps. Carding machines, *left*, untangle the fibers and arrange them into a sheet called a *web*. The web is formed into a narrow rope called a *sliver, center*. The sliver is stretched into a thinner strand, and spinning machines twist it into yarn, *right*.

Weaving of Wool Fabrics is done by large power looms,
above. After a fabric has been made, it goes through various
finishing processes to give it the desired appearance and strength.

Burlington Industries, Inc.

Making Fabric. Wool manufacturers knit or weave
yarn into a variety of fabrics. They use woolen yarns in
making flannel, homespun, melton, Saxony, Shetland,
and tweed fabrics. Worsted yarns are used for such
fabrics as broadcloth, crepe, gabardine, serge, sharkskin,
twill, and whipcord. Almost all wool fabrics except felt
are made from yarn (see FELT).

Wool may be dyed at various stages of the manufacturing process. If the fibers are dyed before spinning,
the process is called *stock dyeing* or *top dyeing*. If they are
dyed after being spun into yarn, it is called *yarn dyeing*,
package dyeing, or *skein dyeing*. If the dyeing does not
take place until the fabric has been made, it is known
as *piece dyeing*. Most fabrics with fancy designs are stock
dyed or yarn dyed. Piece dyeing is used for solid-
colored fabrics. See DYE.

All wool fabrics undergo finishing processes to give
them the desired appearance and feel. The finishing
of fabrics made of woolen yarn begins with *fulling*.
This process involves wetting the fabric thoroughly with
water and then passing it through rollers. Fulling makes
the fibers interlock and mat together. It shrinks the
material and gives it additional strength and thickness.
Worsteds go through a process called *crabbing*, in which
the fabric passes through boiling water and then through
cold water. This procedure strengthens the fabric.

Some wool fabrics tend to shrink when dry-cleaned.
To prevent such shrinkage, some manufacturers pre-
shrink the fabric. One popular process, called London
Shrinking, uses water and pressure to shrink the fabric.
After the various finishing processes, the fabric is made
into clothing and other products.

History. About 10,000 years ago, people in Central
Asia began to raise sheep for food and clothing. The
art of spinning wool into yarn developed about 4000
B.C. and encouraged trade among the nations in the
region of the Mediterranean Sea. Merino sheep were
developed in Spain by A.D. 100. Spain was the only
source of these sheep until the 1700's.

The first wool factory in England was established
about A.D. 50 in Winchester by the Romans. The wool
industry soon played a major part in the nation's
economy. By 1660, the export of wool fabrics accounted
for about two-thirds of England's foreign trade.

During the early 1500's, Spanish explorers brought
sheep to what is now the United States. England discouraged the growth of the wool industry in the American Colonies so the colonists would have to rely on
English goods. But the colonists smuggled sheep from
England. By the 1700's, spinning and weaving were
flourishing in America.

In 1797, the British brought 13 Merino sheep to Australia and started the country's Merino sheep industry.
Spain first sold Merino sheep to the United States in
the early 1800's. Americans bred these animals with
descendants of the sheep that had been brought from
England. In the 1800's, many pioneers brought sheep
with them while traveling to the West. As a result, the
production of wool and wool fabrics spread to nearly all
parts of the United States.   R. CARL FREEMAN

meters) in length. *Combing length fibers* are more than $2\frac{1}{2}$
inches (6.4 centimeters) long.

The natural crimp of wool provides the fibers with
elasticity. This property enables wool fabrics to hold
their shape after being stretched or twisted. The best
wool fibers have many evenly spaced waves.

The color of most wool ranges from white to dark
ivory. White wool is the most desirable because manufacturers may have to bleach darker wool before it can
be dyed.

Making Yarn. The wool is scoured with detergents to
remove the yolk and such impurities as dust and sand.
Wool grease from the yolk is processed into lanolin, a
substance used in hand creams and other cosmetics.

After the wool dries, it is *carded*. The carding process
involves passing the wool through rollers that have thin
wire teeth. The teeth untangle the fibers and arrange
them into a flat sheet called a *web*. The web is then
formed into narrow ropes known as *slivers*.

After carding, the processes used in making yarn vary
slightly, depending on the length of the fibers. Carding length fibers are used in making *woolen yarn*. Combing length and French combing length fibers are made
into *worsted yarn*. The processes used for the two kinds
of yarn are similar. But worsted slivers go through an
additional step called *combing*, which removes impurities and short fibers.

After carding or combing, the slivers are stretched
and slightly twisted to form thinner strands called
roving. Spinning machines then twist the roving into
yarn. Woolen yarn is bulky and fuzzy, with fibers that
lie in different directions. Worsted yarn is smooth and
highly twisted, and its fibers are parallel.

Related Articles in WORLD BOOK include:

Alpaca	Clothing	Llama	Vicuña
Camel	Fiber	Mohair	Weaving
Cashmere	Goat	Sheep	Worsted
Cashmere Goat	Lanolin	Textile	

WOOL WAX. See LANOLIN.

WOOLF, VIRGINIA (1882-1941), was a British novelist and critic. She revolted against what she called the "materialism" of the major British novelists of the early 1900's. She adopted the technique of showing the inner essence of her characters by revealing their thoughts and concentrating on precise detail. Her books show the influence of James Joyce's novel *Ulysses*.

Jacob's Room (1922) was Woolf's first attempt to reveal inner character. She followed this novel with *Mrs. Dalloway* (1925), her first complete success; and *To the Lighthouse* (1927), a novel in which her parents are central figures. *Orlando* (1928) is a fictional review of English history. Her last novels were *The Waves* (1931), *The Years* (1937), and *Between the Acts* (1941). She also wrote many biographical and critical works.

Woolf was born in London. She was the daughter of the scholar Sir Leslie Stephen. In 1912, she married the writer Leonard Woolf. She and her husband founded the Hogarth Press, which provided a center for the *Bloomsbury Group*, an informal group of famous intellectuals. She had mental breakdowns in 1913 and 1915. Fearing a recurrence and the stress it would place on her husband, she drowned herself in 1941.

Leonard Woolf wrote historical and political books. He collected and edited his wife's works, including *A Writer's Diary* (1953), a frank display of the critical intelligence and examining mind of his wife.   JOHN ESPEY

See also BLOOMSBURY GROUP.

WOOLLEY, MARY EMMA (1863-1947), was an outstanding American educator. She served as president of Mount Holyoke College from 1901 to 1937 and was president of the American Association of University Women from 1927 to 1933. Woolley was also active in world peace movements and public affairs. In 1932, she became the first woman to represent the United States at an international disarmament conference. Woolley was born in Norwalk, Conn. In 1894, she became the first woman to receive a bachelor's degree from Brown University.   ALBERT E. VAN DUSEN

WOOLLY MAMMOTH. See MAMMOTH.

WOOLLY MONKEY is a large monkey that lives in the western Amazon Valley of South America. This monkey has the nickname "bag-belly" because it stuffs itself with various wild fruits during the ripening season. Most woolly monkeys have thick, soft, dark fur. There are two species, Humboldt's woolly monkey and Hendee's woolly monkey, also called the yellow-tailed woolly monkey. Hendee's woolly monkey has become rare due to hunting and destruction of its forest home, and biologists consider it an endangered species.

Groups of woolly monkeys move through the trees, feeding on fruits, nuts, leaves, and insects. They usually travel more slowly and deliberately than most monkeys, but they can move swiftly and gracefully.

Adult woolly monkeys weigh from 10 to 20 pounds (4.5 to 9 kilograms) and grow 15 to 23 inches (38 to 58 centimeters) long, not including the tail. The underside of the tail has no fur near the end. This area has ridges similar to human fingerprints, and the rough skin surface helps the monkey grasp. See MONKEY (picture).

Scientific Classification. Woolly monkeys belong to the New World monkey family, Cebidae. They form the genus *Lagothrix*. Humboldt's woolly monkey is *L. lagothricha*; Hendee's is *L. flavicauda*.   NEIL C. TAPPEN

WOOLMAN, JOHN (1720-1772), was a colonial American writer and Quaker minister. He worked to abolish slavery, relieve poverty, obtain better treatment for Indians, and end war.

Woolman was born on a farm near what is now Rancocas, N.J. He worked as a clerk until he was 22 years old, when he became a minister and a tailor. Woolman preached while traveling on foot from New England to North Carolina. He convinced Philadelphia Quakers at their yearly meeting in 1758 to resolve not to keep or deal in slaves. This resolution was the first of its kind in the American Colonies.

When he was about 36 years old, Woolman began to write an account of his life and religious beliefs. His *Journal*, published in 1774, is noted for its sensitive descriptions of his feelings. Woolman also wrote essays condemning slavery and calling for better conditions for the poor.   DEAN DONER

WOOLWORTH is the family name of two American businessmen who were brothers.

Frank Winfield Woolworth (1852-1919) was the principal founder in 1912 of the F. W. Woolworth Company, a chain of five-and-ten-cent stores. When he died, the chain had more than 1,000 stores with annual sales of more than $100 million. In 1913, he built the Woolworth Building in New York City. It was the tallest building in the world at that time.

Woolworth was born in Rodman, N.Y., and he clerked in the village grocery store there. In 1878, while working for the firm of Moore & Smith in Watertown, N.Y., he suggested putting slow-moving merchandise on a counter and selling it for five cents. The venture was so successful that it was continued with new goods. Six store chains grew out of the five-cent counter experiment. All were united in 1912 to form the F. W. Woolworth Company.

Charles S. Woolworth (1856-1947) was co-founder of the F. W. Woolworth Company. He served as vice-president until 1919 and as chairman of the board until 1944, when he retired. He was born in Rodman, N.Y. Woolworth founded 15 stores, which he and his brother united with 581 other stores in 1912 to form the F. W. Woolworth Company.   W. H. BAUGHN

WORCESTER, *WOOS tuhr* (pop. 176,572; met. area pop. 372,144), is a leading New England industrial center and the second largest city of Massachusetts. Worcester lies about 40 miles (64 kilometers) west of Boston, the largest city (see MASSACHUSETTS [political map]).

In 1673, settlers from eastern Massachusetts founded the village of Quinsigamond on what is now the site of Worcester. In 1684, King Charles II of England canceled the charter of the Massachusetts Bay Colony. This action so angered the people of Quinsigamond that they renamed their village Worcester. According to tradition, this name honored the Battle of Worcester (1651), in which Charles suffered a great defeat during the English Civil War.

Description. Worcester, the county seat of Worcester County, covers 39 square miles (101 square kilometers). The city has more than 450 manufacturing plants, which employ about 40 per cent of the workers. Worcester's chief products include iron and steel products; machinery and machine tools; printed materials; wire; and stone, clay, and glass products. Airlines, railroad freight lines, and passenger trains serve the city.

The College of the Holy Cross, the oldest Roman Catholic college in New England, was founded in Worcester in 1843. The city is also the home of Assumption College, Clark University, the University of Massachusetts Medical School, Worcester Polytechnic Institute, and Worcester State College.

The Worcester Art Museum is known for its art objects from many periods of history. The Higgins Armory features an outstanding display of armor and weapons from the Middle Ages. The American Antiquarian Society owns the world's largest collection of early American publications, including newspapers, sheet music, and children's books.

History. Nipmuc Indians lived near what is now the site of Worcester before whites built a village there in 1673. Indians destroyed that settlement and another built in 1684. The whites settled Worcester permanently in 1713 and incorporated it as a town in 1722.

During the Revolutionary War in America (1775-1783), Worcester became the home of the *Massachusetts Spy*, a newspaper famous for its support of the colonists.

Manufacturing became important in Worcester after 1828, when the Blackstone Canal linked the town with Narragansett Bay, an arm of the Atlantic Ocean. Worcester received a city charter in 1848. Through the years, the growing number of industrial jobs in Worcester attracted thousands of immigrants.

The city's population reached a peak of 203,486 in 1950. Since then, a number of companies have moved their factories from the city. In addition, many middle-income families have left Worcester and moved to the suburbs. A downtown development called Worcester Center opened in 1971. The center included two office buildings and nearly 100 restaurants and retail stores. Worcester has a council-manager form of government. CLIF SNICKERS

WORDEN, ALFRED MERRILL (1932-   ), a United States astronaut, was the command module pilot on the Apollo 15 mission. This mission was the first manned moon trip devoted primarily to scientific exploration.

During the Apollo 15 mission, from July 26 to Aug. 7, 1971, Worden orbited the moon in the command module *Endeavour* for six days. He took photographs, operated automatically recording instruments, and launched an 80-pound (36-kilogram) subsatellite into lunar orbit. While Worden orbited the moon, astronauts David R. Scott and James B. Irwin explored the moon. During the return to earth, Worden left the spacecraft for 20 minutes and took the first "walk" in deep space.

Worden was born on Feb. 7, 1932, in Jackson, Mich. He entered the Air Force after graduating from the United States Military Academy in 1955. Worden became an astronaut in 1966. He resigned from the astronaut program in 1972 and took an administrative job in the space program. WILLIAM J. CROMIE

WORDS. See BASIC ENGLISH; DICTIONARY; ETYMOLOGY; LANGUAGE; PRONUNCIATION; SEMANTICS; SLANG; SPELLING; VOCABULARY.

WORDSWORTH, WILLIAM (1770-1850), was an English romantic poet. Many scholars consider *Lyrical Bal-*

lads, by Wordsworth and Samuel Taylor Coleridge, the beginning of the romantic movement in England.

In the preface to the second edition of *Lyrical Ballads* (1800), Wordsworth outlined ideas about poetry that have since been identified with romanticism. He argued that serious poems could describe "situations from common life," and be written in the ordinary language "really used by men." He believed such poems could clarify "the primary laws of our nature." He also insisted that poetry is the imaginative expression of emotions coming from actual personal experience.

Wordsworth has often been praised for his descriptions of nature. But he rightly claimed that his primary interest was the "mind of man." His finest poems, including "Michael," the "Lucy" lyrics, "The Solitary Reaper," and "Resolution and Independence," dramatize how imagination creates spiritual values out of the memory of sights and sounds in nature.

Early Life. Wordsworth was born in Cockermouth, which is now in the county of Cumbria. His mother

Detail of a pencil and chalk drawing (1798) by Robert Hancock; National Portrait Gallery, London

William Wordsworth

died in 1778 and his father died in 1783. Relatives provided for his education. Wordsworth entered Cambridge University in 1787, the year he wrote his first significant poem. During a summer vacation in 1790, he visited France, then in turmoil because of the French Revolution. After Wordsworth graduated from Cambridge in 1791, he returned to France and became a supporter of the revolution. Wordsworth returned to England in December 1792. Although liberal in his youth, he became politically and religiously conservative as he grew older.

Wordsworth met Coleridge about 1795, and *Lyrical Ballads* appeared in 1798. Most of the poems in *Lyrical Ballads* were by Wordsworth, including his famous "Tintern Abbey."

Later Career. Wordsworth married Mary Hutchinson in 1802. They had five children. Wordsworth was deeply saddened by the death of his brother John in 1805. His sadness was reflected in his poem "Elegiac Stanzas Suggested by a Picture of Peele Castle" (1806). By 1806, Wordsworth had completed one of the most famous poems in English literature, "Ode: Intimations of Immortality." In this piece, Wordsworth praised childhood and urged man to rely on his intuition.

Wordsworth's masterpiece is his long autobiographical poem, *The Prelude: Growth of a Poet's Mind*. He wrote it between 1798 and 1805, but it was not published until 1850. In its best passages, *The Prelude* achieves a remarkable combination of simplicity and grandeur. Wordsworth wrote most of his best poetry before 1807. But he wrote several important works later, notably *The Excursion* (1814). This long poem discusses virtue, education, and religious faith. Wordsworth wrote 523 sonnets, and many of them compare with those of Shakespeare and Milton. Queen Victoria honored him in 1843 when she appointed him poet laureate. KARL KROEBER

See also LAKE POETS; ROMANTICISM.

WORK, in physics, is the result of a force moving an object through a measurable distance against a resistance. Two factors determine the amount of work done. One factor is the amount of force applied. The other factor is the distance the object moves. In physics, work is accomplished only when the force is sufficient to move the object. In other words, work is measured by what is done, not by the effort applied in attempting to move an object. A person does work only when lifting, pushing, or sliding an object from one place to another. He does no work when holding an object without moving it, even though he may become tired.

Scientists and engineers measure work in units that represent the measurement of both force and distance. In the customary system of measurement, force is measured in such units as pounds or tons, and distance is measured in feet, inches, miles, or yards. Work can be measured as the product of any distance unit and any force unit. For example, one foot-pound equals the work done when a force of one pound moves something a distance of one foot. If a 50-pound object is lifted 4 feet, the work done is 200 foot-pounds. If, however, a 4-pound object is lifted 50 feet, the work done is still 200 foot-pounds. The foot-pound is the commonly used unit of work in the customary system.

In the metric system, the basic unit of force is the newton, and the basic unit of distance is the meter. Thus, work is measured in newton-meters. Another name for the newton-meter is *joule*. One foot-pound equals 1.35 newton-meters or joules. People who use the metric system also sometimes measure force in *dynes* and distance in centimeters. When these two units are used, work is measured in *dyne-centimeters*, or *ergs*. One dyne-centimeter or erg equals $\frac{1}{10,000,000}$ of a joule.

Work is always done by some agent, such as a person or a machine. The agent produces the force that causes the motion. This motion is always produced against some form of resistance. For example, an automobile produces motion against the friction of the road and the wind.

The units used to measure work are also used to measure energy. Energy is the ability of something to do work (see ENERGY). The rate at which work is done is called *power*. In measuring power, the amount of time needed to do the work is considered along with force and distance. Power is measured in a unit called the *watt*. One watt equals one joule per second. See POWER; WATT. ROBERT L. WEBER

See also FOOT-POUND; JOULE; DYNE; THERMODYNAMICS; KILOGRAM-METER.

WORKER, insect. See ANT (The Ant Colony); BEE (The Honeybee Colony); TERMITE.

WORKERS' COMPENSATION provides pay and medical help for injured workers, and pensions to their dependents in cases where death occurs. Loss of income due to accidents on the job has been a growing problem of workers since the introduction of machine methods to industry. Today, most major countries have laws or private programs for workers' compensation.

The first such laws were passed in Germany in 1883. Austria followed in 1887, and Norway, Finland, France, Denmark, and Great Britain passed laws in the 1890's. During the early 1900's, most other European countries enacted workers' compensation laws.

Employers' liability laws preceded workers' compensation laws. They made an employer responsible for injuries to workers caused by defective machinery or by negligence on the part of management. In 1880, Britain adopted one of the first such laws.

In the United States, Maryland passed the first state compensation law in 1902. But the U.S. Supreme Court declared the Maryland law and other compensation acts of that decade unconstitutional. The cause of workers' compensation was greatly aided when Congress passed the Federal Employees' Compensation Act of 1916. This law provided benefits for certain federal civilian workers, or their survivors, in connection with injuries or death on the job.

Ten states passed workers' compensation laws in 1911. Wisconsin was the first. In 1948, the last of the then 48 states enacted a workers' compensation program. Alaska and Hawaii had such laws when they became states in 1959.

The state workers' compensation laws differ widely in provisions and administration. In general, the laws provide compensation and medical care for injured workers, and death benefits and pensions for the dependents of workers killed on the job. Employers bear the entire cost of workers' compensation, except in a few states where workers contribute small amounts. Most state laws provide training in new jobs for workers who cannot continue in their old work because of injuries. The federal government and almost all the states have laws covering compensation for occupational diseases. Workers' compensation laws exclude most farm workers and domestic servants, and some workers in small firms. A state workers' compensation program may be administered by a state agency, by insurance companies, or by a state agency and insurance companies together. The Office of Workers' Compensation Programs in the Department of Labor administers federal compensation laws.

In the early 1970's, the total premiums paid for workers' compensation amounted to over $5 billion a year, or about one per cent of the wages of covered workers. Total benefits in cash and in medical care were about $3½ billion. The difference between premiums paid and benefits to workers was accounted for by costs of accident prevention work, building up of claims reserves, administrative expenses, and profits of insurance companies. In an average week, about 60 million workers were covered. ROBERT J. MYERS

WORKING CLASS. See SOCIAL CLASS.

WORKING DOG. See DOG (table: Recognized Breeds; color pictures); GUIDE DOG; SHEEP DOG.

WORKING DRAWING is a plan that supplies information to make or assemble something. It may be an *assembly drawing* that shows how various parts of a machine are put together. Other drawings often accompany the assembly drawing to show how the sections are assembled. A *detailed drawing* is a working drawing that guides production workers so that each part of a manufactured item has the right size, shape, finish, and material. See also ARCHITECTURE (How an Architect Designs a Building); BLUEPRINT; RAILROAD, MODEL.

WORKS PROGRESS ADMINISTRATION. See NEW DEAL (The Second Hundred Days); ROOSEVELT, FRANKLIN DELANO (The New Deal); ADULT EDUCATION.

WORLD

WORLD. In all of the enormous universe, our world is only one of millions of heavenly bodies. In fact, the earth is one of the smallest bodies of the universe. But we hardly ever think of the world as just a small planet. To us, the world is the most important part of the entire universe. The earth is the home of human beings, and the source of everything we use or make.

From the very beginning of their life on earth, people have had to learn about the world in order to use it. For thousands of years, people knew only enough to get food and clothing. They lived in caves or in shelters made of branches. People increased their knowledge constantly, sometimes slowly and sometimes rapidly. They learned how to live with others in large groups. They built cities and formed nations. They found ways to control many powerful natural forces. During the last few hundred years, people have made their most rapid progress. Today, we are making more efficient use of the world than any generation of the past. We are even reaching into space to learn more about the rest of the universe.

This article tells about the world as we know it—the home of people today. The story begins with a map of the world. This map shows how people have divided the land surface of the world into countries. The latest information on each country's size and population appears in tables following the world map.

People can live almost everywhere on the land of the world. The geography section of this article explains why some places are more suitable than others for human activities. The great human family—about 4,360,000,000 persons —is described in separate sections of the article. These sections tell where the people of the world live, discuss the world's racial groups, and note the languages that are spoken in various regions.

All human beings share certain needs. But many ways of life have developed in different parts of the world. The similarities and the differences among these cultures are described in a section on the life of the world. Other sections tell about the arts and recreation, education and science, the economy of the world, and the interdependence of nations.

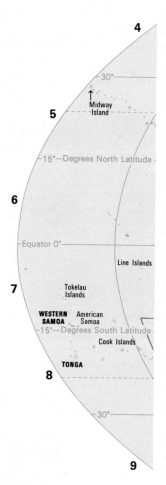

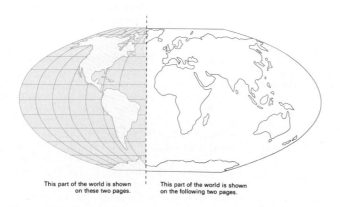

This part of the world is shown on these two pages. | This part of the world is shown on the following two pages.

The names of independent, self-governing countries appear in this kind of type: **CANADA**

The names of areas that do not govern themselves appear in this kind of type: Bermuda

The contributors of this article are Phillip Bacon, Professor of Geography, University of Houston; Paul Bohannan, Professor of Anthropology, University of California, Santa Barbara; Stewart E. Fraser, Director of the Peabody International Center and Professor in International and Comparative Education, George Peabody College for Teachers; and Raymond F. Mikesell, W. E. Miner Professor of Economics, University of Oregon.

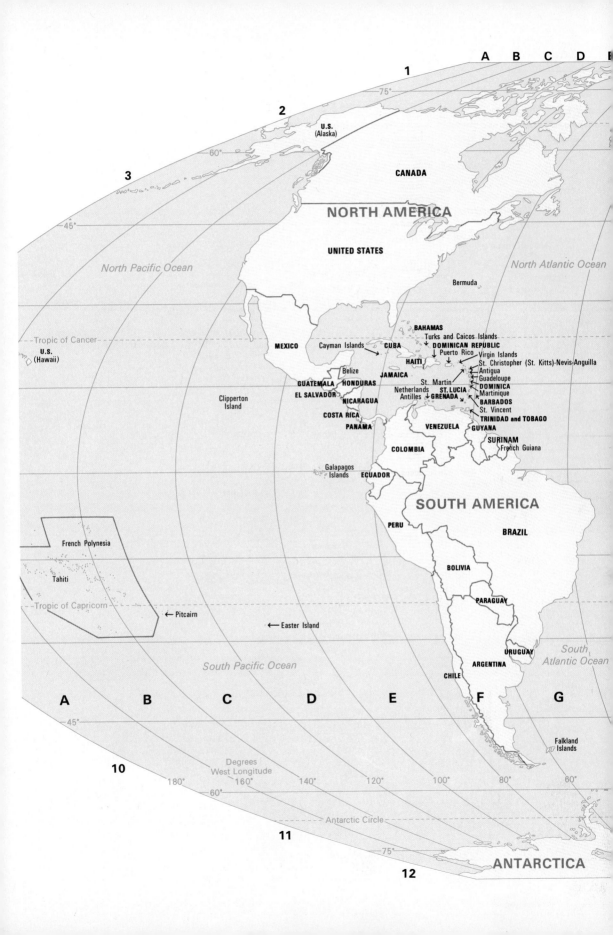

A   B   C   D   E

1

2

U.S.
(Alaska)

3

CANADA

NORTH AMERICA

45°

UNITED STATES

North Pacific Ocean

North Atlantic Ocean

Bermuda

Tropic of Cancer

BAHAMAS

U.S.
(Hawaii)

Turks and Caicos Islands

MEXICO   Cayman Islands   CUBA   DOMINICAN REPUBLIC
                                        Puerto Rico   Virgin Islands
                              HAITI   St. Christopher (St. Kitts)-Nevis-Anguilla
Belize   Antigua
                              JAMAICA   Guadeloupe
GUATEMALA   HONDURAS   St. Martin   DOMINICA
Clipperton   EL SALVADOR   Netherlands   ST. LUCIA   Martinique
Island   Antilles   GRENADA   BARBADOS
              NICARAGUA   St. Vincent
                                                      TRINIDAD and TOBAGO
              COSTA RICA
              PANAMA   VENEZUELA   GUYANA
                                                SURINAM
                          COLOMBIA   French Guiana

Galapagos
Islands   ECUADOR

SOUTH AMERICA

French Polynesia   PERU   BRAZIL

Tahiti   BOLIVIA

Tropic of Capricorn   PARAGUAY

← Pitcairn

← Easter Island   URUGUAY
                                    ARGENTINA
                                                South
                                                Atlantic Ocean
South Pacific Ocean   CHILE

A   B   C   D   E   F   G

45°
                                                Falkland
                                                Islands

10   Degrees
           West Longitude
180°   160°   140°   120°   100°   80°   60°
60°

11   Antarctic Circle

75°

12   ANTARCTICA

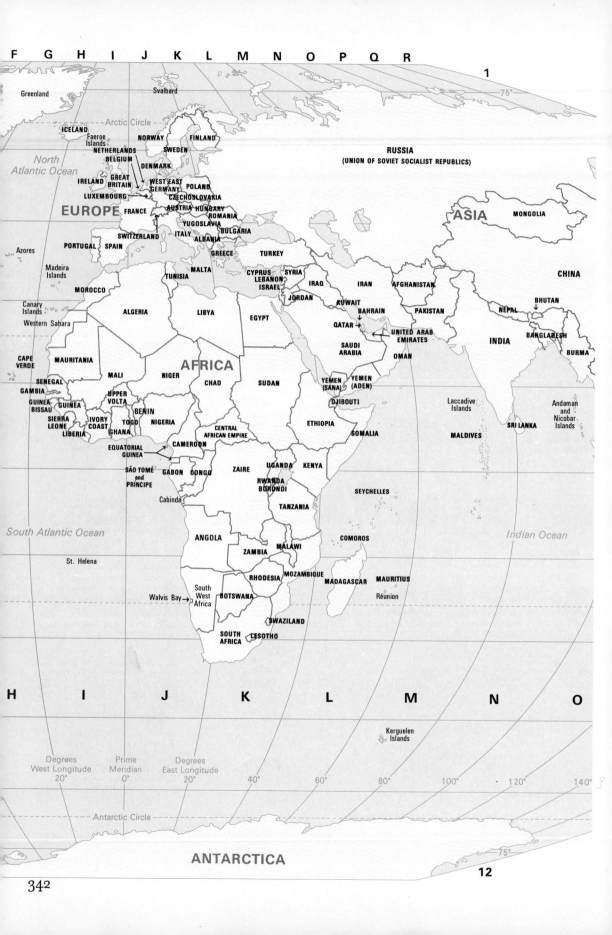

Greenland

Svalbard

Arctic Circle

ICELAND

Faeroe
Islands

NORWAY FINLAND

North
Atlantic Ocean

NETHERLANDS SWEDEN

BELGIUM DENMARK

RUSSIA
(UNION OF SOVIET SOCIALIST REPUBLICS)

IRELAND GREAT
BRITAIN

WEST EAST
GERMANY POLAND

LUXEMBOURG CZECHOSLOVAKIA

EUROPE FRANCE AUSTRIA HUNGARY

ROMANIA

YUGOSLAVIA

ASIA MONGOLIA

SWITZERLAND ITALY BULGARIA

ALBANIA

Azores

PORTUGAL SPAIN

GREECE

TURKEY

CHINA

Madeira
Islands

MALTA

CYPRUS SYRIA

LEBANON

TUNISIA

ISRAEL IRAQ

IRAN AFGHANISTAN

BHUTAN

MOROCCO

JORDAN

NEPAL

Canary
Islands

KUWAIT

PAKISTAN

Western Sahara

BAHRAIN

ALGERIA LIBYA

EGYPT

QATAR

UNITED ARAB
EMIRATES

INDIA BANGLADESH

CAPE
VERDE

MAURITANIA

AFRICA

SAUDI
ARABIA

OMAN

BURMA

SENEGAL

MALI

NIGER CHAD

SUDAN

YEMEN
(SANA)

YEMEN
(ADEN)

GAMBIA

UPPER
VOLTA

DJIBOUTI

Laccadive
Islands

Andaman
and
Nicobar
Islands

GUINEA-
BISSAU GUINEA

BENIN

SIERRA
LEONE IVORY
COAST

TOGO

NIGERIA

ETHIOPIA

SOMALIA

SRI LANKA

LIBERIA GHANA

CENTRAL
AFRICAN EMPIRE

MALDIVES

EQUATORIAL
GUINEA CAMEROON

SÃO TOMÉ
and
PRÍNCIPE GABON CONGO

ZAIRE

UGANDA KENYA

RWANDA
BURUNDI

SEYCHELLES

Cabinda

TANZANIA

South Atlantic Ocean

Indian Ocean

St. Helena

ANGOLA MALAWI

COMOROS

ZAMBIA

RHODESIA MOZAMBIQUE

MADAGASCAR MAURITIUS

Walvis Bay South
West
Africa BOTSWANA

Réunion

SWAZILAND

SOUTH
AFRICA LESOTHO

Kerguelen
Islands

Degrees
West Longitude
20°

Prime
Meridian
0°

Degrees
East Longitude
20°

40°

60°

80°

100°

120°

140°

Antarctic Circle

75°

ANTARCTICA

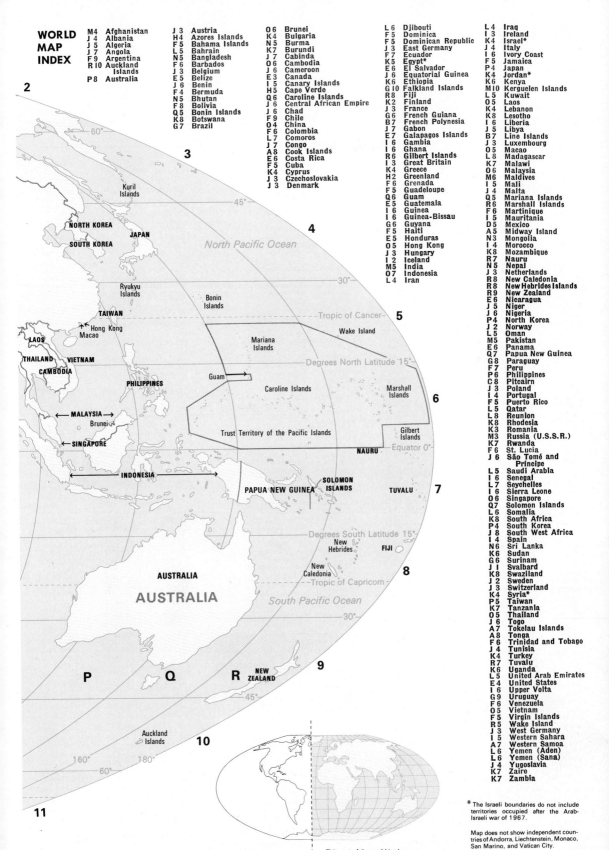

WORLD MAP INDEX

M 4	Afghanistan
J 4	Albania
J 5	Algeria
J 7	Angola
F 9	Argentina
R 10	Auckland Islands
P 8	Australia

J 3	Austria
H 4	Azores Islands
F 5	Bahama Islands
L 5	Bahrain
N 5	Bangladesh
F 6	Barbados
J 3	Belgium
E 5	Belize
J 6	Benin
F 4	Bermuda
N 5	Bhutan
F 8	Bolivia
Q 5	Bonin Islands
K 8	Botswana
G 7	Brazil

O 6	Brunei
K 4	Bulgaria
N 5	Burma
K 7	Burundi
J 7	Cabinda
O 6	Cambodia
J 6	Cameroon
E 3	Canada
I 5	Canary Islands
H 5	Cape Verde
Q 6	Caroline Islands
J 6	Central African Empire
J 6	Chad
F 9	Chile
O 4	China
F 6	Colombia
L 7	Comoros
J 7	Congo
A 8	Cook Islands
E 6	Costa Rica
F 5	Cuba
K 4	Cyprus
J 3	Czechoslovakia
J 3	Denmark

L 6	Djibouti
F 5	Dominica
F 5	Dominican Republic
J 3	East Germany
F 7	Ecuador
K 5	Egypt*
E 6	El Salvador
J 6	Equatorial Guinea
K 6	Ethiopia
G 10	Falkland Islands
R 8	Fiji
K 2	Finland
J 3	France
G 6	French Guiana
B 7	French Polynesia
J 7	Gabon
F 6	Gambia
E 7	Galapagos Islands
I 6	Gambia
I 6	Ghana
R 6	Gilbert Islands
I 3	Great Britain
K 4	Greece
H 2	Greenland
F 6	Grenada
F 5	Guadeloupe
Q 6	Guam
E 5	Guatemala
I 6	Guinea
I 6	Guinea-Bissau
G 6	Guyana
F 5	Haiti
E 5	Honduras
O 5	Hong Kong
J 3	Hungary
I 2	Iceland
M 5	India
O 7	Indonesia
L 4	Iran

L 4	Iraq
I 3	Ireland
K 4	Israel*
J 4	Italy
I 6	Ivory Coast
F 5	Jamaica
P 4	Japan
K 4	Jordan*
K 6	Kenya
M 10	Kerguelen Islands
L 5	Kuwait
O 5	Laos
K 4	Lebanon
I 6	Lesotho
I 6	Liberia
J 5	Libya
B 7	Line Islands
J 3	Luxembourg
O 5	Macao
L 8	Madagascar
K 7	Malawi
O 6	Malaysia
M 6	Maldives
I 5	Mali
J 4	Malta
Q 5	Mariana Islands
R 6	Marshall Islands
F 6	Martinique
I 5	Mauritania
D 5	Mexico
A 5	Midway Island
N 3	Mongolia
I 4	Morocco
K 8	Mozambique
R 7	Nauru
N 5	Nepal
J 3	Netherlands
R 8	New Caledonia
R 8	New Hebrides Islands
R 9	New Zealand
E 6	Nicaragua
J 5	Niger
J 6	Nigeria
P 4	North Korea
J 2	Norway
L 5	Oman
M 5	Pakistan
E 6	Panama
Q 7	Papua New Guinea
G 8	Paraguay
F 7	Peru
P 6	Philippines
C 8	Pitcairn
J 3	Poland
I 4	Portugal
F 5	Puerto Rico
L 5	Qatar
L 8	Reunion
K 8	Rhodesia
K 3	Romania
M 3	Russia (U.S.S.R.)
K 7	Rwanda
F 6	St. Lucia
J 6	São Tomé and Príncipe
L 5	Saudi Arabia
I 6	Senegal
L 7	Seychelles
I 6	Sierra Leone
O 6	Singapore
Q 7	Solomon Islands
L 6	Somalia
K 8	South Africa
P 4	South Korea
J 8	South West Africa
I 4	Spain
N 6	Sri Lanka
K 6	Sudan
G 6	Surinam
J 1	Svalbard
K 8	Swaziland
J 2	Sweden
J 3	Switzerland
K 4	Syria*
P 5	Taiwan
K 7	Tanzania
O 5	Thailand
J 6	Togo
A 7	Tokelau Islands
A 8	Tonga
F 6	Trinidad and Tobago
J 4	Tunisia
K 4	Turkey
R 7	Tuvalu
K 6	Uganda
L 5	United Arab Emirates
E 4	United States
I 6	Upper Volta
G 9	Uruguay
F 6	Venezuela
O 5	Vietnam
F 5	Virgin Islands
R 5	Wake Island
J 3	West Germany
I 5	Western Sahara
A 7	Western Samoa
L 6	Yemen (Aden)
L 6	Yemen (Sana)
J 4	Yugoslavia
K 7	Zaire
K 7	Zambia

* The Israeli boundaries do not include territories occupied after the Arab-Israeli war of 1967.

Map does not show independent countries of Andorra, Liechtenstein, Monaco, San Marino, and Vatican City.

This part of the world is shown on the preceding two pages.

This part of the world is shown on these two pages.

343

WORLD / Nations of the World

In 1979, there were 163 independent countries in the world, and, about 50 other political units, chiefly colonies and territories (also called *dependencies*). An independent country has its own government. A colony or territory is governed by another nation.

The independent countries cover almost all the land area of the world. Their people account for about 4 billion persons—most of the world's population. Only about 16 million live in the dependencies.

The largest country in the world is Russia. It has an area of 8,649,500 square miles (22,402,000 square kilometers). Seven other countries each have an area of over 1 million square miles (2.6 million square kilometers).

INDEPENDENT COUNTRIES OF THE WORLD*

Name	Area In sq. mi.	In km²	Population†	Name	Area In sq. mi.	In km²	Population†
Afghanistan	250,000	647,497	21,859,000	Liberia	43,000	111,369	1,825,000
Albania	11,100	28,748	2,868,000	Libya	679,362	1,759,540	3,002,000
Algeria	919,595	2,381,741	19,628,000	Liechtenstein	61	157	26,000
Andorra	175	453	37,000	Luxembourg	998	2,586	371,000
Angola	481,354	1,246,700	7,538,000	Madagascar	226,658	587,041	9,303,000
Argentina	1,072,163	2,776,889	27,776,000	Malawi	45,747	118,484	5,735,000
Australia	2,966,200	7,682,300	14,480,000	Malaysia	127,316	329,749	13,790,000
Austria	32,374	83,849	7,574,000	Maldives	115	298	148,000
Bahamas	5,380	13,935	243,000	Mali	478,767	1,240,000	6,872,000
Bahrain	240	622	294,000	Malta	122	316	335,000
Bangladesh	55,598	143,998	92,181,000	Mauritania	397,956	1,030,700	1,693,000
Barbados	166	431	254,000	Mauritius	790	2,045	942,000
Belgium	11,781	30,513	10,048,000	Mexico	761,607	1,972,552	71,524,000
Benin	43,484	112,622	3,557,000	Monaco	0.58	1.49	26,000
Bhutan	18,147	47,000	1,311,000	Mongolia	604,250	1,565,000	1,689,000
Bolivia	424,165	1,098,581	5,170,000	Morocco	172,414	446,550	20,070,000
Botswana	231,805	600,372	804,000	Mozambique	302,330	783,030	10,343,000
Brazil	3,286,488	8,511,965	126,497,000	Nauru	8	21	9,000
Bulgaria	42,823	110,912	8,995,000	Nepal	54,362	140,797	14,372,000
Burma	261,218	676,552	34,938,000	Netherlands	15,892	41,160	14,272,000
Burundi	10,747	27,834	4,280,000	New Zealand	103,883	269,057	3,361,000
Cambodia	69,898	181,035	8,540,000	Nicaragua	50,193	130,000	2,543,000
Cameroon	183,569	475,442	7,042,000	Niger	489,191	1,267,000	5,259,000
Canada	3,851,809	9,976,139	24,212,000	Nigeria	356,669	923,768	72,031,000
Cape Verde	1,557	4,033	329,000	Norway	125,182	324,219	4,124,000
Central African Empire	240,535	622,984	3,009,000	Oman	82,030	212,457	894,000
Chad	495,755	1,284,000	4,473,000	Pakistan	310,404	803,943	81,451,000
Chile	292,258	756,945	11,227,000	Panama	29,856	77,326	1,963,000
China	3,678,470	9,527,200	893,873,000	Papua New Guinea	178,260	461,691	3,132,000
Colombia	439,737	1,138,914	27,548,000	Paraguay	157,048	406,752	3,150,000
Comoros	838	2,171	347,000	Peru	496,225	1,285,216	18,180,000
Congo	132,047	342,000	1,540,000	Philippines	115,831	300,000	50,119,000
Costa Rica	19,575	50,700	2,230,000	Poland	120,725	312,677	35,616,000
Cuba	44,218	114,524	10,120,000	Portugal	35,553	92,082	9,904,000
Cyprus	3,572	9,251	662,000	Qatar	4,247	11,000	173,000
Czechoslovakia	49,371	127,869	15,340,000	Rhodesia**	150,804	390,580	7,493,000
Denmark	16,629	43,069	5,155,000	Romania	91,699	237,500	22,317,000
Djibouti	8,494	22,000	250,000	Russia	8,649,500	22,402,000	269,306,000
Dominica	290	751	79,000	Rwanda	10,169	26,338	4,753,000
Dominican Republic	18,816	48,734	5,442,000	St. Lucia	238	616	115,000
Ecuador	109,484	283,561	8,388,000	San Marino	24	61	21,000
Egypt	386,662	1,001,449	41,314,000	São Tomé and Príncipe	372	964	86,000
El Salvador	8,124	21,041	4,619,000	Saudi Arabia	831,313	2,153,090	8,361,000
Equatorial Guinea	10,830	28,051	338,000	Senegal	75,750	196,192	5,791,000
Ethiopia	471,778	1,221,900	31,779,000	Seychelles	108	280	64,000
Fiji	7,055	18,272	623,000	Sierra Leone	27,699	71,740	3,421,000
Finland	130,120	337,009	4,803,000	Singapore	224	581	2,427,000
France	211,208	547,026	54,412,000	Solomon Islands	10,983	28,446	230,000
Gabon	103,347	267,667	1,124,000	Somalia	246,201	637,657	3,614,000
Gambia	4,361	11,295	596,000	South Africa	471,445	1,221,037	28,841,000
Germany (East)	41,768	108,178	16,585,000	Spain	194,885	504,750	37,580,000
Germany (West)	95,934	248,468	61,991,000	Sri Lanka	25,332	65,610	15,568,000
Ghana	92,100	238,537	11,603,000	Sudan	967,500	2,505,813	18,509,000
Great Britain	94,250	244,106	56,326,000	Surinam	63,037	163,265	484,000
Greece	50,944	131,944	9,424,000	Swaziland	6,704	17,363	553,000
Grenada	133	344	98,000	Sweden	173,732	449,964	8,354,000
Guatemala	42,042	108,889	7,014,000	Switzerland	15,941	41,288	6,448,000
Guinea	94,926	245,857	4,980,000	Syria	71,498	185,180	8,649,000
Guinea-Bissau	13,948	36,125	567,000	Taiwan	13,885	35,961	17,696,000
Guyana	83,000	214,969	841,000	Tanzania	364,900	945,087	17,420,000
Haiti	10,714	27,750	4,974,000	Thailand	198,457	514,000	48,711,000
Honduras	43,277	112,088	3,173,000	Togo	21,622	56,000	2,530,000
Hungary	35,919	93,030	10,767,000	Tonga	270	699	92,000
Iceland	39,769	103,000	232,000	Trinidad and Tobago	1,980	5,128	1,137,000
India	1,269,346	3,287,590	662,598,000	Tunisia	63,170	163,610	6,828,000
Indonesia	788,426	2,042,012	154,340,000	Turkey	301,382	780,576	45,794,000
Iran	636,296	1,648,000	38,071,000	Tuvalu	10	26	8,000
Iraq	167,925	434,924	13,494,000	Uganda	91,134	236,036	13,599,000
Ireland	27,136	70,283	3,317,000	United Arab Emirates	32,278	83,600	964,000
Israel	8,019	20,770	3,960,000	United States	3,618,465	9,371,781	222,502,000
Italy	116,314	301,253	58,009,000	Upper Volta	105,869	274,200	6,918,000
Ivory Coast	124,504	322,463	7,847,000	Uruguay	68,037	176,215	2,850,000
Jamaica	4,244	10,991	2,192,000	Vatican City	0.17	0.44	1,000
Japan	145,711	377,389	118,747,000	Venezuela	352,145	912,050	15,081,000
Jordan	37,738	97,740	3,151,000	Vietnam	127,242	329,556	54,763,000
Kenya	224,961	582,646	15,951,000	Western Samoa	1,097	2,842	157,000
Korea (North)	46,540	120,538	19,312,000	Yemen (Aden)	128,560	332,968	1,961,000
Korea (South)	38,025	98,484	40,457,000	Yemen (Sana)	75,290	195,000	7,695,000
Kuwait	7,768	20,118	1,282,000	Yugoslavia	98,766	255,804	22,347,000
Laos	91,429	236,800	3,691,000	Zaire	905,568	2,345,409	28,622,000
Lebanon	4,015	10,400	2,658,000	Zambia	290,586	752,614	5,896,000
Lesotho	11,720	30,355	1,335,000				

*Each country listed has a separate article in WORLD BOOK.
†Populations are 1980 estimates based on the latest figures from official government and United Nations sources.
**Declared itself independent from Great Britain in 1965.

These countries, in order of size, are Canada, China, the United States, Brazil, Australia, India, and Argentina. The smallest independent country is Vatican City, with fewer than 109 acres (44 hectares). Fourteen other countries cover fewer than 250 square miles (647 square kilometers) each. They are Andorra, Bahrain, Barbados, Grenada, Liechtenstein, Maldives, Malta, Monaco, Nauru, St. Lucia, San Marino, Seychelles, Singapore, and Tuvalu.

Throughout history, the political map of the world has changed almost constantly. Most of the important changes have resulted from great wars. During ancient times, the powerful armies of such conquerors as Julius Caesar and Alexander the Great took over country after country. The conquerors built these countries into vast empires. In time, the ancient empires became weak and broke up into many countries again. Other empires rose and fell during later periods of history, and the map changed again and again.

During the 1900's, World Wars I and II caused many important changes on the map. As a result of World War I, several new countries were formed in Europe. They included Austria, Czechoslovakia, Hungary, and Yugoslavia. After World War II, several European na-

tions changed in size, and many new nations were established in Asia. But the greatest change took place in Africa among the colonies of various European nations. A strong movement for independence swept the African continent. About 45 new African nations have been established since the 1950's.

The countries of the world may be grouped in several ways. People often call the countries of the Eastern Hemisphere the *Old World*, and those of the Western Hemisphere, the *New World*. Countries also may be grouped by regions, such as the *Far East*, the *Middle East*, or *Latin America*. Sometimes countries are grouped according to continent, such as *African*, *Asian*, or *European*.

After World War II, Russia and other Communist countries became known as the *Communist World*. The United States and other countries that oppose the spread of Communism are sometimes called the *Free World*. Many nations, including India, Switzerland, and most of the African countries, have not committed themselves to either of these two groups. Such nations are often grouped together as the *neutral* or *nonaligned* nations of the world, and sometimes are called the *Third World*.

CONTINENTS OF THE WORLD*

Name	Area† In sq. mi.	In km²	Population†	Name	Area† In sq. mi.	In km²	Population†
Africa	11,707,000	30,320,000	466,000,000	Europe	4,063,000	10,523,000	688,000,000
Antarctica	5,100,000	13,209,000		North America	9,421,000	24,399,000	369,000,000
Asia	17,012,000	44,062,000	2,565,000,000	South America	6,883,000	17,828,000	†247,000,000
Australia	2,966,000	7,682,000	14,000,000				

*Each continent has a separate article in WORLD BOOK.
†Area figures are rounded to the nearest thousand; and population figures, to the nearest million.

OTHER POLITICAL UNITS OF THE WORLD*

Name	Area In sq. mi.	In km²	Population†	Name	Area In sq. mi.	In km²	Population†
American Samoa (U.S.)	76	197	32,000	Niue I. (N.Z.)	100	259	5,000
Andaman and Nicobar Is. (India)	3,202	8,293	115,133	Norfolk Is. (Austral.)	14	36	2,000
Azores (Port.)	905	2,344	273,400	Pacific Is., Trust Territory of the (U.S.)	717	1,857	119,440
Belize (G.B.)	8,867	22,965	163,000	Caroline Is.	463	1,199	75,394
Bermuda (G.B.)	21	53	60,000	Mariana Is.	184	477	14,335
British Indian Ocean Territory	23	80	2,000	Marshall Is.	70	181	29,511
Brunei (G.B.)	2,226	5,765	217,000	Pitcairn I. (G.B.)	2	5	92
Channel Is. (G.B.)	75	195	133,000	Puerto Rico (U.S.)	3,435	8,897	3,602,000
Cook Is. (N.Z.)	93	241	18,000	Reunion (Fr.)	969	2,510	539,000
Faeroe Is. (Denmark)	540	1,399	41,000	Saint Helena (G.B.)	162	419	6,419
Falkland Is. (G.B.)	4,618	11,961	2,000	Saint Pierre and Miquelon (Fr.)	93	242	5,000
French Guinea	35,135	91,000	67,000	South West Africa (S. Af.)	318,261	824,292	1,027,000
French Polynesia	1,544	4,000	142,000	Tokelau Is. (N.Z.)	4	10	2,000
Gaza Strip (Egypt)	146	378	356,261	Virgin Is. (G.B.)	59	153	12,000
Gibraltar (G.B.)	2.3	6	33,000	Virgin Is. (U.S.)	133	344	104,000
Gilbert Is. (G.B.)	278	720	51,926	Wake I. (U.S.)	3	8	1,647
Greenland (Den.)	840,004	2,175,600	52,000	Wallis and Futuna Is. (Fr.)	106	275	9,000
Guadeloupe (Fr.)	687	1,779	373,000	West Indies Associated States (G.B.)			
Guam (U.S.)	212	549	107,000	Antigua	171	442	75,000
Hong Kong (G.B.)	1,126	2,916	4,790,000	St. Christopher (St. Kitts)- Nevis-Anguilla	138	357	67,000
Johnston I. (U.S.)	0.5	1.3	1,007	St. Vincent	150	388	128,000
Line Is. (G.B., U.S.)	262	679	1,472	Western Sahara**	102,703	266,000	152,000
Macao (Port.)	6	16	286,000				
Madeira (Port.)	308	797	245,000				
Man, Isle of (G.B.)	227	588	65,000				
Martinique (Fr.)	425	1,102	381,000				
Midway I. (U.S.)	2	5	2,220				
Netherlands Antilles	383	993	256,000				
New Caledonia (Fr.)	7,335	18,998	141,000				
New Hebrides Is. (Fr., G.B.)	5,700	14,763	104,000				

*The political units listed are administered by the country shown in parentheses. Each political unit has a separate article in WORLD BOOK.
†Populations are 1980 and earlier estimates based on the latest figures from official government and United Nations sources.
**Claimed by Mauritania and Morocco.

World Cultural Regions

Anglo-America is the cultural region made up of the English-speaking countries of the Western Hemisphere—the United States and Canada. They share laws and customs that came from England, or *Anglia*, the Latin name for *England*.

Latin America includes Mexico and the countries south of it to the southern tip of South America. Latin-American ways of life came largely from Spain, Portugal, or France, and are based on those of ancient Rome, once called *Latium*.

Eastern Europe consists of Communist nations—Albania, Bulgaria, Czechoslovakia, East Germany, Hungary, Poland, Romania, Russia, and Yugoslavia. These countries cover almost two-thirds of Europe.

Western Europe is made up of 25 countries that have non-Communist governments. The nations of Western Europe have formed several organizations for military defense and economic cooperation.

The Middle East lies where Africa, Asia, and Europe meet. Since Biblical times, this region has served as an important link between the three continents. Most of the people are Muslims. Arabic is the chief language of the Middle East.

The Far East is the easternmost region of Asia. It is also called East Asia or the Orient. China and Japan are the chief nations of the Far East. Most of the region's people speak Chinese or a language related to it.

WORLD BOOK maps

344b

WORLD / Geography of the World

The surface of the earth consists of about 196,951,-000 square miles (510,100,000 square kilometers) of land and water. Water covers about 139,692,000 square miles (361,800,000 square kilometers), or about 70 per cent of the world. Land covers about 57,259,000 square miles (148,300,000 square kilometers), or about 30 per cent of the earth's surface.

The water that covers most of the earth's surface is sometimes called the *world ocean*. It is a continuous body of water, made up of three great oceans—the Pacific, the Atlantic, and the Indian. The Pacific is the largest ocean. The Pacific is about twice as large as the Atlantic. The Indian is almost as large as the Atlantic. The waters of the three great oceans come together around Antarctica. The Atlantic and Pacific waters meet again in the world's northernmost region. There, they form the Arctic Ocean. See OCEAN.

The land rises from the world ocean and forms seven continents and many islands. Asia is the largest continent. The others, in order of size, are Africa, North America, South America, Antarctica, Europe, and Australia. Geographers often consider Europe and Asia one continent and call it *Eurasia*. The largest island is Greenland, in the North Atlantic Ocean. More than 30,000 islands lie scattered throughout the Pacific Ocean. Most of them are in the southwestern Pacific. Those islands are grouped under the name *Oceania*.

Except for Antarctica, the continents have many lakes and rivers. The largest inland body of water is a huge lake of salt water called the Caspian Sea. It lies between Asia and Europe, east of the Caucasus Mountains. Lake Superior, one of the Great Lakes of North America, is the largest body of fresh water in the world. The longest river is the Nile River of Africa, which flows 4,187 miles (6,738 kilometers).

The deepest known spot of the oceans is Challenger Deep—36,198 feet (11,033 meters) below the surface of the Pacific. Challenger Deep is southwest of the island of Guam. The highest point on earth is the peak of Mount Everest—29,028 feet (8,848 meters) above sea level. Mount Everest rises in the Himalaya mountain system, on the border between Nepal and Tibet.

People can live almost everywhere on land. But some places are poorly suited for human activities. Most of Antarctica lies buried beneath ice and snow. Scientists have, however, established a few bases there. The principal places where people make their homes are (1) mountains, (2) plateaus, (3) hilly regions, and (4) plains. Most persons live on the plains or in hilly places. Most of those regions have plenty of water and rich soil. The plains and hills are generally good places for people to develop farming, manufacturing, and trade. Relatively few persons live in the high mountains or on plateaus. Some mountain valleys and high grassy plateaus are good places for raising cattle or sheep. But most of the snow-capped mountains and high plateaus are too cold, dry, or rough for comfortable living.

United Press Int.

Fritz Henle, Monkmeyer

Where People Live

People can live almost everywhere on land. But only about 30 per cent of the earth's surface is made up of land, and some of the land is not suitable for human activities. Most of the world's people live on the plains or in hilly regions. These regions are usually good places for farming, manufacturing, or trade.

LAND 30% of world's surface.

WATER 70% of world's surface.

The Ocean covers about 70 per cent of the earth's surface. The ocean has always been a major source of food. Now it is also becoming a source of power, minerals, and drinking water.

Black Star

Harvey Hurtt, Black Star

Farms and Towns usually develop wherever people find plenty of fertile soil and water.

Desert Areas can often be turned into useful lands. Much of Israel's dry Negev area has been changed into rich farmland by irrigation systems.

The Polar Regions are thickly covered by ice and snow during most of the year. The hardy Eskimos have developed a way of life that suits them to the Arctic northland.

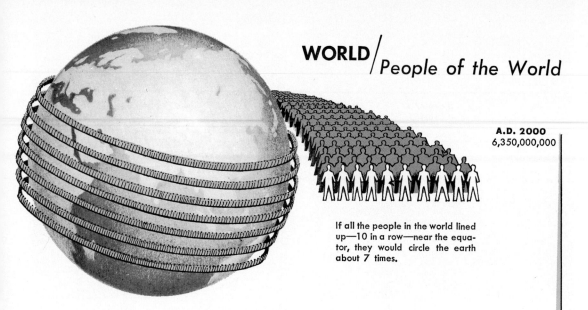

A.D. 2000
6,350,000,000

If all the people in the world lined
up—10 in a row—near the equator, they would circle the earth
about 7 times.

 The Population of the World

The population of the world in 1980 totaled about 4,360,000,000, and it continues to rise rapidly. The yearly rate of increase during the late 1970's was about 1.9 per cent. At that rate, the population of the world will reach about $6\frac{1}{3}$ billion by the year 2000.

If all the people of the world were distributed evenly, there would be about 75 persons for every square mile (29 persons for every square kilometer) of land. But, of course, people are not distributed evenly. The *population density* (the average number of persons who live in a given area) varies greatly. No one lives in most of Antarctica or in parts of some deserts. But there are more than 1,000 persons per square mile (386 persons per square kilometer) living in parts of China, Egypt, India, Indonesia, and other heavily populated countries. Large cities have the highest population densities. Chicago, for example, averages about 14,000 persons per square mile (5,400 persons per square kilometer).

The most densely populated areas of the world are in Europe, and in eastern and southern Asia. North America has clusters of dense populations in some northeastern and midwestern areas, and along the Pacific coast. Africa, Australia, and South America have areas of dense populations near the coasts. The interiors of these three continents are only thinly settled.

The important changes and shifts of the world population throughout history are described in the article on POPULATION. See also the articles on the various countries, states, and provinces for population details.

This chart shows how the world's population has grown since 2000 B.C. The increase was slow until A.D. 1, but by 1000 the population had more than doubled. It doubled again between 1650 and 1850. Between 1850 and 1970, the population tripled. At the present rate of increase, the world's population will be about $6\frac{1}{3}$ billion by the year 2000.

A.D. 1000
275,000,000

2000 B.C.
108,000,000

1000 B.C.
120,000,000

A.D. 1
138,000,000

25 LARGEST COUNTRIES OF THE WORLD IN AREA

Rank	Country	Area In sq. mi.	In km²
1.	Russia	8,649,500	22,402,000
2.	Canada	3,851,809	9,976,139
3.	China	3,678,470	9,527,200
4.	United States	3,618,465	9,371,781
5.	Brazil	3,286,488	8,511,965
6.	Australia	2,966,200	7,682,300
7.	India	1,269,346	3,287,590
8.	Argentina	1,072,163	2,776,889
9.	Sudan	967,500	2,505,813
10.	Algeria	919,595	2,381,741
11.	Zaire	905,568	2,345,409
12.	Saudi Arabia	831,313	2,153,090
13.	Indonesia	788,426	2,042,012
14.	Mexico	761,607	1,972,552
15.	Libya	679,362	1,759,540
16.	Iran	636,296	1,648,000
17.	Mongolia	604,250	1,565,000
18.	Peru	496,225	1,285,216
19.	Chad	495,755	1,284,000
20.	Niger	489,191	1,267,000
21.	Angola	481,354	1,246,700
22.	Mali	478,767	1,240,000
23.	Ethiopia	471,778	1,221,900
24.	South Africa	471,445	1,221,037
25.	Colombia	439,737	1,138,914

25 LARGEST COUNTRIES OF THE WORLD IN POPULATION

Rank	Country	Population
1.	China	893,873,000
2.	India	662,958,000
3.	Russia	269,306,000
4.	United States	222,502,000
5.	Indonesia	154,340,000
6.	Brazil	126,497,000
7.	Japan	118,747,000
8.	Bangladesh	92,181,000
9.	Pakistan	81,451,000
10.	Nigeria	72,031,000
11.	Mexico	71,524,000
12.	West Germany	61,991,000
13.	Italy	58,009,000
14.	Great Britain	56,326,000
15.	Vietnam	54,763,000
16.	France	54,412,000
17.	Philippines	50,119,000
18.	Thailand	48,711,000
19.	Turkey	45,794,000
20.	Egypt	41,314,000
21.	South Korea	40,457,000
22.	Iran	38,071,000
23.	Spain	37,580,000
24.	Poland	35,616,000
25.	Burma	34,938,000

Populations are 1980 estimates based on the latest figures from official government and United Nations sources.

COMPARING THE AREAS AND POPULATIONS OF THE CONTINENTS

This chart shows that Asia has more land and more people than any other continent. Europe is smaller than any continent except Australia, but it has the second largest population. As a result, Europe has the highest population density of any continent—168 persons per square mile (65 persons per square kilometer). Africa, North America, South America, and Australia, in that order, rank after Asia and Europe in size of population.

POPULATION

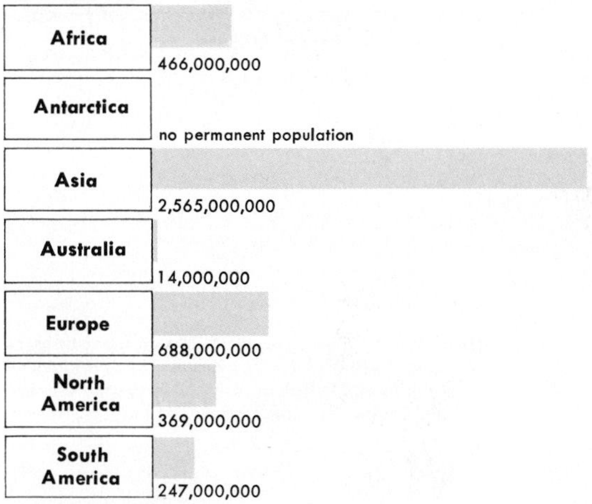

Continent	Population
Africa	466,000,000
Antarctica	no permanent population
Asia	2,565,000,000
Australia	14,000,000
Europe	688,000,000
North America	369,000,000
South America	247,000,000

AREA

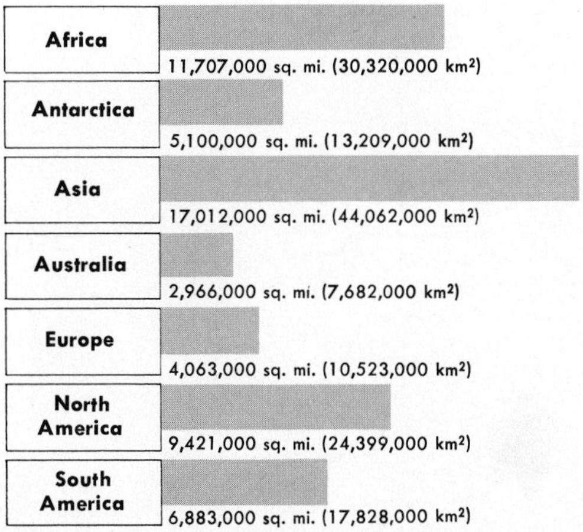

Continent	Area
Africa	11,707,000 sq. mi. (30,320,000 km²)
Antarctica	5,100,000 sq. mi. (13,209,000 km²)
Asia	17,012,000 sq. mi. (44,062,000 km²)
Australia	2,966,000 sq. mi. (7,682,000 km²)
Europe	4,063,000 sq. mi. (10,523,000 km²)
North America	9,421,000 sq. mi. (24,399,000 km²)
South America	6,883,000 sq. mi. (17,828,000 km²)

POPULATION DENSITY

Continent	Density
Africa	39 persons per sq. mi. (15 persons per km²)
Antarctica	no permanent population
Asia	150 persons per sq. mi. (58 persons per km²)
Australia	5 persons per sq. mi. (2 persons per km²)
Europe	168 persons per sq. mi. (65 persons per km²)
North America	39 persons per sq. mi. (15 persons per km²)
South America	36 persons per sq. mi. (14 persons per km²)

Populations are 1980 estimates based on official government and UN sources.

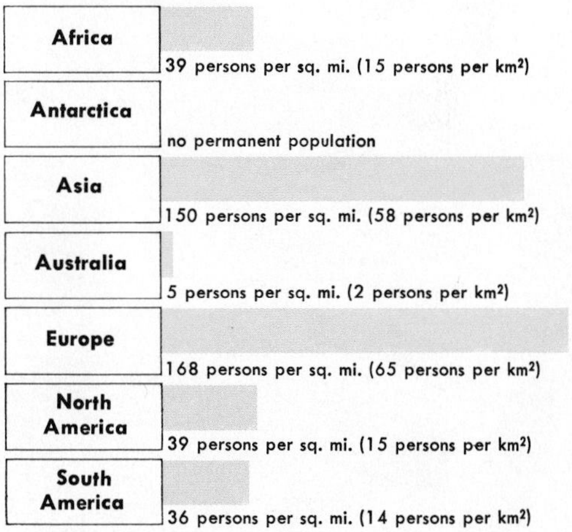

Sudan

Peru

Kuwait

Thailand

Costa Rica

⊕ The Races of the World

The World's People Belong to Many Races.
These Scouts—each from a different country—represent a variety of racial groups.

All human beings are members of the species *Homo sapiens*. But many groups of people have lived apart for long periods of time and have come to differ from one another in various ways. These different groups are called *races*.

The number of races varies according to the classifier and the purposes of the classification. Many scholars recognize 9 or 10 major geographical races and hundreds of local races. The WORLD BOOK article on RACES, HUMAN, recognizes 9 geographical races: (1) African, (2) American Indian, (3) Asian, (4) Australian, (5) European, (6) Indian, (7) Melanesian, (8) Micronesian, and (9) Polynesian.

The World's People Speak Many Languages.
The languages of these newspapers and magazines are, *left to right,* Italian, French, Spanish, Hebrew, Turkish, English, German, Chinese, and Greek.

Most "white" populations are part of the European geographical race. Most blacks, including American blacks, are of African origin. Many people who have light-brown skin, inner eyefolds, and pads of fat over their cheekbones are of Asian ancestry. In Latin America, many blacks, whites, and American Indians have intermarried. The main characteristics of the major races are described in the RACES, HUMAN, article.

Iran

Nigeria

Liechtenstein

Japan

Netherlands

© 1964, National Council
Boy Scouts of America

 ## The Languages of the World

Visitors to the United Nations may listen to translations in any of six languages—Arabic, Chinese, English, French, Russian, and Spanish.

United Nations

Scholars estimate that there are about 3,000 spoken languages. Some of these languages are spoken by only a few hundred persons. Thirteen languages are each spoken by over 50 million persons. More people speak Chinese than any other language. English ranks next, followed by Hindustani, Spanish, Russian, German, and Japanese. The others are Arabic, Bengali, French, Indonesian, Italian, and Portuguese.

The languages of the world can be grouped by families. About half the people of the world speak a language of the Indo-European family. It includes the Germanic languages, such as English, German, and Scandinavian; the Romance languages, such as French, Italian, and Spanish; and the Balto-Slavic languages, such as Russian, Polish, and Lithuanian.

The Sino-Tibetan family, which ranks second in numerical importance, includes Chinese, Thai, Burmese, and Tibetan. The Afro-Asiatic family, which ranks third, includes Arabic and Hebrew.

For the origin and development of the world's languages, see the article LANGUAGE.

The common needs and experiences of people bind them together in the human family. All people know the pull of hunger, the thrill of joy, and the drag of weariness. But different groups of people eat different foods, find enjoyment in different ways, and even sleep on different surfaces. Wherever people live, they have developed a particular way of life that suits them to their particular surroundings.

The Cultures of the World

The many different ways of life followed by groups of people make up a wide variety of *cultures*. The culture of a people consists of all the group's activities, beliefs, customs, traditions, and traits. The people of some cultures prefer rice as their main food. People of other cultures think meat is the only "real food." In still other cultures, the people say the same thing about beans. Their eating customs may differ, but all people must satisfy a common need for food. Other common needs of the human family include the need for companionship, the need for a feeling of security, and the need for opportunities to reproduce. The common needs unify all peoples, in spite of the differences in their cultures.

The important elements of human life that combine in the development of cultures are described in the article CULTURE. For a description of the different ways of life in various parts of the world, see the separate articles on the continents and countries.

The cultures of the world have been developing for thousands of years. Cultures became more complex as people learned more about their surroundings. Ways of life changed—sometimes rapidly and sometimes slowly —whenever a people learned new ways of meeting their needs or achieving their ambitions. Almost all important ideas or inventions developed by one culture spread to other cultures. This spread of ideas, such as democracy or nationalism, and of inventions, such as printing or electric power, changed many cultural patterns. In fact, most human progress has resulted from a continual exchange of ideas and inventions among the cultures of various peoples.

Progress has taken place largely because human beings never lose certain fundamental parts of their culture. For example, after people have used fire to cook their food, they will always find some way to get fire. After people have learned how to farm, they will never go back to a society that lacks an agricultural system. After people have learned how to generate power from natural forces, they will find new ways to produce such energy. The details of a culture—matches, hybrid corn, or the steam engine—may be replaced or even forgotten. But fire, agriculture, and machinery will remain in some form as long as human beings exist.

Most peoples of the world have always been eager to develop new and better ways of doing things. Since the mid-1800's, the rate of change in developed cultures has increased rapidly. This rapid change has gone hand in hand with revolutionary developments of science and technology. During the same period, the exchange of ideas and inventions among the various cultures also has been rapid and widespread. Since about 1920, the airplane, motion pictures, radio, and television have greatly speeded cultural exchange.

Today, the historic process of cultural exchange seems to be producing a trend toward a common world culture. Many differences among people are either disappearing or becoming national symbols. For example, the leaders of many African or Asian countries wear the costumes of their homelands on state occasions or at meetings of the United Nations. But in most African or Asian cities, many people wear Western styles of dress. Different styles of cooking that were once found only in certain countries are becoming common in other countries. Chinese and French cooking have become international, and Indian and Japanese foods are available in many cities throughout the world. American and European foods are familiar to many Africans and Asians.

The trend toward a world culture worries some persons. They fear that a common culture might deprive people of a variety of interesting ways of life. But the belief is growing that the development of a world cul-

The Cities of the World serve as centers of business, industry and government. People who live in cities are accustomed to elbowing their way through crowded streets. This Hong Kong scene is typical of city shopping areas throughout the Far East.

ture would actually spread variety. If the trend continues, the chief features of various cultures would no longer be confined to particular places. They would flourish in all parts of the world, and cultural variety would enrich life everywhere.

🌐 The Religions of the World

All peoples have some form of religion as part of their culture. Religious beliefs meet the need of all people for answers to certain mysteries of life. Most religious teachings emphasize the importance of moral values, especially in person-to-person relationships. The beliefs and teachings of religion help keep life moving smoothly in the various cultures of the world.

The principal religions are practiced in all parts of the world, even though they center in various cultural regions. Christianity is more widespread than any other religion. But most of the world's Christians live in Europe, North America, or South America. Most people of North Africa are Muslims, and follow the religion called Islam. Islam also has large numbers of followers in Asia. Buddhism, Confucianism, Hinduism, Shinto, and Taoism are other important religions of the people of Asia.

In some regions, two or more major religions have large numbers of followers. For example, Hinduism is the religion of the vast majority of the people of India. But millions of other Indians are Muslims. The most important religions of Japan are Shinto and Buddhism. Jews consider Palestine to be the traditional home of their religion, Judaism. But most Jews live in other countries throughout the world.

Many different religions are practiced by the tribal peoples of Africa, Asia, Australia, North and South America, and the Pacific Islands. The religions of these tribal groups are closely linked with such practical needs as food, or the health of animals or crops. Many tribal religions teach morals and ethics that resemble those taught by more widely practiced religions.

For a description of the beliefs, practices, and traditions of the various religions of the world, see the article RELIGION and the separate articles on the different faiths. See also the Religion section of the various country and continent articles.

The Farming Areas that surround most cities are usually quiet places of natural beauty. There, life is unhurried. Most homes in countryside areas are far from each other. Many farmers do their daily work alone, and rarely see their neighbors.

David J. Forbert, Monkmeyer

The Tribal Village is ruled by customs that may be thousands of years old. Tribal people see no reason to change such customs. The tribal system still includes many African peoples, many peoples of the Pacific Islands, and various American Indians.

United Nations

Art Museums in most countries are important cultural centers. There, thousands of persons may enjoy and study masterpieces of painting and sculpture.

WORLD / Arts and Recreation of the World

A world traveler may find that people of various countries enjoy many of the same activities in their leisure time. However, almost every country has certain arts, pastimes, or sports of its own. They usually reflect the national character, talents, or history of the people.

In country after country, most people amuse themselves with radio, television, or motion pictures. These are the most popular forms of entertainment almost everywhere. The people of most nations also take great pride in their art museums, libraries, theaters, and concert halls. These cultural centers preserve the traditional arts of a country.

American tourists hear the jazz music of their homeland almost everywhere they travel. Even in the Communist countries, American music and popular dances are favorites of the young people. They dance to the latest American songs in Belgrade, Moscow, and Warsaw—and also in Capri, Istanbul, and Manila. In the same cities, many persons of all ages still prefer the music and dances that are traditionally Yugoslavian, Russian, Polish, Italian, Turkish, or Filipino.

An American visiting Japan feels at home in a crowded stadium watching Japan's most popular sport —baseball. Large numbers of Japanese know the fine points of baseball. But they also know judo, a tradi-

tional Japanese form of wrestling. In Japanese cities, the tourist sees large audiences at symphony concerts enjoying classical Western music. Many Japanese also enjoy the music that came to their country hundreds of years ago from China and India. Such music is played on drums, flutes, gongs, and guitar-like instruments. It usually accompanies the kabuki dramas that have been favorites in Japan since the early 1600's.

A world traveler probably finds the greatest cultural contrasts in the African countries. An African tribe may prize the transistor radio that serves its village. But it still depends on the *bush telegraph* (messages sent by drums) to communicate with other villages. In many African cities, motion pictures are popular and television is a growing form of entertainment. But crowds still gather around skillful storytellers who recite the folk tales that make up much of Africa's traditional literature. Even more important than folklore to Africans are their music and dances. These activities are vital parts of most African religious ceremonies.

In Latin America, the culture of today is mixed with cultures of the past. The Latin-American cultural mixture can be easily seen in Mexico. There, many of the magnificent, modern buildings are decorated with vivid carvings, mosaics, and paintings. These decorations em-

Soccer ranks as one of the most popular sports in the world. It is the major sport in most of the countries of Europe and South America.

Motion Pictures are a favorite form of entertainment in many countries. Japan produces more movies than any other nation.

The Olympic Games are the world's most important international sports events. The first recorded Olympic race was held in 776 B.C.

phasize Aztec, Maya, or Toltec designs or symbols. Many modern buildings rise next to churches or mansions built in the elaborate style of the Spanish colonial era. From the Spanish conquerors of their land, Mexicans also took much of their basic music and many of their dances. The Mexican love for bullfighting also comes from the Spanish era. Today, Mexico has about 200 bullfighting arenas, including one that seats 50,000 persons—the largest in the world.

For many centuries, Europe has been the center of the arts of Western civilization. The origins of most European literature and drama were in ancient Greece. Europe was the birthplace of today's highly developed forms of symphony, opera, and ballet. European museums exhibit masterpieces of painting and sculpture from all parts of the world. Most European cities have many famous churches and historic palaces. Some of Europe's fashionable boulevards have American-style hamburger stands. But the sidewalk cafes of Paris, and the coffee houses of Vienna still symbolize the traditional leisure-time activities of many Europeans.

The arts, recreation, and sports of each country are described in the WORLD BOOK country and continent articles. See also ART AND ARTS; MUSIC; PAINTING; SCULPTURE; SPORTS.

Erich Hartmann, Magnum

Students of Many Lands attend colleges or universities far from their homes. They take part in the worldwide exchange of educational opportunities conducted by the major countries.

Communications Satellite Corp.

The Communications Satellite has opened the way for the rapid exchange of news and knowledge among all the nations of the world.

WORLD / Education and Science of the World

The search for knowledge has always been a basic activity of human beings. For thousands of years, people have been discovering, classifying, and organizing information about themselves and the world around them. Such scientific knowledge most often is used to satisfy the needs of people and to enrich life everywhere.

Scholars often trace progress through the ages by studying the growth of knowledge from generation to generation. At times, information may accumulate slowly. At other times, some scientific discovery may add greatly to the store of knowledge. The Industrial Revolution resulted from the advances of science and technology during the 1700's and early 1800's. During the mid-1900's, the growth of scientific knowledge was so rapid that it was called the "knowledge explosion."

The rate of scientific development may be seen by comparing the number of technical journals published at various times. Such journals keep scientists and educators up to date on current developments in their fields of knowledge. In 1850, about 1,000 journals were published in the different countries. By 1900, the number had grown to about 10,000. More than 50,000 scientific and technical journals are published today.

The worldwide exchange of knowledge illustrates the extent of international scientific cooperation. Such cooperation includes a wide range of important activities that generally cross political boundaries. Scientists and educators of the most advanced nations constantly exchange information about space travel, the use of nuclear energy, or methods of removing salt from seawater. An outstanding example of such cooperation was the International Geophysical Year (IGY). This program, held in 1957 and 1958, was a joint effort by the scientists of 66 nations. Working together, they made many important discoveries and worked out the first complete world weather maps. See INTERNATIONAL GEOPHYSICAL YEAR (IGY).

International scientific cooperation is vital to the millions of persons who live in the developing countries of Africa, Asia, or Latin America. Scientists and educators of the developed countries conduct many programs to assist their associates in nations where progress has been slow. In the developing countries, educators are helped to teach people to read and write. Doctors are helped to solve health problems, and agriculturists are helped to increase the food supply. See TECHNICAL ASSISTANCE; ILLITERACY.

The international exchange of students is one of the most important activities of worldwide scientific and educational cooperation. During the 1970's, more than 550,000 students a year were studying in countries other than their own. Many of these students were young people of the developing countries. The United States, France, and Canada are among the leading hosts to exchange students. Each year, about 150,000 foreign students enroll in U.S. colleges or universities, about 65,000 in France, and about 55,000 in Canada. The United Nations Educational, Scientific and Cultural Organization (UNESCO) serves as a clearing house for many student exchange programs.

UNESCO is one of many international organizations that promote educational and scientific programs. The United States belongs to more than 50 of these groups.

For the details of the world's educational and scientific development, see the articles on EDUCATION and SCIENCE, and the separate country articles.

350b

Consulate General of Japan, N.Y.

Ministry for Foreign Affairs, Sweden

Bethlehem Steel Corp.

A Large Labor Force is one of the most important elements in the economic life of a developed country. The labor force in Japan includes a large number of skilled workers.

Natural Resources may be a vital factor in the development of a nation's economy. Lumber that has been cut from the vast forests of Sweden is basic to many Swedish industries.

Capital is a chief element in a nation's economy. It includes factories, tools, supplies, and equipment as well as money. The steel mill is an important form of industrial capital.

 ## The Wealth of Nations

Economists generally divide the countries of the world into two groups—rich nations and poor nations. They usually called the rich nations *developed* and the poor nations *developing*. About 20 major non-Communist countries make up the group of developed nations. These countries are also called *industrial nations*, because their economies are based chiefly on manufacturing. They include the United States, Canada, Japan, and the principal countries of Western Europe. More than 85 major countries are generally considered as developing nations. They include most of the countries of Africa, Asia, and Latin America.

The nations are classified largely on the basis of their annual *per capita* (for each person) income, or their per capita Gross National Product (GNP). Income is money, goods, or services received in return for labor or the use of other resources. GNP is the value of all goods and services produced by a country during a year. A nation's per capita income or per capita GNP is its total income or total GNP divided by its entire population.

Among the industrial, developed nations of the world, Liechtenstein in 1978 had the highest per capita GNP—$10,400. The per capita GNP of the United States was about $9,600 in 1978. The developed countries of Western Europe had a combined annual per capita GNP of about $4,800, or about three-fifths that of the United States. In contrast to the developed countries, most of the developing nations had an annual per capita GNP of less than $420.

Russia and the other Communist dictatorships are hard to classify by the same economic yardsticks that are used for non-Communist nations. Under Communism, the government usually owns the property and means of production. However, U.S. economists estimate that in 1978 East Germany had a per capita GNP of about $4,800—the highest among the Communist nations. Russia's estimated per capita GNP was about $4,000.

The per capita income or GNP of a country does not always give a complete picture of a nation's economy. For example, on the basis of per capita GNP, some of the oil-rich Arab countries of the Middle East rank among the world's wealthiest nations. Even so, most of the people of these countries are poor. Most Americans, on the other hand, enjoy a high standard of living. Americans, as individuals, control the income of the United States. The income goes directly to the people, who spend their money—after paying taxes—as they please. Almost all of the income of the oil-producing Middle Eastern countries is earned from selling government-controlled petroleum, and the income goes to the governments. The governments spend much of the money on the education and technical training of the people. With such training, the governments expect to develop a labor force capable of manufacturing a variety of products needed in other countries. After the countries start to manufacture such products, they may be able to build a world trade based on a greater variety of exports. Then, they will no longer need to depend on petroleum for almost all their income.

Although economists usually group nations according to per capita income or GNP, no one can really estimate the wealth of any nation. By wealth, economists mean what people can produce to satisfy their needs and desires. A rich country produces an abundance of food, clothing, shelter, and the goods and services that its people enjoy. A poor country produces so little that many of its people often do not even have enough food.

In every country, people are the central figures in producing wealth. Every nation has some system to organize the production and distribution of products needed by its people. The various kinds of economic systems, and their achievements and problems, are described in the article ECONOMICS.

The nature, quality, and location of a country's natural resources have much to do with its economic strength. Generally, the developed countries of North America and Europe have excellent farmland. Most of these countries also have plentiful supplies of minerals, especially coal and iron ore, that are needed by their manufacturing industries. But such industries use enormous quantities of minerals. Many of the developed nations must import much of their petroleum and other minerals from other countries. Some developing countries have large reserves of minerals.

The size of a country's population may seriously affect its economic development. In most developing countries, for example, the population increases faster than the supply of food, year after year. In Asia, the problem of increasing food production is especially difficult because of the limited amount of farmland. In many parts of Africa and Latin America, much unused fertile soil could be cultivated by clearing, draining, or irrigating the land. In almost every poor country, more food could be grown if farmers planted better seed, and used fertilizer and modern machines. But such improvements require expensive research and large amounts of money, and the developing countries generally lack such funds. Also, their farmers need training in the use of modern agricultural methods. This training takes a good deal of time.

Certain basic economic problems faced by developing countries have been solved by developed countries. Belgium and The Netherlands rank among the richest nations of the world in terms of per capita income. But in one way these countries are like many developing countries—they do not grow enough food to feed their people. To solve this problem, they specialize in manufacturing, using large amounts of capital and the highly developed skills of their workers. Belgium and The Netherlands trade heavily with other nations. They exchange their manufactured goods for the food and raw materials they lack.

All poor countries are trying to increase the ability of their people to produce wealth. The rich nations are sharing in that task. They provide capital and technical advisers to help developing nations help themselves. One of the most important challenges facing the world today is promoting the economic development of the poor countries.

The Work of Nations

The economy of every nation is made up of all the activities that produce wealth. These activities are called *industries*. The chief industries include agriculture, manufacturing, mining, transportation, and many kinds of services needed by the people.

The developed countries have a wide variety of industries. Most of their industries use skilled workers and modern machinery to produce vast quantities of food and manufactured goods. The developing countries are generally agricultural. More than half their people live and work on farms. Almost all developing countries are making progress toward becoming industrialized. Some, including Argentina, Brazil, Chile, India, and Mexico, have reached a fairly advanced stage of industrialization. These countries produce many of the manufactured goods that their people use.

In most developing countries, some farm products are sold to other countries in exchange for manufactured goods that are needed locally. A developing country may also produce certain agricultural products almost entirely for export. Such products grow well in the country's climate and soil. They include the coffee of Brazil and Colombia, the rubber of Malaysia, and the bananas of Central American countries. Similarly, a country with large deposits of copper, iron ore, petroleum, or other minerals may mine those minerals chiefly for export.

The exports of a developing country bring in capital that can be used to develop manufacturing industries. The money received in exchange for the exports helps pay for the machines, equipment, and supplies needed to build and operate factories. Private capital and government aid from the developed countries also help finance industrialization.

The industrial progress of most developing countries is hampered by lack of electric power, inadequate transportation, and a shortage of water supplies. Industrial production is also low because most of the nation's workers have no technical training.

In spite of serious handicaps, most developing countries have established some manufacturing industries. But most of the people in these countries have been little affected by industrialization. The industries are located in a few large cities, and most of the people live in rural areas.

Most industrial progress in the developing countries has occurred since World War II ended in 1945. Today, these nations still produce only a small percentage of the world's manufactured goods. The developed countries still produce most of the goods.

The industries of the developed countries have great advantages over those of the developing countries. About 55 per cent of the world's industrial energy is produced in the United States and Europe. That energy is produced chiefly from coal, oil, natural gas, or water power (see ENERGY). The U.S. factory worker probably uses about 20 times as much industrial energy as does the worker in a developing country. The developed countries also have most of the world's transportation facilities. Of about 760,000 miles (1,220,000 kilometers) of railroads in the world, about 545,000 miles (877,100 kilometers) are in North America, Europe, Australia, and New Zealand. Of about 329 million motor vehicles in the world, approximately 259 million are in the United States, Japan, and Western Europe.

For information about the economies of every country of the world, see the separate country articles in WORLD BOOK. For charts showing the leading crop-growing countries, see the article on AGRICULTURE.

WORLD / The Interdependence of Nations

Basically, each nation is responsible for its own well-being. But each nation also depends on other nations in some ways. Every nation trades with other countries to earn money for its products and to obtain goods it needs. Poor nations receive financial and technical aid from wealthier countries (see INTERNATIONAL TRADE; FOREIGN AID). Some nations with similar political philosophies pledge to support one another in case of attack. Many international organizations have been formed to promote cooperation among nations.

The United Nations (UN) is the largest international organization, and more than 90 per cent of the world's countries belong to it. The UN works to settle disputes among nations and to maintain world peace. It also carries out a variety of programs designed to aid needy people and to improve health and education worldwide. See UNITED NATIONS.

Many international organizations have been formed to promote economic integration among nations of particular regions. They include common markets, customs unions, economic unions, and free-trade associations. All such organizations provide for the removal of tariffs and other trade barriers among member nations. Common markets also provide for the free movement of workers and capital among member nations, and economic unions provide for common economic policies. Important economic integration organizations include the European Economic Community (EEC), the European Free Trade Association (EFTA), the Latin-American Free Trade Association (LAFTA), and the Central American Common Market. See COMMON MARKET; CUSTOMS UNION; EUROPEAN COMMUNITY.

Some nations belong to international military organizations. The North Atlantic Treaty Organization (NATO) is a military alliance of 15 Western European nations and the United States and Canada. It provides for a unified military command among the members. The NATO nations consider an attack against one member to be an attack against all. The Warsaw Pact is a similar organization formed by Russia and other Communist countries of Eastern Europe. Its members operate under a unified command and pledge to support one another in case of attack. See NORTH ATLANTIC TREATY ORGANIZATION; WARSAW PACT.

More than 45 African nations belong to a regional international organization called the Organization of African Unity (OAU). The members work together to promote the region's economic and cultural progress. The United States and most nations of Latin America belong to the Organization of American States (OAS). This international organization provides for the collective defense of member nations and works to promote regional peace and economic progress. See ORGANIZATION OF AFRICAN UNITY; ORGANIZATION OF AMERICAN STATES.   PHILLIP BACON, PAUL BOHANNAN, STEWART E. FRASER, and RAYMOND F. MIKESELL

WORLD / Study Aids

Related Articles. For detailed information about the physical world, see EARTH with its list of Related Articles. For the story of human progress, see WORLD, HISTORY OF; PREHISTORIC PEOPLE with their lists of Related Articles. See also the following:

COUNTRIES AND CONTINENTS

See the separate articles on each continent, country, and dependency listed in the *Nations of the World* section of this article.

REGIONS

Arctic	Far East	Pacific Islands
Balkans	Latin America	Southeast Asia
Central America	Middle East	

OTHER RELATED ARTICLES

Agriculture	Gross National	Olympic Games
Anthropology	Product	Peace
Art and the	Human Being	Population
Arts	Industry	Public Health
Civilization	International Law	Races, Human
Clothing	International	Religion
Communication	Relations	Science
Community	Invention	Shelter
Conservation	Language	Technology
Culture	Law	Trade
Economics	Medicine	Transportation
Education	Migration	United Nations
Food	Multinational	War
Government	Corporation	

Outline

I. **Nations of the World**
II. **Geography of the World**
III. **People of the World**
　A. The Population of the World
　B. The Races of the World
　C. The Languages of the World
IV. **Life of the World**
　A. The Cultures of the World
　B. The Religions of the World
V. **Arts and Recreation of the World**
VI. **Education and Science of the World**
VII. **Economy of the World**
　A. The Wealth of Nations
　B. The Work of Nations
VIII. **The Interdependence of Nations**

Questions

How much of the earth's surface is covered by water?
What is the largest country? The smallest country?
Who made the first complete world weather maps?
What is the largest continent? What is the smallest?
What are some of the languages in the Indo-European language family?
What three oceans make up the *world ocean?*
What is the most densely populated continent?
How are the rich countries helping the poor countries speed their industrial development?
What are the chief industries that contribute to the world's economy?
Why do most people of the world live on plains or in hilly regions?

WORLD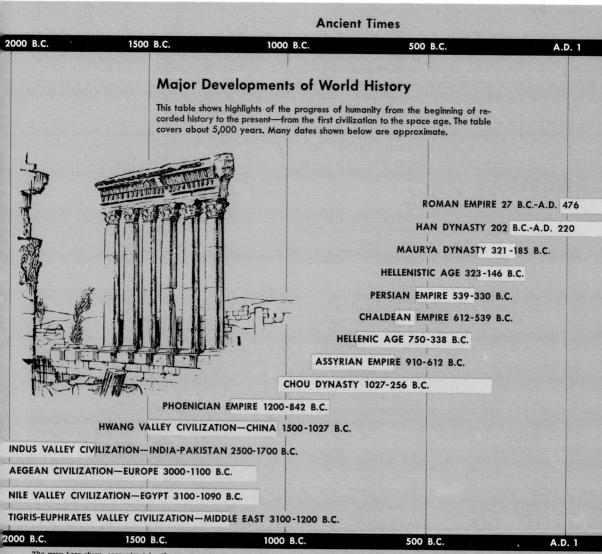

HISTORY

The contributor of this article is T. Walter Wallbank, Professor Emeritus of History at the University of Southern California.

WORLD, HISTORY OF. The history of the world is the story of humanity—from the first civilization to the space age. The story covers a period of about 5,000 years, beginning about 3000 B.C. At that time, or a little earlier, people developed a way to write down their experiences. Those early writings began the record of progress that we study today as world history.

Before the development of writing, human beings had existed for about $2\frac{1}{2}$ million years—over 500 times longer than the total span of recorded history. The long period before writing began is called *Prehistoric Times*. Scientists have pieced together the story of that period. Life during Prehistoric Times is described in the article PREHISTORIC PEOPLE.

World history shows that civilization today is the product of many cultures. For thousands of years, various peoples have borrowed ideas and inventions from

Ancient Times

2000 B.C.	1500 B.C.	1000 B.C.	500 B.C.	A.D. 1

Major Developments of World History

This table shows highlights of the progress of humanity from the beginning of recorded history to the present—from the first civilization to the space age. The table covers about 5,000 years. Many dates shown below are approximate.

ROMAN EMPIRE 27 B.C.-A.D. 476

HAN DYNASTY 202 B.C.-A.D. 220

MAURYA DYNASTY 321-185 B.C.

HELLENISTIC AGE 323-146 B.C.

PERSIAN EMPIRE 539-330 B.C.

CHALDEAN EMPIRE 612-539 B.C.

HELLENIC AGE 750-338 B.C.

ASSYRIAN EMPIRE 910-612 B.C.

CHOU DYNASTY 1027-256 B.C.

PHOENICIAN EMPIRE 1200-842 B.C.

HWANG VALLEY CIVILIZATION—CHINA 1500-1027 B.C.

INDUS VALLEY CIVILIZATION—INDIA-PAKISTAN 2500-1700 B.C.

AEGEAN CIVILIZATION—EUROPE 3000-1100 B.C.

NILE VALLEY CIVILIZATION—EGYPT 3100-1090 B.C.

TIGRIS-EUPHRATES VALLEY CIVILIZATION—MIDDLE EAST 3100-1200 B.C.

2000 B.C.	1500 B.C.	1000 B.C.	500 B.C.	A.D. 1

The gray bars show, approximately, the years covered by each major development. The bars with broken ends indicate continuing developments.

each other. This exchange is called *culture diffusion*. See CULTURE (How Culture Changes).

Throughout most of world history, the most important regions for new ideas and inventions were the Middle East, Egypt, India, and China. But during Modern Times—the period of the last 500 years—Western civilization has made rapid progress, while other civilizations lagged. As a result, the course of culture diffusion changed. During Modern Times, the flow of ideas and inventions has swept from West to East. The development of worldwide systems of communication and transportation conquered barriers of time and distance.

Mankind's progress through the centuries has been marked by many changes, and every generation has faced the challenge of serious problems. Great civilizations have developed, flourished for a time, and then collapsed. International disputes have brought on terrible wars. In every age, millions of persons have suffered hunger and hardship, while others enjoyed prosperity. Today, we live in the greatest civilization of all times. But war and widespread poverty still are the most important problems of mankind. Man has greater knowledge and more technological power than ever before. As a result, he probably has a better chance to meet the challenge of today than any generation of the past.

This article deals broadly with man's progress from Ancient Times to the present. It provides general information on how civilized ways of life developed and advanced in various regions of the world. It describes how these cultures mingled and made lasting contributions to later civilizations. Separate WORLD BOOK articles, especially the articles on each country, provide details about the major events of world history.

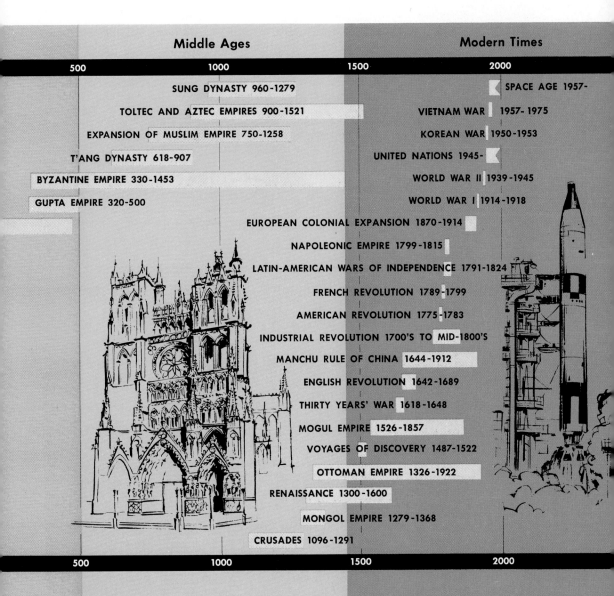

Middle Ages   Modern Times

500   1000   1500   2000

SUNG DYNASTY 960-1279
TOLTEC AND AZTEC EMPIRES 900-1521
EXPANSION OF MUSLIM EMPIRE 750-1258
T'ANG DYNASTY 618-907
BYZANTINE EMPIRE 330-1453
GUPTA EMPIRE 320-500

SPACE AGE 1957-
VIETNAM WAR 1957-1975
KOREAN WAR 1950-1953
UNITED NATIONS 1945-
WORLD WAR II 1939-1945
WORLD WAR I 1914-1918

EUROPEAN COLONIAL EXPANSION 1870-1914
NAPOLEONIC EMPIRE 1799-1815
LATIN-AMERICAN WARS OF INDEPENDENCE 1791-1824
FRENCH REVOLUTION 1789-1799
AMERICAN REVOLUTION 1775-1783
INDUSTRIAL REVOLUTION 1700'S TO MID-1800'S
MANCHU RULE OF CHINA 1644-1912
ENGLISH REVOLUTION 1642-1689
THIRTY YEARS' WAR 1618-1648
MOGUL EMPIRE 1526-1857
VOYAGES OF DISCOVERY 1487-1522
OTTOMAN EMPIRE 1326-1922
RENAISSANCE 1300-1600
MONGOL EMPIRE 1279-1368
CRUSADES 1096-1291

500   1000   1500   2000

The greatest cultural journey of all times took place when man crossed the gulf between barbarism and civilization. The development of civilization was made possible by the invention of farming. After men discovered ways to grow crops and raise animals, they no longer had to roam in search of food. They could settle down in villages. Some became farmers and herdsmen. Others became craftsmen, merchants, religious leaders, teachers, soldiers, or government officials. They developed the skills, tools, beliefs, and laws that produced the early civilizations of mankind. In these civilizations, the first cities were built and the first nations were organized. Some nations of Ancient Times expanded into empires that spread over large parts of the world.

The early civilizations made many contributions to later generations. Probably the most important of these contributions was the invention of a system of writing, sometime before 3000 B.C. At that time, man started to write down a record of his life, and the period called *Ancient Times* or *Ancient History* began. According to most historians, this period ended at about A.D. 476.

The development of Western civilization was strongly influenced by many peoples of Ancient Times. Among them were the Sumerians, Babylonians, Egyptians, Hebrews, Phoenicians, Assyrians, Chaldeans, and Persians. As civilization advanced, the Greeks and the Romans originated many arts and sciences that became basic to Western ways of life. Important cultures also developed in the eastern part of the world—in India and China. Almost from the beginning of Ancient Times, many peoples of the West and the East exchanged ideas and inventions, and the cultures of the world mingled.

Ruins of a Roman Temple in Baalbek, Lebanon

The Oriental Institute, University of Chicago; The Metropolitan Museum of Art, New York, acquired by exchange with J. Pierpont Morgan Library, 1911

Ancient Paintings and Writings tell us much about life in early civilizations. A harvest scene, *above*, was painted on the tomb of an Egyptian public official about 1400 B.C. From such pictures, we learn that the ancient Egyptians were expert farmers. Archaeologists have found many clay tablets inscribed with cuneiform writing in Mesopotamia, the region of the Sumerian civilization. A clay tablet, *right*, inscribed about 2100 B.C., was a grain merchant's business record.

Cradles of Civilization

The Cradles of Civilization: 1. the Tigris-Euphrates Valley, 2. the Nile Valley, 3. the Indus Valley, 4. the Hwang Ho Valley.

The first important civilizations of the world developed in four river valleys. These valleys were (1) the land between the Tigris and the Euphrates rivers in the Middle East, (2) along the Nile River in Egypt, (3) the region watered by the Indus River in Pakistan, and (4) along the Hwang Ho (Yellow River) in China.

The four valleys are generally known as the "cradles of civilization." The valley civilizations of the Middle East and Egypt formed the basis for present-day Western civilization. The Indus civilization formed the basis of the civilization of what is now India and Pakistan. The Hwang Ho civilization developed into the present-day Chinese civilization, and strongly influenced the civilization of Japan.

While civilization was developing in the four valleys, people in most other parts of the world were still following primitive ways of life. Little cultural progress was being made in such regions as northern and central Europe, central and southern Africa, northern and southeastern Asia, or most of North America. In parts of Central and South America, some civilized ways of life were developing. But they did not become advanced civilizations until hundreds of years later.

The Middle East of ancient times was made up largely of the fertile Tigris-Euphrates Valley. The area curved from the southeastern end of the Mediterranean Sea around the Arabian Desert to the Persian Gulf. Because of its shape, the ancient Middle East became known as the Fertile Crescent. Today, this region includes Iraq, Israel, Jordan, Lebanon, and Syria, and part of Turkey. For a description of the ancient region, see FERTILE CRESCENT.

The birthplace of the Middle East civilization was Sumer, in southern Mesopotamia (now Iraq). The Sumerians probably migrated to Mesopotamia from the highlands of what is now Iran or Turkey. By 3000 B.C. they had built an advanced civilization of independent city-states. These city-states had no central government or unified army. As a result, Sumer was unable to resist invasions by envious neighbors. About 2300 B.C., Sumer was conquered by a famous empire builder, Sargon of

Sargon of Akkad was the first great empire builder of history. He conquered Sumer about 2300 B.C. Country after country then fell to Sargon's invading armies until he ruled most of the Middle East.

Directorate-General of Antiquities, Government of Iraq

—————— **MAJOR EVENTS OF ANCIENT TIMES** ——————

c. 3100 B.C. King Menes united Lower and Upper Egypt, and formed one of the world's first national governments.

c. 3000 B.C. Cuneiform writings of the Sumerians began the recorded history of the Middle East.

c. 2500 B.C. The Indus Valley civilization began in what were the cities of Harappa and Mohenjo-daro in Pakistan.

c. 2300 B.C. Sargon of Akkad conquered the Sumerians and united their city-states under his rule.

c. 1750 B.C. Hammurabi established the Babylonian empire.

c. 1600-1400 B.C. The Minoan civilization flourished on the Mediterranean island of Crete.

c. 1500 B.C. The Aryans of central Asia invaded India.

c. 1500 B.C. The Shang dynasty began its 500-year rule of China.

1000's B.C. Latin tribes settled south of the Tiber River, and Etruscans settled in the west central region of the Italian peninsula.

750-338 B.C. Athens, Corinth, Sparta, and Thebes developed as the chief city-states of Greece during the Hellenic Age.

509 B.C. The Latins rebelled against their Etruscan rulers and established the Roman Republic.

338 B.C. Philip II of Macedonia defeated the Greeks and made Greece part of the Macedonian Empire.

331 B.C. Alexander the Great defeated the Persians at Arbela (Irbil), and opened his path of conquest to northern India.

321-185 B.C. The Maurya Empire of northern India spread over almost all of India and part of central Asia.

221-206 B.C. The Ch'in dynasty established China's first strong central government and completed the Great Wall that protected China from invaders.

202 B.C. The Han dynasty began its 400-year rule of China.

146 B.C. The Romans destroyed Corinth and conquered Greece.

55-54 B.C. Julius Caesar led the Roman invasion of Britain.

27 B.C. Augustus became the first Roman emperor.

A.D. 70 Roman forces under Titus captured and destroyed Jerusalem.

50-mid 200's The Kushan empire ruled Afghanistan and northwestern India.

105 The Chinese invented paper.

293 Diocletian divided the Roman Empire into four prefectures and set up two capitals—Nicomedia in Asia Minor, and Milan in Europe.

313 Constantine granted the Christians of the Roman Empire freedom of religion in the Edict of Milan.

320 India began its golden age under the Gupta dynasty.

395 The Roman Empire split into the East Roman Empire and the West Roman Empire.

476 The German chieftain Odoacer deposed Romulus Augustulus, the last emperor of the West Roman Empire.

Akkad. Another invader, Hammurabi, conquered Sumer about 1750 B.C. Hammurabi made Babylon his capital, and the region became known as Babylonia.

Both Sargon and Hammurabi helped preserve and advance the Sumerian civilization. Sargon united the city-states under a strong central government. Hammurabi organized hundreds of laws, most of which were originated by the Sumerians, into one *code* (set) of laws. The *Code of Hammurabi* established what was probably the world's earliest social order based on the rights of the individual. The code influenced the laws of many countries for hundreds of years. See HAMMURABI; SARGON.

The Sumerians also probably invented the first system of writing, called *cuneiform* (wedgelike) writing. With this writing, men started the record of events that make up written history. Many clay tablets with cuneiform writing have been found in the Middle East. These tablets reveal the high development of early Middle East civilization. They include hundreds of financial documents, and many studies in astronomy, mathematics, and medicine. Some of the first literature of world history also was written by the Sumerians and Babylonians. This literature includes the famous *Epic of Gilgamesh*. One of the Gilgamesh stories describes a great flood, similar to the story of a worldwide flood told in the Old Testament. For descriptions of the many achievements of the Babylonians and the Sumerians, see BABYLONIA; SUMER.

For several hundred years after 1200 B.C., no single ruler controlled the Middle East. As a result, several peoples developed important cultures in various parts of the region. Of these peoples, the Hebrews and the Phoenicians had a great influence on future civilizations.

The Hebrews, also called Jews, developed and spread their idea of one God. The Jews worshiped one God during a time when most other peoples worshiped many gods. Judaism also put great emphasis on the ideals of brotherhood, charity, human dignity, and universal peace. These ideals became the chief elements of moral living for many persons of future generations. The Hebrew Bible, or Old Testament, became a basic part of Christianity, the most widespread religion of Modern Times. Islam, the religion of the Muslims, was built on Judaism and Christianity. See JEWS.

The Phoenicians became famous for two achievements—their alphabet and their great colonial empire. The Phoenician alphabet was the basis of the Greek alphabet. All other Western alphabets developed from the Greek alphabet. The colonial empire of the Phoenicians was one of the first links between civilized areas in Ancient Times. The Phoenicians were great explorers and traders. Their ships sailed throughout the Mediterranean Sea and around the west coast of Africa. The Phoenician empire consisted of many colonies and trading posts. One of the most important Phoenician colonies was Carthage. See PHOENICIA.

Three empires rose to power during the period when small nations were important in the Middle East. The first of these empires was built by the Assyrians. By 700 B.C., they had become the masters of the Fertile Crescent. The Assyrians conquered and ruled many peoples by terror. Their cruelty to captives was a form of what is now called *psychological warfare*. The Assyrians were

conquered by the Chaldeans about the year 612 B.C.

Nebuchadnezzar II, the famous ruler of the Chaldeans, rebuilt Babylon as a magnificent city. His royal palace was surrounded by terraced gardens. These gardens, known as the Hanging Gardens of Babylon, became one of the ancient Seven Wonders of the World. The Chaldeans made important discoveries in astronomy and believed they could foretell the future by studying the stars. They probably invented astrology. Chaldean rule of the Middle East ended in 539 B.C. after the Persians captured the city of Babylon.

The Persians ruled about 200 years, and their empire spread over all the Middle East. They built excellent roads that supplied their vast empire with a communications network. Unlike the Assyrians, the Persians ruled the many peoples of their empire sternly but with justice, not by terror. The Persians became famous for developing an efficient system of government. Their theories of justice were guided by the teachings of their religion, Zoroastrianism (see ZOROASTRIANISM).

Egyptian Civilization developed in the rich valley of the Nile River. The kingdoms of that region were united under a single ruler, Menes, about 3100 B.C. Egyptian pharaohs ruled Egypt until about 1090 B.C., except for a period of about 160 years. The Hyksos invaded Egypt during this period (see HYKSOS). After about 1090 B.C., a succession of conquerors ruled Ancient Egypt.

The Egyptians built one of the world's great early civilizations. The huge pyramids near the present site of Cairo show their engineering skill. The Egyptians probably invented post and lintel architecture, the basis of much present-day building (see ARCHITECTURE [table: Architectural Terms (Post and Lintel)]). The Egyptians also were among the first people to use a type of paper, instead of clay tablets, for their records. They wrote on a paper made from the fibers of a water plant called papyrus. The Egyptians were great artists, astronomers, and engineers. They were great merchants, too. Their caravans carried goods throughout the vast desert regions surrounding Egypt. Their ships sailed to the major ports of the world. Egyptian traders spread many elements of their culture among the peoples who lived along the routes of commerce, on both land and sea. See EGYPT, ANCIENT.

The Indus Valley Civilization began about 2500 B.C. in the region that is now Pakistan. Archaeologists have found Sumerian relics in the ruins of the Indus cities of Harappa and Mohenjo-daro. These relics show that the Indus people traded with the people of the Middle East. The Indus Valley cities had buildings made of brick, and efficient sewerage systems. The Indus people also developed a system of writing that has never been translated. The Indus civilization disappeared mysteriously about 1700 B.C. About 1500 B.C., the Aryans, ancestors of the present-day Hindus, invaded India. They came from the plains of Asia through the Himalayan mountain passes. The light-skinned Aryans found many dark-skinned Dravidians living in northern India.

Several features of life in present-day India developed in ancient times. Perhaps the most important was the custom of dividing people into separate social classes, called *castes*. The caste system of India today probably developed from Aryan rules that forbade intermarriage with the Dravidians. See CASTE.

The Hwang Ho Civilization probably began about the same time as the civilizations of the three other cradle valleys. But the earliest Chinese records date from only about 1500 B.C. Under the rule of the Shang dynasty (1500-1027 B.C.), the Chinese had a well-organized government and a system of writing. They worshiped a supreme god and other gods, including ancestral spirits. The early Chinese developed many arts. They were especially skilled at casting beautiful bronzes. The Chou dynasty ruled China from about 1027 to 256 B.C. Many lasting features of Chinese life developed during this period. Probably the most important early Chinese idea was a belief in a "Mandate of Heaven." According to that belief, if a ruler behaved badly, he no longer had the approval of the gods, and could be overthrown. The mandate was one of the first declarations of a people's right to revolt.

 ## Civilization Advances

From the cradle lands, civilized ways of life spread to many other regions of the world. Great civilizations rose in lands where barbarism had been the way of life for thousands of years.

In Europe and Asia, many barbarians became civilized. They took over the ideas and inventions of the cradle civilizations, and also created cultural patterns of their own. In Europe, the Greeks and the Romans developed most of the arts, philosophies, and sciences that became the chief ingredients of Western civilization. In Asia, the Indians and the Chinese developed lasting forms of art, government, and religion.

As civilized cultures advanced and spread, the people of various regions often exchanged ideas or inventions. This mingling of cultures occurred through commerce, conquest, and migration. Traders carried the products of one culture to others over long routes of commerce. The soldiers of conquering armies often settled in lands far from their own. Large groups of people migrated from one region to another, and brought the customs of their homelands with them. Many adopted the ways of life of the people they joined. In this way, the developing cultures of the world often mingled.

The mingling of civilized cultures during Ancient Times was an important development in world history. Ever since, much of mankind's progress has been made by the exchange of ideas among the peoples of the world. See MIGRATION.

The Greeks developed the first advanced civilization on the European mainland, and made many contributions to Western civilization. Their most important contribution probably was the idea of democracy. The ancient Greeks glorified individual freedom. They stressed man's right to criticize, be curious, and be different. The Greeks thought deeply about such questions as: What is the good life? What is beauty? What is truth? In pondering such questions, the Greeks developed the study of philosophy.

The right to think freely was basic in the work of the artists, scientists, and writers of ancient Greece. Democratic ideas were also used in government. The Greek form of democracy in government differed from present-day democracy. But the Greeks set forth certain democratic principles that are still followed today.

Casts from The Oriental Institute, University of Chicago, original in Egyptian Museum, Cairo.

Scenes of Conquest carved on both sides of a slate tablet tell how King Menes united two warring Nile Valley states and established the Egyptian nation about 3100 B.C. Each picture is a symbol of a heroic deed of Menes. Such picture symbols formed the system of hieroglyphic writing developed in ancient Egypt.

Wide World

Ruins of Mohenjo-daro, a center of the ancient Indus Valley civilization, still stand in present-day Pakistan. The brick buildings of the city are at least 4,500 years old.

A Shang Dynasty Bronze shows the skill of ancient Chinese artists who perfected their style of carving during the 1500's B.C. This wine vessel is about 6 inches (15 centimeters) tall.

The Art Institute of Chicago, Lucy Maud Buckingham Collection

352e

In developing their great civilization, the Greeks freed themselves from traditions of the past. As a result, the Greeks produced new and lasting forms of art, politics, and science.

Greek civilization grew out of an early civilization called the Aegean Civilization (3000-1100 B.C.). The most important center of the Aegean Civilization was the Mediterranean island of Crete. The people of Crete built their culture on the ideas and inventions of the cradle civilizations of Egypt and the Middle East.

Crete became the stepping stone of Western civilization. The island linked Europe with Egypt and the Middle East. From about 1600 to 1100 B.C., people from the European mainland often raided Crete. They intermarried with the Cretans and became the people we call Greeks. The Greeks developed their great culture on the European mainland in such city-states as Athens, Corinth, Sparta, and Thebes. See AEGEAN CIVILIZATION; CRETE.

The ancient Greeks called themselves Hellenes, and their homeland was known as Hellas. The period of Greek history from 750 to 338 B.C. is called the Hellenic Age. During this period, Greek culture reached great heights of development. Greek armies and traders colonized many areas along the Mediterranean and Black seas. As ancient Greece expanded, the leaders of the powerful Persian empire tried to take over the country and its colonies. A long war between the two nations ended with the defeat of the Persians in 479 B.C.

After the Persian defeat, Athens became the leading city of Greece. During the Golden Age of Greece (461-431 B.C.), magnificent buildings were constructed and great works of art and literature were produced. No culture has produced so many lasting achievements in such a short period. From the Golden Age of Greece came the great works of men such as Aeschylus, Euripides, Herodotus, Phidias, Socrates, and Sophocles. The period is often called the Age of Pericles, after the brilliant leader of the Athenian government. See GOLDEN AGE; PERICLES.

The progress and riches of Athens were the envy of the other city-states of Greece. Hostility between the Athenians and their fellow Hellenes led to the Peloponnesian War (431-404 B.C.). Athens was defeated in that war. The victorious city-states soon started to quarrel among themselves. However, the political quarrels did not halt the work of Greek scholars. Aristotle and Plato produced their great philosophical works during this period.

In 338 B.C., the quarreling Hellenes were conquered by invaders from Macedonia, led by Philip II. His son, Alexander the Great, became the ruler of Greece. Alexander expanded his empire throughout the Middle East and Egypt, and as far east as northern India. Under Alexander and his successors, Greek culture spread and combined with other cultures. This great period of Greek civilization became known as the Hellenistic Age. The largest city of this period was Alexandria, in Egypt. Alexandria was the home of some of the great scientists of Ancient Times. There, Eratosthenes estimated the circumference of the earth, and Euclid developed the fundamentals of plane geometry. The Hellenistic Age began about 323 B.C. and ended

about 146 B.C., when the Romans conquered Greece.

For a description of life in ancient Greece and the story of how Greek civilization developed, see the article GREECE, ANCIENT.

The Romans were people of the Italian peninsula whose culture had lagged far behind that of the Greeks. It took them more than a hundred years to conquer all the empire that had flourished during the Hellenistic Age. The Romans invaded Greece about 146 B.C. and completed their conquest about 30 B.C. They adopted Greek forms of art and literature, and Greek architectural methods. A culture known as the Greco-Roman culture developed. The Romans built well-planned cities, massive aqueducts and bridges, and vast systems of roads. They became famous for their civic buildings, municipal baths, hospitals, stadiums, and triumphal arches. Greco-Roman sculptors created lifelike statues and portraits in marble. Famous Roman writers included Cicero, Julius Caesar, Livy, Ovid, Tacitus, and Virgil. Latin, the language of the Romans, became the basis of the Romance languages of today.

At the height of their power, the Romans ruled a vast empire. The Roman Empire was truly a "world state." It included many countries with widely different customs. The Romans showed careful respect for these customs, and they won the good will of many of the people they governed. The Romans generally ruled with a strong sense of justice and order.

The Roman legal system became the basis of the legal codes of many present-day European and Latin-American countries. Roman laws were enforced by efficient public officials. Many political terms that are common today originated in Rome. They include such words as *plebiscite, census, consul, municipal,* and *senate.*

One of the most important contributions of the Romans to Western civilization was the preservation of Christianity. Christ was born during the reign of the Emperor Augustus, and was crucified during the rule of Tiberius. The early Christians were persecuted by the Romans. But Christianity eventually became the official religion of the Roman Empire, and spread throughout the world. It became a major ingredient of Western civilization, and the world's most widespread religion.

The development of Roman culture spanned a period

The Triumphal Arch was an outstanding feature of Roman architecture. The famous Arch of Septimius Severus, built in A.D. 203, stood in the Roman Forum, center of government of ancient Rome.

of about 2,500 years. This period probably began about 2000 B.C., when people related to the Greeks migrated from Northern Europe to the Italian peninsula. The period ended in A.D. 476 after a Germanic conqueror overthrew the last emperor of the West Roman Empire. The East Roman Empire continued for another thousand years as the Byzantine Empire. For the dramatic story of how Rome grew from a small village in Italy to become the capital of one of the world's greatest empires, see the article ROMAN EMPIRE.

The Indians of Ancient Times made great progress in developing their civilized culture. They did so chiefly during the years of the Mauryan and the Gupta empires. During the Mauryan period, two of the world's most important religions—Hinduism and Buddhism—developed. The Mauryan civilization reached its highest development under Emperor Asoka, who spread Buddhism throughout India. Buddhism later spread to China and other eastern countries. Hinduism became the chief religion of India after Asoka's death. The teachings of these two religions and their importance to millions of persons throughout Asia are described in the articles BUDDHISM; HINDUISM.

India's golden age developed during the empire of the Gupta dynasty (A.D. 320-about 500). Its center of learning was the city of Nalanda. Indian mathematicians invented the system of numerals that was later taken over by the Arabs and became known as the Arabic system. The Indians also invented the decimal system, with a symbol for the zero. Poets, dramatists, and other writers produced many masterpieces of Indian literature in Sanskrit, the classical Indian language (see SANSKRIT LANGUAGE AND LITERATURE). Indian artists of the period created fine paintings and sculptures. Some of these ancient works may still be seen in Hindu temples and caves throughout India.

The Chinese of Ancient Times, like the Indians, made important cultural progress under the rule of two dynasties. The vast country was unified and protected from invaders by the Great Wall of China during the Ch'in dynasty (221-206 B.C.). The unification of China led to the great advances made under the Han dynasty that followed the Ch'in period.

During the 400 years of the Han period, many basic ways of Chinese life developed. Most of these ways of life came from the teachings of Confucius, one of the world's great philosophers. They included ancestor worship and many rules of conduct that lasted in China until Modern Times. Confucianism became one of the world's most important religions. See CONFUCIANISM.

The Chinese philosophers and scholars of the Han period were among the first to organize the facts of nature into various subjects. These subjects included astronomy, botany, chemistry, and mineralogy. They also compiled one of the first dictionaries, and wrote the first scholarly history of China.

The most famous invention of the Han period was paper, made for the first time from wood. During the same era, the Chinese invented a *seismograph* (an instrument that records earthquakes). Another famous invention of the Han period was the breast-strap harness for beasts of burden. This invention allowed animals to pull heavy loads without choking. The Chinese used the breast-strap harness several hundred years before it became known in Europe or other civilized regions.

American School of Classical Studies at Athens

Ballots Made of Broken Pottery were used by the citizens of ancient Athens to get rid of any politician who began acting like a dictator. Whenever 6,000 or more ballots were cast against an Athenian official, he was sent into exile for 10 years.

Eliot Elisofon, *LIFE* © Time Inc.

A Sculptured Gateway of the Great Stupa at Sanchi, a Buddhist monument in India, was carved about 100 B.C. India was the birthplace of two great religions—Buddhism and Hinduism. Buddhism spread to China. Hinduism became the chief religion of India.

Paper was invented by the Chinese about A.D. 105. The first paper was made from the bark of mulberry trees. This fragment of Chinese paper, a treasure of the British Museum, is about 1,800 years old.

© British Museum

WORLD HISTORY /The Middle Ages

Mankind reached another important cultural landmark during the thousand-year period of the Middle Ages. The ideas and inventions of many peoples were brought together and combined. An important mixture of cultures formed a way of life in Western Europe known as medieval culture. Most historians set the beginning of the Middle Ages at about A.D. 476, the time of the fall of Rome. They end the period in the middle or late 1400's.

Medieval culture was built on the ruins of the Greek and Roman civilizations. Both these civilizations were almost destroyed during the early years of the Middle Ages. Those early years became known as the Dark Ages. During the Dark Ages, many fierce barbarian tribes roamed over the lands of the fallen West Roman Empire. Their conquests even threatened to wipe out civilization in Western Europe.

At the same time that civilization was struggling to survive in Western Europe, civilized cultures were prospering in other regions. In southeastern Europe, the Byzantine Empire enjoyed great wealth. In the Middle East, a new empire—the Muslim Empire—climbed to great power. In the East, China's civilization reached new heights of achievement and Japan enjoyed its golden age. Unlike China, India was unable to continue its earlier important advances. Internal warfare and many invasions slowed progress in India during most of the Middle Ages.

Most regions of the world that were uncivilized during Ancient Times remained uncivilized during the Middle Ages. These uncivilized regions included much of the interior of Africa, and most of North America and South America. However, important civilized cultures were developed by the Aztec, Inca, Maya, and Toltec Indians in parts of Central America and South America.

The Cathedral at Amiens, France

P.I.P. Photos

French Government Tourist Office

Carcassonne, in southwestern France, is the finest example of a medieval walled city in Europe. It stands on the site of a Roman city of the 400's.

Western Europe During The Middle Ages

Christianity was the most important civilizing force in Western Europe during the Middle Ages. After the fall of Rome, the Roman Catholic Church became much more than a religious institution. It became the most powerful political and social influence in the life of Western Europe.

At first, the church converted the Germanic invaders of Rome to Christianity. Later, its missionaries spread Christianity among the barbarians of northern Europe. At the same time, much Greek and Roman scientific knowledge was preserved in the church's monasteries. For hundreds of years, Christian monks were probably the only scholars of Western Europe.

The development of a new political system provided a crude form of law and order during the Middle Ages. This system, called *feudalism*, replaced the governmental units of the Roman Empire. Under feudalism, almost all the land of Western Europe was governed and owned by the church or by powerful nobles. From time to time, landowning nobles gave land to other nobles in return for military assistance. Almost all the people worked as farmers and lived under the protection of the nobles. The ruling nobles quarreled about land almost constantly. In most of these quarrels, the church acted as peacemaker to settle the disputes. See FEUDALISM.

During the 600's, Palestine—the birthplace of Christianity—came under Muslim rule. A desire by the

Empires of the Middle Ages: Byzantine Empire, A.D. 565 (gray); Muslim Empire, 750 (lined); Mongol Empire, 1294 (blue).

—— MAJOR EVENTS OF THE MIDDLE AGES ——

486 Clovis became king of the Franks and founded the Merovingian dynasty, rulers of the first French state.

527-565 Justinian I ruled the Byzantine Empire and developed the famous Justinian Code of law.

622 Muhammad, founder of the Muslim religion, fled from Mecca to Medina. Muhammad's flight, called the *Hegira*, marks the beginning of the Muslim calendar.

661 The Omayyad Caliphate established the capital of the Muslim Empire at Damascus.

711 The Muslims invaded Spain and began an occupation that lasted about 700 years.

732 Charles Martel led the Franks in defeating the invading Muslims at Tours. The victory prevented the Muslims from conquering Europe.

750 The Abbasid Caliphate replaced the Omayyads as rulers of the Muslim Empire, and later established a new capital at Baghdad.

768 Charlemagne became ruler of the Franks.

c. 770 The Chinese invented wood-block printing.

800 Pope Leo III crowned Charlemagne Emperor of the Romans.

843 The Treaty of Verdun divided Charlemagne's empire into three parts, and began the national development of France, Germany, and Italy.

862 Rurik, chief of the Varangians (vikings), established his rule at Novgorod and founded the Russian Empire.

878 Alfred the Great of England defeated the Danes in the Battle of Edington.

969 The Fatimids conquered Egypt and made Cairo the center of the Muslim Empire.

987 Hugh Capet became king of France and founded the Capetian dynasty that ruled until 1328.

c. 1000 Leif Ericson sailed west from Greenland to the North American mainland. He led what was probably the first European expedition to the mainland of America.

1016 Canute became king of England and brought the entire country under Danish rule.

1037 The Seljuk Turks conquered most of the Iranian kingdoms.

1066 Norman forces under William the Conqueror defeated the Anglo-Saxons in the Battle of Hastings, and ended Anglo-Saxon rule of England.

1099 Christian forces captured Jerusalem, ending the First Crusade.

1187 Muslim troops under Saladin recaptured Jerusalem.

1192 Yoritomo became the first shogun to rule Japan.

1215 Barons of England forced King John to grant the Magna Carta.

1279 Kublai Khan led the Mongols in completing the conquest of China.

1368 Ming dynasty established its 300-year rule of China.

c. 1440 Johannes Gutenberg, a German printer, invented movable type.

1453 The Ottoman Turks captured Constantinople (Istanbul) and overthrew the Byzantine Empire.

Bettmann Archive

Medieval Monks copied many manuscripts of Greek and Roman scholars, and preserved the knowledge of Ancient Times.

Muslim Scientists and physicians were the leading scholars of the Middle Ages. They made many discoveries that advanced astronomy and medicine.

Courtesy of Smithsonian Institution

European nobles to free the Holy Land led to several military expeditions against the Muslims. These expeditions, called the Crusades, brought Western Europe into contact with an advanced Muslim civilization (see CRUSADES). Many ideas and inventions of the Muslims were brought back to Europe by the crusaders. The Crusades also spurred European interest in trading with China, India, and other distant lands. This interest in world commerce encouraged explorers to find new trade routes to the East. It also revived European craftsmanship and manufacturing. As a result, many towns were built in Western European countries.

A new class of people developed in the towns of Western Europe. This class consisted of craftsmen, merchants, and traders. Many people moved from the farmlands to the towns. At the same time, many feudal lands were combined and formed large political units. These became states, such as England, France, Portugal, and Spain. As these states were established, nationalism and patriotism developed among their people. Such ideas became important forces in the political development of Europe during Modern Times.

A new civilization was rising in Western Europe. Its moral and spiritual basis was provided by Christianity. Its wealth and thriving cities were supported by widespread commerce. Its education and learning grew with the help of proud and nationalistic monarchies. In the new Western European civilization, the first important universities of Europe were established in Bologna, Cambridge, Heidelberg, Oxford, Paris, and other cities.

There, scholars made important scientific progress, especially in geography, mathematics, and medicine. Much of the scientific progress was based on scholarly achievements of the Muslims. From the Muslims, for example, Europe got its system of numerals and the decimal system. The Muslims had taken over those important systems from the Indian mathematicians of the Gupta dynasty.

During the gradual development of medieval culture, several important European languages came into popular use. Latin remained the language of the Roman Catholic Church and of most scholars. Popular languages such as Italian, French, and Spanish developed from Latin. English came largely from Germanic languages. Much important literature was written in the popular languages. Medieval literature included great epic poems, songs of the troubadours, and ballads about Robin Hood and other folk heroes. Two masterpieces of literature were written—Dante's Divine Comedy and Chaucer's Canterbury Tales.

The most impressive feature of medieval culture was probably Gothic architecture. Gothic cathedrals, such as Canterbury, Chartres, and Notre Dame of Paris, still stand among the finest buildings of the world. They combine many skills of medieval artists and craftsmen. Gothic cathedrals have towering spires, stained glass windows, and ornamental sculptured figures. Gothic architecture largely symbolizes the great power of medieval Christianity and the strong religious feelings in Western Europe during the Middle Ages. For a description of life in Europe during medieval times, see the article MIDDLE AGES.

 ## The Byzantine Empire

Southeastern Europe was the center of a strong empire during the Middle Ages. This empire grew out of the East Roman Empire. Its capital and military stronghold was Constantinople (now Istanbul). Constantinople stood on the site of ancient Byzantium, and the new empire became known as the Byzantine Empire.

The Byzantine Empire was the chief civilizing influence among the Slavic peoples of Eastern Europe. There, civilization was spread mostly by missionaries of the Byzantine Church. Byzantine missionaries converted most of the peoples of the Balkans and Russia to Christianity. The Byzantine Church was united with the church at Rome for many years. But rivalries developed between the two groups, and in 1054 they became separated. The Byzantine Church later became known as the Eastern Orthodox Church. Its members still form the largest Christian group of Eastern Europe, and it has members in many other parts of the world. See EASTERN ORTHODOX CHURCHES.

Byzantine culture was a mixture of several cultures. The power of the Byzantine Empire was built on the Roman traditions of justice and a strong central government. The Byzantine arts, including the famous Byzantine mosaics, combined Greek art forms with strong influences from the Orient. These influences were brought to Constantinople chiefly by Byzantine traders. Their caravans traveled far into Central Asia, and their ships crossed the Black Sea and sailed many miles into the waterways of Russia.

Brown Brothers
Thousands of Crusaders marched through medieval Europe toward Palestine, hoping to free the Holy Land from Muslim rule.

The Byzantine Empire was an important force in defending Western Europe from invasion during the Middle Ages. Many times, the Byzantine armies threw back the Muslims and several barbarian tribes that tried to conquer their empire. If the Byzantine Empire had fallen to such invaders, Western Europe undoubtedly also would have been overrun. The Byzantine civilization flourished until Constantinople fell to the Turks in 1453. See BYZANTINE EMPIRE.

The Muslim Empire

One of the most advanced cultures of the Middle Ages had its center in the Middle East. This important culture originated with the Arabs. They established a new religion, Islam, and converted millions of persons. The Arabs built a huge empire that grew larger than the Roman Empire of Ancient Times. From about 750 to the 1200's, the Islamic empire extended from the Atlantic Ocean to the borders of India. The Islamic empire became known as the Muslim Empire. The term *Muslim* is an Arabic word that means *one who submits* (to God). The religious teachings of Islam are described in the article ISLAM.

The vast expanse of the Muslim Empire brought many cultures together. Muslim culture was a mixture of the ancient cultures of the Middle East, Egypt, India, and China. It also included important contributions of Greek culture that had long been forgotten in Western Europe. For example, many writings of Aristotle and other valuable philosophical works were brought to Spain and Sicily by the Muslims. Such works were then translated into Latin for European scholars.

In addition to gathering and preserving many important cultural works, Muslim scholars produced great works of their own. The Arabs made a number of contributions to the study of algebra. In fact, the word *algebra* is Arabic, and means *reduction* (see ALGEBRA [History]). A medical book written by Avicenna, an Arab scientist, was the chief text used by physicians for over 600 years. Avicenna and other Muslim scientists also wrote important textbooks on astronomy and mathematics. Muslim geographies included the most complete maps of the world during the Middle Ages. Muslim poets, including Omar Khayyam, wrote some of the world's literary masterpieces. Muslim art blended the artistic forms that had developed in Persia, the Byzantine Empire, Egypt, and Spain. This blending created a distinctive style known as Islamic art. Its chief feature was ornamental design. Islamic artists developed forms of design because their religion prohibited the creation of lifelike images of any creatures. The designs were used in painting, weaving rugs, brocading cloth, and decorating leather and fine pottery. The distinctive patterns of Muslim art also appeared in the magnificent tilework that decorated the *mosques* (Muslim houses of worship). See ISLAMIC ART.

Muslim traditions still strongly influence life in certain regions of the world. Most of the Middle East, for example, is known as the *Arab World*. In Southeast Asia, and in such countries as India and Pakistan, Muslim ways of life are followed by millions of people. The development of the Muslim Empire during the Middle Ages is described in the article MUSLIMS.

New York Public Library

Medieval Society in Europe was made up of several classes of people who were ruled by a king or a feudal lord—the central figure in the painting, *above*. At his right stand the clergymen who advised him, and at his left are the noblemen who led his armies. The lower panel shows merchants, *left*, and peasants, *right*.

Justinian I ruled the Byzantine Empire during its Golden Age. He gathered many Roman laws into one legal code. The famous *Justinian* Code became the basis of the laws of most western European countries.

Reproduction from *Byzantine Painting*, courtesy Skira Inc., New York

A Persian Miniature shows Muhammad, founder of the Islamic religion, receiving a message from the angel Gabriel. Muhammad based his teachings on those of Jesus and the Hebrew prophets.

Bettmann Archive

China During The Middle Ages

The civilized culture of ancient China advanced greatly during the Middle Ages. Chinese civilization progressed in spite of many invasions by fierce barbarians, among them the Mongols and the Tartars. Most of the invaders adopted Chinese ways of life. Some, especially the Mongols, spread Chinese civilization to many other lands.

The Mongols conquered all China in 1279, and their famous ruler, Kublai Khan, built a vast empire. The Mongol Empire is often called the largest land empire in all history. It extended more than 4,600 miles (7,400 kilometers), from the Yellow Sea of Asia to the Danube River of Europe.

During Kublai Khan's rule, many Chinese ideas and inventions of the early Middle Ages reached Europe and the Middle East. Kublai Khan encouraged commerce and travel with other civilized peoples. The travels of Marco Polo from Venice to many Far East lands were made chiefly under Kublai Khan's sponsorship (see POLO, MARCO). Soon after the death of Kublai Khan, the Mongols lost control of most of their empire. The Chinese regained control of their own country in 1368, when the Ming dynasty began its 300-year rule of China (see MONGOL EMPIRE).

China's contributions to civilization during the Middle Ages came chiefly during the T'ang dynasty (618-907) and the Sung dynasty (960-1279). The T'ang period became known as the golden age of Chinese civilization. During this period, the Chinese invented printing. The world's oldest printed book is the *Diamond Sutra*, printed in China in 868 (see BOOK [picture]). Chinese arts and literature flourished during the same era. Lasting contributions were made by two of the greatest Chinese poets, Li Po and Tu Fu. Their poems, written in words of great beauty and simplicity, still inspire many poets in all parts of the world.

During the Sung period, the Chinese invented gunpowder, the magnetic compass, and movable type for printing. Scholarly advances also were made during the T'ang and Sung dynasties. Chinese scholars of these periods produced important dictionaries, encyclopedias, and histories.

Japan During The Middle Ages

Japan developed its basic civilization and rapidly advanced to a golden age during the Middle Ages. Little is known of Japan's early days. Buddhist monks and merchants brought civilized ways of life to Japan from China and Korea. By the A.D. 550's, many Japanese were practicing Buddhism. They also were producing arts and crafts similar to those of the Chinese. The Japanese took over the Chinese system of writing, and their scholars produced many works in Chinese styles.

The early Japanese also adopted basic Chinese methods of government. Unlike the Chinese, however, the Japanese thought of their emperor as godlike. They believed an emperor must never be overthrown. The Japanese also developed as important parts of their culture a belief in the superiority of soldiers, and a great respect for stern military conduct.

Civilization developed so rapidly in Japan that a golden age flourished there from the late 700's to about 1150. During Japan's golden age, Kyoto was established as the nation's capital. Kyoto became one of the largest cities of the world during the Middle Ages. At the height of Japan's golden age, the emperor lost much of his political power to the heads of noble families. These noblemen, called *shoguns*, ruled Japan for hundreds of years. But they all ruled in the name of the emperor. Deep respect for the emperors of Japan and strict obedience to military discipline lasted into Modern Times. In fact, these basic elements of Japanese culture became strong influences on the course of history during the early 1900's. See JAPAN (History).

India During The Middle Ages

India was invaded by many peoples during the Middle Ages. As a result, little progress was made in developing the civilization that had flourished in India during Ancient Times.

The most important invaders of India were the Muslims. They pushed into the plains of northern India from Afghanistan and central Asia. Unlike the Mongol invaders of China, the Muslim invaders of India did not unite with the people they conquered. Some Indians gave up their Hindu religion and became Muslims. But most Indians did not accept the Muslim customs or the Islamic religion.

Largely because of their religious differences, the people of India became culturally divided. This deep cultural division has lasted for hundreds of years. It became the basis for the partition of India into two independent countries—India and Pakistan—in 1947.

Other Civilizations During The Middle Ages

Most regions of Africa, North America, and South America remained uncivilized during the Middle Ages. But these continents did have some civilized areas. Northern Africa, of course, had been civilized since the days of ancient Egypt. Some civilizations also existed on the west and east coasts of Africa. Similarly, only a few areas of North and South America were civilized. In parts of Central and South America, some Indian groups developed highly advanced civilizations.

Africa. During the Middle Ages, Arab traders of northern Africa carried Muslim culture to western Africa. There, the Arabs established the state of Ghana. The Negroes of Ghana became converted to the Islamic religion. They also adopted many Muslim ways of life. The Negroes gradually gained control of Ghana and built a large empire. During the mid-1200's, the Malinke people of Kangaba expanded their small state into the Mali empire. The capital of the Mali empire, Timbuktu, became an important African center of trade and Muslim culture. In southern Africa, the Zimbabwe civilization lasted from about 1000 to the early 1800's.

Chinese Printing was a well-established art hundreds of years before Europeans began using movable type in the mid-1400's. The Chinese invented printing about 770, during the T'ang dynasty.

Chicago Sun-Times

Museum of Fine Arts, Boston

Japanese Painting reached a high stage of development during the Kamakura period (1185-1333), when artists recorded the deeds of the *samurai*, a warrior class that controlled feudal Japan.

Ruins of fortresses of that Negro civilization still stand in southern Rhodesia.

The Arabs also established trading settlements on the east coast of Africa, including Kilwa, Mombasa, and Zanzibar. There, Arab goods were exchanged for iron, ivory, and slaves from the African interior.

The Americas. The first people who lived on the North and South American continents probably came from Asia. They were later called Indians. Most Indians of the Americas followed primitive ways of life. But during the Middle Ages, some of these tribal peoples developed civilized societies. Their societies reached about the same cultural level as the cradle civilizations of Ancient Times.

An important Indian civilization was developed by the Maya of Central America. The Maya developed a calendar, a system of writing, and a system of mathematics. They built huge temples that were much like the pyramids of ancient Egypt. The Aztec and the Toltec developed civilizations in what is now Mexico, and the Inca built a magnificent empire in what is now Peru. Most of these Indian civilizations lasted until early Modern Times. They were destroyed by European conquerors. The customs and skills of the Indians were of little interest to the Europeans. But the Europeans learned about many new foods from the Indians. These foods included cocoa, corn, peanuts, potatoes, and tomatoes. See INDIAN, AMERICAN.

Fogg Art Museum

Indian Temples built during the 700's were covered with sculptured figures. The Shore Temple, carved out of granite, stands on the Indian Ocean coast, 30 miles (48 kilometers) from Madras.

Pyramids of the Maya, built about A.D. 1000, are relics of an early civilization of the Americas. *El Castillo,* 75 feet (23 meters) tall, is at Chichén Itzá, in Yucatan.

Charlotte Saikowski

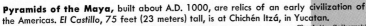

Lee Boltin

Aztec Images of gods or goddesses were decorated with carvings of religious symbols. This stone statue of the goddess Coatlicue is over 8 feet (2.4 meters) tall.

355

WORLD HISTORY / *Modern Times*
Early Period: 1453-1900

Mankind made giant cultural strides during an era that many historians call the early period of Modern Times. They generally date this period from the collapse of the Byzantine Empire in 1453 through the 1800's. It was an era of scientific achievement, industrial revolution, and sweeping political and social change.

The people of Western Europe made almost all the important cultural advances during the new era. Little progress was made in the Middle East, India, or China. As a result, these ancient centers of civilization came largely under the control or influence of Western civilization.

The power of the Western European nations rose on a strong tide of scientific achievements. Some of these achievements made possible long sailing trips and voyages of discovery. Others increased food production and revolutionized manufacturing methods. The European nations sent explorers and military forces throughout the world. They sought markets for European products and raw materials for European industries.

Dutch, English, French, Portuguese, and Spanish colonies were established in the newly discovered lands of the North and South American continents. Thousands of Europeans migrated to these lands, and brought the customs and ideas of Western civilization. Many colonists of the Americas also wanted to develop certain new ideas that were sweeping Europe—democracy, nationalism, and religious toleration.

By the early 1800's, most of the colonists of North and South America had freed themselves from European rule. But European nations still governed large colonial empires in Africa, Asia, and the Middle East. European rule of these regions did not meet serious challenge until the 1900's.

The Clock Tower of the Houses of Parliament, London

The Huntington Library

Ken Lambert, FPG

An Exploration Map of the Caribbean region appears in an atlas published in 1547. It is fairly accurate, but by today's map-making methods, the map shows the region upside down.

The Renaissance

The great advance of Western civilization during Modern Times started during a 300-year period of cultural awakening called the Renaissance. The Renaissance actually began in the early 1300's in Italy. There, artists and scholars supported the idea of individual freedom. They urged people to cast off the ancient customs and rules that governed life during the Middle Ages. The basic Renaissance idea of individual freedom became a cultural force that spread throughout most of northern Europe.

Important cultural achievements resulted from the spirit and vigor of the Renaissance idea. Many world masterpieces of architecture, literature, painting, and sculpture were created. Famous Renaissance artists and writers included Cervantes, Hans Holbein, Leonardo da Vinci, Michelangelo, Raphael, and William Shakespeare. Revolutionary discoveries in astronomy and physics were made by Nicolaus Copernicus and Galileo. Other Renaissance scholars, including Desiderius Erasmus and Saint Thomas More, developed a *humanist* philosophy. This philosophy stressed the importance of man and his enjoyment of life. It influenced many political and social movements of Modern Times. The humanist philosophy also inspired a strong religious movement called the Reformation. The Reformation led to the establishment of Protestant churches in England, Germany, and many other countries. See HUMANISM; REFORMATION.

Exploration and commerce expanded rapidly during the Renaissance. The spirit of the times called for enjoyment of the good things of life—tasty foods, elegant clothes, and elaborate homes. Merchants were en-

The map above shows the European nations and their colonies during the late 1800's (darker areas).

MAJOR EVENTS OF MODERN TIMES—
EARLY PERIOD: 1453-1900

1492 Christopher Columbus reached America and claimed it for Spain.

1492 The Spaniards captured Granada and ended the rule of Spain by the Muslim Moors.

1517 The Reformation began in Germany.

1519-1522 Ferdinand Magellan commanded the first voyage around the world.

1526 Babar, a Muslim ruler, conquered India and established the Mogul Empire.

1532 Francisco Pizarro invaded Peru, beginning the Spanish conquest of the Inca Empire.

1588 The Royal Navy of England defeated the Spanish Armada and established England as a great naval power.

1613 Michael Romanov became Czar of Russia and started the 300-year rule of Russia by the Romanovs.

1644 Manchus conquered China and established their rule that lasted until 1912.

1688 The Glorious Revolution deposed James II of England.

1763 The Treaty of Paris ended the Seven Years' War in Europe, and the French and Indian War in America.

1776 The 13 American colonies of England signed the Declaration of Independence.

1789 The French Revolution began.

1815 Napoleon Bonaparte was defeated at the Battle of Waterloo, ending his attempt to rule Europe.

1824 Armies of Simón Bolívar and Antonio José de Sucre defeated the Spaniards at Ayacucho, ending the Latin-American wars of independence.

1842 The Treaty of Nanking ended the "Opium War" and granted important trading rights in China to Britain.

1847 Liberia was established as the first independent Negro republic of Africa.

1853-1854 Commodore Matthew Perry visited Japan and opened two ports to U.S. trade, ending Japan's isolation.

1858 Great Britain took over rule of India from the East India Company after the Sepoy Rebellion.

1865 Union forces defeated the Confederates in the American Civil War after four years of fighting.

1867 Japanese Emperor Mutsuhito regained his traditional power from the shogun.

1867 The British North America Act established the Dominion of Canada.

1869 The Suez Canal opened.

1871 Germany became united under the Prussian king, who ruled the new empire as Kaiser Wilhelm I.

1882 Great Britain invaded and occupied Egypt.

1885 Leopold II of Belgium established the Congo Free State and controlled it as his personal possession.

1895 Japan took control of Taiwan after the Chinese-Japanese War.

1898 The United States took control of Guam, Puerto Rico, and the Philippines following the Spanish-American War.

The Pierpont Morgan Library

Telescopes Used by Galileo to make revolutionary discoveries in astronomy are displayed in a museum in Florence, Italy. Galileo's chart of the solar system was published in 1632. He has been called the father of modern experimental science.

couraged to bring fine goods of all kinds from distant lands to European markets.

To meet the demands of the merchants, adventurous explorers competed to find the best trade routes to the Far East. Historic voyages were made by Pedro Álvares Cabral, Christopher Columbus, Vasco da Gama, Bartolomeu Dias, Ferdinand Magellan, and others. They opened new sea routes for traders who wanted to avoid the difficult land routes across the Middle East and Asia. An important sea route to Asia was established by way of the Cape of Good Hope. Other sea routes led to the Americas. See EXPLORATION AND DISCOVERY (The Great Age of Discovery).

As goods poured into Europe from distant lands, a commercial revolution developed. Gold and silver imports created a new kind of wealth. Investment opportunities were provided by the creation of *joint-stock companies*. These companies got money to do business by selling shares of stock to a number of individuals. They formed the basis of the corporations of today. The first stock exchanges were also established.

European standards of living rose with the growth of commerce and the use of goods from other countries. European markets were supplied with luxurious chintz fabrics, porcelains, rugs, and silks. Foods from distant lands included bananas, cocoa, coffee, lemons, oranges, and tea. In the same period, a slave trade developed with Africa.

The expansion of overseas commerce led to the establishment of European colonies in many countries. Some of the colonies, chiefly those in tropical countries, were established almost entirely as trading centers. They served as temporary outposts where European manufactured goods were exchanged for raw materials. Many other colonies became permanent. They included the English colony of Virginia, the French colony of Quebec, and the Spanish colonies of New Spain (Mexico) and Peru. These colonies in North and South America formed a pattern for European colonization of many other lands in the years to come.

Life during the Renaissance, and the many cultural achievements of this period of history, are described in the article RENAISSANCE.

 The Age of Reason

During the 1600's and 1700's, an intellectual revolution swept over Western Europe. Traditional principles that had served scholars for hundreds of years were discarded. The leading thinkers of the era insisted that reason was the sole test of truth. The period became known as the Age of Reason.

The most important contribution of the Age of Reason was probably the development of the modern scientific method. Scientists now applied the reasoning process to their studies of basic natural laws. They organized general rules for reaching scientific conclusions that are still followed today (see SCIENCE [How Scientists Work]).

One of the steps of the scientific method was careful experimentation. To carry out such experimentation, scholars needed precise instruments. Their needs were met by inventors of the era. Many important instruments were developed, including the microscope, sextant, slide rule, chronometer, air pump, and adding machine.

With important new instruments to aid them, scientists advanced rapidly. The discoveries of Sir Isaac Newton revolutionized astronomy. Benjamin Franklin and Alessandro Volta discovered the nature of electricity. Robert Boyle, Antoine Lavoisier, and Joseph Priestley founded modern chemistry. René Descartes invented analytic geometry. William Harvey discovered how blood circulates in the human body.

The scientific method was so successful in solving problems of nature that some philosophers applied its principles to human problems. A group of French scholars used the tests of reason in dealing with problems of economics, education, government, and religion. The French scholars, known as the *philosophes*, attacked many evils of the times. These evils included religious

The Study of Human Anatomy opened the way to important medical discoveries in Europe during the 1600's. Rembrandt portrayed this study in his famous painting *The Anatomy Lesson.*
The Royal Gallery, The Hague

Magellan's Ship, *Victoria,* was the first to circle the earth.
Brown Bros.

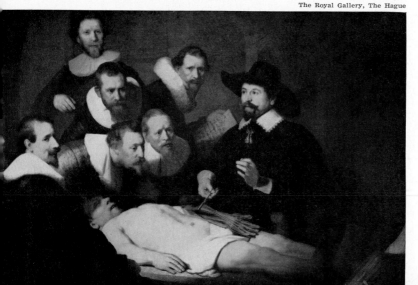

intolerance, superstition, tyranny, unjust laws, and the slave trade. The most famous member of the French group was probably Voltaire. Others included Montesquieu, Denis Diderot, and Jean Jacques Rousseau. Their writings not only attacked evils, but also expressed a basic faith. That faith symbolized the spirit of the era—belief in mankind's ability to solve problems, with reason as the most important tool.

The Age of Reason was also a period of achievement in the arts. The form of the modern novel was developed by Henry Fielding. The poem took on new brilliance in famous couplets written by Alexander Pope. Great painters of the era included Thomas Gainsborough, Francisco Goya, William Hogarth, Rembrandt, Sir Joshua Reynolds, and Antoine Watteau. Many modern forms of music, such as the concerto, opera, symphony, and oratorio, were developed. Outstanding composers of the period included Johann Sebastian Bach, George Frideric Handel, Joseph Haydn, and Wolfgang Amadeus Mozart. See AGE OF REASON.

Democracy and Nationalism

Two powerful political forces—democracy and nationalism—took shape during the 1600's and 1700's. Democracy developed from revolutions that established the right of people to govern themselves. Such revolutions ended *despotism* (absolute control by a ruler) in England, America, and France. Nationalism developed from the strong feelings of national pride that united the people of each country as they fought for their democratic ideals.

The English Revolution of the 1600's was the first important attack in Modern Times on the absolute power of kings. The attack was stimulated by the democratic ideas that developed during the Age of Reason. The English revolution actually was a series of struggles. At one time, the fight was led by the Puritans, a religious group with strong democratic principles. A republic called a commonwealth was established in England in 1649. As a republic, England came under

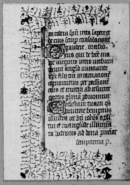
German Consulate General
Page of a Prayer Book of the 1400's, found in France.

Bettmann Archive
Utopia, a mythical country, was described by St. Thomas More.

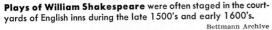
Plays of William Shakespeare were often staged in the courtyards of English inns during the late 1500's and early 1600's.
Bettmann Archive

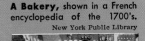
A Bakery, shown in a French encyclopedia of the 1700's.
New York Public Library

the rule of Oliver Cromwell, a Puritan leader. Cromwell ruled as a dictator. The monarchy was restored in 1660. But the English people continued to fight for a strong voice in their government. In 1688, James II was deposed during the Glorious Revolution. The English revolutionary movement ended in 1689. That same year, Parliament adopted the Bill of Rights, assuring the basic rights of the English people, and William and Mary took the throne.

The Bill of Rights took away most powers of the English monarch and guaranteed the liberty of the English people. The document became an important rallying point of English nationalism. The Bill of Rights provided legal grounds for people to revolt against a bad government. This idea spread to many other countries, chiefly through the works of John Locke. Locke, a political scholar, was probably the most influential writer of early Modern Times. See LOCKE, JOHN.

The American Revolution was based chiefly on the right of people to revolt. This right had been established during the English revolution. The American colonists restated it in the Declaration of Independence of July 4, 1776. The Declaration was written by a committee headed by Thomas Jefferson. The committee borrowed from the works of Locke and other political writers, but the language of the Declaration had a special force. Phrases such as "all men are created equal" made the Declaration of Independence one of the most important documents in the history of human liberty. See DECLARATION OF INDEPENDENCE.

British rule in the colonies ended, and a new nation—the United States of America—was formed during the Revolutionary War (1775-1783). The new nation's first system of government, established by the Articles of Confederation, proved unsatisfactory. A new system of government under the United States Constitution was set up in 1789.

The Constitution established the United States as a republic. The Constitution also framed a system of federalism that divided power between the national and state governments. In 1791, the first 10 amendments to the Constitution came into force. These amendments, known as the Bill of Rights, state the basic rights of all citizens. The United States Constitution became a model for the constitutions of many other countries, including most of the Latin-American republics.

During the American revolution and the early years of the republic, strong feelings of democracy developed in the United States. Since then, democracy has become the chief rallying point of American nationalism. Many events of today are influenced by America's support of democracy throughout the world.

The French Revolution (1789-1799) was a great political and social upheaval, marked by disorder and violence. During the First French Republic (1792-1799), most symbols of despotism or privilege in France were wiped out. Titles of nobility were eliminated, and *citizen* became the only French title. The French revolutionists issued a great document of democratic principles—the Declaration of the Rights of Man (see RIGHTS OF MAN, DECLARATION OF THE).

The French revolutionary struggle was climaxed by a reign of terror under the rule of radical leaders such as Georges Jacques Danton and Maximilien Robespierre. The guillotine, a beheading instrument, became a symbol of the French revolution. Thousands of aristocrats, and many citizens who opposed the radicals, were guillotined. During this period, the French armies won many victories against foreign enemies of revolutionary France. In 1794, the period of terror ended. Five years later, the nation came under the stern rule of Napoleon Bonaparte, the great French military genius. The stirring events of the 10-year French revolutionary struggle are described in the article FRENCH REVOLUTION.

Napoleon led France to victory after victory until, in 1812, the French controlled most of Western Europe (see NAPOLEON I). The French soldiers fought to defend and spread the democratic principles in which they believed. Their battle cry of "liberty, equality, and fraternity" stirred the democratic and nationalistic feelings of many peoples. Almost all the European monarchs lost most of their powers in revolutionary movements that swept over much of Europe.

Democratic Reforms and New Nations appeared in Europe after Napoleon was defeated in the Battle of Waterloo in 1815. At the Congress of Vienna (1814-1815), Austria, Great Britain, Prussia, and Russia remade the map of Europe (see VIENNA, CONGRESS OF). For political reasons, the great powers tried to smother the democratic and nationalistic forces that were sweeping over Europe. To hold back democracy, they restored the former monarchies of France, Holland, Spain, and the Italian states. In some areas, to stop nationalism, the great powers joined people of different nationalities under a single ruler. For example, they put the Belgians under the rule of the Dutch king. They agreed to let the Swedish king rule the Norwegians. Most of these efforts failed. Democratic movements succeeded in many countries. During the 1830's, Belgium broke away from the Dutch. In 1875, France established a lasting republican government. By the 1880's, many nations of Western Europe had constitutions as well as some democratic institutions. At the same time, strongly nationalistic people had unified many small states and formed new nations, such as Germany and Italy.

Colonial wars of independence created new nations in Latin America. The colonists were inspired by the principles of democracy and nationalism that had developed in Europe and the United States. By 1830, most of the Latin-American countries had gained independence. New, independent nations included Argentina, Bolivia, Brazil, Chile, Colombia, Ecuador, Mexico, Peru, and Venezuela. See LATIN AMERICA (Struggle for Independence).

 # The Industrial Revolution

During the 1700's and early 1800's, an industrial revolution changed much of Western civilization. Machines replaced many hand tools that civilized man had used for thousands of years. With the new machines, vast quantities of goods could be produced rapidly. Never before had mankind been able to make such great use of the world's natural resources.

The chief ingredients of the industrial revolution were manufacturing machines. The story of their invention,

The English Revolution of the 1600's was the first important attack in Modern Times on the absolute power of kings. Charles I walked to his execution in 1649 during a Puritan rebellion led by Oliver Cromwell.

The American Revolution created the nation that became the leader of the Free World. The Battle of Concord was the second clash between the Americans and the British in the Revolutionary War. The U.S. Constitution became the model of the constitutions of many nations.

The Pennsylvania Packet, *and Daily Advertiser.*

WE, the People of the United States, in order to form a more perfect Union, establish Justice, insure domestic Tranquility, provide for the common Defence, promote the General Welfare, and secure the Blessings of Liberty to Ourselves and our Posterity, do ordain and establish this Constitution for the United States of America.

The French Revolution began on July 14, 1789, with an attack on the Bastille. This famous prison in Paris symbolized the hated government of King Louis XVI.

development, and economic significance is told in the article INDUSTRIAL REVOLUTION.

Industrialism changed the lives of millions of people. When the era began, most families lived in farm areas. Towns and villages served chiefly as market centers for the farmers. As industry developed, factories were built in many towns. These towns grew rapidly into industrial cities. People streamed into the cities to take jobs tending the machines in the factories. Railroads and waterways were built to link many cities. They also provided transportation between the cities and the farmlands, forests, and mines. The invention of the telegraph furnished instant communication between distant places.

The growth of industrialism brought social changes of great importance. A middle class of people appeared. The members of the middle class were neither nobles nor peasants. Most of them were businessmen and wealthy landowners. The middle class grew in size and influence. It owned most of the factories, hired the workers, and operated the banks, mines, railroads, and shops. Most members of the middle class believed that business should be regulated by supply and demand, without government controls. This idea formed the basis of the economic system known as *capitalism*. The principles of capitalism were set forth by the Scotch economist Adam Smith. See CAPITALISM; SMITH, ADAM.

The rapid growth of industrialism produced many problems. Most factory workers were poorly paid and suffered great hardships. They were not permitted to form labor unions, and their working conditions were not regulated by law. The situation led to widespread attacks against the evils of the capitalist system. *Socialism* became the chief rallying point for many persons who opposed the capitalist system. The socialists wanted to put all industrial production under the control of governments. From that basic principle, Karl Marx, a German writer and social philosopher, developed the theories of *communism*. Marx called for the workers to revolt against the middle class and set up state-owned economic systems.

Many reforms supported by members of various social movements were adopted generally during the 1800's. In several countries, workers won the right to form labor unions. Laws regulating working conditions in factories were passed in Great Britain and the United States during the 1830's. Later, many other countries also passed laws that improved the conditions of industrial workers. Great Britain and Germany pioneered in social legislation that provided accident, sickness, and unemployment insurance for industrial employees.

By the late 1800's, most industrial nations had laws that regulated working conditions and also raised the people's standards of living. But the followers of Marx continued to call for a class war and for the violent overthrow of capitalism. The Marxist movement developed into communism in Russia in the early 1900's.

Imperialism. The industrial nations needed large supplies of raw materials for their factories. The vast continents of Africa and Asia had these materials in abundance. Africa and Asia also had millions of people who still used ancient tools of production. These two continents provided good markets for the wide variety of manufactured goods being produced in the industrial nations of Europe.

The European nations established many colonies in Africa and Asia during the 1800's. They did so (1) to insure a flow of raw materials, and (2) to control large markets. European colonial rule extended over most of Africa. Great Britain and France were the leading colonial powers of that continent. Nearly a third of Asia came under the colonial rule of Great Britain, France, The Netherlands, Portugal, and Spain. China had closed most of its ports to Europeans. But they were opened in 1842 after Britain defeated China in the Opium War (see CHINA [The "Unequal Treaties"]).

By the late 1800's, huge European empires had spread over most of the world. The largest empires were those of Great Britain, France, and Germany. Important colonies also were established by Belgium, The Netherlands, and Portugal. This colonial expansion became known as *imperialism*. The United States acted to protect the independent countries of Latin America from European colonial expansion. The protective policy of the United States was set forth in the Monroe Doctrine in 1823. However, the influence of the United States over Latin America was often called imperialism too. See IMPERIALISM; MONROE DOCTRINE.

🌐 The Close of an Era

Industrialism and imperialism climaxed an era of Modern Times that is often called Europe's "wonderful century." Most European nations had become economically wealthy and militarily strong. They ruled vast regions of the world through powerful colonial systems. Their arts, sciences, and scholarship reached high levels of development. The European way of life during the 1800's formed the most advanced civilization the world had ever known. The United States, Canada, and some other countries of the Western Hemisphere were rapidly developing along the European pattern. In contrast, most nations of Africa and Asia remained primitive or at the levels of civilization they had reached during the Middle Ages.

The Opium War with China helped the victorious British to expand their colonial empire in the Orient during the mid-1800's.
Historical Pictures Service

Smoking Factory Chimneys throughout Europe signaled the start of the Industrial Revolution during the 1700's. The rise of industrialism reshaped Western civilization and changed the lives of millions of persons in all parts of the world.

The superior position of the chief European nations met with little challenge during the 1800's. As a result, certain attitudes shaped the basic philosophy of the era. These were:

1. The belief that it was right for millions of colonial peoples to be ruled by European nations.

2. Acceptance of nationalism as the chief political principle of the major European nations.

3. Faith in democracy as a political system that would someday be adopted throughout the world.

4. The certainty that capitalism, although subject to reforms, would develop as the only important economic system.

5. Hopefulness based on the idea that science was a complete blessing to mankind, and that man's progress depended almost entirely on scientific developments.

These were the chief attitudes of Western civilization as a great era of history drew to a close during the early years of the 1900's. All were soon to change.

The Telephone was invented in 1876, and hastened industrial development. Its inventor, Alexander Graham Bell, opened a New York City to Chicago line in 1892.

European Wealth and power were reflected in the elegance of society life during the late 1800's, when the nations of Europe ruled most of the world.

WORLD HISTORY / Modern Times
The 1900's

The first two-thirds of the 1900's was a period of great change—perhaps the most rapid and widespread change in all history. Most of the attitudes of the previous era were shattered. The costliest and most destructive wars in history were fought. Political and social upheavals overturned many long-established governments. At the same time, science made giant advances. Revolutionary technological inventions altered basic ways of life and thrust mankind into the space age.

The 1900's opened with most of the world under the rule of European nations. But by the mid-1960's, the huge European empires had collapsed. Colonialism was a thing of the past. In Africa alone, about 40 new nations established their independence. Traditional European nationalism lost much of its force, and most European countries were trying to solve important problems cooperatively. They were members of organizations set up for their joint defense or for pooling their economic resources. On the other hand, nationalism exploded with full force in Africa and Asia. Nationalism became the chief moving spirit of the newly independent nations.

The 1900's dawned with the idea that democracy and capitalism would spread throughout the world. But that idea proved false. More than a billion persons were living under Communism in the 1970's.

In 1900, it was generally assumed that mankind would use scientific achievements only to build better ways of life. But in 1945, the invention of the atomic bomb demonstrated that man could also use science to produce tremendous destructive power.

By midcentury, the people of an industrialized country hardly realized how much life had changed in 50 years. They took for granted airplanes, atomic energy, automation, radio, refrigerators, color motion pictures, tele-

Men on the Moon. American astronauts made the first lunar landing on July 20, 1969.

NASA

vision, synthetic materials, and superhighways crowded with automobiles. These things had not existed in 1900.

The space age opened in 1957 when Russia launched the first artificial satellite to circle the earth. During the next few years, U.S. and Russian rockets sent many scientific instruments into space. Soon afterward, astronauts of the two countries traveled around the earth in spaceships. In the 1960's, American and Russian scientists solved many problems of extended space travel. In 1968, three American astronauts orbited the moon. The following year, two American astronauts set foot on the surface of the moon. See SPACE TRAVEL.

During the 1900's, people became accustomed to great achievements from medical science. In the first half of the century, many traditional methods of diagnosing, treating, and preventing disease had been revolutionized. The new methods were aided by drugs that previously had been unknown. The new drugs included antibiotics, sulfonamides, and certain serums and vaccines (see DRUG). Rapid medical progress was chiefly responsible for healthier and longer lives in many parts of the world. In 1900, a baby born in the United States had a life expectancy of 47.3 years. By the early 1970's, this figure had increased to 70.6 years.

 World Wars I and II

War—fought on a greater scale than ever before—overshadowed world developments during the early 1900's. World War I raged from 1914 to 1918, and World War II from 1939 to 1945.

Wide World

The Tragedy of World War II was mirrored in the faces of these French people. They are watching as historic French battle flags are paraded out of Marseilles to avoid their capture by advancing German troops. The French government surrendered after France's armies were defeated early in the war.

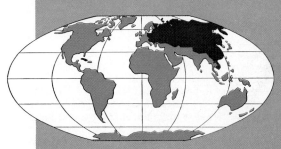

The darker area of the map shows the Communist countries of the world in the 1970's.

MAJOR EVENTS OF THE 1900'S

1901 The Australian states united to form a commonwealth.

1905 Japan defeated Russia in the Russo-Japanese War.

1912 The Republic of China was established.

1914 The assassination of Archduke Francis Ferdinand of Austria-Hungary started World War I.

1917 Revolutionists overthrew Czar Nicholas II and the Bolsheviks seized power in Russia.

1920 The Panama Canal opened.

1920 The League of Nations was established.

1922 The Fascist party seized control of Italy and Benito Mussolini became dictator.

1922 The Union of Soviet Socialist Republics was established.

1923 Mustafa Kemal (Atatürk) established the Republic of Turkey and modernized Turkish institutions.

1933 Adolf Hitler became dictator of Germany.

1935-1936 Italian troops invaded and annexed Ethiopia.

1939 Francisco Franco became dictator of Spain after 32 months of civil war.

1939 Germany invaded Poland, starting World War II.

1941 The Japanese attacked Pearl Harbor, and the United States entered World War II.

1945 The United Nations was established.

1945 The first atomic bombs used in warfare were dropped by U.S. planes on Hiroshima and Nagasaki.

1945 World War II ended in Europe on May 7 and in the Pacific on September 2.

1946 The U.S. granted independence to the Philippines.

1947 Britain granted independence to India and Pakistan.

1948 The U.S. started the European Recovery Program (Marshall Plan) to aid Europe's economic recovery.

1949 The North Atlantic Treaty Organization (NATO) formed by the United States, Canada, and 10 European nations.

1949 The Chinese Communists conquered China.

1950 North Korean Communist troops invaded South Korea, starting the Korean War.

1957 Russia opened the space age by launching Sputnik I, the first artificial satellite to circle the earth.

1957 Communist guerrilla forces of North Vietnam began a terror campaign against U.S.-backed South Vietnam.

1962 Russia agreed to U.S. demands that missiles be removed from Cuba, ending a serious Cold War crisis.

1963 Russia, the United States, and Great Britain signed an agreement banning the testing of nuclear weapons above ground. Other nations signed later.

1965 The Vietnam War expanded. Both the United States and the Communists sent in thousands of troops, and the U.S. began bombing North Vietnam.

1965 The Second Vatican Council ended. Roman Catholic Church leaders had modernized the church.

1967 Israel defeated Egypt, Jordan, Syria, and other Arab states in an Arab-Israeli war.

1969 Two American astronauts became the first men to walk on the moon.

1975 The Vietnam War ended when the non-Communist South Vietnam government surrendered to the Viet Cong.

In World War I, for the first time in history, mankind came to know total war. Entire populations of the fighting nations worked in the war effort. Millions of men, women, and children were killed. Whole cities were destroyed. The fighting forces clashed on vast battlefields—on land, in the air, on the sea, and under the sea. The weapons of total war included bombs and missiles of tremendous destructive power. During World War II, the atomic bomb was developed. Its development led to a bomb a thousand times more powerful—the hydrogen bomb. Thus, mankind's most terrible war helped produce a weapon that could wipe out entire civilizations if used in another total war. The many phases of the two world wars are described in the articles WORLD WAR I and WORLD WAR II.

Out of the horror of each world war came an attempt by mankind to prevent war forever. The first attempt was made after World War I with the creation of the League of Nations (see LEAGUE OF NATIONS). But the League failed to settle many postwar problems. It also was powerless to prevent a rising tide of aggression by Japan, Italy, and Germany during the 1930's. The second attempt was made toward the end of World War II with the establishment of the United Nations (UN). Since 1945, the UN has worked for international peace and security in two chief ways. First, the UN has provided a meeting place where nations can discuss their quarrels peaceably. Second, the UN has conducted worldwide programs to help nations solve problems of health, food shortages, and social injustice. The structure, operations, and accomplishments of the UN are described in the article UNITED NATIONS.

The UN has carried on its peace-keeping tasks in an atmosphere of great tension and unrest. The most important results of World War II were the shift of world power to the United States and Russia, and the collapse of European empires. The shift of power to these two nations produced a bitter struggle that has divided most of the world. The United States and Russia became the leaders of two competing systems of government—democracy and Communism. The collapse of colonial empires brought about the rise of many new nations in Africa, Asia, and the Middle East. These new nations have had many great political, economic, and social problems.

 ## The Rise of New Nations

One by one, the vast European empires collapsed after World War II. Great Britain, France, Belgium, The Netherlands, and the other large colonial powers had been weakened by their losses during the war. They no longer could hold their colonies by force. Furthermore, many Europeans had come to believe that it was morally wrong to rule other people against their will.

The most striking and rapid independence movement took place in Africa. In 1950, there were only four independent countries on the vast African continent. Today, Africa has about 50 independent countries. In Asia, independent governments were established in such countries as Burma, Cambodia, Ceylon (now Sri Lanka), India, Indonesia, Korea, Laos, Malaysia,

Pakistan, the Philippines, and Vietnam since World War II. In the Middle East, the nations that became independent after World War II included Cyprus, Israel, Jordan, Syria, and Yemen (Aden).

Most of the newly independent nations had been under the rule of colonial powers for many years, or even for centuries. In some cases, a colony's land and other natural resources were developed almost entirely for the benefit of the colonial power. Generally, the colonial power gave the people little training in self-government. On the other hand, imperialism brought certain benefits to many colonial peoples. In some lands, tribal wars and certain uncivilized customs were stopped. In many colonies, the ruling powers established modern educational systems and public health services. In several countries, democratic methods of government were introduced by the colonial powers. During the course of their economic development, most of the colonies were equipped with modern communication and transportation systems.

The new nations faced many problems as a result of years of imperialism. But they had been brought in contact with the chief elements of Western progress—education, advanced technology and medicine, and new agricultural and industrial methods.

 ## The Rise of Communism

The challenge of Communism has shaped much of history during the 1900's. Communism's goal is to place all governments under Communist rule. The Communist movement, which achieved its first major success in Russia in 1917, exploded with full force after World War II ended in 1945. During the late 1940's, Russia began to establish Communist dictatorships in Eastern Europe and the Balkans. The democratic nations of the world, led by the United States, fought the spread of Communism. However, Communists also gained control of the government in China—the largest country of Asia—and several other Asian nations.

The great struggle between Communism and democracy became known as the *Cold War*, because it did not lead to direct fighting between the major opponents. The chief weapons of the Cold War included the power of ideas; and economic, political, and technological power. Each side also used these weapons in competing for the support of certain nations that remained neutral in the struggle. These *unaligned*, or *uncommitted*, nations included most of the countries of Africa and Asia that became independent after World War II.

The United Nations became a battleground of the Cold War. The United States supported most UN attempts to settle Cold War disputes. But Russia tried to weaken the authority of the UN.

The most important demonstration of Cold War attitudes on the UN came in 1950, when the UN acted to stop Communist North Korea from invading South Korea. The Korean War (1950-1953) was the first war in which troops of a world organization acted as police to fight an aggressor nation. In the Korean War, strong military units of the United States and many other democratic nations formed the UN army. However, Russia declared that the UN had no right to act at all. Russia aided the North Koreans with war sup-

UN Forces prevented a Communist take-over of South Korea by North Korea. The Korean War (1950-1953) was the first war fought by a world organization to stop aggression.

plies. China sent large forces to fight on the side of North Korea. See KOREAN WAR.

Several incidents of the Cold War became so serious that they could have touched off another world war. Serious incidents occurred from time to time in Berlin, where the Communists built a wall between the two sections of the city. West Berlin is a stronghold of democracy, and East Berlin is the capital of Communist-controlled East Germany. Probably the most serious Cold War incident was the Cuban crisis of 1962. The United States revealed that Russia had installed missiles in Cuba that could launch atomic attacks on U.S. cities. The crisis passed after Russia removed the missiles. See BERLIN; CUBA (The Cuban Missile Crisis).

In spite of other incidents, the Cold War seemed to ease in the late 1950's and the 1960's. Russian leaders talked much of "peaceful coexistence." In 1963, Great Britain, Russia, and the United States signed a treaty banning all nuclear testing except underground tests.

During the mid-1960's, Vietnam became a major battleground of Communist and non-Communist forces. Fighting had begun in 1957 between Vietnamese Communists and South Vietnam government troops. In 1965, North Vietnam began to send thousands of troops to aid the South Vietnamese Communists. Russia and China provided North Vietnam with war materials. At the same time, the United States gave South Vietnam troops and military supplies. The United States withdrew its troops in 1973. Fighting between the Communists and South Vietnam government troops continued until 1975, when South Vietnam surrendered to the Communist forces. See VIETNAM WAR.

The struggle between democracy and Communism is described in the articles COLD WAR and COMMUNISM.

Many New African Nations were born during the 1950's and the 1960's. The flag of Burundi was raised in 1962.

The Vietnam War (1957-1975) resulted in a major victory for Communist forces as North Vietnam helped South Vietnamese Communists win control of South Vietnam. Hundreds of thousands of people had to flee from their homes during the war.

360g

The United Nations, New York

Robert H. Glaze, Artstreet

WORLD HISTORY/The World Today

We live in the most highly developed civilization of all history. At the same time, we face many problems so serious that they could destroy the world as we know it. But there is also hope. Never before has humanity reached our high level of technological power and scientific knowledge. For this reason, we probably have a greater chance of solving the problems of our times than any previous generation.

The most important problem of the times is how to prevent another world war. The struggle between democracy and Communism that started after World War II still continues. But the emergence of China and Western Europe as new centers of power has changed the two-sided nature of the Cold War. As a result, neither the Communist nor the democratic nations have remained united in the struggle.

China—the giant of Asia—has challenged Russia for the leadership of the Communist nations. The Chinese accuse Russia of deserting basic Communist aims. Russia, in turn, accuses the Chinese of misrepresenting the basic Communist aims.

The United States is in a position somewhat like that of Russia. America is no longer the undisputed leader of the democracies. Most European nations have become economically strong and no longer depend on American financial aid. France has urged that Europe also stop depending on America's military might for defense of the continent. France criticized the United States policy in Vietnam, where Americans helped the South Vietnamese fight the Communist forces of North Vietnam.

The problem of preventing war is closely linked with the question of how to rescue millions of persons from poverty. Over half the people of the world do not have enough food to eat. In addition, most of these people cannot read or write. Hunger and illiteracy are widespread in developing nations in Africa, Asia, and Latin America.

The problem of widespread poverty is seriously complicated by a rapidly increasing world population. The increase is so rapid that it is often called the *population explosion*. If the increase continues at its current rate, the present world population of more than $4\frac{1}{3}$ billion will rise to more than $4\frac{3}{4}$ billion by 1985, and will be about $6\frac{1}{8}$ billion by the year 2000. The rate of population growth is generally highest in the developing countries.

A major problem in the developed countries today is how to reduce environmental pollution. The growth of industry and the production of goods in these countries have done much to raise living standards. But these activities have also helped pollute the air, the land, and the water. Poisonous fumes from automobiles and factories have at times endangered public health. The rapid accumulation of garbage and other solid wastes has led to the use of open land for dumps. Industrial wastes that have been emptied into rivers, lakes, and oceans have killed fish and made beaches unsafe for swimming. See ENVIRONMENTAL POLLUTION.

United Press Int.

Food for Hungry Children in many developing countries is often supplied by major developed nations. But the food problem of the world has been complicated by the population explosion in many lands.

WORLD BOOK photo

Environmental Pollution is a major problem in developed countries. Industrial wastes that have been emptied into rivers, lakes, and oceans make swimming unsafe at many beaches.

Other problems that challenged the developed countries in the early 1970's included sharply rising inflation and a fuel shortage. Inflation resulted chiefly because of the failure of producers to meet the demand for goods, plus large-scale spending by governments and citizens of the large industrialized nations. The shortage of fuel was caused partly by a war between Israel and several Arab nations in 1973. The war resulted in greatly reduced oil exports from countries in the Middle East. However, the growing fuel needs of the industrial nations show signs of increasing at a much faster

rate than the development of new supplies of fuel.

Progress in solving the great problems of our times depends chiefly on international cooperation. A large-scale war can be prevented only if the powerful nations settle their quarrels peaceably. If hunger and illiteracy are to be reduced, the developed countries must help the underdeveloped countries. International cooperation has also become vital in fighting pollution.

The United Nations has been a forum for the peaceful settlement of several bitter international quarrels. In addition, UN agencies have helped the developed nations give aid to the underdeveloped nations. Foreign aid programs are the established policies of most of the large countries. Some Western nations have exchanged information on pollution, but the need for more and larger programs is great.   T. WALTER WALLBANK

WORLD HISTORY/Study Aids

Related Articles in WORLD BOOK include:

HISTORY OF COUNTRIES

See the History sections of the country articles, such as ARGENTINA (History). See also the separate articles CANADA, HISTORY OF; UNITED STATES, HISTORY OF THE.

HISTORY OF CONTINENTS OR REGIONS

See the History sections of the following articles:

Africa	Central America	Middle East
Asia	Europe	Pacific Islands
Balkans	Latin America	Southeast Asia

ANCIENT TIMES

Aegean Civilization	Greece, Ancient	Palestine
Ancient Civilization	Hittite	Parthia
Assyria	Indus Valley	Persia, Ancient
Babylonia	Civilization	Phoenicia
Carthage	Jews	Phrygia
Chaldea	Lydia	Roman Empire
Egypt, Ancient	Macedonia	Sumer
Etruscan	Media	Troy
Fertile Crescent	Mesopotamia	

MIDDLE AGES

Aztec	Inca	Mongol Empire
Byzantine Empire	Knights and	Muslims
Crusades	Knighthood	Printing
Feudalism	Maya	(History)
Holy Roman Empire	Middle Ages	Vikings
Hundred Years' War		

MODERN TIMES

Age of Reason	Revolutionary War in
Cold War	America
Exploration and Discovery	Seven Years' War
Foreign Aid	Space Travel
French Revolution	Succession Wars
Industrial Revolution	Thirty Years' War
League of Nations	United Nations
Nuclear Energy	Vienna, Congress of
Reformation	World War I
Renaissance	World War II
Revolution of 1848	

OTHER RELATED ARTICLES

Archaeology	Colonialism
Architecture	Communism
Civilization	Culture

NASA

Joint Space Research between the United States and the Soviet Union symbolizes the efforts of the two countries to promote international cooperation. The picture above shows Russian and U.S. astronauts discussing the Apollo Soyuz Test Project. The project reached a climax when manned U.S. Apollo and Soviet Soyuz space vehicles linked up in space in 1975.

WORLD, HISTORY OF

Democracy
Government
History
Indian, American
Law
Literature
Migration

Music
Painting
Population
Prehistoric
People
Radicalism
Religion

Science
Sculpture
Slavery
Socialism
War
World
Writing

Outline

I. Ancient Times
  A. Cradles of Civilization
  B. Civilization Advances
II. The Middle Ages
  A. Western Europe During the Middle Ages
  B. The Byzantine Empire
  C. The Moslem Empire
  D. China During the Middle Ages
  E. Japan During the Middle Ages
  F. India During the Middle Ages
  G. Other Civilizations During the Middle Ages
III. Modern Times—Early Period: 1453-1900
  A. The Renaissance   D. The Industrial
  B. The Age of Reason   Revolution
  C. Democracy and   E. The Close of an Era
     Nationalism
IV. Modern Times—the 1900's
  A. World Wars I and II   C. The Rise of
  B. The Rise of New Nations   Communism
V. The World Today

Questions

What people developed cuneiform writing? Why is such writing of major importance in world history?

How did the Byzantine Empire help preserve the civilization of Western Europe during the Middle Ages?

What five attitudes shaped the basic philosophy of Europe's "wonderful century"?

How do we know that the Indus Valley people traded with the people of the Middle East in Ancient Times?

Why is environmental pollution one of the world's chief problems today?

What basic idea was championed by the artists and scholars of the Renaissance?

What are the two principal ways in which the United Nations works for peace?

What major contributions to present-day civilization were made by the ancient Hebrews? The Phoenicians?

What people developed the first civilization of the European mainland? What was their most important contribution to Western civilization?

Why did civilization advance in China but not in India during the Middle Ages?

Books for Young Readers

FOSTER, GENEVIEVE S. *George Washington's World.* Scribner, 1941. *Abraham Lincoln's World.* 1944. *The World of Captain John Smith, 1580-1631.* 1959. *The World of Columbus and Sons.* 1965. *Year of Columbus, 1492.* 1969. *Year of the Pilgrims, 1620.* 1969. *Year of Independence, 1776.* 1970. *Year of Lincoln, 1861.* 1970. *Birthdays of Freedom: From Early Egypt to July 4, 1776.* New ed. 1973. *The World of William Penn.* 1973. *The Year of the Horseless Carriage, 1801.* 1975.

HESSEL, MILTON. *Man's Journey Through Time: The Important Events in Each Area of the Earth in Each Period of History.* Simon & Schuster, 1974.

VAN LOON, HENDRIK WILLEM. *The Story of Mankind.* Rev. ed. Liveright, 1972.

Books for Older Readers

BRINTON, CRANE, and others. *A History of Civilization.* 3 vols. 5th ed. Prentice-Hall, 1976.

DURANT, WILL and ARIEL. *The Story of Civilization.* 11 vols. Simon & Schuster, 1935-1975.

FREEMAN-GRENVILLE, GREVILLE S. P. *Chronology of World History: A Calendar of Principal Events from 3000 B.C. to A.D. 1973.* Rowman, 1975.

GARRATY, JOHN A., and GAY, PETER, eds. *The Columbia History of the World.* Harper, 1972.

Great Ages of Man: A History of the World's Cultures. A series of well-illustrated books with titles ranging from *Cradle of Civilization* by Samuel Noah Kramer to *Twentieth Century* by Joel G. Colton. Time Inc., 1965-1968.

LANGER, WILLIAM L., ed. *An Encyclopedia of World History.* 5th ed. Houghton, 1972.

McNEILL, WILLIAM H. *A World History.* 2nd ed. Oxford, 1971.

SNYDER, LOUIS L., and others. *Panorama of the Past: Readings in World History.* 2 vols. Houghton, 1966.

TOYNBEE, ARNOLD J. *A Study of History.* 12 vols. Oxford, 1935-1961.

WALLBANK, T. WALTER, and others. *Civilization Past and Present.* 5th ed. Scott, Foresman, 1978.

WORLD BANK is an international organization that provides loans to countries for development projects. It lends money to member governments and their agencies, and to private organizations in the member nations. The World Bank is a specialized agency of the United Nations. Its official name is the International Bank for Reconstruction and Development. More than 100 countries are members of the bank. The bank gets its loan funds from member countries and by borrowing in the world money market.

The bank operates through a board of governors and 20 executive directors chosen by members. It makes loans to members who cannot obtain money from other sources at reasonable terms. These loans help members develop their national economies. The bank encourages private investment in member countries. It also provides many technical assistance services for members. The bank was founded at an economic conference held in Bretton Woods, N.H., in 1944. It began operating in 1946. Headquarters of the World Bank are in Washington, D.C.

The International Development Association is an organization that was established in 1960 as an affiliate of the World Bank. This association makes loans to less developed member countries on a long-term basis at no interest.

Critically reviewed by
INTERNATIONAL BANK FOR RECONSTRUCTION AND DEVELOPMENT

Related Articles in WORLD BOOK include:

Bretton Woods
Food Supply (Food
  Supply Programs)
International Development
  Association

International Finance
  Corporation
International Monetary
  Fund

WORLD BOOK ENCYCLOPEDIA. See ENCYCLOPEDIA (World Book).

WORLD CALENDAR. See CALENDAR (Calendar Reform).

WORLD COMMUNITY OF ISLAM IN THE WEST. See BLACK MUSLIMS.

WORLD COUNCIL OF CHURCHES is a worldwide organization of more than 260 Protestant, Anglican, Old Catholic, and Orthodox churches. The council works to promote cooperation and unity among all the churches of the world. The churches that belong to the council have about 400 million members in 90 countries and territories.

The Roman Catholic Church, though not a member

of the council, works with the organization in a number of programs. The council has also opened discussions with such non-Christian groups as Buddhists and Muslims.

The council's activities include education; missionary work; aid to refugees, the sick, and underprivileged; and the promotion of world peace and social and interracial justice. It has sponsored studies on the future of human society in an age of scientific and technical progress. It has also studied the role Christians should play in improving government, courts, prisons, and other social institutions.

The World Council of Churches was founded in 1948 in Amsterdam, The Netherlands. The member churches elect six presidents and a 120-member central committee that meets annually to set the council's policies. The council has headquarters in Geneva, Switzerland, and an office at 475 Riverside Drive, New York, N.Y. 10027. Critically reviewed by World Council of Churches

WORLD COURT. See International Court of Justice.

WORLD CUP. See Skiing (Skiing as a Sport).

WORLD GOVERNMENT. Many persons believe that a single authority should dispense justice and maintain law and order for the whole world. They would like to see a world government make the major decisions concerning security and the welfare of individuals that separate national governments now make. World government could come about through conquest, just as the Romans conquered the lands around the Mediterranean Sea. But persons who favor world government think of it as the result of persuasion and agreement.

Some persons began dreaming of a world government as early as the 1300's. The idea did not win wide public support until just before World War II. After that war, many persons accepted the idea. These persons believed that war was inevitable as long as separate national governments existed. They pointed out that war had become a threat to the survival of the whole human race. They argued that countries should give a world government the right to make the final decisions regarding war and peace. Some schemes for world government foresee a federal system, in which subdivisions of the world would continue to perform some governmental functions. Most advocates are unwilling to wait for international organizations to grow slowly into a world government. They want the change to come peacefully, but all at once.

Persons who favor world government are active in most countries of the Western world. But many persons oppose the idea. Critics of world government ask how the peoples of the world could reach agreement on such a topic in the face of acute present conflicts. They point out that, if the conflicts between East and West die down, making agreement on world government attainable, the need for such a government is also diminished.

Some of the questions that must be solved include the problem of finding leaders for a world government, the problem of keeping it from becoming tyrannical, and the problem of avoiding civil wars, often bloodier than international ones. William T. R. Fox

WORLD HEALTH ORGANIZATION (WHO), a specialized agency of the United Nations, works to promote the health of all peoples. WHO helps countries —especially developing ones—build up their public

health services. It fights communicable diseases by organizing campaigns, supporting research, and training technicians. Smallpox, for example, has been nearly eradicated through the efforts of WHO (see Smallpox).

WHO collects and distributes information on epidemics, and develops international quarantine and sanitation rules. The agency carries out biomedical research in cooperation with national research institutions. It also supports projects in many nations to improve waste disposal and ensure a safe water supply.

The agency has a membership of about 150 countries. The principal organs of WHO are the World Health Assembly, the Executive Board, and the Secretariat, which is headed by a director-general. WHO has general headquarters in Geneva, Switzerland, and six regional offices in various parts of the world. WHO was founded in 1948.
Critically reviewed by the World Health Organization

WORLD HOCKEY ASSOCIATION. See Hockey.

WORLD INTELLECTUAL PROPERTY ORGANIZATION is an international agency that works to protect artistic and literary works, inventions, and trademarks against copying. Such creations are known as *intellectual property*. The organization promotes international agreements concerning copyrights, patents, and trademarks. It also furnishes industrial information and other assistance to developing countries. The organization, known as WIPO, is a specialized agency of the United Nations (UN). WIPO has a membership of more than 90 countries. Its headquarters are in Geneva, Switzerland.

WIPO developed from two agencies that were established in the 1880's. One protected copyrights, the other patents and trademarks. The two joined in 1893 to form one organization, which was replaced by WIPO in 1967. The agency became part of the UN in 1974.

WORLD MAP. See World.

WORLD MEDICAL ASSOCIATION is an organization of national medical associations from about 60 countries. Organized in 1947, it has adopted an international code of medical ethics. Headquarters are at 13, chemin du Levant, 01210 Ferney-Voltaire, France.
Critically reviewed by the World Medical Association

WORLD METEOROLOGICAL ORGANIZATION (WMO) is a specialized agency of the United Nations (UN). It sponsors the World Weather Watch program for the rapid exchange of observations to forecast the weather. The program consists of networks of weather stations in all parts of the world, satellites and computers, and a worldwide telecommunications system. The WMO's technical cooperation program helps developing countries set up or improve their meteorological services. The organization also offers advice on how weather conditions affect natural resources and such activities as farming and air and sea transportation.

The organization was founded in 1873 as the International Meteorological Organization. In 1951, it changed its name and became part of the United Nations. WMO headquarters are in Geneva, Switzerland.
Critically reviewed by the World Meteorological Organization

WORLD SERIES. See Baseball (Major Leagues).

WORLD TRADE. See International Trade.

WORLD TRADE CENTER. See New York City (Trade); Skyscraper (table; picture).

WORLD WAR I

WORLD WAR I ranks second only to World War II as the most bloody and most costly war in modern history. Two pistol shots signaled the start of war. An armistice ended the fighting four years later.

Shortly before noon on Sunday, June 28, 1914, crowds gathered in Sarajevo, the capital of the Austrian province of Bosnia. They came to see Archduke Francis Ferdinand, heir to the throne of Austria-Hungary, and his wife Sophie. Suddenly a man jumped on the running board of the royal touring car and fired a pistol. Two shots struck Ferdinand and one hit Sophie, who was trying to shield him. They both died almost immediately. The assassin was Gavrilo Princip, a young Bosnian student who had lived in Serbia.

Austria-Hungary suspected that its small neighbor, Serbia, had approved the plot to kill Ferdinand. As a result, it declared war on Serbia on July 28, 1914. By October 30, the Central Powers—Austria-Hungary, Germany, and the Ottoman Empire—were at war with the Allies—Belgium, France, Great Britain, Russia, and

BRITAIN

FRANCE

RUSSIA

GERMANY

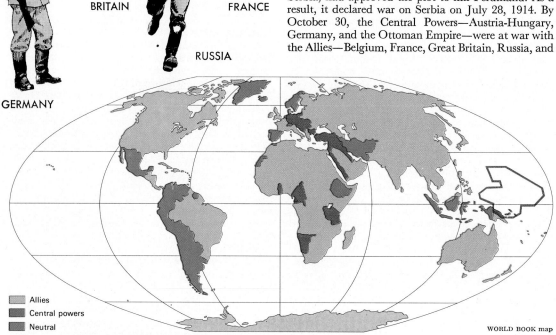

Allies
Central powers
Neutral

WORLD BOOK map

In World War I, Germany and the other Central Powers fought more than 20 Allied nations. The map shows a colony or dependency in the same color as the country governing it.

ITALY

OTTOMAN EMPIRE

UNITED STATES

Allies

Belgium (Aug. 4, 1914)
Brazil (Oct. 26, 1917)
British Empire (Aug. 4, 1914)
China (Aug. 14, 1917)
Costa Rica (May 23, 1918)
Cuba (Apr. 7, 1917)
France (Aug. 3, 1914)
Greece (June 27, 1917)
Guatemala (Apr. 23, 1918)
Haiti (July 12, 1918)
Honduras (July 19, 1918)
Italy (May 23, 1915)

Japan (Aug. 23, 1914)
Liberia (Aug. 4, 1917)
Montenegro (Aug. 5, 1914)
Nicaragua (May 8, 1918)
Panama (Apr. 7, 1917)
Portugal (Mar. 9, 1916)
Romania (Aug. 27, 1916)
Russia (Aug. 1, 1914)
San Marino (June 3, 1915)
Serbia (July 28, 1914)
Siam (July 22, 1917)
United States (Apr. 6, 1917)

Central Powers

Austria-Hungary
    (July 28, 1914)
Bulgaria (Oct. 14, 1915)

Germany (Aug. 1, 1914)
Ottoman Empire
    (Oct. 29, 1914)

The date given after each country's name is the date on which it entered World War I.

Serbia. Other countries later joined in the fighting.

A single act—the shooting of Ferdinand—marked the outbreak of war. But there were several basic causes of World War I. These causes included the growth of nationalism, the system of military alliances that created a balance of power, the competition for colonies and other territory, and the use of secret diplomacy.

At the beginning of the war, Austria-Hungary and Germany planned to conquer new territories and col-

Peter Young, the contributor of this article, is former head of the Military History Department at the Royal Military Academy in Sandhurst, England, and the author of several books and articles on military subjects.

onies. They won early victories on the western and eastern fronts. But, in the First Battle of the Marne, in September, 1914, the Allies stopped the German advance and ended Germany's chances for a quick victory. The opposing armies settled down to trench warfare. The Allies blockaded Germany and seized its colonies.

The United States tried to remain neutral in the early years of World War I. The British angered Americans by searching neutral ships. But Britain, as a nation

and airships fought in the air and bombed soldiers and civilians. Submarines torpedoed merchant ships without warning. More than 5,000,000 Allied servicemen and more than 3,300,000 servicemen of the Central Powers died from wounds, disease, and other causes. In all, the four years of war cost over $337 billion.

Peace agreements after the war changed the map of the world. New governments appeared in Austria, Czechoslovakia, Estonia, Finland, Germany, Hungary, Latvia, Lithuania, Poland, Russia, Yugoslavia, and several countries of western Asia. But World War I did not solve the world's problems. The peace settlement that followed created conditions that plunged the world into another war less than 20 years later.

Causes of the War

The basic causes of World War I went as far back as the early 1800's. Peoples controlled by other countries began to develop feelings of nationalism. Countries grouped together in rival military alliances to advance their own aims. They competed for colonies and other

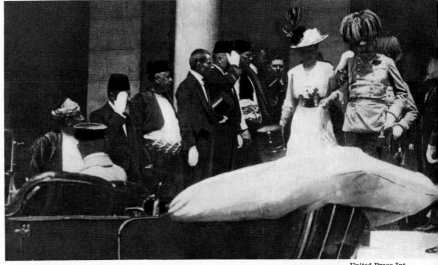

Slaying of Archduke Francis Ferdinand of Austria-Hungary, *right*, triggered World War I. Gavrilo Princip, a student who had lived in Serbia, fired the shots that killed Ferdinand shortly after he entered this car. On July 28, 1914, Austria-Hungary declared war on Serbia to begin World War I.

United Press Int.

at war, had the right to search under international law. Americans turned against the Central Powers when they learned of German submarines sinking unarmed passenger ships, and German atrocities against civilians. Americans decided that by joining the Allies they would help "make the world safe for democracy." American *doughboys*, as the soldiers were called, marched aboard troopships singing George M. Cohan's "Over There." American factories sent a stream of supplies to the fighting forces. The entry of the United States into the war boosted Allied morale, and fresh American troops reinforced the battered Allied armies. The fighting ended with an armistice on Nov. 11, 1918.

Much of the war involved hand-to-hand combat in trenches between the largest armies ever seen up to that time. New and improved weapons gave each side more efficient machines to kill the enemy. Mechanized vehicles—tanks, trucks, automobiles, and motorcycles—speeded the war on land. For the first time, airplanes

lands. Finally, governments clouded international relations by carrying on secret diplomacy.

Nationalism. The French Revolution of 1789 brought about a new feeling of nationalism. French-speaking peoples, German-speaking peoples, Italian-speaking peoples, and others began to feel that they should each have a separate national government in a country where everyone spoke the same language.

After the Napoleonic wars ended in 1815, diplomats at the Congress of Vienna drew the boundaries of Europe to suit their rulers. They often separated people of the same nationality, putting them in different countries instead of uniting them. See VIENNA, CONGRESS OF.

Some decisions of the Congress of Vienna brought violence and some national dissatisfactions. For example, at the end of the Franco-Prussian War in 1871, Germany annexed the province of Alsace and most of Lorraine from France (see FRANCO-PRUSSIAN WAR). Frenchmen looked forward to regaining these provinces.

1914

June 28 Archduke Francis Ferdinand was assassinated.
July 28 Austria-Hungary declared war on Serbia.
July 30 Russia ordered general mobilization.
Aug. 1 Germany declared war on Russia.
Aug. 3 Germany declared war on France.
Aug. 4 Germany invaded Belgium. Great Britain declared war on Germany.
Aug. 26-31 The Germans crushed the Russian Second Army at Tannenberg.
Sept. 1-Oct. 3 The Russians defeated the Austrians in the Battles of Lemberg.
Sept. 6-9 The Allies stopped the Germans in the First Battle of the Marne.
Oct. 21-Nov. 17 Germany failed to reach the English Channel in the First Battle of Ypres.
Oct. 29 The Turks joined the Central Powers.

1915

Feb. 18 Germany started to blockade Great Britain.
Apr. 22 The Germans first used poison gas, in the Second Battle of Ypres.
Apr. 25 Allied troops landed on the Gallipoli Peninsula.
May 2 The Austrians began an offensive in Galicia.
May 7 A German submarine sank the liner *Lusitania*.
May 23 Italy declared war on Austria-Hungary.

1916

Feb. 21 The Germans opened the Battle of Verdun.
Apr. 29 Kut-al-Amara (Al Kūt), with 10,000 British troops, surrendered to the Turks.
May 31-June 1 The British fleet fought the German fleet in the Battle of Jutland.
June 4 Russia began an offensive in eastern Galicia.
July 1-Nov. 18 The Allies advanced in the Battles of the Somme.
Aug. 27 Italy declared war on Germany.
Sept. 15 The British army first used tanks.

1917

Feb. 1 Germany began unrestricted submarine warfare.
Apr. 6 The United States declared war on Germany.
June 26 American troops began landing in France.
July 31-Aug. 9 Germany ended Russia's last offensive.
July 31-Nov. 10 Germany stopped the Allies in the Third Battle of Ypres.
Nov. 7 (Oct. 25 in the old Russian calendar) The Bolsheviks seized power in Russia.
Dec. 9 Jerusalem fell to the Allies.
Dec. 15 Russia signed an armistice with Germany.

1918

Jan. 8 President Woodrow Wilson announced his Fourteen Points as the basis for peace.
Mar. 3 Russia signed the Treaty of Brest-Litovsk.
Mar. 21 Germany launched the first of its final offensives along the Somme.
Apr. 9 Germany launched an offensive at Ypres.
May 27 Germany launched an offensive on the Aisne.
June 15 Austria-Hungary fought its last offensive.
June 23 The Allies occupied Murmansk, Russia.
June 25 American marines captured Belleau Wood.
July 15 Germany launched its last offensive on the Marne.
July 18 France began the Second Battle of the Marne.
July 21 Allied troops recaptured Château-Thierry.
Aug. 8 The British broke the German line at Amiens.
Sept. 26 The Allies began their final offensive on the western front.
Sept. 29 Bulgaria signed an armistice.
Oct. 30 The Ottoman Empire signed an armistice.
Nov. 3 Austria signed an armistice.
Nov. 9 Kaiser Wilhelm II of Germany abdicated.
Nov. 11 Germany signed the armistice.

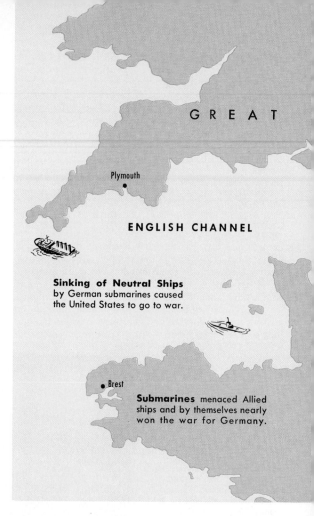

GREAT

Plymouth

ENGLISH CHANNEL

Sinking of Neutral Ships by German submarines caused the United States to go to war.

• Brest

Submarines menaced Allied ships and by themselves nearly won the war for Germany.

Austria-Hungary controlled lands that several of its neighbors thought should belong to them. Serbia, a Slavic nation, wanted the provinces of Bosnia and Hercegovina, because it wanted an outlet to the sea and because so many Slavs lived there. Italy wanted to take the Trentino region and Trieste away from Austria-Hungary, because many Italians lived in these places. The Czechs and the Slovaks also sought to free themselves from Austrian and Hungarian control.

People of many different nationalities lived in Russia, including Estonians, Finns, Latvians, Lithuanians, and Poles. They, too, wanted freedom. In the Balkan Peninsula—often called the *powder keg of Europe* because of many small wars—Bulgarians, Greeks, Romanians, Serbs, and other peoples resented long years of Turkish misrule, and interference by other countries.

The leaders of the Congress of Vienna might have taken care of the national desires of many people in central and eastern Europe if they had wanted to do so. But they decided otherwise.

Some countries had *war cults* (organizations that glorified war). Members of these groups sometimes insulted neighboring peoples, who were quick to take offense. Warmongers sneered at foreign ways of doing things. Often, sensational newspaper stories helped spread their propaganda. Some German leaders vigorously urged commercial and political expansion to the east, especially in Asia. They called this policy of

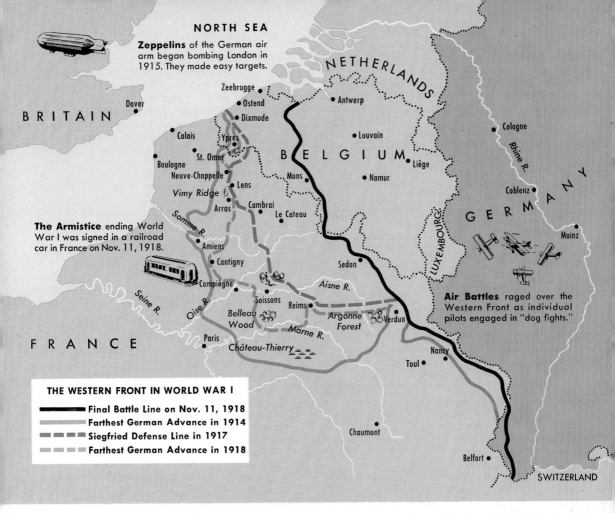

NORTH SEA

Zeppelins of the German air arm began bombing London in 1915. They made easy targets.

NETHERLANDS

BRITAIN

Dover

• Zeebrugge
• Ostend
• Dixmude

• Antwerp

• Louvain

• Calais
Ypres

B E L G I U M

• Liège

Cologne

Rhine R.

• St. Omer

• Boulogne
Neuve-Chappelle
• Lens

• Mons

• Namur

• Coblenz

G E R M A N Y

Vimy Ridge

Arras
• Cambrai
• Le Cateau

Somme R.

The Armistice ending World War I was signed in a railroad car in France on Nov. 11, 1918.

• Amiens

• Cantigny

• Sedan

LUXEMBOURG

• Mainz

Seine R.

Oise R.

Compiègne

Soissons
Reims •

Aisne R.

Belleau
Wood

Argonne
Forest

Verdun

Air Battles raged over the Western Front as individual pilots engaged in "dog fights."

F R A N C E

• Paris
Château-Thierry

Marne R.

Nancy •

Toul •

THE WESTERN FRONT IN WORLD WAR I

━━━━ **Final Battle Line on Nov. 11, 1918**
──── **Farthest German Advance in 1914**
━ ━ ━ **Siegfried Defense Line in 1917**
─ ─ ─ **Farthest German Advance in 1918**

• Chaumont

• Belfort

SWITZERLAND

expansion *Drang nach Osten,* or *"the drive toward the east."*

Military Alliances proved to be another fundamental cause of World War I. After Chancellor Otto von Bismarck unified the German Empire in 1871, he hoped for a period of international peace. Bismarck felt that France's desire to regain Alsace-Lorraine might be the chief threat to peace. He sought allies whose support would discourage other nations from attacking Germany.

The Triple Alliance. In 1882, Germany, Austria-Hungary, and Italy signed a treaty called *the Triple Alliance* (see TRIPLE ALLIANCE). It was designed to protect its members against attack by France or Russia. Germany and Italy feared France, and Germany and Austria-Hungary feared Russia.

The three members of the Alliance formed a powerful bloc in central Europe. But Austria-Hungary and Italy were not really friendly. They quarreled over territory that Italy thought it should have. Both competed for control of the Adriatic Sea. When war broke out in 1914, Italy did not stand by its alliance obligation. It had made a secret treaty with France in 1902. As a result, it remained neutral for a time, then declared war on Austria-Hungary.

The Entente Cordiale. After the formation of the Triple Alliance, the other great countries of Europe found themselves at a disadvantage. In case of an international crisis, Great Britain, France, and Russia would have to act separately, but the countries of the Triple Alliance

could act together. In 1894, France signed a defensive alliance with Russia.

Only Great Britain then remained isolated. It faced growing commercial and naval rivalry with Germany. In 1904, Great Britain and France reached an *Entente Cordiale,* or *cordial understanding.* By the terms of this agreement, they settled their many disagreements about colonies. The two nations became diplomatic partners.

The Triple Entente. Next, France succeeded in bringing Great Britain and Russia together. In 1907, these two nations signed *the Anglo-Russian Entente,* somewhat like the *Entente Cordiale.* The new agreement linking France, Russia, and Great Britain was called *the Triple Entente* (see TRIPLE ENTENTE).

International Disputes. Now Europe was divided into two armed camps, the Triple Alliance opposed to the Triple Entente. Each group attracted a number of smaller allies. Any quarrel between two European countries could quickly involve all six great powers.

One important dispute concerned Morocco, "the Pearl of North Africa." Between 1905 and 1912, France came close to war with Germany several times over control of this large and valuable region. Another trouble spot lay in Bosnia and Hercegovina. Austria-Hungary had occupied these former Turkish provinces in 1878, and formally annexed them in 1908. Russia promised in advance that it would not oppose the annexation. In return, Austria-Hungary agreed to favor giving Russian warships permission to pass freely through the Straits at Constantinople. But Russia could not get the other major countries to approve its plan to open the Straits. It tried to "save face" by insisting on an international conference to confirm Austria-Hungary's action. When Austria-Hungary refused to agree, war seemed near. But France was not ready at this time to support Russia over a Balkan quarrel. But Germany stood willing to support Austria-Hungary. Russia finally gave up its demand for a conference, but encouraged the Serbs in their desire to seize Bosnia and Hercegovina from Austria-Hungary.

Then came the Balkan Wars of 1912 and 1913 (see BALKANS). The Balkan countries fought for more territory, first against Turkey, then against each other. The results weakened Germany's friend, the Ottoman Empire (now Turkey), and doubled the size of Austria-Hungary's enemy, Serbia.

Competition for Colonies. Much of world history during the late 1800's and early 1900's involved rivalry over trade and commerce. The great powers were becoming increasingly industrialized. They competed for markets in which to sell or exchange their products. They quarreled over the control of sources of raw materials. They tried to find and monopolize places in which to invest money. They competed for new sources of food, for new regions to colonize, and for overseas bases from which to supply their ships. Even missionary rivalries played a part in expansion during this period. The British were particularly concerned about German colonial expansion. The growth of the German navy threatened British supremacy on the high seas. The Russians hoped to dominate affairs in the Balkans.

Secret Diplomacy. The nations of the world at this time did not have any international organization to help settle disputes. Sometimes, all the ministers in a cabinet did not know that some of their colleagues had made secret agreements with other countries. Often the cabinet did not keep the legislature fully informed of secret agreements. For example, British Foreign Minister Sir Edward Grey assured France in 1912 that Great Britain would provide naval aid in case of war. But he did not tell Parliament of his promise.

The tense international situation led the German ambassador to France, Wilhelm von Schoen, to remark in 1914: "Peace remains at the mercy of an accident." On June 28, that accident occurred when Gavrilo Princip shot Archduke Francis Ferdinand in Sarajevo.

Men, Battlefronts, and Strategy

At the beginning of World War I, France and Germany had the most important armies. The Central Powers won most of the early victories. But the Allies had time and resources on their side and won the final battles. Germany planned to overwhelm France, then help Austria-Hungary crush Russia. The Allies planned to defeat the Central Powers by hitting from east and west.

Men Under Arms. At the start of the war, Germany had the biggest and best-equipped fighting force in Europe. Its troops were somewhat better trained, and its artillery—especially heavy caliber weapons—was superior. The Central Powers formed a solid land block. They had enemies around them, but not between them. They could speed supplies and reinforcements to any

front. The mobilized strength of the Central Powers reached more than 22,800,000 men and women.

The Allies had far greater manpower and resources of materials than the Central Powers. They took longer to mobilize than Germany did, but they eventually achieved overwhelming strength. They mobilized more than 42 million men and women during the war. The French army had excellent spirit and some good equipment, but was not trained for modern warfare. Russia had the largest army, but it was badly equipped and poorly commanded. The British army, though small, was a superb fighting machine. Britain, however, could not recruit enough men to wage total war until 1915. The British and French found it hard to help Russia because the Central Powers cut off all supply routes. However, the British navy gave the Allies control of the seas, and they could ship much needed supplies.

War Leaders. Herbert H. Asquith and David Lloyd George served as prime ministers of Great Britain. French premiers included René Viviani, Aristide Briand, and Georges Clemenceau. Antonio Salandra, Paolo Boselli, and Vittorio Orlando served as premiers of Italy. Czar Nicholas II ruled Russia. Woodrow Wilson was President of the United States throughout the war. Kaiser Wilhelm II ruled Germany. After Emperor Francis Joseph of Austria-Hungary died in 1916, Charles I became emperor. Other sovereigns of the Central Powers included King Ferdinand I of Bulgaria and Muhammad V of the Ottoman Empire.

The chief Allied military commanders included Marshals Ferdinand Foch, Joseph Joffre, and Henri Philippe Pétain of France; Field Marshals Sir John French and Sir Douglas Haig, Adm. Sir John Jellicoe, and Vice Adm. Sir David Beatty of Great Britain; Generals Luigi Cadorna and Armando Díaz of Italy; Grand Duke Nicholas Nicholaievich of Russia; and Gen. John J. Pershing of the United States. Leading military commanders of the Central Powers included Field Marshals Paul von Hindenburg and August von Mackensen and Generals Erich von Falkenhayn, Erich Ludendorff, and Helmuth Johannes von Moltke of Germany; and Field Marshal Conrad von Hötzendorf and Gen. Arz von Straussenberg of Austria-Hungary.

Battlefronts. Most fighting took place on the western, eastern, and southern battlefronts.

The *western front* at its greatest length stretched about 600 miles (970 kilometers), from the English Channel to the border of Switzerland. Men in trenches faced each other across barbed-wire barriers and *no-man's land.*

The *eastern front* extended over 1,100 miles (1,770 kilometers), from Riga on the Baltic Sea to the shores of the Black Sea. It ran about parallel to the eastern boundaries of Germany and Austria-Hungary in 1914.

The *southern front* ran from Switzerland along the Italian frontier to Trieste for 320 miles (515 kilometers).

Another battlefront extended across the southern Balkans. Other areas that saw fighting included Egypt, Mesopotamia (now Iraq), Palestine, and German colonies in Asia, Africa, and the Pacific Ocean.

Strategy of the War. Count Alfred von Schlieffen, chief of the German General Staff, had planned Germany's basic strategy by 1905. It was modified in 1912. The Schlieffen plan called for German armies to crush France in a quick campaign by sweeping in a great fan-like drive through neutral Belgium. Next, the Germans planned to crush Russia, then force an isolated Great Britain to surrender. After conquering the Balkans, German troops would sweep into Asia. Von Schlieffen expected a two-front war. But he planned for Austria-Hungary and a small German force in East Prussia to handle the eastern front.

Allied strategy called for attacks by the French armies in the Lorraine area immediately upon the outbreak of war. On the eastern front, Russia intended to invade Germany through East Prussia, and attack Austria-Hungary in Galicia. It hoped to strike westward at Germany while Allied armies rolled eastward.

New Weapons and new methods of warfare developed during World War I. In September, 1916, the British army first used the tank (see TANK, MILITARY). The war might have ended sooner if the British had waited to use tanks until they had more available. The Germans, horrified at first by the strange steel monsters, found that field guns were effective against them. Trench warfare forced the fighting nations to develop grenades, trench mortars, and heavy artillery. Effective weapons included field guns such as the German 77 mm. and French 75 mm., and medium artillery such as the German 5.9 inch howitzer. Two famous long range guns were called *Big Bertha*. The Germans used the first Big Bertha against Liège, Belgium, in 1914, and brought up the second in 1918 to shell Paris from 75 miles (121 kilometers) away.

The submarine came into use for the first time on a large scale. The German submarine fleet threatened British naval supremacy. But submarine warfare failed to starve out Great Britain, and Germany's sinking of unarmed ships helped bring the United States into the war on the side of the Allies. See SUBMARINE.

Air warfare also developed in World War I. At the outbreak of the war, each army had several hundred planes. These had no fixed guns, and were intended mainly for reconnaissance. During the war, airplanes directed shellfire, photographed enemy bases, shot at troops, dropped leaflets, and battled each other. By 1917, pursuit planes could travel about 150 miles (241 kilometers) per hour, and bombers could carry about two tons of bombs (see AIR FORCE). The Germans used airships called *Zeppelins* for observation, and for bombing raids (see AIRSHIP).

In 1915, Germany first used poison gas. Soon the Allies began to use it. The effects in the beginning were serious. But both sides developed protective measures and reduced the danger.

The War Begins (1914)

Death of an Archduke. The conflicts between Austria-Hungary and Serbia chiefly concerned ownership of Bosnia and Hercegovina. The Serbs, a nationalistic people, believed they had a natural right to the two provinces. With them, Serbia had a direct outlet to the Adriatic Sea and could ship products, especially hogs, to market without having to cross Austro-Hungarian soil. Austria-Hungary closed its borders whenever Serbian political agitation became too tense. The Serbs called this practice "pig politics."

A group of Serbs formed a secret society called "Union or Death," or "the Black Hand." This group attempted to terrorize Austro-Hungarian officials into satisfying Serbia's territorial aims. Members included high Serbian army officers. The society learned that Archduke Francis Ferdinand, heir to the thrones of Austria and Hungary and nephew of Emperor Francis Joseph, planned to visit neighboring Bosnia in June, 1914. The Black Hand decided to kill him. Some young Bosnian revolutionaries were living in Serbia because the Austro-Hungarian government had exiled them as undesirable. They received training in assassination.

As Ferdinand and his wife rode through Sarajevo, a Bosnian revolutionary threw a bomb at their car. The bomb exploded in the roadway behind the automobile. Later that day, Gavrilo Princip, another of the trained

Imperial War Museum

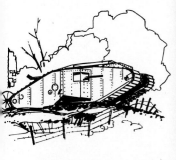

Tanks fought in battle for the first time at Flers-Courcelette, France, in a British offensive in September, 1916.

Automatic Weapons made the war unusually bloody. Gunners wore gas masks in the Battles of the Somme in 1916.

assassins, jumped on the running board and fired the shots that touched off World War I.

The Austro-Hungarian government had no proof that Serbian officials were involved in the murder plot. But Foreign Minister Leopold von Berchtold suspected them. He also wanted to end Serbian agitation against Austria-Hungary. Von Berchtold obtained a promise from Germany that it would support him in any move he might make against Serbia. Then he won Emperor Francis Joseph to his view. On July 23, 1914, von Berchtold sent a harsh ultimatum to Serbia demanding that it allow Austrian officials to take part in the trials of persons involved in the assassination.

Mobilization. Russia hoped to extend its political influence over the Balkans. It assured the Serbs that it would not allow Austrian aggression against their country. Serbia then rejected the demand for Austro-Hungarian officials to take part in the murder trial. Serbia suggested that the conflict be submitted to an international conference for arbitration. Austria-Hungary refused, and declared war on Serbia on July 28, 1914. It realized that it could count on help from Germany if Russia came to Serbia's aid.

Germany and Great Britain tried vainly to keep the war from spreading to other countries. Germany feared that it would have to fight on two fronts—against Russia in the east and against Russia's ally, France, in the west. When the Germans found Russia hastily preparing for hostilities, they knew that war was at hand. On Aug. 1, 1914, Germany declared war on Russia. It asked France to declare its neutrality. When the French an-

swered evasively, it declared war on France on August 3.

The March Through Belgium. Germany's war plans provided for an invasion of Belgium. But, as a political gesture, Germany asked Belgium for permission to send troops across its territory as the easiest road to Paris. Actually, German troops were already moving across the Belgian border. Germany promised to pay after the war for any damage to Belgian property. But King Albert I of Belgium refused permission. He is reported to have declared: "Belgium is a nation, not a road." A treaty which had been signed in 1839 guaranteed that Belgium would always be neutral. When Great Britain asked Germany to respect this treaty, German Chancellor Theobald von Bethmann-Hollweg called it "a scrap of paper." On August 2, German troops moved into Luxembourg, and on August 4 they invaded Belgium. Britain promptly declared war on Germany.

Germany, Austria-Hungary, and their allies became known as the *Central Powers*, because of their position in Europe. The nations opposing them were known as the *Allies*, or the *Associated Powers*.

The small Belgian army resisted courageously. But it could not halt the Germans. The Allies sent British troops and a French army to help the Belgians. After the Belgian cities of Liège and Brussels fell, Gen. Joseph Joffre of France allowed his soldiers to retreat slowly while he assembled more troops. German cavalry pushed to within 15 miles (24 kilometers) of Paris. But as their main forces wheeled eastward to the Marne River, they were attacked from the front and side by the Paris garrison under Gen. Joseph Gallieni, and by a new army under Gen. Michel Joseph Maunoury. The battle halted the Germans and shook their nerve. The Ger-

The Eastern Front developed when Russia invaded Germany and Austria-Hungary at the beginning of the war in 1914. Revolutions in Russia in 1917 weakened that country's war effort, and in 1918 Russia gave up a huge area in the Treaty of Brest-Litovsk.

Allies

Central Powers

Neutral countries

International boundary 1914

Farthest advance westward by Russia

Farthest advance eastward by the Central Powers

✳ Major battle

• City or town

0   300 Miles

0   300 Kilometers

WORLD BOOK map

Trenches protected troops from enemy gunfire. American soldiers in a stone-lined trench, *left*, used hand grenades to drive back advancing enemy troops. The diagram below shows an elaborate trench system constructed by troops in some areas.

Burton Holmes from Ewing Galloway

Barbed wire · 200 yds. (180 m) · 300 yds. (270 m) · Support line · Dugout 30 ft. (9 m) down · H.Q. · Field artillery 500-1,000 yds. (469-910 m) to the rear · Front line · Reserve line · To enemy lines · Communication trench

mans retreated to the Aisne River. More than 1½ million troops fought in the First Battle of the Marne. It marked the first turning point in the war, because it ended Germany's chances for a quick victory.

The Eastern Front. Russia, urged on by France, sent its armies into action before they were ready. In August, the Russian commander in chief, Grand Duke Nicholas Nicholaievich, sent forces across the Galician frontier, and the Russian First and Second armies into East Prussia. German reinforcements rushed to East Prussia from the west under Paul von Hindenburg, a retired general. The Germans were outnumbered, but von Hindenburg was able to deal with the two Russian armies separately because of poor communications between them. In a series of campaigns around Tannenberg and the swampy Masurian Lakes, Von Hindenburg crushed the Russian armies and cleared them from East Prussia. More than 300,000 Russian troops were killed, wounded, or reported missing. But in Galicia, the Russians killed and wounded more than 250,000 Austrian troops, and captured 100,000 others in the Battles of Lemberg during September and October. In the south, Austria-Hungary failed in three attempts to invade Serbia.

The Turks Enter the War. On August 2, the Ottoman Empire (now Turkey) had signed a secret treaty with Germany. The Allies did not know about the treaty, and continued negotiations to keep the Turks neutral. In the last days of October, Turkish warships bombarded Russian ports on the Black Sea. France, Great Britain, and Russia declared war on the Ottoman Empire. Turkish troops fought the Allies in Mesopotamia, Palestine, Sinai, and the Caucasus Mountains in Russia.

The War at Sea. During the first year of fighting, surface ships played the leading role in the war at sea. The British Grand Fleet bottled up the German High Sea Fleet in its home waters near the Kiel Canal. The few German surface ships at sea attacked Allied shipping in the North Seas. But German submarine attacks gradually grew in strength. Vice Adm. Maximilian von Spee's Pacific Ocean Squadron sank two British cruisers near Coronel, Chile, while heading for Germany. In a later battle, the British fleet under Vice Adm. Sir Doveton Sturdee destroyed Spee's fleet off the Falkland Islands.

Colonies Captured. The Allies attacked Germany's overseas colonies shortly after the German invasion of Belgium. New Zealanders captured Samoa, in the Pacific. Australian troops occupied German New Guinea. In late August, Japan declared war on Germany and seized German holdings in China. Japanese forces also occupied German islands in the Pacific, including the Marianas, Carolines, and Marshalls.

The Second Year (1915)

Little ground changed hands on the western front in the second year of World War I. The Central Powers made their main assault on the eastern front. Italy joined the Allies, making easier the Allied control of the Mediterranean Sea and forcing Austria-Hungary to fight a two-front war. The Allies failed to open the Dardanelles for shipments of infantry and weapons to Russia.

Trench Warfare. Fighting on the western front reached a standstill early in 1915. The deadlock continued for almost two years. Both sides dug in and built networks of trenches that stretched for about 600 miles (970 kilometers) across France and Belgium. In some places, less than 100 yards (91 meters) separated the opposing lines.

Between these lines of trenches lay *no-man's land.*

"Over the top!" a battlefront commander would shout. Infantrymen with fixed bayonets climbed out of the trenches and dashed across no-man's land. They flung their grenades, struggled through barbed-wire entanglements, and ran around gaping shell holes. Machine gun fire took a heavy toll and made successful charges almost impossible.

The fighting forces developed trench systems greater than ever built before. They built second and third lines of trenches parallel to the first line. Additional trenches connected these lines, so that troops and supplies could be moved to and from the front. Huge underground caverns served as first-aid stations, supply centers, and living quarters for troops. The trenches protected soldiers from enemy bullets. But troops found life miserable in trenches even when they were not fighting. Rain filled the dugouts with water and mud, and rats swarmed through the vermin-infested trenches. During lulls in the fighting, battle communiqués reported: "All quiet on the western front."

On April 22, the Germans unleashed a new weapon in their drive through Ypres to seize Calais on the French coast. French soldiers found a greenish-white mist drifting toward them from the enemy line. The Germans had released poisonous chlorine gas. Some French troops fled when the gas attacked their eyes and throats. British and Canadian forces moved quickly to seal the gap in the Allied line. But the Germans did not have enough reserve forces to take advantage of the breach. The gas had been used experimentally, and some German commanders had doubted its value. The Second Battle of Ypres was the first action by Canadians in Europe.

On the eastern front, Field Marshal August von Mackensen's German Eleventh Army and Austrian Fourth Army spearheaded a powerful offensive in northern Galicia and eastern Poland. By autumn, the Central Powers had driven the Russians from most of Galicia, Poland, and Lithuania. On October 14, Bulgaria joined the Central Powers. German and Bulgarian troops under von Mackensen later conquered Serbia.

The Dardanelles. Early in January, 1915, Russia asked for an attack that would relieve the pressure on its troops in the Caucasus. The Allies planned to force open the Dardanelles so they could ship supplies to Russia quickly. They formed an expeditionary force to capture the Gallipoli Peninsula and Constantinople (now Istanbul) in Turkey. An Allied fleet destroyed the forts at the entrance of the straits and advanced part way up. But on March 18, the fleet had to turn back after ships struck explosive mines. On April 25, Allied soldiers landed on the peninsula. Unable to push inland, they withdrew at the year's end.

In October, 1915, the Allies had sent troops from Gallipoli through Salonika, Greece, on the only usable road to Serbia. They advanced to the Serbian frontier, but were cut off by Bulgarian soldiers and retreated to Salonika. The Allies advanced into Serbia—as far as Monastir—in November, 1916.

The Italian Front. Italy had been a member of the Triple Alliance, but it did not enter the war immediately. It claimed that the Central Powers were fighting

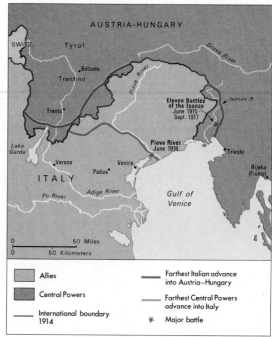

The Southern Front Campaigns began in 1915, when Italy invaded the Trentino and Trieste regions of southern Austria. Austrian and German troops later forced the Italians to retreat.

an offensive war, and that it had not agreed to take part in such a war. Actually, Italy wanted to take some Austrian territories along its border. After long negotiations, Italy signed the secret Treaty of London in 1915 with France, Great Britain, and Russia. Italy agreed to join the Allies in exchange for land in Europe and Africa. Italy declared war on Austria-Hungary in 1915, and on Germany in 1916. As their first offensive action, the Italians advanced all along the border to improve their general position for future operations. This offensive came to a halt after Italy made the gains it wanted, particularly in the Trentino in southern Austria.

Action on the High Seas. Italy's entry into the war helped the Allies control the Mediterranean Sea. On Feb. 4, 1915, Germany declared all waters surrounding the British Isles to be a "war zone." It warned that all enemy merchant ships within the zone would be sunk. The United States announced that it would hold Germany responsible for any loss of American ships and lives in the zone. On May 7, a German submarine sank the British passenger liner *Lusitania* off Queenstown. The death list of 1,198 persons included 128 Americans. After the United States protested, Germany ordered its submarines not to attack neutral or passenger ships.

The War in Africa. The Allied fleet took part in the African campaign by blockading German East Africa. German troops in Cameroon and Southwest Africa surrendered to the Allies in 1915. Turkish troops under German leadership attacked the Suez Canal in February, but British and Indian forces turned them back.

The Third Year (1916)

Great military drives broke out on all fronts in 1916. Germany attacked at Verdun, and the Austro-Hungarians and Italians fought battles along the Isonzo River. The Allies took the offensive along the Somme River in France, and the Russians assaulted Polish Galicia. The fleets of Great Britain and Germany clashed off Jutland in the greatest naval battle of the war. The Central Powers made a bid for peace based on "the map of Europe," keeping what they had won.

The Battle of Verdun. On the western front, Germany tried to pierce the French line with a massive attack on Verdun. Crown Prince Frederick Wilhelm's artillery shelled the city for 24 hours, starting February 21. Then his troops attacked on a 20-mile (32-kilometer) front. A ring of defenses surrounded the fortress city. Gen. Henri Pétain, commanding the French Second Army that defended Verdun, vowed: "They shall not pass!" Wilhelm's troops advanced only about 4 miles (6 kilometers) in six months. They penetrated to within 4 miles of the city by June. Unable to advance farther, the Germans went on the defensive. The French counterattacked. They suffered more than 540,000 casualties, and the Germans lost more than 430,000 men.

The Battles of the Somme. In the north, Gen. Sir Douglas Haig's British troops began an attack on the Somme front on July 1, to relieve pressure on Verdun. In the Battle of Flers-Courcelette, Britain introduced a new weapon, the tank. In the Battles of the Somme, Germany lost more than 500,000 men and the Allies more than 600,000. Kaiser Wilhelm II dismissed Gen. Erich von Falkenhayn as chief of the German General Staff, and appointed Hindenburg in his place. In September, Hindenburg became supreme commander of all Central Powers forces. Gen. Erich Ludendorff continued as his chief assistant.

The Brusilov Offensive. In May, Field Marshal Conrad von Hötzendorf's Austro-Hungarian armies took the offensive in the rocky, mountainous Trentino area. The Italians fell back and called on the Russians for help. In order to divert some Austrian armies from the Trentino, Gen. Alexei Brusilov's Russian troops attacked in Galicia as part of a general Russian offensive. His armies captured more than 400,000 prisoners, and advanced as much as 60 miles (97 kilometers). But the offensive came to a halt when German reinforcements arrived. Russia suffered more than a million casualties. But the Brusilov offensive forced Austria-Hungary to halt its attacks in the Trentino.

On Other Fronts. Austria-Hungary had sent some of its troops from the Trentino to Galicia. Gen. Luigi Cadorna's Italian forces then renewed their offensive along the Isonzo River. But by the end of the year, the troops had dug in for trench warfare.

When Romania saw that the Central Powers were not winning, it decided to join the Allies. On August 17, it signed a secret treaty that promised Romanian rule over Transylvania and the Banat, a region in Hungary. Romanian forces invaded Transylvania. By January, 1917, Austrian, Bulgarian, German, and Turkish troops swept through Romania and captured Bucharest.

The Battle of Jutland. The greatest naval battle of World War I took place on May 31 and June 1, 1916, off the entrance to the Skagerrak Strait, an arm of the North Sea. Adm. Reinhard Scheer, commander in chief of the German High Sea Fleet, felt that he could defeat the British Grand Fleet only if he could divide it and fight each part separately. He directed Vice Adm. Franz

Hipper's scouting squadron to attract a part of the British fleet. His own main battle force would then follow Hipper and destroy the main British fleet. Hipper's ships accidentally came into contact with the British battle cruiser fleet under Vice Adm. David Beatty. Beatty drew the German High Sea Fleet toward the British fleet under Adm. John Jellicoe, who sailed between the German ships and their home port at Kiel.

In the battle that followed, the British lost three battle cruisers, three armored cruisers, eight destroyers, and 6,097 killed. Germany lost one battleship, one battle cruiser, four light cruisers, five destroyers, and 2,551 killed. Germany hailed the battle as a great victory. But Great Britain continued to control the high seas. The German fleet remained almost inactive after the battle.

The War in the Air. Both sides used airplanes for large-scale fighting in the battles of Verdun and the Somme. Air battles became common as each side tried to force the other from the skies. No longer did enemy pilots merely wave to each other as they passed. At first, pilots fired pistols or rifles at one another. Then their planes carried machine guns. Pilots who shot down five or more enemy aircraft were called *aces* (see WAR ACES). Leading aces included Manfred von Richthofen of Germany, René Fonck of France, Billy Bishop of Canada, Albert Ball of Great Britain, and Eddie Rickenbacker of the United States. Toward the end of the war, battles between squadrons of 10 to 50 airplanes replaced combat between single pilots. Before the United States entered the war in 1917, some Americans had volunteered to serve in the French army as pilots. They formed an organization called the *Escadrille Américaine*, later the *Lafayette Escadrille*.

The Germans developed dirigibles as part of their air forces. Beginning in 1915, they sent dirigibles and airplanes to bomb London. But the cigar-shaped airships were fairly easy targets for fighter planes.

The Fourth Year (1917)

Early in 1917, the Central Powers seemed to enjoy a relatively strong position. They occupied Montenegro, Poland, Romania, Serbia, most of Belgium, and northern France. Then the United States entered the war, and the tide began to turn in favor of the Allies.

Baghdad and Jerusalem were captured by the British in 1917. These were the only major Allied gains of the year. A British-Indian force had landed on the Persian Gulf in 1915. The Turks besieged British troops at Kut al-Amara (Al Kūt), south of Baghdad. On April 29, 1916, the entire force of 10,000 British troops surrendered because of threatened starvation. The surrender was a severe blow to British prestige. But in March, 1917, Baghdad fell to the Allies. In December, Gen. Edmund Allenby's forces marched into Jerusalem.

The Siegfried Line. To save manpower and strengthen their position on the western front, the Germans retreated to a specially prepared battle line. Generals Hindenburg and Ludendorff had ordered it built. It was called the *Siegfried Line* by the Germans and the *Hindenburg Line* by the Allies, and it ran behind the existing German trench system from Arras to Laon, France. For 20 months, this line was the most important part of the western front, and most leading German

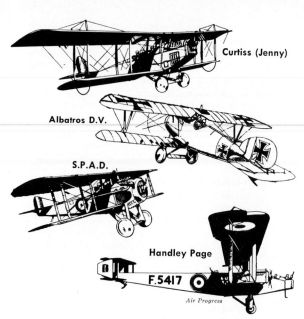

Curtiss (Jenny)

Albatros D.V.

S.P.A.D.

Handley Page

F.5417

Air Progress

Airplanes clashed over the battle lines and tried to sweep the enemy from the skies. Individual pilots fought in *dogfights*. Later battles took place between *circuses*, or groups of aircraft. Pilots who shot down five or more aircraft were called "war aces."

generals served there. In 1917, the Allies carried out the only offensives along the front, including fierce attacks by the British at Passchendaele and Cambrai. But the year ended without important changes in territory.

Revolution in Russia. The Allies faced disaster on the eastern front. The Russians overthrew their government and forced Czar Nicholas II to abdicate in March (February in the Russian calendar then in use). Russia's new government said it would carry on the war. Brusilov's armies advanced in the Carpathian Mountains. But the Germans counterattacked and moved toward Russia's capital, Petrograd (now Leningrad).

Early in November (October in the old Russian calendar), the Bolsheviks under Lenin and Leon Trotsky overthrew the government of Alexander Kerensky and arranged for an armistice with the Central Powers. On Dec. 8, 1917, the new Russian government ended hostilities and began peace talks with Germany.

Propaganda Warfare reached a new high in 1917. Both sides tried to gain additional allies, or to keep other countries neutral. They sought to keep up the spirits of their own people, and to destroy the morale of the enemy. They spread stories of enemy atrocities, such as tales of soldiers cutting off children's hands. Allied propagandists called the Germans "Huns." German propaganda agents claimed that an Allied victory would bring "the end of the German people."

The Submarine Menace also reached its peak in 1917. In January, Germany announced that its submarines would sink any vessel bound into or out of any Allied port. It extended the war zone to cover the high seas. Germany hoped that unrestricted submarine warfare would win a quick victory before the United States could intervene effectively on the side of the Allies.

Both sides had frequently violated the rights of neutral ships. The British regularly seized neutral shipping on the high seas, claiming that it might fall into enemy hands. Germany sank merchant vessels without warn-

ing. The Germans claimed their submarines were fragile and easy targets for ships' guns when on the surface. They said they could not risk stopping ships to check their papers. The Allies used depth bombs, listening instruments, mines, steel nets, and, later, convoys to destroy or escape submarines. In March, Germany torpedoed several American merchant ships without warning. The next month, German submarines sank 900,000 long tons (910,000 metric tons) of Allied shipping, the all-time high for the war.

The United States Enters the War. Germany's unrestricted submarine warfare directly caused the United States to join the Allies. Only three years before, few Americans had thought that they would become involved in the war. The news of the outbreak of the war in 1914 had astonished most Americans. President Woodrow Wilson had declared that the United States would be "neutral in fact as well as in name."

Even after a German submarine torpedoed the *Lusitania* in 1915, killing 128 Americans, Wilson thought the United States would not enter the war. But as a measure of preparation, the government set up military-training camps for men who were willing to spend their vacations learning how to become soldiers.

In June, 1916, Congress increased the size of the army. Three months later, it voted more than $7 billion for national defense, the largest sum appropriated up to that time. Wilson authorized U.S. merchant vessels to carry guns as protection against submarines.

The British intercepted a German message to Mexico in January, 1917, that helped persuade the United States to enter the war. The message, known as the *Zimmerman note*, indicated that Germany had approached Mexico for an alliance in case of war with the United States. As payment, Germany promised to help Mexico recover some land it had ceded to the United States after the Mexican War.

A record number of sinkings of U.S. merchant ships

settled American doubts. On April 2, Wilson read a war message to Congress. "The world must be made safe for democracy," he said. On April 6, the United States declared war on Germany. It associated itself with the Allies, but did not sign a treaty of alliance with them.

Life in America changed from leisure to a feverish pace to win the war. But the country was almost totally unprepared. The government adopted a selective-service act that required all men between 21 and 30 to register for the draft. Its committee on public information sought to make the Allied cause known in almost every city, town, and village. "Four-minute" men promoted the sale of Liberty bonds and support for the draft. Billboards shouted slogans such as "Food Will Win the War." A stern-looking Uncle Sam appeared on army recruiting posters to announce "I Want *You.*" Soldiers and civilians alike sang "Over There" to let the world know that the Yanks were coming.

Mobilizing for War. Six major wartime agencies mobilized the country's economic and industrial system for war. A War Industries Board under Bernard Baruch controlled war production. The Shipping Board tried to get ships built faster than the Germans could sink them. A Food Administration urged people in the country to save food. It promoted "meatless" days. A Rail Administration operated the railroads. A Fuel Administration directed the civilian uses of gasoline. The War Trade Board controlled exports and imports.

Feelings against Germany grew stronger as the war progressed. Schools stopped offering courses in German language and literature. Anyone who criticized the war effort was suspected of working for the enemy. The Department of Justice received wide powers to investigate espionage and sedition cases.

Espionage. On July 30, 1916, German saboteurs set off an explosion at the Black Tom Island ammunition shipping station, near Jersey City, N.J. The year before, Heinrich Friedrich Albert, an agent of the German government, had carelessly left a briefcase in a New York elevated railway car. From secret documents in the briefcase, the United States traced propaganda and sabotage plans to the German and Austrian embassies.

"Lafayette, We Are Here!" American Expeditionary Forces under Gen. John J. Pershing began landing in France on June 26, 1917. Remembering that the French had aided the colonists in the Revolutionary War, Col. Charles E. Stanton, one of Pershing's staff officers, announced on July 4: "Lafayette, we are here!" During the war, the government inducted more than 2,800,000 men into military service. The American armed forces totaled 4,800,000 men. About 2 million American soldiers served in France. The first units entered the trenches in October. Pershing opposed the use of American soldiers as individual replacements. He insisted that they fight as units. These units formed the American First Army.

The American Expeditionary Forces took part in 13 major operations of World War I. The Saint Mihiel

Submarines attacked Allied ships, sometimes stopping them first. The Germans declared a war zone around Great Britain, and warned Americans of the danger. In 1917, they began unrestricted submarine warfare, sinking Allied ships anywhere. The United States then declared war on Germany.

Bettmann Archive

Dancing in the Streets of many American cities greeted the news that the armistice ending the war had been signed.

The New York Times.

ARMISTICE SIGNED, END OF THE WAR!
BERLIN SEIZED BY REVOLUTIONISTS;
NEW CHANCELLOR BEGS FOR ORDER;
OUSTED KAISER FLEES TO HOLLAND

battle of September, 1918, was the first distinctly American offensive of the war. In this operation, Brig. Gen. Billy Mitchell directed the war's largest aerial assault, with 1,481 Allied airplanes taking part. U.S. naval forces in European waters helped the Allied fleets fight German submarines. Under the command of Rear Adm. William S. Sims, they also convoyed troops and transported war materials.

The Final Year (1918)

The Allies won final victory in 1918. Bulgaria, the Ottoman Empire, Austria-Hungary, and Germany signed armistices.

The Fourteen Points. On January 8, Wilson announced his Fourteen Points as the basis for a postwar peace settlement. The Fourteen Points included freedom of navigation, an end to secret diplomacy and trade barriers, a reduction in armaments, an adjustment of colonial claims, the evacuation of Central Powers troops from Allied countries, the re-establishment of Poland, the creation of an association of nations to work for permanent peace, independence for the subject peoples of Austria-Hungary, and home rule for the non-Turkish parts of the Ottoman Empire. Allied planes dropped thousands of copies of the Fourteen Points over enemy countries. The Fourteen Points gave hope to many enemy peoples for a just peace settlement, and encouraged them to overthrow their governments.

The Last Campaigns. After a quiet winter on the western front, the Central Powers planned to overwhelm the Allied armies before the full benefit of American aid could arrive. Hindenburg had promised the German people that he would be in Paris by April 1. In March, German armies under Ludendorff struck along a 50-mile (80-kilometer) front, and the Allies gave way. In April, the Allies finally formed a unified command. They appointed Marshal Ferdinand Foch as General-in-Chief of the Allied Armies in France.

On May 31, the Germans reached the banks of the Marne. The U.S. 4th Marine Brigade made strong attacks in Belleau Wood, on the road to Paris. It lost nearly 7,800 men. France later renamed the spot "the Wood of the Brigade of Marines" to honor their heroic stand. American troops blocked an enemy offensive at Château-Thierry, and helped prevent the Germans from crossing the Marne to Paris. Then Foch began a series of hammering blows between Reims and the

North Sea. Five major battles raged at the same time. After July 18, the Allied offensive never stopped until the armistice. On August 8, the Allies, led by Canadian and Australian troops, attacked at Amiens. A Canadian corps advanced 14,000 yards (12,800 meters) in one of the war's deepest advances made in a single day. On August 26, the Germans began retreating to the Siegfried Line. Ludendorff described this battle as "the Black Day" in the history of the German army. In September, the Allies swept toward Saint Mihiel and the Meuse-Argonne region. American soldiers took over a large portion of the battle line, and helped break through the fortified Siegfried Line. About 1,200,000 Americans fought in the Battle of the Meuse-Argonne. About one of every ten was killed or wounded.

The Collapse of Russia. In February, peace negotiations broke down between Germany and Russia, and the Germans continued their invasion. On March 3, the Russians signed the humiliating Treaty of Brest-Litovsk. By its terms, Russia gave up Finland, the Baltic States, Poland, and the Ukraine. Russia surrendered to Turkey the districts of Kars, Batum, and Ardahan south of the Caucasus Mountains.

A few months later, Romania also made peace with the Central Powers. It agreed to grant oil concessions and give up some territory.

In April, 1918, Allied forces landed in Vladivostok, Siberia, to help 60,000 Czechs and Slovaks who had been prisoners of war in Russia. In August, the Allies occupied Archangel to protect supplies there from Bolshevik troops. The following summer, other Allied soldiers landed in Murmansk to fight against the Bolsheviks in the Russian civil war (see RUSSIA [History]).

The End of the Central Powers. Austria-Hungary also planned a huge drive to make Italy withdraw from the war. But floods and resistance by Gen. Armando Díaz's Italian troops halted the advancing Austro-Hungarian armies in June. In October, Díaz launched an offensive to the northeast across the Piave River. He split the Austro-Hungarian armies in two and destroyed them.

Allied forces from Salonika broke the Bulgarian front in September. Bulgaria signed an armistice at Salonika on September 29. Another member of the Central Powers, the Ottoman Empire, signed an armistice on October 31. The Austro-Hungarian Empire was crumbling rapidly. In the fall of 1918, the Hungarians, Czechs, Slovaks, and Poles declared their independence. On

November 3, representatives of Emperor Charles I agreed to an armistice. Germany stood alone.

The Armistice. Sailors in the German High Sea Fleet at Kiel mutinied in late October. As the news spread, revolts broke out in other parts of Germany. Small mutinies flared among German troops as food and munitions supplies dwindled. Hindenburg told Kaiser Wilhelm II that, to avoid a catastrophe, Germany must seek an immediate armistice with the Allies. The Kaiser appointed Prince Max of Baden as Chancellor with the task of seeking an armistice. Prince Max appealed to President Wilson for armistice terms. On November 7, the world received a premature news story that the Germans had signed an armistice. This has been called "the false armistice."

A German armistice delegation went to Foch's headquarters near Rethondes in the Forest of Compiègne on November 7. Foch outlined the armistice terms: the Germans were to (1) evacuate all occupied territory, (2) surrender their arms and warships, (3) withdraw all forces from west of the Rhine, (4) return Allied prisoners, and (5) permit Allied troops to occupy German territory. Foch gave the Germans 72 hours to accept the terms. In Berlin, German socialists under Friedrich Ebert proclaimed a German Republic on November 9. Kaiser Wilhelm abdicated and fled to neutral Netherlands.

In a drizzling rain, the German delegates entered a railway car in the Compiègne Forest, and at 5 A.M. November 11, signed the armistice. Foch signed for the Allies and Secretary of State Matthias Erzberger signed for Germany. Foch ordered fighting to stop on all battlefronts at 11 A.M. World War I had ended.

At the time of the armistice, Allied troops stood about 120 miles (193 kilometers) from the Rhine River in northern Germany. The Allies established a neutral zone 6 miles (10 kilometers) wide along the river's east bank. British and Belgian troops occupied a bridgehead at Cologne. American forces had headquarters at the Koblenz bridgehead. French occupation forces held the bridgehead in the Mainz area. From these three points, the Allies commanded the Rhine valley. In 1923, the last American troops in Germany withdrew. The last Allied soldiers, French and Belgian, left in 1930.

Results of the War

The peace settlements after World War I healed many old wounds. But they inflicted new ones. The Allies had emphasized the principle of *self-determination* (the right of each nation to choose its own form of government). This caused the flame of nationalism to burn even more brightly than it had before 1914. The Allies formed the League of Nations and a World Court as agencies to settle disputes peacefully. But member nations did not always support these agencies in international disputes. The United States did not join the League of Nations (see LEAGUE OF NATIONS).

War Losses. World War I took the lives of twice as many men as all major wars from 1790 to 1913 put together. About 63 of every 100 servicemen who died came from the Allied armed forces. The number of civilian deaths in areas of actual war totaled about 5,000,000. Starvation, disease, and exposure accounted for about 80 of every 100 of these civilian deaths. Spanish influenza, which some persons blamed on the war, caused tens of millions of other deaths.

World War I cost more than $337 billion. Of this amount, about $186 billion paid the direct cost of carrying on the war. The Allies spent about two-thirds of the money used to buy guns, food, ammunitions, and other war materials. During the first three years of war, the fighting nations spent more than $85,000 every minute, and twice that amount in 1918. None of these figures includes the additional economic loss involved in servicemen crippled, the billions of dollars needed to pay interest on war debts, or the pensions paid to veterans and their families.

About $8 of every $10 spent for the war came from borrowed funds. The warring countries sold bonds to individuals and firms. For example, the United States borrowed money from its citizens through Liberty Loans. It also raised money by new taxes such as the excess-profits tax and the luxury tax. Tax receipts totaled about $11,280,000,000 in 1917 and 1918. The United States loaned more than $10 billion to the Allies (see WAR DEBT).

The Home Front in Europe came under intense bombing and shelling in areas of military operations. The war destroyed the industrial and community lives of many cities, towns, and villages in these areas. It closed or destroyed schools, factories, roads, and railroads. In many countries, people had to depend on food supplied by their governments.

In eastern Europe and the Balkans, millions of persons fled their homes in terror of invasion. Refugees moved helplessly from place to place in search of food, shelter, and clothing. They sought shelter in the ruins of blasted buildings and houses. After the war, those who tried to return to their homes often found that their towns or villages no longer existed.

During and immediately after the war, the Allies sent food and supplies to war-shattered countries. The United

— MILITARY CASUALTIES IN WORLD WAR I (1914-1918) —

	Total Casualties	Dead	Wounded	Prisoners or Missing
THE ALLIES				
Belgium (including colonials)	126,154	45,550	78,624	73,976
British Empire (including Canada, Ireland, and colonials)	2,384,860	942,135	2,110,933	197,874
France (including colonials)	4,968,000	1,368,000	3,600,000	557,000
Greece	38,310	23,098	14,145	1,067
Italy	2,197,000	680,000	947,000	600,000
Japan	13,245	1,344	11,901	(X)
Montenegro	*50,000	*3,000	*10,000	*7,000
Portugal	22,929	8,145	14,784	(X)
Romania	*405,545	*300,000	*105,000	*80,000
Russia	*9,150,000	*1,700,000	*4,950,000	*2,500,000
Serbia	*331,106	*45,000	*133,148	*152,958
United States	320,518	116,516	204,002	4,500
THE CENTRAL POWERS				
Austria-Hungary	4,820,000	1,200,000	3,620,000	2,200,000
Bulgaria	256,250	87,495	155,026	13,729
Germany	6,251,000	1,935,000	4,216,058	990,000
Ottoman Empire	2,290,000	725,000	1,565,000	(X)

From official estimates provided by respective embassies or military attachés.
* Unofficial. (X) Unavailable.

	The German Empire before the war
	Austria-Hungary before the war
	The Russian Empire before the war
	Serbia before the war
	Montenegro before the war
·······	Boundaries after the war

The Peace Treaties. The Allies signed separate peace treaties with Austria, Bulgaria, Germany, Hungary, and Turkey. The treaty with Germany was called *the Treaty of Versailles*. The Allies signed *the Treaty of Saint Germain* with Austria and *the Treaty of Trianon* with Hungary. Bulgaria signed *the Treaty of Neuilly*, and Turkey *the Treaty of Sèvres*. All five treaties together were called *the Peace of Paris*. The United States did not ratify the Treaty of Versailles, but signed a separate treaty with Germany.

Many historians consider the Treaty of Versailles particularly harsh. The agreement declared that Germany was solely responsible for World War I, and reduced Germany's

States supplied food, clothing, and medicine. Herbert Hoover directed Allied relief and reconstruction. He organized the American Relief Administration to care for children in liberated and former enemy territory.

Peace Aims. The peacemakers who met in Paris in 1919 hoped to create a new and better world. But the Allied nations had not agreed on a common peace program during the war. France, Great Britain, and Italy did not protest against President Woodrow Wilson's Fourteen Points when he announced them (see WILSON, WOODROW [World War I Begins]). But they did not officially accept them. Wilson tried to wipe out the grievances that had helped to bring on the war. He tried to ignore secret treaties, such as the London Treaty of 1915, which followed the theory that "to the victor belong the spoils." In the end, the peacemakers disregarded about half of Wilson's program. But Wilson hoped that the League of Nations would correct any injustices and mistakes in the final peace settlements.

The Paris peace conference arranged for the evacuation of enemy troops from Allied countries and gave independence to the subject peoples of Austria-Hungary. The peacemakers took colonies away from Germany and provinces from Turkey, but did not adjust all colonial claims. The Allies disarmed the Central Powers.

size by one-eighth and its population by 6,500,000. The treaty took away all Germany's colonies and overseas investments, a sixth of its farm land, an eighth of its livestock, and a tenth of its factories. It cut down Germany's merchant fleet, abolished its navy, and limited its army to about the size of the Belgian army. See VERSAILLES, TREATY OF.

The treaties with the other Central Powers followed closely the one with Germany. Germany's allies had to limit their armaments, pay reparations, admit guilt in starting the war, and give written promise that they would treat minority groups within their borders fairly.

Each peace treaty contained the Covenant of the League of Nations. It gave the League responsibility for enforcing the treaty provisions. The Paris conference created a mandate system to be administered by the League (see MANDATED TERRITORY). Many former possessions of Germany and the Ottoman Empire became League mandates under one of the Allied nations.

Changes in the World's Map. The world, particularly Europe, took on a new look after the war. Three independent countries—Austria, Czechoslovakia, and Hungary—emerged from the old Austro-Hungarian Empire. Allied diplomats made a new Poland out of Austrian, German, and Russian territory. They formed

Yugoslavia by adding to Serbia large portions of Austria-Hungary, Bulgaria, and Montenegro. Romania was doubled in size. The peace conference awarded additional territory to Greece and Italy. The Ottoman Empire lost Armenia (now mostly parts of Turkey and Russia), Palestine (later divided between Jordan and Israel), Mesopotamia (now Iraq), Syria, and territorial claims in Africa. In 1917-1918, Estonia, Finland, Latvia, and Lithuania declared their independence from Russia.

A wave of republicanism swept Europe after the war. In 1914, only five nations had republican forms of government where elected representatives governed the country. By 1932, this number had increased to 16. Germany, Austria, and the Ottoman Empire replaced their imperial rulers with republican governments.

World War I and its aftermath led to the greatest economic depression in history during the early 1930's. The consequences of the war and the problems of adjustment to peace led to unrest in almost every nation. In some European nations, conditions allowed dictators to seize power (see COMMUNISM; FASCISM; NAZISM).

The victorious Allies of World War I made no real effort to cooperate in enforcing the peace. They allowed their own military power to decline, so that they were unprepared for World War II.   PETER YOUNG

Related Articles. See the History sections of WORLD BOOK articles on the countries that took part in World War I. See also the following articles:

BATTLE AREAS

Alsace-Lorraine	Jutland, Battle of	Verdun, Battles
Balkans	Rijeka	of
Flanders Field	Saar	Vimy Ridge,
Gallipoli Peninsula	Siegfried Line	Battle of

ALLIED MILITARY LEADERS

Albert I	Jellicoe, Sir John R.
Allenby, Lord	Kitchener, Horatio H.
Beatty, David	March, Peyton C.
Bishop, Billy	Mitchell, Billy
Byng, Julian H. G.	Pershing, John J.
Currie, Sir Arthur W.	Pétain, Henri Philippe
Foch, Ferdinand	Piłsudski, Józef
French, John D. P.	Rickenbacker, Eddie
Haig, Earl	York, Alvin C.

ALLIED CIVILIAN LEADERS

Asquith, Herbert H.	Nicholas (II) of Russia
Baruch, Bernard M.	Orlando, Vittorio E.
Clemenceau, Georges	Poincaré, Raymond
Grey, Edward	Venizelos, Eleutherios
Hoover, Herbert C.	Wilson, Woodrow
Lloyd George, David	

CENTRAL POWERS MILITARY LEADERS

Hindenburg, Paul von	Tirpitz, Alfred von
Ludendorff, Erich F. W.	

CENTRAL POWERS CIVILIAN LEADERS

Bethmann-Hollweg,	Wilhelm (II)
Theobald von	Zeppelin, Count von

OTHER BIOGRAPHIES

Atatürk, Kemal	Lawrence, T. E.
Cavell, Edith L.	Lenin, V. I.
Constantine (I)	Mata Hari

FORCES, MATERIALS, AND WEAPONS

Air Force	Artillery	Chemical-Biological-
Air Force, U.S.	Automobile	Radiological
Airship	(History)	Warfare
Army	Aviation	Machine Gun
Army, U.S.	Camouflage	Navy

Navy, U.S.	Submarine	Tank, Military

ORGANIZATIONS

American Legion	Gold Star Mothers, American
American Legion	Red Cross
Auxiliary	

TREATIES

Neuilly, Treaty of	Sèvres, Treaty of
Rapallo, Treaties of	Trianon, Treaty of
Saint Germain, Treaty of	Versailles, Treaty of

OTHER RELATED ARTICLES

Fourteen Points	Neutrality	Unknown Soldier
League of Nations	Refugee	Veterans Day
Lusitania	Stars and Stripes	War Aces
Mandated	Triple Alliance	War Crime
Territory	Triple Entente	War Debt

Outline

I. Causes of the War
  A. Nationalism   C. Competition for Colonies
  B. Military Alliances D. Secret Diplomacy

II. Men, Battlefronts, and Strategy
  A. Men Under Arms   D. Strategy of the War
  B. War Leaders   E. New Weapons
  C. Battlefronts

III. The War Begins (1914)
  A. Death of an Archduke E. The Turks Enter
  B. Mobilization   the War
  C. The March Through F. The War at Sea
    Belgium   G. Colonies Captured
  D. The Eastern Front

IV. The Second Year (1915)
  A. Trench Warfare   D. Action on the
  B. The Dardanelles   High Seas
  C. The Italian Front   E. The War in Africa

V. The Third Year (1916)
  A. The Battle of Verdun E. The Battle of Jut-
  B. The Battles of the Somme land
  C. The Brusilov Offensive F. The War in the
  D. On Other Fronts   Air

VI. The Fourth Year (1917)
  A. Baghdad and Jerusalem E. The Submarine
  B. The Siegfried Line   Menace
  C. Revolution   F. The United States
    in Russia   Enters the War
  D. Propaganda Warfare G. "Lafayette, We Are
      Here!"

VII. The Final Year (1918)
  A. The Fourteen Points D. The End of the
  B. The Last Campaigns   Central Powers
  C. The Collapse of Russia E. The Armistice

VIII. Results of the War
  A. War Losses   D. The Peace Treaties
  B. The Home Front   E. Changes in the
  C. Peace Aims   World's Map

Questions

What were four basic causes of World War I?
When did the war officially end?
What battle was the first turning point in the war?
Where were the major battlefronts?
What country had the most military casualties?
What country first used poison gas in the war? What country first used tanks?
What peace treaties were signed after the war?
How many American soldiers fought in France?
What directly caused the U.S. to join the Allies?
How did the warring countries raise the money to pay for the war?

Reading and Study Guide

See *World War I* in the RESEARCH GUIDE/INDEX, Volume 22, for a *Reading and Study Guide*.

WORLD WAR II

War Began on Sept. 1, 1939, when German aircraft, tanks, and motorized troops attacked Poland. Many Polish cities soon lay devastated. By early 1942, all major countries of the world were involved in the most destructive war in history.

WORLD WAR II killed more persons, cost more money, damaged more property, affected more people, and probably caused more far-reaching changes than any other war in history. It opened the atomic age, and brought sweeping changes in warfare. Trucks sped infantrymen to the battle front after aerial bombing, giant tanks, and pinpoint artillery had "softened" the enemy. Bombers and ballistic missiles rained death and destruction on soldiers, sailors, and civilians alike. Airplanes, warships, and ground forces worked together with split-second timing in amphibious attacks. Paratroops dropped from airplanes or landed in gliders.

The number of people killed, wounded, or missing between September, 1939, and September, 1945, can never be calculated. More than 10 million Allied servicemen and nearly 6 million military men from the Axis countries died in the war. World War II cost more than $1,150,000,000,000. More than 50 countries took part in the war, and the whole world felt its effects.

Men fought in almost every part of the world. The chief battlegrounds included Asia, Europe, North Africa, the Atlantic and Pacific oceans, and the Mediterranean Sea.

On Sept. 1, 1939, Germany attacked Poland. After this successful test of its *blitzkrieg* (lightning war) methods, the German war machine crushed six countries—Denmark, Norway, Belgium, Luxembourg, The Netherlands, and France—in three months in 1940. Adolf Hitler, the dictator of Germany, failed in his attempts to knock out Great Britain by bombing and submarine blockades. In 1941, Hitler's armies conquered Yugoslavia and Greece—which Italy had attacked after entering the war against France in 1940—and then marched into Russia. Japan's plans for expansion in the Far East led it to

War Ended on Sept. 2, 1945, less than a month after the Allies dropped atomic bombs on Hiroshima and Nagasaki, Japan.

Theodore Ropp, the contributor of this article, is Professor of History at Duke University and author of War in the Modern World. *The article was reviewed by Admiral Chester W. Nimitz and General Carl Spaatz.*

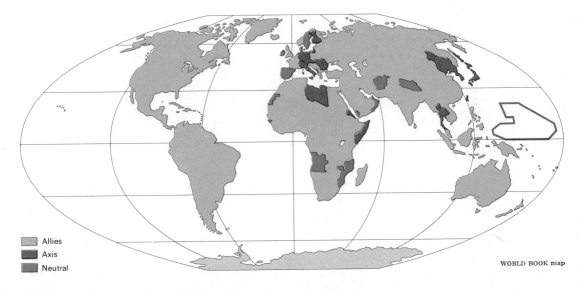

Allies
Axis
Neutral

In World War II, about 50 Allied nations joined forces against Germany, Japan, and the other Axis powers. Few countries remained neutral. The map shows a colony or dependency in the same color as the country governing it.

attack Pearl Harbor on Dec. 7, 1941, bringing the United States into the war. After a series of disasters, the Allies took the offensive. They halted Axis advances at El Alamein in North Africa, off Midway Island in the Pacific, and at Stalingrad (now Volgograd) in Russia. Amphibious invasions of Pacific islands brought the Allies to Japan's doorstep. In Europe, Allied armies landed in Italy and France, then swept into Germany. Italy surrendered on Sept. 3, 1943, Germany on May 7, 1945, and Japan on Sept. 2, 1945. An uneasy peace, more like a cease-fire, returned to a war-weary world.

The Allies called the conflict *a war for survival*. Even before the guns were stilled, new threats to world peace arose. Russia sought to impose Communist dictatorships and stir up revolutions throughout the world. The atomic bomb and the ballistic missile served notice that any future world war would be even more destructive than World War II.

Causes of Conflict

The three main causes of World War II were: (1) the problems left unsolved by World War I, (2) the rise of dictatorships, and (3) the desire of Germany, Italy, and Japan for more territory.

Historians do not agree on the exact date when World War II began. Many consider the German invasion of Poland on Sept. 1, 1939, as the beginning of the war. Some say that it started when the Japanese invaded Manchuria on Sept. 18, 1931. Others even regard World Wars I and II as parts of the same conflict, with only a breathing spell between.

The world did not enjoy total peace from 1918 to 1939. Acts of aggression and "little wars" flared during this period, and dictators seized power in Russia, Italy, Germany, and other countries.

Problems Left by World War I

The Versailles Treaty. Many historians trace the roots of World War II to the Treaty of Versailles and

The Allies

Argentina (Mar. 27, 1945)
Australia (Sept. 3, 1939)
Belgium (May 10, 1940)
Bolivia (Apr. 7, 1943)
Brazil (Aug. 22, 1942)
Canada (Sept. 10, 1939)
Chile (Apr. 11, 1945)
China (Dec. 8, 1941)
Colombia (Nov. 26, 1943)
Costa Rica (Dec. 8, 1941)
Cuba (Dec. 9, 1941)
Czechoslovakia
   (Dec. 16, 1941)
Dominican Republic
   (Dec. 8, 1941)
Ecuador (Feb. 2, 1945)
Egypt (Feb. 24, 1945)
El Salvador (Dec. 8, 1941)
Ethiopia (Dec. 14, 1942)
France (Sept. 3, 1939)
Great Britain
   (Sept. 3, 1939)
Greece (Oct. 28, 1940)
Guatemala (Dec. 9, 1941)
Haiti (Dec. 8, 1941)
Honduras (Dec. 8, 1941)
India (Sept. 3, 1939)

Iran (Aug. 25, 1941)
Iraq (Jan. 17, 1943)
Lebanon (Feb. 27, 1945)
Liberia (Jan. 27, 1944)
Luxembourg (May 10, 1940)
Mexico (May 22, 1942)
Mongolian People's Republic
   (Aug. 9, 1945)
Netherlands (May 10, 1940)
New Zealand (Sept. 3, 1939)
Nicaragua (Dec. 11, 1941)
Norway (Apr. 9, 1940)
Panama (Dec. 7, 1941)
Paraguay (Feb. 7, 1945)
Peru (Feb. 12, 1945)
Poland (Sept. 1, 1939)
Russia (June 22, 1941)
San Marino (Sept. 21, 1944)
Saudi Arabia (Mar. 1, 1945)
South Africa (Sept. 6, 1939)
Syria (June 8, 1941)
Turkey (Feb. 23, 1945)
United States (Dec. 8, 1941)
Uruguay (Feb. 15, 1945)
Venezuela (Feb. 15, 1945)
Yugoslavia (Apr. 6, 1941)

The Axis

Albania (June 15, 1940)
Bulgaria (Mar. 1, 1941)
Finland (June 25, 1941)
Germany (Sept. 1, 1939)
Hungary (Apr. 10, 1941)

Italy (June 11, 1940)
Japan (Dec. 7, 1941)
Romania (Nov. 23, 1940)
Thailand (Jan. 25, 1942)

Dates are those on which each country entered the war.

other peace settlements that followed World War I. The Allies occupied part of Germany. They forced it to disarm, give up land, pay reparations, and admit its guilt in starting the war (see VERSAILLES, TREATY OF). Germany suffered from widespread unemployment, runaway currency inflation, and food and raw materials shortages caused by the Allied blockade. The Germans

381

found it easy to blame the Versailles Treaty for their troubles. They called it the *Versailles Dictate*. Germany set up a republican form of government at Weimar in 1919. But many Germans blamed the new government for accepting the hated treaty. Workers who could not find jobs drifted into the Communist and National Socialist parties. The National Socialists loudly demanded revision of the treaty and an overthrow of the Weimar republic.

The League of Nations was set up by the treaties that ended World War I. The heads of member states wanted the League to help nations settle their disputes peacefully. But the League had no international police force that could snuff out sparks of war. It did settle some arguments. In 1926, Germany became a member of the League. But the United States did not join the League, and the organization gradually grew weaker each year (see LEAGUE OF NATIONS).

Most countries of western Europe were too occupied with their own problems to pay much attention to Germany, although its officials pleaded for help. The German people decided that their government could do nothing to help them. This general discontent, and the worldwide depression that began in 1929, hastened the death of the republic. As the government lost power, Adolf Hitler and his National Socialist, or Nazi, party grew stronger (see HITLER, ADOLF; NAZISM).

Attempts at Disarmament. The Allies disarmed Germany after World War I, and promised to work for general disarmament. In 1921, the Washington Naval Conference agreed to limit the number and size of major warships of the leading naval powers. Naval conferences held in 1927 and 1930 met with less success, and nothing was done about general disarmament. Many countries held discussions about disarmament, but none of them took positive steps.

The League of Nations called a conference of 60 nations at Geneva, Switzerland, in 1932. Chancellor Heinrich Brüning of Germany announced that his country would be willing to stay at the armament level set by the Versailles Treaty if other countries would reduce their armaments to that level. But France refused to disarm until an international police system could be established. The Geneva conference ended in failure. Brüning's government collapsed. Within eight months, Hitler became chancellor of Germany. Almost immediately, he withdrew Germany from the conference and the League of Nations. See DISARMAMENT.

Economic Problems were among the fundamental causes of World War II. Germany, Italy, and Japan considered themselves unjustly handicapped in trying to compete with other nations for markets, raw materials, and colonies. They believed that such countries as Belgium, France, Great Britain, The Netherlands, and the United States unfairly controlled most of the world's wealth and people. In prosperous times, Germany, Italy, and Japan could find markets for their products. But these markets were closed in times of economic depression. Other governments put high tariffs and low quotas on imports. So Germany, Italy, and Japan looked for lands to conquer in order to get what they considered their share of the world's resources and markets.

The problem of war debts and reparations troubled many countries during this period. In World War I, the Allied nations had borrowed from each other to finance the war. Some countries began demanding that these loans be repaid (see WAR DEBT). Germany and the other defeated countries had to pay reparations for damages they caused during the war. The Allies demanded $33 billion in reparations from Germany alone.

Nationalism hindered international cooperation before World War II as it had before World War I. For a time during the 1920's, it appeared that international cooperation might reduce national rivalries. But, with the depression of 1929, nations again became concerned chiefly with solving only their own problems, instead of cooperating with their neighbors. Each sought security for itself in the form of rearmament and alliances.

Some countries faced additional problems of nationalism from the minorities within their borders. For example, a number of German-speaking citizens lived in the Sudetes Mountains region of Czechoslovakia. Some Sudeten Germans had left Germany to escape the growing tyranny there. Others demanded the right to be governed by Germany or have their own government.

The Rise of Dictatorships

Many countries had liberal, democratic governments after World War I. But dictatorships developed during the 1920's and 1930's, and destroyed democratic rights. Totalitarian governments found fertile fields for growth in Russia, Italy, Germany, and other countries. For a more detailed discussion of how such dictatorships developed, see the *History* section of RUSSIA, ITALY, and GERMANY.

Communism in Russia came to power in the revolution of November, 1917 (see COMMUNISM). The Communists under Lenin promised a "dictatorship of the proletariat," or working people. But they set up a one-party dictatorship instead. First Lenin and then Joseph Stalin ruled Russia. The government seized all types of private property. It outlawed all political parties other than its own—the Communist party.

Fascism in Italy. Benito Mussolini founded the Fascist party in 1919 (see FASCISM; MUSSOLINI, BENITO). After he became prime minister of Italy in 1922, he quickly seized all powers of government and transformed the country into a totalitarian state. During the peace settlements of World War I, many Italians had blamed the liberal government for not pressing Italy's claims to more land. The country faced inflation and a huge public debt. Mussolini promised to restore Italy to its ancient greatness, when Rome was the center of a mighty empire.

Nazism in Germany. The National Socialist, or *Nazi*, party came to power in 1933. Adolf Hitler had clearly revealed his plans in 1925 in his book *Mein Kampf*. He urged the use of armed force to remove the restrictions of the Versailles treaty. In a program his party adopted in 1920, he called for rearmament and a union of all German-speaking peoples into a "Greater Germany." See NAZISM.

As soon as Hitler became chancellor of Germany, he crushed all political opposition and started to rebuild Germany's armed strength. German schools, from kindergarten up, began teaching children the glories of military might. Boys and girls were required to join *Hitler Youth* groups, which stressed military discipline.

Militarism in Japan had long been part of the country's traditions. The people held the *samurai* (warrior class) in the highest regard. War and conquests, according to the Japanese militarists, were the highest human achievements. Japan had a liberal government for a brief period during the 1920's. But by 1931 the militarists again began to dominate the government. They revived as a national slogan *Hakko Ichiu* (*Bringing the Eight Corners of the World Under One Roof*). Japan's military leaders strengthened their power by invading Manchuria on Sept. 18, 1931. Many historians consider this act the real start of World War II, because aggression was not halted.

Aggression on the March

Manchuria. The Japanese found Manchuria a particularly inviting goal because of its abundant natural resources. From Manchuria, Japan could go on to control all northern China. After Japan had established its leadership in China, it could expand elsewhere.

The Japanese struck at a time when most countries were more concerned with the depression than with an invasion in far-off China. The League of Nations did nothing but condemn Japan formally. The United States introduced the doctrine of *nonrecognition*, simply declaring that it would not recognize Japan's conquest.

China. The Japanese invaded China near Shanghai in 1932, but later withdrew. Then they began an economic campaign against Chinese commerce. Fighting broke out on July 7, 1937, after the Japanese staged an "incident" near Peiping (now Peking). The undeclared war between Japan and China quickly spread to most of eastern China. By December, 1938, the Japanese controlled most of China's major ports and industrial and rail centers. Chungking, the wartime Chinese capital, was far up the Yangtze River. Japan placed an economic blockade on China. Some countries gave a little aid and sympathy to China, but most nations continued to sell war supplies to Japan.

Ethiopia and Spain. In 1935, Mussolini's troops swept into Ethiopia. The Italians slaughtered the crudely equipped and poorly trained Ethiopian forces. In 1936, they completed the conquest (see ETHIOPIA [History]). The League of Nations voted economic sanctions against Italy, but later withdrew them.

The Spanish Civil War broke out in 1936. Both Mussolini and Hitler sent men and supplies to help the rebel forces of Francisco Franco. Russia gave aid to the Spanish Loyalists. Franco overthrew the Spanish government and in 1939 organized an absolute dictatorship similar to the ones in Germany and Italy (see SPAIN [World War II]). Historians often call the war in Spain the *testing ground of World War II*, because the Germans, Italians, and Russians tested some weapons and military tactics there.

The Rhineland. In 1935, Hitler established military conscription for all German men, created an air force, and began to build submarines. The Treaty of Versailles limited Germany to a 100,000-man army, but Hitler soon had 600,000 men under arms. Some European governments protested these violations of the treaty. But Great Britain agreed to scrap the limitations of the Versailles Treaty and to allow Germany to build an air force and navy.

In another violation of the treaty, Hitler sent troops into demilitarized districts west of the Rhine River in March, 1936. This act brought German soldiers to the French border. Some French leaders wanted to send troops to force the Germans back. But it was felt that such an act might lead to total war, and Europe shrank from the risk. So Hitler won again.

Late in 1936, Germany and Japan signed an anti-Comintern pact to oppose Communism (see COMINTERN). In 1937, Italy signed the pact. The three countries became allied in what was known as the *Rome-Berlin-Tokyo Axis* (see AXIS). They signed a military-aid pact in 1940.

Austria. Confident of success, Hitler turned to his next objective: uniting Austria with Germany. The peace settlements of 1919 had forbidden such a union. Hitler falsely claimed that Germany "has neither the wish nor intention . . . to annex or unite with Austria." But he had secretly encouraged and supported a revolutionary Nazi movement in Austria. In 1934, Nazi conspirators had assassinated Chancellor Engelbert Dollfuss of Austria, but had failed to seize his country. In March, 1938, German troops marched triumphantly into Austria.

Czechoslovakia. Hitler's swift and bloodless conquest of Austria frightened Czechoslovakia. The Germans now faced the Czechs on three sides. Within the country lived $3\frac{1}{2}$ million Sudeten Germans. Many had joined a pro-German party that took orders from Hitler.

Hitler demanded that the Sudeten Germans be placed under his rule. But the Czechs stood ready to fight. France vowed to stand by its treaty obligations to the Czechs. Russia also gave assurances. Britain pledged to support France. With Europe on the brink of war, Hitler promised that the Sudetenland was "the last territorial claim I have to make in Europe." Prime Minister Neville Chamberlain of Britain and Premier Edouard Daladier of France conferred with Hitler and Mussolini in Munich. The Germans did not allow Czech representatives to attend the conference. Chamberlain and Daladier finally gave in to the dictators' demands. Under the Munich agreement of Sept. 29, 1938, Czechoslovakia lost the Sudetenland to Germany. When Chamberlain returned to London, he said the pact meant "peace for our time." See MUNICH AGREEMENT.

Poland. Hitler then made another "last claim" in violation of his promise. He secretly ordered Poland to hand over a strip of territory across the Polish Corridor to link Germany proper with East Prussia. He also wanted to unite Danzig (now Gdańsk) with Germany (see GDAŃSK; POLISH CORRIDOR).

In March, 1939, Hitler's army occupied the rest of Czechoslovakia. Next, he seized Memel (now Klaipėda) from Lithuania. In April, Italy occupied Albania.

In the west, the Germans worked at frantic speed to complete the Siegfried Line fortifications opposite the French Maginot Line (see MAGINOT LINE; SIEGFRIED LINE). Hitler's broken promises finally convinced Great Britain and France that he intended to conquer all eastern Europe. The policy of *appeasement* (giving in) had proved to be a complete failure. When Hitler again demanded Danzig and a pathway across the Polish Corridor, Chamberlain announced that Great Britain would support Poland if it resisted a German attack.

EUROPEAN THEATER

ATLANTIC
OCEAN

SWEDEN

FINLAND

Battle of the Atlantic
Sept., 1939-May, 1945

NORWAY
Apr. 9-June 9, 1940

NORWAY

BALTIC
SEA

Leningrad
Jan. 21-27, 1944

ESTONIA

LATVIA

Moscow

NORTH
SEA

Denmark
Apr. 9, 1940

DENMARK

LITHUANIA

Danzig

EAST
PRUSSIA
(Germany)

GREAT
BRITAIN

V-Weapons Attacks
June 13, 1944-Mar. 21, 1945

The Netherlands
May 10-15, 1940

GERMANY

Berlin
Apr. 22-May 2, 1945

Warsaw
Jan. 11, 1945

RUSSIA

London

THE
NETHERLANDS

Poland
Sept. 1-28, 1939

Russia Invaded
June 22, 1941

Battle of Britain
July 10, 1940-Oct., 1940

BELGIUM

Belgium
May 10-28, 1940

POLAND

Battle of
the Bulge
Dec. 16-27, 1944

Luxembourg
May 10, 1940

CZECHOSLOVAKIA

Nov. 19, 1942-Jan.31, 1943

Stalingrad

Normandy Invaded
June 6, 1944

Paris

Surrender
at Reims
May 7, 1945

Vienna
Apr. 13, 1945

AUSTRIA

Budapest
Feb. 13, 1945

SWITZERLAND

HUNGARY

France
June 5-22, 1940

ROMANIA

Sevastopol
Nov. 1, 1941-July 1, 1942

FRANCE

ITALY

Yugoslavia
Apr. 6-18, 1941

Southern France
Invaded
Aug. 15, 1944

Italy
Sept. 3, 1943-
May 2, 1945

YUGOSLAVIA

BULGARIA

BLACK SEA

PORTUGAL

Rome

ALBANIA

GREECE

TURKEY

SPAIN

MEDITERRANEAN
SEA

Sicily
July 10-Aug. 17, 1943

Greece
Oct. 28, 1940-
Apr. 27, 1941

MOROCCO

TUNISIA

North Africa
Nov. 7-8, 1942-May 12, 1943

Tobruk
June 18-21, 1942

ALGERIA

El Alamein
Oct. 23-Nov. 3, 1942

SAUDI ARABIA

LIBYA
(Italian territory)

EGYPT

RED
SEA

THE WAR AGAINST GERMANY AND ITALY

Axis Victory   Allied Victory

(- - - - - - - - - - -) Extent of battle lines

HIGHLIGHTS OF THE WAR IN EUROPE AND AFRICA

1939

Sept. 1	German troops invaded Poland.
Sept. 3	Britain and France declared war on Germany.
Nov. 30	Russian troops invaded Finland.

1940

Apr. 9	Germany attacked Denmark and Norway.
May 10	Germany invaded Belgium, Luxembourg, and The Netherlands.
June 10	Italy declared war on Britain and France.
June 22	France surrendered to Germany.
Aug. 4	Italy invaded British Somaliland.
Oct. 28	Italy attacked Greece.
Nov. 20	Hungary joined the Axis.
Nov. 23	Romania joined the Axis.

1941

Jan. 15	British soldiers invaded Ethiopia.
Mar. 1	Bulgaria joined the Axis.
Apr. 6	Germany invaded Greece and Yugoslavia.
June 22	Axis forces invaded Russia.
July 7	United States troops landed in Iceland.
Aug. 14	The Atlantic Charter was announced.
Dec. 11	Germany and Italy declared war on the United States. The United States declared war on Germany and Italy.

1942

June 5	The United States declared war on Bulgaria, Hungary, and Romania.
June 21	German troops seized Tobruk in North Africa.
July 2	The British halted the Germans at El Alamein.
Sept. 16	German forces entered Stalingrad (now Volgograd) in Russia.
Oct. 23	The British began an offensive at El Alamein.
Nov. 7-8	Allied forces landed in North Africa.
Nov. 11	French resistance in North Africa ended.
Nov. 12	British troops captured Tobruk.
Nov. 19	The Russians counterattacked at Stalingrad.
Nov. 27	The French scuttled their fleet at Toulon.

1943

Jan. 31	Field Marshal Friedrich von Paulus surrendered to the Russians.
May 7	Tunis and Bizerte fell to the Allies.
May 12	Organized Axis resistance in Africa ended.
July 10	Allied forces invaded Sicily.
Sept. 3	The Allies landed in Italy.
Sept. 3	Italy signed a secret armistice with the Allies.
Oct. 13	Italy declared war on Germany.
Nov. 6	The Russians recaptured Kiev.

1944

Jan. 27	The Russians broke the siege of Leningrad.
Mar. 19	German troops swept into Hungary.
June 6	The Allies landed in Normandy, France.
June 13	The first V-1 guided missile fell on London.
July 25	United States forces broke out of Normandy.
Aug. 15	Allied troops landed in southern France.
Aug. 25	Romania declared war on Germany.
Sept. 9	Bulgaria declared war on Germany.
Sept. 10	Finland signed an armistice with Russia.
Dec. 16	The Germans began the Battle of the Bulge.
Dec. 27	The Allies halted the German offensive.

1945

Jan. 11	Russian soldiers entered Warsaw, Poland.
Jan. 21	Hungary declared war on Germany.
Feb. 13	Russian forces occupied Budapest.
Apr. 13	Vienna fell to invading Russian troops.
Apr. 22	The Russians reached the suburbs of Berlin.
Apr. 25	U.S. and Russian forces met at Torgau.
May 2	German troops in Italy surrendered.
May 2	Berlin surrendered to Russian troops.
May 7	Germany surrendered to the Allies.
July 26	The Allies issued the Potsdam Declaration.

Axis Empire at Its Height (November, 1942) extended from Norway to North Africa and France to western Russia.

Normandy Invaded (June, 1944). The Allies pierced Germany's *Fortress Europe* with an amphibious attack.

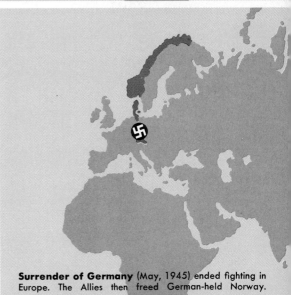

Surrender of Germany (May, 1945) ended fighting in Europe. The Allies then freed German-held Norway.

Hitler complained that Chamberlain's guarantees to Poland encouraged the Poles to be "unreasonable." German newspapers screamed about the "frightful maltreatment" of the German-speaking peoples in Poland. Hitler renounced a treaty of friendship with Poland. Conflict between the Germans and the Poles in Danzig increased. Tension grew as rumors of war filled the air.

Prelude to War. Early in the spring of 1939, Hitler decided definitely to attack Poland in September. His high command prepared plans for the invasion under the code name of *Case White*. The British and French had been negotiating with the Russians to gain support for the Poles. At the same time, Russia was negotiating with Germany for better commercial and trade relations.

Some historians believe that Russia knew in the spring or early summer of 1939 that Germany planned to invade Poland in September. Knowing this, Russia signed a nonaggression pact with Germany on August 23. The Russians promised to remain neutral in case Germany went to war. They also made a secret agreement to divide Poland with the Germans after the conquest.

Hitler assumed that Great Britain and France would not go to war to support Poland. At dawn on Sept. 1, 1939, German troops smashed into the country. Britain and France at once ordered Hitler to withdraw his forces, warning that they would go to war if he refused. Hitler paid no attention. On September 3, Britain and France declared war on Germany.

Men and Strategy

As in World War I, Great Britain, France, and the countries siding with them became known as the *Allies*. The Allies totaled about 50 nations during World War II. Germany and its eight allies were known as the *Axis*. At the beginning of the war, the Axis nations had the advantages. They had trained more powerful armed forces than the Allies. They had organized their factories to produce war materials. But after the war became a truly global conflict in 1941, the Allies cooperated to outfight the Axis on the battlefields and to outproduce them in the factories.

Wartime Leaders

The Allies. The heads of government of China, Great Britain, Russia, and the United States became known as the *Big Four*. Two of the Big Four powers had the same heads of government throughout the war. Chiang Kai-shek ruled China, and Joseph Stalin directed Russia's war efforts. In Great Britain, Winston S. Churchill replaced Neville Chamberlain as prime minister in 1940, and Clement R. Attlee succeeded Churchill in July, 1945. Franklin D. Roosevelt was re-elected President of the United States in November, 1944, but died in April, 1945. Vice-President Harry S. Truman succeeded him. During the war, the Big Four leaders conferred several times. Churchill met with Roosevelt in Washington, D.C., Casablanca, Malta, and Quebec. The two conferred with Chiang Kai-shek in Cairo, and with Stalin at Teheran and Yalta. Churchill, Attlee, Stalin, and Truman met at Potsdam.

After 1942, Great Britain and the United States worked out the broad strategic outlines of the war through the Combined Chiefs of Staff. This group included the United States Joint Chiefs of Staff and the British Chiefs of Staff Committee. Officers who served on it during most of the war included Generals of the Army George C. Marshall and Henry H. Arnold, and Fleet Admirals William D. Leahy and Ernest J. King of the United States; and Field Marshals Sir John G. Dill and Sir Alan F. Brooke, Marshal of the Royal Air Force Sir Charles Portal, and Admirals of the Fleet Sir Dudley Pound and Sir Andrew B. Cunningham of Great Britain.

The principal Allied battle commanders included Field Marshals Sir Harold Alexander and Henry M. Wilson in the Mediterranean, General of the Army Dwight D. Eisenhower in North Africa and Europe, General of the Army Douglas MacArthur in the Southwest Pacific, Admiral Lord Louis Mountbatten in Southeast Asia, and Fleet Admiral Chester W. Nimitz in the Central Pacific. Chiang Kai-shek and Stalin had the titles of Generalissimo of military forces.

The Axis. Among the three chief Axis powers, only Emperor Hirohito of Japan ruled throughout the war. Japan had several premiers. General Hideki Tojo, the most important, held dictatorial powers from October, 1941, to July, 1944. Victor Emmanuel was king of Italy during the war, but the real head of the government, Benito Mussolini, resigned in 1943. Adolf Hitler, the German chancellor, committed suicide in April, 1945.

The chief Axis field commanders included German Field Marshals Karl Gerd von Rundstedt, Albert Kesselring, and Erwin Rommel; Marshal Rodolfo Graziani of Italy; and General Tomobumi Yamashita and Admiral Isoroku Yamamoto of Japan.

Strategy of the War

Global Warfare. Historians have found no evidence that Germany, Italy, and Japan had any formal joint strategic plans for winning World War II. Germany intended to build up a powerful empire by occupying territory to the east and south. Then, after overrunning France, it expected to use air assaults to force Britain to make peace. German troops would then defeat Russia, capture the Caucasus oilfields, and organize Hitler's plan for a European *New Order*. Italy hoped to take advantage of German successes to grab territory for itself.

Japan intended to cripple the U.S. Pacific Fleet at Pearl Harbor, then overrun Thailand, Malaya, the Philippines, and the Netherlands Indies. It would then complete its conquest of China, and unite all East Asia under Japanese domination in a *Greater East Asia Co-Prosperity Sphere*. Japan expected that a two-ocean war would exhaust the Allies and make them willing to let Japan keep the territories it had seized. Japan had no plans for invading the United States mainland.

"Germany First." The Allies agreed upon basic strategy once the war began. Roosevelt and Churchill at their first wartime conference, in December, 1941, decided to concentrate on Germany first and then on Japan. They considered Germany the greater and closer enemy. The Allies planned to invade western Europe to relieve German pressure on the Russians. Driving east-

Allied "Big Three" were Britain's Winston Churchill, Franklin D. Roosevelt of the United States, and Russia's Joseph Stalin.

Axis Leaders Adolf Hitler of Germany and Benito Mussolini of Italy failed to win their dream of a great world empire.

Wide World; United Press Int.

ward, Allied armies would crush Germany against the Russian forces rolling westward. The Allies planned to knock Italy out of the war by invading it from North African bases.

In order to defeat Japan, the Allies planned to seize key Pacific islands and to build bomber bases in China. Using China and the Pacific islands as springboards, the Allies could then invade Japan.

Mobilization

When war began in 1939, Germany had the advantage of being substantially mobilized. It had already organized its industrial plants for wartime needs. The Allies, after war broke out, had to draft and train men for the armed forces, transform factories and plants for war production, and adopt strategic plans.

Hitler had a well-balanced *wehrmacht*, or armed force, of 106 combat divisions, with powerful tanks, motorized vehicles, and heavy artillery. Great Britain, France, and Poland had greater reserves of manpower. But their armies were not so well trained and equipped as those of the Germans. Germany had about 12,000 military air-craft, compared to about 8,000 for the Allies. The Allies had larger navies, with about five tons of ships to every one for the Germans. But the Allies also had to patrol wide areas of the world, and Germany could restrict its fleet activities to the North Sea and the nearby Atlantic. In addition, German submarines seriously threatened Allied vessels carrying troops and war materials.

From the time Germany attacked Poland until Japan surrendered six years later, the Axis mobilized about 30,000,000 men and women in their armed forces. The Allies mobilized about 62,000,000 men and women.

Early Stages of the War

The overwhelming power of the Axis won a series of major conquests during the first two years of war. In turn, Poland, Denmark, Luxembourg, The Netherlands, Belgium, Norway, France, Yugoslavia, and Greece fell before the Axis war machine. Germany gained active allies in Italy, Hungary, Romania, and Bulgaria. The Germans tried to bomb Britain into sur-

render, but failed. German armies then invaded Russia.

Blitzkrieg

Poland Crushed. The German high command planned the Polish campaign with great care. It pioneered a new method of warfare called *blitzkrieg*, or lightning war. On Sept. 1, 1939, German *Stuka* dive bombers attacked Polish troops, and heavier bombers struck at fortifications and industrial plants. On the ground, tanks and infantry raced through the Polish lines. The British and French could not give direct help to the Poles.

In August, Germany and Russia had agreed secretly to divide Poland. On September 17, with the Polish armies ready to collapse, Russian armies invaded eastern Poland against little opposition. The Russians claimed that they wanted to "protect their own frontiers." Most Polish resistance ended within three days.

387

But the people of Warsaw fought on. Without food and supplies, the city had to surrender on September 27. The next day, Germany and Russia divided Poland.

For seven months after the Polish campaign of 1939, the Germans and the Allies fought no important land battles. The French dug in behind the Maginot Line, and the Germans sat behind their Siegfried Line, awaiting the next order to attack. Each side conducted small raids, took aerial photographs, and dropped propaganda leaflets. Newspapers called the war in the west the *phony war*. But on the Atlantic Ocean the German pocket battleships *Admiral Graf Spee* and *Deutschland* raided Allied convoys.

Denmark and Norway had excellent bases from which submarines could operate in the North Sea. Ships carrying Swedish iron ore to Germany steamed through these waters. The Germans decided to invade Denmark in order to make an invasion of Norway easier. At dawn on April 9, German warships carrying troops slipped into Copenhagen, Denmark, and into Bergen, Oslo, and other coastal cities in Norway. Denmark surrendered almost immediately. German troops seized airfields at Oslo and near Stavanger. A Norwegian *fifth column* of spies and other German sympathizers, led by Vidkun Quisling, helped the invaders. Quisling became head of the puppet government in Norway.

After the first shock of the invasion, the Norwegians began to fight back. Great Britain and France sent troops to Norway, but could not furnish adequate air support. The Germans gained strength, particularly in airpower, and finally drove the Allied forces from Norway in June. The British navy meanwhile inflicted heavy losses on German warships.

As a result of this British defeat, Winston S. Churchill succeeded Neville Chamberlain as British prime minister in May, 1940. Churchill told his people that he could offer them nothing but "blood, toil, tears, and sweat."

Retreat to Dunkerque. Hitler next unleashed his terrifying war machine in western Europe. On May 10, 1940, German troops plunged into Belgium, Luxembourg, and The Netherlands. Generals Fedor von Bock, Wilhelm von Leeb, and Karl Gerd von Rundstedt commanded the three invading army groups. The Allies thought the Germans would use the same maneuver that they tried in World War I. Instead, armored units, paratroops, and dive bombers struck at Luxembourg and the heavily wooded Ardennes Forest. The Germans raced to the coast and isolated the Allied forces in Belgium from the main body in France. Luxembourg fell in one day, and The Netherlands in five days. On May 19, Gen. Maxime Weygand of France replaced Gen. Maurice Gamelin as Allied commander in chief. Weygand began to set up a defense line on the south banks of the Somme and Aisne rivers. On May 28, King Leopold III surrendered the Belgian army and became a prisoner.

Belgium's surrender left the remaining Allied forces under Gen. Lord John Gort in a desperate situation. They retreated to Dunkerque, the only escape port on the northern French coast. German armored units were close to the port, but they halted about 20 miles (32 kilometers) from Dunkerque. As the tiny Royal Air Force formed an aerial umbrella to repel German bombers, more than 336,000 British, French, and Belgian troops waded out to British rescue ships that included fishing boats and motorboats. Some historians believe that Hitler allowed the Allied soldiers to escape, because he felt it would be easier to negotiate a peace with Britain if he spared them.

The Fall of France. On June 5, the Germans launched a new offensive against France. In four days, the French were in hopeless retreat. Mussolini decided that the time had come for Italy to get a share of the spoils. On June 10, he told Britain and France that Italy would enter the war on Germany's side. The Italians did little except to invade a small part of the coast of southern France. But some of France's best troops were tied down guarding the Italian border against just such an attack. The Germans entered Paris on June 14, and pierced the Maginot Line from Germany two days later.

The German victory caused a major split in the French government. One group wanted to move the government to North Africa and continue the war. Winston Churchill offered to unite Britain with France under a single government, if the French would continue to fight. But Premier Henri Philippe Pétain of France decided to surrender.

France signed an armistice with Germany on June 22. Hitler forced the French to surrender in the historic railway car in the Compiègne Forest where Germany had surrendered to the Allies in 1918. The Germans then divided France into two zones. German troops occupied the northern and western part of the country. In the unoccupied southern part, Pétain set up a government at Vichy. Thousands of Frenchmen fled to North Africa and to Britain, and continued to fight the Germans. Brig. Gen. Charles de Gaulle became leader of a Free France movement with headquarters in London.

The Battle of Britain. France's surrender left Great Britain with no allies in western Europe. Germany had crushed six countries in three months, and Hitler boasted that he would march into London in two more months. He ordered his high command to plan an invasion of the British Isles, called *Operation Sea Lion*. But Hitler hoped he could force Britain to surrender without invasion.

In July, the German *Luftwaffe* (air force) began to blast British airfields and ports. The Royal Air Force, outnumbered but with better planes and pilots, shot down so many aircraft that the Germans were forced to give up daylight attacks. In September, Reich Marshal Hermann Goering took command of the air assaults. His Luftwaffe switched to night raids. The British used radar, a carefully guarded secret development, to track the attacking planes. From Sept. 7, 1940, through May 10, 1941, German planes blasted London nearly every night. These raids became known as the *London Blitz*. The Germans also bombed other cities. Hitler offered to negotiate a peace, but the British did not reply.

By the middle of 1941, Germany gave up its attempts to conquer Britain by air raids, after dropping more than 190,000 short tons (172,000 metric tons) of bombs. But it continued the raids into 1944. Historians consider the Battle of Britain one of the turning-points of the war, because the British showed that they could defeat the Luftwaffe. German aircraft losses at the height of the battle had totaled more than 2,600 planes.

Assaults in Africa. About the time that Germany and Britain clashed in the air over the British Isles, Italy opened up other battle fronts. In August, 1940, Italian troops in Africa pushed eastward from Ethiopia and overran British Somaliland. In September, Marshal Rodolfo Graziani's Italian forces in Libya advanced eastward into Egypt. By February 1941, an Allied army under Gen. Sir Archibald P. Wavell had thrown the Italians back into Libya as far west as Benghazi. Wavell captured more than 130,000 prisoners. Hitler then sent the *Afrika Korps*, a highly motorized and armored army under Gen. Erwin Rommel, to aid the Italians.

Rommel caught the British army by surprise. Within two weeks, the Afrika Korps had recovered all the territory the Italians had lost, and had driven the British back to the Nile Delta in Egypt. But the Germans could not protect Italian Somaliland and Ethiopia. British Commonwealth forces recaptured British Somaliland and occupied all Italian East Africa by the end of 1941.

Fighting in Eastern Europe

The Balkans. When Germany and Italy failed to smash the Allies in Britain and Africa, they quickly changed their strategy. In October 1940, German troops marched into Romania on the pretext of protecting its oil fields and reorganizing its army.

Mussolini demanded the right to use bases in Greece, but the Greek government refused. Without notifying Hitler, Mussolini sent his armies across the Greek border from Albania. But the Greeks fought back savagely, forcing the Italians back into Albania, and seizing one fourth of that country.

Hungary and Romania joined the Axis in November, and Bulgaria joined a short time later. Yugoslavia also signed the Axis pact, but the people revolted against their pro-German ministers. German troops poured into Yugoslavia from the surrounding Axis countries. In 12 days, the Germans destroyed the Yugoslav army. But guerrilla forces in the mountains, called *Chetniks* and *Partisans*, continued to fight the Germans and the Italians (see MIHAILOVICH, DRAŽA; TITO, JOSIP BROZ).

Hitler used Yugoslavia as a base to help the Italians in their Greek campaign. German troops entered Athens on Apr. 27, 1941, and handed the country over to the Italians. The British had sent troops to Greece, but most of them escaped to Egypt and Crete before Athens surrendered. Then German paratroops and men in air transports made the first airborne invasion in history by landing on Crete. They wiped out most of the British forces on the island. Germany and Italy now controlled the Balkan nations.

The Invasion of Russia. Germany and Russia proved to be uneasy and suspicious partners. In a drive to strengthen their borders and obtain more naval bases in the Baltic, the Russians attacked Finland on Nov. 30, 1939. After severe fighting, the Finns surrendered in March 1940. In the summer of 1940, Russia seized the Baltic countries of Estonia, Latvia, and Lithuania.

Many signs pointed to a German invasion of Russia. After Rudolf Hess, Hitler's deputy, flew to Great Britain in May 1941, the British repeated their earlier warnings that Germany would soon invade Russia. But the Russians did not act on the warning. See HESS, RUDOLF.

On June 22, 1941, over 150 German and other Axis divisions swept across the Russian border in *Operation Barbarossa*. The 3-million-man force faced about 2 million Russian troops. The battle line stretched 2,000 miles (3,200 kilometers) from the Arctic to the Black Sea.

British Information Services

DUNKERQUE

Evacuation of Allied troops escaping from Dunkerque in 1940 was carried out by British rescue ships.

LONDON BLITZ

Air Raids hit London nightly during the Battle of Britain. The Germans tried to bomb the British into surrender.

United Press Int.

Commanding the invading forces were the three army group commanders who had conquered France, Field Marshals Von Bock, Von Leeb, and Von Rundstedt.

Hitler announced that he had ordered the attack "to save the entire world from the dangers of Bolshevism." Germany needed Russia's vast supplies of foods, petroleum, and other raw materials. The Germans confidently expected another blitzkrieg. They made no preparations for a long struggle, and did not even issue winter uniforms to the troops.

For almost five weeks, the Germans drove the Red Army back, and captured thousands of prisoners. Most of the world expected Russia to collapse. As the Germans advanced, the Russians burned or destroyed factories, dams, railroads, food supplies, and everything else they could not move. Bands of Russians fought behind the German lines. The government began moving factories and machinery to comparative safety east of the Ural Mountains. It hurried troops westward from Siberia. Great Britain and the United States shipped lend-lease supplies to Russia through the Arctic Ocean and the Persian Gulf. They lost many ships in the Arctic to German planes and submarines operating from Norway on the icy Murmansk convoy run.

America Joins the War

After war began in Europe in 1939, people in the Americas debated whether their countries should take part or stay out. Canada declared war on Germany almost at once. The United States shifted its policy from neutrality to preparedness. It began to expand its armed forces, build defense plants, and give the Allies all-out aid short of war. Japan's attack on Pearl Harbor in 1941 brought the United States into the war on the Allied side. Every country in the Americas eventually declared war on the Axis. But only Brazil, Canada, Mexico, and the United States actually provided fighting forces.

Defending the Americas

Isolation or Intervention? The threat of war in the 1930's had sharply divided public opinion in the United States. Most Americans hoped the Allies would win, but they also hoped to keep the United States out of war. A second group, called *isolationists*, wanted the country to stay out of the war at almost any cost. A third group, called *interventionists*, wanted the United States to do all in its power to aid the Allies.

The outbreak of war in 1939 also split the people of Canada. Many Canadians had criticized the British and French policy of appeasing Hitler in the middle 1930's. After Britain declared war on Germany, many Canadians felt that Canada's interests lay with those of Britain and the Commonwealth. But others felt that Canada should remain neutral. Canada declared war on Germany on Sept. 10, 1939, and on Japan on Dec. 8, 1941.

The Arsenal of Democracy. The United States remained neutral when Germany invaded Poland in 1939. But the government stopped all shipments of American arms to warring nations. Later, it allowed the Allies to buy goods on a "cash and carry" basis. By the end of 1940, Great Britain had almost used up its funds to buy arms. China, in a death struggle with Japan, had already exhausted its funds. In September, the United States gave Great Britain 50 over-age destroyers in return for the right to lease bases for 99 years in Bermuda, Newfoundland, and the British West Indies.

President Roosevelt called upon the United States to be "the great arsenal of democracy," and to supply war materials to the Allies through sale, loan, or lease. The lend-lease bill became law on March 11, 1941 (see LEND-LEASE). During the next four years, the United States sent more than $50,000,000,000 worth of war materials to the Allies. About half went to Britain and one fourth to Russia.

Canada contributed its own form of lend-lease, called *mutual aid*. Under the Mutual Aid Act of 1943, Canada

390

sent about $2 billion worth of supplies to the Allied countries, over and above what they could pay for.

Manpower

Expanding the Armed Forces. In 1939, the United States had about 174,000 men in the army; 126,400 in the navy; 26,000 in the army air corps; 19,700 in the marine corps; and 10,000 in the coast guard. At the height of its strength in 1945, the United States had 6 million in the army; 3,400,000 in the navy; 2,400,000 in the army air forces; 484,000 in the marine corps; and 170,000 in the coast guard. In 1939, the United States had about 2,500 airplanes and 760 warships. By 1945, it had about 80,000 airplanes and 2,500 warships.

Canada's military forces went through a similar expansion. In September, 1939, Canada had 4,500 men in the army, 1,774 in the navy, and 4,000 in the air force. The peak strength of the Canadian Army was 481,500, the navy 92,900, and the air corps 206,300.

The United States and Canada used draft laws to build their armed forces. The United States Selective Training and Service Act became law on Sept. 16, 1940 (see DRAFT, MILITARY). The Canadian conscription law went into effect in June, 1940. Parliament amended it on July 23, 1942, to allow the government to send drafted soldiers overseas.

Women in the Services. As in World War I, women other than nurses joined the U.S. armed forces. They enlisted in the Women's Army Auxiliary Corps (WAAC), which later became the Women's Army Corps (WAC); the Women Appointed for Voluntary Emergency Service in the Navy (WAVES); the Women's Auxiliary Ferrying Command (WAF); the Women's Reserve of the Coast Guard Reserves (SPARS); and the Marine Corps Women's Reserves. Women had a more important role than in World War I, when most of them were clerks. See SPARS; WAC; WAF; WAVES.

The newly created Women's Army Corps of Canada reached a peak strength of 20,020. Canadian women

also enlisted in the Royal Canadian Air Force Women's Division, which grew to 15,153 members. The Women's Royal Canadian Naval Service had 5,853 members.

Women in the U.S. armed forces served in almost every theater of war, while Canadian women served mostly in Canada, Europe, and the United States. Women became clerks, cooks, mechanics, and drivers and filled other positions to release men for combat.

The Battle of the Atlantic

Blockade and Convoys. The war in the Atlantic Ocean began on Sept. 3, 1939, when the British announced a naval blockade of Germany. On September 11, the Germans ordered a counter-blockade of the Allies with the aim of preventing shipments of food and war materials from reaching Britain and France.

The British set up a convoy system for merchant ships sailing from Halifax, in Canada, to the British Isles. Air patrols helped protect convoys by covering much of this route. On September 4, the U.S. Navy received orders to shoot on sight at any vessel that threatened American ships or any ships escorted by American vessels. On Oct. 31, 1941, a German submarine torpedoed the destroyer *Reuben James*, making it the first American naval vessel to be lost by enemy action in the war.

In March, 1943, the Allied high command gave the British and Canadian navies the primary job of protecting North Atlantic convoys. The United States had chief responsibility for convoys in the central Atlantic and the Caribbean Sea. As the time for the invasion of Normandy drew near in 1944, the Canadian fleet took over the task of escorting North Atlantic convoys.

U-Boats, or German submarines, constantly menaced Allied shipping. The small German surface fleet also caused much trouble. The German pocket battleships were smaller but faster than Allied battleships. Germany also had the biggest ships in the Atlantic—the *Bismarck*

STALINGRAD

Russian Soldiers inched forward in house-to-house fighting. The Germans lost almost an entire army at the Battle of Stalingrad.

Sovfoto

PEARL HARBOR ATTACKED

and the *Tirpitz*. The "unsinkable" *Bismarck's* armor by itself outweighed an entire pocket battleship. In May, 1941, the *Bismarck* slipped into the North Atlantic between Iceland and Greenland. It sank the old British battlecruiser *Hood* and damaged the new battleship *Prince of Wales*. British carrier planes, cruisers, battleships, and destroyers gave chase, and finally sank the *Bismarck* about 400 miles (640 kilometers) from the coast of France. This ended Germany's use of giant ships against convoys in that part of the Atlantic.

Rear Adm. Karl Doenitz, the German submarine fleet commander, formed his U-boats into "wolf-packs" of 8 or 9, and sometimes 20 or more, to attack Allied ships. By the spring of 1943, as many as 235 U-boats were in action. During the war, the Allies lost 23,351,-000 gross tons of shipping. U-boats destroyed more than half of this total. In November, 1942, alone, the Allies lost a record 807,754 gross tons.

The Allies fought the submarines by bombing U-boat bases and factories. They spotted U-boats with sonar and radar devices, and attacked them with destroyer escorts and escort carriers (see SONAR). Land-based aircraft attacks on submarines proved highly successful. During the last two years of the war, the Allies sank submarines faster than the Axis could build them.

War Comes to the United States

Conflicts with Japan. Since 1937, Japan had been buying cotton, gasoline, scrap iron, and aircraft equipment from the United States. It sold large quantities of silk to the United States to create the credit for its purchases. After the "undeclared war" between Japan and China began in 1937, most Americans sympathized with the Chinese. In 1938, the United States extended $25 million in credit to China. It also placed a "moral embargo" on exporting aircraft to Japan. After Japan occupied Indochina in 1940, the United States stopped shipping gasoline, iron, steel, and rubber to Japan, and froze all Japanese assets in the United States.

The Axis countries turned to Latin America for war materials. In 1941, the United States government pro-hibited American companies from doing business with German, Italian, and Japanese firms in Latin America.

Relations between Japan and the United States became increasingly tense in the fall of 1941, when a new Japanese cabinet took office. Lt. Gen. Hideki Tojo, leader of the extremist Japanese military group, became premier. His cabinet began planning for war with the United States. Tojo sent a special representative, Saburo Kurusu, to help Ambassador Kichisaburo Nomura negotiate with Secretary of State Cordell Hull. The two countries argued over U.S. aid to China, Japanese troops in Indochina, Japan's frozen assets, and its exploitation of resources in the Netherlands East Indies. In November, the Japanese cabinet council accepted Tojo's decision to go to war against the United States, Great Britain, and The Netherlands.

The Attack on Pearl Harbor. In October, the Japanese Army and Navy had completed their plans to bomb Pearl Harbor in Hawaii, and to invade Thailand, the Malay peninsula, and the Philippines. Early in November, Adm. Isoroku Yamamoto, commander in chief of the Japanese Combined Fleet, set Monday, December 8 (Japanese time), as the approximate day of the attack. While the Japanese negotiated with Hull, their 33-ship fleet secretly steamed eastward.

About 7:55 A.M., Dec. 7, 1941 (Hawaii time), the first bombs fell on Pearl Harbor. About 360 Japanese planes attacked Pacific Fleet units at the naval base, and army aircraft at Hickam Field and other nearby military installations. Fortunately for the United States, no aircraft carriers were tied up at the base during the attack. When the assault ended nearly two hours later, the Pacific Fleet had lost 8 battleships, 3 light cruisers, 3 destroyers, and 4 other vessels. Among the losses were the battleships *Arizona, California, Oklahoma*, and *West Virginia;* the mine layer *Oglala;* and the target ship *Utah*. Except for the *Arizona, Oklahoma*, and *Utah*, all ships sunk were later repaired and returned to service. The attack also destroyed about 170 U.S. planes. The Japanese had concentrated on ships and planes, leaving repair facilities, the submarine base, and fuel oil stor-

The Attack on Pearl Harbor on Dec. 7, 1941, plunged the United States into war. Japanese aircraft sank 18 ships and killed or wounded about 3,700 persons, including civilians. President Franklin D. Roosevelt signed the declaration of war.

age facilities relatively undamaged. They had dealt the Pacific Fleet and Hawaii's air defense a crippling blow. But the attack united U.S. public opinion against Japan, and forced the U.S. Navy to think of its aircraft carriers as its major counter weapon. See PEARL HARBOR NAVAL BASE.

In Tokyo, the Japanese government immediately declared war on the United States and Great Britain. The following day, President Roosevelt asked Congress for a declaration of war against Japan. He called December 7 "a date which will live in infamy." Only Jeannette Rankin, Congresswoman from Montana, voted against the declaration. On December 11, Germany and Italy declared war on the United States, and Congress then declared war on Germany and Italy.

The question of responsibility for the losses at Pearl Harbor aroused a great controversy. Associate Justice Owen J. Roberts of the Supreme Court of the United States led one investigation, in addition to one by the Navy Department, one by the War Department, and one by a special joint committee of Congress. The Congressional investigators reprimanded the senior commanders at Pearl Harbor, Adm. Husband E. Kimmel (1882-1968) and Lt. Gen. Walter C. Short (1880-1949), for "errors of judgment." They said the United States was not alert to the threat of a sudden attack.

The Allies Attack in Africa and Europe

Allied defeats in Europe came to a halt in late 1941. The Russians took the offensive along the eastern front. The Allies invaded North Africa in 1942, and forced Italy to sign an armistice in 1943. Then Allied troops swarmed ashore in northern France in 1944 in the largest amphibious operation in history. Attacks from all sides finally forced Germany to surrender in 1945.

On the Russian Front

The turn of the tide on the eastern front came with the bitter Russian winter of 1941-1942. Snow, mud, cold, and darkness stalled the German armies. Von Bock's troops advanced almost to the city of Moscow,

but Russian defenders in the surrounding forests threw them back. Then Gen. Georgi K. Zhukov, the defender of Moscow, launched a counteroffensive. By Dec. 16, 1941, the Germans had been forced back into winter defensive positions.

The Russian offensive continued into the spring of 1942. In May, the Germans resumed their attack. They captured Sevastopol on the Black Sea after besieging the city for eight months. In late August, the German Sixth Army drove south toward the important oil-distribution center of Stalingrad on the Volga River. But Stalingrad held firm and Russian troops finally broke a two-month German assault. Col. Gen. Andrei I.

WORLD WAR II

Yeremenko's armies from the south and Col. Gen. Konstantin K. Rokossovsky's armies from the north surrounded the Sixth Army and destroyed it. When Field Marshal Friedrich von Paulus, the Sixth Army commander, surrendered on Jan. 31, 1943, only 90,000 of his original force of more than 350,000 soldiers were still alive. The victory at Stalingrad, boasted Stalin, "signified the decline of the German-fascist army." See STALINGRAD, BATTLE OF.

The North African Campaign

The British fought a seesaw campaign against the Germans and Italians in North Africa, taking and losing ground over and over again. In May, 1942, Rommel's Afrika Korps, aided by Italian troops, began a powerful offensive. Capturing Tobruk in Libya, they moved toward Egypt. By July, strong British resistance and Rommel's supply shortage had halted the Axis attacks at El Alamein, Egypt. In October, the British Eighth Army under Gen. Sir Bernard L. Montgomery took the offensive, and rolled on to Tripoli and southern Tunisia. This victory was a major turning point of the war.

Landings. Along with the British offensive in Tunisia, the Allies planned an invasion of French North Africa with the code name of *Operation Torch*. They hoped to force the Axis armies out of Africa, and also to relieve pressure on the hard-pressed Russian forces, which were reeling under a new German offensive. Lt. Gen. Dwight D. Eisenhower commanded an Allied force that landed on the coast of Algeria and Morocco on Nov. 8, 1942. About 500 troop and supply ships, escorted by more than 350 warships, transported Allied troops from the United States and the British Isles. The invasion caught the German high command completely by surprise.

The Allies made elaborate preparations to capture French North Africa with as little fighting as possible. Allied diplomats plotted with French patriotic groups, and Maj. Gen. Mark W. Clark secretly landed in North Africa from a submarine to plan with the French. French forces resisted the landings, but Adm. Jean Darlan, the Vichy French leader, ordered them to stop fighting.

Final Collapse. As soon as Hitler learned about the Allied landings in North Africa, he ordered German troops to occupy all France. The Germans tried to capture the main French fleet at Toulon, but the French managed to sink about 50 ships. An assassin shot Darlan on Dec. 24, 1942, and Gen. Henri Giraud succeeded him as chief of state in North Africa.

Early in 1943, President Roosevelt and Prime Minister Churchill conferred at Casablanca, Morocco. They announced that the Allies would accept nothing less than unconditional surrender from the Axis nations. While U.S. troops pushed eastward across Algeria, the British Eighth Army advanced into southern Tunisia. On May 12, 1943, the last organized Axis army force in Africa surrendered. The Allies had killed, wounded, or captured about 350,000 Axis soldiers, and had suffered about 70,000 casualties in the North African campaign.

The War in the Mediterranean

Allied control of North Africa ended Axis threats to Egypt and the Suez Canal, and to British oil resources in the Middle East. In June, 1941, British troops had forced the German-sponsored government in Iraq out of office. British and Russian soldiers jointly occupied Iran. Free French and British forces took over Syria and Lebanon from Vichy French troops.

Sicily. The Allies moved swiftly to take advantage of their African victory. On July 10, 1943, Gen. Sir Harold Alexander's Fifteenth Army Group landed on Sicily. During the fighting, Mussolini fell from power in Italy. On July 25, Marshal Pietro Badoglio became premier of Italy. The Italian government imprisoned Mussolini, but a daring band of German paratroopers later rescued him. The Allies occupied all Sicily on August 17, after a 39-day campaign. Badoglio's government signed an armistice with the Allies on September 3, and announced it five days later.

Italy. British and Canadian forces of the Eighth Army used Sicily as a springboard for invading the toe of the Italian peninsula. On Sept. 3, 1943, the British Eighth Army crossed the Strait of Messina and landed in Calabria in southern Italy. Lt. Gen. Mark W. Clark's U.S. Fifth Army, which had sailed from Africa, landed at Salerno on September 9. A German counterattack threatened to push the Fifth Army back to the sea. After intense fighting, Clark's troops swept out of the marshy beachhead and linked with the Eighth Army.

North Africa fell to Allied control in 1943. Tanks battled in the fierce desert heat. British Eighth Army soldiers, *left*, stormed the Axis lines, armed with rifles and kukri knives.

Italy became a "co-belligerent" and declared war on Germany on October 13. The Allies hoped that Italian soldiers would attack German garrisons. But most Italians allowed themselves to be disarmed by the Germans. The Germans continued to fight Allied advances.

The Allied drive up the Italian boot proved to be a slow struggle against a 400,000-man German army led by Field Marshal Albert Kesselring. The Allies also faced floods, mud, mountains, and winter cold.

Early in November, 1943, the Allies reached a line about 75 miles (121 kilometers) south of Rome, but they could not pierce the German defenses. Naples had fallen to the Allies after landings near Salerno. Late in January, 1944, the Allies tried to outflank the German lines by landing troops near Anzio, 33 miles (53 kilometers) south of Rome. But the Germans held the high ground and hemmed in the invaders on a small beachhead. The town of Cassino stood about halfway between Naples and Rome. The Allies bombed the famous monastery on top of Monte Cassino, thinking that Germans were using it. The Germans later claimed they had not used the monastery until after the bombing. The Allies finally captured Cassino and pushed northward. The Italians made Rome an *open city* by announcing that they would not defend it. On June 4, it became the first Axis capital to fall.

Two months later, the Allies captured Florence. The Mediterranean Allied Air Forces supported the ground forces by attacking German troops and supply centers. The Allies finally reached the Gothic Line, a German defense system 4 miles (6 kilometers) deep across northern Italy.

The Air War in Europe

The Allied Air Offensive played a major role in defeating Germany and Italy. The Germans had designed the *Luftwaffe*, their air force, to work closely with ground forces in blitzkrieg campaigns. German combat aircraft included the *Messerschmitt* and *Focke-Wulf* fighter planes, the *Junker*, *Dornier*, and *Heinkel* bombers, and the *Stuka* dive bomber.

The Allies concentrated on developing bombers that could fly long distances. Allied air forces grew until they could make almost daily raids over Europe. By 1942, as many as 1,000 Allied bombers made such raids.

The Royal Air Force Bomber Command, under Air Chief Marshal Sir Arthur T. Harris, favored *saturation bombing* by night. This technique meant dropping a large load of bombs in the general area of a target with the belief that enough bombs would hit the target to destroy it. British airmen flew such planes as the *DeHavilland Mosquito*, a medium bomber; the *Avro Lancaster*, a heavy bomber; and the *Hawker Hurricane* and *Supermarine Spitfire*, both fighters.

The U.S. Eighth Air Force favored *pin-point bombing*. This strategy involved dropping bombs on important targets from high altitudes by daylight. Eighth Air Force pilots flew the *Flying Fortress* and *Liberator* heavy bombers, and the *Thunderbolt*, *Lightning*, and *Mustang* fighters.

In 1944, Lt. Gen. Carl Spaatz became commander of the U.S. Strategic Air Forces in Europe. His command included Lt. Gen. James H. Doolittle's Eighth Air Force, based in England, and the Fifteenth Air Force, based in Italy under Maj. Gen. Nathan F. Twining. Lt. Gen. Hoyt S. Vandenberg commanded the U.S. Ninth Air Force in western Europe.

Crippling German Industries. Allied *strategic* air forces blasted Axis military and industrial targets. The *tactical* air forces supported ground troops and attacked enemy aircraft and airfields.

For five days in late February, 1944, Allied air forces in overwhelming strength bombed German aircraft industries. Gen. Henry H. Arnold, commanding general of the U.S. Army Air Forces, reported that "those five days changed the history of the air war." Allied bombers blasted German aircraft plants and other factories at Bernberg, Brunswick, Leipzig, and Schweinfurt. Other planes raided Augsburg, Regensburg, and Stuttgart. Reichsmarshal Hermann Goering, commander in chief of the Luftwaffe, had boasted that Allied bombers would never reach Berlin. But they did, beginning as early as August, 1940. In August, 1944, Allied bombers hammered at the rich oil fields in Ploiești, Romania, in the attack that finally stopped production there.

Instead of attempting to destroy entire industries, the Allies tried to knock out key targets. For example, bombers destroyed dams in the Ruhr Valley, depriving many German industries of their power sources. They

British Information Services

hit ball-bearing plants, slowing down the production of machinery, aircraft, and tanks. The Allies destroyed more than 56,000 German aircraft, and dropped about 2,700,000 short tons (2,450,000 metric tons) of bombs in Europe. American pilots flew over 750,000 bomber and nearly a million fighter sorties. The British flew nearly 700,000 bomber and 1,700,000 fighter sorties.

The Invasion of Europe

In their first wartime meeting, in December, 1941, Roosevelt and Churchill had adopted a "Defeat Germany First" strategy. The Allies considered an assault across the English channel as early as 1942. The Russians demanded that the Allies open a second battle front to relieve German pressure on their troops in eastern Europe. Gen. George C. Marshall, Chief of Staff of the U.S. Army, had long insisted that the main drive against Germany should come in northern France, and that an invasion would bring a decisive victory.

In August, 1942, the Allies launched a major raid on Dieppe, on the northern coast of France. About 5,000 Canadian, 1,000 British, and 50 United States troops held parts of the coast for nine hours. The Canadians suffered extremely heavy casualties, but the raid provided valuable information on amphibious tactics.

Preparations for the invasion of the Normandy coast began early in 1943, when the Allies set up a planning staff under Lt. Gen. Frederick E. Morgan of Great Britain. The invasion plan received the code name of *Operation Overlord.* Roosevelt and Churchill selected Gen. Dwight D. Eisenhower as supreme commander of the Allied Expeditionary Force. Hitler had appointed Field Marshal Karl Gerd von Rundstedt as commander in chief of the western front to defend *Festung Europa* (Fortress Europe). The Germans built the *Atlantic Wall,* fortifications stretching from Norway to Spain.

D-Day. The British, Canadians, and Americans assembled almost 3 million men, and stored 16 million short tons (14.5 million metric tons) of supplies in Britain for the great invasion. The Allies had 5,000 large ships, 4,000 smaller landing craft, and more than 11,000 aircraft. Months before the invasion, Allied bombers pounded the Normandy coast to prevent the Germans from building up their military strength. The invasion had been set for June 5, but storms forced Eisenhower to postpone it one day. Paratroopers went ahead to cut railroad lines, blow up bridges, and seize landing fields. Gliders brought in men, jeeps, light artillery, and small tanks. Allied warships rained shells on the German coastal batteries.

Eisenhower told his forces: "You are about to embark upon a great crusade." The first wave of infantry and armored troops, commanded by Montgomery, crossed the choppy English Channel under an overcast sky. They waded ashore on a 50-mile (80-kilometer) front at 6:30 A.M. on D-Day, June 6, 1944. There was no air opposition because the Allied air forces had subdued the German air force. To the west, U.S. First Army troops landed on both sides of the Vire River. To the east, British and Canadian infantrymen of the British Second Army pushed ashore near Caen. Allied engineers devised prefabricated harbors in which to unload troops and supplies. These harbors and floating piers

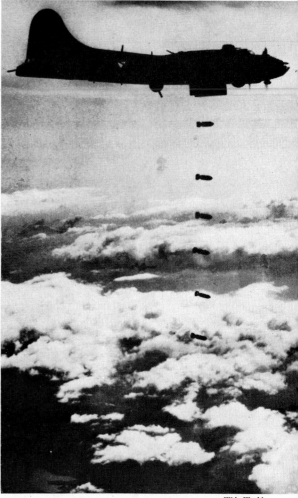

Wide World

AIR
POWER

Bombers, *above,* hit industrial and military targets. Fighters, *right,* attacked enemy aircraft, troops, and ships. Air power proved decisive in the outcome of World War II.

were assigned the code name of *Mulberry.* See D-DAY.

While Von Rundstedt's forces bitterly resisted the Allied landings, Hitler opened a new age in air warfare. On June 13, he sent the first flying bombs over London. The Germans called their new secret weapon the *Vergeltungswaffe* (Vengeance Weapon), or V-1. The British called it the *buzz bomb.* The Germans also developed the V-2 (see GUIDED MISSILE).

The Breakthrough. The capture of Cherbourg on June 27 gave the Allies an excellent harbor. The Allies also had an oil pipeline, called *Pluto,* that ran under the English Channel to Cherbourg. Saint Lô fell to Allied troops on July 18. This opened the way for Lt. Gen. Omar N. Bradley's U.S. First Army to break out of the Normandy peninsula and sweep across France. During the assault, a misdirected bomb from a U.S. Army Air Forces plane killed Lt. Gen. Lesley J. McNair, commander of the U.S. Army Ground Forces.

On July 20, as the climax of a plot by German military leaders, Col. Count Klaus von Stauffenberg placed a time-bomb under Hitler's table during a staff meeting in a hut. The bomb exploded, but only injured Hitler.

Bradley and Montgomery became army group commanders on August 1. By August 6, tanks of Lt. Gen. George S. Patton's U.S. Third Army had raced south and cut off the Brittany Peninsula. After capturing Caen, Canadian forces rolled toward Falaise. They linked with U.S. First Army units under Lt. Gen. Courtney H. Hodges and trapped or killed 60,000 German troops. Those who escaped the trap included Field Marshal Günther von Kluge, who had recently replaced Von Rundstedt as commander in chief.

On August 15, Lt. Gen. Alexander M. Patch's U.S. Seventh Army and Gen. Jean de Lattre de Tassigny's French First Army made an amphibious landing near Cannes in southern France in *Operation Anvil*. French soldiers and other American First Army forces from the northwest entered Paris on August 25.

In the north, Allied armies smashed forward from the Seine River to cross the Somme and Marne rivers and the Belgian border. Brussels fell to British and Canadian troops early in September. Eisenhower hoped to capture Antwerp and knock out many of the V-2 rocket launching sites. He gave supplies to his northern armies, and hard-driving Third Army armored units were halted in Lorraine for a short time. Montgomery's forces pushed into The Netherlands. Hodges' First Army advanced into Luxembourg and crossed the German border on September 12. In the largest airborne operation ever attempted, Lt. Gen. Lewis H. Brereton's First Allied Airborne Army dropped three paratroop divisions from 4,500 planes and gliders into The Netherlands to seize bridges in advance of the ground forces. They achieved only part of their objectives.

Allied troops swept up the Rhône Valley from south-ern France, joining the Third Army near Dijon on September 15. Montgomery's men seized Walcheren Island in the North Sea, suffering heavy casualties. Fierce enemy resistance forced the First Army to battle savagely for Aachen and the Huertgen Forest in Germany.

The Battle of the Bulge. Before the Allies could cross the Rhine, they had to face a last-stand German onslaught in the Ardennes Forest. Hitler personally planned a swift breakthrough to capture Antwerp and split the Allied armies. Field Marshal Walter Model, army ground commander under Von Rundstedt, directed the assault, which had the code name *Watch on the Rhine*. Under cover of fog, 38 German divisions struck along a 50-mile (80-kilometer) front on December 16. Mechanized units overran several First Army positions.

Model's armies drove the Allies almost to the Meuse River, and surrounded Bastogne in the southern Ardennes. Asked to surrender, Brig. Gen. Anthony C. McAuliffe of the 101st Airborne Division at Bastogne replied: "Nuts." Third Army armored units pierced the German lines from the south and relieved Bastogne. This attack became known as the *Battle of the Bulge*, because of the bulging shape of the battleground on a map. By early January, 1945, the Allies had recovered all ground lost in the battle. The Germans had 110,000 men taken prisoner, and about 100,000 other casualties.

Early in February, the Allies cleared the west bank of the Roer River, west of the Rhine. After capturing Cologne, First Army troops advanced toward Remagen. On March 7, they found the Ludendorff Bridge that crossed the Rhine at Remagen still intact. German soldiers tried to destroy the bridge, but not all their charges exploded. First Army units raced across to set up a bridgehead east of the Rhine. A few days later, the Third Army crossed the Rhine to the south and then

U.S. Coast Guard; U.S. Army

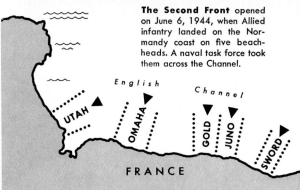

English Channel

UTAH OMAHA GOLD JUNO SWORD

FRANCE

Talking to the Troops, Supreme Allied Commander Dwight D. Eisenhower met black-faced airborne troops before they dropped into France behind the German lines on D-Day.

three Allied armies crossed the river to the north. On April 1, the First Army and Lt. Gen. William H. Simpson's Ninth Army made contact near Paderborn. This action isolated the rich Ruhr Valley and trapped more than 300,000 enemy soldiers.

The Russian Advance. As the Allies raced toward the heart of Germany, Russian armies rolled toward Berlin from the east. The last major German offensive in Russia, in July, 1943, had failed. Within a year, the Russians had recaptured the Ukraine, the Crimea, White Russia, eastern Poland, and most of Lithuania. Russian troops drove into Romania, Bulgaria, and the Baltic states. In October, 1944, Finland again surrendered to the Russians, and declared war on Germany. Russian armies swept into eastern Hungary and joined forces with Tito in Yugoslavia. They swung north and captured Vienna and eastern Austria. In five months, Russia knocked the four Axis satellites—Romania, Bulgaria, Finland, and Hungary—out of the war.

Early in January, 1945, the Red Army crashed into Warsaw and Kraków. The people of Warsaw had expected the Russians to continue westward, and rebelled against the Germans. But the Russians halted east of the city, and the Germans put down the rebellion.

For the final assault on Germany in April, the Russians assembled more than 4 million men. Marshal Georgi Zhukov's First White Russian and First Ukrainian Army groups drove toward Berlin, and Marshal Konstantin Rokossovsky's Second White Russian Army group marched into northern Germany. Hitler appointed Col. Gen. Heinz Guderian to head the fast-crumbling German eastern front.

Victory in Europe. From all directions, Allied armies closed in on the Germans. Canadian troops under Gen. Henry D. G. Crerar liberated The Netherlands, and Lt. Gen. Miles C. Dempsey's British Second Army headed for Bremen in the north. Bradley's group of four armies raced eastward to the Elbe River to meet the Russians. In the south, Allied armies under Gen. Jacob L. Devers rolled toward Austria and Czechoslovakia. They hoped to cut off Berlin from the Bavarian Mountains, where it was rumored that many determined Germans hoped to make a last-ditch stand.

Late in April, Heinrich Himmler, head of the German home guard and the dreaded *Gestapo* (secret police), tried to negotiate a peace with Great Britain and the

United States. The Allies demanded that German troops on all fronts surrender. On April 25, First Army patrols and Red Army units joined forces at Torgau, on the Elbe River. Three days later, Italian partisans captured and executed Mussolini, who had tried to escape into Switzerland. German forces in Italy surrendered on May 2.

On May 1, the German radio announced that Hitler had died while defending Berlin against the Russians, and had named Grand Adm. Karl Doenitz as his successor. Allied investigators later learned that Hitler and his wife, Eva Braun, had committed suicide in Berlin on April 30, and that their bodies had been burned. Berlin

finally fell to the invading Russian armies on May 2.

Early on the morning of May 7, Col. Gen. Alfred Jodl of the German high command entered Allied headquarters in a red school building at Reims, France. There, on behalf of his government, he signed the terms of unconditional surrender. Lt. Gen. Walter B. Smith, Eisenhower's chief of staff, signed for the Allies. The free world celebrated May 8 as V-E (Victory in Europe) Day. On May 9, a ceremony in Berlin ratified the surrender terms. After five years, eight months, and seven days, the European phase of World War II had ended.

The War in Asia and the Pacific

War had raged in Asia since Japan's attack on China in 1937. The war in Europe opened the way for Japan to turn south. In September, 1940, its troops marched into French Indochina as part of its plan for a *Greater East Asia Co-Prosperity Sphere* similar to Hitler's *New Order* in Europe. By 1942, the Japanese had overrun Burma, Malaya, the Netherlands East Indies, the Philippines, and Thailand. Japan's steady expansion came to a halt in the summer of 1942. After a series of island-hopping campaigns, air bombardments, and submarine attacks, the Allies forced Japan to surrender unconditionally on Sept. 2, 1945, and end World War II.

Early Japanese Victories

Japan Sweeps Ahead. Within a few hours after attacking Pearl Harbor on Dec. 7, 1941, Japanese bombers struck at American bases on the islands of Guam, Midway, and Wake. They also bombed Manila and Singapore. More than 56,000 Japanese troops under Lt. Gen. Masaharu Homma landed on Luzon in the Philippines between December 10 and 22. Hong Kong, defended partly by Canadians, was seized. The Japanese also occupied Guam and Wake islands.

Instead of storming the stronghold of Singapore by sea, as the British expected, Japanese forces advanced through the thick jungles of the Malay Peninsula and attacked the city from the rear. On Feb. 16, 1942, the

British were forced to surrender Singapore to Japan.

Japanese troops quickly overran New Britain, New Ireland, and the Admiralty and Solomon islands. The Japanese routed an Allied fleet in the Battle of the Java Sea, opening their way to the Netherlands East Indies.

Burma and the Philippines fell to Japan early in 1942. As the invaders approached, Gen. Douglas MacArthur, commander of U.S. Army Forces in the Far East, declared Manila an open city. He withdrew his troops to the Bataan Peninsula. The enemy entered Manila on January 2. American and Philippine troops in Bataan stoutly resisted Japanese assaults. On March 11, MacArthur left the Philippines by torpedo boat at President Roosevelt's order, then flew to Australia to command the Southwest Pacific Area. He put Lt. Gen. Jonathan M. Wainwright in charge of the defenders of Bataan, and promised the Filipinos: "I shall return." The shortage of food and medical supplies forced Bataan's surrender on April 9. The 11,000-man garrison on Corregidor, a rocky fortress in Manila Bay, held out until May 6. The Japanese forced about 60,000 prisoners to march 70 miles (110 kilometers) to prison camps. In the *Bataan Death March*, about 10,000 of the prisoners died from starvation or maltreatment.

In Burma, the Japanese also met stubborn resistance. The country had rich resources of oil and tin. By conquering Burma, the Japanese could close the Burma

GERMAN SURRENDER

Unconditional Surrender of German forces came on May 7, 1945, at Allied headquarters in Reims, France. Alfred Jodl, *center,* signed for the German High Command.

Road, the last land route open to China. The British evacuated Rangoon on March 7. Chinese troops under Lt. Gen. Joseph W. Stilwell tried to hold Mandalay and protect the Burma Road, but the Japanese were too strong. He and a handful of men tramped 140 miles (230 kilometers) through mountains and jungles to India.

The Allies Strike Back

Hit-and-Run Raids. After Japan conquered the western and southern Pacific, it expected the Allies to seek peace. But the Japanese soon realized that the Allies would never allow them to keep their newly-conquered territories. Early in 1942, a U.S. carrier task force raided the Marshall, Gilbert, and Marcus islands. On April 18, a fleet of 16 B-25 army bombers led by Lt. Col. James H. Doolittle took off from the carrier *Hornet*, about 650 miles (1,050 kilometers) east of Honshu, Japan. The bombers hit Tokyo and other cities. The raid astounded the Japanese who had believed that Allied planes could never reach their homeland. Fifteen of the planes crashed when they ran out of fuel and could not reach bases in China. One landed in Siberia. The Chinese underground helped Doolittle and 63 of his fliers to escape. The Japanese executed two pilots.

The Battle of the Coral Sea. The Doolittle raid helped convince the Japanese that they would have to expand their defense boundaries. They planned to seize Port Moresby in southeastern New Guinea. Then they hoped to cut Allied shipping lanes to Australia, and perhaps even invade Australia. But Rear Adm. Frank J. Fletcher's task force intercepted a Japanese fleet headed for Port Moresby in the Coral Sea. The two forces fought a four-day battle from May 4 to 8, in which aircraft did all the fighting. The battle was an important Allied strategic victory. It blocked Japan's push southeastward and ended its threat to Port Moresby.

The Battle of Midway. The most important objectives in Japan's resumed offensive were the capture of Midway Island and of the Aleutian Islands, west of Alaska. Midway lies 1,000 miles (1,600 kilometers) northwest of Hawaii. Yamamoto hoped that, by seizing Midway, he could draw the Pacific Fleet away from Hawaii and win a decisive victory with his larger force.

Before Pearl Harbor, the United States scored one of its greatest triumphs by cracking Japan's secret codes.

This feat enabled Adm. Chester W. Nimitz, who had succeeded Adm. Husband E. Kimmel as commander in chief of the Pacific Fleet, to know about Yamamoto's plans in advance. On June 4, 1942, aircraft from the Japanese fleet began blasting Midway. Nimitz' task force commanders, Rear Admirals Frank J. Fletcher and Raymond A. Spruance, launched aircraft from the carriers *Enterprise*, *Hornet*, and *Yorktown*. At the end of the two-day battle, Japan had lost four carriers and a major part of its air arm. Enemy submarines sank the *Yorktown*. The Battle of Midway proved to be one of the most decisive victories in history. It ended Japanese threats to Hawaii and to the United States.

Although Japan failed to seize Midway, its troops occupied Kiska and Attu, at the tip of the Aleutian chain, on June 7. In July, they captured Agattu. Japan had no plans to attack Alaska. In the spring of 1943, U.S. troops drove the Japanese from Attu and the enemy withdrew from Agattu and Kiska.

The South Pacific

Allied strategy in the South Pacific had three major objectives: (1) to recapture the Philippines, (2) to cut Japan's lines of communications with its overseas bases, and (3) to set up bases from which to attack Japan itself. But first the Allies had to capture or neutralize Rabaul, an important enemy base on New Britain Island, north of Australia. They planned an invasion of the nearby Solomon Islands, while other Allied forces approached Rabaul by way of New Guinea.

Guadalcanal. On Aug. 7, 1942, the Allies began their first offensive action in the Pacific. U.S. Marines under Maj. Gen. Alexander A. Vandegrift landed on Guadalcanal in the Solomon Islands. The fighting was bitter, and control of the island seesawed for several months. In February, 1943, army troops under Maj. Gen. Alexander M. Patch finally cleared Guadalcanal. By November, other Allied forces had advanced up the Solomons chain to Bougainville Island.

The Allies learned many lessons during the Solomons campaign. They gradually perfected the technique of amphibious warfare, which involved air, land, and sea forces working as a team. Allied soldiers encountered the fanatical code of *bushido*, which requires Japanese soldiers to fight to the death. The Japanese believed

A Convoy escorted by Allied warships dots the Pacific as it steams toward an enemy-held island. Ships brought in troops and supplies.

Antiaircraft Guns, carried as cargo, blast away on a convoy run. Japanese *kamikazes,* or suicide planes, flew into Allied ships, causing much damage.

U.S. Navy; United Press Int.

that surrender meant disgrace, and often preferred suicide to capture. The Japanese mistreated many Allied prisoners.

In the Solomons, the Allies fought the first of many jungle campaigns. Heavy rains made roads unusable. Troops waded knee deep through thick, black mud. In the green half-light, soldiers often could not distinguish their own battle lines from the enemy's. Malaria and other jungle diseases took a terrific toll. Japanese snipers lurked everywhere.

New Guinea. Japanese bases in New Guinea threatened Allied airfields in Australia. Late in 1942, Japan launched an overland campaign against the Allied base at Port Moresby. Its troops came within 32 miles (51 kilometers) of the town. American, Australian, and Dutch forces then took the offensive.

Allied troops under MacArthur inched their way to Buna, Gona, Salamaua, and Lae, the main enemy positions in New Guinea. But Japanese planes based on nearby Rabaul continued to attack Allied shipping.

Encirclement. In December, 1943, Allied troops landed on the nearby island of New Britain. After brief enemy resistance, the Admiralty Islands fell to the Allies in March, 1944.

Allied forces continued to make a series of jumps in their march up the New Guinea coast. They invaded such important bases as Aitape (April 22), Hollandia (April 22), Wakde (May 17), and Biak (May 27).

Island Hopping

While Allied forces in the South Pacific followed one road toward Japan, Allied forces in the Central Pacific took another route. The Japanese Empire had reached its height in August, 1942. It controlled the Gilbert, Marshall, Caroline, and Mariana islands that stretched halfway across the Pacific. These islands served as *unsinkable aircraft carriers,* bases for airplanes.

Allied strategists believed that the central Pacific fortress of Japan could be cracked. They did not intend to seize each island separately. This would be too costly and take too long. Instead, they decided on a plan of *island hopping,* or seizing key islands from which to attack the next target, bypassing other targets.

Tarawa. Nimitz selected the Gilbert Islands as the first major objective in his island-hopping campaign.

On Nov. 20, 1943, Spruance's Central Pacific Force (later Fifth Fleet) landed U.S. Marines on Tarawa and army troops at Makin. Makin fell in three days.

The marines encountered fierce opposition and an intricate system of fortifications on Tarawa. The Japanese had studded the island with barricades, concrete pillboxes, gun emplacements, and bombproof underground shelters. They had been ordered to resist to the bitter end. Of the 3,000 enemy troops and 1,800 civilian laborers on the island, the marines captured only 147 Japanese and Koreans alive. The United States suffered 3,110 casualties in one of the war's most savage battles.

Kwajalein, one of the world's largest atolls, lies in the Marshall Islands. In January, 1944, Rear Adm. Marc A. Mitscher's Task Force 58 began a series of raids on Japanese bases in the Marshalls. His command included the U.S. Navy's fastest carriers, battleships, and cruisers. It operated as part of the 1,200-ship Cen-

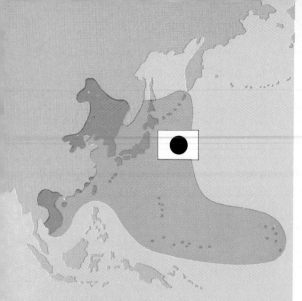

Pearl Harbor Attacked (December, 1941). Japan's conquests included Indochina, Manchuria, and parts of China.

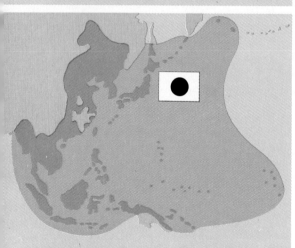

Japan's Empire at Its Height (August, 1942) stretched from the Netherlands East Indies to parts of the Aleutians.

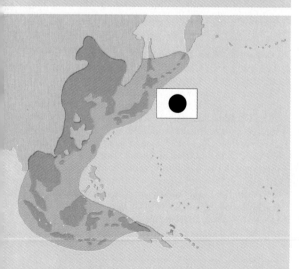

Surrender (August, 1945). When Japan surrendered, ending World War II, it still occupied parts of eastern Asia.

HIGHLIGHTS OF THE WAR IN ASIA AND THE PACIFIC

1931
Sept. 18   Japan invaded Manchuria in North China.

1937
July 7   Japan invaded China.

1940
Sept. 22   Japan pushed into French Indochina.

1941
Apr. 13   Japan and Russia signed a non-aggression pact.
June 8   British and French troops invaded Syria.
Aug. 25   Russian and British forces invaded Iran.
Dec. 7   The Japanese attacked Pearl Harbor.
Dec. 8   The United States declared war on Japan.
Dec. 9   China declared war on Germany, Italy, and Japan.
Dec. 10   Guam surrendered to the Japanese.
Dec. 23   Wake Island surrendered to the Japanese.
Dec. 25   British troops at Hong Kong surrendered.

1942
Jan. 2   Manila fell to invading Japanese forces.
Jan. 11   The Japanese landed in the Netherlands East Indies.
Feb. 1   U.S. ships raided the Marshalls and Gilberts.
Feb. 15   Singapore surrendered to the Japanese.
Feb. 27   The Allies lost the Battle of Java Sea.
Mar. 7   The Japanese occupied the Netherlands East Indies.
April 9   Bataan surrendered to the Japanese.
Apr. 18   U.S. carrier-based aircraft bombed Tokyo.
May 4-8   The Allies won the Battle of the Coral Sea.
May 6   The Japanese occupied Corregidor.
June 4-6   The Battle of Midway ended Japan's expansion eastward.
Aug. 7   U.S. marines landed on Guadalcanal.

1943
Mar. 2-5   The Allies defeated a Japanese naval force in the Battle of the Bismarck Sea.
Mar. 13   Japanese troops retreated across the Yangtze.
May 30   Organized Japanese resistance on Attu ended.
Oct. 2   Allied forces captured Finschhafen.
Nov. 1   U.S. troops landed on Bougainville Island.
Nov. 20   U.S. marines invaded Tarawa and Makin.
Nov. 22   The Allies conferred at Cairo in Egypt.

1944
Jan. 31   U.S. troops attacked Kwajalein atoll.
Feb. 17   U.S. naval forces raided Truk Island.
Feb. 29   Allied soldiers landed in the Admiralties.
Mar. 22   Japanese troops crossed the border of India.
Apr. 22   Allied forces landed at Hollandia.
June 15   U.S. marines invaded Saipan Island.
June 15   B-29 Superfortresses raided Japan.
June 19-20   U.S. forces won the Battle of the Philippine Sea.
July 21   U.S. troops landed on Guam Island.
Sept. 15   U.S. marines invaded Peleliu Island.
Oct. 20   U.S. Army forces landed on Leyte.
Oct. 23-26   The U.S. Pacific Fleet crushed the Japanese fleet in the Battle for Leyte Gulf.

1945
Jan. 9   Allied troops invaded Luzon, Philippines.
Jan. 22   The Allies reopened a land route to China.
Feb. 19   U.S. marines stormed Iwo Jima Island.
Apr. 1   U.S. troops landed on Okinawa Island.
Aug. 6   U.S. dropped an atomic bomb on Hiroshima.
Aug. 9   U.S. dropped an atomic bomb on Nagasaki.
Aug. 10   Japan opened peace negotiations.
Aug. 14   Japan accepted the Allied surrender terms.
Sept. 2   Japan signed the terms of surrender.
Sept. 8   Japanese forces in China surrendered.
Sept. 12   Japanese troops in Southeast Asia surrendered.

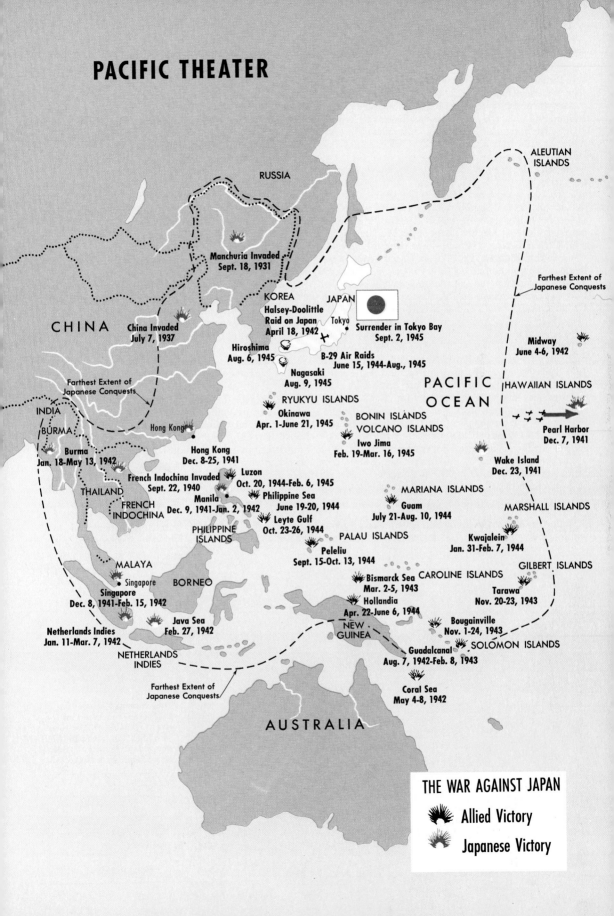

PACIFIC THEATER

ALEUTIAN
ISLANDS

RUSSIA

Manchuria Invaded
Sept. 18, 1931

Farthest Extent of
Japanese Conquests

KOREA   JAPAN

Halsey-Doolittle
Raid on Japan
April 18, 1942

CHINA   China Invaded
July 7, 1937

Tokyo
Surrender in Tokyo Bay
Sept. 2, 1945

Midway
June 4-6, 1942

Hiroshima
Aug. 6, 1945

B-29 Air Raids
June 15, 1944-Aug., 1945

Nagasaki
Aug. 9, 1945

PACIFIC
OCEAN

HAWAIIAN ISLANDS

Farthest Extent of
Japanese Conquests

INDIA

RYUKYU ISLANDS

Okinawa
Apr. 1-June 21, 1945

BONIN ISLANDS

VOLCANO ISLANDS

Pearl Harbor
Dec. 7, 1941

BURMA

Hong Kong

Burma
Jan. 18-May 13, 1942

Hong Kong
Dec. 8-25, 1941

Iwo Jima
Feb. 19-Mar. 16, 1945

Wake Island
Dec. 23, 1941

THAILAND

French Indochina Invaded
Sept. 22, 1940

FRENCH
INDOCHINA

Luzon
Oct. 20, 1944-Feb. 6, 1945

Manila
Dec. 9, 1941-Jan. 2, 1942

Philippine Sea
June 19-20, 1944

MARIANA ISLANDS

Guam
July 21-Aug. 10, 1944

MARSHALL ISLANDS

PHILIPPINE
ISLANDS

Leyte Gulf
Oct. 23-26, 1944

PALAU ISLANDS

Kwajalein
Jan. 31-Feb. 7, 1944

MALAYA

Singapore

Peleliu
Sept. 15-Oct. 13, 1944

GILBERT ISLANDS

BORNEO

Bismarck Sea
Mar. 2-5, 1943

CAROLINE ISLANDS

Tarawa
Nov. 20-23, 1943

Singapore
Dec. 8, 1941-Feb. 15, 1942

Java Sea
Feb. 27, 1942

Hollandia
Apr. 22-June 6, 1944

Bougainville
Nov. 1-24, 1943

Netherlands Indies
Jan. 11-Mar. 7, 1942

NEW
GUINEA

SOLOMON ISLANDS

NETHERLANDS
INDIES

Guadalcanal
Aug. 7, 1942-Feb. 8, 1943

Farthest Extent of
Japanese Conquests

Coral Sea
May 4-8, 1942

AUSTRALIA

THE WAR AGAINST JAPAN

Allied Victory

Japanese Victory

tral Pacific Force. The carriers launched hundreds of navy planes, including the *Corsair*, *Dauntless*, and *Hellcat*.

Marines and infantrymen landed on Kwajalein and Majuro on January 31, and occupied the two atolls after a week's fighting. Enewetak atoll, 360 miles (579 kilometers) northwest of Kwajalein, came under Allied control on February 21.

Saipan. The Mariana Islands lay within long-range bomber distance of Japan. The army air forces had developed B-29 superfortress bombers that were half again as large as the B-17 bombers being used to blast Germany. It wanted bases in the Central Pacific for these bombers. The four biggest islands of the Marianas—Saipan, Tinian, Rota, and Guam—lie at the southern end.

Vice Adm. Richmond K. Turner's amphibious forces landed troops on Saipan on June 15. Lt. Gen. Holland M. Smith directed the marine and army forces. His troops occupied Saipan on July 9, after suffering about 16,500 casualties and killing over 28,000 enemy soldiers. Premier Hideki Tojo of Japan could not face criticism for the loss of Saipan. He resigned on July 18.

Japanese carriers went into action for the first time since early 1943. In the Battle of the Philippine Sea on June 19-20, near Guam, the Japanese lost 395 carrier planes. Tinian fell to the Allies in late July.

Army and marine forces under Maj. Gen. Roy S. Geiger invaded Guam on July 21. The Japanese fought bitterly. More than 10,000 of them died before Geiger announced on August 10 that organized resistance had ended. American casualties in Guam totaled 7,800.

The army air forces promptly built huge bases in the Marianas for B-29 bombers. The first superfortress raid on Japan from these bases came on November 24.

Return to the Philippines

With the Marianas occupied, Allied forces stood within 1,600 miles (2,570 kilometers) of Tokyo and Manila. In preparation for attacks on the Philippines and Japan, Adm. William F. Halsey's Third Fleet put to sea. Vice Adm. John S. McCain commanded his fast carrier task forces. On September 15, marines landed on Peleliu in the Palau Islands. Army troops attacked Morotai Island in the Netherlands East Indies. Conquest of the two islands put the Allies within 400 miles (640 kilometers) of the Philippines.

Landings on Leyte. Air, ground, and naval forces had all worked together to bring the Allies to the Philippines. On October 20, Lt. Gen. Walter Krueger's U.S. Sixth Army won two beaches on the central island of Leyte. It faced a 270,000-man Japanese army and air force in the Philippines, commanded by Field Marshal Count Hisaichi Terauchi. MacArthur and his staff waded ashore at Tacloban about five hours after the first landings. He had kept his promise to return. By December, the Sixth Army had occupied Leyte.

The Battle for Leyte Gulf. The Japanese Navy decided to muster its remaining strength to try to drive the Allies from Leyte. The Battle for Leyte Gulf was the biggest naval engagement in history from the standpoint of naval tonnage involved. It consisted of actions in four separate areas: (1) in the Sibuyan Sea, (2) in Surigao Strait, (3) off Samar, and (4) off Cape Engano.

The Japanese planned to send their northern force under Adm. Jisaburo Ozawa south from Japan. They wanted to lure the Third Fleet toward this force and away from the Philippines. Adm. Takeo Kurita's central force would sail east from Borneo through the San Bernardino Strait and head for Leyte Gulf. Vice Adm. Shoji Nishimura and a southern force would sail from Borneo and drive for Surigao Strait, south of Leyte. Vice Adm. Kiyohide Shima's attack force would proceed south from the Pescadores Islands and join with the other ships to attack the Leyte beachheads.

Sibuyan Sea. The Battle for Leyte Gulf began on October 23, when U.S. submarines torpedoed two cruisers in Kurita's force. The following morning, fliers

TARAWA

U.S. Marines crawled up a shell-raked beachhead on Tarawa in the Gilberts. The Allies' island-hopping campaign began with landings in the Solomon Islands in August, 1942.

Wide World

LEYTE GULF

Shells Burst around American carriers in the Battle for Leyte Gulf in 1944. A weak Japanese force (black line) lured one U.S. fleet north (dotted line) as other forces steamed toward Leyte Gulf.

from Halsey's Third Fleet spotted Kurita's ships near the Sibuyan Sea and Nishimura's force to the south near the Mindanao Sea. They attacked the central force and sank the giant battleship *Musashi*. They then sighted Ozawa's carriers heading south. Halsey decided to attack Ozawa. This left the San Bernardino Strait unguarded. He felt that his fleet could dash back to the strait if Kurita tried to go through it. The Japanese succeeded in drawing him north to Ozawa's force.

Surigao Strait. Kurita turned eastward, slipped through San Bernardino Strait, and headed toward Leyte Gulf. Offshore, Vice Adm. Thomas C. Kinkaid's Seventh Fleet stood guard. When Kinkaid learned that Nishimura's southern force was approaching the gulf through Surigao Strait to the south, he formed a task force under Rear Adm. Jesse B. Oldendorf to block the strait. As Nishimura's warships sailed up the strait, Oldendorf's warships sank two enemy battleships and four destroyers.

Samar. As Kurita steamed southward along the Samar coast, he came upon a Seventh Fleet escort carrier task group. The Japanese forces got to within three hours' sail from Leyte Gulf and sank an Allied escort carrier and two destroyers, but then retired northward.

Cape Engano. As the Seventh Fleet battled off Samar, Halsey's Third Fleet pursued Ozawa's force, which had swung north. His battleships came within 45 miles (72 kilometers) of the enemy. After Kinkaid appealed for help, Halsey ordered some fast battleships and carriers to turn south. But he lost all chances of destroying the northern force. The Third Fleet raced back to San Bernardino Strait, too late to wipe out the remainder of Kurita's force.

The Battle for Leyte Gulf was a decisive victory for the United States. At the end of the battle on October 26, Japan had lost 3 battleships, 4 carriers, 10 cruisers, and 9 destroyers. The Allies lost 1 light and 2 escort carriers, 2 destroyers, and a destroyer escort. In desperation, the Japanese began on October 25 to strike with

kamikazes, or suicide planes. Enemy fliers flew their planes into Allied warships, knowing they would be killed (see KAMIKAZE).

On to Manila. The Eighth Army under Lt. Gen. Robert L. Eichelberger took over mop-up operations on Leyte. On Jan. 9, 1945, the Sixth Army landed in Lingayen Gulf, about 110 miles (177 kilometers) north of Manila on the island of Luzon. Third Fleet carriers roamed the South China Sea with almost no opposition, cutting Japan's last supply line with its empire in the south.

Japanese troops fiercely resisted the Allied advance toward Manila, and destroyed part of the Philippine capital. By the end of February, the Allies had largely cleared Manila and Luzon of enemy forces. However, scattered Japanese resistance continued in the Philippines until the end of the war.

The China-Burma-India Theater

Control of the Philippines gave the Allies another base from which they could invade the Japanese-held Chinese mainland. Some Allied strategists favored using the Philippines as a direct springboard to Japan. But they also felt that China had to be kept in the war. The Chinese pinned down thousands of Japanese troops.

Burma played a vital role in the Allied plan of keeping China in the war. War materials to China had once flowed over the Burma Road (see BURMA ROAD). After Japan seized Burma, it promptly cut off the road. In 1943, the Allies began a campaign to reopen the road and restore land communications with China. They hoped to drive through northern Burma and build a road that would connect the railway in northeast India with the Chinese end of the old Burma Road. This road was completed in January, 1945. It became known as the *Ledo Road.* The road later became known as the *Stilwell Road.*

American, British, and Chinese troops in northern Burma had to hack through thick jungles and climb

Supplies pile up on Iwo Jima Island as U.S. Marines push inland. The bloody Iwo campaign was one of the last major land battles in the Pacific.

Hiroshima lay in ruins after the Allies blasted the city with an atomic bomb on Aug. 6, 1945. A second atomic bomb destroyed Nagasaki on Aug. 9.

Wide World; United Press Int.

steep mountains. The Allies organized guerrilla groups, including Merrill's Marauders and Wingate's Raiders (see MERRILL'S MARAUDERS; WINGATE'S RAIDERS). Stilwell's Chinese troops advanced south, seeking to hold the Chinese end of the Burma Road.

The Japanese tried to cut the new Ledo Road. Early in 1944, they began a drive to capture Allied airfields in northeast India. American, British, Chinese, and Indian troops halted their advances. Heavy rains, tropical diseases, and a shortage of supplies also hindered the Japanese. On Feb. 4, 1945, the first Allied convoy rolled into China over the Stilwell Road. British Commonwealth forces recaptured Mandalay on March 20, and forced the Japanese to evacuate Rangoon on May 3.

China had been isolated from most of the world when the Japanese cut the Burma Road. Supplies could come only through the air. The U.S. Air Transport Command flew the dangerous 500-mile (800-kilometer) route, known as the *Hump*, over the Himalaya between Assam in India and the Yunnan plateau in western China.

In the early 1940's, the United States began building air bases in China. The American Volunteer Group, known as the *Flying Tigers*, became a full-fledged air force under Maj. Gen. Claire L. Chennault. In 1944, the Japanese began a determined drive to capture Allied air bases. They drove south in Hunan province, past Changsha to Hangchow. Turning southwest, they seized most of the major airfields there. The Japanese also captured the important bases of Liu-chou and Kuei-lin. At one point, they swept to within 200 miles (320 kilometers) of the Chinese wartime capital of Chungking. But they pushed ahead faster than their supply lines could move, and had to retreat. By early 1945, Chinese forces had regained most of the lost territory.

Target Tokyo

Allied strategy to end the war called for an invasion of Japan with the code name of *Operation Olympic*. It would be launched from islands near Japan, or from bases in China and Korea. Allied warships would continue to raid Japanese shipping and coastal areas, and Allied bombers would increase their attacks.

Air Attacks on Japan by long-range B-29 bombers had begun on June 15, 1944, from bases in China. The superfortresses bombed steel mills at Yawata. Through-

out the summer of 1944, the U.S. Twentieth Air Force raided Japan, Taiwan, and Japanese-held Manchuria about once a week. B-29's in the Marianas joined with bombers based in China to raid Tokyo on November 24.

In March, 1945, B-29's commanded by Maj. Gen. Curtis E. LeMay began incendiary bombing at night from a low altitude of about 7,000 feet (2,100 meters). This allowed bombers to carry a heavier bomb load, because they did not need so much gasoline. As many as 800 superfortresses took part in these attacks. Three raids wiped out the heart of Tokyo, and one attack destroyed most of Yokohama. The army air forces flew more than 15,000 missions against 66 major Japanese cities, and dropped more than 100,000 short tons (91,-000 metric tons) of incendiary bombs. The Allies held such superiority in the air that early in July, 1945, Gen. Carl Spaatz, who assumed command of the U.S. Army Strategic Air Forces in the Pacific after the war ended in Europe, publicly announced in advance the names of cities to be bombed.

The Sea Road. Naval aircraft joined in raids on Japanese cities and transportation. Without ships, Japan could not long survive. It needed ships to link the widespread parts of its empire, and to transport troops and supplies. Allied submarines increased their activity in Japanese coastal waters, where they had been operating since 1942. By 1945, Japan's shipping tonnage had been reduced to about 1½ million short tons (1.4 million metric tons) compared with 10 million short tons (9.1 million metric tons) early in 1942. Submarines accounted for over half of Japan's losses in merchant ships.

In April 1945, carrier planes operating in the East China Sea sank the Japanese battleship *Yamato*. The *Yamato* and the *Musashi*, which had been sunk in 1944, were the largest battleships ever built. The U.S. Third Fleet, joined by the British Pacific Fleet, moved to within a short distance of Japan to bombard its cities.

Iwo Jima lay halfway between Guam and Japan. Capture of this tiny island would place the Allies within 750 miles (1,210 kilometers) of Tokyo. For seven months before the invasion, the army air forces and navy bombed or shelled the island almost daily. The Japanese built a system of concrete fortifications and underground defenses on Iwo Jima.

On Feb. 19, 1945, Maj. Gen. Harry Schmidt's Fifth Marine Amphibious Corps landed on Iwo Jima. The 60,000 marines met savage opposition from the troops of Lt. Gen. Tadamichi Kuribayashi. On February 23, marines scaled the steep slopes of Mount Suribachi and hoisted the American flag. In Nimitz' words, "uncommon valor was a common virtue" during the 26 days of heavy fighting before Iwo fell to the Allies on March 16. The marines and the navy killed more than 20,000 enemy troops at the cost of more than 6,000 killed.

Okinawa. The Joint Chiefs of Staff selected Okinawa as the next step on the road to Tokyo. This island in the Ryukyus chain lies about 350 miles (563 kilometers) from Kyushu, the southern Japanese home island. It would provide a base for landings in China or Japan.

On Easter Sunday, April 1, 1945, two corps of army and marine troops under Lt. Gen. Simon B. Buckner, Jr., invaded Okinawa. The Japanese fought desperately. By the end of the campaign in mid-June, their *kamikazes* (suicide planes and missiles) had sunk 36 vessels and damaged 332 others (see KAMIKAZE). Organized Japanese resistance on the island ended on June 21. During the ground fighting, Buckner was killed. The Allies had suffered 49,000 casualties. More than 109,000 Japanese were killed. The fighting on Okinawa proved to be the last major land battle of the war.

Invasion Plans. The Allies planned to invade the Japanese home island, Kyushu, in November. This invasion, given the code name *Operation Olympic*, was to be followed in March 1946 with an assault on the Tokyo plain of eastern Honshu, the main home island.

In July 1945, the heads of government in Britain, Russia, and the United States conferred at Potsdam, Germany. Stalin reported that he had received a message indicating Japan's willingness to negotiate a peace and unwillingness to accept unconditional surrender. On July 26, the heads of state of the United States, Great Britain, and China issued an ultimatum calling for unconditional surrender and a just peace. They planned to occupy Japan, restrict Japanese authority to the home islands, disarm the country, and bring its war criminals to trial. When Japan ignored the ultimatum, the United States decided to use the atomic bomb.

The Atomic Bomb helped make an invasion of Japan unnecessary. On August 6, a B-29 called "Enola Gay" dropped the first atomic bomb used in warfare on the city of Hiroshima (see ATOMIC BOMB). More than 92,000 persons were killed or missing. Three days later, an atomic bomb dropped on Nagasaki killed at least 40,-000. Injuries from the two bombings were about equal to the deaths. Others would later die from radiation sickness. The Japanese realized that they were helpless,

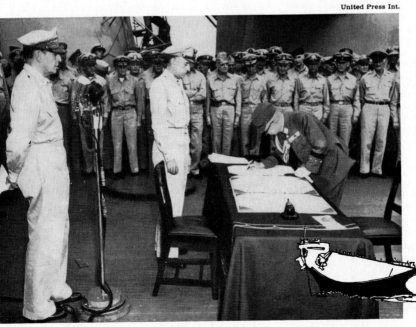

Surrender marking the end of World War II came aboard the U.S.S. *Missouri* in Tokyo Bay, on Sept. 2, 1945. Gen. of the Army Douglas MacArthur, *far left*, signed for the Allies. Gen. Yoshijiro Umezu signed for the Japanese army.

if one atomic bomb could cause so much damage.

On August 8, the Russians had declared war on Japan, and invaded Manchuria. They met little opposition, because many Japanese troops had been moved to other fronts. They also occupied the Japanese half of Sakhalin Island, north of Japan.

Victory in the Pacific. On August 10, the Japanese government asked the Allies if unconditional surrender meant that Emperor Hirohito would have to give up his throne. The Allies replied that the Japanese people would decide his fate. On August 14 (in the United States), the Allies received a message from Japan accepting the Potsdam terms. The Allies appointed MacArthur supreme commander for the Allied Powers.

On September 2 (Tokyo time), aboard the battleship *Missouri* in Tokyo Bay, the Allies and Japan signed the surrender agreement. MacArthur signed for the Allied Powers, Nimitz for the United States, and Foreign Minister Mamoru Shigemitsu for Japan. President Truman proclaimed September 2 as V-J (Victory Over Japan) Day. Three years, eight months, and 22 days after Japan bombed Pearl Harbor, World War II ended.

The Secret War

Armies of men and women fought behind the battle lines throughout World War II. Spies sought to steal secrets from other governments. Saboteurs tried to disrupt transportation and production on the home front. Underground resistance movements harassed occupation troops. Psychological-warfare experts tried to win the battle for people's minds with propaganda.

Spies and Saboteurs

Most countries operated networks of men and women engaged in espionage and sabotage. The Germans landed eight saboteurs on the east coast of the United States in June, 1942. The Federal Bureau of Investigation arrested all eight. Six were executed and two were given prison terms after a trial by a military court.

The Germans bought secret information from a spy called *Cicero*, who was employed in the British Embassy in Turkey. Richard Sorge, a Communist agent, worked in the German Embassy in Tokyo. For nine years, he directed a Russian spy ring before the Japanese police caught him in 1941. The British broke Germany's code for messages and read thousands of German military orders as soon as or before they reached leaders in the field. Norwegian and British commandos damaged Germany's secret heavy-water plant in Norway, and British bombers later attacked a key shipment from the plant. The water could have been used with uranium to make atomic bombs.

The Office of Strategic Services (OSS), a wartime agency of the United States government, trained its own spies, conducted sabotage, and worked with underground movements. OSS agents secretly radioed reports on enemy troop movements and defenses. Their activities ranged from stealing the German plans for resisting an Allied invasion of North Africa to organizing Burmese guerrilla fighters against the Japanese.

Underground Resistance

Underground resistance movements sprang up in every occupied country. Many patriots "went underground" to hide. They derailed trains and blew up bridges, passed out illegal newspapers and leaflets, and killed enemy officials. At first, most attacks were spontaneous and performed by individuals. Later, huge organizations developed, including the *French Forces of the Interior*, or *maquis*, which helped Allied operations in occupied France, and the *Polish Home Army*, which rebelled unsuccessfully in Warsaw. *Partisan* and *Chetnik* forces won large areas of Yugoslavia. Underground fighters in German-occupied Russia rose up in the forests to carry on guerrilla warfare and sabotage. Resistance leaders rescued Allied fliers, hid spies and saboteurs, and aided the Allied armed forces in other ways.

Psychological Warfare

The use of propaganda to hurt the enemy's morale reached a high state of development during World War II. Psychological-warfare teams went with Allied armies as they pushed forward. They used propaganda to create disunity in the enemy and confidence in their own forces. Their tools included public address systems, radios, loudspeakers, and mobile printing presses.

Allied propaganda agencies included the British Ministry of Information and the United States Office of War Information (OWI). The OWI operated radio stations in Europe and the Pacific. In attempts to destroy morale on the enemy home front, the OWI, the British Broadcasting Corporation, and Radio Moscow made long-range propaganda broadcasts. Paul Joseph Goebbels, German minister of propaganda, fought back with short-wave broadcasts. The Japanese broadcast propaganda over Radio Tokyo.

After the war, the Allies brought to trial a number of persons who had served the Axis cause. They included William Joyce, who had made propaganda broadcasts for Germany and became known as *Lord Haw-Haw*. A British court found him guilty of treason, and he was hanged. Americans convicted of treason and sent to prison included Mildred Gillars, who broadcast for the Nazis and became known as *Axis Sally*, and Iva D'Aquino, who broadcast for Japan and was known as *Tokyo Rose*. In 1977, President Gerald R. Ford granted a pardon to D'Aquino, who claimed that the Japanese had forced her to make the broadcasts.

The Home Front in the United States and Canada

People on the home front helped win World War II. They built weapons, produced food and clothing, paid taxes, and bought war bonds. The people in the United States and Canada did not suffer hardships comparable to those of the fighting forces or of peoples in war-torn areas. But they provided the tools that gave the Allies victory.

Producing for War

Many historians believe that war production was the

real key to Allied victory. The Allies not only mobilized more men and women in their armed forces, but also outproduced the Axis in weapons and machinery. The avalanche of war materials from the home front in the United States alone included 296,429 airplanes, 86,333 tanks, and 11,900 ships.

Converting Industries. Plants in the United States and Canada converted from civilian to war production with amazing speed. Private industry and the government rapidly built new plants. Firms that had made vacuum cleaners before the war began to make machine guns. Automobile factories turned out airplanes, engines, and tanks. American organized labor adopted a *no-strike* pledge to insure an uninterrupted flow of goods. New and old industries expanded. For example, Canadian aircraft firms that had manufactured about 14 airplanes a year were producing 4,000 a year by the end of the war. Opportunities for work in war industries caused people to move about. Industries on the Pacific Coast attracted more than 1,200,000 newcomers.

Strategic Raw Materials. The United States had vast resources of such basic materials as chemicals, coal, copper, cotton, iron ore, lead, nitrates, petroleum, and wool. But it had to import such strategic raw materials as antimony, quinine, rubber, silk, and tin. It also needed aluminum, cork, graphite, optical glass, and platinum. In the late 1930's, the government began building stockpiles of all these raw materials.

When Japan conquered the Netherlands East Indies in 1942, it cut off a source of many strategic materials needed by the Allies. The United States and Canada began to manufacture synthetic rubber (see RUBBER). Rayon and nylon replaced silk. Doctors used atabrine instead of quinine to control malaria.

Women in War Work. As men went into the armed forces, women took their places in war plants. By 1943, more than 2 million women were working in American war industries. In shipyards and aircraft plants, *Rosie the riveter* became a common sight. In 21 key industries, officials discovered that women could perform the duties of 8 of every 10 jobs normally done by men.

In Canada, more than 260,000 women worked in war industries. Another 780,000 women worked on farms to raise the crops needed by the Allies. Women took part in civil defense and worked with agencies such as the American Red Cross and United Service Organizations (USO). Many served as nurses' aides.

Government Controls

Rationing. Urgent requirements for war materials caused many shortages in consumer goods. Most governments, both Allied and Axis, had to ration the amount of consumer goods each person could use (see RATIONING). In the United States, rationed items included meats, butter, sugar, fats, oils, coffee, canned foods, shoes, and gasoline. Canada began rationing coffee, butter, gasoline, sugar, and tea in 1942, and later added meats and preserves. The Canadian government also limited the amount of some civilian goods that industries could manufacture.

Price Controls were used with rationing as weapons to combat inflation (see PRICE CONTROL). Congress gave the President power to freeze prices, salaries, and wages at their levels of Sept. 15, 1942. On July 1, 1943, rents were frozen. In December, 1941, Canada established an over-all price ceiling for all retail sales. For the first two years of the war, it controlled prices on certain foods, including butter and sugar. The Canadian government also froze rents and wages.

Censorship. Each government warned its people not to give away information that might be of value to the enemy. Well-known slogans in the United States included *Loose talk costs lives* and *A slip of the lip may sink a ship.* The government set up an Office of Censorship that had power to censor all communications between the United States and other countries. A Code of Wartime Practices guided newspapers and radio stations. Canada centralized its censorship activities under a Director of Censorship in May, 1942. He controlled all cable and transoceanic radio messages.

War Agencies. The U.S. government set up agencies to handle such wartime problems as communications, economic stabilization, housing, labor, manpower, mobilization, price controls, rationing, and transportation. Canadian agencies handled labor relations, purchasing, prices, and manpower.

The United States and Canada established several joint boards to handle problems of food, materials, mutual aid, and production. The Joint Board on Defense studied the defense of North America. The two governments built the Alaska Highway through northwest Canada, and an oil pipeline from the Mackenzie Valley to the Yukon Territory to supply fuel for U.S. troops in Alaska and Canada (see ALASKA HIGHWAY). In 1942, the United States and other American republics formed an Inter-American Defense Board to

On the Home Front, the governments of the United States and Canada rationed scarce civilian goods to assure fair distribution. Civilians were issued ration books allowing them to buy such goods.

Wide World

study measures for collective security. It also set up joint defense commissions with Brazil and Mexico.

Financing the War

War Loans. The U.S. government conducted seven war loans and a victory loan to raise funds for fighting the war and for controlling inflation. It sold more than $156,893,000,000 in bonds, certificates, notes, and stamps to individuals and firms (see SAVINGS BOND). Canada's two war loans and nine victory loans raised more than $12 billion. It also sold more than $370 million in war-savings certificates and stamps.

Taxation. The United States imposed a special excise tax on such luxury products as jewelry and cosmetics. The government also levied an excess-profits tax on corporations. Canadians paid wartime tax increases in customs and excise duties. Canada also taxed luxury items and imposed an excess-profits tax on corporations. Both income and spending increased tremendously as the war progressed. In the United States, income and excess-profits tax receipts rose from $2,188,-757,000 in 1939 to $35,173,051,000 in 1945. Government expenditures amounted to $8,765,338,000 in 1939, and $100,404,597,000 in 1945.

Security Measures

Civil Defense. The U.S. government set up a civil-defense system to protect the country from attack (see CIVIL DEFENSE). Many cities practiced "blackouts." Cities on the Atlantic and Pacific coasts dimmed their lights. Ordinarily, the glare from their lights made ships near the shore easy targets for submarines.

Internment of Aliens. Shortly after Japan attacked Pearl Harbor, the Federal Bureau of Investigation took over 1,700 enemy aliens into custody. Of the 4 million aliens in the United States, 1,100,000 citizens of Germany, Italy, and Japan were classified as *enemy aliens*.

The steps taken against aliens affected the Japanese living on the Pacific Coast more strongly than any other group. In 1941, the country had 40,869 Japanese aliens and 71,484 *nisei*, or American-born Japanese, living in California, Oregon, and Washington. Public opinion against all Japanese became strong after Pearl Harbor. Early in 1942, the government moved all Japanese from the Pacific Coast to relocation camps in Arkansas, Colorado, Utah, and other states. In February, 1942, Canada began to move about 23,000 Japanese out of areas west of the Cascade Mountains to camps in Alberta, Manitoba, and Ontario.

Science in Wartime

Scientific inventions and discoveries helped shorten the war. The United States organized its scientific resources in the Office of Scientific Research and Development under Vannevar Bush. This government agency invented or improved radar, flame throwers, rocket launchers, jet engines, amphibious assault boats, long-range navigational aids, devices for detecting submarines, and radar bombsights.

Scientists made it possible to produce large quantities of penicillin to cure a wide range of diseases. They developed the insecticide DDT to fight jungle diseases caused by insects. Other medical advances included the use of blood plasma for the wounded. American, British, and Canadian scientists cooperated to build the first atomic bomb (see ATOMIC BOMB). In Canada, the National Research Council coordinated the work of Canadian scientists.

The Germans made the greatest progress in the field of missiles and rockets. Their V-1 and V-2 missiles were the first guided missiles used in wartime (see GUIDED MISSILE). The Germans also developed the first successful jet-propelled fighter planes (see JET PROPULSION). Other important Axis weapons included the antitank rifle, the heavy *Tiger* and *Panther* tanks, and smokeless and flashless gunpowder.

The Aftermath of War

World War II was the mightiest struggle that mankind had ever seen. It caused major changes and developments in every country. The Allies divided Austria and Germany into occupation zones after the war. Russia annexed Estonia, Latvia, and Lithuania early in the war. It received land from Finland, Germany, Japan, Poland, and Romania. Czechoslovakia got territory from Hungary, Bulgaria from Romania, Poland from Germany, and Romania from Hungary. Italy had to give up land to France, Greece, and Yugoslavia. Countries occupied by Germany and Italy regained their independence. In Asia, the Allies occupied Japan and Korea. The former Japanese islands—Carolines, Marshalls, Marianas, and Palaus—became United States trust territories. Ten countries in Asia gained their independence within five years after the war ended.

The war solved some problems, but it created as many as it solved. Dictators no longer ruled Germany and Italy, and militarists no longer dominated Japan. But Russia moved quickly to replace Germany as the most powerful country in Europe. Russia also sought to take Japan's place as the dominant power in Asia. The Communists took over mainland China by the fall of

1949. Russia and China sought to set up satellite nations under their rule.

The Price of Peace

War Costs. Historians find it difficult to measure the costs of World War II. They can only estimate. No assessor can count the individual cost of personal property lost in bombings and shellings. No person can measure the cost in human suffering and loss of life. Only a rough estimate of damage can be given.

Casualties. World War II took the lives of more persons than any other war in history. It has been estimated that civilian and military dead totaled 55 million. Eastern Europe and East Asia suffered the heaviest losses. Germany and Russia, and the nations that had been ground between them, may have lost as much as a tenth of their populations. Figures on Chinese deaths are inaccurate, but they numbered in the millions. Civilians suffered the greatest losses, except in the United States, Britain, Canada, and a few other countries. Most civilian deaths were from bombings, massacres, forced migrations, epidemics, and starvation.

Cost in Money. World War II was the most expensive

war in history. It has been estimated that the cost of the war totaled $1,154,000,000,000, and the cost of property damage amounted to more than $239 billion. The United States spent about 10 times as much as it had spent in all its previous wars put together. The national debt rose from $42,968,000,000 in 1940 to $269,-422,000,000 in 1946. Many countries will continue to pay for the war in years to come through repaying loans and caring for veterans. In 1962, the United States established a $500 million fund to repay its citizens for losses suffered in the war. Damage to key industries, transportation, and housing in World War II was far greater and covered much wider areas than in World War I. Bombing, artillery fire, and street fighting devastated such major cities as Berlin, Budapest, Coventry, Dresden, Frankfurt, Hamburg, Hiroshima, Leningrad, London, Manila, Milan, Munich, Nagoya, Nanking, Rotterdam, Stuttgart, Tokyo, and Warsaw.

Filling the Vacuum. Germany had been the dominant power on the European continent. Japan had held this role in Asia. Their defeat in World War II immediately left open positions of leadership. Allied strategy allowed Russia a free hand in eastern Europe during the war. Some strategists had proposed that the Allies invade the Central Mediterranean and the Balkans, called *the soft underbelly of Europe*. They believed that Russia's occupation of Hungary and Romania, and Russian influence in Yugoslavia, would threaten the future peace of the world. But unfavorable geographic conditions in eastern Europe forced the Allies to invade northern and southern France instead. Europe was thus divided into a Communist-controlled East and free West.

In Asia, the Russians moved quickly to take over Japan's position. The long struggle between Chinese Communists and Nationalists ended in 1949, with the Communists ruling all mainland China. After Japanese

armies moved out of Southeast Asia and the southwest Pacific, revolutionists quickly took over. With China, France, and Great Britain devastated and financially exhausted by the war, the United States and Russia became the two major powers of the world.

Population Changes

The war left millions in Europe and Asia without adequate food, shelter, or clothing. They lacked fuel, machinery, raw materials, and money. Their farms lay devastated. Infant mortality and disease were high. The United Nations Relief and Rehabilitation Administration (UNRRA) and many private social agencies provided aid for the starving and homeless (see UNITED NATIONS RELIEF AND REHABILITATION ADMINISTRATION).

The war caused vast population shifts. Millions fled their homes because of their race, religion, or political beliefs, or were sent to isolated areas as slave laborers. At the end of the war, many became DP's, or displaced persons (see DISPLACED PERSON). Returning soldiers and prisoners of war added to the problems of adjustment. About 10 million refugees had to move from their homes. Some returned to their homelands. Others migrated to other countries.

In some countries, whole groups were uprooted. The Poles moved westward from Russian-occupied eastern Poland. Millions of Chinese fled westward from the Japanese, and had to return. Many Arabs were forced out of Palestine, and Germans had to leave the Baltic states, East Prussia, Silesia, and the Sudetenland. Nearly 6 million European Jews died in German concentration camps. Refugees by the thousands moved to the United States, Canada, Latin America, and Israel. See IMMIGRATION AND EMIGRATION; MIGRATION; CONCENTRATION CAMP.

The United Nations

Organizing the Peace. The Allies were determined not to repeat the mistakes of World War I. The Allies failed to set up an organization to enforce the peace until after World War I ended. In June, 1941, nine European governments-in-exile joined with Great Britain and the Commonwealth countries in signing the *Inter-Allied Declaration*. This document called for nations to cooperate and work for lasting peace. In August, 1941, President Roosevelt and Prime Minister Churchill issued a statement of postwar objectives that became known as the *Atlantic Charter* (see ATLANTIC CHARTER).

Shortly after the Pearl Harbor attack, 26 countries signed a *Declaration by United Nations* in Washington, D.C. They pledged to fight the Axis and make no separate peace agreements. In October, 1943, the foreign ministers of China, Great Britain, Russia, and the U.S. met at Moscow and suggested an international organization in their *Moscow Declaration*.

Birth of the United Nations. The Dumbarton Oaks conference, held in Washington, D.C., in 1944, developed the idea of creating a postwar international organization (see DUMBARTON OAKS). A conference of 50 countries met in San Francisco on April 25, 1945, and prepared a charter for a United Nations organization (see SAN FRANCISCO CONFERENCE).

The United Nations was born on Oct. 24, 1945. Its

MILITARY CASUALTIES IN WORLD WAR II (1939-1945)
(Official Estimates)

	Total Casualties	Dead	Wounded	Prisoners or Missing
THE ALLIES				
Belgium (including colonials)				
	(X)	11,240	(X)	198,321
China	3,086,442	1,324,518	1,761,924	130,172
France (excludes forces in IndoChina under Vichy Government)				
	640,813	200,240	429,600	1,798,543
India	107,078	49,466	57,612	(X)
Poland	327,000	107,000	210,000	636,000
Russia	(X)	*7,500,000	(X)	(X)
United Kingdom (including colonials)				
	610,904	271,320	284,049	236,242
United States	1,215,954	405,399	670,846	139,709
Other	**304,310	*145,159	**227,815	**44,364
THE AXIS				
Austria	(X)	247,000	(X)	(X)
Bulgaria	(X)	*10,000	(X)	(X)
Finland	99,308	51,808	47,500	6,445
Germany	8,156,000	2,916,000	5,240,000	1,858,000
Hungary	(X)	*140,000	(X)	(X)
Italy	(X)	159,957	(X)	(X)
Japan (from July, 1937)				
	2,391,736	2,144,507	247,229	(X)
Romania	(X)	*200,000	(X)	(X)

Official estimates provided by respective embassies or military attachés. *Unofficial. **Incomplete. (X) Unavailable.

first sessions were held the following January in London. The United Nations also set up organizations to deal with agriculture, monetary problems, health, civil aviation, and other matters (see UNITED NATIONS).

The Peace Treaties

The preparation of peace treaties took many months of conferences. The foreign ministers of China, France, Great Britain, Russia, and the United States drew up the treaties, which were then submitted to the United Nations for approval. The wartime Allies first met in London in late 1945. The treaties with Italy, Bulgaria, Hungary, Romania, and Finland were signed in Paris in 1947. Disagreements between Russia and the West delayed the peace treaties for Austria, Germany, and Japan. Most of the Allies signed the treaty with Japan in 1951, and with Austria and Germany in 1955. Russia signed only the treaty with Austria.

Axis Satellites. On Feb. 10, 1947, the Allies signed peace treaties with Bulgaria, Hungary, Romania, and Finland. The United States did not sign a treaty with Finland, because the two countries had not been at war. Allied occupation troops were required to leave Bulgaria within 90 days. The peace treaties contained guarantees against racial and religious discrimination, and banned the formation of fascist parties in the satellite countries. Each nation had to repay two-thirds of the value of Allied property lost in the country as a result of the war. The Allies also limited the size of each nation's military forces.

Italy fought on the side of the Allies after 1943, but it had been a leading Axis partner. The peace treaty with Italy was also signed in Paris on Feb. 10, 1947. It provided for the withdrawal of Allied occupation forces within 90 days after the treaty came into force. The treaty limited the size of Italy's armed forces, and it required Italy to pay $360 million in reparations within seven years. The treaty required Italy to give up African colonies, to give some border areas to France and Yugoslavia, and to give the Dodecanese Islands to Greece. Italy had to recognize the independence of Albania and Ethiopia, and Trieste as a free city.

Japan came under Allied occupation within two weeks after it surrendered. General MacArthur, as supreme commander for the Allied Powers, ruled Japan during the occupation. Russia and the United States set up occupation zones in Korea, and Russian and Chinese troops rushed into Manchuria (see MANCHURIA [History]).

Representatives of 52 countries met in San Francisco in September 1951, to draw up a peace treaty with Japan. On September 8, diplomats from 49 of these countries signed the treaty. Czechoslovakia, Poland, and Russia opposed the terms of the pact and refused to sign. The treaty required Japan to give up its former possessions outside its four home islands. The Allies claimed reparations of more than $100 million. The treaty gave Japan the right to rearm for self-defense, to develop industries, and to negotiate defense and trade agreements. The United States officially ended its war with Japan on Apr. 28, 1952. With the end of the occupation, Japan signed treaties with the major Allies, allowing their troops to remain in Japan. In December

1956, Japan and Russia signed an agreement ending the state of war between them.

Germany and Austria. The Allies divided Germany into four occupation zones. Russia controlled the eastern zone, Great Britain the northwestern zone, France the Rhineland and the Saar Valley, and the United States the southwestern zone. Germany gave up the northern half of East Prussia to Russia, and Danzig, Silesia, and land east of the Oder River to Poland. Belgium, Czechoslovakia, and France also received territory. Berlin came under four-power rule.

The Allies also divided and occupied Austria, after its liberation from Germany. Austria received its independence on May 15, 1955, after signing the Austrian State Treaty with France, Great Britain, Russia, and the United States.

Russia was given the right to remove for reparations all machinery in its German zone that was not necessary for the German peacetime economy. The other Allies also provided some equipment from their zones. Leading Nazis were tried for war crimes at Nuremberg, and each occupying country held war-crime trials in its zone (see NUREMBERG TRIALS).

The United States formally ended hostilities with Germany on Oct. 19, 1951. On May 5, 1955, the western Allies signed a treaty making West Germany an independent republic and permitting it to raise a 500,000-man defense force. The western Allies received the right to station troops in West Germany. This treaty was not a general German peace treaty because Russia refused to sign it, and because West Germany would accept neither the division of Germany nor East Germany's frontiers.　　　　　　　　　　　　THEODORE ROPP

Critically reviewed by CHESTER W. NIMITZ and CARL ANDREW SPAATZ

Related Articles. See the History section of articles on countries that took part in World War II. Additional related articles in WORLD BOOK include:

Spaatz, Carl
Spruance, Raymond A.
Stilwell, Joseph W.
Taylor, Maxwell D.
Van Fleet, James A.

Vandenberg, Hoyt S.
Wainwright, Jonathan M.
Wavell, Archibald P.
Weygand, Maxime
Zhukov, Georgi K.

AXIS MILITARY LEADERS

Doenitz, Karl
Goering, Hermann W.
Heydrich, Reinhard
Jodl, Alfred
Keitel, Wilhelm

Kesselring, Albert
Rommel, Erwin
Rundstedt, Karl R. G. von
Yamamoto, Isoroku
Yamashita, Tomobumi

ALLIED POLITICAL FIGURES

Attlee, Clement R.
Beneš, Eduard
Chamberlain (Neville)
Chiang Kai-shek
Churchill, Sir Winston L. S.
Daladier, Édouard
De Gaulle, Charles A. J. M.
Eden, Anthony
Giraud, Henri H.
Haile Selassie I
Hull, Cordell

Knox, Frank
Leopold (III)
Mihailovich, Draža
Molotov, Vyacheslav M.
Morrison, Herbert S.
Roosevelt, Franklin D.
Stalin, Joseph
Stimson, Henry L.
Tito, Josip Broz
Truman, Harry S.

AXIS POLITICAL FIGURES

Badoglio, Pietro
Boris III
Eichmann, Adolf
Goebbels, Paul Joseph
Hess, Rudolf
Himmler, Heinrich
Hirohito
Hitler, Adolf

Konoye, Prince
Laval, Pierre
Mussolini, Benito
Pétain, Henri P.
Quisling, Vidkun A. L.
Ribbentrop, Joachim von
Rosenberg, Alfred
Tojo, Hideki

OTHER BIOGRAPHIES

Bonhoeffer, Dietrich
Dollfuss, Engelbert
Frank, Anne
Kaiser, Henry J.
Krupp (family)

Mauldin, Bill
Pyle, Ernie
Schuschnigg,
   Kurt von

CONFERENCES AND TREATIES

Casablanca Conference
Munich Agreement
Pan-American Conferences
Potsdam Conference

San Francisco Conference
Teheran Conference
Yalta Conference

FORCES, MATERIALS, AND WEAPONS

Air Force
Aircraft Carrier
Airplane
Ammunition
Amphibious
   Warfare
Army
Atomic Bomb
Aviation
Bazooka
Blitzkrieg
Bomb
Bulldozer
Camouflage
Coast Guard,
   United States
Commando

Convoy
Fifth Column
Guided Missile
Helmet
Hostage
Intelligence
   Service
Jeep
Jet Propulsion
Kamikaze
Lend-Lease
Marine
Mine Warfare
Minesweeper
Navy
Propaganda
PT Boat

Radar
Radio Control
Rationing
Rocket
Savings Bond
Sniperscope
Sonar
Submarine
Tank,
   Military
Tank Destroyer
Torpedo
Walkie-Talkie
War Aces
War
   Correspondent
Warship

ORGANIZATIONS

American Legion
American Legion Auxiliary
Amvets
Gold Star Mothers,
   American
Red Cross
Strategic Services, Office of
United Nations

United Nations Relief
   and Rehabilitation
   Administration
United Service
   Organizations
Veterans of Foreign Wars
   of the United States

OTHER RELATED ARTICLES

Alaska Highway
Atabrine
Atlantic Charter
Azores
Burma Road
D-Day
Displaced Person
Draft, Military
Four Freedoms
Gestapo
Graf Spee

Jews (The
   Holocaust)
Korean War
Maquis
Neutrality
Nuremberg Trials
Partisan
Polish Corridor
Refugee
Stars and Stripes
V-E Day

V-J Day
Underground
United States,
   History of the
   (pictures)
Unknown Soldier
War Crime
War Debt
World War I
Yank

Outline

I. Causes of Conflict
   A. Problems Left by World War I
   B. The Rise of Dictatorships
   C. Aggression on
      the March

II. Men and Strategy
   A. Wartime Leaders
   B. Strategy of the War
   C. Mobilization

III. Early Stages of the War
   A. Blitzkrieg   B. Fighting in Eastern Europe

IV. America Joins the War
   A. Defending the Americas
   B. Manpower
   C. The Battle of the Atlantic
   D. War Comes to the
      United States

V. The Allies Attack in Africa and Europe
   A. On the Russian Front
   B. The North African Campaign
   C. The War in the Mediterranean
   D. The Air War in Europe
   E. The Invasion of Europe

VI. The War in Asia and the Pacific
   A. Early Japanese Victories
   B. The Allies Strike Back
   C. The South Pacific
   D. Island Hopping
   E. Return to the
      Philippines
   F. The China-Burma-
      India Theater
   G. Target Tokyo

VII. The Secret War
   A. Spies and Saboteurs
   B. Underground Resistance
   C. Psychological Warfare

VIII. The Home Front in the United States and Canada
   A. Producing for War
   B. Government Controls
   C. Financing the War
   D. Security Measures
   E. Science in Wartime

IX. The Aftermath of War
   A. The Price of Peace
   B. Population Changes
   C. The United Nations
   D. The Peace Treaties

Questions

How did the Geneva Conference in 1932 fail to correct conditions that helped cause World War II?

Why was the Spanish Civil War considered the *testing ground of World War II?*

Why did newspapers call the seven months following the defeat of Poland the *phony war?*

What was the *blitzkrieg? Kamikaze?* Why were they used?

Why did the French sink about 50 of their own ships at Toulon in 1942?

What was the first Axis capital to fall into Allied hands? When did it fall?

What was the *Vengeance Weapon* used by the Germans shortly after the Allied invasion of France?

What battle in World War II was the biggest naval engagement in history? Where was it fought and what were the results?

What was the strategy behind the island-hopping campaign of Allied forces in the Pacific?

What was the last major land battle of World War II?

Reading and Study Guide

See *World War II* in the RESEARCH GUIDE/INDEX, Volume 22, for a *Reading and Study Guide.*

WORLD WEATHER WATCH PROGRAM. See WORLD METEOROLOGICAL ORGANIZATION.

WORLD'S COLUMBIAN EXPOSITION observed the 400th anniversary of Christopher Columbus' arrival in America. It was held in Chicago in 1893, a year later than originally planned. It exhibited such wonders of its time as the expansion engine, Pullman cars, and the linotype. It used more electricity than the whole city of Chicago at that time. The first Ferris wheel was created for the exposition (see FERRIS WHEEL [picture]).

Canals and lagoons laced the grounds, which covered 666 acres (270 hectares). The main buildings were finished in plaster and fiber, and shone like white marble in the sunlight. They were often called *The White City.* The Transportation Building represented early experiments in functional design in architecture. The Building of Manufacturers and Liberal Arts, spanning nearly 40 acres (16 hectares), was the largest exposition building constructed up to that time. The Palace of Fine Arts now houses Chicago's Museum of Science and Industry.   HERBERT J. DOTTEN

WORLD'S FAIR. See FAIRS AND EXPOSITIONS.

WORM is any of several kinds of animals that have a soft, slender body and no backbone or legs. There are thousands of kinds of worms. The largest species measure many feet or meters long, and the smallest ones cannot be seen without a microscope. Some worms live in water or soil. Many of these free-living worms eat small plants and animals, and others feed on decaying matter. Still other worms live as parasites in various animals and plants. They cause a number of diseases.

Many people believe that such wormlike animals as caterpillars and grubs are worms. But these animals are insects in their *larval* (juvenile) stage and do not resemble worms after they mature.

Most kinds of worms have a well-developed sense of touch, as well as special organs that respond to chemicals in their surroundings. Many species have a sense of sight, with eyes or eyespots located on the head.

There are four main groups of worms: (1) flatworms, or *Platyhelminthes;* (2) ribbon worms, or *Nemertea;* (3) roundworms, or *Nematoda;* and (4) segmented worms, or *Annelida.* The study of parasitic worms is called *helminthology.*

Flatworms are the simplest kinds of worms. Some look like oval leaves, and others resemble ribbons. Flatworms include both free-living and parasitic species.

Most free-living flatworms live in the sea. But many freshwater species, called *planarians,* live among algae and stones along the shores of lakes and ponds. They eat tiny animals. *Flukes* and *tapeworms* are parasitic flatworms that infect human beings and many other animals. In human beings, they cause serious blood and intestinal disorders.

Ribbon Worms resemble flatworms, but many species are larger. Most kinds of ribbon worms live in the sea. One, the *bootlace worm,* grows several feet or meters long. Ribbon worms are also called *proboscis worms.* They have a long *proboscis* (tubelike structure) that they shoot out from their head to capture prey. These worms feed on a variety of animals, including other worms and mollusks.

Roundworms make up the largest group of worms. There are more than 10,000 species. Roundworms have a long, cylindrical body that resembles a piece of thread. Some, including *filariae, hookworms,* and *trichinae,* are parasites that cause disease in human beings and other animals and in plants. Free-living roundworms make

Some Common Worms There are several thousand kinds of worms. The illustrations below show representatives of each of the four major groups of worms. The sizes listed are approximate because many species can stretch to unusually great lengths. For example, bootlace worms are normally no more than 6½ feet (2 meters) long. But scientists measured one bootlace worm that was stretched to nearly 90 feet (27 meters). The illustrations are not drawn to scale.

WORLD BOOK illustrations by Patricia J. Wynne

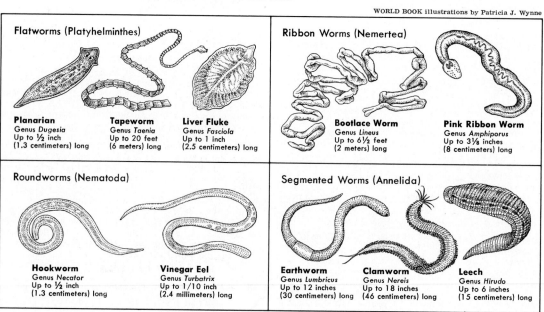

Flatworms (Platyhelminthes)

Planarian
Genus *Dugesia*
Up to ½ inch
(1.3 centimeters) long

Tapeworm
Genus *Taenia*
Up to 20 feet
(6 meters) long

Liver Fluke
Genus *Fasciola*
Up to 1 inch
(2.5 centimeters) long

Ribbon Worms (Nemertea)

Bootlace Worm
Genus *Lineus*
Up to 6½ feet
(2 meters) long

Pink Ribbon Worm
Genus *Amphiporus*
Up to 3⅛ inches
(8 centimeters) long

Roundworms (Nematoda)

Hookworm
Genus *Necator*
Up to ½ inch
(1.3 centimeters) long

Vinegar Eel
Genus *Turbatrix*
Up to 1/10 inch
(2.4 millimeters) long

Segmented Worms (Annelida)

Earthworm
Genus *Lumbricus*
Up to 12 inches
(30 centimeters) long

Clamworm
Genus *Nereis*
Up to 18 inches
(46 centimeters) long

Leech
Genus *Hirudo*
Up to 6 inches
(15 centimeters) long

their home in water or on land and eat small plants and animals.

Segmented Worms are the most highly developed worms. Their body consists of a number of similar segments that give the worms a ringed appearance. This group includes *polychaete worms, oligochaete worms,* and *leeches.*

Polychaete worms, the largest group of segmented worms, live in the sea and along the shore. Many of these worms have *tentacles* (feelers) on their head and a pair of leglike projections called *parapodia* on each body segment. The parapodia are used in crawling. They have many *setae* (bristles) that help the worms grip the surface on which they are moving. Many polychaete worms live among algae or burrow in mud or sand. Some live in tubes attached to the sea floor. A worm makes its tube from sand or from material secreted by its body. Some polychaete worms eat small plants and animals. Others feed on decaying plant and animal remains.

Oligochaete worms include earthworms and many freshwater species. They have a few setae but no parapodia. Most of these worms eat decaying plant matter.

Leeches make up the smallest group of segmented worms. They grow from $\frac{3}{4}$ to 8 inches (2 to 20 centimeters) long and have a flat body with a sucker at each end. Most leeches live in water and feed on the blood of fish and other water creatures.   ROBERT D. BARNES

Related Articles in WORLD BOOK include:

Earthworm	Hair Snake	Nematoda	Roundworm
Eelworm	Hookworm	Pinworm	Tapeworm
Filaria	Leech	Planarian	Trichina
Flatworm	Lobworm	Ribbon Worm	Vinegar Eel
Fluke			

WORMS, *vawrms* (pop. 78,000), a city in West Germany, lies along the Rhine River. It is located between Mannheim and Mainz (see GERMANY [political map]).

The city of Worms is over 2,000 years old. Its famous Romanesque cathedral, which dates from the 1300's, escaped destruction during World War II. See ARCHITECTURE (Romanesque [picture]). Worms gained historical importance as the meeting place of many German *diets* (imperial councils). Martin Luther appeared before Emperor Charles V of the Holy Roman Empire at the Diet of Worms in 1521 to defend his stand on Protestantism (see LUTHER, MARTIN). Worms is the scene of the legendary story told in the epic poem *Nibelungenlied* (see NIBELUNGENLIED).   FRANK O. AHNERT

WORMS, EDICT OF, was the sentence pronounced upon Martin Luther by the Diet of Worms in 1521. The Edict proclaimed Luther a heretic and cast him outside the protection of the law.

See also LUTHER, MARTIN (Reformation Leader).

WORMWOOD is a large group of plants that give off pleasant odors. Often the term applies to an entire group of about 250 different kinds of plants of the genus *Artemisia.* The wormwood shrub grows mostly in the Northern Hemisphere and is most abundant in arid regions. The most important wormwood in commercial use is a perennial plant that grows in Europe and North Africa. This kind of wormwood supplies an essential oil used in the manufacture of absinthe and medicine. Europeans grow common wormwood, or *mugwort,* for seasoning and medicinal purposes. People in eastern Canada and the northeastern United States consider

J. Horace McFarland

The Leaves of the Wormwood Yield a Valuable Oil.

this plant a weed. Several kinds of shrubby wormwoods are called *sagebrush* in the western United States.

The Bible mentions wormwood in several places. The plants called "hemlock" in the books of Amos and Hosea probably refer to the wormwood plant.

Scientific Classification. Wormwood belongs to the composite family, *Compositae.* Wormwood yielding oil for absinthe is genus *Artemisia,* species *A. absinthium.* Common wormwood is *A. vulgaris.* The common sagebrush is *A. tridentata.* The wormwood in the Bible is *A. judaica* and possibly *A. arborescens.*   HAROLD NORMAN MOLDENKE

WORRY. See ANXIETY.

WORSHIP. See RELIGION; COLONIAL LIFE IN AMERICA (Why the Colonists Came to America); FREEDOM OF RELIGION; GOD; IDOL; PRAYER.

WORSTED is a smooth, shiny, strong wool yarn. Its name came from Worstead, a town in England where the yarn was first made. The yarn is spun from long wool that has been combed to lay the fibers parallel. The word *worsted* also describes cloth woven with worsted yarns. Worsted cloths look smooth and hard. Poplin and serge fabrics are often worsted. See also SERGE.

WOTAN. See ODIN.

WOUK, *wohk,* **HERMAN** (1915-   ), an American novelist, won a Pulitzer prize in 1952 for *The Caine Mutiny.* The book became one of the most discussed works about World War II. Part of the novel was made into a play, *The Caine Mutiny Court Martial,* in 1954. The book appealed to many readers because it depicted the resistance of a junior officer to the insane tyranny of his commanding officer on a ship in the Pacific. It

WOUND

appealed to every person's desire for justice, but was in no way intended to represent typical navy life. Wouk also wrote two related novels about World War II, *The Winds of War* (1971) and *War and Remembrance* (1978). Other novels written by Wouk include *Aurora Dawn* (1947), *The City Boy* (1948), *Marjorie Morningstar* (1955), and *Youngblood Hawke* (1962). Wouk was born in New York City.

Editta Sherman

Herman Wouk

GEORGE J. BECKER

WOUND. See FIRST AID (First Aid for Bleeding).

WOUNDED KNEE, BATTLE OF. See SOUTH DAKOTA (Territorial Days).

WOVOKA, *wo VO kuh* (1856?-1932), founded the Ghost Dance religion of the western American Indians. While sick with a fever in 1889, he dreamed that he was lifted into the sky where the Great Spirit talked to him. He also saw all the old-time Indians living a happy life. The Great Spirit taught him some songs and a new dance, and told him to teach the Indians to stop fighting and to lead a good life. Then no one would ever grow old, be sick, or go hungry. All the dead Indians and the buffalo would come back to life.

Wovoka was a Paiute Indian, born in Nevada. His father had been a prophet before him. Adopted as a boy by a white settler named David Wilson, he was also known as Jack Wilson. E. ADAMSON HOEBEL

WPA was the Works Progress Administration. See NEW DEAL (The Second Hundred Days); ROOSEVELT, FRANKLIN D. (The New Deal); ADULT EDUCATION.

WRANGEL, *RANG gul*, **FERDINAND VON** (1794-1870), BARON VON WRANGEL, was a Russian naval officer and colonial administrator. He led an expedition into the Siberian Arctic between 1820 and 1824 which greatly increased knowledge about the region. He became governor of Alaska in 1830. As the Russian minister of marine, he opposed the sale of Alaska and had to retire. Wrangel Island is named for him. He was born in what is now Latvia. WILLIAM P. BRANDON

WRANGEL ISLAND, *RANG gul*, lies in the Arctic Ocean, about 90 miles (140 kilometers) north of the northeastern corner of Siberia (see RUSSIA [physical map]). It covers 2,819 square miles (7,301 square kilometers), and has a population of about 50. It is owned by Russia. The island is barren, granite rock locked in most of the year by ice. Lichen and grass grow in the summer. Birds, polar bears, seals, and walruses live there. The people fish, hunt, and trap furs. There is also a meteorological station on the island.

Wrangel Island was named for the Russian explorer Baron Ferdinand von Wrangel, who searched for it in 1823 after Siberian natives had reported its existence. But Wrangel never found the island. American whalers discovered it in 1867, and named it for Wrangel. Claimed by the United States, Canada, and Russia, the island was finally left to Russia in 1924. Russia sent settlers there in 1926. THEODORE SHABAD

WRECKING MACHINES. See BUILDING AND WRECKING MACHINES.

WREN is a small, active bird found in most parts of North America. Wrens have slender bills, rounded wings, and dull brown or gray feathers. They often hold their tails erect instead of straight out behind as do other birds. Wrens like to live near the ground. They seem to be always moving about and never at rest. Wrens can sing melodiously, but they can also make disagreeable chattering sounds. There are 63 species of wren, most of which live in Asia and the Americas. Only one species of wren lives in Europe.

The *house wren*, also known as the *common wren*, the *jenny wren*, and the *brown wren*, is the most familiar of all the wrens. It is about 5 inches (13 centimeters) long and often lives in cities. It will nest in wren houses built for it. It lays five to seven eggs, white in color and thickly dotted with salmon spots. The wren is valuable to farmers and gardeners because it eats insects.

Karl Maslowski, Photo Researchers

The House Wren often builds its nest in a birdhouse built for it. The entrance is about the size of a quarter.

Bewick's Wren
Thryomanes bewickii
Found from southern Canada to Mexico
Body length 5½ inches (14 centimeters)

WORLD BOOK illustrations by Guy Tudor

416

The largest wren in the United States is the *cactus wren*. It may be 7 inches (18 centimeters) long. This wren lives in the dry regions of the Southwest. Its breast is heavily spotted. The *rock wren* lives in the western part of the United States. It builds its nest under rocks in the dry foothills of the Rocky Mountains. It is mostly gray in color. The *Carolina wren* lives in the southern United States. It often nests in farm buildings. The Carolina wren measures about 5½ inches (14 centimeters) long. *Bewick's wren* likes to live around people's homes. It has a white-edged tail and a white line over its eyes. The *winter wren* is one of the smallest wrens. It builds its nest in the wild forests of the northern United States and Canada. The winter wren has a melodious song. The *long-billed* and the *short-billed marsh wrens* build their nests among reeds and cattails in marshes. The long-billed marsh wren has a gurgling, liquid song. The song of the short-billed marsh wren is like the sound made by striking two pebbles rapidly together. The long-billed is the more common of the two marsh wrens. Its tail stands up straight, or forward over its back.

Scientific Classification. Wrens are in the wren family, *Troglodytidae*. The cactus wren is genus *Heleodytes*, species *H. brunneicapillus;* the rock wren is *Salpinctes obsoletus;* the Carolina wren is *Thryothorus ludovicianus;* the winter wren is *Troglodytes troglodytes;* and the house wren is *Troglodytes aëdon*. The long-billed marsh wren is *Telmatodytes palustris;* and the short-billed marsh wren is *Cistothorus stellaris*.   LEONARD W. WING

See also BIRD (table: State Birds; Territories of Birds; color pictures: Birds' Eggs, Favorite Songbirds, Other Bird Favorites).

Winter Wren
Troglodytes troglodytes
Found in the Northern Hemisphere
Body length 4 to 5 inches
(10 to 13 centimeters)

Riverside Wren
Thryothorus semibadius
Found in Costa Rica and Panama
Body length 5½ to 5¾ inches
(14 to 15 centimeters)

Band-Backed Wren
Campylorhynchus zonatus
Found from Mexico to western Panama
and western Ecuador
Body length 7¾ to 8¼ inches
(20 to 21 centimeters)

Short-Billed Marsh Wren
Cistothorus stellaris
Found in eastern North America
Body length 4 inches
(10 centimeters)

Rock Wren
Salpinctes obsoletus
Found from southwestern Canada and
western United States to
northwestern Costa Rica
Body length 5 to 6 inches
(13 to 15 centimeters)

Long-Billed Marsh Wren
Telmatodytes palustris
Found from southern Canada
to central Mexico
Body length 4 to 5½ inches
(10 to 14 centimeters)

A. F. Kersting

The Two Domes of Sir Christopher Wren's Greenwich Hospital flank a long courtyard. Wren emphasized the repetition of columns and arches in many of his most famous buildings.

WREN, SIR CHRISTOPHER (1632-1723), was an English architect, scientist, and mathematician. After the Great Fire of London in 1666, he redesigned part or all of 55 of the 87 churches that had been destroyed. The most famous one is St. Paul's Cathedral (1710). The grace and variety of many of Wren's church spires are still a feature of the London skyline. His other major buildings include the churches of St. Bride (about 1678) and St. James (about 1684), Chelsea Hospital (about 1691), and Greenwich Hospital (about 1715).

Wren was born in the village of East Knoyle in the county of Wiltshire. His early interests and training were in science and mathematics. From 1641 to 1646, he attended Westminster School in London, where the poet John Dryden and the philosopher John Locke were fellow students. Wren received his B.A. degree from Oxford University in 1651 and his M.A. degree there in 1653. In 1657, Wren was appointed professor of astronomy at Gresham College in London. His lectures in Latin and English became popular and helped spread his reputation among European scientists.

In 1661, King Charles II appointed Wren to the important architectural position of assistant surveyor-general. In 1663, Wren attracted attention with his proposal for a unique roofing system over the Shel-

Sir Christopher Wren
Detail of an oil portrait (1711) by Sir Godfrey Kneller; National Portrait Gallery, London

donian Theatre in Oxford. Unlike other English architects of his day, Wren never went to Italy to gain firsthand knowledge of classical architecture. He did visit France in 1665, and the architecture he saw there probably influenced his later work.

Wren was a founding member of the Royal Society in 1660 and served as its president from 1680 to 1682. According to a biography written by his son, Wren was responsible for 53 inventions, experiments, and theories. For an example of Wren's architecture, see LONDON (picture: Saint Paul's Cathedral).   J. WILLIAM RUDD

See also ARCHITECTURE (Baroque: picture); ENGLAND (The Arts).

WREN, PERCIVAL CHRISTOPHER (1885-1941), was a British novelist. *Beau Geste* (1924), as a novel, play, and motion picture, brought him international renown. *Beau Geste* is a romantic adventure story about life in the French Foreign Legion. Wren followed it with *Beau Sabreur* (1926), *Beau Ideal* (1928), *The Good Gestes* (1929), and *Two Feet from Heaven* (1940). However, he never quite repeated his first success.

Wren was born in Devon, England. He was graduated from Oxford University, and then toured the world. His first novels dealt with India, where he served in a government post for 10 years.   R. W. STALLMAN

Percival Wren
United Press Int.

WRESTLING, *REHS lihng*, is a sport in which two opponents try to *pin* (hold) each other's shoulders to a mat on the floor. Wrestlers use maneuvers called *holds* to grasp their opponents and control their movements.

Successful wrestling demands strength, speed, coordination, balance, physical conditioning, and knowledge of body leverage. A clever wrestler can often defeat a stronger and heavier opponent.

There are more than 50 kinds of wrestling. Each has its own rules. Some kinds do not require a pin for victory. In Japanese *sumo* wrestling, for example, a wrestler tries to throw his opponent to the ground or force him outside a 15-foot (4.6-meter) circle.

Amateur Wrestling

Amateur wrestling is one of the fastest-growing sports in schools in the United States. Every year, students in junior high school, high school, and college take part in wrestling matches. National and world championship competitions are held annually. Wrestlers also compete in the Summer Olympic Games every four years.

Chief Forms of Wrestling. The two most popular forms of wrestling in the world are (1) *Greco-Roman* and (2) *free-style*, or *catch-as-catch-can*. Greco-Roman is the older of the two forms. Both styles use the same general rules, and Olympic competition is held in both. Greco-Roman is the more popular form throughout most of Europe, but free-style is more popular in the United States. Japanese, Russian, and Turkish wrestlers are known for their skill in both styles.

In Greco-Roman wrestling, a wrestler may not grasp his opponent's legs or use any hold below the waist. A wrestler may use his legs only for support, not to hook, trip, or lift an opponent.

In free-style wrestling, a wrestler may use his legs as scissors to grasp an opponent's arm or leg. But he cannot close the scissors around the opponent's head or body. A wrestler may also trip or tackle his opponent's legs. Rules forbid holds that could injure an opponent or cause him great pain.

High School and Intercollegiate Wrestling. There are 12 weight classes in high school wrestling in the United States. There are 10 intercollegiate classes. A wrestler may weigh no more than the weight in his class, though he may weigh less. The high school classes are 98 pounds, 105 pounds, 112 pounds, 119 pounds, 126 pounds, 132 pounds, 138 pounds, 145 pounds, 155 pounds, 167 pounds, 185 pounds, and heavyweight. The intercollegiate classes are 118 pounds, 126 pounds, 134 pounds, 142 pounds, 150 pounds, 158 pounds, 167 pounds, 177 pounds, 190 pounds, and heavyweight.

High school matches are divided into three periods of two minutes each. Intercollegiate matches begin with a two-minute period. The remaining two periods last three minutes each. Matches take place on a cushioned mat with a wrestling area at least 24 feet (7 meters) square or 28 feet (8.5 meters) in diameter. At least 5 feet (1.5 meters) of mat must surround the wrestling area. The match begins with the wrestlers standing and facing each other. If a *fall* (pin) occurs, the match is over. If no fall occurs, the second period begins with the wrestlers in the *referee's position*. One wrestler takes a *defensive position* on his hands and knees. The other wrestler takes an *offensive position* at his opponent's side or with one foot behind the opponent. The wrestler in the offensive position puts an arm around his opponent's waist and a hand on his elbow. The referee flips a coin to determine which wrestler takes each position. If no fall occurs, the third period follows. The wrestlers reverse positions at the start of this period.

Wrestlers receive points for skillfully executing various holds and maneuvers. They may also win points if their opponent commits a technical error, uses an illegal hold, or breaks a rule. The match ends when

Chicago Sun-Times

An Amateur Wrestling Match is a test of strength and skill between the two opponents. Each wrestler tries to win the match by *pinning* (holding) his opponent's shoulders to the floor for one second. The referee, *left,* watches for a pin, awards points for skillful maneuvers, and penalizes wrestlers for illegal holds or tactics.

WRESTLING

a wrestler gains a fall by holding his opponent's shoulders to the mat. The opponent's shoulders must be held for two seconds in a high school match and for one second in an intercollegiate match. If no fall occurs, the wrestler with the most points wins by a *decision*. The referee is sometimes assisted by judges.

The National Collegiate Athletic Association (NCAA) publishes an annual *Official Wrestling Guide*. It contains scholastic and collegiate rules and a survey of the preceding year's wrestling activities in U.S. high schools and colleges.

Professional Wrestling

Professional wrestling has become more of an entertainment spectacle than a sport governed by accepted rules. Showmanship often replaces skill in professional matches. Most matches are called exhibitions and take place in a roped and padded ring similar to a boxing ring. Many wrestlers wear fantastic costumes and use unusual names. Many matches pair a "hero" against a "villain," who may kick, bite, or gouge his opponent.

History

Wrestling dates back to prehistoric times. In French caves, carvings and drawings 15,000 to 20,000 years old show more than 500 wrestlers in various holds and leverage positions. According to the Old Testament, Jacob wrestled God in the form of a man. Wrestling was introduced into the Olympic Games in Greece in about 708 B.C. The Greek philosopher Plato won many prizes for wrestling when he was a young man. Wrestling became popular in England during the early Middle Ages.

In America, Indians wrestled as part of their sports activities before Europeans arrived in the New World. Presidents George Washington and Abraham Lincoln were skillful wrestlers.   KARL A. KITT

HOW POINTS ARE SCORED

Individual Match Points

Near Fall	3 points
Takedown	2 points
Reversal	2 points
Predicament	2 points
Time Advantage (1 minute)	1 point
Escape	1 point

Dual Meet Points

Fall	6 points
Forfeit	6 points
Default	6 points
Disqualification	6 points
Decision (by 10 or more points)	4 points
Decision	3 points
Draw	2 points

WRESTLING HOLDS AND POSITIONS

These illustrations show some basic holds and positions amateur wrestlers use. Most wrestling holds and positions are used to pin an opponent or to control his movements.

WORLD BOOK illustrations by Anthony Ravielli

A Match Begins when the wrestlers approach each other from opposite sides of the mat. Each wrestler then tries to outmaneuver his opponent in an effort to seize him and toss him to the mat.

A Cross-Ankle Pickup is one method used to take an opponent down to the mat. A wrestler grabs his opponent's ankle with one hand and uses his body to drive him backward. These combined actions force the opponent down.

A Tie-Up occurs when two wrestlers come to grips while in a standing position. Many grips can be used. The tie-up is the starting position for several methods of forcing an opponent to the mat.

A Ride is one of several methods by which a wrestler earns points through controlling the movements of his opponent. An offensive wrestler might ride his opponent by gripping an ankle to limit his maneuverability.

The Referee's Position starts the second and third periods. The top wrestler is on offense, and the bottom man is on defense. This position tests the wrestlers' ability to use an advantage or to escape from a bad position.

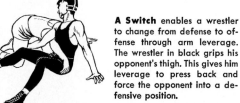

A Switch enables a wrestler to change from defense to offense through arm leverage. The wrestler in black grips his opponent's thigh. This gives him leverage to press back and force the opponent into a defensive position.

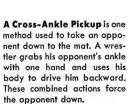

A Sit-Out is a defensive maneuver often performed by the bottom man from the referee's position. He goes into a sitting position, which gives him a chance to escape holds or to maneuver himself into an offensive position.

A Fall ends a wrestling match. To gain a fall, a wrestler must pin his opponent's shoulders to the mat for one second. The top wrestler has pinned his opponent by using a crotch and half-nelson hold.

418

WRIGHT, FRANK LLOYD (1867-1959), was one of America's most influential and imaginative architects. During his career of almost 70 years, he created a striking variety of architectural forms. Wright's works ranged from traditional buildings typical of the late 1800's to ultramodern designs, such as his plan for a skyscraper 1 mile (1.6 kilometers) high.

Wright became internationally famous as early as 1910, but he never established a style that dominated either American or European architecture. His influence was great but generally indirect. It was spread as much by his speeches and writings as by his buildings and designs. Wright's *Autobiography* (1932, revised 1943), one of the great literary self-portraits of the 1900's, provides insights into his philosophy of architecture.

Early Career. Wright was born in Richland Center, Wis. He studied engineering briefly at the University of Wisconsin in the mid-1880's. In 1887, Wright moved to Chicago, where he became a draftsman in the office of Joseph Lyman Silsbee, a noted Midwestern architect. Wright designed his first building while working for Silsbee.

Later in 1887, Wright joined the staff of the famous Chicago architects Dankmar Adler and Louis Sullivan. He soon became their chief draftsman. Wright left Adler and Sullivan in 1893 to establish his own practice. Wright's work after 1893 reflected Sullivan's influence, especially in attempts to harmonize a building's form with its function. See SULLIVAN, LOUIS H.

Wright's first distinctive buildings were homes designed in his famous *prairie style*. In a typical prairie house, open spaces inside the home expand into the outdoors through porches and terraces. Because of their low, horizontal form, the homes seem to grow out of the ground. This effect was emphasized by Wright's use of wood and other materials as they appear in nature.

Wright designed many prairie houses in and around Chicago. The Willitts house (1902) in Highland Park, Ill., was shaped like a cross, with the rooms arranged so they seemed to flow into one another. The Robie house (1909) in Chicago looks like a series of horizontal layers floating over the ground.

Karsh, Ottawa
Frank Lloyd Wright

Wright's major nonresidential designs of the early 1900's included the Larkin Soap Company administration building (1904) in Buffalo, N.Y., and Unity Temple (1906) in Oak Park, Ill. The core of the Larkin building was a large, skylighted court. Unity Temple was the first public building in the United States that showed its concrete construction. In earlier buildings, the concrete had been covered with other materials.

In 1910, a German publishing firm published a luxurious volume of illustrations of Wright's drawings and plans. A second volume appeared in 1911. These books and later publications of Wright's works strongly influenced the development of architecture in Europe from about 1913 through the 1920's. European architects were especially impressed by Wright's complex use of cubic shapes.

During the 1920's, Wright designed several houses in southern California that are noted for the use of precast concrete blocks. He also planned the Imperial Hotel complex (1922) in Tokyo. The hotel was designed to withstand the earthquakes common in Japan and was one of the few undamaged survivors of a severe earthquake that struck Tokyo in 1923.

Later Career. In 1932, Wright founded the Taliesin Fellowship. This fellowship was made up of architectural students who paid to live and work with Wright. The students worked during the summer at Taliesin, Wright's home near Spring Green, Wis., and during the winter at Taliesin West, his home in Scottsdale, Ariz. For a color picture of Taliesin, see WISCONSIN (A Visitor's Guide).

Wright's projects of the 1930's included the Kauf-

Ed Kumler, Tom Stack & Assoc.

Wright's Marin County Civic Center was one of his final and most imaginative designs. This series of futuristic structures stretches along several hills near San Francisco.

Wright's Robie House is an example of his prairie style. He tried to blend the structure with its natural surroundings.

mann "Falling Water" house (1936) at Bear Run near Uniontown, Pa., and the Johnson Wax Company administration building (1939) in Racine, Wis. The Kaufmann house was dramatically perched over a waterfall and became a symbol for the general public of far-out modern architecture. The Johnson Wax building featured a smooth, curved exterior of brick and glass. The design expressed the streamlined style common in automobiles and other products of the late 1930's. A laboratory tower designed by Wright was added later. For a color picture of the Johnson buildings, see ARCHITECTURE (What Makes Great Architecture).

During his final years, Wright designed two of his most famous projects—the Guggenheim Museum (completed in 1960) in New York City and the Marin County, California, Civic Center. The interior of the museum is dominated by a spiral ramp that runs from the floor almost to the ceiling. For an interior view of the museum, see NEW YORK (Education). The Marin County Civic Center is a series of futuristic structures built on three hills. About nine buildings are planned for the center, which is expected to be completed by the year 2000.   DAVID GEBHARD

For additional pictures of Wright's work, see ARIZONA (Education); FLORIDA (Education); ARCHITECTURE (picture: Greek Orthodox Church). For a *Reading and Study Guide*, see *Wright, Frank Lloyd*, in the RESEARCH GUIDE/INDEX, Volume 22.

WRIGHT, JAMES CLAUDE, JR. (1922-   ), a Texas Democrat, was elected majority leader of the United States House of Representatives in 1976. As majority leader, Wright led the efforts to pass his party's programs in the House.

Wright was born in Fort Worth, Tex., and attended Weatherford College and the University of Texas. He left the university in 1941, during World War II, to enlist in the Army Air Force and served until 1945.

From 1947 to 1949, Wright was a member of the Texas House of Representatives. Then, at the age of 26, he was elected mayor of Weatherford, Tex., and became the state's youngest mayor. He headed the city's government until 1954, when he won election to the U.S. House of Representatives.

In Congress, Wright supported generous spending for defense and highway construction. He was also a strong supporter of water conservation. He wrote several books, including *The Coming Water Famine* (1966), a discussion of water pollution and shortages.   NANCY H. DICKERSON

WRIGHT, JOHN JOSEPH CARDINAL (1909-1979), was appointed a cardinal of the Roman Catholic Church in 1969 by Pope Paul VI. That same year, the pope named Wright *prefect* (head) of the Vatican Congregation of the Clergy, which is responsible for the spiritual welfare of Roman Catholic clergy.

Cardinal Wright was born in Boston. He was ordained a priest in 1935. From 1950 to 1959, he served as the first bishop of Worcester, Mass. He became bishop of Pittsburgh in 1959.   THOMAS P. NEILL

WRIGHT, RICHARD (1908-1960), was a black author who gained immediate fame with his dramatic first novel, *Native Son* (1940). The novel tells the story of Bigger Thomas, a young black of the Chicago slums. It describes his attempts to live within the discouraging pattern of black-white relationships in the city.

Wright's other novels include *The Outsider* (1953) and *The Long Dream* (1958). He wrote his autobiography, *Black Boy* (1945), in the form of a novel. This work is considered important for an understanding of the life of blacks in America. Wright continued his story in *American Hunger* (published in 1977, after his death). He also wrote about his experiences and ideas in *Black Power* (1954) and *White Man, Listen!* (1957), and in *The God That Failed* (1949), a collection of essays by former Communists.

Wright was born near Natchez, Miss. After living with relatives in several places, he moved to Chicago about 1927, and then to New York City in 1937. Wright's first published fiction was *Uncle Tom's Children* (1938), a collection of four long stories. He lived in Paris from 1946 until his death.   DEAN DONER

WRIGHT, SEWALL (1889-   ), developed a mathematical theory of biological evolution, based on the Mendelian laws of heredity. His theory of *genetic drift* stated that in small populations, chance, rather than natural selection, is an important evolutionary agent. Wright was born in Melrose, Mass. MORDECAI L. GABRIEL

WRIGHT, WILLARD H. See VAN DINE, S. S.

WRIGHT BROTHERS, WILBUR (1867-1912) and ORVILLE (1871-1948), invented and built the first successful airplane. On Dec. 17, 1903, they made the world's first flight in a power-driven, heavier-than-air machine at Kitty Hawk, N.C. Orville Wright piloted the plane, having won the privilege by the toss of a coin. He flew 120 feet (37 meters) and remained in the air for 12 seconds. The brothers made three more flights that day. The longest, by Wilbur, was 852 feet (260 meters) in 59 seconds. Five persons besides the Wrights witnessed the flights. Only three or four newspapers reported the event the next morning, and their accounts were inaccurate. The *Journal* in the Wrights' home city of Dayton, Ohio, did not even mention it. The first scientific description of the machine and its flights appeared the following March in a magazine entitled *Gleanings in Bee Culture*. The Wrights did not foresee how greatly the airplane would change civilization. They did not believe at first that it would ever be possible to fly at night.

Early Life. Wilbur Wright was born Apr. 16, 1867, on a small farm 8 miles (13 kilometers) from New Castle, Ind., and Orville Wright was born Aug. 19, 1871, in Dayton, Ohio. Their father was a bishop of the United Brethren Church. The boys went through high school, Wilbur in Richmond, Ind., and Orville in Dayton, but neither received a diploma. Wilbur did not bother to go

Underwood & Underwood

Orville Wright   **Wilbur Wright**

possible for them to design a machine that could fly.

The brothers built a third glider and took it to Kitty Hawk in the summer of 1902. This glider, based on their new figures, had aerodynamic qualities far in advance of any tried before. With it, they solved most of the problems of balance in flight. They made nearly 1,000 glides in this model, and, on some, covered distances of more than 600 feet (180 meters). Their basic patent, applied for in 1903, relates to the 1902 glider.

First Airplane. Before leaving Kitty Hawk in 1902, the brothers started planning a power airplane. By the fall of 1903, they completed building the machine at a cost of less than $1,000. It had wings $40\frac{1}{2}$ feet (12 meters) long and weighed about 750 pounds (340 kilograms) with the pilot. They designed and built their own lightweight gasoline engine for the airplane.

The Wrights went to Kitty Hawk in September, 1903, but a succession of bad storms and minor defects delayed their experiment until December 17. They were so sure of the accuracy of their calculations that they showed no surprise when the machine flew.

The Wrights continued their experiments at a field near Dayton in 1904 and 1905. In 1904, they made 105 flights, but totaled only 45 minutes in the air. Two flights lasted five minutes each. On Oct. 5, 1905, the machine flew 24.2 miles (38.9 kilometers) in 38 minutes, 3 seconds. When the Wrights first offered their machine to the U.S. government, they were not taken seriously. But by 1908 they closed a contract with the U.S. Department of War for the first military airplane. Meanwhile, they resumed experimental flights at Kitty Hawk which newspapers reported at great length.

Immediately after these trials, Wilbur went to France, where he aroused the admiration and enthusiasm of thousands. He made flights to altitudes of 300 feet (91 meters) and more. He arranged with a French company for the construction of his machine in France. When he returned to the United States, he made demonstration flights from Governors Island, N.Y., around the Statue of Liberty, up to Grant's Tomb, and back.

While Wilbur was in France, Orville made successful flights in the United States. On the morning of Sept. 9, 1908, he made 57 complete circles at an altitude of 120 feet (37 meters) over the drill field at Fort Myer, Va. He remained in the air one hour and two minutes, and set several records on the same day. On Sept. 17, however, while he was flying at 75 feet (23 meters), a blade of the right-hand propeller struck and loosened a wire of the rear rudder. The wire coiled about the blade and snapped it across the middle. The machine became dif-

to the commencement exercises, and Orville took special subjects rather than a prescribed course in his final year. Mechanics fascinated them even in childhood. To earn pocket money they sold homemade mechanical toys. Orville started a printing business, building his own press. They later launched a weekly paper, the *West Side News*, with Wilbur as editor. Wilbur was 25 and Orville 21 when they began to rent and sell bicycles. Then they began to manufacture them, assembling the machines in a room above their shop. They built the "Van Cleve" bicycle.

Flying Experiments. After reading about the death of pioneer glider Otto Lilienthal in 1896, the brothers became interested in flying. They began serious reading on the subject in 1899, and soon obtained all the scientific knowledge of aeronautics then available. That same year they experimented for a day or two with a 5-foot (1.5-meter) biplane kite.

On the advice of the Weather Bureau (now the National Weather Service) in Washington, D.C., the Wrights selected for their experiments a narrow strip of sand called Kill Devil Hill, near the settlement of Kitty Hawk, N.C. In 1900, they tested their first glider that could carry a person. The glider measured 16 feet (5 meters) from wing tip to wing tip, and cost $15 to build. They returned to Kitty Hawk in 1901 with a larger glider. They showed that they could control sidewise balance by presenting the right and left wings at different angles to the wind. But neither the 1900 or 1901 glider had the lifting power they had counted on.

The Wrights concluded that all published tables of air pressures on curved surfaces must be wrong. They set up a 6-foot (1.8-meter) wind tunnel in their shop and began experiments with model wings. They tested more than 200 wing models in the tunnel. From the results of their tests, the brothers made the first reliable tables of air pressures on curved surfaces. These tables made it

Culver

The Wright Brothers' First Airplane reached a speed of about 30 miles (48 kilometers) per hour on its first flight in December, 1903.

ficult to manage and plunged to the earth. Orville suffered a broken thigh and two broken ribs. His passenger, Thomas E. Selfridge, died within three hours of a fractured skull. This accident was the most serious in the Wright brothers' career. Orville reappeared at Fort Myer the next year, fully recovered. He completed official tests with no evidence of nervousness.

In August, 1909, the Wrights closed a contract with some wealthy men in Germany for the formation of a German-Wright Company. Later that year, they formed the Wright Company in New York City to manufacture airplanes. They earned some money, but they were troubled with imitators, infringements on their patents, conflicting claims, and lawsuits.

After Wilbur's Death. Three years later, just as the airplane was beginning to make great advances, Wilbur Wright died of typhoid fever. Orville worked on alone, and in 1913 won the Collier Trophy for a device to balance airplanes automatically. He sold all his interest in the Wright Company and retired in 1915.

Wright continued work on the development of aviation in his own shop, the Wright Aeronautical Laboratory. In 1929, he received the first Daniel Guggenheim Medal for his and Wilbur's contributions to the advancement of aeronautics. Wilbur was elected to the Hall of Fame in 1955, and Orville in 1965.

Orville sent the original plane flown at Kitty Hawk to the Science Museum in South Kensington, London, in 1928, after a dispute with the Smithsonian Institution. The Science Museum sent the plane to the United States in 1948, and it is now in the National Air and Space Museum in Washington, D.C. Basic principles of that machine are used in every airplane that flies. The Kill Devil Hill Monument National Memorial in North Carolina became the Wright Brothers National Memorial in 1953.   WELMAN A. SHRADER

See also AIRPLANE (The Wright Brothers; pictures); GLIDER (History).

WRIGHT-PATTERSON AIR FORCE BASE, Ohio, is the *logistics* (supply) headquarters of the U.S. Air Force. It is also a major research and development center. The 8,242-acre (3,335-hectare) base lies about 10 miles (16 kilometers) from Dayton, Ohio. The Air University operates the Air Force Institute of Technology there. The base also houses the Air Force Museum and two divisions of the Air Force Systems Command. The base is named for the Wright brothers and Lt. Frank S. Patterson, who died in a plane crash in 1918. See also OHIO (Places to Visit).   RICHARD M. SKINNER

WRIST is the joint that connects the hand and the forearm. A person uses the wrist to move the hand up, down, and sideways. The word *wrist* also refers to an area of the upper part of the hand. This area includes eight small bones called *carpals*.

The carpal bones extend across the hand in two rows of four bones each. Strong tissues called *ligaments* bind the carpals in place, but they also permit movement. Three carpals of the upper row join the *radius*, one of the two bones of the forearm, to form the wrist joint. The *ulna*, the other bone of the forearm, does not connect with the carpals. It forms a joint with the radius just above the wrist. This joint permits the wrist to rotate and thus helps turn the palm of the hand up and down.

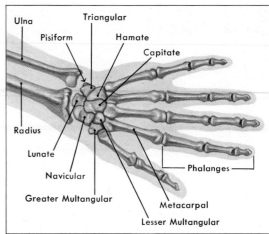

WORLD BOOK illustration by Lou Barlow

The Wrist includes eight small, irregularly shaped bones located between the ulna and radius, the bones of the forearm, and the metacarpals, the bones of the palm.

Cordlike tissues called *tendons* extend through the carpal area and connect the finger bones with muscles in the arm. When these arm muscles contract, they pull the tendons and make the fingers move. The tendons on the palm side of the carpals bend the fingers. Those on the back of the hand straighten the fingers.

A fall on an outstretched arm may fracture one of the carpals, called the *navicular* bone, or the radius's lower end. Either injury is called a broken wrist. Many athletes suffer such fractures.   LEONARD MARMOR

See also HAND.

WRIT is generally used in its legal meaning to describe the written orders of a court of law. Many kinds of orders have specific names. For instance, if a court orders the sheriff to seize property which has been wrongfully taken, it gives the sheriff a *writ of replevin*. A *writ of habeas corpus* is designed to protect persons taken into custody unlawfully. A *writ of error* is an order to a court to send records of a proceeding to a superior or appellate court, so that the judgment may be examined for errors of law. Early English-speaking people called anything in writing a writ. Even today, some persons call the Bible the *Holy Writ*.   ERWIN N. GRISWOLD

Related Articles in WORLD BOOK include:

Attachment	Injunction	Replevin
Certiorari, Writ of	Mandamus	Subpoena
Habeas Corpus	Quo Warranto	Summons

WRIT OF ASSISTANCE. In colonial days the British government provided customs officials in America with general search warrants called *writs of assistance*. The officials used them to enforce the collection of import duties and to seize goods upon which no duty had been paid. The writs were different from ordinary search warrants, which authorized the officers to seize only specified goods at a certain time and place. With writs of assistance they could search for suspected goods at any time in any place. In 1767, Parliament declared the writs legal. But the colonists opposed them, and they were seldom used. In modern law, a writ of assistance is a court order to a sheriff, commanding the sheriff to turn over certain real estate to the person entitled to it. See also SEARCH WARRANT.   JOHN R. ALDEN

WRITING, as a career, attracts more people than any other field in the arts. Writing seems both simple and glamorous to many people, and it can offer great rewards. A writer needs only a few tools—paper, a typewriter, and pencils—and may achieve fame and wealth. Written works may be read long after the author's death and thus give a kind of immortality. But many beginning authors spend hundreds of hours perfecting their skills before they can sell any of their works.

There are two main kinds of writers, *staff writers* and *free-lance writers*. Most professional writers are staff writers, who work for a salary. Many work as editors for book publishers, magazines, or newspapers. They write articles and also improve the work of other writers. Many staff writers earn a living as newspaper reporters or columnists. Others work as *technical writers*, who express the complex ideas of engineers and scientists in words that a nonexpert can understand.

Free-lance writers have no employer and earn no salary. They get paid only if a publisher buys their work. Free-lancers write most books—both fiction and non-fiction—dramas, poems, screenplays, and short stories, as well as many magazine and newspaper articles. Many staff writers create free-lance material in addition to their regular work.

This article discusses the chief types of free-lance writing and tells how to submit works for publication. For some information on how to write, see the WORLD BOOK article on COMPOSITION.

Preparing for a Writing Career. A person who wants to be a writer should critically read the many kinds of writing encountered every day. New items, textbooks, poems, novels, and even cookbooks and repair manuals each communicate with a particular audience in a certain style. A beginner who carefully analyzes why a piece of writing seems stimulating, puzzling, or boring can learn to develop a fresh, lively style. A person who finds ambiguous statements in any kind of writing has taken a long step toward understanding the importance of clear, concise expression.

Beginning writers should also scan popular magazines to learn what subjects seem to appeal to various groups of readers. These groups include business persons, children, homemakers, scientists, and teachers. The study of great novels can provide insight into how authors create believable characters, plots, and settings.

A wise beginner sets aside some time to write every day. Learning to express ideas effectively in writing takes a great deal of practice. Some professional writers spend months polishing a poem or a short story. The beginner may ask a teacher to point out faulty grammar, poor organization, or other writing problems. Gradually, a promising writer develops the ability to evaluate and revise his or her own work.

High schools and colleges offer many learning opportunities for young writers. Most students study composition and literature in English courses. They may also take creative writing and journalism courses to sharpen their writing skills. Many students work on literary magazines, newspapers, and yearbooks published by their school. These young people may write short stories, edit articles, and gain other kinds of editorial experience. Some high schools and colleges have a creative writing club that invites professional writers to discuss career opportunities and on-the-job experiences.

Beginners can also gain experience and recognition by entering various writing contests. Civic organizations in most communities sponsor essay contests on a wide range of topics. So do companies whose products appeal especially to young people. Entrants who express their ideas in a convincing, logical style may win a prize and have their picture appear in the local newspaper. Such rewards give a beginner confidence and provide encouragement to continue writing. Many magazines, including *The Atlantic Monthly*, *Mademoiselle*, and *Seventeen*, offer cash awards to promising young authors whose works they publish.

Free-Lance Markets. About 16,500 magazines are published in the United States. They range from general-interest publications to specialized periodicals that appeal to relatively few readers. Most magazines welcome free-lance material. Many editors send a sample copy of their magazine and a free list of editorial guidelines to anyone who requests them. This material can help free-lancers decide whether the content and style of their work would appeal to readers of a certain publication.

A reference book called *Writer's Market* lists the name, address, and editorial needs of more than 5,000 magazines, book and play publishers, and other literary markets. *Writer's Market* is revised annually and can be found in most public libraries. Articles in such monthly magazines as *The Writer* and *Writer's Digest* offer helpful tips on how to write and sell nearly every kind of manuscript.

A writer whose article or short story appears in a magazine may be paid from $\frac{1}{2}$ cent per word to more than $1 per word. Book publishers pay authors a *royalty* (commission) of 10 to 15 per cent of the book's price for each copy sold.

Some writers hire a *literary agent* to find markets for their works. An agent reads a client's manuscript and suggests ways to improve it. The agent then tries to sell the manuscript to a publisher. If the manuscript is sold, the agent receives a commission of 10 per cent of the author's income for that piece of writing. Beginning writers should try to sell their own works. Many agents work only with writers who have been recommended by editors or professional authors. *Writer's Market* lists about 100 agents in the United States.

Nonfiction ranks as the largest market for free-lance writers. Book publishers buy about 10 times as many nonfiction manuscripts as novels. In most magazines, nonfiction articles greatly outnumber poems and short stories. Nonfiction articles range in length from a few hundred words to a book-length piece. Long articles may be *serialized* (published in installments) in several issues of a magazine.

Several kinds of publications accept nonfiction from free-lancers. General-interest magazines contain articles on current, popular subjects that appeal to a wide audience. Such magazines attract many professional writers. Payment for an article ranges from less than $100 to several thousand dollars. Readers of specialized publications share a common interest, such as a hobby, a political viewpoint, or membership in a professional organization. Many beginners succeed in selling articles to these magazines, which attract relatively few well-known writers. These magazines pay from 1 cent to about 10 cents per word. Trade journals, designed for workers in a specific occupation or kind of business, buy free-lance articles related to that field. Payment varies among such publications.

Writers should choose a topic that readers want to know more about. Then they can select the *format* (kind of presentation) best suited for their audience and their subject. A free-lancer who writes about money might offer an article called "How to Find a Part-Time Job" to *Seventeen*. Another article, called "Stretching Your Food Dollars," might be sent to *Family Circle*, and a third, entitled "Tips on Canoe Camping in British Columbia," to *Field & Stream*. A writer must always be sure to use reliable sources so that the article presents accurate information.

Poetry and Fiction. Poetry is one of the most challenging and lowest-paying types of writing. A poet whose works appear in a literary magazine may win honor and recognition. But even such top publications as *The Atlantic Monthly* and *Harper's Magazine* pay only about $2 per line for poetry. Some magazines pay poets by giving them copies of the issue in which their work appears. Most beginners publish their work in literary and poetry magazines and in university periodicals. Some newspapers, religious magazines, and trade journals also publish poetry. Short poems of 20 lines or less can be sold more easily than longer works. A poet should study several issues of poetry magazines to determine the preferred length, style, and subject matter for each publication.

Fiction sold by free-lance writers includes short stories of various kinds—adventure and confession tales, mysteries, romances, science fiction, and westerns. Markets include many general-interest publications and fiction and literary magazines. Payment generally ranges from 1 cent to 10 cents per word.

A writer who wants to sell a novel should study the catalogs of various publishers. These catalogs offer guidance on which publishers are most likely to buy a particular kind of work. Some writers submit an entire manuscript to a publisher. Most editors respond within two months. Other writers prefer to submit only the first few chapters of a novel, plus a one- or two-page summary of the plot. This method usually brings a response in about three weeks.

Literature for Children includes adventure stories, mysteries, and articles about folklore, nature, science, and famous people. Payment ranges from $\frac{1}{2}$ cent to 5 cents per word. Many children's magazines also buy quizzes, puzzles, and riddles. Free-lance authors write about 90 per cent of the approximately 2,000 juvenile books published yearly in the United States. Most publishing firms that specialize in children's books prefer to receive complete manuscripts.

Other Kinds of Writing. Most plays produced on Broadway in New York City are written by established playwrights. Some off-Broadway, community, and school groups perform plays written by beginners. A playwright may submit a script to a publisher or directly to a play producer. Professional productions usually pay a percentage of the total box-office receipts as royalties. Royalties from amateur productions range

from $10 per performance to $75 on opening night and $25 for each succeeding performance.

Many motion-picture screenplays and television scripts are written by free-lance writers. Free-lancers should hire an agent to sell such material because movie and television producers rarely deal directly with an author. The size of the royalty depends on the writer's professional reputation and the quality of the script. Such newspapers as *Daily Variety* and *The Hollywood Reporter* help writers by reporting various trends in the film and television industries.

Preparing and Submitting a Manuscript. All manuscripts should be neatly typed on white, high-quality paper that measures $8\frac{1}{2}$ by 11 inches (22 by 28 centimeters). The typist should doublespace and leave a margin of about $1\frac{1}{4}$ inches (3.2 centimeters) at the top, bottom, and sides of every page. The number of each page should be at the center of the top margin. The author's name and address appear in the upper left-hand corner of the title page. The article title and the author's *by-line* should be centered about halfway down the page. A by-line is the author's name as the author wants it to appear in the published article.

A writer may enclose a *cover letter* that briefly describes his or her qualifications for writing about the subject. Some editors prefer that a free-lancer send a *query letter* that summarizes the manuscript before submitting the entire work. The writer should always enclose a stamped, self-addressed envelope for the editor to use to return the manuscript.   ROBERT ANDERSON

Related Articles in WORLD BOOK include:

Book	Literature for Children	Publishing
Book Review	Magazine	Science Fiction
Criticism	Motion Picture	Short Story
Drama	(The Writer)	Television
Essay	Novel	(Writers)
Literature	Poetry	

WRITING is a system of human communication by means of visual symbols or signs. The most primitive stages of "writing," or marking on objects, date almost from the time of the earliest human beings. However, the first fully developed systems of word writing appeared only about 5,000 years ago.

Counting Sticks have been used in all parts of the world. A shepherd could record the exact number of sheep in the flock by cutting one notch in a stick for each sheep. The Inca of Peru tied knots in strings of various lengths and colors to keep accounts. Such a string was called a *quipu*. These methods of keeping accounts could not easily be adapted to actual writing.

Rock Drawings conveyed a clearer meaning, but were not so useful for counting. A simple rock drawing was found near a dangerously steep trail in New Mexico. The design shows a mountain goat and a man riding a horse. The mountain goat stands on all fours, but the horse and rider are upside down. The design warns a horseman that a mountain goat can climb the rocky trail, but that his horse cannot.

Ideographs. The characteristic feature of this Indian drawing, and of any primitive drawing, is that it expresses a group of ideas without any clear connection with any language. Any other person can understand it, whether or not he speaks the language of the man who drew it. This way of expressing ideas, not necessarily in words, is called *ideography*. Pictures drawn for the purpose of communication differ only slightly from pictures drawn for artistic purposes. Communication pictures are simplified and stereotyped, with no details that are not needed as part of the communication.

Logographs. Man took the decisive step in developing real writing when he learned that he could express ideas indirectly. He did this by using signs that stood for the words in his language, not the ideas the words stood for. This kind of writing is called *logography*. To see how it works, take such a message as "The king killed a lion." In ideography, the message would include two drawings, one showing a man with the insignia of his office, such as a crown, holding a spear in his hand, and the other showing a lion. Logography, or word writing, would express the same message by signs that stand for the words themselves. One picture, of a man wearing a crown, stands for the word "king." A spear stands for the word "kill," and a drawing of a lion stands for "lion." If the king had killed three lions, the phrase "three lions" would be expressed in word writing by two signs, one standing for the numeral "three" and the other for "lion." In ideography, the message would have to contain pictures of three lions.

Early in the development of this kind of writing, the pictures became *conventional*, or simplified and formal. They often showed only a part for the whole, such as a crown for the word "king." But pictures cannot represent words like "the" or "a," nor can they represent grammatical endings like the "-ed" of "killed."

The Sumerians, who lived in southern Mesopotamia, were the first people to reach the stage of a primitive word writing, sometime before 3000 B.C. They kept records with such simple entries as "10 arrows" and the sign for a personal name, or "5 cows" and the sign for another name. They could easily use signs for numbers and for items such as arrows or cows. But they had difficulty in writing names and abstract ideas.

Phonetization. To overcome these problems, the Sumerians found that they could use word-symbols of objects that were easy to picture, like "arrow," to stand for words that sounded similar, but were hard to picture. The sign for "arrow" could also stand for "life," because the word *ti* means both things in Sumerian. This principle of *phonetization*, often called the *rebus* principle, is the most important single step in the history of writing (see REBUS). If the arrow sign could stand for both "arrow" and "life," because they are both pronounced *ti*, why not use the arrow sign for the sound *ti* wherever it occurs, regardless of its meaning? The Sumerian language was made up largely of one-syllable words, so it was not difficult for the people to work out a *syllabary* of about one hundred phonetic signs.

Sumerian writing is called *logo-syllabic*, or word-syllabic. It uses both *logograms*, or word signs, and *syllabograms*, or syllabic signs. Logograms expressed most of the words in the language, and syllabograms expressed rare and abstract words and proper names. Sumerian writing gradually developed the wedgelike appearance we call *cuneiform*. The Babylonians and Assyrians took cuneiform from the Sumerians, and the Hittites and other peoples learned it from them (see CUNEIFORM).

The Egyptians developed another important word-syllabic writing, *hieroglyphic*, about 3000 B.C. It resembled Sumerian in using word-signs, but differed in the choice of syllabic signs. The Sumerians regularly indicated differences in vowels in their syllabic signs,

but the Egyptians did not. The Hittites also had a writing of their own, *hieroglyphic Hittite*, that was related to some of the systems used in the lands around the Aegean Sea. See HIEROGLYPHIC.

The Chinese, perhaps about 1300 B.C., began the most highly developed word writing in the world. The peoples of the Middle East usually had only a few hundred word signs, but the Chinese may have as many as 50,000. They use some of these signs for the syllables in proper names or in foreign words.

The Alphabet. Men gradually simplified the older word-syllable systems. From the complicated Egyptian system, the Semites of Syria, especially the Phoenicians, developed simple systems of from 22 to 30 signs, each standing for a consonant followed by any vowel. The Japanese worked out a syllabic system with symbols for an initial consonant and different vowels. They also used many word symbols borrowed from Chinese. The alphabet was the next step. The Greeks were the first to evolve a system of vowel signs, creating the first alphabetic system of writing.   I. J. GELB

Related Articles. See the articles on letters of the alphabet. See also the following articles:

Aegean Civilization	Egypt, Ancient	Manuscript
Alphabet	(Language)	Pictograph
Babylonia	Hittite	Rune
Chinese Language	Inca	Sumer

WRITING ROCK. See NORTH DAKOTA (Places to Visit).

WROCŁAW, *VRAW tslahf* (pop. 527,600), is a city that lies in southwestern Poland on the Oder River. For location, see POLAND (political map). Wrocław serves as a rail center and river port. Leading products of Wrocław include computers, machinery, and textiles. The city has two universities and a cathedral that dates from the 1100's. Wrocław became part of Poland in the 900's. Austria took over the city in 1526 and Prussia seized it in 1742. Wrocław became part of Germany in 1871. The city's German name was *Breslau*. When World War II ended in 1945, Poland again gained control of the city.   ADAM BROMKE

WROUGHT IRON. See IRON AND STEEL (Kinds of Iron and Their Uses); ALLOY (Alloys of Iron).

WRYNECK. See RHEUMATISM.

WRYNECK, or SNAKEBIRD, is a small, mottled-brown bird that lives in Europe. Three of its species also live in Africa. The bird nests in the hollows of trees. When disturbed, it thrusts its head and neck out of its nest and hisses. Its name comes from the twisting motion of its neck when it does this. The wryneck has a cone-shaped beak and a horny-tipped tongue.

The Wryneck, or Snakebird
Eric Hosking

Scientific Classification. The European wrynecks belong to the woodpecker family, *Picidae*. They are in the genus *Jynx*, species *J. torquilla*.   ARTHUR A. ALLEN

WU, CHIEN-SHIUNG (1912?-   ), an American experimental physicist, helped disprove the law of the conservation of parity (see PARITY [in physics]). For about 30 years, most physicists had accepted this law as a universal principle of nature. But in 1957, Wu performed an experiment that showed it to be incorrect.

The law stated, in part, that electrons called *beta particles*, which are emitted by a radioactive nucleus, would fly off in any direction, regardless of the spin of the nucleus. Using atoms of cobalt-60, Wu showed that beta particles were more likely to be emitted in a particular direction that depended on the spin of the cobalt nuclei. Her experiment confirmed a theory proposed in 1956 by two Chinese-born American physicists, Tsung Dao Lee and Chen Ning Yang. Lee and Yang shared the 1957 Nobel prize in physics for their theory.

Wu was born in Liu Ho, China, near Shanghai. She moved to the United States in 1936 and received a Ph.D. degree from the University of California at Berkeley. Wu became a professor of physics at Columbia University in 1957.   STANLEY GOLDBERG

WU TAO-TZU (A.D. 700's) was a famous Chinese painter. He painted chiefly religious subjects on the walls of Buddhist and Taoist temples in the Chinese capital of Ch'ang-an (now Sian). He usually worked on a very large scale in black and white. His murals were destroyed, and we can only imagine his style from descriptions and inferior copies. He was born near Loyang, in Honan.   ALEXANDER C. SOPER

WUCHANG. See WUHAN.

WUHAN (pop. 4,250,000) is the collective name for the adjacent cities of Hankow, Hanyang, and Wuchang in Hupeh province of China (see CHINA [political map]). The cities are considered a single political and economic unit. Wuchang lies on the south bank of the Yangtze River. Hankow and Hanyang are on the north bank. The Han River separates Hankow and Hanyang. The Han River bridge and ferries provide transportation between these two cities. The Yangtze bridge links Wuchang with Hanyang. Wuhan, an industrial center, was the birthplace of the Chinese Revolution in 1911.   THEODORE H. E. CHEN

WULFENITE. See MINERAL (picture); MOLYBDENUM; LEAD (How Lead Is Obtained).

WUNDT, *VOONT,* **WILHELM** (1832-1920), a German philosopher, became known as the *Father of Modern Psychology.* He founded the first laboratory for experimental psychology in 1879. He believed the methods for studying psychology included both laboratory experimentation and *introspection* (self-observation). Wundt was born in Neckarau, in Baden. See also PSYCHOLOGY (History).   KENNETH E. CLARK

WUPATKI NATIONAL MONUMENT, *woo PAT kih,* is in northern Arizona. It contains prehistoric dwellings, built by farming Indians. The Hopi Indians are believed to be partially descended from the Indians who built these dwellings. The monument was established in 1924. For its area, see NATIONAL PARK SYSTEM (table: National Monuments).

See also NATIONAL PARK SYSTEM (picture).

WYATT, SIR THOMAS (1503?-1542), was an English poet. His most important works are lyrics he wrote for lute accompaniment. Through his lyrics and sonnets, he helped make English poetry more personal, harmonious, and graceful than it had been. Wyatt also helped bring the Renaissance to England. He translated works by many writers, including Plutarch. Wyatt and Henry Howard, Earl of Surrey, are credited with introducing Petrarch's sonnet techniques into English literature.

Wyatt was born in Kent. He received a good education, and traveled in Spain, France, and Italy as a diplomat for King Henry VIII. Wyatt is usually linked in literary history with the Earl of Surrey because their poems were first published together in *The Book of Songs and Sonnets* (1557). This book is usually called *Tottel's Miscellany.* See SURREY, EARL OF.   THOMAS A. ERHARD

WYCHERLEY, WILLIAM (1640?-1716), an English playwright, ranks with Sir George Etherege and William Congreve as a leading author of witty satires called *comedies of manners* during the Restoration period of English literature. Wycherley's style is coarse, his satire often brutal, and his attitude toward people venomous.

Wycherley's first plays, *Love in a Wood* (1671) and *The Gentleman Dancing Master* (1672), are light comedies of intrigue. *The Country Wife* (1675), in which all the characters are fools or villains, best reveals Wycherley's attitude toward life. Although the plot is taken from a Latin comedy, the greatest fool in the play, Margery Pinchwife, is wholly original and a memorable comic character. *The Plain Dealer* (1676) is based partly on plays by Shakespeare and Molière, but it is more savage in its presentation of humanity.   ALAN S. DOWNER

WYCLIFFE, *WIK lif,* **JOHN** (1320?-1384), was a leading English philosopher in religion and politics during the Middle Ages. His challenges to existing religious and political practices remained influential long after his death.

Little is known of Wycliffe's life before 1356, when he was on the faculty of Merton College at Oxford University. Except for brief absences, he was connected with Oxford until he retired about 1382. At Oxford, he became famous as a professor of philosophy.

Wycliffe felt driven to become a reformer because of conditions in Europe during his time. A form of bubonic plague called the *black death* killed about a fourth of Europe's population during the 1300's. The Hundred Years' War between England and France began in 1337. Throughout the 1300's, violent struggles for power occurred between the popes and clergy on one side, and the kings and their nobles on the other. Both sides seemed corrupt and dominated by self-interest, and neither apparently cared about the common people.

The conditions in Europe raised many questions in people's minds. Was the pope lord over kings? Could a civil government punish a wicked bishop or priest? Could a civil government tax the church, or could the church demand that the government support it? Did church rulers or civil rulers have the right to make laws merely because they wished to, or did their laws have to be fair? Wycliffe dealt with these issues in his lectures and books. His most important political idea was summarized in the statement, "Dominion is founded in grace." He meant that unjust rulers could not claim that people must obey them because obedience was God's will. After Wycliffe applied this idea to the popes and bishops, he was brought to trial several times in church courts. Each time, the English royal family saved him from condemnation.

Dry-brush tempera (1954); collection of Mr. and Mrs. Joseph E. Levine

Teel's Island by Andrew Wyeth shows how the artist created a haunting mood of isolation out of a commonplace subject. Wyeth painted the scene while visiting a friend on an island in Maine.

By about 1371, Wycliffe had become a writer for the royal family and its supporters against the bishops and their followers. He evidently felt that there was more hope of reform from the royal family. Wycliffe tried to show that the claim to authority by popes and bishops was founded on false ideas of the superiority of priests over lay people. He denied the doctrine of transubstantiation, which he regarded as the basis of the clergy's claim to superiority. According to this doctrine, priests changed bread and wine into the body and blood of Jesus Christ during the Mass. In Wycliffe's later writings, he declared that the Bible, not the church, was the authority for Christian beliefs.

Wycliffe's followers, with his help and inspiration, translated the Bible into English about 1382. They completed an improved version about 1388, after his death. Wycliffe's followers, called *Lollards*, were severely persecuted in England (see LOLLARDS). The upper classes felt that Wycliffe's ideas encouraged the poor to demand better lives.

Wycliffe's writings influenced a number of reformers, including John Huss of Bohemia. Many early English Protestants regarded the teachings of Wycliffe as forerunners of those of the Reformation. They considered him the first great English reformer.   L. J. TRINTERUD

WYETH, ANDREW (1917-   ), probably ranks as the most popular American painter of his time. He is best known for his realistic and thoughtful pictures of people and places in rural Pennsylvania and Maine.

Wyeth's paintings show uncrowded rural scenes that are reminders of earlier American life. His works include pictures of old buildings with bare windows and cracked ceilings, and abandoned boats on deserted beaches. Such scenes portray the remains of past activity rather than the accomplishments of the present.

Wyeth's style follows the tradition of Thomas Eakins and Winslow Homer, two realistic American painters of the 1800's. His work is often extremely detailed, almost photographic. Wind and fog seem as real as actual objects in Wyeth's work. All his figures are portraits of real people—especially his family and neighbors. Wyeth paints in *egg tempera*, a medium which gives his pictures a smooth, delicate, detailed surface. He also

uses a water color medium called *dry brush*. His painting *Albert's Son* appears in the PAINTING article.

Wyeth was born in Chadds Ford, Pa., near Philadelphia. His father, N. C. Wyeth, was a noted illustrator of children's books (see LITERATURE FOR CHILDREN [picture: A Modern Edition of a Medieval Classic]). He gave Andrew an appreciation and a knowledge of disciplined drafting skills. Andrew Wyeth's son Jamie is also a painter.   ALLEN S. WELLER

WYLER, WILLIAM (1902-   ), is a motion-picture director, whose films have a high artistic quality and wide popular appeal. He won Academy Awards for his directing in three films: *Mrs. Miniver* (1942), *The Best Years of Our Lives* (1946), and *Ben-Hur* (1959). His other important films include *These Three* (1936), *Dodsworth* (1936), *Dead End* (1937), *Wuthering Heights* (1939), *The Letter* (1940), *The Little Foxes* (1941), *The Heiress* (1948), *Detective Story* (1951), *Roman Holiday* (1953), *The Desperate Hours* (1955), *Friendly Persuasion* (1956), *The Collector* (1965), and *Funny Girl* (1968).

Wyler was born and educated in France. He was a film publicist in Europe before coming to Hollywood in 1920 as an assistant director. He became a director and a United States citizen in 1928.   HOWARD THOMPSON

WYLIE, ELINOR (1885-1928), was an American poet. Although her poetry explores a wide range of subjects, much of her best work combines descriptions of nature with moral reflections. She could write of the "austere, immaculate" New England landscape, of the "red noonday" of the South, of an eagle's flight, or of the burrowing of a mole. She found significance in each of these subjects that affected both herself and others.

Wylie experimented widely with poetic forms, and was equally at home using the quatrain, sonnet, rondeau, or blank verse. Her style is notable for a rich, exact vocabulary, and for brilliant word pictures. She also wrote several novels, including a minor classic, *Jennifer Lorn* (1923).

Elinor Wylie was born in Somerville, N.J. She married the poet William Rose Benét, her third husband, in 1924. Her beauty and wit made her popular in literary society. After her death, Benét edited her *Collected Poems* (1932) and *Collected Prose* (1933).   CLARK GRIFFITH

427

Jack Zehrt, Publix

Jackson Hole Valley in the Teton Mountains of Western Wyoming

Herding Sheep in the Bighorn Mountains

Petroleum Refinery in Cody

WYOMING

THE EQUALITY STATE

WYOMING is a state famous for the beauty of its mountains. The peaks of the Rocky Mountains tower over the landscape. They provide the setting for the nation's largest and the world's oldest national park—Yellowstone. Wyoming also has the first national monument in the United States, Devils Tower, and the first national forest, Shoshone. Another famous scenic wonder, Grand Teton National Park, includes some of the West's most beautiful mountains. Millions of tourists visit Wyoming each year to enjoy its scenery and historic places.

Not all of Wyoming is mountainous. Between the mountain ranges lie broad, flat, treeless basins. Some of these basins are dotted with rugged, lonely towers of rock called *buttes*. In the eastern part of the state, a flat, dry plain stretches westward toward the mountains.

Wyoming's wealth—cattle and oil—comes from its land. About 95 per cent of the state's land is used for grazing. Thousands of oil wells dot the prairies. Visitors may see a white-face steer cropping the grass near a pumping oil well. Petroleum, natural gas, coal, and other minerals make Wyoming an important mining state. Wyoming also ranks as a leader in the production of bentonite, a special clay used in oil well drilling; trona, a mineral with wide use in the chemical industry; and uranium, the raw material of atomic power.

The contributors of this article are James M. Flinchum, Jr., editor of the Wyoming State Tribune *of Cheyenne; T. A. Larson, Professor Emeritus of History and American Studies at the University of Wyoming; and J. David Love, supervisor of the Laramie, Wyo., office of the U.S. Geological Survey. Photographs are* WORLD BOOK *photos by James R. Simon unless otherwise indicated.*

The federal government owns almost half the land in Wyoming. Since the state depends mostly on its land, this makes the government especially important in Wyoming's economy. Federal agencies control grazing, logging, and mining on the government land.

Wyoming has attracted travelers since the earliest days of white settlement. Three of the great pioneer trails cross Wyoming. The California, Mormon, and Oregon trails all took the covered wagons through South Pass. This pass became famous as the easiest way for the pioneers to cross the mountains.

Millions of persons have crossed Wyoming, but relatively few have stayed. Of the 50 states, only Alaska has fewer people, according to the 1970 census. Wyoming's capital and largest city, Cheyenne, has a population of less than 50,000.

The word *Wyoming* comes from a Delaware Indian word meaning *upon the great plain*. Wyoming is nicknamed the *Equality State* because Wyoming women were the first in the nation to vote, hold public office, and serve on juries. In 1870, Wyoming's Esther H. Morris became the nation's first woman justice of the peace. In 1924, Wyoming voters elected the first woman governor, Mrs. Nellie Tayloe Ross.

For the relationship of Wyoming to the other states in its region, see ROCKY MOUNTAIN STATES.

——— FACTS IN BRIEF ———

Capital: Cheyenne.

Government: *Congress*—U.S. senators, 2; U.S. representatives, 1. *Electoral Votes*—3. *State Legislature*—senators, 30; representatives, 62. *Counties*—23.

Area: 97,914 sq. mi. (253,596 km²), including 711 sq. mi. (1,841 km²) of inland water; 9th in size among the states. *Greatest Distances*—east-west, 365 mi. (587 km); north-south, 275 mi. (443 km).

Elevation: *Highest*—Gannett Peak in Fremont County, 13,804 ft. (4,207 m) above sea level. *Lowest*—Belle Fourche River in Crook County, 3,100 ft. (945 m) above sea level.

Population: *Estimated 1975 Population*—374,000. *1970 Census*—332,416; 49th among the states; distribution, 60 per cent urban, 40 per cent rural; density, 3 persons per sq. mi. (1 person per km²).

Chief Products: *Agriculture*—beef cattle, sugar beets, wheat, sheep, dry beans, hay. *Manufacturing*—petroleum and coal products; food products; stone, clay, and glass products; lumber and wood products; printed materials. *Mining*—petroleum, trona, coal, natural gas, uranium, natural gas liquids, clays, iron ore, sand and gravel.

Statehood: July 10th, 1890, the 44th state.

State Abbreviations: Wyo. (traditional); WY (postal).

State Motto: *Equal Rights*.

State Song: "Wyoming." Words by Charles E. Winter; music by G. E. Knapp.

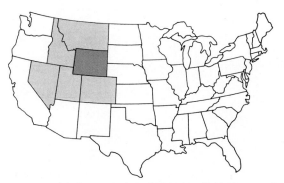

Wyoming (blue) ranks ninth in size among all the states, and fourth in size among the Rocky Mountain States (gray).

Constitution. Wyoming is still governed under its original constitution, which was adopted in 1889. The constitution has been *amended* (changed) 41 times. Amendments must be approved by a majority of the people voting in that particular election. Amendments may be proposed by a two-thirds vote of both houses of the legislature, or by a constitutional convention. Such a convention must be approved by two-thirds of the legislators of each house, and by a majority of the voters.

Executive. The governor of Wyoming is elected to a four-year term and may be re-elected an unlimited number of times. The governor is paid $37,500 a year.

Much of the governor's power lies in the right to appoint other important state officials. For example, the governor appoints the attorney general and the heads of the budget and personnel departments. For a list of all the state's governors, see the *History* section of this article.

The voters elect four other high state officials to four-year terms. These are the secretary of state, auditor, superintendent of public instruction, and treasurer. The treasurer may not serve two consecutive terms, but there are no limits on re-election of the others.

Wyoming does not have a lieutenant governor. If the governor dies in office or resigns, the secretary of state serves as governor until a new governor is elected.

Legislature consists of a 30-member senate and a 62-member house of representatives. Senators are elected to four-year terms and representatives are elected to two-year terms. The two houses of the legislature meet each year. General sessions of the legislature begin on the second Tuesday of January in odd-numbered years. Budget sessions begin on the fourth Tuesday in January in even-numbered years. The legislature may not meet more than 40 legislative days in any year or more than 60 days in each two-year period. The governor may call special legislative sessions.

Courts. The highest court in Wyoming is the Supreme Court. This court has five justices who are appointed to eight-year terms. The justices elect one of their num-

The State Legislature meets in the Capitol each year. Members of the house of representatives, above, assemble in the east wing of the Capitol, and senators meet in the west wing.

ber to serve as chief justice. The Supreme Court usually hears only appeals from lower courts.

Most major civil and criminal trials in the state are held in district courts. Wyoming has nine judicial districts, each with either one or two district judges. District judges are appointed to six-year terms. The governor appoints all Supreme Court judges. The governor chooses them from nominees of the Wyoming Judicial Nominating Commission. Other courts in Wyoming include police courts, municipal courts, and justice-of-the-peace courts.

Local Government. Wyoming has 23 counties, each governed by a board of three commissioners. The commissioners are elected to four-year terms. Most Wyoming cities have the mayor-council form of government. Casper and Laramie employ city managers. By state law, a city must have 4,000 residents. Communities with

The Governor's Mansion stands in northwestern Cheyenne. This 13-room, ranch-style house was built by the state and completed in 1976. It replaced a governor's mansion that dated from 1905.

The State Seal

The State Flag

Symbols of Wyoming. On the seal, the woman and the motto symbolize the equal rights women have had in the state. The two men represent Wyoming's livestock and mining industries. The dates are those on which Wyoming became a territory and a state. The seal was adopted in 1893. The flag, adopted in 1917, shows the seal on a buffalo to represent the branding of livestock. The red border symbolizes Indians and the blood of the pioneers.

Bird and flower illustrations, courtesy of Eli Lilly and Company

populations between 150 and 4,000 are called towns.

Taxation provides slightly more than half the state government's income. Sales taxes, license fees, and property taxes, in that order, bring in the most money. Almost all the rest of the state government's income comes from federal grants and other U.S. government programs.

Politics. In state and local elections, Republicans have won two-thirds of the contests since 1890, but Democrats often win major offices. The cities of southern Wyoming are a major source of Democratic strength. Republicans usually get more votes from the northern counties, which are largely rural.

In presidential elections, Wyoming has given its electoral votes to Republican and Democratic candidates about equally since the early 1930's. For Wyoming's electoral votes and voting record in presidential elections, see ELECTORAL COLLEGE (table).

State Capitol in Cheyenne is a massive sandstone building. The dome is 50 feet (15 meters) in diameter and towers 145 feet (44 meters) above the ground. Cheyenne became the capital of Wyoming in 1869.

The State Bird
Meadow Lark

The State Flower
Indian Paintbrush

The State Tree
Cottonwood

WYOMING Political Map

Legend:

- ⊛ State capital
- ● City or town
- ◉ County seat
- UINTA County name
  County boundary
- State boundary
- Park or other recreation area
- Forest or other conservation area
- Military or other federal area
- Indian reservation

- ✛ Point of interest
- Water
- River
- Waterway
- Intermittent river
- Intermittent lake

Highways:
- ═══ Expressway
- ─── Other road
- (41) Interstate
- (66) U.S.
- (84) Other

Lambert conformal conic projection
WORLD BOOK map ©Field Enterprises Educational Corporation

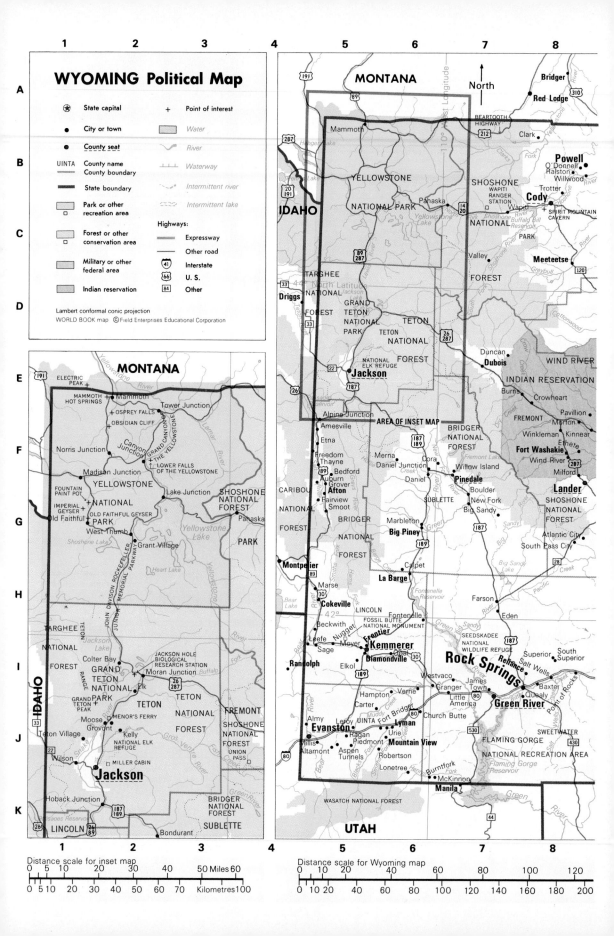

Distance scale for inset map
0 5 10 20 30 40 50 Miles 60
0 5 10 20 30 40 50 60 70 Kilometres 100

Distance scale for Wyoming map
0 10 20 40 60 80 100 120
0 10 20 40 60 80 100 120 140 160 180 200

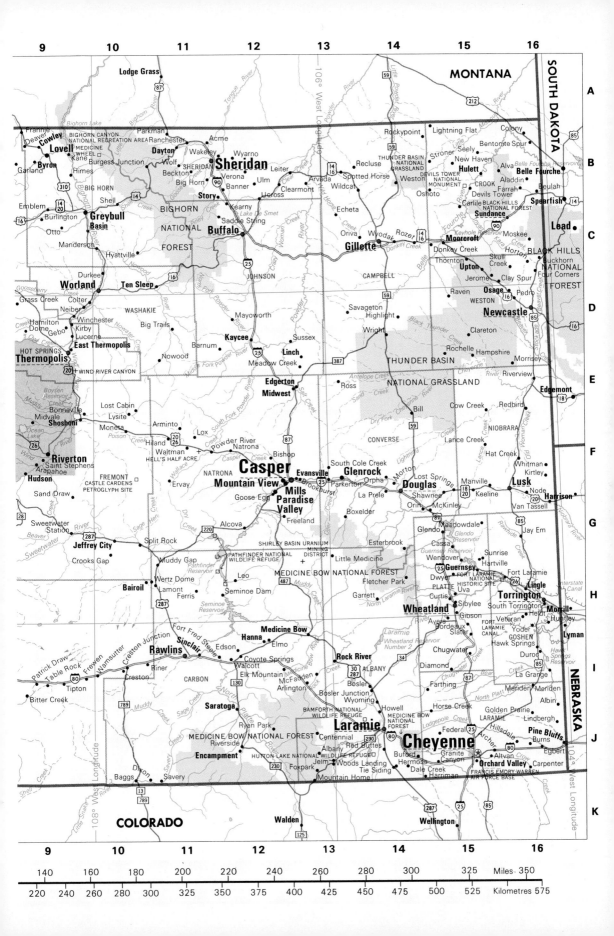

Population

374,000	Estimate	1975
332,416	.Census.	1970
330,066	"	1960
290,529	"	1950
250,742	"	1940
225,565	"	1930
194,402	"	1920
145,965	"	1910
92,531	"	1900
62,555	"	1890
20,789	"	1880
9,118	"	1870

Counties

Albany .....26,431..I 14
Big Horn ..10,202..B 10
Campbell ..12,957..D 14
Carbon ....13,354..I 11
Converse ..5,938..F 14
Crook .....4,535..B 15
Fremont ...28,352..F 7
Goshen ...10,885..I 16
Hot Springs .4,952..E 9
Johnson ....5,587..D 12
Laramie ...56,360..J 15
Lincoln ....8,640..H 5
Natrona ...51,264..F 11
Niobrara ...2,924..F 15
Park ......17,752..C 7
Platte .....6,486..H 15
Sheridan ..17,852..B 11
Sublette ...3,755..G 6
Sweetwater .18,391..I 8
Teton ......4,823..D 6
Uinta ......7,100..J 5
Washakie ...7,569..D 10
Weston .....6,307..D 15

Cities and Towns

Acme ....B 11
Afton ....1,290..G 5
Aladdin ....B 16
Albany ....J 13
Albin ....118..J 16
Alcova ....G 12
Almy ....J 5
Alpine Junction ...F 5
Altamont ....J 5
Altvan ....J 15
Alva ....B 16
Amesville ....F 5
Arapahoe ....F 9
Archer ....J 15
Arlington ....I 13
Arminto ....F 11
Arvada ....B 13
Aspen Tunnels .....I 8
Atlantic City .....G 8
Auburn ....F 5
Ayers ....H 15
Baggs ....146..K 10
Bairoil ....H 10
Banner ....B 12
Barnum ....E 12
Basin ....1,145..C 10
Baxter ....I 8
Beckton ....B 11
Beckwith ....H 5
Bedford ....F 5
Bentonite Spur ....B 16
Beulah ....B 16
Big Horn ....B 11
Big Piney .....570..G 6
Big Sandy ....G 7
Big Trails ....D 11
Bill ....E 14
Bishop ....I 9
Bitter Creek ......I 9
Bondurant ....K 2
Bonneville ....E 10
Bordeaux ....H 15
Bosler ....I 14
Bosler Junction ...I 14
Boulder ....G 7
Boxelder ....G 13
Brookhurst ....F 13
Buckhorn ....C 16
Buffalo ......3,394..C 12
Buford ....J 14
Burgess Junction ..B 10
Burlington ....C 9
Burns ....185..J 16
Burntfork ....K 6
Burris ....E 8
Byron ....397..B 9
Calpet ....F 6
Canyon Junction ...F 2
Carlile ....C 15
Carpenter ....J 16
Carter ....J 5
Casper .....39,361..F 13
Cassa ....G 15
Centennial ....I 13
Cheyenne ...40,914..J 15
Chugwater .....187..I 15
Church Butte ......J 6
Clareton ....D 15
Clark ....D 7
Clay Spur ....D 16
Clearmont .....141..B 12
Cody ....5,161..C 8
Cokeville .....440..H 5
Colony ....B 16
Colter ....D 10

Colter Bay ....I 2
Cora ....F 6
Cow Creek ....E 15
Cowley ....366..B 9
Coyote Springs ....I 12
Creston ....I 10
Creston Junction ..I 10
Crooks Gap ....G 10
Crowheart ....E 8
Curtis ....H 15
Dale Creek ....J 14
Daniel ....F 6
Daniel Junction ...F 6
Dayton ....396..B 11
Deaver ....112..B 9
Devils Tower ......B 15
Diamond ....I 15
Diamondville ..485..I 5
Dixon ....72..K 10
Donkey Creek ......C 15
Douglas ......2,677..G 14
Dubois ....898..E 7
Duncan ....E 7
Durkee ....C 10
Duroc ....H 15
Dwyer ....H 15
East
  Thermopolis .316..E 9
Echeta ....C 13
Eden ....H 7
Edgerton ......350..E 13
Edson ....I 12
Egbert ....J 16
Elk ....I 2
Elk Mountain .127..I 12
Elkol ....I 5
Elmo ....53..I 12
Emblem ....C 9
Encampment ...321..J 12
Ervay ....F 11
Esterbrook ....G 14
Ethete ....F 8
Etna ....F 5
Evanston ....4,848..J 5
Evansville ..2,185..F 13
Fairview ....G 5
Farrah ....B 16
Farson ....H 7
Farthing ....I 15
Federal ....J 15
Ferris ....H 11
Fletcher Park .....H 14
Fontenelle ....H 6
Fort Bridger ......J 5
Fort Fred Steele ..I 11
Fort Laramie ..197..H 16
Fort Washakie .....F 8
Four Corners ......C 16
Fox Farm* ...1,329..J 15
Foxpark ....J 13
Frannie ....139..B 9
Freedom ....F 5
Freeland ....G 12
Frewen ....I 10
Frontier ....I 5
Garland ....B 9
Garrett ....H 14
Gebo ....D 9
Gibson ....H 15
Gillette ....7,194..C 14
Glendo ....210..G 15
Glenrock ....1,515..F 13
Golden Prairie ....J 16
Goose Egg ....G 12
Granger ....137..I 6
Granite Canyon ....J 15
Grant Village .....G 2
Grass Creek ....D 9
Green River .4,196..I 7
Greybull ....1,953..C 10
Grover ....F 5
Grovont ....J 2
Guernsey ......793..H 15
Hamilton Dome .....D 9
Hampshire ....E 15
Hampton ....I 6
Hanna ....460..I 12
Harriman ....K 14
Hartville .....246..H 15
Hat Creek ....F 16
Hawk Springs ......I 16
Heldt ....H 16
Hermosa ....I 15
Highlight ....D 14
Hiland ....F 11
Hillsdale ....J 16
Himes ....B 9
Hoback Junction ...K 2
Horse Creek ....J 15
Horton ....C 16
Howell ....J 14
Hudson ....381..F 9
Hulett ....318..B 15
Huntley ....H 16
Hyattville ....C 10
Jackson .....2,688..E 5
James Town ....I 7
Jay Em ....G 16
Jeffrey City ......G 10
Jelm ....J 13
Jerome ....D 15
Kane ....B 9
Kaycee ....272..D 12
Kearny ....C 12
Keeline ....G 15
Kelly ....J 2
Kemmerer ....2,292..I 5

Kinnear ....F 8
Kirby ....75..D 9
Kirtley ....F 16
La Barge ......204..H 6
La Grange .....189..I 16
Lake Junction .....G 2
Lamont ....H 11
Lance Creek ....F 15
Lander ......7,125..F 8
La Prele ....G 14
Laramie ....23,143..J 14
Leefe ....I 4
Leiter ....B 13
Leo ....H 12
Leroy ....J 5
Lightning Flat ....A 15
Linch ....E 13
Lindbergh ....J 16
Lingle ....446..H 16
Little America ....I 7
Little Medicine ...G 13
Lonetree ....J 6
Lost Cabin ....25..E 10
Lost Springs ...2..G 15
Lovell ......2,371..B 9
Lox ....F 11
Lucerne ....D 9
Lusk ....1,495..F 16
Lyman ....2,002..J 6
Lysite ....E 10
Madison Junction ..F 1
Mammoth ....A 5
Manderson .....117..C 10
Manville ......92..F 15
Marbleton .....223..G 6
Marse ....H 5
Mayoworth ....D 12
McFadden ....I 13
McKinley ....G 15
McKinnon ....K 6
Meadow Creek ......E 13
Meadowdale ....H 15
Medicine Bow 455..I 13
Meeteetse .....459..C 8
Meriden ....I 16
Merna ....F 6
Midvale ....F 9
Midwest ....459..E 13
Milford ....F 8
Millis ....F 11
Mills ....1,593..F 12
Moneta ....F 10
Moorcroft .....981..C 15
Moose ....J 2
Moran Junction ....I 2
Morrisey ....E 16
Morton ....F 8
Morton ....F 14
Moskee ....C 16
Mountain Home .....I 13
Mountain View 597..J 6
Mountain
  View ......1,641..F 12
Moyer ....I 5
Muddy Gap ....H 11
Natrona ....F 12
Neiber ....D 10
New Fork ....G 7

New Haven ....B 15
Newcastle ...3,432..D 16
Node ....G 16
Norris Junction ...F 2
Nowood ....E 11
Nugget ....I 5
O'Donnell ....B 8
Old Faithful ......G 1
Opal ....34..I 6
Orchard
  Valley ....1,015..J 15
Orin ....1,015..G 14
Oriva ....C 14
Orpha ....F 14
Osage ....D 16
Oshoto ....B 15
Otto ....C 9
Pahaska ....C 6
Paradise
  Valley* ...1,764..F 13
Parkerton ....F 13
Parkman ....B 11
Patrick Draw ......I 9
Pavillion .....181..E 8
Pedro ....D 16
Piedmont ....J 5
Pine Bluffs ...937..J 16
Pinedale ......948..F 6
Point of Rocks ....I 8
Powder River ......F 11
Powell ......4,807..B 8
Quealy ....J 15
Ragan ....J 5
Ralston ....C 8
Ranchester ....345..B 11
Raven ....B 13
Rawlins .....7,855..I 11
Recluse ....B 13
Red Buttes ....J 14
Redbird ....E 16
Reliance ....I 8
Riner ....I 10
Riverside .....46..J 12
Riverton ....7,995..F 9
Riverview ....E 16
Robertson ....J 5
Rochelle ....E 15
Rock River ....344..I 13
Rock
  Springs ...11,657..I 8
Rockypoint ....B 14
Ross ....E 13
Rozet ....C 14
Ryan Park ....J 12
Saddle String .....C 12
Sage ....I 5
St. Stephens ......F 9
Salt Wells ....I 8
Sand Draw ....G 9
Saratoga ....1,181..J 12
Savageton ....D 13
Savery ....K 11
Seely ....B 15
Seminoe Dam ......H 12
Shawnee ....G 15
Shell ....C 10
Sheridan ...10,856..B 11
Shoshoni ......562..F 9

Sibylee ....H 15
Sinclair ......445..I 11
Skull Creek ....C 16
Slater ....I 15
Smoot ....G 5
South Cole Creek .F 13
South Pass City ...G 8
South Superior 197..I 8
South Torrington ..H 16
Split Rock ....G 10
Spotted Horse .....B 13
Story ....B 12
Stroner ....B 15
Sundance ...1,056..C 16
Sunrise ....G 15
Superior ....I 8
Sussex ....D 13
Sweetwater Station .G 9
Table Rock ....I 9
Ten Sleep .....320..D 10
Teton Village .....J 1
Thayne ....195..F 5
Thermopolis .3,063..E 9
Thornton ....C 15
Tie Siding ....J 14
Tipton ....I 9
Torrington ..4,237..H 16
Tower Junction ....E 2
Trotter ....B 8
Ucross ....B 12
Ulm ....B 12
Upton ....987..C 15
Urie ....J 5
Uva ....H 15
Valley ....C 7
Van Tassell ...21..G 16
Verne ....I 6
Verona ....B 12
Veteran ....H 16
Wakeley ....B 12
Walcott ....I 12
Waltman ....F 11
Wamsutter .....139..I 10
Wapiti ....C 7
Warren* .....4,527..J 15
Wendover ....H 15
Wertz Dome ....H 11
West Thumb ....G 2
Weston ....B 14
Westvaco ....I 7
Wheatland ...2,498..H 15
Whitman ....F 16
Wildcat ....B 13
Willow Island .....F 7
Willwood ....B 8
Wilson ....J 1
Winchester ....D 9
Wind River ....F 8
Winkleman ....F 8
Wolf ....B 11
Woods
  Landing ....J 13
Worland .....5,055..D 11
Wright ....D 14
Wyarno ....B 12
Wyodak ....C 14
Wyoming ....I 14
Yoder ....101..H 16

Van Cleve Photography

Rodeo Fans in Pinedale, Wyo., watch the saddle-bronc riding event. The people of Wyoming sponsor many exciting rodeos every year to show their pride in the pioneer and "Wild West" heritage of the state.

434 °County seat.
*Does not appear on the map; key shows general location.

Sources: Latest census figures (1970 and special censuses). Places without population figures are unincorporated areas and are not listed in census reports.

WYOMING/People

The 1970 United States census reported that Wyoming had 332,416 persons. This was an increase of about 0.7 per cent over the 1960 United States census figure of 330,066. The U.S. Bureau of the Census estimated that by 1975, the state's population had reached about 374,000.

About three-fifths of Wyoming's people live in cities. Most of the cities are small compared with those in other states. Cheyenne, the capital and largest city, and Casper, the second largest city, both have fewer than 50,000 persons. The next three cities, in order of size, are Laramie, Rock Springs, and Sheridan. About three-tenths of the state's people live in cities and towns along a single major highway and rail line in southern Wyoming. See the separate articles on the cities of Wyoming listed in the *Related Articles* at the end of this article.

About 98 out of 100 persons in Wyoming were born in the United States. Wyoming has about 5,000 Indians, most of whom live on the Wind River reservation near Riverton.

Roman Catholics make up Wyoming's largest religious group. Mormons and Protestants also form large groups in the state.

POPULATION

This map shows the *population density* of Wyoming, and how it varies in different parts of the state. Population density means the average number of persons who live in a given area.

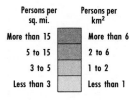

Persons per sq. mi.	Persons per km²
More than 15	More than 6
5 to 15	2 to 6
3 to 5	1 to 2
Less than 3	Less than 1

```
0      50      100 Miles
0   50   100 Kilometers
```

WORLD BOOK map

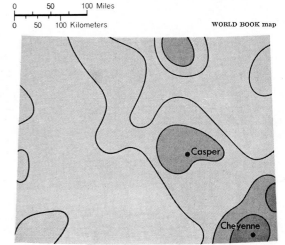

WYOMING/Education

Schools. The first school in Wyoming was founded at Fort Laramie in 1852. William Vaux, the chaplain of the fort, started the school. In 1860, a school was built at Fort Bridger, and its students began their studies the same year. In 1869, the territorial legislature passed a law providing tax support for schools. There were district schools in many communities after 1870. The first high school in Wyoming opened in Cheyenne in 1875.

Wyoming's public school system is supervised by an elected state superintendent of public instruction. A nine-member board of education makes school policies. The governor, with the approval of the senate, appoints board members to six-year terms. Most of the money for Wyoming's schools comes from property taxes. Income from certain state-owned land also is used to support schools.

Children are required to attend school either between the ages of 7 and 16, or until they complete the eighth grade. Wyoming has one of the highest percentages in the United States of persons who can read and write. For the number of students and teachers in Wyoming, see EDUCATION (table).

The University of Wyoming is the state's only university. It is accredited by the North Central Association of Colleges and Schools. The university was founded in Laramie in 1886, and is supported by the state.

Libraries and Museums. In 1886, Wyoming's territorial legislature passed laws providing for a system of free county libraries. Today, each of Wyoming's 23 counties has a public county library. The Wyoming Territorial Library was established in Cheyenne in 1871. It is now called the Wyoming State Library. The most important libraries at the University of Wyoming include the William Robertson Coe Library and a geological library.

Wyoming has about 50 museums. Most of them feature pioneer and Indian relics. Outstanding collections in the state include the exhibits at the Wyoming State Museum in Cheyenne, the Fort Caspar Museum in Casper, the Fort Bridger State Museum in Fort Bridger, and the Wyoming Pioneers' Memorial Museum in Douglas.

Other museums have exhibits about particular areas or points of interest. For example, the Fort Laramie National Historic Site has relics from the days of the old pioneer wagon trains. The Jackson Hole Museum in Jackson has displays about the early days of the area. The National Park Service operates the Fur Trade Museum at Moose. It also operates the Colter Bay Museum, which features a fine collection of Indian art. This museum is located in Grand Teton National Park.

The Buffalo Bill Museum in Cody displays possessions of the famous hunter and showman, Buffalo Bill Cody. Also in Cody are the Whitney Gallery of Western Art, which features paintings and sculpture by famous Western artists, and the Plains Indian Museum.

The University of Wyoming Geological Museum has fine collections of fossils, minerals, and rocks. It also features exhibits about prehistoric times.

Wyoming's tourist attractions rank among the most spectacular in the nation. Each year about 8 million persons visit the state. Yellowstone and Grand Teton national parks are the chief attractions. These parks have beautiful mountain scenery and many kinds of animals. Wilderness trails challenge the hiker's skill. Thousands of visitors also come to Wyoming to hunt big game animals or to fish in the lakes and streams. In 1904, the Eaton Ranch, near Sheridan, became the first dude ranch in the West.

Old Faithful, Yellowstone National Park   Frontier Days in Cheyenne

Lake Solitude, Grand Teton National Park

Devils Tower National Monument

PLACES TO VISIT

Following are brief descriptions of some of Wyoming's many interesting places to visit.

Devils Tower National Monument, in northeastern Wyoming, is a volcanic tower that stands 865 feet (264 meters) above its base, which is 415 feet (126 meters) high. In 1906, President Theodore Roosevelt established Devils Tower as the nation's first national monument.

Fort Laramie National Historic Site, near the town of Fort Laramie, was a fur trading center and later a military post. The fort helped protect pioneer wagon trains on the Oregon Trail. Some of the original buildings have been restored.

Fossil Butte National Monument, 10 miles (16 kilometers) west of Kemmerer, have the remains of fishes that lived in the water which covered the area about 50 million years ago.

Grand Teton National Park lies in northwestern Wyoming. The majestic Teton Mountains rise sharply from the floor of a beautiful valley called Jackson Hole. Several lakes lie along the east side of the mountains. Visitors can see many kinds of wild animals, which are protected there. See GRAND TETON NATIONAL PARK.

Hell's Half Acre, near Casper, is a rugged 320-acre (129-hectare) depression where wind and water have created unusual rock gullies, ridges, and towers. The canyon is near the South Fork of the Powder River.

Wildlife Refuges. Wyoming has six major wildlife refuge areas where visitors can watch animals and birds in their natural surroundings. The largest area is the National Elk Refuge near Jackson. Jackson Hole Wildlife Park is near Moran Junction. Federal waterfowl refuges include Pathfinder near Leo, Bamforth and Hutton Lake near Laramie, and Seedskadee near Green River.

Wind River Canyon, south of Thermopolis, offers motorists a scenic drive between the Bridger and Owl Creek mountains. Cliffs rise 2,000 feet (610 meters) above the river. The canyon walls are interesting because of the rock formations exposed where the river cut through the mountains.

Yellowstone National Park, in northwestern Wyoming, is the nation's largest, and the world's oldest national park. Its spectacular beauty and unusual attractions were recognized by early explorers. It be-

Lower Falls of the Yellowstone, Yellowstone National Park

Wyoming Travel Commission

Fort Laramie National Historic Site

Jack Zehrt, Publix

All American Indian Days in Sheridan

came a national park in 1872, and the earliest tourists faced danger from Indians. Major features of the park include the world's largest geyser area, towering waterfalls, hot springs, canyons, excellent fishing, and playful, but dangerous, bears. See YELLOWSTONE NATIONAL PARK.

National Forests. Ten national forests in Wyoming provide timber and serve as recreation areas. Shoshone, in northwestern Wyoming, is the largest forest. Other forests entirely in Wyoming are Bighorn near Sheridan, Bridger near Kemmerer, Medicine Bow near Laramie, and Teton near Jackson.

Wyoming shares Black Hills forest with South Dakota, Caribou with Idaho and Utah, Targhee with Idaho, and Ashley and Wasatch with Utah. For the areas and chief features of these national forests, see NATIONAL FOREST (table).

State Parks. Wyoming has set aside a number of historic sites, parks, and recreation areas. For information on the state parks and facilities in Wyoming, write to Director, Wyoming Recreation Commission, Cheyenne, Wyo. 82002.

ANNUAL EVENTS

Wyoming's most popular annual event is the Frontier Days celebration in Cheyenne, which has been staged since 1897. It is held during the last full week in July. Other annual events include the following.

January-April: Cutter (horse-drawn sleigh) races near Afton, Big Piney, Jackson, and Pinedale (January).

May-August: Days of '49 in Greybull (June); Pioneer Days in Lander (July 3-4); Rodeos in Buffalo, Cody, Sheridan, and other towns (July 4); Jubilee Days in Laramie (second week of July); Green River Rendezvous in Pinedale (second Sunday in July); Indian Sun Dances in Ethete and Fort Washakie (late July); Central Wyoming Fair and Rodeo in Casper (late July or early August); Fine Arts Festival in Jackson Hole (July and August); All American Indian Days in Sheridan (early August); Indian pageant in Thermopolis (early August); Wyoming State Fair in Douglas (late August or early September).

September-December: Governor's Challenge Cup Canoe Race in Jackson (early September); Oktoberfest in Worland (late September); Evanston Cowboy Days (Labor Day).

437

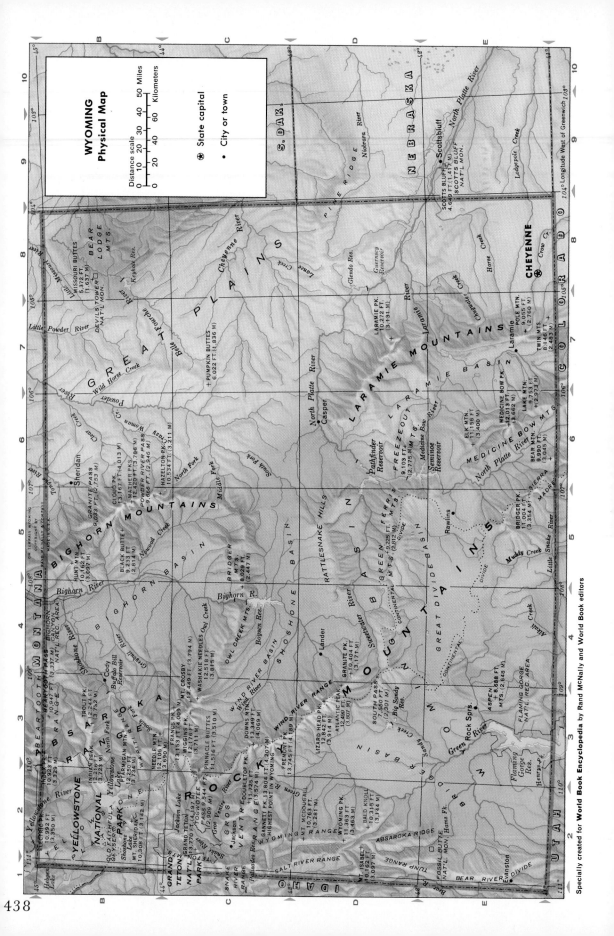

WYOMING
Physical Map

Distance scale

| 0 | 10 | 20 | 30 | 40 | 50 Miles |

| 0 | 20 | 40 | 60 Kilometers |

⊛ State capital
• City or town

MONTANA

IDAHO

UTAH

COLORADO

NEBRASKA

S. DAK.

GREAT PLAINS

BEAR LODGE MTS.

MISSOURI BUTTES 5,372 FT. (1,637 M)
DEVILS TOWER NAT'L MON.

Keyhole Res.

Little Missouri River

BIGHORN MOUNTAINS

Sheridan

GRANITE PASS 9,033 FT. (2,753 M)

CLOUD PK. 13,167 FT. (4,013 M)
POWDER RIVER PASS 9,666 FT. (2,946 M)
MATHER PKS. 12,420 FT. (3,786 M)
HAZELTON PK. 10,534 FT. (3,211 M)

PUMPKIN BUTTES 6,022 FT. (1,836 M)

Powder River

HUNT MTN. 10,162 FT. (3,097 M)

BLACK BUTTE 9,233 FT. (2,814 M)

BIGHORN BASIN

BRIDGER MTS. 8,029 FT. (2,447 M)

Bighorn River

Cheyenne River

Belle Fourche River

North Platte River

Casper

LARAMIE MOUNTAINS

LARAMIE PK. 10,272 FT. (3,131 M)

LARAMIE BASIN

Laramie

POLE MTN. 9,055 FT. (2,760 M)

Horse Creek

CHEYENNE

TWIN MTS. 8,146 FT. (2,483 M)

Scottsbluff
SCOTTS BLUFF 4,649 FT. (1,417 M)
SCOTTS BLUFF NAT'L MON.

PINE RIDGE

Niobrara River

Lodgepole Creek

Horse Creek

ABSAROKA RANGE

YELLOWSTONE NATIONAL PARK

OLD FAITHFUL GEYSER
Yellowstone Lake
Shoshone Lake
MT. SHERIDAN 10,308 FT. (3,142 M)

BEARTOOTH PASS

TROUT PK. 12,244 FT. (3,732 M)

INDIAN PK.

Buffalo Bill Reservoir

Cody

PTARMIGAN MTN. 12,250 FT. (3,734 M)

FRANCS PK. 13,153 FT. (4,009 M)
WIGGINS PK. 12,176 FT. (3,711 M)

MT CROSBY 12,449 FT. (3,794 M)

WASHAKIE NEEDLES 12,518 FT. (3,815 M)

PINNACLE BUTTES 11,516 FT. (3,510 M)

OWL CREEK MTS.

Boysen Res.

SHOSHONE BASIN

WIND RIVER BASIN

Wind River

Lander

GRANITE PK. 12,404 FT. (3,177 M)

RATTLESNAKE HILLS

Pathfinder Reservoir

GREEN MTS. 9,225 FT. (2,812 M)

FREEZEOUT MTS. 9,103 FT. (2,775 M)

Seminoe Reservoir

Medicine Bow River

ELK MTN. 11,156 FT. (3,400 M)

Rawlins

GREAT DIVIDE BASIN

CONTINENTAL DIVIDE

MEDICINE BOW

MEDICINE BOW PK. 12,013 FT. (3,662 M)

LAKE MTN. 9,751 FT. (2,973 M)

BEAR MTN. 9,900 FT. (3,045 M)

SIERRA MADRE

Muddy Creek

Little Snake River

BRIDGER PK. 11,004 FT. (3,354 M)

GRAND TETON NAT'L PARK

Jackson Lake
GRAND TETON 13,770 FT. (4,197 M)
TOGWOTEE PASS

GROS VENTRE RANGE
Jackson
Gros Ventre River

DOUBLETOP PK. 11,725 FT. (3,574 M)

GANNETT PK. 13,804 FT. (4,207 M) HIGHEST POINT IN WYOMING

WIND RIVER RANGE

DOWNS MTN. 13,349 FT. (4,069 M)

FREMONT PK. 13,745 FT. (4,189 M)

LIZARD HEAD PK. 12,842 FT. (3,914 M)

ATLANTIC PEAK 12,490 FT. (3,807 M)

SOUTH PASS 7,550 FT. (2,301 M)

Big Sandy River

GREEN RIVER BASIN

Green River

Rock Sprs.

ASPEN MTS. 8,688 FT. (2,648 M)

FLAMING GORGE NAT'L REC. AREA
Flaming Gorge Res.

Henrys Fk.

SNAKE RIVER RANGE

SALT RIVER RANGE

WYOMING RANGE

MT. McDOUGALL 10,763 FT. (3,281 M)

BALD KNOLL 12,283 FT. (3,744 M)

ABSAROKA RIDGE

FOSSIL BUTTE NAT'L MON.

Hams Fk.

Bear River

TUNP RANGE

MT. ISABEL 10,162 FT. (3,097 M)

Evanston

BEAR RIVER DIVIDE

ROCKY MOUNTAINS

WIND RIVER

NEEDLE MTN. 12,106 FT. (3,690 M)

Little Powder River

Wild Horse Creek

Clear Creek

North Fork

Middle Fork

South Fork

Nowood Creek

Greybull River

Shoshone River

North Fork

Wapiti

WAPITI RANGE

Snake River

Green River

North Platte River

Sweetwater River

Chugwater Creek

Crow Cr.

Horse Creek

Glendo Res.

Guernsey Reservoir

Lance Creek

Crazy Woman Cr.

Little Powder River

Tongue River

Crazy Woman Creek

438

Specially created for **World Book Encyclopedia** by Rand McNally and World Book editors

Land Regions. Wyoming lies where the Great Plains meet the Rocky Mountains. The Continental Divide winds through Wyoming from the northwest corner to the south-central edge of the state (see CONTINENTAL DIVIDE). Water on the east side of the divide flows to the Atlantic Ocean. Water on the west side goes into the Pacific Ocean. Wyoming has an average elevation of 6,700 feet (2,042 meters), and is higher than any other state except Colorado. Wyoming has three major land regions: (1) the Great Plains, (2) the Rocky Mountains, and (3) the Intermontane Basins.

The Great Plains cover the eastern part of the state. This region is part of the vast interior plain of North America that stretches from Canada to Mexico. In Wyoming, short, tough grass covers much of the land and provides good grazing for cattle and sheep. Cottonwoods and thickets of brush grow along the rivers. Little rain falls on the plains, but irrigation has turned portions of this region into valuable farmland.

A portion of the famous Black Hills lies in the northeastern part of the state. About a third of the Black Hills area lies in Wyoming, and the rest is in South Dakota.

The Rocky Mountains sweep across Wyoming in huge ranges, most of which extend from north to south. In the north, the Bighorn Mountains form the front range of the mountain area. The Laramie range stretches north from Colorado. Between these two front ranges lies a wide plateau. In the 1800's, pioneers traveled westward on trails through this area. The Absaroka Range rises along the east side of Yellowstone National Park. The rugged Wind River Range to the south includes nine peaks that tower above 13,000 feet (3,960 meters). Among them is the highest mountain in Wyoming, 13,804-foot (4,207-meter) Gannett Peak. The Granite Mountains extend eastward from near the southern tip of the Wind River Range. The Gros Ventre, Salt River, Snake River, Teton, and Wyoming ranges are near the western border. The scenic Tetons rise nearly straight up for more than 1 mile (1.6 kilometers) from the Jackson Hole Valley. Other major ranges include the Medicine Bow and Sierra Madre in southern Wyoming.

There is one special link between the flat land of the plains and the heights of the mountains. It is in south-

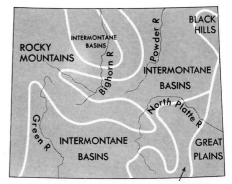

Land Regions of Wyoming

eastern Wyoming, where a narrow finger of land rises gently from the plains to a point high in the Laramie Mountains. Along the slope are major rail and highway routes that quickly bring a traveler from the plains to the mountains. This finger of land, sometimes called the *Gang Plank,* is only about 100 yards (91 meters) wide.

The Intermontane Basins include several fairly flat areas between Wyoming's mountain ranges. The word *intermontane* means *between mountains.* The major basins include the Bighorn and Powder River basins in the north, and the Wind River Basin in central Wyoming. The Green River, Great Divide, and Washakie basins are in southwestern Wyoming.

The basins are mostly treeless areas which get less rainfall than the mountains. Short grasses and other low plants make most of the basins good areas for grazing sheep and cattle. The Great Divide Basin is an exception. It lies along the Continental Divide, but has no drainage of water either to the Atlantic or the Pacific. The divide splits and runs around the 3,000 square miles (7,800 square kilometers) of this basin. The little rain that falls there soaks quickly into the dry ground. Part of the Great Divide Basin, and the area to the south of it, are sometimes called the *Red Desert.* A few prong-

---

Map Index

*Does not appear on the map; key shows general location.

439

Lake Marie lies in the Rocky Mountains of southern Wyoming.

Farmers Harvest Corn near the Wind River in the Intermontane Basins of central Wyoming.

Ten Sleep Creek rushes through the thickly wooded Bighorn Mountains.

Large Herds of Elk graze in the meadows and foothills of the National Elk Refuge near Jackson. Each autumn, thousands of these animals migrate from the snow-covered mountains of northwestern Wyoming to the refuge, where they spend the winter.

horns and wild horses feed on the thinly scattered plant growth. Sometimes sheep are grazed in the area.

Rivers and Lakes. Parts of three great river systems start in the mountains of Wyoming. These systems are the Missouri, the Colorado, and the Columbia.

The tributaries of the Missouri flow both north and east. The Yellowstone, Clarks Fork, Bighorn, Tongue, and Powder rivers flow north. The Cheyenne, Niobrara, and North Platte rivers flow east.

The Green River, the major source of the Colorado River, rises in the Wind River Mountains and flows south across western Wyoming into Utah. The Snake River is part of the Columbia River system. It starts in the Absaroka mountains south of Yellowstone Park. It flows into the park, then turns south. The Snake leaves Wyoming through a magnificent canyon that cuts through three mountain ranges. The Snake is joined by the Salt River, and eventually reaches the Columbia. Bear River, in the southwestern corner of Wyoming,

flows into the Great Salt Lake of Utah.

Many of the rivers have cut beautiful canyons, and some plunge over steep cliffs in spectacular waterfalls. The most interesting canyons include the Laramie River Canyon, the Grand Canyons of the Snake and the Yellowstone, Platte River Canyon, Shoshone River Canyon, and the Wind River Canyon. The most dramatic waterfalls are the Upper and Lower falls of the Yellowstone River.

Wyoming has hundreds of clear, cold, mountain lakes. Among the largest are Fremont, Jackson, Shoshone, and Yellowstone lakes. The major man-made lakes include Alcova, Boysen, Buffalo Bill, Glendo, Guernsey, Keyhole, Pathfinder, and Seminoe reservoirs. Two new dams outside the state formed major lakes in Wyoming. Yellowtail Dam in Montana created a large lake in northeastern Wyoming. Flaming Gorge Dam in Utah backs up water of the Green River 30 miles (48 kilometers) inside Wyoming.

Wyoming has a dry, sunny climate. Winters are cold and the summers are warm. The dry air makes the climate more comfortable than the temperatures would indicate. Differences in altitude create large differences in temperature in various parts of the state. At Casper, in central Wyoming, the average January temperature is 22° F. (−6° C), and the average July temperature is 71° F. (22° C). Near Yellowstone Lake, at a higher elevation, the January average is 12° F. (−11° C), and the July average is 59° F. (15° C). In the high mountains, freezing temperatures can occur any time of the year.

Wyoming's highest recorded temperature was 114° F. (46° C) at Basin on July 12, 1900. Moran had the lowest temperature, −63° F. (−53° C), on Feb. 9, 1933.

The average annual *precipitation* (rain, melted snow, and other forms of moisture) ranges from about 5 inches (13 centimeters) at Hyattville in the Bighorn Basin to about 50 inches (130 centimeters) in the Yellowstone Park area. Snowfall varies from 15 to 20 inches (38 to 51 centimeters) in the Bighorn Basin to about 260 inches (660 centimeters) in the northwestern mountains.

On the Great Plains, and in some open areas of southern Wyoming, the wind blows during the afternoons, usually from the west or southwest. If dry snow is on the ground, the wind may whip it into a *ground blizzard*. A person cannot see straight ahead in the swirling snow, even though the sky may be blue and the sun shining.

SEASONAL TEMPERATURES

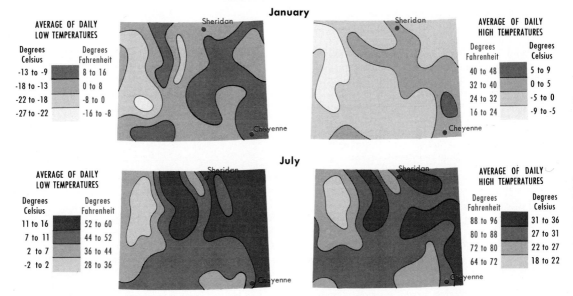

AVERAGE YEARLY PRECIPITATION
(Rain, Melted Snow, and Other Moisture)

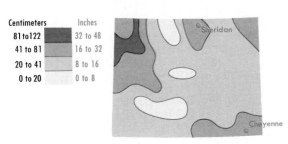

WORLD BOOK maps

AVERAGE MONTHLY WEATHER

	CHEYENNE					SHERIDAN				
	Temperatures				Days of Rain or Snow	Temperatures				Days of Rain or Snow
	F°		C°			F°		C°		
	High	Low	High	Low		High	Low	High	Low	
JAN.	37	14	3	-10	7	33	7	1	-14	8
FEB.	40	16	4	-9	6	36	11	2	-12	9
MAR.	44	20	7	-7	9	43	20	6	-7	12
APR.	54	29	12	-2	10	56	31	13	-1	11
MAY	63	37	17	3	13	66	40	19	4	13
JUNE	74	47	23	8	11	75	48	24	9	11
JULY	83	54	28	12	11	86	55	30	13	7
AUG.	81	53	27	12	10	84	53	29	12	7
SEPT.	72	43	22	6	7	73	43	23	6	8
OCT.	60	33	16	1	6	61	32	16	0	7
NOV.	47	23	8	-5	6	46	21	8	-6	8
DEC.	40	17	4	-8	5	37	12	3	-11	8

Wyoming's economy depends almost entirely on its land. The land provides the state's most important product—petroleum. In addition, it provides grazing for countless cattle and sheep. Most of Wyoming's manufacturing plants depend on the land. They process the products of mines, farms, and forests. Millions of tourists come to Wyoming to see its scenic beauty.

The federal government owns almost half the land in Wyoming. The government has an especially important part in Wyoming's economy because it controls grazing, logging, and mining on this huge area. The area includes national forests and parks, Indian lands, and other public lands.

Natural Resources. Wyoming's most important natural resources are mineral deposits, grazing land, scenery, and water.

Soil. Wyoming does not have large areas of fertile soil. Much of the state has sandy soil formed from sandstone rock that lies beneath the surface. The most fertile soils of Wyoming are those deposited in the major river valleys by floodwaters. Wind-blown dirt called *loess* also has formed fertile soil in some areas.

Minerals. Wyoming's reserves of bentonite, coal, petroleum, trona, and uranium rank among the nation's largest. The mineral reserves are found mostly in the basin areas of the state.

Experts estimate that Wyoming's petroleum reserves total about 900 million barrels. Natural gas occurs in many of the oil fields. About 40 per cent of the state has coal under it. Trona is found in the southwestern portion of the state. The largest uranium deposits are in the Powder River, Shirley, and Wind River basins. Bentonite is a type of clay used in oil drilling and in foundries. The largest bentonite reserves are in the northeast and north-central sections.

Major deposits of iron ore lie in several locations in the southern half of Wyoming. The western mountains contain quantities of phosphate rock. The southwestern part of Wyoming has a major deposit of oil shale, a potential source of petroleum. Wyoming also has gemstones, particularly agate and jade. Other mineral resources include building stone, gypsum, limestone, pumice, sulfur, vanadium, and vermiculite.

Forests cover about 10 million acres (4 million hectares), or nearly a sixth of Wyoming's land. Most of the forests grow in the mountain areas. About half of the forests are available for commercial use. About 2½ million acres (1 million hectares) have been set aside in parks and other reserves. The rest of the forests may be either too poor in quality or too far from transportation to be cut profitably. The federal government controls about 80 per cent of the commercial forest land.

The principal commercial trees are lodgepole pine, Engelmann spruce, Douglas fir, and ponderosa pine. Other trees include alpine fir, aspen, cottonwood, and limber pine.

Plant Life. Bluegrass, wheat grass, tufted fescues, and redtops grow on much of the state's approximately 50 million acres (20 million hectares) of grazing lands. Cactus and sagebrush are found in the drier regions. Areas with poor soil produce greasewood brush, which campers and herders use as firewood. Mountain wild

Production of Goods in Wyoming

Total value of goods produced in 1975—$2,271,023,000

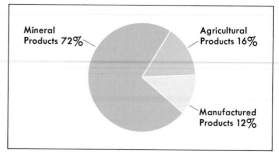

Percentages are based on farm income, value added by manufacture, and value of mineral production.

Sources: U.S. government publications, 1976-1977.

Employment in Wyoming

Total number of persons employed in 1976—171,200

		Number of Employees
Government	👤👤👤👤👤👤👤👤👤	36,200
Wholesale & Retail Trade	👤👤👤👤👤👤👤👤	34,700
Community, Social, & Personal Services	👤👤👤👤👤👤	23,000
Mining	👤👤👤👤👤	20,500
Agriculture	👤👤👤👤	15,800
Construction	👤👤👤👤	14,700
Transportation & Public Utilities	👤👤👤	12,800
Manufacturing	👤👤	8,400
Finance, Insurance, & Real Estate	👤👤	5,100

Sources: *Employment and Earnings*, September 1977, U.S. Bureau of Labor Statistics; *Farm Labor*, February 1977, U.S. Dept. of Agriculture.

flowers include the arnica, buttercup, evening star, five-finger, flax, forget-me-not, goldenrod, saxifrage, sour dock, and windflower.

Animal Life. The forests of Wyoming shelter many kinds of wild animals. The most common larger animals include antelopes, black bears, elk, and mule deer. Moose are common in the northwestern forests, and mountain sheep live among the rocky peaks of the higher mountains. Grizzly bears, lynxes, and mountain lions are seen occasionally. Smaller fur-bearing animals include beavers, martens, raccoons, and otters.

Pronghorn antelopes are common in the open areas of the basins. Other animals in the basin areas include badgers, cottontail and jack rabbits, coyotes, foxes, skunks, and wildcats. Hunters seek such game birds as ducks, geese, grouse, pheasants, sage hens, and wild turkeys. Wyoming also is the home of bald and golden eagles. The bald eagle builds its nest in tall pines near mountain streams or lakes. The golden eagle usually chooses a home farther from water.

Mining accounts for about $1½ billion, or about three-fourths of the annual value of goods produced in Wyoming.

Petroleum is by far the most important mineral product. It provides about three-fifths of the mineral value. Wyoming produces about 132 million barrels of petroleum a year. This production has an annual value

FARM, MINERAL, AND FOREST PRODUCTS

This map shows where the leading farm, mineral, and forest products are produced. The major urban areas (shown in red) are the important manufacturing centers.

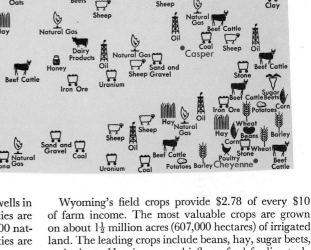

0	25	50	75	100 Miles
0	50	100		150 Kilometers

WORLD BOOK map

of about $1 billion. Oil comes from about 8,700 wells in Wyoming. Campbell, Natrona, and Park counties are the top oil producers. The state also has about 900 natural gas wells. The leading gas-producing counties are Campbell, Fremont, Sublette, and Sweetwater.

Coal mining is expanding rapidly, chiefly in the northeastern Powder River Basin and in the areas around Kemmerer in Lincoln County and north of Sheridan. Wyoming produces about 31 million short tons (28 million metric tons) of coal annually.

Wyoming leads the states in uranium production. Most of the uranium mined in Wyoming comes from the Gas Hills and Crooks Gap areas of Fremont County, and the Shirley Basin area of Carbon County. *Trona*, a white mineral containing sodium carbonate, is also an important mineral product. Trona is used in making glass and detergents. Mines in Fremont and Platte counties produce iron ore.

A special clay called bentonite is another major mineral product of Wyoming. Bentonite swells to several times its normal size when wet, and is used in oil-well drilling. Other important mineral products include natural gas liquids such as butane and propane, and sand and gravel, limestone, building stone, and phosphate rock.

Agriculture provides products worth about $360 million a year, or 16 per cent of the annual value of goods produced in the state. Wyoming has about 8,000 farms. They average about 4,000 acres (1,600 hectares) in size.

Ranching is by far the most important agricultural activity in Wyoming. Of every $10 of income from farm products, $7.22 comes from livestock and livestock products. Beef cattle provide $6.05; sheep, 52 cents; and milk, 25 cents. Eggs, hogs, honey, poultry, and wool produce the rest of the income from livestock. Wyoming ranks second only to Texas in the production of sheep and wool. About 95 per cent of Wyoming's land area is used to graze cattle and sheep. This includes millions of acres of U.S. land leased to ranchers.

Wyoming's field crops provide $2.78 of every $10 of farm income. The most valuable crops are grown on about 1½ million acres (607,000 hectares) of irrigated land. The leading crops include beans, hay, sugar beets, and wheat. Hay is grown chiefly as feed for livestock. Little of the hay is marketed. Certified seed potatoes, which must be unusually free of disease, are raised in Goshen and Laramie counties. Farmers use dry farming methods on the Great Plains (see DRY FARMING). The most important crops raised on these farms include hay, and wheat and other small grains.

Manufacturing, including processing, accounts for 12 per cent of the value of goods produced in Wyoming. Goods manufactured in the state have a *value added by manufacture* of about $265 million a year. This figure represents the value created in products by Wyoming's industries, not counting such costs as materials, supplies, and fuel.

The production of petroleum and coal products, Wyoming's most important industry, accounts for about two-fifths of the value added. Casper leads in petroleum refining and has three refineries. Others are in Cheyenne, Cody, Cowley, La Barge, Lusk, Newcastle, and Sinclair. Wyoming ranks fifth in the nation in crude oil production. The state has about 35 plants that process natural gas. Six refineries produce sulfur as a by-product of gas processing.

Other plants also process Wyoming mineral products. Uranium mills in Shirley Basin process the ores of mines in the Gas Hills. Four companies mine trona and produce soda ash near Green River. One plant uses trona to make chemicals for detergents. Plants that produce pellets of iron from ore are in Atlantic City and Sunrise. A nitrogen fertilizer plant operates in Cheyenne. Cement is manufactured in Laramie. About 10 plants process bentonite clay. Plants in Cody and near Lovell produce gypsum wallboard.

Plants in Lovell, Torrington, and Worland refine sugar from sugar beets. Other food processing industries

440c

make cheese and meat products. Printing and publishing are also important to Wyoming's economy.

About 50 sawmills and a number of other plants in Wyoming handle logs from the state's forests. Sawmills in Wyoming cut about 188 million board feet (444,000 cubic meters) of lumber a year.

Electric Power. Coal-burning power plants generate about 75 per cent of the state's electric power. These plants burn low-sulfur coal that is plentiful in the state. Major plants operate near Gillette and in Glenrock, Kemmerer, and Rock Springs. Water power provides most of the rest of Wyoming's electricity. The largest hydroelectric plants are at Alcova, Boysen, Fremont Canyon, Kortes, and Seminoe dams.

Transportation. Wyoming has about 35,000 miles (56,300 kilometers) of roads and highways. About a

third of them are surfaced. The state also has about 90 airports. Casper and Cheyenne have the busiest commercial airports. Wyoming's first railroad was the Union Pacific. It was built across the territory in 1867 and 1868. Today, railroads operate on about 2,400 miles (3,860 kilometers) of track. Three lines provide freight service, and passenger trains connect six Wyoming cities and towns to other areas of the United States.

Communication. The first newspaper in Wyoming was the *Daily Telegraph*, published at Fort Bridger in 1863. Today, Wyoming has about 40 newspapers, including 10 dailies. Newspapers with the largest circulations include the *Casper Star Tribune*, and the *Wyoming State Tribune* and *Wyoming Eagle*, both of Cheyenne. The state's first radio station, KDFN (now KTWO), began broadcasting at Casper in 1930. The first television station was KFBC-TV (now KYCU-TV) in Cheyenne, which started operating in 1954. Today, the state has about 40 radio stations and 3 TV stations.

WYOMING/History

Indian Days. The first people who lived in the Wyoming area were Indian hunters of at least 11,000 years ago. Later, huge herds of buffaloes roamed the prairies. This rich source of meat attracted many Indians to the area. When white people arrived they found Arapaho, Bannock, Blackfeet, Cheyenne, Crow, Flathead, Nez Percé, Shoshoni, Sioux, and Ute Indians living in what is now Wyoming.

Exploration. French trappers may have entered the Wyoming region in the mid-1700's. However, exploration of the area did not begin until after 1800. The United States bought most of the region from France in 1803, as part of the Louisiana Purchase. After that, American trappers came to the area to find furs. In 1807, a trapper named John Colter became the first white man to discover the geysers and hot springs of the Yellowstone area. Five years later, in 1812, a party of fur traders from Oregon crossed the area from west to east. The group, led by Robert Stuart, discovered a relatively easy way across the mountains through South Pass. This route became important in pioneer travel to the West.

During the 1820's and 1830's, the fur trade became more highly organized. General William Ashley established an annual *rendezvous* (gathering) of trappers. At these gatherings, his company traded ammunition, food, and other supplies for furs. The first rendezvous took place in 1824 on the Green River, near the present Wyoming-Utah border. The yearly rendezvous became important to the trappers not only for trading, but for exchange of news and as a social event.

A trapping and trading party of more than a hundred men came to the Wyoming area in 1832. The group was led by Captain Benjamin L. E. de Bonneville. Bonneville's party discovered an oil spring in 1833 in the Wind River Basin. In 1834, traders William Sublette and Robert Campbell established Fort William in what is now eastern Wyoming. This fort, later called Fort Laramie, was the area's first permanent trading post. Jim Bridger, one of the great western trappers and scouts, founded Fort Bridger in southwestern Wyoming

--- IMPORTANT DATES IN WYOMING ---

1807 John Colter explored the Yellowstone area.

1812 Robert Stuart discovered South Pass across the Rocky Mountains.

1833 Captain Benjamin L. E. de Bonneville mapped the Wyoming area and discovered oil east of the Wind River Mountains.

1834 William Sublette and Robert Campbell established Fort William (later Fort Laramie).

1843 Scout Jim Bridger established Fort Bridger.

1867 The Union Pacific Railroad entered Wyoming.

1868 Congress created the Territory of Wyoming.

1869 The Wyoming territorial legislature gave women the right to vote and hold elective office.

1872 Yellowstone became the first national park.

1883 Wyoming's first oil well was drilled in the Dallas Field, near Lander.

1890 Wyoming became the 44th state on July 10.

1892 The Johnson County War broke out after a dispute over cattle rustling.

1906 President Theodore Roosevelt made Devils Tower the first national monument.

1910 Engineers completed Shoshone (now Buffalo Bill) Dam.

1925 Nellie Tayloe Ross became the first woman governor in the United States.

1929 Grand Teton became a national park.

1938-1939 Engineers completed Alcova and Seminoe dams.

1951-1952 Major uranium deposits were found in several parts of Wyoming.

1960 The United States' first operational intercontinental ballistic missile base opened near Cheyenne.

1962 Iron mining revived the ghost town of Atlantic City.

1965 Minuteman missile sites were completed near Cheyenne.

1974 The Jim Bridger Power Plant in Rock Springs began operating.

in 1843. After trading posts were established, the rendezvous became less important. The last of these colorful gatherings was held in 1840.

In 1842 and 1843, Lieutenant John C. Frémont explored the Wind River Mountains. His party was

HISTORIC WYOMING

The First National Park.
Trapper John Colter discovered
Yellowstone in 1807. It was
made a national park in 1872.

Johnson County Cattle War
of 1892 involved ranchers and
rustlers who battled each other
for control of the cattle ranges.

First National Monument.
Devils Tower, in the Black Hills
region, became a national monument in 1906. The tower of rock
is 865 feet (264 meters) high.

Fur Trade began in 1806,
when trapper John Colter found
rich pelts in the Wyoming area.

Petroleum was discovered in
the Wind River Basin in 1833 by
Captain Benjamin de Bonneville.
It was first used as axle grease.

Fort Laramie ●

Feminine Firsts in Wyoming. Women won
the right to vote in 1869. In 1870, Esther H.
Morris became the first woman justice of the
peace in the United States. In 1925, Nellie
Tayloe Ross became the first woman governor.

Fort Bridger ●

Fort Laramie and Fort Bridger offered protection from Indians in Wyoming. Thousands
of travelers crossed the state in covered wagons on overland trails between 1840 and 1870.

The Treaty of Fort Laramie
brought peace with the Sioux in
1868, when they agreed to give
up their lands. Father De Smet, a
missionary, arranged the treaty.

guided by the famous scout Kit Carson. After Frémont made his report, Congress voted in 1846 to establish forts along the Oregon Trail to protect settlers moving west. In 1849, the government bought Fort William. This fort, also known as Fort John, was renamed Fort Laramie by the army.

At various times, parts of what is now Wyoming were in the territories of Louisiana, Missouri, Nebraska, Oregon, Washington, Idaho, Utah and Dakota. Part of southern Wyoming, south of the 42nd parallel, belonged to Spain from the 1500's to the 1800's. Mexico owned it in the early 1800's, but lost it to the Republic of Texas in 1836. This area became part of the United States in 1845 when Texas joined the Union.

The Great Trails. By 1850, pioneers were streaming west through the Wyoming area on three famous trails. These were the California Trail, the Mormon Trail to Utah, and the Oregon Trail to the Pacific Northwest. All three trails took South Pass through the mountains. Beyond the pass, the Oregon Trail turned northwest, and the Mormon and California trails went southwest. Thousands of settlers traveled through Wyoming, but few of them stayed.

The Plains Indians watched this stream of settlers with growing alarm. The white settlers killed or frightened away the game. Their carelessness with fire caused roaring blazes on the prairie, and their diseases killed or crippled countless Indians. The angry warriors began to attack the wagons.

Indian Troubles. The Plains Indians were expert horsemen and brave fighters. They raided the wagon trains, and fought the soldiers sent to protect the wagons. In one fight near Fort Laramie in 1854, Lieutenant John Grattan and 29 troopers were killed.

Gold was discovered in Montana in the 1860's, and settlers began moving north up the Bozeman Trail to Montana. This trail crossed a different area of the Indian land, and the tribes fought with new fury.

To keep the Bozeman Trail open, the army built Fort Phil Kearny near the Bighorn Mountains in the summer of 1866. The Sioux hated this fort. Led by Red Cloud, they put war parties around it in what was called the *Circle of Death*. During the first six months, about 150 men were killed. Captain W. J. Fetterman and 81 of his men died in a single battle. Finally, in 1868, Red Cloud and other Indian leaders signed a treaty. The army agreed to give up Fort Phil Kearny and two other forts and leave northeastern Wyoming to the Indians. In return, the Indians agreed not to interfere with the construction of the Union Pacific Railroad through southern Wyoming.

A troubled peace lasted until 1874, when prospectors discovered gold in the Black Hills. Thousands of white people violated the treaty by moving into the area. The Sioux considered the Black Hills sacred, and fought the new invasion. Sioux and Cheyenne warriors won two bitter battles with U.S. soldiers in what is now Montana. However, the Indian force broke up to flee from other troops. Some Indians went to Canada, and others agreed to move to reservations. Serious Indian fighting ended in the summer of 1876, and Wyoming settlers finally had peace.

Territorial Progress. Even before the Indian troubles ended, southern Wyoming was developing rapidly. The Union Pacific Railroad entered the area in 1867. Towns were founded as the "end of track" moved west. Cheyenne, Laramie, Rawlins, Rock Springs, Green River, and Evanston grew up in turn. Towns also appeared along the route of the great trails. In 1868, Congress created the Territory of Wyoming. President Ulysses S. Grant appointed Brigadier General John A. Campbell as the first governor of the territory.

On Dec. 10, 1869, the territorial legislature granted women the right to vote, hold office, and serve on juries. The new law was the first of its kind in the United States. Women first served on juries in 1870, in Laramie. That same year, Mrs. Esther H. Morris of South Pass City became the nation's first woman justice of the peace.

Ranching supported the new territory's economy. Large numbers of longhorn cattle were driven north from Texas to Wyoming. Wealthy ranchers controlled huge areas of the territory and ruled the affairs of the territorial government until 1887. That year, thousands of cattle died in the howling blizzards and freezing temperatures of a bitterly cold winter. Many ranchers were ruined financially, and lost much of their political power.

The foundations of Wyoming's minerals industry were laid long before the area became a territory. In 1833, the Bonneville party greased its wagon axles at a spot where oil seeped from the ground in the Wind River Basin. Jim Bridger sold oil at his fort, and pioneers mixed it with flour to use as axle grease. Gold was found at South Pass in 1842, but the discovery aroused little interest. In 1867, a more promising strike attracted many prospectors to the area. Several boom towns, such as Atlantic City and South Pass City, sprang up.

In 1883 and 1884, interest in oil was revived because of profitable drilling elsewhere. The first successful well was drilled in 1883 in the Dallas Field, near Lander. Plans were made for exploration of several areas near

Wind River Indian Reservation was presented to the famous Chief Washakie in 1868 by the U.S. government. The Shoshoni received the reservation as a reward for their friendliness to the white man and their help in fighting tribes hostile to settlers. W. H. Jackson took this picture in 1870. His photographs form a vivid record of Wyoming history during the late 1800's.

Casper. But the industry developed slowly, and several years passed before oil activity prospered.

Wyoming's tourist industry also got its start during the territorial days. In 1872, Congress created Yellowstone National Park. The nation's first national park immediately attracted tourists.

Statehood. Wyoming became the 44th state of the Union on July 10, 1890. Francis E. Warren, a Republican, became the first state governor on September 11. He resigned in November after being elected to the U.S. Senate. Settlers flocked to Wyoming, and trouble started almost immediately. Many settlers built homes on the prairies and tended small herds of cattle. The powerful cattlemen who had used the range for years grew angry when the settlers started fencing their small ranches. Some of the newcomers built their cattle herds by stealing cattle from the established ranches.

The Johnson County War. Violence broke out in north-central Wyoming in 1892. The established cattlemen were convinced that their herds were being looted. They had no proof to identify the rustlers, but they had strong suspicions. The operators of the large ranches prepared a list of suspects and decided to kill the men on the list. They brought in about 25 gunmen from

Texas, and made up a force of about 55 men. This force, called the Invaders, raided the Kaycee Ranch near Buffalo and killed two men.

Information about the killings reached Buffalo, the seat of Johnson County, and a group of armed men was formed to stop the Invaders. The two forces met on the TA Ranch, but federal troops arrived in time to prevent a bloody battle. The Invaders were taken to Cheyenne for trial. However, important witnesses failed to appear at the trial. The Invaders were released, and the "war" ended.

Trouble again broke out on the range in the early 1900's. Cattlemen and sheepmen argued over grazing rights. The cattlemen claimed that their animals would not feed on land that had been grazed by sheep. A feud developed as the number of sheep increased. The climax came when cattlemen killed three sheepmen near Ten Sleep in 1909. But tempers cooled, and sheep became an important Wyoming product.

Progress as a State. After 1900, Wyoming's population grew rapidly. The Homestead acts of 1909, 1912, and 1916 provided free land for settlers under certain conditions. The construction of dams along major streams brought irrigation water to some areas of the

THE GOVERNORS OF WYOMING

	Party	Term		Party	Term
1. Francis E. Warren	Republican	1890	15. Frank C. Emerson	Republican	1927-1931
2. Amos W. Barber	Republican	1890-1893	16. Alonzo M. Clark	Republican	1931-1933
3. John E. Osborne	Democratic	1893-1895	17. Leslie A. Miller	Democratic	1933-1939
4. William A. Richards	Republican	1895-1899	18. Nels H. Smith	Republican	1939-1943
5. DeForest Richards	Republican	1899-1903	19. Lester C. Hunt	Democratic	1943-1949
6. Fenimore Chatterton	Republican	1903-1905	20. Arthur Griswold Crane	Republican	1949-1951
7. Bryant B. Brooks	Republican	1905-1911	21. Frank A. Barrett	Republican	1951-1953
8. Joseph M. Carey	Democratic	1911-1915	22. C. J. Rogers	Republican	1953-1955
9. John B. Kendrick	Democratic	1915-1917	23. Milward L. Simpson	Republican	1955-1959
10. Frank L. Houx	Democratic	1917-1919	24. J. J. Hickey	Democratic	1959-1961
11. Robert D. Carey	Republican	1919-1923	25. Jack R. Gage	Democratic	1961-1963
12. William B. Ross	Democratic	1923-1924	26. Clifford P. Hansen	Republican	1963-1967
13. Frank E. Lucas	Republican	1924-1925	27. Stanley K. Hathaway	Republican	1967-1975
14. Nellie Tayloe Ross	Democratic	1925-1927	28. Edward J. Herschler	Democratic	1975-

Guided Missile Launching Site near Warren Air Force Base symbolizes Wyoming's important role in the defense of the United States. During the 1960's, many missiles were installed in underground *silos* (storage places) near the base.

prairie. Crops grown on this land increased the agricultural wealth of the state. Tourism became more important after President Theodore Roosevelt in 1906 made Devils Tower the first national monument.

Wyoming's first oil boom came in 1912 in the Salt Creek Field north of Casper. Pipelines and refineries were built to handle the crude oil. By 1918, Casper had become a bustling center of business and finance.

In 1924, Wyoming voters elected the United States' first woman governor, Mrs. Nellie Tayloe Ross. In 1933, Mrs. Ross became the first woman director of the U.S. Mint.

Wyoming suffered less than most of the other states during the Great Depression of the 1930's. The state's economy was helped by increasing oil production, and by various government construction projects. These included the Kendrick Project, which provided both irrigation water and new hydroelectric capacity. The project, on the North Platte River, included Alcova, Kortes, and Seminoe dams.

The Mid-1900's. Wyoming's economy boomed during World War II (1939-1945). The war brought great demands for the state's coal, lumber, meat, and oil. Economic development continued after the war, and tourism increased. New industrial growth resulted from the mining of two minerals, trona and uranium. Sodium carbonate, the key ingredient of trona, has many uses in the chemical industry.

Oil drilling in southwestern Wyoming had shown that trona lay over 1,500 feet (457 meters) under the surface of the earth in the Green River Basin. A mine shaft was sunk there in 1947, and mining of trona began. Output increased rapidly during the 1950's. During the 1960's, two chemical companies built huge plants near the town of Green River for the mining of trona and the production of sodium carbonate.

The first major uranium discovery in Wyoming occurred in 1951. Large deposits were found in the Powder River area. After the findings were published early in 1952, uranium was discovered in many of Wyoming's main river basins. By the late 1950's, Wyoming ranked third among the states in known uranium reserves.

Many companies expanded their operations in Wyoming during the 1960's. A steel company built a new iron ore processing plant near Sunrise. Another firm revived the ghost town of Atlantic City by opening an iron mine and building a processing plant there. Trona operations near Green River continued to grow. Oil exploration also expanded, with the greatest activity in the Powder River Basin. A group of oil companies experimented with the production of oil from oil shale.

Two electric power companies built generating plants —at Glenrock and Kemmerer—that use Wyoming's huge coal deposits as fuel. Coal production, which had dropped during the 1950's, rose again in 1959.

In 1960, Wyoming became the headquarters of the first operational long-range missile squadron in the United States. The squadron ranks as one of the largest missile installations in the world. The control center is Francis E. Warren Air Force Base in Cheyenne.

Wyoming Today faces the problems of a large state with a small population. Wyoming has no major population centers to provide markets for its manufactured goods. As a result, its products must be shipped long distances to be sold. Business and political leaders in the state, aided by the Wyoming Department of Economic Planning and Development, are working to attract new industries. This department was created in 1969. It replaced the Wyoming Natural Resources Board.

Mining continues to be the major source of economic growth in the state. The fuel shortage that struck the nation in the early 1970's spurred further development of Wyoming's coal deposits. Coal companies planned new mines and shipping facilities. Several power companies announced plans to expand coal-fueled generating plants and to build new plants. In 1971, construction began on the Jim Bridger Power Plant in Rock Springs. This plant, one of the largest electric power plants in the West, began operating in 1974. By 1976, it had three 500,000-kilowatt units. An additional unit is scheduled for completion about 1980. This expansion assured a steady market for the state's coal.

During the 1970's, Wyoming's mining regions began experiencing some problems of industrial and population growth. The state legislature approved new taxes on minerals to provide funds to help communities deal with these problems.

JAMES M. FLINCHUM, JR., T. A. LARSON, and J. DAVID LOVE

WYOMING/*Study Aids*

Related Articles in WORLD BOOK include:

BIOGRAPHIES

Bridger, James
Laramie, Jacques
Morris, Esther H.
Pollock, Jackson
Ross, Nellie Tayloe
Spotted Tail
Washakie

CITIES

Casper   Cheyenne   Laramie   Sheridan

HISTORY

Bozeman Trail
Homestead Act
Indian, American
Indian Wars
(Death on the Plains)
Oregon Trail
Pony Express
Trails of Early Days
Western Frontier Life

PHYSICAL FEATURES

Bighorn River
Black Hills
Devils Tower National
  Monument
Fossil Butte National
  Monument
Grand Teton National Park
Great Plains
Powder River
Rocky Mountains
Teton Range
Yellowstone National
  Park
Yellowstone River

PRODUCTS

For Wyoming's rank among the states in production, see the following articles:

Bean   Sheep   Wool
Petroleum   Uranium

OTHER RELATED ARTICLES

Buffalo Bill Dam
Cowboy
Ranching
Rocky Mountain States
Wyoming, University of

Outline

I. Government
  A. Constitution
  B. Executive
  C. Legislature
  D. Courts
  E. Local Government
  F. Taxation
  G. Politics
II. People
III. Education
  A. Schools
  B. Libraries and Museums
IV. A Visitor's Guide
  A. Places to Visit
  B. Annual Events
V. The Land
  A. Land Regions
  B. Rivers and Lakes
VI. Climate
VII. Economy
  A. Natural Resources
  B. Mining
  C. Agriculture
  D. Manufacturing
  E. Electric Power
  F. Transportation
  G. Communication
VIII. History

Questions

What three famous pioneer routes crossed Wyoming in the mid-1800's?

What part of Wyoming once belonged to the Republic of Texas?

What was the first national park established in the United States?

Why was the construction of the Union Pacific Railroad important to the development of cities in Wyoming?

Why was the result of Wyoming's election for governor in 1924 so unusual?

What is Wyoming's leading mineral product?

What was the first U.S. national monument?

Why is Wyoming nicknamed the *Equality State?*

Who were the Invaders?

What was a fur trappers' *rendezvous?*

Books for Young Readers

BURT, NATHANIEL. *War Cry of the West: The Story of the Powder River.* Holt, 1964.

CARPENTER, ALLAN. *Wyoming.* Childrens Press, 1966.

CARR, MARY JANE. *Children of the Covered Wagon.* Rev. ed. Crowell, 1957. Fiction.

FISHER, LAURA H. *Charlie Dick.* Holt, 1972. Fiction.

GAGE, JACK R. *Geography of Wyoming.* Prairie Publishing Co., 1965.

KIRK, RUTH. *Yellowstone: The First National Park.* Atheneum, 1974.

O'HARA, MARY. *My Friend Flicka.* Lippincott, 1941. *Thunderhead.* 1943. *Green Grass of Wyoming.* 1946. All are fiction.

WHITTENBURG, CLARICE T. *Wyoming's People.* Old West Publishing Co., 1958.

Books for Older Readers

BARTLETT, RICHARD A. *Nature's Yellowstone.* Univ. of New Mexico Press, 1974.

BRAGG, BILL. *Wyoming's Wealth: A History of Wyoming.* Big Horn Books, Box 750, Basin, Wyo. 82410, 1976.

CALKINS, FRANK. *Jackson Hole.* Knopf, 1973.

HEDGPETH, DON. *Spurs Were A-Jinglin': A Brief Look at the Wyoming Range Country.* Northland, 1975.

HUNTER, RODELLO. *Wyoming Wife.* Knopf, 1969. Life in Wyoming as seen through the eyes of a city girl.

LARSON, TAFT A. *History of Wyoming.* Univ. of Nebraska Press, 1965. *Wyoming: A Bicentennial History.* Norton, 1977.

OLSON, TED. *Ranch on the Laramie.* Little, Brown, 1973. Memories of Wyoming ranch life before World War I.

SMITH, HELENA H. *The War on Powder River.* Univ. of Nebraska Press, 1967.

TRENHOLM, VIRGINIA C. *The Arapahoes: Our People.* Univ. of Oklahoma Press, 1970.

TRENHOLM, VIRGINIA C., and CARLEY, M. *The Shoshonis: Sentinels of the Rockies.* Univ. of Oklahoma Press, 1964.

WOODS, LAWRENCE MILTON. *The Wyoming Country Before Statehood: Four Hundred Years Under Six Flags.* Worland Press, Worland, Wyo., 1971.

WYOMING, UNIVERSITY OF

WYOMING, UNIVERSITY OF, is a state-controlled coeducational school at Laramie, Wyo. It has colleges of agriculture, arts and sciences, commerce, education, engineering, law, nursing, and pharmacy; and a graduate school. The University of Wyoming has ROTC and AFROTC units.

The university is noted for its geology program, its American Studies program, and its large manuscript and printed collections on Western economic history. The school has a science camp in the Medicine Bow Mountains, a biological research station at Moran, and six agricultural substations in the state. The university was founded in 1886. For the enrollment of the University of Wyoming, see UNIVERSITIES AND COLLEGES (table).   WILLIAM D. CARLSON

WYOMING VALLEY is a section of northeastern Pennsylvania about 3 miles (5 kilometers) wide and 20 miles (32 kilometers) long. It lies along the north branch of the Susquehanna River near Wilkes-Barre. The Wyoming Valley has rich deposits of *anthracite* (hard coal).

The valley is a historic gateway to central Pennsylvania from New England and New York. Many settlers entered the valley during colonial days. In the 1770's, it became the center of a boundary controversy between Connecticut and Pennsylvania. Congress settled the dispute in favor of Pennsylvania. In 1778, the Wyoming Valley was the scene of a bloody massacre (see WYOMING VALLEY MASSACRE).   S. K. STEVENS

WYOMING VALLEY MASSACRE, one of many tragedies of the American Revolutionary War, occurred in what is now Luzerne County, Pennsylvania. In 1778, it was an incorporated county in the colony of Connecticut. At that time, most of the inhabitants of the Wyoming Valley believed in the American cause of independence from Great Britain. However, some of the valley's residents were Tories, and they remained loyal to Great Britain.

As the war went on, the Tories were driven out of the community, and joined other Tory and Indian bands. In the summer of 1778, these bands attacked Wyoming Valley. The inhabitants fled for safety to Forty Fort, near the site of the present city of Wilkes-Barre, Pa. About 300 men defended the fort. An army of 800 fighters, led by a British officer, opposed them. Six hundred of the attackers were Indians.

On July 3, the two groups met in a hard-fought battle. The attackers defeated the settlers, and killed more than two-thirds of them. The Indians tortured many of them to death. The survivors were left to find their way to the nearest settlements, and many of them died before they could reach help. The attackers completely destroyed the village and left the rest of the valley in ruins.   JOHN R. ALDEN

WYSS, *vees,* is the family name of a Swiss clergyman and his sons. Together they produced the story *The Swiss Family Robinson.* JOHANN DAVID WYSS (1743-1818), the father, wrote the story. His son JOHANN RUDOLPH (1781-1830) edited and published it. Another son, JOHANN EMMANUEL (1782-1837), illustrated it. *The Swiss Family Robinson* tells of the adventures of a family shipwrecked on a *desert* (uninhabited) island in the Pacific Ocean. It is perhaps the best of the many stories written in imitation of Daniel Defoe's *Robinson Crusoe* (see DEFOE, DANIEL).

The Wyss family liked to read and discuss adventure stories such as *Robinson Crusoe.* They pretended they had been shipwrecked on a desert island, and told each other tales of their imaginary life there. Johann David wrote down these tales as the family told them, and his son Johann Emmanuel illustrated them with drawings and water colors. Some years later, Johann Rudolph edited the stories. He published them in Switzerland in 1812 and 1813 as *The Swiss Robinson.* The book has been translated from German into many languages, including the English version *The Swiss Family Robinson* (1813). Johann Rudolph Wyss also wrote "My Country Calls," a national song of Switzerland.

WYSZYŃSKI, *vih SHIHN skee,* **STEFAN CARDINAL** (1901-   ), is the head of the Roman Catholic Church in Poland. Several months after Wyszyński became a cardinal in 1953, Poland's Communist government imprisoned him for his fight against its antireligious policies.

Wyszyński has led the opposition to the government since his release from prison in 1956. However, he has followed a policy of compromise. For example, Wyszyński has spoken out for religious freedom and other personal rights. But he has avoided open conflict with the Communists, especially when he thought it might lead to Russian intervention in Poland. During the 1970's, his policies helped improve relations between the church and the government.

Keystone

Cardinal Wyszyński

Wyszyński was born in Zuzela, near Warsaw. He was ordained a priest in 1924 and earned a doctorate in sociology from Catholic University in Lublin. Wyszyński took part in the resistance movement against the Nazi occupation of Poland during World War II (1939-1945). He became an archbishop in 1948.   ADAM BROMKE

WYTHE, *wihth,* **GEORGE** (1726-1806), an American statesman, was a signer of the Declaration of Independence. He was also a well-known lawyer and judge, and a patron of Thomas Jefferson and other distinguished Virginians (see JEFFERSON, THOMAS [Education]). He wrote the original Virginia protest against the Stamp Act in 1764. It was so fiery that it had to be rewritten in a softer tone. He participated in the Constitutional Convention of 1787.

Wythe served in the Second Continental Congress in 1775 and 1776. Later he helped draft the Virginia constitution. He became a judge of the court of chancery of Virginia in 1778, and, in 1786, he became chancellor of the state.

Wythe was born at Back River, Va., and attended the College of William and Mary. He was admitted to the bar in 1757, and entered the Virginia House of Burgesses a year later. In 1779, Wythe was appointed to the nation's first law professorship. The professorship was established that year at William and Mary by Thomas Jefferson.   CLARENCE L. VER STEEG

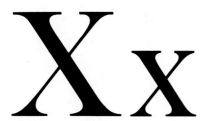

X is the 24th letter of our alphabet. It came from a letter used by the Semites, who once lived in Syria and Palestine. They named it *samekh*, their word for *fish*, and adapted an Egyptian *hieroglyphic*, or picture symbol, used to represent fish. The Greeks later took the symbol into their alphabet, and used it to represent the sound of *ch*. The Romans used the letter to represent the same sound, but changed its shape slightly. See ALPHABET.

Uses. *X* or *x* is about the 23rd most frequently used letter in books, newspapers, and other printed material in English. *X*, used alone or in combination with other letters, often stands for the word *Christ*, as in *Xmas*. *X* is the Roman numeral for *ten*. *X* is used in physical science and in mathematics to denote an unknown quantity, or a quantity that was at first unknown, as in *X ray*. In arithmetic problems, *x* is the sign of multiplication. In describing measurements, *x* represents the word *by*, as in *9′ x 12′*, or *nine by twelve feet*.

Pronunciation. In English, *x* has six sounds: *ks*, as in *six; gz*, as in *examine; ksh*, as in *luxury; gzh*, as in *luxurious; sh*, as in *anxious;* and *z*, as in *xylophone*. In some cases, such as *luxury*, the *x* is not voiced. In *luxurious*, the *x* is voiced. In Spanish, *x* may be pronounced as the English *s* or as the English *h*. In most other European languages, *x* has the same sounds as it has in English. See PRONUNCIATION. I. J. GELB and JAMES M. WELLS

Development of the Letter X

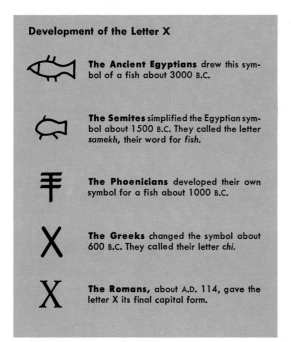

The Ancient Egyptians drew this symbol of a fish about 3000 B.C.

The Semites simplified the Egyptian symbol about 1500 B.C. They called the letter *samekh*, their word for *fish*.

The Phoenicians developed their own symbol for a fish about 1000 B.C.

The Greeks changed the symbol about 600 B.C. They called their letter *chi*.

The Romans, about A.D. 114, gave the letter X its final capital form.

The Small Letter x developed about A.D. 800 from Roman writing. By the 1500's, the letter had the form that is used today.

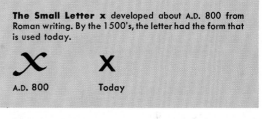

A.D. 800   Today

Special Ways of Expressing the Letter X

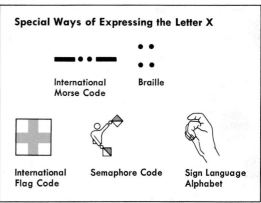

International Morse Code

Braille

International Flag Code

Semaphore Code

Sign Language Alphabet

Common Forms of the Letter X

Handwritten Letters vary from person to person. Manuscript (printed) letters, *left*, have simple curves and straight lines. Cursive letters, *right*, have flowing lines.

Roman Letters have small finishing strokes called *serifs* that extend from the main strokes. The type face shown above is Baskerville. The italic form appears at the right.

Sans-Serif Letters are also called *gothic letters*. They have no serifs. The type face shown above is called Futura. The italic form of Futura appears at the right.

Computer Letters have special shapes. Computers can "read" these letters either optically or by means of the magnetic ink with which the letters may be printed.

445

X RAYS

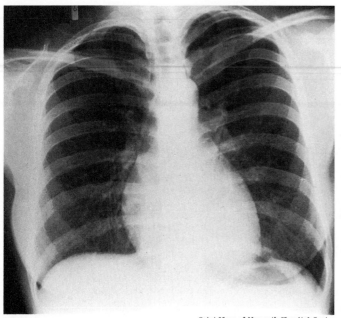

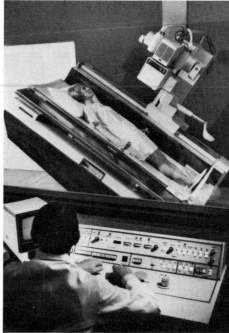

A Chest X Ray, *left,* reveals the shadows of the heart, the lungs, and the ribs. It can help physicians detect lung disease, broken bones, and other abnormal conditions inside a patient's body. X-ray pictures are produced by an X-ray machine, *right,* operated by a technologist.

X RAYS are one of the most useful forms of energy. They were discovered in 1895 by Wilhelm K. Roentgen, a German physicist. Roentgen called the rays *X rays* because at first he did not understand what they were. *X* is a scientific symbol for the unknown.

Scientists now know that X rays are a kind of *electromagnetic radiation*, which also includes visible light, radio waves, and gamma rays. X rays and visible light, for example, have many characteristics in common. X rays travel at the speed of light—186,282 miles (299,792 kilometers) per second. Both X rays and light travel in straight lines in the form of related electric and magnetic energy, called *electromagnetic waves*. In addition, X rays darken photographic film in much the same way that light does.

However, X rays and light differ in terms of *wavelength*, the distance between two crests of an electromagnetic wave. The wavelengths of X rays are much shorter than those of light. For this reason, X rays can penetrate deeply into many substances that do not transmit light. The penetrating power and other characteristics of X rays make them extremely useful in medicine, industry, and scientific research.

X rays can cause biological, chemical, and physical changes in substances. If the rays are absorbed by a plant or animal, they may damage or even destroy living tissue. For this reason, X rays can be dangerous. In human beings, an overdose of X rays may produce cancer, skin burns, a reduction of the blood supply, or other serious conditions. Dentists and *radiologists* (physicians who work with X rays) must take special care not to overexpose their patients or themselves to the rays.

In nature, X rays are produced by the sun, other stars, pulsars, and certain other heavenly bodies. Most X rays from sources in space are absorbed by the atmosphere before they reach the earth.

Man-made X rays are produced chiefly with *X-ray tubes*, a principal part of X-ray machines. Devices that accelerate atomic particles also produce X rays. Such devices include *betatrons* and *linear accelerators* (see BETATRON; LINEAR ACCELERATOR).

Uses of X Rays

In Medicine, X rays are widely used to make *radiographs* (X-ray pictures) of the bones and internal organs of the body. Radiographs help physicians detect abnormalities and disease conditions, such as broken bones or lung disease, inside a patient's body. Dentists take X-ray pictures to reveal cavities and impacted teeth.

A radiograph is made by passing a beam of X rays through the patient's body onto a piece of photographic film. The bones absorb more of the rays than do muscles or other organs, and so the bones cast the sharpest shadows on the film. Other parts of the body allow more X rays through than the bones do and cast shadows of varying density. The shadows of the bones show up clearly as light areas on a radiograph, and the organs are seen as darker areas. Radiologists can see a patient's organs actually functioning by means of an X-ray device called a *fluoroscope*. The rays cause a special screen in the fluoroscope to *fluoresce* (glow) when they strike it. See FLUOROSCOPE; FLUORESCENCE.

Sometimes a harmless substance is injected into the body to make certain organs stand out clearly on a radiograph or fluoroscopic image. For example, a doctor may give a patient a solution of barium sulfate to swallow before making an intestinal X ray. The barium sulfate absorbs X rays, and so the intestines show up clearly on the X-ray image.

X rays are widely used to treat cancer. They kill cancer cells more readily than they kill normal cells. A cancerous tumor can be exposed to a limited dose of X rays. In many cases, the X rays eventually destroy the tumor but do less damage to nearby healthy tissue.

X rays also serve other purposes in medicine. For example, they are used to sterilize such medical supplies as plastic or rubber surgical gloves and syringes. These materials would be damaged by exposure to intense heat and cannot be sterilized by boiling.

In Industry, X rays are used to inspect products made of various kinds of materials, including aluminum, steel, and other cast metals. Radiographs reveal cracks and other defects in these products that are not visible on the surface. X rays are also used to check the quality of many mass-produced products, such as transistors and other small electronic devices. Some metal detection devices work by means of X rays. They include the scanners used at airports to check for weapons in luggage.

Manufacturers treat certain kinds of plastics with X rays. The rays cause a chemical change in these substances that makes them stronger. Powerful X rays have been used to help control an insect pest called the *blowfly*. Male blowflies cannot produce young after being exposed to X rays. In addition, X rays have been used to cause *mutations* (changes in cell structure) in barley. Mutated barley has produced new varieties of the grain. Some of these varieties can be raised in poor soil that cannot support regular barley.

In Scientific Research. X rays have been used to analyze the arrangement of atoms in many kinds of substances, particularly crystals. The atoms in crystals are arranged in planes, with regular spacing between each plane. When a beam of X rays travels through a crystal, the planes of atoms act as tiny mirrors that *diffract* (spread out) the rays into a regular pattern. Each type of crystal has a different diffraction pattern. Scientists have learned much about the arrangement of atoms in crystals by studying the various diffraction patterns. The study of how crystals diffract X rays is known as *X-ray crystallography*. Scientists also use X rays to help analyze the structure and makeup of many complex

Hewlett Packard

Police Officers Use X Rays for detection purposes. The X-ray picture shown above reveals a supply of narcotics and a hypodermic needle, *center*, hidden in the heel of a shoe.

chemical substances, such as enzymes and proteins.

Archeologists have used X rays to examine ancient objects that are covered by a heavy crust of dirt or corrosion. This method allows researchers to see an image of the object without attempting to remove the crust, which could damage the specimen. X rays also are used to reveal a painting covered by other paintings.

Characteristics of X Rays

Electromagnetic radiation with short wavelengths has higher energy than radiation with long wavelengths. X rays have some of the shortest wavelengths and highest energies among all the kinds of electromagnetic radiation. The wavelengths of X rays range from about

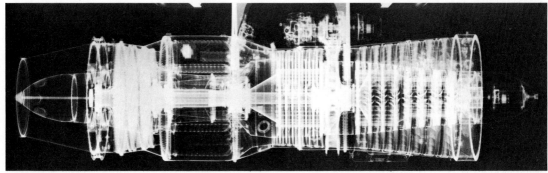

Eastman Kodak Company

X Rays Have Many Industrial Uses because of their tremendous penetrating power. They can be used to check the construction of a jet airplane engine, *above*. An X-ray picture of this kind can uncover cracks and other structural defects that may not be visible on the surface.

$\frac{1}{100}$ of an *angstrom unit* to 100 angstrom units. An angstrom unit equals about $\frac{4}{1,000,000,000}$ of an inch (0.00000001 centimeter). By comparison, the wavelengths of visible light range from about 4,000 to 7,000 angstrom units. The WORLD BOOK article on ELECTROMAGNETIC WAVES has a diagram that compares X rays with other kinds of electromagnetic radiation.

Many of the special characteristics of X rays result from their short wavelengths and high energy. The behavior of X rays can be compared with the behavior of visible light. For example, X rays can penetrate matter more deeply than light can because their energy is much higher than the energy of light. Also, X rays cannot be reflected easily by a mirror, as light can. Because of their high energy, X rays usually penetrate the mirror instead of being reflected by its surface.

X rays do not *refract* (bend) much when they travel from one material into another, as light does when it travels from air into a glass lens. Light is refracted by a lens because the light waves interact with the electrons in the atoms of the lens. But X rays have such short wavelengths that they pass through many substances without interacting with the electrons.

X rays are absorbed by a substance when they strike electrons in the atoms of the substance. The number of electrons in an atom equals its *atomic number* (see ATOM [Atomic Number]). Therefore, substances that have atoms of a high atomic number generally absorb more X rays than do substances with atoms of a low atomic number. Lead, which has an atomic number of 82, absorbs more X rays than most substances do. It is often used to make X-ray shields. Beryllium, which has an atomic number of 4, absorbs relatively few X rays. X-ray absorption also depends on the density of the substance and on other complex factors. High-density substances absorb more X rays than do low-density substances.

If the X rays absorbed by a substance have enough energy, they knock electrons out of the atoms of the substance. Whenever an electrically neutral atom gains or loses electrons, it becomes an electrically charged particle called an *ion*. This process is called *ionization*. Ionization causes the many kinds of biological, chemical, and physical changes that make X rays both useful and dangerous.

How X Rays Are Produced

X rays are produced whenever high-energy electrons suddenly give up energy. Machines produce the rays by accelerating electrons to extremely high speeds and then crashing them into a piece of solid material called a *target*. There, the electrons rapidly slow down because they collide with atoms in the target, and part of their energy is changed into X rays. Physicists call such X rays *bremsstrahlung*—from the German word for *braking radiation*.

Some of the high-energy electrons knock other electrons out of their normal positions in the atoms of the target. When these dislodged electrons fall back into place, or are replaced by others, other X rays may be produced. Physicists call such X rays *characteristic X rays*. Bremsstrahlung has a wide range of wavelengths, but each characteristic X ray has a particular wavelength, depending on the electronic structure of the atom it came from (see ATOM [Electronic Structure]).

X rays are produced by high-vacuum X-ray tubes for many medical and industrial uses. Such tubes consist of an airtight glass container with two electrodes—one positive and one negative—sealed inside (see ELECTRODE). The *cathode* (negative electrode) has a small coil of wire. The *anode* (positive electrode) consists of a block of metal. In most X-ray tubes, the anode and cathode consist of tungsten or a similar metal that can withstand high temperatures.

When an X-ray tube is in operation, an electric current flows through the cathode, causing it to glow white-hot. The heat releases electrons from the cathode. At the same time, an extremely high voltage is applied across the cathode and the anode. This high voltage forces the free electrons to travel at extremely high speeds toward the anode, which serves as the target. The electrons move easily through the space between the cathode and the target because the tube contains almost no air to block their motion. When the electrons strike the target, X rays and heat are produced.

The X rays scatter in many directions from the target. But most of them are absorbed by the *tube housing*, a metal case that surrounds the tube. One side of the

WORLD BOOK diagram

How an X-Ray Machine Works

An electric current flows through the cathode, causing it to become extremely hot. The heat releases electrons from the cathode. At the same time, a high voltage is applied across the cathode and the anode. This voltage forces the electrons to travel at high speeds toward the tungsten target. X rays are produced when the electrons strike the target.

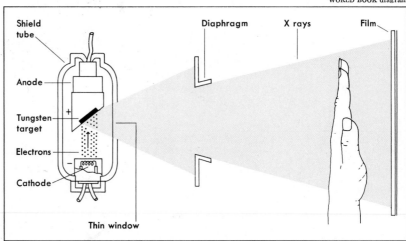

Shield tube
Anode
Tungsten target
Electrons
Cathode
Thin window
Diaphragm
X rays
Film

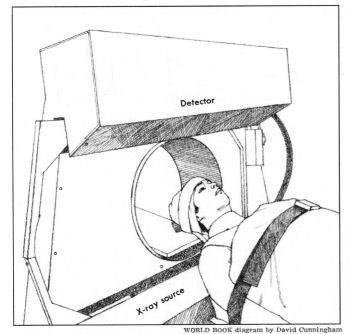

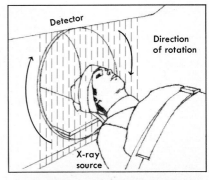

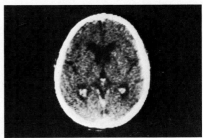

WORLD BOOK diagram by David Cunningham

Pfizer Inc.

A Tomographic Scanner is an X-ray machine that makes a cross-sectional view of the brain and other internal organs. It shoots X rays through a patient's body from many angles. An X-ray detector measures the rays that penetrate. A computer reads the data from the detector and then forms an image on a screen. The scanner thus produces a detailed picture of the brain, *right*.

housing has a small window. A narrow beam of X rays escapes from the tube through this window. The beam can be aimed at whatever object is to be X-rayed. The tube housing has a lead lining to absorb stray X rays. It also may contain oil or water to insulate and cool various parts of the tube.

The voltage across the cathode and target of an X-ray tube determines the energy, or penetrating power, of the rays it produces. A high voltage slams the electrons into the target at a higher energy level than does a low voltage. The X rays become more penetrating as the speed of the electrons increases. The voltage in an X-ray tube can be raised or lowered by means of a control box.

The voltage in most X-ray tubes ranges from about 20,000 to 250,000 volts. Such voltages produce X rays powerful enough for most medical purposes. However, voltages of 300 million electron volts (300 MeV) or higher can be achieved in betatrons and linear accelerators. X rays produced by these machines are used for medical and other scientific research.

History

After Roentgen discovered X rays in 1895, he experimented with them and soon demonstrated most of their characteristics. The discovery caused a sensation among scientists and the public. Within a few months, doctors were using X rays to examine broken bones.

In 1896, the American inventor Thomas A. Edison improved the fluoroscope so it could be used to view X-ray images. During the next 17 years, various scientists and inventors refined the X-ray tube. In 1913, the American physicist William D. Coolidge devised a way to make a more efficient X-ray tube. Mod-

ern X-ray tubes are basically the same as Coolidge's.

In the 1970's, radiologists began to use a new process for recording X-ray pictures. It records the image on a sheet of clear plastic instead of on photographic film. The new method, called *xeroradiography*, is cheaper and requires less X-ray exposure than the old process.

Also in the 1970's, radiologists started using a kind of X-ray machine that makes a cross-sectional view of a patient's body. This device, called a *computerized tomographic scanner*, shoots a pencil-thin beam of X rays through the patient's body from many angles. An X-ray detector on the opposite side of the body measures the rays that come through. Then a computer reads data from the detector and constructs an image on a television screen. This technique enables physicians to see detailed pictures of various organs, especially the brain, that cannot be seen well by conventional X-ray techniques. RAYMOND L. TANNER

Related Articles in WORLD BOOK include:

Betatron
Bragg, Sir William
Compton,
 Arthur H.
Gamma Ray

Laue,
 Max T. F. von
Radiation
Roentgen,
 Wilhelm K.

Siegbahn,
 Karl, M. G.
Synchrotron

XANTHIPPE, *zan TIP ee*, or XANTIPPE, was the wife of Socrates. She may have been 40 years younger than the great philosopher, and some historians say she belonged to the family of Pericles. Later generations believed that she had a poor disposition and a bitter tongue, and that Socrates married her simply to discipline himself and acquire self-control. But there is no proof of this. See also SOCRATES. C. BRADFORD WELLES

XANTHOPHYLL. See LEAF (Why a Leaf Turns Color).

449

St. Xavier College

St. Francis Xavier Was a Roman Catholic Missionary.

XAVIER, *ZAY vih ur,* **SAINT FRANCIS** (1506-1552), was a Jesuit missionary. He is also called the *Apostle of the Indies.* Most of his work was done in the Far East.

Saint Francis Xavier was born Francisco de Xavier near Sangüesa, Spain. His study in Paris brought him acquaintance with Ignatius of Loyola, with whom he helped to found the Society of Jesus. He accompanied Ignatius to Italy, doing hospital and missionary work, and was ordained a priest in 1537. He remained in Rome as secretary to the Jesuit society until 1540.

Xavier was sent in that year by John III of Portugal to spread Christianity in the Portuguese possessions in India. He landed in Goa, on the Malabar Coast, in 1542. His preaching in Travancore, in Malacca, and in Japan gained many converts to the Roman Catholic Church. He planned a mission to China, but died on the island of Shangchwan (Saint John Island) while trying to gain admission to the mainland. His body lies in a shrine in Goa. He was declared a saint in 1622.

Xavier was credited in his own day with possessing the gift of tongues, but he strongly denied it. Many miracles were credited to him. He was one of the greatest missionaries and explorers in the Far East, and his converts numbered hundreds of thousands. Saint Francis Xavier was an efficient organizer and a very capable man. His feast day is December 3. FULTON J. SHEEN

See also JAPAN (Foreign Relations); JESUITS.

XAVIER UNIVERSITY is a Roman Catholic coeducational liberal arts school in Cincinnati, Ohio. It is controlled by members of the Society of Jesus. Xavier offers undergraduate and graduate degrees. The university was founded in 1831. For enrollment, see UNIVERSITIES AND COLLEGES (table). PAUL L. O'CONNOR

XAVIER UNIVERSITY OF LOUISIANA is a coeducational Roman Catholic school in New Orleans. It is the only Catholic university in the Western Hemisphere with a predominantly Negro student body. The university has colleges of pharmacy and of arts and sciences. It also has a graduate school.

Xavier was founded in 1925 by the Sisters of the Blessed Sacrament. For the enrollment of Xavier University of Louisiana, see UNIVERSITIES AND COLLEGES (table). NORMAN C. FRANCIS

XENON, *ZEE nahn,* is a chemical element that makes up about one part in 20 million of the earth's atmosphere. The British chemists Sir William Ramsay and Morris W. Travers discovered it in 1898. Industry uses xenon in filling flash lamps and other powerful lamps. Xenon is also used to make *bubble chambers,* in-

Xenophon Gave Thanks to the Gods As His "Ten Thousand" Finished Their Long Retreat to the Bosporus.

Xerxes I Grimly Witnessed the Defeat of His Fleet at the Battle of Salamis. The Greek ships drove into the heart of the Persian fleet and wiped it out. Xerxes was enraged, because this defeat meant the end of his plan of conquest.

struments used by physicists to study nuclear particles. Xenon is obtained from liquid air.

Xenon is a colorless, odorless, tasteless gas. It is classed as an inert gas because it does not react readily with other substances. Its symbol is Xe. It has the atomic number 54, and an atomic weight of 131.30. Scientists once believed that xenon could not form chemical compounds. But today, xenon is known to form compounds with two chemical elements, fluorine and oxygen. FRANK C. ANDREWS

See also RAMSAY, SIR WILLIAM.

XENOPHON, *ZEHN oh fun* (?434 B.C.-?355 B.C.), was a Greek soldier and historian. Although a man of action, he is best known as a writer.

Xenophon was born in Athens of a noble family. He studied under Socrates, but was more interested in military subjects than in philosophy. In 401 B.C., he joined a band of Greek adventurers, led by the Persian prince, Cyrus the Younger. Cyrus wanted to seize the throne of Persia from his brother Artaxerxes. But Cyrus was killed in the battle of Cunaxa, and the Greek commanders were killed soon afterward. The 10,000 Greek adventurers were stranded in a strange country without commanders. They chose Xenophon to lead their retreat. Xenophon described this 1,500-mile (2,410-kilometer) march in *Anabasis*, a history of the expedition.

After months of hardships, the adventurers reached Trapezus, a city on the Black Sea. They served for a time with a Thessalian king, then joined a Spartan army in a battle against the Persians. In the last campaign, Xenophon captured a wealthy Persian and forced him to pay an enormous ransom. The Persian's ransom made Xenophon financially independent for the rest of his life. He settled in the district of Elis and devoted himself to writing. Xenophon wrote *Hellenica*, a history of Greece; *Memorabilia of Socrates*, an account of the life and teachings of Socrates; and *Cyropaedia*, a life of Cyrus the Great. C. BRADFORD WELLES

XEROGRAPHY. See DUPLICATOR (Electrostatic Copiers); PRINTING (Electrostatic); XEROX CORPORATION.

XEROPHYTE. See PLANT (Where Plants Live).

XEROX CORPORATION, a leading United States company, ranks as one of the world's largest industrial organizations. It developed the first automatic copier that makes dry copies of printed or written materials on ordinary paper. It also works in aerospace and medical technology and provides various educational products and services.

The corporation was founded in 1907 as The Haloid Company, a manufacturer of photocopying and photographic papers. After World War II ended in 1945, it began work on *xerography*, a process that makes copies without ink or pressure (see PRINTING [Electrostatic Printing]). This process was perfected by 1960 and soon revolutionized office work. The corporation, which has headquarters in Stamford, Conn., adopted its present name in 1961. For the sales, assets, and number of employees of the Xerox Corporation, see MANUFACTURING (table). THOMAS C. ABBOTT

XERXES, *ZURK seez*, was the name of two kings of Persia.

Xerxes I (519?-465 B.C.) was the son of Darius I (see DARIUS [I]). He came to the throne in 485 B.C. His first act was to put down a revolt in Egypt. Then he devoted himself to the conquest of Greece to avenge his father's defeat at Marathon. Xerxes also wanted to punish the Greeks for their part in the Ionian rebellion. In 483 B.C., he collected perhaps the largest army that had ever been assembled. It included over 180,000 men drawn from all parts of the empire. Xerxes set out with an immense fleet that the Phoenicians had assembled for him. He used a double line of ships to form two bridges across the Hellespont, and cut a canal through the isthmus of Mount Athos Peninsula. In 480 B.C., Xerxes sent his warriors across the Hellespont and invaded Greece. See GREECE, ANCIENT (The Persian Wars).

Xerxes won a victory at Thermopylae (see THERMOPYLAE). He entered Athens and burned all the houses and temples. But in 480 B.C., his fleet was crushed at the

Battle of Salamis (see SALAMIS). Xerxes feared that his supply line would be cut. He returned to Persia, but left a force in Greece under his brother-in-law, Mardonius. The next year, the Greeks defeated Mardonius at Plataea.

The Greek sources, however, probably present a one-sided picture of Xerxes. His venture in Greece was a failure, but it was offset by such successes as the recovery of Egypt and a series of other victories. He was also a great builder and a wise administrator. His son, Artaxerxes I, succeeded him to the throne.

Xerxes II (450?-424 B.C.) came to the throne of Persia in 424 B.C., after the murder of his father, Artaxerxes I. But the reign of Xerxes lasted for only 45 days. His half-brother, Sogdianus, murdered him and seized the throne. Sogdianus himself was murdered soon afterward.   RICHARD NELSON FRYE

See also AHASUERUS.

XMAS. See CHRISTMAS (History).

XOCHIMILCO. See LAKE XOCHIMILCO.

XYLEM. See STEM; TREE (Trunks and Branches; picture).

XYLOPHONE, *ZY loh fohn,* is a percussion musical instrument. Players produce tones by striking the wooden sounding bars with hard mallets. The xylophones used now have a metal resonating, or sounding, tube under each bar. The lack of resonators in the first xylophones and their higher pitch were the chief distinguishing features between this instrument and the marimba. The xylophone has a range of three octaves or more. Musicians in orchestras and bands use it for special effects and occasionally for solo playing. Two similar instruments are the vibraphone and the orchestra bells. The vibraphone has metal bars and resonators. An electric motor operates a butterfly valve at the top of each resonator. These valves help the vibraphone produce a rich, brilliant tone. *Danse Macabre,* by the French composer Saint-Saëns, requires a xylophone.

The xylophone is an old instrument. It is related to many Oriental instruments and was common among the Slavic peoples. The sounding bars of the early instruments were often made of glass or pinewood. Rosewood is more commonly used now.   CHARLES B. RIGHTER

See also MARIMBA; ORCHESTRA BELLS.

XYZ AFFAIR was the name given to an exchange of diplomatic proposals between France and the United States. In 1798, relations between the governments of the United States and France were strained. The French government grew bitter because the United States refused to help France in its war against Great Britain. French leaders became furious when the United States signed the Jay Treaty with Great Britain in 1794. This treaty brought to a peaceful settlement various American-British problems which arose from boundary and trade disputes. The angry French seized cargoes from United States ships, and forced United States seamen to serve on French vessels. The Directory then governing France refused to receive the U.S. Minister, General Charles Cotesworth Pinckney, whom President George Washington had appointed.

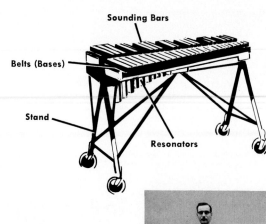

Sounding Bars
Belts (Bases)
Stand
Resonators

The **Xylophone** is a percussion instrument played by striking wooden bars with mallets. Orchestras and bands often use xylophones for special effects.

Chicago Symphony Orchestra

The next President, John Adams, had no desire to declare war on France. So he sent three special ambassadors to France to seek a peaceful settlement. The ambassadors were Pinckney, John Marshall, and Elbridge Gerry. The French Foreign Minister, Prince Talleyrand, stalled the discussions for some weeks. Then he appointed three agents to deal with the Americans. The agents insulted the Americans with various dishonorable proposals. One proposal demanded a loan for France and a large gift, or bribe, for Talleyrand. Another required payment for certain critical remarks that President Adams had made to Congress about France. When asked for his reply, Ambassador Pinckney said, "It is No! No! Not a sixpence." The slogan "Millions for defense, but not one cent for tribute" is often credited to Pinckney. It was actually written by Robert Goodloe Harper in a magazine article.

President Adams made an official report of these proposals to the United States Congress. He did not name Talleyrand's agents, but simply referred to them as X, Y, and Z. President Adams told Congress: "I will never send another minister to France without assurance that he will be received, respected, and honored as the representative of a great, free, powerful, and independent nation."

The United States did not declare war on France, but did take steps to raise an army. American privateers received permission to attack armed French vessels. The XYZ Affair aroused indignation among citizens of both France and the United States. In 1800, a second American commission arranged for a friendly settlement with France.   EUGENE C. BARKER

See also ADAMS, JOHN (Difficulties with France); GERRY, ELBRIDGE; MARSHALL, JOHN; PINCKNEY (Charles Cotesworth); TALLEYRAND.

Yy

Y is the 25th letter of our alphabet. It came from a symbol used by the Semites, who once lived in Syria and Palestine. They named it *waw*, their word for *hook*, and adapted an Egyptian *hieroglyphic*, or picture symbol. *Waw* was also the origin of *F, U, V,* and *W.* The Greeks later took the symbol into their alphabet, and gave it its capital Y form. They called it *upsilon.* The Romans used the letter when writing words taken from Greek. See ALPHABET.

Uses. *Y* or *y* is about the 17th most frequently used letter in books, newspapers, and other printed material in English. *Y* represents the word *young* in many abbreviations, such as *YMCA* for *Young Men's Christian Association.* In archaic words, such as *ye* in *Ye Olde Tea Shoppe, y* represents a discarded Anglo-Saxon character called *thorn.* The thorn resembled *y* in appearance, and had the sound of *th.* In chemistry, *Y* represents the metallic element *yttrium.*

Pronunciation. *Y* or *y* may be either a vowel or a consonant. In English, a person pronounces the consonant *y* by placing the front of his tongue near his hard palate, and then gliding his tongue into position to make the sound of the vowel that follows. The velum, or soft palate, is closed, and the vocal cords vibrate. As a vowel, the letter *y* may have the sound of long *i* as in *my* and *fly;* that of short *i* as in *myth* and *nymph;* that of *u* as in *myrtle;* or that of long *e* as in *baby.* See PRONUNCIATION.

I. J. GELB and JAMES M. WELLS

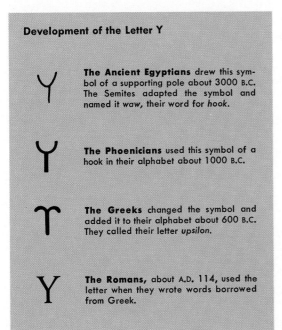

Development of the Letter Y

The Ancient Egyptians drew this symbol of a supporting pole about 3000 B.C. The Semites adapted the symbol and named it *waw,* their word for *hook.*

The Phoenicians used this symbol of a hook in their alphabet about 1000 B.C.

The Greeks changed the symbol and added it to their alphabet about 600 B.C. They called their letter *upsilon.*

The Romans, about A.D. 114, used the letter when they wrote words borrowed from Greek.

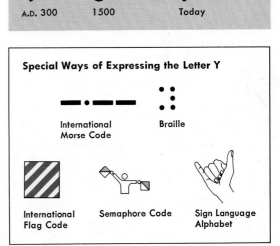

The Small Letter y developed during the A.D. 300's from Roman writing. By the 1500's, the letter had the form that is used today.

A.D. 300   1500   Today

Special Ways of Expressing the Letter Y

International Morse Code

Braille

International Flag Code

Semaphore Code

Sign Language Alphabet

Common Forms of the Letter Y

Handwritten Letters vary from person to person. Manuscript (printed) letters, *left,* have simple curves and straight lines. Cursive letters, *right,* have flowing lines.

Roman Letters have small finishing strokes called *serifs* that extend from the main strokes. The type face shown above is Baskerville. The italic form appears at the right.

Sans-Serif Letters are also called *gothic letters.* They have no serifs. The type face shown above is called Futura. The italic form of Futura appears at the right.

Computer Letters have special shapes. Computers can "read" these letters either optically or by means of the magnetic ink with which the letters may be printed.

Y-INDIAN GUIDES

Y-INDIAN GUIDES is a national program of father-and-son clubs sponsored by the Young Men's Christian Association (YMCA). The program aims at fostering understanding and companionship between boys who are 6 to 8 years old and their fathers.

Knowledge of American Indian culture and traditions forms a basic part of the Y-Indian Guide program. Each club, called a *tribe*, has from five to nine father-son teams. Fathers and sons must attend meetings together. Activities include camping, ceremonies, crafts, games, service projects, storytelling, and outings.

Boys who are 9 to 11 years old and their fathers may join Y-Trail Blazers. This program emphasizes mental and spiritual growth, outdoor activities, physical fitness, service projects, and vocational exploration.

Critically reviewed by the YOUNG MEN'S CHRISTIAN ASSOCIATION

Y-INDIAN MAIDENS is a program of clubs in the United States for girls 6 to 8 years old and their mothers. The clubs, sponsored by the Young Men's Christian Association (YMCA), encourage companionship and understanding between mother and daughter.

The program's theme is based on American Indian culture. Each club, called a *tribe*, has from six to nine mother-daughter teams. Activities of the tribes include learning crafts, songs, and stories; outings; and service projects.

Critically reviewed by the
YOUNG MEN'S CHRISTIAN ASSOCIATION

Y-INDIAN PRINCESSES is a program of clubs in the United States for girls 6 to 8 years old and their fathers. The program encourages companionship and love between father and daughter. The Young Men's Christian Association (YMCA) sponsors the Y-Indian Princesses.

American Indian culture forms a basic part of the program. Each club, called a *tribe*, has from six to nine father-daughter teams. They learn crafts, ceremonies, games, songs, and stories. Other activities include camping, service projects, and outings.

Critically reviewed by the YOUNG MEN'S CHRISTIAN ASSOCIATION

Y-TEENS is a program for members of the Young Women's Christian Association who are of junior high or high school age. The program aims to serve the educational, health, recreational, and social needs of teen-age women. Members work to promote understanding among all people and to end racism.

Y-Teens began as the Little Girls' Christian Association in Oakland, Calif., in 1881. It was a model for other girls' clubs throughout the United States. In 1918, the program became known as Girl Reserves, and its name was changed to Y-Teens in 1947. The program has more than 200,000 participants. Headquarters are at 600 Lexington Avenue, New York, N.Y. 10022.

Critically reviewed by the YOUNG WOMEN'S CHRISTIAN ASSOCIATION

YABLONOVYY MOUNTAINS, *yih bluh nuh VOY*, or YABLONOI MOUNTAINS, lie east of Lake Baykal in Siberia. For location, see RUSSIA (physical map). The range extends northeast from northern Mongolia for about 1,000 miles (1,600 kilometers) until it joins the Stanovoy Mountains. The Yablonovyy range is the dividing line between the rivers that flow into the Arctic Ocean and those that flow into the Pacific. Mount Sokhondo (8,199 feet, or 2,499 meters) is the highest peak. Some of Russia's largest tin mines are in these mountains. THEODORE SHABAD

YACHT, *yaht*, is a vessel, usually a small one, that is used only for pleasure. A yacht may be any kind of vessel, from a small sailing craft to a steam-powered ocean-going ship. Modern yachts originated in The Netherlands, where they were called *jaght boats*, or *hunting boats*. For more information on yachts, see BOATING. See also SAILING. CARL D. LANE

YADKIN RIVER. See PEE DEE RIVER.

YAFO. See TEL AVIV-YAFO.

YAHWEH. See JEHOVAH.

YAJUR-VEDA. See VEDAS.

YAK, *yak*, is the wild ox of Asia. It inhabits the cold, dry plateaus of Tibet, often more than 16,000 feet (4,870 meters) above sea level. The wild yak stands over 6 feet (1.8 meters) high at the shoulders. But it carries its head low with the nose almost touching the ground. It may weigh from 1,100 to 1,200 pounds (499 to 544 kilograms). The yak is covered with black or brownish-black hair. The hair is especially long and silky on shoulders, flanks, and tail. The yak is agile in spite of its bulk and its heavy forequarters. It can slide down icy slopes, swim swift rivers, and cross steep rock slides. If forced to defend itself, it charges furiously. Excessive hunting has resulted in the killing of so many wild yaks that the animal is in danger of extinction.

New York Zoological Society

The Yak of Asia is a relative of the American bison. Yaks thrive in the high, cold mountains of Tibet.

The domestic yak, often called the *grunting ox* because of the sounds it makes, is the result of many generations of careful breeding. It is often white or piebald instead of black like the wild yak. Smaller and much more docile than the wild yak, it is useful in many ways. As a pack animal, it can carry a heavy load 20 miles (32 kilometers) a day. In Tibet, the yak carries travelers and mail. It provides rich milk. Its flesh is dried or roasted for food. The soft hair of the domestic yak is used to make cloth, and the coarser hair for mats and tent coverings. Saddles, whips, boots, and other articles are made from the hide. The bushy tail is used as a fly chaser at ceremonial processions in India, and as an ornament for a tomb or shrine.

Scientific Classification. The yak belongs to the bovid family, *Bovidae*. It is in the genus *Bos*, and is species *B. grunniens*. DONALD F. HOFFMEISTER

YAKIMA, Wash. (pop. 45,588; met. area pop. 145,-212), is a food-processing and shipping center. It lies in the Yakima Valley of south-central Washington, about 140 miles (225 kilometers) southeast of Seattle. For location, see WASHINGTON (political map). Many irrigated valley farms furnish fruits, potatoes, hops, sugar beets, wheat, poultry, and dairy products for the city's processing and packing plants. Manufacture of farm machinery, agricultural chemicals, clay products, packing boxes, and lumber are major industries in Yakima. The city is the eastern gateway to the recreational areas of the Cascade Mountains. Yakima is the name of the confederation of 14 Indian tribes that live on the nearby 1-million-acre (400,000-hectare) Yakima reservation. Yakima is the seat of Yakima County. It has a council-manager government. HOWARD J. CRITCHFIELD

YAKUBOVSKY, *yah koo BAHV skee,* **IVAN IGNA-TIEVICH** (1912-1976), was deputy defense minister of Russia from 1967 to 1976. In 1967, he also was selected to command the Warsaw Pact forces—the combined armed forces of the Communist nations of Eastern Europe.

Yakubovsky was born in Zaytsevo, near Minsk, and began his military career in 1932. He joined the Communist Party in 1937. During World War II (1939-1945), he commanded Russian tank corps and armored units. Yakubovsky commanded the Russian troops in East Germany from 1960 to 1961 and from 1962 to 1965. In 1961, he was elected to the Central Committee of the All-Union Party Congress, one of the top units of the Communist Party in Russia. WALTER C. CLEMENS

YALE, ELIHU (1649-1721), was an official of the East India Company and a benefactor of Yale University. During 27 years' service in India, from 1672 to 1699, he acquired a large fortune and became governor of Fort Saint George in Madras.

After returning to England, Yale made many gifts to churches, schools, and missionary societies. He gave books and other valuable goods to the Collegiate School which was founded in 1701 by the Congregationalists in Connecticut. In 1718, in recognition of his generosity, the trustees changed the name of the school to Yale College. Yale was born in Boston, but was taken to England when he was three years old. He joined the East India Company in 1670. ROBERT H. BREMNER

Chicago Historical Society
Elihu Yale

YALE, LINUS, JR. (1821-1868), an inventor and manufacturer, is best known for his inventions of locks. He began to assist his father in developing bank locks in 1849. He gained a wide reputation as an authority on these complicated devices, and held a number of patents. After about 1862, Yale introduced several combination safe locks and key-operated cylinder locks which set the pattern for future development. In 1868, he established a lock factory. He was born in Salisbury, N.Y. See also LOCK AND KEY. ROBERT P. MULTHAUF

YALE UNIVERSITY is a coeducational, privately endowed, nonsectarian school in New Haven, Conn. Chartered in 1701, Yale is the third oldest institution of

Yale News Bureau
Yale's Harkness Tower is part of the Memorial Quadrangle. The Gothic structure towers 201 feet (61 meters) in the air. The building was named for Charles W. Harkness, who was a graduate of Yale University and a benefactor of the school.

higher learning in the United States. Only Harvard University and the College of William and Mary are older.

Yale graduates have always played a major role in American life. Many graduates have become leaders in government, business and industry, the arts, and community services. The presidents of about 70 U.S. universities and colleges graduated from Yale.

The Yale Campus covers about 175 acres (71 hectares). Connecticut Hall, built in 1752, is the oldest building. This red brick building is the only structure left on the campus from colonial days. In recent years, famous American architects have constructed more than 25 buildings at Yale, including a science center.

Freshmen live on the *Old Campus*, the site of the original school. Sophomores, juniors, and seniors live in 12 residential colleges. Each college houses about 280 students and some faculty members. Each college has its own library, common rooms, and dining hall. The colleges compete with each other in several sports. The residence plan started in 1933 through the gifts of Edward S. Harkness, a Yale graduate.

The Yale library, containing about 6 million volumes, is one of the largest libraries in the world. Yale's Beinecke Rare Book and Manuscript Library was dedicated in 1963. It is one of the largest buildings in the world devoted to rare books and manuscripts.

Yale's Peabody Museum of Natural History is one of the oldest university-related museums in the United States. It has many world-famous fossil exhibits. Yale's art gallery is the oldest university art gallery in the nation. The Yale Center for British Art and British Studies has an excellent collection of British paintings and drawings, and related books and papers.

The *Yale Daily News*, established in 1878, is the

oldest college daily newspaper in the United States. The *Yale Literary Magazine*, founded in 1836, was the first undergraduate magazine published in the nation.

Educational System. Yale has 12 divisions, each under the supervision of its own dean and faculty. The divisions of the university include Yale College; the graduate school; and the schools of art, architecture, divinity, drama, forestry, law, medicine, music, nursing, and organization and management.

The Corporation of Yale University governs the school. The corporation consists of the university president, the governor and lieutenant governor of Connecticut, and 16 *fellows* (trustees).

History. Yale was founded in 1701, when 10 Connecticut clergymen met in the village of Branford and made a gift of books to found a college. Later that year, the General Assembly of Connecticut approved a charter for the *Collegiate School*. From 1702 to 1707, classes met in the home of Rector Abraham Pierson at Killingworth (now Clinton).

Classes were held in Milford and then Saybrook before the school moved to New Haven in 1716. Two years later, the school's only college building was still unfinished because of a lack of funds. Elihu Yale, a retired merchant in London, contributed money to the school in 1718 (see YALE, ELIHU). Yale is sometimes called *Old Eli*. The same year, the school adopted its present name in honor of Yale. The undergraduate school, known as Yale College, was open only to men until 1969. For the enrollment of the university, see UNIVERSITIES AND COLLEGES (table).

Critically reviewed by YALE UNIVERSITY

See also CONNECTICUT (picture); LIBRARY (picture: A Rare Book Collection); UNITED STATES (picture: Beinecke).

YALOBUSHA RIVER. See YAZOO RIVER.

YALOW, ROSALYN. See NOBEL PRIZES (table: Nobel Prizes for Physiology or Medicine—1977).

YALTA, *YAHL tuh* (pop. 63,000), is a seaport in the Ukrainian Soviet Socialist Republic, a republic of Russia. It is a favorite Russian winter resort. The city is at the southern tip of the Crimean Peninsula beside the Black Sea. For location, see RUSSIA (political map).

YALTA CONFERENCE was a meeting held early in 1945, between the leaders of the "Big Three" Allied nations. On February 4, President Franklin D. Roosevelt of the United States, Prime Minister Winston Churchill of Great Britain, and Premier Joseph Stalin of Russia met at the Livadia, an estate near Yalta, a famous Black Sea resort in the Crimea.

On February 11, the three leaders issued a statement. They agreed on plans to occupy Germany, set up a new Polish government, and hold the San Francisco Conference to form the United Nations. They again endorsed the Atlantic Charter.

Later reports of the Conference revealed that Stalin had promised that Russia would declare war on Japan within three months after Germany's surrender. In return for this promise, Russia was promised the Kuril Islands and the southern part of Sakhalin Island, which Japan then controlled, as well as other concessions. Russia did declare war on Japan, but only after the first atomic bomb had fallen on Hiroshima. It also seized

Manchuria and North Korea, and set the stage for the Korean War. The Russians did not allow free elections to be held in Poland as they had agreed, and they used the Yalta agreements to enslave millions of people.

The Conference led to much political controversy in the United States. In March, 1955, the Department of State released the Yalta Papers, which told the full story of the Conference. PAYSON S. WILD

See also SAN FRANCISCO CONFERENCE.

YALU RIVER, *YAH LOO*, rises from the highest peak of the Changpai Shan, or Long White Mountains, of Manchuria. The river forms most of the boundary between North Korea and Manchuria as it flows 500 miles (800 kilometers) to the Yellow Sea. The river became important during the Korean War (1950-1953). Chinese Communists crossed the Yalu in mid-October, 1950, to aid North Korea in the war. J. E. SPENCER

YAM is a plant that has thick roots much like those of the sweet potato. For this reason, juicy varieties of sweet potatoes are often wrongly called yams. The thick roots of yams are a major food crop in many tropical countries. They contain mostly water. Most of the solid matter is starch and sugar. The root has less starch than the white potato, but more sugar. Some kinds of yams are not fit to eat, but they produce substances called *sapogenins* that can be used to make drugs such as cortisone.

A. W. Ambler, National Audubon Society

Yams

Yam plants are climbing vines that bear small, green flower clusters. Cuttings of the vine or sections of roots are usually planted to start new vines. Cuttings should be planted in widely spaced rows to give the roots room to grow. Yams require a long growing season and hot, moist weather.

About 20 million short tons (18 million metric tons) of yams are grown for food each year. About half of them are grown in western Africa. Yams are also grown in India and in the countries of Southeast Asia and the Caribbean Sea. Few yams are grown for food in the United States, because the weather is too cold and the growing season is too short. See also SWEET POTATO.

Scientific Classification. Yams belong to the yam family, *Dioscoreaceae*. The edible yam is genus *Dioscorea*. A common species is *D. alata*. TEME P. HERNANDEZ

YAMACRAW BLUFF. See GEORGIA (Places to Visit).

YAMAMOTO, *YAH muh MOH toh*, **ISOROKU** (1884-1943), commanded the Japanese combined fleet at the time of the attack on Pearl Harbor in 1941. He was one of Japan's great admirals, with a long and distinguished career in war and peace. He opposed the policies that led to war with the United States. But he sponsored the planning that led to the Pearl Harbor attack as Japan's only chance of victory. Yamamoto was born in Niigata. He was killed in 1943 when his plane was shot down in the South Pacific. MARIUS B. JANSEN

YAMASHITA, *yuh MAH shee tah*, **TOMOBUMI** (1885-1946), a Japanese general in World War II, was executed for "violation of the laws of war." A brilliant field commander, Yamashita advanced rapidly in Korea and Manchuria. He became famous for the campaign against Malaya and Singapore in 1942. Later, he served in Manchuria until he took charge of the defense of the Philippines in 1944. Yamashita was born in Kōchi prefecture.　　　　　　　　MARIUS B. JANSEN

YAMATO PERIOD was the time in Japanese history from about A.D. 200 to 646. During this period, Japan's emperors ruled from the Yamato area, the area around what is now the city of Nara. They controlled much of central Japan and parts of southern Korea during the 200's and 300's. Japan's royal family traces its ancestry to the Yamato emperors, and so the entire nation is sometimes called *Yamato*.

Chinese culture and Buddhism greatly influenced the development of art, literature, and government in Japan during the Yamato period. Buddhism became popular among Japan's rulers and leading families. However, Shinto remained a chief religion. The Yamato period ended in 646, when the emperor began a program called the Taika Reform to establish a central government (see TAIKA REFORM).　　　　　　　TETSUO NAJITA

See also JAPAN (Early History).

YANCEY, WILLIAM LOWNDES (1814-1863), an American statesman, was often called "The Orator of Secession." He served in the United States House of Representatives as a Democrat from Alabama from 1844 to 1846. He devoted himself after leaving Congress to arousing the South to defend its rights.

Yancey's "Alabama Platform" demanded that southerners have the right to take their slaves into western territories. He opposed the Compromise of 1850. In 1858, he tried to organize a League of United Southerners to work for Southern rights in both political parties.

Yancey opposed Stephen A. Douglas' candidacy for the Democratic presidential nomination in 1860, and supported John C. Breckinridge. He drew up Alabama's Secession Ordinance. Later he was a Confederate commissioner to Europe, and a Confederate senator from Alabama. Yancey was born in Warren County, Georgia. He practiced law and edited a newspaper in Greenville, S.C., before moving to Alabama.　　W. B. HESSELTINE

YANG, CHEN NING (1922-　　), a Chinese-born physicist, shared the 1957 Nobel prize in physics with Tsung Dao Lee (see LEE, TSUNG DAO). They received the award for their contributions to the laws of fundamental particles. They disproved the law of *conservation of parity*, which concerned the physical interactions of fundamental nuclear particles. Yang was born in Ho-fei, Anhwei, China. He was a staff member at the Institute for Advanced Study in Princeton, N.J., from 1949 to 1965. He became director of the Institute for Theoretical Physics at State University of New York at Stony Brook in 1965. See also PARITY; NOBEL PRIZES (picture).　　　　　　　　RALPH E. LAPP

YANGTZE RIVER, *YANG SEE*, or YANGTZE KIANG, is the world's third longest river, and the longest and most important river in China. To most Chinese, the Yangtze is known as the *Ch'ang Chiang*, or *long river*. It rises in the Kunlun Mountains of Tibet, 16,000 feet (4,880 meters) above sea level. The river flows east, southeast, and then south into the province of Yünnan. From here it winds in a great double curve and flows northeast across Szechwan Province. It then follows an irregular course east through central China and enters

Eastfoto
The Yangtze River is the longest river in China. Thousands of small boats carry people and goods on this important waterway.

the Yellow Sea 3,434 miles (5,526 kilometers) from its source. The Yangtze and its branches drain nearly 706,-000 square miles (1,829,000 square kilometers).

The high mountains at the Yangtze's source cause it to flow rapidly for most of its length. The great gorges in its upper parts above I-ch'ang make it one of the most beautiful rivers in the world. Just above I-ch'ang is perhaps the largest potential hydroelectric site in the world. In places, mountains over 1 mile (1.6 kilometers) high form the river's banks. About half of China's ocean trade is distributed over the Yangtze and its branches. Ocean steamers reach Hankow, 680 miles (1,090 kilometers) by river from the coast. Smaller boats can go 1,000 miles (1,600 kilometers) farther inland.

Thousands of Chinese live on the Yangtze on sailing craft called *junks*. Millions of Chinese live on the banks of this great river. Occasional summer floods temporarily drive many people from their homes. Among the great cities along the Yangtze River are Shanghai, Nanking, An-ch'ing, I-ch'ang, Chungking, and the twin cities of Hankow and Wu-ch'ang.　　J. E. SPENCER

See also RIVER (chart: Longest Rivers).

YANK was a weekly magazine for soldiers published during World War II by the United States Army. *Yank* was written and edited by a staff of enlisted men. *Yank* contained excellent features, and was credited with many exclusive stories on the course of the war. The first issue appeared on June 17, 1942. *Yank* was discontinued at the end of 1945. Over 2,600,000 soldiers read *Yank*. It was printed in 21 regional editions, which reached such distant places as Iran, India, Egypt, England, and France.　　　　　　　　EARL F. ENGLISH

YANKEE. People of other countries often call any person from the United States a Yankee. In the southern United States, the word *Yankee* means a Northerner, or someone who comes from north of Mason and Dixon's line. But most of the people of the United States use the word *Yankee* to mean a New Englander.

People often say that someone is "shrewd as a Yankee" or "clever as a Yankee." The people of early New England had to develop great shrewdness and cleverness as they struggled to make homes and create industries in the rocky wilderness. "Yankee peddlers" roamed far and

457

wide through early American communities, selling the articles made by Yankee craftsmen. These peddlers won a great reputation for getting high prices.

No one is certain where the word *Yankee* came from. Some dictionaries state that the English word *Yankee* comes from the Scottish word *yankie*. A *yankie* is a sharp and clever woman. Other dictionaries suggest that *Yankee* is an Indian pronunciation of the word *English*, or of the French word for *English*, which is *Anglais*. The word *Yankee* may have had a Dutch origin. Early Flemish people sometimes called persons from The Netherlands *Jan Kees*, which was short for the common Dutch names *Jan* and *Cornelis*. Some authorities believe that the people of Flanders gave the same name to Netherlanders who lived in North America.

The first person to use the word Yankee very widely was a farmer of Cambridge, Mass., named Jonathan Hastings. He used the word in the early 1700's to express the idea of excellence, speaking of a "Yankee good horse," or "Yankee cider." Harvard students who hired horses from Hastings began to use the expression. The word was widely used during the Revolutionary War, when British soldiers made fun of New England troops by calling them Yankees. During the Civil War, Confederate soldiers called Federal troops "Yankees." When United States troops arrived in Paris in 1917, the French press hailed them as Yankees or Yanks. Europeans have continued to use the word as a name for American soldiers.   JOHN R. ALDEN

See also YANKEE DOODLE.

YANKEE DOODLE is a song that has been popular in America since colonial days. The tune is an old one. It may have begun in southern Europe in the Middle Ages. About 1500 it was popular in Holland, where the harvesters sang it. The verses began with the meaningless words:

> Yanker dudel doodle down.

The song was sung to small children in England during Shakespeare's time. Later the tune was used for a rhyme that began:

> Lucy Locket lost her pocket,
> Kitty Fisher found it;
> Nothing in it, nothing in it,
> Save the binding round it.

Another English form of the Yankee Doodle tune was sung by the Cavaliers in the 1600's. They made up words to poke fun at Oliver Cromwell when he rode down from Canterbury to take charge of the Puritan forces.

> Yankee Doodle came to town
> Upon a Kentish pony,
> He stuck a feather in his cap
> And called it macaroni.

At that time, some people used the word *macaroni* to refer to the young men of London who dressed in odd Italian styles.

The words of "Yankee Doodle" known in the United States were written by an English army surgeon, Dr. Richard Schuckburgh. The song made fun of the untrained American troops during the French and Indian War in 1755.

But the American troops liked "Yankee Doodle" and the song soon became popular. "Yankee Doodle" was

well known all through the American colonies by the time of the Revolutionary War. The first printed notice of it in America appeared in the New York *Journal* on October 12, 1768. The words of the song are:

> Father and I went down to camp,
>   Along with Captain Goodwin,
> And there we saw the men and boys,
>   As thick as hasty puddin'.
>
> Chorus: Yankee Doodle keep it up,
>   Yankee Doodle dandy,
>   Mind the music and the step,
>   And with the girls be handy.
>
> And there was Captain Washington,
>   Upon a slapping stallion,
> And giving orders to his men,
>   I guess there was a million.
>
> And then the feathers on his hat,
>   They looked so 'tarnal finy
> I wanted peskely to get,
>   To give to my Jemina.
>
> And then they had a swamping gun,
>   As big as a log of maple,
> On a deuced little cart,
>   A load for father's cattle.

"Yankee Doodle" was sung and played in every patriot camp. American soldiers often whistled it in battle. The British heard it so often during their retreat from Concord that General Gage is said to have exclaimed, "I hope I shall never hear that tune again!" But the British did hear it again. American bands played it as the British left after the surrender at Yorktown.   RAYMOND KENDALL

YANKEE TERRIER. See AMERICAN STAFFORDSHIRE TERRIER.

YANKTON, S.Dak. (pop. 11,919), is a wholesale and retail center on the Missouri River in southeastern South Dakota (see SOUTH DAKOTA [political map]). It was first settled in 1858, and named for the Yankton tribe of the Sioux Indians. It became the capital of the Dakota Territory, organized in 1861 to include North Dakota, South Dakota, and all land west to the Rockies. Mount Marty and Yankton colleges are located in Yankton. Yankton is the seat of Yankton County. It has a council-manager government.

YANKTON COLLEGE. See UNIVERSITIES AND COLLEGES (table).

YAOUNDÉ, *YAH OON DAY* (pop. 274,399), is the capital of Cameroon. For location, see CAMEROON (map). It is a center of commerce and transportation for the area. Yaoundé was founded in 1888 and became the capital of Cameroon in 1922.

YAP ISLANDS form an island group in the western Pacific Ocean. The group is part of the Caroline Islands. It lies about 1,000 miles (1,600 kilometers) east of the central Philippines and about 2,000 miles (3,200 kilometers) south of Yokohama, Japan. For location, see PACIFIC ISLANDS (map). The Yap Islands are the chief islands of Yap District, one of six administrative districts of the Trust Territory of the Pacific Islands. Yap District has a population of about 7,900 and covers 46 square miles (119 square kilometers). The Yap Islands include four large islands and 10 smaller islands. The main islands are Yap (the largest), Gagil-Tomil, Map, and Rumung. The island group covers 39 square miles (101 square kilometers) and has a population of about 5,100. The islands are composed of ancient crystalline rocks and have a rugged surface. Long, narrow channels separate the islands, and coral reefs surround them. One large break in the reefs allows small vessels to enter a natural harbor.

The people are Micronesians with mixtures of Indonesian stock. The women do most of the work in the fields. Taro, bananas, yams, coconuts, and tropical fruits are the main crops. The men dive under water with spears to catch fish.

Spaniards first discovered and controlled Yap. In 1899, Spain sold the islands to Germany. In 1905, Yap became internationally important as a cable station between the United States, the Netherlands Indies (now Indonesia), and Japan. After World War I, the League of Nations put Yap under Japanese mandate. The United States protested this action. In 1921, the two nations signed a treaty by which the United States recognized the Japanese mandate. In return, Japan granted the United States equal rights to cable and radio service through Yap, and allowed U.S. citizens free entry there.

During World War II, the Japanese used the island group as a naval and air base. American troops occupied Yap after the war ended, and in 1947 the islands came under control of the United States, as a trusteeship under the United Nations.   EDWIN H. BRYAN, JR.

See also CAROLINE ISLANDS; PACIFIC ISLANDS, TRUST TERRITORY OF THE; RACES, HUMAN (picture: Micronesian).

YAQUI INDIANS, *YAH kee*, are a tribe that lives in Mexico, Arizona, and California. They are noted for their religious ceremonies, which blend concepts of Roman Catholicism with ancient tribal customs. On holy days, the Yaqui perform ancient dances and rituals in honor of Jesus Christ, the Virgin Mary, and tribal patron saints.

The ancient Yaqui lived along the Yaqui River in northwestern Mexico. They raised beans, corn, and squash. They also hunted game and gathered wild plants. The Yaqui lived in small, scattered villages and had no central government.

Yaqui warriors defeated the Spanish invaders who entered their territory in 1533 and 1609. In 1610, the Yaqui made a treaty with the Spaniards and asked for Jesuit missionaries to settle in their villages. The Yaqui wanted the Jesuits to teach them how to raise wheat, fruit, and livestock.

The Jesuits arrived in 1617, and the Yaqui lived prosperously for the next 120 years. They learned the Roman Catholic religion and blended it with their own culture. The Jesuits helped the Yaqui organize the villages into eight towns, which became centers of Yaqui religion and government.

In the 1730's, many Yaqui became dissatisfied with the Jesuits and the Spanish colonial government. Some of the Indians sought independence. The tribe fought Spanish and Mexican troops in a series of bloody wars that lasted until the 1900's. During these wars, the Mexican government forced many Yaqui to leave their homeland and settle in other parts of Mexico. Some Yaqui fled into the United States.   DON D. FOWLER

YARD is a unit of length. It is equal to 3 feet, or 36 inches. One yard equals 0.9144 meter. See also WEIGHTS AND MEASURES.   E. G. STRAUS

YARMOUTH. See GREAT YARMOUTH.

YARMOUTH, *YAHR muth,* Nova Scotia (pop. 7,801), lies at the entrance to the Bay of Fundy. For location, see NOVA SCOTIA (political map). Yarmouth, county seat of Yarmouth County, is a summer resort and an agricultural center. Its industries include lobster fishing, fish processing, textile manufacturing, and lumbering. Some historians believe that Yarmouth was the site of the first settlement of Norsemen in North America, about A.D. 1000. New England settlers founded Yarmouth in 1761.   THOMAS H. RADDALL

YARMOUTH BLOATER. See GREAT YARMOUTH; HERRING (Uses).

YARN. See COTTON (Spinning); WOOL.

YATES, ELIZABETH (1905-   ), an American author, won the Newbery medal in 1951 for *Amos Fortune, Free Man,* a biography of an American slave who purchased his freedom. Her other works include *High Holiday* (1938); *Once in the Year* (1947); *A Place for Peter* (1952); *An Easter Story* (1967); and *With Pipe, Paddle and Song* (1968). She was born in Buffalo, N.Y.

YAW. See AIRPLANE (Flying an Airplane; diagram).

YAWATA, *yah wah tah,* is the chief center of Japan's heavy industry. It lies on the coast of northern Kyushu. Japanese government mills there make pig iron from imported ore and produce much of Japan's steel. The city is near coal mines and has coke plants. It is part of the city of Kitakyushu (see KITAKYUSHU). Yawata was the target of the first United States B-29 air raid on Japan, June 15, 1944.   HUGH BORTON

YAWL is a two-masted sailboat. Its back mast, called the *jigger, mizzen,* or *dandy,* is usually placed behind the rudder post, and is less than half the height of the main-mast.

See also SAILING (picture: Types of Sailboats).

YAWNING is the act of opening the mouth wide, or *gaping.* The usual yawn is due to drowsiness or fatigue. It is a sign that the body needs sleep. Yawning is an involuntary reflex. After the act has started, it is almost impossible to stop it. The mouth can be held closed, but the yawning muscles still contract.

People and animals yawn when oxygen is slowly cut

Ford Motor Co.

The Legal Yard in the time of King Henry I of England was the distance from the king's nose to about the end of his thumb.

off from them, and when the muscles are thoroughly relaxed. A person who yawns often is probably not getting enough oxygen. He may need better ventilation, or exercise. He will generally stop yawning if he drinks a beverage, or bathes his face with cold water. Scientists are not sure what part of the nervous system controls yawning, but it may be the *mesencephalon* (midbrain) in the brain. One purpose of yawning may be to awaken a person by stretching the muscles and helping the blood to circulate.   ARTHUR C. GUYTON

YAWS, also called FRAMBESIA, is a disease that attacks chiefly children of humid tropical regions. Various kinds of *lesions* (skin eruptions) appear and disappear during the course of the disease, which may last several years. Yaws attacks the skin and bones, but it causes death in only rare cases.

Bacteria called *spirochetes* cause yaws. The spirochetes, which resemble those that cause syphilis, enter the body through a break in the skin. In most cases, a person catches the disease from contact with an infected individual.

Three to four weeks after infection, a small, yellow-red, pimplelike lesion forms where the spirochetes entered the body. Other lesions, some of which resemble raspberries, break out weeks or months later. Painful sores often form on the soles of the feet and make walking difficult. Still later, tumorlike lesions may develop. The disease may gradually destroy the cartilage of the nose and cripple bones and joints.

Yaws can be cured by injections of penicillin. The widespread use of this drug has greatly reduced the number of cases of yaws since the 1950's. THOMAS H. WELLER

YAZOO FRAUD. In 1795, Georgia's general assembly sold state-owned land on the Yazoo River to speculators. Most of the legislators were bribed. The people became indignant, and the legislature passed a Rescinding Act in 1796. But the speculators refused to give up their bargain. The Supreme Court ruled in 1810 that the Rescinding Act was unconstitutional. But, by this time, Georgia had sold its western lands to the federal government. Congress appropriated over $4,200,-000 to settle the Yazoo claims in 1814.   ALBERT B. SAYE

YAZOO RIVER, *YAZ oo*, a tributary of the Mississippi, drains 13,400 square miles (34,710 square kilometers) in the state of Mississippi (see MISSISSIPPI [physical map]). The Tallahatchie and Yalobusha rivers unite to form the Yazoo River near Greenwood, Miss. The Yazoo River flows south for 188 miles (303 kilometers) and flows into the Mississippi River near Vicksburg, Miss.

Light draft vessels can sail up the Yazoo-Tallahatchie river system for about 230 miles (370 kilometers). Four flood-control reservoirs were built on Yazoo tributaries between 1940 and 1954. They have greatly reduced flood damage in the Yazoo Delta.   M. W. MYERS

YEAGER, CHARLES ELWOOD (1923-   ), was the first man to fly faster than the speed of sound. He accomplished this on Oct. 14, 1947, in a Bell X-1 rocket airplane. He set another speed record on Dec. 12, 1953, by flying $2\frac{1}{2}$ times the speed of sound in a Bell X-1A. Yeager was born in Myra, W.Va. During World War II (1939-1945), he served as a fighter pilot. In 1975, Yeager retired from the military with the rank of brigadier general.   ROBERT B. HOTZ

YEAR is the time the earth takes to make one complete revolution around the sun. There are two different kinds of years which are used by astronomers. The *solar, equinoctial,* or *tropical* year is the time between two passages of the sun through the vernal equinox, which occurs in March. This year is 365 days, 5 hours, 48 minutes, and 46 seconds long. This year is used for all practical and astronomical purposes. It is the basis of our common or calendar year.

The *sidereal* year is made up of 365 days, 6 hours, 9 minutes, and 9.5 seconds. This is the time it takes the earth to return to the same place in its orbit, with reference to the fixed stars. The sidereal year is longer than the solar year because of the *precession of the equinoxes*. The sidereal year is seldom used except in the calculations of astronomers.

The Calendar Year is only 365 days long, and so we have to add an extra day every four years to correct the difference in time between the calendar year and the solar year. This fourth year is called *leap year*, and the extra day is February 29. Adding an extra day every fourth year makes the average calendar year 11 minutes, 14 seconds too long. So, the day is not added in the century years, except in those divisible by 400. The years 1700, 1800, and 1900 have had only 365 days. The year 2000 will contain 366 days. Thus the difference between calendar and solar years will vary only one day over a period of several thousand years.

The *lunar year* is made up of 12 lunar months. The ancient Greeks used this year. It contained 354 days.

In most Christian nations the calendar year begins on January 1. During the Middle Ages, however, most European nations considered March 1 or March 25, Annunciation Day, as the first day of the calendar year. By 1600, nearly all civilized countries except England recognized January 1 as the first day of the year. England adopted the Gregorian calendar, which recognized January 1 as the beginning of the year, on September 14, 1752.

The Church Calendar, which is used in the Roman Catholic and in most Protestant churches, is regulated partly by the solar and partly by the lunar year. This causes a difference between the fixed feast days, which always fall on the same day every year, and movable feasts such as Easter, whose dates vary from year to year. The fixed feast days are determined by the solar year, and the movable feast days, by the lunar year.

In ancient Roman times, before the Julian calendar was adopted, the year began on March 1. The Jewish year begins near the time of the autumnal equinox, around the 22nd of September. The Islamic year, however, is based on the changing phases of the moon and lasts for 354 days. Therefore, the beginning of the Islamic year continually falls earlier in the seasons. Thirty Islamic years make up a cycle during which there are 11 leap years. These leap years occur at irregular intervals.   PAUL SOLLENBERGER

Related Articles in WORLD BOOK include:

A.D.	Christian Era	Olympiad
B.C.	Equinox	Season
Calendar	Leap Year	

YEAR OF CONFUSION. See CALENDAR (The Julian Calendar).

YEARDLEY, SIR GEORGE. See HOUSE OF BURGESSES.

YEAST, *yeest.* The yeast with which people are most familiar is a substance that bakers put in dough to make it rise. This yeast contains a mass of tiny, one-celled plants called *yeasts*. Yeasts are among the simplest kinds of plants. Like mushrooms, they belong to the group of plants called *fungi*.

Yeasts increase very rapidly, and the tiny plants float in the air almost everywhere. Some yeasts form new plants by a process called *budding*. A small part of the cell wall swells out, and a wall of cellulose soon shuts off this new growth from the parent plant. It becomes an independent cell, and soon grows other buds. Sometimes all the cells cling together in chains that later break up. Some yeast plants increase simply by dividing in two. This process is called *fission*.

What Yeast Does. The French scientist Charles Cagniard de la Tour (1777-1859) discovered in 1857 that yeasts are living plants which increase by budding. He also found that these plants can act on sugar to change it to alcohol. This important chemical change is part of a process of fermentation, which yeasts produce in organic substances. It is a result of the way yeast plants get their food. While each cell is growing, it produces substances known as *enzymes*, or *ferments*. Yeasts may form various enzymes, including *diastase*, *invertase*, and a group of enzymes called *zymase*. These enzymes cause fermentation by breaking down starch and sugar in solution. Diastase breaks down starch. Invertase causes one sugar to form another sugar. Zymase breaks down the sugar. Zymase and invertase can work only in the right moisture and temperature—about 80° to 85° F. (27° to 29° C).

Types of Yeast. Bakers use two forms of commercial yeast—dry and compressed. Dry yeast is made by mixing yeast mass and corn meal into cakes, and drying them. In this form, the yeast cells are inactive. They will keep indefinitely, and become active only when they are mixed with the right material. Compressed yeast contains enough starch and moisture to start fermentation in a short time. It cannot be stored long, and must be kept cool until used.

Mixing yeast with dough to ferment it is called *leavening* the dough. With dry yeast, the baker must first make a *sponge*. This is a mixture of yeast, flour, and water. Sugar may be added to hasten the fermentation. The sponge is allowed to stand a few hours—sometimes overnight. Then it is mixed with flour and more liquid—water, milk, potato water, or whey—to make the dough. This dough is kneaded thoroughly, covered, and set to "rise." With compressed yeast, the baker does not have to prepare a sponge.

Yeast Makes Bread Dough Rise. At left, the yeast has just been added to the dough. In about two hours it has caused the dough to rise, center, to about twice its original size. At the right is the baked loaf of crusty, tasty bread.

Fred Korth, Wheat Flour Institute

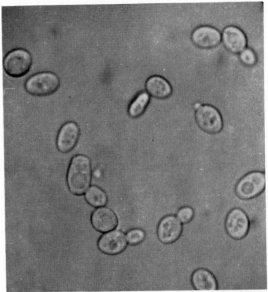

Red Star Yeast & Products Co.

Budding of Yeast Cells to form new plants can be seen in this highly magnified picture of the simple, one-celled plants.

How Yeast Works. Enzymes from the yeast cells attack the starch in the flour, and change it to sugar. The sugar is then changed to alcohol and carbon dioxide gas. The gas bubbles up through the mixture, forming the familiar bubbles in bread dough, and making the mass light and porous. When the bread is baked, the alcohol evaporates and the yeast plants are destroyed. If bread is baked properly, it should have no taste of alcohol or yeast. Sometimes dough is left to rise too long, and the fermentation forms acid. This condition results in sour bread. Fermentation by yeast is also important in making alcoholic beverages, such as beer and ale.

Making Yeast. In the days before yeast cakes were sold in the stores, homemakers made their own yeast. They prepared a batter of flour, potato water, salt, and sugar, and left it uncovered for several hours. Yeast cells in the air furnished the enzymes. This process was uncertain, because types of yeast not suitable for bread sometimes lodged in the batter. Some housekeepers still like to use this old-fashioned liquid yeast. But they may also buy prepared yeast and add a small amount to make sure of the quality. The mixture will keep a long time in a cool place.

Commercial yeast is prepared by grinding corn and rye to a mash and mixing it with filtered water. Sprouted barley, or malt, is then added. The malt changes the starch in the grain to malt sugar. Next, a culture of the bacteria which turn milk sour is added to the mixture. The mash is then filtered. The liquid, called *wort*, is then ready to serve as food for living yeast cells. The yeasts increase rapidly in this liquid. When the fermentation of the wort is violent, the yeast is skimmed off. It is pressed to free it from water. Finally the mass is molded, and cut into cakes. Starch is usually added to compressed yeast before the pressing, but it must be mentioned on the label.   LEWIS HANFORD TIFFANY

See also BREAD; BREWING; ENZYME; FERMENTATION; GLUTEN.

YEATS, *yayts,* **WILLIAM BUTLER** (1865-1939), an Irish poet and dramatist, won the 1923 Nobel prize for literature. Many critics consider him the greatest poet of his time. Yeats led the Irish Literary Revival, a movement of the late 1800's and early 1900's that stimulated new appreciation of traditional Irish literature. It also encouraged the creation of new works written in the spirit of Irish culture, as distinct from English culture.

Yeats developed elaborate theories about history as a recurring cycle of events. He expressed his personal views about history and life through the use of old Irish tales and the facts and legends of Irish history.

Ewing Galloway
William Butler Yeats

His views also reflect his belief in the supernatural. Yeats published his theories in *A Vision* (1925), a book that is useful as a guide to some of his more difficult poems.

Yeats was born in Dublin and lived in London for part of his childhood. He spent many holidays in Sligo, a county in western Ireland that he loved and often wrote about. In 1898, he joined the authors Lady Gregory and Edward Martyn in establishing the Irish Literary Theatre. It was reorganized in 1904 as the Abbey Theatre, which became world famous.

The Irish Literary Theatre was founded partly to support Irish nationalism by encouraging the writing and production of plays about Irish life. The theater performed most of Yeats's 26 plays, and he served until his death as one of the directors who managed the institution. The theater's first production was Yeats's *The Countess Cathleen,* written in 1891. This play was inspired in part by the author's love for Maud Gonne, a beautiful Irish nationalist leader. She became the subject of many of his plays and love lyrics.

Yeats's verse, unlike that of most poets, improved as he grew older. He wrote much of his best work during the last 10 years of his life. His most important works were published in *Collected Poems* (1950) and *Collected Plays* (1952). *Memoirs,* a collection of autobiographical writings, was published in 1973. DARCY O'BRIEN

YEDO, or EDO. See TOKYO (History).

YELLOW is one of the basic colors found in light and pigments. It lies about in the middle of the spectrum of visible light. It is considered a primary color in pigments and a complementary color in light. Mixed with blue pigment, yellow forms green. Mixed with red pigment, it makes orange. Because the sun looks yellow, some primitive tribes consider the color sacred. Yellow is the national color of China. Strong light makes yellow appear more intense, although it dims most other colors. Early peoples made yellow dye from saffron in the crocus plant. Artists often use gamboge yellow, made from gum resin.

See also COLOR.

YELLOW DAISY. See BLACK-EYED SUSAN.

YELLOW-DOG CONTRACTS were agreements between employers and employees in which workers promised not to join a union, assist a union, or take part in any group action against the employer. A yellow-dog contract, backed by court injunctions, was a device that employers used to oppose union organization in their plants.

The Norris-La Guardia Act of 1932 made it impossible to enforce such contracts in federal courts. The National Labor Relations Act of 1935 gave employees the right to join unions of their choice. GERALD G. SOMERS

YELLOW FEVER is a virus disease carried by certain mosquitoes. The virus damages many tissues in man's body, but especially the liver. As a result of this damage, the liver cannot function properly and yellow bile pigments gather in the skin. These pigments make the skin look yellow and give the disease its name.

In most cases, the *Aëdes aegypti* mosquito carries the yellow fever virus from one person to another. Some monkeys and sloths may also be infected. When the mosquito bites an infected person or animal, the virus enters the insect's body, where it develops rapidly. After 9 to 12 days, the bite of the mosquito can produce yellow fever. A mosquito that is infected with the virus can transmit the disease for the rest of its life.

Symptoms. The first stage of yellow fever begins from three to six days after a person has been bitten. The victim develops a fever, headache, and dizziness, and his muscles ache. In many persons, the disease progresses no further. But in others, the fever drops for a day or two and then rises steeply. The skin turns yellow and the patient bleeds from the gums and from the lining of the stomach.

Many patients recover from this stage. But some become delirious and go into a coma. Death follows the coma in most cases. Only from 2 to 5 per cent of all cases of yellow fever result in death, though the figure may be higher during an epidemic. Patients who recover have lifelong immunity to the disease.

Prevention. Yellow fever was once widespread throughout Central America, parts of South America, Africa, and some tropical islands. Today, it is under control in most areas. A U.S. Army physician, William Gorgas, developed mosquito control measures that eliminated the disease as a major health menace in the Panama Canal Zone. The disease can also be prevented with a vaccine developed in 1937 by Max Theiler, a South African research physician.

The conquest of yellow fever was one of the great achievements of modern medicine. In 1881, Carlos Finlay, a Cuban physician, suggested that a mosquito transmitted the disease. Walter Reed, a U.S. Army doctor, proved that yellow fever was carried by a mosquito. Reed suggested that the cause was a microorganism. In 1927, three research physicians proved that the microorganism was a virus. A. WILLIAM HOLMES

Related Articles in WORLD BOOK include:
Finlay, Carlos Juan
Gorgas (William C.)
Lazear, Jesse W.
Panama Canal (Victory Over Disease)
Reed, Walter
Tennessee (Reconstruction)
Theiler, Max

YELLOW FLAG. See QUARANTINE.

YELLOW GOLD. See ALLOY (Costly and Ornamental Alloys).

YELLOW JACKET is a small wasp with black and yellow stripes. Yellow jackets belong to the group called the social wasps, and are relatives of the hornets. Yellow jackets, like hornets, make their nests of paper. They form the paper by chewing up old wood and plant fibers. Yellow jackets produce a finer paper than hornets. The nests have several stories of cells inside a thick paper covering. There are three classes among these wasps. They are the workers, queens, and the males, or drones. In this respect, the wasps resemble the bees.

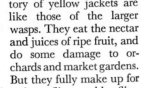

Yellow jackets sometimes hang their nests from trees or bushes. Sometimes they build them in the ground, in holes dug by gophers or field mice. Sometimes they build nests in the hollows of stumps or stone fences.

The habits and life history of yellow jackets are like those of the larger wasps. They eat the nectar and juices of ripe fruit, and do some damage to orchards and market gardens. But they fully make up for this damage by destroying houseflies, stable flies, caterpillars, and other harmful insects.

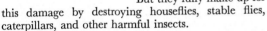
Gayle Pickwell
Queen Yellow Jacket

Scientific Classification. Yellow jackets are in the colonial wasp family, *Vespidae*. The common yellow jacket is genus *Vespula*, species *V. pennsylvanica*.   DALE W. JENKINS

YELLOW JASMINE. See GELSEMIUM.

YELLOW JOURNALISM. See JOURNALISM (History); OUTCAULT, RICHARD FELTON.

YELLOW POPLAR. See TULIP TREE.

YELLOW PUCCOON. See GOLDENSEAL.

YELLOW RACE. See RACES, HUMAN (The Three-Race Theory).

YELLOW RIVER. See HUANG HO.

YELLOW SEA is an arm of the Pacific Ocean extending inland for about 400 miles (640 kilometers) between the east coast of China and Korea. The waters along the banks here are a yellow, muddy color, and the Chinese have named this part of the ocean the *Huang Hai* (Yellow Sea). The Yellow Sea gets its name from deposits of yellow earth (*huang-tu*) brought to the sea by the Huang and Yangtze rivers. For location, see CHINA (political map). The sea is about 300 feet (91 meters) deep in its deepest part. It covers 480,000 square miles (1,243,194 square kilometers).

Tsingtao lies on the Chinese coast of the Yellow Sea, on the southern shore of the Shan-tung Peninsula. Port Arthur and Dairen are at the southern end of China's Liao-tung Peninsula. The Korea Strait connects the Yellow Sea with the Sea of Japan. At the north, the Yellow Sea forms Lai-chou Bay, the Po Gulf, the Liao-tung Gulf, and Korea Bay.   BOSTWICK H. KETCHUM

YELLOW TREFOIL. See SHAMROCK.

YELLOWFIN. See TUNA.

YELLOWHAMMER is the popular name of two North American birds, the *yellow-shafted flicker* and the *great crested flycatcher*. The yellow-shafted flicker is a brown woodpecker with an ashy-gray head (see FLICKER). It ranges from the northernmost forests of Canada to southern Illinois and North Carolina. The yellow-shafted flicker spends much time on the ground, searching for ants. The great crested flycatcher ranges from South Carolina to Central America. The bird is about 8½ inches (22 centimeters) long, and is olive brown with yellow underneath.

Scientific Classification. The yellow-shafted flicker belongs to the woodpecker family, Picidae. It is genus *Colaptes*, species *C. auratus*. The great crested flycatcher belongs to the tyrant flycatcher family, Tyrannidae. It is classified as *Myiarchus crinitus*.   LEON A. HAUSMAN

See also BIRD (picture: Birds That Help Us [Yellow-Shafted Flicker]).

YELLOWHAMMER STATE. See ALABAMA.

YELLOWKNIFE (pop. 8,256) is the capital and largest city of Canada's Northwest Territories. It lies on the shores of Yellowknife Bay, a projection at the northern end of Great Slave Lake. See NORTHWEST TERRITORIES (map). Yellowknife is a mining center. Its industries include gold mining, prospecting, transportation, and tourism. Yellowknife was founded in the mid-1930's. It was incorporated as a city in 1970.

YELLOWLEGS is the name of two kinds of shore birds. They have black and white markings and long yellow legs. They live along shores and marshes during their flight north in the spring. They nest in northern North America. In the winter, they fly as far south as southern Chile, in South America. The two kinds of yellowlegs differ only in size. The *greater yellowlegs* averages 15 inches (38 centimeters) in length, while the *lesser* averages a little over 10 inches (25 centimeters). Yellowlegs lay four buff or tan eggs. They have a flutelike whistle that hunters imitated to entice them to decoys. At one time, they became rare, because so many people hunted them. Now, federal laws protect them and they are again becoming common.

Scientific Classification. Yellowlegs belong to the sandpiper family, Scolopacidae. The greater yellowlegs is classified as *Tringa melanoleuca;* the lesser yellowlegs is *T. flavipes*.   ALFRED M. BAILEY

See also BIRD (picture: Water Birds).

YELLOWS is a name for jaundice in dogs, sheep, and other animals. Jaundice is due to an improper flow of bile. Two common forms occur in dogs, one due to an abrupt stoppage by gallstones, the other to inflammation and hardening of the liver, which is often seen after distemper. The mucous membrane, skin, and whites of the eyes turn yellow. Other symptoms are vomiting, constipation, and green or deep yellow urine. Treatment should begin by feeding a scant diet free from fat. Baking soda taken by mouth or as an enema acts as a laxative to help remove the obstruction.

An infectious form of yellows is sometimes called canine typhus. It is caused by spirochetes, which are thought to be carried by rats. Besides the yellow color, the dog has a high fever, bleeding gums, and poor appetite. It may vomit and show bloody bowel discharges. A serum and a vaccine for this disease are sometimes useful. In fighting the disease it is important to control rats, because the disease is carried from rats by ticks. The living quarters of infected dogs should also be disinfected to destroy the ticks.   R. C. KLUSSENDORF

See also BILE; JAUNDICE.

Yellowstone's Natural Wonders include sparkling lakes and hot spring terraces. Yellowstone Lake, *left*, is the largest high-altitude lake in North America. The gently flowing waters of Minerva Terrace, *right*, deposit minerals that build up large rock terraces, one above the other.

YELLOWSTONE NATIONAL PARK, the oldest national park in the United States, is world famous for its many natural wonders. The park has more geysers and hot springs than any other area in the world. Yellowstone's scenic attractions include deep canyons, thundering waterfalls, sparkling lakes, and great expanses of evergreen forests broken by rolling meadows. Yellowstone is also the largest wildlife preserve in the United States. Bears, elk, and *bison* (American buffaloes) roam the park freely, and bald eagles, trumpeter swans, and white pelicans nest there.

Yellowstone lies in the northwest corner of Wyoming and spreads into Idaho and Montana. It covers 2,219,-823 acres (880,330 hectares). A series of high plateaus extends across the park, and mountains rise along Yellowstone's northern, eastern, and western boundaries. The highest point, Eagle Peak, rises 11,353 feet (3,460 meters) in the Absaroka Range in the east.

Most of Yellowstone's landscape was created by periodic volcanic eruptions more than 60,000 years ago. A large mass of molten rock still lies beneath the surface of the park. This rock, called *magma*, furnishes the heat for the park's geysers and hot springs. Yellowstone has more than 200 active geysers and thousands of hot springs.

The government established Yellowstone in 1872. More than 2 million persons visit the park yearly. Most of them drive through Yellowstone, but many explore large wilderness areas that can be reached only by foot or on horseback. The park has more than 300 miles (480 kilometers) of roads and over 1,000 miles (1,600 kilometers) of trails.

Touring Yellowstone

There are five entrances into Yellowstone National Park—two from Wyoming and three from Montana. Each entrance road connects with the Grand Loop, a

Yellowstone National Park

- Park boundary
- State boundary
- Road
- ▪ Point of interest

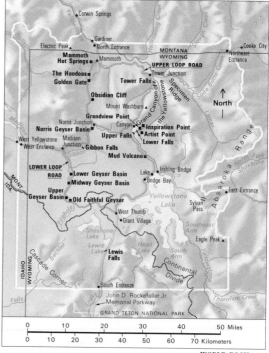

WORLD BOOK map

464

143-mile (230-kilometer) road that leads to major points of interest. The Grand Loop consists of the southern Lower Loop and the northern Upper Loop.

The Lower Loop. The west entrance road joins the Lower Loop at Madison Junction. Southbound, the Lower Loop leads to several geyser basins. The Lower Geyser Basin includes the Fountain Paint Pots, a series of hot springs and bubbling pools of mud called *mudpots* or *paint pots*. The mudpots are formed by steam and other gases that rose from holes in the ground and changed the surrounding rock into clay. Minerals in the clay give the mud various colors. Great Fountain Geyser, also in the Lower Geyser Basin, erupts from the center of a large pool. Its powerful bursts of water sometimes spout 200 feet (61 meters) above the pool.

Grand Prismatic Spring, in Midway Geyser Basin, is the largest hot spring in Yellowstone. Its pool, which has a deep blue center ringed with pink, measures 370 feet (113 meters) in diameter. Small water plants called *algae* give the edge of the pool its color.

The Upper Geyser Basin has a large group of geysers. Old Faithful, the most famous geyser in the park, erupts on an average of every 65 minutes. The actual intervals between eruptions vary from about 30 to 90 minutes. The geyser sends a stream of boiling water more than 100 feet (30 meters) into the air (see WYOMING [picture]). Other geysers in the area include Castle, Giantess, Grand, and Grotto. Morning Glory Pool, one of the most beautiful hot pools in the basin, resembles the morning-glory flower in color and shape.

Yellowstone Lake, which lies 7,733 feet (2,357 meters) above sea level, is the largest high-altitude lake in North America. It measures about 20 miles (32 kilometers) long and 14 miles (23 kilometers) wide. The lake has a shoreline of more than 100 miles (160 kilometers). Geysers and hot springs occur along the shore at West Thumb. The Lower Loop follows the shoreline of Yellowstone Lake for 21 miles (34 kilometers), providing a view of the lake's islands and the rugged mountains of the Absaroka Range.

The Grand Canyon of the Yellowstone cuts across the landscape for about 20 miles (32 kilometers). This canyon reaches a depth of about 2,000 feet (610 meters) in some places. The park was named for the yellow rock of the canyon walls. The Yellowstone River runs through the canyon, creating two waterfalls. The Lower Falls plunges 308 feet (94 meters) and the Upper Falls 109 feet (33 meters) into the canyon. Views of the canyon are especially beautiful from Artist Point, Grandview Point, and Inspiration Point. See NATIONAL PARK SYSTEM (picture: *Grand Canyon of the Yellowstone*); YELLOWSTONE RIVER.

The Upper Loop leads north from Canyon with a climb through the mountains of the Washburn Range. Mount Washburn rises 10,243 feet (3,122 meters) on the east. Specimen Ridge, which can be seen from the road leading to the northeast entrance, has some of the park's most famous petrified forests. The trees of these forests were buried by lava ash during volcanic eruptions over 60,000 years ago. Minerals from the ash seeped into the trees and turned them into stone.

At Mammoth Hot Springs, beautiful terraces are formed by gently flowing waters. The waters deposit a form of limestone called *travertine*, building large terraces one above the other. Algae and bacteria give some of the terraces various colors. Minerva Terrace and Opal Terrace are among the most beautiful in the area. The terraces change continually through the years as the waters build them up. Some springs die, and the terraces become gray and lifeless. The Hoodoos are the remains of old hot-spring terraces broken up by landslides.

Obsidian Cliff is a mountain of black glass that was formed by molten lava. Rootless plants called *lichens* now cover the glass in many places.

Norris Geyser Basin consists of hundreds of geysers, hot springs, and pools. It is the hottest and most active thermal area in Yellowstone. The temperature of the water in some of the springs reaches more than 200° F. (93° C). Several of the geysers may erupt at the same time. Steamboat Geyser set a world record by hurling its water 400 feet (120 meters) into the air.

Plants and Wildlife

Evergreen forests and mountain meadows cover most of Yellowstone. The most abundant tree is the lodgepole pine. Forests of Douglas fir, Engelman spruce, limber pine, and subalpine fir grow in some areas. During the summer, the mountain meadows display a variety of wildflowers, including the fringed gentian, Indian paintbrush, monkey flower, and mountain bluebell.

More than 200 species of birds and over 40 kinds of other animals live in Yellowstone. Trumpeter swans, blue herons, white pelicans, bald eagles, and gulls feed on fish in the park's lakes and rivers. These fish include cutthroat trout, grayling, mountain whitefish, and rainbow trout.

Elk are the most common of the large animals in the park. Approximately 20,000 elk live in the park in summer. About half of them stay there through the winter, but the rest wander south to warmer areas. Yellowstone has about 1,000 bison. These animals were widely hunted in the United States during the 1800's. The protection provided by the park helped save them from being killed off completely. About 250 grizzly bears also live in the park. Other large animals in Yellowstone include black bears, cougars, moose, and mule deer.

In Yellowstone, the balance of nature is maintained through natural controls such as disease, weather, and competition for food (see BALANCE OF NATURE). For example, if the park's elk population becomes too large, many of the animals die during winters when food is scarce. In addition, park regulations protect the animal and plant life from human interference. The feeding of bears is prohibited not only because it is dangerous but because it disrupts their natural feeding habits.

Recreational Activities

More than 1,000 miles (1,600 kilometers) of trails provide a wide choice of hiking routes through Yellowstone. Park naturalists offer free guided hikes and evening campfire programs. The Yellowstone Park Company has a program of bus tours, horseback trips, stagecoach rides, and cookouts in summer.

Fishing in the park's rivers and lakes is controlled by special regulations, and a permit is required. Hunting and the use of firearms are prohibited. Boats and canoes may be used on most of the lakes, but they are not allowed on the rivers. Visitors must obtain a permit to use any type of boat or canoe.

Campgrounds are located at Canyon, Madison Junction, Mammoth, Norris Junction, and other sites. A few major sites, including Canyon, Old Faithful, and Lake, have cottages, cabins, and hotels. Visitors who want to camp in the wilderness must have a permit.

During the winter, a heavy snow covers the park. All park roads, except the one connecting the north and northeast entrances, are closed. Snowmobiles may be used on the unplowed roads. Cross-country skiers can also travel over the trails through the park.

Further information may be obtained by writing Superintendent, Yellowstone National Park, Wyoming 82190.

History

Yellowstone's landscape was shaped by the action of volcanoes and glaciers through millions of years. A large mass of magma, which lies about 2 miles (3.2 kilometers) below the surface of the park, has erupted more than 27 times during the past 2 million years.

A major volcanic eruption occurred in the Yellowstone area about 2 million years ago. About 600,000 years ago, another explosion of magma and gas created a huge crater about 40 miles (64 kilometers) long and 30 miles (48 kilometers) wide. Yellowstone Lake now occupies part of this crater. During the eruption, lava covered more than 1,000 square miles (2,600 square kilometers) and formed the broad plateaus that characterize Yellowstone today.

Glaciers once covered much of the Yellowstone area. The last ones melted about 10,000 years ago and filled Yellowstone Lake. Outflow from the lake drained northward and helped shape the Grand Canyon of the Yellowstone.

One Indian tribe, the Sheepeaters, are known to have lived in the area of the present-day park. Other tribes, including the Bannock, the Crow, and the Blackfeet, crossed the area to hunt bison and elk.

The government obtained the Yellowstone region in 1803 as part of the Louisiana Purchase. John Colter, a member of the Lewis and Clark expedition, was probably the first white person to see Yellowstone. He traveled alone on foot through the area in 1807 and 1808 (see COLTER, JOHN). Many other trappers explored the area during the 1830's and 1840's. They returned with stories of spouting geysers, hot springs, and bubbling mudpots, but no one believed them.

In 1870, General Henry D. Washburn, the surveyor general of the Montana Territory, led an expedition to check out the reports of the trappers. In 1871, a government expedition led by Ferdinand V. Hayden, a geologist, documented the unusual features of the area.

In 1872, Congress passed a bill to establish the park and preserve its natural resources. Civilian superintendents administered the park for the first few years, but they were unable to stop widespread hunting and trapping there. The Army took over control of the park in 1886 and began to protect the wildlife. A detachment of cavalry occupied the park until 1916, when Congress established the National Park Service.

Today, the National Park Service manages Yellowstone. A superintendent, appointed by the director of the service and assisted by park rangers, naturalists, and a maintenance staff, administers the park. Park headquarters are at Mammoth.

Critically reviewed by YELLOWSTONE NATIONAL PARK

YELLOWSTONE RIVER rises near the Continental Divide in northwestern Wyoming and flows north into Yellowstone National Park. For location, see WYOMING (physical map). There it forms Yellowstone Lake, which covers 137 square miles (355 square kilometers) at an elevation of 7,731 feet (2,356 meters). The lake is the largest high-elevation lake in North America. North of the lake, the river plunges 109 feet (33 meters) over its upper falls and 308 feet (94 meters) over its lower falls into Yellowstone Canyon. Then it flows northeast across the Great Plains of Montana, where it is used for irrigation. The Yellowstone flows a total distance of 671 miles (1,080 kilometers) and joins the Missouri River on the Montana-North Dakota line. See also MONTANA (picture). JOHN H. GARLAND

YELLOWTAIL DAM. See BIGHORN RIVER; MONTANA (The Mid-1900's; picture).

YELLOWTHROAT is a common wood warbler that lives in North America. Yellowthroats grow about the size of a small wren. They live in wet grassy or marshy areas, where they can hide among the tall reeds. They have olive-green backs, and bright orange-yellow throats. The male has a black mask on its face, with a white border above it. These birds nest on or near the ground. The female usually lays four eggs.

Scientists recognize 12 *races* (subspecies) of common yellowthroat. These groups differ slightly in color and size. Yellowthroats breed within an area stretching from Ontario and southeastern Alaska south to Mexico. They generally spend the winter in an area extending from the Gulf States into Central America.

Belding's yellowthroat is slightly larger, with solid yellow underparts and a yellow border on the black mask of the male. It lives in Baja California, Mexico.

Scientific Classification. Yellowthroats belong to the wood warbler family, *Parulidae.* The common yellowthroat is genus *Geothlypis*, species *G. trichas.* Belding's yellowthroat is *G. beldingi.* GEORGE E. HUDSON

Ron Austing, Photo Researchers

The Yellowthroat is about as big as a wren. It is usually found in swampy areas with high grass, where it can hide easily.

Yemen (Aden)

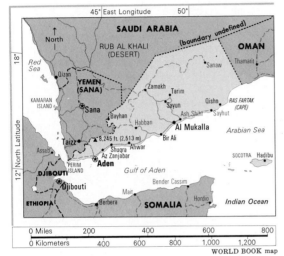

- ⊛ Capital
- • Other city or town
- —— Road
- – – – Trail
- ▲ Mountain peak

WORLD BOOK map

YEMEN (ADEN) is an independent country on the southern edge of the Arabian Peninsula. It extends from the mouth of the Red Sea eastward along the Indian Ocean about 740 miles (1,191 kilometers) to the boundary of Oman. Three islands—Socotra in the Indian Ocean, and Kamaran and Perim in the Red Sea—are part of the country. About 90 per cent of the people of Yemen (Aden) are Arabs. The rest are Indians, Pakistanis, or East Africans.

Most of Yemen (Aden) is hot and dry. There are only a few fertile areas where the land can be farmed. Aden is the nation's capital and largest city. It is also an important port and oil center.

Yemen (Aden) gained independence from Great Britain on Nov. 30, 1967. The country's full name in Arabic, the official language, is JUMHURIYYAT AL-YEMEN ASH-SHAABIYYAH AL-DIMUGRATIYYAH (PEOPLE'S DEMOCRATIC REPUBLIC OF YEMEN). The nation is often called *Yemen (Aden), South Yemen,* or *Southern Yemen* to distinguish it from Yemen (Sana)—its neighbor to the northwest.

Government. Yemen (Aden) is governed by the United Political Organization National Front (UPONF), the country's only political party. A three-member Presidential Council made up of UPONF leaders heads the government. A Cabinet appointed by the council's

chairman helps carry out government operations.

The country is divided into six areas called *governorates.* Each is headed by a governor. Yemen (Aden) is a member of the United Nations and the Arab League.

People. About 1,969,000 people live in Yemen (Aden). About 90 per cent are Arabs of various tribes. The rest are Indians, Pakistanis, or East Africans. Almost all the people are Muslims of the Shafii sect.

The British brought Western ways of life to Aden, and some of the people there live much as Europeans do. They wear Western-style clothing, live in modern houses or apartments along broad streets, and shop in supermarkets. Others follow an older way of life. They live in thick-walled houses along narrow, twisting alleys, and they shop in open-air markets. Most of the men wear the striped *futa* (kilt). On their heads, the men wear skullcaps, turbans, or tall round hats called *tarbooshes.* Women appear in public in veils and dark, shapeless clothing.

Each street in Aden's market district has its own trade. Workers produce handicrafts in small, one-room shops. They make inlaid *jambiyas* (daggers), wooden chests, brassware, and jewelry.

Aden has many cafes where the men sit and drink strong, bitter coffee. In the afternoon, many men meet in cafes and chew the leaves of the qat plant. These leaves contain a drug that gives people a feeling of contentment.

On the coast and on Socotra Island, the people live by fishing. The men spear fish near the shore from dugout canoes called *sambuqs,* or in deeper water from single-sail *dhows.* Inland are valleys and a few scattered oases where the people live by farming. Some farm families live in towns, such as Sayun, that have mudbrick houses standing three or four stories high. Others live in small villages close to the land they farm. Most families outside Aden have at least one member working as a trader or merchant in India, Java, or Sumatra.

In the desert, the people are herders. They travel constantly in search of water and food for their sheep and goats. Most of the men own nothing but their clothes and their curved jambiya. Women are unveiled.

─────── **FACTS IN BRIEF** ───────

Capital: Aden.

Official Language: Arabic.

Area: 128,560 sq. mi. (332,968 km²). *Coastline*—about 740 mi. (1,191 km).

Elevation: *Highest*—Jabal Thamir, 8,245 ft. (2,513 m). *Lowest*—sea level.

Population: *Estimated 1980 Population*—1,969,000; distribution, 63 per cent rural, 37 per cent urban; density, 16 persons per sq. mi. (6 persons per km²). *1973 Census*—1,590,275. *Estimated 1985 Population*—2,294,000.

Chief Products: *Agriculture*—barley, cotton, dates, millet, sorghum, wheat. *Industry*—dyeing, fishing, oil refining, ship refueling, tanning, weaving.

Flag: Red, white, and black horizontal stripes with a red star on a blue triangle at the mast. See FLAG (color picture: Flags of Asia and the Pacific).

Money: *Basic Unit*—dinar.

William Spencer, the contributor of this article, is Professor of History at Florida State University and the author of several books about the Arab world.

Many are tattooed on their faces and arms with tribal marks.

Rice, bread, lamb, and fish are the chief foods in Yemen (Aden). But most of the country's desert people live on bread and on ilb nuts, which they gather from wild thorn trees.

The British established the first public schools in Yemen (Aden). In the early 1970's, the nation had 905 elementary schools, 66 intermediate schools, 10 high schools, and 5 teacher training schools. The law requires all children to go to school for seven years. But some areas have no schools, and many children receive little or no education. About 10 per cent of the people can read and write.

Land. Yemen (Aden) covers 128,560 square miles (332,968 square kilometers), an area a little larger than that of New Mexico. The mainland part of the country has three regions: (1) the Coastal Plain, which is mostly sand but has a few fertile areas; (2) a dry, hilly plateau cut by deep valleys called *wadis* that have some rich farmland; and (3) the Empty Quarter, a stony desert that extends into Saudi Arabia. Socotra has a narrow coastal plain and a steep, rugged interior.

Yemen (Aden) is hot most of the year. Temperatures range from 61° to 106° F. (16° to 41° C) in Aden and climb to 130° F. (54° C) in the desert. Rainfall averages 3 inches (7.6 centimeters) a year.

Economy. Aden's oil refinery and port provide Yemen (Aden) with most of its income. The oil refinery can process about 50 million barrels of oil a year. Ships of many nations use the port for refueling, repairs, and transferring cargoes.

Outside of Aden, the economy is largely undeveloped. The country has no known mineral resources. Agriculture is limited to the few areas that have underground water for irrigation. Farmers grow three or four crops a year of millet, sorghum, sesame, wheat, and barley.

History. In ancient times, southern Arabia grew rich because it lay along important trade routes between Europe, Asia, and Africa. Cities were built and the land was irrigated. But fighting among local leaders and invasions from the north and east brought widespread destruction. In the 600's, the Prophet Muhammad's son-in-law, Ali, introduced Islam to the people.

Great Britain seized Aden in 1839, after people from the town robbed a wrecked British ship. Aden became an important refueling stop for British ships going to India by way of the Suez Canal and the Red Sea. Aden was a part of British India until 1937, when it became a British crown colony.

To protect Aden from Yemen, which claimed the town, Britain extended its control to the tribal states in the region around Aden. Britain signed treaties with the tribal leaders, promising protection and aid in return for loyalty. The region came to be known as the Aden Protectorate.

In 1959, six tribal states in the protectorate formed the Federation of the Arab Emirates of the South. Britain signed a treaty with the federation, promising to grant independence. The date for independence was later set for 1967. Meanwhile, the British controlled the federation's foreign policy and provided military

WORLD BOOK photo by Henry Gill

An Open-Air Shop in Aden sells a wide variety of goods. The clerks are wearing the *futa* (kilt).

protection and economic aid. In 1962, the name of the federation was changed to the Federation of South Arabia. By 1965, Aden and all but four of the tribal states in the protectorate had become members of the federation.

In the early 1960's, Britain tried to form a representative government that would rule the federation after independence. But Arab nationalist leaders in Aden and tribal leaders in the protectorate both wanted to rule. The nationalists began a terror campaign against the British and the tribal leaders. Two nationalist groups, the National Liberation Front (NLF) and the Front for the Liberation of Occupied South Yemen (FLOSY), also fought each other.

In late 1967, the federation government collapsed. Britain announced that it would withdraw its troops and give power to any group that could set up a government. The NLF emerged as the most powerful group in the federation. On Nov. 30, 1967, the last British troops were withdrawn, and the NLF formed a government and proclaimed the federation an independent country.

In 1975, the NLF and smaller political groups merged and formed the United Political Organization National Front. The leaders of Yemen (Aden) favor some political principles of Karl Marx, one of the founders of Communism. The leaders of neighboring Yemen (Sana) oppose such principles. Border clashes took place between Yemen (Aden) and Yemen (Sana) from time to time during the 1970's. In February 1979, the fighting became widespread. An armistice ended the fighting between the two countries in March.　　WILLIAM SPENCER

See also ADEN; ARAB LEAGUE; SOUTH ARABIA, FEDERATION OF; MADINAT ASH SHAB.

Yemen (Sana)

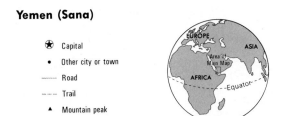

★   Capital

●   Other city or town

——   Road

- - -   Trail

▲   Mountain peak

WORLD BOOK map

YEMEN (SANA) is a country in the southwestern corner of the Arabian Peninsula. It borders on the Red Sea on the west. Yemen (Sana) covers 75,290 square miles (195,000 square kilometers), and is about the same size as South Dakota. Sana is its capital. See SANA.

The country's fertile high interior is the most beautiful and best cultivated part of Arabia. Almost as many people live there as in the rest of the peninsula.

The people of Yemen (Sana) are farmers and craftworkers. The country is famous for its Mocha coffee. The Yemeni have been famous for their textiles, leather work, and iron work since ancient times.

The country's full name in Arabic, the official language, is AL-JUMHURIYAH AL ARABIYAH AL YAMANIYAH (THE YEMEN ARAB REPUBLIC). The country is often called *Yemen* (*Sana*), *North Yemen*, or *Northern Yemen* to distinguish it from Yemen (Aden)—its neighbor to the southeast.

Douglas D. Crary, the contributor of this article, is Professor Emeritus of Geography at the University of Michigan.

Government. From A.D. 897 to 1962, an *imam* (ruler) was the political and religious leader, although Egyptians and Turks sometimes controlled the country. In 1962, a group of military officers overthrew the imam and set up a republic. The 1970 Constitution provided for a Cabinet, headed by a prime minister, and for a Republican Council, elected by the legislature. But in 1974, army leaders suspended the Constitution and dissolved the legislature. A council composed of military leaders took control of the government. The head of the council serves as the nation's president.

People. Most of the people of Yemen (Sana) are Arabs. The Hashid, Khawlan, and Baqil are the largest and most powerful tribes. The men wear cotton breeches and shirts. The women wear long robes and black shawls and veils on their heads. In the High Yemen, the people build mud or stone houses. In the Tihamah, most people live in straw huts. People in the cities often build one-story mud brick houses. Wealthy Yemenis live in houses that are two to six floors high. They wear white silk robes, turbans, and leather sandals.

The tribes are divided into two main groups according to their Muslim beliefs. The largest group is the Shiites of the Zaydi sect. Many of them live in the High Yemen and Sana. The imams were Zaydis. A group of Zaydis called the Sayyids served in the government, administered the courts, and collected taxes. The Zaydis claimed that they were chosen by God to govern, because they are descendants of Muhammad. The people in the southern part of Yemen (Sana), especially those in Taizz and the Tihamah ports, are Sunnites of the Shafi sect. This sect has a powerful merchant class that controls commerce. The division between the politically powerful Zaydis and the wealthy Shafis has caused bitterness between them. The Zaydis emphasized education. But schooling was often limited to reading, writing, and studying Muslim law and tradition. Only about 15 per cent of the Yemeni can read and write.

Land. Yemen (Sana) has three land regions: a coastal plain, a cliff region, and a high interior.

A plain called the *Tihamah* extends inland from the Red Sea for 20 to 50 miles (32 to 80 kilometers). It is hot and humid, but receives less than 10 inches (25 centimeters) of rain a year. Temperatures range from

―――――――――― FACTS IN BRIEF ――――――――――

Capital: Sana.

Official Language: Arabic.

Form of Government: Military rule.

Area: 75,290 sq. mi. (195,000 km²). *Coastline*—about 280 mi. (451 km).

Elevation: *Highest*—12,336 ft. (3,760 m). *Lowest*—sea level.

Population: *Estimated 1980 Population*—7,695,000; distribution, 91 per cent rural, 9 per cent urban; density, 101 persons per sq. mi. (39 persons per km²). *1975 Census*—6,471,893. *Estimated 1985 Population*—8,921,000.

Chief Products: *Agriculture*—coffee, fruits, grains, qat, vegetables. *Manufacturing*—handicrafts.

National Anthem: "Assalam Alwatani Al-Gumhuri" ("Republican National Anthem").

Flag: Red, white, and black horizontal stripes, with a green star in the center. These colors are traditional Arab colors. See FLAG (picture: Flags of Asia).

Money: *Basic Unit*—rial. See MONEY (table).

YEMEN (SANA)

Wide World

The Market Place In Sana, the capital of Yemen (Sana), bustles with activity. Here craftworkers sell handmade goods.

68° to 130° F. (20° to 54° C). Few people live there.

A few rocky hills border the Tihamah on the east. Then, cliffs rise steeply. The cliffs get as much as 30 inches (76 centimeters) of rain a year. The rains have cut into the cliffs, forming short, steep valleys.

East of the cliffs is the high interior, called the *High Yemen.* Broad valleys and plateaus lie 6,000 feet (1,800 meters) above sea level. They are surrounded by steep mountains that rise as high as 12,336 feet (3,760 meters). The high altitude makes the region much cooler than the Tihamah. The High Yemen gets 10 to 15 inches (25 to 38 centimeters) of rain a year. East of the mountains, the land slopes to the desert in Saudi Arabia.

Economy of Yemen (Sana) depends on farming, and the hills and highlands are the most productive part of the country. Farmers there raise such food grains as wheat, barley, and *dura* (a sorghum). They also raise a great variety of fruits, including citrus fruits, apricots, bananas, grapes, papayas, and pomegranates. They raise beans, lentils, onions, and tomatoes in gardens at the edges of towns and villages. People on the Tihamah raise dura and some dates and cotton.

Coffee and qat are the main cash crops. Coffee is a major export. Coffee trees grow on terraces cut into the hillsides. Ancient *aqueducts* (water channels) carry water to the terraces. In recent years, wind-blown sand has filled the coffee port of Mocha (Al Mukha).

Qat, or kat, a woody shrub, grows in the highlands, and is now probably the leading cash crop. Qat leaves contain a narcotic that produces a mild form of intoxication or *euphoria* (state of well-being) when chewed. Thousands of people in this part of Arabia chew qat.

Yemen (Sana) has almost no industry. Most goods are made by hand. The people weave and dye cloth, make rope, glassware, harness, saddles, and pottery. They sell their goods in the village *bazaars* (market places).

Most of the people use camels, donkeys, and horses for transportation. Gravel roads link Mocha, Taizz, and Sana. An asphalt road links Al Hudaydah and Sana. Most other towns are linked by trails.

History. According to Arab tradition, Semitic people invaded what is now Yemen (Sana) about 2000 B.C. They brought farming and building skills to the herdsmen who lived in Yemen. About 1400 B.C., an important trade route began forming. Caravans carrying pearls and spices passed through Yemen. Cities, castles, temples, and dams were built during this time. The Queen of Sheba ruled the Yemeni during the 900's B.C. She visited King Solomon about 950 B.C.

Yemen's prosperity ended after the time of Christ. Local chieftains fought among themselves, and Abyssinia (Ethiopia) invaded Yemen. The next 1,300 years were marked by fighting between Yemeni tribes and religious groups, and against invading Egyptians and Turks.

The Ottoman Empire, centered in Turkey, had varying degrees of control over Yemen from 1517 to 1918. The Treaty of Lausanne freed Yemen from the Turks in 1924.

On Sept. 26, 1962, a group of military officers supported by Egypt overthrew the imam and set up a republic. The imam's forces—called *royalists*—fought from their bases in the mountains to try to regain control of the government. They were supported by Saudi Arabia. But the republicans, supported by Egypt, controlled most of Yemen. The fighting between the republicans and royalists ended in 1970. The republicans then set up a new government that included both republican and royalist officials.

In 1974, army leaders took control of the government of Yemen (Sana). The leaders of the country are conservatives who oppose Communism. The leaders of neighboring Yemen (Aden) favor some political principles of Karl Marx, one of the founders of Communism. Some border clashes took place between Yemen (Sana) and Yemen (Aden) during the 1970's. In February 1979, the fighting became widespread. An armistice ended the fighting in March.   DOUGLAS D. CRARY

YEN is the chief unit of Japanese money. Japanese coins are minted in five denominations: 1, 5, 10, 50, and 100 yen. Paper money is printed in denominations of 100; 500; 1,000; 5,000; and 10,000 yen. The *sen* and *rin,*

Chase Manhattan Bank Money Museum

Face, *left,* **and Reverse Side of the Yen**

smaller denominations of the yen, were removed from circulation in 1954. But they are still used as units for calculation. For the value of the yen in dollars, see MONEY (table: Exchange Rates).   LEWIS M. REAGAN

YENISEY RIVER, *YEN uh SAY,* drains an area of more than 1 million square miles (2.6 million square kilometers) in Siberia. The Yenisey travels 2,566 miles (4,130 kilometers) from its origin in the Sayan Mountains of southern Siberia to its mouth on the Arctic coast. After the river leaves the Sayan Mountains, it flows in a general northerly direction. It enters the Arctic Ocean through an *estuary* (broad river mouth) about 200 miles (320 kilometers) east of the Bay of Ob. Ocean steamers go 400 miles (640 kilometers) up the river to Igarka, a lumber port.

During the early 1960's, the Russian government built a large hydroelectric station near Krasnoyarsk, where a railroad crosses the Yenisey River. Timber, gold, coal, and graphite are taken along the Yenisey's banks. THEODORE SHABAD

See also RIVER (color chart: Longest Rivers).

YEOMAN, *YO mun,* was a *retainer* (dependent) of a feudal lord in early England. In the 1400's, the name *yeomen* came to mean English foresters, or small freeholders on a feudal manor. Later, the yeomen became an independent class of small landowners and farmers. They were famous for their sturdiness and patriotism. Yeomen formed their own volunteer cavalry groups, called *yeomanry,* after 1761.

The Yeomen of the Guard form a bodyguard to the king or queen of Great Britain. King Henry VII first organized this group in 1485. Today, the Yeomen still serve as royal bodyguards on formal occasions. The officers wear contemporary uniforms, but the men wear colorful costumes and carry weapons that date back to the Tudor period. Their tunics are red and have blue and gold facings, and they wear red knee breeches and flat-topped hats. Years ago, the Yeomen Warders of the Tower of London were nicknamed *beefeaters.* This may have started in Tudor days, when servants ate their masters' beef in large quantities.

An appointment to the Yeomen of the Guard is honorary. Officers and enlisted men for the Guard are chosen from Great Britain's regular armed forces. But the job no longer requires any fighting ability.

In the United States Navy, petty officers performing clerical work have the rating of *Yeoman.* Their insignia show sets of crossed quills. ROBERT S. HOYT

See also TOWER OF LONDON.

YEPISHEV, *YEHP ee shehv,* **ALEXEI ALEXEYEVICH** (1908-   ), is chief of the Main Political Directorate of Russia's armed forces. The Communist Party uses the *directorate* (group of managers) to maintain political control over Soviet military forces.

Yepishev was born in Astrakhan, Russia. He joined the Communist Party in 1929. He served in the army from 1930 to 1938, and graduated from the Military Academy of Mechanization and Motorization in 1938. Yepishev held military and political administrative posts during World War II. He was Soviet ambassador to Romania from 1955 to 1960, and ambassador to Yugoslavia from 1960 to 1962. Yepishev became chief of the directorate in 1962. WALTER C. CLEMENS, JR.

YERBA MATÉ. See MATÉ.

YEREVAN, *YEH reh VAHN* (pop. 791,000), capital of the Armenian Soviet Socialist Republic, lies at the foot of Mount Ararat in southwestern Russia. Yerevan's industries include aluminum, chemical, machinery, and food-processing plants. The city has several universities and museums. It was founded in the 600's. For the location of Yerevan, see ARMENIA (map).

YERKES, ROBERT MEARNS (1876-1956), an American psychologist, became best known for his studies of the behavior of apes. His most important work is *The Great Apes* (1929). He energetically promoted a center for the biological and psychological study of primates, the Yerkes Laboratories for Primate Biology in Orange Park, Fla. This center is now in Atlanta and called the Yerkes Regional Primate Research Center. Yerkes was born in Breadysville, Pa. In World War I, he promoted the development and administering of intelligence tests to make better use of U.S. manpower.

YERKES OBSERVATORY is the astronomical observatory of the University of Chicago. The observatory is located 76 miles (122 kilometers) north of Chicago, at Williams Bay on Lake Geneva in Wisconsin. It has three major telescopes—two reflecting telescopes with lenses 40 and 24 inches (102 and 61 centimeters) across, and a refracting telescope with a lens 40 inches (102 centimeters) across. The refracting telescope, which is 63 feet (19 meters) long and weighs 760 pounds (345 kilograms), is the largest of its kind in the world. It is adjusted by delicate electrical devices. The floor below the instrument may be raised or lowered so the observer can use the eyepiece when the telescope is placed at an angle. A dome 90 feet (27 meters) in diameter accommodates the instrument.

Yerkes Observatory is famous for work done there on the distances of the stars by the American astronomer Frank Schlesinger. It also won fame for advances in solar physics made by its first director, George E. Hale, and for studies of stellar spectra, stellar photometry, and theoretical astrophysics. Hale founded the observatory in 1895 with a large donation made by the Chicago businessman Charles T. Yerkes.

Critically reviewed by YERKES OBSERVATORY

See also HALE, GEORGE ELLERY.

YERMAK. See SIBERIA (History).

YESHIVA UNIVERSITY is a private school in New York City. Founded in 1886, it was the first university in the United States under Jewish auspices. Yeshiva has separate undergraduate colleges for men and women. They provide general studies programs and courses in Jewish learning. The university has coeducational graduate schools of humanities and social sciences, natural sciences, Semitics, and social work, and a graduate college of medicine. For enrollment, see UNIVERSITIES AND COLLEGES (table). SAM HARTSTEIN

YETI. See ABOMINABLE SNOWMAN.

YEVTUSHENKO, YEVGENY (1933-   ), is a Russian poet. In his poems, he sets out to be the spokesman of the generation of Russians who grew up after World War II. He became famous outside Russia as one of the first writers to be openly critical of aspects of Russian society. However, he regards himself as a Communist poet. His poems are simple and direct. His works include *Third Snow* (1955), *Longbow and Lyre* (1959), *A Sweep of an Arm* (1962), and *Bratsk Station and Other New Poems* (1967). One of his best-known poems, "Babi Yar" (1961), commemorates Jews massacred by the Germans in World War II, and attacks anti-Semitism. Yevtushenko was born in Zima, near Irkutsk.

YEW is the name of a group of evergreen trees and shrubs. The leaves of yews are flat, pointed needles, dark-green on top and pale-green beneath. They spread apart in two rows along the stem. The bark is reddish-brown and scaly. Yews bear scarlet seeds that look like berries. The trunk of the yew may grow large,

YIDDISH LANGUAGE AND LITERATURE

T. H. Everett; New York Botanical Garden

The Shrublike Japanese Yew, *left,* thrives in rocky soil. The foliage of the yew, *right,* remains a rich dark-green throughout the year. In autumn, the yew bears scarlet seeds that look like berries. The seeds, needles, and bark of the yew are poisonous. Yew trees sometimes live for hundreds of years.

and yew trees sometimes live for hundreds of years.

The *English yew* grows in Europe, Asia, and Africa. There are a great many yews near the English Channel, where the chalky soil seems to further their growth. The famous English archers who defeated the French knights during the wars of the Middle Ages used longbows made of yew wood. Yew trees often grew in English churchyards. Branches of the trees served as funeral decorations, and were twined into wreaths for the heads of the mourners. For this reason, the yew often symbolizes sadness.

The yew has a tough elastic wood, and a grain almost as beautiful as that of mahogany. Yew is polished and made into tables. The heartwood has an orange-red color. The bark, needles, and seeds are poisonous.

Several different kinds of yews grow in America. One is the tall *western,* or *Pacific, yew.* The wood of this tree is valued for use in cabinetwork and for canoe paddles. The *Japanese yew* grows more in the form of a shrub. The *American yew,* or *ground hemlock,* is a low, straggling shrub. People often use the branches of the American yew for Christmas decorations.

Scientific Classification. The yews belong to the yew family, *Taxaceae.* The English yew is classified as genus *Taxus,* species *T. baccata;* the western yew is *T. brevifolia;* the Japanese yew is *T. cuspidata;* and the American yew is *T. canadensis.*　　　　　JOHN T. BUCHHOLZ

See also CONE-BEARING TREES; PLANT (picture: Japanese Yew).

YIDDISH LANGUAGE AND LITERATURE. Millions of Jews throughout the world speak and write in the Yiddish language. Yiddish is about a thousand years old. It grew from German dialects of the Middle Ages, and includes elements from Hebrew and Aramaic; Romance languages, such as Old French and Italian; and Slavic languages, such as Polish and Ukrainian. Yiddish folklore is rich in songs, tales, and proverbs.

Early Yiddish literature was made up mainly of long stories, poems, and religious writings. The literature declined in the early 1800's, but was revived in the 1860's in a new movement that began in Eastern Europe. Leaders included the novelist Mendele the Bookseller (Solomon Jacob Abramowitsch, 1836-1917), the poet

and short-story writer Isaac Loeb Peretz (1851-1915), and the humorist Sholom Aleichem (Solomon Rabinowitz, 1859-1916). Since then, hundreds of prose writers, dramatists, and poets have contributed to Yiddish literature.　　　　　URIEL WEINREICH

See also ASCH, SHOLEM; SHOLOM ALEICHEM.

YMCA. See YOUNG MEN'S CHRISTIAN ASSOCIATION.

YMHA. See JEWISH COMMUNITY CENTERS.

YMIR. See MYTHOLOGY (Teutonic Mythology).

YO-YO is a kind of grooved top attached to a person's finger by a loop at the end of a string. The opposite end of the string is attached inside the groove of the yo-yo.

By maneuvering the string, the operator can make the yo-yo run up and down the string. An accomplished operator can make the yo-yo perform intricate loops.

YODEL is a warbling type of singing which is most commonly heard among the Alpine mountaineers of Switzerland and northern Italy. It is also heard in rural areas of the United States. Yodeling is done by changing a normal singing tone to falsetto and then back again in quick succession.　　　　　RAYMOND KENDALL

YOGA is a term that has two meanings. It is both (1) a school of thought in the Hindu religion and (2) a system of mental and physical exercise developed by that school. Followers of the yoga school, who are called *yogis* or *yogins,* use yoga exercise to achieve their goal of isolation of the soul from the body and the mind. Many non-Hindus in Western countries practice some form of yoga exercise in hope of improving their health and achieving peace of mind. The word *yoga* means *discipline* in Sanskrit, the classical language of India.

According to the yoga school, every human being consists of *prakrti* and *purusha.* Prakrti includes a person's body, mind, and *ego* (conscious self). Purusha is pure, empty consciousness—the soul. The yoga school teaches that the soul is completely separate from the rest of a person, but that the person does not realize it. Man suffers because he wrongly believes that his soul is bound to his body and mind. The yoga school, through yoga exercise, aims to give man *prajna* (understanding) of the meaning of his soul. After a person has obtained this understanding, his soul will gain *moksha* (release) from the *samsara* (cycle of rebirth) in which Hindus believe.

A yogi, under the guidance of a *guru* (teacher), goes through eight stages of training on the way to moksha. The yogi learns: (1) disciplined behavior, called *yama;* (2) self-purification (*niyama*); (3) bodily postures, such as the lotus position (*asana*); (4) control of breathing (*pranayama*); (5) control of the senses (*pratyahara*); (6) fixing of the mind on a chosen object (*dharana*); and (7) meditation (*dhyana*). The eighth stage, called *samadhi,* is a state of concentration in which the yogi realizes that his soul is pure and free, and empty of all content. A yogi who has completed these eight stages has reached *kaivalya.* Kaivalya is total isolation of the soul from the body, from all other souls, and from all of nature.

In addition to the practices of the yoga school, other popular forms of yoga exist in the religious traditions of India. One form, called *bhakti-yoga,* involves the dedication of all actions and thoughts to a chosen god. Another form, *karma-yoga,* involves doing one's duty without caring about reward. A third form, *hatha-yoga,*

Sivananda Yoga Center

Yoga includes exercises and postures that its followers believe help isolate the soul from the body and mind. The yogi shown above is meditating while sitting in the lotus position.

YOKOHAMA, *YOH kuh HAH muh* (pop. 2,714,966), is a leading Japanese port and a major center of commerce and industry. Among the cities of Japan, only Tokyo has more people. Yokohama lies about 20 miles (32 kilometers) south of Tokyo, on the island of Honshu (see JAPAN [political map]). Yokohama is the capital of Kanagawa Prefecture. A prefecture in Japan resembles a state in the United States.

The City covers 163 square miles (421 square kilometers) on the western shore of Tokyo Bay and on the slopes of the surrounding hills. Downtown Yokohama occupies a triangular plain, bordered by narrow streams on two sides and by the bay on the third side. Residential areas lie among the hills beyond the harbor.

Yokohama has a number of gardens, libraries, parks, and theaters. Universities in the city include Kanagawa University, Kanto Gakuin University, Yokohama Municipal University, and Yokohama National University.

The city faces such problems as air and water pollution and lack of space. Overcrowded harbor conditions led to the construction of a $111-million pier that opened in 1970. The pier has special loading and unloading machinery to speed the handling of cargo.

People. Most Yokohamans are Japanese, though many Americans, Chinese, and Europeans also live in the city. Most of the people wear clothing similar to that worn in the United States and Canada. Some men and women occasionally wear a *kimono*, a traditional long robe tied with a sash. Many Yokohamans live in large apartment buildings similar to those in Western cities. Others live in one- or two-story wooden houses.

Economy. Yokohama is Japan's second largest port. Only Kobe handles more cargo. Ships leaving the city

stresses difficult bodily postures and breathing techniques, with better health as the main goal.

Various forms of yoga have become popular in the United States and Europe. One form, Transcendental Meditation, requires less mental concentration than does the yoga of Hinduism. Members of the Hare Krishna movement practice bhakti-yoga by devoting themselves to the supreme god Krishna. Hatha-yoga has been called a method of gaining perfect health. But medical research has shown that it provides little more than does any good athletic program. GERALD JAMES LARSON

See also HINDUISM.

YOGURT, or YOGHURT, is a smooth, semisolid dairy product made from milk. It has a high acid content and thick curd. Yogurt ranks as a popular food in many parts of the world. People in Iran, Turkey, and some other countries of the Middle East have eaten yogurt for thousands of years.

Yogurt may be made from the milk of buffaloes, cows, goats, or other cud-chewing animals. In the United States, commercial yogurt is made from cows' milk. Yogurt makers add two types of bacteria to milk to make yogurt. These bacteria, called *Lactobacillus bulgaricus* and *Streptococcus lactis*, multiply at carefully controlled temperatures and cause milk to *ferment* (ripen). During fermentation, the bacteria change milk sugar into a syrupy substance called *lactic acid*. Lactic acid causes fluid milk to thicken, resulting in yogurt.

The high acid content of yogurt gives the product a sour taste that many people enjoy. However, many others prefer yogurt that has been sweetened with fruit flavoring. Yogurt has the same nutritional elements as milk. Some unflavored yogurt contains only a few calories per serving and is popular for low-calorie diets.

Some people make yogurt at home. They use commercial yogurt or bacteria from special laboratories to start the fermentation process. Several firms manufacture yogurt-making machines for home use. C. L. NORTON

YOHO NATIONAL PARK. See CANADA (National Parks).

M. Tonooka, Bruce Coleman Inc.

Yokohama is one of Japan's largest ports. Its modern harbor facilities have helped make it a major distribution center for products manufactured in Tokyo and other nearby industrial regions.

carry many products manufactured in Tokyo and other nearby industrial regions. Rail lines link Yokohama with such other major cities as Kobe, Osaka, and Tokyo. Shipbuilding is a major industry in Yokohama, and the city also produces automobiles, chemicals, electric equipment, iron and steel, and machinery.

History. Until 1854, the area that is now Yokohama was little more than a seashore with a few houses. That year, Commodore Matthew C. Perry of the U.S. Navy signed an agreement with the Japanese opening Japan to trade with the United States. Traders from a number of countries established offices in Yokohama in 1859. In time, Yokohama became a major seaport.

The city has twice been almost destroyed. On Sept. 1, 1923, one of the worst earthquakes in history killed more than 23,000 Yokohamans. In 1945, during World War II, U.S. bombers dropped thousands of fire bombs on Yokohama. The war ended that same year, and the city was rebuilt a second time.

In 1973, a new Yokohama law took effect that regulates the construction of new buildings. This law requires that no structure be built that allows sunlight to fall on the surrounding neighborhood fewer than four hours a day. LEWIS AUSTIN

YOLK. See EGG.

YOLK. See WOOL (Types of Wool).

YOM KIPPUR, *yahm KIHP uhr,* or *YOHM kee POOR,* is the Jewish day of atonement. In the Jewish civil calendar, Yom Kippur falls on the tenth day of the first month, Tishri. Jews observe it as a day of fasting and worship. Yom Kippur is the most important and sacred Jewish holy day. On this day devout Jews think of their sins, repent, and ask forgiveness from God. In ancient times, the high priest held a service in the Temple in Jerusalem, and sacrificed certain animals as a ceremonial offering. The service was the main event of the day. Today, Jews fast, do no work, and attend services in the synagogue or temple on Yom Kippur. The holiday begins at sunset on the ninth day and lasts until sunset on the tenth day. The laws about Yom Kippur are found in Leviticus 16; 23:26-32; 25:9, and Numbers 29:7-11. LEONARD C. MISHKIN

See also ATONEMENT; AZAZEL; SCAPEGOAT.

YONKERS, N.Y. (pop. 204,297), is an important manufacturing center that forms part of the New York City metropolitan area. Yonkers lies between the Bronx and Hudson rivers in the southeastern corner of the state. For location, see NEW YORK (political map).

Yonkers covers 18 square miles (47 square kilometers). The city is the home of Sarah Lawrence College and St. Joseph's Seminary and College. Museums in Yonkers include Philipse Manor Hall and the Hudson River Museum.

The city has more than 400 manufacturing plants, and they employ about 20 per cent of the work force. The chief products include chemicals, corn syrup and molasses, elevators, and wire goods.

Manhattan Indians once lived in the area that is now Yonkers. In 1646, Adriaen Van der Donck, a Dutch nobleman, received a land grant that included the site. He built a sawmill near the junction of the Nepperhan and Hudson rivers, where he could use the Nepperhan's water power. Van der Donck was called *De Jonk-*

heer (young gentleman). The settlement that grew up around the mill became known as De Jonkheer's land and, later, as Yonkers.

In 1693, a merchant named Frederick Philipse gained possession of much of the Yonkers area. He rented land to farmers, and, by the 1800's, the community consisted chiefly of farmers. The Hudson River Railroad opened in 1849, which encouraged the development of new industries in the area. Elisha G. Otis opened an elevator manufacturing shop in Yonkers in 1853, and his business grew into a leading industry. Yonkers became a village in 1855 and a city in 1872.

Industrial expansion continued in Yonkers during the early 1900's. The jobs created by the industries attracted many immigrants, and the city's population increased from 79,803 in 1910 to 190,634 in 1960.

In the mid-1970's, Yonkers planned a government center complex, including an administration building, a public library, and a parking garage. Construction of the garage began in 1975, but financial problems delayed the rest of the project. Yonkers has a council-manager form of government. GWEN HALL

YORK (pop. 104,750) was the principal center of northern England in the Middle Ages. It stands at the junction of the rivers Ouse and Foss (see GREAT BRITAIN [political map]). Romans founded York and called it *Eboracum.* York Minster Cathedral is one of the finest English churches. The archbishop of York is second in authority to the archbishop of Canterbury in the Church of England. FRANCIS H. HERRICK

YORK, Pa. (pop. 50,335; met. area pop. 329,540), is an industrial and distribution center for one of the nation's richest farm areas. It lies in southeastern Pennsylvania, near Harrisburg (see PENNSYLVANIA [political map]). Factories there make machinery, paper, textile goods, cement, lime, candy, furniture, and cigars.

York is the oldest settlement in Pennsylvania west of the Susquehanna River. The town was laid out in 1741 under the authority of the Penn family, the proprietors of Pennsylvania. During the Revolutionary War, the Continental Congress met there after the British took Philadelphia. The Congress met there from September, 1777, to June, 1778. Congress accepted the Articles of Confederation at York. York became a borough in 1777 and a city in 1887. It has a commission government and is the seat of York County. S. K. STEVENS

YORK is a branch of the English royal family of Plantagenet. The House of York won the English throne from the House of Lancaster during the Wars of the Roses (1455-1485). Members of the House of York ruled England from 1461 to 1485, with a brief interruption in the early 1470's. See WARS OF THE ROSES.

Richard, duke of York, the leader of the Yorkist party, was descended, through his mother, from the third son of King Edward III. Henry VI, the reigning king, was descended from Edward III's fourth son, John of Gaunt, duke of Lancaster. Because he was descended from an older son, the duke of York claimed that he had a better right to the throne than Henry VI.

Open warfare broke out in 1455, when Henry VI was defeated at the first battle of St. Albans. In December, 1460, the duke of York was killed at the Battle of Wakefield. But, the following year, King Henry's forces were decisively beaten, and York's eldest son was crowned Edward IV, the first Yorkist king. Edward lost his throne in 1470, but regained it in 1471 after the battles of Barnet and Tewkesbury. He ruled until 1483.

He was succeeded by his 12-year-old son, Edward V. Shortly afterward, the boy's uncle, Richard, duke of Gloucester, seized the crown as Richard III, and imprisoned Edward and his younger brother. The boys were never heard of again.

In 1485, Henry Tudor, earl of Richmond, a descendant of the House of Lancaster, defeated and killed Richard III at Bosworth Field. He was crowned Henry VII, first ruler of the Tudor dynasty. Henry married Edward IV's daughter, Elizabeth, and so at last united the rival houses of Lancaster and York. PAUL M. KENDALL

See also EDWARD (IV; V); HENRY (VI; VII) of England; LANCASTER; RICHARD (III).

YORK, ALVIN CULLUM (1887-1964), an outstanding American soldier of World War I, killed more than 20 Germans and forced 132 others to surrender on Oct. 8, 1918. York was a member of a patrol sent to silence German machine-gun nests. He shot more than 20 Germans and forced a German major to order the entire group to surrender. York received the Congressional Medal of Honor for his deed. Marshal Ferdinand Foch called it "the greatest thing accomplished by any private soldier of all the armies of Europe." Although he became famous as Sergeant York, he was a corporal at the time of his incredible feat.

York was born in Fentress County, Tennessee, and grew up on a mountain farm. He developed amazing marksmanship with the rifle and pistol during his boyhood. He became deeply religious and was reluctant to go to war, but his pastor persuaded him that it was his duty to do so. H. A. DeWEERD

United Press Int.
Alvin C. York

YORK, CAPE. See CAPE YORK.

YORK RITE. See MASONRY (The Lodges and Degrees).

YORK RIVER. See VIRGINIA (Rivers and Lakes).

YORK UNIVERSITY is a coeducational university in Toronto, Ont. It is supported mainly by the province. York has faculties of administrative studies, arts, education, environmental studies, fine arts, law, science, and graduate studies. It also includes Atkinson College for part-time students and Glendon College, a bilingual liberal arts school. York grants bachelor's, master's, and doctor's degrees. It was founded in 1959. For enrollment, see CANADA (table: Universities and Colleges).

Critically reviewed by YORK UNIVERSITY

YORKSHIRE TERRIER is a bright-eyed toy dog that weighs 4 to 8 pounds (1.8 to 3.6 kilograms). Weavers in northern England developed the breed in the 1850's. They wanted a dog bold enough to kill rats, but small enough to be carried in a pocket. The dog has long, silky hair. Its coat is steel blue with a golden tan. See also DOG (picture: Toy Dogs). JOSEPHINE Z. RINE

YORKTOWN, Va. (pop. 311), is a historic village on the York River (see VIRGINIA [political map]). In 1781, Lord Cornwallis surrendered to General George Washington at Yorktown in the final British defeat of the

YOSEMITE NATIONAL PARK

Revolutionary War. Today, several historic homes in Yorktown are part of Colonial National Historical Park. This park includes the Yorktown Battlefield; much of Jamestown Island; and Colonial Parkway, a drive that connects Jamestown and Yorktown and passes through historic Williamsburg. The Cape Henry Memorial at Cape Henry is another part of the park. FRANCIS B. SIMKINS

YORKTOWN, BATTLE OF. See REVOLUTIONARY WAR IN AMERICA (Surrender at Yorktown; picture).

YOSEMITE FALLS, *yoh SEHM ih tee,* in California's Yosemite National Park, is one of the world's highest waterfalls. It is formed by Yosemite Creek as it plunges 2,425 feet (739 meters) down a rock wall of Yosemite Valley. Yosemite Falls has three parts: Upper Falls, 1,430 feet (436 meters) high; the intermediate cascade, 675 feet (206 meters); and Lower Falls, 320 feet (98 meters). See also WATERFALL (chart). JOHN W. REITH

YOSEMITE NATIONAL PARK, *yoh SEHM ih tee,* is a great wilderness in east-central California. It lies in the Sierra Nevada mountains about 200 miles (320 kilometers) east of San Francisco (see CALIFORNIA [physical map]). It has about 700 miles (1,100 kilometers) of trails. Most of the trails lead to the "High Sierra," a region of sparkling lakes, rushing streams, and jagged mountain peaks. The Yosemite Museum in the park has a collection of Indian displays, and exhibits of the area's wildlife. For the area of the park, see NATIONAL PARK SYSTEM (table: National Parks).

Over 60 kinds of animals and more than 200 species of birds live in the forests and on the mountain slopes.

U.S. Department of the Interior
Upper and Lower Yosemite Falls are a favorite scenic attraction in Yosemite National Park. They rank among the 10 highest waterfalls in North America. The two falls and the cascade that connects them have a combined height of 2,425 feet (739 meters).

473

YOSEMITE NATIONAL PARK

Bears and deer are numerous. Yosemite has over 30 kinds of trees and more than 1,300 varieties of plants. There are three groves of the famous *Sequoiadendron giganteum* or *Big Trees*. The best known is the Mariposa Grove, 35 miles (56 kilometers) south of Yosemite Valley. The grove includes the Grizzly Giant Tree, whose base measures over 34 feet (10 meters) in diameter.

In 1864, Congress gave Yosemite Valley to California for use as a public park and recreation area. John Muir, a naturalist, first saw the area in the 1860's. His enthusiastic reports of the beauties of the region aroused interest in the Yosemite Valley. Congress created Yosemite National Park in 1890. But the park did not include Yosemite Valley and the Mariposa Grove. California ceded these areas back to the federal government, and they were added to the park in 1906. The park has many tourist accommodations. Skiing is popular in the High Sierra. Other activities include horseback riding, fishing, golf, tennis, hiking, and swimming.

Yosemite Valley. Much of the park's most spectacular scenery is in the Yosemite Valley. The valley lies at a 4,000-foot (1,200-meter) elevation in the heart of the park. A group of explorers on their way to the Pacific Coast in the 1830's were probably the first white people to see the valley. But white people did not enter it until 1851. In that year, members of the Mariposa Battalion, a volunteer fighting force, set out to capture a group of Yosemite Indians. Tenaya, the Yosemite chief, had been leading his tribe in raids on white settlers in the foothills of the Sierra Nevada. The battalion captured Tenaya, but the whites eventually let him return to the valley, which was named for his tribe.

Millions of years ago, California's Sierra Nevada was formed by a gradual series of earth upheavals. As the mountains rose, the westward-flowing Merced River accelerated to torrential speed and carved the narrow, V-shaped Merced Canyon. Later, massive glaciers flowed down the canyon. The glaciers ground and polished the canyon to a smooth U-shaped valley, nearly 1 mile (1.6 kilometers) wide and almost 1 mile deep in places. Tributary streams did not carve their canyons as deep as Merced Canyon. Glaciers sheared off these canyons, leaving them as "hanging valleys." Today, the world's greatest concentration of free, leaping waterfalls pours from these valleys.

Waterfalls. Bridalveil Fall is the first waterfall seen by most Yosemite visitors. It graces the southern wall of the valley with a 620-foot (189-meter) descent. Nearby, the Illilouette Falls also tumbles over the side of the valley. Yosemite Falls is formed by Yosemite Creek, leaping free from its hanging valley 2,425 feet (739 meters) above the valley floor. The Upper Falls is 1,430 feet (436 meters) high, and the Lower Falls measures 320 feet (98 meters) high. The cascades between the two tumble another 675 feet (206 meters). The total height of Yosemite Falls is about ½ mile (0.8 kilometer), about twice the height of the Empire State Building.

Vernal and Nevada falls pour over giant steps formed by glaciers. Vernal Falls, 317 feet (97 meters) high, is famous for the rainbows that sparkle in the heavy mist at its base. About 1 mile (1.6 kilometers) upstream is 594-foot (181-meter) Nevada Falls. It is so violent that the Indians called it *Yo-wipe* or *The Twisted Fall*.

Some of the park's falls burst forth during the high-water season in spring. These include the slender 1,612-foot (491-meter) Ribbon Falls, the erratic Sentinel Falls which drops 2,000 feet (610 meters), and the 1,170-foot (357-meter) Silver Strand Falls.

Rock Masses. A number of rock masses rise sharply from the valley floor. The Half Dome rises to an 8,852-foot (2,698-meter) elevation at the head of the valley. El Capitan, which is a gigantic mass of unbroken granite, rises vertically 3,600 feet (1,100 meters) above the canyon. From Glacier Point, one can look down more than 3,000 feet (910 meters) into the valley. Cloud's Rest, the highest point in Yosemite Valley, stands more than 1 mile (1.6 kilometers) above the valley floor.

Hetch Hetchy Valley lies in the northwestern part of the park. It was carved by the Tuolumne River and ancient glaciers in much the same manner as Yosemite Valley. A reservoir now covers the floor of the valley. The Grand Canyon of the Tuolumne River is above Hetch Hetchy, to the east. The river rushes through the canyon at great speed, dropping 4,000 feet (1,200 meters) in 4 miles (6 kilometers). It creates many cascades and waterfalls, including the Waterwheel Falls, a series of amazing pinwheels of water. Some of the pinwheels rise as high as 40 feet (12 meters). The pinwheels are formed when the river, cascading down a steep granite apron, strikes rocky obstructions.

The Tuolumne River flows through Tuolumne Meadows, a vast grassland. The meadows have an elevation of about 8,500 feet (2,590 meters). Tourists camp there and the area is also used as a base camp by mountain climbers. Tenaya Lake, which lies near Tuolumne Meadows on the Tioga Road, is the largest and the most beautiful of the more than 300 lakes in Yosemite.

Transportation. Yosemite is a year-round park. Most roads remain open throughout the winter. However, snows close roads in the High Sierra region from about mid-autumn until late spring.　　　ROBERT D. THOMSON

Related Articles in WORLD BOOK include:

Bridalveil Fall	Nevada Falls	Sequoia
Muir, John	Ribbon Falls	Yosemite Falls

YOUNG, ANDREW JACKSON, JR. (1932-　　), was the first black to serve as United States ambassador to the United Nations (UN). Young, a former civil rights leader, became known for his outspoken comments on world affairs. He strongly supported black majority rule in Africa.

Young was born in New Orleans. He graduated from Howard University and from the Hartford Theological Seminary. In 1955, Young was ordained a minister in what is now the United Church of Christ. He served as pastor of several churches in Alabama and Georgia.

In 1960, Young joined the Southern Christian Leadership Conference (SCLC), a civil rights organization led by Martin Luther King, Jr. Young became one of King's chief aides and served as execu-

United Nations
Andrew Young, Jr.

tive director of the SCLC from 1964 to 1970. He was jailed in Selma, Ala., and St. Augustine, Fla., for taking part in civil rights demonstrations.

Young, a Democrat from Georgia, won election to the U.S. House of Representatives in 1972. He was the first black elected to Congress from the South since 1901. He held the seat until President Jimmy Carter appointed him to the UN in 1977.   NANCY H. DICKERSON

YOUNG, BRIGHAM (1801-1877), led the Mormons from Illinois to what is now Utah, and established their church there. Young was the second president of the Mormon church, which is officially called the CHURCH OF JESUS CHRIST OF LATTER-DAY SAINTS. He became the Mormon leader in 1844, after Joseph Smith, the church founder, was shot to death.

Young was a stocky man, and a tireless worker. A strong will, engaging personality, and deep convictions made him an outstanding leader.

Early Life. Young was born in Whitingham, Vt. His father, a farmer, had fought under George Washington during the Revolutionary War. In 1804, Young's father took the family to western New York. Young spent most

Brigham Young

of his early years on his father's farm. He attended school only about 12 days. As a young man, he worked as a painter, glazier, and carpenter. In 1829, Young settled in Monroe County, New York, near Joseph Smith's home. He studied Smith's religious teachings and was baptized into the church in 1832. In 1833, he joined the Mormon settlement at Kirtland, Ohio.

Mormon Leader. The Kirtland community broke up and non-Mormons (called "gentiles" by the Mormons) drove them from Independence, Mo., in the 1830's. Young, Smith, and other church members then settled in Far West, Mo. Anti-Mormonism also developed there, and non-Mormons imprisoned Smith and other leaders on what Mormons believe were false charges in 1838. But Young led about 15,000 Mormons to safety in Illinois.

Young was one of the church's most successful missionaries. From 1839 to 1841, as a missionary in Great Britain, he converted many persons to his faith and arranged for them to come to the United States. Young was preaching in New England in 1844, when Joseph Smith was shot by a mob at Carthage, Ill. Young hurried back to Illinois. He made a powerful speech that rallied the church members. He was the undisputed leader of the Mormons from that time until his death.

Settles in Utah. Non-Mormons forced the Mormons to leave Illinois in 1846. Starting in mid-winter, Young led his followers on a long journey across the Mississippi River and through Iowa to Winter Quarters, Nebr., near present-day Omaha. But Young decided that there could be no lasting peace for his people until they were completely separated from the gentiles. So, in 1847, Young led an advance party of 148 Mormons west to a previously planned refuge in the Great Basin. When they arrived in the Great Salt Lake valley in what is

now Utah, Young said, "This is the place." He supervised the migration of thousands of other Mormons to the valley. He was formally elected church president in 1847.

The Mormons prospered in Utah. Under Young's leadership, they developed irrigation techniques, and parts of the barren desert blossomed into rich and fruitful land. The United States government established the Territory of Utah in 1850 and appointed Young its first governor. Young still found time to direct missionary work and to establish hundreds of Mormon settlements in the West.

But the move to Utah did not end the Mormons' troubles. Gentiles came to the territory, and some who opposed them held political posts under the United States government. False reports circulated that the church was in rebellion against the government. These reports alarmed the federal government. In 1857, President James Buchanan replaced Young with a gentile governor and sent troops to Utah. The Mormons prepared to defend themselves, and the Utah War (also called the Mormon War) followed. The "war" was bloodless. No engagements were fought. Although the Mormons raided some troop wagon trains as a delaying action, they then temporarily abandoned Salt Lake City to the army. The troops established a camp near the western mountains. During the winter of 1857 and 1858, Young and the federal troops discussed peace terms. The hostilities ended in 1858 when Young accepted the new governor and President Buchanan fully pardoned all concerned. Even though Young stepped down as governor, he remained the most powerful man in Utah until his death.

Young's Place in History. Critics have accused Young of intolerance to opposition. Many persons opposed his practice of polygamy, which led him to take 27 wives. But Young's leadership and pioneering efforts rank him as one of the most important colonizers of the American West. Mormon history records that Young brought 100,-000 persons to the mountain valleys, founded over 200 cities, towns, and villages, and established many schools and factories. A statue of Young represents Utah in Statuary Hall in Washington, D.C.   Critically reviewed by the
CHURCH OF JESUS CHRIST OF LATTER-DAY SAINTS

See also MORMONS; UTAH; SMITH, JOSEPH; LATTER DAY SAINTS, REORGANIZED CHURCH OF JESUS CHRIST OF.

YOUNG, CHARLES AUGUSTUS (1834-1908), an American astronomer, did pioneer studies in the physics of the sun. During a total eclipse of the sun in Iowa in 1869, he made the first observation of the spectrum of the sun's corona. At the 1870 eclipse, he observed the flash spectrum and proved the existence of the chromosphere, a region in the sun's gaseous shell. Young also determined the rate of rotation of the sun on its axis. His book, *The Sun*, was published in 1881. Young was born in Hanover, N.H., and studied at Dartmouth College. He taught, and directed the observatory at Princeton University from 1877 to 1905.   HELEN WRIGHT

YOUNG, CY (1867-1955), was one of baseball's greatest right-handed pitchers. He won a record 511 major-league games between 1890 and 1911. Young pitched for the Cleveland Spiders, St. Louis Nationals, Boston Red Sox, Cleveland Indians, and Boston

YOUNG, EDWARD

Braves. Denton True Young was born in Gilmore, Ohio. He was elected to the National Baseball Hall of Fame in 1937. JOSEPH P. SPOHN

YOUNG, EDWARD (1683-1765), was an English poet. His later verse was part of a trend from the witty, imitative poetry of England's Augustan age, to the more passionate, imaginative poetry of the romantic period.

Two works established Young's reputation. *The Complaint: or Night Thoughts on Life, Death, and Immortality* (1742-1745) is a series of nine meditative blank verse poems defending Christianity against freethinkers. *Conjectures on Original Composition* (1759) is a critical essay claiming that originality in literature is superior to the imitation of ancient writers. Young was born in Upham, near Winchester. He served as *rector* (clergyman in charge of a parish) at Welwin in Hertfordshire from 1730 until his death. MARTIN C. BATTESTIN

YOUNG, ELLA FLAGG (1845-1918), was the first woman to serve as superintendent of schools in a large city. She held this position in Chicago from 1909 to 1915. Her chief contribution was to introduce practical studies such as home economics and manual training. She was born in Buffalo, N.Y. CLAUDE A. EGGERTSEN

YOUNG, JOHN WATTS (1930-   ), is a United States astronaut. He has made more space flights than any other astronaut. On March 23, 1965, Young and Virgil I. Grissom made the first flight in the Gemini program. They circled the earth three times and became the first space pilots to change their orbit.

Young and Michael Collins flew the Gemini 10 space mission from July 18 to 21, 1966. Young was the command pilot. The astronauts performed two *rendezvous* (meetings) with unmanned spacecraft.

Young, Eugene A. Cernan, and Thomas P. Stafford went into orbit around the moon during the Apollo 10 space flight of May 18 to 26, 1969. Young remained in orbit in the command module while Cernan and Stafford flew to within 10 miles (16 kilometers) of the moon in the lunar module. This mission cleared the way for the first moon landing, two months later.

From April 16 to 27, 1972, Young commanded the Apollo 16 flight to the moon. Young and Charles M. Duke, Jr., explored in the Descartes region of the moon's central highlands while Thomas K. Mattingly II piloted the command module.

Young was born in San Francisco. He graduated from the Georgia Institute of Technology in 1952. He joined the Navy that year and became a test pilot. He became an astronaut in 1962. WILLIAM J. CROMIE

See also ASTRONAUT.

YOUNG, LESTER WILLIS (1909-1959), a tenor saxophonist, developed one of the most imitated styles in jazz history. More than any other jazz instrumentalist, Young was responsible for the transition from the "hot jazz" style in the 1930's to the more relaxed, behind-the-beat approach usually known as "cool." He did his best work while playing with the Count Basie band from 1936 to 1940.

Young was born in Woodville, Miss. He was nicknamed "Prez." He played with King Oliver, Walter Page, and Fletcher Henderson before joining Basie. In the 1940's and 1950's, Young often played on "Jazz at the Philharmonic" concert tours. The last years of his life were tragic. He had a nervous breakdown and was often hospitalized. LEONARD FEATHER

YOUNG, THOMAS. See COLOR (The Three-Component Theory); INTERFEROMETER; LIGHT (Interference).

YOUNG, WHITNEY MOORE, JR. (1921-1971), was an American civil rights leader. He served as the executive director of the National Urban League from 1961 until his death. Young helped thousands of black Americans obtain jobs. He started on-the-job training programs, and established Head Start and tutoring centers.

Young was born in Lincoln Ridge, Ky. He graduated from Kentucky State College (now Kentucky State University) and earned a master's degree at the University of Minnesota. From 1947 to 1953, he worked for the Urban League in St. Paul and Omaha. Young was dean of the Atlanta University School of Social Work from 1954 to 1960. He taught at the University of Nebraska School of Social Work, and served on federal commissions concerned with social welfare or race relations. Young wrote several books, including *To Be Equal* (1964). C. ERIC LINCOLN

YOUNG ADULT. See ADOLESCENT.

YOUNG ITALY. See MAZZINI, GIUSEPPE.

YOUNG MEN'S CHRISTIAN ASSOCIATION (YMCA) is a worldwide service organization based on Christian principles. The YMCA provides programs that encourage the development of body, mind, and spirit. Its goals include eliminating racism, improving mental and physical health, promoting world peace, strengthening family life, and spreading Christian values.

The YMCA has more than 100 million members in over 85 countries. Membership is open to people of every age, creed, nationality, and race. In the United States, more than 9 million persons—including about $3\frac{1}{2}$ million women and girls—belong to the approximately 1,800 local associations. Canada has about 125 local associations that have a total membership of about 1 million.

Programs. Local associations offer physical fitness programs for the entire family. More than 800,000 persons learn to swim annually through the YMCA's aquatic program. Boys and girls learn basketball skills and personal values in the YMCA's Youth Basketball Association. Local associations also provide camping programs, classes and groups for hobbyists and persons with special interests, and leadership training programs. Some YMCA's have residential facilities.

The association sponsors HI-Y clubs for young people and offers several parent-child programs to strengthen family relationships. The YMCA also sponsors the National Youth Program Using Minibikes and other programs that fight delinquency.

The YMCA is a founding agency of the United Service Organizations (USO) and provides assistance to military personnel through Armed Services YMCA's. The association also sponsors citizenship and community action programs.

The organization's education program ranges from informal classes on such subjects as carpentry and yoga to college-level courses that lead to degrees. The college program includes schools of commerce, engineering, law, liberal arts, physical education, and trade and business.

The YMCA has a publishing arm called Association Press that prints books on adult education, crafts, religion, sports, and many other subjects. The YMCA also publishes several magazines for its members, staff, and lay leaders.

History. The YMCA was founded in 1844 by a young London clerk named George Williams and a group of his friends. They established the organization to spread Christianity among young men.

The YMCA movement grew rapidly and spread to other countries. The greatest development took place in the United States and Canada. In 1851, groups of young men formed YMCA's in Boston and Montreal. The first convention of North American YMCA's met in Buffalo, N.Y., in 1854. Thirty-seven delegates from 19 associations attended the convention. The YMCA held its first World Conference in 1855 in Paris. By that time, the movement had grown to 379 associations in seven countries, with a total of 30,360 members.

In 1869, the New York City YMCA erected its own building. For the first time, all its activities were held in the same place. The San Francisco YMCA admitted the association's first women members in 1874.

YMCA activities for members of the armed forces began during the Civil War (1861-1865). These services increased with each later war and reached their fullest development during World War II (1939-1945). The YMCA maintained more than 450 clubs for the Allied armed forces. It also raised more than $12 million to aid about 6 million war prisoners of all nations.

In the United States, the National Council of YMCA's has headquarters at 291 Broadway, New York, N.Y. 10007. The National Council of YMCA's of Canada is at 2160 Yonge Street, Toronto, Ont. M4S 2A9. The YMCA's international headquarters are in Geneva, Switzerland.

Critically reviewed by the YOUNG MEN'S CHRISTIAN ASSOCIATION

See also HI-Y CLUB; Y-INDIAN GUIDES; Y-INDIAN MAIDENS; Y-INDIAN PRINCESSES.

YOUNG MEN'S HEBREW ASSOCIATION. See JEWISH COMMUNITY CENTERS.

YOUNG PLAN. See WAR DEBT.

YOUNG PRETENDER. See SCOTLAND (Union with England).

YOUNG TURKS. See TURKEY (History).

YOUNG WOMEN'S CHRISTIAN ASSOCIATION (YWCA) is the world's oldest and largest multiracial women's organization. The YWCA, which is based on the teachings of Christianity, is open to women and girls of all faiths and backgrounds. The organization tries to meet the needs of its members with a program that combines services and social action. The YWCA works to increase the power of women, minority groups, and young people. Since 1970, its chief goal has been the elimination of racism.

The YWCA has more than 2½ million members. This total includes about 320,000 men and boys, who may become YWCA associates. The organization employs approximately 23,000 national and local staff members, and it also has about 160,000 volunteer workers. The YWCA cooperates with, but is not related to, the Young Men's Christian Association (YMCA).

Programs. The YWCA conducts programs in more than 5,000 locations throughout the United States—in cities, towns, and rural communities; and on college campuses. Local YWCA's offer a wide range of activities and services. They feature child-care centers, classes

on various subjects, discussion programs, food services, and health education. They also provide counseling, job placement services, leadership training programs, recreational activities, and residential facilities.

The association sponsors programs to fight crime and delinquency. Many local YWCA's have a Y-Teen program for teen-age members (see Y-TEENS). As a member agency of the United Service Organizations (USO), the YWCA assists military personnel and their families.

History. In 1855, a group of London women led by Emma Robarts organized a young women's association. Their purpose was to find housing for nurses who had returned from the Crimean War (1853-1856). At about the same time, another women's group in London organized prayer circles. The two groups united in 1877 as the Young Women's Christian Association.

In the United States, The Ladies' Christian Association, an organization similar to the London groups, was founded in New York City in 1858. The first Young Women's Christian Association was organized in Boston in 1866. The movement grew rapidly, especially in industrial cities, where the YWCA provided housing for single working women. Later, the YWCA became active on college campuses. The first student YWCA was founded in 1873 at Illinois State Normal University (now Illinois State University) in Normal, Ill. Separate organizations arose in the Midwest and in the East. In 1906, these groups united as the Young Women's Christian Associations of the United States of America.

From its beginnings, the United States YWCA worked with women of other nations. The first American secretary in foreign service was sent to India in 1894. Today, the YWCA works in more than 80 countries. It provides services and training that help women become equal partners with men in the continual development of their nations. The YWCA of the United States has headquarters at 600 Lexington Avenue, New York, N.Y. 10022. It is a member of the World Young Women's Christian Association, which has headquarters in Geneva, Switzerland.

Critically reviewed by the YOUNG WOMEN'S CHRISTIAN ASSOCIATION

YOUNGSTOWN, Ohio (pop. 140,909), is one of the world's great steel-producing centers. It ranks fourth among steel centers in the United States.

Youngstown lies in the northeastern part of Ohio. It is midway between Cleveland and Pittsburgh, and midway between New York and Chicago. For location, see OHIO (political map). With Warren, it forms a metropolitan area of 537,124 persons.

Youngstown has many parks and recreation areas. Mill Creek Park has over 2,300 acres (931 hectares) and is one of the nation's most beautiful natural parks. Youngstown institutions include the Youngstown Public Library and its branches, Youngstown State University, Butler Institute of American Art, Stambaugh Auditorium, Youngstown Symphony Center, and the Youngstown Playhouse.

Youngstown steel products include coils, sheets, pipe, bars, and stainless steel. The city has foundries, machine shops, metal fabricators, and mill equipment suppliers. Youngstown factories also produce aluminum products, automotive parts, electric light bulbs, electronic equipment, leather products, office equipment, paints, paper products, plastics, rubber goods, and textile products.

Youngstown was settled in 1797 and named in honor of John Young of New York, who bought the site of the future city from the Connecticut Land Company. The town was incorporated in 1848. It has a mayor-council form of government. Youngstown is the seat of Mahoning County. JAMES H. RODABAUGH

YOUTH. See ADOLESCENT.

YOUTH, ALLIED. See ALLIED YOUTH.

YOUTH FOR CHRIST INTERNATIONAL is a nonprofit organization specializing in teen-age evangelism. Founded in 1944, it has more than 300 local groups in the United States, Canada, and about 45 other countries. Its local interdenominational groups sponsor youth rallies, high school clubs, and camps designed to supplement the work of local churches. Its headquarters are at N. Main St., Wheaton, Ill. 60187. Its official publication is *Campus Life* magazine.

Critically reviewed by YOUTH FOR CHRIST INTERNATIONAL

YOUTH HOSTEL is an overnight lodging place constructed for members of American Youth Hostels, Inc. The association encourages inexpensive travel as a means of recreation and exercise. Members may bicycle, hike, ride horseback, or canoe from one hostel to another. Hostels are usually located about 25 to 35 miles (40 to 56 kilometers) apart.

Hostels are found in most parts of the United States, Canada, and Europe. There are many special *loops* (circuits) of hostels in the United States for tours of such scenic districts of the country as New England, the Great Lakes region, the Rocky Mountains, and the Pacific Coast. Other hostels are situated so that members can travel for months at a time throughout countries.

Each hostel is supervised by houseparents who provide sleeping quarters. Sometimes they also provide

American Youth Hostels, Inc.
Youth Hostels in many parts of the world provide inexpensive lodging for young travelers. Many youth hostel associations also sponsor bicycle trips, hikes, and other group activities. The cyclists shown above are resting at a hostel in Truro, Mass.

meals at low cost. Most hostels have a common kitchen, a dining room, and a recreation room. The time anyone can stay at one hostel is usually three days.

Youth hostels were originated by Richard Schirrmann, a German schoolteacher of Altena, Germany, in 1910. He founded hostels in the former state of Westphalia, Germany. His idea was to encourage people to spend more of their time outdoors. The plan became popular and quickly spread to most European countries.

The first youth hostel in North America was established in a tent in 1933 at Bragg Creek, Alberta, Canada, by two sisters, Mary and Catherine Barclay. They founded Canadian Youth Hostels. In the United States, Isabel and Monroe Smith introduced the first hostel, at Northfield, Mass., in 1934. The American Youth Hostels, Inc., has its National Campus at Delaplane, Va. 22025. JUSTIN J. CLINE

YOUTH MOVEMENT was the term used after World War I for organized groups of young people who began to seek political influence through various planned campaigns. In Europe, Fascist and Communist governments often directed youth movements.

YPRES, *E pr'*, or, in Dutch, IEPER, *YAY per* (pop. 21,306), is a Belgian city in West Flanders that lies 35 miles (56 kilometers) southwest of Ostend. For location, see BELGIUM (political map). Linen and lace are made in Ypres from the flax of Flanders.

Ypres became famous as a center of the textile industry about 1300. At that time, its population was about 20,000, almost as great as London's. In World War I, Ypres was the scene of severe fighting, and it was almost destroyed. It was rebuilt, but again became a battleground during World War II. DANIEL H. THOMAS

YTTERBIUM, *ih TUR bee um*, is a soft silvery metal. Small amounts of ytterbium are used in metallurgical and chemical experiments. In 1878, the Swiss chemist Jean de Marignac gave the name *ytterbium* to a substance that he found in a mineral called *yttria*. In 1907, the French chemist Georges Urbain separated de Marignac's substance into two chemical elements, *lutetium* and *ytterbium*. Several minerals, such as monazite, gadolinite, and xenotime, contain ytterbium.

Ytterbium is a rare-earth element. Its chemical symbol is Yb and its atomic number is 70. Seven ytterbium isotopes are stable. Their average atomic weight is 173.04. The metal melts at 824° C (1515° F.) and boils at 1466° C (2671° F.). FRANK H. SPEDDING

See also ELEMENT, CHEMICAL (table); LUTETIUM; RARE EARTH.

YTTRIUM, *IH tree um*, is a silvery metallic chemical element used in electronics and in medicine. In 1794, the Finnish chemist Johan Gadolin discovered yttrium in a mineral called *yttria* found near Ytterby, Sweden. Most yttrium now is found in minerals called monazite and xenotime mined throughout the world.

Yttrium oxides or phosphates combine with rare-earth europium compounds to form a red phosphor used in color television screens. Yttrium oxide and iron oxide combine to form a crystal called *garnet* used in radar equipment. Yttrium resembles the rare-earth elements and is often associated with them. Its chemical symbol is Y. Its atomic number is 39 and its atomic weight is 88.905. Yttrium melts at 1523° C (2773° F.) and boils at 3337° C (6039° F.). FRANK H. SPEDDING

See also ELEMENT, CHEMICAL (table); RARE EARTH.

YUAN, *yoo AHN*, is the Chinese word for *dollar*. In Taiwan, people refer to the *New Taiwan Dollar* as a *yuan*. China uses the yuan as its basic unit of currency. It is divided into 10 *chiao*, each worth 10 *fen*. In 1914, China established the yuan as a silver coin with 23.4934 grams of pure silver. The yuan usually circulates now as paper money with little silver backing.   LEWIS M. REAGAN

YUCATÁN, *yoo kuh TAHN*, is a Mexican state on a level plain at the northern end of the Yucatán Peninsula. It has a population of 758,355 and covers 16,749 square miles (43,380 square kilometers). The state has no rivers but wells provide water for the people. Henequen is the chief farm product, and forests produce chicle and hardwood lumber. Mérida is the capital. Yucatán was one of the original states of Mexico. For the location of Yucatán, see MEXICO (political map). See also MÉRIDA.   CHARLES C. CUMBERLAND

YUCATÁN CHANNEL. See GULF OF MEXICO.

YUCATÁN PENINSULA, *yoo kuh TAHN*, includes the southeastern Mexican states of Campeche, Quintana Roo, and Yucatán; Belize; and part of El Petén, a department of Guatemala. The peninsula separates the Gulf of Mexico from the Caribbean Sea. It covers over 75,000 square miles (194,000 square kilometers). For location, see MEXICO (physical map).

The peninsula is a low, rolling tableland of coral and limestone covered by a thin layer of soil. It has a hot, humid climate. Tropical rain forests cover the lowlands. The chief cities include Mérida, capital of Yucatán; Campeche, capital of Campeche; and Progreso, Yucatán, the peninsula's chief port.

Quintana Roo and Belize lie along the eastern coast of the peninsula. The state of Yucatán is in the northern part of the peninsula. The state of Campeche lies south and west of Yucatán. Part of El Petén in Guatemala is inland in the peninsula's southern part.

Most of the people, called *Yucatecos*, are descendants of the Maya Indians who lived in Yucatán hundreds of

WORLD BOOK maps

The Yucatán Peninsula separates the Gulf of Mexico from the Caribbean Sea. It lies in southeastern Mexico, and in northern Guatemala and Belize.

years before the Spaniards arrived (see MAYA). Ancient ruins of the Mayan civilization have been discovered at Chichén Itzá in Yucatán. Most Yucatecos are farmers. Northern Yucatán is one of the chief henequen-raising areas of the world. Henequen is used in making rope and twine. Other crops of the Yucatán Peninsula include cacao, chicle, coffee, corn, cotton, sugar cane, and tobacco.

Francisco Fernández de Córdoba, a Spaniard, came

YUCCA HOUSE NATIONAL MONUMENT

to the peninsula in 1517. By 1542, Francisco de Montejo the Younger had set up Spanish rule over half of Yucatán and established the cities of Campeche and Mérida. Some of the Indians became slave laborers on henequen plantations. During the 1800's and 1900's, the Indians revolted several times against the Mexican government. They won most of the land in Campeche and Yucatán from the Mexican landlords. Salvador Alvarado and Felipe Carillo, who served as governors of Yucatán in the early 1900's, introduced many reforms.

See also BELIZE; CAMPECHE; MÉRIDA; QUINTANA ROO.

YUCCA, *YUK uh*, is the name of a group of shrubs or trees of the agave family. The yucca plant has a striking appearance. It is an evergreen plant, and does not shed its leaves each year. There are many varieties of the yucca plant.

Some yucca plants have short stems and others have tall woody and scaly trunks. The leaves of the yucca plants are usually pointed, stiff, and narrow, with saw-like or fibrous edges. They grow along the stem or in clusters at the end of a stem. The yucca plant has flowers shaped somewhat like bells. Certain varieties of the yucca have whitish-green flowers, while others have white or cream-colored flowers. These flowers grow in a cluster on a stem which springs up from the center of a cluster of leaves. Some of these flowers give off a strong fragrance when they open at night. The yucca has large fruits that may be either fleshy or dry. They contain many small, flat, black seeds.

Yuccas grow most abundantly in the southern and southwestern parts of the United States. They also grow in the desert highlands and plateaus of Mexico. Most of the species are low shrubs. But in deserts of the southwestern United States, and in Mexico, there are several species that become large, picturesque trees. The Joshua Tree National Monument in California contains important collections of yucca trees. The popular northern species of yucca is called *Adam's needle*.

The Indians found many uses for yucca plants. They made rope, sandals, mats, and baskets from the leaf fibers. They ate the buds and flowers raw or boiled. The Indians dried the fleshy fruits and ate them during the winter. They also made a fermented drink from the fruits. The roots and stems of the yucca make a soap. Some kinds of yucca are known as *soapweed*. Yuccas serve as decorative plants in gardens throughout the United States. They are often grown as border plants.

Scientific Classification. Yuccas belong to the agave family, *Agavaceae*. The common yucca tree or Joshua tree is genus *Yucca*, species *Y. brevifolia*. Another common species, *Y. baccata*, is found in the dry areas of the United States and Mexico. The soapweed, *Y. glauca*, is found from New Mexico to the Dakotas. The Adam's needle yucca is *Y. filamentosa*.   EDMUND C. JAEGER

See also FLOWER (color picture: Flowers of the Desert); SPANISH BAYONET.

YUCCA HOUSE NATIONAL MONUMENT stands on the eastern slope of Sleeping Ute Mountain, 10 miles (16 kilometers) southwest of Cortez, Colo. It contains ruins and relics of prehistoric inhabitants. The 10-acre (4-hectare) monument was established in 1919. It is not open to the public because of its inconvenient location, and because it has not been excavated.

Shostal

Rugged Mountains Cover Most of Yugoslavia. The mountains above tower over the town of Kotor, a historic seaport on the Adriatic Sea in southern Yugoslavia.

YUGOSLAVIA

YUGOSLAVIA, or JUGOSLAVIA, is a mountainous country in southeastern Europe. It lies on the Balkan Peninsula along the Adriatic Sea. The country is a little larger than Oregon, but it has about 10 times as many people as that state. Belgrade is the nation's capital and largest city.

The name *Yugoslavia* means *Land of the Southern Slavs.* The name comes from the fact that Slavic peoples make up most of the country's population. These peoples belong to six major nationality groups: Bosnian Muslims, Croats, Macedonians, Montenegrins, Serbs, and Slovenes. The country also has many minority groups, such as Albanians, Germans, Hungarians, Slovaks, and Turks.

Yugoslavia is organized into six regions, called *socialist republics,* according to the historical boundaries of its major nationality groups. These republics are Bosnia and Hercegovina, Croatia, Macedonia, Montenegro, Serbia, and Slovenia. Serbia includes the *autonomous* (self-governing) provinces of Kosovo and Vojvodina, which have numerous ethnic minorities.

Yugoslavia's many nationality groups have given the country a rich variety of cultures. But differences in religion, language, and customs have also led to bitter disputes among the groups and made unity difficult.

Joseph Velikonja, the contributor of this article, is Associate Professor of Geography at the University of Washington.

Yugoslavia has three major religions, three official languages, and two alphabets. But it has only one political party—the Communist Party.

After centuries of separate development, the regions that now make up Yugoslavia were united as an independent kingdom in 1918. In 1945, Yugoslavia became a Communist state under the leadership of Josip Broz Tito. However, the country developed its own form of

--------------------- FACTS IN BRIEF ---------------------

Capital: Belgrade.

Official Languages: Serbo-Croatian, Slovenian, and Macedonian.

Official Name: *Socijalistička Federativna Republika Jugoslavija* (Socialist Federal Republic of Yugoslavia).

Form of Government: Socialist republic.

Area: 98,766 sq. mi. (255,804 km²). *Greatest Distances—* north-south, 415 mi. (668 km); east-west, 475 mi. (764 km). *Coastline—*490 mi. (789 km) along the Adriatic Sea.

Elevation: *Highest—*Mount Triglav, 9,393 ft. (2,863 m) above sea level. *Lowest—*sea level.

Population: *Estimated 1980 Population—*22,347,000; distribution, 54 per cent rural, 46 per cent urban; density, 225 persons per sq. mi. (87 per km²). *1971 Census—* 20,522,972. *Estimated 1985 Population—*23,371,000.

Chief Products: *Agriculture—*corn, livestock, potatoes, sugar beets, wheat. *Manufacturing—*automobiles, chemicals, food products, machinery, metal products, textiles, wood products.

National Anthem: "Hej Sloveni" ("Hey Slavs").

Money: *Basic Unit—*dinar. For its value in U.S. dollars, see MONEY (table: Exchange Rates).

480

Communism, independent of control by the Soviet Union. Tito became a leader of the Third World nations—those countries which side with neither the Communist powers nor the Western democracies.

Before the Communists gained control of Yugoslavia, most of the people were poor farmers. But the Communists have encouraged industrial growth and have worked to raise living standards. They developed an unusual system of economic self-management under which the workers themselves run the industries.

Government

Yugoslavia is a federation of socialist republics. The nation's Constitution was adopted in 1946, and it has been revised several times since.

All Yugoslav citizens 18 or older may vote for delegates to local assemblies. These delegates, in turn, elect the members of higher legislative bodies. Political activity in Yugoslavia centers in the Socialist Alliance of the Working People of Yugoslavia and the Confederation of Trade Unions. The Communist Party controls both organizations.

The Communist Party is the only political party permitted in Yugoslavia. Its official name is the *League of Communists of Yugoslavia*. About 6 per cent of the Yugoslav people belong to the party. They play a major role at all levels of government. Tito serves as president of the League of Communists.

The National Government of Yugoslavia is headed by a nine-member council called the *Presidency*. It is the country's chief policymaking body. The council has one representative from each republic and province. Tito serves as president of the council and as Yugoslavia's head of state.

Yugoslavia has a two-house legislature called the *Federal Assembly*. The 88 members of the Chamber of the Republics and Autonomous Provinces are elected by the assemblies of the republics and provinces. The Federal Chamber has 220 delegates. They are chosen by local assemblies. In addition to passing laws for the nation, the Federal Assembly elects the members of the cabinet, called the *Federal Executive Council*. Council members administer the departments of the national government.

Shostal
Parliament Building houses Yugoslavia's legislature, the Federal Assembly. The building stands in Belgrade, the capital.

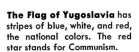

The Flag of Yugoslavia has stripes of blue, white, and red, the national colors. The red star stands for Communism.

Coat of Arms has a torch for each of the nation's six republics. The date marks the start of Communist rule in Yugoslavia.

The president of the council, called the *premier*, is Yugoslavia's head of government.

Republican Government. The government of each republic and province is modeled on the federal system. Each has an assembly elected by local legislatures and an executive council chosen by the assembly.

Local Government. Yugoslavia's republics and provinces are divided into 508 districts called *communes*. Each commune has an assembly and a communal council. Assembly delegates are elected by the residents of cities and towns; by members of social and political organizations; and by workers in individual factories, farms, and other places of work.

Courts. Yugoslavia has civil, criminal, and military courts at each level of government. Special economic courts called *self-management courts* settle disputes between business organizations.

The Armed Forces of Yugoslavia have about 250,000 men. They serve in the Yugoslav People's Army, which consists of air, ground, and naval forces and frontier guard units. Men may be drafted at age 18.

People

Ancestry and Population. About 85 per cent of Yugoslavia's people belong to six Slavic nationality groups. These groups, in order of size, are Serbs, Croats, Slovenes, Bosnian Muslims, Macedonians, and Montenegrins. Other nationalities in Yugoslavia include Al-

WORLD BOOK map
Yugoslavia is a country in southeastern Europe. It lies along the Adriatic Sea and forms part of the Balkan Peninsula.

Yugoslavia Political Map

⎯⎯⎯ International boundary	⎯⎯⎯ Railroad
⎯⎯⎯ Republic boundary	⊛ National capital
⎯⎯⎯ Expressway	★ Republic capital
⎯⎯⎯ Road	• Other city or town

↑ North

WORLD BOOK map

0   100   200 Miles
0   100   200   300 Kilometers

Republics

Bosnia and Herce-
  govina .4,029,000..C 3
Croatia .4,530,000..B 2
Mace-
  donia .1,784,000..F 6
Montenegro 565,000..D 5
Serbia ..8,860,000..D 6
Slovenia .1,792,000..B 2

Cities and Towns

Apatin ...17,565..B 4
Arande-
  lovac* ..15,545..C 5
Bačka
  Palanka ..21,104..B 5
Bačka
  Topola* .15,989..B 5
Banja Luka 90,831..C 3
Bar ....3,612..E 4
Batajnica* .14,567..C 5
Bečej ....26,722..B 5
Belgrade (Beo-
  grad) ..746,105..C 5
Bežanija* ..15,617..C 5
Bihać ....24,060..B 2
Bijeljina ..24,761..C 4
Bileća ....4,033..D 4
Bitola ....65,035..F 6
Bjelovar ..20,998..B 3
Blato ......5,912..D 3

Bor ....29,118..C 6
Bosanski
  Petrovac ..4,016..C 3
Brčko ....25,377..C 4
Čačak ....38,244..C 5
Celje ....31,305..A 2
Cetinje ..11,876..E 4
Ćuprija ...17,564..C 6
Đakovica ..29,653..E 5
Đakovo ...15,987..B 4
Derventa ..11,824..C 4
Doboj ....18,264..C 4
Dubrovnik .31,182..E 4
Foča ......9,257..D 4
Gevgelija ..9,414..F 6
Gnjilane* .21,258..E 6
Gospić ....8,046..C 2
Gostivar ..19,467..E 6
Hercegnovi ..6,705..E 4
Indija* ...17,892..C 5
Ivangrad ..11,164..D 5
Jajce .....9,127..C 3
Jesenice ..17,394..A 1
Karlobag ...508..C 2
Karlovac ..47,543..B 2
Kavadarci .18,170..F 7
Kičevo ...15,393..F 6
Kikinda ..37,576..B 5
Kladanj ...3,379..C 4
Knin ......7,300..C 3
Kočani ...17,257..E 7
Konjic ....9,584..D 4
Koper ....17,116..B 1
Koprivnica .16,483..A 3

Kosovska
  Mitrovica 42,160..D 6
Kragujevac .71,049..C 6
Kraljevo ..27,839..C 6
Kranj ....27,211..A 1
Kruševac ..29,509..D 6
Kula .....17,245..B 5
Kumanovo .46,363..E 6
Leskovac ..45,478..D 6
Livno .....7,207..D 3
Ljubljana .173,853..A 1
Loznica ...13,871..C 5
Metković ..7,117..D 4
Maribor ..96,895..A 2
Mladenovac 15,858..C 6
Mostar ...47,802..D 4
Negotin ..11,166..C 7
Nikšić ...28,527..D 4
Niš .....127,654..D 6
Nova
  Gradiška .11,580..B 3
Nova Varoš .5,718..D 5
Novi Bečej* 16,075..B 5
Novi Pazar .28,950..D 6
Novi Sad .141,375..B 5
Novo Mesto .9,668..B 2
Ogulin ....9,923..B 2
Ohrid ....26,369..F 6
Opatija ...8,995..B 1
Osijek ...94,672..B 4
Pančevo ..54,444..C 5
Paraćin ..21,511..C 6
Peć ......41,853..E 5
Pirot ....29,298..D 7

Pljevlja ...13,865..D 5
Ploče .....4,662..D 3
Požarevac .32,828..C 6
Priboj ...13,034..D 5
Prijedor ..22,223..B 3
Prilep ...48,202..F 6
Priština ..69,514..E 6
Prizren ..41,681..E 6
Prokuplje* .20,104..D 6
Pula .....47,498..C 1
Rijeka
  (Fiume) 132,222..B 1
Rovinj ....8,871..B 1
Ruma .....23,933..B 5
Šabac* ...42,075..C 5
Sarajevo .243,980..D 4
Senj ......4,906..B 2
Senta ....24,723..B 5
Šibenik ..30,066..C 2
Šid ....11,823..B 5
Sisak ....38,458..B 3
Sivac ....10,469..B 5
Skopje ..312,980..E 6
Slavonska
  Požega ..18,184..B 3
Slavonski
  Brod ....38,705..B 4
Slunj .....1,858..B 2
Smederevo .40,192..C 6
Smederevska
  Palanka* 18,687..C 5
Sombor ...44,100..B 4
Split ....152,905..D 3
Srbobran ..14,189..B 5

Sremska
  Mitrovica 31,986..C 5
Stara
  Pazova* .13,776..C 5
Štip .....27,224..E 7
Struga ...11,475..F 6
Strumica ..23,034..F 7
Subotica ..88,813..A 5
Svetozarevo .27,658..C 6
Tetovo ...35,745..E 6
Titograd ..54,822..E 5
Titov Veles 35,980..E 6
Titovo
  Užice ...34,555..C 5
Travnik ..12,977..C 4
Trbovlje ..16,659..A 2
Trogir .....6,717..D 3
Tuzla ....53,926..C 4
Uroševac ..22,239..E 6
Valjevo ...26,293..C 5
Varaždin ..34,312..A 3
Vinkovci ..29,106..B 4
Virovitica .16,378..B 3
Vranje ...25,653..E 6
Vrbas ....22,496..B 5
Vršac ....34,256..B 6
Vukovar ..30,222..B 4
Zadar ....43,087..C 2
Zagreb ..566,224..B 2
Zaječar ..27,599..C 6
Zarkovo* ..29,204..C 5
Železnik* .16,510..C 5
Zenica ...51,263..C 4
Zrenjanin .59,630..B 5

*Does not appear on map; key shows general location.

Sources: 1976 official estimates for republics; 1971 census for cities and towns.

banians, Germans, Gypsies, Hungarians, Slovaks, and Turks.

Groups of Slavs began to migrate to the Balkan Peninsula from what are now southern Poland and Russia during the A.D. 500's. Each Slavic group had its own leaders and culture. Relations among the various nationality groups—especially between Serbs and Croats—have always been tense.

Yugoslavia has a population of about 22 million. About 46 per cent of the people live in cities and towns. However, the percentage of urban dwellers is rising constantly as more and more countrypeople move to the cities to seek jobs in industry. About 746,000 persons live in Belgrade, the capital and largest city. Yugoslavia has eight other cities with more than 100,000 persons. They are, in order of population, Zagreb, Skopje, Sarajevo, Ljubljana, Split, Novi Sad, Rijeka, and Niš.

Languages. Yugoslavia has three official languages and two alphabets. The languages—Serbo-Croatian, Slovenian, and Macedonian—are closely related. Serbo-Croatian is the most common of the three languages. Serbs, Montenegrins, and most Bosnians write it in the Cyrillic alphabet. Croats write it in the Roman alphabet. Slovenian is written in Roman letters, and Macedonian in Cyrillic letters.

Each minority group in Yugoslavia also has its own language. The Yugoslav Constitution guarantees citizens the right to use their native language in business, in the courts, and in schools. Many Yugoslavs speak more than one language.

Way of Life. Yugoslavs have a higher standard of living than do the people of most other Eastern European countries. Many families own an automobile, a television set, and various other luxury items. Yugoslavs also have greater personal freedom than do the citizens of other Communist nations. For example, Yugoslavs may travel about their country freely. They also may travel abroad and even work in other countries. All citizens receive free medical care, and workers are given a pension on retirement.

Many city dwellers in Yugoslavia live in modern apartment buildings. Numerous others live in older apartments or houses. In most families, both the husband and the wife have a full-time job. Government day-care centers look after preschool children. Yugoslav cities have a severe housing shortage, largely because so many rural people keep moving to them. New apartment buildings are being constructed—but not fast enough to meet the demand.

Many rural families live in small stone or wooden houses. The size and style of the homes vary from region to region. About three-fourths of all rural homes in Yugoslavia have electricity.

In the cities, most people wear Western-style clothing. They wear traditional costumes only on holidays. Such costumes are more common in rural areas. But in Slovenia and Croatia, even countrypeople wear mainly Western-style clothes.

Food and Drink. Each region of Yugoslavia has its own special foods. For example, Serbs like grilled meats, particularly a spicy meatball dish called *čevapčiči* (pronounced *cheh VAHP chee chee*). Fish stew and other seafood dishes are popular in the coastal areas. Macedonians eat many lamb dishes. Yugoslavia's national

Jerry Frank, DPI

Belgrade is Yugoslavia's largest city. Modern buildings line the broad, busy streets of the downtown section.

drink is plum brandy, called *slivovitz*. Yugoslavs also like wine and coffee.

Recreation. In the evening, many Yugoslavs take part in an old custom called the *korzo*. They stroll along the main street of their city or town and stop to chat with friends they meet. Coffee houses, called *kafanas*, are popular gathering places throughout Yugoslavia. Many city people enjoy motion pictures, concerts, operas, and stage plays.

Sports events, especially soccer games, draw huge crowds. In winter, many people ski in the mountains of Slovenia and Bosnia. In summer, they enjoy fishing, swimming, and other water sports in the Adriatic Sea and in the country's many mountain lakes.

Religion is important in the lives of most Yugoslavs, but especially rural people. About one-third of all Yugoslavs, including the majority of Macedonians, Mon-

William Parker

Folk Dancers in Traditional Costumes perform every Sunday in Cilipi, a village near Dubrovnik. Each of Yugoslavia's many nationality groups has preserved its rich folk traditions.

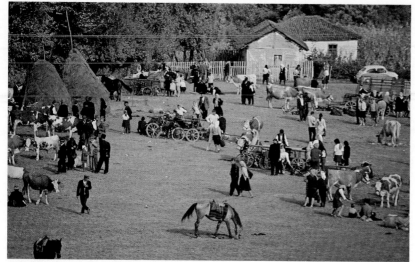

A Rural Fair in the republic of Serbia attracts countrypeople from neighboring villages and towns. Farmers come to the fair to buy and sell livestock and other products.

tenegrins, and Serbs, belong to Eastern Orthodox churches. About 25 per cent of the people are Roman Catholics. They include most Croats and Slovenes. About 10 per cent of the Yugoslavs are Muslims. Most of them live in Bosnia and Macedonia.

The government tries to reduce the influence of religion in Yugoslavia. But it generally does not interfere with the religious practices of the people. However, religious organizations may not take part in politics.

Education. About 85 per cent of the Yugoslav people can read and write. Education is free. The law requires children from ages 7 through 14 to attend elementary school. The students are taught in their native language. After completing elementary school, students may enter either a vocational school or a four-year secondary school. Yugoslavia's major universities are in Belgrade, Ljubljana, Sarajevo, Skopje, Titograd, and Zagreb. The Communist Party controls all Yugoslav schools, and teachers are expected to support party policies.

The Arts. Much of Yugoslavia's art reflects the rich folk traditions of the country's nationality groups. These traditions go back hundreds of years. They have been preserved in colorful costumes, dances, tales, songs, and handicrafts. Many modern Yugoslav writers, composers, and artists use elements of folk traditions in their works.

Until the 1800's, most of the people who lived in what is now Yugoslavia could not read or write. They handed down their culture orally from generation to generation. Religious writings were the only form of literature in most of the area before the 1800's. Then nonreligious literature began to develop. Most writers followed Western European styles, but many also borrowed themes from folk stories and songs.

After the Communists came to power in 1945, they strictly controlled what Yugoslav authors could publish. But since the mid-1950's, writers have had greater freedom. Ivo Andrić, the best-known Yugoslav writer of the 1900's, won the 1961 Nobel prize for literature.

The Coastal Region of Yugoslavia has many rocky cliffs and steep mountains that rise abruptly from the Adriatic Sea. The walled city shown here is Dubrovnik, which has been a major port for centuries. It is one of Yugoslavia's most popular tourist attractions.

Other leading writers of the 1900's include Ivan Cankar, Dobrica Ćosić, Oskar Davičo, Miroslav Krleža, and Oton Župančič.

Wall paintings decorate many Serbian churches built in the Middle Ages. These paintings are the most important examples of early Yugoslav art. Since the early 1800's, most Yugoslav painters have followed Western European styles. The so-called primitive paintings of untrained peasant artists have gained increasing praise from some art critics.

During the early 1900's, Ivan Mestrovic became Yugoslavia's most famous sculptor. His highly patriotic and religious works can be seen in many parts of the world. Large commemorative sculptures stand throughout Yugoslavia. They memorialize events in the lives of the people during World War II (1939-1945).

The Land

Yugoslavia occupies 98,766 square miles (255,804 square kilometers) on the Balkan Peninsula. Mountains cover most of the country. Yugoslavia has three main land regions: (1) the Coastal Region, (2) the Interior Highlands, and (3) the Pannonian Plains.

The Coastal Region is a narrow, rocky strip of land along the Adriatic Sea. The region also includes more than 600 islands. In many areas, steep mountains and cliffs rise abruptly from the sea. The sharply indented coastline provides many excellent natural harbors. The region's beautiful scenery and sunny beaches attract millions of vacationists each year.

The Coastal Region is made up of a type of limestone called *karst*. The surface is mostly barren rock with patches of fertile soil.

The Interior Highlands rise from the Coastal Region and consist of a number of mountain ranges. The ranges extend from northwestern to southeastern Yugoslavia.

The Julian Alps lie in the northwest corner of the country. Mount Triglav, Yugoslavia's highest peak, rises 9,393 feet (2,863 meters) in this range. The Julian Alps have many ski resorts and are Yugoslavia's winter playground.

The Dinaric Alps parallel the Adriatic coast. Like the Coastal Region, the Dinaric Alps consist mostly of karst and have little fertile land. The area has many caves with fantastic rock formations. The cave at Postojna, near Ljubljana, is world famous. In eastern and southeastern Yugoslavia, mountain ranges extend into Romania, Bulgaria, and Greece.

The Interior Highlands are a barrier between the Coastal Region and the Pannonian Plains. In the past, the mountains often helped protect the country from invasion. But they also made communication and transportation difficult within Yugoslavia. Today, many roads and railroads cut through the mountains.

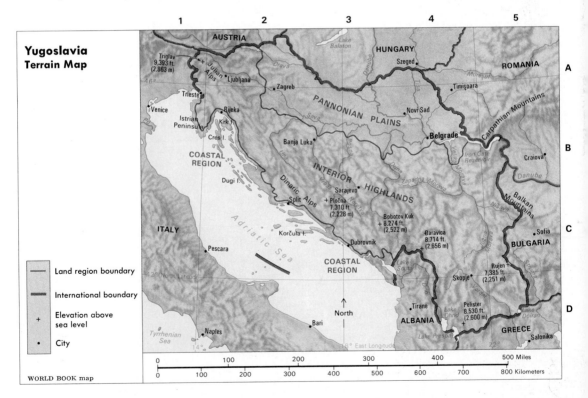

Yugoslavia Terrain Map

WORLD BOOK map

Physical Features		
Adriatic Sea ......C 2		
Bobotov Kuk		
(Mountain) ......C 3		
Bosna (River) .....B 3		
Cres Island ....B 1		
Danube (River) ....A 3		
Đaravica (Mountain) C 4	Istrian Peninsula ..B 1	Lake Scutari ......C 3	Triglav (Mountain) A 1
Dinaric Alps	Julian Alps	Neretva (River) ....C 3	Una (River) ....B 2
(Mountains) ....B 2	(Mountains) ....A 1	Nišava (River) .....C 5	Vardar (River) ....D 5
Drava (River) .....A 2	Južna Morava	Pelister (Mountain) D 4	Velika Morava
Drina (River) .....B 3	(River) ....C 5	Ploćna (Mountain) .C 3	(River) ....B 4
Dugi Island ....B 2	Korčula Island ....C 2	Rujen (Mountain) ..C 5	Vrbas (River) .....B 3
Iron Gate	Krk Island ....B 2	Sava (River) ....B 3	Zapadna Morava
Reservoir ....B 4	Lake Ohrid ....D 4	Tisa (River) ....A 4	(River) ....B 4

Yugoslav Farmers use both modern equipment and farm animals to work their fields. About 85 per cent of Yugoslavia's farms are privately owned. But the government limits the size of these farms to 25 acres (10 hectares).

Earthquakes frequently strike the highlands. In 1963, a violent earthquake leveled most of Skopje. In 1979, a major earthquake badly damaged towns and villages in the southern Interior Highlands and caused even more damage in the southeastern Coastal Region.

The Pannonian Plains lie in north-central Yugoslavia. The region is mostly flat, with some low hills. It has the richest soil in Yugoslavia and is the country's chief agricultural area.

Rivers and Lakes. Yugoslavia's most important river is the Danube. It enters the country from Hungary and flows through the Pannonian Plains. It then enters Romania through a gorge called the Iron Gate. The Danube's main tributaries in Yugoslavia are the Drava, Morava, Sava, and Tisa rivers. They serve as shipping routes, and many major cities lie along their banks. Other important Yugoslav rivers include the Bosna, Drina, Neretva, Nišava, and Vardar.

The Interior Highlands are dotted with hundreds of small, beautiful lakes that attract many tourists. Yugoslavia's largest lake, Lake Scutari, extends into Albania. Yugoslavia also shares Lake Ohrid with Albania, Lake Doiran with Greece, and Lake Prespa with both Albania and Greece.

Climate

The Coastal Region has a mild climate. In winter, the temperature rarely falls below freezing along most of the coast. But the northern area is often hit by strong, cold winds that blow in from the mountains. Summers are sunny, hot, and dry.

The Interior Highlands have exceptionally cold winters with much snow. Heavy rains fall in early summer. Summers are warm in the mountain valleys but cool at higher elevations.

The Pannonian Plains have cold winters with a freezing wind called a košava. Summers are dry and extremely hot. Temperatures often rise to about 100° F. (38° C). Heavy rains in spring and autumn frequently cause floods along the Danube and its tributaries. These floods sometimes do great damage.

Economy

Since World War II, the Communists have worked to develop Yugoslavia from an agricultural country into an industrial nation. The government introduced economic programs to encourage industrial growth and raise living standards. At first, the programs were developed and carried out by government agencies. But in the 1950's, the government began a system of *self-management*. Under this system, economic planning is done by workers in individual enterprises, such as factories and mines. A workers' council in each enterprise determines production goals, prices, and wages—all based on government guidelines.

Before World War II, agriculture accounted for half the value of all goods and services produced in Yugoslavia. About three-fourths of all workers were farmers. Today, agriculture accounts for about 20 per cent of the country's total production, compared with 40 per cent for industry. Agriculture still employs about two-fifths of all workers. But the number of farm workers is declining steadily as more and more of them seek higher-paying jobs in the cities.

Natural Resources. Farmland covers about 58 per cent of Yugoslavia, and forests cover about 35 per cent. The nation's mineral resources include rich deposits of bauxite, chromite, coal, copper, iron, and lead. Yugoslavia also has some deposits of natural gas and petroleum.

Hydroelectric plants generate more than half the nation's electricity. Coal is also widely used to produce electric power. A large nuclear power plant is being built near Zagreb. The plant is scheduled for completion in 1980.

Industry. Socialist factories produce about 85 per cent of Yugoslavia's industrial output. Privately owned businesses account for the rest. The government limits the size of private businesses.

Most of Yugoslavia's industries are in Slovenia and Croatia. These industries produce automobiles, chemicals, machinery, metal and wood products, processed foods, and textiles. Factories in the Pannonian Plains produce flour, refined sugar, textiles, and tobacco products. The coastal cities of Rijeka and Split are shipbuilding centers.

Craftworkers in small, privately owned shops make baskets, carpets, woodcarvings, and various other handicraft items. Yugoslavia's handicraft industry has grown rapidly with the increase in the number of foreign tourists. Many of these tourists prize handmade objects that reflect native cultures.

Agriculture. About 85 per cent of Yugoslavia's farms are privately owned. The government limits the size of these farms to 25 acres (10 hectares) and controls the prices that farmers may get for their products. Large farms are organized into *cooperative* and *state* farms. On cooperative farms, the workers decide what to produce and share the earnings. State farms are owned and operated by the government, and the workers receive a salary. Cooperative and state farms have modern equipment, but many private farmers use primitive methods and tools. As a result, cooperative and state farms account for a higher percentage of the nation's agricultural production.

Yugoslavia's leading farm products include corn, sugar beets, and wheat, which grow chiefly on the Pannonian Plains. Farmers in the Interior Highlands grow barley, oats, and potatoes and raise cattle and sheep. Tobacco and grapes, olives, plums, and other fruits are grown in the Coastal Region.

Trade. Yugoslavia trades mostly with Western European nations, especially Italy and West Germany. The amount of trade between Yugoslavia and other Communist countries depends on how friendly their political relations are. Yugoslavia's chief imports include coal, crude oil, machinery, motor vehicles, and textiles. Its main exports include forest products, livestock, machinery, metals, plastics, and textiles.

Yugoslavia spends more money on imports than it earns on exports. Income from the foreign tourist business partly makes up for this poor balance of trade. In addition, many Yugoslav citizens who work abroad send money home. Yugoslav cargo ships also bring in money by transporting goods for other countries. The total earnings from these three sources equal the value of Yugoslavia's exports.

Transportation. Yugoslavia has approximately 61,000 miles (98,200 kilometers) of roads, about half of which are paved. Some 6,400 miles (10,300 kilometers) of railroad track crisscross the country. Trains haul most of the nation's freight. Trains also carry passengers, but most Yugoslavs travel about the country by bus. For local transportation, many people have a bicycle, car, or motorcycle.

The government controls Yugoslavia's airlines, and 12 Yugoslav cities have an international airport. The country's leading ports include Bar, Dubrovnik, Koper, Ploče, Rijeka, and Split. The Danube River and its tributaries are major shipping routes.

Communication. Yugoslavia publishes about 25 daily newspapers. The official government paper, *Borba*, is printed in the Cyrillic alphabet in Belgrade and in the Roman alphabet in Zagreb. Many newspapers and magazines are published in local languages.

The government controls radio and television broadcasting. Each republic has its own stations, which broadcast in the local language. Owners of radio and TV sets pay an annual fee to help finance the programs.

History

People have lived in what is now Yugoslavia for at least 100,000 years. The first settlers in recorded history were Illyrians and Thracians, who lived in the area about 3,000 years ago. The Greeks established colonies along the Adriatic Sea coast during the 600's B.C. Celtic tribes moved into the area 100 years later.

The Romans began to invade the Balkan Peninsula during the 300's B.C. By the time of Christ's birth, they had conquered the entire peninsula. In A.D. 395, the Roman Empire was divided into two parts. The West Roman Empire included what are now Croatia, Slovenia, and part of Bosnia. The East Roman, or Byzantine, Empire included what are now Macedonia, Montenegro, and Serbia. The division of the empire influenced the region's history to the present time. People in the areas ruled by the Byzantine Empire adopted the Eastern Orthodox faith and the Cyrillic alphabet. People in the other areas became Roman Catholics and used the Roman alphabet.

The Slavs. Groups of Slavs began to move into the Yugoslav area in the 500's. They migrated from what are now southern Poland and Russia and became known as *southern Slavs.* Each Slavic group formed its own independent state. For example, the Croats established Croatia, and the Serbs founded Serbia. But by 1400, foreign powers controlled nearly all the lands of the southern Slavs. Austria ruled Slovenia, and Hungary ruled Croatia. The Turks controlled Serbia, which included what are now Macedonia and Montenegro. The Turks also ruled Bosnia and Hercegovina. The Venetians controlled the coastal region of Dalmatia, which is now part of Croatia.

The Movement for Slavic Unity began in the early 1800's. Slovenia and Croatia were united from 1809 to 1815 under the rule of Emperor Napoleon I of France. This brief period of unity inspired the Slovenes and Croats to work for a single, independent nation of all southern Slavs. Serbia, which gained independence from Turkey in 1878, was also interested in such a union. But Austria-Hungary, which ruled Slovenia and Croatia, refused to grant them independence. In addition, the country extended its control of the area by gaining Bosnia and Hercegovina.

During the early 1900's, the movement to unite the southern Slavs became inflamed. On June 28, 1914, a

Shostal

Factory Workers in Slovenia assemble parts for electronic equipment. Slovenia leads the other Yugoslav republics in industrial output. But industry is growing rapidly throughout the nation.

483

YUGOSLAVIA

Bosnian patriot assassinated Archduke Francis Ferdinand of Austria-Hungary in Sarajevo. Austria-Hungary believed that Serbia had planned the killing and declared war on it, which marked the start of World War I. Austria-Hungary was defeated in 1918. The southern Slavs were then free to form their own state. See WORLD WAR I.

A New Nation called *the Kingdom of the Serbs, Croats, and Slovenes* was formed on Dec. 1, 1918. It consisted of Bosnia and Hercegovina, Croatia, Dalmatia, Montenegro, Serbia, and Slovenia. King Peter I of Serbia became king of the new nation. However, he was old and sick, and so his son Alexander served as regent. Peter died in 1921, and Alexander became king.

Problems soon developed in the kingdom. The Slovenes and Croats believed that the Serbs had too much power in the government. They demanded greater control over their local affairs. In addition, the many nationality groups made unity difficult.

The nation's Constitution, adopted in 1921, provided for a constitutional monarchy. But in 1929, King Alexander abolished the Constitution and began to rule as a dictator. He changed the name of the country to Yugoslavia and tried to unite the nationality groups by enforcing the use of only one language. He also created new political divisions that ignored the groups' historical boundaries. He banned political parties and restricted the press. Alexander's actions only worsened relations between the nationality groups. He was assassinated in 1934 by Croatian terrorists. His 11-year-old son, King Peter II, was too young to rule. Alexander's cousin, Prince Paul, ruled in the boy's place. Paul carried on Alexander's policies, however, and the disputes among the groups continued.

World War II began in 1939 as a struggle between the Axis powers, led by Germany and Italy, and the Allies, led by Great Britain and France. Yugoslavia was unprepared for war, and so its government wanted to be friendly with both sides. Under pressure from the

Germans, the Yugoslav government joined the Axis on March 25, 1941. But the Yugoslav people rebelled. The army overthrew Paul's government, and 17-year-old Peter took the throne. On April 6, Germany invaded Yugoslavia. The Yugoslav armed forces surrendered 11 days later. Peter and government leaders fled to London and formed a government-in-exile.

German and other Axis troops occupied Yugoslavia. A resistance movement spread among the Yugoslav people. Some of them joined the *Partisans*, a group led by Josip Broz Tito and the Communist Party. Other Yugoslavs fought with the *Chetniks*, a group led by Draža Mihailovich. The Partisans wanted to establish a Communist government in Yugoslavia. The Chetniks supported the government of King Peter.

The two resistance groups fought each other, as well as the occupation forces. At first, the Allies provided the Chetniks with weapons and supplies. But they switched their support to the Partisans in 1943 because Tito's forces were more effective against the Axis.

Communist Rule. The Partisans quickly gained the support of the Yugoslav people. The Communists set up a temporary government in Jajce in November 1943. Aided by Soviet troops, the Partisans freed Belgrade from occupation in 1944. The Communists then began to govern from the capital. By the time World War II ended in Europe in May 1945, Tito and the Communists firmly controlled all Yugoslavia.

On Nov. 29, 1945, Yugoslavia became a republic. It was called the Federal People's Republic of Yugoslavia and was organized according to the present-day republics and provinces. The monarchy was abolished, and King Peter never returned to Yugoslavia. Opponents of the Communist government were either imprisoned or exiled. Mihailovich was executed in 1946. The archbishop of Zagreb, Aloysius Stepinac, was imprisoned the same year on charges of having aided the enemies. The government permitted only one political party, the Communist Party, and took control of farms, factories, and other businesses.

Yugoslavia was a close Soviet ally, but Tito refused to let the Soviet Union control the country. In June 1948, the Soviet dictator, Joseph Stalin, broke off relations with Yugoslavia. The Cominform, an organization of Communist nations, expelled Yugoslavia and withdrew all aid. Yugoslavia turned to the United States and other Western nations for help. Beginning in 1951,

WORLD BOOK map

The Formation of Yugoslavia began with the union of the territories dated 1918. Other territories were added in 1919, 1920, and 1947. The red line shows Yugoslavia's present borders.

the United States provided Yugoslavia with military and economic aid.

After the split with the Soviet Union, Yugoslavia began to develop its own type of Communist society. The republics and provinces received greater control over local matters. A system of self-management, under which the workers run the industries, began about 1950. It became the basis of the Yugoslav economic system.

However, disagreements arose among Yugoslav Communist leaders. Some of them sided with the Soviet Union in the 1948 split and were imprisoned. Milovan Djilas, a high government official, was expelled from the party in 1954 for his writings, which criticized the Communist system. Djilas was imprisoned from 1956 to 1961 and again from 1962 to 1966.

In 1955, two years after Stalin's death, Soviet and Yugoslav leaders reopened relations. However, Tito refused to take sides in the Cold War between the Communist nations and the Western democracies. Instead, he became a leading speaker for the uncommitted nations of the world.

Yugoslavia Today. Since 1974, a nine-member council called the *Presidency* has headed the Yugoslav government. The Presidency was established to provide leadership after Tito's retirement or death. However, many Yugoslavs fear that a power struggle will then take place which could lead to increased Soviet influence over their country.

In 1971 and 1974, changes in the Yugoslav Constitution gave more political power to the republics. But many Croats want complete independence. During the 1960's and 1970's, some Croatian groups used terrorist methods to publicize their demands. In the early 1970's, several Croatian Communist leaders were expelled from the party for supporting the independence movement.

The government is working to build up industry in the underdeveloped regions of Kosovo, Macedonia, and Montenegro. It hopes to raise the standard of living in these regions. In addition, the growth of manufacturing would slow the migration of Yugoslav workers to the industrialized cities of the northwest and to foreign countries.   JOSEPH VELIKONJA

Related Articles in WORLD BOOK include:

BIOGRAPHIES

Alexander I   Peter II
Mestrovic, Ivan   Stepinac, Aloysius Cardinal
Mihailovich, Draža   Tito, Josip Broz
Peter I

CITIES

Belgrade   Sarajevo
Ljubljana   Skopje
Novi Sad   Split
Rijeka   Zagreb

HISTORY

Albania (History)   Little Entente   Trieste
Austria-Hungary   Rapallo,   World War I
Balkans   Treaties of   World War II
Hungary (History)

REGIONS AND PHYSICAL FEATURES

Alps   Danube River
Dalmatia   Istria

REPUBLICS

Bosnia and Hercegovina   Montenegro
Croatia   Serbia
Macedonia   Slovenia

OTHER RELATED ARTICLES

Christmas   Lead (graph)   Slavs
(In Yugoslavia)   Para

Outline

I. Government
  A. The Communist Party   D. Local Government
  B. The National   E. Courts
     Government   F. The Armed Forces
  C. Republican Government
II. People
  A. Ancestry and Population   E. Recreation
  B. Languages   F. Religion
  C. Way of Life   G. Education
  D. Food and Drink   H. The Arts
III. The Land
  A. The Coastal Region   C. The Pannonian Plains
  B. The Interior   D. Rivers and Lakes
     Highlands
IV. Climate
V. Economy
  A. Natural Resources   D. Trade
  B. Industry   E. Transportation
  C. Agriculture   F. Communication
VI. History

Questions

Who were the *Partisans*? The *Chetniks*?

What are the six main nationality groups in Yugoslavia?

What is the *korzo*?

How did the division of the Roman Empire influence Yugoslavia's history?

How does the Yugoslav economic system of self-management operate?

What does the name *Yugoslavia* mean?

Why has Yugoslavia's handicraft industry grown rapidly?

What is Yugoslavia's chief agricultural region?

Who became the best-known Yugoslav writer of the 1900's?

What is a *cooperative farm*? A *state farm*?

YUIT. See ESKIMO.

YUKAWA, *YOO kah wah*, **HIDEKI** (1907-   ), a Japanese physicist, became famous for his contributions to theoretical nuclear physics. He won the 1949 Nobel prize for physics. He was the first Japanese so honored. He won the award for a theory he worked out in 1935. The theory predicted the existence of the *meson*. This elementary nuclear particle has a mass greater than that of the electron and less than that of the proton. The British physicist Cecil F. Powell provided experimental proof for Yukawa's theory in 1947. Powell discovered a particle in cosmic rays that had the properties of the particle predicted by Yukawa's theory.

Yukawa was born in Tokyo and studied at Kyoto University. He became a lecturer at Kyoto in 1932 and a professor there in 1939. From 1933 to 1936, he was a lecturer in nuclear physics at Osaka University.

Yukawa came to the United States in 1948, at the invitation of J. Robert Oppenheimer, to act as a visiting professor and work at the Institute for Advanced Study in Princeton, N.J. He became professor of physics at Columbia University in 1950. In 1953, he became the first director of the Research Institute for Fundamental Physics at Kyoto University. Yukawa has written books on advanced physics, but he is better known as an essayist.   R. T. ELLICKSON

See also ANDERSON, CARL DAVID; MESON.

YUKON RIVER

YUKON RIVER, one of the longest rivers in North America, flows through Alaska and the Yukon Territory of Canada. The river rises in Canadian soil, but two-thirds of its course is in Alaska. Its total length, from its mouth on the Bering Sea to its headwaters in British Columbia, is 1,770 miles (2,849 kilometers). This is about as far as the distance between Boston and Denver, or between Montreal and Edmonton in Canada. The Yukon drains more than 330,000 square miles (855,000 square kilometers). About half of this area lies in Alaska.

The Yukon is navigable for almost its entire length. Before World War II, wood-burning stern-wheelers traveled from its mouth to Dawson in the Yukon Territory. The Yukon was the principal transportation route during the early mining days of Alaska and the famous Klondike Gold Rush. But decreased mining activities and the convenience of air transportation have made shipping by boat unprofitable. Villagers along the river still use boats to transport freight and other necessities. The Yukon is frozen up to seven months of the year. Many of the small tributaries contain gold-bearing gravels. The eastern part has hot springs.

The Course of the Yukon. The Yukon rises from a series of small lakes in northwest British Columbia. It flows northwest and joins the Pelly River at Fort Selkirk. The Yukon continues past Dawson, and crosses the U.S.-Canada border near Eagle, Alaska. The river continues to flow northwest to Ft. Yukon, where it begins flowing southwest. It then curves and flows northwest to the Bering Sea. The Yukon Valley is divided into

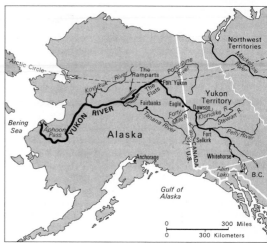

WORLD BOOK map
Location of the Yukon River

two regions, the Upper Yukon and the Lower Yukon.

Upper Yukon. The principal tributaries of the Upper Yukon are the Selwyn, White, Stewart, Klondike, and Forty-Mile rivers. The first important discoveries of gold in this region were made on Forty-Mile Creek in 1895. But these were overshadowed a few years later by the richness of the Klondike field. Dawson, the largest settlement on the Upper Yukon, and capital of Yukon Territory until 1951, stands at the meeting point of the Klondike River and the Yukon.

After flowing northwest for 450 miles (724 kilometers), the Yukon turns almost at right angles and flows southwest for 200 miles (320 kilometers) through the famous "Flats." These are level areas of sand bars and low islands, covered with spruce, willow, and birch. There the river channel constantly shifts, and at seasons of high water it increases from a normal width of 10 miles (16 kilometers) to more than 40 miles (64 kilometers). The "great bend" of the Yukon is about 3 miles (4.8 kilometers) north of the Arctic Circle.

The "Flats" end at the Ramparts, a gorge that extends 110 miles (177 kilometers) to the mouth of the Tanana River. In this part, the Yukon Valley is 1 to 3 miles (1.6 to 4.8 kilometers) wide. The Tanana, which is the Yukon's largest tributary entirely in Alaska, flows northwest for about 400 miles (640 kilometers), roughly parallel to and about 125 miles (201 kilometers) west of the Upper Yukon.

Lower Yukon. The Ramparts gorge ends at the mouth of the Tanana River. The river then enters a lowland about 25 miles (40 kilometers) wide. From this point to the sea, 800 miles (1,300 kilometers) away, the river valley is never less than 2 miles (3.2 kilometers) wide.

The Yukon delta covers nearly 9,000 square miles (23,000 square kilometers). The river has more than 20 outlets over 600 feet (180 meters) wide. But most of them are shallow and filled with sand bars. Steamers enter the delta through the Aphoon Pass, which is only 4 feet (1.2 meters) deep at low water.   LYMAN E. ALLEN

See also RIVER (chart: Longest Rivers).

Bob and Ira Spring
A Yukon River Cruise takes passengers through Miles Canyon, above, in the Yukon Territory of Canada. The river begins in British Columbia and flows across the Yukon Territory and Alaska.

Yukon Territory

⊛	**Capital**
•	Other City or Town
—	Road
+—	Rail Line
▲	MOUNTAIN
⌒	*River*

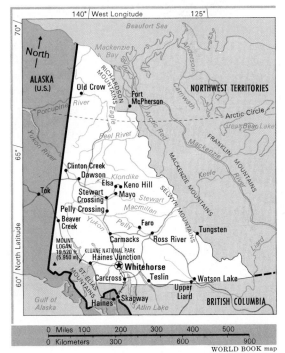

WORLD BOOK map

YUKON TERRITORY, *YOO kahn,* is a region in northwest Canada. It is part of a vast subarctic region, with long, cold winters and short, warm summers. Rich mineral deposits have been developed there. Many prospectors hurried to the territory during the Klondike Gold Rush in 1897 and 1898. Today, mining remains the most important industry. Whitehorse is the capital.

The Land and Its Resources

Location, Size, and Description. The Yukon Territory covers 207,076 square miles (536,324 square kilometers) in the shape of a rough triangle. The base rests on the border of British Columbia, and the peak on the Arctic Ocean. Alaska lies to the west of the territory, and the Northwest Territories lies to the east. The Yukon Territory is about one-third the size of Alaska.

Ranges of the largest mountain system of North America almost entirely cover the Yukon Territory. The Rockies form part of this system, but spread out into smaller chains in the southeast, near the Liard River. The highest peaks rise in the Saint Elias Mountains in the southwest. Mount Logan (19,520 feet, or 5,950 meters) is the highest point in Canada.

The territory derives its name from the Yukon River.

The word Yukon probably had its origin in the Indian word *Youcon* (*greatest* or *big river*). The Yukon River drains over half of the territory. Most of the rest is drained into the Mackenzie River through the Peel and Liard river systems. Two bridges span the main section of the Yukon River—the Robert Campbell Bridge at Whitehorse and the Carmacks Bridge at Carmacks.

Natural Resources. The territory has large deposits of asbestos, coal, copper, gold, lead, nickel, silver, and zinc. Valuable forests of white spruce cover much of the land. Other trees include birch, fir, pine, and poplar.

Varieties of almost all fur-bearing animals live in the Yukon Territory. Animals of the region include bear, caribou, Dall (white) sheep, moose, and mountain goats. Among the game birds are grouse, ptarmigan, and waterfowl. Grayling, northern pike, lake and rainbow trout, salmon, and whitefish swim in streams and lakes.

Climate. The territory's temperatures vary greatly. Average January temperatures are 5° F. (−15° C) at Whitehorse and −16° F. (−27° C) at Dawson. The coldest temperature ever recorded in North America was −81° F. (−63° C), at Snag Airport near the Alaska border on Feb. 3, 1947. Summer temperatures average from 50° F. (10° C) in the north to 60° F. (16° C) in the south. The territory's record high temperature, 95° F. (35° C), occurred in Dawson and Mayo on June 18, 1950. Annual snowfall varies from 40 inches (100 centimeters) in the north to over twice as much in the south. Rainfall averages from 9 to 13 inches (23 to 33 centimeters) per year.

The People and Their Work

The People. The Yukon Territory has a population of 21,836. Most of the inhabitants are white, but the

---
FACTS IN BRIEF

Capital: Whitehorse.

Government: *National*—members of the Senate, 1; members of the House of Commons, 1. *Territorial*—members of the territorial council, 16.

Area: 207,076 sq. mi. (536,324 km²), including 1,730 sq. mi. (4,481 km²) of inland water. *Greatest Distances*—north-south, 666 mi. (1,072 km); east-west, 600 mi. (966 km).

Elevation: *Highest*—Mount Logan in the Saint Elias Mountains, 19,520 ft. (5,950 m) above sea level. *Lowest*—sea level, along the Beaufort Sea.

Population: *1976 Census*—21,836; distribution, 61 per cent urban, 39 per cent rural; density, 11 persons per 100 sq. mi. (4 persons per 100 km²).

Chief Products: *Fishing Industry*—salmon, whitefish, lake trout. *Fur Industry*—lynx, muskrat. *Manufacturing*—chemicals, food products, printed materials, wood products. *Mining*—zinc, copper, lead, silver, gold.

Flag: The flag has three vertical panels. The left panel is green for the forests, the center panel is white for the snows, and the right panel is blue for the lakes. On the center panel is the territory's coat of arms above a wreath of the official flower, the fireweed. The coat of arms has a crest bearing a black and white malamute dog. The coat of arms also has a shield. The shield consists of a wavy blue vertical stripe representing the Yukon River, red "steeples" referring to the mountains, gold balls representing the mineral resources, and a Cross of St. George symbolizing the fur trade of the early English explorers. The flag was adopted in 1967. See FLAG (picture: Flags of Canada).

Whitehorse, the capital and largest city of the Yukon Territory, lies in an important mining region. Offices of the territorial government are in the Administration Building, *center.*

number also includes about 2,700 Indians. About three-fifths of the territory's people live in the Whitehorse area. Most of the rest live near mining camps. Most Yukoners work in government, mining, tourism, or other service activities. Almost all of the people speak English. Anglicans and Roman Catholics make up the largest religious groups in the Yukon Territory.

Way of Life. The people of the Yukon Territory must wear warm clothing in order to survive the cold winters. Some people bank the side walls of their homes with snow during the winter to provide added insulation from the cold. But in the many modern, well-insulated houses having basements and force-draft oil furnaces, this is not necessary. Daily air, rail, and trucking services bring perishable foods to the territory. Shipments of food also come from Vancouver, B.C. These shipments go to Skagway, Alaska, by ocean steamer and reach the Yukon Territory by rail.

Cities. Whitehorse (pop. 13,311) is the territory's capital. Other Yukon settlements and their populations include Faro (1,544), Dawson (838), Watson Lake (808), Mayo (448), and Haines Junction (268).

Mining. Most of the people in the Yukon Territory work in mining or related activities. Mining provides an annual income of about $125 million. Zinc is the great-

est source of this income, providing about $40 million a year.

For many years after the Klondike Gold Rush, gold mining ranked as the chief industry. By the mid-1900's, it had been surpassed by the mining of ores containing lead, silver, and zinc. These minerals come from mines in the Elsa and Faro areas. Copper is mined at Whitehorse.

Tourism ranks as the second greatest source of income in the Yukon Territory. It provides an annual income of about $25 million. Every year thousands of people travel across the Yukon Territory on the Alaska Highway. The Yukon section is considered by many to be the most scenic portion of the entire highway. Tourists also visit the territory to see the scenes of the famous Klondike Gold Rush. Dawson has preserved many landmarks of that era.

Many visitors to the Yukon Territory have read the works of Robert William Service, who wrote his first famous poems in Whitehorse. The MacBride Museum at Whitehorse is another tourist attraction. In 1972, Kluane National Park was established in the Yukon Territory.

Manufacturing. The Yukon has several small manufacturing industries. Goods manufactured there have a

Territorial Coat of Arms

Dawson, a boom town in the Yukon Territory during the Klondike Gold Rush in 1897 and 1898, lies at the mouth of the Klondike River. Mining is still its most important industry.

Canadian Government Travel Bureau

value added by manufacture of about $687,000 a year. This figure represents the value created in products by Yukon industries, not counting such costs as materials, supplies, and fuels. Plants in Whitehorse refinish furniture, produce soft drinks, and make lenses for glasses. Whitehorse also has several printing and newspaper companies. Other industries in the Yukon make explosives, gold jewelry, and such wood products as canoes, dogsleds, and snowshoes.

Fur Industry. Fur trapping provides an annual income of about $430,000. The chief animals trapped are lynx, marten, and muskrat.

Fishing Industry. A small amount of commercial fishing takes place on the Yukon River for chum and coho salmon. Whitefish and trout are caught in Lakes Labarage and Teslin.

Agriculture. Because of the short summer, agriculture is of little importance, except for the production of quick-growing vegetables. Excellent vegetables can be grown in greenhouses during the long hours of sun in the early spring and summer.

Transportation and Communication. The White Pass & Yukon Route railway stretches for about 110 miles (177 kilometers) from Whitehorse south to Skagway, Alaska. Boats sail regularly from Skagway to Vancouver, B.C. Four airlines serve the Yukon Territory. They connect it with Alaska, Alberta, British Columbia, and the Northwest Territories. The Alaska Highway extends for about 600 miles (970 kilometers) through the Yukon Territory. Bus service provides connections to cities in Alaska, Alberta, and British Columbia. The Canadian Broadcasting Corporation (CBC)

has a radio station at Whitehorse. Automatic relays transmit its programs to nearly all of the territory. A private radio station and cable television company also serve Whitehorse. Live CBC television service is provided to nearly all Yukon communities via communications satellite. Telephone and telegraph service are provided in most of the territory. Newspapers are published in Dawson, Faro, Watson Lake, and Whitehorse.

Education and Social Services

Education. The territorial government maintains schools at the population centers. There are public high schools (grades 8 through 12) in Faro, Mayo, Watson Lake, Dawson, and Whitehorse. The Roman Catholic Church also operates schools in Whitehorse.

Social Services. Resident doctors live in Clinton Creek, Dawson, Elsa, Faro, Mayo, Watson Lake, and Whitehorse. Resident dentists have offices in Whitehorse and visit other settlements periodically. Nurses travel through the territory. Dawson, Watson Lake, and Whitehorse have hospitals. Other settlements have nursing stations.

Government

The Canadian government appoints a commissioner for the Yukon Territory. The commissioner serves an indefinite term as chief executive officer of the territorial government. The Legislative Council of the Yukon Territory consists of 16 members, who are elected to four-year terms. The council has the chief responsibility for most of the territory's local matters, which include education, public works, social services, and taxation.

489

YUKON TERRITORY

The people elect one representative to the Canadian House of Commons. The Yukon Territory is also represented by one member in the Canadian Senate.

History

In the 1840's, Robert Campbell, a British fur trader of the Hudson's Bay Company, became the first white person to explore the Yukon region. He named the Pelly River and a portion of the Yukon River which he called the *Lewes* (renamed the Yukon in 1949). Campbell built a trading post on the Pelly River at Fort Selkirk in 1848. But Chilkat Indians looted and burned the post a short time later. The Yukon River valley was a part of the company's fur-trading empire until 1870, when it became part of the Northwest Territories.

On Aug. 17, 1896, George Carmack and his Indian friends Skookum Jim and Tagish Charlie made a gold strike on Bonanza Creek. This led to the Klondike Gold Rush of 1897 and 1898. The creek is a tributary of the Klondike River, near the present site of Dawson. Thousands of prospectors poured into the Yukon when news of the rich discovery reached the rest of the world. Simple methods of hand mining produced $22,275,000 worth of gold in 1900. A fleet of gold dredges soon began digging gold. Dredges still dig about $2,000,000 worth of gold annually from the rich deposits.

The miners who lived in the Yukon were often rough and unruly. At the beginning of the gold rush, a detachment of the North-West Mounted Police entered the region to preserve order. The influx of prospectors increased the Yukon's political importance. In 1898, the Yukon became a territory, and Dawson became the capital.

At the height of the Klondike Gold Rush in 1898, an estimated 35,000 persons lived in the Yukon Territory. Records of the North-West Mounted Police (now the Royal Canadian Mounted Police) show that 7,080 boats passed down the Yukon River in 1898, carrying 28,000 people. An estimated 5,000 people reached the gold fields by other routes.

After much of the surface ore had been exhausted by simple hand-mining methods, many prospectors sold their claims and drifted away from the Klondike area. Whitehorse had railroad service. Because of this, it became the distributing point for the entire territory, and grew more rapidly than Dawson. Whitehorse became the capital in 1951.   WALTER A. WOOD

Related Articles in WORLD BOOK include:

Alaska Highway	Mount Lucania
Hudson's Bay Company	Service, Robert
King Peak	Silver (graph)
Klondike	Whitehorse
Lead (graph)	Yukon River
Mount Logan	

YULE, *yool,* is an old name for the Christmas season. The term comes from the Anglo-Saxon word for the months of December and January. The Anglo-Saxons called December "the former Yule," and January, "the after Yule." The early pagans of Scandinavian countries held yule festivals near the end of each year. After Christianity spread into Europe, these festivals became Christmas celebrations. The custom of burning a yule log started in pagan times. The early Vikings honored Thor, their god of war, by burning a yule log during the yule season. This custom has become part of the present celebration of Christmas, especially in England.   ELIZABETH HOUGH SECHRIST

See also CHRISTMAS.

YUMA, *YOO muh,* Ariz. (pop. 30,081), is a trading center in southwestern Arizona. It lies on the Colorado River opposite the site of old Fort Yuma, Calif. (see ARIZONA [political map]). The river irrigates surrounding farmlands. These farmlands produce alfalfa, citrus fruits, cotton, hay, lettuce, and melons. A ferry was established at what is now Yuma in 1849. It took emigrants across the river on their way to the California gold fields. The town was laid out in 1854, and was named Colorado City. Later, the name was changed to Arizona City. The name was finally changed to Yuma, after the Yuma Indians.

The first railroad to enter Arizona crossed the Colorado River at Yuma in 1877. Yuma is the seat of Yuma County. A United States Army installation and a United States Marine Corps air station are located in Yuma. Gila and Yuma irrigation projects cover about 165,000 acres (66,770 hectares) nearby. These farmlands were opened to homesteaders in 1947. Yuma has a mayor-council government. For the monthly weather in Yuma, see ARIZONA (Climate).

YUNGA. See BOLIVIA (Land Regions).

YUNGKIA. See WENCHOW.

YURT. See SHELTER (In Asia).

YWCA. See YOUNG WOMEN'S CHRISTIAN ASSOCIATION.

Brown Bros.

Rugged Miners packed their belongings in sleds and hurried to the gold fields during the Klondike Gold Rush in 1897.

Zz

Z is the 26th and last letter in our alphabet. Historians believe that it came from a symbol used by the Semites, who once lived in Syria and Palestine. They named it *zayin* and adapted an Egyptian *hieroglyphic*, or picture symbol, for an arrowlike object. The Greeks later made the symbol the sixth letter of their alphabet, and called it *zeta*. They gave it the capital Z form which we use. The Romans used *z* only when writing words borrowed from Greek, and moved the letter to the end of their alphabet. In Canada and Great Britain, *z* is called *zed*. In some English dialects it is called *izzard*. See ALPHABET.

Uses. Z or *z* is the letter least frequently used in books, newspapers, and other printed material in English. Z is often used to denote the last of anything, as in the phrase "from A to Z." Z is used to denote *atomic number* in chemistry and *zenith distance* in astronomy. *Zone* and *zero* are also represented by *z*.

Pronunciation. In English, a person pronounces the normal consonant *z* sound, as in *zone*, by placing his tongue blade near the edges of his upper front teeth, with a narrow chink left over the tip. His velum, or soft palate, is closed, and his breath is expelled through the chink and against his front teeth. The vocal cords vibrate. The letter *z* may also have a *zh* sound, as in *azure* or *glazier*. In German, *z* has a *ts* sound. In most other European languages, *z* sounds are like those in English. See PRONUNCIATION. I. J. GELB and JAMES M. WELLS

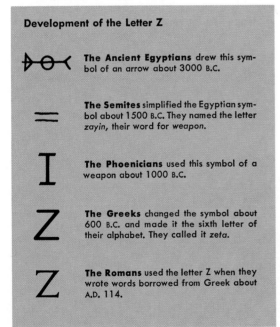

Development of the Letter Z

The Ancient Egyptians drew this symbol of an arrow about 3000 B.C.

The Semites simplified the Egyptian symbol about 1500 B.C. They named the letter *zayin*, their word for *weapon*.

The Phoenicians used this symbol of a weapon about 1000 B.C.

The Greeks changed the symbol about 600 B.C. and made it the sixth letter of their alphabet. They called it *zeta*.

The Romans used the letter Z when they wrote words borrowed from Greek about A.D. 114.

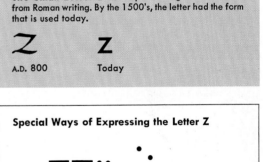

The Small Letter z developed during the A.D. 800's from Roman writing. By the 1500's, the letter had the form that is used today.

A.D. 800   Today

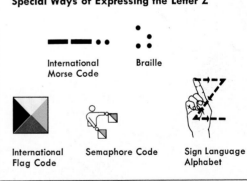

Special Ways of Expressing the Letter Z

International Morse Code   Braille

International Flag Code   Semaphore Code   Sign Language Alphabet

Common Forms of the Letter Z

Handwritten Letters vary from person to person. *Manuscript* (printed) letters, *left*, have simple curves and straight lines. Cursive letters, *right*, have flowing lines.

Roman Letters have small finishing strokes called *serifs* that extend from the main strokes. The type face shown above is Baskerville. The italic form appears at the right.

Sans-Serif Letters are also called *gothic letters*. They have no serifs. The type face shown above is called Futura. The italic form of Futura appears at the right.

Computer Letters have special shapes. Computers can "read" these letters either optically or by means of the magnetic ink with which the letters may be printed.

491

ZACATECAS, *SAH kah TAY kahs,* is a state of Mexico. It covers 28,973 square miles (75,040 square kilometers) on Mexico's central plateau. For location, see MEXICO (political map).

Mining provides the chief source of income for the state's 951,462 people. Zacatecas produces gold, lead, silver, and zinc. The chief crops include corn, maguey, peppers, potatoes, and wheat. Goats, sheep, and other livestock graze on the plains. Zacatecas is noted for such handmade items as *serapes* (blankets worn as shawls) and elaborately decorated spurs. The city of Zacatecas is the capital. CHARLES C. CUMBERLAND

ZACHARIAS. See ELIZABETH, SAINT.

ZAGREB, *ZAH greb* (pop. 566,224), is the second largest city in Yugoslavia and a major trade and industrial center. Only Belgrade, the nation's capital, is larger. Zagreb serves as the capital of Croatia, one of Yugoslavia's six republics. The city stands on the Sava River, about 230 miles (370 kilometers) northwest of Belgrade (see YUGOSLAVIA [map]). Industries in the city manufacture leather, machinery, paper, and textiles.

Zagreb is one of Yugoslavia's most important centers of culture. The city has art galleries, museums, and theaters. It is also the home of Zagreb University.

A Slavic tribe settled an area in present-day Zagreb in the A.D. 600's. A religious community was founded nearby in 1094. In 1557, the two towns merged into one city, called Zagreb. ALVIN Z. RUBINSTEIN

ZAGROS MOUNTAINS. See IRAN (Land Regions).

ZAHARIAS, BABE. See DIDRIKSON, BABE.

ZAIRE, *zah IHR,* is a large country in the heart of Africa. It is more than three times as big as the state of Texas. A narrow strip of Zaire borders the Atlantic Ocean. But most of the country lies deep in the interior of Africa, slightly south of the center of the continent. The equator runs through northern Zaire.

One of the world's largest and thickest tropical rain forests covers about a third of Zaire. The mighty Congo River (called the Zaire River in Zaire) flows through the forest and is one of the country's chief means of transportation. A variety of fascinating wild animals live in Zaire. They include antelope, crocodiles, elephants, giraffes, gorillas, hippopotamuses, leopards, lions, monkeys, rhinoceroses, and zebras.

The vast majority of Zaire's people are black Africans. Most of the people live in small rural villages and farm the land for a living. But each year, many villagers move to Zaire's cities, and so the cities are growing rapidly. Kinshasa is Zaire's capital and largest city.

Belgians ruled Zaire from 1885 until it became an independent nation in 1960. The nation was called Congo until 1971, when it took its present name. Europeans greatly influenced Zaire's economic and cultural life at the time of independence. In addition, deep divisions existed among Zaire's people, and the country faced severe economic problems. Since independence, Zaire's leaders have worked to reduce European influence, unite the people, and improve the economy.

Government

Zaire's Constitution provides for a presidential form of government. It gives the nation's president almost complete control over the government.

National Government. The president makes all major government policy decisions in Zaire and also appoints the officials who carry out the operations of the government. The president is elected by the people to a five-year term. By law, the president may serve only two terms. But Mobutu Sese Seko, who has been president since 1965, is allowed by a special provision to serve an unlimited number of terms.

The *Mouvement Populaire de la Révolution* (Popular Movement of the Revolution) is Zaire's only political

M. Crawford Young, the contributor of this article, is Professor of Political Science at the University of Wisconsin at Madison, and the author of Politics in the Congo.

Jacques Jangoux

Zaire is a country in the heart of Africa. Many of its rural areas lack good roads as well as bridges across waterways. The rural children at the left use boats to cross a swampy area in order to get to school. Their school buildings stand in the background.

party. Commonly called the MPR, it exists to support and promote the president's policies. All Zairian citizens belong to the party. Citizens may not openly criticize the government. Instead, they must privately pass their criticisms on to MPR officials. Zaire's president heads the MPR. The president's key assistants make up the party's Political Bureau, which has from 15 to 30 members.

About 20 executive departments direct the operations of Zaire's national government. A commissioner appointed by the president heads each department. Zaire's legislature, called the National Legislative Council, meets for a few weeks each year to debate details of the government's budget and to pass laws proposed by the president. The council has 240 members. MPR leaders choose all candidates for council seats. The people elect the council members to five-year terms.

Local Government. Zaire is divided into eight regions, plus the separate district of Kinshasa, for purposes of local government. The regions are divided into about 30 subregions, and the subregions into about 150 zones. An administrator governs each of these local government units. All the administrators are appointed by the president. Zaire's zones are divided into hundreds of smaller units called collectivities, in which tribal chiefs are responsible for maintaining order.

Courts. The Supreme Court is Zaire's highest court. It hears appeals from lower courts. The president appoints its members. Zaire also has three other appeals courts and a variety of lower courts.

Armed Forces. Zaire has one of the largest armed forces in Africa. Its army, navy, and air force have a total of about 70,000 members.

People

Population and Ancestry. Zaire has a population of about 28,622,000. About three-fourths of its people live in rural areas, and about one-fourth live in urban areas. Kinshasa, the largest city, has about 2 million people.

More than 99 per cent of Zaire's people are black Africans. Most of them are descendants of people who began moving to the area from other parts of Africa about 2,000 years ago. At that time, other black Africans called pygmies lived in what is now Zaire. The

Editorial Photocolor Archives, Inc.

Kinshasa is the capital, largest city, and main business center of Zaire. It has many wide boulevards and tall, modern buildings.

Zaire's Flag was adopted in 1971. The torch stands for progress and honors those who died in the nation's conflicts.

The Coat of Arms, adopted in 1971, bears a leopard's head and the French words for justice, peace, and work.

───────── FACTS IN BRIEF ─────────

Capital: Kinshasa.

Official Language: French.

Form of Government: Presidential regime.

Area: 905,568 sq. mi. (2,345,409 km²). *Greatest Distances*—north-south, about 1,300 mi. (2,090 km); east-west, about 1,300 mi. (2,090 km). *Coastline*—25 mi. (40 km).

Elevation: *Highest*—Margherita Peak, 16,762 ft. (5,109 m) above sea level. *Lowest*—sea level along the coast.

Population: *Estimated 1980 Population*—28,622,000; distribution, 77 per cent rural, 23 per cent urban; density, 31 persons per sq. mi. (12 persons per km²). *1955-1958 Census*—12,768,706. *Estimated 1985 Population*—32,860,000.

Chief Products: *Agriculture and Forestry*—cassava, cocoa, coffee, cotton, corn, palm oil, rice, rubber, tea, timber. *Manufacturing*—beer, cement, soap, soft drinks, steel, textiles, tires. *Mining*—cadmium, cobalt, copper, gold, industrial diamonds, manganese, oil, silver, tin, zinc.

Money: *Basic Unit*—zaire. See MONEY (table: Exchange Rates).

WORLD BOOK map

Zaire is a large country that lies near the center of Africa. The equator runs through the northern part of the country.

492a

pygmies, known for their small size, number about 50,000 in Zaire today (see PYGMIES). About a million black African refugees—chiefly from Angola, Burundi, and Rwanda—live in Zaire. The population also includes about 50,000 Europeans, mostly Belgians.

Zaire's people belong to many different ethnic groups. At times, conflicts between groups have flared up. Since 1965, Zaire's government has made progress toward overcoming ethnic divisions and giving the people a sense of national unity.

Languages. Most of Zaire's ethnic groups have their own local language. About 200 local languages are spoken in the country. Most of them belong to the

Bantu language group and are closely related (see BANTU). Most Zairians also speak at least one of the country's four regional languages—Kikongo, Lingala, Swahili, and Tshiluba. French is Zaire's official language. Government officials often use French in their work, and many students learn it in school.

Way of Life. Most rural Zairians live in small villages that range in size from a few dozen to a few hundred people. The vast majority of the village families farm a small plot of land for a living. They raise almost all their own food, including cassava, corn, and rice. Some rural people also catch fish for food. Few families can afford any farm machinery, and so most of them use hand tools in their work. As a result, farm production is low, and most farm families are poor.

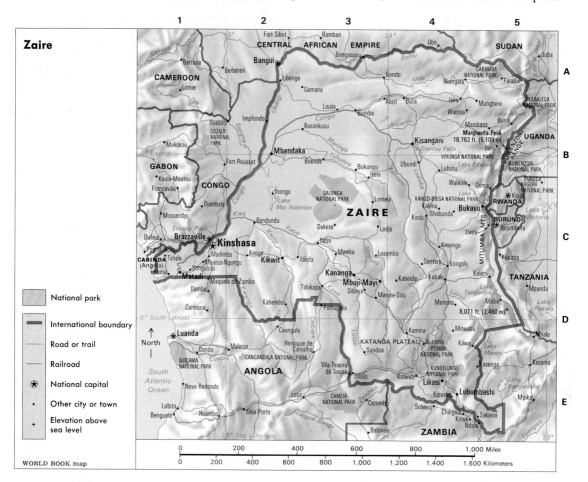

Zaire

National park
International boundary
Road or trail
Railroad
National capital
Other city or town
Elevation above sea level

North

WORLD BOOK map

| 0 | 200 | 400 | 600 | 800 | 1,000 Miles |
| 0 | 200 | 400 | 600 | 800 | 1,000 | 1,200 | 1,400 | 1,600 Kilometers |

Cities and Towns

Aketi	A 3
Bandundu	.74,467..C 2
Basankusu	B 2
Beni	B 5
Boende	B 3
Bokungu	B 3
Boma	.79,230..D 1
Bondo	A 3
Bukama	D 4
Bukavu	.181,774..C 5
Bumba	B 3
Bunia	B 5
Buta	A 4
Dekese	C 3
Dibaya	D 3
Dilolo	E 3
Faradje	A 5

Gemena	A 2
Goma	B 5
Idiofa	C 2
Ikela	B 3
Ilebo	C 3
Inongo	C 2
Isiro	A 4
Kabalo	D 4
Kabinda	D 4
Kahemba	D 3
Kalemi	.86,687..D 5
Kalima	C 4
Kamina	.114,804..D 4
Kananga	.601,239..D 3
Kasenga	E 5
Kasongo	C 4
Kenge	C 2
Kikwit	.150,253..C 2
Kilwa	D 4

Kindu	C 4
Kinshasa 2,008,352..C 1
Kipushi	E 4
Kisangani .310,705..B 4
Kolwezi	.70,558..E 4
Kongolo	C 4
Libenge	A 2
Likasi	.150,000..E 4
Lisala	B 3
Lodja	C 3
Lubum-	
bashi	.403,623..E 4
Lubutu	B 4
Lusambo	C 3
Madimba	C 1
Mambasa	B 5
Manono	D 4
Matadi	.143,598..D 1
Mbandaka 134,495..B 2

Mbanza-Ngungu ...C 1
Mbuji-	
Mayi ...336,654..D 3
Moba	D 5
Mungbere	A 5
Mweka	C 3
Mwene-Ditu	D 3
Niangara	A 4
Sakania	E 5
Sandoa	D 3
Sentery	C 4
Shabunda	C 4
Songololo	C 1
Tshela	C 1
Tshikapa	D 3
Ubundi	B 4
Uvira	C 5
Walikale	B 4
Wamba	B 4

Physical Features

Aruwimi (River)	B 4
Congo (River)	C 2
Kasai (River)	D 3
Katanga Plateau	D 4
Lake Albert	B 5
Lake Edward	B 5
Lake Kivu	C 5
Lake Mai-Ndombe	C 2
Lake Mweru	D 5
Lake Tanganyika	D 5
Lomami (River)	B 4
Lualaba (River)	B 4
Margherita Peak	B 5
Mitumba Mountains	C 5
Stanley Falls	B 4
Stanley Pool	C 1
Ubangi (River)	B 2

Sources: Latest official estimates (1967–1974).

Small Rural Villages dot Zaire's countryside. Most of the village families farm a small plot of land for a living. They live in small houses with thatched roofs, like the one above.

Zaire's Cities are growing at a rapid rate. City people often shop in outdoor marketplaces. The busy marketplace shown above is in Goma, a city in eastern Zaire.

Since 1960, large numbers of Zairians—especially young people—have moved from rural areas to cities. They have been attracted to the cities by the opportunity for jobs in business, industry, and government. The rapid growth of cities has led to such problems as unemployment and crowded living conditions. Also, many people who have jobs earn low wages and find it difficult to support themselves and their families.

During the period of Belgian rule, few Zairian women received more than a few years of education or held a job outside the home. Since independence, the government has increased educational and job opportunities for women.

Housing. Most rural Zairians live in houses made from mud bricks or dried mud and sticks. The majority of the houses have thatched roofs. The houses of some well-to-do rural families have metal roofs.

In Zaire's cities, important government officials, business managers, and merchants—as well as many Europeans—live in attractive bungalows. But large numbers of factory and office workers live in crowded areas of small, cheap houses and apartments made from cinder blocks or baked mud bricks. Since independence, the government and major businesses have built many housing units in an effort to improve living conditions for city dwellers.

Clothing. Zaire's government discourages people from wearing Western-style clothing as part of its program to reduce European influence. Since independence, most Zairian men who hold important jobs have adopted a kind of "national costume." They wear a collarless suit without a shirt or tie. Most male workers and farmers wear either long or short trousers with a shirt. Zairian women usually wear a long, one-piece dress of colorful cotton cloth or a blouse and long skirt.

Food and Drink. Corn, rice, and *manioc meal*—which is made from cassava—are the basic foods of most of the people. Zairians serve these foods mostly as a thick porridge flavored with a spicy sauce. They add fish or meat to the porridge when they can afford to do so.

Beer is a popular beverage among adults. The diet of many Zairians lacks important nutritional elements, especially protein. As a result, many people suffer from malnutrition.

Recreation. Rural Zairians enjoy social gatherings that feature drum music and dancing. Many city people spend much leisure time in barrooms. There, they dance and listen to Zairian jazz provided by a phonograph or small band. Soccer ranks as the country's most popular spectator sport. Large crowds attend Sunday afternoon soccer matches in Zaire's main cities.

Religion. About 60 per cent of Zaire's people practice traditional African religions based on the worship of many gods and spirits. Christians make up approximately 40 per cent of the population. About four-fifths of the Christians are Roman Catholics, and about a fifth are Protestants. About 1 per cent of Zaire's people are Muslims.

Education. Zairian children are not required to attend school by law. But since independence, most parents have come to value education as a key to a better life for their children. The percentage of children who attend elementary school has risen from about 65 per cent in 1960 to about 80 per cent today. During the same period, secondary school enrollment has risen from approximately 1 per cent to 8 per cent. A secondary school student must pass a nationwide examination in order to receive a diploma. Schools in Zaire's remote rural areas are poorly equipped compared with those in other parts of the country. Many students from those areas fail the examination.

Zaire has a single university system. Called the National University of Zaire, the system includes campuses in several parts of the country. Each campus specializes in one area of study, such as education, medicine, or social science. Since independence, the number of Zairian university students has increased from a few hundred to about 15,000.

The Arts. Carved wooden statues and masks are the best-known Zairian works of art. Many art critics have

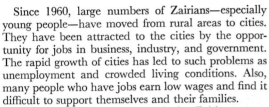

492c

Jacques Jangoux

Zaire's Tropical Rain Forest is an area of thick vegetation. Its weather is hot and humid throughout the year. Because of the weather and lack of open space, few people live in the forest.

praised these works for their delicate form and balance and rich symbolism. Music is also a major art in Zaire. The rhythm of drums dominates Zairian music. Urban Zairians have developed their own form of jazz. This music blends elements of modern jazz and traditional Zairian music.

Land and Climate

Zaire covers 905,568 square miles (2,345,409 square kilometers). Among Africa's countries, only Sudan and Algeria are larger than Zaire. Zaire's land includes three distinct kinds of regions: (1) a tropical rain forest, (2) savannas, and (3) a highland.

The Tropical Rain Forest covers most of the northern part of Zaire. It is one of the world's largest and thickest rain forests and has an extraordinary variety of trees and other plants. The forest is so thick that sunlight seldom reaches parts of its floor. The equator runs through the center of the rain forest, and the area has hot, humid weather throughout the year. Daytime temperatures average about 90° F. (32° C). Annual rainfall often totals 80 inches (203 centimeters) or more. Much of the rain falls in heavy thunderstorms. Because of the climate and a lack of open land, few people live in the rain forest.

Savannas. A savanna covers much of southern Zaire. Another savanna covers a strip of land north of the rain forest. The savannas are chiefly grasslands, and a variety of grasses grow there. Small groups of trees are scattered throughout the savannas, and forests grow in some valleys. Daytime temperatures in the savannas average about 75° F. (24° C). The savannas receive little or no rain for several months each year. Annual rainfall averages about 37 inches (94 centimeters).

The Highland is an area of plateaus and mountains along Zaire's eastern and southeastern borders. Plant life in the highland varies with the elevation. Margherita Peak, the highest point in Zaire, rises 16,762

feet (5,109 meters) there. Daytime temperatures in the highland average about 70° F. (21° C). Annual rainfall totals about 48 inches (122 centimeters).

Rivers and Lakes. The Congo River is Zaire's most important waterway. It rises near the southeast corner of the country. It flows northward to northern Zaire and is called the Lualaba River until it reaches Stanley Falls near the equator. The river then flows westward across northern Zaire. Finally, it flows southwestward until it empties into the Atlantic Ocean in far western Zaire. The world's sixth longest river, the Congo flows for 2,716 miles (4,371 kilometers). The Congo carries more water than any other river except the Amazon. Many other rivers branch out from the Congo. They include the Ubangi and the Aruwimi to the north and the Lomami and Kasai to the south.

Several deep lakes lie along Zaire's eastern border. The largest is Lake Tanganyika.

Animal Life. Zaire has a spectacular variety of wild animals. Baboons, chimpanzees, gorillas, and many kinds of monkeys live in areas of trees. Antelope, giraffes, leopards, lions, and zebras roam open areas. Crocodiles, hippopotamuses, and rhinoceroses live in and near water. Through the years, hunters have killed many animals in Zaire and have endangered some species. As a result, the government has set aside large areas of land as part of a national park system where animals are protected from hunters. Many wild animals also still live outside the parks, especially in thinly populated areas in the east.

Economy

Zaire is a poor country with a developing economy. But it has many valuable resources that give it the

Agence Hoa-Qui from Tom Stack & Assoc.

The Congo River is Zaire's main waterway and the sixth longest river in the world. The people in the picture above are setting traps in the Congo in order to catch fish.

Agence Hoa-Qui from Tom Stack & Assoc.

A Huge Copper Mine operates near Likasi, in southeastern Zaire. Copper is Zaire's chief product.

potential of becoming a wealthy nation. Mining ranks as Zaire's most important economic activity.

Mining. Copper is Zaire's most important mineral. The country ranks among the world's leading copper-producing nations. Zaire leads the world in the production of industrial diamonds, its second most important mineral. Zaire produces oil from deposits off its coast. Its other economically valuable minerals include cadmium, cobalt, gold, manganese, silver, tin, and zinc.

Agriculture and Forestry. Agriculture in Zaire centers around small plots, where families struggle to produce enough food for their own needs. The chief food crops include cassava, corn, and rice. Crops raised for sale include cotton, coffee, and tea. The trees of Zaire's rain forest yield cocoa, palm oil, rubber, and timber.

Manufacturing. Zaire produces relatively small amounts of manufactured goods. Its chief products include beer, cement, soap, soft drinks, steel, textiles, and tires. Since independence, manufacturing has grown in importance in Zaire.

Foreign Trade. Copper is Zaire's chief export by far. Other exports include cobalt, coffee, industrial diamonds, and palm oil. Imports include food, oil, textiles, and manufactured goods. Zaire trades chiefly with nations of Western Europe, especially Belgium.

Transportation and Communication. Zaire has about 24,000 miles (40,000 kilometers) of usable roads. Many roads in the country are in poor condition.

The Congo River plays an important role in Zaire's transportation system, especially in the rain forest where there are few good roads. The river and its many branches are navigable for about 7,200 miles (11,500 kilometers) in the country.

Zaire has about 3,000 miles (4,800 kilometers) of railroads. Matadi is the country's main seaport. A national airline serves Zaire's major cities and towns. It also has flights to and from a number of African and European countries.

The development of inexpensive transistor radios since the mid-1900's has made radio the most important means of communication in Zaire. Even remote villages

have at least one transistor radio. In some rural areas, people communicate from village to village by means of drum signals. Television broadcasts serve Zaire's largest cities, but few people can afford TV sets. Only about 7,000 Zairians own a TV. Four daily newspapers are published in Zaire.

History

Early Days. Pygmies were the first known inhabitants of what is now Zaire. They have lived there since prehistoric times. About 2,000 years ago, people from other parts of Africa moved into the area. In the A.D. 700's, well-developed civilizations grew up in southeastern Zaire. In the 1400's—or perhaps earlier—several separate states developed in the savanna south of the rain forest. The largest were the Kongo, Kuba, Luba, and Lunda kingdoms. In the 1600's or 1700's, other kingdoms grew up near the eastern border. The kingdoms carried on long-distance trade with people on the east and west coasts of Africa.

The Coming of the Europeans. In 1482, Portuguese seamen began stopping at the mouth of the Congo River. Portugal soon established diplomatic relations with the Kongo kingdom, which then ruled the coastal region. Representatives of the kingdom visited Portugal and the Vatican—the headquarters of the Roman Catholic Church—in the late 1400's. The kingdom soon adopted Roman Catholicism as its religion, and many Kongo men became Catholic priests.

In the early 1500's, the Portuguese began enslaving black Africans. They bought many of the slaves from the leaders of the Kongo kingdom. Other Europeans soon began taking part in the slave trade. From the early 1500's to the early 1800's, thousands of people were enslaved in the Zaire area. Most of them were sent to North or South America.

In 1876, Henry M. Stanley, a British explorer, crossed Zaire from east to west. Other explorers crossed the area at about the same time. The explorations gave Europeans and Americans their first detailed information about the interior of what is now Zaire.

Belgian Rule. In 1878, King Leopold II of Belgium hired Stanley to set up Belgian outposts along the Congo River. Through skillful diplomacy, Leopold persuaded other European leaders to recognize him as the ruler of what is now Zaire. The recognition stated that Leopold himself—not the Belgian government—was the ruler. The area became Leopold's personal colony

--- **IMPORTANT DATES IN ZAIRE** ---

A.D. 700's Well-developed civilizations grew up in what is now Zaire.

c. 1400 The Kongo and other kingdoms were established in the area.

Early 1500's The slave trade began in what is now Zaire.

1885 King Leopold II of Belgium took control of the area and named it the Congo Free State.

1908 The Belgian government took control of the Congo Free State and renamed it the Belgian Congo.

1960 The Belgian Congo gained independence from Belgium and was renamed Congo.

1965 A five-year period of civil disorder ended.

1971 The country's name was changed to Zaire.

1977 and 1978 Katanga rebels invaded Zaire from Angola, but were defeated.

on July 1, 1885, and was named the Congo Free State.

The people of the Congo Free State suffered under Leopold's rule. The king's agents treated the people cruelly and forced them to work long hours at such jobs as collecting rubber in forests and building a railroad. Many of the people died as a result of the harsh treatment. Leopold's rule brought many protests, especially from Great Britain and the United States. In response, the Belgian government took over control of the Congo Free State from Leopold in 1908. Belgium renamed the colony the Belgian Congo. The Belgian government's rule was often harsh, but the government improved working and living conditions somewhat.

By the 1920's, Belgium was earning great wealth from the Belgian Congo's copper, diamonds, gold, palm oil, and other resources. The worldwide Great Depression of the 1930's crippled the colony's economy as prices and demand for its resources fell sharply. In 1940, Belgium entered World War II on the side of the Allies. During the war, the Belgian Congo provided the Allies with valuable raw materials.

After World War II ended in 1945, the Belgian Congo's economy again developed rapidly as prices for its exports soared. The Belgians made efforts to improve education and medical care for the colony's people. But they refused to allow the people to have a voice in their government.

Independence. In the 1950's, many Africans in the Belgian Congo began calling for independence from Belgium. In 1957, Belgium allowed the colony's people to elect their own representatives to local government councils. But the demand for independence continued. In 1959, rioting broke out against Belgian rule. On June 30, 1960, Belgium granted the colony independence. The new country was called Congo.

In Congo's first general elections—held about a month before independence—nine political parties won seats in the national legislature. No party received a majority. This splitting of votes weakened the power and unity of Congo's government. In a compromise on the eve of independence, two opposing leaders agreed to share power. Joseph Kasavubu became president and Patrice Lumumba became prime minister.

Civil Disorder broke out in the country following independence. Belgian officers still held power in Congo's army, and many Belgians retained important posts in the government. Five days after independence, Congolese army troops near Léopoldville (now Kinshasa) revolted against their Belgian officers. The revolt spread throughout the country. Most Belgian government workers then fled the country.

In July 1960, Katanga Province (now the Shaba Region) *seceded* (withdrew) from the new nation and declared itself independent. This copper-producing province in the south ranked as Congo's wealthiest area. The diamond-producing province of Kasai seceded in August. In September, President Kasavubu dismissed Prime Minister Lumumba. Lumumba was imprisoned and, in 1961, he was assassinated. Lumumba's supporters established a rival government to that of Kasavubu and claimed to rule the country.

Fighting broke out between the rival groups in Congo. United Nations (UN) troops—at the invitation of Kasavubu's government—were sent to the country to restore order in 1960. In August 1961, the rival groups reached a compromise that united all of the country except Katanga Province. Cyrille Adoula headed the new government as prime minister.

UN troops finally brought an end to the Katanga secession in January 1963. Many of the Katanga rebels then fled to neighboring Angola. The UN forces were withdrawn from Congo in June 1964. In a surprising political settlement in July, Moise Tshombe, who had led the Katanga secession movement, became prime minister of the reunited country. At about the same time, a wave of new revolts broke out in Congo. White *mercenaries* (hired soldiers) helped the Congolese government end the revolts by 1965.

National elections were held in March 1965. A loose coalition headed by Tshombe gained control of the government. But the coalition soon fell apart, and disagreements among the leaders brought government operations to a standstill. In November, the Congolese army took control of the government. General Joseph Désiré Mobutu became president.

Rebuilding the Nation. The civil disorder of the early 1960's severely damaged Congo's economy. The fighting among the country's people resulted in bitterness and deep divisions.

After taking office, President Mobutu took steps to try to solve the country's problems. He set up a strong national government that extended its authority throughout the nation. The government's authority helped end fighting among people and lessen the ethnic divisions of earlier years. The economy improved steadily in the late 1960's. Mobutu also tried to strengthen the nation by encouraging pride in its African heritage and reducing European influence. Many cities, towns, and physical features in the country had European names. Mobutu's government gave all of these African names. In 1971, the government changed the country's name from Congo to Zaire. The government also required all Africans in the country who had European names to adopt African names. Mobutu changed his own name from Joseph Désiré Mobutu to Mobutu Sese Seko in 1972.

Zaire Today. In the early 1970's, the worldwide problems of recession and inflation caused new economic hardships in Zaire. The price of copper fell sharply, greatly reducing the country's revenues. At the same time, the prices of food and oil—which Zaire imports—rose dramatically. A civil war in Angola closed a railroad there that Zaire had used for the shipment of goods. Zaire provided much financial aid to the losing side in the Angolan war.

In 1977, Katanga rebels who had been living in Angola invaded Zaire in an attempt to take over the former Katanga Province. By then, the province had been renamed the Shaba Region. Zairian government troops, aided by Moroccan troops and French military equipment, defeated the rebels. Katanga rebels invaded Zaire again in 1978, but were defeated. French and Belgian troops played a leading role in helping the Zairian forces turn back the invasion.

In spite of its problems, however, Zaire still has great economic potential. Its valuable natural resources give it the possibility of becoming one of Africa's wealthiest nations.   M. CRAWFORD YOUNG

Related Articles in WORLD BOOK include:

Outline

I. Government
  A. National Government
  B. Local Government
  C. Courts
  D. Armed Forces

II. People
  A. Population and Ancestry
  B. Languages
  C. Way of Life
  D. Housing
  E. Clothing
  F. Food and Drink
  G. Recreation
  H. Religion
  I. Education
  J. The Arts

III. Land and Climate
  A. The Tropical Rain Forest
  B. Savannas
  C. The Highland
  D. Rivers and Lakes
  E. Animal Life

IV. Economy
  A. Mining
  B. Agriculture and Forestry
  C. Manufacturing
  D. Foreign Trade
  E. Transportation and Communication

V. History

Questions

What is Zaire's most important economic activity?

What problems has Zaire faced since it gained independence from Belgium?

Why is farm production low in Zaire?

Why has Zaire's government discouraged the wearing of Western-style clothing?

What is the role of Zaire's only political party?

What were the roles of Henry M. Stanley and King Leopold II in the area's history?

What is the chief river in Zaire?

Why do few people live in Zaire's tropical rain forest?

What is the most important means of communication in Zaire?

How has the government sought to protect wild animals in Zaire?

ZAMA, BATTLE OF. See ARMY (table: Famous Land Battles of History); SCIPIO.

ZAMBEZI RIVER, *zam BE zih*, is the fourth largest river in Africa. Only the Nile, the Niger, and the Congo are larger. It rises in Zambia, near the border between Zaire and Angola. The river follows a winding 1,600-mile (2,570-meter) course, separating Zambia from Rhodesia and crossing Mozambique to empty into the Mozambique Channel (see AFRICA [map]). The Zambezi has many branches, and drains more than 500,000 square miles (1,300,000 square kilometers).

The upper course of the river lies in level land, where the water supply depends on equatorial rains which fall from October to March. From this plateau, the Zambezi plunges to a lower level over Victoria Falls, a mighty cataract of water. A hydroelectric plant has been in operation there since 1938. Kariba Dam, completed in 1959, lies in Kariba Gorge, about 200 miles (320 kilometers) downstream. It forms a lake that covers 2,000 square miles (5,200 square kilometers).

Early geographers knew of the Zambezi region, probably through Arab traders. The first European to explore the Zambezi River was David Livingstone. He explored it in the 1850's and 1860's. HARRY R. RUDIN

See also STANLEY AND LIVINGSTONE; VICTORIA FALLS.

ZAMBIA is a landlocked country in south-central Africa. It ranks as one of the largest producers of copper. The busy copper mines help make Zambia one of the richest countries in Africa. Without copper, it would be one of the poorest.

Zambia is a little larger than the state of Texas, but Texas has about 2½ times as many people. The country takes its name from the Zambezi River, which forms most of its southern border. Mighty Victoria Falls, one of the world's most beautiful waterfalls, lies on the river. The great Kariba Dam, largest hydroelectric project in Africa, and Kariba Lake also are located on the Zambezi, serving both Zambia and Rhodesia.

Zambia was formerly a British protectorate called *Northern Rhodesia.* From 1953 to 1963, it formed part of the Federation of Rhodesia and Nyasaland with Nyasaland (now Malawi) and Southern Rhodesia (now Rhodesia). It became the REPUBLIC OF ZAMBIA in 1964. Zambia's relations with Rhodesia have been strained since 1965, when Rhodesia declared itself independent. Lusaka, a city of about 348,000 persons, is the capital of Zambia.

The contributor of this article, Richard Hall, is Syndication Manager of the Financial Times *of London and author of* Zambia *and* Kaunda, Founder of Zambia.

Zambia

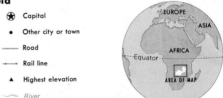

⊛ Capital
• Other city or town
—— Road
+—+ Rail line
▲ Highest elevation
~~~ River

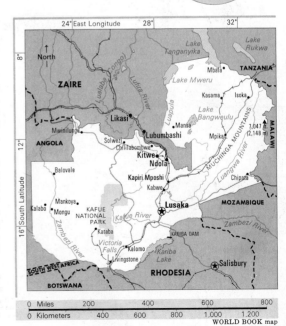

ZAMBIA

──────── **FACTS IN BRIEF** ────────

Capital: Lusaka.

Official Language: English.

Form of Government: Republic.

Area: 290,586 sq. mi. (752,614 km²). *Greatest Distances*—east-west, 900 mi. (1,448 km); north-south, 700 mi. (1,127 km).

Population: *Estimated 1980 Population*—5,896,000; distribution, 68 per cent rural, 32 per cent urban; density, 21 persons per sq. mi. (8 per km²). *1969 Census*—4,056,995. *Estimated 1985 Population*—7,003,000.

Chief Products: *Agriculture*—cassava, cattle, corn, cotton, millet, tobacco. *Fishing*—perch, whitebait. *Manufacturing and Processing*—cement-making, copper-smelting, sawmilling. *Mining*—cobalt, copper, lead, zinc.

Flag: The flag has an orange eagle in the upper right corner over three vertical stripes of red (for freedom), black (for the people), and orange (for mineral wealth) on a field of green (for natural resources). See FLAG (color picture: Flags of Africa).

Money: *Basic Unit*—kwacha. See MONEY (table: Exchange Rates).

Marc & Evelyne Bernheim, Woodfin Camp, Inc.

Copper and Copper Products, such as the wire manufactured in the factory above, make up nine-tenths of Zambia's exports.

Government. The people of Zambia elect the president as head of state and government. The people also elect 125 members of the National Assembly, the country's legislature. The president nominates 10 extra assembly members to represent particular interests. Assembly members serve five-year terms. The president appoints the Cabinet from among the Assembly. All citizens over the age of 18 may vote.

The country is divided into eight provinces. Each province is administered by a provincial minister.

People. Most Zambians are black Africans who speak Bantu languages (see BANTU). There are more than 70 ethnic groups represented and eight major local languages spoken in Zambia. Many people also speak English, the official language.

In remote parts of Zambia, village life goes on much as it has for hundreds of years. The people live in circular, grass-roofed huts, and raise food crops on the surrounding land. But the development of mining has caused thousands of people to move to mining towns.

Maize (corn) is the main food. A favorite dish is *nshima*, a thick porridge made from maize. In the *bush* (rural areas), where most Zambians live, the people plant their crops in November and December. They plant maize, millet, cassava, and pumpkins. They store the maize crop in bins set up off the ground on poles so rats and other pests cannot get at it.

Most Zambians are Christians, but traditional local beliefs still have a strong hold on the village people. However, witchcraft and old customs such as *polygyny* (marrying several wives) and *bride price* (paying the parents for a bride) are slowly dying out in the towns.

Until 20 years ago, there was little chance for education. Primary education is now available for nearly all children, however, and more than 20 high schools were opened in 1966. The University of Zambia was founded in 1965. Zambia also has several trade and technical schools.

Land. Most of Zambia is flat and covered with trees and bushes. It lies on a plateau about 4,000 feet (1,200 meters) above sea level. The plateau is broken by the 7,000-foot (2,100-meter) Muchinga Mountains in the northeast. In the south, the trees are smaller, and there are large open areas. The Zambezi River flows south through western Zambia, and forms much of the southern border. Every year it floods a broad, sandy plain in Western province in the southwest.

Because of its altitude, Zambia has a milder climate than might be expected. The hot season lasts only from September through November. Midday temperatures then range between 80° and 100° F. (27° and 38° C). From November through April, Zambia has a rainy season. Violent storms flood the rivers by March. From

Keystone

Lusaka, Zambia's Capital and Commercial Center, has a broad main street lined by offices and shops.

May through August, temperatures range from 60° to 80° F. (16° to 27° C). Northern Zambia gets about 50 inches (130 centimeters) of rainfall a year. The south gets 20 to 30 inches (51 to 76 centimeters).

Economy. Copper accounts for about 90 per cent of Zambia's export earnings. Four large copper mines and several smaller mines lie in an area called the *copperbelt*, along Zambia's border with Zaire. South of the copperbelt, Zambia has a lead and a zinc mine at Kabwe, and large coal deposits near Kariba Lake. Much of Zambia's soil is poor, but there are large pockets suitable for growing tobacco and cotton.

Zambia has no outlet to the sea. Railroads connect it with seaports in Angola, Mozambique, and Tanzania. The railroad to Angola passes through Zaire, and the one to Mozambique passes through Rhodesia. The railroad to Tanzania was built in the early 1970's with millions of dollars of aid from China.

History. In 1851, the Scottish missionary David Livingstone crossed the Zambezi from the south. He spent nearly 20 years exploring the region.

In the late 1800's, Cecil Rhodes's British South Africa Company made treaties with African chiefs in the area. The company named the area Northern Rhodesia to distinguish it from the region south of the Zambezi, which they called Southern Rhodesia.

In 1924, the British government took over the administration of Northern Rhodesia and appointed a governor. The discovery of large copper ore deposits during the late 1920's brought a rush of Europeans to the area. Ten years later, mining was an established industry.

After World War II, the Europeans asked Great Britain for greater control of the government. Many wanted the merger of Northern Rhodesia with Southern Rhodesia. The Africans of Northern Rhodesia opposed these demands. But in 1953, Britain formed a federation of Northern Rhodesia, Southern Rhodesia, and Nyasaland. The Africans opposed the federation, because the European minority controlled the government in Southern Rhodesia. Britain dissolved the federation in 1963 (see RHODESIA AND NYASALAND, FEDERATION OF). On Oct. 24, 1964, Northern Rhodesia became independent. Kenneth Kaunda was elected president in 1964. He was re-elected in 1968, 1973, and 1978. See KAUNDA, KENNETH D.

In 1965, Rhodesia (Southern Rhodesia) declared its independence in defiance of Great Britain. Relations between Zambia and Rhodesia became severely strained, because Rhodesia's white minority government refused to give the African majority a greater voice in government.

Zambia faced economic problems in the 1970's. In 1973, Rhodesia prohibited Zambia from shipping goods across its territory, eliminating one of Zambia's main outlets to the sea. Rhodesia soon lifted the ban. But until 1978, Zambia refused to ship goods across Rhodesia. The price of copper fell sharply in the 1970's, causing a drop in the revenue earned by Zambia's main industry.   RICHARD HALL

See also COPPER (graph); LAKE BANGWEULU; LUSAKA; VICTORIA FALLS; ZAMBEZI RIVER.

ZAMBOANGA, *SAHM boh AHNG gah* (pop. 240,066; met. area pop. 250,300), is a beautiful city in the Philip-

pines. It lies on the western tip of Mindanao Island, 550 miles (885 kilometers) south of Manila (see PHILIPPINES [map]). The city is the chief port and trading center for a region that produces abacá, rubber, coconuts, lumber, and rice. The Spaniards built a fort at Zamboanga in 1635. The city served as a Japanese base in World War II.   RUSSELL H. FIFIELD and CARLOS P. ROMULO

ZAMENHOF, LUDOVIC L. See ESPERANTO.

ZAMIA. See CYCAD.

ZANE'S TRACE. See OHIO (Transportation).

ZANGWILL, *ZANG wil*, **ISRAEL** (1864-1926), a British novelist and dramatist, made his reputation with the novel, *The Children of Israel* (1892), a sympathetic story of Jewish life. He also wrote the novels, *Ghetto Tragedies* (1893), and *Dreamers of the Ghetto* (1898). He won success with the dramatization of *The Children of Israel* in 1899, with light comedies such as *Merely Mary Ann* (1904), and with social plays such as *The Melting Pot* (1908) and *The War God* (1911). Zangwill was born in London, and was a leader in the Zionist movement.   R. W. STALLMAN

ZANZIBAR. See TANZANIA.

ZANZIBAR (pop. 68,490) is the capital of Zanzibar, an island that is part of Tanzania. The city exports cloves, copra, chili peppers, citrus fruit, clove oil, coconut oil, and soap. Zanzibar was founded in the 1500's as a Portuguese trade center.

ZAPATA, EMILIANO (1880?-1919), was a leader of the Mexican Revolution. He was an Indian, and his main objective was to gain land for his people. After forced service in the army, he joined the revolt in 1910 against President Porfirio Díaz. Zapata refused to lay down his arms until the revolutionary leader, Francisco Madero, distributed land. He also refused to recognize Victoriano Huerta, Madero's assassin. With Pancho Villa, he occupied Mexico City in 1914. Zapata was murdered by Colonel Jesús Guajardo in 1919. He was born in Anenecuilco, Morelos.   DONALD E. WORCESTER

See also MEXICO (The Constitution of 1917).

ZAPOTEC INDIANS, *SAH poh tehk*, formed one of the main Indian groups in southern Mexico. They occupied most of the eastern half of the present state of Oaxaca. They developed one of the major Mexican civilizations, but owed many of their ideas to the Maya. The Zapotec farmed, followed a calendar, and used a form of hieroglyphic writing. Their magnificent tombs indicate that the Zapotec believed in an afterlife.

Many ancient ruins in Oaxaca are attributed to the Zapotec. The best known site is that of Monte Albán, just west of the city of Oaxaca. The Zapotec built most of this mountaintop "city" between A.D. 1 and 900. Ruins include great plazas and temples, rich tombs, and *stelae* (carved stone slabs). The Mixtec, a large Indian group from western Oaxaca, occupied the city before and after this time. Thousands of pure-blooded Zapotec still live in the mountain region of Oaxaca. They speak the Zapotec language.   GORDON F. EKHOLM

ZARAGOZA. See SARAGOSSA.

ZARATHUSTRA. See ZOROASTER.

ZAUDITU. See ETHIOPIA (History).

ZBB. See ZERO-BASE BUDGETING.

ZEALOTS. See SIMON THE CANAANITE, SAINT.

ZEBEDEE. See JAMES (Saint James the Greater); JOHN, SAINT.

ZEBRA

ZEBRA is a striped, horselike animal found wild in Africa. It stands 4 to 5 feet (1.2 to 1.5 meters) high at the withers. The zebra differs from all other members of the horse family because of its startling color pattern. It has parallel black or dark-brown stripes on a whitish background arranged in exact designs. These stripes run all over its body, meeting diagonally down the sides of the head. The lines may appear even on the zebra's long ears, short thick mane, and down its tail to the tuft of hair. The lines help to hide the zebra from its enemies. The zebra's chief foe is the lion. Some kinds of zebras live on open grassy plains, and some in rough mountains. Zebras are grazing animals. They live in small bands, each of which is led by a stallion. Zebras are savage fighters. They are difficult to tame and train to work. They are sometimes tamed in South Africa because they appear immune to *nagana*, a disease that attacks most domesticated animals in Africa. Nagana is carried by the tsetse fly (see TSETSE FLY).

Great numbers of zebras once lived over most of the eastern part of Africa, from southern Egypt to Cape Colony. They were killed for their meat and hides. Their meat is said to have an excellent taste and their hides are used to make a tough leather. Some kinds of zebras are nearly extinct, but others are numerous.

Scientific Classification. The zebra belongs to the horse family, *Equidae*. It is classified as genus *Equus*. The three species of zebras are *E. zebra*, *E. bontequagga*, and *E. grevyi*.   E. LENDELL COCKRUM

Giuseppe Mazza

Zebras resemble horses but have a wild nature and are difficult to tame. Most zebra mares have one colt every spring.

ZEBU. See CATTLE (Beef Cattle).

ZEBULUN, *ZEHB yoo luhn*, was the name of one of the 12 tribes of Israel. It occupied an area in southwestern Galilee just north of the Plain of Esdraelon. In the 1100's B.C., Zebulun, together with neighboring tribes, played a leading part in the defeat of the Canaanites by Deborah and Barak (Judges 4-5). Later, it was a part of the northern kingdom of Israel. In 733 B.C., Zebulun was taken by the Assyrians along with the rest of Galilee. Jesus' home, Nazareth, lay in what had once been the territory of Zebulun. Zebulun was named for the tenth son of Jacob, the sixth and youngest born to him by Leah (Genesis 30:20). The tribe claimed that it descended from him.   JOHN BRIGHT

ZECHARIAH, *ZEHK uh RY uh*, was the name of several persons in the Old Testament. The name means *the Lord remembers*. Probably the best-known Zechariah was the prophet who lived about 520 B.C. His name is given to the second from the last of the Old Testament books in the English Bible. Zechariah was probably born in Babylonian captivity, but he worked in Jerusalem. He urged the people of Jerusalem to rebuild the Temple, and encouraged the Jews to believe that soon they would be a free nation. He preached against the social and religious evils of his day, and related many visions, interpreted to him by an angel. His prophecy is in the first eight chapters of his book. Scholars believe the last chapters are later additions.   WALTER G. WILLIAMS

ZED. See Z.

ZEEMAN, *ZAY mahn*, **PIETER** (1865-1943), a Dutch physicist, became well known for his discoveries in spectroscopy. In 1896, he discovered what is now called the *Zeeman effect*, the splitting of spectral lines by a magnetic field (see ZEEMAN EFFECT). The theory for this phenomenon was developed by Hendrik A. Lorentz, and the two scientists shared the 1902 Nobel prize in physics for their work (see LORENTZ, HENDRIK A.). It is by means of the Zeeman effect that astronomers can measure the strength of the magnetic field on the surface of the sun or other stars. Zeeman was born in Zonnemaire, in Zeeland, The Netherlands.   R. T. ELLICKSON

ZEEMAN EFFECT is the splitting of a spectral line when a source of light is placed in a magnetic field. Spectral lines of light are produced when the electrons in atoms change from one energy level to another (see LIGHT [Sources of Light]). The pattern of spectral lines thus indicates the energy levels of the atoms. Because the lines split into two or more parts when the atoms are in a magnetic field, the Zeeman effect indicates that the energy levels of the atoms have changed.

The Zeeman effect was first observed in 1896 by Pieter Zeeman, a Dutch physicist. Scientists did not completely understand its importance until the development of quantum mechanics in the 1920's. Physicists can learn about such things as the magnetic properties of atoms and the electrons in them by observing the split spectral lines. The Zeeman effect can also be used to study molecules and nuclei.   GERALD FEINBERG

See also ZEEMAN, PIETER.

ZEIN. See CORN (Processing Corn).

ZELAYA, JOSÉ SANTOS. See NICARAGUA (History).

ZEMACH, MARGOT (1931-   ), is an American illustrator of children's books. She won the 1974 Caldecott medal for her pictures for *Duffy and the Devil* (1973). Her husband, Harve Zemach, adapted the story from an English folk tale. The story tells about a girl named Duffy who outwits the devil.

Margot and Harve Zemach worked together on several children's books, including *Salt; a Russian Tale* (1965) and *A Penny a Look* (1971), which are adaptions of folk tales. In addition, Margot Zemach has illustrated children's books by other authors. She was born in Los Angeles.   ZENA SUTHERLAND

ZEMI. See INDIAN, AMERICAN (Indians of the Caribbean).

ZEN is an intuitive school of Buddhist meditation. It is not a philosophy or religion in the proper sense. It has nothing to teach and no rituals. Zen is a method of self-training that leads to an understanding of reality. Its basic idea is that people can discipline the mind so that they come in touch with the inner workings of their being. They aim to grasp intuitively what they cannot grasp rationally. This larger "awareness" cannot be taught. Individuals must find it for themselves. Zen was founded in China in 520 by Bodhidharma, who called it *Ch'an*. A Zen movement flowered in Japan in the 1100's and 1200's.   GEORGE NOEL MAYHEW

See also BUDDHISM (Buddhist Schools).

ZEND-AVESTA. See PARSIS.

ZENER CARD. See EXTRASENSORY PERCEPTION.

ZENGER, JOHN PETER (1697-1746), gained the first major victory for freedom of the press in the American Colonies. Friends established Zenger, a printer, as editor and publisher of the *New York Weekly Journal* in 1733. These friends, including Chief Justice Lewis Morris, belonged to the Popular Party, and used the *Journal* to oppose the Government Party. In 1734, when the British governor William Cosby abruptly dismissed Morris from his office, the *Journal* criticized Cosby severely.

The British arrested Zenger, and tried him in 1735 for criminal libel. Zenger's lawyers were disbarred, and he was left almost defenseless. Finally, Andrew Hamilton, a famous Philadelphia lawyer, came to New York to aid Zenger. Hamilton presented a brilliant and powerful speech that persuaded the jury to find Zenger "not guilty" by arguing that Zenger had printed the truth, and that truth is not libelous. See FREEDOM OF THE PRESS (In the United States; picture). After his acquittal, Zenger published *A Brief Narrative of the Case and Tryal of John Peter Zenger* (1736).

Zenger was born in Germany, and came to New York at the age of 13. He was apprenticed to a printer, and set up his own printing shop in 1726. The Zenger Memorial Hall in Federal Hall, New York City, was dedicated in 1953.   KENNETH N. STEWART

ZENITH, *ZE nith*, is a term in astronomy that refers to the point in the heavens directly overhead. The zenith is opposite to the *nadir*, or the point directly below. A straight line could be drawn connecting the zenith, the center of the earth, and the nadir. The zenith provides a means for making certain calculations in astronomy and geography. For example, the location of a star can be computed by determining the distance between the zenith and the star. Astronomers call this distance the *zenith distance*. See also NADIR.   OLIVER J. LEE

ZENO, an emperor. See ODOACER.

ZENO, *ZEE noh* (335?-265?B.C.), was the founder of Stoic philosophy in Athens. He was born in Citium on the island of Cyprus. It is reported that he was originally a merchant, but was shipwrecked and lost all his property traveling to Athens in 314 B.C. He stayed there, and took up the study of philosophy, meeting his students on a *stoa* (porch), from which the name *stoic* came (see STOIC PHILOSOPHY).

Zeno taught that it is foolish to try to shape circumstances to our desires. The world process is not like a blindly running machine. Instead, a divine intelligence guides and governs it, and directs all things ultimately toward what is good. Wise people will "follow nature" and fit their desires to the pattern of events. They will find happiness in freedom from desire, from fear of evil, and in knowing that they are in tune with the divine purpose directing all things. The Stoic philosophy spread to Rome and flourished there for several centuries after the birth of Christ.   LEWIS M. HAMMOND

ZEOLITE, *ZEE oh lyt*, is the name of a group of minerals that have their atoms arranged in an open crystal framework. Zeolites can hold other atoms or molecules in this framework much as a sponge holds water. Scientists call zeolites *hydrous* because they contain up to 20 per cent water. They release this water easily when heated. The name *zeolite* comes from two Greek words meaning *boiling stone*.

Zeolite crystals occur in nature or they can be manufactured. They consist of aluminum, oxygen, silicon, and one other metal, usually calcium, potassium, or sodium. Zeolites are widely used as water softeners. They exchange their water and sodium for almost all the metal *ions* (electrically charged atoms), such as those of calcium, that make water hard.   CECIL J. SCHNEER

See also WATER SOFTENING.

ZEPHANIAH, *ZEHF uh NY uh*, was an ancient Hebrew prophet. He probably lived during the reign of Josiah, who ruled in Judah from about 639 to 608 B.C. His name was given to a book of the Old Testament. This book has only three chapters. The first two were written by Zephaniah. He prophesied that Judah and several other nations were doomed because their people had done evil. The end of the book tells of the happy state of those who have been purified by God and reunited with Him. The book is famous for its description of the coming "Day of the Lord."   WALTER G. WILLIAMS

ZEPPELIN. See AIRSHIP (The Zeppelins).

ZEPPELIN, *ZEHP uh lihn* or *TSEHP uh LEEN*, **FERDINAND VON** (1838-1917), was a famous German pioneer in lighter-than-air vehicles. He designed aircraft that were primarily gas bags, supported internally by a light framework. Engines powered and controlled his aircraft. These aircraft soon were named after him. Germany used zeppelins in air raids against Great Britain during World War I. These were the first planned air raids against a civilian population in history (see AIRSHIP).

Zeppelin was born in Constance, Baden, and was trained to be an army officer. He visited the United States during the Civil War and went up in balloons with the Union forces. The balloons convinced him of the usefulness of aircraft. Zeppelin served in the Franco-Prussian War in 1870. After he retired from the army in 1891, he devoted himself to aeronautics. He had spent most of his savings when Kaiser Wilhelm II became interested in his work and offered some financial support.   ROBERT B. HOTZ

ZERNIKE, FRITS. See NOBEL PRIZES (table: Nobel Prizes for Physics—1953).

ZERO, a Japanese plane. See AIR FORCE (picture).

ZERO, in arithmetic, is the name of the digit, 0. It is used to indicate the absence of quantity. A zero is needed in a positional numeral system, such as the familiar system commonly used by most peoples today. In a *positional* system, the *position*, or place, of a digit determines the digit's value. Thus, in the numeral 246, the digit 2 stands for two hundred, the digit 4 stands for four tens (or forty), and the digit 6 stands for six units, or ones. The numeral represents the number two hundred forty-six. In order to write the number two hundred six, a symbol is needed to show that there are no tens. The digit 0 serves this purpose, and the number is written 206. Zero added to or subtracted from any number gives the original number. A number multiplied by zero gives zero. Division by zero is undefinable.

On most scales, zero marks the starting point or the neutral position. Positive numbers are placed to the right or above zero, and negative numbers to the left or below zero. On some scales, the zero point is set arbitrarily. For example, on a Celsius thermometer, zero is set at the temperature at which water freezes.

Scholars do not know when the zero was invented. It was used before the A.D. 800's, and may have been used as early as 600. The Hindus probably originated it. The word *zero* probably came from *ziphirum*, a Latinized form of the Arabic word *sifr*. *Sifr* is a translation of the Hindu word *sunya* (void or empty).　　HOWARD W. EVES

See also DECIMAL NUMERAL SYSTEM; DIGIT; MAYA (Science and Learning).

ZERO-BASE BUDGETING (ZBB) is a technique used to reduce spending in business and government. ZBB requires each department of an organization to justify annually every dollar it wishes to spend during the next year. The technique differs from *incremental budgeting*, which requires departments to justify only proposed changes from the previous year's *base* (budget). With ZBB, department managers regard a program as though it never existed before—in other words, that it has a base of zero dollars.

Departments of organizations that use ZBB prepare annual outlines called *decision packages*, which describe each program. The outlines set forth a program's current spending level and its proposed high and low spending levels. Using the outlines, executives decide how much money to spend on each program.

ZBB was introduced in the 1960's by Texas Instruments, Incorporated, an electronics company. In 1977, President Jimmy Carter planned to extend ZBB to all federal agencies. At the same time, various state legislatures began to adopt procedures called *sunset laws* to control spending.　　ROBERT T. GOLEMBIEWSKI

See also SUNSET LAWS.

ZERO POPULATION GROWTH. See BIRTH AND DEATH RATES; EHRLICH, PAUL RALPH.

ZEUS was the king of the gods and the supreme ruler of people in Greek mythology. He originally was a god of the sky. In time, the Greeks regarded him as the only god who concerned himself with the entire universe. They also associated Zeus with justice and believed that he punished the wicked and rewarded the good. He had the same powers as the Roman god Jupiter.

Zeus was the son of Cronus and Rhea, who belonged to a mythological race called the Titans.

Vatican Museums, Rome
(Viollet, Paris)

Zeus

Zeus and the other children of Cronus overthrew their father during a war against the Titans. Zeus then took Cronus' place and ruled from Mount Olympus. He headed a family of 12 major gods and goddesses called the Olympians. Zeus's brothers were the gods Hades and Poseidon. Hades ruled the underworld, and Poseidon controlled the seas. The goddesses Demeter, Hera, and Hestia were Zeus's sisters. Zeus married Hera, who became queen of the gods. They had two children, the gods Ares and Hephaestus.

Zeus had many love affairs with goddesses and mortal women. His children by them included the gods Apollo, Dionysus, and Hermes; the goddess Artemis; and the heroes Heracles (Hercules in Latin) and Perseus. In addition, Zeus gave birth to the goddess Athena, who sprang full-grown from his head. Zeus and the goddess Mnemosyne were the parents of the Muses, the nine goddesses of the arts and sciences. According to some myths, Zeus and the goddess Themis were the parents of the Fates, three goddesses who controlled human destiny.

Artists have shown Zeus as a bearded and majestic man. His symbols were the eagle, the oak tree, the royal scepter, and the thunderbolt.　　ROBERT J. LENARDON

See also MYTHOLOGY (Greek); JUPITER; DODONA; HERA; OLYMPIA; OLYMPUS; PERSEPHONE; TITANS.

ZEUS, STATUE OF. See SEVEN WONDERS OF THE WORLD (Ancient Wonders; picture: The Statue of Zeus).

ZHIVKOV, TODOR. See BULGARIA (Communist Rule).

ZHUKOV, *ZHOO kawf,* **GEORGI KONSTANTINOVICH** (1896-1974), became a Russian military hero during World War II (1939-1945). He organized the defense of Moscow in 1941 and the Russian victory at Stalingrad in 1942 and 1943. He led the Russian forces that captured Berlin in 1945. Zhukov became a marshal—the highest rank in the Russian army—in 1943.

Russian dictator Joseph Stalin feared Zhukov's popularity after the war and assigned him to minor posts. Stalin died in 1953, and Zhukov rose to the post of defense minister in 1955.

Zhukov helped Nikita S. Khrushchev increase his power in the Russian Communist Party in June, 1957. Khrushchev made Zhukov a member of the party's *Presidium* (now called *Politburo*), the highest Russian governing body. But Khrushchev came to fear Zhukov's influence, and removed him from his high positions in the fall of 1957. Zhukov was born in Strelkovka, near Moscow. He fought in World War I.　　ALBERT PARRY

ZIEGFELD, *ZIG feld,* **FLORENZ** (1869-1932), was an American theatrical producer. He became famous for musical spectacles which featured beautiful women, scenery, and costumes, and sometimes excellent comedians. In 1907, Ziegfeld produced the first of his annual *Ziegfeld Follies*. He also produced musical comedies such as *Show Boat*. He was born in Chicago. BARNARD HEWITT

ZIEGLER, KARL. See NOBEL PRIZES (table: Nobel Prizes for Chemistry—1963).

ZIGGURAT. See ARCHITECTURE (Beginnings).

ZIM, HERBERT SPENCER (1909-　　), is an author and educator. He wrote more than 60 children's science books, including *Elephants* (1946), *Dinosaurs* (1954), *The Universe* (1961), and *Sharks* (1966).

Zim was born in New York City. He earned B.S., M.A., and Ph.D. degrees from Columbia University.

He taught science courses at a private school in New York City from 1932 to 1950 and at the University of Illinois from 1950 to 1957.   ELOISE RUE

ZIMBABWE, *zihm BAH bway,* or GREAT ZIMBABWE, was the capital of two southern African empires—the Mwanamutapa Empire in the 1400's and the Changamire Empire from the late 1400's to the early 1800's. The ruins of the city lie near Fort Victoria, Rhodesia. They include a tower 30 feet (9 meters) high and part of a wall that measures 800 feet (240 meters) around and up to 32 feet (10 meters) high. The structures at Zimbabwe were made of huge granite slabs, most of which were fitted together without mortar.

Shona farmers and herders were living in Zimbabwe by the 1000's or 1100's. During the 1400's, a branch of the Shona, called the Karanga, established the Mwanamutapa Empire and made Zimbabwe its capital. The word *zimbabwe* means *dwelling of a chief* in the Shona language. The Mwanamutapa Empire included all of what are now Rhodesia and western Mozambique. At eastern African ports, the Karanga traded ivory, gold, and copper for porcelain from China and cloth and beads from India and Indonesia. The Rozwi, a southern Karanga group, rebelled in the late 1400's and founded the Changamire Empire. This empire became stronger than the Mwanamutapa Empire, and the Rozwi took over Zimbabwe. The Rozwi built the city's largest structures. The Changamire Empire was prosperous and peaceful until Nguni people from the south conquered the empire in the 1830's. Zimbabwe was then abandoned.   LEO SPITZER

ZIMBABWE RHODESIA. See RHODESIA.

ZIMBALIST, EFREM (1889-   ), is a well-known violinist. He made his debut in Berlin in 1907, and his first appearance in the United States in 1911. Later he became a United States citizen. In 1941 he was appointed director of the Curtis Institute of Music in Philadelphia. Zimbalist was born in Rostov, Russia.   DOROTHY DeLAY

ZINC, a chemical element, is a shiny, bluish-white metal. It is important in industry. A coating of zinc applied to metals such as iron or steel prevents them from rusting. The coated metal, called *galvanized* iron or steel, is used in such products as roof gutters and tank linings. Zinc is also used in electric batteries.

Zinc can be combined with other metals to form many *alloys* (mixtures). For example, brass is an alloy of copper and zinc. Bronze is copper, tin, and zinc. Nickel silver is copper, nickel, and zinc. Zinc is also used in *solders* (easily melted alloys used for joining metals). Zinc and its alloys are used in *die-casting* (forming objects from liquid metal in molds), *electroplating* (coating an object by use of electricity), and *powder metallurgy* (forming objects from metal powder).

Moist air *tarnishes* (discolors) zinc with a protective coating of zinc oxide (ZnO). Once a thin layer of this coating forms, air cannot tarnish the zinc below it. White powdery zinc oxide is one of industry's most useful chemicals. It is used in the manufacture of cosmetics, plastics, rubber, skin ointments, and soaps. It is also used as a *pigment* (coloring matter) in paints and printing inks. Zinc sulfide (ZnS) glows when ultraviolet light, X rays, or *cathode rays* (streams of electrons) shine on it. It is used on luminous dials for clocks. It is also used to coat the inside of television screens and fluorescent lamps. Zinc chloride (ZnCl$_2$) in a water solution pre-

Leading Zinc-Mining Countries

Tons of zinc mined in 1974

Country	
Canada	1,278,100 short tons (1,159,500 metric tons)
Russia	750,000 short tons (680,400 metric tons)*
Australia	499,900 short tons (453,500 metric tons)
United States	499,900 short tons (453,500 metric tons)
Peru	437,800 short tons (397,200 metric tons)

*Estimate.
Source: *Minerals Yearbook, 1974,* U.S. Bureau of Mines.

serves wood from decay and protects it from insects.

Zinc metal is never found pure in nature. It occurs combined with sulfur in a mineral called *zinc blende* or *sphalerite.* Other zinc-containing minerals include *calamine, franklinite, smithsonite, willemite,* and *zincite.* Zinc metal is hard and brittle at room temperature, but it softens when it is heated above 100° C (212° F.). It is taken from its ores by heating them in the air to convert them to zinc oxide. The oxide is converted to zinc by heating it with carbon.

The chemical symbol for zinc is Zn. Its atomic number is 30 and its atomic weight is 65.37. Zinc has a melting point of 419.58° C. The element boils at 907° C. The earliest complete study of zinc was published in 1746 by Andreas Sigismund Marggraf, a German chemist.   ALAN DAVISON

Related Articles in WORLD BOOK include:

Alloy
Australia (picture: Miners Transport Zinc Ore)
Ductility
Element, Chemical
Galvanized Iron and Steel
Malleability

ZINC CHLORIDE. See CHLORIDE.

ZINCITE. See ZINC.

ZINJANTHROPUS. See LEAKEY; AUSTRALOPITHECUS.

ZINNEMANN, FRED (1907-   ), is a motion-picture director whose films are noted for their skillful character portrayal. He won Academy Awards for his directing of *From Here to Eternity* (1953) and *A Man for All Seasons* (1966). His other major films include *The Seventh Cross* (1944), *The Search* (1947), *The Men* (1950), *The Member of the Wedding* (1952), *High Noon* (1952), *Oklahoma!* (1955), *The Nun's Story* (1958), *The Sundowners* (1960), *The Day of the Jackal* (1973), and *Julia* (1977).

Zinnemann was born in Vienna, Austria. He learned film techniques while working in Paris. He moved to Hollywood in 1929, and gained his first success as a director of short subjects. His short *That Mothers Might Live* (1938) won an Academy Award. Zinnemann became a director of full-length movies in 1942. HOWARD THOMPSON

ZINNIA, *ZIHN ee uh,* is a genus of garden plants of the composite family. There are about 16 species. The zinnias are native to Mexico and the southwestern United States. The best-known zinnia is a garden plant that blooms in a wide variety of colors. Its stiff, hairy stem may grow 2 feet (61 centimeters) tall. The flowers are in tones of red, yellow, scarlet, crimson, pink, salmon, and bronze. This zinnia is one of the most successful summer annual flowers. It grows in three types. One is *youth-and-old-age*, which grows as high as 3 feet (91 centimeters). Another has golden, starlike flowers. The third is a miniature hybrid. Zinnias grow well in warm, sunny climates. They are grown from seed.

Scientific Classification. Zinnias are in the composite family, *Compositae*. Youth-and-old-age is genus *Zinnia*, species *Z. elegans*. The starlike flower is *Z. linearis;* the small hybrid, *Z. angustifolia.*   ALFRED C. HOTTES

See also FLOWER (picture: Summer Garden Flowers).

ZINZENDORF, COUNT OF. See MORAVIAN CHURCH.

ZION is a word with many different meanings. It comes from the Hebrew word *Tsīyōn*. Originally, it was the name of a hill in the city of Jerusalem. After the Israelites captured the city from the Jebusites, Zion became the place where the royal palace of King David stood and where Solomon later built the Temple. It was the seat of Jewish worship and government. The name Zion also refers to the Israelites themselves. After their exile from the Holy Land, the word Zion meant to them their homeland, with Jerusalem, the Temple, and all Palestine's ancient glory. Among Christians, the name Zion means the church ruled by God, or a heavenly city or heavenly home. See also ZIONISM.

ZION NATIONAL PARK lies in southwestern Utah. It has many colorful canyons, some of which are extremely narrow and have steep, plunging walls. Rock formations range in color from dark red and orange to light purple and pink. These colors change continuously with the reflection of light. Wild animal and plant life flourish in the park. Mule deer, bighorn sheep, and other animals live there.

Zion Canyon is the main feature of the park. It is about 15 miles (24 kilometers) long and from $\frac{1}{2}$ mile (0.8 kilometer) to less than 50 feet (15 meters) wide. Its walls tower as high as 3,000 feet (910 meters), in some places almost straight up and down. The canyon contains many unusual rock formations.

The park was set aside in 1909 as Mukuntuweap National Monument. In 1918, the park was enlarged and in 1919 it became Zion National Park. Zion National Monument, a vast area of rugged land adjoining the park, was added in 1956. For the area of the park, see NATIONAL PARK SYSTEM (table: National Parks). For the location of Zion National Park, see UTAH (political map).   CARLOS S. WHITING

See also UTAH (picture).

ZIONISM is a movement aimed at establishing a national Jewish state in Palestine, the ancient Jewish homeland. Active Zionism began in the 1800's and led to the establishment of Israel in 1948. Zionism now supports various projects in Israel and acts as a cultural bridge between Israel and Jews in other countries. Zionists work to revive the national Jewish language and culture, and to establish the political and social institutions needed to re-create national Jewish life. *Zion* is the Hebrew poetic name for Palestine.

Movement to Palestine. A series of *pogroms* (organized persecutions of the Jews) in Russia in the 1800's spurred the first significant wave of Jewish emigration from Europe. In 1882, groups of Jewish youths calling themselves *Hoveve-Zion* (Lovers of Zion) formed a movement to promote immigration to Palestine. The Hoveve-

Zion started what was called *practical Zionism*, which favored establishing Jewish settlements in Palestine. Theodor Herzl, an Austrian journalist, developed *political Zionism*, which worked for political recognition of the Jewish claim to a Palestine homeland.

Herzl was a reporter at the famous trial in 1894 of Alfred Dreyfus, the French army officer falsely convicted of treason. The Dreyfus affair convinced Herzl that, if anti-Semitism could be an active force in a country as enlightened as France, Jews could not assimilate in non-Jewish society. To him, the only remedy was to create an independent Jewish state.

Herzl organized the Zionist movement on a worldwide scale at the First Zionist Congress in Basel, Switzerland, in 1897. Since that time, Zionism has been opposed by those Jews who claim that (1) only God can restore the Jews to their homeland; and (2) the Jews are a religious denomination, not a national group.

Practical Zionism dominated the movement until World War I. But the movement gained political recognition when Great Britain liberated the Middle East, including Palestine, from Turkish domination in World War I. Scientist Chaim Weizmann, who later became the first president of Israel, helped persuade the British government to issue the Balfour Declaration in 1917.

The Balfour Declaration pledged British support for a national homeland for the Jews in Palestine. It was included in the British *mandate* (order to rule) over Palestine that was approved by the League of Nations in 1922. Arabs fought against a Jewish state in Palestine, and severe fighting broke out several times in the 1920's and 1930's. The mandate recognized an organization called the Jewish Agency as the representative of the Jews in Palestine. The agency developed economic and cultural facilities, set up educational and scientific institutes, and encouraged Jews to settle there.

In 1939, the British began restricting Jewish immigration to Palestine to gain Arab support for the Allies during World War II. Palestine's Jews fought bitterly against the restrictions after World War II, and the British submitted the problem to the United Nations. In 1947, the UN approved the partition of Palestine into an Arab and a Jewish state. The Zionists proclaimed the State of Israel in 1948. Arab states attacked Israel almost immediately. Arab-Israeli fighting has broken out several times since then.   JOEL L. KRAEMER

See also PALESTINE; ISRAEL; HERZL, THEODOR; SHAZAR, SCHNEOR ZALMAN; WEIZMANN, CHAIM.

ZIP CODE is a code system used to speed the sorting and delivery of mail in the United States. The name stands for *Zoning Improvement Plan*.

The ZIP system uses five numerals that appear after an address. In the ZIP number 22207, for example, the first numeral—2—designates one of 10 geographical areas. Area 2 consists of the District of Columbia, Maryland, North Carolina, South Carolina, Virginia, and West Virginia. The second two numerals—22—indicate a metropolitan area or sectional center. In this case, the mail is going to the Arlington area of Virginia. The last two numerals—07—represent a small town or delivery unit from which the mail will be delivered.

The Post Office Department (now the United States Postal Service) introduced the ZIP Code in 1963. By that time, the volume of the mail in the United States had increased almost 900 per cent since 1900. The

State or Area	Abbreviation	State or Area	Abbreviation	State or Area	Abbreviation	State or Area	Abbreviation
Alabama	AL	Illinois	IL	Nebraska	NE	South Carolina	SC
Alaska	AK	Indiana	IN	Nevada	NV	South Dakota	SD
Arizona	AZ	Iowa	IA	New Hampshire	NH	Tennessee	TN
Arkansas	AR	Kansas	KS	New Jersey	NJ	Texas	TX
California	CA	Kentucky	KY	New Mexico	NM	Utah	UT
Colorado	CO	Louisiana	LA	New York	NY	Vermont	VT
Connecticut	CT	Maine	ME	North Carolina	NC	Virgin Islands	VI
Delaware	DE	Maryland	MD	North Dakota	ND	Virginia	VA
District of Columbia	DC	Massachusetts	MA	Ohio	OH	Washington	WA
Florida	FL	Michigan	MI	Oklahoma	OK	West Virginia	WV
Georgia	GA	Minnesota	MN	Oregon	OR	Wisconsin	WI
Guam	GU	Mississippi	MS	Pennsylvania	PA	Wyoming	WY
Hawaii	HI	Missouri	MO	Puerto Rico	PR		
Idaho	ID	Montana	MT	Rhode Island	RI		

mail had also changed in nature from chiefly personal to about 80 per cent business correspondence.

Many companies use mechanized addressing systems. To help these firms, the Post Office Department in 1963 introduced two-letter abbreviations for states and some other areas. These abbreviations enable mechanized addressing systems to save space by putting a ZIP Code on the same line of an address as the city and state.

The ZIP Code especially speeds up the handling and delivery of *bulk mail* (a huge number of identical pieces). Several other nations also use code systems for mail processing. Critically reviewed by the U.S. POSTAL SERVICE

ZIPPER is a term often used to mean any kind of slide fastener. These fasteners have two edges of teeth and hollows which fit into each other snugly. A slide draws the edges together and meshes the teeth into the hollows. The edges remain fastened until the slide is drawn back, unmeshing the teeth. Slide fasteners are used in such articles as clothing and brief cases.

Whitcomb L. Judson of Chicago patented the first slide fastener in 1893. It was a series of hooks and eyes that fastened together with a slider. Gideon Sundback obtained a patent on the meshed-tooth type of slide fastener in 1913. In 1922, the B. F. Goodrich Company gave the trade name *Zipper* to galoshes with slide fasteners. WILLIAM H. DOOLEY

ZIRCON is a semi-precious stone that occurs in many shades of red, green, and blue. A colorless variety is often used as a diamond substitute. The best examples of zircon have been found along the beaches and river beds of California, Florida, and North Carolina in the United States. Large amounts of zircon are found in Australia, Malaysia, and Madagascar. Zircon is a December birthstone (see BIRTHSTONE). Zircon gems are large crystals of the mineral *zircon*, a source of zirconium. See also GEM (picture).

ZIRCONIUM, *zur KOH nee uhm,* is a rare, grayish-white metal. It is used to make the cores of nuclear reactors because it resists corrosion and does not readily absorb neutrons. *Zircaloy* is an important *alloy* (mixture of metals) developed for many nuclear applications, such as a coating for fuel parts. *Baddeleyite,* a compound of zirconium and oxygen, can withstand extremely high temperatures. It is used for laboratory *crucibles* (melting pots for metals) and the linings for high-temperature furnaces.

Zirconium is found in many minerals, such as zircon and baddeleyite. Zirconium has the chemical symbol Zr. Its atomic number is 40, and its atomic weight is 91.22. It melts at 1852° (±2°) C and boils at 3578° C. Martin Heinrich Klaproth, a German chemist, discovered it in 1789. ALAN DAVISON

ZITHER is a stringed instrument that has musical tones much like those of a harp, lute, or guitar. The zither has from 29 to 42 strings, which the player plucks with the fingers of both hands. The strings are stretched over a thin, flat box rounded at one end. The zither probably developed from an ancient Greek lutelike instrument called a *cithara*. The instrument is particularly popular in central European countries. However, the zither was quite widely played in the United States during the late 1800's. CHARLES B. RIGHTER

Wide World

The Zither

ZOAR VILLAGE. See OHIO (Places to Visit).

ZÓCALO. See MEXICO CITY (Famous Landmarks).

ZODIAC is the name for a band of stars that appears to encircle the earth. *Astrologers* (persons who tell fortunes by studying the stars) believe that the zodiac influences the lives of people. Astrologers use a representation of the zodiac to draw a chart called a *horoscope.* The chart supposedly reveals a person's character or future.

The Signs of the Zodiac. The zodiac consists of 12 divisions called *signs.* The signs are named for certain groups of stars called *constellations.* For example, the zodiac includes Aries (the Ram) and Taurus (the Bull). Astrologers believe that a person comes under the influence of a particular sign, depending on the person's date of birth. For example, persons born during the period from June 22 to July 22 have Cancer as their sign. For the names of all the signs of the zodiac and their related dates, see the illustration with this article.

The Influence of the Signs. According to astrologers, the zodiac's influence on a person comes from several sources. Some of this influence comes from the planets. Each sign gets its main characteristics from a particular planet called its *ruling* planet. For example, the planet Jupiter rules Sagittarius. Astrologers consider Jupiter

499

ZODIACAL LIGHT

"friendly" and "generous." Therefore, persons born under the sign of Sagittarius supposedly also are friendly and generous.

The zodiac also receives some of its influence from four "substances" called *elements:* air, earth, fire, and water. Ancient astrologers thought that all matter was made up of these four elements. Each element has certain qualities that it gives to three signs of the zodiac. For example, fire—considered forceful and restless—influences Aries, Leo, and Sagittarius.

History. Astrologers developed the idea of the zodiac more than 2,000 years ago. They observed the changing position of the stars that accompanied the change in seasons. They knew that if the stars could be seen in daytime the sun would appear to move through a series of constellations, entering a new one each month. These constellations made up the zodiac.

Ancient peoples believed there was a connection between seasonal changes and the constellations of the zodiac. At that time, for example, spring began when the sun was "in" Aries. Thus, Aries became associated with the energetic forces of spring. In time, astrologers developed ways to explain the supposed influence of the zodiac on people's lives.

The position of the earth in space has changed since ancient times. As a result, the dates for each sign no longer represent the time when the sun is in the related constellation. For example, on March 23, a date associated with Aries, the sun is actually in Pisces. However, most modern astrologers still use the traditional dates. CHRISTOPHER MCINTOSH

See also ASTROLOGY; CONSTELLATION; HOROSCOPE; HOUSE (in astrology); and the articles on signs of the zodiac, such as ARIES.

ZODIACAL LIGHT, *zoh DY uh kuhl,* is a cone-shaped glow of faint light which is seen in the Northern Hemisphere. It appears soon after twilight on spring evenings, and just before dawn in the autumn. It extends upward and southward from the position of the sun. In the tropics the zodiacal light can be seen both evening and morning throughout the year. The light is brightest near the sun and shades off gradually. It can easily be traced halfway across the sky. Some observers have said they can trace it completely around the sky. They say they notice a brighter area just opposite the sun, called the *Gegenschein,* which means *counterglow.*

The zodiacal light is so named because it is seen against the zodiacal constellations which lie along the *ecliptic* (the sun's apparent path around the earth). The accepted explanation of the light is that large numbers of small particles of material scattered about the inside of the earth's orbit reflect sunlight and become visible when the earth is dark. OLIVER J. LEE

ZOLA, ÉMILE (1840-1902), made naturalism the leading form of literature in France in the late 1800's. He described life as he saw it, and his books and his life demonstrate his courage, intelligence, and sense of justice. Zola's open letter *J'accuse* (1898) helped win a new trial for Alfred Dreyfus, a French army officer unjustly convicted of spying. Zola was convicted of libel after publication of the letter. He fled to England for a year, but he later became a national hero for his part in the affair. Zola also tried to win acceptance for artist Edouard Manet and other impressionist painters who broke with artistic tradition.

Zola was born in Paris. He began his career as a journalist and novelist in the 1860's. His first novel of merit was *Thérèse Raquin* (1867). After the Franco-Prussian War of 1870, he started working on a long series of novels, *The Rougon-Macquart.* Zola subtitled the series the "natural and social history of a family in the Second Empire." Each of the 20 novels in the series describes the adventures of one or several members of the Rougon-Macquart family, and each treats a different profession, trade, or class of society.

The Belly of Paris (1873), the third volume in the

The Signs of the Zodiac Astrologers believe that every person is influenced by a particular sign, depending on his birthday. The chart below shows the dates and some of the characteristics associated with each sign.

500

series, gives a vivid picture of the central markets of Paris. *The Grog Shop* (1877) is a terrifying portrait of the effects of alcoholism on industrial workers in Paris. *Nana* (1880), a study of prostitution and other vice, caused a scandal when it was published. *Germinal* (1885) is probably Zola's best novel and perhaps the finest novel ever written on the life of miners. *The Crash* (1892) describes France's defeat by Germany in 1870.

Zola wrote a second series, *The Three Cities*, dealing with religious and social problems. A third series, *The Four Gospels*, was still unfinished at his death.

In his fiction, Zola tried to practice the scientific method. He argued that the novels of *The Rougon-Macquart* showed the effects of heredity and environment on society. However, the scientific basis of Zola's work is weak. But he used the documentary style skillfully and his novels are still valid portraits of various aspects of French life from 1860 to 1890.

Each of Zola's major novels is dominated by a symbol, such as the mine in *Germinal*. His style is somewhat heavy, but he excelled in writing descriptions, especially of crowds. Zola's characters often lack complexity, but they perform vividly in dramas of death and destruction.

Zola wrote several works of criticism defending the naturalist movement. These include *The Experimental Novel* (1880), *The Naturalistic Novelists* (1881), and *Naturalism in the Theater* (1881).　　　ROBERT J. NIESS

See also NATURALISM; DREYFUS, ALFRED.

ZOLLVEREIN, *TSAWL fur INE,* is the German word for *customs union.* It was the name of the commercial union, or trading arrangement, which Prussia and all the other states of Germany except Austria set up in the 1800's. The Zollverein prepared the way for the unification of Germany in 1871.

At the close of the Napoleonic Wars, Germany was made up of 39 separate states (including four city republics). Each state gloried in its own independence. Each had its own tariff system, and charged customs duties on all trade. Trade was thus very difficult. In 1818, the Prussian government abolished its internal tariffs and invited the other German states to join Prussia in eliminating their tariffs against each other. The German states were attracted by the advantages of free trade and most entered the Zollverein. By 1866 only Austria, which had not been allowed to join, and a few other states were not members.

When the German Empire was established in 1871, the Imperial Customs Union replaced the Zollverein. This union included all the German states except the free ports of Bremen and Hamburg. Bremen and most of Hamburg became members in 1888.　　　HAROLD J. HECK

See also CUSTOMS UNION.

ZOMBA, *ZAHM buh* (pop. 19,666), is a city in Malawi, in eastern Africa. It lies about 70 miles (110 kilometers) south of Lake Nyasa. For location, see MALAWI (map). Zomba is the center of a tobacco- and cotton-raising region. The city served as Malawi's capital until 1975, when the capital was moved to Lilongwe in central Malawi.　　　HIBBERD V. B. KLINE, JR.

ZONE, *zohn,* is a section or division of the earth's surface, usually in the form of a band or strip.

Climatic Zones are five geographic belts that encircle the earth. Each of these zones is bounded by a parallel of latitude. The *Torrid Zone* lies across the equator, extending 23°27' north to the Tropic of Cancer and

23°27' south to the Tropic of Capricorn. The northern and southern *Temperate Zones*, each nearly 43° in width, lie between the tropics and the polar circles. The *Frigid Zones*, each about 23½° in width, lie north of the Arctic Circle and south of the Antarctic Circle.

These five zones were defined by the early Greeks, who thought climatic conditions remained constant along parallels of latitude. Scientists know this is not true. Today, climatic zones or regions are marked out by lines of equal temperature and rainfall. The position of these lines is affected by latitude, altitude, and distance from the sea. See CLIMATE (Describing and Classifying Climates; Why Climates Differ; map).

Time Zones are slightly irregular north-south belts that extend from pole to pole. The boundaries of these zones are based in general on meridians of longitude. Each zone is about 15° wide and represents an hour of time (see TIME [Time Zones; map]).

Other Zones. Cities are often divided into zones, commonly called commercial, residential, and industrial. Postal zones help speed mail delivery in large cities and determine parcel post charges.　　　SAMUEL N. DICKEN

See also ANTARCTIC CIRCLE; ARCTIC CIRCLE.

ZONE, POSTAL. See PARCEL POST (Parcel Post Rates); POST OFFICE (Your Letter Goes on Its Way).

ZONE MELTING is a method of removing impurities from solid materials that are used in industry and in research. Germanium metal was the first material to be refined commercially by zone melting. Germanium can be purified by zone melting until it contains only 1 atom of an impurity in every 10 billion atoms. If a boxcar of sugar were this pure, it would contain only one grain of impurity. Extremely pure germanium and other substances are used in making semiconductor electronic devices such as transistors.

The apparatus used for zone melting consists of a row of ring-shaped heaters that move slowly along a tube containing the solid to be purified. Each heater melts a narrow band of the material, forming a liquid "zone" that moves along with the heater. After each heater passes, the liquid cools and freezes. The impurities tend to stay in the liquid zone and are carried to one end of the tube. The material melts again when the next heater passes, and it becomes purer with each melting and freezing. Scientists have found that many substances have unexpected properties in a highly pure state. Impurities in these substances had affected their properties in unsuspected ways.　　　KENNETH SCHUG

ZONING. See CITY PLANNING (Governmental Authority).

ZONING IMPROVEMENT PLAN (ZIP). See ZIP CODE.

ZONTA INTERNATIONAL is a service organization of executive women in business professions. It has more than 630 clubs in the United States and about 45 other countries. Zonta International works to improve the economic, legal, political, and professional status of women. The organization awards Amelia Earhart fellowships annually to women graduate students in aerospace sciences. Zonta International was founded in 1919 in Buffalo, N.Y. It publishes a magazine, *The Zontian.* Headquarters are at 59 E. Van Buren St., Chicago, Ill. 60605. Critically reviewed by ZONTA INTERNATIONAL

Robert H. Glaze, Artstreet

WORLD BOOK photo

Zoos Acquaint City-Dwellers with Nature. Visitors at Brookfield Zoo near Chicago, *left,* can see polar bears and other rare animals. Children's zoos, such as the one at the Milwaukee County Zoo, *right,* give youngsters an opportunity to see and touch various animals.

ZOO is a place where wild animals are kept and displayed. Most large zoos exhibit mammals, birds, reptiles, and amphibians from all parts of the world. Some also feature fish and insects. Many zoos have beautiful gardens and wide, tree-lined paths that lead from one animal display to another. The word *zoo* is a short form of *zoological garden.*

Man has put wild animals on display since ancient times. Today, almost every large city has at least one zoo, and many smaller communities also have one. The Zoological Society of San Diego operates the two largest zoos in the world. The San Diego Zoo, which has about 5,100 animals of 1,600 species and subspecies, owns the largest zoo collection. The San Diego Wild Animal Park, which covers 1,800 acres (728 hectares), ranks as the largest zoo in terms of area.

Size does not necessarily determine the quality or importance of a zoo. For example, the Arizona-Sonora Desert Museum in Tucson, Ariz., ranks as one of the finest zoos in the United States. Most of the animals in this small zoo come from the Sonora Desert. But the zoo's imaginative display techniques have been copied throughout the world.

The Purposes of Zoos

Entertainment and Education. People of all ages enjoy visiting zoos. They delight in viewing creatures that they would never otherwise see face-to-face. But zoos provide more than just recreation. They help keep people aware of the beauties of nature and of the need to preserve wildlife.

Many zoos offer educational tours and lectures for schoolchildren and other groups. Most large zoos include a special *children's zoo,* where youngsters can pet and perhaps even feed some animals.

Scientific Research. Zoos have long served as living zoology laboratories. Zoologists have learned much about animal habits and diseases by studying them in zoos. Studies of live zoo animals, together with examinations of those that have died, have provided information about the structure and function of animal bodies.

Zoos also function as collecting centers for facts about animals. The London Zoo, for example, has the largest zoological library in the world. Since 1864, this zoo has published *The Zoological Record,* a yearly index of zoological writings. Scientists in all parts of the world use this book.

Wildlife Conservation has become one of the most important jobs of zoos. The breeding of animals in captivity may offer the only means of survival for many species that face extinction in nature. Zoos breed endangered species and subspecies in the hope that these creatures may someday be returned to the wild. Such breeding has saved the European bison, the Hawaiian goose, Père David's deer, and Przhevalski's horse from extinction. At least two of these species, the European bison and the Hawaiian goose, have been returned to the wild. In the future, zoo breeding programs may help save such creatures as the orang-utan, the pygmy hippopotamus, and the tiger.

Caring for Zoo Animals

The life of most zoo animals differs greatly from that of their relatives in the wild. For example, zoo animals receive regular meals and medical care. Trained zookeepers take care of the animals' needs, and *curators* (zoologists employed by the zoo) carefully watch the animals. Also, zoo animals need not fear enemies called *predators*, which would eat them or their young. In zoos, predators and prey are kept apart.

On the other hand, the advantages of zoo life can become disadvantages. Regular care and safety make some animals less alert, and boredom causes many to become sluggish or nervous. A number of species will not breed in zoos.

Many institutions have acted to remedy the problems of zoo life. Zoologists, using their increased knowledge of animal behavior, have designed zoos that encourage animals to act as they would in the wild. This emphasis on naturalism has resulted in lively, more active animals. It also has increased the number of species that breed in zoos.

Display. Zoos exhibit animals in a variety of natural settings. One of the most widely used naturalistic display techniques is based on a moat. Heavy-bodied animals, such as bears, lions, and tigers, cannot jump far, and so zoos need not cage them. These creatures can be displayed in an outdoor area surrounded by a deep moat. Such displays not only encourage animals to behave more naturally, but also provide a better view of them. Leopards, mountain lions, and certain other animals that can jump long distances are usually kept in cages.

Many animal exhibits, both indoors and outdoors, include plants, play equipment, and pools and waterfalls. These features relieve the boredom of captivity and encourage the animals to act more as they would in nature.

Other display techniques include a cold barrier for reptiles. This method, developed by the Antwerp Zoo in Belgium, features a refrigerated area that separates the animals from the viewers. Reptiles are cold-blooded and cannot maintain their body temperature in cold surroundings. They will not normally enter the refrigerated zone, and for this reason they do not have to be caged.

Many animals, such as owls and raccoons, are usually active only at night, and they often appear sluggish to zoo visitors. But the Bronx Zoo in New York City developed a lighting system that enables these animals to be viewed under nighttime conditions. At night, a bright white light is shone in the animals' cages. The light causes the animals to sleep, as they normally would do during the day. In the daytime, when people come to the zoo, the cages are lit only with red or blue light. The animals can barely detect these colors of light, and they behave as they would at night.

During the late 1960's, drive-through zoos began to be developed. These zoos do not display their animals in cages, but they do keep predators and prey apart. Visitors ride through the zoo in their automobile or aboard a bus or a monorail train. In a well-planned drive-through zoo, the animals live in spacious, naturalistic settings. But some drive-through zoos crowd the animals into smaller areas than traditional zoos do.

Wild-animal parks resemble drive-through zoos because the animals are not caged. But these parks are larger than most drive-through zoos, and they have less interest in exhibiting animals. They serve largely as breeding farms for many species of zoo animals because they provide the natural surroundings required for mating. The San Diego Wild Animal Park, the first such establishment in the United States, opened in 1972. Animals in this huge park roam over large areas under

Robert H. Glaze, Artstreet

Kenneth W. Fink, Bruce Coleman Inc.

Zoos Vary Greatly in Size and Kinds of Animals. The enormous San Diego Wild Animal Park, *above,* features animals from many parts of the world, such as these African elephants. The much smaller Arizona-Sonora Desert Museum, *right,* exhibits only animals, including this coati, that live in the Sonora desert.

Tigers and Deer at the Milwaukee County Zoo live in areas that are side-by-side. A deep moat, which visitors cannot see, prevents the tigers from attacking the deer.

WORLD BOOK photo

the close watch of curators. Visitors may ride a monorail train that travels through the park. The train's route is designed to skirt the areas where animals live, thus disturbing the herds as little as possible. Wild-animal parks have succeeded in breeding such animals as cheetahs and rhinoceroses, which do not breed well in traditional zoos.

Feeding. Zoo kitchens prepare meals designed to meet each animal's nutritional needs. The kinds and amounts of food given to different creatures vary greatly. Some reptiles are fed only once a week, but certain birds and small mammals eat several meals a day.

Zoo kitchens keep a variety of foods, including eggs, fish, fruit, meat, seeds, and vegetables. They also have such unusual items as insects and earthworms. Food supplements, such as vitamins and bone meal, are used to ensure a nutritious diet for every animal. Many animals receive cakes or pellets that consist of various foods and supplements mixed together. These mixtures assure a balanced meal for each animal.

An animal's diet may vary under certain conditions. A male deer receives special food during the summer, when he grows antlers. Pregnant females and mothers nursing their young also require a special diet.

Flip Schulke, Black Star

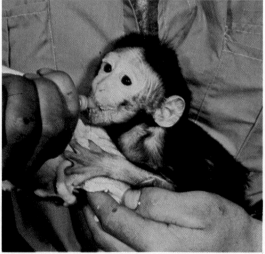

Terence Spencer, Colorific

Zoo Animals Receive Expert Care. A zookeeper feeds milk to an infant monkey at Gerald Durrell's Zoo, *above*, on the British island of Jersey. An employee in the kitchen of the London Zoo, *right*, prepares carefully balanced meals for the animals.

Some zoos have set aside areas where visitors may feed prepared foods to the animals. Except in these areas, people should not feed zoo animals. Candy, popcorn, and similar foods can make an animal sick. Thoughtless visitors often throw wrappers, tinfoil, and other objects to the animals. If an animal swallows these things, it could become ill, or it might even die.

Medical Care. Nearly all large zoos employ a full-time staff veterinarian to care for their animals. The veterinarian examines the animals regularly and treats sick or injured creatures. Most large zoos have an animal hospital, complete with a nursery for zoo babies. Many smaller zoos employ a veterinarian on a part-time basis.

How Zoos Obtain Animals

Zoos buy most of their animals from persons called *animal dealers.* An animal dealer obtains specimens from other zoos and dealers, or from hunters who specialize in capturing wild animals. A dealer sends a list of his animals to different zoos. If a zoo wants any of the animals, it buys them from him. Zoos also deal directly with one another, buying and trading animals.

The United States government severely restricts the import of many animals, especially endangered species and those that may transmit diseases to livestock. Because of these restrictions, zoos must rely increasingly on breeding programs as a source of animals.

History

The earliest known zoo was established by Queen Hatshepsut of Egypt about 1500 B.C. About 500 years later, the Chinese emperor Wen Wang founded the Garden of Intelligence, an enormous zoo that covered about 1,500 acres (607 hectares). Between 1000 and 400 B.C., kings from northern Africa, India, and China established many small zoos. These zoos were designed to display the wealth and power of the ruler.

The ancient Greeks established public zoos as places for the study of animal and plant life. Greek students visited the local zoo as part of their education. The Romans had many private zoos. They also kept a large public collection of wild animals for use in the bloody fights in the Colosseum (see COLOSSEUM). During the Middle Ages, from about A.D. 400 to 1500, zoos became rare in Europe. The world's largest zoo at this time was in China.

By the end of the 1400's, global exploration and an increased interest in learning had renewed the desire of Europeans for zoos. Explorers brought back strange creatures from the New World. But these adventurers found more than just animals. In 1519, the Spaniards discovered a huge zoo built by the Aztec Indians in what is now Mexico.

During the next 250 years, a number of zoos were established in Europe. Some of them amounted to nothing more than small exhibits called *menageries.* These consisted of a few bears, lions, or tigers in small, gloomy cages or pits. Many people became disgusted with this treatment of animals and refused to visit menageries. Through the years, menageries were replaced by larger collections of animals that received better care. These institutions became centers of research as well as ex-

Thomas Nebbia, DPI

Captured Animals, such as this giraffe, are exhibited in many zoos. But shrinking wildlife populations have caused zoos to rely increasingly on animals bred in captivity.

hibitions of animals, and they developed into the first modern zoos. The oldest zoo still in existence is the Schönbrunn Zoo, which opened in Vienna, Austria, in 1752. The Madrid Zoo in Spain was established in 1775, and the Paris Zoo, the third oldest zoo in continuous operation, opened in France in 1793. The Berlin Zoo, which became a leader in research of animal behavior, opened in Germany in 1844.

The development of zoos in the United States began with the chartering of the Philadelphia Zoological Society in 1859. But the Civil War (1861-1865) delayed construction of the Philadelphia Zoo, which did not open until 1874. The Central Park Zoo in New York City opened in 1864, followed by the Buffalo Zoo in New York in 1870 and Chicago's Lincoln Park Zoo in 1874. In 1889, Congress established the National Zoological Park in Washington, D.C. This zoo is the only one operated by the federal government (see NATIONAL ZOOLOGICAL PARK). The first Canadian zoo opened in Toronto in 1887.

In 1907, a German animal dealer named Karl Hagenbeck developed the moat technique of displaying animals (see HAGENBECK, KARL). The first children's zoo in the United States opened at the Philadelphia Zoo in 1938.

By the mid-1940's, zoologists knew that many species of animals faced extinction in the wild. Zoos realized that they could help preserve some of these species and began to develop breeding programs. Previously, most zoos had tried to display at least one member of as many different species as possible. Few zoos owned more than one or two animals of a rare species. Today, as a result of the policy of developing breeding herds, many zoos own several animals of the same species. CLYDE A. HILL

ZOOGEOGRAPHY. See ZOOLOGY (Branches).

ZOOLOGICAL GARDEN. See ZOO, with pictures; SAN DIEGO (picture).

ZOOLOGY

ZOOLOGY, *zoh AHL oh jih*, is the science or study of animal life. Together with *botany*, the study of plant life, it forms the science of *biology*, the study of living things. See BIOLOGY.

Man himself belongs to the animal kingdom, although his intellectual development sets him apart. Facts learned from the study of animals give man a better knowledge of himself. Man has gained much understanding of the human body by studying animals that have organs and body processes similar to his own.

Branches of Zoology

Zoology is such a vast subject that most zoologists specialize in some part of the field. Many branches of the zoological science have been established. Some deal with special groups of animals. *Entomology*, for example, deals with insects. *Ornithology* deals with birds. Other branches deal with special aspects of all the animal groups. *Taxonomy* is the science of naming and classifying animals. *Morphology* examines animal form and structure. *Pathology* deals with the nature of diseases. Pathologists can apply knowledge gained from animal diseases to the struggle to cure human ills.

Comparative anatomy, which compares the body structures of different animals, is closely related to evolutionary studies. *Histology* deals with the fine structures of the body tissues. *Cytology* studies the structure of individual body cells.

Genetics, the science of heredity, offers many interesting lines of research. Parents pass on a combination of their own characteristics to their offspring. Much information about heredity has come from careful study of these combinations. Still more knowledge has come from breeding experiments. These have led to valuable improvements in breeds of domestic animals, and have shed much light on human heredity.

Embryology studies the development from an egg to a fully-formed young animal. Embryologists have observed growth stages in a great variety of animals. Many embryologists are now trying to discover the complicated physical and chemical processes that underlie development.

Physiology deals with bodily functions. Physiologists study such problems as how nerve fibers transmit impulses, how muscles contract, and how the body absorbs, circulates, and uses various food substances. *Biochemistry* and *biophysics* study chemical and physical processes that can explain bodily functions.

Psychology is the study of the mind. Our interest centers mainly on man, but investigating animal psychology has helped us to understand the human mind and human behavior better.

Ecology studies the environment in which animals live. Ecologists also study the factors that cause an animal to flourish in one type of surrounding and perish in another. *Zoogeography* is associated with ecology. It deals with the distribution of animals in the various regions of the world. Zoogeographers try to answer such questions as: Why do polar bears live only near the North Pole, and penguins only near the South Pole? Why do opossums live in the Western Hemisphere, but not in the Eastern Hemisphere?

Paleontology, a biological field, borders on the science of geology. It deals with animals of past ages. *Vertebrate fossils* (fossils that have backbones) have furnished much knowledge about the evolution of the higher animals.

For more detailed information on branches of zoology, see the separate articles listed at the end of this article.

The Development of Zoology

Earliest man knew about and observed the animal life around him. Cave paintings by Stone Age artists show close knowledge of animal subjects. Aristotle was the first true scientist whose studies of animals have come down to us. He lived in Greece more than 300 years before Christ was born. Aristotle wrote several works on animals. They show that he was a keen and accurate observer. Some of his accounts on animal development and structure stood unequaled for nearly 2,000 years. Galen was a second great figure in ancient science. He practiced medicine in Rome in the A.D. 100's. He also described many features of the structure of higher animals. After the decline of Rome, about the A.D. 400's, zoology and other sciences went into a decline that lasted a thousand years. See ARISTOTLE; GALEN.

Zoology and other scientific inquiry enjoyed a rebirth in the 1500's. Andreas Vesalius of Belgium studied the structure of higher animals and man. He shocked people by finding errors in Galen's work. Swiss scientist Konrad Von Gesner made a detailed study of the kinds of plants and animals found in Europe.

During the 1600's and 1700's, knowledge of zoology expanded greatly. Explorations brought strange new animals to Europe from other continents. Tiny forms of life appeared under the microscope. Scientists established the major fields of taxonomy and morphology during this period.

Carolus Linnaeus, a Swedish naturalist, founded modern taxonomy. So many animals were known by the 1700's that it created a need for a method of classifying them. Linnaeus devised a reasonable classification scheme. See LINNAEUS, CAROLUS; CLASSIFICATION.

Baron Cuvier, a French naturalist, connected earlier studies of the structure of various animals with his own observations. He pointed out that almost all forms of animals belong to one or another of a few existing basic body patterns. Cuvier's work stimulated further studies in animal structure, and led to the discovery of evidence for evolution. See CUVIER, BARON.

Scientists found close resemblances between many kinds of animals. Charles Darwin of Great Britain was the first to collect evolutionary evidence. This evidence indicated that blood relationships or common ancestors might account for the resemblances. In his book *The Origin of Species* (1859), Darwin assembled observations and facts that had accumulated for decades before him. This data showed the reality of evolutionary processes, and explained how they operate. Many zoologists feel that Darwin's explanations of evolution are incomplete. But they accept almost universally the reality of evolution itself. See DARWIN (Charles R.); EVOLUTION.

Careers in Zoology

Each branch of the zoological sciences offers vocational opportunities. Zoologists may work in many fields, ranging from public health and animal hus-

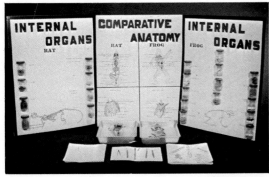

WORLD BOOK photo

The purpose of this science project is to learn how the body structures of one animal compare with those of another. Zoologists use such comparisons as one way of determining how to group animals for scientific classification.

MATERIALS

You can buy all the materials needed for this project from a company that sells biological supplies. The animals come ready for dissection. In this project, a rat and a frog are used. Materials include two dozen small jars with lids, a box of straight pins, several towels, and formalin. CAUTION: Formalin is extremely irritating to the eyes and nose. Handle it with care and wash your hands after using it. A comparative anatomy textbook will help you identify the parts, and a biology laboratory manual will give additional information on how to remove them.

Instruments, *left,* include a medium-sized scalpel with an extra blade, two dissecting probes (one with a hooked end), a medium-sized tissue forceps, and a small tissue forceps. Ordinary tweezers may be used for the small forceps.

Dissecting Pan. You can buy a dissecting pan, *below,* or you can make one from a cake pan. To make the pan, melt equal amounts of beeswax and paraffin. Pour this mixture into the pan to a depth of about ¼ inch (6.4 millimeters).

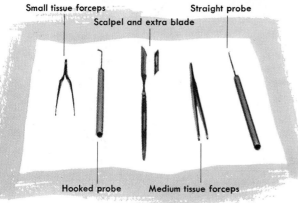

Small tissue forceps
Scalpel and extra blade
Straight probe
Hooked probe
Medium tissue forceps

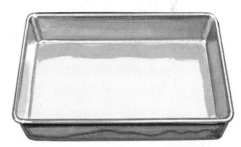

PREPARING THE SPECIMENS

Stretch the Animal on its back in the pan, fastening it in place with straight pins. Use the scalpel to make an incision down the center of the exposed part of the animal. Hold the scalpel loosely and stroke the tip of the blade along the skin. After the skin separates, put the scalpel aside.

Remove the Specimens, using the tissue forceps, the probes, and your fingers. Separate the various internal organs from the tissues that surround them and hold them in place. Do not cut away the tissues with the scalpel unless you cannot remove the organs by using the blunt intruments.

Identify the Body Parts. As you remove each specimen, identify it by comparing it with illustrations from the anatomy textbook. Place the specimen in a jar containing enough formalin to cover it. Label the jar and screw the lid on tightly to prevent the formalin from evaporating.

PRESERVING THE SKELETONS

Remove as much tissue as possible from the bones. Then soak the skeleton for about two hours in hot, soapy water. Scrub the bones with a stiff brush, *left,* and rinse well. Arrange the skeleton in the position you want for display, *right.* Let it dry thoroughly. The cartilage will stiffen as it dries and will hold the bones in place.

WORLD BOOK illustrations by Bill Fleming

bandry to teaching and research. A bachelor's degree is sufficient for some positions, but most require advanced training. Zoological management offers many opportunities, such as managing wildlife preserves, conducting expeditions, and supervising laboratories and museums. Museum work involves classifying animals, preparing exhibits, and preserving specimens. The federal government and many states offer special civil service positions to trained zoologists.   PETER GRAY

Related Articles. See ANIMAL with its list of Related Articles. See also the following:

BIOGRAPHIES

Broom, Robert	Lankester, Sir Edwin R.
Cuvier, Baron	Medawar, Sir Peter
Dana, James Dwight	Osborn (family)
Frisch, Karl von	Schaller, George B.
Goodall, Jane	Swammerdam, Jan
Haeckel, Ernst H.	Tinbergen, Nikolaas
Huxley (Thomas)	

ANIMAL GROUPS

Amphibian	Flatworm	Nematoda
Arachnid	Insect	Protozoan
Arthropod	Invertebrate	Reptile
Bird	Mammal	Rotifer
Coelenterate	Metazoan	Vertebrate
Crustacean	Mollusk	Worm
Echinoderm		
Fish		

BRANCHES OF ZOOLOGY

Anatomy	Entomology	Ichthyology
Biochemistry	Ethology	Morphology
Bionics	Evolution	Ornithology
Biophysics	Genetics	Paleontology
Cytology	Helminthology	Pathology
Ecology	Herpetology	Physiology
Embryology	Histology	

OTHER RELATED ARTICLES

Classification, Scientific	Taxidermy
Fauna	Vivisection
Order	Zoo

ZOOM LENS. See TELEVISION (The Cameras); CAMERA (Motion Picture Cameras).

ZORACH, *ZOHR ahk,* **WILLIAM** (1887-1966), became one of the leading American sculptors in the 1930's. He exhibited at the Whitney Museum and the Museum of Modern Art. He designed the sculpture for the Post Office and Department of Justice buildings in Washington. Born near Kaunas, Lithuania, Zorach came to the United States as a child, and later studied painting and drawing.   CHARLES SEYMOUR, JR.

ZOROASTER, *ZAWR oh AS tuhr,* was an ancient Persian prophet and religious teacher who founded the religion called *Zoroastrianism.* He probably lived from the early 600's B.C. to the mid-500's B.C., though he may have lived even earlier. Zoroaster's real name was Zarathustra. *Zoroaster* is the Greek form of his name.

Historians know little about Zoroaster. They have constructed a general outline of his life based on the legends of Zoroastrianism. Zoroaster probably lived in what is now northeastern Iran and, at the age of 20, left home on a search for religious truth. After wandering and living alone for 10 years, he had a revelation. Zoroaster had six more revelations during the next 10 years. In each revelation, he spoke with God and the

chief angels. Zoroaster was told to call all people together to worship God, called Ahura Mazda. Zoroaster was also told to gather people together to fight Angra Mainyu, the spirit of evil and Ahura Mazda's enemy.

For many years, Zoroaster tried to convert others to his religion, which was based on the belief in Ahura Mazda. But he failed to do so. When Zoroaster was 42 years old, he converted King Vishtaspa, who ruled an area that is now part of Afghanistan. Other Persians then joined the faith. At the time of Zoroaster's death, his teachings were beginning to have a strong influence in Persia.   KENDALL W. FOLKERT

See also ZOROASTRIANISM.

ZOROASTRIANISM, *ZAWR oh AS tree uh nihz uhm,* is a religion founded in the 500's B.C., or perhaps earlier, by a Persian prophet named Zoroaster. Zoroastrianism teaches a belief in one God, called Ahura Mazda, who created all things. All people must seek and obey Ahura Mazda, who will judge them at the end of time.

A Winged God named Ahura Mazda is the symbol of Zoroastrianism. He was the chief god of the ancient Persians.

Zoroastrianism teaches that Ahura Mazda has an enemy called Angra Mainyu, who is the spirit of evil. Zoroastrians believe that the world and the lives of everyone in it represent a battleground. A great struggle takes place there between good, represented by Ahura Mazda, and evil, represented by Angra Mainyu. All people are called on to join the battle on the side of the good, which will win at the end of time. Each person is judged at death according to the side that he or she chose. A sacred book called the *Avesta* contains basic teachings of Zoroastrianism.

Zoroastrianism thrived in Persia from about 550 to 330 B.C. The religion then seems to have lost some of its vitality, but it revived in new forms from the A.D. 200's to the mid-600's. About 650, the Muslims conquered Persia and forbade the practice of Zoroastrianism. But some people continued to follow it. Today, Zoroastrianism is practiced only by a small group in Iran and by a people in India called Parsis.   KENDALL W. FOLKERT

See also MAGI; MITHRAS; PARSIS; PERSIA, ANCIENT (Religion); TOWER OF SILENCE; ZOROASTER.

ZOUAVES, *zoo AHVZ,* were soldiers of certain infantry regiments in the French Army. The name *Zouave* came from that of the *Zouaoua* tribe of Kabyles in Algeria, where the French first recruited Zouaves in 1830. At first, the Zouave regiments were battalions made up of tribesmen and Frenchmen. Later, the army separated the races, but the French Zouaves continued to wear their tribal dress. The Algerian regiments were called *Turcos.* The Zouaves fought with Free French forces in North Africa during World War II (1939-1945).

Napoleon III organized a group called the Papal Zouaves in 1860 for the protection of the Papal States. They were disbanded in 1871.   THOMAS E. GRIESS

ZSIGMONDY, RICHARD. See NOBEL PRIZES (table: Nobel Prizes for Chemistry—1925).

ZUGSPITZE is a mountain peak. See GERMANY (The Bavarian Alps).

ZUIDER ZEE. See NETHERLANDS (introduction).

ZULU are one of the main Bantu-speaking peoples of Africa. Most Zulu live in the province of Natal in the Republic of South Africa. Many Zulu live in urban areas. Others live in Kwazulu (Zululand), a homeland assigned to them by the South African government. The government subjects the Zulu to severe discrimination under a policy of racial segregation called *apartheid*.

During the early 1800's, a Zulu king named Shaka led his nation in a series of military conquests of the neighboring peoples. In 1838, the Zulu clashed with invading Dutch settlers, called *Boers*. The Zulu remained independent until the British conquered them in 1879.

Before the British conquest, the Zulu were farmers and cattle herders. They lived in cone-shaped houses made of finely matted reeds and straw. They arranged these houses in circles to form villages. The Zulu had a powerful monarch and a well-disciplined army.

The Zulu have traditionally practiced *polygamy*, the custom of a man's having more than one wife at the same time. A traditional Zulu family consists of a man, his wives, his unmarried children, and his married sons and their wives and children. In urban areas, however, polygamy is becoming less common, and most families are smaller.   PIERRE L. VAN DEN BERGHE

See also BANTU; SOUTH AFRICA.

ZUÑI INDIANS, *ZOO nyee*, are a tribe that lives in northwestern New Mexico near the Arizona border. Many live in adobe and stone houses in the pueblo village of Zuni, but others have modern houses. The Zuñi are best known for their handcrafted jewelry made from coral, silver, and turquoise. Many Zuni raise livestock.

The Zuñi are descendants of the Anasazi Indians (see CLIFF DWELLERS [History]). Most of the early Zuñi were farmers. The tribe first came in contact with foreigners in 1539. That year, a Spanish expedition discovered six Zuñi villages while searching for the imaginary Seven Cities of Cibola (see CIBOLA, SEVEN CITIES OF). The Zuñi resented the invasion of their territory by foreigners and killed the leader of the expedition, a black explorer named Estevanico (see ESTEVANICO).

The Zuñi came under the authority of the United States after the Mexican War ended in 1848. That year, the United States acquired land from Mexico, including regions that later became parts of Arizona and New Mexico.

In 1969, the tribe established the Zuñi Comprehensive Development Plan to create jobs and improve education and living conditions. In 1970, as a result of this plan, the Zuñi became the first Indians to assume supervision of all the programs the U.S. Bureau of Indian Affairs had set up for them.

Many tourists attend a colorful Zuñi ceremony called *Shalako*. It is held annually between Thanksgiving and mid-December to bless new homes.   ROBERT E. LEWIS

See also INDIAN, AMERICAN (picture: The Southwest Indians).

ZUNZ, *tsoonts,* **LEOPOLD** (1794-1886), has been called the founder of the scientific study of Judaism. He was the first scholar to make a scientific study of the prayers and poetry used in the services of the synagogue. He also studied the intellectual life of European Jews. Zunz was born in Detmold, Germany, and spent most of his life in Berlin.   CLIFTON E. OLMSTEAD

ZURBARÁN, *zur ba RAHN,* **FRANCISCO** (1598-1664), was a Spanish painter of the 1600's. His calm, almost classical paintings seem simple, but they are carefully and intricately composed. Zurbarán was unsurpassed in his ability to create sculptural forms through the use of broad areas of light and shadow or color. His favorite subjects for paintings included meditating monks, female saints, and still life objects such as earthenware jugs.

Zurbarán was born in Fuente de Cantos in the province of Estremadura. Many scholars believe the severity of the Estremadura landscape influenced his style. However, the paintings of Michelangelo Caravaggio, Jusepe de Ribera, and Diego Velázquez were probably more important in Zurbarán's development as an artist. Zurbarán's finest works were done between 1629 and 1645, principally for monasteries. His severely simple style made him the foremost interpreter of monastic life. In his own day, Zurbarán's paintings were exported to Latin America, where they had a decisive influence on colonial painting.   MARILYN STOKSTAD

See also MOOR (picture).

ZURICH, *ZOOR ik* (pop. 396,300; met. area pop. 720,800), is the largest city and the manufacturing, commercial, and banking center of Switzerland. For location, see SWITZERLAND (map). This city at the north end of Lake Zurich has steep, narrow streets

Conzett & Huber

The Stately Grossmünster Cathedral in Zurich, *left,* **founded by Charlemagne in the 700's, towers above the Limmat River.**

and old-fashioned houses that contrast with its newer sections. The Limmat River divides Zurich into two parts called the *Little City* and the *Great City*. Eleven bridges cross the river to connect the two parts.

Many famous buildings dot Zurich. The National Museum contains relics of the republic. The famous Swiss reformer, Huldreich Zwingli, once was pastor at the Romanesque cathedral built there in the 1000's. Zurich, a center of learning, has the canton university. It also has the Federal Institute of Technology and many other excellent schools.   FRANKLIN CARL ERICKSON

ZWAANENDAEL MUSEUM. See DELAWARE (Places to Visit).

ZWEIG, *tsvyk,* **STEFAN** (1881-1942), was a well-known Austrian writer of psychological novels, stories, biographies, and poems.

Stefan Zweig

Schaal, Pix

His best-known novels include *Amok* (1922), *Conflicts* (1926), and *Beware of Pity* (1939). Some of his best biographies are *Romain Rolland* (1921), *Marie Antoinette* (1932), and *Erasmus of Rotterdam* (1934). Zweig was born in Vienna. The Nazis forced him to leave Austria because of his Jewish ancestry, and from 1934 to 1940 he lived in London. He and his wife committed suicide in Brazil because of depression over world affairs. He described the tragic conflicts of his life in his autobiography, *The World of Yesterday* (published in 1946, after his death).   GOTTFRIED F. MERKEL

ZWINGLI, *TSVING lee,* **HULDREICH** (1484-1531), was a leader of the Protestant Reformation. His career centered in Switzerland, but he influenced the Reformation in Germany, The Netherlands, and England.

His Life. Zwingli was born in the Wildhaus Valley near St. Gall, Switzerland. In 1506, he was ordained a Catholic priest. By 1514, Zwingli had become an enthusiastic follower of the Dutch humanist Desiderius Erasmus. Zwingli studied Erasmus' edition of the Greek text of the New Testament and adopted the program of the Christian humanists for reforming the church. This program tried to follow what the humanists felt was the simple faith of the New Testament and of the early Christians.

In 1518, Zwingli was chosen to be a priest of the cathedral in Zurich. He became a forceful reform preacher, following the views of Erasmus. Soon he was reading works by the reformer Martin Luther. By 1520, Zwingli had worked out a Protestant theology unlike that of Luther. After the Catholic bishop of Zurich tried to silence Zwingli, the civil magistrates took charge of all the city's religious affairs. In 1523, the magistrates called a public meeting to decide between Catholicism and Zwingli's new Protestantism. Zwingli's side won. During the next two years, the magistrates abolished religious images such as statues, adopted a Protestant liturgy, closed the monasteries, and substituted the Lord's Supper for the Mass. By 1528, the major German-Swiss cities had followed Zurich's lead, though rural areas remained Catholic. In 1531, Zwingli, serving as a chaplain with the Protestant troops, was killed during a war with Catholics.

His Ideas. Zwingli agreed with other early reformers on many issues. These issues included salvation by faith rather than by good works, the supremacy of the Bible as the sole authority for Christianity, and the universal priesthood of all believers. The concept of universal brotherhood declared that all believers were considered priests. The Catholic Church had various ranks of priests that were separate from lay people.

Luther and Zwingli disagreed on certain points, especially the Lord's Supper. Luther regarded this sacrament as a means by which God gave people His grace. Zwingli considered the Lord's Supper a thanksgiving to God for grace already given in other ways, especially through God's gift of the Gospel. Luther was primarily concerned about individual salvation. Zwingli had greater concern about what he called the "renaissance of Christendom." By this he meant the total rebirth of humanity and society. He thus became active in politics and in social reform. He supported radical changes in the church and worked successfully for the right of the people to control the church.   L. J. TRINTERUD

See also LUTHER, MARTIN; REFORMATION.

ZWORYKIN, *ZWOHR ih kin,* **VLADIMIR KOSMA** (1889-   ), is a Russian-born American physicist and electronics engineer. He is responsible for many advances in radio, television, and the electron microscope.

He came to the United States in 1919. After learning to speak English, he went to work in 1920 for the radio tube department of the Westinghouse Electric Company in Pittsburgh, Pa. He studied at the University of Pittsburgh, where he received his Ph.D. degree in 1926.

At Westinghouse, Zworykin was put in charge of a group of young engineers to help develop the television camera and picture tube. His most important work there was the practical development of the *iconoscope*, an electronic tube that converts light rays into electric signals. The signals can then be changed into radio waves.

Zworykin was also largely responsible for developing and perfecting the electron microscope (see ELECTRON MICROSCOPE). In 1929, he became director of electronics research for the Radio Corporation of America (now RCA Corporation). He was made vice-president of the company in 1947.

RCA

Vladimir Zworykin

Zworykin was born in Murom, Russia, and was graduated from the Petrograd Institute of Technology in 1912 with a degree in electrical engineering. He then went to Paris, where he did X-ray research with the physicist Paul Langevin at the College of France. At the outbreak of World War I in 1914, Zworykin returned to Russia, and served for the next four years as a radio officer. After traveling around the world twice, Zworykin settled in the United States.   G. GAMOW

See also ELECTRONICS (picture: A Pioneer of Television).

ZYGOTE. See FERTILIZATION.

ZYMASE. See YEAST.